# TOURISM

## PRINCIPLES AND PRACTICE

## PEARSON

At Pearson, we take learning personally. Our courses and resources are available as books, online and via multi-lingual packages, helping people learn whatever, wherever and however they choose.

We work with leading authors to develop the strongest learning experiences, bringing cutting-edge thinking and best learning practice to a global market. We craft our print and digital resources to do more to help learners not only understand their content, but to see it in action and apply what they learn, whether studying or at work.

Pearson is the world's leading learning company. Our portfolio includes Penguin, Dorling Kindersley, the Financial Times and our educational business, Pearson International. We are also a leading provider of electronic learning programmes and of test development, processing and scoring services to educational institutions, corporations and professional bodies around the world.

Every day our work helps learning flourish, and wherever learning flourishes, so do people.

To learn more please visit us at: **www.pearson.com/uk**

# TOURISM
## PRINCIPLES AND PRACTICE

**Fifth Edition**

**John Fletcher**
**Alan Fyall**
**David Gilbert**
**Stephen Wanhill**

**PEARSON**

Harlow, England • London • New York • Boston • San Francisco • Toronto • Sydney
Auckland • Singapore • Hong Kong • Tokyo • Seoul • Taipei • New Delhi
Cape Town • São Paulo • Mexico City • Madrid • Amsterdam • Munich • Paris • Milan

**PEARSON EDUCATION LIMITED**
Edinburgh Gate
Harlow CM20 2JE
United Kingdom
Tel: +44 (0)1279 623623
Web: www.pearson.com/uk

First published 1993 (print)
Second edition published 1998 (print)
Third edition published 2005 (print)
Fourth edition published 2008 (print)
**Fifth edition published 2013** (print and electronic)

ISBN:    978-0-273-75827-3 (print)
         978-0-273-75835-8 (PDF)
         978-0-273-78106-6 (eText)

**British Library Cataloguing-in-Publication Data**
A catalogue record for the print edition is available from the British Library

**Library of Congress Cataloging-in-Publication Data**
Tourism : principles and practice / John Fletcher, Alan Fyall, David Gilbert, Stephen Wanhill. — Fifth
    edition. pages cm.
 Includes bibliographical references and index.
 ISBN 978-0-273-75827-3 (alk. paper)
1. Tourism. I. Fletcher, John.
 G155.A1T5892 2013
 338.4'791—dc23

                                                                          2013010882

10 9 8 7 6 5 4 3 2 1
17 16 15 14 13

Print edition typeset in 10/12 Minion Pro
Print edition printed and bound by L.E.G.O S.p.A., Italy

NOTE THAT ANY PAGE CROSS REFERENCES REFER TO THE PRINT EDITION

# BRIEF CONTENTS

SYDNEY 7553 MILES
SOUTH SOUTH EAST
NEW YORK 7386 MILES
NORTH NORTH WEST
TOKYO 7005 MILES
NORTH EAST
BERLIN 4016 MILES
NORTH NORTH WEST
NAIROBI 113 MILES
NORTH EAST
LONDON 4299 MILES
NORTH NORTH WEST.

# CONTENTS

Photograph, left: Ngorongoro Crater, Tanzania, Africa © Graham Meyer

## Companion Website

For open-access **student resources** specifically written to complement this textbook and support your learning, please visit **www.pearsoned.co.uk/fletcher**

## Lecturer Resources

For password-protected online resources tailored to support the use of this textbook in teaching, please visit **www.pearsoned.co.uk/fletcher**

# GUIDED TOUR

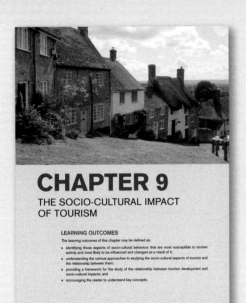

## CHAPTER 9
### THE SOCIO-CULTURAL IMPACT OF TOURISM

**LEARNING OUTCOMES**

The learning outcomes of this chapter may be defined as:

- identifying those aspects of socio-cultural behaviour that are most susceptible to tourism activity and most likely to be influenced and changed as a result of it;
- understanding the various approaches to studying the socio-cultural aspects of tourism and this relationship between them;
- providing a framework for the study of the relationship between tourism development and socio-cultural impacts; and
- encouraging the reader to understand key concepts.

Photograph: Shaftesbury, Dorset, UK © Peter Worwall

**◄** Every chapter opens with **learning outcomes** that let you know what you will gain from that section of the book.

**Introductions** concisely describe the themes and issues explored through the rest of the chapter.

**Key terms** are highlighted throughout the text. Definitions for all these terms are included in a full glossary at the end of the book, creating a particularly useful revision tool.

**◄** **Mini case studies** concentrate on specific destinations and organisations to illustrate the theory and practice of contemporary tourism and how they can lead to issues and controversies.

**Self-check questions** at the end of chapters allow you to review material and track your progress.

Links are included to **YouTube**, highlighting some of the most interesting travel videos available online.

**References and further reading** lists offer helpful starting points for continued study of the chapter material.

Extensive, colourfully illustrated and up-to-date **case studies** conclude each chapter by applying what you've just read to real-life tourism situations.

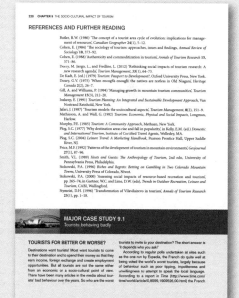

**Practitioners' views** are included in each part of the book, giving a fresh insight from someone who understands the real world of tourism.

# CASE MATRIX

| Mini | Major | Case No. | Case Title | Destination | Page |
|:---:|:---:|:---:|---|---|:---:|
| ● | | 11.1 | A strategy and action plan for sustainable tourism in the Broads, 2011–2015 | UK | 267 |
| | ● | 11.1 | Republic of Kenya Ministry of Tourism Strategic Plan 2008–2012 | Kenya | 285 |
| ● | | 12.1 | March 2011, disaster in Japan | Japan | 291 |
| | ● | 12.1 | Is there more than a risk of sunburn in the Middle East? | Middle East | 305 |
| ● | | 13.1 | Savonlinna Opera Festival | Finland | 317 |
| ● | | 13.2 | Big build projects: Titanic Belfast | Northern Ireland | 328 |
| | ● | 13.1 | Developing a theme park | | 343 |
| ● | | 14.1 | Farm and rural-based tourism accommodation | | 353 |
| | ● | 14.1 | Hilton worldwide | | 369 |
| ● | | 15.1 | The story of Beach Break Live – then and now | UK | 379 |
| | ● | 15.1 | Bournemouth Air Festival | UK | 386 |
| ● | | 16.1 | TripAdvisor | | 398 |
| | ● | 16.1 | Thomas Cook Group plc – a changing landscape | | 413 |
| ● | | 17.1 | Tourism and the environment: mixed signals from the government | | 440 |
| | ● | 17.1 | The cruise ship industry | | 444 |
| ● | | 18.1 | The United Nations World Tourism Organization (UNWTO) | | 452 |
| | ● | 18.1 | Tourism project assistance from the European Union | | 475 |
| ● | | 19.1 | New York set for boom in gay weddings | New York, USA | 509 |
| | ● | 19.1 | The case of Malta as a competitive tourist destination | Malta | 518 |
| ● | | 20.1 | Tourism in a post-enchanted world | | 525 |
| | ● | 20.1 | Disneyland® Resort Paris | Paris, France | 545 |
| ● | | 21.1 | The rise of accessories tourism | | 579 |
| | ● | 21.1 | The portrayal of indigenous identity in Australian tourism brand advertising: engendering an image of extraordinary reality or staged authenticity? | Australia | 586 |
| ● | | 22.1 | Internet and social media role in democracy and political movements | Egypt | 593 |

# AUTHORS AND CONTRIBUTORS

## AUTHORS

**Professor John Fletcher** is Professor of Tourism and Director of the International Centre for Tourism and Hospitality Research at Bournemouth University. John is Editor in Chief of the *International Journal of Tourism Research*, a Fellow of the International Academy for the Study of Tourism and a Fellow of the Tourism Society. He has undertaken tourism development and impact studies throughout the Caribbean, the South Pacific, the Indian Ocean and across Europe on behalf of national governments, local authorities and international agencies. John has led research projects funded by the EU, UNEP, USAID, UNWTO, WTTC, WWF and international development banks. In his efforts to improve the accessibility of tourism impact research he pioneered the development of interactive economic and environmental impact models in the 1990s and is author of more than 130 articles, official reports and book chapters on tourism impacts. He has also written on the place of tourism in national accounts and presented to the British Association for the Advancement of Science.

**Alan Fyall** is Professor at the Rosen College of Hospitality Management, University of Central Florida, USA. Prior to arriving in the USA, Alan was Professor in Tourism and Deputy Dean Research & Enterprise in the School of Tourism, Bournemouth University in the UK. He has published widely in his fields of expertise and is the author of over 100 articles, book chapters and conference papers as well as 14 books. Alan has organised a number of international conferences and workshops for academic, professional and governmental audiences and is frequently invited to deliver keynote addresses. He is Co-Editor of Elsevier's *Journal of Destination Marketing & Management* and Co-Editor of Goodfellow Publishers' Contemporary Cases Online. He also sits on the editorial boards of *Annals of Tourism Research*, *Journal of Heritage Tourism*, *International Journal of Tourism Research* and *Anatolia*, and is a Visiting Professor at the University of Ulster and Edinburgh Napier University in the UK and the Université d'Angers in France. Alan's current research interests lie in destination management and emerging destination management structures and the impact of generational change on patterns of buying behaviour in the context of attractions and destinations. Alan is a former Member of the Bournemouth Tourism Management Board and Board of Solent Synergy Limited, and has conducted numerous consulting and applied research projects across the UK and overseas for the likes of the European Union, Commonwealth Secretariat, Grant Thornton and the Malaysian Ministry of Tourism.

**David Gilbert** is Emeritus Professor of Marketing at the Surrey Business School, Surrey University as well as a Visiting Professor at the Universities of Dongbei University of Finance and Economics and Bournemouth. He has 27 years' academic experience in higher education and over eight years' operational marketing experience for the private sector, having worked as a Product Manager and as a Marketing Manager for Rank Leisure. He specialises in the teaching of marketing related to: Relationship Marketing, Consumer Behaviour, e-Business, Market Research, Research Methods and the functions of Marketing Management and was the founder of both the MSc in Tourism Marketing at Surrey and the DBA programme. His main research is in the field of services marketing and his publications, which number over one hundred, also include a book on retail marketing management. Alongside his academic duties he has worked with several government and private organisations and consultancies on tourism or marketing project work, as well as having planned and provided training in 20 overseas' countries. He was the founder and research director of the Thomas Cook Research Centre at the University of Surrey and has an in-depth knowledge of marketing in relation to the service industry.

**Stephen Wanhill** is Professor of Tourism Economics, University of Limerick and Emeritus Professor of Tourism Research, Bournemouth University and a Visiting Professor at the Universities of Nottingham and Swansea. He is a Director of Global Tourism Solutions (UK) and his principal research interests are in the field of tourism destination development. To this extent he has acted as a tourism consultant to a number of UK planning and management consulting firms, and has undertaken a wide range of tourism development strategies, tourism impact assessments, lecture programmes and project studies from airports to cultural attractions, both in the UK and worldwide, covering some 50 countries. Steve has written extensively on public sector intervention in tourism, tourism impact methodology, and project appraisal and development in academic journals and edited books, which brought him recognition in terms of acting as tourism policy advisor to the Select Committee on Welsh Affairs for a period of five years in the House of Commons. He has been a board member of the Wales Tourist Board with responsibilities for the development and research divisions. In this capacity, he spent much time reviewing and recommending grant applications for projects that encompass accommodation, restaurants and pubs, attractions and public facilities, such as country parks, visitor centres and infrastructure improvements. He is the Editor of *Tourism Economics* and has served as an Editorial Board Member for *Acta Touristica*, *The Service Industries Journal*, *European Journal of Tourism Research*, *Tourism Management*, the *International Journal of Tourism Research* and the *Journal of Travel Research*.

## CONTRIBUTORS

**Dr Bas Amelung** is an assistant professor at the Environmental Systems Analysis group at Wageningen University in the Netherlands. Bas holds an MSc degree in environmental economics from the Free University of Amsterdam and a PhD degree in integrated assessment from Maastricht University (2006). His research is centred around the interface between tourism and sustainable development, with three main foci: climate change and tourism; polar tourism; ecosystem services and tourism. Bas teaches two undergraduate courses: Environment and Tourism, and Tourism Systems Analysis.

**Professor Dimitrios Buhalis** is a Strategic Management and Marketing expert with specialisation in Technology and Tourism. He is currently Established Chair in Tourism, Director of the eTourism Lab and Deputy Director of the International Centre for Tourism and Hospitality Research (ICTHR) at the School of Tourism at Bournemouth University and Professorial Observer at the Bournemouth University Senate. He is also the President of the International Federation of Information Technology for Travel and Tourism (IFITT). He previously worked at the Universities of Surrey, Westminster and the Aegean whilst he had visiting appointments at ESSEC in France, Hong Kong Polytechnic University, China University of Aveiro, Portugal, and the Modul University in Vienna, Austria. He is regarded as an expert in the impacts of ICTs in the tourism industry, the management of tourism distribution channels as well

as in strategic tourism marketing and management. He has recently included accessible tourism in his research portfolio. He has worked around the world and has written 14 books, including *Tourism Business Frontiers and Tourism Management Dynamics* published by Elsevier, *eTourism: Strategic Information Technology for Tourism* published by Pearson (Prentice Hall/Financial Times) and *Tourism Distribution Channels* (Thomson) and more than 100 articles. Dimitrios is still an active tourism practitioner, listing the positions of Marketing Manager and Web Master for his family hotel, Board of Directors of Aquis Hotels and Resorts SA, the fastest growing hotel chain in Greece managing 13 hotels in January 2010; Marketing Advisor for the Aliathon Holiday Village among his activities. He has also been advising private sector organisations such TUI, Opodo.com and YouTravel.com on the strategic aspects of their business. Dimitrios has been involved with a number of European Commission FP5, FP6, FP7 projects and regularly advises the World Tourism Organization, the World Tourism and Travel Council and the European Commission on eTourism. Dimitrios represents Bournemouth University as a Vice President on the Board of Affiliate Members of the United Nations World Tourism Organization (UNWTO).

**Dr Mary Beth Gouthro** is former Programme Leader for BA (Hons) Events Management at the School of Tourism at Bournemouth University and now oversees Graduate and Professional Engagement on behalf of the Events course with industry. Mary Beth delivers on the first year and final year of the events management undergraduate degree, overseeing Events Context and International Events Management. Before embarking on an academic career, Mary Beth's thirteen years of industry experience spanned charity, corporate private and public sector positions in Marketing Communications/Events. This combined with her passion for education in the field of events management feeds research and practical interests in the events field more broadly e.g. managing/creating optimal event experiences, as well as an interest in Event Management research, particularly qualitative methods. She has advised industry associations such as the UK Chapter of ISES (International Special Event Society) in building a programme for their membership to gain more mutually beneficial initiatives between event management courses and UK universities.

**Dr Yeganeh Morakabati** is a Tourism Risk Analyst, Middle East and Research Methods Specialist. She is currently Senior Lecturer in the School of Tourism at Bournemouth University. Yeganeh read for her doctorate degree on the topic of travel risk perceptions at

Bournemouth University before being appointed as a lecturer in 2008 and then moved to Plymouth Business School in 2011. Following a successful period at Plymouth Business School where she continued her research for organisations such as the UNWTO and the Gibraltar Government she returned to Bournemouth University as a Senior Lecturer in 2012. Yeganeh was the owner and Managing Director of a successful major travel agency in Tehran prior to moving to the UK to study for her Master's degree in Tourism Management and Marketing. Since graduating she has undertaken a wide variety of research projects for the University including economic impact studies, the construction of a major database for the Commonwealth Tourism Centre, national and local governments. She also provides research methodology support and training to the postgraduate and PhD students.

**Derek Robbins** trained as a transport planner and is currently Senior Lecturer in Transport and Tourism in the School of Tourism at Bournemouth University. He has developed specialist units at both undergraduate and postgraduate level in aviation, tourism transport, and tourism's contribution to climate change. He has published widely on the relationship between transport and tourism and specific research interests include the deregulation of transport services, most notably the bus and coach industry, transport for tourists within the destination, sustainable transport, cycle tourism, cruise ship tourism, slow travel and tourism and climate change. He co-authored a special tourism edition of the *Journal of Transport Geography* in 2007 and was commissioned to contribute open learning materials for professional courses by a partnership of the Euro Arab Institute Foundation and the UNWTO. Derek chaired the Leisure and Tourism stream of the European Transport Conference for four years, which attracts around 400 transport practitioners and researchers, and he remains a member of the programme committee. He is also an active member of the Chartered Institute of Logistics and Transport.

**Dr Debbie (Deborah) Sadd** is an academic in the School of Tourism at Bournemouth University, teaching Olympic Studies, Strategy and Leadership and Marketing on both the Undergraduate and Postgraduate Events Programmes. She also has undertaken guest lectures within the Sports Management programme, both in the UK and overseas. Debbie completed a Tourism Management and Planning Masters degree in September 2004 with distinction. The research for her Masters was undertaken in Weymouth and Portland, Dorset, prior to the successful 2012 Olympic Bid. This research project is on-going. She also completed in 2006 a Masters in Event Management. Her research interests include social impacts of events, urban regeneration opportunities from events, community identification, legacy planning and in particular the opportunities to be gained for the local communities from the hosting of London 2012. For her PhD, she used both Sydney and Barcelona as case studies to develop a framework of best practice for London 2012 in relation to stakeholder identification. Debbie was awarded an ESRC funded scholarship as part of the STORMING initiative to undertake research into Sporting Events Carrying Capacity including travelling to Tampa, Florida to undertake further research.

# PREFACE

Welcome to the fifth edition of *Tourism: Principles and Practice*. This edition is the latest manifestation of the textbook that we published 20 years ago because we could not find a text that met the needs of our undergraduate and postgraduate students at that time. The past 20 years have witnessed enormous changes in the world, and tourism principles and practice have also changed in that time, reflecting the dynamics of the world in which we now live. This edition contains new features and content to ensure that the book keeps pace with the changing world of tourism and tourism education. We have completely revised and streamlined this edition to make the content more accessible and up to date. Practitioner insights have been added, as well as extensive case studies, with clear intended learning objectives, all set in a colourful and user-friendly format. This fifth edition uses a collaborative approach between academics and practitioners to help students, organisations and practitioners understand and apply current principles and practice to the exciting subject area of tourism.

## THE FEATURES OF THIS BOOK

This new edition expands on the concept of tourism satellite accounts to reflect their growing role in the management and planning of tourism around the world. There are also new chapters introduced, one on events and another on disaster management, which add further insight to the key aspects that made earlier editions so successful. In an increasingly challenging and volatile business world, and with the dynamics of social change facing the world, we offer readers fundamental and underlying principles to study the world of tourism, within four distinct but related Parts: **Tourism Demand**, **The Tourism Destination**, **The Tourism Sector** and **Marketing For Tourism**. Chapters have all been updated to reflect the developments and changing significance of various aspects, such as the economic/environmental/socio-cultural impacts of tourism, climate change, and concerns for the safety and security of tourists.

While the underlying structure of this edition follows earlier successful editions, we have updated, refined and improved all subject areas, added new concepts where necessary and added practitioner comments on tourism, new case studies and examples throughout. The text retains the features that have made it so reader-approachable over the past 20 years, as well as containing some new features. Features include:

- **Learning Outcomes** at the beginning of every chapter to orientate the reader and to focus their mind in respect of the key concepts that underpin each chapter.

- The use of **Major** and **Mini Case Studies** within each chapter to allow the reader to link the theory of the chapter to contemporary issues and practice. Each of these case studies, together with accompanying questions, have been specially selected for this edition.

- The introduction of practitioner '**As I See It**' stories to illustrate important aspects of tourism and its development.

- The identification of key texts and web-based material in a section of **References and Further Reading** at the end of each chapter. Here we have provided the key sources to guide the reader through the increasingly complex maze of tourism literature. These bibliographic signposts will act as the first port of call for assignments and presentations and provide an opportunity for guided specialised investigations where core concepts are reviewed in more detail and from which the reader may derive a deeper understanding.

- The use of **hyperlink addresses** which allow the viewing of supporting evidence such as videos or other forms of communication which will help reinforce the chapter content.
- The updated **Glossary** of key terms to guide the reader through the specialist terminology used in the chapters.
- The use of **photographs** to bring the material to life and the use of colour in the presentation of the text to make the book more attractive and its content more accessible.

This text started out on its journey of development and refinement two decades ago and was based on the research experience of the authors as they undertook projects for national governments, industry and international agencies across all continents of the world. The authors have continued that practice through all five editions, and this current edition reflects their more recent research undertaken to meet the needs of the changing economic, social, environmental and security demands of tourism. When the first edition was written, world international tourist arrivals were around the 500,000 level; in 2012 this number had increased to more than one billion and is predicted to reach 1.8 billion by 2030. This growth in tourism presents many challenges for those people charged with its management. We hope you find that this edition captures your imagination and helps you set out on your journey of discovery as you research into one of the world's largest and most rapidly growing industries.

# PUBLISHER'S ACKNOWLEDGEMENTS

We are grateful to the following for permission to reproduce copyright material:

**Figures**

Figure 1.1 from *International Recommendations for Tourism Statistics (IRTS). Department of Economics and Social Affairs, Statistics Division.*, UNWTO (2008) UNWTO; Figure 1.3 from The framework of tourism, *Annals of Tourism Research 6(4)*, 6(4), 390–407 (Leiper 1979), Annals of tourism research by Elsevier Science. Reproduced with permission of ELSEVIER SCIENCE via Copyright Clearance Center.; Figure 1.4 from A comparison of tourism output and employment in Ireland and the UK: some TSA-based results, *Global Business & Economics Anthology*, 1, 445–460 (Deegan, J., Kenneally, M., Moloney, R. and Wanhill, S. 2006), Business & Economics Society International; Figure 3.8 from *Tourism: Economic, Physical and Social Impacts*, Longman, London (Mathieson, A. & Wall, G. 1982) Pearson Education; Figure 3.9 from *Tourism: Economic, Physical and Social Impacts*, Longman, London (Mathieson, A. and Wall G. 1982) Pearson Education; Figure 3.10 from A general model of traveller destination choice, *Journal of Travel Research*, 27, 8–14 (Woodside, A. and Lysonski, S 1989), Business Research Division, College of Business and Administration, University of Colorado; Figure 3.11 from Understanding vacation destination choice through travel motivation and activities, *Journal of Vacation Marketing*, 2(2), 109–22 (Moscardo, G., Morrison, A.M., Pearce, P.L., Lang, C.T. and O'Leary, J. 1996), by SAGE PUBLICATIONS LTD., Reproduced with permission of SAGE PUBLICATIONS LTD., via Copyright Clearance Center; Figure 5.6 from *Demand forecasting in tourism & recreation* (Witt & Martin 1989) © 1989 John Wiley & Sons Limited, reproduced with permission; Figure 6.1 from *The competitive destionation: a sustainable tourism perspective* CABI publishing (Ritchie & Crouch 2003) CABI Publishing, used with permission; Figures 7.3, 7.4 from http://www.ausstats.abs.gov.au/ausstats/subscriber.nsf/0/3E281CC5A71E3F91CA25796C00143363/$File/52490_2010–11.pdf Australian Bureau of Statistics; Figure 8.3 from http://www.coolantarctica.com/antarctica%20fact%20file/science/threatstourism.htm Accessed 29th Mar 2012 Paul Ward coolantarctica.com; Figure 8.4 from http://www.coolantarctica.com/antarctica%20fact%20file/science/threatstourism.htm, Paul Ward coolantarctica.com; Figure 9.1 from *Domestic and International Tourism* Wellesley MA: Institute of Certified Travel Agents (Plogg 1977) copyright © Dr Stanley Plog; Figure 11.2 from http://www.broads-authority.gov.uk/broads/live/authority/strategy/Tourism_Strategy_for_the_Broads_2011.pdf Page 28. Last accessed 6th June 2012., Broads Authority; Figure 11.3 from *Progress in Tourism, recreation and hospitality management* (Cooper,C. 1991) copyright ©, 1991 John Wiley & Sons Limited, reproduced with permission.; Figures 12.1, 12.2 from http://statistics.unwto.org/sites/all/files/pdf/tsa_data.pdf, UNWTO; Figure 12.8 from Towards a destination tourism disaster management framework: longterm lessons from a forest fire disaster, *Tourism Management*, 29, 151–162 (Hystad PW and Keller PC 2008), Reproduced with permission of ELSEVIER SCIENCE via Copyright Clearance Center.; Figure 13.1 from *The Geography of Travel & Tourism Heinemann*, London (Boniface & Cooper 1987) Elsevier reproduced with permission; Figure 13.2 from *Managing Visitor Attractions: New Directions*, Butterworth Heinemann, Oxford (Leask, A, 2008) 3–15, Elsevier; Figure 13.5 from *Managing Visitor Attractions: New Directions*, 2e, Elsevier (Wanhill, S. 2008) 16–35, Elsevier reproduced with permission; Figure 13.6 from *Managing Visitor Attractions: New Directions*, 2ed (Wanhill, S. 2008) 16–35, Elsevier reproduced with permission; Figure 13.7 from *Managing Visitor Attractions: New Directions*, 2ed, Elsevier (Wanhill, s. 2008) 16–35, Elsevier reproduced with permission; Figure 15.1 from *Special Events: Event Leadership for a New World*, 5ed, John Wiley & Sons: Hoboken (2008) John Wiley & Sons: Hoboken; Figure 15.2 adapted from *Event Management and Event Tourism*, Cognizant Communication Corporation Cognizant Communications Group; Figure 16.2 from WTO, 2002; Figure 16.4 from *Tourism Distribution Channels: Practices, Issues & Transformations.* Thomson Learning (Hudson, Snaith & Miller 2001) Cengage Learning Services copyright © Cengage Learning; Figure 19.5 The Profitable Part of Service Recovery? by Christopher W.L.Hart, James L.Heskett, and W.Earl Sasser, Jr., Harvard Business Review, July-August 1990.; Figure 19.6 from *Strategic Management and Marketing in the Service Sector* Gronroos (Gronroos 1982) Hanken, Swedish

School of Economic and Business Administration copyright © Hanken, reprinted with permission; Figure 20.3 Adapted with the permission of The Free Press, a Division of Simon & Schuster, Inc., from COMPETITIVE STRATEGY: Techniques for Analyzing Industries and Competitors by Michael E. Porter. Copyright © 1980 by the Free Press. All rights reserved.; Figure 21.13 from *Marketing Services* (Donnelly & George, Booms & Bitner 1981) copyright © American Marketing Association; Figure 22.1 from The Internet Economy in the G-20: The $4.2 Trillion Growth Opportunity © 2012, The Boston Consulting Group.; Figure 22.3 from *Empowering Inspiration: The future of travel Search*, (Rheem, C. 2012) PhoCusWright, USA; Figure 22.4 from *Empowering Inspiration: The future of travel Search* (Rheem, C. 2012) PhoCusWright, USA; Figure 22.6 from *Technology and Independent Distribution in European Travel Industry*, PhoCusWright, European Technology and Travel Services Association (Merlino, D., Quinby, D., Rasore, P., Sileo, L., 2010) PhoCusWright USA; Figure 22.7 from SITA, 2012, Airline IT Trends Survey 2012, http://www.sita.aero/file/8068/airline-it-trends-2012-executive-summary-pdf; Figure 22.8 from SITA, 2012, Airline IT Trends Survey 2012, http://www.sita.aero/file/8068/airline-it-trends-2012-executive-summary-pdf.

### Screenshots and Misc.

Screenshot on p. 399 from www.tripadvisor.co.uk, Excerpt from Tripadvisor.com, © 2013, TripAdvisor, LLC. All rights Reserved. Used with permission.

### Tables

Table 1.1 from *International Recommendations for Tourism Statistics (IRTS)*, UNWTO (2008) UNWTO; Table 1.3 from 2008 Tourism Satellite Account: Recommended Methodological Framework (TSA: RMF 2008), Luxembourg, Madrid, New York, Paris, http://unstats.un.org/unsd/statcom/doc08/BG-TSA.pdf, EUROSTAT; Table 2.1 adapted from *The Economic Geography of the Tourist Industry: A Supply Side Analysis*, Routledge (Uysal, M. 1998) 79–95, Routledge, London; Table 4.4 from Long-term forecasts for international Tourism, *Tourism Economics*, 10(2), 145–166 (Smeral, E. 2004), IP publishing; Tables 4.5, 4.7 from www.world-tourism.org, UNWTO; Table 4.6 from www.-world-tourism.org, UNWTO; Table 4.8 from www.world-tourism.org; Table 5.5 from *Forecasting in Business and Economics*, 2ed., Emerald Group Publishing (Granger, C.W.J. 1986) Copyright 1986. Reproduced with permission of EMERALD GROUP PUBLISHING LIMITED via Copyright Clearance Center.; Tables 7.1, 7.4 from *World Tourism Barometer* (2012) UNWTO; Table 7.2 from *World Tourism Barometer* (2102); Table 7.3 from *WWTC Economic Impact Reports* (2011) WWTC;

Table 11.2 from *Tourism and Employment: Enhancing the Status of Tourism Professions*, WTO, Madrid (1980) UNWTO; Table 15.1 from http://www.juliasilvers.com/embok.htm, Julia Silvers; Table 17.1 from *Tourism and Climate Change Mitigation: Methods, greenhouse gas reductions and policies* (Peeters, P. 2007) 11–26, NHTV, Breda; Table 17.4 from ec.europa.eu/eurostat, Eurostat, http://epp.eurostat.ec.europa.eu © European Union, 1995–2012; Tables 17.5 from *Cruise Industry Overview: marketing edition* (2006) copyright © 2007 Cruise Lines International Association Inc; Table 17.5 from *Cruising at the Crossroads – A worldwide analysis to 2025*, Seatrade Communications Ltd, Colchester (Peisley, T. 2010) Seatrade Communications Ltd; Tables 17.6 from *Cruise Industry Overview: marketing edition*(2006) copyright © 2007 Cruise Lines International Association Inc; Table 21.5 from European product purchase methods and systems *The service industries journal* 10(4), 644–79 (Gilbert, D.C. 1990), by ROUTLEDGE. Reproduced with permission of ROUTLEDGE via Copyright Clearance Center.; Table 22.2 from What Is Web 2.0: Design Patterns and Business Models for the Next Generation of Software, http://www.oreillynet.com/pub/a/oreilly/tim/news/2005/09/30/what-is-web-20.html, Copyright © 2005 O'Reilly Media, Inc.; Table 22.4 from http://www.iresearchchina.com/news/4004.html, iresearch consulting group; Table 22.5 from *Social media as a destination marketing tool: its use by national tourism organisations, Current Issues in Tourism*, Taylor & Francis (Hays, S., Page, S., Buhalis, D 2012) Reprinted by permission of TAYLOR AND FRANCIS LTD, http://www.tandf.co.uk/journals via Copyright Clearance Center.

### Text

General Displayed Text 2. from Lindsay W. Turner, Professor of International Trade, Victoria University Lindsay W. Turner; Case Study 3.1 from Splendid Isolation, *Financial Times*, 26/11/2011 (Tom Robbins), Financial Times, © The Financial Times Limited. All Rights Reserved.; Case Study 4.1 from www.world-tourism.org, UNWTO; Case Study 4.1 adapted from *The UK Tourist*, National Tourist Boards of England, Northern Ireland, Scotland and Wales; Case Study 6.1 adapted from A tourism strategy for Greater Manchester 2008–2013, Paul Simpson, MD, Visit Manchester; Box 8. from Applications of the Delphi technique in tourism, *Annals of Tourism Research*, 17, 270–9 (Green, D.H., Hunter, C.J. and Moore, B. 1990), Annals of tourism research by Elsevier Science. Reproduced with permission of ELSEVIER SCIENCE via Copyright Clearance Center.; Case Study 8.1 from http://www.coolantarctica.com/antarctica%20fact%20file/science/threatstourism.htm, Paul Ward coolantarctica.com; Mini Case Study 9.1 from APOLINARI TAIRO, ETN | AUG 26, 2010, http://

www.eturbonews.com/18140/travel-philanthropy-course-benefit-maasai-people-tanzania last accessed 6th June 2012. eturbonews.com; Major Case Study 9.1 'China's Campaign for Civilized Tourism: What to do When Tourists Behave Badly', reproduced by permission of the American Anthropological Association from *Anthropology News*, Volume 51, Issue 8, pages 14–15, November 2010. Not for sale or further reproduction; General Displayed Text 10. from Geoffrey Lipman, President ICTP International; Case Study 10.1 from http://www.iied.org/sustainable-tourism-srepok-wilderness-area-cambodia last accessed 7th June 2012, International Institute for Environment and Development; General Displayed Text 11. from Professor Terry Stevens MD Stevens Associates, International Tourism Consultant; Case Study 11.1 from http://www.broads-authority.gov.uk/broads/live/authority/strategy/Tourism_Strategy_for_the_Broads_2011.pdf Page 28. Last accessed 6th June 2012.; Major Case Study 11.1 from http://www.tourism.go.ke/ministry.nsf/doc/STRATEGIC_PLAN_2008%20-%202012.pdf/$file/STRATEGIC_PLAN_2008%20-%202012.pdf Republic of Kenya, Ministry of Tourism; Case Study 12.1 from http://statistics.unwto.org/sites/all/files/pdf/tsa_data.pdf, UNWTO; General Displayed Text 13. from Paul Simpson, Managing Director – Visit Manchester Paul Simpson, Managing Director – Visit Manchester; Case Study 13.1 from *Managing Visitor Attractions: New Directions*, 2ed, Elsevier (Wanhill, S. 2008) 59–79, Elsevier reproduced with permission; Case Study 13.2 from Professor Stephen Boyd, Department of Hospitality and Tourism Management, University of Ulster; Case Study 16.1 from www.TripAdvisor.c.uk (accessed 29 May 2012), Excerpt from Tripadvisor.com, © 2013, TripAdvisor, LLC. All rights Reserved. Used with Permission.; Case Study 19.1 adapted from Place Marketing, Strategic. Planning and Competitiveness: The Case of. Malta, *European Planning Studies*, 17(9), 1357–1378 (Metaxas, Theodore 2009), Reprinted by permission of TAYLOR AND FRANCIS LTD, http://www.tandf.co.uk/journals via Copyright Clearance Center.; Case Study 20.1 from *e-Review of Tourism Research*, John Wiley & Sons (Tarlow, P. 2003) Dr Peter Tarlow; Case Study 21.1 adapted from The rise of accessories tourism, *Financial Times*, 13/10/2011 (Vanessa Friedman), FT, © The Financial Times Limited. All Rights Reserved.; Case Study 21.1 from The portrayal of Indigenous identity in Australian tourism brand advertising: Engendering an image of extraordinary reality or staged authenticity?, *Place Branding and Public Diplomacy* 7(3), 165–174 (Pomering, A. and White, L. 2011), Place Branding and Public Diplomacy, published 2011 reproduced with permission of Palgrave Macmillan.

**Photographs**

(Key: b-bottom; c-centre; l-left; r-right; t-top)

**Alamy Images:** Ace Stock Ltd 76, All Canada Photos 449, Archimage 531b, Blaine Harrington III 230, Caro 531t, Corbis Bridge 353, Corbis RF 45, Danita Delimont Creative 215, Eye Ubiquitous 241, Greg Balfour Evans 50, Image broker 265t, Image Source 507, Jeremy Hogan 297, Marka 354, Peter Scholey 146, PYMCA 204, Steve Vidler 153, Tommy Trenchard 540, Travel Pictures 28, Werner Dieterich 85; **Andrew Muller:** 1, 65, 117, 450, 482; **BAA Aviation Photo Library:** 421; **European Parliament:** 476; **Getty Images:** Chris Conway 141, Peter Phipp 91; **Graham Meyer:** vi, 24, 144, 308, 588; **Helen Savill:** 112, 224, 288, 389, 521, 547; **Joanna Milner:** 386; **John Foxx Images:** 31; **Kelly Miller:** xxv, 20, 86, 175, 258, 372, 416; **Mary Beth Gouthro:** 379; **Rex Features:** Keystone USA-Zuma 343, Ros Drinkwater 329; **Shutterstock.com:** AISPix by Image Source 37, Ammit Jack 554, Andrey Bayda 6, Gordon Bell 315, Holbox 298, Lee Yiu Tung 131, Luciano Mortula 107, Mohamed Elsayyed 465, Pichugin Dmitry 567, Spirit of America 193, Think4photop 181, tuan0989250402 130, Yolka 265b; **Sundus Pasha:** xi, 313, 348; **Thomas Cook Archives:** 393; **Tina Cadle-Bowman:** 39; **UK Government Departments:** 489; **Peter Woowat:** iii, 197, 487.

Cover images: *Front*: **Getty Images:** Gerad Coles.

In some instances we have been unable to trace the owners of copyright material, and we would appreciate any information that would enable us to do so.

# ABBREVIATIONS

**AA** Automobile Association
**AAA** American Automobile Association
**ABS** Australian Bureau of Statistics
**ABTA** Association of British Travel Agents
**ADS** Additional shares
**AOC** Air Operator's Certificate
**APEX** Advanced purchase excursion fare
**APT** Advanced passenger train
**ARC** Airlines Reporting Corporation
**ASAs** Air service agreements
**ASEAN** Association of South East Asian Nations
**ASP** Application service provider
**ASTA** American Society of Travel Agents
**ATB** Area tourist board
**ATC** Air traffic control
**ATMs** Air traffic movements
**ATOL** Air Travel Organisers' Licence
**AWES** Automatic website evaluation system

**B2B** Business-to-business
**B2C** Business-to-consumer
**BA** British Airways
**BCG** Boston Consulting Group matrix
**BHTS** British Home Tourism Survey
**BRIC** Brazil, Russia, India and China
**BTSM** British Tourism Survey Monthly

**CAB** Civil Aeronautics Board
**CGE** Computable general equilibrium
**CLIA** Cruise Line International Association
**CPGI** Country potential generation index
**CPI** Consumer Price Index
**CRO** Central reservations office
**CRS** Computerised reservation system
**CSF** Community support framework
**CSR** Corporate social responsibility
**CTO** Caribbean Tourism Organisation
**CUC** Cuban convertible peso
**CVB** Convention and visitor bureau

**DAGMAR** Defining Advertising Goods for Measured Advertising Results
**DICIRMS** Destination integrated computer information reservation management system
**DMO** Destination management/marketing organisation

**DMS** Destination management system
**DPUK** Destination Performance UK
**DRC** Democratic Republic of the Congo

**EAFRD** European Agricultural Fund for Rural Development
**EAP** Environmental action programme
**EAP** East Asia and the Pacific
**EBRD** European Bank for Reconstruction and Development
**EC** European Community
**ECAA** European Common Aviation Area
**ECPAT** End Child Prostitution, Child Pornography and Trafficking of Children for Sexual Purposes
**ECSC** European Coal and Steel Community
**ECTAA** European Travel Agents & Tour Operators Association
**EEB** European Environmental Bureau
**EIA** Environmental impact assessment
**EIB** European Investment Bank
**EIS** Environmental impact statement
**EMBOK** Event Management Body of Knowledge
**EMS** Environmental management system
**EPA** Environmental Protection Agency
**EPS model** Extended problem-solving model
**ERDF** European Regional Development Fund
**ESF** European Social Fund
**ETC** European Travel Commission
**ETS** Emissions Trading Scheme
**EU** European Union
**eWOM** Electronic word-of-mouth

**FBP** Family brand performance
**FIT** Fully-inclusive tour
**FLC** Family life cycle
**FTE** Full-time equivalent

**GA** General admission
**GAAP** Generally accepted accounting principles
**GATS** General Agreement on Trade in Services
**GATT** General Agreement on Tariffs and Trade
**GBTS** Great Britain Tourism Survey
**GCET** Global Code of Ethics for Tourism
**GDP** Gross domestic product
**GDS** Global distribution system

**GHG** Greenhouse gas
**GNI** Gross national income
**GNP** Gross national product
**GRASP** Great Apes Survival Partnership
**GVA** Gross value added
**gwt** Gross weight tonnage

**IAAPA** International Association of Amusement Parks and Attractions
**IAATO** International Association of Antarctic Tour Operators
**IADB** Inter-American Development Bank
**IATA** International Air Transport Association
**IBRD** International Bank for Reconstruction and Development
**ICAO** International Civil Aviation Organisation
**ICT** Information communication technology
**IDD** International direct dial
**IFC** International Finance Corporation
**IIED** International Institute for Environment and Development
**IIPT** International Institute for Peace through Tourism
**IIT** Independent inclusive tour
**ILO** International Labour Organization
**IMC** Integrated marketing communications
**IMF** International Monetary Fund
**IMO** International Maritime Organization
**IO** input–output
**IPCC** Intergovernmental Panel on Climate Change
**IPEX** Instant purchase fares
**IPS** International passenger survey
**ISIC** International Standard Industrial Classification
**IUOTO** International Union of Official Travel Organisations

**KM** Knowledge management

**LAC** Limits of acceptable change
**LCCs** Low-cost carriers
**LDC** Less developed countries
**LPS models** Limited problem-solving models
**LTV** Lifetime value

**MA** Moving average
**MAPE** Mean absolute percentage error
**MARPOL** International Convention for the Prevention of Pollution from Ships
**MDGs** Millennium Development Goals
**MEPs** Members of the European Parliament
**MICE** Meetings, incentives, conferences and exhibitions
**MVIC** Manchester Visitor Information Centre

**NAFTA** North American Free Trade Association
**NATS** National Air Traffic Services

**NGO** Non-governmental organisation
**NSRF** National Strategic Reference Framework
**NTO** National tourist organisation
**NYSE** New York Stock Exchange

**OAS** Organization of American States
**OECD** Organisation for Economic Co-operation and Development
**OECS** Organization of East Caribbean States
**OPEC** Organization of Petroleum Exporting Countries
**ONS** Office of National Statistics
**OPs** Operational Programmes
**ORM** Online reputation management

**PATA** Pacific Asia Travel Association
**PBP** Product brand performance
**PEST** Political, Economic, Social and Technological
**PESTEL** Political, Economic, Social, Technological, Environmental and Legal
**PMS** Property management system
**PNR** Passenger name record
**POP** Pay-one-price
**PPC** Pay per click
**PPT** Pro-poor tourism
**PR** Public relations
**PRC** People's Republic of China

**QSCV** Quality, service, cleanliness and value

**RM** Relationship marketing
**RMSE** Root mean square error
**RMSPE** Root mean square percentage error
**ROI** Return on investment
**RTB** Regional tourism board
**RTO** regional tourism organisation

**SAM** Social accounting matrices
**SARS** Severe acute respiratory syndrome
**SAS** Scandinavian Airlines System
**SBU** Strategic business unit
**SCH** Scotland's Commended Hotels
**SDNs** Sustainable development networks
**SEO** search engine optimisation
**SIC** Standard industrial classification
**SIDS** Small Island Developing States
**SITA** Société Internationale de Télécommunications Aéronautiques
**SMART** Specific, measurable, achievable, realistic, time limits
**SME** Small and medium-sized enterprise
**SPD** Single programming document
**STB** Scottish Tourist Board
**STEP** Social, technological, economic and political factors

**ST–EP** Sustainable tourism–eliminating poverty
**SWOT** Strengths, weaknesses, opportunities and threats

**TA** Travel agency
**TALC** Tourist area life cycle
**TAT** Tourist Authority of Thailand
**T&T** Travel and tourism
**TCSP** Tourism Council for the South Pacific
**TDC** Tourist Development Corporation
**TERN** Tourism Emergency Response Network
**TFC** Tourism Forecasting Committee
**TFCTC** Tourism Forecasting Committee technical committee
**TGV** Train à Grande Vitesse
**TIC** Tourist information centre
**TIP** Tourist information point
**TO** Tour operator
**TOP** Thomson Open-Line Programme
**TPI** Tourism Penetration Index
**TQM** Total quality management
**TSA** Tourism satellite account

**UFTAA** United Federation of Travel Agents' Associations
**UGC** User generated content
**UKTS** United Kingdom Tourism Survey
**UN** United Nations
**UNCTAD** United Nations Conference on Trade and Development

**UNDP** United Nations Development Programme
**UNEP** United Nations Environment Programme
**UNESCO** United Nations Educational, Scientific and Cultural Organization
**UNISDR** United Nations Office for Disaster Risk Reduction
**UNSD** United Nations Statistical Division
**UNSTAT** United Nations Statistical Commission
**UNWTO** United Nations World Tourism Organization
**USTTA** United States Travel and Tourism Administration

**VAT** Value Added Tax
**VFR** Visiting friends and relatives
**VR** Virtual reality

**WCS** Wildlife Conservation Strategy
**WCTE** World Committee on Tourism Ethics
**WHO** World Health Organization
**WTO** World Tourism Organization
**WTP** Willingness to pay
**WTTC** World Travel and Tourism Council
**WWF** World Wide Fund for Nature
**WWW** World Wide Web
**WYSE** World Youth, Student and Educational

**YHA** Youth Hostel Association
**YM/WCA** Young Men's/Women's Christian Association

# CHAPTER 1

## AN INTRODUCTION TO TOURISM

### LEARNING OUTCOMES

In this chapter we focus on the definitions, concepts and frameworks that underpin the study of tourism to provide you with:

- a basic understanding of how tourism is defined;
- a comprehension of the issues associated with the academic and practical study of tourism as a concept;
- an appreciation of the components which when combined comprise a conceptual framework for tourism;
- a knowledge of the role of markets and basic supply-side and demand-side issues; and
- the operational framework for tourism supply and demand as embodied in the Tourism Satellite Account (TSA).

Photograph: Chateau Chillon, Switzerland © Andrew J. Müller

## INTRODUCTION

In a world of change, one constant since 1950 has been the sustained growth and resilience of tourism as both an activity and an economic sector. It is therefore clear that tourism is a major force in the economy of the world, an activity of global importance and significance. The World Travel and Tourism Council (WTTC) have demonstrated the tremendous scale of the world's tourism sector (WTTC, 2011). In 2011 the travel and tourism industry's direct contribution to the Gross Domestic Product (GDP) of the world was estimated at US$1,850 billion and in total, by taking account of the re-spending of tourist dollars, US$5,992 billion. This amounts to a direct contribution of 2.9% and a total contribution of 9.1% to world GDP. From a human perspective, the world travel and tourism industry directly supported 99 million jobs and a further 160 million jobs indirectly, some 8.8% of total world employment.

The dimensions of these figures presented by WTTC make it clear that tourism has now become a major economic sector in its own right, but when examined it is found to be a complex multi-sectoral industry demanding high-level planning and co-ordination, with many and varied agents involved, as the contents of this text testify. In this chapter, starting with definitions, we aim to give the overview of tourism as an activity, so as to provide a structure to contain the many different issues discussed in the rest of this text.

## DEFINING TOURISM

Travel as an aspect of human activity has a pedigree going back thousands of years, but the idea of travel for leisure, educational or health purposes really came to prominence during the eighteenth century 'Age of Enlightenment', with the development of the 'Grand Tour' in Europe. Destinations then organised themselves to provide facilities for these temporary visitors, who we now know as tourists, taking a round trip or tour. The costs of such travel prohibited these trips to all but the wealthy, and it was not until the coming of the railways in the nineteenth century that opportunities were opened up for the general population, albeit limited to domestic tourism, which gave rise to the growth of the seaside resorts in Europe and the USA that can be found all around the coastlines of these continents. During the first half of the twentieth century expansion was curtailed by two world wars, so it would be safe to say that the tourism we see today has its roots in the 1950s, when what is now the United Nations World Tourism Organisation (UNWTO) set about introducing a statistical definition of international tourism, and later domestic tourism, for the purposes of collecting information.

### Operational classification

From the standpoint of gathering statistical information, definitions need to be clear, relevant to the subject of study and measurable. The starting point from the official UNWTO perspective is the inbound traveller to the destination (UNWTO, 2008), who is someone moving between different geographic locations, for any purpose and any duration. The inbound visitor is a traveller who is included in tourism statistics through taking a trip to a main destination outside his/her usual environment, for less than a year, for any main purpose, as indicated in Figure 1.1, other than to be employed by a resident entity or organisation within the country or locality visited. Thus tourism refers to the activity of visitors as illustrated in Figure 1.1. It is therefore a subset of travel and visitors are a subset of travellers, whose activities are not solely concerned with the popular notion of pleasure travel, but also those who travel for the purposes of business, visiting friends and relatives, and several other reasons. This is relevant to users of tourism statistics: passenger transport carriers require the broad range of travellers to be recorded, while hoteliers

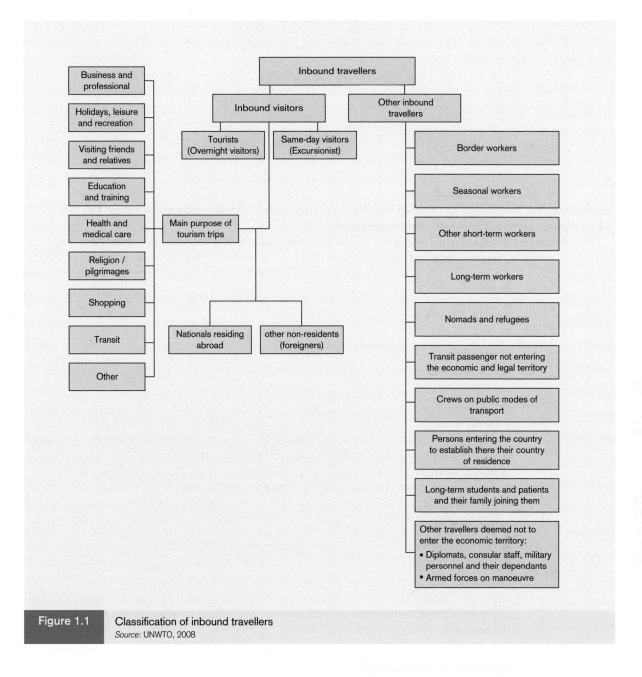

| Figure 1.1 | Classification of inbound travellers |
| --- | --- |
| | *Source*: UNWTO, 2008 |

are interested in tourists, especially business travel because of the relatively high revenue the latter generates for them.

The term 'usual environment' is critical for separating the visitor from the traveller, and hence tourism. It is defined as the geographical area (though not necessarily a continuous one) within which an individual conducts his/her regular life. The purpose of introducing this concept is to exclude from visitors those travellers commuting regularly between their place of usual residence and place of work or study, or frequently visiting places within their current life routine, for instance homes of friends or relatives, shopping centres, religious, health care or any other facilities that might be a substantial distance away or in a different administrative area but are regularly and frequently visited. Thus, for international visitors, place of usual residence rather than nationality is the defining characteristic of their origin, as with domestic tourism. Recognising the significance of second homes in today's tourism, this aspect has particular relevance, for trips to vacation homes are usually tourism trips, but should not be so frequent and the duration of the stay so long so as to turn the secondary dwelling into the principal dwelling of the visitor.

A further essential aspect in defining tourism is the separation of visitors into tourists or overnight visitors, when the trip includes an overnight stay, and same-day visitors or excursionists otherwise. When the definitions of tourism were first discussed in the early 1950s, the volume of day visits was nothing like it is today, and virtually negligible when international tourism was considered. However, modern transport and communication developments have made day trips an increasingly important economic activity through ease and speed of access both within a country and internationally, so they cannot be ignored in the assessment of tourism.

### Forms of tourism

Dispelling common perceptions that tourism is mainly about international travel, official classifications put forward by the UNWTO recommend that three basic forms of tourism for a country should be distinguished:

- Domestic tourism, which comprises the activities of a resident visitor within the country of reference either as part of a domestic trip or part of an outbound trip, and is the predominant form (some 80%) of tourism activity;
- Outbound tourism, which consists of the activities of a resident visitor outside the country of reference, either as part of an outbound trip or as part of a domestic trip;
- Inbound tourism, which encompasses the activities of a non-resident visitor within a country on an inward trip.

For the resident visitor it is the main destination of a tourism trip, namely the place visited, that is central to the decision to take the trip, and which forms the dividing line between domestic and outbound. An outbound tourism trip might include visits to places within the country of residence in the same way as a domestic trip might include visits outside the country of residence of the visitor. The nature of a visit supposes that there is a stop, so entering a geographical area without stopping there does not qualify as a visit to that area.

Combinations of the basic three forms above lead to a further set of tourism categories used to identify visitors:

- Internal tourism, which includes domestic tourism and inbound tourism – that is, the activities of resident and non-resident visitors within a country as part of domestic or international trips;
- National tourism, which is the sum of domestic tourism and outbound tourism – that is, the activities of resident visitors within and outside the reference country as part of either domestic or outbound trips;
- International tourism, which covers inbound tourism and outbound tourism – namely, the activities of resident visitors outside the country of reference either as part of domestic or outbound trips and the activities of non-resident visitors within the country of reference on inbound trips.

These last definitions are significant for the TSA, which, since it was first approved by the United Nations Statistical Division (UNSD) in 2000, now provides the standard framework for assessing the activity of tourism (UNSD, 2008).

## TOURISM AS A CONCEPT

As a field of study and research, the complexity of tourism draws in a wide range of perspectives from a variety of disciplines, as illustrated in Figure 1.2, where tourism can be observed from different standpoints due to its near relationship to other social sciences. The economic

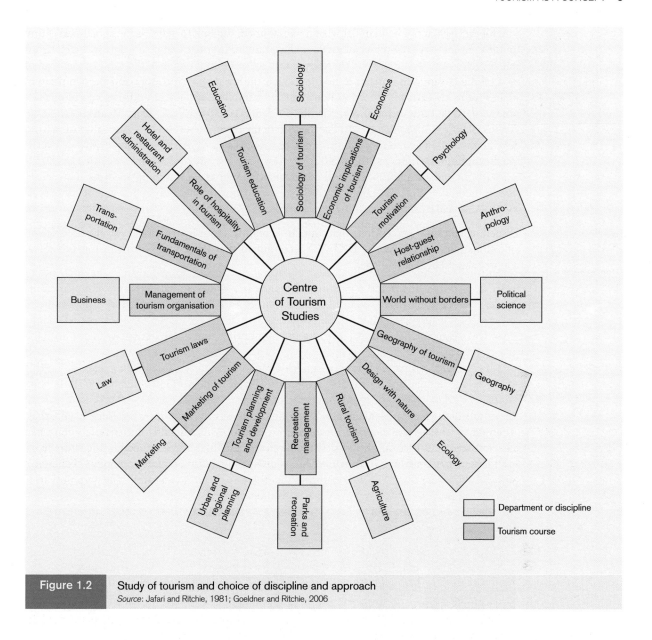

| Figure 1.2 | Study of tourism and choice of discipline and approach |
|---|---|

*Source*: Jafari and Ritchie, 1981; Goeldner and Ritchie, 2006

importance of modern tourism and its impact upon environments and societies are seen as meriting its inclusion as a domain of studies in its own right, but the operational definitions examined above can be rightly criticised for reducing tourism to a set of activities or economic transactions instead of analysing the significance, meaning and role of tourism to individuals. (These latter aspects are discussed in Chapter 3 and in Part 4.) However, some would argue that as an element of human behaviour, it is questionable that tourism should be seen as a separate field of study, as witnessed by the fact that in many universities tourism is simply one aspect of scholarship within an existing single discipline department (Franklin and Crang, 2001).

However, it would be naïve to suppose that organisations drawing up operational definitions are unaware that tourism is about human behaviour that consists of many sundry aspects and uncertainties. They recognise tourism as a social, cultural and economic phenomenon related to the movement of people to places outside their usual place of residence, for which pleasure is the usual motivation. But having more and reliable statistics is essential for policy makers to make effective decisions. Only with sufficient and adequate data that generate credible statistics is it possible to undertake different types of analysis of tourism.

Gilbert (1990) commented that what makes tourism difficult to define is the very broad nature of the concept as well as the need for so many goods and services inputs. Tourism also envelops other sectors and industries and therefore has no clear boundary due to the expansive spread of activities it covers. With this in mind others have added supply-side aspects to the definition of tourism so as to incorporate the visitor's impact (economic, social, cultural and environmental) on the destination (Goeldner and Ritchie, 2006; Lieper, 1979, 1990, 2008; Tribe, 1997, 2006). Tribe's view (1997) was that tourism is 'the sum of the phenomena and relationships arising from the interaction, in generating and host regions, of tourists [visitors], business suppliers, government, communities and environments'.

Within an academic discipline, the benefit of having an overarching theoretical structure is the methodological direction that it bestows. To put it simply, practice without theory is blind. As a field of academic study, various writers, as indicated above, have noted that tourism lacks the theoretical underpinnings that govern other social sciences, giving rise to conceptual weaknesses and lack of clarity. On the other hand many disciplines have their own imprisoning theories in which esoteric arguments have no known reality, thus rendering them sterile. Scientists have found that the behaviour of natural systems do not conform to the doctrines of reductionism that theoretical structures demand. They have shown that small simple actions could never be counted on to have small outcomes and frequently they cascaded into multiple outcomes of unsuspected intensity. Such systems are termed chaotic and chaos theory demands adaptive management, continual learning and monitoring, and frequent reviews to deal with the uncertainty arising.

Chaos theory has parallels in tourism, which has been subject to several disasters so far this century, for example, the destruction of the World Trade Center on 11 September 2001, the wars in Iraq and Afghanistan, the bombings of the London and Madrid railway systems, Tsunamis on the coasts of Sri Lanka, Thailand and Japan, the 'Arab Spring', and the Global Financial Crisis. These are events over which the actors had no control, which in turn have raised interest in chaos theory and its relation to crisis management. Adaptability is the key, for chaos theory postulates a system which has periodic bouts of instability that facilitate change as their states

**Photograph 1.1**    Tourism has become an increasingly popular area of study for many students as the subject gains acceptability in the academic community.
*Source*: Andrey Bayda/Shutterstock.com

are transformed in an evolutionary and adaptive manner. Interdisciplinary tourism, whether a science, a discipline or not, underpinned by a good working knowledge of the subject, is thought likely to show much more promise than anything else so far conceived. It suggests an open-minded approach to tourism that acknowledges the contribution of differing subjects and disciplines to explaining tourism. This has been termed a 'post-disciplinary' approach (Coles et al., 2006), that breaks through the parochial boundaries of the various disciplines to study how the diverse components of tourism interact, adapt and come together as a **tourism system** which is forever evolving as a construct and in the provision of the tourist experience.

## A CONCEPTUAL FRAMEWORK FOR TOURISM

Having discussed the concept of tourism, the next step is to offer a framework or model that can provide a basis for encompassing the different approaches to the study of tourism. A highly regarded model in the literature is that proposed by Leiper in 1979 (Figure 1.3), which we have adapted to be in accord with the definitions given in this chapter. The general term 'traveller' is maintained because this is the measure used in passenger transport services. It is at the destination that the data separation between visitors and other travellers takes place.

There are three basic elements to Leiper's model:

1. **Visitors**, who, as travellers in this system, initiate the demand for travel for tourism purposes;
2. **Geographical elements**, which Leiper calls the 'traveller-generating region', the 'tourism destination region' and the 'transit route region';
3. **The tourism industry**, which Leiper initially took to be all those firms, organisations and facilities that exist to serve the specific needs and wants of visitors (Leiper, 1979), but because the idea of a single tourism industry is debatable, replaced it later with the expression 'tourism industries' (Leiper, 2008).

Taking account of the spatial aspects, the traveller-generating region represents the source market for tourism and can be thought of as providing the 'push' to stimulate and motivate travel. It is from here that the tourist searches for information, makes the booking and departs. The tourism destination region is the *raison d'être* for tourism, with a range of special places distinguished from the everyday by their cultural, historic or natural significance (Rojek and

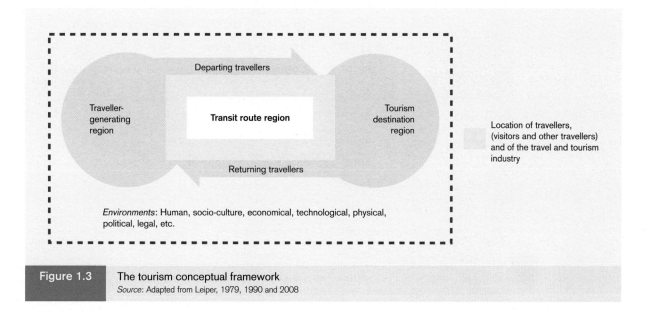

| Figure 1.3 | The tourism conceptual framework |
|---|---|

*Source*: Adapted from Leiper, 1979, 1990 and 2008

Urry, 1997). The 'pull' to visit destinations activates the whole tourism system and creates demand for travel in the generating region. It is at the tourism destination that the full impact of tourism is experienced and product innovation takes place, together with visitor management and planning processes so as to take account of the effects on host communities. (These aspects are discussed in depth in Part 2.)

The transit route region does not simply represent the short period of travel to reach the destination, but must include intermediate places which may be visited en route, if it is to be registered as part of a visitor's trip: 'There is always an interval in a trip when the traveller feels they have left their home region but have not yet arrived . . . [where] they choose to visit' (Leiper, 1990: 22).

The issue as to whether tourism is an industry rests on the definition of an industry within a country's national accounts. These use internationally accepted classifications to produce output measures in accordance with a country's industrial structure. In these terms, an industry is a collection of firms that use similar processes to produce relatively homogeneous goods and services. On the other hand, the tourism product is an amalgam of a multiplicity of goods and services that is configured to meet visitors' demands and drawn from a range of industries, from transport to retailing. In establishing the TSA, the UNWTO (2000 and 2001) decided to label tourism as a sector made up of a number of industries as defined by international standards and these are listed fully in Table 1.1 so as to show the range of businesses directly included in tourism. Yet on a practical level, those engaged in the tourism business and their trade associations commonly use the term 'tourism industry' when representing their views to governments and dealing with issues amongst themselves. Noting this, we will use the terms 'tourism sector' and 'tourism industry' synonymously throughout this text.

| Table 1.1 | Tourism industries as defined by the UNWTO | |
|---|---|---|
| **Tourism industries** | **SIC2007** | **Description** |
| Accommodation | 55100 | Hotels and similar accommodation |
| | 55202 | Youth hostels |
| | 55300 | Recreational vehicle parks, trailer parks and camping grounds |
| | 55201 | Holiday centres and villages |
| | 55209 | Other holiday and other collective accommodation |
| | 55900 | Other accommodation |
| | 68209 | Other letting and operating of own or leased real estate |
| | 68320 | Management of real estate on a fee or contract basis |
| Restaurants and similar | 56101 | Licensed restaurants |
| | 56102 | Unlicensed restaurants and cafes |
| | 56103 | Take-away food shops and mobile food stands |
| | 56290 | Other food services |
| | 56210 | Event catering activities |
| | 56301 | Licensed clubs |
| | 56302 | Public houses and bars |
| Railway passenger transport | 49100 | Passenger rail transport, interurban |

| Table 1.1 | (Continued) | |
|---|---|---|
| **Tourism industries** | **SIC2007** | **Description** |
| Road passenger transport | 49320 | Taxi operation |
| | 49390 | Other passenger land transport |
| Water passenger transport | 50100 | Sea and coastal passenger water transport |
| | 50300 | Inland passenger water transport |
| Air passenger transport | 51101 | Scheduled passenger air transport |
| | 51102 | Non-scheduled passenger air transport |
| Transport equipment rental | 77110 | Renting and leasing of cars and light motor vehicles |
| | 77341 | Renting and leasing of passenger water transport equipment |
| | 77351 | Renting and leasing of passenger air transport equipment |
| Travel, tour and guide services | 79110 | Travel agency activities |
| | 79120 | Tour operator activities |
| | 79901 | Activities of tour guides |
| | 79909 | Other reservation service activities |
| Cultural activities | 90010 | Performing arts |
| | 90020 | Support activities for the performing arts |
| | 90030 | Artistic creation |
| | 90040 | Operation of arts facilities |
| | 91020 | Museums activities |
| | 91030 | Operation of historical sites and buildings and similar visitor attractions |
| | 91040 | Botanical and zoological gardens and nature reserves activities |
| Sporting and recreational activities | 92000 | Gambling and betting activities |
| | 93110 | Operation of sports facilities |
| | 93199 | Other sports activities |
| | 93210 | Activities of amusement parks and theme parks |
| | 93290 | Other amusement and recreation activities |
| | 77210 | Renting and leasing of recreational and sports goods |
| Country-specific tourism characteristic activities | 82301 | Activities of exhibition and fair organisers |
| | 82302 | Activities of conference organisers |
| | 68202 | Letting and operating of conference and exhibition centres |

*Source*: UNWTO

The benefits of Lieper's tourism system lie in its generality in bringing together the demand and supply for tourism in spatial terms at any scale from international to local tourism. It permits an interdisciplinary approach to the study of tourism and allows for the positioning of different industry components within the framework. Thus, intermediaries such as travel agents and tour operators are mostly found in the traveller-generating region, accommodation, restaurants and attractions are found in the destination region, while passenger transport is largely represented in the transit route region.

The framework proposed by Leiper is also flexible in that it provides a backdrop against which the various categories of tourism trips may be examined. Mini Case Study 1.1 shows how the demand and supply aspects of the growing popularity of eco-tourism can be evaluated within Leiper's model, for example, the Great Apes Survival Partnership (GRASP), through involving the local communities in Rwanda, Uganda and the Democratic Republic of the Congo (DRC), has seen the gorilla population rising in numbers. From a business perspective, this is identifying tourism as a series of markets bringing buyers and sellers together to sell a range of tourist products from sun and beach tourism to more focused offers such as medical, cultural and sports tourism. To appreciate this we will look briefly at the role of markets in economic activity and the issues that arise from them, which are fundamental to understanding the various parts of this text.

## MINI CASE STUDY 1.1
Characteristics of elements of the eco-tourism system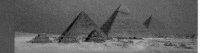

## GENERATING REGION

**Demand for eco-tourism:**

- is purposeful and currently growing two or three times faster than the tourism industry as a whole;
- desires first-hand experience/contact with nature/culture;
- has the motive to study, admire and/or enjoy nature/culture;
- is tempered by the need to consume tourism responsibly and offset carbon emissions;
- can be segmented in many ways including by level of commitment, level of physical effort, motives; and
- comes from those who are more likely to be well educated, have a higher income and be slightly older than the average tourist.

## DESTINATION REGION

**Destinations for eco-tourism:**

- are relatively natural areas which are undisturbed and/or uncontaminated;
- have attractions of scenery, flora, fauna and/or indigenous culture;
- allow eco-tourism to deliver economic and conservation benefits to the local people;
- provides an incentive to local communities to take care of their environment;
- develop eco-tourism with a view to conserving/enhancing/maintaining the natural/cultural system;
- apply integrated planning and management techniques;
- apply environmental impact and auditing procedures to all elements of the tourism destination (such as accommodation facilities);
- attempt to be carbon neutral;
- encourage local ownership of facilities;
- local businesses can deliver up to 90% or more of visitor expenditure into the local economy.

## TRANSIT ZONE

**Transport for eco-tourism:**

- should be of low impact to the environment in terms of noise, carbon emissions, congestion, fuel consumption and waste;
- should monitor emissions and environmental impacts;
- should promote the conservation ethic;
- should be used as a management tool;
- should encourage use of public transport;
- should encourage the use of locally owned transport companies; but
- reaching a long-haul eco-tourism destination may consume large amounts of aircraft fuel and be more damaging to the environment than the tourist realises.

*Source*: Cooper et al., 2008, p.10

## DISCUSSION QUESTIONS

1. Do the principles of eco-tourism apply equally to each of the elements of the eco-tourism system?
2. Should eco-tourists be true to their beliefs and offset their carbon emissions?
3. Tourism trade associations establish environmental charters to foster eco-friendly policies amongst their members. How can such charters be propagated and enforced?

### Role of markets

It will be apparent that for most towns and cities around the world, their populations go to bed each night without being in fear that the morning will bring a breakdown in the elaborate economic processes upon which their existence depends. Yet in a system of free enterprise no one individual or organisation is consciously concerned with the fundamental economic problems of what to produce, how to produce and for whom to produce. What resolves this somewhat paradoxical situation is the concept of 'the market' that puts consumers in touch with producers. In times gone by, markets were physical places of critical importance to towns and cities, but in today's developed world the market square and traders therein often hold more value as visitor attractions serving tourists and residents alike – for example, Covent Garden in central London. Modern information and communication technologies (ICT) have created virtual markets allowing the potential tourist to create his/her own market by contacting suppliers at the destination directly via the Internet to assemble the tourism trip.

In a free enterprise system the prices set in the market serve to adjust demand and supply for goods and services. This is explained in Table 1.2 where at a price of 600 currency units potential tourists only want to purchase 2,000 of the holidays on offer, whereas at that price tour operators are willing to provide 8,000. Clearly there is a mismatch between supply and demand, so the price will have to be reduced to bring the market into equilibrium, at the same time curtailing supply. This is achieved at a price of 400 currency units where demand now equals supply and the market is said to be 'cleared'. At prices below 400 demand is greater than the number of holidays on offer, while at 200 there is no offer since costs are such that tour operators are unwilling to supply holidays at this price. To clear the market and satisfy demand, price will have to rise by 400 currency units. Thus, as this example shows, the prices set in the market serve to reward sellers and ration the supplies on offer amongst buyers, at the same time relaying information between both parties: forwards from tour operators indicating relative costs of production, or value in exchange, and backwards from tourists showing their relative preferences, or value in use, by what they are willing to pay.

| Table 1.2 | Market demand for holiday packages | |
|---|---|---|
| **Unit price** | **Quantity demanded** | **Quantity supplied** |
| 600 | 2,000 | 8,000 |
| 500 | 3,000 | 6,000 |
| 400 | 4,000 | 4,000 |
| 300 | 5,000 | 2,000 |
| 200 | 6,000 | 0 |

*Source*: Author

When countries attempt to abolish the market system, as was the case in Russia and China under their old Communist regimes, then the state has to take over the role of what to produce, how to produce and for whom to produce. The extraordinary inefficiencies and associated corruption that this entailed resulted in such severe disillusionment with state provision amongst the population that it contributed to the collapse of the Soviet Union in the 1990s and the liberalisation of markets in China and Cuba, despite the general adherence to what are perceived as socialist principles in respect of state control of the economy. For Cuba, the development of tourism has been seen as a major collector of foreign exchange ('hard' currency) for the Cuban economy, but this has produced parallel currencies in its largely state–planned economy. Visitors exchange their money for the Cuban convertible peso (CUC), which gives them access to tourism amenities in the usual manner. Residents are paid in the national Cuban peso and have ration books which are used when purchasing items in government shops. Only if residents have CUCs, say from working in the tourism industry, are they able to use tourist shops and restaurants. Common services such as taxis charge residents and visitors the same price irrespective of the currency used, though the black market price for CUCs is considerably above the national peso. Even in North Korea, where free markets are illegal, since they reflect badly on state provision, casual street markets arise quite often to alleviate severe shortages of food and consumer goods, and the authorities turn a 'blind eye' to them.

## Issues with markets

Today, the common description of Western societies is that they are 'mixed economies' in which both public and private enterprise exist. State intervention takes place because free markets do not always work optimally in the allocation and use of resources. Increasing industrial concentration has shifted the balance of power from consumers to suppliers, as witnessed by the current global financial crisis. The financial system, through lack of transparency as to its activities, was able to immunise itself from the market penalties associated with failure, until the financial 'bubble' burst, when financial institutions had to be rescued by the state on the grounds that they 'were too big to fail'. The state's response to monopoly power is to regulate markets so as to make them behave competitively and to pass consumer protection legislation, which is particularly important in tourism as the visitor is buying the product unseen and untested beforehand.

On the other hand, some goods such as the natural and physical environment produce social benefits which are not captured in the marketplace and so need protection to prevent their degradation, which is the essence of the sustainable development issues discussed in Chapter 10. There also exists in society a range of products, referred to as 'public goods', for which free markets would not provide in adequate amounts, if at all, because it is difficult to enforce payment. If they are to be provided at all, they must be shared by everyone, as in the case of city and national parks, so provision for them has to be made out of general taxation. Akin to such facilities are commodities which have a meritorious element such that their consumption should be encouraged. These are termed 'merit goods' and they differ from public goods in that payment is enforceable, but as the object is to foster wide consumption they are either provided free at the point of use or are heavily subsidised. Museum services, sports and recreation, galleries and the performing arts fall under this category as well as social tourism provided for the needy. Need and demand are separate notions: the former has to do with social justice, while the latter is about the ability as well as the willingness to pay.

## AN OPERATIONAL FRAMEWORK FOR TOURISM – THE TOURISM SATELLITE ACCOUNT (TSA)

The operational aspects of Leiper's tourism system from the destination perspective are embodied in the TSA, which is a synthesis of tourism statistical provision to provide a means of separating and examining both tourism supply and tourism demand within the general framework of a country's system of national accounts. We have seen that tourism is not a 'traditional' industry and is, therefore, not measured in standard economic accounting systems. 'Industry' is a *supply-side* concept: typically, the focus is on *what* is being produced. But 'Tourism' is a *demand-side* concept: the focus is on *who's* buying products – the traveller, or visitor. Tourism demand affects parts of many industries, hence the need to measure tourism in a way that enables benchmarking with other sectors.

The importance of a TSA to a destination is that it:

- measures tourism's contribution to the economy and allows it to be compared with other economic sectors. The TSA provides much greater detail and accuracy than any other approaches in measuring the economic contribution of tourism. By evaluating and using this information, both public bodies and tourism enterprises will increase their capacity to influence decision making at all levels. By tying the TSA to standard national accounting practices, credible and reliable estimates of the importance of tourism will be produced allowing valid comparisons with other industries both domestically and internationally;

- governs the relevant statistics that need to be collected;

- identifies industries that benefit from tourism and to what extent, particularly industries that are not traditionally associated with tourism – the weight of tourism activity in terms of outputs for tourism-related industries;

- shows how different forms of tourism (inbound, outbound and domestic) interact in the national economy and generates the ability to gauge the weight of the tourism expenditure incurred by the various visitor categories;

- indicates tourism's contribution to government revenues: tax is an important factor in terms of convincing municipal, provincial, regional and national authorities to design policies for boosting tourism investments;

- provides information on employment: improvement of knowledge concerning jobs generated by tourism and their characteristics, without which the creation of really useful employee training programmes in more characteristic tourism activities (e.g. hotels, travel agencies, car rental firms, tourism information services, etc.) can prove to be a haphazard exercise.

When a TSA was first constructed for Canada, Meis (1999) reported that for the first time they could see the totality of tourism consumption. In the past they had statistics from various surveys of domestic demand, travel nationally, household expenditure and other tourism indicators, but they were not able to put them into what they thought was a credible additive total. By commissioning a TSA, they found that the share of value added broken down into each of the tourism components was a real revelation. Other industries, which they did not consider in the tourism sector, were actually contributing about 25% to total value and GDP. For example,

| Table 1.3 | Structure of a TSA |
|-----------|--------------------|

| Table number | Contents |
|--------------|----------|
| TSA 1 | Inbound tourism consumption by products and categories of visitor |
| TSA 2 | Domestic tourism consumption by products and ad hoc sets of resident visitors |
| TSA 3 | Outbound tourism consumption by products and categories of visitor |
| TSA 4 | Internal tourism consumption by products and categories of visitor (TSA 1 + 2) |
| TSA 5 | Production accounts of tourism characteristics and other industries |
| TSA 6 | Domestic supply and internal tourism consumption by products |
| TSA 7 | Employment in the tourism industrial sectors |
| TSA 8 | Gross fixed capital expenditure in the tourism industries and other related industries |
| TSA 9 | Tourism expenditure by governments and other public authorities |
| TSA 10 | Non-monetary indicators such as the volume of tourist trips and nights, and the number of businesses |

*Source*: UNSD, 2008

in the retail sector they did not realise how significant that was and subsequently set about new ways of trying to harness some of that money and that activity for tourism development.

## The structure of a TSA

In total the TSA system consists of 10 tables and these are listed in Table 1.3. TSA 6 which features domestic supply and internal tourism consumption by products is the core of the TSA system. It may be seen that the TSA presents a formidable array of information gathering and its completion depends on the statistical infrastructure of the country concerned. The UNWTO acknowledges that supply-side data are the most difficult to obtain and suggests the focus should be on the demand tables TSA 1 to TSA 4, and TSA 7 and TSA 10 in the first instance.

It is in TSA 6 that supply and demand aspects at the destination are measured, where the contribution of tourism to GDP and its component parts can be estimated, as indicated by the WTTC statistics at the beginning of this chapter. To obtain effective measurement of the level of these activities, detailed statistics on sales and purchases by firms need to be collected to build a transactions account of the economy. These efforts will vary from country to country given the extent and focus of the central statistical office.

The significance of TSA 6 is in estimating the share of tourism consumption that is attributable to the various supplying industries that serve to meet the demands of visitors. The approach to this is to layer tourism consumption in order of its importance, as illustrated in Figure 1.4, which splits the categories of tourism consumption into three: characteristic products which take a high proportion of that industry's sales, connected products with a lesser proportion and non-specific products at the lowest level. The appearance of retail sales as non-specific might seem surprising as we all know that visitors on holiday are 'compulsive' shoppers, but the point is that for large economies their effect on retail sales in total is likely to be small. However, there are no hard and fast rules and for small, say, island destinations where sales of souvenirs and other retail goods are a key of the economy, shopping may be included as a characteristic product.

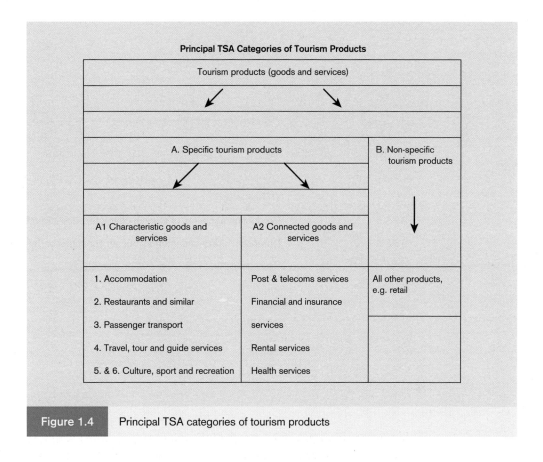

**Figure 1.4**    Principal TSA categories of tourism products

Understanding TSA 6 is best realised by taking a numerical example, as shown in Table 1.4. It is based on an actual research study carried out as part of a team (Deegan et al., 2006) by the author, but considerably simplified for pedagogic purposes. To set it in context, the number of inbound visitors' trips is just over 2.3 million, while domestic visitors' trips amount to 31.8 million, the majority being same-day visitors given the relatively small size of the region as a destination. The last column looks at the ratio of internal tourism consumption to domestic supply at the purchase prices paid by inbound and domestic visitors at the destination, and that part of expenditure by outbound visitors that is paid to local suppliers. This represents tourism's share of the outputs of the various products by the industry groups listed in Figure 1.4.

It is to be noted that the outputs by industry are in basic prices. The *basic price* is the amount receivable by the producer from the purchaser for a unit of a good or service produced as output minus any tax payable, and plus any subsidy receivable, on that unit as a consequence of its production or sale; it excludes any transport charges or trading margins invoiced separately by the producer. Summing down the columns yields total output by the industries associated with tourism at basic prices. From these values input purchases by the respective businesses (which now include product taxes net of subsidies) are then deducted to give the value added by the associated industries in the production of goods and services. The reason for using gross value added (GVA) as a measure of the value of goods and services produced in an area or sector of the economy is technical: it is linked as a measurement to GDP, as both are measures of output. If we sum up the GVA for each sector of the economy as a whole, add on taxes and take off subsidies, we will get to GDP at market prices. As the total aggregates of taxes and subsidies are normally only available at whole economy level, GVA is commonly used for measuring output for entities smaller than the whole economy.

It may be seen from Table 1.4 that the tourism GVA for this economy is 378 + 44 + 108 = 530 million currency units. Going across the table it may be observed that total internal tourism

**Table 1.4**   TSA 6 domestic supply and internal tourism consumption by outputs for a small economy (currency units in millions)

Table six

| Products | Tourism industries | | Connected industries | | Other industries | | Domestic supply (basic prices) | Net taxes on products | Domestic supply (purchasers' prices) | Tourism consumption (purchasers' prices) | Tourism ratios % |
|---|---|---|---|---|---|---|---|---|---|---|---|
| | All | Tourism share | All | Tourism share | All | Tourism share | | | | | |
| **A. Specific products** | | | | | | | | | | | |
| **A.1 Characteristic products** | | | | | | | | | | | |
| 1. Accommodation | 158 | 99 | | | | | 158 | 15 | 173 | 108 | 62% |
| 2. Restaurants and similar | 665 | 377 | | | | | 665 | 68 | 733 | 415 | 57% |
| 3. Passenger transport | 672 | 97 | | | | | 672 | 0 | 672 | 97 | 14% |
| 4. Travel, tour and guide services | 350 | 175 | | | | | 350 | 8 | 358 | 179 | 50% |
| 5 & 6. Culture, sport and recreation | 639 | 84 | | | | | 639 | 57 | 696 | 91 | 13% |
| **A.2 Connected products** | | | | | | | | | | | |
| 1. Renting and business services | | | 1,503 | 62 | | | 1,503 | 52 | 1,555 | 64 | 4% |
| **B. Non specific products** | | | | | | | | | | | |
| 1. Retail | | | | | 5,357 | 421 | 5,357 | 296 | 5,653 | 444 | 8% |
| Total output (at basic prices) | 2,484 | 832 | 1,503 | 62 | 5,357 | 421 | 9,344 | 496 | 9,840 | 1,398 | 14% |
| Total inputs (at purchasers' price) | 1,541 | 454 | 446 | 18 | 3,981 | 313 | 5,968 | | | | |
| Gross Value Added (at basic prices) | 943 | 378 | 1,057 | 44 | 1,376 | 108 | 3,376 | | | | |

Source: Author

consumption at purchasers' prices sums to 1,398, which at basic prices is $832 + 62 + 421 = 1,315$. This implies that net taxes on products paid from tourism amount to $1,398 - 1,315 = 83$ million currency units. Adding this value to the tourism GVA of 530 results in the direct contribution of tourism to GDP of 613 million currency units. It might at first sight seem unusual in Figure 1.4 that net taxes on passenger transport are given a value of zero, for it is well known that governments around the world levy airport taxes on passenger movements (see Chapter 18), but governments also subsidise domestic passenger transport, so in this instance the net effect on that sector is approximately zero. Where there is a marked disparity in the tax positions of inbound and domestic visitors then appropriate adjustments need to be made.

Total GDP in this economy happens to be just under 22 billion currency units, which means that tourism's direct contribution to GDP is about 2.8%. It is in this manner that the WTTC calculates the impact of tourism in the various regions and countries of the world. The total impact is assessed by examining the causal relationships in Table 1.4 to account for the re-spending of money earned from tourism in the local economy by building an economic model to simulate these effects. These aspects are discussed in detail in Chapter 7.

## CONCLUSION

As a human activity modern tourism has experienced unprecedented growth rates since the early 1950s, and its economic importance is something few governments can ignore. But as a field of study it remains relatively new, lacking in the maturity of other subject areas and disciplines. This lack of maturity is manifested in arguments over how tourism should be studied and the appropriate framework to examine tourism demand and supply. Embodied in this are the dynamics of developing new tourism products in response to changing tastes and more diverse interests as society alters its patterns of consumption and value systems. In a practical sense this has led to new definitions and classifications of tourism, and its most recent formal recognition in the establishment of a Tourism Satellite Account, though even here countries have some latitude as to what should be listed as a characteristic tourism product. For those working in our industry the dynamics of change offer both challenges and opportunities in creating new products, for example space tourism, managing the increasing volume of tourism flows, and ensuring that the expansion that this entails is sustainable at both at the global and local level.

## SELF-CHECK QUESTIONS

1. Review the major methods used to classify tourists.
2. Which of the following can be counted as tourists in the official definitions?
   a) military personnel
   b) space shuttle pilots
   c) international conference delegates
   d) travelling diplomats
   e) students
   f) immigrants
3. What is the role of markets in economic activity?
4. Review the major elements of the tourism system – how do they relate to each other?
5. How does a TSA classify tourism products?

# YOUTUBE

**www.youtube.com/watch?v=CV1JtM9fTa4**

Taylor's University Deputy Vice Chancellor, Pradeep Nair, live on 'Hello on Two' talking about the hospitality and tourism industry in the twenty-first century.

**www.youtube.com/watch?v=0gp-nfhWY0E**

Discussion of what tourism is and how is it a part of the islands of Trinidad and Tobago.

**www.youtube.com/watch?v=dsgJYfDpLm4**

Tourism as a system, which features Singapore.

# REFERENCES AND FURTHER READING

Coles, T., Hall, C.M. and Duval, D.T. (2006) 'Tourism and post-disciplinary enquiry', *Current Issues in Tourism* **9**(4–5), 293–319.

Cooper, C., Fletcher, J., Fyall, A., Gilbert, D. and Wanhill, S. (2008) *Tourism Principles and Practice*, 4th edn, Pearson Education, London.

Deegan, J., Kenneally, M., Moloney, R. and Wanhill, S. (2006) 'A comparison of tourism output and employment in Ireland and the UK: some TSA-based results', *Global Business & Economics Anthology*, **1**, December, 445–60.

Dwyer, L., Forsyth, P. and Dwyer, W. (2010) *Tourism Economics and Policy*, Channel View Publications, Bristol. An excellent and very readable textbook that offers a thorough coverage of the different business issues facing the tourism industry.

Franklin, A. and Crang, M. (2001) 'The trouble with tourism and travel theory', *Tourism Studies* **1**(1), 5–22.

Gilbert, D. (1990) 'Conceptual issues in the meaning of tourism', pp. 4–27 in Cooper, C. (ed.), *Progress in Tourism, Recreation and Hospitality Management*, Belhaven Press, London.

Goeldner, C.R. and Ritchie, B. (2006) *Tourism: Principles, Practices, Philosophies*, 10th edn, Wiley, New York.

Jafari, J. (2001) *The Encyclopedia of Tourism*, Routledge, London. A wide-ranging volume with definitive statements on every tourism term, written by the leading expert in each field.

Jafari, J. and Ritchie, J.R.B. (1981) 'Towards a framework for tourism education', *Annals of Tourism Research* **8**(1), 13–34.

Leiper, N. (1979) 'The framework of tourism. Towards a definition of tourism, tourist and the touristic industry', *Annals of Tourism Research* **6**(4), 390–407.

Leiper, N. (1990) 'Tourism systems', Massey University Department of Management Systems Occasional Paper 2, Auckland.

Leiper, N. (2008) 'Why "the tourism industry" is misleading as a generic expression: the case for the plural variation "tourism industries"', *Tourism Management* **29**(2), 237–51.

Meis, S.(1999) 'The Canadian experience in developing and using the tourism satellite account', *Tourism Economics* **5**, (4), 331–44.

Rojek, C. and Urry, J. (1997) *Touring Cultures – Transformations of Travel Theory*, Routledge, London.

Tribe, J. (1997) 'The indiscipline of tourism', *Annals of Tourism Research* **24**(3), 638–57.

Tribe, J. (2006) 'The truth about tourism', *Annals of Tourism Research* **33**(2), 360–81.

UNSD, The Statistical Office of the European Communities (EUROSTAT), Organisation for Economic Co-operation and Development (OECD), and UNWTO (2008) *2008 Tourism Satellite Account: Recommended Methodological Framework* (TSA: RMF 2008), Luxembourg, Madrid, New York, Paris. Available at **http://unstats.un.org/unsd/statcom/doc08/BG-TSA.pdf**

United Nations World Tourism Organization (UNWTO) (2000) *General Guidelines for Developing the Tourism Satellite Account (TSA): Measuring Tourism Demand*, Madrid.

United Nations World Tourism Organization (UNWTO) (2001) *Conclusions of the International Conference on Tourism Satellite Accounts*, Madrid.

UNWTO (2008) *International Recommendations for Tourism Statistics (IRTS)*. Department of Economics and Social Affairs, Statistics Division. Available at **http://unstats.un.org/unsd/ trade/IRTS/IRTS%202008%20unedited.pdf**

WTTC (2011) *Travel and Tourism Economic Impact: World*, World Travel and Tourism Council, London.

## Websites

**http://www.world-tourism.org**

An all-embracing website providing the official United Nations' tourism definitions, statistics and forecasts, as well as policies on tourism issues such as tourism ethics, pro-poor tourism, women in tourism, taxation and many more aspects affecting the industry.

**http://www.wttc.org**

A comprehensive website from the private sector's representative body for tourism with up-to-date statistics and reports on the tourism industry and its economic contribution to different countries of the world.

# PART 1

## TOURISM DEMAND

# INTRODUCTION

This part of the text provides you with a comprehensive introduction to tourism demand. It aims to provide you with five key knowledge areas:

1. The factors affecting tourism demand.
2. The theoretical aspects of tourism demand.
3. Consumer behaviour in tourism.
4. How tourism demand is measured and reported.
5. Tourism demand modelling.
6. Tourism demand forecasting.

This part is organised into four chapters, each covering one or more of the key knowledge areas above. Each chapter explores the area of knowledge in depth and is structured to meet a set of learning outcomes which are provided at the beginning of the chapter. In addition, we identify and annotate selected reading in order to provide an introduction to the substantive literature on measuring and evaluating tourism demand. Various case examples are used to confirm the concepts and theoretical issues examined in the chapters, while self-check questions in each chapter allow you to review and test your understanding of the material.

In the introduction to this text we saw how tourism is defined and discussed Leiper's tourism system as an effective structural framework for tourism, where the operational aspects of Leiper's tourism system from the destination perspective are embodied in the Tourism Satellite Account (TSA). Tourism demand originating from Leiper's generating region is effectively the subject of this section of four chapters. In Chapter 2 – The Nature of Tourism Demand – we introduce the factors affecting tourism demand and show how these may vary according to different stages taking place during a person's life span: on this point we provide a mini case study of the family life cycle and tourism demand, and a major case example on youth tourism. The second theme of the chapter is the exposition of the theoretical aspects of tourism demand to show how the transition is made from individual demand schedules into market demand in preparation for the empirical measurement aspects that are the subject of Chapter 4.

Chapter 3 – Tourism Consumer Behaviour – allows for a fuller understanding of demand by providing the concepts and relationships of the consumer decision-making process in tourism. The subject matter of this chapter provides, first, an understanding of the components of the tourism consumer decision process and, secondly, some of the important models of the process. We show that there is a range of factors that influence travel decisions – factors such as motivation, attitudes, perceptions and images. The chapter provides you with a number of key tourism authors' approaches and covers their ideas and the major literature debates. In addition, a number of the consumer behaviour factors outlined have been drawn together and presented in the form of models of consumer decision making. For tourism, these models have been adapted from more general approaches in the consumer marketing literature. It is important when reading this chapter to question whether these models are purely an academic exercise or if they have a practical use for tourism managers in a changing world. Finally, the chapter draws these threads together in a major case study providing you with the task of applying the concepts learnt to solving a case study of a Japanese ski resort which suffers from low demand.

In Chapter 4 – Measuring and Modelling Tourism Demand – we return to the TSA with the specific intentions of showing how the demand tables are formulated, since these govern the approaches used to measure demand for both international and domestic tourism, and assessing their effectiveness. We go on to consider the variety of ways used for collecting tourism data and discuss the principles of sampling tourism populations, as a prelude to building economic models of tourism demand for understanding visitor behaviour and forecasting. The chapter ends with a major case study that provides a historical perspective of tourism demand by major world regions as defined by the UNWTO.

Chapter 5 – Forecasting Tourism Demand – focuses on the need for and different methods of tourism forecasting. It will be readily appreciated that accurate forecasts in tourism are essential to inform decision making in both governments and the tourism industry. We begin with a general overview and then follow two directions in forecasting practice, namely quantitative and qualitative forecasts, and indicate how they are related. We reinforce this with case examples of good practice. Modern computing power has enabled researchers to develop very sophisticated statistical forecasting techniques, but the methods explained in this chapter are those that can be undertaken with the use of a hand-held calculator or a basic computer spreadsheet. The final section of this chapter deals with simple procedures for evaluating forecasting performance.

## A FORECASTING PRACTITIONER'S VIEW

### By Lindsay W. Turner, Professor of International Trade, Victoria University, Melbourne and Research Consultant PATA

The Pacific Asia Travel Association (PATA) is the oldest travel association in the world with its head strategic office in Bangkok, Thailand. In 2012 the Association is celebrating its 60th anniversary. The PATA is a networking, lobby and research organisation that produces industry-directed research outputs such as impact analyses, city and country trend research and, since 1999, forecasts of tourist arrivals. I undertake the quantitative forecast modelling and the expert opinion stage is assisted by Professor Stephen Witt from Surrey University.

In forecasting tourist arrivals and many other series that display variability, it is not possible to know in advance which statistical method will accurately forecast the series. Additionally, it is not possible to forecast many years ahead accurately, although sometimes this is done regardless of accuracy. Although forecasts can be based upon requiring accuracy, they can have the dual purpose of setting a standard. Competent forecasting can set a benchmark against which the impact of change such as a political, terror or financial crisis can be measured.

For one forecast series it is possible to simply try several models, and determine within sample how accurately a particular model can predict the last section of the sample data. For the PATA forecasts this is not so easy (in terms of cost) because some 2,400 individual series are forecast annually. A system has been created whereby the data is forecast using only time series models first and then independent causal variables are added later to those series where such data is available and potentially will improve accuracy. For series such as 'Other Europe' the forecast remains time series modelling regardless. If the time series forecasts are highly accurate then there is no point moving to an econometric model for PATA because there is no need to explain the causal impact, the industry just wants to know 'how many will arrive' from each source country to the 44 odd Asia Pacific markets including North America.

The forecasts are re-done annually with a three-year forecast horizon and keep overall accuracy below 15% error, expanding on average from 5% in year one to 10% in year two, to 15% in year three. This high accuracy level requires additional processes. The accuracy for each series has been watched for several years and those models that work best were focused upon for particular series. Interestingly, approximately 60% of accuracy is derived from time-series models alone, although often including interventions (dummy variables) while 40% use econometric models yielding higher but not often statistically significantly higher accuracy.

Despite the huge work in quantitative modelling the overall average accuracy relies significantly upon expert opinion. Professor Witt and I spend as much time going over the quantitative forecasts and checking them against opinions from various authorities in national tourism offices as we do in undertaking the modelling. The fact is that somewhere between 25% and 40% of the final overall accuracy depends upon changes made as a result of consultation with knowledgeable professionals in the local markets.

# CHAPTER 2
## THE NATURE OF TOURISM DEMAND

### LEARNING OUTCOMES

In this chapter we focus on the basic concepts and determinants of tourism demand to provide you with:

- the theoretical background to understanding the nature of tourism demand;

- an awareness of the factors affecting tourism demand;

- a comprehension of the purpose of demand schedules and an understanding of how to interpret them; and

- an understanding as to how individual demand translates into market demand.

## INTRODUCTION

In this chapter we introduce the theoretical approaches to tourism demand that underpin its management. There is no doubt that managing tourism demand is one of the challenges for tourism in this century as the volume of tourism continues to grow and the remotest corners of the world are visited. In Leiper's model and in the operational framework of the TSA, demand is the fundamental driver of the tourism system and defines the proportion of businesses in the supplying industries that may be said to be involved in tourism. Thus interpreting the observable phenomenon governing tourism demand is critical to understanding how markets will behave. To this end, it is important to understand the nature of demand in terms of the various components that affect it and how they impinge on the business aspects of tourism and measures to regulate visitors' flows.

## INDIVIDUAL TOURISM DEMAND

The market demand identified within Leiper's tourism system discussed in Chapter 1 is the outcome of activities and decisions made by individuals in the generating region (see Figure 1.3). Knowledge of individual behaviour and how it relates to the market makes it possible to predict future trends for planning and visitor management purposes, and enables suppliers to correctly read the signals given in the marketplace so as to provide the right tourism products. Equally it is important for government policy, for example in terms of taxation or influencing visitors' behaviour. In the latter respect, the perceptions of demand have changed over the years with early pronouncements such as the UN's Universal Declaration of Human Rights encouraging everyone to travel as a 'right', to the present day when the tourist is urged to travel 'responsibly' and to offset his or her carbon emissions generated from air travel, though airlines have found that these voluntary schemes attached to ticket prices have not had much take-up.

To benefit the destination, the UNWTO (1999) has produced a *Global Code of Ethics for Tourism*, which requests visitors to observe the laws, practices and customs in the countries they visit. In other words, if individuals demand tourism they should take responsibility for the environment and host societies at the destination and the hosts have a right to expect this. In tourism development work this is part of what is known as the 'triple bottom-line', namely, taking account of the economic, social and environmental situation at the places where visitors stay. In economic terms this implies guidance to encourage visitors to support local businesses. (These aspects are covered in much greater detail in Part 2 of this text.)

Unlike most other goods and services, consumption of the tourism product by an individual involves purchasing a bundle of goods and services that are consumed at the destination, which is the point of supply. Given this complexity and to be comprehensive, Uysal (1998) has produced a most helpful listing of the major influences on tourism demand that also draws in psychological aspects of motivations, tastes and perceptions, and demographics such as population size, age distribution, gender, education, occupation and family composition/life cycle (Mini Case Study 2.1), under the heading social-psychological factors: this is shown in Table 2.1. The exogenous factors are those outside the individual's control, which Uysal regards as the environment in which tourism transactions take place.

It is to be expected that different subject disciplines (see Figure 1.1) will approach the matter of tourism demand in alternative ways, but in general, for ease of exposition, when looking at demand for the tourism product we will divide the factors influencing demand into motivations on the one hand and determinants on the other. Motivations deal with Uysal's psychological factors as to why people travel and what needs they are trying to satisfy. They are important for the study of consumer behaviour, which is the topic of Chapter 3. Understanding motivational priorities and their role in decision making are necessary for establishing the potential demand

| Table 2.1 | The major influences on tourism demand | |
| --- | --- | --- |
| **Economic factors** | **Social-psychological factors** | **Exogenous factors** |
| Disposable income | Demographic factors | Availability of supply resources |
| GNP per capita income | Motivations | Economic growth and stability |
| Private consumption | Travel preferences | Political and social environment |
| Cost of living (CPI) | Benefits sought | Recession |
| Tourism prices | Images of destinations | Technological advancements |
| Transportation costs | Perceptions of destinations | Accessibility |
| Cost of living in relation to destinations | Awareness of opportunities | Levels of development, infrastructure and superstructure |
| Exchange rate differentials | Cognitive distance | Natural disaster |
| Relative pricing among competing destinations | Attitudes about destinations | Epidemics |
| Promotional expenditures | Amount of leisure time | War, terrorism |
| Marketing effectiveness | Amount of travel time | Social and cultural attractions |
| Physical distance | Paid vacations | Degree of urbanisation |
| | Past experience | Special factors/Olympic Games, mega events |
| | Life span | Barriers and obstacles |
| | Physical capacity, health and wellness | Restrictions, rules and laws |
| | Cultural similarities | |
| | Affiliations | |

*Source*: Adapted from Uysal, 1998

for a new tourism offer and removing barriers to travel at the destination end, for example visa restrictions, perceptions on security and concerns about the tourism infrastructure, particularly accommodation and transport. Security is a major concern but potential visitors frequently do not discriminate between one country and another, thus the 'Arab Spring' which commenced in 2011 had dramatic consequences for visitor numbers to neighbouring countries such as Jordan, with its world class attractions in the rose city of Petra and the Dead Sea, where security was not an issue. (Dealing with these aspects of tourism is the subject of Chapter 12.)

Determinants are factors influencing demand which can be economic, sociological, demographic, political and geographical. The latter has a spatial context, in the sense that distance when expressed in both travel time and cost serves to limit travel from the generating region to the destination, as noted in Leiper's model. As a rule, most destinations find that their near neighbours generate the largest volume of international visitors and this tails off with distance. But, as is well known, if we were to redraw the map of the world based on airfares between countries some very unusual configurations would be the result, since due to different competitive practices in the airline industry the pricing of air tickets does not necessarily correspond to the distance travelled (see Chapter 17). Within countries domestic airfares are often several times more than the equivalent distance when flying internationally.

# MINI CASE STUDY 2.1
## Family life cycle (FLC) and tourism demand

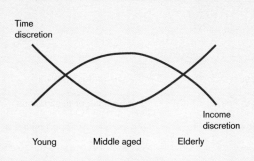

| Figure 2.1 | FLC and changes in demand for the tourism product |

The demographics of the FLC are aspects that are of considerable interest to tourism providers, because not only do the factors listed in Table 2.1 change in importance, but also a person's value systems and tastes are almost certain to change. Figure 2.1 illustrates how two factors – namely available leisure time and discretionary income (income that is available after meeting what may be considered as essential expenses) – may move over an individual's life cycle. Using age as a basis for classification it is possible to draw up different behavioural scenarios.

## YOUNG

When a person is a child, decisions are normally taken for them in terms of holidays. However, children do have a significant influence upon both their parents' decisions and their satisfaction levels at the destination and as a result children are of interest to tourism researchers. For example, owners of theme parks know very well that if the children have a good day out then so will the parents. Resort parks provide evening entertainment for parents combined with child care facilities.

By the age of 10 or 11 years some children have already taken organised holidays with school or youth groups and day trips are common, but typically holidays independent of parents begin at around 15 years, constrained by lack of finance. The latter is compensated by having few other commitments, no shortage of free time, and a curiosity for new places and experiences. By their late teens and early 20s, young people have a high propensity to travel, mainly on budget holidays using low-cost travel and self-catering accommodation. Here the preoccupation is simply to 'get away' – the destination is not always that important, and is often associated with rites of passage such as the American 'Spring Break'. At this stage, sometimes known as the bachelor stage, young single people not living at home have a preoccupation for independence, socialising and a search for identity. In recent years, however, we are seeing more of this group living at home later than before due to longer periods in education and housing costs.

## MIDDLE AGED

The advent of marriage can have a number of options. For example, newly married couples who are young and with no children may have few constraints on travel. Before the arrival of children young couples often have a high income and few other ties, giving them a high travel propensity, frequently overseas. With the raising of a family the combination of factors listed in Table 2.1 are completely reshaped. At this point in an individual's life, previous constraints and influences upon holiday-taking are totally changed as holidays become more organised around the children's needs and less about 'jetting off' to new places. Companies such as Disney utilise

| Photograph 2.1 | At certain stages of the domestic life cycle the needs and demands of children determine the family's holiday decisions.<br>*Source*: Travel Pictures/Alamy Images |
| --- | --- |

this FLC concept to win children as customers at an early age in order to retain them into later life. With the decline in birth rates in the developed world it is important to create hotel, activity and restaurant products that will socialise children to want to take certain types of activity holidays so as to encourage continual demand.

For many, the arrival of children coupled with the responsibility of a home may mean that constraints of time and money depress travel propensity. Holiday preferences switch to domestic destinations, self-catering accommodation, and visiting friends and relatives. This is known as the full nest stage and constraints on travel will depend on the age of the children. The global financial crisis initiated in 2008 exacerbated this situation, introducing the concept of the 'staycation' to the travel trade, focusing on domestic holidays.

As children grow up, reach the young adult stage and begin to travel independently, constraints of time and finance are lifted from parents and their travel propensity increases in what is termed the 'empty nest' phase. This is often linked to lifestyle variables when in married middle age holiday entitlement, income and mobility are often at a maximum and this is reflected in the level of holiday-taking (see Figure 2.1). This is a time for long-haul travel – the cruise market typically comprises this group which extends into older age provided the level of discretionary income is maintained.

## ELDERLY

The emergence of early retirement at 50 or 55 years is creating an active and mobile group in the population of many countries who will demand both domestic and international travel. However, it is too simplistic to view senior travellers as homogeneous and there are many different categories – partly defined by the tension between physical health and financial resources. In later retirement, lack of finance, infirmity and often the loss of a partner act to offset the increase in free time experienced by this group. Holidays become more hotel-based and travel propensity decreases, switching to the domestic market, commonly coaching holidays.

## CONCLUSIONS

The explanatory framework provided by the FLC approach is a powerful one in that it helps us to understand how situation-specific life-stage conditions exert a great influence on tourism demand. It has implications for providers, for the analysis of market needs of particular population groups (for example, the growing numbers of relatively wealthy elderly people in Western countries and the expansion of the cruise industry) and has clearly been used as a basis for market segmentation by tour operators and wholesalers.

The cycle is not just a progression by phase or age but represents likely fluctuations in discretionary income and changes in social responsibilities. The single stage represents an individual living away from home with few responsibilities but with the need for affiliation with others and the likelihood of purchases of leisure and entertainment, personal care items and clothes. It is also useful in explaining many barriers to travel – energy and social ties tend to decline with age, while women with young children demonstrate lower levels of travel. Equally it highlights the importance of discretionary income which may be very limited for the poorer groups in society and hence the need for social provision of holidays for the less well-off, particularly those who have some permanent disability.

*Source*: Updated from Cooper et al., 2008

## DISCUSSION QUESTIONS

1. How may tour operators use the FLC to segment their products?
2. Examine typical holidays at different periods of the FLC.
3. Using the checklist in Table 2.1, consider the barriers to tourism that might be experienced at each stage of the FLC.

## Economic considerations

The economic analysis of tourism demand focuses on factors which affect an individual's willingness to pay and ability to pay. Typically the demand for travel goods and services by a person, say, the $i$th individual may be expressed as:

$$q^i = f^i(P_t, P_1, \ldots \ldots, P_m, y^i, z^i) \tag{2.1}$$

where

$q^i$ = a quantity measure of the individual's tourism demand and is functionally $f^i$ related to the following:

$P_t$ = the price of the tourism product;

$P_1 \ldots \ldots, P_m$ = the prices of alternative goods and services which are making claims on the visitor's budget;

$y^i$ = the person's income;

$z^i$ = sociological and demographic factors that characterise this individual's demand as in Table 2.1. These are taken to change slowly over time.

By holding each of the explanatory factors or variables in equation (2.1) that are not of interest constant, known as the *ceteris paribus* assumption, it is possible to specify the relationship between $q^i$ and its own price, $P_t$. Equation (2.1) thus becomes:

$$q^i = f^i(P_t, \textit{ceteris paribus})$$
$$= f^i(P_t) \tag{2.2}$$

This relationship is illustrated in Figure 2.2, in which *DD* is termed a *demand schedule*, and refers to the quantities of the tourism product that an individual wishes to purchase at different prices at a given point in time. Generally, the form of this relationship between price and quantity purchased is an inverse one, i.e. the higher the price of the product, the lower is the demand; the lower the price, the greater is the demand.

It is normal to characterise the demand schedule in Figure 2.2 by an appropriate measure which expresses the responsiveness of quantity to changes in price. Such a measure is termed

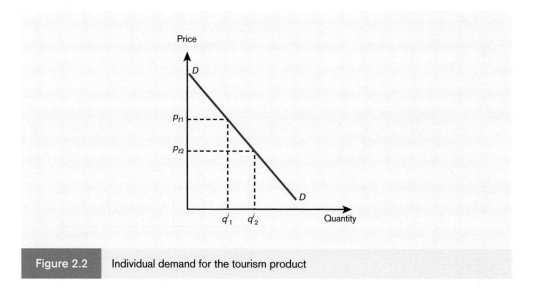

| Figure 2.2 | Individual demand for the tourism product |
|---|---|

the 'elasticity of demand' and in terms of equation (2.2), the own-price elasticity of demand ($e^i$) measures the ratio of the percentage change in quantity ($q^i$) to the percentage change in price ($P_t$), i.e.:

$$e^i = \frac{\% \text{ change in quantity } (q^i)}{\% \text{ change in own price } (P_t)} \tag{2.3}$$

Looking at Figure 2.2 it may be seen that for a movement down the demand schedule, equation (2.3) becomes

$$e^i = \frac{\dfrac{(q_2^i - q_1^i)}{q_1^i}}{\dfrac{(P_{t2} - P_{t1})}{P_{t1}}} \tag{2.4}$$

Since quantity and price move in opposite directions the value of $e^i$ when measured from actual data is negative, but it is conventional to consider $e^i$ in its absolute or positive value; thus we refer to an own price elasticity of demand as 1.0, 2.0, 3.0, etc., and not $-1.0$, $-2.0$ or $-3.0$. The critical value of $e^i$ is 1.0; for goods that have an own-price elasticity greater than 1, demand is said to be elastic. Products exhibiting this property are goods that are normally viewed as luxury items – overseas holidays or dining out. Typically international travel has an own price elasticity of between 1.2 and 1.5, which implies that a 10% fall in price will produce a 12–15% increase in demand. When a good has an own-price elasticity of demand of less than 1 it is classed as a necessity. For necessities, quantity adjustments respond sluggishly to price changes since they are considered essential purchases, as in the case of food, clothing and utilities such as gas, electricity and water. These items attract lower rates of taxation or even subsidy from governments and price rises often become political issues.

If we now repeat the above in a similar manner, but with respect to alternative goods and service competing for the visitor's budget, we have:

$$q^i = f^i(P_1, \ldots \ldots, P_m) \tag{2.5}$$

By examining the relationship between $q^i$ and, say, $P_m$ we are able to derive what are described as cross-price elasticity effects:

$$e_x^i = \frac{\% \text{ change in quantity } (q^i)}{\% \text{ change in } m\text{th price } (P_m)} \tag{2.6}$$

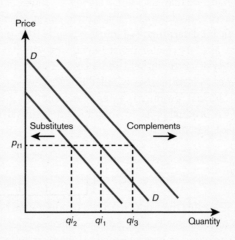

Figure 2.3 depicts a Price–Quantity graph showing demand curves with labels for Substitutes (arrow pointing left) and Complements (arrow pointing right), with $p_{t1}$ on the price axis and $qi_2$, $qi_1$, $qi_3$ on the quantity axis.

| Figure 2.3 | Effects of substitutes and complements on the tourism product |

When the $m$th good or service is a substitute for choosing a tourism trip, then the effect of a reduction in its price is to cause the demand for $q^i$ to fall. In Figure 2.3 this is represented by a shift in the demand schedule to the left as $q_1^i$ falls to $q_2^i$. This implies that $e_x^i$ takes on a positive value. Conversely, if the $m$th good or service is a complement, then a fall in its price will induce the demand for $q^i$ to increase from $q_1^i$ to $q_3^i$, in which case $e_x^i$ is negative in value.

| Photograph 2.2 | Price is a real constraint on demand for tourism, particularly for expensive holidays such as winter sports. |

*Source*: AL RF (John Foxx Images)/Pearson Online Database

Finally, we may also plot $q^i$ against $y^i$, the individual's income. This is most important, because in practice income experiences the greatest variation amongst potential visitors and is the most significant determinant of tourism trends. The graph traced out by this plot is known as an Engel curve, after its creator Ernst Engel, who was the first person to study the relation between the quantity of a product sold and income. His findings that the percentage of income spent on food declines as income rises is called Engel's Law.

A 'normal' product is where consumption increases as income rises: if the converse is true then the product is called 'inferior'. Analogous to equation (2.6) we may define the income elasticity of demand as:

$$e_y^i = \frac{\text{\% change in quantity}\,(q^i)}{\text{\% change in income}\,(y^i)} \tag{2.7}$$

If $e_y^i$ is greater than one, then the product may be considered a 'luxury', and if positive but less than one in value it is regarded as a 'necessity'. When $e_y^i$ is negative the product is considered an 'inferior' good or service, since as income rises less is consumed. Examples of these relationships are shown in Figure 2.4 and empirically holiday travel has revealed itself, as a rule, to be a luxury product.

Typically the average values of $e_y^i$ for overseas holidays from the major tourism generating countries are in the region of $+1.8$ to $+2.0$, thus ensuring that volume will respond more than proportionately for unit changes in income. It appears that despite various bouts of recession in the advanced economies since the development of modern tourism in the 1950s, the volume of pleasure travel has continued to rise. Observers of this phenomenon have explained this as a 'ratchet effect' or 'habit persistence': once people participate in tourism they seem to want more and are loath to put aside their vacation in the face of an economic downturn. Often adjustments are made in terms of the length of trip, the choice of where to stay, and the type of accommodation, as in the recent concept of the 'staycation' arising from the uncertainties generated by the global financial crisis dating from 2008. But in the main, past recessions have not affected the industry to any great extent. This is not to suggest that holiday travel is a necessity, rather that

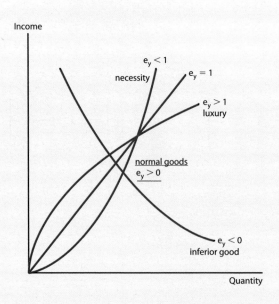

| Figure 2.4 | Effects of income changes on consumption – Engel curves |

once consumers have acquired a taste for it they seem to place it higher on their list of priorities than other luxuries.

## MARKET TOURISM DEMAND

In Chapter 1, for the purpose of constructing the TSA, our concern was with the market for tourism products, not just individuals. Since individual tourists make up the market, it is reasonable to suppose that market demand curves respond in a similar fashion to individual curves, hence a first approach is to sum the individual demand schedules to arrive at the market schedule. This is illustrated in Figure 2.5, which supposes that there are only two individuals in the market. The market demand is derived from the horizontal summation of the two individual schedules. We can see that the market schedule has a distinct 'kink' where the two individual demands join: this arises because the market is assumed to consist of only two persons. As the number in the market increases so any kinks are ironed out and a more or less smooth schedule results. If we designate $p$ as the population of visitors, then summing $q^i$ in equation (2.1) for all visitors, holding income and all other determinants save prices constant, gives the market demand $Q$ as:

$$Q = \sum_{i=1}^{p} q^i = \sum_{i=1}^{p} f^i(P_t, P_1, \ldots \ldots, P_m)$$
$$= F(P_t, P_1, \ldots \ldots, P_m) \tag{2.8}$$

Equation (2.8) tells us that since all individuals broadly face the same set of prices we can model total tourism demand (summed over all visitors, where the Greek sigma $\Sigma$ represents summation) as a function of prices in the marketplace, from which we can calculate own price and cross-price elasticities as in equations (2.4) and (2.6), but this time they are market averages as opposed to individual values.

However, if we now introduce the income variable, sociological and demographic factors from equation (2.1) into equation (2.8) the relationship is not so simple:

$$Q = F(P_t, P_1, \ldots \ldots, P_m, y^1, y^i, y^p, z^1, z^i, z^p) \tag{2.9}$$

Equation (2.9) tells us that to correctly represent a market demand schedule, we need to know the personal circumstances of each individual purchaser of the tourism product and their

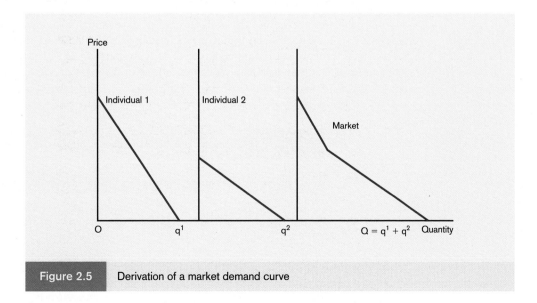

**Figure 2.5**  Derivation of a market demand curve

incomes. This is clearly an impossible task, so in practice in order to estimate market demand approximations have to be made. Looking first at personal circumstances, the $z^i$ factors, we can

- assume that they alter slowly, for example working hours or holidays with pay;
- segment the visitor market into specific groupings in accordance with a range of demographics or social factors (see Chapter 20), such as occupation, age group within the FLC or region of origin;
- use a general variable that gives weight to the most salient characteristic of the visitors we are considering, say, educational attainment.

The most common practice when dealing with the income variable is to replace all individual incomes by their total sum $Y$, so having made any adjustments for personal circumstances, equation (2.9) simplifies to:

$$Q = F(P_t, P_1, \ldots \ldots, P_m, Y) \qquad (2.10)$$

This equation forms the basis of much of the econometric estimation that is discussed in Chapter 4, which looks at measuring visitor demand. There is still however a complication that is implicit in equation (2.10), and this relates to the distribution of income amongst individuals. In any period of time, alterations in the current distribution of income will mean that market demand curves will behave differently to individual ones, invalidating the summation action that gave us equation (2.10). This is known as the aggregation problem and is illustrated in Table 2.2, which lists the demand of two individual visitors with similar tastes. If we let the total income shared between the two visitors amount to no more or less than 3,000 currency units, that is:

$$Y = y^1 + y^2 = 3,000 \qquad (2.11)$$

Suppose in the first instance that both persons have the same income of 1,500, then:

$$Q = q^1 + q^2 = 14 + 14 = 28 \qquad (2.12)$$

Now, let $y^1 = 1,000$ and $y^2 = 2,000$, thus maintaining the income constraint given by equation (2.11). Once again summing visitors' demands yields:

$$Q = q^1 + q^2 = 10 + 16 = 26 \qquad (2.13)$$

Comparing equations (2.12) and (2.13) indicates that for the same aggregate income levels, but different distributions, the level of tourism consumption changes, which is in accordance with reality. This has implications for the discussions on measurement in Chapter 4, in that the doubling of income makes little difference to empirical demand models provided the distribution of income shares do not change much. Evidence supports this notion, but it should by now be apparent through comparing equation (2.9) with equation (2.10) that statistical demand relationships are only approximations or 'caricatures' of the real world.

| Table 2.2 | Demand and the distribution of income |
|---|---|
| **Quantity demanded** | **Income level** |
| $q^1$ and $q^2$ | $y^1$ and $y^2$ |
| 10 | 1,000 |
| 14 | 1,500 |
| 16 | 2,000 |

## CONCLUSION

The generating regions of Leiper's tourism system are influential in shaping the nature and scope of tourism flows around the world. As the tourism industry has developed in volume and importance, the techniques and approaches outlined in this chapter are increasingly applied to evaluating tourism demand. The factors or determinants affecting tourism demand are many and different disciplines consider the subject from a range of viewpoints. Economists discuss demand in terms of models and markets, so as to bring supply and demand together as in Leiper's system. Other fields of study offer a more qualitative appreciation, as in the case of responsible tourism, in other words, visitors exercising their 'right' to travel but doing so in a 'responsible' way. It is thought that this will become increasingly of consequence if the integrity of destinations, societies and the globe itself is to be preserved. Such qualitative considerations help to give context to the available statistical information on tourism, for by understanding the various determinants of demand, it is possible to identify the barriers preventing people from travelling. This is significant, not just from the welfare standpoint of increasing society's access to travel, but also from a commercial point of view in increasing the viability of enterprises. Finally, this chapter has outlined the assumptions that are required to translate the behaviour of individual demand schedules into market demand in preparation for empirical measurement aspects, which are the subject of Chapter 4.

## SELF-CHECK QUESTIONS

1. What do you consider are the top 10 factors affecting tourism demand?
2. Suggest ways in which travel to a destination can be carbon neutral.
3. List some of the reasons why an individual may not participate in tourism.
4. Review the concepts of demand substitutes and complements in respect of a leisure break to a city destination and provide two examples of each.
5. Identify some typical holiday patterns that occur at different stages of the family life cycle.

## YOUTUBE

**http://www.youtube.com/watch?v=dYz-LWR2gGg**

The balance between national and international travel as credit-squeezed holiday makers stay at home.

## REFERENCES AND FURTHER READING

Cooper, C., Fletcher, J., Fyall, A., Gilbert, D. and Wanhill, S. (2008) *Tourism Principles and Practice*, 4th edn, Pearson Education, London.

Dwyer, L., Forsyth, P. and Dwyer, W. (2010) *Tourism Economics and Policy*, Channel View Publications. A comprehensive textbook on tourism economics that gives many examples covering issues on tourism demand.

Jafari, J. (2001) *The Encyclopedia of Tourism*, Routledge, London. A number of entries providing a definitive view of elements of tourism demand, the gravity model and other concepts, written by the leading expert in each field.

United Nations World Tourism Organization (UNWTO) (1999) *Global Code of Ethics for Tourism*, Madrid at **http://www.unwto.org/code_ethics/eng/global.htm**

Uysal, M. (1998) 'The determinants of tourism demand: a theoretical perspective', pp. 79–95, in Ioannides, D. and Debbage, K.G. (eds) *The Economic Geography of the Tourist Industry: A Supply Side Analysis,* Routledge, London.

### Websites

**http://www.tourismconcern.org.uk**

One of the first pressure groups for the responsible consumption of tourism and a comprehensive resource.

**http://www.world-tourism.org**

The UNWTO's site is an excellent source for new initiatives concerning tourism demand and the Global Code of Ethics.

# MAJOR CASE STUDY 2.1
## Young people and tourism

There are 1.7 billion people on Earth today who are 15–30 years old. They busily buzz about the world in massive numbers. They descend on locations and immediately fill the space with intense colour, sound and what could easily be described as a hive of activity. They carry on their backs the wings of their mobility, their backpacks. The sharpness of their minds, words, and texts can be stinging in their often vowel-less expression. And yet their youthful nature can be as sweet as honey. Some destinations tend to (wrongly) view them as pests, overtaking the image and peacefulness of the places they arrive into. Others, visionaries of the global travel and tourism (T&T) world, see these travellers buzzing about like busy bees not as a nuisance, but as a fundamental necessity. Because it is these travellers, youth travellers, who, through their journeys, are pollinating the future of the industry. Without them, there is no hope of our sector blossoming, of the future of T&T growing across the globe.

Still, sadly, the eye can judge based on packaging before the mind understands the value of the contents within. What value can these young people from nations across the globe, typically between the ages of 16 and 29, travelling on their own or with a few mates, often without set itineraries, and carrying their worldly possessions in a small sack snugly positioned on their back for easy transporting whether sitting on a plane, a local bus, a rickshaw or a train, possibly bring to a global sector shaped by the creation of infrastructure, accessibility, investment and promotion? How can the contribution of these young people be of such significance when standing alongside grown-ups?

What value, indeed. What is so often overlooked is that those small backpacks carry deep within them Blackberries, cutting-edge technology and well-fed credit cards that turn these floating travellers of today into formidable shapers of the future of tourism. Their current contribution to global tourism activity is strong, double-digit strong. In 2011, the youth travel segment accounted for a huge 20% of international arrivals. As the global T&T sector as a whole reaches 1 billion travellers in 2012, at current rates of growth and contribution, youth travel is estimated to reach a remarkable 200 million according to the World Youth, Student and Educational travel confederation (WYSE, 2012). In the words of this segment, OMG!

## CREDIT WHERE IT IS DUE

While the numbers are staggering, what is often absent in statistics is the heartbeat of the people that make up the metrics. The global T&T sector takes great pride in the various dimensions of impact that travel has. As all T&T professionals know, it is about so much more than simply measuring arrivals. T&T has become a key that is actively, excitedly and ambitiously being used by nations across the globe to unlock their economies, societies and identities. In so doing, nations are opening their people up to the possibilities of the future.

Youth travel offers a number of other key strategic benefits that align directly to the core mandates of tourism authorities around the globe, including:

- The youth market is a US$136 billion enterprise.
- Spends more than those in other travel sectors.
- Year-round visitation: unconstrained by holiday periods, able to travel during off-peak seasons when more competitive rates and availabilities allow for longer stays.

- Take four times longer travelling to a destination than the average visitor.

- The average young traveller spends US$2,600 per trip.

- They have a higher lifetime value than other travel sectors because the backpackers and students of today are tomorrow's honeymooners, family, business and leisure travellers.

- Increase in length of stay: average length of stay is 53 days.

- Increase in revenues: making a higher level of financial contribution to local enterprises (especially SMEs) as more inclined to eat, sleep and shop at local establishments.

- Are more resilient to economic downturns and are less risk averse than mainstream travellers.

- Are trend-setters and pioneers in exploring tourism frontiers and opening up new markets.

- Communicate their experiences to a wide audience through their use of social media. Vietnam and other Asian markets are examples of areas that developed from the backpacker's market.

- Are leaders in environmental and socially conscious causes.

- Dispersion throughout the destination and region: goes without saying, whether self-guided or on youth travel tourism (i.e. Contiki, one of the world's largest and most successful youth travel companies, that really 'gets it').

- Direct participation of, and contribution to, local communities: mixing visitation, work assignments, volunteering and education.

But the benefits go even further than just the fulfilment of strategic priorities and political mandates. The innate 'insider' quest of a youth traveller turns this segment into a vital force of qualitative growth and development as destinations, and as a sector, as a whole. The youth travel segment, young people from nations across the globe who cross borders to create a borderless community of global citizens sharing experiences, provides an invaluable contribution, not only quantitatively, but also in terms of how it creates and champions emerging trends, as well as responds to emerging issues facing the sector. Not only do these travellers bring their own freshness of spirit, imagination and opportunity to the places they visit and people they connect with (through an increasing number of powerful, pervasive and personal-sharing mediums), they also possess an inner courage and curiosity when it comes to locations of natural, political or social crisis. They want to go see, understand and even help.

For youth travellers, the motivations of travel goes far beyond the quest for sun, sand, sea and stories. At the

**Photograph 2.3**    The volume of young people travelling continues to rise.
*Source*: AISPix by Image Source/Shutterstock.com

heart of youth travel is a wonderfully personal, positively selfish, desire of the traveller to be a more active participant in the world. The travel is about them – their experiences, their learning, their time, their sharing (e- and otherwise). They are travelling with purpose, choosing to put themselves 'out there' to be able to experience the world unvarnished, unpackaged, unedited and unafraid.

For many travel segments, cultural and environmental awareness and appreciation comes implicitly through travel experiences chosen – locations, accommodation, tours, transport methods. The youth travel segment, however, is composed of hundreds of millions of individuals who explicitly seek to learn, to explore, to be immersed, to be involved and to make an impact. And, importantly, these are not travellers interested in simply dabbling in ways of improving the world, they are insisting on being a real part of them. Youth travellers view 'responsible tourism' as a verb, not a noun. To travel the world with only a backpack is an explicit expression of 'I want to be a part of where I am through how I travel, where I eat, where I sleep, who I meet and what stories we share'. A backpack is an overt statement of 'I am open'.

## SAME PLANET, DIFFERENT WORLDS

One of the world's strongest, most passionate advocates of the power of the youth travel segment to global T&T is David Jones, the former Secretary General of the World Youth, Student & Educational Travel Confederation (WYSE). Few international business leaders are able to seemingly reverse-age as they grow wiser in their chosen field of expertise. David has found the source of T&T's fountain of youth. And while no longer WYSE's lead voice, he remains a vital messenger of the power of this often under-estimated, under-credited segment.

Jones is clear in his belief that youth travellers – travellers who distinctly do not wish to be referred to as 'tourists' – provide a compass for future tourism sector growth. 'Understanding the characteristics and trends of the youth market offers an insight on future mainstream market trends. Youth travellers opened many of today's most popular destinations and led the trend to independent travel that has now spread through the industry', Jones said. Importantly, Jones emphasises the need to be careful in classifying all youth travellers as simply back-pack carrying, Internet café visiting, solo adventurers.

'Youth market demand has been driven by the growth of popular international activities. In the 80s &
90s, demand was driven by a massive growth in "backpacking" and in the 90s by the new student working holiday opportunities. The biggest growth sector in youth travel 2000–2010, was voluntary experiences. Acts of community service are increasingly important to young people, and the motivation to do some good in the world created a massive demand for international voluntary experience programmes in the first decade of the 21st century. This is a demand that continues today', Jones added.

It is critical that today's T&T leaders look closely at, and appreciate, the youth travel segment and its evolving areas of interest. It is not simply kind sentiment, it is smart strategy. Jones continued, 'Destinations that work to build and maintain their appeal to the youth market are future proofing their brand for the next generation of travellers. Those destinations that deliver on the interests of the youth market, including the potential for discovery, cultural interaction, heritage exploration, and action, will be the market leading brands now and into the future'.

Yes, today's youth can be intimidating. It can be daunting knowing just how sharp and capable these future leaders of the world are. Even attempting to understand what they understand can be deeply humbling. Any adult trying to figure out how their new mobile phone apps work knows the feeling. Yet it is when the power of youth is harnessed – when we hand over our phones and ask for help – that the possibilities become endless.

In this spirit, the T&T sector needs to embrace the invaluable contribution that youth travel makes to one of the world's fastest growing, and most widely beneficial, economic sectors. Whether they are young, traditional 'Western' (i.e. American, Canadian or European) travellers carrying backpacks, or young Asian travellers carrying Burberry bags, youth travellers are defining the direction of our world on the move. With a billion people travelling the globe, all types of travellers and travel choices are needed to ensure that the power of the tourism economy is leveraged across all segments and regions. T&T needs the guided tours and all-inclusive resorts as much as it needs the business traveller hotels and backpacker lodges. There is no 'right or wrong', no 'best way', no 'more authentic', no 'more valuable'. It is all about shaping the future of the T&T sector through enabling travellers to live out their travel dreams today.

*Source*: Adapted from Anita Mendiratta, CNN Task Group/ETN, Mar 01, 2012, and WYSE Travel Confederation (2012) *Youth and Student Travel Market – Pricing, Industry Review No. 2*, WYSE, London

# CHAPTER 3
## TOURISM CONSUMER BEHAVIOUR

### LEARNING OUTCOMES

This chapter provides an understanding of how different factors and influences, when combined, will generate a consumer's demand for tourism. By reading this chapter you will:

- have a knowledge of the main elements influencing the buyer decision process in tourism;

- have an understanding of the theory of motivation applied to tourism;

- be able to identify the roles and psychographics of tourists and how these are associated with specific forms of tourism and tourist needs; and

- have an awareness of the strengths and weaknesses of the key models that seek to explain the decision-making process for the purchase of tourism products.

Photograph: The Taj Mahal, Agra, India © Tina Cadle-Bowman

# INTRODUCTION

In the previous chapter we outlined basic definitions and concepts of demand and showed how the management of demand has changed in the past 70 years. This chapter examines additional factors of demand by providing an overview of the consumer decision-making process in tourism. The dynamics of group and individual consumer decision processes are an important aspect of all consumption patterns. Demand for tourism at the individual level can be treated as a consumption process that is influenced by a number of factors. These may be a combination of needs, motivation and desires, availability of time and money, images, perceptions and attitude or roles. In this chapter we review the major approaches surrounding these concepts in order to explain how these factors influence individual behaviour in tourism. For tourism, the models utilised have been adapted from more general approaches in the consumer marketing literature. As we will see, this creates some issues in terms of the practical use of these models and their ability to capture the particular nature of the tourism purchasing decision.

## THE INDIVIDUAL DECISION-MAKING PROCESS

At the individual level it is clear that the factors influencing demand for tourism are closely related to models of consumer behaviour. No two individuals are alike and differences in attitudes, perceptions, images and motivation have an important influence on travel decisions. It is important to note that:

- **attitudes** are learned predispositions of response and are related to an individual's perception of the world;
- **perceptions** are mental impressions which help us organise our world based upon many input factors from childhood, family, work experiences, education, books, television programmes and films and promotional images. Perception involves the encoding of information by individuals and has a major influence on attitude and behaviour towards products;
- **travel motivators** explain the dynamics of why people want to travel based upon the inner urges that initiate travel demand as part of need-satisfying goals; and
- **images** are sets of beliefs, ideas and impressions relating to companies, products and destinations.

## THE FUNDAMENTALS OF CONSUMER BEHAVIOUR AND TOURISM

It is important to understand the factors that shape tourism consumer behaviour in order to appreciate the way in which tourism consumers make decisions and act in relation to the consumption of tourism products. While the term 'consumer' would seem to indicate a single concept of demand, the reality is that there is a diversity of psychological, sociological and economic aspects related to consumer behaviour leading to decision making. We need to study the consumer behaviour of tourists to be aware of:

- the needs, purchase motives and decision process associated with the consumption of tourism;
- the influence of the different effects of various promotional tactics, including the Internet;
- the different types of perception of risk for tourism purchases, including the impact of terrorist incidents;
- the different market segments based upon purchase behaviour; and
- how managers can improve their chance of marketing success.

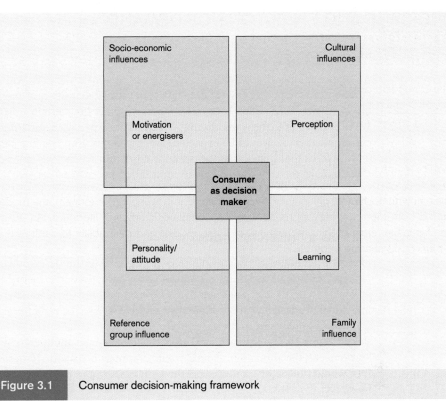

| Figure 3.1 | Consumer decision-making framework |
|---|---|

Many variables will influence the way consumption patterns differ. Patterns will change based upon the different products available and the way individuals have learnt to purchase tourism products. The variations are complex and therefore it is more practical to deal with general behavioural principles. These are often dealt with in a framework that includes the disciplines of psychology, sociology and economics. Figure 3.1 provides a simplification of some of the main influences affecting the consumer as decision maker. These are discussed within this chapter.

It is possible to view the tourism consumer decision process as a system made up of four basic elements which can be found in Figure 3.1:

1. **Energisers of demand.** These are the forces of motivation that lead a tourist to decide to visit an attraction or go on a trip.

2. **Effectors of demand.** The consumer will have developed ideas of a destination, product or organisation by a process of learning, attitudes and associations from promotional messages and information. This will affect the consumer's image and knowledge of a tourism product, thus, serving to heighten or dampen the various energisers that lead to consumer action.

3. **Roles and the decision-making process.** Here, the important role is that of the individual or group/family member as to their involvement in the different stages of the purchase process and the final resolution of decisions about the when, where and how of the overall tourism product.

4. **Determinants of demand.** In addition, the consumer decision-making process for tourism is underpinned by the determinants of demand. Even though motivation may exist, demand is filtered, constrained or channelled due to economic (e.g. discretionary income), sociological (reference groups, cultural values) or psychological (perception of risk, personality, attitudes) factors. We further review the determinants of demand in Chapter 4.

# ENERGISERS AND EFFECTORS OF DEMAND

## Motivation

An understanding of motivation is the key essential to tourist behaviour as it helps answer the question of why people travel. The classic dictionary definition of motivation is derived from the word 'motivate', which is to cause a person to act in a certain way or to stimulate interest. We can also refer to the word 'motive', which is concerned with initiating movement or inducing a person to act. As would be expected, tourism motivation is a key concept as motivation is a driving force that impels and influences a trip and is a starting point of consumer behaviour. If we look at the way tourists satisfy unfulfilled needs then general theories, such as that by Maslow, discussed below, allows us some insight into the levels of demand related to different need states.

## Maslow's hierarchy model

Maslow's hierarchy of needs (Figure 3.2) is probably the best-known theory of motivation, perhaps because of its simplicity and intuitive attraction. The theory of motivation proposed by Maslow (1970) is in the form of a universal ranking, or hierarchy, of the arrangements of individual needs which are in mutually exclusive levels. The early humanistic values of Maslow seem to have led him to create a model where self-actualisation is valued as the level 'man' should aspire to. He argued that if none of the needs in the hierarchy was satisfied, then the lowest needs, the physiological ones, would dominate behaviour. If these were satisfied, however, they would no longer motivate and the individual would be motivated by the next level in the hierarchy.

Maslow identified two motivational types, which can be greatly simplified as:

1. deficiency or tension-reducing motives; and
2. inductive or arousal-seeking motives.

Maslow maintained that his theory of motivation is holistic and dynamic and can be applied to both work and non-work spheres of life. He treats his levels of need as universal and innate, yet of such instinctual weakness that they can be modified, accelerated or inhibited by the environment. He also stated that while all the needs are to some extent innate, only those behaviours that satisfy physiological (biogenic) needs are unlearned and other acquired needs (psychogenic) are developed after birth. Although a great deal of tourism demand theory has been built upon Maslow's approach, there are a number of questions that Maslow does not answer:

- It is not clear from his work why he selected five basic needs or why the needs are ranked as they are.
- The stress of the model is only on satisfaction and not dissatisfaction as the driving force.

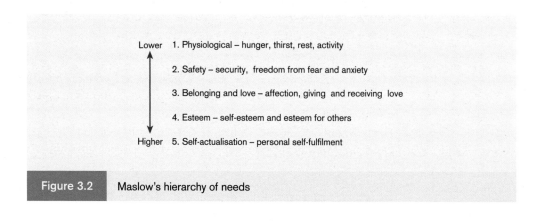

| Figure 3.2 | Maslow's hierarchy of needs |

- How could he justify his model when he did not carry out sufficient research to generalise the model, or provide the measure of what level does satisfaction need to be in order to make the next level of need operative?

- Why did he never try to expand the original set of motives given the needs are simple and generic?

Tourism authors have borrowed extensively from Maslow, simply because he has provided a convenient set of containers that can be relatively easily labelled. The notion that a comprehensive coverage of human needs can be organised into an understandable hierarchical framework is of obvious benefit to tourism theorists.

Within Maslow's model, human activity is wired into predetermined, understandable and predictable aspects of action. This is very much in the behaviourist tradition of psychology as opposed to the cognitive approach, which stresses the concepts of irrationality and unpredictability of behaviour. However, Maslow's theory does allow for humans to transcend the mere embodiment of biological needs that sets them apart from other species.

To some extent the popularity of Maslow's theory can be understood in moral terms. It suggests that, given the right circumstances, people will grow out of their concern for the materialistic aspects of life and become more interested in 'higher' things.

## The study of motivation in tourism

The study of motivation has been derived from a range of social science fields, which has resulted in a diversity of approach in tourism. This diversity is reflected in the approaches of various authors' discussions of how motivation influences tourists' consumer behaviour as outlined below.

### Dann

Dann (1981) has pointed out that there are seven elements within the overall approach to motivation:

1. **Travel as a response to what is lacking yet desired.** This approach suggests that tourists are motivated by the desire to experience phenomena that are different from those available in their home environment.

2. **Destination pull in response to motivational push.** This distinguishes between the motivation of the individual tourist in terms of the level of desire (push) and the pull of the destination or attraction.

3. **Motivation as fantasy.** This is a subset of the first two factors and suggests that tourists travel in order to undertake behaviour that may not be culturally sanctioned in their home setting. The tourist can, as part of this, be freer and more liberated when undertaking the trip.

4. **Motivation as classified purpose.** A broad category which invokes the main purposes of a trip as a motivator for travel. Purposes may include pleasure, novelty or change as part of visiting friends and relatives, enjoying leisure activities, or study.

5. **Motivational typologies.** This approach is internally divided into:

   **a)** behavioural typologies such as the motivators 'sunlust' (search for a better set of amenities than are available at home) and 'wanderlust' (curiosity to experience the strange and unfamiliar) as proposed by Gray (1970); and

   **b)** typologies that focus on dimensions of the tourist role.

6. **Motivation and tourist experiences.** This approach is characterised by interpreting the behaviour of the tourist. It would include how a tourist relates to the authenticity of tourist experiences and how this depends upon beliefs about types of tourist experience.

7. **Motivation as auto-definition and meaning.** Here the emphasis is placed on how tourists judge the host people and define the situation they find. This suggests that the way in which tourists define their situations will provide a greater understanding of tourist motivation than simply observing their behaviour.

Dann suggests that these seven identified approaches demonstrate a 'definitional fuzziness' which, if not clarified, may make it difficult to discover 'whether or not individual tourism researchers are studying the same phenomenon'. Dann utilises a push rather than adding the development of a pull approach, and draws mainly from sociology to develop his concepts, and in doing this has been criticised for not taking a more psychological approach to the understanding behind his concepts.

## McIntosh, Goeldner and Ritchie

McIntosh, Goeldner and Ritchie (1995) utilise four categories of motivation:

1. **Physical motivators:** those related to refreshment of body and mind, health purposes, sport and pleasure. This group of motivators are seen to be linked to those activities which will reduce tension.

2. **Cultural motivators:** those identified by the desire to see and know more about other cultures, to find out about the natives of a country, their lifestyle, music, art, folklore, dance, etc.

3. **Interpersonal motivators:** this group includes a desire to meet new people, visit friends or relatives, and to seek new and different experiences. Travel is an escape from routine relationships with friends or neighbours or the home environment, or it is used for spiritual reasons.

4. **Status and prestige motivators:** these include a desire for continuation of education (i.e. personal development, ego enhancement and sensual indulgence). Such motivators are seen to be concerned with the desire for recognition and attention from others, in order to boost the personal ego. This category also includes personal development in relation to the pursuit of hobbies and education.

## Plog

In 1974, Stanley Plog developed a theory based upon his research related to why a large section of the US population of that time did not fly and how could they be encouraged to fly. This allowed him to classify the US population into a series of interrelated psychographic types. The initial research found that personality types exhibited: (i) territory boundness – where individuals had not travelled often; (ii) generalised anxieties – being insecure; (iii) sense of powerlessness – having little control over one's life. This group led to his definition of the tendency toward pyschocentrism and those who travel less and was characterised as being different to allocentrics, who are venturesome and self-assured.

These types were then described as having a range of two extremes:

1. The 'psychocentric' type is derived from 'psyche' or 'self-centred', where an individual centres thoughts or concerns on the small problem areas of life. These individuals tend to be conservative in their travel patterns, preferring 'safe' destinations and often taking many return trips. For this latter reason, market research in the tour-operating sector labels this group as 'repeaters'.

2. The 'allocentric' type derives from the root 'allo' meaning 'varied in form'. These individuals are adventurous and motivated to travel/discover new destinations. They rarely return to the same place twice, hence their market research label 'wanderers'.

The majority of the population fall in between these extremes in an area which Plog termed 'midcentric'. Plog also found that those who were at the lower end of income scales were more likely to be psychocentric types whereas at the upper income band there was more of a likelihood

| Photograph 3.1 | Tourists now live in a web-enabled world. |
| --- | --- |

*Source*: Corbis RF/Alamy Images

of being allocentric. In a later study it was observed that middle-income groups exhibited only a small positive correlation with psychographic types. This created a problem because there were a number of psychographic types who could not, through income constraint, choose the type of holiday they preferred even if they were motivated towards it; after all, to be a wanderer around the globe can be expensive.

Plog's theory closely associates travel motivation to types of destination and can help in providing reasons for the rise and fall of destinations. Allocentrics, for example, will prefer destinations at the frontier of tourism, unspoilt and undiscovered by the travel trade. Psychocentrics, on the other hand, desire the comfort of a well-developed and 'safe' destination. While this is a useful way of thinking about tourists and destinations, it is more difficult to apply it. For example, tourists will travel with different motivations on different occasions. A second holiday or short-break weekend may be in a nearby psychocentric-type destination, whereas the main holiday may be in an allocentric-type destination.

Smith (1990) tested Plog's model, utilising evidence from seven different countries. He concluded that his own results did not support Plog's original model of an association between personality types and destination preferences. Smith questioned the applicability of the model to countries other than the USA. In answer to Smith, Plog (1990) questioned the validity of Smith's methodology.

As we have shown, the concept of motivation as a major determinant of tourism behaviour is widely used by tourism authors. Yet most authors fail to provide a definitive study or sound scientific basis for their motivation categories, or provide a clear indication of the proportion of tourists who would exhibit one type of motivation rather than another. An exception to this is shown in Figure 3.3. Here motivators were identified by research of a sample based upon a quota sample matched to the British Tourist Authority profile for overseas travel from the UK. The response involved individuals providing evidence of a cluster of motives, each of which is important as a determinant of demand.

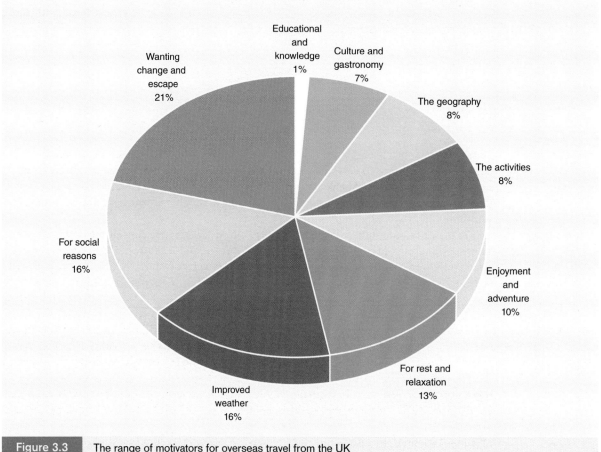

| Figure 3.3 | The range of motivators for overseas travel from the UK |
|---|---|
| | *Source*: Gilbert, 1992 |

## A summary of the concept of motivation

We can see that the dimensions of the concept of motivation in the context of travel are difficult to map. In summary they can be seen to include:

- the idea that travel is initially need-related and that this manifests itself in terms of wants and the strength of motivation or 'push' and 'pull' as the energiser of action;

- motivation is grounded in sociological and psychological aspects of acquired norms, attitudes, culture, perceptions, etc., leading to person-specific forms of motivation; and

- the image of a destination created through various communication channels will influence motivation and subsequently affect the type of travel undertaken.

The motivation literature is still evolving in tourism and there is no doubt that motivation is an essential concept in the explanation of tourist demand. A survey of the literature indicates that most theories are based on the motivation to escape and leave behind something but there are other approaches based upon the seeking of recreational rewards from travel. However, we should remember that while motivation can be stimulated and activated in relation to the 'want' to travel, 'needs' themselves cannot be created. Needs are dependent upon the human element through the psychology and circumstances of the individual. There is also the crucial question of what types of motivation may be innate in us all (curiosity, need for physical contact) and what types are learned because they are judged as valuable or positive (status, achievement). In addition, the situation of the tourist in terms of their own day-to-day lifestyle may motivate toward less or more stimulation based upon whether they have a full life with high levels of well-being or alternatively live in a poor neighbourhood with more pressures on well-being.

# ROLES AND THE DECISION-MAKING PROCESS IN TOURISM

## Tourist typologies

Tourists can be characterised into different typologies or roles which exercise motivation as an energising force linked to personal needs. Utilising this approach, roles can be studied in relation to goal-orientated forms of behaviour or holiday choice activity. Therefore, some appreciation of tourist roles provides us with a deeper understanding of the choice process of different consumer segments.

The majority of authors who have identified tourist roles have concentrated on the assessment of the social and environmental impact of tourism or the nature of the tourist experience. Any definition or interpretation of tourist roles, such as those of motivation, varies according to the analytical framework used by the individual author. The initial ideas of role developed from the work of sociological theorists such as Goffman (1959). He suggested that individuals behave differently in different situations in order to sustain impressions associated with those situations. Just as actors have different front- and backstage performances, participants in any activity vary their behaviour according to the nature and context of that activity. Consequently individual roles can be identified and managed according to social circumstances. Whereas tourists may vary considerably in type and activity, we can recognise a pattern of roles from the literature. Theoretical studies focusing on the sociological aspects of tourism role were developed in the 1970s through the work of Cohen (1972, 1974, 1984), MacCannell (1976) and Smith (1990).

The interaction of personality attributes such as attitude, perceptions and motivation allow different types of tourist role to be identified. One classification by Cohen is particularly useful and this is presented in Figure 3.4. He uses a classification based on the theory that tourism combines the curiosity to seek out new experiences with the need for the security of familiar reminders of home, thus reflecting Plog's ideas. Cohen proposes a continuum of possible combinations of novelty and familiarity. Cohen described the first two roles as institutionalised (organised group/individual mass tourist) and as non-institutionalised (explorers/drifters). Whereas the former is related to the individual's quest for familiarity, the latter is characterised by novelty seeking. By breaking up this continuum into combinations of these two elements, a fourfold classification of tourists is produced.

While destinations may be enjoyed as novel, most tourists prefer to explore them from a familiar base. The degree of familiarity of this base underlies Cohen's typology in which the author identifies four tourist roles: organised mass tourist, individual mass tourist, explorer and drifter (see Figure 3.4). Cohen was interested in classifying groups in order to understand not only demand, but the effects or impact of institutionalised forms of tourism. He found these to be authenticity issues, standardisation of destinations, festivals and the development of facilities. He also identified the impact of non-institutionalised forms of tourism upon the destination, which he found acts as a 'spearhead for mass tourism' as well as having a 'demonstration effect' on the lower socio-economic groups of the host community.

Cohen's typology assists in formulating operational approaches to tourism research and forms a framework for management practice. Although it is not complete and cannot be applied to all tourists at all times, it does afford a way of organising and understanding different types of tourist activity. For example, Elsrud (2001) in studying backpackers and their narratives found that their accounts of adventurous experiences were an attempt to distinguish themselves from conventional mass tourists.

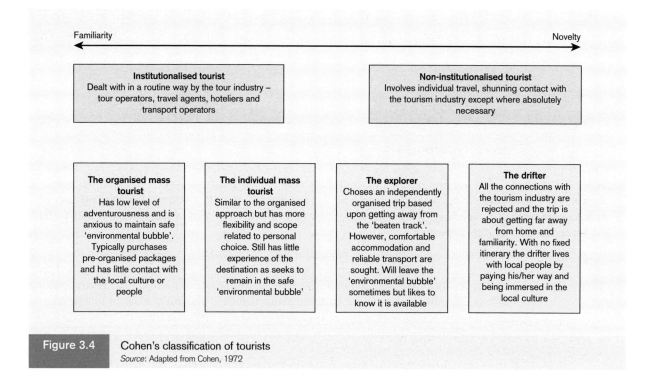

Familiarity ←――――――――――――――――――――――――――――――→ Novelty

**Institutionalised tourist**
Dealt with in a routine way by the tour industry –
tour operators, travel agents, hoteliers and
transport operators

**Non-institutionalised tourist**
Involves individual travel, shunning contact with
the tourism industry except where absolutely
necessary

**The organised mass tourist**
Has low level of adventurousness and is anxious to maintain safe 'environmental bubble'. Typically purchases pre-organised packages and has little contact with the local culture or people

**The individual mass tourist**
Similar to the organised approach but has more flexibility and scope related to personal choice. Still has little experience of the destination as seeks to remain in the safe 'environmental bubble'

**The explorer**
Choses an independently organised trip based upon getting away from the 'beaten track'. However, comfortable accommodation and reliable transport are sought. Will leave the 'environmental bubble' sometimes but likes to know it is available

**The drifter**
All the connections with the tourism industry are rejected and the trip is about getting far away from home and familiarity. With no fixed itinerary the drifter lives with local people by paying his/her way and being immersed in the local culture

**Figure 3.4**    Cohen's classification of tourists
*Source*: Adapted from Cohen, 1972

## Role and family influence

As the fundamental social unit of group formation in society, the influence of a family on tourism demand is extremely important. A family often acts as the purchasing unit which may be supplying the needs of perhaps two or more generations. In addition, it socialises children to adopt particular forms of purchasing and acts as a wider reference group. Given the importance of family behaviour in the purchase of leisure products, we may want to question the preponderance of literature which treats consumer behaviour as an individual model of action. For example, the concept of motivation has been presented as essentially an individual one, yet the idea of 'shared motivators' takes into account that family and friends often influence holiday decisions.

Each member of a family fulfils a special role within the group. He or she may act as husband/father, wife/mother, son/brother and daughter/sister. Family decision making assigns roles to specific members of the family and decision making may be shared, or conducted by one person. One member of the family may be the facilitator, while information may be gathered by another. The family acts as a composite buying unit with the different role patterns leading to particular forms of tourism product purchasing. We can also see the influence of younger family members on travel behaviour and, in particular, the different generations as they mature, as Mini Case Study 3.1 shows.

## The importance of image

An individual's awareness of the world is made up of experiences, learning, emotions and perceptions, or, more accurately, the cognitive evaluation of such experiences, learning, emotions and perceptions. Such awareness can be described as knowledge producing a specific image of the world. This image is critically important to an individual's preference, motivation and behaviour towards tourist products and destinations, as it will provide a 'pull' effect resulting in different demand schedules.

## MINI CASE STUDY 3.1
### Generations X and Y

## INTRODUCTION

Both generations X and Y represent the future of tourism demand for the next 50 years, and yet little in-depth research has been done about their attitudes to travel, or their travel consumer behaviour. Instead, the research has been focused on the current active travel generation – the baby boomers. However, Generation X will soon take their place, with Generation Y following quickly behind (Y generally taken as time for births from 1980 to 2003). For example, the forecast boom in outbound travel from China and India will be led in part by generations X and Y but operators do not understand how they will behave, the intermediaries that they will use, or their tourism product preferences. This case study examines the characteristics of generations X and Y and the implications for tourism behaviour.

## DO GENERATIONS IMPACT UPON CONSUMER BEHAVIOUR?

In terms of tourism consumer behaviour, there are divided opinions as to whether there are generational differences:

- Some support the fact that generations X and Y will have differing travel behaviour from, say, their parents. This is because each generation grows up as a cohort within a particular environmental and social system, where the media, culture and world events shape their behaviour, including tourism demand. Effectively, we can define a generation socially as well as demographically.

- Others, however, argue that generations are too large a group to be helpful in explaining different consumer behaviour. Also, that these groups need to be studied on a cross-national basis because different country cultures will affect behaviour. This is made worse by the fact that with changing social trends people are marrying and having children later in life, extending generational spans: while in the past the traditional definition of a generation as the years between the birth of parents and the birth of their children tended to average around 20 years, it is now nearer 30 years. Within this time span, of course, there will be significant changes in technology and social values. Finally, there are cusp times when generations change from X to Y and therefore the question is, do these cusp groups share a mix of cohort characteristics?

## THE CONSUMER BEHAVIOUR OF GENERATIONS X AND Y

The two generations are very different. Generation Y, for example, are sometimes known as the 'millennial generation', 'connexivity kids' or the 'dot-com generation', suggesting a techno and connected generation. In contrast, Generation X were raised in less secure economic times and tend to be more mobile than the younger generation. They have married and had children later in life than their parents, and are traditional in their family values and behaviour, while careful in their financial management.

**Generation Y** were born into a period dominated by the information age and technology which offers the ability to be permanently connected to friends and peers and to utilise daily social networking. Media via the use of a screen are important to this generation, particularly broadband Internet and television, in terms of reality television and the spontaneous availability of programming. They tire of well-known brands quickly and they enjoy finding adverts in other media, such as the Internet, rather than in the usual press and television placement. For tourism, this means that successful tourism products and destinations must 'connect' with these consumers. It is less important to build products *for* them, than to build products *with* them. One aspect of their life is the emphasis placed upon the reduction of risk and the need for safety as they will have witnessed via the media the reality of the terrorist attacks of 2001 on the World Trade Center twin towers as well as other world crisis events.

**Generation X**, in contrast, are less concerned with the idea of having products built for them and are more interested in being able to afford new authentic experiences. These are preferably in fresh destinations

| Photograph 3.2 | Young people will grow up with a culture based upon their experiences. |
| --- | --- |

*Source*: Greg Balfour Evans/Alamy Images

and will satisfy their curiosity for other countries and cultures in a memorable way. While they are less technologically savvy than Generation Y, they are good at processing and understanding information, and they are catching up with their younger counterparts in their use of the Internet for searching and booking travel. This makes them a challenge for marketers as their demand behaviour demonstrates a lack of brand loyalty – they are more footloose than Generation Y. At the same time their strong family values and financial conservatism means that they seek value for money travel – using low cost carriers for example – and holiday with the family.

Both these generations will be mature, adventurous and active travellers. It is thought: they will travel more often; provide more demand for exploration of new areas and forms of travel; search for more information prior to the trip; mainly use the Internet for all their travel needs. They represent the demand patterns and consumers of the future and their behaviour will be distinctive, driven by technology and underpinned by their considerable formal education levels which make them aware of opportunities, world geography and tourism destinations.

## DISCUSSION QUESTIONS

1. Draft a table summarising 10 characteristics of each generation. How will these characteristics impact upon tourist activity such as that proposed in the Cohen model in Figure 3.4?

2. Make a list of the advantages and disadvantages of taking a generational approach to tourism consumer behaviour.

3. Given their technological orientation, what will the tourism industry need to develop as part of the marketing mix for generations X and Y?

There are various kinds of definition adopted to describe the word 'image' in different fields. For example, the UNWTO defines image as follows:

- the artificial imitation of the apparent form of an object;
- form resemblance, identity (e.g. art and design); and
- ideas, conceptions held individually or collectively of the destination.

Following the work of Gunn (1972), the UNWTO suggests that the tourist image is only one aspect of a destination's general image, with the two being closely interrelated. Nobody is likely to visit a destination for tourism if for one reason or another he or she dislikes it. Conversely, a tourist discovery may lead to knowledge of other aspects of an economic, political or cultural nature of that destination. The UNWTO further adds that the presentation of a **destination image** must allow for the fact that it is generally a matter not of creating an image from nothing but of transforming an existing image.

Echtner and Ritchie (1991) propose that destination images are perceived in terms of both an attribute-based and a holistic component. They indicate a dual aspect of image whereby destination images should be understood in terms of both individual attributes (such as climate and accommodation facilities) and also holistic impressions (mental pictures or imagery of the destination). They reinforce this by stressing that there are functional and psychological characteristics of an image. The functional characteristics refer to directly observable or measurable components such as price levels, attractions and accommodation facilities, whereas the psychological characteristics are intangibles such as friendliness and safety. The psychological impression is described as the atmosphere or mood of the destination.

Echtner and Ritchie further stress that destination images can range from images based on common to unique features whereby the image itself can be more unique if sufficient positive differences to other destinations are present.

Tourist behaviour both of individuals and groups depends upon their image of immediate situations and the world. The notion of image is closely related to behaviour and attitudes. Attitudes and behaviour become established on the basis of a person's derived image and are not easily changed unless new information or experience is gained.

## The holiday image

Mayo (1973) examined regional images and regional travel behaviour. Among other things he indicated that the image of a destination area is a critical factor when choosing a destination. Mayo further concluded that, whether or not an image is in fact a true representation of what any given region has to offer the tourist, what is important is the image that exists in the mind of the vacationer.

The tourist may possess a variety of images in connection with travel. These include the image he or she has formed of the destination, of the term 'holiday' itself, of the mode of transport he or she wishes to utilise, of the tour operator/wholesaler or travel agency and of his or her own self-image. For example, it is probable that the term 'holiday' evokes different images for different people. However, it is likely that similar images of a particular holiday experience are held by people within the same segment of society and who have experienced a similar lifestyle or education.

Gunn (1972) identifies two levels of image. Viewed in terms of a country or destination, the 'organic' image is the sum of all information that has not been deliberately directed by advertising or promotion of a country or destination; this information comes from television coverage, radio reports, geography books, history books, what other people have said about the area, newspapers and magazines or the Internet. An imaginary picture is built up which is the result of all this information. The individual, following from the approaches described in Gestalt psychology, attempts to make sense of it by forming a pattern or a picture of what he or she imagines the area to be like.

The second level of image is the 'induced' image. This is formed by deliberate portrayal and promotion by various organisations involved with tourism.

It is important to distinguish between these two levels since the induced image is controllable while it is more difficult to influence the organic image. Equally, the source of information is a significant influence upon a consumer's perception of its value. We can identify four stages in the development and establishment of a holiday image:

1. The first is a vague, fantasy type of image created from advertising, education and word of mouth and is formed before the subject has thought seriously about taking a holiday. This belief may be that people engage in taking holidays as a desirable activity.

2. The second stage is when a decision is made to take a holiday and then choices must be made regarding time, destination and type of holiday. This is when the holiday image is modified, clarified and extended. On completion of the holiday plans, the anticipatory image is crystallised.

3. The third stage is the holiday experience itself, which modifies, corrects or removes elements of the image that prove to be invalid and reinforces those that are found to be correct.

4. The fourth stage is the after-image, the recollection of the holiday which may induce feelings of nostalgia, regret or fantasy. This is the stage that will mould an individual's holiday concepts and attitudes and will promote a new sequence of holiday images influencing future holiday decisions.

# MODELS OF CONSUMER BEHAVIOUR IN TOURISM

One approach to understanding tourism demand is to identify and evaluate the broader theories and models of consumer behaviour linked to purchasing behaviour. This is not easy given we are faced with a proliferation of research within a subject area that has displayed significant growth and diversity. Perhaps the major utility of these models is to demonstrate the interrelationships of the key factors influencing consumer behaviour in tourism. We also have to understand the particular characteristics of a tourism purchasing decision as opposed to other products, and this includes the implications of tourism as a service activity. We can identify three phases that characterise the development of consumer behaviour theory:

1. **The early empiricist phase** covered the years between 1930 and the late 1940s and was dominated by empirical commercial research. This research was characterised by attempts in industry to identify the effects of distribution, advertising and promotion decisions. The basis for these models came mainly from economic theories relating to the company.

2. **The motivational research phase** in the 1950s was an age where stress was placed on Freudian and drive-related concepts. There was a greater emphasis placed upon in-depth interviews, focus groups, thematic apperception tests and other projective techniques. Activity was directed at uncovering 'real' motives for action which were perceived to lie in the deeper recesses of the consumer's mind. Much of the theory was based around the idea of there being instinctual needs which reside in the 'id' and are governed by the 'ego' which acts to balance unrestrained instincts and social constraints. The 'super ego' in turn was seen to embody values but to limit action on the basis of moral constraint. The major problem was the focus on unconscious needs which are by definition extremely difficult to prove empirically. Furthermore, they do not always translate into effective marketing strategies.

3. **The formative phase** of the 1960s can be seen as the formative years of consumer behaviour modelling. The first general consumer behaviour textbook became available in 1968 (Engel, Kollat and Blackwell) and other influential books such as Howard and Sheth (1969) followed soon after. The Howard–Sheth model of buyer behaviour is perhaps the most influential one, as it identifies the inputs to the consumer's decision-making process. During the formative phase, models of behaviour proved useful as a means of organising disparate knowledge of social action. The major theorists developed 'grand models' of consumer behaviour which have been subsequently utilised or transformed by authors interested in the tourism choice process.

These grand models can be found to share several commonalities:

- They all exhibit consumer behaviour as a decision process. This is integral to the model.
- They provide a comprehensive model focusing mainly on the behaviour of the individual consumer.
- They share the belief that behaviour is rational and hence can, in principle, be explained.
- They view buying behaviour as purposive, with the consumer as an active information seeker, both of information stored internally and of information available in the external environment. Thus, the search and evaluation of information is a key component of the decision process.
- They believe that consumers limit the amount of information taken in, and move over time from general notions to more specific criteria and preference for alternatives.
- All the 'grand models' include a notion of feedback, that is, outcomes from purchases will affect future purchases.
- The models envisage consumer behaviour as multi-stage triggered by the individual's expectation that a product will satisfy their needs.

## THE BUYING DECISION PROCESS IN TOURISM

Figure 3.5 demonstrates that consumer behaviour is normally conceived as a process of stages. As part of this approach the decision to travel is the involvement of some or all of the following stages. The starting point is where a need is recognised and the individual is energised into becoming a potential customer. The stages can be thought of as:

- need arousal;
- recognition of the need – the prerequisite stage;
- level of involvement – amount of time and effort invested in the decision process, e.g. degree of search for information;

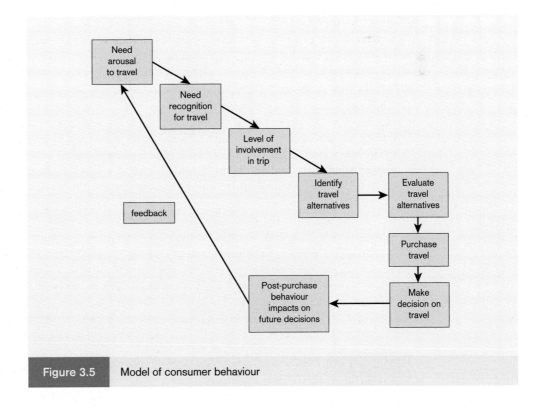

**Figure 3.5**   Model of consumer behaviour

- identification of alternatives – brands that initially come to mind when considering a purchase are referred to as the evoked set. However, friends, shop assistants, merchandise, leaflets, advertisements, etc. may provide a consideration step;
- evaluation of alternatives – comparisons are made of the salient attributes based upon criteria of the potential purchaser;
- decision choice made;
- purchase action; and
- post-purchase behaviour – the feelings and individual experiences after the purchase.

Quite often with important purchases, such as travel, the purchaser will doubt the wisdom of their choice and have a need for reassurance to what is known as dissonance or disequilibrium. This psychological state is reduced by the means of guarantees or telephone helplines to deal with queries. It is also reduced by the 'welcome back' communication made to someone on their return from their trip or experience.

Consumer behaviour models are designed to attempt to provide an overall representation of the consumer behaviour process and to identify the key elements of the process and their inter-relationships. Engel, Blackwell and Miniard (1986) classified models according to the degree of search or problem-solving behaviour by the consumer:

1. **Limited problem-solving models (LPS models)** are applicable to repeat or mundane purchases with a low level of consumer involvement. Apart from short trips near to home these are not applicable to tourism.

2. **Extended problem-solving models (EPS models)** apply to purchases associated with high levels of perceived risk and involvement, and where the information search and evaluation of alternatives plays an important part in the purchasing decision. Models of tourist behaviour fall into this category.

Given the high cost, risk factor and involvement of a tourism purchase, a number of models of consumer behaviour which seek to explain low involvement purchase behaviour are less relevant and therefore not considered here. The following models are all examples of EPS models.

## Wahab, Crampon and Rothfield

One of the first attempts to provide some understanding of tourism purchase behaviour is to be found in the work of Wahab, Crampon and Rothfield (1976). These authors presented the consumer as purposeful and conceptualised his or her buying behaviour in terms of the unique-ness of the buying decision:

- no tangible return on investment;
- considerable expenditure in relation to earned income;
- purchase is not spontaneous or capricious; and
- expenditure involves saving and pre-planning.

They presented a model of the decision-making process based upon the preceding 'grand models' of consumer behaviour and having the stages outlined in Figure 3.6.

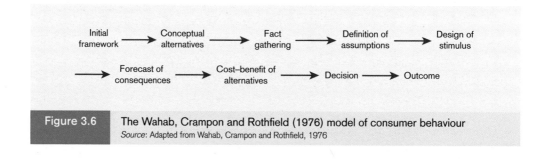

| Figure 3.6 | The Wahab, Crampon and Rothfield (1976) model of consumer behaviour |
| --- | --- |

*Source:* Adapted from Wahab, Crampon and Rothfield, 1976

## Schmoll

Schmoll (1977) argued that creating a model of the travel decision process was not just a theoretical exercise, for its value could be found in its aid to travel decision making. His model was based on the Howard–Sheth (1969) and Nicosia (1966) models of consumer behaviour – see Figure 3.7.

Schmoll's model is built upon motivations, desires, needs and expectations as personal and social determinants of travel behaviour. These are influenced by travel stimuli, the traveller's confidence, destination image, previous experience and cost and time constraints. The model has four fields, each of which exerts some influence over the final decision – according to Schmoll (1977): 'The eventual decision (choice of a destination, travel time, type of accommodation, type of travel arrangements, etc.), is in fact the result of a distinct process involving several successive stages or fields.'

- **Field 1: Travel stimuli.** These comprise external stimuli in the form of promotional communication, personal and trade recommendations.

- **Field 2: Personal and social determinants.** These determine customer goals in the form of travel needs and desires, expectations and the objective and subjective risks thought to be connected with travel.

- **Field 3: External variables.** These involve the prospective traveller's confidence in the service provider, destination image, learnt experience and cost and time constraints.

- **Field 4: Destination characteristics.** These consist of related characteristics of the destination or service that have a bearing on the decision and its outcome.

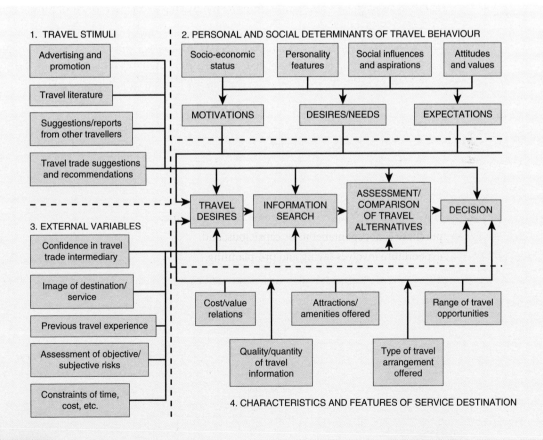

| Figure 3.7 | The Schmoll model |
|---|---|
| | *Source*: Adapted from Schmoll, 1977 |

The model (with the exception of some changes which incorporate the word 'travel' in the headings and the location of previous experience in Field 3) has been borrowed directly from the 'grand models' already discussed. In Schmoll's model there is no feedback loop and no input to attitude and values, and therefore it is difficult for us to regard the model as dynamic. However, Schmoll does highlight many of the attributes of travel decision making which, while not unique in themselves, do influence tourism demand. We can include here decisions regarding choice of a mix of services which make up the product: high financial outlay, destination image, the level of risk and uncertainty, necessity to plan ahead and difficulty of acquiring complete information.

Schmoll, while highlighting some of the characteristics associated with the problem-solving activity of travel, simply reiterates the determinants of cognitive decision-making processes. Within Schmoll's work we are introduced again to the importance of image, which plays a significant part in the demand process.

## Mayo and Jarvis

Mayo and Jarvis (1981) have also borrowed from the grand theorist models. They have taken the basic Howard–Sheth three-level decision-making approach where problem solving is seen as extensive, limited or routinised.

Mayo and Jarvis follow the earlier theories by describing extensive decision making (destination purchase for them) as being characterised as having a perceived need for an information search phase and needing a longer decision-making period. The search for, and evaluation of, information is presented as a main component of the decision-making process whereby the consumer moves from general notions to more specific criteria and preferences for alternatives.

Mayo and Jarvis argue that travel is a special form of consumption behaviour involving an intangible, heterogeneous purchase of an experiential product, yet they then fail to develop an activity-based theory.

## Mathieson and Wall

Mathieson and Wall (1982) offer a five-stage process of travel-buying behaviour (see Figure 3.8). Their framework (as shown in Figure 3.9) is influenced by four interrelated factors:

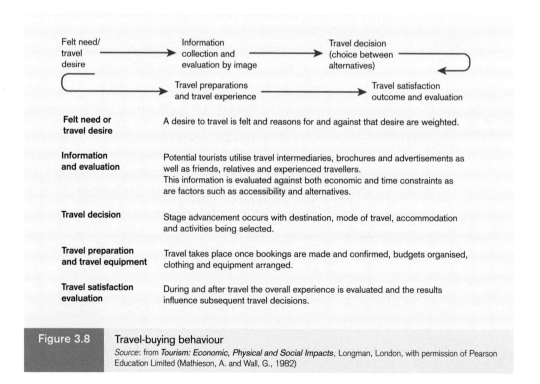

| | |
|---|---|
| **Felt need or travel desire** | A desire to travel is felt and reasons for and against that desire are weighted. |
| **Information and evaluation** | Potential tourists utilise travel intermediaries, brochures and advertisements as well as friends, relatives and experienced travellers. This information is evaluated against both economic and time constraints as are factors such as accessibility and alternatives. |
| **Travel decision** | Stage advancement occurs with destination, mode of travel, accommodation and activities being selected. |
| **Travel preparation and travel equipment** | Travel takes place once bookings are made and confirmed, budgets organised, clothing and equipment arranged. |
| **Travel satisfaction evaluation** | During and after travel the overall experience is evaluated and the results influence subsequent travel decisions. |

Figure 3.8     Travel-buying behaviour

*Source*: from *Tourism: Economic, Physical and Social Impacts*, Longman, London, with permission of Pearson Education Limited (Mathieson, A. and Wall, G., 1982)

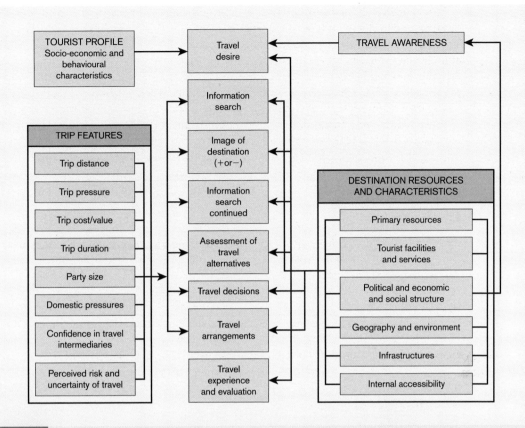

| Figure 3.9 | The Mathieson and Wall model |
| --- | --- |

*Source*: from *Tourism: Economic, Physical and Social Impacts*, Longman, London, with permission of Pearson Education Limited (Mathieson, A. and Wall, G., 1982)

1. Tourist profile (age, education, income attitudes, previous experience and motivations).
2. Travel awareness (image of a destination's facilities and services which are based upon the credibility of the source).
3. Destination resources and characteristics (attractions and features of a destination).
4. Trip features (distance, trip duration and perceived risk of the area visited).

In addition, Mathieson and Wall recognise that a holiday is a service product with the characteristics of intangibility, perishability and heterogeneity, which in one way or another affect the consumer's decision making. However, apart from pointing out that consumption and evaluation will occur simultaneously, the basis of their model relies on the previously reviewed grand models. This is not to say that the model reflects the depth of insight of these models; on the contrary, it only incorporates the idea of the consumer being purposive in actively seeking information and the importance of external factors. The model omits important aspects of perception, memory, personality and information processing, which is the basis of the traditional models. The model they provide focuses more on a product-based perspective rather than that of a consumer behaviourist.

## Woodside and Lysonski

Woodside and Lysonski's (1989) model considers two types of inputs:

1. the marketing inputs of product, promotion, place and price as the key external inputs; and
2. the tourist's internal variables, including experience, socio-demographic variables, lifestyle and values.

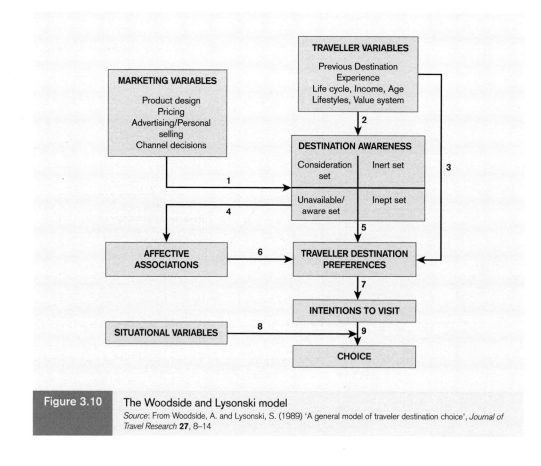

**Figure 3.10** The Woodside and Lysonski model

*Source*: From Woodside, A. and Lysonski, S. (1989) 'A general model of traveler destination choice', *Journal of Travel Research* **27**, 8–14

The model traces the tourist's unfolding awareness of the destination or product from initial awareness to choice and purchase (Figure 3.10). Woodside and Lysonski's contribution lies in factoring into the model the emotions associated with destination or product choice, the fact that tourists may rank the options, and the perceived likelihood of purchase and situational variables such as the environment. Tourists' ranking of options is seen in Figure 3.10. The categories are:

1. Consideration set – destinations or products considered likely to purchase. Woodside and Lysonski suggest this set ranges from three to five options.
2. Unavailable set – destinations or products not considered for purchase. This includes 'inept destinations', rejected on the grounds of, say, lack of relevant attractions.

## Moscardo et al.

Moscardo et al. (1996) have provided a different approach to consumer behaviour by stressing the importance of activity preference as a critical link between the tourist motivation and travel and destination choice. They argue that motives provide travellers with expectations for activities, and destinations are seen as offering these activities. Figure 3.11 demonstrates this approach as an activities model of destination choice. In this model, Moscardo *et al.* have provided a useful applied approach for the use of these models by marketers. They argue that activity-based traveller segments can be linked to destination activities through product development and communication strategies.

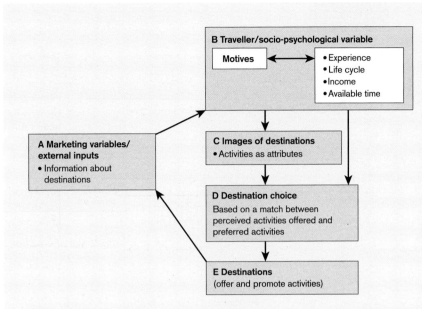

Box A: Contextual or social influence process providing information on the activities available at destinations.
Box B: Travel motives are connected to other socio-demographic variables including life cycle and travel experience.
Box C: How the travel motive groups perceived destinations.
Box D: How the travel motive groups related activity-based images to destination choice.
Box E: Activities available at destinations.

| Figure 3.11 | An activities-based model of destination choice |
|---|---|
| | *Source*: Moscardo et al., 1996 |

## THE WAY FORWARD

Consumer decision-making models have tended to be based on a view that tourist consumer behaviour is rational and sequenced. The generic 'grand models' are also designed for the purchase of tangible goods rather than services, and assume individual rather than group purchase, making them less than ideal to explain tourism behaviour which is often based upon a group or family decision. There is also a danger that these models are too generalised and simplified to explain, first, the richness of tourism behaviour and, secondly, the changed tourism marketplace of the twenty-first century. Decrop (2000) argues that what is needed is an approach that captures both the situational and experiential nature of tourist behaviour, effectively including the complexity of everyday life. In addition we believe that tourism is highly complex given it is based upon many different segments representing different needs and the choice of a whole variety of destinations that can satisfy such needs. This complexity will demand deep and meaningful research into behaviour, utilising methodologies to deliver insights as to how decisions are made and how influences such as current well-being, destination image, attitudes and prior tourist experience may influence behaviour.

| Table 3.1 | Considerations for the consumer purchase stages and the relevant marketing approach | |
|---|---|---|
| **Issues at particular purchase stages** | **Consumer considerations** | **Marketing considerations** |
| **Pre-purchase stage** | How does a consumer decide that he/she needs a travel product? | How are consumer attitudes towards travel products formed and/or changed? For example, why is the mass tourism experience, so popular in the 1970s, now less popular? |
| | What is the level of involvement/commitment on the part of the purchaser of a travel product? | What cues does the consumer use to infer which products are superior to others – a critical piece of information for promotion and positioning of travel products. |
| | What are the best sources of information to learn more about alternative choices, and, given the intangible nature of the travel product, which sources have more authority and influence? | |
| **Purchase stage** | Is acquiring a product a stressful or pleasant experience and does this influence the nature of intermediary used – or indeed whether an intermediary is bypassed? | How do situational factors such as time pressure, family pressure or travel agent displays affect the consumer's purchase decision? |
| | What does the destination and type of holiday arrangement purchased say about the consumer? | |
| **Post-purchase stage** | Does the travel product provide pleasure or perform its intended function? | What determines whether a consumer will be satisfied with the travel experience or whether he/she will buy it again? |
| | How is the travel product consumed and are there environmental or social consequences to the travelling activity? | Does this person tell others about his/her travel experiences and therefore affect their purchase decisions? |

*Source*: Adapted from Swarbrooke and Horner, 1999; Solomon, 1996

## CONCLUSION

Tourism marketing will become more effective if it develops a fuller understanding of what influences the tourist's consumer behaviour. This need has been highlighted following events in 2001 with the realisation that we could not predict travel demand response to shocks to the system. To do this we require an appreciation of the way consumers behave and the way they recognise specific needs for travel, search for and evaluate information, make purchases and then evaluate what has been consumed as part of the tourism experience. This involves the need to understand some of the approaches to how motivation may function, the roles we adopt as tourists and how sociological changes will affect demand.

The understanding of the consumer is enhanced by the incorporation of these different variables into simplified models. Although these need improvement, they act as a guide to current thinking of how tourism demand may function. Nonetheless, these models of consumer behaviour in tourism remain at a relatively early stage of their development and significant levels of research are still required to clarify what are, effectively, subjective psychological influences upon buying processes in tourism. Indeed, they have been criticised on the grounds that they are too theoretical and offer little assistance to the tourism marketer. This said, they do perform a useful role in clarifying our thinking about the tourist decision-making process and in particular help us to understand the interrelationships of a range of complex variables.

## SELF-CHECK QUESTIONS

1. Draft a list of images you have of tourist destinations and thinking of your last experiences of a destination, which aspects of image may have changed from in the past?
2. Consider tourist typologies that predominate at a tourist destination with which you are familiar.
3. Review the process you or your family went through in the purchase decision process for the last holiday you took.
4. What important consumer behaviour factors are similar or different in the choice and purchase of tourism based upon the 20, 40 and 60 year age groups in the population?
5. Consider a tourism product such as a tour operator's brochure – what clues are there to suggest the market targeted by the company?

## YOUTUBE

**http://www.youtube.com/watch?v=L1C1chw1I4U&feature=results_main&playnext=1&list=PL9 4633A6F390BE60E**
The link allows an understanding of tourism demand trends

**http://www.youtube.com/watch?v=VpVw0g5doAo**
A hospitality and generation Y talk, delivered by Ioannis S. Pantelidis, Senior Lecturer of Hospitality at the University of Brighton.

**http://www.youtube.com/watch?v=ugIDVARaTNU**
A quick explanation of how to segment your customer groups for better targeting within your strategic plan.

**http://www.youtube.com/watch?v=WocW6gcLkgw**
Morocco focuses on carving its niche as a tourism destination.

**http://www.youtube.com/watch?v=sWwRsclX44M**
Are there going to be even more unusual tours for young people?

## REFERENCES AND FURTHER READING

Cohen, E. (1972) 'Towards a sociology of international tourism', *Social Research* **39**(1), 164–82.
Cohen, E. (1974) 'Who is a tourist? A conceptual clarification', *Sociological Review* **22**(4), 527–55.
Cohen, E. (1984) 'The sociology of tourism: approaches, issues, findings', *Annual Review of Sociology*, 1984, 373–92.
Dann, G.M.S. (1981) 'Tourist motivation: an appraisal', *Annals of Tourism Research* **8**(2), 187–219.
Decrop, A. (2000) 'Tourists' decision-making and behaviour processes', pp. 103–33, in Pizam, A. and Mansfield, Y. (eds) *Consumer Behaviour in Travel and Tourism*, Haworth, New York.

Decrop, A. (2006) *Vacation Decision Making*, CABI Publishing, Wallingford. A thorough overview of leisure and vacation decision-making processes.

Echtner, C.M. and Ritchie, J.R.B. (1991) 'The meaning and measurement of destination image', *Journal of Tourism Studies*, **2**(2), 2–12.

Elsrud, T. (2001) 'Risk creation in traveling: backpacker adventure narration', *Annals of Tourism Research* **28**, 597–617.

Engel, J.F., Blackwell, R.D. and Miniard, P. (1986) *Consumer Behavior*, Dryden Press, New York.

Engel, J.F., Kollat, D.J. and Blackwell, R.P. (1968) *Consumer Behavior*, Holt, Reinhardt & Winston, New York.

Gilbert, D.C. (1992) A Study of Factors of Consumer Behaviour Related to Overseas Holidays from the UK, Unpublished PhD Thesis, University of Surrey, Guildford.

Goffman, E. (1959) *The Presentation of Self in Everyday Life*, Pelican, London.

Gray, H.P. (1970) *International Travel – International Trade*, Heath Lexington Books, Lexington, KY.

Gunn, C. (1972) *Vacationscape – Designing Tourist Regions*, University of Texas Press, Austin.

Howard, J.A. and Sheth, J.N. (1969) *The Theory of Buyer Behavior*, Wiley, New York.

MacCannell, D. (1976) *The Tourist: A New Theory of the Leisure Class*, Macmillan, London.

Maslow, A.H. (1970) *Motivation and Personality*, 2nd edn, Harper & Row, New York.

Mathieson, A. and Wall, G. (1982) *Tourism: Economic, Physical and Social Impacts*, Longman, London.

Mayo, E. (1973) 'Regional images and regional travel consumer behavior', pp. 211–18, in *TTRA Conference Proceedings*, Idaho.

Mayo, E. and Jarvis, L. (1981) *The Psychology of Leisure Travel*, CBI Publishing, Boston.

McIntosh, R.W., Goeldner, C.R. and Ritchie, J.R.B. (1995) *Tourism Principles, Practices, Philosophies*, Wiley, New York.

Moscardo, G., Morrison, A.M., Pearce, P.L., Lang, C.T. and O'Leary, J. (1996) 'Understanding vacation destination choice through travel motivation and activities', *Journal of Vacation Marketing* **2**(2), 109–22.

Nicosia, F.M. (1966) *Consumer Decision Processes: Marketing and Advertising Implications*, Prentice Hall, Englewood Cliffs, NJ.

Pearce, P. (2005) *Tourist Behaviour: Theories and Conceptual Schemes*, Channel View, Clevedon. An excellent research-based text reviewing the major theories and concepts of tourist behaviour.

Pizam, A. and Mansfield, Y. (eds) (2000) *Consumer Behavior in Travel and Tourism*, Haworth, New York. A useful edited volume covering all the main elements of consumer behaviour.

Plog, S.C. (1974) 'Why destination areas rise and fall in popularity', *Cornell Hotel and Restaurant Quarterly* **14**(4), 55–8.

Plog, S.C. (1990) 'A carpenter's tools: an answer to Stephen L.J. Smith's review of psychocentrism/allocentrism', *Journal of Travel Research* **28**(4), 43–5.

Plog, S.C. (2001) 'Why destinations rise and fall in popularity: an update of a Cornell restaurant quarterly classic', *Cornell Hotel and Restaurant Quarterly* **42**(3), 13–24.

Schmoll, G.A. (1977) *Tourism Promotion*, Tourism International Press, London.

Smith, S.L.J. (1990) 'A test of Plog's allocentric/psychocentric model: evidence from seven nations', *Journal of Travel Research* **28**(4), 40–43.

Solomon M.R. (1996) *Consumer Behavior*, 3rd edn, Prentice Hall, Englewood Cliffs, NJ.

Swarbrooke, J. and Horner, S. (1999) *Consumer Behaviour in Tourism*, Butterworth Heinemann, Oxford.

Wahab, S., Crampon, L.J. and Rothfield, L.M. (1976) *Tourism Marketing*, Tourism International Press, London.

Woodside, A. and Lysonski, S. (1989) 'A general model of traveler destination choice', *Journal of Travel Research*, **27**, 8–14.

# MAJOR CASE STUDY 3.1
## Splendid isolation

## THE JAPANESE ISLAND OF HOKKAIDO GETS HUGE QUANTITIES OF SNOW BUT VERY FEW SKIERS

If Chamonix, Aspen and Whistler are at one end of the ski resort spectrum, then Niseko Weiss is at the opposite extreme. The resort has seen better days. The big restaurant is half in darkness; the posters on the walls show skiing stars from years ago. Through the windows we watch as two workers clear snow from a piste basher, then gesture for us to come out and join them. This is to be our means of transport up the mountain as none of the lifts are working. It isn't a temporary malfunction, and is not connected to March's earthquake and tsunami (Hokkaido was almost unaffected). In fact, the lifts haven't worked for a decade. As we ride up to the top of the mountain, shivering on the back of the piste basher, we pass the broken remains of lift stations: the tangled cables, engines and concrete supports already half-erased by the ever-rising snow. Niseko Weiss is a ghost resort.

## PROBLEM

For the past 30 years, Japan's ski industry has been on something of a roller coaster. In the economic boom years of the 1980s, skiing enjoyed a sudden surge in popularity. Office workers became suki-kichigai, ski crazy, pouring out of the cities by train on Friday nights, skiing all weekend, then rushing back to their desks on Monday morning. A hit 1987 film, *Take Me Skiing*, fanned the flames still further, and skier numbers grew from 8.6 million in 1981 to 17.7 million in 1993. Investment flooded in and between 1980 and 1993, 236 new resorts were created, taking the total to at least 600 – more than any other country in the world.

But just as suddenly as it had arrived, the craze began to pass, helped on its way by recession and the rise of an alternative pastime, the computer game. By the time the Winter Olympics came to Nagano in 1998, many resorts were struggling with dwindling numbers, and some, such as Niseko Weiss, closed their lifts altogether. By 2006, the number of skiers and snowboarders had tumbled to 10.3 million.

It all sounds rather depressing until you remember, entirely selfishly, that empty slopes are the stuff of skiers' dreams. At the top of the hill we climb down from the piste basher, windmill our arms to restore circulation, then clip into our skis. Spread out before us is a private ski resort, covered in more than a metre of fresh, untouched snow. While it may lack the money to repair its lifts, this place has other riches – typically 14 metres of snow falls in this area each winter. Compare that with Val d'Isère in France, which last season managed less than 3 metres. And, on a busy day, Val d'Isère can get more than 10,000 skiers.

We take three glorious runs down the mountain, all for ¥3,500 (£29), starting off on the piste, then switching to routes through snow-laden trees. It is a wonderful way to spend a day but the slopes aren't really steep or extensive enough to hold your attention much longer. Besides, it's time for us to move on to the next stop on our week-long tour of Hokkaido's slopes.

'Middle-aged and retired people still ski but the young Japanese just want to play around with computers', says Mitsuhiko Maeda, director of Kamui Ski Links, a small resort in central Hokkaido. Set up in 1984 by a golf company (hence the strange name), it was taken over by the local government when visitors numbers started to fall. Today it gets 1,500 skiers on a busy day, 300 off peak. 'Young people don't have the money for it any more, and they complain about the cold. The resort isn't in the red but it's certainly hard.'

Most of the other guests have come not to ski but to bathe in the onsen, or hot springs, attached to the hotel. Japan's onsen obsession is long-standing and deeply ingrained, and, unlike skiing, shows no signs of abating. The previous day we had hiked up another volcano, Tokachidake, then skied down to Fuki Age Onsen, a natural hot spring in the woods, surrounded by mounds of snow. We hadn't seen a soul on the mountain all day but at least eight other people were poaching in the steam of the pool. We stripped off layer after layer of ski gear, hung it on branches and hurriedly jumped in.

The largest ski area in central Hokkaido is Furano but even here skiing isn't the number one draw. More tourists come in summer to look at the lavender fields, visit locations used in long-running television series *From the Northern Country*, and eat the town's famous omelette curry in as many restaurants as possible. With agriculture still bigger than tourism, Furano feels like a laid-back rural town rather than a resort. We arrive in time to watch 'Saturday Night Live', a wonderfully homespun show put on by townspeople to welcome tourists. A women's dance class performs a pop routine, then a harpist and a bamboo flute player take to the stage to recite a piece called 'The Delusion of the Plover Bird'. The show ends with a raffle and the excited MC calls out the prizes: 'Two jam packs from our friends at the the Furano jam factory! One entry ticket for the museum of art!' The only downside to Furano is the authorities' extreme nervousness about skiing off-piste. Anyone who wants to leave the marked runs must first register at the police station, and even then it's unclear exactly what is allowed. But Furano's pistes are excellent and it makes a good base for trips to resorts where off-piste is allowed, such as Kamui and Tomamu.

Only one Hokkaido resort has convincingly bucked skiing's downward trend. Niseko, 20 minutes' drive from Niseko Weiss, has managed to replace the falling numbers of Japanese with an influx of foreigners. In 2000, fewer than a thousand foreigners came to Niseko; by 2008, more than 13,000 came here from Australia alone. Today it stands on the brink of a new boom. Investors are pouring money into the resort, hoping to create a destination for the nascent ski market in China, Malaysia and Singapore.

Some are already speaking disparagingly of how it has lost its Japanese identity. Compared to Furano it undoubtedly has, and on busy days there is a feeling,

familiar from resorts such as Verbier or Chamonix, that if you don't get to the powder early, someone else will get there first. Nevertheless, you'd be mad to miss Niseko. The slopes are by far the most extensive in Hokkaido and there are sensational views of Mount Yotei. The lifts run until 9pm and huge floodlights on the mountain mean you can ski deep powder in the trees long after dark.

*Source*: Tom Robbins, *FT*, 25 November 2011

## DISCUSSION QUESTIONS

1. Examine the concepts of consumer behaviour in this chapter and the evidence from the above case and explain why the ski resort is not attracting sufficient numbers of tourists.

2. From a consumer point of view discuss whether the demand can be increased and if so what needs to happen to achieve this.

3. Provide a plan of the tourist segments that need to be targeted in order to achieve longer term success for the ski resort area – You can research articles on skiing.

# CHAPTER 4

## MEASURING AND MODELLING TOURISM DEMAND

### LEARNING OUTCOMES

In this chapter, we review the key issues associated with the measurement of tourism demand and the process of applying the theory of demand discussed in Chapter 2 to the construction of empirical models. Our aim is to provide you with:

- an understanding of TSA demand tables and the reasons why we measure both international and domestic demand for tourism;

- an overview of the main methods used to measure tourism demand and what is measured in respect of tourism activity;

- an appreciation of the difficulties of researching tourism markets and aspects of sampling; and

- modelling tourism demand and estimating elasticity measures.

Photograph: Herstmonceux Castle, East Sussex, UK © Andrew J. Müller

# INTRODUCTION

Following on from previous chapters dealing with tourism concepts, demand analysis and consumer behaviour, we now turn to methods for measuring inbound, outbound and domestic tourism commensurate with the needs of the TSA. In this chapter we begin by taking up the TSA structure introduced in Chapter 1 and critically appraise the measurement of demand for both international and domestic tourism. We treat these separately for convenience, although it is recognised that international and domestic movements may be considered essentially matching activities. We examine the rationale for measuring tourism demand and which statistics are normally compiled. Emphasis is placed on the sampling methods commonly used to gather data by place and process, with an indication of their strengths and weaknesses.

In the last part of this chapter we discuss the measurement and importance of measuring own price elasticity of demand and outline how empirical models of international tourism demand for leisure purposes are derived and estimated. Based on work by Smeral (2004) we illustrate own price and income demand elasticities for a range of countries.

## TOURISM SATELLITE ACCOUNT REQUIREMENTS

In Chapter 1 we based our analysis of tourism supply and demand firmly in the procedures of the TSA. To match Table 1.4, we show a simplified demand side of the tourism economy in Table 4.1, which details the different measures of tourism consumption that are internationally recognised and were defined in Chapter 1. Each column measures all visitors' expenditure by product category, while at their foot volume statistics are recorded by trips and overnights. Trips are not counts of different individuals, but the number of inbound, outbound or domestic movements, so to find out the former one would need to know the average number of trips per person. From the perspective of accommodation establishments it is the number of overnights that is a key measure of performance, which is related to the volume of tourist trips by the average length of stay. On the other hand, from the standpoint of attractions, retail and food and beverage providers it is the volume of trips that is most significant, especially same-day visits as can be seen in the disproportionate amount of trips taken by residents travelling within the country when compared to overnights. The retail expenditure included in Table 4.1 is actual purchases at market prices, so the total of 757 million currency units for TSA 4 is made up of the retail margin of 444 million, as in Table 1.4, which is the value added or output measure, and product purchases for resale of 313 million, which appear as inputs to the retail industry in Table 1.4.

What is clear from Table 4.1 is that measuring the volume and values of international and domestic tourism movements is fundamental to any tourism system, but many statistical collections are incomplete in this respect, notably in gathering information on domestic tourists and day visitors. Conversely, the recording of international tourism has a long history in that governments found it necessary to monitor and attach measures to the movement of people into and out of their countries. This was done for a variety of reasons, many of which have nothing whatsoever to do with tourism, such as security, health and immigration control. The measurement of tourism movements, however, has increasingly been seen as important because of the effects of tourism activity on a country's balance of financial payments arising from international trade and the UN requirement for the reporting of these values.

Table 4.1 demonstrates the typical pattern of a small country in high latitudes where there is an imbalance between inbound tourism consumption (which counts as an export in the balance of payments) and outbound tourism consumption (which counts as an import). The latter is caused by main long holidays being taken in warmer latitudes, as for example the movements from Northern Europe to the Mediterranean in the summer months. Nevertheless, as may be seen from column four, not all expenditure by residents travelling abroad ends up as import payments, particularly when there is a sophisticated local travel trade that packages the trips for residents.

| Table 4.1 | TSA Tables 1–4 Measurements of tourism demand (currency units in millions) | | | | |
|---|---|---|---|---|---|
| Tables 1 to 4 | TSA 1 Inbound tourism consumption | TSA 2 Domestic tourism consumption | | TSA 3 Outbound tourism consumption | TSA 4 Internal tourism consumption |
| Products | Same-day + Tourists = All visitors | By residents travelling only within the country | By residents[a] travelling abroad | By residents[b] travelling abroad | TSA 1 + TSA 2 |
| **A. Specific products** | | | | | |
| **A.1 Characteristic products** | | | | | |
| 1. Accommodation | 69 | 39 | | 323 | 108 |
| 2. Restaurants and similar | 96 | 307 | 12 | 301 | 415 |
| 3. Passenger transport | 36 | 52 | 9 | 471 | 97 |
| 4. Travel, tour and guide services | 15 | 48 | 116 | 31 | 179 |
| 5 & 6. Culture, sport and recreation | 21 | 70 | | 156 | 91 |
| **A.2 Connected products** | | | | | |
| 1. Renting and business services | 6 | 40 | 22 | 39 | 68 |
| **B. Non specific products** | | | | | |
| 1. Retail | 135 | 597 | 25 | 257 | 757 |
| **TOTAL** | 378 | 1,153 | 184 | 1,578 | 1,715 |
| Number of trips (000s) | 2,319 | 31,814 | | 4,623 | 34,133 |
| Number of overnights (000s) | 8,693 | 5,360 | | 21,827 | 14,053 |

*Source*: Author

[a] This refers to those resident visitors whose trip will take them outside the economic territory of the country of reference. These columns will include their consumption expenditure before departure or after their return.

[b] As for (a) but refers to expenditure only incurred outside the economic territory of the country of reference.

After deductions of fares paid to international carriers, which go into the transport account of the balance of payments, the remaining inbound and outbound tourism expenditure in columns two and five are put into what is known as the travel account for the country of reference. A negative travel account means that spending by incoming visitors is less than spending abroad by outgoing visitors, and the combined effect will be to the detriment of the balance of payments. Politically, a negative imbalance is often looked at pejoratively as a measure of the performance of the domestic tourism industry, given the importance attached to foreign exchange earnings, and national tourist administrations are often urged to do better in attracting inbound visitors. Such a view is naïve as the imports and exports of travel services are often strongly differentiated or non-competitive products, say city breaks versus summer sun holidays. What is a more sensible alternative is to evaluate the net foreign exchange yield from inbound tourism, namely earnings less the foreign exchange cost of servicing this tourism. This is known as the tourist propensity to import which can range from more than 50% for small island destinations to 10–15% for major developed countries. This matter is given further consideration in Chapter 7.

While governments are supportive in measuring the movement of international tourism, especially incoming tourism because of its economic benefits and the concomitant need to prepare and evaluate national marketing campaigns (see Part 4), many still do not have effective volume and value measures of domestic tourism. Yet, as Table 4.1 indicates, the volume of tourism by residents travelling only within their country can be many times greater than international tourism. One argument is that it will happen anyway, and another is that they do not achieve prominence because they are not major users of the commercial accommodation industry (domestic tourists often stay with friends and relatives), as column three in Table 4.1 will testify, but knowing the volume and value of domestic tourism has a number of important implications:

- measuring the contribution of tourism to the overall economy;
- regional development policies;
- market intelligence for local businesses;
- additional public sector infrastructure provision, as in the case of seaside resorts, to compensate for influxes of visitors;
- understanding the holiday-taking habits of residents in order to deliver social tourism assistance to the underprivileged in society.

## MEASUREMENT METHODS

The early recording of international travel movements came from the completion of disembarkation and embarkation cards at ports of entry and exit, along with the passenger statistics collected by international carriers. Such complete tallies are known as a census since all movements in and out are counted. Such procedures used at entry and exit points have normally been determined on the basis of administrative control and other reasons not specifically related to tourism. Tourism statistics are thus a by-product of the process rather than its main aim. Nevertheless, there are many countries that do make counts and collect information at frontiers for tourism-related purposes. While these methods are relatively easy to apply in the case of destinations where there are limited points of entry by sea or air, as in the case of islands, they have proved to be unworkable for countries that are either landlocked or have extensive land borders with many roads and rail links passing through them. Traditionally such countries have relied on the registration of hotel nights as a measure of tourism flows, but as noted above not all tourists stay in commercial accommodation, and there is usually a minimum hotel size, say 20 rooms, below which overnights are not collected, so such records are only partial in their coverage. Similarly, earlier approaches to gathering value statistics for inbound and outbound tourism were exercised through foreign exchange controls. Controls allow the central bank to monitor currency movements in and out of the country from various sources.

However, over time agreements on travel movements between countries have seen a reduction in the use of count data methods, save in the case of selected countries where aspects of control for security and immigration are deemed important. Equally, restrictions on currency movements have been increasingly relaxed, so that foreign exchange statistics are no longer a reliable indicator of the value of international tourism. In view of this it is becoming more common to collect information directly from the visitors themselves, through surveying a sample (as opposed to a census) of the relevant population by asking visitors:

- who they are;
- what they do at the destination;
- what they think about the places they visit; and
- how much they spend.

By this means tourism authorities are able to establish detailed profiles of their visitors for market intelligence purposes. Smith (1996) has provided a helpful checklist, albeit with a North American approach, of the kinds of information that can be asked for on a sample survey questionnaire, depending upon the objectives, type, cost and time available for the survey, matters which are considered in the next section.

| Table 4.2 | Checklist of relevant information to be collected through tourism surveys |
|---|---|

| | Levels of measurement |
|---|---|
| **Socio-economic variable** | |
| 1  Age | Collect by single years. It may be convenient to summarise by age cohorts. |
| 2  Sex | Male/female. Age–sex cohorts may also be useful. |
| 3  Education | Given the diversity of educational systems in North America, a basic four-part classification may be most useful: elementary, secondary, post-secondary, non-university and university. It may be useful in other circumstances to distinguish between completion of secondary or post-secondary programmes and partial work (drop-out before completion). |
| 4  Occupational status | Categories can include employed full-time, employed part-time, retired (some reference to former occupation may be desired), homemaker, student, unemployed. If employed, refer the respondent to the next question, 'occupation'. |
| 5  Occupation | This is best determined through an open-ended question. Responses can be summarised according to the *Occupation Classification Manual* or other comparable national statistical coding system such as the *Canadian Classification and Dictionary of Occupations*. These codes refer to the type of industry in which the traveller is employed. |
| 6  Annual income | This is an especially sensitive subject; some of the concern over reporting income can be reduced by using income categories. The specific categories should be based on those used in the most recent national census. Household income is often the most relevant measure of income, although the respondent's income may be useful in special circumstances. |
| 7  Family composition | This can be an especially important variable if the purpose of study includes some analysis of the effect of travel party composition on travel behaviour. One possible classification is:<br>Single individual living alone<br>Husband–wife family<br>No children under 18 years<br>No children at home or no children at all<br>Adult children or other adult relatives living at home<br>With children under 18 years<br>With no other adult relatives<br>With other relatives<br>Single-parent families<br>Male head<br>Female head<br>All other families |
| 8  Party composition | This is closely related to the previous variable for many travelling parties. Levels include:<br>One person alone<br>One family with children<br>Two families with children<br>Organised group<br>One couple<br>Two or more couples<br>Group of friends (unorganised group)<br>Other |

| Table 4.2 | *(Continued)* |
| --- | --- |

| | Levels of measurement |
| --- | --- |
| **Trip variable** | |
| 1 Season or trip period | Calendar quarters:<br>    January to March<br>    April to June<br>    July to September<br>    October to December<br>If the trip overlaps two or more quarters, the following convention is often used: for household surveys, use the quarter in which the trip ends; for exits or re-entry surveys, use the date of the survey.<br>It is sometimes desirable to distinguish weekend trips from other trips. |
| 2 Trip duration | Both days and nights are used as the unit of measurement. The number of nights is usually one less than the number of days; a three-day weekend lasts 'two nights'. The actual number of days or nights up to one week is often collected. Periods longer than one week are often measured as ranges, e.g. 8–15 days (or 7–13 nights). |
| 3 Trip distance | This should be based, in part, on the threshold distance required for definition of a trip. Narrow ranges for lowest levels are desirable to permit aggregating or exclusion of data so that comparisons can be made between surveys using different distance thresholds. A possible classification would be:<br>    25–49 miles<br>    50–99 miles<br>    100–499 miles<br>    500–999 miles<br>    1000–1499 miles<br>    More than 1500 miles (2400 km)<br>Metric conversion is usually necessary for international comparisons; however, international travel is normally not measured by distance. |
| 4 Purpose of trip | Very simple classifications are used, such as business versus pleasure. This dichotomy is normally inadequate for analytical purposes and is too simplistic to represent the purposes of many trips. More precise classifications would include:<br>    Conventions or other business meetings<br>    Buying, selling, installation or other business<br>    Recreation/vacation<br>    Touring/sightseeing<br>    Attending cultural/sporting events<br>    Participating in cultural/sporting events<br>    Visiting friends or relatives<br>    Other family or personal matters<br>    Shopping<br>    Study tour<br>    Health/rest<br>Many trips involve more than one purpose, so it may be useful to specify 'primary' purpose. |
| 5 Mode of transportation | Private automobile<br>Rental automobile<br>Bus/motor coach<br>Train |

| Table 4.2 | (Continued) |
|---|---|

| | | Levels of measurement |
|---|---|---|
| **Trip variable** | | |
| | | Scheduled airline<br>Chartered airline<br>Private aeroplane<br>Boat/ship (additional categories for ferries, cruise ships, private boats may be added as necessary)<br>Some trips involve multiple modes, such as a combination of scheduled airline and rental car. These combinations may be specified or a primary mode may be requested. |
| 6 | Expenditures | Transportation (broken down by mode, if desired)<br>Accommodation (including camping fees, but not park entrance fees)<br>Food and beverages (restaurant meals may be separated from food purchased at a store)<br>Convention or registration fees<br>Admission fees and other entertainment, including park admissions, licence fees for hunting and fishing<br>Souvenirs<br>Other purchases |
| 7 | Type of accommodation | Hotels and inns<br>Motels and motor inns<br>Resorts<br>Campgrounds<br>Hostels<br>Commercial cottages<br>Institutional camps<br>Private cottages<br>Bed and breakfast/tourist home<br>Homes of friends or relatives<br>Other<br>Additional classifications could be based on size of accommodation, price, public versus private ownership, function (e.g. fishing camp, ski resort), type of location (e.g. airport strip; downtown), availability of liquor and so on. |

*Source*: Tourism Research Planning Committee, 1975; and from *Tourism Analysis: A Handbook*, Harlow, Longman with permission of Pearson Education Limited (Smith, 1989)

## Sample surveys

At one time it was thought that the only way to guarantee accurate information about the population we are interested in was to conduct a census. This might be relatively easy when the reference population is relatively small, say a group of hotels, but with large tourism flows at a national level this would be both time-consuming and very costly, with reporting often some years after the data collection due to the time taken for processing the raw data into useable information. Moreover, with a population that is itself changing in response to events, it may never stay stationary long enough to allow for complete measurement of its characteristics.

Fortunately for researchers the statistical theory of sampling permits inferences to be drawn about a population that are representative of its characteristics by randomly drawing a subset or sample of the population to interview. Randomness in statistics does not mean haphazard, but rather that every member of the populace has an equal chance of being selected. In this way, as the mathematics assures us, the sample will mirror the population from which it is taken. However, the estimates obtained from the sample will be subject to error, the amount of which will depend upon the variation in the characteristics being observed and the size of the sample taken. The latter is inversely related to the amount of variation in the population being considered: fewer interviews need to be undertaken when dealing with a very similar population. The degree of sampling error may be calculated to give confidence limits within which the true values may be said to lie. For example, the UK International Passenger Survey records the number of visitors to the UK with a sampling error of around plus or minus 3% of the true value.

In any sampling procedure there is always a trade-off between sample size, method and cost. Strict random sampling is a costly method but has the benefits that the sample should be unbiased, permits the calculation of confidence limits for the true values and provides sample weights for grossing up to total values. Thus if, say, one in every 50 of the population is sampled using a counting system after a random start, then multiplying the results of the sample survey by 50 will give the estimate for the whole population.

Where prior information about the population is available and the need is to profile certain types of visitors, then it is common in market research to use what are described as 'convenience' sampling techniques. These are non-random methods and are undertaken to reduce survey expense, of which the most frequently used is 'quota' sampling. The researcher is given a target or quota of people to select, say young travellers, who will be directly approached rather than go through a strict counting system. The latter would result in considerable redundancy as the person selected at random may not be a young traveller. The principal disadvantage of convenience sampling is that the statistical mathematics for estimating confidence limits no longer apply, though if the quota method is well controlled, researchers still make these calculations as an approximation. The other issue to guard against is selection bias: this introduces a systematic error into the results which cannot be eliminated no matter how large the sample.

It should now be clear that with random sampling from a given population, the greater the size of the sample the smaller will be the sampling error applied to estimate values, and the narrower the range of confidence limits within which the true value may be said to lie. Yet the mathematics of sampling yield a further complication in that raising sample size and reducing sampling error are not directly proportional. Changing the sample size by a factor of, say, $n$ leads to a change in confidence limits by a factor $\frac{1}{\sqrt{n}}$. Thus the reduction in the width of confidence limits by one-half would require a fourfold increase in the sample size. This is fundamental to the costs of obtaining a representative sample of visitors through random selection and no amount of ingenuity is able to get around this.

# SAMPLING BY PLACE

## Frontier surveys

These are undertaken at points of entry and exit, normally by personal interview after the traveller has passed through border controls. Given that locations are known, the sample is stratified by airports, seaports and land routes, though, as noted earlier, for landlocked countries with open borders frontier surveys have not proved to be cost-efficient ways of collecting visitor information. By stratifying the sample according to transport mode of entry, the design effect is to reduce sampling error. However, it is common not to sample all points of entry and departure at any one time. While countries need to include their main airports, seaports and land routes (if possible) in the sample with certainty, the remainder are often grouped into clusters from which a few will be randomly drawn for sampling. The assumption is that one or two regional airports, for example, will be representative of similar facilities. The design effect of clustering is to increase the sampling error, so it will be appreciated that calculating confidence limits for such large-scale surveys is complex. Once the sample is in the appropriate weighting, factors are applied to yield gross totals. These can then be checked against the recorded passenger statistics of transport carriers for accuracy.

For frontier surveys time is of the essence, so the questionnaire is usually fairly brief, asking travellers their country of residence and nationality (for migration statistics), purpose of visit, length of stay, places where they stayed (which provides the regional spread of visitors) and how much in total they spent in the country. This usually takes less than five minutes, but more detailed information (most common being expenditure patterns and the different accommodation used) can be obtained if researchers are given permission to interview passengers while they are waiting in airline or seaport lounges.

## Household surveys

Most governments carry out a census of their population, normally every 10 years, to identify the demographics and socio-economic characteristics of their people. A census form is delivered to every household by an enumerator and completion is mandatory. In between times government statistical offices run general household sample surveys to monitor economic and social trends, and the section on consumption patterns in the questionnaire is likely to include questions on tourism activity. The sampling procedure for such surveys is one of stratifying the country into known administrative areas, say by postcode or election districts, so that the sample population is known, and then allocating the sample size in proportion to the population in each strata before making random drawings of households. However, it may still be too costly to interview a sample of households scattered across a wide area such as a city, so the final selection may be made after first dividing the city into clusters. A random choice of clusters is then taken from which the appropriate sample of households is drawn. Dedicated domestic tourism or national travel surveys, as discussed in Mini Case Study 4.1, follow the same method. Such surveys can be used to provide information on both domestic and national tourism, in the latter case by including questions on foreign trips, and also information on those who have not taken any tourism-related trip.

## MINI CASE STUDY 4.1
The United Kingdom Tourism survey

## INTRODUCTION

While inbound and outbound visitor flows into the UK are collected officially by the Office of National Statistics (ONS) through the International Passenger Survey (IPS) as part of border controls, the measurement of domestic tourism by volume and value was left to the national tourist boards of England, Northern Ireland, Scotland and Wales. Prior to 1989, in view of its separate location, Northern Ireland gathered in its own statistics on tourism, while the remaining tourist boards joined forces to finance the British Tourism Survey Monthly (BTSM). Given that dedicated randomly drawn sample surveys conducted by personal interview are very costly, the tourism authorities decided to buy questions on a commercially available household consumer omnibus survey so as to economise on the budget.

Yet while the BTSM and its annual publication the British Home Tourism Survey (BHTS) gave tolerably accurate estimates in terms of sampling errors for all Britain and England, the results were not sufficient for Scotland and Wales where tourism was becoming an increasingly significant part of each nation's economy. Thus in 1989 all four tourist boards came together again with the formation of the United Kingdom Tourism Survey (UKTS), using the same procedure as before, but with a far larger sample size of over 70,000, so as to give greater confidence in the results and permit more detailed coverage of the activities of domestic tourists.

## THE UNITED KINGDOM TOURISM SURVEY

The UKTS covers trips away from home lasting one night or more taken by UK residents for the purpose of holidays, visits to friends and relatives, business and conferences or any other purpose. Tourism is measured in terms of volume (trips taken, nights away) and value (expenditure on trips) and collects the following key information:

- purpose of trip;
- number of nights away;
- accommodation used;
- transport used;
- activities undertaken;
- type of location;
- month trip started;
- booking method;
- demographics (age, gender etc.).

## METHOD

The UKTS is an example of how survey methodology changes to address both financial and technological change, but not necessarily for the better. The survey method for the 10 years from 1989 to 1999 was an in-home personal interview. Each month, continuously, interviews were conducted face to face in the homes of a fresh representative sample of UK adults aged 16 or more. The sampling frame used was the UK's electoral register, leading to named persons for interview who were asked about tourism trips within the last two months. Up to four recalls were made at different times and on different days of the week: no substitutes were used in the sample, since this would lead to selection bias. This method garnered in some 20,000–25,000 completed trips, which illustrates the considerable redundancy in random sampling. But the survey was able to produce confidence limits of about 2% for England, just under 6% for Scotland and Wales and 12% for Northern Ireland.

Between 2000 and 2004 the method changed to landline telephone interviewing and the sample was reduced to 50,000 adults. The sampling was achieved through random digital dialling with the interviewing spread evenly throughout the year. Unfortunately such a sampling frame is incomplete due to households registering not to receive commercial calls and those not having a landline, some relying on mobile phones. Furthermore, the response rate was affected by the survey length and fell to around 30%, with non-response being connected to the characteristics of the person sampled. Changing the sampling methodology will alter the results, but by 2004 it became clear that the estimates did not conform to supply-side indicators from the tourism industry and were systematically biased downwards, so this method was abandoned.

As a result of this experience, the previous methodology was reinstated in 2005, more than doubling the sample size and cutting trip recall to one month. However, this is at the cost of being able to compare year-on-year trends as the change in methodology has meant that the current results are not comparable to previous years. In 2011 the UKTS became the GBTS as Northern Ireland decided to collect its own data about trips taken by its residents.

To conclude, a final word of caution is in order. While a national survey of this kind will record trips to every part of the country, it is unrealistic to expect it to produce robust statistics for areas smaller than the regions of the UK, in view of the mathematics of sampling error. For regions the confidence limits are about 10% on average, while for less frequented localities they can be as much as 40%. As a point of reference, domestic tourism to London estimated from the UKTS has a confidence limit of plus or minus just under 8%.

*Source*: Adapted from *The UK Tourist*, published jointly by the national tourist boards of England, Northern Ireland, Scotland and Wales.

## DISCUSSION QUESTIONS

1. Trip recall is a critical element of this type of survey – see if you can remember tourism trips in the last three months in sufficient detail to answer the checklist of questions asked by the UKTS above.

2. Examine ways by which domestic tourism statistics may be best disseminated and may be used in support of local destinations.

3. Consider the differences between personal and telephone interviewing.

### En route surveys

En route surveys are surveys of travellers during the course of their journey once in the destination country. Strategic points are selected on key transport routes to stop or approach people, who are then either interviewed or given a questionnaire or other documentation to complete in their own time for return by post. A major problem with this type of survey is how representative the sample might be because of incomplete knowledge of traffic movements within a country.

### Destination surveys

Surveys are often conducted at popular tourist destinations or in areas where there are high levels of tourist activity. They typically take the form of personal interviews by teams of interviewers. It is difficult to construct with confidence a representative sample of visitors at a tourism destination because visitors are often dispersed over a large area. The golden rule is to spread the sample out as much as possible, hence it is conventional to sample proportionately to the seasonal nature of demand time of year, notably in peak months, and to conduct interviews at a wide range of sites which visitors are likely to frequent, namely attractions and places of interest, accommodation establishments, shopping centres, transport termini and similar.

### Surveys of suppliers

One of the issues with demand surveys is their timeliness, in that acquiring, processing and publishing such extensive volumes of information involves a considerable effort, even with modern technologies, so that the results may not appear until a half-year or more has passed. For business users of these statistics this is often too late, although authorities try to counter this by producing rolling monthly and quarterly statistics. Surveys of the suppliers of tourism services are much more immediate and, although partial in coverage, they can be used as indicators to monitor trends. There is a range of indicators for which regular collection from a statistically determined sample of businesses is impracticable but can be collected from panels of businesses organised by tourist boards. Evidence on short-term trends in such indicators is beneficial for marketing and for monitoring the impact of any sudden shocks to the tourism system. International passenger movements are readily available from aviation authorities, while at the destination indicators may include:

- accommodation occupancy data;
- business confidence surveys;
- attendance at visitor attractions;
- state of the market indicators such as average revenue achieved per available room, average cheque for restaurants and achieved gate prices for attractions;
- key performance indicators collected from best practice forums.

# ADMINISTERING THE SAMPLE

The most common ways in which a sample survey is administered are through personal or telephone interview, a self-completion questionnaire sent by post, via the Internet, a mobile phone app or completed at sampling points at the destination or during the return journey, as in the case of business surveys by holiday companies. The choice as to which to use depends on the nature of the research concerned, the available budget, the need to ensure randomness in selection and the completeness of the sampling frame as in the case of Internet use. As noted in the mini case study, there is no doubt that using trained interviewers to collect survey data is the best recommendation when dealing with lengthy and often complex questionnaires. Interviewer presence is essential in qualitative market research studies to obtain insight and understanding into consumers' perceptions, awareness and motivations in 'focus' group studies, where between six and ten people, chosen to be representative of the target market, are led into open discussion of their preferences. Equally, in-depth interviews or discussions with managers of tourism enterprises can be very helpful in profiling the different characteristics of visitors from key tourism generating countries coming to a destination.

| Photograph 4.1 | In drafting a survey questionnaire before piloting it, it is beneficial to take in colleagues' views. |
| --- | --- |
| | *Source*: Ace Stock Ltd/Alamy Images |

Telephone interviewing has become increasingly popular because it is low cost and the response rate is likely to be good if the interview is kept short and the questions uncomplicated. On the other hand, people are becoming somewhat fatigued by 'cold' calls, particularly when the 'end game' of the interview is about selling. Non-response bias (hanging up) is a difficulty, as noted in Mini Case Study 4.1, and this also applies to self-completion questionnaires. For the latter, using the postal system enables the researcher to reach the majority of people or businesses within a country and delivery of the survey form may be followed up with telephone interviews to ensure completion, and personal visits to a sample of non-respondents to ensure that their lack of response is not related to the contents of the questionnaire.

Technological development has given rise to the regular use of Internet survey packages. These surveys are very low cost and benefit from immediacy in delivery and response, particularly for post-purchase appraisal. From a business perspective, social media networks have been escalating in importance for researching visitors' preferences and communicating their message, in contrast to traditional promotional methods, but the usual caveats about just being convenience samples and non-response bias still apply.

## MEASURING OWN PRICE ELASTICITY

When measuring own price elasticity for travel products there are two possibilities to consider in the first instance: one is **point** elasticity of demand and the other is **arc** elasticity of demand. These possibilities are illustrated in Table 4.3, which extends the example of the demand for package holidays that was first introduced in Table 1.1. Columns four and five show the percentage change in quantity demanded with respect to the percentage change in price when moving down the demand schedule. Dividing column four by column five yields the own price

| Table 4.3 | | Market demand for holiday packages | | | | | |
|---|---|---|---|---|---|---|---|
| Unit price P | Quantity demanded Q | Revenue P × Q | Percentage change Q | Percentage change P | Point elasticity downwards | Point elasticity upwards | Arc elasticity |
| 600 | 2000 | 1200000 | | | | | |
| | | | 50% | 17% | 3.00 | 1.70 | 2.20 |
| 500 | 3000 | 1500000 | | | | | |
| | | | 33% | 20% | 1.67 | 1.00 | 1.29 |
| 400 | 4000 | 1600000 | | | | | |
| | | | 25% | 25% | 1.00 | 0.60 | 0.78 |
| 300 | 5000 | 1500000 | | | | | |
| | | | 20% | 33% | 0.60 | 0.33 | 0.45 |
| 200 | 6000 | 1200000 | | | | | |

*Source*: Author

elasticities shown in column six, while on the other hand, if we move from the bottom upward in the demand schedule a different set of elasticities is derived, as shown in column seven. This arises because the base on which each percentage change in the movements of price and quantity varies depending on whether we move down the schedule or up the schedule. The solution to this dilemma is given in column eight, and is known as arc elasticity because it averages the movement between one point on the schedule and the next, and is therefore invariant of the direction taken, whether up or down. For example if the price of a package holiday is reduced from 500 to 400 currency units, then:

$$\text{Arc Elasticity} = \frac{1000/(3000 + 4000)}{100/(500 + 400)} = 1.29$$

The above measure of elasticity value is now invariant of the direction of movement along the demand schedule.

The revenue column of Table 4.3 reveals an interesting practical consequence of elasticity. It may be observed that when the elasticity is greater than unity, cutting price increases revenue, but upon elasticity falling below unity overall revenue declines, since it fails to expand proportionately to the price cut. The effect of this phenomenon when the situation is one of oversupply is to cause product to be put into stock or, where it is perishable, as in the case of agricultural commodities, simply 'dumped' so as to keep up prices. In a world where large numbers of the populace do not have enough food, such actions are difficult to comprehend for many people. In the tourism industry this aspect of demand combined with modern ICT leads to sophisticated revenue management strategies so as to maintain earnings. This relies on dealing with different market segments in which secondary trading is either not allowed (the product sold to a named person) or difficult to accomplish. It allows the travel trade to offer last minute availability for surplus holiday packages, late discounting of hotel rooms and half-price 'on the day' tickets in theatres, without affecting the previous selling price. The more people book online the easier it becomes for tourism businesses to use 'real time' revenue management in which the price offered for a given product will vary according to the time of booking, the time of consumption and how well the product is selling.

## MODELLING TOURISM DEMAND

Given the significance of international tourism and the importance attached to its export earnings by governments, it is not unexpected that there have been many empirical country studies on international tourism flows. Globally the UNWTO monitors international arrivals on a continual basis as reviewed in Major Case Study 4.1, while at the country level the demand for international travel is treated in much the same way as the demand for imports and exports of commodities, save that importing refers, as noted previously, to expenditure by domestic residents in foreign countries and conversely for exports, which are demands for international travel made by people abroad.

When estimating demand functions for international travel it must be remembered that the data points that are collected through surveys are not that of a demand schedule, but rather observed market equilibrium positions between demand and supply. For such observations to trace out a demand function requires supply to be continually responding to changing market conditions. The supporting evidence for this is that over time the real cost of travel has been falling, which in turn has encouraged continuous growth in demand (see Major Case Study 4.1) and a commensurate expansion of supply.

It remains to make operational the general demand function given by equation (2.10) that was derived in Chapter 2, and reproduced below:

$$Q = F(P_t, P_1, \ldots \ldots, P_m, Y) \tag{4.1}$$

where,

$P_t =$ the price of the tourism product;

$P_1, \ldots \ldots, P_m =$ the prices of alternative goods and services which are making claims on the visitor's budget;

$Y =$ the sum of individual incomes in the market.

The most frequent analysis of international travel is to interpret equation (4.1) for inbound arrivals, and the export function is simplified by assuming that consumers have a two-stage budgeting process. First they allocate their expenditure over broad categories of goods and services such as food, clothing, housing, transport, holidays, and so on. These groups are separable in the sense that they are not directly substitutable and it is only after allocations have been made that the consumer decides where to go for his/her holiday. This allows researchers to draw up a fairly simplified export demand function for international arrivals at the destination from each tourism-generating country:

$$Q^* = F(P_t, Y^*) \tag{4.2}$$

where,

$Q^* =$ measure of inbound visitor demand;

$P_t =$ the price of the tourism product;

$Y^* =$ the sum of inbound visitor incomes for this market.

A number of measures of $Q^*$ have been used by researchers, which include the number of visitors, total expenditure by all inbound visitors in constant value (real) terms, per capita real expenditure by visitors and the visit rate, the latter being the number of visitors from the originating country divided by the population of that country. Of these, total expenditure adjusted by a consumer price index to remove purely inflationary movements and give real values tends to be most popular. Business travel needs to be treated in a different way to leisure trips, because much of it may be regarded as an intermediate demand to do with the volume of trade and investment between various countries.

For $Y^*$ there are again a number of possibilities of which the simplest measures are GDP or GDP per capita in the country of origin at constant prices. Some researchers have used personal income after taxation, while the two-stage budgeting process noted earlier suggests that total tourism expenditure to all countries by inbound visitors from the country of reference would be appropriate. In most instances data availability restricts researchers to GDP measures which do perform satisfactorily.

However, it is the price measure that presents the greatest difficulty because of the general lack of adequate data for empirical work. Ideally what is needed is an indicator of the relative price of the tourism product as between the origin and the destination, and between the destination of interest and likely competing locations. Given ever widening choice, pricing is necessarily comparative, so more and more purchasing decisions are based on relative prices and not actual or specific prices. In practice $P_t$ is broken down into two main components: the round-trip cost of travel or fare $FA$, and the comparable cost of stay, which is shown by the cost-of-living index in the two countries, usually the consumer price index, adjusted for exchange rate changes. Thus re-writing equation (4.2) gives:

$$Q^* = F\left(FA, \frac{C/E}{C^*}, Y^*\right) \tag{4.3}$$

where,

$C =$ the consumer price index in the destination country;

$E =$ the destination country exchange rate in terms of units of local currency per unit of the visitors' currency;

$C^* =$ the consumer price index in the tourism generating country.

Some researchers include $E$ as a separate variable from $\frac{C}{C^*}$ in equation (4.3) on the grounds that visitors are more likely to know $E$ as a price signal than any comparison of the costs of stay. Where competing destinations are considered to be significant, then similar expressions such as $\frac{C/E}{C^*}$ can be inserted into equation (4.3), as well as particular variables to cover for known events and even marketing campaigns levelled at increasing awareness and realising new demand (see Chapter 21).

While equation (4.3) is an export demand function, dealing with inbound tourism, outbound tourism or import demand functions are simply the reverse:

$$Q = F\left(FA^*, \frac{C^*/E^*}{C}, Y\right) \tag{4.4}$$

where,

$Q =$ measure of outbound (resident) tourism demand;

$C =$ the consumer price index in the home country;

$E^* =$ the home country exchange rate in terms of units of foreign currency per unit of the domestic currency;

$C^* =$ the consumer price index in the destination country.

$Y =$ the sum of residents' incomes in the market.

Table 4.4 shows aggregate own price and income elasticities derived from imports end export demand functions of the kind presented in equations (4.3) and (4.4). The price elasticities are shown as their true negative values since quantity and price move in opposite directions. Since the measures shown in Table 4.4 refer to all inbound and outbound tourism in the respective countries the statistics used for estimating them are weighted averages of the relevant variables. For example, the average of $Y^*$ will usually be real GDP of the leading 'customer' countries for the destination, weighted by the share of each country in the total export receipts shown in the travel account of that destination.

To conclude this section it only remains to consider the functional form that equations (4.3) and (4.4) may take for statistical estimation purposes. In the absence of any prior knowledge, the common procedure is to estimate them as additive linear or multiplicative, but linear in logarithms. Thus equation (4.3), and similarly for equation (4.4), may be represented as:

$$Q^* = \beta_0 + \beta_1 FA + \beta_2\left[\frac{C/E}{C^*}\right] + \beta_3 Y^* + u \tag{4.5}$$

| Table 4.4 | Overall country own price and income elasticities | | | |
|---|---|---|---|---|
| | **Own price elasticities** | | **Income elasticities** | |
| **Countries** | **Import functions** | **Export functions** | **Import functions** | **Export functions** |
| Austria | −0.58 | −1.34 | 1.12 | 1.08 |
| Belgium | −1.73 | −0.57 | 1.83 | 0.74 |
| Czech Republic | −1.36 | – | 9.23 | 3.93 |
| Denmark | −0.99 | −0.31 | 1.75 | 0.53 |
| Finland | −1.50 | −1.06 | 1.80 | 0.61 |
| France | −1.12 | −1.00 | 2.06 | 1.00 |
| Germany | −0.74 | – | 1.21 | 0.76 |
| Greece | −0.74 | −1.22 | 2.18 | 0.47 |
| Hungary | −1.81 | −0.66 | 3.96 | 1.38 |
| Ireland | −0.42 | −2.03 | 1.57 | 1.32 |
| Italy | – | −1.43 | 4.75 | 1.13 |
| Netherlands | −0.93 | −1.14 | 1.20 | 0.81 |
| Norway | −1.55 | −0.50 | 0.81 | 0.70 |
| Poland | – | – | 4.46 | 2.86 |
| Portugal | −3.61 | −0.79 | 2.18 | 1.30 |
| Slovenia | – | −2.89 | 2.41 | – |
| Spain | −1.58 | −0.91 | 2.11 | 1.09 |
| Sweden | −1.32 | −1.75 | 3.18 | 1.09 |
| Switzerland | −0.88 | −0.45 | 1.55 | 0.79 |
| United Kingdom | −1.04 | −0.62 | 2.61 | 0.81 |
| Australia | −1.28 | −0.47 | 1.38 | 1.41 |
| Canada | −2.18 | −0.69 | 2.00 | 0.69 |
| Japan | −0.73 | – | 1.98 | 0.72 |
| Mexico | −0.64 | −0.72 | 2.51 | 0.34 |
| USA | −0.56 | −0.40 | 1.50 | 0.55 |
| *Arithmetic mean* | *−1.24* | *−1.00* | *2.45* | *1.09* |

*Source*: Smeral, 2004

or

$$Q^\star = \beta_0 FA^{\beta_1}\left[\frac{C/E}{C^\star}\right]^{\beta_2} Y^{\star\beta_3}u \tag{4.6}$$

where $\beta_0$ is the constant term, and $\beta_1$ to $\beta_3$ are coefficients of the explanatory variables of inbound tourism movements to be estimated using statistical multiple regression analysis, with $u$ being the error term. The latter is assumed to be random and normally distributed with a mean of zero, so that the estimates will be unbiased. Multiple regression analysis (which will be discussed further in Chapter 5) is readily available in most statistical computer packages.

Taking logarithms of equation (4.6) will convert it into the linear format of equation (4.5) for estimation purposes. The advantages of this procedure are twofold: often the data for each of the variables are in very different dimensions, so by transforming them into logarithms puts them on the same scale; secondly, the coefficients $\beta_1$ to $\beta_3$ so estimated turn out to be constant value elasticities, which is how the statistics in Table 4.4 were measured.

## CONCLUSION

It is now clear to all governments that the activity generated by the demand for tourism is extensive. Its measurement has always been problematic, but the requirements of the TSA have imposed a discipline on the collection of data. However, many countries still collect their tourism statistics as secondary to other needs, with the balance often distorted to international arrivals and neglecting outbound and domestic tourism. As a consequence, much of tourism demand modelling is confined to inbound tourism, but in reality all forms of tourism are significant for destination planning, management and marketing. The measurement of tourism activity and an understanding of the factors that influence visitors' behaviour provide a wealth of information for such purposes.

## SELF-CHECK QUESTIONS

1. Examine the data requirements for the demand tables of a TSA and see whether they can be completed from the available information in your country.
2. What might be some of the key problems in comparing tourism statistics from different areas and regions of the world?
3. Review the different methods of collecting tourism statistics.
4. List the key questions you would ask in a domestic tourism survey.
5. How does the concept of elasticity help our understanding of tourism demand?

## YOUTUBE

http://www.youtube.com/watch?v=MvfHBqhdXBg
Conducting an airport passenger survey.

## REFERENCES AND FURTHER READING

Lennon, J. (ed.) (2003) *Tourism Statistics: International Perspectives and Current Issues*, Continuum, London. An in-depth and excellent international overview of the many issues associated with tourism statistics.

Ryan, C. (2003) *Recreational Tourism Demand and Impacts*, Channel View, Clevedon. An approachable and complete overview of tourism demand.

Smeral, E. (2004) 'Long-term forecasts for international tourism', *Tourism Economics* **10**(2), 145–66.

Smith, S.L. (1989) *Tourism Analysis: A Handbook*, Longman, Harlow.

Smith, S.L. (1996) *Tourism Analysis*, 2nd edn, Longman, Harlow.

Song, H., and Witt, S.F. (2000) *Tourism Demand Modeling and Forecasting: Modern Econometric Approaches*, Amsterdam: Pergamon. An advanced text for those wishing to delve deeper into the modelling of tourism demand.

Veal, A.J. (2005) *Research Methods for Leisure and Tourism: A Practical Guide*, Pearson Education, Harlow. A non-technical guide to researching tourism.

World Tourism Organization (2000) *Data Collection and Analysis for Tourism Management, Marketing and Planning*, WTO, Madrid. A comprehensive practical guide to collecting and analysing tourism information within a disciplined and coherent framework of statistics.

UNWTO (annual) *Tourism Highlights* WTO, Madrid.

UNWTO (2008). International Recommendations for Tourism Statistics (IRTS). Department of Economics and Social Affairs, Statistics Division. This not only offers a definitive explanation of concepts and definitions, but also recommendations on the collection of data. It is available at http://unstats.un.org/unsd/trade/IRTS/IRTS%202008%20unedited.pdf

## Websites

**http://www.world-tourism.org**

An all-embracing website providing the official United Nations' tourism definitions, statistics and forecasts, as well as policies on tourism issues such as tourism ethics, pro-poor tourism, women in tourism, taxation and many more aspects affecting the industry.

**http://www.wttc.org**

An all-inclusive website from the private sector's representative body for tourism with up-to-date statistics and reports on the tourism industry and its economic contribution to different countries of the world.

# MAJOR CASE STUDY 4.1
World patterns of demand for tourism

## PATTERNS OF DEMAND: THE HISTORIC TREND

Since World War II, there has been rapid growth worldwide in international tourism (as may be seen from Table 4.5). After the war increasing proportions of the populations of the industrialised nations were in possession of both the time (in the form of paid leave from employment) and the money (with post-war economic recovery in the 1950s) to engage in international travel. Supply to meet this increased demand for leisure tourism in particular was developed mainly in the form of the volume package tour, which was priced to get around foreign exchange controls. This was made possible by the availability of surplus transport aircraft and further cost-cutting with the conversion from propeller-driven to jet aircraft in 1958, and by the general availability of cheap oil. Furthermore, economic recovery boosted international business travel.

As one would expect, the fastest growth in world arrivals took place in the earlier years, so between 1950 and 1970 the average rate was about 9.9% per annum, doubling every seven years. The 1970s started off well but was hit by the rising price of oil in late 1973, which in a short space of time went up four times. The setback this caused to the major tourism-generating countries saw growth in world arrivals fall back to 5.3% between 1970 and 1980. Nevertheless, international tourism continued to expand on a worldwide scale, demonstrating a robustness against economic adversity and the ingenuity of the travel industry in overcoming difficulties. Generally, in times of economic growth, demand for travel has increased; on the other hand, during times of recession, demand has either remained constant or has soon recovered, in both cases due to new travellers entering the market and existing travellers taking more frequent trips.

## THE 1980s

In addition to growth, the market has diversified as it has matured, with an extensive growth in the array of destinations available. As the market matured, so the average annual growth rate has tended to decrease, as would be expected, implying that the rapid advance in the early post-war period of international travel was unlikely to be repeated.

The early part of the 1980s was a continuance of the recession in the late 1970s, which acted to dampen international travel, and volume did not really recover until 1984 – 1984 and 1985 were record years, with European destinations doing particularly well. However, the accident at the nuclear power plant in Chernobyl, in the then Soviet Union, combined with terrorist activity, the Libyan bombing incident and the weakening of the US dollar against other major currencies all conspired to

| Table 4.5 | International tourism trends: worldwide arrivals 1950–2010 | | |
|---|---|---|---|
| Year | Arrivals (millions) | Year | Arrivals (millions) |
| 1950 | 25.3 | 2005 | 798.0 |
| 1960 | 69.3 | 2006 | 842.2 |
| 1970 | 165.8 | 2007 | 897.7 |
| 1980 | 277.1 | 2008 | 916.9 |
| 1990 | 434.5 | 2009 | 882.1 |
| 2000 | 674.5 | 2010 | 939.8 |

*Source*: UNWTO, annual

contribute to the depressing of demand for tourism. As a result, international travel was severely affected. The effect was not so much in terms of total numbers, which were up on the previous year anyway, but in terms of tourism flows and changes in types of trip taken. Many destinations suffered badly, whereas others gained. The second half of the decade saw a return to some sort of normality, in terms of both growth rates and types of trip taken, but all told the decade achieved less than what had gone before at 4.6% a year.

## THE 1990s

The 1990s commenced with the Gulf War and further economic recession, leading to great uncertainty for international tourism. In the short term, the build-up to the Gulf War, the war itself and the aftermath led initially to the virtual cessation of travel to the Gulf, the Eastern Mediterranean and North Africa. It not only depressed international tourism further afield, but also the economic recession experienced by the majority of industrialised countries was aggravated by it. The lessons of earlier years were that international tourism would recover and develop, with new products, destinations and generating markets; and indeed this has been the case, with tourism responding well to the growth in economic and social conditions and little or no slowdown was seen in international tourism flows in the 1990s. In particular the decade was characterised by the growth of overseas travel by residents of developing countries and the acceleration of multiple, but short-haul, trips from travellers in industrialised countries.

## THE NEW MILLENNIUM

Tourism in the early years of the new millennium has been characterised by contrast. Based on 1995 data the UNWTO predicted over 1 billion international arrivals for 2010, at an average annual growth rate of 4.1%. The outturn was somewhat lower, as indicated in Table 4.5, representing a growth rate of 3.4%, for while the millennium opened with optimism and the success of the Sydney Olympic Games, considerably boosting arrivals to Australia, a series of adverse happenings over the last decade were responsible for keeping growth down.

The attacks on the World Trade Center on 11 September 2001 saw international tourism arrivals decline by 0.5% over 2000. 9/11, as it is commonly known, was followed by the Bali bombings of 2002, the commencement of wars in Iraq and Afghanistan and the SARS outbreak in Asia, which gave rise to a three-year period of stagnant growth. Despite the Indian Ocean tsunami of 2004, this year saw a considerable rebound in international arrivals, with only two sub-regions not breaking their previous records, namely North America and Western Europe. Terrorist attacks

on surface transport in both Spain and the UK severely affected the pattern of tourism demand, and tightened security at both borders and in the airline industry prompted consumers to holiday at home rather than internationally.

However, tourism demand has shown itself to be robust and arrivals and receipts recovered in general by 2005, with growth restored for the next few years before the effects of the global financial crisis began to be felt in late 2008 and 2009. In 2010, world tourism recovered more strongly than expected from the financial shock it had received, with the exception of Europe which was locked into difficulties with the euro and government debts.

## REGIONAL DIMENSIONS

The changes in the share of international tourism worldwide for the different regions over the period 1950 to 2010 are shown in Table 4.6. It may be seen that the global experience of almost uninterrupted growth is not equally shared by all regions but when viewed in the context of an expanding total even a constant share represents substantial gains.

Europe, notably the EU, and to a lesser extent the Americas, under the influence of USA and Canada, have for some time dominated the international travel scene in terms of numbers of arrivals and receipts. But these are mature markets and it is only to be expected that they will lose market share to emerging destinations in Asia and the Pacific, and more recently the Middle East. For the latter, the key factors have been the support of most governments, the permanent development of tourism infrastructure, significant public and private sector investment in tourism, the low-cost airline phenomenon and the increasing cooperation regarding border facilities among the countries in the region. But the political activities identified as 'Arab Spring' that began in 2011 have reversed this trend. In all this it must be remembered that approximately four-fifths of international travel is within each region (intraregional) so that long-haul or interregional travel only accounts for some 20% of the total. The latter is one of the first to be affected by downturns in the market and equally one of the first to recover. One of the consequences of uncertainty caused by terrorist actions is to curtail travel to within the visitor's own region of familiarity.

Of all the regions, Europe was hit hardest by the global financial crisis, yet it still accounts for just over half of all international tourist arrivals. The factors that explain this on the demand side have been in place for a considerable time, namely a high per capita GDP, paid leave from work and a growing attachment to the annual foreign holiday in the main generating countries of Germany, France and the UK. On the supply side,

| Table 4.6 | Regional distribution of international tourism 1950–2010 |
| --- | --- |

| Region | 1950 | 1960 | 1970 | 1980 | 1990 | 2000 | 2010 |
| --- | --- | --- | --- | --- | --- | --- | --- |
| **Arrivals (millions)** | | | | | | | |
| Africa | 0.3 | 0.8 | 2.4 | 7.2 | 14.8 | 26.5 | 49.4 |
| Americas | 7.6 | 16.7 | 42.3 | 62.1 | 92.8 | 128.2 | 149.8 |
| Europe | 16.7 | 50.4 | 113.0 | 177.8 | 261.5 | 385.6 | 476.5 |
| Asia & the Pacific | 0.5 | 0.8 | 6.2 | 22.9 | 55.8 | 110.1 | 203.8 |
| Middle East | 0.2 | 0.6 | 1.9 | 7.1 | 9.6 | 24.1 | 60.3 |
| World | 25.3 | 69.3 | 165.8 | 277.1 | 434.5 | 674.5 | 939.8 |
| **Share of arrivals (percentages)** | | | | | | | |
| Africa | 1.2 | 1.2 | 1.4 | 2.6 | 3.4 | 3.9 | 5.3 |
| Americas | 30.0 | 24.1 | 25.5 | 22.4 | 21.4 | 19.0 | 15.9 |
| Europe | 66.0 | 72.7 | 68.2 | 64.2 | 60.2 | 57.2 | 50.7 |
| Asia & the Pacific | 2.0 | 1.2 | 3.7 | 8.3 | 12.8 | 16.3 | 21.7 |
| Middle East | 0.8 | 0.9 | 1.1 | 2.6 | 2.2 | 3.6 | 6.4 |
| World | 100.0 | 100.0 | 100.0 | 100.0 | 100.0 | 100.0 | 100.0 |
| **Average annual growth rates (percentages)** | 1950–1960 | 1960–1970 | 1970–1980 | 1980–1990 | 1990–2000 | 2000–2010 | |
| Africa | 10.3 | 11.6 | 11.6 | 7.5 | 6.0 | 6.4 | |
| Americas | 8.2 | 9.7 | 3.9 | 4.1 | 0.8 | 1.6 | |
| Europe | 11.7 | 8.4 | 4.6 | 3.9 | 2.6 | 2.1 | |
| Asia & the Pacific | 4.8 | 22.7 | 14.0 | 9.3 | 6.9 | 6.4 | |
| Middle East | 11.6 | 12.2 | 14.1 | 3.1 | 8.5 | 9.6 | |
| World | 10.6 | 9.1 | 5.3 | 4.6 | 3.4 | 3.4 | |

*Source*: UNWTO, annual

ease of access, a sophisticated travel industry, a wealth of attractions and a common currency in the euro have all facilitated tourism trips. Nonetheless, the financial turmoil has exposed structural economic weaknesses in having a common currency between different sovereign states, which have posed questions as to the future of the euro in terms of the number of countries joining or staying within the eurozone. History has dictated that political union comes before a common currency, from which then follows fiscal union and the free movement of labour. Europe has done the reverse in creating the euro, so it is not surprising that there is considerable dissension in the face of a major economic downturn.

A number of these factors are equally applicable to North America, but the sheer size of the USA and Canada means that the majority of their populations prefer to take domestic trips. Nevertheless, there are substantial numbers of North Americans who do engage in foreign travel each year, not merely within their own continent but also in long-haul trips.

As may be observed from Table 4.6, the rising star in the last three decades has been the Asia and Pacific region in response to economic development. The most significant destination has been China, which has been consistently moving up the rank of the world's major destinations. Table 4.7 shows the most recent ranking of

| Table 4.7 | Top ten international destinations (millions of arrivals) |
| --- | --- |

| Country | 2005 | Country | 2010 |
| --- | --- | --- | --- |
| France | 75.9 | France | 76.8 |
| Spain | 55.9 | USA | 59.7 |
| USA | 49.2 | China | 55.7 |
| China | 46.8 | Spain | 52.7 |
| Italy | 36.5 | Italy | 43.6 |
| UK | 28.0 | UK | 28.1 |
| Mexico | 21.9 | Turkey | 27.0 |
| Germany | 21.5 | Germany | 26.9 |
| Austria | 20.0 | Malaysia | 24.6 |
| Russian Federation | 19.9 | Mexico | 22.4 |

*Source*: UNWTO, annual

**Photograph 4.2**    Asia is becoming a significant generator of international tourism.
*Source*: Werner Dieterich/Alamy Images

the top ten destinations in the world. France has occupied the top spot for many years, but we now see China as number four and Malaysia has also entered the list as the weight of economic development has shifted in favour of Asia and Australasia.

## UNWTO VISION

International tourism will continue to grow in the period 2010–2030, but at a more moderate pace than in the past decades, with the number of international tourist arrivals worldwide increasing by an average 3.3% a year. It is difficult to contemplate this at a time when most of the leading tourism generating countries are suffering from economic recession without a clear view of recovery and further growth. Even under conditions of lower increases in GDP and a shift from falling to rising transport costs, it is felt that there is still potential for substantial expansion in the coming decades. Thus, by 2030, arrivals are expected to reach about 1.8 billion, as shown in Table 4.8, meaning that in two decades' time, 5 million people every day will be crossing international borders for leisure, business or other purposes such as visiting friends and family.

International arrivals in emerging economy destinations are expected to continue growing at double the pace of advanced countries, at 4.4% per annum compared to 2.2% a year. In absolute terms, the emerging economies of Asia, Latin America, Central and Eastern Europe, Eastern Mediterranean Europe, the Middle East (given a return to more normal times) and Africa will gain an average 30 million arrivals a year, compared to 14 million in the traditional destinations of

| Table 4.8 | UNWTO vision (millions of arrivals) | |
|---|---|---|
| **Region** | **2020** | **2030** |
| Africa | 80 | 126 |
| Americas | 196 | 252 |
| Europe | 598 | 738 |
| Asia & the Pacific | 334 | 540 |
| Middle East | 94 | 144 |
| World | 1302 | 1800 |

*Source*: UNWTO, annual

the advanced economies of North America, Europe and Asia and the Pacific. Equally, with large populations and rising affluence, it is expected that Brazil, Russia, India and China will become significant tourism generating countries for the traditional destinations.

*Source*: www.world-tourism.org

## DISCUSSION QUESTIONS

1. Consider the circumstances that point to Asia and the Pacific region becoming a major destination in the world.

2. With reference to Chapter 12 examine the impact of political unrest on international tourism demand patterns.

3. International tourism growth was phenomenal during the twentieth century. Identify some constraints to tourism in the twenty-first century that might slow this growth.

# CHAPTER 5
## FORECASTING TOURISM DEMAND

### LEARNING OUTCOMES

The purpose of this chapter is to introduce and discuss the various approaches to forecasting. We develop some basic statistical methods and introduce qualitative or judgemental techniques, drawing together this analysis with practical examples and case studies. This chapter is designed to provide you with:

- an overview of tourism forecasting;
- an understanding of the need for forecasting and the different time periods involved;
- some basic modelling techniques for forecasting tourism demand;
- a knowledge of econometric models of tourism demand;
- an understanding of qualitative and combined approaches to forecasting;
- an appreciation of forecasting errors; and
- an awareness of the role of forecasting in market planning.

Photograph: Siesta Key, Sarasota, Florida, USA © Kelly Miller

## INTRODUCTION

This chapter builds upon our previous discussion of the determinants of tourism demand and the theoretical appraisal of demand models. It goes on to show how an understanding of these underlying influences is important for predicting future tourism in both a quantitative and qualitative sense. Case studies are used to indicate how these two approaches are combined in practice to generate what are termed 'hybrid' forecasts that can be used by the tourism industry for market planning.

The emphasis in this chapter is on basic model building and linking this to the time period for which the forecast is likely to be made and the availability of information. There is no doubt that forecasts are necessary, despite the fact that some might argue from a chaos theory perspective (as in Chapter 1) that the volatile nature of our industry operating in a world of rapid and unexpected change makes forecasts increasingly irrelevant. As the case examples will show, forecasters counter this issue by taking account of a wide spectrum of opinions and techniques in settling upon their final predictions.

## AN OVERVIEW OF TOURISM FORECASTING

Set against a background of increasing liberalisation in terms of border controls and international trade growing at twice the rate of world GDP, tourism has verified the nature of demand illustrated in textbooks on economics, namely that a combination of higher incomes and lower prices brings forth an increased volume. As discussed in Major Case Study 4.1, tourism has demonstrated its resilience in the past to adverse events, with their impacts usually being discounted within three years of normal operating conditions being restored, and even here the spill-over effects are not all negative, since market share is relatively easily switched from troubled regions to other destinations. Even in the face of the global financial crisis, with the uncertainty about the euro, the UNWTO (2011) is predicting a long-term growth trend for international tourism of 3.3% per annum over the period 2010–2030. This is a more moderate pace than in past decades. It is based on a scenario of lower increases in GDP and a shift from falling to rising transport costs, yet continuing innovation in the travel industry. International income elasticities of demand for the major countries are in the region of +1.8 to +2.0 (see Chapter 2), while own price elasticities are around 1.2 to 1.5, thus ensuring that volume will respond more than proportionately to unit changes in these economic variables. Thus, by 2030 international arrivals are expected to reach a level of 1.8 billion.

At the individual country level, demand forecasts have their importance in planning tourism investments and managing visitor flows as destinations and businesses need to know in advance who will come. In the short term they are also of value to firms for planning revenue yields (Frechtling, 2001). In an industry with such an array of different, but complementary suppliers the role of forecasting is to give direction and this task is typically taken on by the appropriate tourism authority at the destination (see Mini Case Study 5.1). A particular issue that lays emphasis on accuracy in forecasting arises from the nature of tourism as a 'perishable' service industry, implying that surpluses cannot be stored. Thus supply has to be calculated around peak demand, though not the very peak as this would result in excessive capacity, but rather an average busy time during peak holiday months. This is necessary to avoid unwarranted expense, but does mean that every business may experience times when there is heavy congestion or overloading of facilities.

At the firm level, one of the major drawbacks to forecasting is the availability of quantitative data of the kind that is at the disposal of an NTA. Breaking down national data to the local level is not very practical because of the resulting size of sampling errors. In the main businesses rely on their own management accounts, polling their sales force and advanced bookings in their reservations systems. Apart from their own experiences, they will also draw on destination indi-

## MINI CASE STUDY 5.1
### Forecasting at a National Tourism Administration

Given the many influences on the demand for tourism, experience indicates that successful market planning at the NTA level requires knowledge of:

1. current demand and supply position;
2. historic trends that have produced this;
3. factors influencing tourism;
   a) exchange rates;
   b) GDP;
   c) personal disposable income;
   d) unemployment,
   e) airfares;
   f) petrol costs;
   g) accommodation costs at home and abroad;
   h) holiday entitlement.
4. decisive factors and bottlenecks in the sector;
5. current importance of tourism;
6. tourism product that is offered;
7. market outlook for this product.

The need for such information is determined by the complex and sometimes volatile nature of tourism demand. While everyday monitoring of trends may be drawn from business indicators, for the longer term the NTA will produce typically a ten-year forecast; annually for the first five years, with just target figures for the tenth year. Longer term forecasts will be set against likely scenarios to produce high, central and low targets that might be achievable. It is often difficult to quantify some of the influences listed above, either due to measurement difficulties, for example the future of space tourism, or the costs of collecting such information in relation to the available budget. A common difficulty is how to measure the effects of promotional spend, and the accepted wisdom is that this may be best represented through changes in market share rather than absolute visitor numbers.

NTAs will normally layer their markets in order of importance and in relation to the tourism products on offer, termed a 'product-fit table', paying most attention to the major sources of origin of visitors and those showing new potential. There is an old forecasting adage to deal with uncertainty which says: 'Give them a number or give them a date but never both!' This is to avoid being tied down to absolute numbers on a given date some way into the future. Customary practice is to put forward scenarios for each market with likely targets supported by qualitative analysis of the influences that affect them, so that the probabilities of change may be thoroughly understood. This will enable plans to be drawn up to make rational responses to changes when and where they occur.

## DISCUSSION QUESTIONS

1. With reference to a destination of your choice construct a product-fit table.
2. How might an NTA organise a response to a violent disturbance such as a riot or terrorist attack in its capital city?
3. How would you evaluate the impact of a large rise in oil prices on international travel?

cators provided by the local tourist boards (as suggested in Chapter 4) and any anticipatory data, such as holiday intentions surveys. But while such information will be sufficient for short-term forecasting over two years, it is inadequate for project development which depends on long-term assessment in order to determine whether the capital costs will or will not be recovered. This is particularly difficult for 'new-to-the-world' products where there is little prior knowledge to hand (a matter that is looked at in more detail in Chapter 18, covering attractions).

## Time periods

It should be apparent that the time period over which the forecast has to be made will affect the approach and methodology. Forecasters conventionally divide time into short-, medium- and long-term phases, and then what may be considered futuristic planning that looks at the evolution of past and present innovations so as to assess when the next likely breakthrough will occur and what would be its consequences. By and large there tends to be an optimism bias in these matters, which goes with the nature of human society. Governments have been shown to have a poor track record in this respect, pouring vast sums of money into 'seemingly never ending' projects on the promise that the solution is 'just around the corner' before they are finally abandoned. On the other hand, history has revealed that the prophets of 'doomsday' have not been too successful either.

The short term is considered to last up to one or two years and represents a period in which nothing much can be done apart from mobilising unused capacity to meet changes in visitor flows; indeed it is often desirable that not much should be done until such time as these changes are seen to be permanent. The medium term is considered to be up to five years and corresponds to the development plan of most tourist boards. In this time phase it is feasible to build models of supply and demand to assess the effects of alternative policies, such as restructuring prices, taxes and subsidies, regulations, organising events or festivals, for it will now be possible to make alterations to the tourism infrastructure that will carry into the longer term covering the next 5–15 years.

Model building is still valid in the longer term provided that there are no major changes in the social, economic and technical factors of the kind listed in Table 2.1. It is these that form the basis of scenario writing as far as futuristic planning is concerned. In essence, scenario writing is 'story-telling' about the future. The objective may not necessarily be about prediction, but rather to raise awareness of the factors or variables that might alter the future and how they could combine. Forecasting requires a deep understanding of the prime movers of change as they affect visitor flows and how to interpret them. With the aid of long-term projections of underlying trends, different scenarios are drawn up on the basis of what the 'world' might look like in 15 or more years' time, selecting the most likely occurrence and then working backwards to the present to indentify the bottlenecks that need to be eliminated for the forecast targets to be realised.

An essential strategy for future planning is to try to keep options open so that the final decision as to when capital funds should be invested in fixed assets such as hotels, restaurants, transport and recreation facilities is made in the medium term when the most recent information on underlying trends is available. It follows therefore that a good information system is a very necessary part of a forecaster's 'toolkit'.

# FORECASTING METHODS

There is a wide variety of methods available for forecasting tourism demand at very different levels of sophistication that are supported by advanced computer packages (Song and Witt, 2000; Frechtling, 2001). Two basic approaches may be adopted – quantitative and qualitative – but as should be apparent from the discussion in the last section these are not mutually exclusive. Most applied forecasters use a combination of these two methods, utilising the strengths or relative strengths of each. A key factor is the availability of quantitative data and the further we look into the future the more reliance we tend to place on qualitative assessments.

## Quantitative forecasting

Again, there are numerous quantitative aspects to forecasting demand, ranging from the simple to the highly technical. At the level of this text we will confine ourselves to basic techniques that may easily be implemented on a hand-held calculator or a spreadsheet. Techniques that do not involve a great deal of mathematics, provided they are effective, are easier to explain to the end user. If the latter has a good appreciation of how they work then this gives more confidence in their use for decision making.

### Time series models

These models rely on extrapolating future trends from the past by taking the variable to be forecast as being solely a function of one explanatory variable, time. As such these relationships are known as 'univariate' models. Thus equation (4.1) in Chapter 4 becomes

$$Q^* = F(t) \tag{5.1}$$

where,

$Q^* =$ measure of inbound tourism demand;

$F(t) =$ the functional relationship explaining $Q$.

The simplest approach is the 'one-step' no-change model, which essentially says that the next period is going to be very much like this one, so this year's value is the best approximation of what might happen next year. To guard against fluctuations some will take a further step in using average values from the most recent years as a basis for forecasting, but a method which is eminently suitable for short-term forecasting at the firm or country level is where the dependent variable is broken down into its component parts, namely the trend $T$, a cyclical component $C$, a seasonal component $S$ and an error term $u$. The latter is assumed to be random and normally distributed with a mean of zero (see Chapter 4), so that the estimates will be unbiased. It is therefore the non-systematic part of the time series which will always be unaccounted for.

This procedure for separating a time series into its component parts is known as 'classical decomposition'. There are two structural forms for undertaking this, additive and multiplicative:

$$Q^* = T + C + S + u \tag{5.2}$$
$$Q^* = TCSu \tag{5.3}$$

A representative time series pattern is illustrated in Figure 5.1 with the trend component also shown separately as a straight line. The choice as to whether to use equation (5.2) or equation (5.3) for the modelling process depends on the behaviour of the data. In an additive system

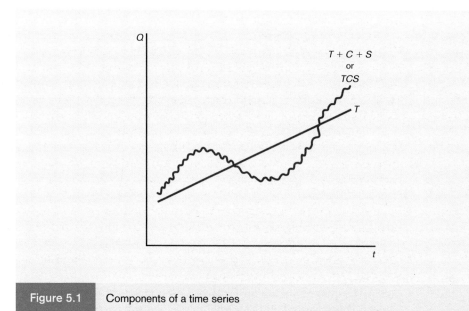

| Figure 5.1 | Components of a time series |

| Photograph 5.1 | Understanding seasonal visitor flows is essential for capacity planning in tourism |
|---|---|

*Source*: Peter Phipp/Getty Images

the components are independent amounts, while with a multiplicative process, the components are proportional to fluctuations in the data. The latter tends to correspond more closely to reality, so multiplicative models are those most frequently used for practical forecasting. Their use is best explained through a worked example, which is the subject matter of Table 5.1.

The second column in Table 5.1 corresponds to equation (5.3) and shows the monthly visitor data taken from a destination that has an all-year-round tourism industry. Nine years of data are available, but for short-term forecasting the most recent three years have been taken for model building. From inspection it can be seen that the destination does have a peak summer season, but the difference between winter and summer demand is not as marked as in other tourist areas, for example islands in the Caribbean where demand from North America is heavily concentrated in the winter season. Being able to fill the off-season has important economic benefits for a destination in terms of employment, accommodation occupancy and the use of tourism facilities in general.

The first step in analysing data of this kind is to inspect it for 'outliers'. These are out of the ordinary happenings, say a festival that is unlikely to be repeated, and should be replaced in the data with a commensurate average so as not to skew the results. Once the data have been prepared, it is then necessary to remove the irregular and seasonal components via a '*moving average*' (MA) with length equal to the seasonal effect, which is 12 months. A moving average is a series of arithmetic means constructed by taking a rolling average of the data 12 months at a time by successively dropping the first observation in the series and adding the next one. The result

| Table 5.1 | | Classical time series decomposition, visitor data (000s) | | | | | |
|---|---|---|---|---|---|---|---|
| Time | $Q^* = TCSu$ | MA(12) | MA(2) = TC | $Su = Q^*/TC$ | Unadjusted $S$ | Adjusted $S$ | $Q^*_s = Q^*/S$ |
| Year 7 Jan | 251 | | | | | | 306 |
| Feb | 242 | | | | | | 313 |
| Mar | 284 | | | | | | 315 |
| Apr | 309 | | | | | | 321 |
| May | 347 | | | | | | 327 |
| Jun | 364 | 323 | | | | | 324 |
| Jul | 392 | 325 | 324 | 1.210 | | | 324 |
| Aug | 395 | 326 | 325 | 1.214 | | | 325 |
| Sep | 349 | 328 | 327 | 1.067 | | | 325 |
| Oct | 341 | 330 | 329 | 1.037 | | | 327 |
| Nov | 311 | 331 | 330 | 0.942 | | | 330 |
| Dec | 290 | 332 | 332 | 0.875 | | | 331 |
| Year 8 Jan | 273 | 335 | 334 | 0.819 | 0.819 | 0.820 | 333 |
| Feb | 259 | 337 | 336 | 0.771 | 0.773 | 0.773 | 335 |
| Mar | 305 | 339 | 338 | 0.902 | 0.900 | 0.901 | 338 |
| Apr | 328 | 342 | 341 | 0.963 | 0.963 | 0.964 | 340 |
| May | 361 | 344 | 343 | 1.053 | 1.059 | 1.060 | 341 |
| Jun | 385 | 346 | 345 | 1.117 | 1.122 | 1.123 | 343 |
| Jul | 418 | 348 | 347 | 1.206 | 1.208 | 1.209 | 346 |
| Aug | 423 | 350 | 349 | 1.214 | 1.214 | 1.215 | 348 |
| Sep | 378 | 352 | 351 | 1.078 | 1.073 | 1.074 | 352 |
| Oct | 370 | 354 | 353 | 1.049 | 1.043 | 1.044 | 354 |
| Nov | 334 | 357 | 355 | 0.940 | 0.941 | 0.942 | 355 |
| Dec | 314 | 360 | 358 | 0.876 | <u>0.875</u> | <u>0.876</u> | 358 |
| Year 9 Jan | 296 | 363 | 361 | 0.819 | 11.990 | 12.000 | 361 |
| Feb | 282 | 366 | 364 | 0.774 | | | 365 |
| Mar | 330 | 369 | 367 | 0.899 | | | 366 |
| Apr | 356 | 371 | 370 | 0.963 | | | 369 |
| May | 396 | 373 | 372 | 1.064 | | | 374 |
| Jun | 422 | 375 | 374 | 1.128 | | | 376 |
| Jul | 452 | | | | | | 374 |
| Aug | 459 | | | | | | 378 |
| Sep | 412 | | | | | | 384 |
| Oct | 398 | | | | | | 381 |
| Nov | 362 | | | | | | 384 |
| Dec | 338 | | | | | | 386 |

is shown in column three of Table 5.1, where the first mean 323 is the monthly average of the data in Year 7 from January to December, the second 325 is the monthly average from February of Year 7 to January of Year 8, and so on in a rolling manner until the data series is all used. This process has three consequences:

1. fluctuations in the data are smoothed out;

2. 11 observations are lost, the general rule being that the number is the order of the moving average less one; and

3. the data need to be repositioned as the mid-point of a year is between June and July.

Thus the next step is to calculate a two-period moving average of the moving average. This is done to centre the average to a month. The result is shown in column four, which is the measure of $TC$ or $T+C$ according to whether the series is multiplicative or additive.

As the centred moving average in column four represents the trend and cyclical components, it is now possible to calculate $Su$, by dividing the original series $Q^*$ in column two by the centred moving average. The result is a 24-month seasonal index as shown in column six that contains elements of the error or irregular component. The latter may be eliminated by averaging the seasonal factors for each month as in column six. The results are unadjusted seasonal factors, for by definition they should add to 12, so a further minor adjustment is necessary as indicated in column seven. The final column in Table 5.1 is the seasonally adjusted value $Q_s^*$, which is derived by dividing the original date series in column two by the appropriate monthly adjusted seasonal factors in column seven.

Column seven still contains $C$, which would be a gradual wavelike movement in the series around the trend $T$. The easiest approach is to fit a trend line to $Q_s^*$ of the kind shown in Figure 5.1, as follows:

$$T = \beta_0 + \beta_1 t \tag{5.4}$$

The Excel spreadsheet has an in-built function TREND which may be used to estimate equation (4), but an algorithm which is relatively easy to use on a hand calculator to estimate trends, though not necessarily optimal, is the three-point method (Granger, 1986). The methodology follows from the basic notion that two parameter (coefficient) trends such as equation (5.4) require two data points, three parameter trends three data points and so on.

When the number of observations N is below 10 we take the weighted average of the first three terms and the last three terms. Thus:

$$F = (Q_1^* + 2Q_2^* + 3Q_3^*)/6 \tag{5.5}$$

$$L = (Q_{N-2}^* + 2Q_{N-1}^* + 3Q_N^*)/6 \tag{5.6}$$

From which the parameters of equation (5.4), the proofs for which may be found in Granger (1986), are:

$$\beta_1 = \frac{L - F}{N - 3} \tag{5.7}$$

and

$$\beta_0 = F - \frac{7}{3}\beta_1 \tag{5.8}$$

Substituting into the above formulas the data from column seven of Table 5.1:

$$\beta_1 = (384.56 - 312.92)/33 = 2.17$$

and

$$\beta_0 = 312.92 - (7/3) \times 2.17 = 307.86$$

hence,

$$T = 307.86 + 2.17t \tag{5.9}$$

With a long series as is the case in Table 5.1, we can take an average of five terms:

$$F = (Q^*_1 + 2Q^*_2 + 3Q^*_3 + 4Q^*_4 + 5Q^*_5)/15 \tag{5.10}$$

$$L = (Q^*_{N-4} + 2Q^*_{N-3} + 3Q^*_{N-2} + 4Q^*_{N-1} + 5Q^*_N)/15 \tag{5.11}$$

From which the appropriate formulas are:

$$\beta_1 = \frac{L - F}{N - 5} \tag{5.12}$$

and

$$\beta_0 = F - \frac{11}{3}\beta_1 \tag{5.13}$$

From which, as before

$$\beta_1 = (383.70 - 319.82)/31 = 2.06$$

and

$$\beta_0 = 319.82 - (11/3) \times 2.06 = 312.27$$

and

$$T = 312.27 + 2.06t \tag{5.14}$$

The TREND function in Excel estimates equation (5.4) by the process of 'least squares regression'. This method regresses the dependent variable $Q^*$ on the independent variable $t$ and positions the trend line in Figure 5.1 in such a way as to minimise the squared deviations between the trend and the data series. The trend parameters are derived from solving two equations:

$$\sum Q^* = N\beta_0 + \beta_1\sum t \tag{5.15}$$

$$\sum tQ^* = \beta_0\sum t + \beta_1\sum t^2 \tag{5.16}$$

where the sign $\sum$ refers to the summation of all values of the N observations.

As before we solve first for $\beta_1$:

$$\beta_1 = \frac{N\sum tQ^* \, | \, (\sum t)(\sum Q^*)}{N\,\Sigma t^2 - (\Sigma t)^2} \tag{5.17}$$

If we then divide equation (5.15) through by N it produces mean values so that we can solve for $\beta_0$ in terms of the means in the time series:

$$\beta_0 = \text{mean}(Q^*) - \beta_1\,\text{mean}(t) \tag{5.18}$$

The calculations undertaken by the least squares method are shown in Table 5.2. It will be noticed that the line is not being fitted through all observations, but rather the mean monthly values for each of the three years presented in Table 5.1. This is a perfectly acceptable procedure, for in any statistical series the mean is a representative measure, and since the seasonal variation

| Table 5.2 | Classical time series decomposition, visitor data (000s) | | | |
|---|---|---|---|---|
| Year | $t$ | $Q^*$ | $t^2$ | $tQ^*$ |
| 7 | 6.50 | 322.92 | 42.25 | 2,098.96 |
| 8 | 18.50 | 345.67 | 342.25 | 6,394.83 |
| 9 | 30.50 | 375.25 | 930.25 | 11,445.13 |
| | $\sum t = 55.50$ | $\sum Q^* = 1,043.84$ | $\sum t^2 = 1,314.75$ | $\sum tQ^* = 19,938.92$ |

cancels itself in one year, the mean monthly values will provide the correct indication of the trend. Note that the value of time is given in months, so the mean monthly value for the first year falls between June and July, hence $t = (6 + 7)/2 = 6.5$. Placing the values from Table 5.2 into equations (5.17) and (5.18) yields the trend line

$$T = 307.60 + 2.18t \tag{5.19}$$

In Table 5.3. we match the predicted values from the trend lines given by equations (5.9), (5.14) and (5.19) against the deseasonalised data $Q_s^*$. If we now divide the latter by the trend line then this will produce the cyclical component $C$. However, by inspection of the trend values it will be appreciated that the deviations from the trend in $Q_s^*$ are negligible, indicating the cyclical component is of little consequence, certainly within the period for which such analysis will be used for forecasting. It will be further observed from Table 5.3 that while each statistical method produces a slightly different trend line, as is to be expected, their predicted values of $Q_s^*$ are broadly the same. This then raises the question as to how the best trend line might be evaluated.

The recommended test of 'goodness of fit' is the root mean square error (RMSE) $= \sqrt{\sum_{t=1}^{N} \frac{(Q_{st}^* - T_t)^2}{N - k}}$. This statistic is derived by summing the squared differences between the deseasonalised observations on visitor numbers and their trend estimate. The resulting sum

| Table 5.3 | Classical time series decomposition, visitor data (000s) | | | |
|-----------|------|------|------|------|
| **Month** | $Q_s^*$ | **3-term prediction** | **5-term prediction** | **Least squares** |
| 1 | 306 | 310 | 314 | 310 |
| 2 | 313 | 312 | 316 | 312 |
| 3 | 315 | 314 | 318 | 314 |
| 4 | 321 | 317 | 321 | 316 |
| 5 | 327 | 319 | 323 | 319 |
| 6 | 324 | 321 | 325 | 321 |
| 7 | 324 | 323 | 327 | 323 |
| 8 | 325 | 325 | 329 | 325 |
| 9 | 325 | 327 | 331 | 327 |
| 10 | 327 | 330 | 333 | 329 |
| 11 | 330 | 332 | 335 | 332 |
| 12 | 331 | 334 | 337 | 334 |
| 13 | 333 | 336 | 339 | 336 |
| 14 | 335 | 338 | 341 | 338 |
| 15 | 338 | 340 | 343 | 340 |
| 16 | 340 | 343 | 345 | 342 |
| 17 | 341 | 345 | 347 | 345 |
| 18 | 343 | 347 | 349 | 347 |
| 19 | 346 | 349 | 351 | 349 |
| 20 | 348 | 351 | 353 | 351 |

| Table 5.3 | (Continued) | | | |
|-----------|-------------|---|---|---|
| Month | $Q^*_s$ | 3-term prediction | 5-term prediction | Least squares |
| 21 | 352 | 353 | 356 | 353 |
| 22 | 354 | 356 | 358 | 356 |
| 23 | 355 | 358 | 360 | 358 |
| 24 | 358 | 360 | 362 | 360 |
| 25 | 361 | 362 | 364 | 362 |
| 26 | 365 | 364 | 366 | 364 |
| 27 | 366 | 366 | 368 | 366 |
| 28 | 369 | 369 | 370 | 369 |
| 29 | 374 | 371 | 372 | 371 |
| 30 | 376 | 373 | 374 | 373 |
| 31 | 374 | 375 | 376 | 375 |
| 32 | 378 | 377 | 378 | 377 |
| 33 | 384 | 379 | 380 | 380 |
| 34 | 381 | 382 | 382 | 382 |
| 35 | 384 | 384 | 384 | 384 |
| 36 | 386 | 386 | 386 | 386 |

is then divided by the value of $N - k$, where $k$ is the number of parameters, which in this case is 2. The value $N - k$ is termed 'the degrees of freedom' of the estimate, hence the model has 34 degrees of freedom. The last step is to take the square root of the derived value to standardise the error to the same order as the estimates. Applying this procedure results in an RMSE of 2.88 for equation (5.9), 4.28 for equation (5.14) and 2.87 for equation (5.19), indicating that the least squares procedure is the most accurate. However, it will be seen from Table 5.4 that each method generates similar forecasts for the next year. The latter are constructed by projecting the trend and then multiplying by the seasonal factors to give *TS*. This may be repeated for succeeding years provided the researcher is confident in the stability of the market over the required forecasting period. A common practice is to produce a rolling forecast by updating the estimates every time new data become available.

## Econometric models

Without the help of intentions surveys or leading indicators, it is not possible for pure time series models to predict changes or turning points in the direction of tourism flows. On the other hand (as noted in the last part of Chapter 4), econometric models attempt to explain tourism demand by estimating the latter as a function of influencing variables. They provide the opportunity to predict turning points, in the sense that it is possible to demonstrate the outcomes of different scenarios through asking 'what if?' questions, but are very data using. This is one of their major difficulties, since their development has been generally constrained by data availability in the tourism sector. Below we restate the multiplicative form for measuring inbound tourism demand $Q^*$ from a particular country of origin.

$$Q^* = \beta_0 FA^{\beta_1} \left[ \frac{C/E}{C^*} \right]^{\beta_2} Y^{*\beta_3} u \qquad (5.20)$$

| Table 5.4 | Classical time series decomposition, visitor data (000s) |

| | | | Monthly Trend Forecast | | | Monthly Seasonal Forecast | | |
|---|---|---|---|---|---|---|---|---|
| Year 10 | $t$ | Seasonal index | Three terms | Five terms | Least squares | Three terms | Five terms | Least squares |
| Jan | 37 | 0.82 | 388 | 389 | 388 | 318 | 318 | 318 |
| Feb | 38 | 0.77 | 390 | 391 | 390 | 302 | 302 | 302 |
| Mar | 39 | 0.90 | 393 | 393 | 393 | 354 | 354 | 354 |
| Apr | 40 | 0.96 | 395 | 395 | 395 | 380 | 380 | 381 |
| May | 41 | 1.06 | 397 | 397 | 397 | 421 | 420 | 421 |
| Jun | 42 | 1.12 | 399 | 399 | 399 | 448 | 448 | 448 |
| Jul | 43 | 1.21 | 401 | 401 | 401 | 485 | 485 | 485 |
| Aug | 44 | 1.21 | 403 | 403 | 404 | 490 | 489 | 490 |
| Sep | 45 | 1.07 | 406 | 405 | 406 | 435 | 435 | 436 |
| Oct | 46 | 1.04 | 408 | 407 | 408 | 426 | 425 | 426 |
| Nov | 47 | 0.94 | 410 | 409 | 410 | 386 | 385 | 386 |
| Dec | 48 | 0.88 | 412 | 411 | 412 | 361 | 360 | 361 |

where

$FA$ = the round trip travel cost or fare variable;

$C$ = the consumer price index in the destination country;

$E$ = the destination country exchange rate in terms of units of local currency per unit of the visitors' currency;

$C^*$ = the consumer price index in the tourism generating country;

$Y^*$ = the sum of inbound visitor incomes for this market; and

$\beta_0$ is the constant term, and $\beta_1$ to $\beta_3$ are coefficients of the explanatory variables of inbound tourism movements to be estimated using statistical multiple regression analysis, with $u$ being the error term.

The estimation of equation (5.20) requires the dependent variable $Q^*$ to be regressed on multiple independent variables. There are specific statistical packages designed to do this and Excel has the LINEST function, which again uses the least squares method to calculate a straight line that best fits the data set. But to be able to undertake this in the case of equation (5.20) would require the function to be made linear in logarithms by converting the data set to give:

$$\text{Log}Q^* = \text{Log}\beta_0 + \beta_1\text{Log}FA + \beta_2\text{Log}\left[\frac{C/E}{C^*}\right] + \beta_3\text{Log}Y^* + \text{Log}u \qquad (5.21)$$

The Excel spreadsheet contains the two most commonly used logarithmic functions, LN and LOG10. The former transforms the data into natural logarithms to the exponential base $e$, where $e = 2.718$ approximately, while the latter converts the data to common logarithms to the base 10. A logarithm to the base, say $a$, is the power to which the base $a$ must be raised in order to be equal to the number, hence the value of $\text{Log}_3 9 = 2$, for $3^2 = 3 \times 3 = 9$. Natural logarithms are also known as Napierian logarithms after John Napier who originated the concept. The exponential base $e$ is used because it is a mathematical constant irrespective of the nature of the analysis being undertaken: it is known as a transcendental constant. The benefit of using logarithms is seen in changing multiplication to addition.

To allow for habit persistence in tourism trip-taking most researchers use lagged as well as current values of the independent variables shown in equation (5.21). This gives a multi-period or dynamic time dimension to the forecast equation and produces what is termed a distributed lag model of tourism trends. These are complex models, for example Witt et al. (2004) estimate such a model for Denmark in the form:

$$\text{Ln}Q^*_{it} = \text{Ln}\beta_0 + \beta_1\text{Ln}Q^*_{it-1} + \beta_2\text{Ln}Y^*_{it} + \beta_3\text{Ln}Y^*_{it-1} + \beta_4\text{Ln}\left[\frac{C/E}{C^*}\right]_{it} + \beta_5\text{Ln}\left[\frac{C/E}{C^*}\right]_{it-1}$$

$$+ \beta_6\text{Ln}\left[\frac{Cs/Es}{C^*}\right]_{ist} + \beta_7\text{Ln}\left[\frac{Cs/Es}{C^*}\right]_{ist-1} + \beta_8T + dummies + \text{Ln}u_{it} \qquad (5.22)$$

Where

$Q^*_{it} =$ tourism consumed per capita at time $t$ measured by the expenditure-weighted number of nights spent by tourists from country $i$ in Denmark: the weights reflect the different daily spending for tourists in different accommodation types;

$Y^*_{it} =$ real private consumption expenditure per capita in country $i$;

$\left[\dfrac{C/E}{C^*}\right]_{it} =$ represents the real cost of stay for tourists in Denmark relative to country $i$;

$\left[\dfrac{Cs/Es}{C^*}\right]_{ist} =$ weighted average of tourism prices in substitute destinations;

$T =$ a time trend; and

$dummies =$ dummy variables to account for 'spikes' in the data caused by two oil scares, the first Gulf War, German unification and a dummy for Chernobyl/the US bombing of Libya.

The construction of demand models of the kinds shown by equation (5.22) involve considerable time and effort. An illustration of the model-building process is presented in Figure 5.2. Witt et al. estimated six different model specifications through imposing certain restrictions on the parameters

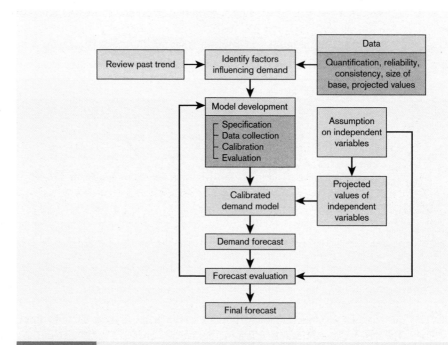

**Figure 5.2**  Building an econometric model

in equation (5.22) and examined their performance over one-, two- and three-year forecasts to discover the best fit structure. The reasons for this complexity lie in the disappointing performance of econometric forecasts in the past, even against the most simple of time series extrapolations. While the availability of data is one hindrance, it has been noticed that fluctuations in the data are not internally consistent, giving rise to unreliable model estimation. To cope with this, researchers have introduced a range of demand models in order to produce more stable long-run relationships for forecasting purposes. What is interesting about equation (5.22) is that the travel cost variable is omitted as it was found to be insignificant in the empirical analysis. Relative destination prices reveal themselves to be the more important signal in consumers' decision making.

## Long-term projections

At this level, the data resource difficulty is further exaggerated, given that we are looking at time periods covering the next 5–15 years, or more when project evaluation is being considered, though situations longer than this are regarded as 'futurism'. Causal models require the future values of independent variables to be known at the time of forecasting, which is highly improbable, so we tend to focus on univariate annual trend analysis as a qualitative judgement aid. In order to produce the best representation of the trend, we need a range of equations that may be classified into:

**Two parameter curves:**

- Straight line $\quad\quad\quad\quad\quad\quad Q^{\star} = \beta_0 + \beta_1 t$
- Exponential $\quad\quad\quad\quad\quad Q^{\star} = \beta_0 \beta_1{}^t$
- Hyperbola $\quad\quad\quad\quad\quad\, Q^{\star} = 1/(\beta_0 + \beta_1 t)$

**Three parameter curves:**

- Parabola $\quad\quad\quad\quad\quad\quad Q^{\star} = \beta_0 + \beta_1 t + \beta_2 t^2$
- Modified exponential $\quad\; Q^{\star} = \beta_0 + \beta_1 \beta_2{}^t$
- Gompertz $\quad\quad\quad\quad\quad Q^{\star} = \beta_0 \beta_1{}^{\beta_2{}^t}$
- Logistic $\quad\quad\quad\quad\quad\quad Q^{\star} = 1/(\beta_0 + \beta_1 \beta_2{}^t)$

An illustration of the trend drawn out by the two parameter curves is given in Figure 5.3. Three parameter curves are capable of producing more varied shapes: examples for the parabola

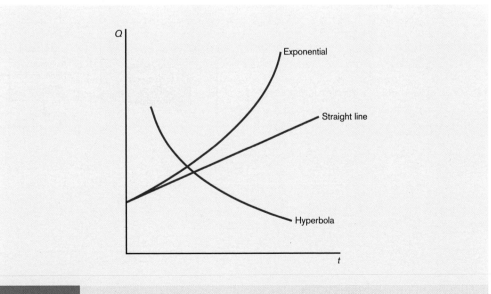

| Figure 5.3 | Two parameter curves |

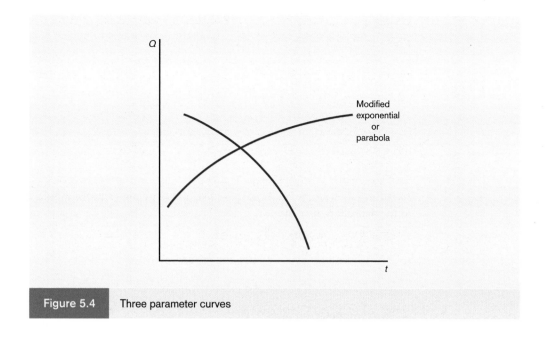

| Figure 5.4 | Three parameter curves |
| --- | --- |

or modified exponential are shown in Figure 5.4, while the Gompertz and logistic curves produce the familiar S-shaped trend, as presented in Figure 5.5. S-curves have often been used to illustrate the tourism life-cycle of destinations. This is because as the value of $t \rightarrow \infty$ they approach limiting values of $\beta_0$ and $\frac{1}{\beta_0}$ respectively, and so they are appropriate for a time series that has an upper limit that may be interpreted as maximum market penetration.

## Estimation

Most people today would use a computer software package to fit these trend curves to the available data and some basic shapes are available as set functions in modern spreadsheets. However, the three-point method discussed earlier may also be developed for calculating these curves. For two parameter curves the formulas are the same as for a straight line, but for

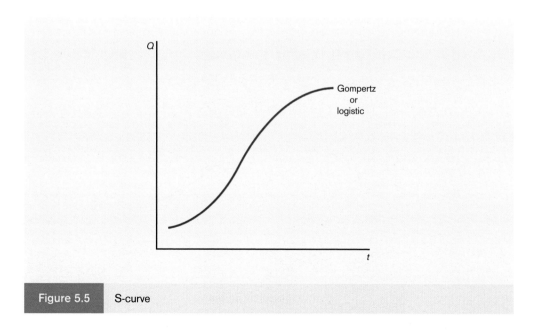

| Figure 5.5 | S-curve |
| --- | --- |

$Q^* = \beta_0\beta_1{}^t$ and $Q^* = 1/(\beta_0 + \beta_1 t)$ we have to transform the data, so the exponential becomes $LogQ^* = Log\beta_0 + tLog\beta_1$ and the hyperbola $\frac{1}{Q^*} = \beta_0 + \beta_1 t$.

Of the three parameter curves, it is the parabola that is set apart from the others, as it has a squared '$t$' term. The other three curves are all of the same family, as in the two parameter case, once the dependent variable is transformed for estimation purposes:

- Modified exponential $\qquad\qquad Q^* = \beta_0 + \beta_1\beta_2^t$
- Gompertz $\qquad\qquad\qquad LogQ^* = Log\beta_0 + Log\beta_1\beta_2^t$
- Logistic $\qquad\qquad\qquad\quad \dfrac{1}{Q^*} = \beta_0 + \beta_1\beta_2^t$

Furthermore, the fact that there are three coefficients to compute means that it is necessary to have three data points. So in addition to F and L, we now take the middle terms M, three or five as the data allow, namely:

$$M = (Q^*_{j-1} + 2Q^*_j + 3Q^*_{j+1})/6 \qquad\qquad\qquad (5.23)$$

or

$$M = (Q^*_{j-2} + 2Q^*_{j-1} + 3Q^*_j + 4Q^*_{j+1} + 5Q^*_{j+2})/15 \qquad\qquad (5.24)$$

where $j = (N + 1)/2$, hence the need for dropping the earliest term when the data series is an even number so as to allow the average to fall on a specific data point. The relevant formulas for estimating three parameter curves are presented in Table 5.5. They are shown in sequential order of calculation. Note that the algorithms for the Gompertz and logistic curves are exactly the same as for the modified exponential, save that for the former we use logarithms of the data when forming F, L and M, and for the latter the reciprocals of the data.

Once again the use of trend curves may be best illustrated through worked examples so we return to the data from Table 5.1, but this time using the nine years of annual statistics, to which an exponential and modified exponential trend will be fitted. The results are shown in Table 5.6 together with annual projections for the next 10 years. The second column in Table 5.6 has the

| Table 5.5 | Algorithms for estimating three parameter trend curves | |
|---|---|---|
| **Three-point method** | **Three terms** | **Five terms** |
| Parabola | $\beta_2 = \dfrac{2(F + L - 2M)}{(N - 3)^2}$ | $\beta_2 = \dfrac{2(F + L - 2M)}{([N - 5)]^2}$ |
| | $\beta_1 = \dfrac{L - F}{N - 3} - \dfrac{\beta_2(3N + 5)}{3}$ | $\beta_1 = \dfrac{L - F}{N - 5} - \dfrac{\beta_2(3N + 7)}{3}$ |
| | $\beta_0 = F - \dfrac{7}{3}\beta_1 - 6\beta_2$ | $\beta_0 = F - \dfrac{11}{3}\beta_1 - 15\beta_2$ |
| Modified exponential Gompertz logistic | $Log\,\beta_2 = \dfrac{2}{N - 3}\,Log\left(\dfrac{L - M}{M - F}\right)$ | $Log\,\beta_2 = \dfrac{2}{N - 5}\,Log\left(\dfrac{L - M}{M - F}\right)$ |
| | $m = \dfrac{6}{\beta_2 + 2\beta_2^2 + 3\beta_2^3}$ | $m = \dfrac{15}{\beta_2 + 2\beta_2^2 + 3\beta_2^2 + 4\beta_2^4 + 5\beta_2^5}$ |
| | $\beta_1 = \dfrac{m(M - F)^2}{F + L - 2M}$ | $\beta_1 = \dfrac{m(M - F)^2}{F + L - 2M}$ |
| | $\beta_0 = \dfrac{LF - M^2}{F + L - 2M}$ | $\beta_0 = \dfrac{LF - M^2}{F + L - 2M}$ |

*Source*: Granger, 1986

actual data, while the third column presents the natural logarithms of this same data for the purposes of estimating the two parameter exponential curve. Using the formulas in equations (5.7) and (5.8):

$$\text{Ln}\beta_1 = (8.36 - 7.89)/(9 - 3) = 0.078$$

and

$$\text{Ln}\beta_0 = 7.89 - (7/3) \times 0.078 = 7.71$$

hence,

$$\text{Ln}Q^* = 7.71 + 0.078\,t \tag{5.25}$$

If we take anti-logarithms of equation (5.25) by raising the base $e$ to the power of the values shown (in Excel there is an EXP function that does this), then the actual exponential trend is

$$Q^* = 2227(1.081)^t \tag{5.26}$$

The predicted values of $Q$ may be calculated from equations (5.25) or (5.26) by substituting in the values for time as shown in the first column of Table 5.6, though if the former is used then the resulting estimates will be in logarithms and will require conversion back to actual values.

| Table 5.6 | Annual trend in visitor arrivals, visitor data (000s) | | | |
|---|---|---|---|---|
| Year | Data | Log data | Exponential | Modified exponential |
| | Actual | Ln values | Three terms | Three terms |
| 1 | 2,397 | 7.7820 | 2,408 | 2,409 |
| 2 | 2,612 | 7.8679 | 2,604 | 2,605 |
| 3 | 2,815 | 7.9427 | 2,816 | 2,816 |
| 4 | 3,052 | 8.0236 | 3,045 | 3,045 |
| 5 | 3,285 | 8.0971 | 3,293 | 3,292 |
| 6 | 3,562 | 8.1781 | 3,561 | 3,560 |
| 7 | 3,875 | 8.2623 | 3,850 | 3,849 |
| 8 | 4,148 | 8.3304 | 4,163 | 4,163 |
| 9 | 4,503 | 8.4125 | 4,502 | 4,502 |
| 10 | | | 4,868 | 4,869 |
| 11 | | | 5,264 | 5,265 |
| 12 | | | 5,692 | 5,695 |
| 13 | | | 6,155 | 6,159 |
| 14 | | | 6,655 | 6,662 |
| 15 | | | 7,196 | 7,205 |
| 16 | | | 7,782 | 7,794 |
| 17 | | | 8,414 | 8,430 |
| 18 | | | 9,099 | 9,118 |
| 19 | | | 9,839 | 9,863 |

The use of natural logarithms in estimation has an added benefit in that $Ln\beta_1$ measures the annual growth rate of visitor arrival in Table 5.6, which is about 7.8%. This may be used to advantage by forecasters through the 'Rule of 70': if 70 is divided by the growth rate of $Q^*$ in percentage terms, it will tell you how long it will take in years for the current value to double. This acts as a useful 'common sense' check on the forecast, as well as being helpful for comparative purposes in setting realistic goals. Thus if $Q^*$ is growing at 7.8% per annum, then the current value of 4.503 million visitors will double in just under nine years' time, which occurs towards the end of Year 18 in Table 5.6.

Turning now to the modified exponential, this is calculated by applying the formulas shown in Table 5.5 in sequence, but using the actual data in column two of Table 5.6 and not the logarithmic data in column three. From this it follows that

$$Ln\beta_2 = 0.79$$

hence

$$\beta_2 = 1.082$$

and

$$m = 0.83$$

and

$$\beta_1 = 2205$$

and

$$\beta_0 = 24$$

which gives:

$$Q^* = 24 + 2205(1.082)^t \tag{5.27}$$

As one might expect, it turns out that equations (5.26) and (5.27) are very similar in parameters and also in their forecasting ability, as shown in Table 5.6. To discriminate between the two we apply the RMSE procedure, which gives a value of 12.84 for equation (5.26) and 14.07 for equation (5.27). Fitting an extra parameter in equation (5.26) results in an additional loss of one degree of freedom for no improvement, therefore the simpler exponential curve is to be preferred. In practice forecasters will augment their statistical techniques by observing the pattern of the data before specifying the functional form of the trend curve and use judgement in respect of the causal logic behind the trend. Testing the reliability of long-run forecasts can be undertaken by using the Rule of 70 and examining what happens when the time value becomes very large, in order to see whether the forecasts are within an acceptable range. If they do not seem credible in terms of what is theoretically possible then they must be reconsidered. These are the qualitative aspects of forecasting, which are the subject of the next section in this chapter.

## Qualitative forecasting

Qualitative methods may be used solely or in combination with statistical forecasts by providing a reasoned scenario for likely outcomes. Qualitative methods come into their own when data are scarce, which is the case when predicting long-term trends. From the practitioner's standpoint it makes sense to combine the best of quantitative and qualitative forecasting so as to produce an integrated approach to future planning. This makes drawing distinctions between different approaches somewhat arbitrary, but for the purposes of exposition we will consider the most common qualitative methods, namely by analogy to what has happened elsewhere, the Delphi technique and scenario writing.

### Analogy

Most countries produce macro-economic data which may be used to interpret the relative wealth, economic health and the stage of economic development in the country (see

Chapter 11). The purpose of international comparisons is to use available data to place the country of reference on a general trend line so an assessment may be made of what demand might be given appropriate conditions. The main points to watch when selecting countries for analysis are the comparability of the qualitative factors influencing tourism demand and uniformity in data definitions. Boniface and Cooper (1987) have identified a few tourism indicators to aid comparisons:

- The *gross travel propensity,* which gives the total number of tourism trips taken as a percentage of the population. This is a measure of the penetration of trips, and not individual travellers. The relevance of this can be found in developed economies where second and third holiday-taking are increasingly common.

- The *net travel propensity,* which refers to the percentage of the population that takes at least one tourism trip in a given period of time. This is a measure of the penetration of travel among 'individuals' in the population. Simply dividing gross travel propensity by net will give the *travel frequency,* which is the average number of trips taken by those participating in tourism during a given time.

- Finally, they offer the '*country potential generation index*' (CPGI) as a measure:

$$\text{CPGI} = \frac{N_e / N_w}{P_e / P_w}$$

where

$N_e$ = number of trips generated by the country;

$N_w$ = number of trips generated in the world or region of interest;

$P_e$ = population of the country;

$P_w$ = population of the world or region of interest.

- Countries with an index greater than unity are generating more tourists than expected by their population and conversely for countries with an index below one.

### Delphi models

As the name suggests, the Delphi technique relies upon finding an 'oracle' to predict future trends and events. The oracle in this case is a panel of experts chosen according to the nature of the research question and asked to deliver a consensus view of the future. Unlike everyday panels or committees, the essence of a Delphi study is anonymity, so the participants never meet. This is to avoid opinions being influenced by the pressures of group discussion where one or a group of individuals may have strong opinions that can assert considerable influence on the consensus forecast that is reached.

The procedure for undertaking a Delphi study is outlined in Figure 5.6. The experts communicate only with the coordinator through successive rounds of questionnaires. Those holding extreme views, that is views outside the interquartile range, which is defined as plus or minus a distance of 25% from the median or middle value, are invited to give their reasons. At the end of the first round the replies are summarised by the coordinator and returned to the panel members who are invited to revise their opinions in view of the information feedback to them. This process is repeated through a number of iterations until it is clear that a consensus has emerged or is not likely to emerge. Three rounds are normally considered sufficient for this.

### Scenarios

From the discussion in this chapter it should now be apparent that although scenarios may stand alone, scenario writing has an important part to play in integrated forecasting through clarifying the issues involved. The steps in scenario writing involve in the first instance

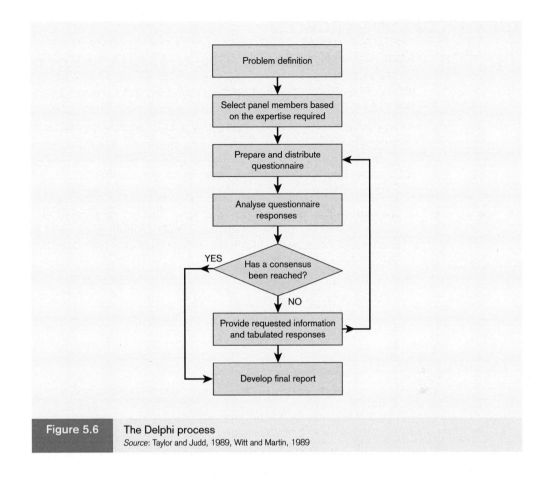

**Figure 5.6**    The Delphi process
*Source*: Taylor and Judd, 1989, Witt and Martin, 1989

establishing a baseline with some specific patterns relating to the current situation in order to build up a logical sequence of events to indicate how some future state might arise. Next a range of future scenarios are drawn up, followed by the exploration of networks of events that will define the pathway to each future state of affairs. Technological forecasts are often included into scenario writing so as to comprehend factors that might cause major shifts in travel patterns or behaviour.

While most attention is given to the more probable scenarios, one issue that frequently arises is how critical incident or disaster planning, say an explosion, earthquake, fire or crash, may be built into planning tourism projects for the future. These factors are very difficult to account for in a quantitative manner in the appraisal process, as this example will show. Suppose, when matched against a catastrophe, the probability of achieving positive net economic benefits of 50 over a project's lifetime is 99%, leaving the probability of some accident as 1%. Presume that this accident would result in the loss of the investment in the project of 200, all the net benefits of 50 and compensation of 50. Then the expected value of the net economic benefits is $0.99 \times 50 - 0.01 \times (200 + 50 + 50) = 46.5$, and so the possibility of a catastrophe has very little bearing in a quantitative sense on the worth of the project. Nonetheless, these low-probability but high-impact scenarios cannot be ignored as they tend to be featured by the media and colour public opinion. What happens in practice is that safeguards are built into the project design and management to ensure that such accidents are avoided. Major incidents are rare, but when they occur they can usually be put down to the simultaneous failure of a number of preventative measures, arising from some combination of human error, design flaws, and natural occurrences that are difficult to guard against with 100% certainty.

# THE FORECASTING PROBLEM

Figure 5.7 poses the question as to whether A or B is the better forecast? Any measure of forecast accuracy both at $t$ and $t + 1$ would rank $A > B$, because of A's tracking ability, which implies that Model A is better than Model B. Yet it is clear that B is the most useful because of its ability to predict accurately the turning point in the actual data series at $t$. Thus the evaluation of a forecast must consider two aspects: the ability to predict turning points and the ability to track closely the original series.

All in all we are prepared to sacrifice tracking for the benefit of predicting turning points. For although forecast B consistently underestimates the actual series, if year-on-year changes are taken they will show that B follows the data very closely. The importance of this may be realised by the fact that forecasters are interested in finding leading indicators that will enable them to predict changes in the economic variables they are studying. For the calculation of turning point errors, it is essential to take changes in the actual data and the forecast, either absolute, or in percentage terms. When comparing forecast values against outcomes, we can use the familiar:

$$\text{RMSE} = \sqrt{\left[ \sum_{t=1}^{f} \frac{(A_t - P_t)^2}{f} \right]} \tag{5.28}$$

where

$A_t$ = actual data;

$P_t$ = predicted data;

$f$ = the length of the forecast period.

Alternatively we may use a percentage error calculation:

$$\text{RMSPE} = \sqrt{\left[ \frac{1}{f} \sum_{t=1}^{f} \frac{(A_t - P_t)^2}{A_t^2} \right]} \times 100 \tag{5.29}$$

But a more common measure is the mean absolute percentage error, namely,

$$\text{MAPE} = \frac{1}{f} \sum_{t=1}^{f} \left[ \left( \text{ABS} \frac{A_t - P_t}{A_t} \right) \right] \times 100 \tag{5.30}$$

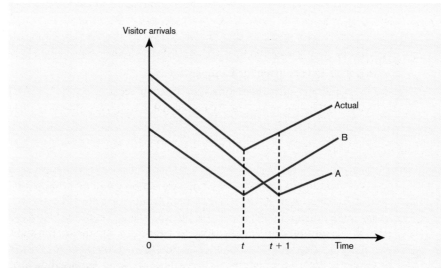

| Figure 5.7 | Which forecast? |

Photograph 5.2 | Propensities for travel in the developing world are generally higher for those living in the cities than for rural areas.
*Source*: Luciano Mortula/Shutterstock.com

The absolute value ignores the sign of the number so there is no need to square the differences in equation (5.30) to avoid plus and minus values cancelling themselves when summed. The popularity of MAPE over RMSPE relates to the fact that the latter penalises outliers in the forecast heavily, when average performance may be satisfactory.

## MARKET PLANNING

It will now be appreciated that the measurement and forecasting of tourism demand are an essential component of market planning for businesses, destinations and government bodies, particularly where investment in infrastructure that requires long lead times is concerned. Irrespective of the organisation involved market scheduling follows along these lines:

- identification of current demand;
- taking and inventory of existing supply and its capacity;
- matching existing supply and demand to determine whether there is currently too much or too little capacity;
- forecasting future demand, noting the lead times required for future investment; and
- planning future supply.

(Further aspects of market planning are discussed in more detail in Chapters 11 and 20.)

Of the different industries engaged in tourism, it is generally the transport and commercial accommodation sectors that pay most attention to demand forecasting, since they are the principal facilitators for tourism. Attractions, unless they are destinations in their own right, as in the case of Disney World in Orlando, Florida, tend to compete for visitor numbers once they are at the destination. Each supplier will have its own particularities, thus airports will be looking at passenger movements and matching these to the type of aircraft, which in turn affects runway capacity and terminal provision.

At the destination the commercial accommodation sector will be relating demand to the provision of rooms. As for any other supplier this does require some adaptation to the forecasted volume of visitors $Q^*$. In order to produce a forecast for rooms we need the following additional information about supply:

- The proportion of visitors who are tourists in that they stay overnight, say $p$.
- The proportion of tourists using commercial accommodation, say $a$, since many tourists stay with friends and relatives.
- The average length of stay in nights, say $l$.
- The time period for which the above apply, which would commonly be a year, but could be the main season or the peak month.
- The effective occupancy rate, say $\theta$, for 100% occupancy is unlikely year-round due to seasonal fluctuations in demand but very possible in the peak month. Thus it relates to the time period being considered.
- The expected room density, say $d$, which is the average number of persons per room and is derived from the ratio of the number of bed nights sold to room nights. In hotel terms it is a measure of the degree of double occupancy compared to single occupancy.

Putting the above together gives the following formula for calculating the number of rooms required $R$:

$$R = \frac{p \cdot Q^* \cdot a \cdot l}{365 \cdot \theta \cdot d} \tag{5.31}$$

The numerator in equation (5.31) determines the number of commercial bed nights demanded, thus using the example in Table 5.6 we note that in 10 years' time according to the forecast there will be just over 9.8 million inbound visitors. We estimate that some 85% of these will be staying visitors, of which 65% will be requiring commercial accommodation, staying an average of 5.5 nights, hence the number of bed nights demanded $= 0.85 \times 9.839 \times 0.65 \times 5.5 = 29.898$ million. Given the degree of seasonality it is expected that the year-round effective occupancy rate would be at the most 80%, and with an average room density of 1.6 persons per room, giving $R = (29.898 \text{ million})/(365 \times 0.80 \times 1.6) = 63,995$. From this value current stock and developments already planned need to be deducted to arrive at additional new build targets.

## CONCLUSION

As outlined in the overview to this chapter, forecasting is an activity which is undertaken by organisations at all levels with the primary purpose of giving directions as to the future. The methodology of forecasting can be divided into quantitative and qualitative approaches for predicting the flows and patterns of demand. It so happens these are bound up with a time dimension in that the further we look into the future the less likely it is that supportive data are available for building numerical models of prediction. Consequently more reliance is placed on qualitative assessment such as scenario writing and expert opinion where long-term forecasts are concerned.

The case studies in this chapter reveal that in order to counter uncertainty practitioners base their forecasts on a combination of quantitative and qualitative methods to produce a hybrid prediction. The conceptual thinking behind this approach is to take account of as wide a range of information sources as possible and also to reach a consensus amongst industry participants upon which to base future planning.

Forecasting logic dictates that detailed estimates are prepared for the short term, with greater aggregation and a range of options in the longer term. By instituting a rolling forecasting plan practitioners are able to update their forecasts as new information becomes available and the long term turns into the short term, requiring concrete planning decisions to be made. When looking back at previous forecasts priority should be given to methods and models which have the ability to predict changes in direction of the reference data, rather than tracking ability alone.

## SELF-CHECK QUESTIONS

1. Consider how the time period chosen affects the choice of techniques in forecasting the demand for tourism.
2. Review the key determinants of demand at an aggregate level and their importance for econometric models.
3. List three advantages of quantitative approaches to demand forecasting and three advantages of qualitative approaches.
4. Summarise the experiences of practitioners in developing procedures for tourism demand forecasting.
5. Taking a destination of your choice list the steps you would take to plan for future demand.

## YOUTUBE

**http://www.youtube.com/watch?v=0hAEfrHwZc8&feature=related**
Demand forecasting for San Antonio.

**http://www.youtube.com/watch?v=eZG0bUqX48M&feature=related**
Examines sales forecasting accuracy.

## REFERENCES AND FURTHER READING

Boniface, B. and Cooper, C. (1987) *The Geography of Travel and Tourism*, Heinemann, London.

Frechtling, D. (2001) *Forecasting Tourism Demand: Methods and Strategies*, Butterworth Heinemann, Oxford. A very user-friendly account of the techniques and issues of tourism demand forecasting.

Granger, C. (1986) *Forecasting in Business and Economics*, 2nd edn, Emerald Group Publishing, Bingley, UK.

Song, H., and Witt, S. (2000) *Tourism Demand Modeling and Forecasting: Modern Econometric Approaches*, Amsterdam: Pergamon. An advanced text for those wishing a thorough and technical review of tourism demand forecasting.

Taylor, R.E. and Judd, L.L. (1989) 'Delphi Forecasting', pp. 535–9, in Witt, S.F. and Moutinho, L. (eds) *Tourism Marketing and Management Handbook*, 2nd edn, Prentice Hall, Hemel Hempstead.

UNWTO (2001) *Tourism 2020 Vision – Global Forecasts and Profiles of Market Segments*, WTO, Madrid. A comprehensive, but now somewhat dated, review of future patterns of tourism demand and the key changes in determinants across the world.

UNWTO (2011) *Tourism towards 2030 – Global Overview*, WTO, Madrid.

Witt, S.F. and Martin, C.A. (1989) 'Demand forecasting in tourism and recreation', pp. 4–32 in Cooper, C.P. (ed.), *Progress in Tourism, Recreation and Hospitality Management*, Vol. 1, Belhaven, London.

Witt, S., Song, H., and Wanhill, S. (2004) 'Forecasting tourism generated employment: the case of Denmark', *Tourism Economics* **10**(2), 167–76.

# MAJOR CASE STUDY 5.1
## The Australian Tourism Forecasting Committee

## ORGANISATION

Tourism forecasting plays an important role in providing awareness and support for future development of the Australian tourism industry. Australia's Tourism Forecasting Committee (TFC) was established in 2004 to provide the Australian tourism sector with accurate forecasts of tourism. The TFC is an independent body charged with providing present and potential tourism investors, industry and governments with 'consensus forecasts' across the tourism sectors. By consensus is meant that the various members of the Committee have agreed them. The Committee is independent but funded by Tourism Research Australia, which is a business unit of Tourism Australia that produces the *Forecast* publication twice a year, giving a selection of inbound, domestic and outbound forecasts available for the next 10 years, which are also available online.

The TFC is a consultative body that draws upon a wide range of expertise to formulate its forecasts. The Committee is wide-ranging in its make-up to ensure representation across relevant tourism stakeholders in both the public and private sectors. It comprises the following members:

### The Tourism Forecasting Committee

- Accounting and management consultants KPMG
- Tourism Australia
- Queensland Tourism Industry Council
- Tourism & Transport Forum
- ANZ Bank
- Department of Resources, Energy and Tourism
- Australian Tourism Export Council
- Tourism Western Australia
- Qantas Airways Limited

The TFC is supported by a technical committee (TFCTC) which also has a mixture of private and public sector representation and relevant experience to inform decision making:

### The Tourism Forecasting Committee Technical Committee

- Tourism Research Australia
- Tourism & Transport Forum

- Airport Coordination Australia
- Australian Bankers' Association
- Jones Lang LaSalle
- Tourism Australia
- Qantas Airways Limited
- Department of Resources, Energy and Tourism

## PRINCIPAL OBJECTIVES OF THE TFC

The three main objectives of the TFC are to: improve private and public sector investment and marketing decision-making; provide an understanding of changing industry dynamics, including times of increasing uncertainty; and assist in the formulation of public policy at national and regional levels within the Australian tourism sector. In order to achieve these objectives, the Committee is assisted by the TFCTC and a forecasting and analysis section within Tourism Research Australia. Working with these groups the TFC is charged with:

- developing and enhancing forecasting techniques on both the demand and the supply side;
- recommending dissemination strategies and products to improve the tourism sector's use of forecasts; and
- engaging with other tourism research providers to assist in achieving the committee's objectives.

In this way the TFC reduces its dependence upon econometric modelling through consultation to ensure that aspects of a qualitative nature are accounted for. By engaging with the tourism industry the TFC not only gathers in a diverse range of influences, but also gives credibility to the forecasts for management decision-making. The aim is to ensure that TFC's forecasts are both disseminated to and used by Australian tourism businesses.

## THE FORECASTING PROCESS

The forecasts have a firm base due to the implementation by the Australian Bureau of Statistics (ABS) of an annual TSA in accordance with international standards, which in turn is underpinned by Australia's key tourism surveys – the International Visitor Survey and the National Visitor Survey. The approach is to undertake three iterative rounds of consultation. The first round generates initial forecasts produced by Tourism Research Australia based on econometric and time series modelling, incorporating variables such as aviation capacity, price comparisons, incomes, populations and seasonality as well as significant events affecting source markets.

In the next round the TFCTC then reviews the forecasts addressing methods and technical matters affecting the models, such as GDP projections, relative price changes and movements in exchange rates. Adjustments are made using qualitative information to take account of uncertainty, competitors' marketing, market conditions, travel propensity, aviation trends and inter-country agreements in terms of travel movements and trade relations. These are influences that no statistical model can encompass and are used to adjust the outputs to produce a consensus as to the most likely outcomes.

The last round rests with the TFC to assess the strategic direction of the industry and provide consensus growth rates to determine the final forecasts to be published. The TFC takes the view that this integrative or hybrid approach delivers the forecasts that are the most probable outcomes, given historic data, current trends, and the impact of policy and industry events. The rolling nature of the forecasting process generates the best available estimates of future activity at a given time.

*Source*: http://www.tra.australia.com

## DISCUSSION QUESTIONS

1. Suggest ways in which these forecasts might be used by tourism enterprises.

2. Download the TFC's latest forecast and consider its user friendliness.

3. It is evident that the TFC takes advice from a wide range of sources. Which organisation would you like to see on a committee of this kind in your country or region?

# PART 2

## THE TOURISM DESTINATION

Photograph: Old City Damascus, Syria © Helen Savill

# INTRODUCTION

Part 2 of this text focuses on the destinations in which tourism activity takes place and the impacts associated with that activity on the economy, environment and culture. This part also includes an examination of how those impacts can be managed during the planning process and what should be done in the event of a shock to the tourism system. Unlike most goods or services, tourism brings the consumers to the place of production and that creates a wide range of impacts, both positive and negative and these impacts need to be understood and built into planning processes and systems if tourism development is to be optimal. The chapters in this part examine the concept of destinations and how this term is fluid and can be applied to single attraction sites and to regions of the world. The chapters also identify and scope out the impact issues and then examine the multitude of models and approaches that have been used to address them in order to facilitate sound tourism planning. Each chapter examines a specific aspect of destinations, impacts and planning. The models that have been used to measure impacts are examined and the final two chapters of this part address the planning processes and the ways in which disaster management can be used to improve the resilience of tourism destinations when incidents occur.

Tourism development, although often driven by economic needs such as foreign exchange earnings, job creation or economic diversification, cannot be considered without examining the environmental and socio-cultural impacts that such development may bring. Tourism, as a development option, must be considered in the light of its *net* impacts, its sustainability and the vulnerability to which the destination may be exposed if it chooses tourism as a major part of its economy. When assessing the positive and negative impacts of tourism development it is important that they are examined within a common framework so that the direct and indirect effects of development can be fully considered in a way that allows sensible planning decisions to be made. Therefore, one of the major learning outcomes of this part of the book is to demonstrate the breadth and depth of impacts associated with tourism development and the ways in which they can be considered within a single analytical framework. It is acknowledged in this part of the text that the main driving force that explains the strong, resilient growth of the global tourism industry over the past century is money; money in the form of foreign exchange earnings, income and investment – i.e. the contribution that tourism makes to a destination's gross domestic product (GDP). In effect destinations are selling some of their environment and culture in return for the economic benefits associated with tourism and planning is intended to secure the best net result for destinations.

Chapter 6 looks at the central role of destinations in the tourism system. The definition, scope and range of destinations are explored, and the way destinations are a fluid concept that refers to the economy, environment and society within which tourism takes place. It can be a region of the world, a national economy, a sub-national region or a resort. Because tourism has many secondary effects associated with it, some positive and some negative, the definition used to identify the 'destination' is vital because the wider the economy the more comprehensive the indirect or secondary effects become. The destination concept is crucial for the management and marketing of tourism and thus its competitiveness and resilience.

Chapter 7 examines how important (the significance) tourism is to the economies in which it takes place and how the full significance can be measured. It then goes on to look at the methodologies that have been used in an attempt to measure the economic impact associated with a change in the level of tourism activity within an economy.

To measure the economic significance of tourism it is necessary to identify the structure of the destination's economy and the level of economic dependence that exists upon the income, employment and foreign exchange earned from tourism. Where the level of economic dependence is high there may be concerns that the economy is vulnerable because of tourism's sensitivity to factors outside the control of the destination. This is particularly important following the past decade or more of enhanced terrorist activities and the more recent global economic and financial crises. The ability to measure the economic significance of tourism using accounting practices such as tourism satellite accounts (TSA) provides governments with the ability to understand the importance of the sector but offers little scope to help with specific policy decisions. In order to provide economic policy and planning guidance it is necessary to turn attention to the economic, environmental and socio-cultural impact models that have been constructed to determine the nature of the impacts and how these relate to the volume and characteristics of tourism activity.

The economic impact of tourism can be measured using a number of techniques of which ad hoc, input–output (IO) and Computable General Equilibrium (CGE) multiplier models have been the most important over the past 30 years or so. Chapter 7 examines the advantages and weaknesses of each type of economic impact model and looks at their practical use to policy makers. Finally, this chapter looks at the often overlooked economic costs associated with tourism and its development and stresses the need for policy makers to focus on the net economic benefits.

Chapter 8 examines the relationship between tourism activity and the environment in which it takes place. One of the major issues with respect to tourism development is the way in which the environment is often seen as a 'free' (not priced) input to the tourism product. Tourism is often discussed in terms of its negative environmental impacts, whereas in fact it has both negative and positive environmental attributes. A range of environmental issues is discussed in order to examine tourism's relationship with the environment in which it takes place and how this need not be solely a negative result. The importance of looking wider than purely the direct environmental effects is also stressed, together with ways of looking at the secondary environmental consequences associated with production in general and tourism production in particular. The chapter concludes by examining some of the environmental tools that have been used such as environmental impact assessments (EIAs) and environmental audits, drawing distinctions between them and the roles that each can play in enhancing resilience both of the environment and tourism activity.

The socio-cultural aspects of a destination and their relationship with tourism activity are examined in Chapter 9. The various approaches that have been used to study the development of tourism are examined, together with their implications for socio-cultural impacts in the destination. An overview of the major models that have been used to explain the development of tourism is employed to demonstrate the commonality of the models and also to highlight the inadequacy of the framework to produce solutions within a dynamic world. The chapter draws out some fundamental issues with respect to the socio-cultural impact of tourism on host communities and critically examines their implications for tourism development. Both positive and negative impacts are discussed and some high-profile negative issues such as crime, sex tourism and displacement are examined in further detail. The chapter concludes by looking at some of the sources of data that are available for the study of the socio-cultural impacts.

Sustainable tourism has become commonplace in the literature but the concept is subject to a variety of interpretations and is often misunderstood. The definitions and concepts are examined in Chapter 10 together with their implications for tourism development. Different types of sustainability are considered and the fundamental rationality of sustainability is brought into question. Factors that work towards some form of sustainable tourism and those that work against it are reviewed before moving on to the main ways forward to improve the resilience of the industry and the destination. The limits to development are discussed using terms such as carrying capacity and limits of acceptable change together with the strengths and weaknesses of such approaches. Concern is expressed about the use of the term sustainability as a marketing strategy rather than a commitment to resilience, and then different types of tourism products are examined, including eco-tourism, to examine if they are robust in practice. The chapter finishes by looking at the issue of climate change, and scopes out the likely relationship between climate change and tourism followed by an examination of mitigation and adaptation strategies and policies.

Several competing models that have been put forward to explain the process of general economic development and some of the main theories are examined, together with an assessment of the role that tourism can play within such models. Chapter 11 starts by briefly looking at each of the main models and the role of tourism before looking at the characteristics of tourism that make it such an attractive development option for many destinations. Tourism planning is a process that can take place at different levels from the international (such as the Caribbean or Europe) through to national and then to local planning levels. Planning at each of these levels is discussed prior to looking at the planning process and its key stages. The importance of each stage is considered, followed by a brief look at the expertise needed to construct successful tourism development plans. The chapter concludes by looking at what can go wrong and the reasons that can bring about plan failure.

Finally, tourism operates in a dynamic world and, whereas there are many forces that drive tourism forward to higher volume and deeper penetration, there are also forces outside a destination's control that can suddenly deter people from travelling to specific places or, like the events of 9/11 in 2001 can change the way in which some aspects of tourism activity are conducted. Therefore, tourism development strategies must also consider how best to deal with the negative forces that can switch off tourism activity overnight or work against tourism growth. Chapter 12 concludes this part by examining crises that can hinder tourism activity and the disaster management processes that can mitigate some of the damage caused by negative events.

## AN IMPACT ASSESSMENT PRACTITIONER'S VIEW

## By David J. James, Managing Director, Global Tourism Solutions (UK) Ltd

In 1985, following the establishment of Canada's National Task Force on Tourism Data, Frank Hart and I were appointed co-Chairmen of the Working Party to consider local area statistics. This work focused on the city of Edmonton, Alberta, Canada, and became the first attempt to develop the effective use of supply-side-generated local area tourism statistics drawing on the model developed in Saskatchewan in 1981. This research provided much-needed data for the city councils and convention bureaus on the impact of tourism, which is the principal subject matter of this part of *Tourism: Principles and Practice*.

In 1988, I was appointed Director of Tourism and Amenities for Scarborough Borough Council and it was in that context that the model was transferred to the UK. The model was first run on behalf of Scarborough Borough Council in 1990, becoming known as the 'Scarborough Tourism Economic Activity Monitor' (STEAM), and has subsequently been adopted by many local authorities in the UK.

STEAM approaches the measurement of tourism at the local level from the supply side, which has the benefit of immediacy and relative inexpensiveness. It is not a statistically estimated model in the manner of an input–output model of the local economy, but rather uses the output of such models as discussed in this section, particularly multiplier values arranged by location and industrial sector as pioneered by the authors of this text. In effect STEAM is a spreadsheet model that is more of a process in which the values of the relationships or equations defined on the spreadsheet are specified at each stage by the user. Thus, although the logic of the model is constant, the nature of data input will alter from area to area depending on the amount of survey material available and qualitative expert opinion concerning the structure of tourism in the local economy. In this way the model builds in both quantitative and qualitative assessments to arrive at local volume and value measures of tourism.

# CHAPTER 6

## DESTINATIONS

### LEARNING OUTCOMES

The focus of the chapter is on the destination and its role in the tourism system. By the end of this chapter, therefore, you will understand:

- the nature and roles of destinations in the wider tourism industry;

- the range of destinations that exist and the context within which they are planned and developed on the one hand, and compete with other destinations on the other;

- the number of forces in the external environment impacting on a destination's future;

- the ways in which destinations are managed and marketed; and

- the collaborative nature of destinations and the organisational and governance structures advocated for their effective management.

Photograph: Golden Gate Bridge, San Francisco, USA © Andrew J. Müller

# INTRODUCTION

In this chapter we show that the destination lies at the core of the travel and tourism system. Destinations come in all shapes and sizes and can be found in a variety of geographical settings such as in urban, rural and coastal environments. Destinations can be countries or a collection of countries, a distinct state, county or province, or in fact represent a local city, town or resort, national park, area of outstanding natural beauty or coastline. As with other parts of the tourism system they can be viewed in both a supply and demand context in that destinations can be seen to represent a mix of products and services that come together to meet the needs of the tourist (supply) or as places where tourists travel to in order to experience particular features or experiences (demand). The geographical location of destinations is, for reasons that will become clearer as you proceed through the chapter, particularly significant as often they do not sit comfortably in convenient political, administrative and/or legislative-bound locations. More often than not, destinations are in fact subject to artificial divides that ignore the more consumer-driven needs and expectations of the tourist. As will become evident throughout this chapter, destinations are traditionally viewed as particularly difficult entities to manage due to the complex relationships of stakeholders that come together to make them work and the multiple objectives that they seek to achieve.

This chapter outlines the relationship between the destination and the wider tourism industry before introducing the context within which destination policy, planning and development takes place. The chapter continues by identifying a number of trends impacting on destinations and provides a useful framework which facilitates understanding. The chapter then introduces a range of issues relating to the management and marketing of destinations before concluding with a series of thoughts for the future.

# THE NATURE AND ROLE OF DESTINATIONS

The destination sits at the core of the wider tourism system in that it represents an amalgam of tourism products that collectively offer a destination 'experience' to visitors. For many consumers (day visitors or tourists), particularly in leisure tourism, the destination is the principal motivating factor behind the consumer's decision and expectations. In this context it is somewhat surprising to find that, even to many experts in the field, the destination remains conceptually difficult to define. One of the principal barriers in neatly defining destinations is the 'inconvenient' nature of boundaries, be they administrative, political or simply geographical, and the means by which they do not always sit comfortably with the perceptions of the destination to consumers. For example, although London represents an 'iconic' global destination, the wider destination is made up of 33 local authorities which incorporate two cities: the City of London and the City of Westminster. However, for the purposes of tourism, especially international visitors, 'tourist' London is essentially the inner core, often referred to as that area within the Circle Line of London's Underground system. Also in the UK, this time in Dorset on the south coast of England, the three destinations of Christchurch, Bournemouth and Poole – although often viewed by visitors as a single 'destination' – represent three different boroughs managed by three different local authorities despite the fact that they 'share' a 12-kilometre beach which to many visitors represents a single destination.

With respect to arriving at a definition of a destination, it is necessary to introduce both supply- and demand-side perspectives. So, while supply-side definitions identify the destination as 'a well-defined geographical area which is understood by its visitors as a unique entity, with a political and legislative framework for tourism marketing and planning' (Buhalis, 2000: 98), demand-side definitions define destinations as 'places towards which people travel and where they choose to stay for a while in order to experience certain features or characteristics' (Leiper, 1995: 87 in Buhalis, 2000: 98). In reality, whether one views the destination as a 'tourist place', a 'tourism product' or a 'system of products' very much depends on the purpose of defining it and the perceptions of the stakeholders either directly and/or indirectly involved with its management. Despite this definitional haze, the UNWTO considers the destination to be the fundamental unit of analysis in tourism (WTO, 2002a). The destination is complex and difficult to manage, but their importance for the entire tourism system is such that the effective and efficient management of destinations is one of the key priorities for tourism professionals across the world. For this reason alone, it is imperative that a systematic and interdisciplinary approach is adopted for the analysis, planning, management and control of destination development (Manente and Minghetti, 2006: 230). The adoption of a systematic approach to the understanding of destinations has been advocated for some time in that those responsible for destinations are fully aware of the interactions among destination stakeholders and the impact(s) exerted by the competitive environment on the destination 'system'.

## Destination types

There are many types of destinations that can be identified but the most basic classification is threefold:

- coastal destinations, epitomised in the ever popular seaside resort that has undergone many changes since its modern-day emergence in the mid-eighteenth century with advocacy of inland spas and sea bathing for health cures;
- urban destinations in that major cities have been cultural attractions from ancient times onwards and some, such as Venice, which was popularised in the period of the Grand Tour by Europe's aristocracy, have continued as tourist cities long after their commercial function has diminished;
- rural destinations that range from the ordinary countryside to national parks, wilderness areas, mountains and lakes.

From a planning perspective, the designation of a tourist destination should provide the basis for integrated development to generate the balance of amenities and facilities required by tourists. It also allows for the staging of tourism from one locality to another, opening up new areas as others become saturated, therefore the definition of a destination is a dynamic concept even for a particular geographical area where neighbouring areas can be encompassed as and when they are brought into the tourism offer or tourists recognise them as such.

It follows from the discussion so far that the key features of a tourist destination are:

- logical geographical unit recognised by visitors;
- contains visitor attractions;
- access or possible provision of access;
- internal transport network;
- tourist infrastructure and superstructure are present or can be developed;
- administratively possible to plan and manage.

When planning tourist destinations it is often desirable to establish a tourist centre that acts as the hub and gateway to various parts of the area. This allows the public and private sectors to concentrate facilities and obtain economies of development scale. Access is also a key factor in determining the development of tourism and this can be clearly seen with the development of transport infrastructure and services that have heralded the development and spread of tourism nationally and internationally. Economic distance becomes an important factor in determining which locations/destinations are within the scope of a potential tourist (economic distance in this sense is the geographical distance, taking into account the cost of travel in terms of actual costs and time). As transport developments took place, first with the development of the railways, then the ownership of cars to the development of low-priced air travel, tourists have travelled further and more frequently, not only for the traditional longer stay leisure vacations but also for the shorter stay and weekend breaks.

## Coastal

In Britain, as in the rest of Europe, although 'taking the waters' was popularised by the Romans through the building of luxurious *thermae* over hot springs, the foundation of spa towns, the peak periods for seeking cures at spas or at the seaside took place during the Georgian and Victorian eras of the eighteenth and nineteenth centuries. Initially for the wealthy, it was the industrial growth in the north of Europe and on the east coast of the USA, together with the advent of the railways, that popularised coastal resort development. A classic example of this is Brighton, located on the south coast of England. The community was formerly a fishing village, known as Brighthelmstone, but the construction between 1784 and 1787 of an Asian-style Royal Pavilion as a residence for the Prince Regent, later King George IV, initiated the transformation of the village into a fashionable resort town. By 1841 Brighton became accessible by rail, and it grew rapidly thereafter.

The development of the railway networks helped bring about the growth of seaside resorts during the latter half of the nineteenth century in Europe and the USA, and this growth can be seen as the result of a partnership between the public and private sectors. The local authorities invested in the promenades, piers, gardens and so on, while the private sector developed the revenue-earning activities, which increased the value of property in the area and thus the associated property tax receipts for the authorities, and enhanced local income and employment opportunities. Pier building was a particularly British phenomenon; 78 were constructed between 1860 and 1910, while very few were built on mainland Europe. However, the development of seaside resorts was paralleled in Europe and the USA with the expansion of the amusement park industry. Although New York's Coney Island had started up in the 1870s, and its rides and games entertained countless visitors, it was Captain P. Boynton's Sea Lion Park, which opened on the Island in 1895, that set the trend and inspired numerous amusement parks throughout the United States, including the three Great Coney Island Parks: Luna Park (1903–1947), Dreamland (1904–1911) and Steeplechase (1897–1964). Although travelling fairs in Britain have a history that dates them back to the twelfth century, the amusement arcades were a late nineteenth and early twentieth century attraction that tended to be confined to the ends of piers, but in 1896 the American 'revolution' crossed the Atlantic with the founding of Blackpool Pleasure Beach.

It was not until the 1950s, with the growth of air travel, that the dominance of the seaside resorts of northern Europe over the traditional summer break began to face the challenge of the warm water resorts in southern Europe. This left them facing a different future, to which some have adapted by investing in new markets, for example, the conference trade and the growth in short breaks. In Europe the latter are more likely to be taken within the home country, whereas the ideal main holiday today is often considered to be abroad, mainly short haul, but also being made easier by developments in long-haul overseas travel to more exotic destinations. Another major change has been increased residential settlement in these resorts, simply because they are 'nice places to live'. This has generated local conflict in terms of allocating resources to tourism use versus residential use, and over time has altered the demographic and economic base of the resort, because the priorities of local representatives have changed and they remain not as seaside resorts but as coastal towns.

Typical stereotypes of resorts that have become urban settlements are seaside towns that now have a population where the proportion of pensionable age residents is above the national average; low levels of economic activity; seasonal employment opportunities; considerable commuting; a high percentage of second homes; and a high percentage of communal living in apartment blocks and retirement homes. The policy of NTOs in these circumstances is to focus their attention on regenerating a few key resorts that are willing and able to maintain their position in the marketplace. One of the fundamental lessons to learn from the development of coastal resorts, whether new or old, is the importance of the public–private sector partnership. Embodied in the tourist product are common goods and services, which are either unlikely to be provided in sufficient quantity if left to the market mechanism, or are available without cost, as is the case with natural resources.

The principal concern for the environment is that indiscriminate consumption, without market regulation, will cause irreversible damage that cannot be compensated by increasing the stock of other capital (see Chapter 10 on sustainability). The upshot is that the single-minded pursuit of private profit opportunities within tourism may be self-defeating, as many older resorts have found to their cost. The outcome may not be the integrated tourism development which distils the essence of the country in its design, but a rather crowded, overbuilt and place-less location with polluted beaches – one that is totally out of keeping with the original objectives set by the country's tourism policy. As a number of Mediterranean resorts have discovered, the lack of public involvement in tourism has resulted in overbuilding by the accommodation sector, since this tends to be the major revenue-earning activity where there are substantial short-term profits to be made during the early stages of development. Such building has often been at the expense of the aesthetic quality of the natural landscape and also, when it has been overlaid onto an existing town or village, it may severely disrupt the lifestyle of the local community. For example, the major hotel developments that took place in the resorts of southern Spain during the 1960s and early 1970s were completed under laissez-faire expansionism with little considera-tion given to planning or control. In general, the public infrastructure was overloaded and, since the second half of the 1980s, there has been a continual programme to correct this imbalance by refurbishing the resort centres to give more 'green' space in the form of parks and gardens, and pull down older hotels, as in the Balearic Islands.

It is evident that the public is becoming more aware of the perceived adverse effects of tourism on the environment and it has become fashionable to 'go green'. Green tourism, eco-tourism or alternative tourism (the words are often used synonymously) is in essence small-scale solutions to what is a large-scale problem, namely the mass movements of people travelling for leisure purposes. Thus, there is a requirement to continue to maintain large 'resortscapes' capable of managing high density flows, such as sun, sea and sand family groups, and it is important that the local economy, whilst being sustainable, is kept in balance with the coastal environment. Local people should be involved in the decision making, but the 'last settler syndrome' of incoming residents opposing new developments in the seaside economy, which has hampered the regen-eration of many older resorts, should be avoided.

## Urban

During the last half of the twentieth century, the troubles caused by the move of manufacturing industries from urban areas to cheaper rural locations and the continued flight of the middle classes to the suburbs severely affected the image of industrialised cities, already dented by issues of congestion and pollution. This has forced local authorities, policy makers and busi-ness groups to revive their cities by attracting new industries, residents and visitors through the application of modern city management and marketing systems founded on longer term plans. North American cities, where the revitalisation trend was referred to as 'city boosterism', were the first to practise city marketing strategies with the support of both public and private organisations, for example, Toronto, Baltimore and Boston. Tourism has thrived in the regen-eration of run-down industrial and dock areas, at the same time acting as a catalyst to attract new industries, belying the previously held notions that cities are just places where people live and work.

From the early 1980s, major cities have been taking tourism development more seriously and trying to strengthen the sector with strategic plans and tactics hinged upon the existence of quintessential factors for tourism development. While such factors include the social, cultural, economic and environmental endowments of urban areas, their use as tourism assets depends heavily on the success of public and private authorities in integrating tourism development into overall town planning. The characteristics of such tourism derive from both the distinctive nature of urban structures and the manifestation of tourism in such intricate settlements. Some of the common characteristics of city destinations drawn from the empirical and theoretical research available in the literature are:

- Urban destinations are both multi-sold and multi-bought, through offering a range of tourist products and services that create diverse product packages. Shoppers, cultural visitors, visi-tors on education trips, business visitors, short-break trips, domestic visitors and overseas visitors can all be found in many major city destinations.

- City destinations are often the tourism gateways to their surrounding region. Locations that associate themselves with a major city destination may benefit from the latter's high volumes of visitors, by drawing day trips from tourists basing themselves in the city.

- The sheer scale of heterogeneous products and services sold to visitors and locals in urban areas make each city destination a unique tourism product cluster. Therefore, while there may be some similarities between some urban functions and tourist services, as in accommodation and transport, each city destination is different when it comes to their size, location, heritage, and economic and social functioning.

- Developing and marketing the product clusters of city destinations cannot be directed by a single authority. Residents, private and public tourism stakeholders and other urban authorities need to cooperate to initiate development projects and to effect marketing activities by creating a one-voice strategy. The 'over-fragmentation' of tourism stakeholders in urban areas makes partnerships, alliances and cooperation imperative in the process of developing the tourism economy.

- Despite the fact that tourism-related products and services in cities are manifold, visitors usually concentrate on certain locations and create invisible boundaries that define tourist zones or districts.

- Tourism in urban areas, compared to traditional holiday resorts, is an all-year-round activity with limited seasonality. This is principally due to the diversified demand and supply aspects of city destinations.

- By their very nature, cities embrace more than one economic industry. Hence their economic function depends on the coexistence of various manufacturing and service operations. Whether the economic and social richness of urban areas is tourism-related or not, sustainable tourism development and management can only be fulfilled through the success of local authorities in being able to integrate tourism into the overall urban economic structure. Neither tourism nor other industries should hamper each other's functioning. Opposition to tourism may arise from residents and businesspeople if concentrated tourist flows in certain districts impair the living standards of the city.

## Rural

The product strengths of many rural areas lie in their strong natural environments – for example, hills, mountains and lakes, and remoteness – which make them increasingly attractive for tourism development at a time when an increasing proportion of the world's population are becoming urban dwellers and where environmental guilt brings 'green tourism' into vogue. Benefits are seen in the rural way of life, physical activity from hill walking to adventure sports, tranquillity, aesthetics of the landscape and so forth. Within Europe, as in many other regions, the promotion of rural tourism is part of a greater convergence and cohesion policy. In many rural locations, the outlook for small farmers and therefore the fabric of the landscape, culture and way of life of the rural economy is bleak without the expenditure of substantial sums of public money for little return. Supporting farm tourism is just one of a number of ways in which essential and inevitable subsidies can be paid to farmers, and it seems to be among the more cost-effective measures. Policies aimed at developing this sector, especially those seeking to improve the qualitative characteristics such as suitable transport infrastructure, accommodation facilities, cultural activities in the form of festivals, and food quality, are intended to generate higher tourism revenues, which would be beneficial to sustaining local income growth. However, although every location has some tourism potential, it would be naïve to suppose that tourism development could be effective in every region. Increasing market segmentation will generate niche markets for some areas, but the cost of supplying these markets could be prohibitive, for in higher latitudes the lack of tourist infrastructure in rural areas is compounded by weather conditions, which limit the length of the season, as in so many of the outlying regions of the world.

On the other hand, there is concern for the social impact of tourism on small, close-knit communities and the environmental threat to undisturbed wilderness. Scenic areas may be protected by zoning landscape for different use patterns, creating intermediate or buffer zones and limiting tourist flows, which is the purpose of creating national parks and designating areas of outstanding natural beauty. This is to protect them from inappropriate developments, so as to preserve the landscape and rural structure.

As a rule, when considering the impact of tourism on the local community, the greater the difference in lifestyles between rural hosts and tourists, and the less the former have been exposed to visitors, then the longer should be the period of adaptation. Phasing development over time and space is a fundamental underlying principle, but any programme for growth is made all the harder when the community lacks the necessary skills, capital, organisation structures and information sources to progress the plan. Solutions for such difficulties could include bringing in 'flagship' projects from outside and inviting the operators to invest long term in the community, forming a development corporation or taking a low-key approach by running a small business extension service backed up by development grants. Although there is always the risk with outside companies that they might, in response to commercial pressures, revert to short-term profit goals, there is no guarantee that local owners will not be even keener to exploit tourism opportunities, particularly when they have the necessary political representation to do so.

## Destination policy, planning and development

Prior to the closer examination of those forces in the external environment that are impacting on the future management of destinations, it is advisable to set destinations more broadly, and their management, within the context of tourism policy and planning and the wider context of 'competitiveness'. In essence, all aspects of tourism sit within the broader context of tourism policy. According to Ritchie and Crouch (2003) tourism policy focuses on macro-level policies, is long term in orientation, and concentrates on how critical and limited resources can best respond to perceived needs and opportunities in a changing environment. Tourism policy is significant as it defines the so-called 'rules of the game', sets out the activities and behaviours that are acceptable, and provides common direction and guidance for all tourism stakeholders within a destination. In a strategic sense it facilitates consensus around the specific vision, strategies and objectives for a given destination while it also provides a suitable framework for public and private discussions on the role of the tourism sector and its contributions to the economy and to society in general. In its broadest sense, tourism policy allows tourism to interface with other industrial sectors within the wider economy and link more effectively into other more general strategies such as national and regional economic strategies, spatial strategies and integrated national and regional strategies. Destination management, on the other hand, represents

## YOUTUBE
### Trends: new destinations

Introduction to Baku, Azerbaijan
**http://www.youtube.com/watch?v=PFV4pkG_QSg**

Libya
**http://www.youtube.com/watch?v=Q6o9teX4b1s**

Gaza
**http://www.youtube.com/watch?v=W4xObOaJgCl**

Space, the ultimate future destination?
**http://www.youtube.com/watch?v=UWQWpuO0QsQ;**
**http://www.youtube.com/watch?v=vZHRdOcjeWg**

a more micro activity in 'which all the many resident and industry stakeholders carry out their individual and organisational responsibilities on a daily basis in efforts to realize the macro-level vision contained in policy, planning and development' (Ritchie and Crouch, 2003: 147).

### Destination competitiveness

Destinations are managed within a broader context of 'competitiveness' and 'stewardship' which relate to the deployment of 'management' resources to both develop and enhance the destination and at the same time protect and conserve its core resources respectively. Hence, the competitiveness of a destination refers to its ability to compete effectively and profitably in the marketplace, while the successful management of a destination involves a balance between traditional economic and business management skills with an increasing need for sensitive environmental management capabilities. The comparative advantage of a destination, meanwhile, refers to a destination's ability to manage its natural and man-made resources effectively over the long term. Fundamental to achieving competitive advantage for its tourism industry, any destination must ensure that 'its overall "appeal", and the tourist experience offered, must be superior to that of the alternative destinations open to potential visitors' (Dwyer and Kim, 2003: 369). One of the particular challenges in defining competitiveness in the context of destinations is that, as already stated, the destination represents an amalgam of many industrial services, such as accommodation, transportation, attractions, entertainment, recreation and food services. This fragmented and highly disparate 'product' clearly does not make the management of the visitor experience an easy task. Despite difficulties of definition, it is sensible for destinations to focus attention on long-term economic prosperity as the yardstick by which they are to be assessed competitively (Ritchie and Crouch, 2003).

In order to remain competitive, destinations need to be aware of both demand and supply factors. With regard to demand, those managing destinations need to take note of the nature, timing and magnitude of demand. At the same, they need to be aware of those products, services, amenities and attractions that are necessary components for a satisfactory destination 'experience'. Ritchie and Crouch (2003: 60) propose a conceptual model of destination competitiveness as a vehicle to facilitate understanding of what is essentially a quite complex issue, the model depicting the 'structure of interrelationships between separate constructs or factors which help to explain a higher-order concept'.

Figure 6.1 demonstrates the open nature of the tourism system in that it is subject to many (micro) influences and pressures arising from the system itself. In addition, numerous (macro) forces exist externally that are profound in their implications for tourism. Although the attractiveness of a destination may remain relatively constant, the means by which competition changes indicate that a constant reassessment of the destination's strengths, weaknesses, opportunities and threats is necessary. The work by Porter (1998) is useful here in that those managing destinations need to understand the contributions of factor conditions, demand conditions, related and supporting industries, and firm strategy, structure, organisation and rivalry in determining destination success. Building on the work of Porter, Figure 6.1 refers to the global (macro) environment; the competitive (micro) environment; core resources and attractors; supporting factors and resources (such as infrastructure, accessibility and hospitality); destination policy, planning and development; destination management; and qualifying and amplifying determinants. In reality, all destinations, irrespective of size, location and market, need to adapt continually, not simply because they need to modernise but because they need to retain and build on their overall competitiveness over other destinations.

# DESTINATION TRENDS

The challenges facing destinations are significant, with a whole host of issues that impact on their management and marketing. The global economic crisis only served to increase those challenges as the patterns of distribution of tourism activity changed to accommodate the effects of falling real income levels for many tourists. Both the macro and micro environments are in a

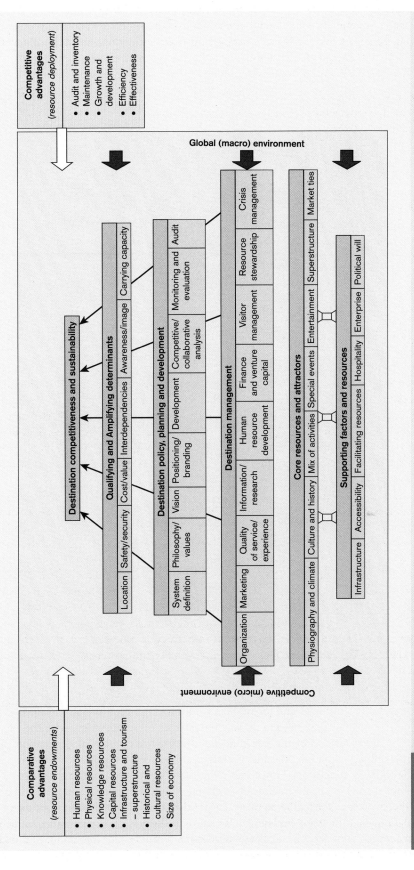

**Figure 6.1**

Model of destination competitiveness

*Source:* Ritchie, J.R.B. and Crouch, G. (2005), p. 62, Fig. 3.1 'Conceptual model of destination competitiveness'

constant state of change and evolution and, as such, those managing destinations are encouraged to migrate from their traditional 'inward looking' nature and recognise more fully the true magnitude of events and their impact on how destinations are to be managed in the future. Two studies which set the context well for the future management of destinations are those by Bennett (1999) and King (2002). Bennett (1999) also highlighted the need to take into account the needs, wants and expectations of more mature and knowledgeable customers; the need for more up-to-date and reliable information upon which to base such decision making; and the considerable pressures caused by the sustained presence and influence of intermediaries, as well as the parallel imbalance of channel power for destinations in the tourism system. With regard to transportation and technological pressures, developments in useful destination management systems have taken place which now afford them necessity status, while the systematic growth of discount airlines and the surplus of new destinations continues to ensure severe competition among destinations for tourist spend. Of all these forces, however, it is, according to Bennett, the long-standing 'dividing line' between the public and private sectors that remains the prime catalyst for change, a dividing line considered to have been holding back the potential of destination marketing for far too long.

King (2002), whilst acknowledging the existence of a number of pressures, also raises the scenario of the traditional distribution channels being increasingly bypassed in the future with more direct contact between the consumer and the supplier taking place. He also suggests that a reduction in booking lead times is likely to occur, as is a steady downturn in the demand for mass tourism products, leading to a greater pressure for the destination to deliver satisfaction and meet expectations of an increasingly independent tourist. King is very critical of many existing **destination management organisations** (DMOs), in that the majority remain focused on 'what the destination has to offer' and continue to use 'mass marketing techniques more suited to the passive customer' (King, 2002: 106). He develops this theme by alluding to the fact that the customer is now very much an active partner in the marketing process. For destinations to be a success, marketers will need to engage the customer as never before, as well as to be able to provide them with the types of information and experience they are increasingly demanding.

In the same study, King advances a number of so-called 'new realities' for destination marketers. These include the need for even greater emphasis on a strong brand image, with clearly identified and projected brand values that resonate with key target segments; more direct engagement with the customer to identify their holiday motivations, anticipate their needs and fulfil their aspirations; the establishment of ongoing, direct, two-way and networking consumer communication channels, and for key customer relationship strategies to take place with the eventual development of mass customisation marketing and delivery capabilities; greater emphasis to be given to the creation and promotion of holiday experiences that link key brand values and assets with the holiday aspirations and needs of key customers; and a move away from a relatively passive promotional role to include greater intervention, facilitation and direction in the conversion process.

## The 15 Cs framework

In recognition of the dynamic context within which destinations are being managed now, and are to be managed in the future, Fyall et al. (2006) propose a framework which provides a 'route map' for professionals and researchers working in the field (see also Fyall, 2011). Although in a developmental phase, and in no way intended to represent a definitive list, Figure 6.2 provides a suitable synthesis of the key challenges facing the domain of destination management and marketing for the next decade. Clearly their degree of importance will vary according to the destination in question. However, the omission of even one of the challenges in the design and implementation of destination management and marketing strategies is likely to hinder the effectiveness of the final plan or strategy in that an inadequate understanding of the wider destination environment is evident. Nevertheless, identifying future issues and strategic challenges is a common practice. The challenge for destinations is to take due notice of the forces at play and to manage destinations accordingly.

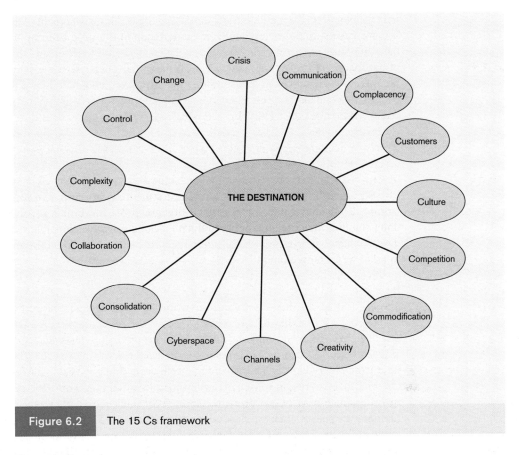

| Figure 6.2 | The 15 Cs framework |

## Complexity

The complexity of the destination product is not in dispute as all destinations to varying degrees are comprised of multiple stakeholders, multiple components and multiple suppliers, and convey multiple meanings to multiple markets and market segments. Perhaps the issue most pressing in the context of complexity is the pressure for the public sector to increase revenue from private sector sources at a time when considerable pressure is being put on the public purse within the context of emerging destination management structures and the increasing devolution and regionalisation of tourism organisation and funding, most notably in the UK. The complexity of a destination is particularly marked when the consumer and community dimensions are taken into consideration (see Wang, 2008). For example, consumers will often differ in their perceptions, expectations and desired satisfactions of the 'tourism place'. Only a minority, if at all, will view the destination as a neatly encapsulated bundle of suppliers.

## Control

The adoption of a strategic approach to marketing destinations based on destination branding is often undermined due to the inherent difficulties of destination coordination and control. For example, campaigns can be frequently undertaken 'by a variety of tourist businesses with no consultation or coordination on the prevailing message or the destination values being promoted' (Scott et al., 2000: 202). This issue is one that has contributed to London's historical struggle to make a sustained impact in terms of brand positioning. Much has, however, changed with considerable budget increases awarded to Visit London in recent years. In addition, the top-down nature of making strategy and the large sums made available to 'make things happen' have afforded a step change in marketing activity within the capital and a greater ability for the tourism authorities to retain a sense of control over how the destination is positioned and marketed.

One of the consequences of a greater top-down orientation is the tendency to ignore the smaller players, many of whom in the past were members of previous forms of destination management structures and tourist boards. For the wider management of destinations, however, it is recognised that developments are being made in the need to bring tourism's information base up to date as there is considerable evidence to suggest that 'the design and implementation of destination management systems (DMSs) are taking place to the extent that for most destinations, rather than being an aspirational element of their marketing armoury, they are now deemed essential and represent a very real opportunity for destination marketers to gain greater control of their product' (Fyall et al., 2006: 77–8).

### Change

The migration from the traditional division that has historically existed between the public and private sectors is perhaps that element of change most needed in that it has often been perceived as holding back the potential of destinations. To date, however, most countries around the world retain a strong public bias in their organisational and funding structures. Not only does this result in the retention of a predominantly public 'organisational' mindset but it serves as a barrier to the raising of additional funding and the speed with which DMOs can react to forces in the external environment.

### Crisis

The majority of destinations around the world, either directly or indirectly, are to some extent affected by crises, be they natural or man-made. Crises often impact on established tourism flows and their related spend and accommodation requirements (Fletcher and Morakabati, 2008). Unfortunately, the external environment is predictable in its unpredictability. For example, political turmoil in Sri Lanka and Thailand in recent years, and the recent Arab Spring, among others, continue to impact negatively on many destinations around the world. It is clear that the future for many destinations is inherently uncertain due to a whole myriad of natural and man-made crises, the one type that is often overlooked being economic crises in the major generating countries, which are economically far more damaging for tourist-receiving countries than more high-profile, media-hungry events such as 9/11. For these reasons alone, any destination management organisation that does not now incorporate some form of crisis management planning into its strategic marketing planning cycle can be accused of grossly ignoring the realities of modern tourism.

### Complacency

The crises mentioned above are all significant in that although many destinations clearly suffered from very rapid drops in demand, among other negative impacts, tourists continued to travel, albeit intra-regionally or domestically. For destinations everywhere, irrespective of scale and geographic location, fear of crises ought to be sufficient to prevent complacency among those managing and marketing destinations. For many destinations, however, specific markets have been such reliable sources of custom over many years (Fyall and Leask, 2007). However, although in the past destinations could perhaps be excused for being slow to react to forces in the external environment, this clearly is no longer the case. Although as a broad phenomenon tourism has proven to be particularly robust, travel and spending patterns do change. Tourism in its broadest sense has consistently proved to be a highly robust phenomenon in that although travel patterns may change the act of travelling remains steadfast and for many markets it is now a necessity rather than a luxury, especially in the developed world.

### Customers

The task of managing destinations is never going to be an easy one and destinations urgently need to develop suitable strategies to accommodate what may be referred to as Poon's 'new tourist': that is, tourists who are flexible, segmented, diagonally integrated and environmentally conscious, who seek quality, flexibility and value for money (Poon, 1993). Every year that passes, destination marketers need to be more innovative in their adoption of marketing techniques and strategies in meeting the needs of more demanding customers (Li and Petrick, 2008). For example, the highly competitive global market for tourists serves as a catalyst for tourism destinations to seek more innovative 'relationship' marketing strategies so as to engender a degree of loyalty and stimulate lucrative repeat business among their visitor base. That said, in a context of many destinations competing in price-driven, low-margin markets, the costs and benefits to be derived from relationship marketing require significant research before tourism destinations are able to accept the concept as a new paradigm or potential solution to maintain/expand their share of the market for visitors. In view of the inherent imbalance of power, resources and experience between tourism destination 'actors', generating cohesion, mutual trust and respect within the tourism system stand as significant challenges for those marketing tourism destinations in the future.

## Culture

Although the cultural division between the public and private sectors within tourism continues to represent a barrier for progress across many countries, on the demand side culture represents a significant opportunity for destinations, especially those that have acquired 'commodity' status in recent years, to differentiate themselves in the future via the development of niche tourism strategies. With respect to aspects of supply, the cultural division between the public and private sectors is considerable by the very nature of their respective roles in providing for the tourist experience. Destinations are for the most part reliant on 'public goods' as part of their wider tourism appeal – which in turn raises the issue of who is to pay for the upkeep of these 'public goods' in the future: the local community or visitors? Despite the pressure in many countries for a greater financial contribution to the costs of developing and managing destinations, the rationale for continued public sector intervention remains strong. For the most part, governments continue to recognise the economic value of tourism (which in turn has contributed to the proliferation of DMOs worldwide) while the 'one-industry' concept of tourism recognises that although businesses have individual goals, the success of the tourism industry relies on effective interrelationships between the public and private sector (Pike, 2004).

## Competition

One interesting indirect dimension to competition is the exponential growth in the ownership of second homes, most notably in countries such as France and Spain. The phenomenon of second-home ownership is a significant threat in that an increasing percentage of the market now no longer needs variety in their choice of destinations as with their purchase of a second home they have expressed some indication of their loyalty, albeit to varying degrees, to a particular destination. Work by Pedro (2006) has explored this phenomenon in greater depth and evaluated the true impact on the management of destinations. Some of the key outcomes include the fact that second-home tourism is not labour intensive, involves visitors with lower expenditure patterns and represents competition for the traditional hospitality sector. It also involves visitors who do not pay tourism taxes and are not subject to the legislation often associated with tourism accommodation although they may well pay taxes on their properties. Finally, the phenomenon inadvertently puts pressure on the price of land and contributes to price inflation in the house and consumer goods markets. One notable fact is that, as evidenced recently, competition is at its most cut-throat post-crisis, with evidence from recent disasters suggesting that, although the overall volume of trips taking place remains relatively static, the shift in travel patterns is significant in that domestic and intra-regional travel to more familiar and perceived 'safe' destinations has become the norm.

## Commodification

According to Fyall et al. (2006: 80), one of the 'outcomes of commodification of the destination product is the continual downward pressure on prices'. The reduction in prices, although beneficial to tourists, reduces the destination-wide yield and poses a considerable challenge for destination marketers in that increasingly more marketing, and marketing spend, is necessary to generate a decreasing yield from tourists. Niche tourism developments are a means to counter such a trend – as best demonstrated by marketing strategies adopted by the Tourism Authority of Thailand and their development of the Amazing Thailand brand and its annual niche-orientated marketing 'straplines'. One of the principal means to counter commodification is via the use of festivals and events, as evidenced in Mini-Case Study 6.1 on Hong Kong and its WinterFest as a key differentiator in the international marketplace.

## MINI CASE STUDY 6.1
Hong Kong WinterFest: enhancing destinations via festivals, events and shopping!

One of the principal means by which destinations are able to differentiate themselves in an increasingly crowded marketplace is via the use of festivals and events to enhance their overall destination offer. Although the use of mega or hallmark events are a key event strategy for large, world-city destinations such as London, Rio de Janeiro, Johannesburg and Sydney, such destinations also benefit from many smaller events that collectively create much energy and excitement in the destination, add much to the destination experience, and serve as critical vehicles to generate first-time and repeat visitation among both domestic and international visitors. One such destination is Hong Kong in South East Asia where visitors are able to enjoy a consistent deluge of festivals, events, conventions, exhibitions, performances and competitions throughout the year. Such events not only take place throughout the day and night but are also major drivers of visitation in traditionally quieter off-peak periods. In a recent poll by CNN, Hong Kong was in fact voted as one of the top 10 destinations in the world to spend your Christmas! The Hong Kong WinterFest, which runs from the end of November to the beginning of January, includes a vast mix of events against a backdrop of a stunning waterfront location and a large supply of festive lighting and illuminations! Victoria Harbour dazzles while the city's restaurants and shops are full of seasonal dishes and festive gifts. With very competitive packages for a variety of visitors, the WinterFest has proved very popular. In fact, at times it has perhaps become too popular, with enormous traffic jams, claustrophobic nightclubs and overbooked restaurants proving challenging for the authorities in their endeavour to maintain and enhance the energy, variety and depth of Hong Kong's visitor experience.

Much of Hong Kong's appeal as a destination can be attributed to its vast retail provision, much of it at the high end of the spectrum, with shopping, it would appear, almost a national and international pastime! In fact, practically all of Hong Kong is a shopper's paradise. Year-round, you'll find many sales in and around the Central district on Hong Kong Island and limitless bargains to be had in Mongkok, on the Kowloon side of the city. Designer shops and exclusive labels are everywhere, with visitors from all over the world restocking and updating their wardrobes. It is not only the well-known international labels that prove popular as several markets across Hong Kong offer silk products, Chinese artwork, collectibles and curios at affordable prices with further opportunities for the more intrepid visitor to seek further retail therapy in Macau and Shenzhen in Mainland China!

| Photograph 6.1 | Shopping as a pastime in Hong Kong. |

*Source*: tuan0989250402/Shutterstock.com

| Photograph 6.2 | The ubiquity of festivals in Hong Kong. |
| --- | --- |
| | *Source*: Lee Yiu Tung/Shutterstock.com |

## DISCUSSION QUESTIONS

1. What are some of the principal challenges facing a destination of your choice when deciding upon an extensive programme of year-round festivals and events to enhance its appeal to visitors?

2. In what ways can festivals and events be used by destinations to enhance the visit 'experience'?

3. Retail is a major component of destinations but very often is managed separately. How do retail and tourism cross over and what are some of the many benefits to be derived from a cohesive retail tourism strategy at the destination level?

### Creativity

The considerable challenges that confront those tasked with developing destination brands helps to explain why there is such a paucity of brand innovation in the destination sector as compared to other sectors within the tourism industry (Hankinson, 2007).

### YOUTUBE
#### Destination branding

Helsinki destination branding for tourists
**http://www.youtube.com/watch?v=8nGm8_3S4dQ**

Singapore
**http://www.youtube.com/watch?v=_4XAW-QqWm0**

Hans van Driem on Destination Branding
**http://www.youtube.com/watch?v=s1sMXOyy2xo**

## Communication

In view of the competitive forces at play, there is a strong argument for more varied approaches to the development of communication strategies for destinations. According to King (2002), much greater emphasis needs to be given to the creation and communication of holiday experiences that link key brand values and assets with the holiday aspirations and needs of key customers. In parallel King advocates a move away from a relatively passive promotional role to include greater intervention, facilitation and direction in the conversion process. The migration to an economy based on 'experience' opens the door to the establishment of ongoing, direct, two-way and networking consumer communication channels, and for key customer relationship strategies to take place with the eventual development of mass customisation marketing and delivery capabilities.

## Channels

Although there have been significant developments with regard to computer reservation systems and global distribution systems, for the destination it is the growth of destination management and marketing systems that are the principal competitive tools in their quest for gaining greater control over the distribution of the destination product. Irrespective of the location, scale and type of destination in question, the development of a suitable destination management system, whether unilaterally or with other destinations, is a priority that can no longer be ignored.

## Cyberspace

The emergence of the Internet and its application in the domains of tourism, travel and hospitality is significant. It has underpinned significant changing patterns of consumption, and has affected the entire buying processes and the means by which tourism, travel and hospitality products are packaged and sold. The complexity of the destination product and the coordinating role practised by destination marketers clearly makes the development, implementation and management of destination-wide websites particularly challenging. However, as with the rest of the wider tourism industry, it is a challenge that destinations cannot afford to ignore.

## Consolidation

Greater consolidation has impacted significantly on the global tourism industry, most notably in the domains of travel in the form of airlines, hospitality in the form of large international hotel groups, and tourism in the form of intermediaries. For destinations this issue throws open a number of challenges in their attempt to counter the power imbalance that often results from such developments.

## Collaboration

Destinations are difficult to organise as there are often numerous stakeholders involved, all with their own aims, goals and motivations, which have to coexist. Whether one is referring to intra-destination networks, inter-destination collaboration, relational brands or forms of collaboration governance, this move towards the need for greater collaboration is referred to by King (2002) as the 'network economy', in that DMOs will probably enter into strategic relationships with industry partners who can together provide a seamless experience for the customer. This is because it will be the 'relevance of the experience they offer the customer, rather than the destination they promote, which will be the key ingredient for success in the future' (King, 2002: 108). In this context, collaboration is not considered a luxury but a necessity for destinations to survive in the face of considerable competition and environmental challenges. A number of benefits to be derived from cooperative public–private sector tourism organisations are provided by Poetschke (1995: 57–8). These include the reduction in antagonism through representation of all stakeholders; the avoidance of duplication through enhanced communication channels between represented sectors; and the bringing together of expertise. Benefits can also include increased funding potential through the reduction in duplicated efforts as well as industry-based taxes; the creation of a win/win situation through an increase in industry profitability and ensuing increase in government tax revenue; and the provision of infrastructure and investment funds.

# DESTINATION MANAGEMENT AND MARKETING

## Destination collaboration

Destination management is predominantly a micro-level activity in which 'all the stakeholders carry out their individual and organisational responsibilities on a daily basis in efforts to realise the macro-level vision contained in policy, planning and development' (Ritchie and Crouch, 2003: 111). However, the fact that destinations are comprised of so many products, stakeholders, and complex management and political relationships contributes to their being regarded as one of the most difficult 'products' to manage and market. To best manage the complexities and 'imperfections' inherent within destinations it is accepted that destinations need to bring together all parties to collaborate rather than to compete, and to pool resources towards developing an integrated management and delivery system. Referred to by King as the 'network economy' (2002), destination management organisations are, in the future, recommended to enter into strategic partnerships that can collectively deliver a seamless visitor experience to customers. This is likely to occur because it is the significance of the experience that they offer the customer, rather than the destination they promote, which will be the key constituent for success in the years to come.

The UNWTO (WTO, 2002b) also recognises that there is a growing need for destinations to develop alliances with a broad range of organisations, even on occasion with potential competitors. Despite this sense of currency and urgency, collaboration among and between destinations is not a new phenomenon. For example, various forms of destination collaboration have taken place in Bali and the Caribbean. In the case of Bali, collaboration was deemed essential in overcoming the island's perceived migration 'downmarket', while in the Caribbean cooperation among the public and private sectors in tourism was not merely desirable but a necessity in view of the particular characteristics of the tourism industry. Further studies, such as those by Darrow (1995) in the Caribbean, and Henderson (2001) in the Greater Mekong Subregion, explore the means by which destinations can work in partnership with other destinations in improving the interregional, interstate and interdestination product. Fyall and Garrod (2005: 289–90) highlight a number of advantages that exist with respect to collaboration within and among destinations. These include:

- Reduction in risk through strength in numbers and interconnectedness within and across destinations.
- Efficient and effective exchange of resources for perceived mutual benefit.
- The generation of increased visitor flows and positive economic impacts.
- The potential for collaborative initiatives to counter the threat of channel intermediary powers.
- In peripheral locations, collaboration serving as a significant vehicle to broaden the destination domain.
- The ability to counter greater standardisation in the industry through the use of innovative collaboration marketing campaigns.
- The potential to develop destination-wide reservation systems and two-way dialogue with customers through technological collaboration, whereby the emerging technologies can facilitate relationship building and customer relationship management programmes.
- Further collaboration on the Internet, so affording DMOs the ability to reach large numbers of consumers, to transmit information and offer products at a relatively low cost, to provide complete and more reliable information, to make client reservations quickly and efficiently, and to reduce the costs associated with producing and distributing printed materials.

In addition, such activity may be particularly useful when a country's tourism product is underdeveloped or when existing products are in an advanced stage in the product life cycle. Similarly, collaboration in a promotional sense often starts at the 'national' stage of the resort development spectrum, which involves joint campaigns by state and local government and local businesses together with campaigns by hotels and major attractions (Prideaux, 2000). Destination collaboration is, however, far from widespread. Indeed, there remain a number of constraints and drawbacks to collaboration both within and between destinations. These include:

- General mistrust and suspicion among collaborating partners due to governance or structures that are inappropriate for moving the shared project forward.
- Inability of various sectors within the destination to work together due to excuses of a political, economic or even interpersonal nature.
- Instances where particular stakeholders fail to recognise the real value of collaboration and remain closed to the benefits of working together.
- The frequent lack of interest in collaboration from 'honey-pot' attractions, where the need to work more closely together is discounted due to their own individual success in the marketplace.
- Competition between municipal authorities that administer separate geographical regions within a recognised destination resulting in inertia (Fyall and Garrod, 2005: 290).

Despite the above shortcomings, inter-organisational collaboration, often in the form of public–private sector partnerships, is a popular strategy for tourism destinations. In their comparative study of the management of tourism on the Gold Coast and Sunshine Coast, both in Queensland, Australia, Prideaux and Cooper (2002: 49) concluded that 'where there is strong co-operation between the private sector and LGAs at representative DMO level and where all key stakeholders in the tourism industry have supported a single brand strategy, the destination can anticipate considerable growth, as demonstrated by the Gold Coast'. Conversely, they concluded that 'where there is a lack of unity or where there are multiple marketing bodies with multiple brands representing the same primary destination there is considerable danger that primary market research will not be undertaken and that marketing strategy will degenerate into unco-ordinated selling campaigns' (Prideaux and Cooper, 2002: 49). Although the situation in the Sunshine Coast appears to have persisted over a long time, Heath and Wall (1992) suggest that problems related to collaboration between local authorities and destination marketing organisations can be overcome, or at least reduced, by establishing greater consensus between stakeholders on the domain 'sense of purpose' as part of a more participative management approach. Greater collaboration is, therefore, viewed as a precondition for effective brand building, which, in turn, becomes a catalyst for further growth of destinations.

## Destination management organisations

Destination management organisations (DMOs) represent a recent conceptualisation of the organisation function for the management of destinations, where the 'M' emphasises total management rather than just marketing. This refocused philosophy represents a more holistic approach to the management of destinations whereby the DMO is responsible for the well-being of all aspects of the destination. According to Ritchie and Crouch (2003: 73–4) it 'emphasizes the provision of a form of leadership in destination development that makes extensive use of teamwork in all DMO-led initiatives. Destination promotion is no longer the sole purpose of the DMO. While this modified role presents many new challenges, it also provides a much broader range of opportunities for ensuring destination competitiveness'. One can now legitimately argue

**YOUTUBE**
Destination marketing

DMAI, 97th Annual convention – Destination Marketing = Passion, Impact, Innovation
**http://www.youtube.com/watch?v=f0dR3n1aW3s**

that the DMO is the most appropriate organisational arrangement to meet fully the experiential needs of visitors. Ritchie and Crouch (2003: 175) argue that a DMO may be either a 'public sector agency or a private sector-driven organisation'. Buhalis (2000: 99), meanwhile, suggests that DMOs tend to be 'part of the local, regional or national government and have political and legislative power as well as the financial means to manage resources rationally and to ensure that all stakeholders can benefit in the long term'. Irrespective of their nature, Ritchie and Crouch (2003: 175) advocate that DMOs are constituted in a manner that provides them with the following characteristics. They must:

- Be clearly identifiable as the organisation responsible for coordinating and directing the efforts of the many parts of the diverse and complex tourism system.
- Command the support of all important sectors and all major actors in the tourism system.
- Be capable of influencing the decisions and actions of the many public sector agencies/departments and private firms that directly determine the nature and quality of the tourism experience provided to visitors.
- Possess the tools necessary to stimulate and encourage the type and amount of supply development that is required by the overall tourism megapolicy.
- Be sufficiently independent and flexible to develop innovative strategies that can be implemented in a timely manner in response to rapidly evolving market and environmental conditions.

Although the scope of DMOs varies, in most cases they exist to build the destination, to support and bring together the trade, to help minimise business failures, particularly among SMEs, to manage the public realm, to build and develop the destination brand, represent the interests of the trade at national, regional and sub-regional organisations, to develop skills and training for the trade, and to deliver an input into the planning process and wider economic development plan. Ultimately, the role of a DMO must be to enhance the long-term competitiveness of the destination.

## Roles and structures

Despite the importance and significance of DMOs across the world, it is therefore surprising that no real 'blueprint' exists. That said, most DMOs, although varying in their roles and tasks undertaken, demonstrate an effective internal and external focus, especially with regard to marketing. In all reality, DMOs identify and manage stakeholders, manage community relations and develop suitable publication programmes. More importantly, they stress the need to expand the number of roles and tasks to include all that is necessary to manage the destination in its entirety. Ritchie and Crouch (2003: 188) argue that in 'the past, the importance of the marketing and promotion roles of the DMO were of such priority that the DMO label was understood to

### YOUTUBE
Destination marketing organisations

Aspen as a destination
http://www.youtube.com/watch?v=waeUcpgZLLl

Destination Germany
http://www.youtube.com/watch?v=_fqEwv_NRIM

Destination India campaign
http://www.youtube.com/watch?v=rNWeBVBqo2c

Destination India winning world travel award
http://www.youtube.com/watch?v=xJ9dP0svBjg

mean "destination *marketing* organisation". It is only in recent years that DMOs have acknowledged how significant their non-marketing roles are in developing, enhancing and maintaining destination competitiveness. Nearly all progressive and effective DMOs in today's world now appreciate the importance of their more broadly based mandate and use DMO to mean "destination *management* organisation". '

According to South West Tourism (SWT) (2005: 10), a DMO can be responsible for the coordination of all those properties that define the destination for visitors through the following functions. Although each will have varying degrees of direct and/or indirect impact, roles could include any mix of the following:

- strategy and planning/policy;
- representation of interest;
- product development;
- marketing;
- skills/training;
- infrastructure development;
- collection and management of information and research;
- sustainability;
- business support and advice;
- coherence, communication and the management of quality; and
- the creation of a strong unified voice for the local industry.

According to SWT (2005: 10), these 'functions' 'represent the key elements that are requirements of a competitive destination'. To achieve these functions clearly requires a large number of stakeholders working towards attaining a structure that delivers them in a mutually beneficial and efficient way.

Despite the above inclusive list of roles/functions, for many DMOs marketing remains a core focus of its activity. In this context, Pike (2004) excludes separate government departments and a number of regional bodies that are responsible for planning and policy. That said, it is difficult to make sweeping generalisations as so many national tourism organisations (NTOs), regional tourism organisations (RTOs) and convention and visitors bureaux (CVBs) vary in the roles undertaken and structures adopted. One of the challenges of comparing and contrasting the roles and structures of DMOs is the significant paucity of information on DMOs generically. Although Pike (2004) provides a worthy historical overview of their development, his text is isolated and represents one of the very few works that explore this phenomenon in any significant depth. Pike is passionate about the role of DMOs, both now and in the future, and, irrespective of their title, argues that while a 'myriad of private and public sector organisations have vested interests in different aspects of society relating to tourism, no other entity has such an active and holistic interest in the quality of the traveller experience, the host community's sense of place, and the profitability of tourism businesses' (2004: 19).

Buhalis (2000) is equally passionate and argues that DMOs should all meet four generic strategies if they are to be a success. He argues that they should:

- enhance the long-term prosperity of local people;
- delight visitors by maximising their satisfaction;
- maximise profitability of local enterprises and maximise multiplier effects; and
- optimise tourism impacts by ensuring a sustainable balance between economic benefits and socio-cultural and environmental assets.

Buhalis (2000: 109) continues by suggesting that DMOs have an overall responsibility 'for the entire destination product and through incentives and policies facilitate the development of products, which is desirable from the demand side, and at the same time does not jeopardise local resources'. In essence, he is arguing that it is the DMO that should serve as the guardian of the image and resources of the destination. One additional area where DMOs will increasingly be looked upon to take the lead is in managing the information and research needs of the destination. Related to this is the need for a suitable framework to analyse/evaluate the effectiveness of the DMO itself, work undertaken in the UK by Destination Performance UK (DPUK), representing a small beginning in what remains an under-researched area.

While the basic roles of a DMO are generally similar at all destination levels, structures put in place will depend on numerous factors, in particular the nature and type of the destination and the level of funding that is forthcoming to meet both operational and strategic targets and ensure ongoing long-term success. Although structures can vary slightly at the national regional/state/provincial level, principal differences in structure can be found at the urban/municipal/city-state level. Some DMOs are membership-based while others tend to represent a loosely connected 'federation' of supporting organisations. It is also the case that the structures of yet others are such that in all reality they merely represent a department or section of local government. With regard to the balance between the public and private sectors in the UK, it is usual for a local authority tourism department to remain in public hands, while convention and visitor bureaux are often privately controlled. Interestingly, very few, if any, countries or regions have experimented with more novel forms of organisation lying somewhere between the public and the private models. For the most part, the public sector remains 'crucial in ensuring optimal use of public tourism resources/services and a balanced sharing of costs and benefits among all the actors involved' (Manente and Minghetti, 2006: 234). For the most part, the involvement of the public sector is critical in order to preserve the local environment, the residents' quality of life, the tourists' quality of experience, and the identity of the destination as a whole. In essence, the public sector serves as an agent for development in that it creates the conditions necessary to succeed. Pike (2004) concludes that ultimately the key goals for DMOs should be to enhance destination image, increase industry profitability, reduce seasonality and ensure suitable long-term funding. To achieve this he advocates that DMOs should be responsible for industry coordination, the monitoring of service and quality standards and the enhancing of community relations.

## Governance, funding and effectiveness

In view of the considerable diversity apparent with regard to roles and structures, it perhaps comes as no surprise that governance also varies considerably. That said, Poetschke (1995: 62–3) identifies four critical factors for success with regard to the governance of DMOs of globally competitive destinations:

1. a significant level of private sector control over spending;
2. understanding of the need to incorporate public sector objectives to achieve a balance between marketing and new product development;
3. a dedicated revenue stream that is not subject to annual government control; and
4. a broad, integrated mandate encompassing a function critical to developing a strong tourism industry, such as marketing, education, research and infrastructure development.

Although the orientation of the principal decision-making body, most probably a board, is also important in that orientations will vary quite considerably between an official public board, a private board, or a public–private sector partnership, each body will have to come to terms with considerable diversity, the likelihood of some representatives being unable to grasp the wider 'domain' picture, suspicions of others' sectoral interests, the probability of a cumbersome organisational name to reflect all areas covered, a regional community not fully informed on the advantages of tourism and a paucity of current and reliable statistics.

Irrespective of their structure, the majority of DMOs, at all levels, rely to a large extent on public support, i.e. funding. This proved to be particularly problematical for the former area tourist boards (ATBs) in Scotland where they crossed local political and administrative boundaries and were thus forced to lobby several councils for funding. Sources of funding for DMOs vary considerably, although the gradual reduction in funding from the public sector serves as a principal catalyst for change with greater emphasis on the need to source funds from alternative avenues. One alternative is to increase membership fees for industry members. Although a very logical and laudable rationale, it is frequently unsuccessful due to the propensity for too many stakeholders within the destination benefiting from 'free-rider' activity. One further option is the imposition of a local hotel tax. However, although relatively easy to administer, it is arguably one-sided, unfair and in essence not representative of the wider visitor economy. Conceptually logical but impractical to put into practice is a tourism/recreation tax whereby the cost of implementation often outweighs the benefit to be gained from its imposition. Finally, there is the private sector sponsorship alliance which, although considered successful in the short term, does not represent a sustainable vehicle for the longer term funding of destinations. In addition, it has been suggested that various types of user fees and more importance placed on partnership and buy-in programmes be advocated.

Related to the above, there are also various means by which a budget, most notably in the public sector, can be determined, for example by the size of the host population, visitor numbers, as a ratio of visitor spend, by the number of commercial accommodation beds/rooms, and/or the number of taxpayers/ratepayers. Pike (2004: 51–2) suggests that each of these will be influenced by the local situation vis-à-vis the local political situation, the stage of the destination in the tourism area life cycle (TALC) and the state of maturity of the local industry, the economic importance of tourism relative to other industries, and the overall history of the DMO and its current structure.

One of the perennial problems of destination management has been the extent to which the contribution of DMO efforts to the overall success of the destination can be measured. Pike (2004: 36) argues that the 'lack of suitable data leaves the industry open to attack from politicians and other industries seeking justification for funding from the public purse'; and adds that 'isolating and quantifying a DMO's contribution to destination competitiveness is currently an impossible task. Ultimately the success of a destination will be as a result of a combination of factors, many of which will be exogenous to the DMO' (Pike, 2004: 190).

## CONCLUSION

Given the foremost position of destinations in the tourism system it is a little surprising that the UNWTO waited so long to conduct an international forum on destination management and that so few academic texts have explored the operations and dynamics of DMOs to date (WTO, 2002a). This is also true of academic research published in journals where there remains a distinct paucity of material that explores the origins, nature, organisational and governance structures, sources of funding and overall performance aspects of DMOs (Wang and Pizam, 2011). Further areas lacking research rigour in this domain include strategic planning and implementation, destination competitiveness, destination positioning, human resource management, destination brand management and integrated marketing communications (Pike, 2004).

One of the common themes emerging throughout this chapter is the issue of collaboration. For collaboration to succeed the DMO needs to act as a strong unifying force that is able to bring all component parts of the destination together and develop it in its entirety. Effective collaboration is key while the need to remain cognisant of all those issues and forces impacting on their future direction is vital if destinations are to keep abreast of competitors. In many ways destinations have not changed over the years; they have always been difficult products to manage. What has changed is the quite significant forces for change existing in the macro and micro environments and their long-term impact on the future management of destinations. According to Pike (2004: 2) the vast majority of DMOs, irrespective of where they are in the world, share 'a common range of political and resource-based challenges not faced by private sector tourism businesses'. The most notable challenge is that of year-on-year reductions in contributions from the public purse. This factor alone represents a significant catalyst for change which single-handedly may change how the industry and general public view destinations, especially with regard to boundaries.

DMOs are clearly emerging as the 'glue' that bonds together stakeholders at the destination in their search for increasing competitiveness and long-term sustainability. Costa and Buhalis

(2006: 245) add that 'DMOs will play a critical role in ensuring that business opportunities are planned and managed within the context of regional development, and therefore will be contributing to optimization of economic, physical and social impacts' in the years ahead. Nevertheless, evidence suggests that many tourism destinations, whether at a national, regional or local level, still retain a narrow perspective of their process of evolution (Manente and Minghetti, 2006). The same authors continue by asking whether traditional tourism destinations in the mature phase of their life cycle will be able to make an evolutionary leap, or whether in fact competition will be driven by new emerging destinations that see tourism as an important factor of economic development and can learn from other territorial experiences. To conclude, although present across many countries, DMOs are a relatively new phenomenon in many parts of the world where their rationale for establishment, roles and structures, and governance and funding remain unclear. In theory at least, however, they serve as the most appropriate organisational structures for the effective management of destinations.

## SELF-CHECK QUESTIONS

1. What are the principal differences in the markets attracted to different types of destinations?
2. What are the differences between 'competitive' and 'comparative' advantage in the context of destinations?
3. Identify five key trends impacting future visitation patterns to urban and coastal destinations.
4. Why is the management of rural destinations particularly challenging?
5. What is the difference between a destination management organisation and a destination management partnership?

## REFERENCES AND FURTHER READING

Bennett, O. (1999) 'Destination marketing into the next century', *Journal of Vacation Marketing* **6**(1), 48–54.

Buhalis, D. (2000) 'Marketing: the competitive destination of the future', *Tourism Management* **21**(1), 97–116.

Costa, C. and Buhalis, D. (2006) 'Conclusion: tourism futures', pp. 241–6 in Buhalis, D. and Costa, C. (eds) *Tourism Business Frontiers: Consumers, Products and Industry*, Elsevier Butterworth Heinemann, Oxford.

Darrow, K. (1995) 'A partnership model for nature tourism in the eastern Caribbean islands', *Journal of Travel Research* **33**(3), 48–51.

Dwyer, L. and Kim, C. (2003) 'Destination competitiveness: determinants and indicators', *Current Issues in Tourism* **6**(5), 346–69.

Fletcher, J. and Morakabati, Y. (2008) 'Tourism activity, terrorism and political instability within the Commonwealth: the case of Fiji and Kenya', *International Journal of Tourism Research* **10**(6), 537–56.

Fyall, A. (2011) 'Destination management: challenges and opportunities', pp. 340–57 in Wang, Y. and Pizam, A. (eds) *Destination Marketing and Management: Theories and Applications*, CABI, Oxford.

Fyall, A. and Garrod, B. (2005) *Tourism Marketing: A Collaborative Approach*, Channel View, Clevedon.

Fyall, A., Garrod, B. and Tosun, C. (2006) 'Destination marketing: a framework for future research', pp. 75–86 in Kozak, M. and Andreu, L. (eds) *Progress in Tourism Marketing*, Elsevier, Oxford.

Fyall, A. and Leask, A. (2007) 'Destination marketing: future issues – strategic challenges', *Tourism & Hospitality Research* **7**(1), 50–63.

Hankinson, G. (2007) 'The management of destination brands: five guiding principles based on recent developments in corporate branding theory', *Brand Management* **14**(3), 240–54.

Heath, E. and Wall, G. (1992) *Marketing Tourism Destinations: A Strategic Planning Approach*, Wiley, New York.

Henderson, J. (2001) 'Strategic alliances and destination marketing in the Greater Mekong Subregion', *Pacific Tourism Review* **4**(4), 149–59.

King, J. (2002) 'Destination marketing organisations: connecting the experience rather than promoting the place', *Journal of Vacation Marketing* **8**(2), 105–8.

Leiper, N. (1995) *Tourism Management*, TAFE Publications, Collingwood, Victoria.

Li, X. and Petrick, J.F. (2008) 'Tourism marketing in an era of paradigm shift', *Journal of Travel Research* **46**, 235–44.

Manente, M. and Minghetti, V. (2006) 'Destination management organisations and actors', pp. 228–37 in Buhalis, D. and Costa, C. (eds) *Tourism Business Frontiers: Consumers, Products and Industry*, Elsevier Butterworth Heinemann, Oxford.

Pedro, A. (2006) 'Urbanization and second-home tourism', pp. 85–93 in Buhalis, D. and Costa, C. (eds) *Tourism Business Frontiers: Consumers, Products and Industry*, Elsevier Butterworth Heinemann, Oxford.

Pike, S. (2004) *Destination Marketing Organisations*, Elsevier, Oxford.

Poetschke, B. (1995) 'Key success factors for public/private sector partnerships in island tourism planning', in Conlin, M.V. and Baum, T. (eds) *Island Tourism*, Wiley, Chichester.

Poon, A. (1993) *Tourism, Technology and Competitive Strategies*, CABI, Oxford.

Porter, M. (1998) 'Clusters and the new economics of competition', *Harvard Business Review* (Nov–Dec), 77–90.

Prideaux, B. (2000) 'The resort development spectrum: a new approach to modelling resort development', *Tourism Management* **21**(3), 225–40.

Prideaux, B. and Cooper, C. (2002) 'Marketing and destination growth: a symbiotic relationship or simple coincidence?', *Journal of Vacation Marketing* **9**(1), 35–51.

Ritchie, J.R.B. and Crouch, G.I. (2003) *The Competitive Destination: A Sustainable Tourism Perspective*, CABI, Oxford.

Scott, N., Parfitt, N. and Laws, E. (2000) 'Destination management: co-operative marketing, a case study of Port Douglas Brand', pp. 198–221 in Faulkner, B., Moscardo, G. and Laws, E. (eds) *Tourism in the 21st Century*, Continuum, London.

SWT (2005) *South West Tourism: Destination Management Organisation Delivery Plan*, South West Tourism, Exeter.

Wang, Y. (2008) 'Collaborative destination marketing: roles and strategies of convention and visitors bureaus', *Journal of Vacation Marketing* **14**(3), 191–209.

Wang, Y. and Pizam, A. (2011) *Destination Marketing and Management: Theories and Applications*, CABI, Oxford.

WTO (2002a) *Thinktank*, WTO, Madrid.

WTO (2002b) *Tourism in the Age of Alliances, Mergers and Acquisitions*, WTO, Madrid.

# MAJOR CASE STUDY 6.1
## Manchester – an original modern visitor destination

## INTRODUCTION

Although at first glance Manchester, located in the North West of industrial England, does not spring to mind as a tourist destination when compared to the likes of Orlando in Florida (USA), Paris in France and Bangkok in Thailand, with just under 10 million staying visitors a year and about 1.2 million international visitors, Manchester is a thriving destination. The economic value of tourism to the Manchester economy is a highly impressive £6 billion with up to 81,000 full-time-equivalent jobs now attributed to tourism. With a little help from its two football teams, Manchester United and Manchester City, a burgeoning business and conference product,

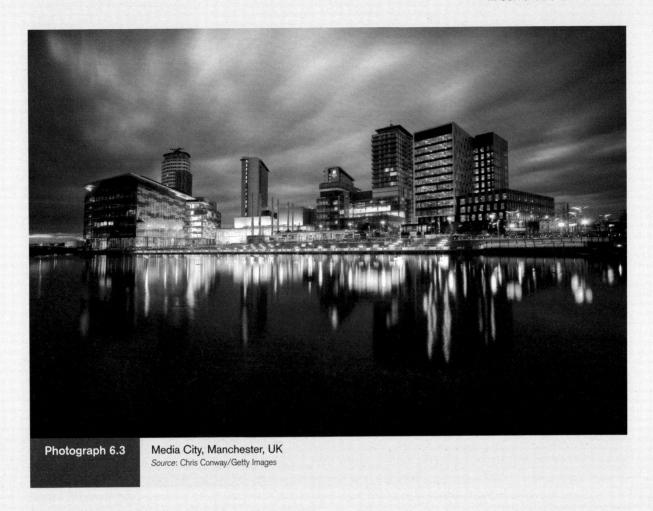

**Photograph 6.3**  Media City, Manchester, UK
*Source*: Chris Conway/Getty Images

an impressive night-time economy and the recent relocation of much of the BBC to MediaCity:UK in nearby Salford, Manchester is very much a force in the world of tourist destinations both in the UK and beyond and is, for the most part, no longer viewed as an old grey industrial city. Today, Manchester is the third most visited city in the UK by international visitors, behind London and Edinburgh, while its ever-growing airport now serves around 200 destinations worldwide and connects to 16 airports in the UK; Manchester is very much a destination with an upward trajectory of growth!.

## A PERIOD OF SUSTAINED GROWTH AND IMPROVEMENT

Manchester's growth and success in recent years is, however, no accident. Over the past five years, those managing and marketing Manchester set a number of key priorities so as to help develop Manchester into a truly memorable and distinguishable destination. The first priority, *enhancing the image*, involved much interaction with the world media with over 500 international journalists being hosted from a number of its key international

markets, including the USA, China and India, to name but a few, in addition to the development of a highly proactive relationship with key publications such as *Lonely Planet* and the *New York Times*. Along with many other city destinations around the world, Manchester benchmarks its progress with the Anholt City Brands Index, with a very positive shift in perceptions registered in recent years from both domestic and international markets. This said, there still remain in some markets negative perceptions of Manchester so the need to continue targeted press coverage and marketing campaigns is as relevant as ever in the search to inspire potential visitors into coming to Manchester, be they local, regional, national or international.

The need to continue to *promote Manchester to both national and international visitors* represents the second priority with a seasonal, multi-faceted and multi-channel approach adopted. With a strong focus on 'families' as well as the more traditional audience of 'cosmopolitan couples and discoverers', a variety of thematic campaigns have been adopted such as 'Modern History' and 'Manchester's Countryside'. Wherever possible, international marketing campaigns are delivered in partnership with airlines and destination airports, leveraging match funding and extending the reach of seasonal campaign messages to key leisure tourism markets. For the future, the strategy is focused on increasing the number of visitors to Manchester, encouraging them to stay longer and, it is hoped, spend more money in the local economy. To achieve this it is critical to ensure the survival of existing key air routes and attract leisure visitors from new and developing markets.

The third priority is to *create a leading conference and business tourism destination*. Business tourism has always been a priority for Visit Manchester, the agency responsible for marketing Manchester, which has a very focused approach to targeting international and national association conferences in partnership with key stakeholders. For example, in recent years Manchester has hosted many high-profile events including Conservative and Labour Party Annual Conferences, the Soccerex European Forum and the World Youth Student Tourism Congress. It is estimated that the conference sector alone contributes almost £600 million to the local economy. To support and further develop this component of the destination, significant investment is ongoing across the city with many of its venues, including Manchester Central and Lancashire County Cricket Club Old Trafford, having undertaken major improvements since 2008. For the future, Manchester seeks to further increase the value and volume of business tourism, increase the number of international business tourism and conference visitors, and above all improve the perception of Manchester as a conference destination.

The fourth priority, *improving the provision of information to visitors*, has benefited significantly since 2010 from the opening of the all-new Manchester Visitor Information Centre (MVIC). With its new location, the MVIC is now accessing a much higher proportion of visitors as well as local residents and is scoring higher in most categories in the visitor satisfaction surveys. The MVIC is the first visitor centre in Europe to use interactive Microsoft Surface Tables which allow people to interact directly with the information available and discover a wide range of information independently. A Manchester Twitter feed also streams onto screens while a 12-screen video wall advertises local and regional attractions. The primary asset of the MVIC remains the experienced team of staff who 'walk' the centre freely, welcoming an annual footfall of over 232,000! In addition, **visitmanchester.com** has undergone a complete redevelopment, with unique visitors growing from 785,000 in 2008 to a level that will exceed 2 million by the end of 2011/12. Rather than using traditional approaches to website design, the new website incorporates real-time information from real people, delivering a genuine, honest interpretation of the city. For the future it is hoped that Manchester will increase visitor dispersal, motivate longer stays and repeat visits, make it easier for those visiting the destination to discover what it has to offer and improve the destination's welcome. It also seeks to enhance and add value to the visitor experience, provide the 'right' information to visitors through the channel most relevant and appropriate for their needs and support and encourage the quality and breadth of the visitor offer and visitor experience.

The need to *develop and enhance the destination product* represents the fifth priority with well over 1,000 people and almost 900 businesses benefiting from subsidised customer service, leadership and management, marketing and young chefs training and skills programmes since 2008. Interestingly, the Commonwealth Games in 2002 served as a major catalyst for the staging of events in the city, with Manchester being named as the 'World's Best City for Sport' at the Sports Business Awards in November 2008! Although with a very strong sporting pedigree, Manchester has also invested in its more traditional attractions such as the People's History Museum and Manchester Art Gallery while the MediaCity:UK development goes from strength to strength and now includes new hotels, retail, food and drink and leisure provision. One notable success for Manchester has been its ability, despite the ongoing economic challenges in the UK, to continue to encourage leading accommodation providers into the destination with the likes of Crowne Plaza City Centre (228 rooms), Park Inn by Radisson (252 rooms), Holiday Inn Express Manchester Arena (192 rooms) and Ramada Manchester Salford Quays (142 rooms), just some of the new providers in the town since 2008. For the future, Manchester is seeking to ensure that the visitor experience meets expectations and delivers quality on all levels as it aims to continue to develop the appeal, profile and impact of events and festivals. It also aims to support tourism businesses to help improve their productivity and profitability as well as supporting signature projects where there exists both a gap in the market and sufficient demand to ensure success! Finally, in its endeavour to meet the principles of sustainability, it seeks to improve the quality and reputation of the food and drink offer and support the use of local foods and suppliers.

The final strategic priority for the destination is to *improve the infrastructure* such as the airport (which has recently benefited from an £80 million investment in the redevelopment of both Terminal 1 and 2) and the redevelopment of Manchester's Medieval Quarter. For the future, Manchester has hopes to improve the quality of the public realm in key destinations across Greater Manchester, particularly encouraging the development of green space and blue corridors wherever possible, and to develop strategies to open up the city and towns during evenings and nights to a wider audience. It also seeks to support the development of 'icons' and so increase the attractiveness of the tourism offer. Finally, it hopes to improve sustainable transport options and integration for visitors, and provide better information and easier ticketing options.

## A RESIDENT-FRIENDLY DESTINATION

Rather than focus entirely on the tourist or visitor, one of the very interesting features of Manchester's strategy for 2008–2013 is the provision of a destination that delivers a better quality of life for its residents. Quite simply, the pervading philosophy is that if Manchester is 'fit' for its residents then it ought to be a destination that is of significant appeal to visitors from all over the world who have a thirst for discovery. To achieve this, Manchester seeks to set itself apart from competing destinations by becoming what is termed an *Original, Modern Destination.* Not only does it wish for residents to be proud of the physical environment including its culture, entertainment and food, but it wishes to create a genuine buzz across the destination through drive and differentiation rather than focusing on incremental improvement. To achieve this 'experiential buzz' across the destination it wishes to create globally recognised and iconic events, developments, initiatives and opportunities which include people or collectives rather than just places, and build on those original themes from which Manchester developed its initial appeal, namely: industry, innovation, pop culture, sport, radicalism and independence. It also seeks to meet the expectations of its visitors through the provision of a holistic experience where all the individual components of the destination are connected, with all suppliers empowered to engage fully with the aspirations and ambitions of the destination.

With particular regard to its local resident population, the future of Manchester as a destination is all about improving the quality of life for the host community. In particular, through its development of tourism and the visitor economy Manchester is seeking to ensure that the quality of life for the wider community improves, with accessibility and diversity, a more inclusive night-time economy, and the need to boost physical activity, health and mental well-being key aspirations for the future development of the destination. To achieve this highly laudable goal, it is essential that all contributors to the destination 'product' and 'experience', such as the local authorities, businesses and employees, transport providers and, of course, residents themselves, work in collaboration with those tasked to take the destination forward.

As with all destinations, however, Manchester is faced with a number of pressing challenges as it seeks to continue to develop into a quality, 'must see' destination. The most pressing challenge without doubt is the current economic situation in the UK and in much of the Western world, where economic hardship is slowly becoming the norm. With less disposable income at their disposal, fuel costs rising and increasing job insecurity, Manchester is well placed to benefit from the 'staycation' effect but, with no sign to date of the 'beginning of the end' of the economic problems, there is a very real sense of caution as to how quickly things will recover. That said, much can be achieved through improved connectivity across the destination, a more balanced night-time economy, yet more 'iconic' developments and greater clarity of communicating what Manchester stands for and what differentiates it from other destinations.

## DISCUSSION QUESTIONS

1. What are the particular challenges for Manchester as it seeks to appeal to national and international leisure and business markets and at the same time seek to improve the quality of life and well-being of local residents?

2. Festivals and events are adopted by many destinations across the world as they seek differentiation in the marketplace. To what extent is such an approach sustainable in the challenging economic climate being experienced by so many countries in the West?

3. Sport tourism offers many attractive opportunities for many destinations. With its high-profile football clubs, world-class stadia and excellent transportation infrastructure what more can Manchester do to leverage benefit from its reputation as an outstanding sporting destination?

*Sources*: A Tourism Strategy for Greater Manchester 2008–2013; Greater Manchester Destination Management Plan: The Visitor Economy Action Plan 2012–13; Mr Paul Simpson, Managing Director, Visit Manchester.

# CHAPTER 7
## THE ECONOMIC IMPACT OF TOURISM

### LEARNING OUTCOMES

This chapter focuses on the economic impacts of tourism and aims to provide you with:

- an understanding of the economic contribution of tourism locally, nationally and internationally;

- an understanding of the methods used to estimate tourist expenditure and the way in which the significance of tourism can be measured;

- an appreciation of the positive and negative economic impacts of tourism activity; and

- a general knowledge of the approaches that may be used to measure the economic impacts of tourism and the strengths and weaknesses associated with each approach.

Photograph: Tadapani, Nepal © Graham Meyer

# INTRODUCTION

This chapter examines the economic significance of tourism as well as the economic impacts associated with the industry. In the same way that the literature tends to exaggerate the negative impacts of tourism upon host societies and environments, so the positive impact of tourism upon economies is often overstated. Therefore the positive and negative economic impacts of tourism will be discussed. An integral part of this chapter is a critical assessment of the methods of measuring economic impact drawing, particularly, on the application of multiplier analysis, tourism satellite accounts (TSAs) and computable generalised equilibrium models. All the multiplier models that are outlined in this chapter generate information that is valuable to policy makers and planners. It should also be noted that, within known limitations, multiplier analyses provide powerful and valuable tools for estimating and analysing the economic impact of tourism and comparing the performance of tourism with that of alternative industries.

## OVERVIEW

In spite of the many altruistic and well-meaning reasons sometimes put forward to support the case for tourism development, such as those originally proposed in the Manila Declaration (WTO, 1980a), it is the economic benefits that provide the main driving force for tourism development. Foreign exchange earnings, income and employment generation are the major motivations for including tourism as part of a development strategy. Tourist expenditure is as 'real' as any other form of consumption and international tourist expenditure can be seen as an **invisible export** from the host country, whereas domestic tourism can be seen as an 'export' from the hosting region to the other local regions. Domestic tourism can also, in some instances, be seen as an import substitute for the national economy. Tourism activity can be seen as import substitution when tourists choose to take their vacation within the national economy rather than travel abroad.

In spite of the fact that domestic tourism is far more prevalent in terms of volume and spending than its international counterpart, international tourism activity is often easier to measure because it frequently involves custom/immigration procedures and currency exchange. Many countries collect information from visitor arrivals at the frontier and this provides a good source of data relating to the volume of arrivals, country of origin and purpose of visit. Currency exchange information is collected and monitored by central banks and this provides some useful information, but is by no means ideal, relating to tourist spending. Tourist expenditure can only be estimated with some degree of accuracy by undertaking specific visitor expenditure surveys, normally at exit points. Such surveys tend to be time-consuming and costly. Some countries attempt to estimate the level and patterns of tourist spending from central bank statistics, while others try to economise by collecting tourist expenditure data at infrequent intervals (say, every five years). In order to use economic impact analyses for the purpose of tourism planning and development strategies it is important to have reliable flows of expenditure data. Therefore, visitor expenditure data should be collected by exit surveys each year, or at least every other year. This information can be collected along with demographic data and other variables that will help underscore other important surveys for, say, the market research referred to in Part 4 of this text.

During the past few decades many economies have experienced growth in their service sectors, even when the more traditional agricultural and manufacturing sectors have been subject to **stagnation** or decline. The global importance of the service sectors can be identified by the introduction of the General Agreement on Trade in Services (GATS) following the Uruguay Round of negotiations. Tourism is the largest service-based industry and, as such, has been partly responsible for this service sector growth. In **developing countries** the service sector is responsible for around 40–50% of **GDP**, while in the most industrialised economies it is responsible for more than 70–80% of GDP. In spite of its economic importance, the service sector has not been given adequate prominence in economic textbooks, which have tended to concentrate on the more traditional manufacturing industries. The dearth of material on service-based industries in the major textbooks can be, in part, explained (if not excused) by the lack of available and comparable statistics for service-based sectors. This shortfall in data is improving but, in general, it is tradition that has dictated the content of such books rather than pragmatism. The latter half of the 1980s saw a growing interest in the operation and performance of service industries. In 1985, it was observed that, because of the strength of **intersectoral linkages**, the service sector generally performs a more important function in the process of development than that suggested merely by looking at the service sector's contribution to a country's GDP. From the mid-1990s, the international world has been dominated by the service industries and they have also been responsible for the accelerated drive towards **globalisation**. International tourism activity enjoyed strong growth throughout the 1990s, often growing faster than other commercial services and at a rate that was almost twice as fast as international trade. If the 1990s were characterised by strong relentless growth in arrivals, like much of the second half of the twentieth century, the twenty-first century has to date been quite volatile. Global growth rates of arrivals ended the twentieth century with a 3.7% year on year growth rate and the new millennium got off to a bright start, recording a 7.9% growth in arrivals in the first year of the twenty-first century. However, the optimism generated by this performance was short-lived and the events of 9/11 brought confidence down to the ground and 2001 saw a decline in tourist arrivals of 0.1%. Tourism bounced back in 2002 (3%) only to be dashed again in 2003 with the onset of the Iraq War causing arrivals to decline (−1.6%). This was followed by a period of strong growth from 2004 to 2007 riding on an economic boom that was noted by the UNWTO in its market trends assessment in 2007. However, the onset of the global financial crisis in 2008 caused a downturn in tourism activity that was far more dramatic than those caused by terrorist attacks and natural disasters. Tourist arrival growth was well below the long-term average rate in 2008 at 2.1% only to decline by 3.8% in 2009. The advanced economies have suffered more from the global financial crisis than the emerging economies as real incomes have been hit sharply. Nevertheless tourist arrivals reached a shade under 940 million in 2010, 980 million in 2011 and passed the billion threshold in 2012.

Recognition of the importance of the service sector to the world economy came in the form of the establishment of the General Agreement on Trade in Services (GATS). **GATS** grew out of the World Trade Organization's Uruguay Round of the General Agreement on Tariffs and Trade (GATT). The main declared purpose of GATS is the liberalisation of services. However, a brief examination of the slowdown in the growth of trade might suggest that GATS was introduced because the strong growth in service industries would accelerate the World Trade Organization's processes and influence.

| Photograph 7.1 | The tourism industry is affected by stock market performance. |

*Source:* Peter Scholey/Alamy Images

Along with the movement towards the liberalisation of international trade has been the growth of *globalisation*. Globalisation refers to the result of a collection of forces that tend to change the way that the economic, political and cultural worlds operate. As the world becomes economically smaller, the concept of globalisation has taken on a more central position on the stage of global politics. From the earliest days when the world economy first started to transform from subsistence farming and fishing towards a market-based economy there has been a sustained growth in the geographical reach of businesses. However, this process of globalisation accelerated throughout the latter half of the last century. It has been referred to as a process in which the geographical distance between economic factors, producers and consumers becomes a factor of diminishing significance.

Tourism, as a major element of the service economy, has for some time been applauded for its sustained and rapid growth. However, in spite of the damage that has clearly been done to the growth of tourism activity following the onset of the 2008 global financial crisis, not even its most ardent supporters would have forecast just how resilient tourism has been in the face of enormous economic pressures – pressures that have severely damaged many of the world's major industries where car manufacturers, computing and electronic giants and even financial service organisations have either rationalised their activities or ceased trading. Although the purpose of this chapter is to examine the economic impact of tourism, it is useful to examine the economic significance of tourism to a number of countries, most notably the prime generators and/or recipients of international tourists. The economic significance of tourism is determined not only by the level of tourism activity that is taking place, but also by the type and nature of the economy being considered. For instance, the economic significance of tourism activity to a developing country may well be measured in terms of its ability to generate an inflow of foreign exchange or to provide a means for creating greater price flexibility in its export industries, whereas, for a developed or industrialised economy, the researcher may be looking at tourism's ability to assist **diversification** strategies and to combat regional imbalances.

The significance of tourism may be assessed in terms of the proportion of total global visitors attributable to individual countries, for here one can assess the relative importance of single countries in determining the volume of world travel. On the other hand, the significance of tourism may be examined with respect to the importance of tourist activity to the economy of each destination. This chapter examines both aspects in order to establish how some countries are extremely important as tourist generators and how other countries are highly dependent upon such tourism activity.

## International tourism in selected countries

Events that have happened throughout the 1990s and the first decade or so of the 2000s have had a profound effect on the patterns and flow of international tourism. How permanent these effects will be depends, to a large extent, on the future political and economic stability of the world. The global financial crisis has affected not only the flow of activity but also the geographical patterns. The events of 11 September 2001 fundamentally changed air transport services and the subsequent conflicts in the Middle East, which have not abated, and the Arab Spring still leaves that region of the world in an uncertain state. Therefore, the global and regional figures for international tourist arrivals and spending are characterised by volatility in the twenty-first century together with the rapid rise of new economic powerhouses such as China and India, with China entering the top five tourist-generating list for the first time in 2009.

The selection of countries for inclusion in tables of top generating and top recipient countries is at best difficult and at worst arbitrary. However, the countries selected in Tables 7.1 and 7.2 (China, France, Germany, Italy, Spain, UK and USA) have been included because they are among either the top five tourist-generating countries with respect to tourist expenditure and/or the top five countries with respect to tourism receipts.

Table 7.1 shows the principal tourist-generating countries, with respect to the level of their international tourist expenditure, over the time period from 2000 to 2010. It can be seen that, over the years covered by the table, the proportion of the world's total tourist expenditure

| Table 7.1 | Principal tourist-generating countries, 2000–2010: expenditure (US$ billion) | | | | |
|---|---|---|---|---|---|
| Country | 2000 | 2005 | 2008 | 2009 | 2010 |
| Germany | 53.0 | 74.4 | 91.0 | 81.2 | 78.1 |
| United States | 65.4 | 69.9 | 80.5 | 74.1 | 75.5 |
| China | 13.1 | 21.8 | 36.2 | 43.7 | 54.9 |
| United Kingdom | 38.4 | 59.6 | 68.5 | 50.1 | 50.0 |
| France | 22.6 | 31.8 | 41.1 | 38.4 | 38.5 |
| Top five countries | 192.5 | 257.5 | 317.3 | 287.5 | 297.0 |
| Rest of world | 282.5 | 421.5 | 622.7 | 564.5 | 629.0 |
| World total | 475.0 | 679.0 | 940.0 | 852.0 | 926.0 |
| Top five as percentage of world total | 40.5 | 37.9 | 33.8 | 33.7 | 32.1 |

*Source*: Derived from UNWTO World Tourism Barometer, January 2012

attributable to the top five generating countries continues to fall as emerging countries take a more active role in tourism generation and has declined from the 40.5% level recorded in 2000 (the corresponding figure in 1990 was 50.3%) to just a little over 32% in 2010. It can also be seen that Germany re-established itself as the prime tourism-generating country, in terms of tourist expenditure, in 2005. The UK peaked in terms of expenditure during this period in 2008 at 68.5 US$ billion and its expenditure diminished in the following two years as a result of the economic conditions. China as a tourism-generating country has been nothing short of sensational, coming into the top five in fourth place in 2009 and rising to third in 2010 and is clearly on course to be the world's top tourism-generating country.

The start of the new millennium saw the proportion of the world's total tourism receipts from international tourism activity attributable to the top five countries fall below 40% for the first time (see Table 7.2). By the end of the first decade the top five tourism receipt countries

| Table 7.2 | Principal destinations in terms of tourism receipts, 2000–2010: tourism receipts (US$ billion) | | | | |
|---|---|---|---|---|---|
| Country | 2000 | 2005 | 2008 | 2009 | 2010 |
| United States | 82.9 | 82.2 | 110.4 | 94.2 | 103.5 |
| Spain | 30.0 | 48.0 | 61.6 | 53.2 | 52.5 |
| France | 33.0 | 44.0 | 56.6 | 49.5 | 46.6 |
| China | 16.2 | 29.3 | 40.8 | 39.7 | 45.8 |
| Italy | 27.5 | 35.4 | 45.7 | 40.2 | 38.8 |
| Top five countries | 189.6 | 238.9 | 315.1 | 276.8 | 287.2 |
| Rest of world | 285.4 | 440.1 | 624.9 | 575.2 | 638.8 |
| World total | 475.0 | 679.0 | 940.0 | 852.0 | 926.0 |
| Top five as percentage of world total | 39.9 | 35.2 | 33.5 | 32.5 | 31.0 |

*Source*: Derived from UNWTO World Tourism Barometer, January 2012

accounted for just 31% of total world receipts. This demonstrates not only the wider dispersion of tourism activity as more countries compete for tourism receipts but also the effects of the global financial crisis on advanced economies, where receipts for all countries except China peaked in 2008 and had not recovered that level by 2010. Similarly, total world tourism receipts peaked in 2008 at 940 US$ billion and had not recovered to that level by 2010.

A fact that becomes clear when examining the top tourist expenditure generating and receiving countries is the high degree of correlation between the listings. Tourism does not perform well as a global redistributor of income and wealth in the same way as it does for sub-national income redistribution. This is particularly true if the relationship between developed and developing countries is considered. It is the developed and industrialised countries that tend to populate the lists in both the top generators of tourist expenditure and the top recipients.

The division between the performance of developed and developing countries is of additional significance when it is considered that, on average, the industrialised countries are responsible for 70% of total world exports and yet receive over 70% of all tourism receipts, which contrasts with developing countries that are responsible for less than 30% of all world exports and received less than 30% of all tourist receipts. It is also interesting to note that, in 2010, the top three countries in terms of the highest proportion of total world trade included China, Germany and USA.

## Dependence upon tourism

Table 7.3 provides another way of examining the economic significance of tourism for countries by looking at dependence on tourism receipts (**economic dependence**) relative to total gross domestic product (GDP), employment, export earnings and investment for 2011. Travel and tourism's contribution is shown as a percentage of each indicator both as a direct significance, i.e. the first round effect of international tourism receipts, and as a total contribution which takes into account the secondary effects of travel and tourism spending as it runs through the supporting sectors. It can be seen that even among these industrialised economies, there is significant variation, with tourism's contribution to GDP ranging from Spain's 14.4% to Germany's 4.6%. In terms of export earnings travel and tourism accounts for 15.5% of Spain's total exports but only 1.6% of total exports for Japan.

Two major problems that exist when making international comparisons of tourism expenditure and receipts are that the data are generally expressed in current prices and are standardised in US dollars. The problems created by this form of presentation is that (1) it does not take into account the effects of **inflation**, and (2) movements in the value of the dollar exchange rate (which have been both frequent and dramatic over the past decade or so) will appear to be changes in the local value of tourist receipts and expenditure. This is particularly true in the somewhat volatile economic state that has characterised the twenty-first century to date. Also, the US dollar has suffered as a result of its massive **trade deficit** and its involvement in the conflicts in Afghanistan and Iraq, and, finally, the sharp increases in demand for oil and mineral resources that have accompanied the rapid development of the economies of China and India are putting enormous pressures on world resources and hence causing price inflation.

Table 7.4 examines the relationship between tourism receipts and expenditures in order to establish the net effect of travel on selected countries of the world. In 2010 the USA, Italy, France and Australia all had positive tourism balance sheets. That is, they earned more from international tourism receipts than their national residents spent as tourists outside of the country. However, China, Canada, Japan, the Russian Federation, the UK and Germany were all subject to a negative tourism balance sheet. That is, the residents of those countries spent more abroad on international tourism than the countries received from international tourism receipts.

There have been various attempts at finding consistent ways to measure the level of demand or the significance of tourism activity to any individual country. The most universally accepted approach is through the construction of tourism satellite accounts.

| Table 7.3 | Travel and tourism's contribution to GDP, employment, exports and investment, 2011 (%) | | | |
|---|---|---|---|---|
| Country | As % of total GDP | As % of total employment | As % of total exports | As % of total investment |
| **Spain** | | | | |
| Direct contribution | 5.1 | 2.6 | 15.5 | 5.4 |
| Total contribution | 14.4 | 12.7 | | |
| **Australia** | | | | |
| Direct contribution | 3.3 | 5.7 | 12.4 | 5.5 |
| Total contribution | 13.0 | 16.2 | | |
| **France** | | | | |
| Direct contribution | 3.9 | 4.5 | 8.1 | 3.0 |
| Total contribution | 9.1 | 10.2 | | |
| **United States** | | | | |
| Direct contribution | 2.6 | 3.9 | 8.5 | 5.3 |
| Total contribution | 8.8 | 10.5 | | |
| **Italy** | | | | |
| Direct contribution | 3.2 | 3.7 | 8.1 | 4.1 |
| Total contribution | 8.6 | 9.7 | | |
| **China** | | | | |
| Direct contribution | 2.5 | 2.9 | 2.9 | 3.3 |
| Total contribution | 8.6 | 8.2 | | |
| **United Kingdom** | | | | |
| Direct contribution | 2.4 | 3.1 | 5.7 | 3.9 |
| Total contribution | 6.9 | 7.6 | | |
| **Japan** | | | | |
| Direct contribution | 2.2 | 2.3 | 1.6 | 3.1 |
| Total contribution | 6.8 | 7.1 | | |
| **Russian Federation** | | | | |
| Direct contribution | 1.4 | 1.4 | 3.2 | 2.1 |
| Total contribution | 5.9 | 5.5 | | |
| **Germany** | | | | |
| Direct contribution | 1.7 | 1.8 | 3.0 | 3.1 |
| Total contribution | 4.6 | 4.9 | | |

*Source*: WTTC Country Reports 2011

| Table 7.4 | Tourism balance sheets for the top ten tourist spenders, 2010 | | |
|---|---|---|---|
| Country | International tourism receipts (US$ billion) | International tourism expenditure (US$ billion) | Balance (US$ billion) |
| United States | 103.5 | 75.5 | 28.0 |
| Italy | 38.8 | 27.1 | 11.7 |
| France | 46.6 | 38.5 | 8.1 |
| Australia | 29.6 | 22.2 | 7.4 |
| China | 45.8 | 54.9 | − 9.1 |
| Canada | 15.7 | 29.6 | − 13.9 |
| Japan | 13.2 | 27.9 | − 14.7 |
| Russian Federation | 9.0 | 26.5 | − 17.5 |
| United Kingdom | 32.4 | 50.0 | − 17.6 |
| Germany | 34.7 | 78.1 | − 43.4 |

*Note*: A minus balance indicates where the country spends more than it receives through tourism activity.

*Source*: Derived from UNWTO, World Tourism Barometer, January 2012

## Tourism satellite accounts

One approach to determining the economic significance of tourism to an economy is to construct **tourism satellite accounts**. This methodology was approved and adopted by the United Nations and the World Tourism Organization in 2000. Tourism satellite accounts (TSAs) perform a different role from economic impact models that attempt to estimate the net economic benefits associated with a change in tourism activity. To be of use TSAs must be built around an **input–output model** and they take a demand-orientated approach rather than the supply-orientated approach that is associated with input–output models. As the TSA name suggests, they are a set of accounts that can be used to determine the size or significance of tourism within an economy, but not the impact of tourism. They are based on the national accounts data but this information is rearranged so that the full magnitude of tourism activities can be taken on board. Like input–output models, they also provide a means whereby tourism can be viewed in parallel with other industries and across international boundaries. The underpinning philosophy of TSAs is to add credibility to tourism, which suffers because it does not fit into a single industry and its socio-economic impact is often difficult to measure.

In terms of the discussions in this chapter, the multiplier models are used to determine the economic impact of changes in tourist spending on the income, employment, government revenue and foreign exchange of any economy. They can also be used to identify **opportunity costs** by examining the effects of comparable changes in other industries. TSAs, on the other hand, offer a way of improving the estimation of the significance of tourism to an economy.

The concept of tourism satellite accounts is based on the need for a framework that provides consistency over time and between countries and comparability between industries when calculating the significance of tourism to an economy. Providing the accurate and extensive data needs can be met in a timely manner the accounts should do much to promote the importance of tourism globally and within countries. There have been some serious concerns, however, that tourism satellite accounts require more data than are often available, resulting in data being estimated or 'imported' from other economies to be used as a proxy for the TSA.

Thus, TSAs may be constructed using data that are not accurate and this will only undermine the confidence that can be attached to these accounts and harm the reliability of the estimates derived from them. The framework for Tourism Satellite Accounts is aptly demonstrated in the 10 Excel spreadsheets from the UN Statistics office (**http://unstats.un.org/unsd/tradeserv/ TSA%20RMF%202008%20edited%20whitecover.pdf**). These TSA spreadsheets show the composition of the various tables and the most useful, from this chapter's perspective, is Table 6 (reproduced in Chapter 1 as Table 1.4).

| | |
|---|---|
| TSA 1 | Inbound tourism expenditure; an element of aggregate demand |
| TSA 2 | Domestic tourism expenditure; part of total consumption |
| TSA 3 | Outbound tourism expenditure |
| TSA 4 | Internal tourism final consumption |
| TSA 5 | Production accounts of tourism industries and other industries |
| **TSA 6** | **Domestic supply and internal consumption by products** |
| TSA 7 | Employment in tourism industries |
| TSA 8 | Tourism gross fixed capital formation |
| TSA 9 | Tourism collection consumption by functions and levels of government |
| TSA 10 | Non-monetary indicators of tourism |

## MINI CASE STUDY 7.1
### Tourism as a redistribution mechanism of wealth

Tourism has been lauded as an excellent vehicle for redistributing income from rich areas with abundant employment opportunities to poorer areas where employment opportunities are scarce. Consider domestic tourism in an economy such as France. The tendency is for people from the relatively affluent urbanised areas of, say, Paris to travel to less populated, poorer and more scenic rural areas. This results in a transfer of demand from the wealthier urban areas to the sparsely populated rural areas. Such transfers can stimulate investment and act as a catalyst for general economic development.

The same redistributive qualities of tourism have not been so apparent at the international level where the vast majority of tourism activity takes place between the wealthy industrialised economies (see e.g. **http:// www.youtube.com/watch?v=uGEgItNDTC**). Tourism has done little to bridge the North–South divide. Indeed, it has been argued quite convincingly that tourism can exacerbate the income inequalities between rich countries such as the USA and less rich countries such as Kenya. The drive towards globalisation by some of the key elements of the tourism industry adds further substance to this belief.

The existence of economies of large-scale production, **comparative advantage** and the global nature of communications might suggest that any attempt to redress the imbalances will result in a misallocation of resources.

### DISCUSSION QUESTIONS

1. Explain why tourism may act as an effective means of redistributing wealth at national level but often fails to do so at regional levels within an economy.

2. If the natural market forces are left to their own devices will tourism result in income redistribution that works in favour of the poorer segments of the population (nationally and internationally)?

3. What actions could be taken to encourage tourism to assist in redressing income inequalities without damaging the development of the industry?

# THE GENERATION OF ECONOMIC IMPACTS BY TOURIST SPENDING

Tourists spend their money on a wide variety of goods and services provided by a wide range of businesses. For example, tourists purchase accommodation, food and beverages, transport, communications, entertainment services, goods from retail outlets and tour/travel services. This money may be seen as an injection of demand into the host economy, i.e. demand that is created by people from outside the area of the local economy. In the case of international tourism, the tourist expenditure is a result of non-nationals spending within the national economy. In the case of domestic tourism, the tourist expenditure is a result of spending by people that do not live within the local area in which the money is spent. However, the total value of international and domestic tourist expenditure represents only a partial and sometimes misleading picture of the economic impact. The full assessment of economic impact must take into account other aspects such as:

- **leakages** of expenditure out of the local economy;
- indirect and induced effects; and
- **displacement** and opportunity costs.

# LEAKAGES OF EXPENDITURE OUT OF THE LOCAL ECONOMY

When tourists make expenditures within an economy the amount of money that stays within that economy depends upon the extent of leakages that occur. For instance, if a tourist purchases a carved wooden souvenir from a gift shop in Beijing, the extent of leakages will depend upon whether the carving was imported or made locally. If the carving was imported the tourist is really only buying the **value added** that was created within the local economy,

| Photograph 7.2 | Tourist expenditure locally is an important aspect of economic activity. |

*Source*: Steve Vidler/Alamy Images

i.e. the value of local transport, import, wholesale and retail margins, government taxes and duties, etc. The extent of leakages can result from demand-side factors such as the fact that different types of tourist and different types of tourist activity tend to be associated with differences in propensities to purchase imported goods. The leakages can also be associated with supply-side factors, particularly in developing economies where the local capacity to supply the needs of tourists may be small and there is consequently a high proportion of demand met through imported goods and services. Wherever money flows out of circulation, either by being spent on goods and services from outside or simply being withdrawn through savings, this constitutes a *leakage*.

# THE MEASUREMENT OF ECONOMIC IMPACT

The measurement of the economic impact of tourism is far more involved than simply calculating the level of tourist expenditure. Indeed, estimates of the economic impact of tourism based on tourist expenditure or receipts can be not only inaccurate, but also very misleading. Before examining how the economic impact is measured, it is necessary to look at the different aspects of the economy that are affected by tourism expenditure.

To begin with, a difference can be drawn between the economic impact associated with tourist expenditure and that associated with the development of tourism. The former refers to the ongoing effects of, and changes in, tourist expenditure, whereas the latter is concerned with the one-off impact of the construction and finance of tourism-related facilities. The difference between these two aspects of impact is important because they require different methodological approaches. The calculation of the economic impact of tourist expenditure is achieved by using multiplier analysis and the estimation of the economic impact of tourism development projects is often achieved by resorting to **project appraisal** techniques such as **cost–benefit analysis**.

The measurement of the economic impact of tourist expenditure, if it is to be meaningful, must encompass the various effects of tourist spending as it impacts throughout the economy. That is, the direct, indirect and induced effects associated with tourist expenditure need to be calculated.

## Direct, indirect and induced economic effects

Tourist expenditure has a 'cascading' effect throughout the host economy. It begins with tourists spending money in 'front-line' tourist establishments, such as hotels, restaurants and taxis, and then permeates throughout the rest of the economy. It can be examined by assessing the impact at three different levels – the direct, indirect and induced levels.

### Direct effects

The direct level of impact is the value of tourist expenditure *less* the value of imports necessary to supply those 'front-line' goods and services. Thus, the direct impact is likely to be less than the value of tourist expenditure except in the rare case where a local economy can provide all of the tourist's wants from its own productive sectors.

### Indirect effects

The establishments that directly receive the tourist expenditure also need to purchase goods and services from other sectors within the local economy, for example hotels will purchase the services of builders, accountants, banks, food and beverage suppliers, electricity and water, etc. Furthermore, the suppliers to these 'front-line' establishments will also need to purchase goods and services from other establishments within the local economy and so the process continues. The generation of economic activity brought about by these subsequent rounds of expenditure is known as the indirect effect. The indirect effect will not involve all of the monies spent by tourists during the direct effect since some of that money will leak out of circulation through imports, savings and taxation.

### Induced effects

Finally, during the direct and indirect rounds of expenditure, income will accrue to local residents in the form of wages, salaries, distributed profit, rent and interest. This addition to local income will, in part, be re-spent in the local economy on goods and services and this will generate yet further rounds of economic activity.

It is only when all three levels of impact (direct *plus* indirect *plus* induced) are estimated that the full positive economic impact of tourism expenditure is fully assessed. However, there can be negative aspects to the economic impact of tourist expenditure.

## Measuring the economic impact of tourist expenditure

At a national level, the UNWTO publishes annual tourist statistics for countries throughout the world. These statistics include figures relating to tourist expenditure, but these figures do not reflect the economic impact of tourist expenditure. These figures only show how much tourists spend in a destination. They take no account of how much of that sum leaks out of the economy (paying for imported goods and services) or how much additional impact is experienced through the 'knock-on' effects of this tourist spending.

At a sub-national level the availability of accurate and consistent tourist expenditure data is much more difficult to find. Some countries, such as the UK, undertake visitor expenditure surveys (for example, International Passenger Survey (IPS) and United Kingdom Tourist Survey (UKTS)) which allow expenditure estimates to be made at the national level and these figures lose some of their accuracy when examined at the regional level. It is often necessary to undertake specific tourist expenditure surveys to establish the tourist spend in particular areas. This is a very important point given that investment and planning decisions are often taken at the local level where such data are not freely available.

In order to translate tourist expenditure data into economic impact information the appropriate multiplier values have to be calculated. The term *multiplier* is one of the most quoted economic concepts in the study of tourism. Multiplier values may be used for a variety of purposes and are often used as the basis for public sector decision making.

# THE MULTIPLIER CONCEPT

The concept of the multiplier is based upon the recognition that sales for one firm require purchases from other firms within the local economy, i.e. the industrial sectors of an economy are interdependent. This means that firms purchase not only primary inputs such as labour and imports, but also intermediate goods and services produced by other establishments within the local economy. Therefore, a change in the level of final demand for one sector's output will affect not only the industry that produces that final good/service but also other sectors that supply goods/services to that sector and the sectors that act as suppliers to those sectors as well.

Because firms in the local economy are dependent upon other firms for their supplies, any change in tourist expenditure will bring about a change in the economy's level of production, household income, employment, government revenue and foreign exchange flows (where applicable). These changes may be greater than, equal to or less than the value of the change in tourist expenditure that brought them about. The term 'tourist multiplier' refers to the ratio of two changes – the change in one of the key economic variables such as output (income, employment or government revenue) to the change in tourist expenditure.

Therefore, there will be some value by which the initial change in tourist expenditure must be multiplied in order to estimate the total change in output – this is known as the *output multiplier*. In the same way, there will be a value that, when multiplied by the change in tourist expenditure, will estimate the total change in household income – this is known as the *income multiplier*. The reason why the initial change in tourist spending must be subject to a multiplier effect can be seen from Figure 7.1.

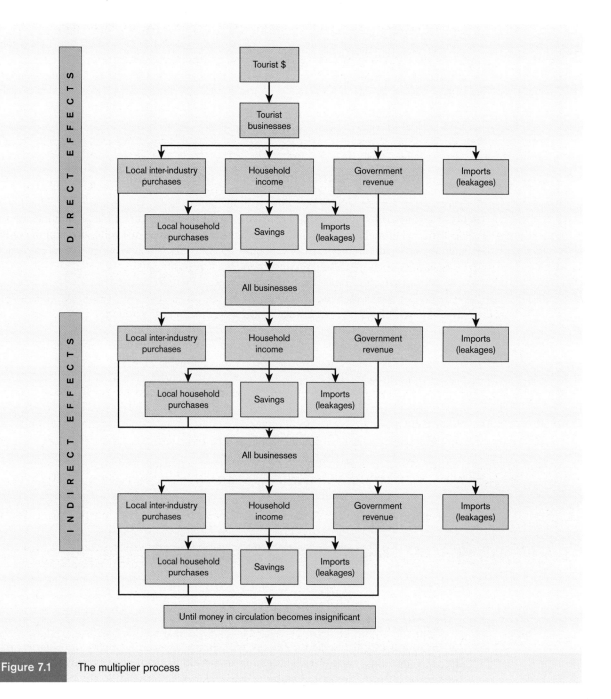

**Figure 7.1**    The multiplier process

Figure 7.1 shows that the tourist expenditure goes, initially, to the front-line tourist establish-ments that provide the tourists with their goods and services. This money will be re-spent by the firms that receive it. A proportion of the money will leak directly out of the economy in the form of imports and savings (the tan boxes in the diagram). These imports may be in the form of food and beverages that the tourist consumes but are not provided locally, or in respect of services provided to the establishment by individuals or firms located outside the economy being analysed. Where the tourist consumes a product that has been imported into the local economy, they are only consuming the value added (**distributive trade**, importation, transport, local taxes, etc.) rather than the full cost of the product. The money paid to persons outside the economy cannot have any further role in generating economic activity within the local economy and, thus, the value of tourist expenditure that actually circulates in the local economy is immediately reduced. The remaining sum of money will be used to purchase locally produced goods and services, labour and entrepreneurial skills (wages, salaries and profits) and to meet government taxes, licences and fees. These effects are all known as the direct effects.

We can see from Figure 7.1 that money will flow from the tourism-related establishments to other local businesses. This money will also be re-spent, some of it leaking out as imports, some of it leaking out of circulation through savings and some going to the government. The remainder will be spent on labour and entrepreneurial skills and purchases from other businesses for goods and services. The businesses that receive money in payment for their goods/services will also make purchases locally, import goods and services and pay government taxes. These effects are known as the indirect effects.

During each round of expenditure, some proportion of money accrues to local residents in the form of income (wages, salaries and profits). Some of this money will be saved (by either households or businesses) and will cease to circulate in the economy, i.e. a leakage. The income that accrues to local households and is not saved will be re-spent. Some of it will leak out of the system as imports and some of it will go to the government as tax. The remainder will be re-spent as household consumption. This spending of income accrued as a result of the initial tourist expenditure will generate further rounds of economic activity – this effect is known as the induced effect.

The value of any tourism multiplier is meaningless unless it is qualified by both the methodology used to estimate it and the type of multiplier involved.

# TYPES OF MULTIPLIER

There are a number of multipliers in regular use and each type has its own specific application. However, considerable confusion and misleading conclusions can be derived if they are misused or misinterpreted. This issue will be discussed later in this chapter. The major types of multipliers are as follows:

- A **transactions (or sales) multiplier** that measures the amount of additional business revenue created in an economy as a result of an increase in tourist expenditure. Similar to this in concept is the output multiplier.

- An **output multiplier** that measures the amount of additional output generated in an economy as a result of an increase in tourist expenditure. The principal distinction between the two multipliers is that output multipliers are concerned with changes in the actual levels of production and not with the volume and value of sales. Not all sales will be related to current production (some sales may have been made from inventories and some productive output may not be sold within the time-frame of the model and, therefore, result in an increase in inventories). Therefore, the value of an output multiplier may well be larger or smaller than the value of the corresponding transactions multiplier.

- An **income multiplier** which measures the additional income (wages and salaries, rent, interest and profits) created in the economy as a result of an increase in tourist expenditure. Such income can be measured either as *national income* (*regional* in the case of domestic tourism) or as *disposable income*, i.e. the income that is actually available to households either to spend or to save. However, as mentioned earlier, the income which accrues to non-nationals who have been 'imported' into the area should be excluded because the incomes that they receive cannot be considered to be benefits to the area. On the other hand, the secondary economic effects created by the re-spending of non-nationals' incomes within the area *must* be included within the calculations.

- An **employment multiplier** which is a measurement of either the total amount of employment generated by an additional unit of tourist expenditure or the ratio of the total employment generated by this same expenditure to direct employment alone. Employment multipliers provide a useful source of information about the secondary effects of tourism, but their measurement involves more heroic assumptions than in the case of other multipliers and care is needed in their interpretation.

- A **government revenue multiplier** that measures the impact on government revenue, from all sources, associated with an increase of tourist expenditure. This multiplier may be expressed in gross terms, that is, the gross increase in government revenue as a result of an increase in tourist spending, or in net terms when the increase in government revenue is reduced by the increase in government expenditures associated with the increase in tourist activity.

Since the different types of multiplier are calculated using the same database they are closely interrelated. However, the concepts involved in each of the above multipliers are very different, as are the magnitudes of each of the different multipliers calculated for the same economy. Some examples of these multiplier values are shown later in this chapter. Given the number of different multiplier concepts that are available it is not surprising to find that there has been some confusion over their interpretation. This confusion has been compounded by the fact that there are also a variety of methods that may be used to calculate each of the above multipliers.

# METHODOLOGICAL APPROACHES

There are five major techniques that have been employed to measure the economic impact of tourism. Although they are often viewed as alternative approaches by many authors, with the exception of the base theory approach, each of the other methodologies plots out the natural evolution of a single concept as it struggles to overcome the inherent weaknesses and limitations. The five approaches are:

- base theory models;
- Keynesian multiplier models;
- ad hoc models;
- input–output analysis; and
- computable general equilibrium (CGE) models.

## Base theory models

The basic assumption underlying base theory models is that there exists a stable relationship between each of the export sectors and the local sectors of an economy, so that changes in the level of tourist expenditure will create predictable and measurable changes in the level of activity in local sectors. An example of this approach is given under the following sub-heading. Base theory multipliers are normally oversimplified formulations and are now rarely used.

### Multiplier analysis using base theory

One early and interesting application of the technique by R.R. Nathan and Associates (1966) was used to calculate the short-run employment effects created by tourism expenditure in each of 375 counties and independent cities of Appalachia. The final model used took the form:

$$\frac{E}{E_{rx2}} = \frac{1}{1 - E_r/E_r} \tag{7.1}$$

where $E_r$ is total local employment, $E_{rc}$ is local employment servicing local consumer demand and $E_{rx2}$ is the direct change in employment created by a change in tourism expenditure.

Nathan Associates developed the multiplier model further, to measure long-term effects, by incorporating investment activity. This model took the form:

$$\frac{E_r}{E_{rx2}} = \frac{1 + i_2}{1 - E_{rc}/E_r} \tag{7.2}$$

where $i_2$ is a statistically estimated parameter (the value of which lies between 0 and 1) which relates the change in investment to the change in tourism activity.

This model is far too simplistic to be accurate in calculating tourism multiplier values.

## Keynesian multiplier models

These multipliers are designed to measure the income created in an economy by an additional unit of tourist expenditure. The Keynesian multipliers were the first rigorous attempt at measuring the economic impact of an **exogenous change in demand**. The simplest formulation of the multiplier ($k$) is shown in equation (7.3):

$$k = \frac{1}{1 - c + m} \tag{7.3}$$

where 1 is the additional unit of tourism expenditure and leakages are the proportion of this expenditure which goes into savings ($1 - c$) and imports ($m$), i.e.:

$$k = \frac{1}{\text{leakages}}$$

To develop this model into a long-term formulation, which takes investment into account, is shown in equation (7.4):

$$k = \frac{1}{1 - c + m - i} \tag{7.4}$$

where $i$ is the marginal propensity to invest.

Similarly the effects of the re-spending of money accruing to the public sector can be built into the model, and this is shown in equation (7.5):

$$k = \frac{1}{1 - c + m - i - g} \tag{7.5}$$

where $g$ is the marginal propensity of the public sector to spend.

A typical Keynesian short-term multiplier model is shown in equation (7.6). The derivation of this model is given in Archer (1976):

$$k = \frac{1 - L}{1 - c(1 - t_i)(1 - t_d - b) + m} \tag{7.6}$$

where $L$ = first round leakages out of the economy, $t_i$ = the marginal rate of indirect taxation, $t_d$ = the marginal rate of taxation and other deductions and $b$ = the marginal rate of transfer payments.

The difference in the value of the multiplier created by applying exactly the same data to the short-term models shown in equations (7.3) and (7.6) highlight the dangers of relying on a model whose structure is too simplistic. For example, if we let $L = 0.5$, $c = 0.9$, $m = 0.7$, $t_i = 0.16$, $t_d = 0.2$ and $b = 0.2$ and calculate the income multipliers using, first, the model shown in equation (7.1) and then, again, using the more developed model shown in equation (7.6), the results are:

$$\frac{1}{1 - c + m} = \frac{1}{1 - 0.9 + 0.7} = 1.25$$

and

$$\frac{1 - L}{1 - c(1 - t_i)(1 - t_d - b) + m} = \frac{1 - 0.5}{1 - 0.9(1 - 0.16)(1 - 0.2 - 0.2) + 0.7} = 0.40$$

The two multiplier values derived from the same database are very different and would result in very different policy implications. However, even the more developed model shown in equation (7.6) is far too simplistic and is unable to measure variations in the form and magnitude of **sectoral linkages** and leakages out of the destination's economy during each round of transactions. Even the most complex and comprehensive Keynesian models developed for some studies are unable to provide the level of detail that is required for policy making and planning. One practical solution is to use ad hoc models.

## Ad hoc models

The next step in the evolution of the multiplier approach was intended to overcome the 'broad brush' approach adopted by the Keynesian model wherein each sector was treated in an identical manner. The ad hoc models, although similar in principle to their Keynesian counterparts, are constructed specifically for each particular study. The simplest form of ad hoc model, using matrix algebra, is shown in equation (7.7):

$$A*\frac{1}{1-BC} \tag{7.7}$$

where $A =$ the proportion of additional tourist expenditure remaining in the economy after first-round leakages, i.e. $A$ equals the $(1 - L)$ expression in the Keynesian model, $B =$ the propensity of local people to consume in the local economy and $C =$ the proportion of expenditure by local people that accrues as income in the local economy.

The ad hoc model shown in equation (7.7) is too simplistic for serious application but more advanced models have been developed and used widely to calculate tourist multipliers to estimate the effect of tourist expenditure on income, public sector revenue, employment and imports. One such model, developed in the early 1970s (by Archer and Owen, 1971) is:

$$\sum_{j=1}^{N}\sum_{i=1}^{n}Q_jK_{ij}V_i\frac{1}{1-c\sum_{i=1}^{n}X_iZ_iV_i} \tag{7.8}$$

where $j =$ each category of tourist $j = 1$ to $N$, $i =$ each type of business establishment $i = 1$ to $n$, $Q_j =$ the proportion of total tourist expenditure spent by the $j$th type of tourist, $K_{ij} =$ the proportion of expenditure by the $i$th type of tourist in the $j$th category of business, $V_i =$ the direct and indirect income generated by unit of expenditure by the $i$th type of business, $X_i =$ the pattern of consumption, i.e. the proportion of total consumer expenditure by the residents of the area in the $i$th type of business, $Z_i =$ the proportion of $X_i$ which takes place within the study area and $c =$ the **marginal propensity to consume**.

The multiplicand equation (7.8) measures the direct and indirect effects of tourist expenditure while the multiplier measures the induced effects. In order to trace the flows of expenditure through successive rounds, separate equations are estimated for a range of $V_i$ values. Examples of these are provided in the literature (see, for example, Archer and Owen, 1971).

Multiplier studies using ad hoc models are commonly used and examples can be found in the USA, the UK, South Pacific islands, Caribbean and elsewhere. More recent models have achieved even greater levels of **disaggregation**, even down to the levels of individual establishments.

Although models of this type can produce a large quantity of detailed and accurate information for policy making and planning purposes, they are unable to provide the wealth of data yielded by the final methodological approach to be discussed, input–output analysis.

## Input–output analysis

In order to overcome the subjectivity inherent in the ad hoc multiplier approach and to provide a more encompassing estimate of economic impact, the multiplier models commonly being used adopted the input–output framework. The input–output model approach presents a general equilibrium, rather than the partial equilibrium approach used in ad hoc models, to studying economic impacts. Input–output analysis begins with the construction of a table, similar to a table of national/regional accounts, which shows the economy of the destination in matrix form. Each sector of the economy is shown in each column as a purchaser of goods and services from other sectors in the economy, and in each row as a seller of output to each of the other sectors. The structure of an input–output table is shown in Figure 7.2. The table may be subdivided into three major quadrants. First, the inter-industry matrix (located in the top left-hand quadrant) details the sales and purchases that take place among the various sectors of the economy (for example, $X_{11}, X_{12}, X_{13}$, etc. are the sales of sector 1 to all other sectors within

| SALES TO | INTERMEDIATE DEMAND Productive sectors | | | | | | FINAL DEMAND Final demand sectors | | | | TOTAL OUTPUT |
|---|---|---|---|---|---|---|---|---|---|---|---|
| PURCHASES FROM | Industry | | | | | | H | I | G | E | |
| | 1 | 2 | 3 | 4 | ... | m | H | I | G | E | |
| Industry 1 | $X_{11}$ | $X_{12}$ | $X_{13}$ | $X_{14}$ | ... | $X_{1m}$ | $C_1$ | $I_1$ | $G_1$ | $E_1$ | $X_1$ |
| Industry 2 | $X_{21}$ | $X_{22}$ | $X_{23}$ | $X_{24}$ | ... | $X_{2m}$ | $C_2$ | $I_2$ | $G_2$ | $E_2$ | $X_2$ |
| Industry 3 | $X_{31}$ | $X_{32}$ | $X_{33}$ | $X_{34}$ | ... | $X_{3m}$ | $C_3$ | $I_3$ | $G_3$ | $E_3$ | $X_3$ |
| Industry 4 | $X_{41}$ | $X_{42}$ | $X_{43}$ | $X_{44}$ | ... | $X_{4m}$ | $C_4$ | $I_4$ | $G_4$ | $E_4$ | $X_4$ |
| ... | . | . | . | . | ... | . | . | . | . | . | . |
| ... | | | | | | | | | | | |
| Industry m | $X_{m1}$ | $X_{m2}$ | $X_{m3}$ | $X_{m4}$ | ... | $X_{mm}$ | $C_m$ | $I_m$ | $G_m$ | $E_m$ | $X_m$ |
| Wages and salaries | $W_1$ | $W_2$ | $W_3$ | $W_4$ | ... | $W_m$ | $W_C$ | $W_I$ | $W_G$ | $W_E$ | $W$ |
| Profits/ dividends | $P_1$ | $P_2$ | $P_3$ | $P_4$ | ... | $P_m$ | $P_C$ | $P_I$ | $P_G$ | $P_E$ | $P$ |
| Taxes | $T_1$ | $T_2$ | $T_3$ | $T_4$ | ... | $T_m$ | $T_C$ | $T_I$ | $T_G$ | $T_E$ | $T$ |
| Imports | $M_1$ | $M_2$ | $M_3$ | $M_4$ | ... | $M_m$ | $M_C$ | $M_I$ | $M_G$ | $M_E$ | $M$ |
| Total inputs | $X_1$ | $X_2$ | $X_3$ | $X_4$ | ... | $X_m$ | $C$ | $I$ | $G$ | $E$ | $X$ |

Productive sectors (row label for industries); Primary inputs (row label for wages, profits, taxes, imports)

where:
$X$ = Output
$C$ = Consumption (households)
$I$ = Investment (private)
$G$ = Government expenditure

$E$ = Exports
$M$ = Imports
$W$ = Wages and salaries
$P$ = Profits and dividends
$T$ = Taxes

Final demand sectors:
$H$ = Household consumption sector
$I$ = Investment expenditure sector
$G$ = Government expenditure sector
$E$ = Exports sectors

**Figure 7.2** Basic input–output transactions table

the economy, whereas $X_{11}, X_{21}, X_{31}, X_{41}$, etc., represent the purchases of sector 1 from all other sectors within the economy). Secondly, the bottom left-hand quadrant shows each sector's purchases of primary inputs (such as payments to labour, $W$, profits, $P$, taxes, $T$ and imported goods and services, $M$). Thirdly, the right-hand quadrant shows the sales made by each sector to each source of final demand.

The simplest formulation is shown in equations (7.9) and (7.10) where, for ease of explanation, all forms of final demand are represented by a column vector (**Y**).

$$X = AX + Y$$
$$X - AX = Y \tag{7.9}$$
$$(I - A)X = Y$$

$$X = (I - A)^{-1}Y$$
$$\Delta X = (I - A)^{-1}\Delta Y \tag{7.10}$$

where $X$ = a vector of the total sales of each sector of the economy, i.e. $[x_1 + x_2 + x_3 + x_4]$, **A** = a matrix of the inter-industry transactions within the economy, **Y** = a vector of final demand sales, **I** = an identity matrix (equivalent to 1 in simple algebra) and $\Delta$ = a change in a variable.

A change in the level of final demand (**Y**) will create an increase in the level of activity within the economy which manifests itself as changes in the output and sales of each sector. Further sub-models are required to calculate the effects on business revenue, public sector revenue, imports, employment and income. The model shown in equation (7.10) is still too simplistic for practical application and must be developed further.

For instance, in the simplified model discussed above, the imports of the economy are shown as a single row vector. However, the robust and flexible framework of input–output models allows the researcher to incorporate a matrix of import functions in order to draw distinctions between competitive and non-competitive imports. This is an extremely useful distinction because competitive imports are, by their very nature, far less predictable than non-competitive imports.

Incorporating an import function matrix which examines the trade-off between domestic production and competitive imports results in equation (7.10) being revised as follows:

$$\Delta X = (I - K^*A)^{-1}\Delta Y \tag{7.11}$$

where $\mathbf{K}^*$ = a matrix where the diagonal values reflects the level of competitive imports associated with each sector which, when applied to the $\mathbf{A}$ matrix, reduces the domestic component of output by the required amount.

In this manner, changes in primary inputs ($\Delta\mathbf{P}$) created by a change in tourist expenditure ($\Delta\mathbf{T}$) will be given by:

$$\Delta P = B(I - K^*A)^{-1}\Delta T \tag{7.12}$$

where $\mathbf{B}$ = an $m \times n$ matrix of primary inputs.

Furthermore, the input–output model can be developed in order to provide information with respect to changes in employment levels brought about by changes in tourism expenditure. Let $\Delta\mathbf{L}$ represent the change in employment and $\mathbf{E}$ be an $m \times n$ matrix of employment coefficients. The model will now take the form shown in equation (7.13):

$$\Delta L = E(I - K^*A)^{-1}\Delta T \tag{7.13}$$

Using this procedure, the labour usages of each productive sector can be incorporated on either a skill or educational requirement basis and this will allow the multiplier model to provide human resource planning information. Thus, multiplier models can provide information which will inform the future training needs for the destination.

In general, the input–output model can be as comprehensive as data, time and resources allow. Notwithstanding the fact that input–output analysis has been subject to criticism because of its general approach and the aggregation of firms into 'whole industries', the sectors of the model can be disaggregated to achieve the highest level of detail – even down to the level of individual establishments.

There are several weaknesses and limitations apparent with input–output models and most of them are the result of the restrictive assumptions upon which the model is based. For instance, the input–output model as discussed so far implicitly assumes that there are no such things as **supply constraints**. Supply constraints can inhibit the ability of an economy to supply the quantity and quality of goods and services needed to accommodate an increase in tourism expenditure. If capacity is inadequate to meet the additional demand and if insufficient factors of production, especially labour, are available, then additional tourism expenditure creates inflation and additional goods and services may have to be imported. Thus the size of the multiplier, if measured by an appropriate model, will fall. Within the input–output model framework the existence of supply constraints can be incorporated by building in a restrictions matrix that will channel unsupportable supply requirements into the import matrix. Such a way of working around this problem has the disadvantage that it tends to act as a switch in the sense that it will either be 'on' or 'off'. The reality of supply constraints is that there are likely to be some inflationary pressures that build as supply capacity is approached and such inflationary pressures may bring about other undesirable effects on the production function of many sectors within the economy. This is always a problem when the model that is being used is static rather than dynamic.

Most multiplier models are static in nature but can be made dynamic. Static models assume that:

- production and consumption functions are linear and the intersectoral expenditure patterns are stable;

- all sectors are able to meet any additional demands for their output; and
- relative prices remain constant.

The first of these assumptions is that any additional tourism expenditure occurring will generate the same impact on the economy as an equivalent amount of previous tourism expenditure. Thus, any additional production in the economy is assumed to require the purchase of inputs in the same proportions and from the same sources as previously required. Similarly, any consequential increase in consumer demand is assumed to have exactly the same effect upon the economy as previous consumer expenditure. These anomalies arise because of the use of average rather than marginal production coefficients. The difference between the two often comes down to the existence or otherwise of economies of large-scale production and the stability of the production functions themselves.

With respect to the stability of the production functions, tourism, being a labour-intensive personal service, tends to be associated with fairly stable production functions. Thus, the use of average technical coefficients and the assumption of **linear homogeneity in production** tends not to be a serious drawback when using input–output analysis to study service-based economies. However, the problems of not being able to handle price changes are a major drawback of static systems.

Computable general equilibrium (CGE) models have been developed to overcome some of these limitations.

## Computable general equilibrium (CGE) models

Input-output (IO), Social Accounting Matrices (SAM) and CGE all have their roots embedded in the same economy-wide approach to economic analysis, popularly referred to as general equilibrium models. However, IO and SAM models have restrictions imposed by their assumptions, the most serious being the simplifying assumptions that ignore the behavioural responses that agents or actors make to changes in prices, together with the forces that generate such price changes. CGE models, which started to emerge in the 1970s with international trade simulations, build on the IO and SAM framework by constructing a series of relationship equations that reflect the behaviour of economic agents (production and consumption agents) to changes in prices and then go on to map out the repercussions of that behaviour on the prices of inputs influenced by that change in behaviour.

CGE models relating to the effects of policy changes on the tourism sectors started to take shape during the latter half of the 1990s. If constructed properly, CGE models allow for the effects of interaction between all elements of the economy, unlike the input–output models that focus upon the supply side through output changes. For instance, CGEs can allow prices to vary and for resources in an economy to be reallocated from one sector to others. Furthermore, the CGE approach, because it is based upon a series of equations that explain the behaviour of individual sectors that are then simultaneously solved for the economy, means that changes from a wide range of sources (such as tax, price inflation, interest rate, exchange rate changes, etc.) can be analysed.

Although the addition of the dynamic aspects offered by CGE modelling to the input–output framework are clearly welcome, there is much work to be done, particularly in terms of the availability of reliable data, before such models can make significant improvements to the accuracy of impact estimates. To create realistic models, the data requirements of CGE models are enormous and at the end of the day there has to be some trade-off between accuracy and cost. Also, the approach of CGE modelling often presents itself as a black box approach where it is frequently difficult to see where the impacts take place within an economy other than the final effects. This is not because the model does not trace them, but is more related to the way in which the results of such model are disseminated. Also, there is the danger, as with TSAs, of making assumptions with respect to price elasticities of demand, substitution propensities, etc., that are not appropriate to the economy being examined and this can lead to wildly inaccurate results.

# WEAKNESSES AND LIMITATIONS OF MULTIPLIER MODELS

Each of the multiplier model approaches outlined above contains several inherent problems that need to be overcome if they are to produce meaningful results. The majority of these problems stem from two distinct areas: the assumptions necessary to apply the models and the data needs.

## Restrictive assumptions

Every economic model is founded upon a series of assumptions. The realism of those assumptions is clearly crucial to the model's performance – unrealistic assumptions will provide unrealistic results. During the early attempts at multiplier analysis the assumptions used were very restrictive. Sectors were all assumed to have the same propensities to import, employ labour, pay taxes and they were all assumed to be producing homogeneous output. As the models have become more sophisticated, one by one these assumptions have been replaced with more realistic ones. The homogeneity of output can be overcome by the sectoral disaggregation, the differential needs for imports, tax liabilities and labour requirements can all be catered for within the post-Keynesian model structures. However, the greatest obstacles to improving the accuracy of estimates are found in the dynamics of the model. Most impact models are static in nature, providing a snapshot of an economy at one point in time. If the model is static it will not be able to reflect the effects of changes in relative prices, changes in production and consumption functions as a result of changes in relative prices and/or supply constraints. To build these bridges and enhance the accuracy of the estimates, it is necessary to calculate price and income **elasticities of demand and supply**, relative returns on investment within dynamic capital markets and the effects of changes in interest and foreign exchange rates. In order to achieve this, it is necessary to know whether each sector is operating close to operational capacity because, as they move towards full capacity, pressure will be placed on the prices of some resources and this will affect other sectors as they compete for resources, and so on. This leads to the second category of problems – that is, those associated with data deficiencies.

Recent attempts to build in such enhanced assumptions by using CGE models have not been too successful in overcoming these weaknesses and limitations. For instance, it is not uncommon for CGE models to assume that economies are always in full equilibrium at all times. This is clearly unrealistic for most economies. Many economies have some unemployment and are not populated by sectors that are all running at full capacity. Therefore models using such an assumption are likely to underestimate the true economic impact of an increase in tourism activities. Furthermore, CGE models tend to be based on assumptions that reflect developed market systems with relative prices constantly adjusting to reflect demand and supply circumstances. This is not always the case and can lead to inaccurate estimates. Finally, as pointed out by authors such as Miller (2002) and Cooper and Wilson (2002), most CGE models are heavily constrained by theory in the way that the dynamics are included and they typically do not perform well when subjected to statistical tests.

## Data deficiencies

Secondary data (published and unpublished data) are rarely adequate to meet the requirements of the more demanding and advanced models. This means that researchers need to spend considerable time, effort and money collecting data for multiplier purposes.

Other data difficulties arise out of the nature of tourism itself as a multi-product industry directly affecting a large number of sectors in an economy. Tourist expenditure is spread across several sectors of an economy and accurate surveys of visitor expenditure are required in order to obtain an acceptable breakdown of this expenditure into its various components, e.g. accommodation, meals, beverages, transportation and shopping.

Furthermore, problems often arise when attempting to integrate this visitor expenditure into the categories disaggregated in the input–output table. Rarely are pre-existing input–output tables produced in a form sufficiently disaggregated to accept the detailed data derived from visitor expenditure surveys. In such cases, either the tourist expenditure data have to be compressed to fit the sectors already identified in the input–output table, with a consequent loss in the accuracy of the results, or else much time and effort has to be expended on disaggregating the existing input–output table.

If, however, an input–output (or alternative) model is constructed especially for the study, then the matrix can be arranged in a form which fits the tourist expenditure pattern and the data can be fed directly into the model. The development of the CGE models demonstrates the need to enhance the dynamic nature of the models but adds considerable pressures to the data needs of the models. Rarely do we have sufficient information to calculate the effects of relative price changes on the allocation of resources within an economy. The movement of people from region to region as the relative prosperity of regions changes is, itself, a dynamic event and is determined by a host of economic, social and environmental factors. Foreign exchange rate data need to be considered on a global basis because international tourism is a global industry. Therefore, the data demands associated with making the models dynamic and sensitive to economic interactions between sectors and regions are formidable.

As economic impact models become more sophisticated and are able to reflect some of the dynamic processes it will be possible to estimate the 'net' economic benefits of tourism in a more meaningful way. As with any change in economic output, there are likely to be positive as well as negative economic impacts. To date the negative economic impacts have been sadly neglected by most model structures.

These negative economic impacts can manifest in a number of ways ranging from the misallocation of resources, an increase in the demand for public goods and infrastructure as a result of urbanisation, through to the displacement of existing business.

## Negative economic impacts

The production of tourist goods and services requires the commitment of resources that could otherwise be used for alternative purposes. For instance, the development of a tourism resort in Spain may involve the migration of labour from rural to urban areas which brings with it economic implications for both the rural and urban areas – the former losing a productive unit of labour and the latter implying additional infrastructure pressure for health, education and other public services. If labour is not in abundance then meeting the tourists' demands may involve the transfer of labour from one industry (such as agriculture or fishing) to tourism industries, involving an opportunity cost that is often ignored in the estimation of tourism's economic impact. Furthermore, if there is a shortage of skilled labour then there may be a need to import labour from other countries such as Morocco and this will result in additional economic leakages as income earned from this imported labour may, in part, be repatriated (**repatriated income**).

Similarly, the use of capital resources (which are often scarce) in the development of tourism-related establishments precludes their use for other forms of economic development. To gain a true picture of the economic impact of tourism it is necessary to take into account the opportunity costs of using scarce resources for tourism development as opposed to alternative uses.

Where tourism development substitutes one form of expenditure and economic activity for another, this is known as the displacement effect. The displacement effect should be taken into account when the economic impact of tourism is being estimated. Displacement can take place when tourism development is undertaken at the expense of another industry and is generally referred to as the opportunity cost of the development. However, it is more commonly referred to when a new tourism project is seen to take away custom from an existing facility. For instance, if a destination such as St Lucia finds that its all-inclusive hotels are running at high occupancy levels and returning a reasonable yield on the investment, the construction of an additional all-inclusive hotel may simply reduce the occupancy levels of the existing establishments. This means that the destination may find that its overall tourism activity has not increased by as much as the new business from the development. This is displacement.

## The size of multiplier values

The size of multiplier values will vary under different circumstances because it is dependent upon the patterns of tourist expenditure, the nature of an area's economy and the extent to which the various sectors of the economy are linked in their trading patterns.

| Table 7.5 | The range value of tourism output multipliers for selected destinations |
|---|---|

| Country or region | Tourism output multiplier |
|---|---|
| Medium to large industrialised economies | 2.00–3.40 |
| Selection of US states | 1.57–2.20 |
| City/urban economies | 1.24–1.51 |
| Rural area economies | 1.12–1.35 |

*Source*: Compiled by the author from published articles and unpublished reports to governments

A large number of tourism multiplier studies have been carried out since the 1960s. Table 7.5 shows the range of values of tourism output multipliers for a selection of industrialised countries, US states, cities and rural areas. The figures are provided only to give an indicative view of the relative size of output multipliers. Of course, the values will also depend upon the methodology used to calculate them and the following multiplier values were derived from the average of studies that used the unorthodox multiplier (output change as a result of a change in tourist expenditure) at the direct, indirect and induced level, using input–output analysis.

For policy making and planning purposes, income multipliers are often seen to be the most useful because they provide information about national or local income rather than merely business output or turnover. Table 7.6 shows the range of income multiplier values for a variety of types of destinations. Care must be taken when comparing multiplier values between countries. First, the analyses may be undertaken over different time periods and, even though multiplier values tend not to be subject to drastic changes even over two decades, they do tend to increase as economies develop and improve their sectoral linkages. Secondly, and more importantly, using the different methodologies can make a significant difference to the values. For instance, input–output models, because they are based upon a general equilibrium approach, tend to yield significantly higher multiplier values than ad hoc models and, depending upon the level of comprehensiveness and detail achieved in the ad hoc models, this difference may be as high as 30%. It has been suggested that input–output based multipliers often return higher multiplier values than their CGE counterparts (Dwyer et al., 2003) because they may not pick up the negative effects created by relative price changes or demand displacement. However, there is a tendency for CGE models to underestimate the economic impact of tourism when they are based on assumptions of full capacity and market equilibrium.

It is also noticeable from Table 7.6 that the size of the income multiplier values tends to be correlated with the size of the economy. In general, the larger the economy, the higher will be the multiplier value, although there will obviously be some exceptions to this. The reason for this correlation is that larger economies tend to have a more developed economic structure which

| Table 7.6 | The range of tourism income multipliers for selected types of destinations |
|---|---|

| Country or region | Income multiplier |
|---|---|
| National economies | 1.23–1.98 |
| Small island economies | 0.39–1.59 |
| US states and counties | 0.44–1.30 |
| UK regions and counties | 0.29–0.47 |
| UK cities and towns | 0.19–0.40 |

*Source*: Compiled by the author from published articles and unpublished government reports

means that they have stronger intersectoral linkages and lower propensities to import in order to meet the demands of tourists, the tourist industry, non-tourist industries and the local population. The higher the propensity to import in order to meet local and tourist demand, the lower the income multiplier.

In addition to calculating the levels of output, income, employment and government revenue generated by additional units of tourist expenditure, multiplier analysis provides valuable information concerning its impact on a country's net foreign exchange flows. The impact model can be used to determine not only the direct import requirements necessary to meet the tourists' demands but also the indirect and induced imports required or generated as a result of the initial tourist expenditure. When all import requirements are summed and deducted from the international tourist expenditure the result will be the net foreign exchange flow. This can be further explored by examining the expenditure of local people when travelling abroad and a travel and tourism trade balance can be calculated.

The multipliers most vulnerable to criticism (and inaccuracies) are the employment multipliers. Therefore great care must be exercised in their interpretation. The data used for their measurement and the assumptions underlying the model constructions are more heroic for employment than for any other type of effect. The two major problems relate to the fact that:

- in the majority of studies employment is assumed to have a linear relationship with either income or output, whereas the available evidence suggests that this relationship is non-linear; and

- multiplier models assume that employment in each sector is working at full capacity, so that to meet any increase in demand will require additional employment. In practice, this is unlikely to be true and increases (or decreases) in the level of tourist expenditure will not generate a corresponding increase (or decrease) in the number of people employed.

In consequence, tourism employment multipliers should be interpreted as only an *indication* of the number of full-time equivalent (FTE) job opportunities supported by changes in tourist expenditure. Whether or not these job opportunities will materialise depends upon a number of factors, most notably the extent to which the existing labour force in each sector is fully utilised, and the degree to which labour is able to transfer between different occupations and between different sectors of the economy.

Table 7.7 shows the employment multipliers for several countries and regions. We can see that these employment multipliers are of a different magnitude from those relating to either output or income. This reflects the need for considerably larger amounts of tourist spending to generate one new full-time equivalent job opportunity.

Unlike the income and output multipliers, it is not possible to compare employment multipliers between different destinations when they are presented in this form. This is because the table figures show the number of full-time equivalent job opportunities created by 10,000 units of tourist expenditure where that unit is expressed in the local currency. Thus, differences

| Table 7.7 | Tourism employment multipliers for selected destinations per 10,000 units of tourist expenditure (i.e. dollars, pounds or lira) |
|---|---|
| **Country/city** | **Employment multiplier** |
| Bermuda | 0.44 |
| Fiji | 0.79 |
| Jamaica | 1.28 |
| Malta | 1.59 |
| UK (Edinburgh) | 0.37 |

| Table 7.8 | Standardised employment multipliers for selected destinations |
| --- | --- |
| Country | Employment multiplier |
| Jamaica | 4.61 |
| Mauritius | 3.76 |
| Bermuda | 3.02 |
| Gibraltar | 2.62 |
| Solomon Islands | 2.58 |
| Malta | 1.99 |
| Western Samoa | 1.96 |
| Republic of Palau | 1.67 |

in the unit value of local currencies will provide employment multipliers of different magnitudes. A more sensible way of making international comparisons of employment multipliers is to express them as a ratio of total employment generated to direct employment. Examples of this latter type of employment multiplier are shown in Table 7.8.

Table 7.8 shows that in Jamaica, for every new full-time employee directly employed as a result of an increase in tourist expenditure, a further 4.61 full-time equivalent job opportunities are created throughout the Jamaican economy. Again, we can see that the more developed the tourism economy, the larger the employment multiplier.

# THE POLICY IMPLICATIONS OF MULTIPLIER ANALYSIS

Tourism multipliers measure the present economic performance of the tourism industry and the short-term economic effects of a change in the level or pattern of tourism expenditure. They are particularly suitable for studying the impact of tourist expenditure on business turnover, incomes, employment, public sector revenue and the **balance of payments**.

In the 1970s some economists argued strongly in favour of rejecting multiplier analysis as an appropriate technique for studying impact on the grounds that these models yield 'no useful guideline to policy makers as regards the merits of tourism compared with alternatives' (Bryden, 1973: 217), yet a number of writers have shown that this is precisely the type of information which multiplier analysis can provide in a short-term context. For example, Diamond (1976) used an input–output model of the Turkish economy to measure sectoral output multipliers (for tourism and other sectors) in relation to four policy objectives that reflected Turkish planning priorities. His work demonstrated that multiplier analysis deals effectively with problems associated with short-term **resource allocation**.

Resource allocation is not the primary use of multiplier analysis. The technique is most frequently used to examine short-term economic impacts where policy objectives other than the efficiency of resource allocation are considered important. A detailed input–output or CGE model, for example, can yield valuable information about the structure of an economy, the degree to which sectors within the economy are dependent upon each other, the existence of possible supply constraints and the relative capital and labour intensities of each sector.

Detailed multiplier models are suitable for:

• analysing the national or regional effects of public or private sector investment in tourism projects;

- simulating the economic impact, sector by sector, of any proposed tourism developments and hence determining the future requirements of factors of production, such as labour needs;
- examining the relative magnitudes of the impacts made by different types of tourism and by tourism compared with other sectors of the economy; and
- identifying the optimal tourism mix (those associated with relatively high net benefits).

For instance, a tourism input–output study of Jamaica examined the economic impact of tourism expenditure by purpose of visit, winter or summer visit, first and repeat visit in order to determine which tourists generated the highest level of income, employment and government revenue per unit of expenditure. This type of information can be used to target future markets to maximise the benefits derived from tourism.

## CONCLUSION

The economic impact of tourism on a host economy is generally positive but also carries with it some negative aspects. The literature is biased towards the positive aspects of economic impacts. It is important to establish how significant tourism spending is to an economy because this allows policy makers and planners to determine dependency and to develop strategies for the future. Of particular note is the fact that the majority of tourism spending tends to take place between the richer, industrialised countries rather than between industrialised and non-industrialised countries.

Tourism satellite accounts have been derived in order to present a clearer picture of the economic significance of tourism to a given destination. Built along similar lines to national accounts, such tables provide insight into the contribution that tourism makes towards gross national product and the proportion of demand that is attributable to tourism activity. Such tables tend to be based around input–output models in order to provide an accurate picture and to help determine optimal policy decisions.

There are several models that have been used to estimate the economic impact of tourism but only the ad hoc, input–output and CGE models are of sufficient accuracy and of policy use. The input–output and CGE methods provide the most comprehensive picture of tourism's economic impacts and also information that is useful to the tourism development planners. However, these models are also the most expensive type of impact model because of their data requirements. The impacts are measured in terms of income, employment and government revenue multipliers as well as demonstrating the import requirements per unit of tourist spending. All of these different forms of economic impacts can be estimated at the direct, direct plus indirect and direct plus indirect plus induced levels of impact. This information has been successfully used to target market segments in order to enhance the economic benefits associated with tourist spending. Recent developments in the estimation of tourism impact analyses include the combining of economic, environmental and social impact models with forecasting techniques all within a common framework to provide a comprehensive planning tool. There are weaknesses associated with economic impact models but most of these can be alleviated by the adoption of various procedures.

## SELF-CHECK QUESTIONS

1. What is the difference between the economic significance of international tourism and the economic impact of international tourism? What methods would you use to determine each effect?
2. What are the different levels of economic impact associated with international tourism and how might a destination try to improve the economic benefits it gets from international tourism?

3. Domestic tourism in the world is many times larger than international tourism, yet the literature has mainly focused on the economic impacts of international tourism. Discuss why you feel the literature has had such a focus.

4. Tourism has been seen to be effective at redistributing income within industrialised countries, from the relatively wealthy areas to the relatively poor areas. Why has this type of income redistribution not been apparent at the international level?

# YOUTUBE

### Tourism Satellite Accounting

Launch of South Africa's Tourism Satellite Account at this Year's South Africa Tourism Indaba Parts 1–2

http://www.youtube.com/watch?v=pJMIQt8f9AM

http://www.youtube.com/watch?v=pBQ31Pqj_0M

### Tourism research and data collection

Professor Wolgang Arlt - UQ School of Tourism China Tourism Research Symposium Parts 1–3

http://www.youtube.com/watch?v=n8beC7xEu6A

http://www.youtube.com/watch?v=fA5gNPr222U

http://www.youtube.com/watch?v=1ne0XqXE6Ng

### Economic impacts

Tourism Alliance: Tourism is one of the largest industries in the UK, generating revenue of £125bn per annum and employing 2.7m people

http://www.youtube.com/watch?v=NyVI2tiRBeE

David Scowsill launches WTTC Economic Impact Research 2011

http://www.youtube.com/watch?v=Z6jJkKxYAJ0

2010 Cruise Economic Impact Study–NYCEDC President Seth Pinsky

http://www.youtube.com /watch?v=u0WHwRX4M3Y

The Executive Director of the Arizona Office of Tourism, Sherry Henry, talks about the latest Arizona tourism industry statistics.

http://www.youtube.com/watch?v=t1WeUDNgFLs

China Tourism to Help U.S. Economy–Microblog Buzz: Apr. 6 – BON TV China

http://www.youtube.com/watch?v=X0mQkMB_eaU

Tourism Spend with Mandy Lamb

http://www.youtube.com/watch?v=Fpdp6id2xFk

Airports Economic Impact Trends

http://www.youtube.com/watch?v=Uhq9ogJE3R0

'Good Point'–The Economic Impact of Illinois Tourism

http://www.youtube.com/watch?v=76s9OW-JE8M

UHERO: Economist reaction to positive tourism numbers

http://www.youtube.com/watch?v=0q4JoWg3WPs

# REFERENCES AND FURTHER READING

Archer, B.H. (1976) 'The anatomy of a multiplier', *Regional Studies* **10**, 71–7.

Archer, B.H. (1982) 'The value of multipliers and their policy implications', *Tourism Management* **3**(2), 236–41.

Archer, B.H. and Fletcher, J.E. (1990) *Multiplier Analysis*, Les Cahiers du Tourisme, Series C, No. 130, April.

Archer, B.H. and Owen, C. (1971) 'Towards a tourist regional multiplier', *Regional Studies* **5**, 289–94.

Bryden, J.M. (1973) *Tourism and Development: A Case Study in the Commonwealth Caribbean*, Cambridge University Press, Cambridge.

Cooper, A. and Wilson, A. (2002) 'Extending the relevance of TSA research for the UK: general equilibrium and spillover analysis', *Tourism Economics* **8**(1), 5–38.

Diamond, J. (1976) 'Tourism and development policy: a quantitative appraisal', *Bulletin of Economic Research* **28**(1), 36–50.

Dwyer, L., Forsyth, P., Spurr, R. and VanHo, T. (2003) 'Tourism's contribution to a state economy: a multi-regional general equilibrium analysis', *Tourism Economics* **9**(4), 431–48.

Fletcher, J.E. (1989) 'Input–output analysis and tourism impact studies', *Annals of Tourism Research* **16**(4), 541–56.

Fletcher, J.E. and Archer, B.H. (1991) 'The development and application of multiplier analysis', pp. 28–47, in Cooper, C. (ed.), *Progress in Tourism, Recreation and Hospitality Management*, Vol. 3, Belhaven, London.

Fletcher, J.E. and Snee, H.R. (1985) 'The need for output measurements in the service industries: a comment', *Services Industries Journal*, **5**(1), 73–8.

Fletcher, J.E. and Snee, H.R. (1985) 'The service industries and input–output analysis', *Service Industries Review* **2**(1), 51–79.

Frechtling, D. (2010) 'The tourism satellite account: a primer', *Annals of Tourism Research*, **37**(1), 136–53.

Leontief, W. (1966) *Input–Output Economics*, Oxford University Press, New York.

Miller, R. (2002) 'Preface to Cooper, A. and Wilson, A.' *Tourism Economics* **8**(1), 5–38.

Milne, S.S. (1987) 'Differential multipliers', *Annals of Tourism Research* **14**(4), 499–515.

Nathan, R.R. and Associates, 1966 Recreation as an Industry, A Report Prepared for the Appalachian Regional Commission, Washington D.C.

OECD (2001) *National Accounts*, OECD, Paris.

Sinclair, M.T. and Sutcliffe, C.M.S. (1982) 'Keynesian income multipliers with first and second round effects: an application to tourist expenditure', *Oxford Bulletin of Economics and Statistics* **44**(4), 321–38.

Sinclair, M.T. and Stabler, M.J. (2010) *The Economics of Tourism*, 2nd edn, Routledge, New York

Smeral, E. (2009) 'The impact of the financial and economic crisis on European tourism', *Journal of Travel Research*, **48**(1), 3–13.

TCSP (1992) *The Economic Impact of International Tourism on the National Economy of Fiji*, a report published by the Tourism Council for the South Pacific, Suva, Fiji.

UNWTO (2007) *Yearbook of Tourism Statistics*, UNWTO, Madrid.

Wanhill, S.R.C. (1988) 'Tourism multipliers under capacity constraints', *Service Industries Journal* **8**(1), 136–42.

WTO (1980a) *Manila Declaration on World Tourism*, WTO, Madrid.

WTO (1980b) *Tourism and Employment: Enhancing the Status of Tourism Professions*, WTO, Madrid.

WTO (1988) *Yearbook of Tourism Statistics*, WTO, Madrid.

WTO (1992, 1997, 2002a) *Yearbook of Tourism Statistics*, WTO, Madrid.

WTO (2000b) *The Tourism Satellite Account (TSA): A Strategic Project for the World Tourism Organization*, Report by the Secretary-General, Madrid, November 2000.

WTO (2003) *Yearbook of Tourism Statistics*, WTO, Madrid.

WTTC (2006) 'The impact of travel and tourism on jobs and economy', available at
**http://www.oxfordeconomics.com/OE_Tourism.asp#**

# MAJOR CASE STUDY 7.1
## Australian Tourism Satellite Accounts

The following figures are extracted from the Australian Tourism Satellite Accounts published in December 2011. They show the significance of tourism to the Australian economy. Examine the data shown in the tables and figures and reflect upon their use and importance to tourism planners, policy makers and analysts. Then respond to the questions asked at the end of the case study.

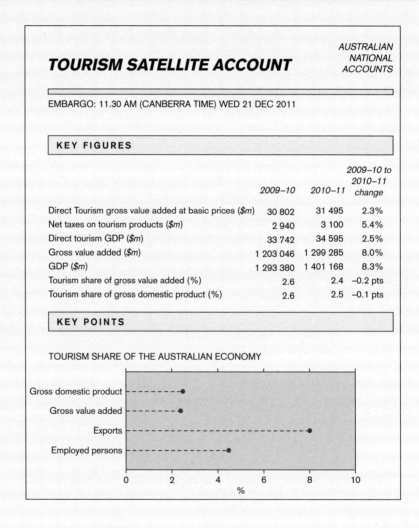

### TOURISM SATELLITE ACCOUNT

AUSTRALIAN NATIONAL ACCOUNTS

EMBARGO: 11.30 AM (CANBERRA TIME) WED 21 DEC 2011

**KEY FIGURES**

|  | 2009–10 | 2010–11 | 2009–10 to 2010–11 change |
|---|---|---|---|
| Direct Tourism gross value added at basic prices ($m) | 30 802 | 31 495 | 2.3% |
| Net taxes on tourism products ($m) | 2 940 | 3 100 | 5.4% |
| Direct tourism GDP ($m) | 33 742 | 34 595 | 2.5% |
| Gross value added ($m) | 1 203 046 | 1 299 285 | 8.0% |
| GDP ($m) | 1 293 380 | 1 401 168 | 8.3% |
| Tourism share of gross value added (%) | 2.6 | 2.4 | –0.2 pts |
| Tourism share of gross domestic product (%) | 2.6 | 2.5 | –0.1 pts |

**KEY POINTS**

TOURISM SHARE OF THE AUSTRALIAN ECONOMY

**GDP**
- Tourism share of GDP fell 0.1% points to 2.5%
- Direct tourism GDP increased by 2.5% to $34,595m

**INDUSTRY GROSS VALUE ADDED**
- Tourism share of gross value added fell 0.2% points to 2.4%
- Direct tourism gross value added increased by 2.3%  to $31,495m

**TOURISM CONSUMPTION**
- Internal tourism consumption (total domestic and international consumption in Australia) increased by 2.6% to $95,653m
- Domestic tourism consumption increased by 2.1% to $71,972m
- Tourism exports (international tourism consumption in Australia) increased by 4.4% to $23,681m
- Tourism imports (tourism consumption by Australian residents on outbound trips) increased by 11.0% to $30,901m

**TOURISM EMPLOYMENT**
- Tourism share of total employment remained at 4.5%
- Tourism employed persons increased by 2.7%, or 13,500 persons

**Figure 7.3**    Australian TSA

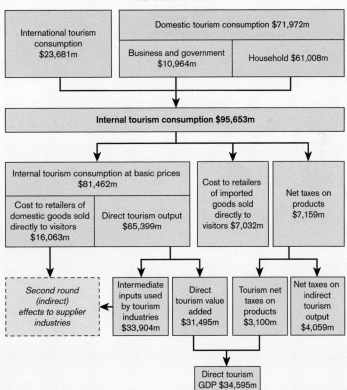

**Figure 7.4**    Flow of tourism consumption through the Australian economy (year ended June 2011)

*Source*: http://www.ausstats.abs.gov.au/ausstats/subscriber.nsf/0/3E281CC5A71E3F91CA25796C00143363/$File/52490_2010-11.pdf

## DISCUSSION QUESTIONS

1. Why do we need to measure the significance of tourism economic activity?

2. What are the problems likely to be encountered in many countries when attempting to create a consistent set of tourism satellite accounts and how can they be addressed?

3. What useful information do the Australian Tourism Satellite Accounts shown in this Case Study give to the policy maker? Read the linked report to see the nature of information that can be derived from TSAs before considering your answer.

# CHAPTER 8

## THE ENVIRONMENTAL IMPACT OF TOURISM

### LEARNING OUTCOMES

The objective of this chapter is to provide you with:

- an understanding of the physical impacts of tourism on the environment, both direct and indirect, positive and negative;
- a review of strategies and techniques that may be implemented to measure and quantify the impacts of tourism on the environment such as an environmental impacts assessment;
- an appreciation of the difficulties of assessing environmental impacts; and
- real-life examples to encourage the application of theory to practice.

Photograph: Half Dome, Yosemite National Park, California, USA © Kelly Miller

## INTRODUCTION

Any form of industrial development will bring with it impacts upon the physical environment in which it takes place. In view of the fact that tourists must visit the place of production in order to consume the output, it is inevitable that tourism activity will be associated with environmental impacts. The identification of the need to follow an environmentally compatible pattern of tourism development is now well into its third decade but in spite of the fact that environmental issues are high profile, little has been achieved to ensure that future developments are environmentally sound.

# ENVIRONMENTAL IMPACT

At the end of the 1970s the **OECD** set out a framework for the study of environmental stress created by tourism activities. This framework highlighted four main categories of stressor activities including permanent environmental restructuring (major construction works such as highways, airports and resorts); waste product generation (biological and non-biological waste which can damage fish production, create health hazards and detract from the attractiveness of a destination); direct environmental stress caused by tourist activities (destruction of coral reefs, vegetation, dunes, etc. by the presence and activities of tourists); effects on the population dynamics (migration, increased urban densities accompanied by declining populations in other rural areas).

In 1992, the United Nations Conference on the Environment and Development, held in Rio de Janeiro, added further impetus to a debate that was growing stale and a new maxim emerged where 'Only whatever can be sustained by nature and society in the long term is permissible'. This new impetus was given the title **Agenda 21** to reflect the fact that it was a policy statement aimed at taking the world into the twenty-first century. What made Agenda 21 significant was the fact that it represented the first occasion when a comprehensive programme of environmental actions was agreed to be adopted by 182 governments. The Agenda was based around a framework of themes that were aimed at providing an overall strategy to transform global activity onto a more sustainable course. The matters addressed within Agenda 21 were not solely environmental because they included aspects such as human development and the redressing of the imbalance between rich and poor nations. However, many of the matters discussed and the strategies recommended were environmentally based.

Now, in the twenty-first century and in spite of the programme's elegance and simplicity, the adoption of this maxim requires enforcement that is still far beyond the reach of most legislative frameworks and none of the recommendations made in Agenda 21 were legally binding on the 182 nations that approved its adoption. Furthermore, the implementation of this maxim requires that those charged with the construction of the necessary legislative framework be fully informed of the environmental repercussions of productive and consumptive activities. To date this is not the case. The literature on the environmental impacts of tourism is often biased, painting highly negative pictures of tourism with respect to its associated environmental impacts. In this chapter we examine the nature of environmental impacts, how they can be identified and measured and how this information can be integrated into the tourism planning process.

## Tourism and the environment

The environment, whether it is natural or artificial, is the most fundamental ingredient of the tourism product. However, as soon as tourism activity takes place, the environment is inevitably changed or modified either to facilitate tourism or through the tourism production process. Environmental preservation and improvement programmes are now an integral part of many **development strategies** and such considerations are treated with much greater respect than they were during the first two-thirds of the last century. Relatively little research has been undertaken within a standardised framework to analyse tourism's impact on the environment. The **empirical studies** that have taken place have been very specific case studies – such as the impact of tourism on the wildlife of Africa, the pollution of water in the Mediterranean or studies of particular coastal areas and mountains. But the diverse areas studied, the varying methods used to undertake those studies and the wide range of tourism activities involved makes it difficult to bring these findings together in order to assemble a comprehensive standardised framework within which to work.

In order to study the physical impact of tourism it is necessary to establish:

- the physical impacts created by tourism activity as opposed to other activities;
- what conditions were like before tourism activity took place in order to derive a baseline from which comparisons can be made;
- an inventory of flora and fauna, together with some unambiguous index of tolerance levels to the types of impact created by different sorts of tourism activity; and
- the secondary levels of environmental impact that are associated with tourism activity.

The environmental impacts associated with tourism development, just like the economic impacts, can be considered in terms of their direct, indirect and induced effects. Again some of the impacts can be positive and some negative. It is not possible to develop tourism without incurring environmental impacts, but it is possible, with correct planning, to manage tourism development in order to minimise the negative impacts while at the same time encouraging the positive impacts.

## Positive environmental impacts

On the positive side, the direct environmental impacts associated with tourism include:

- the preservation/restoration of ancient monuments, sites and historic buildings, such as the Great Wall of China (PRC), the Pyramids (Egypt), the Taj Mahal (India), Stonehenge and Warwick Castle (UK);
- the creation of national parks and wildlife parks, such as Yellowstone Park (USA), the Amboseli National Park and the Maasai Mara National Reserve (Kenya), Las Canadas (Tenerife), the Pittier National Park (Venezuela) and the Fjord Land National Park (New Zealand);
- protection of reefs and beaches, such as the Great Barrier Reef (Australia), Grand Anse (Grenada); and
- the maintenance of forests, such as the New Forest (UK) and Colo I Suva (Fiji).

**Conservation** and **preservation** may be rated highly from the point of view of researchers, or even the tourists. However, if such actions are not considered to be of importance from the hosts' point of view, it may be questionable as to whether they can be considered to be positive environmental impacts. When evaluating the net worth of preservation and conservation activities the opportunity costs associated with such activities must also be taken into account. African wildlife parks, such as Etosha National Park in Namibia, may result in the grazing lands of nomadic tribes being limited and hence constrain food production capability.

## Negative environmental impacts

On the negative side, tourism may have direct environmental impacts on the quality of water, air and noise levels. Sewage disposal into water will add to pollution problems, as will the use of powered boats on inland waterways and sheltered seas. Increased usage of the internal combustion engine for tourist transport, oil burning to provide the power for hotels' air conditioning and refrigeration units all add to the diminution of air quality. Noise levels may be dramatically increased in urban areas through nightclubs and other forms of entertainment as well as by increased road, rail and air traffic.

Physical deterioration of both natural and built environments can have serious consequences:

- hunting and fishing have obvious impacts on the wildlife environment;
- sand dunes can be damaged and eroded by over-use;
- vegetation can be destroyed by walkers;
- camp fires may destroy forests;
- ancient monuments may be disfigured and damaged by graffiti, eroded or literally taken away by tourists (the Byzantine Fort in Paphos, Cyprus, for instance, is a World Heritage Site subject to pilfering);
- the construction of a tourism superstructure utilises real estate and may detract from the aesthetics; and
- the improper disposal of litter can detract from the aesthetic quality of the environment and harm wildlife.

Examples of direct negative environmental impacts include:

- the erosion of paths to the Pyramids at Giza, Egypt by the camels used to transport tourists;
- the dynamiting of Balaclava Bay (Mauritius) to provide a beach for tourist use; and
- the littering of Base Camp on Mount Everest, Nepal by tourists and the erosion of the pathway to this site.

The building of high-rise hotels on beach frontages is an environmental impact of tourism that achieves headline status. This kind of obvious environmental rape is now less common than it was during the rapid growth periods of the 1960s and 1970s. In a number of countries, particularly island economies, the issue of land usage is often high on the agenda of planning meetings. Regulations have been introduced to restrict beachfront developments to a height no greater than that of the palm trees (as for example in Mauritius), or restrict development to a certain distance back from the beach (as in some parts of India).

Tourism activities can put scarce natural resources, such as water, under severe pressure. Tourists tend to be far more extravagant with their use of water than they are at home with estimates of up to 440 litres per person per day being made for areas around the Mediterranean. To put this into context, this is up to twice the normal usage of residents in urban areas of Spain or Italy. Some activities, such as swimming pools and golf courses, require intensive use of these scarce resources and the latter can add further to the environmental impacts if fertilisers and weeding chemicals are used. Tourism Concern has estimated that the average golf course in tropical countries like Thailand requires 1,500 kg of fertilisers, pesticides and other treatments per annum and uses the same amount of water that would be consumed by approximately 60,000 village residents. Similar physical depletion can be witnessed in terms of deforestation as trees are cleared for land use and fuel.

Tourism is responsible for high levels of air and noise pollution through the transportation networks and leisure activities. Air transport is claimed to be a significant factor in global warming and tourism is responsible for the vast majority of international air transport. At the local level air transport near urban areas can cause severe pollution problems along with ground transport systems such as tour buses that use up resources in an attempt to maintain climate control for their passengers. Other forms of transport, such as jet skis, quad bikes and snowmobiles, can create excessive noise pollution in coastal areas, national parks and areas of outstanding natural beauty. The noise from snowmobiles (particularly the older models) can be really intrusive when the area is a place of natural beauty. For instance, at the Yellowstone National Park the *Idaho News* reported in 2006 that a survey showed that snowmobile noise could be heard for 70% of the time available at 11 out of 13 sampling sites. This noise and the pollution from snowmobiles adds further pressure on the wildlife and vegetation. Furthermore, the construction of additional roads and car parking facilities encroaches on wildlife habitats and the pollution from vehicles can be so severe that at times areas such as Yosemite Valley are enshrouded in smog and not visible from the air. The smog is harmful to all species of animal and vegetable (UNEP, 2004).

The problems associated with littering (such as the high profile given to the littering by tourists at Base Camp on Mount Everest) present significant danger to wildlife as well as being unsightly and expensive to clear. Similarly, solid waste disposal, if not undertaken properly, can be a major despoiler of the environment in coastal areas, rivers, lakes and roadsides. Such pollution can also give rise to serious health risks to humans as well as wildlife. Nowhere is this type of direct environmental impact more obvious than with respect to cruise ships. Cruise ships have grown in size over the past century and are now equivalent to floating cities or towns. They visit near coastal areas where water quality is vital for the marine life and the safety of bathers and although they are subject to regulations such as the use of advanced water treatment systems, these are often violated because of a lack of monitoring and such violations have resulted in some areas such as British Columbia being referred to as the 'toilet bowl' of the Western Coast of the USA (**http://www.cruiselawnews.com/2010/08/articles/pollution-1/cruise-ships-turn-british-columbia-waters-into-toilet-bowel-of-raw-sewage/**). A typical 3,000-passenger cruise ship will produce nearly 200,000 litres of sewage every day and the maximum capacity of the largest cruise ship in 2011 is 6,360 passengers (*Allure of the Seas* and *Oasis of the Seas*), which results in double that volume of sewage. Furthermore, the sewage systems on cruise ships are often not as water-intensive as land-based flushing; consequently the effluent that gets pumped into the sea is some-times four or five times more concentrated than effluent discharged from land systems. This can introduce hazardous levels of bacteria into the sea. *Our Planet* magazine reported that the wider Caribbean region received 63,000 port calls from ships on an annual basis and that this activity alone resulted in 82,000 tons of rubbish. Given that cruise ships are responsible for 77% of the total waste generated this represents a major pollution problem for the islands where the cruise ship passengers create four times more daily rubbish than their local resident counterparts (*Our Planet* (UNEP), 2006, vol. 10, no. 3).

## MINI CASE STUDY 8.1
Environmental impacts of tourism

## EFFECTS OF OTHER INDUSTRIES ON TOURISM

**BP Gulf oil spill's impact on tourism estimated at three years, nearly $23 billion**

By now you've probably seen the ads: Come to Florida/Another Gulf Coast state, our beaches are still beautiful (despite the worst oil spill in US history). It's a sign that the states are losing visitors, and tourism dollars. A new analysis by Oxford Economics projects the BP oil spill will impact Gulf Coast tourism for at least three years, and cost the region $22.7 billion. That's a lot of zeros, and based on history and current trends, researchers say. The study demonstrates that natural assets like blue water and sandy beaches are hard to replace. Does it make better sense to try to replace our fossil-fueled economy instead? Congress?

The Oxford Economics analysis, done for the US Travel Association, says a $500 million marketing effort to attract visitors to the Gulf Coast could reduce the total economic impact by $7.5 billion. Not as many zeros. The $500 million would come from BP, with a marketing effort supervised by the federal government.

This may be a good investment if the money is spent on telling people the truth, rather than a Photoshopped version of the truth (speaking of BP). If efforts to (finally) halt the spill and clean up beaches are having an effect, let's highlight that. But let's not engage in false advertising.

'Travel is a perception business and the impact of disasters like the BP oil spill on the industry is actually predictable', says Roger Dow, president and CEO of the US Travel Association.

'We know from this research that the oil spill will have long-term effects on businesses and jobs in the Gulf Coast region unless we counteract the usual course of events with an unprecedented response.'

The US Travel Association says 400,000 travel industry jobs hang in the balance, and they've released a 10-point 'Road to Recovery'. The plan calls on feds to:

- Create a $500 million, BP-funded marketing program;

- Develop a 'one-stop shop' online portal where consumers can obtain up-to-the-minute information about which areas are safe and open for travel and business;

- Provide tax deductions in a disaster-affected area to give travelers added incentive to travel to and do business in that region;

- Intervene to provide increased access to capital, low interest loans and tax incentives that allow businesses to remain open and retain employees.

Residents, travelers, what do you think? Is it time to urge people to return to the Gulf Coast states for tourism, or urge them to donate money and time toward a cleanup? US President Barack Obama is urging people to vacation in the Gulf Coast. He's taking his family there in August.
Can we trust BP with the truth?

*Source*: http://www.treehugger.com/natural-sciences/bp-gulf-oil-spills-impact-on-tourism-estimated-at-3-years-nearly-23-billion.html, 26 July 2010 (accessed 29 March 2012)

## DISCUSSION QUESTIONS

1. 'The tourism industry is a relatively "clean" industry and just gets a bad press.' Discuss this statement with respect to the environmental impact of tourism.

2. 'Environmental damage is simply a part of the twenty-first century and there is no point in trying to clean up the tourism industry unless all industries are brought into line.' Discuss.

3. Where high environmental risk industries, such as oil extraction, are located in or near areas of tourism activity should there be a tourism indemnity policy to protect tourism in the event of a disaster? Discuss the pros and cons of such a scheme.

4. Are certification schemes likely to succeed in 'greening' the tourism industry?

It is also important to note that many environmental factors are interdependent – often in ways that are not yet fully understood. Damage to coral reefs by divers, cruise ship anchors, or through the construction of coastal developments will reduce the local diversity and population of fish and other creatures that may feed off the coral. This, in turn, may reduce the numbers of birds that feed on the fish and so on. In order to determine the full impact of environmental changes accurately, the **ecological system** and the way in which it responds to environmental stress must be understood.

The effect of any loss to **biological diversity** is an increased threat to the food chain, can imbalance species and soil formation, and result in less ability to absorb greenhouse gases. A loss of biodiversity also hinders nature's ability to withstand the natural shocks caused by droughts, earthquakes, floods and hurricanes. Finally, it reduces the enjoyment that tourists experience when visiting areas by reducing the variety and wealth of flora and fauna available.

## ENVIRONMENTAL IMPACT ASSESSMENT

There are no generally accepted models for environmental impact assessment (EIA). In many environmentally sensitive tourism destinations the need for EIAs has become more frequent and expected when considering tourism development and its relationship with the environment. Many countries have now incorporated the need for EIAs within their planning legislation but even the absence of legislation to support environmental planning should not deter tourism planners from undertaking their own environmental impact assessments on proposed developments. Environmental protection is so much easier and less costly than environmental correction even when such remedial action is possible.

It is important to understand the motivation that underlies a particular environmental impact assessment before an appropriate methodology is selected. For instance, an EIA may be undertaken in order to determine a development's impact upon a specific ecology or even upon a single 'rare' species. This type of assessment may not require the evaluation of the environmental impacts in monetary terms. However, other EIAs may be instigated for the express purpose of determining the financial implications of environmental correction in order to reflect accurately the net economic returns of tourism activity or in an attempt to retrieve some of these costs from the industry. Furthermore, EIAs may be required in order to compare alternative developments so as to allocate resources in a manner that maximises the economic benefits of development while minimising the negative environmental impacts. In this case there is a need to take a general equilibrium approach which enables the researcher to compare and contrast development options not only between various tourism strategies but also between different industrial structures.

Finally, EIAs may be required simply to raise the profile of environmental issues. That is, future developments should not be evaluated solely in economic terms but in a more holistic manner that includes the effects upon the local environment. This approach allows the democratic processes of development choice to be fully informed. It also highlights the fact that environmental impacts and environmental audits should become a way of life for business organisations as well as governments and individuals.

**Photograph 8.1**    Oil spills can be disastrous for the local tourism industry as well as for the environment.
*Source*: Think4photop/Shutterstock.com

Once the environmental consequences of our actions are recognised this information can be incorporated at every decision-making level to ensure the effective use of the planet's finite resources. Environmental awareness during the production and consumption processes may also bring long-term economic and social benefits. For instance, the effective use of scarce resources, particularly energy-related resources, can result in lower marginal costs of production. On the other hand, the careless or reckless use of resources during the production or consumption processes can add to social resentment of tourism development. This may hinder future development and will certainly detract from the effective use of resources.

In spite of the fact that there is no single accepted framework for conducting EIAs, the true scope of environmental impacts should not be underestimated. Most forms of industrial development impact upon land use, energy consumption and other direct forms of physical impacts. However, to assess the overall environmental impact it is necessary to take into account the consequential impacts brought about by the direct productive activity. In the same way that the economic impacts associated with tourism development can be direct and indirect, the same must be said for environmental impacts. If tourism activity requires the production of output from a diverse range of industries, including those that do not supply tourist goods and services directly, then the environmental impact associated with the output and production processes of these supporting industries should also be included in the overall evaluation. For example, if the level of tourism increases, and this causes hotels to increase their purchases from the building and construction industry, then the environmental damage created by that increased building and construction must also be included. This is also true with respect to the effects of the quarries that supply the builders and the transport system that facilitates it.

The direct and indirect environmental impacts can be estimated with the input–output framework (discussed in Chapter 7). By constructing a matrix of environmental coefficients relating to a variety of indicators, the change in tourist expenditure can be used to estimate the change in output of each productive sector and this in turn can be used to determine the likely environmental impact brought about by those changes. (This is discussed in greater detail under the sustainability heading in Chapter 11.)

Attempts have been made in some areas to construct tourism/environment balance sheets to assess the net effect of tourism development with respect to the environment. One such approach for Scotland concluded that tourism is an important sector of the Scottish economy and that, although there are widespread environmental impacts associated with tourism activity, they were only regarded as being serious in a few specific locations and that careful management could overcome these problems in the wider tourism areas. In 1991 the UK Department of Employment set up a task force to examine the relationship between tourism and the environment in England and the report published under this same title supported the major views expressed by the Scottish Tourism Coordinating Group. However, this suggests that in places where the environmental impacts are serious over a wider range of areas then careful management may not be able to overcome these problems. In this latter case it may be questionable as to whether tourism development should be considered at all.

## THE EIA PROCESS

It is important to identify environmental impacts associated with tourism development at an early stage because:

- it is easier to avoid environmental damage by either modifying or rejecting developments than it is to rectify environmental damage once a project has been implemented; and
- projects that rely heavily upon areas of outstanding beauty may become non-viable if such developments degrade the environment.

There are a variety of methods that may be used for EIA including checklists and network systems, but generally the EIA is a process that enables researchers to predict the environmental consequences associated with any proposed development project. To draw up a checklist of environmental impacts it is necessary to establish what potential impacts can occur as a result of tourism activity and Green's checklist, even though compiled 20 years ago still represents a fine example of the scope of what is involved.

## Green's checklist of the environmental impacts caused by tourism

### THE NATURAL ENVIRONMENT

(a) Changes in floral and faunal species composition

- Disruption of breeding habits
- Killing of animals through hunting
- Killing of animals in order to supply goods for the souvenir trade
- Inward or outward migration of animals
- Destruction of vegetation through the gathering of wood or plants
- Change in extent and/or nature of vegetation cover through clearance or planting to accommodate tourism facilities
- Creation of a wildlife reserve/sanctuary

(b) Pollution

- Water pollution through discharges of sewage, spillage of oil/petrol
- Air pollution from vehicle emissions
- Noise pollution from tourist transportation and activities

(c) Erosion

- Compaction of soils causing increased surface run-off and erosion
- Change in risk of occurrence of land slips/slides
- Change in risk of avalanche occurrence
- Damage to geological features (e.g. tors, caves)
- Damage to river banks

(d) Natural resources

- Depletion of ground and surface water supplies
- Depletion of fossil fuels to generate energy for tourist activity
- Change in risk of occurrence of fire

(e) Visual impact

- Facilities (e.g. buildings, chairlifts, car parks)
- Litter

### THE BUILT ENVIRONMENT

(a) Urban environment

- Land taken out of primary production
- Change of hydrological patterns

(b) Visual impact

- Growth of the built-up area
- New architectural styles
- People and belongings

**(c)** Infrastructure

- Overload of infrastructure (roads, railways, car parking, electricity grid, communications systems, waste disposal and water supply)
- Provision of new infrastructure
- Environmental management to adapt areas for tourist use (e.g. sea walls, land reclamation)

**(d)** Urban form

- Changes in residential, retail or industrial land uses (move from houses to hotels/boarding houses)
- Changes to the urban fabric (e.g. roads, pavements)
- Emergence of contrasts between urban areas developed for the tourist population and those for the host population

**(e)** Restoration

- Reuse of disused buildings
- Restoration and preservation of historic buildings and sites
- Restoration of derelict buildings as second homes

**(f)** Competition

- Possible decline of tourist attractions or regions because of the opening of other attractions or a change in tourist habits and preferences

*Source*: Green et al., 1990 (with permission from Elsevier Science)

In spite of the apparent comprehensiveness of this checklist it is evident that the listed aspects focus primarily on direct tourism activities and development. This is an inadequate approach because the indirect consequences must also be assessed. It is also important that environmental resources should be utilised efficiently. This means not only that they should be effectively used within the tourism industry but that this effectiveness should also be evaluated in relative terms in comparison with alternative economic development strategies. Only then can fully informed and sound rational planning decisions be made.

Once the potential impacts have been considered, a checklist consisting of the fundamental elements at risk can be assembled. This checklist can then be used to form the basis of an evaluation matrix which will assess the impact of proposed developments on each of the fundamental elements according to whether the development will have no impact, minor impacts, moderate impacts or major impacts.

An EIA will examine:

- environmental auditing procedures;
- limitations to natural resources;
- environmental problems and conflicts that may affect project viability; and
- possible detrimental effects to people, flora and fauna, soil, water, air, peace and quiet, landscapes, cultural sites, etc. that are either within the proposed project area or will be affected by it.

Figure 8.1 sets out a typical process which an environmental impact assessment would adopt. A proposed development is put forward by a developer and this is initially assessed using the destination's environmental policy document as a performance indicator. Following this initial evaluation the proposal moves forward to site selection and undergoes a preliminary environmental impact assessment. This assessment can then be compared in more detail with the environmental performance indicators identified in the policy legislation/regulations in order to investigate potential conflicts.

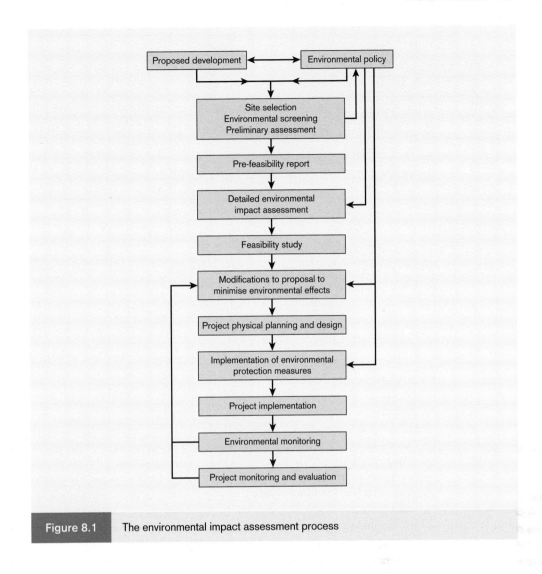

| Figure 8.1 | The environmental impact assessment process |

## Environmental indicators

There is a wide range of environmental indicators that can be used. However, few countries have instigated data collection procedures to monitor these environmental variables. The OECD (2004) provides an ongoing programme that highlights core environmental indicators. The development of harmonised environmental indicators with its member countries is pursued under the belief that there is no one universal set of environmental indicators but rather several sets intended to meet the needs of different purposes and audiences. More emphasis is now given to the conceptual framework of environmental indicators. The framework should include indicators that meet the criteria initially set out by the OECD in 1994 when it subdivided indicators into the following categories:

- climate change and ozone layer depletion;
- eutrophication;
- acidification;
- toxic contamination;
- urban environmental quality;
- biodiversity;

- cultural landscapes;
- waste;
- water resources;
- forest resources;
- fish resources;
- soil degradation;
- material resources; and
- socio-economic, sectoral and general indicators.

The criteria for indicator selection are that they should:

- provide a representative picture of conditions or society's response;
- be simple, easy to interpret and able to show trends over time;
- be responsive to changes in the environment and related human activities;
- provide a basis for international comparisons;
- be either national in scope or applicable to regional environmental issues of national significance; and
- have a threshold or reference value against which to compare it.

These criteria should be expanded further to allow for intersectoral comparisons if they are to facilitate future development planning and the optimum use of resources. Environmental indicators should not be confined to a role of simply measuring what we do, they should also provide information as to what we *should* do.

Once the preliminary assessment has been completed, a pre-feasibility study is undertaken followed by a detailed EIA that attempts to evaluate specific environmental costs and benefits. Again the results of the impact assessment are compared with the environmental policy and, if no serious conflicts arise, the proposal can move forward to a full feasibility study and modifications can be introduced to minimise any negative environmental impacts and bring the project in line with policy.

The physical planning and design of the project can then take place together with the introduction of measures designed to protect the environment in line with environmental policy. At this stage the project can be implemented and the project's development can then be monitored in terms of its future environmental impact.

However, if the EIA is undertaken in order to estimate the economic costs of correcting for the environmental impacts, or to compare the environmental performance of various industries, the above approach requires some modification. To examine impacts within a cohesive framework it is important that economic and environmental indicators are combined within a single model. This approach to EIA has been undertaken by researchers from Bournemouth University (UK) in studies for the government of Mauritius (1994) and the Wales Tourist Board (2002). The integration of economic, environmental and social impacts is essential if tourism strategies and choices are to be well informed and steps taken to prevent tourism development exceeding the carrying capacity of the destination. The Mauritius and Welsh models utilise the economic linkage information acquired during the input–output analysis (see Chapter 5) to provide the framework for estimating the indirect and induced environmental impacts associated with an industry's output level. The model relies only upon quantifiable environmental indicators in order to maintain objectivity. By constructing a set of environmental indicator coefficients that relate output by sector to environmental effects, planners are able to identify the environmental impact of any given change in the pattern or volume of production. The direct, indirect and induced environmental consequences of production in each industry can be assessed in exactly the same way that economic effects are measured. By utilising the economic linkage information to trace the consequential environmental effects of production, the model can provide a uniform framework for comparing not only the different types of tourism activity but also tourism with other forms of industrial activity. The confinement to measurable environmental indicators provides a platform for at least regional and national comparisons, and at best international comparisons. Because of the reliance on quantifiable variables the financial implications of production and consumption can also be estimated. Finally, because such models are constructed as interactive computer-based models, they are ideal for facilitating the **environmental auditing** process required of developments into the future.

# ENVIRONMENTAL AUDITING

Unlike EIAs which focus on the effects of any given change in demand, environmental auditing represents a way of life; a way of doing business; a modus operandi; an ongoing process of monitoring and evaluation. The major differences between EIAs and environmental auditing are:

- environmental audits are generally voluntary in nature while EIAs tend to be written into the legislation and required as part of the planning approval process;
- environmental audits are part of an ongoing process – even a sense of attitude – rather than the one-off EIA studies; and
- environmental audits are concerned with performance and focus on how well a process is functioning. In this sense the environmental audit should become part of the organisational structure of private and public sector bodies alike.

However, one of these distinguishing features, the voluntary nature of environmental auditing, is also its Achilles heel. Without the necessary legislation and regulation required to enforce the implementation and quality of environmental auditing, it is unlikely to be an effective environmental protector. Also, because tourism is a fragmented industry with no clear boundaries, the environmental auditing needs to be economy-wide rather than solely aimed at tourism establishments. There is also an argument that common standards of environmental audits and performance indicators should be adopted on a universal basis because of the dangers of conflict if different industries pursue different environmental goals. All of these factors point to a single conclusion, namely, that environmental auditing is a macro rather than micro issue and that the distinction between EIAs and environmental auditing is becoming narrower. A more satisfactory solution is to adopt the general equilibrium EIA approach which encompasses all industrial output and consumption and facilitates the identification of consequential as well as direct impacts. In this way the EIA model can be a subset of the environmental audit process and be used to generate relative performance indicators that will act as benchmarks for each of the productive sectors within the economy. Legislation could then be drafted in such a way as to reward businesses that perform better than their industry average, thereby rewarding best practice.

Where environmental legislation and regulations are in force, then environmental auditing should be used to ensure that these legal and planning requirements are fulfilled. Where there are no legal or regulatory requirements, then environmental auditing should still be implemented in order to secure the long-term benefits associated with the effectiveness of appropriate development.

The environmental auditing process involves three distinct aspects:

1. An assessment of the system, how it functions and the implications of its operation.
2. A rigorous testing of the system to see how its performance compares with some optimal ideal or benchmark performance.
3. The certification of the results from the above comparisons.

Environmental auditing can take place at establishment and corporate levels for national and multinational businesses. However, with the recognition by many countries that the public sector has a vested interest in the development of tourism, environmental auditing should not only be incorporated into the legislation for private sector businesses, but it should also be part of the operational remit of public sector divisions and departments. The adoption of environmental auditing can effect good use of resources as well as help create a good marketing image.

Finally, neither the public nor the private sector owns the environment. It is important that all of the stakeholders should be consulted when there are any proposals to implement development policies that will impinge or detract from the environmental store. These consultations can take many forms but should be undertaken well in advance of any implementation to allow proper time to consider and evaluate opposition and alternative strategies. The public announcement shown in Figure 8.2 demonstrates how such consultative procedures can be organised. In this example, the proposal for a second airport in Sydney, Australia, was under consideration and the public was being informed of the preparation of an EIA. It is commendable to note that the public were invited to attend preliminary information seminars prior to the release of the draft environmental impact assessment report. The airport development has not gone ahead but the consultation process did open up the forum for debate.

Having progressed through the 'cautionary platform' of tourism research, the major thrust of experienced researchers is now one of acceptance. That is, there is an acceptance that destinations should not have the ideological stances of 'puritan' researchers imposed upon them. Indeed, destinations should have sovereignty over their own economic and environmental

## Second Sydney Airport proposal

The Commonwealth Government is assessing Badgerys Creek and the Holsworthy Military Area as potential sites for the Second Sydney Airport. An Environmental Impact Statement is being prepared to consider the impact of these proposals. Preliminary information is available on:

- **Flight Paths** information prepared by Airplan
    - **Master Plan**
        - **Road and Rail Access to the Sites**
            - **Assessing the Impact of Noise**
                - **Air Traffic Forecasts** information prepared by
                    Commonwealth Department of Transport and Regional Development;
to assist you to understand these proposals. When the Draft EIS has been completed it will be released for public comment.

**Come to a preliminary information session prior to the release of the Draft EIS**

**Helensburgh**
Helensburgh Community Centre
Walker Street, Helensburgh
Tuesday 22 July, 6.00 pm – 9.30 pm

**Penrith**
Penrith Civic Centre
High Street, Penrith
Saturday 26 July, 10.00 am – 2.30 pm

**Telephone Information Line: 1800 818 017**

**HOW TO FIND OUT MORE**

- Fax the Community Access Centre on (02) 9600 9741
- Look up the Internet at http://www.magnet.com.au/2sydair and e-mail us at 2sydair@magnet.com.au

**Figure 8.2**   Public announcement for the new Sydney Airport
*Source:* Advertisement from the *Sun Herald*, 6 July 1997, p. 9 © Commonwealth Department of Transport and Regional Development

destiny providing that destiny does not impinge upon the destiny of others. Thus, if it is decided that tourism is an appropriate catalyst for economic development, it should not be suffocated under a barrage of concern for environmental conservation. Where tourism researchers can best help these destinations is in providing the framework for environmental auditing so that development may move forward in an optimal manner.

# ENVIRONMENTAL ACTION PROGRAMMES

In addition to the development of viable and acceptable environmental impact assessment models, there has been a wide range of environmental initiatives undertaken in order to enhance the net effects of tourist activities and move towards some consideration of environmental sustainability. There are environmental protection agencies located at regional (for example, EU) and national levels throughout the world and further tiers of agencies at sub-national levels. Within Europe, the European Commission produces policy directives and guidelines in the form of **environmental action programmes** (EAPs) as well as commissioning wide-ranging research projects into the specifics of environmental issues. The latest EAP is the sixth such plan and will direct environmental policy throughout the first decade of this century. The European EAP targets four priority areas for urgent action with seven thematic strategies. These four areas are climatic change; environment, health and quality of life; natural resources and issues relating to waste; nature and biodiversity. These are very broad areas and are impacted on by tourism in all of its forms. The European Environmental Bureau (EEB) sees the sixth plan as being particularly important in view of the fact that it will oversee the period of enlargement of the EU. These projects range from the sewage and waste disposal problems created by youth tourism in the eastern cantons of Belgium, through the more widely applicable case studies relating to coastal zone management and transport systems to the more specialised analysis of golf tourism and its ecological implications.

Within the USA the Environmental Protection Agency (EPA) provides national environmental policies while state EPAs provide local directives. The US EPA's declared role is to protect human health and to safeguard the natural environment. The national agency works to develop regulations and enforce their implementation as well as commissioning research into environmental issues and providing support (policy and financial) to state EPAs.

In spite of the proliferation of environmental protection agencies since the 1980s there is still no consensus on the way that the environment should be protected from the activities of tourism. This in part may be the result of the fact that tourism's environmental impacts tend to be most obvious in specific areas rather than across nations. Unlike its position with respect to agriculture, energy and transport, the EU has so far failed to produce a comprehensive environmental policy with respect to tourism and much of the policy has been left to individual member countries.

Environmental impact assessments (EIAs) and environmental impact statements (EISs) are studies that estimate the potential or expected environmental impacts of proposed actions or developments. In many countries EIAs or EISs are required (by legislation) for developments that exceed some minimum threshold level. For instance, in Mauritius an EIA is required on any tourism real estate development where more than nine tourism bungalows are to be built. In Ghana EIAs are required if a planned hotel construction involves more than 40 rooms or if it is to be located within a national park, reserve, hilltop or island. However, the criteria for determining whether or not an EIA or EIS is required vary from always to only when there are significant environmental implications. The vagueness of the latter approach often renders environmental legislation impotent and even when there are detailed criteria there are quite often ways of circumventing the requirement, such as developing multiple adjacent sites where each site may be below the prescribed threshold and yet the development as a whole may vastly exceed that criteria.

To be effective, environmental legislation must be enforceable, rigorous and given the same serious consideration as the financial aspects of the proposed development. The UNWTO produced a tourism and environmental publication in 1992 that illustrated 'an integrated approach to resort development' (Inskeep and Kallenberger, 1992) by referring to six case studies. These case studies covered a wide variety of resorts in Indonesia, the Republic of Korea, Mexico, the Dominican Republic, Turkey and the Canary Islands of Spain.

In spite of the range of countries included in the case studies some general conclusions and recommendations could be noted. One major conclusion was that serious environmental problems can be prevented by the adoption of sound planning and development. The recommendations made by the authors encompassed not only the physical needs of integrated planning such as adequate infrastructure, the implementation of appropriate design standards and the need to integrate the resort planning exercise into the local or regional planning process, but also the organisational structures and training of human resources.

However, EIAs and EISs tend to apply to new developments. What can be done to mitigate the damage that is being done by the operation of existing sites? A survey undertaken by the United Nations Environment Programme (UNEP) revealed that more than 100 codes of conduct exist for national tourism organisations, the industry and tourists. For instance, environmental codes of conduct have been adopted by the Tourism Industry Association of Canada and the American Society of Travel Agents as well as by national bodies and individual companies that are targeting the environmentally aware tourists and/or operating in particularly fragile areas. International organisations such as the World Tourism Organization and the World Travel and Tourism Council also promote environmental codes of conduct to the tourism industry.

While some countries have attempted to create an economic framework that will encourage best practice from an environmental point of view, and examples of these can be found in the national parklands of New Zealand, Africa and the Great Barrier Reef Marine Park of Australia, others have attempted to produce comprehensive environmental guidelines for developers. The UNWTO, UNEP and the EU have all published guidelines for the development of tourism in protected areas such as national parks.

Some players within the private sector have been notable in their attempts to drive home greater environmental awareness and the pursuit of best practice. Large private sector businesses have adopted environmental management systems which contain four distinct elements:

1. An environmental review – baseline impact studies that produce environmental inventories of the businesses activities and functions.
2. An environmental policy – a publicly stated set of identifiable and achievable objectives.
3. The design of an implementation and environmental system – setting out the mechanisms by which the objectives will be pursued.
4. An environmental audit – which can be used to measure the business's actual performance against its declared objectives.

Individual airlines have been striving to improve their environmental performance and IATA has released its 'Global Approach to Reducing Aviation Emissions' which it claims has been endorsed by the whole aviation industry as they strive to become carbon neutral by 2020. Southwest Airlines (USA) has adopted its 2010 Environmental Stewardship programme which ranges from seeking enhanced fuel efficiency from its fleet, changing idling speeds on the ground, using recyclable and greener material inside the aircraft to the engagement of its crews and ground staff in the environmental goals.

Disney has been effective in driving forward environmental initiatives and claims a 60-year pedigree of environmental programmes and conservation (**http://corporate.disney.go.com/ citizenship/environment.html**) . The European operations of CenterParcs claim to be a flagship of environmental initiatives in the leisure industry (**http://www.centerparcs.co.uk/company/ environment/index.jsp**) and have been noted for their car-free resorts which provide a healthier environment for guests and, while the Maya Mountain Tours Company of Belize provides teaching facilities for students and researchers into environmental ethics, the Grecotel hotel chain ensures that all of its staff are trained in environmental issues. The Greek National Tourist Office uses policies of spatial zoning, visitor management plans, financial incentives and awareness campaigns in an attempt to drive home the need for better environmental management.

There are also dangers embodied in the growing awareness of environmental issues. With imperfect information the tourist can easily be misled into believing that specific tourist products are environmentally sound. This may encourage tourists to purchase tour operators' packages that are anything but environmentally friendly.

It is only the largest of private sector businesses that normally have the expertise and resources to implement their own environmental management systems. Given the fact that the tourism industry is dominated by **SMEs**, the full impact of environmental management systems will be relatively minor.

There are some areas of the planet that are extremely fragile, where even very small numbers of tourists can have a very high environmental impact. The United Nations Environment Programme (UNEP) noted the rapid rise in tourism to the polar regions in 2007, with tourism activity growing rapidly both in terms of visits from cruise ships and land-based tourists. In such fragile areas one could question the environmental viability of any amount of tourism irrespective of how low-key or what activities they undertake when in these areas. Tourism in the Arctic and Antarctic regions has grown dramatically over the past few decades and poses serious threats to the local populations and the integrity of the environment. It has grown to sufficient proportions to attract the larger tourism businesses and this increase in the level of tourism brings new hazards to tourists and to the environments they visit. Small aircraft have been known to run into problems when taking tourists sightseeing in the Antarctic and the debris of crashed vehicles is sometimes left behind as it is not economically viable to recover the remnants. The pollution caused by increased vehicular activity in the region adds to the pressures being imposed on the environment. Major Case Study 8.1 at the end of the chapter highlights the scale of tourist numbers and activities in Antarctica in order to provide some insight into the growing problems involved in conserving the polar regions.

However, to temper this view, a more positive statement was issued by Achim Steiner, UN Under-Secretary General and UNEP Executive Director, who said:

> The fragility of some of these unique and biologically rich ecosystems may be impacted by the number of visitors and the activities undertaken. Yet, tourism is an activity that if sustainably managed and with profits and revenues fairly shared can contribute to the conservation of the polar environment as well as the well-being and livelihoods of local communities in the Arctic.
>
> (http://www.unep.org/Documents.Multilingual/Default.asp?DocumentID=512&ArticleID=5593&l=en)

Tourism in such areas is often characterised by very marked seasonality patterns. Although where these areas have an indigenous population tourism can bring much-needed revenue and employment opportunities, it can also damage the fragile stability of the economy, driving them to become dependent upon ever-increasing levels of tourist activity, with the environmental and socio-cultural damage that comes with this growth. Where the areas do not have indigenous human populations the presence of tourists and their associated activities can have serious repercussions on the flora and fauna and the impacts of tourists can bring about permanent and irrecoverable damage to the environment.

# CONCLUSION

Environmental impacts are not unique to tourism and tourism receives a disproportionate share of criticism for its negative environmental impacts. Environmental impacts manifest themselves at the direct, indirect and induced levels and all three levels of impact should be taken into account during the process of assessment. The methods of assessment available to researchers have been developed in a piecemeal fashion, limiting their usefulness to generalisations. However, the adoption of a matrix approach, utilising input–output modelling structures, provides the most promising outlook for a universally acceptable framework for the study of such impacts. International agencies, through statements such as Agenda 21, have declared their intentions to develop an environment-friendly approach to policy making. Similarly, national governments are responding to the pressures from these international bodies, as well as from their own populations, to move towards a more environmentally friendly development path. Finally, the private sector (at least as represented by the larger businesses) is responding to pressures by implementing environmental management systems.

Environmental issues have captured many headlines in the tourism world over the past decade and in response organisations such as UNEP have launched a variety of initiatives. UNEP has recently launched the Global Partnership for Sustainable Tourism (**http://www.GlobalSustainableTourism.com**) to help drive home sustainable tourism principles in tourism policies, development and the industry's operations.

There is an overwhelming need to bring some credibility to the study of environmental impacts and this can be achieved by focusing upon the objective environmental indicators, such as those listed by the OECD, IADB, UNEP and other organisations, rather than subjective data sets that may only have local relevance. There is also a need to bring together the various types of impacts associated with tourism (economic, environmental and socio-cultural) so that they can be assessed and considered within a single framework. Only then can policy decisions be made on the basis of informed choice (such an approach is discussed in Chapter 11).

## SELF-CHECK QUESTIONS

1. With respect to the environmental impacts associated with tourism activity, list three positive and negative impact examples at the (a) direct (b) indirect, and (c) induced levels of impact.
2. What made Agenda 21 so unique?
3. Explain briefly the difference between environmental impact assessments (EIAs) and environmental audits.
4. What are the major difficulties associated with trying to identify the environmental impacts caused by tourism activity?
5. How would you define eco-tourism?

## YOUTUBE

### Environmental impacts

Galapagos: managing tourism in
**http://www.youtube.com/watch?v=jBiLFjK_Ztw**

Sustainable Tourism Video News Release
**http://www.youtube.com/watch?v=pVSaVwcTiec**

Responsible tourism definition
**http://www.youtube.com/watch?v=_08Nxj-7RSQ**

Impact of tourism on dolphins – The Changing Oceans Expedition
**http://www.youtube.com/watch?v=-aW-mSa4ngU**

Polar Tourism
**http://www.youtube.com/watch?v=0Desa9FzBjQ**

## REFERENCES AND FURTHER READING

Burnett, G.W. and Conover, R. (1989) 'The efficacy of Africa's national parks: an evaluation of Julius Nyerere's Arusha Manifesto of 1961', *Society and Natural Resources* **2**, 251–60.

Cohen, E. (1978) 'The impact of tourism on the physical environment', *Annals of Tourism Research* **5**(2), 215–37.

De Kadt, E. (ed.) (1979) *Tourism: Passport to Development?*, Oxford University Press, New York.

Getz, D. (1986) 'Models in tourism planning', *Tourism Management* **7**(1), 21–32.

Green, D.H., Hunter, C.J. and Moore, B. (1990) 'Applications of the Delphi technique in tourism', *Annals of Tourism Research*, **17**, 270–79.

Inskeep, E. (1991) *Tourism Planning: An Integrated and Sustainable Development Approach*, Van Nostrand Reinhold, New York.

Inskeep, E. and Kallenberger, M. (1992) *An Integrated Approach to Resort Development: Six Case Studies*, WTO, Madrid.

Lorch, J. and Bausch, T. (1995) 'Sustainable tourism in Europe', in *Tourism and the Environment in Europe*, EU, Brussels.

Mathieson, A. and Wall, G. (1982) *Tourism: Economic, Physical and Social Impacts*, Longman, Harlow.

OECD (1994) *Environmental Indicators*, OECD core set and Paris.

OECD (2004) **http://www.oecd.org/searchResult/0,2665,en_2649_34283_1_1_1_1_1,00.html**

UNEP (2004) **http://www.uneptie.org/pc/tourism/sust-tourism/env-3main.htm**

Welford, R. and Gouldson, A. (1993) *Environmental Management and Business Strategy*, Pitman, London.

# MAJOR CASE STUDY 8.1
## The environmental impact of tourism in Antarctica

## THE IMPACT OF VISITORS

Antarctica doesn't have any 'residents' in that everyone who goes is a visitor for a short time. There are two groups of visitors who can have an impact on Antarctica: tourists and those who go as part of a national Antarctic programme.

**Photograph 8.2**   Tourists observing penguins in Paradise Harbor, Antarctica.
*Source*: Spirit of America/Shutterstock.com

In terms of numbers, tourists greatly outnumber national programme personnel – 46,069 as against 5,000 in the peak season so far in the 2007/08 season for instance (tourist numbers were up 14% on the previous year leading to calls to limit the number of tourists allowed to go). The most recent figures for the 2010/11 season show that there were 33,824 visitors. The national programme personnel clock up far more man-days, however, and impacts are difficult to compare directly. This figure will probably be the peak visitor number for some time to come (see **http://www.ttnworldwide.com/ articles.aspx3id=1386&artid=9860**).

While tourists may only only spend a relatively small time on landings, it is by its nature relatively 'high-impact' time – compared to scientists or electricians, say, who probably spend most of their time on a permanent or semi-permanent base. Tourists also, by their nature, will want to visit the most picturesque and wildlife-rich areas of Antarctica, and they tend to do so in numbers far greater than the entire complement of many Antarctic bases.

Those national programmes that are supplied by ship (as the majority are) have relatively few visits from those ships, whereas in the season the great majority of all shipping activity in Antarctica is of tour ships. There have been accidents with ships being grounded on uncharted rocks and there have been oil-spills. With the best safeguards in the world (and it has to be said that marine regulations for Antarctic ships, both statutory and self-imposed, are as good as they get), the more ships there are, the more accidents there will be.

Tourism in Antarctica is at present self-regulated by the International Association of Antarctic Tour Operators (IAATO). This is an organisation that applies strict guidelines to its member tour operators and ships. Such guidelines limit the size of the ships that can cruise Antarctic waters and also how many people can be landed at sites around Antarctica. So far IAATO is perceived as being successful in its aims and in regulation for Antarctic protection — though there are always those who would have no tourism at all.

Another threat comes from smaller expeditions by individuals and small parties that are becoming increasingly common. Antarctica requires careful planning and a series of fail-safe rescue procedures if anyone gets into difficulty. These smaller expeditions often fail to do this adequately and resort to 'humanitarian' requests for aid from shipping or nearby national bases when they get into difficulty. In recent years, for example, a small helicopter crashed into the sea off the Antarctic Peninsula, requiring rescue, and an attempt to fly across Antarctica via the pole in a small aircraft ended by the aircraft crashing and the pilot being rescued by nearby base personnel.

There is no guarantee that derelict or crashed vehicles left by private expeditioners will be removed from Antarctica as they should be.

## LARGER SHIPS

In 2009 the IMO (International Maritime Organization) approved an amendment to MARPOL (International Convention for the Prevention of Pollution from Ships –

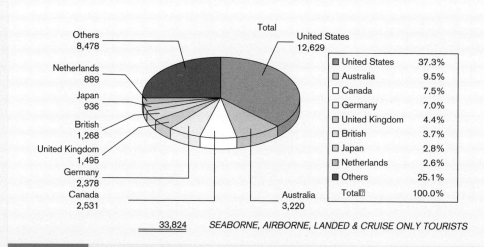

33,824    *SEABORNE, AIRBORNE, LANDED & CRUISE ONLY TOURISTS*

| Figure 8.3 | Antarctica tourist visitor numbers, 2010/11 |

MARPOL being short for Marine Pollution) banning the use and carriage of heavy and intermediate fuel oils for all shipping in the Antarctic Treaty Area.

This ban will largely affect large cruise ships that operate 'cruise-only' tourism. These ships carry 500+ passengers and do not offer landings in Antarctica. As a result of this it is expected that overall tourism numbers for the 2011/12 austral summer will be about 26,775 (down from 47,225 in 2006/07), with the difference due largely to the large passenger ships leaving the Antarctic market.

These larger ships have long posed the biggest potential threat to Antarctica from fuel leaks as they carry so much and from potential sinkings, especially as they are not ice-strengthened; if they no longer sail to Antarctica the risk is reduced greatly.

## ACCIDENTS

Fortunately there have been no major pollution incidents or losses of life in Antarctica as a result of tourism, though there was a very close call in November 2007 with the holing and subsequent sinking by an iceberg of the M/V *Explorer* in the Bransfield Strait.

Fortunately for the passengers and crew of the *Explorer* the collision occurred in calm conditions, so everyone was able to get off the ship safely and into lifeboats. It was doubly fortunate as, having done so, they found that some of the boats were inadequate in that they were open and not large enough for all on board to sit down and three out of four of the powered boats' engines didn't work.

The passengers and crew spent about four hours in the lifeboats before being rescued by other cruise ships in the area and about 15 hours after this the ship sank in around 1,500 metres (4,920 feet) of water. This was despite the ship having an experienced captain and crew and having a double-reinforced hull to withstand submerged ice.

The ship sank carrying approximately 178 cubic metres of diesel, 24 cubic metres of lube oil and 1,200 litres of gasoline. A surface oil slick 1.5 kilometres long and covering 2.5 square kilometres was reported by the Chilean navy a few days afterwards, which grew to about 5 square kilometres though this represents only a few cubic metres of oil. Further slicks were seen in the days following, implying there was a slow leak from one or more tanks.

While the lower temperatures in the Antarctic mean that spills may persist longer than in warmer climates, it seems that the generally rougher seas help to disperse spills more quickly. The *Explorer* was well away from the nearest land, so the slick was dispersed before it came ashore.

The factors of a relatively small ship, calm weather and sinking in deep water well away from land meant that this shipwreck was nowhere near as damaging as it might have been for the people involved and also for the environment – these factors however were as much to do with luck as was the ship hitting the iceberg that holed it in the first place.

*Source:* http://www.coolantarctica.com/antarctica%20fact%20file/science/threats_tourism.htm (accessed 29 March 2012)

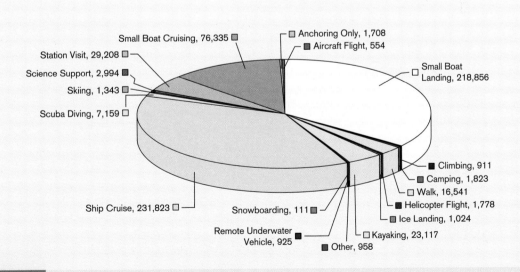

| Figure 8.4 | Tourist activities in Antarctica, 2007/8 |

## DISCUSSION QUESTIONS

1. 'Tourism in the most fragile areas of the planet should not be allowed.' Discuss this statement with respect to the positive and negative aspects of tourism in fragile areas.

2. What could be done to minimise the environmental impact of tourism to fragile environments in general and Antarctica in particular?

3. 'Having rules and regulations regarding the activities and behaviour of tourists while in Antarctica is one thing, enforcing them is a different matter.' Discuss.

# CHAPTER 9

## THE SOCIO-CULTURAL IMPACT OF TOURISM

### LEARNING OUTCOMES

The learning outcomes of this chapter may be defined as:

- identifying those aspects of socio-cultural behaviour that are most susceptible to tourism activity and most likely to be influenced and changed as a result of it;

- understanding the various approaches to studying the socio-cultural aspects of tourism and the relationship between them;

- providing a framework for the study of the relationship between tourism development and socio-cultural impacts; and

- encouraging the reader to understand key concepts.

Photograph: Shaftesbury, Dorset, UK © Peter Woowat

# INTRODUCTION

A core aspect of tourism is that it creates an arena where different cultures interact. That interaction can be through the act of delivering the tourism product, it can be incidental, or even the motivation for travel. The results of such cultural interaction can be either positive or negative, with respect to both the host and tourist cultures. There is a wide range of **service industries** in the world, but there is often no need for the consumer to visit the place of production in order to consume the product, such as when buying insurance or financial services. The fact that tourists must visit a location for tourism consumption to take place means that cultural interaction is inevitable. The implications of this for the destination's population is that not only will it be subject to the changes created by the stimulation and change in direction of the local economy, it will also be subject to change from coming into contact with an alien population. Changes in economic growth and development will always be associated with changes in the socio-cultural characteristics of an area. As the population becomes wealthier and healthier, their wants and needs change and this influences their spending choice and lifestyles. However, because tourism brings visitors into contact with the local population it adds further dimensions to the socio-cultural change.

The contact between visitors and local residents can be beneficial or detrimental to the host population depending upon the difference in cultures and the nature of the contact. Much of the literature on social impacts is biased in that it focuses attention upon the negative impacts of tourism on the host population. In reality socio-cultural impacts tend to contain a mixture of both positive and negative strands and these impacts affect both hosts and guests. Similarly, little attention has been paid to the fact that there can also be socio-cultural impacts on the tourist population, which can again be either positive or negative.

# THE NATURE OF SOCIO-CULTURAL IMPACTS OF TOURISM

The aim of this chapter is to outline the nature of socio-cultural impacts, and to examine those contacts that are positive and those that may be deemed to be negative. In order to do this it is important to include an examination of the process of tourism development because the speed and nature of development can be a major influence on the magnitude and direction of socio-cultural changes. The chapter will also investigate the causal factors for socio-cultural impacts, suggest possible methods for measurement and outline some policy implications.

It is not possible for tourism to occur without there being some form of socio-cultural impact because, by its very nature, tourism is about bringing people from one culture and background to co-exist temporarily alongside people from a different socio-cultural background. That difference may be slight, as is the often the case with domestic tourism where there may be regional variations in dialect, eating habits and dress codes, or it may be significant in the case of international tourism where there may be differences in language, religion, dress and behaviour codes. The range of impacts is enormous and ranges from the arts and crafts through to the fundamental behaviour of individuals and collective groups. The impacts can be positive, such as the case where tourism preserves or even resurrects the craft skills of the population or where there is a positive cultural exchange between two distinct populations. The impacts can also be negative, such as the **commercialisation and bastardisation** of arts, crafts and ceremonies/rituals of the host population. The impacts can also detract from cultural exchange by presenting a limited and distorted view of one of the populations.

A factor often overlooked by researchers is the socio-cultural impact of tourism on the visitor population. For instance, the growth of UK tourists visiting Spain throughout the 1960s and 1970s resulted in culinary and beverage changes in the UK (paella and Rioja wine being two Spanish products that benefited from this exchange). Visitors to Australia would often find it hard to resist adopting the beach-based lifestyle and the barbecue when they returned home. There is evidence of socio-cultural impacts, ranging from the clothes we wear, the food we eat and our general lifestyles and attitudes, which can all be influenced by places we visit.

There is a tradition of viewing the socio-cultural impacts as a combined effect because of the difficulty in distinguishing between sociological and cultural impacts. This distinction is also somewhat artificial given the fact that sociological and cultural effects overlap to a large extent. There is also a tradition of examining the socio-cultural impacts of tourism purely in terms of the contact that takes place between the host and visiting populations: this is a very limited approach. The true socio-cultural impact of tourism is far-reaching and encompasses direct and indirect effects in a manner similar to the economic impacts. Again, some of these consequential impacts may be beneficial while others may be seen as detrimental. These matters will be explored in greater detail below.

# APPROACHES TO THE STUDY OF SOCIO-CULTURAL IMPACTS OF TOURISM

The relationships between tourism development and socio-cultural and socio-economic changes can be examined in a variety of ways. Authors such as Cohen (1984) looked at the study of socio-cultural impacts from four different but overlapping viewpoints:

1. Tourism impact studies.
2. Host–guest interaction.
3. Tourist systems.
4. Tourists and their behaviour.

The studies that have taken place have ranged from those that have attempted to provide formal models to explain tourism development and the host–guest interaction (such as those by Butler (1980), Doxey (1975) and Smith (1989)). Although none of these models has met with a great deal of success, they have created frameworks within which researchers can examine appropriate issues. Many of the other studies relating to the socio-cultural impact of tourism have been specific case study approaches which have lacked the universal rigour that allows the development of an overarching theoretical understanding. One of the major handicaps that has prevented major breakthroughs in fully understanding the nature and characteristics of the social impacts of tourism is the reliance upon quantitative methods. Socio-cultural impacts, both positive and negative, tend to be more subjective and qualitative in nature. This is a point highlighted by Deery et al. (2012) when they argue for a new framework for research into socio-cultural impacts.

The development of the tourist product is inextricably linked to the contribution that tourism development can make to general economic development. In fact, the relationship between tourism development and general economic development can be studied under the heading of dependency or core–periphery theory, which relates to the enrichment of metropolitan areas at the expense of underdeveloped peripheral areas. Studies of dependency theory often cite examples of the Caribbean and the South Pacific to highlight not only the economic and political dependence resulting from tourism activity, but also the socio-cultural dependence. However, the issues are more far-reaching than the effects upon small island developing states (SIDS) and we find that all countries that are in the tourism business experience socio-cultural changes as a result of tourism activity. In some countries, such as Spain, the dynamics of socio-cultural change have been found to be surprisingly rapid, as the effects of tourism development in the Costa Brava demonstrated in the late 1960s and early 1970s.

The development of the tourism product will, to some extent, be determined by the type of tourism activity that takes place. This, in turn, will be partly determined by the nature of the destination and the socio-economic characteristics of the tourists. Similarly, the magnitude and direction of the economic and sociological impact of tourism on the host population will be partly determined by the type of tourism product.

The impact brought about by the interaction of hosts and tourists is a well-documented phenomenon, and the findings of researchers, such as Smith (1989) in her book on the **anthropology of tourism**, have rapidly gained acceptance in the academic world. The categorisation of tourists into **typologies** is now accepted as an orthodox tool in the study of socio-cultural impacts. Authors such as Doxey (1975) have explored the changing relationship between guests and hosts through the construction of his Index where that relationship travels from a state of euphoria, through apathy to annoyance, and ends up with a state of open antagonism as the visitor presence becomes more and more pronounced. Plog (1977) and Butler (1980) both used the dynamics of change as part of their explanatory models, but here they were looking at the changing fortunes of the destination as the visitors revised their perceptions.

## The typology of tourists

Typology is a method of sociological investigation that seeks, in this instance, to classify tourists according to a particular phenomenon, usually motivations or behaviour. A simple example of a typology which has implications for the development of the tourism product is shown in Table 9.1.

- Package tourists – usually demand Western amenities, are associated with rapid growth rates and often lead to the restructuring of the local economy.
- Independent tourists – usually fit in better with the local environment and social structure, are associated with relatively slow growth rates and often lead to local ownership.

A more detailed typology, such as the one devised by Valene Smith, relates the type of tourist to volume and adaptation levels.

Before examining the different approaches that can be used to study the socio-cultural impacts of tourism it is important to consider some fundamental matters relating to these impacts that are often ignored by researchers. In spite of the fact that some researchers regard socio-cultural change as one of the evils of tourism development, any form of economic development will, by definition, carry with it implications for the social structure and cultural aspects of the host population. This is true for both international and domestic tourism development. To condemn tourism development because it will inevitably bring with it socio-economic change is tantamount to consigning a destination to a cultural museum. This choice can only come from the host population and not from external researchers who become too embroiled in the sociological resources that are used in the tourist transactions. Furthermore, to criticise researchers for forecasting future growth levels of tourism and human resource requirements on the grounds that such forecasts ignore the fact that these employees are members of families is to deny the whole essence of sound tourism planning. Successful tourism development can only be achieved by undertaking rigorous quantitative and qualitative research.

| Table 9.1 | Typology of tourism: frequency of types of tourist and their adaptations to local norms |
|---|---|

| Types of tourist | Number of tourists | Adaptation to local norms |
|---|---|---|
| Explorer | Very limited | Accepts fully |
| Elite | Rarely seen | Adapts fully |
| Off-beat | Uncommon but seen | Adapts well |
| Unusual | Occasional | Adapts somewhat |
| Incipient mass | Steady flow | Seeks Western amenities |
| Mass | Continuous flow | Expects Western amenities |
| Charter | Massive arrivals | Demands Western amenities |

*Source*: Smith, 1989. Reprinted by permission of the University of Pennsylvania Press

The speed and concentration of tourism development are also important influences on the magnitude and direction of social impacts and must be taken into account when attempting to attribute the cause of socio-cultural impacts. The nature of the tourism development process and its impact on the host population can be categorised into a variety of subsets and the analyses of each of these subsets can shed additional light on the type and source of impacts attributable to tourism development.

With respect to the speed of development a broad analytical approach would suggest that if tourism develops rapidly, the accompanying change to the economy would create a new power structure. In contrast, slow tourism development tends to be associated with small, locally owned developments with less change to the power structure.

## THE TOURISM DEVELOPMENT PROCESS

Studies that look at the socio-cultural impact of tourism on specific types of destinations according to their resource base are quite common (see for example, Gill and Williams (1994), Price (1992), Stokowski (1996)). Although tourism development can take place in a wide variety of forms, a typical development scenario considers the tourism product as it grows from infancy to maturity and looks something like this:

- A few tourists 'discover' an area or destination.
- In response to this discovery, local entrepreneurs provide new or special facilities to accommodate the growing number of visitors and service their needs. More importantly, they provide the means to attract more visitors in the future.
- The public sector provides new or improved infrastructure to cater for the inflow of visitors.
- Finally, **institutionalised or mass tourism** is developed, which is commonly resort-based and sold as a package. It is based upon large-volume production techniques in order to exploit economies of large-scale production in marketing, accommodation and transport, such as high payload factors for aircraft.

Many regional and national tourism development plans have attempted to shortcut the above tourism evolution cycle by aiming for the final stage of mass tourism straightaway, but few destinations can make this leap without first securing outside capital and expertise and incurring severe social stress.

Unfortunately, there is no single coherent body of knowledge or theory that comprehensively explains tourism development. Evidence, such as it is, is rather piecemeal and comes from a number of disparate case studies. Furthermore, the situation is compounded by the fact that different disciplines approach the subject matter in different ways, and although many aspects of the studies may overlap, it is difficult to tie the different conclusions together into a single body of thought.

The different approaches may be categorised under the following headings:

- psychological;
- sociological;
- socio-economic.

## THE PSYCHOLOGICAL BASIS OF TOURISM DEVELOPMENT

In Chapter 2 we introduced Stanley Plog's (1977) approach to a typology of tourists and in this chapter we have reiterated how useful such typologies can be in the study of socio-cultural impacts. Plog devised his classification in terms of **psychographic analysis,** and in this way attempted to explain why resort destinations appear to follow a pattern that causes them to rise through a period of development and then fall into a period of decline. He saw a continuum of market segments with two diametrically opposed groups occupying either pole (see Figure 9.1).

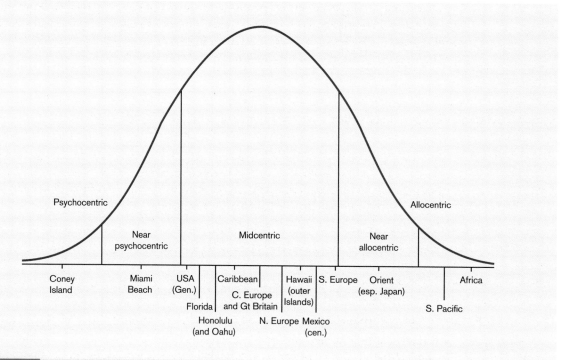

| Figure 9.1 | Psychographic positions of destinations |
| --- | --- |
| | Source: Plog, 1977 |

In 2004, Stanley Plog revisited his earlier work and modified the categories of tourists, replacing the allocentrics with venturers and the psychocentrics with dependables (Plog, 2004). Plog also updated his chart in 2003.

Plog's theory suggests that the tourist segments can be divided into different psychographic traits, i.e. allocentrics, near allocentrics, midcentrics, near psychocentrics and psychocentrics. The polar extremes of these groups can be described as exhibiting the following characteristics:

- **Allocentrics** seek cultural and environmental differences from their norm, belong to the higher income groups, are adventurous and require very little in the way of tourism plant.

- **Psychocentrics** seek familiar surroundings, belong to the lower income groups, are unadventurous and demand a high level of tourism plant.

According to Plog's framework, a resort may typically begin by attracting a small number of allocentrics (trendsetters), similar to Smith's explorers, but will soon develop in order to attract larger numbers of visitors. Using Plog's terminology, this development will move the resort into and through the near allocentrics and then into the midcentrics. During this process the allocentrics will be alienated and they will move on to look for new destinations to 'discover'.

Resorts that have a strong competitive advantage, in terms of climate, location or top-quality tourism plant, such as Disneyland in Florida, USA, may continue to thrive in the midcentric market. However, many resorts will tend to lose favour (perhaps because they are considered by tourists to be too commercialised) and continue their drift towards the psychocentric markets by offering lower tariffs, more comprehensive packaging and more scheduling of activities – the complete 'no-surprise vacation'.

Contrary to thoughts concerning Plog's original theory, this process of rise and decline is not immutable. Such a process may have seemed inevitable for many resorts in the past but, once decision makers realise that limited tourism development can be an attractive means of growth, they may develop tourism plant that is compatible with the environment and the indigenous characteristics of a region, and target them at the 'desired' market segments. Alternatively, recognition of the importance of quality tourism plant can allow destinations to maintain a midcentric position in the market continuum. Classic examples of this would include Disney resorts, which have maintained their positioning over the years.

# THE SOCIOLOGICAL BASIS OF TOURISM DEVELOPMENT

The sociological basis of tourism development can be subdivided into (a) the social phenomenon of tourism and (b) the socio-economic basis underlying tourism development.

Several factors of the modern world can be identified as the seeds from which international tourism has grown into an inescapable social phenomenon:

- Population growth.
- Increasing urbanisation and the overwhelming pressures of urban life which create the desire to escape.
- Growth in communications and information technology, creating awareness and stimulating interest.
- Changes in mobility and accessibility, brought about largely by the growth of air transport and private motor car ownership.
- Increased leisure time and longer periods of vacation, together with rising real incomes in the wake of sustained economic growth.
- Increases in world trade for business tourism.

When examining the factors that are associated with tourism development it is interesting to note that they can also be categorised according to whether they are *push* factors or *pull* factors. By this we mean that some factors generate a desire to escape (*push*) such as urbanisation, overcrowding, pollution or even tedium, whereas other factors such as specific events (Olympics) or climate and natural phenomena generate a magnetism that attracts tourists (*pull*). There are a number of factors that will influence the attitude of people towards tourism at both domestic and international levels. These include the following:

- **Age.** The age of the tourist will, within certain boundaries, influence the type of tourism activity pursued. For instance, there is likely to be less demand from the elderly for trekking and mountaineering vacations than from other age groups. Similarly, the greatest demand for tourist destinations with a hectic nightlife is likely to be from the 18–35-year age group. Of course there are always exceptions to these rules.
- **Education.** There is a tendency to associate the more adventurous and independent vacations with the more educated portion of the population. These would include Plog's allocentrics as well as Smith's explorers and elite travellers.
- **Income levels.** Income levels have an obvious influence on the decision of people to travel, the location to which they travel, the nature of the activities undertaken while away and the mode(s) of transport utilised.
- **Socio-economic background.** The previous experiences of people will play an important role in determining the type of holiday they will consume in future time periods. For instance, children from the higher **socio-economic groups**, who are accustomed to frequent trips abroad, are likely to continue this pattern throughout adulthood.

In addition to the socio-economic characteristics of the tourists, the tourism development process, together with its implications for socio-cultural impacts, should be examined. This approach encompasses all three approaches discussed so far – the psychological basis, the sociological basis and the socio-economic basis for tourism development. In general there is a

**Photograph 9.1**    Clubbing in Ibiza.
*Source*: PYMCA/Alamy Images

*direct* socio-cultural impact which occurs as a result of the contact between the host population and the visitors. De Kadt (1979) suggests that there are three broad categories of such contact:

1. When the tourists buy goods and services from the hosts.
2. When the hosts and tourists share a facility such as the beach, a train or bus, a restaurant or bar, etc.
3. When tourists and hosts come together for the prime purpose of cultural exchange.

The first two of these types of contact are associated with the majority of the negative aspects of social contact, whereas the third type of contact is generally considered to be positive in nature. To draw comparisons between this work of de Kadt and the typology-based research of Smith, it is evident that the explorer/adventurer tourist is most likely to take part in the latter, positive type of interaction – providing a favourable association between this type of tourist and their socio-cultural impacts. However, the mass and charter tourist is more likely to be predominantly concerned with the first two types of contact, thereby making their presence generally unfavourable from a socio-cultural impact point of view. A crude conclusion can be drawn from this somewhat simplistic approach – the negative types of interaction are by far the most common and the positive types of contact are relatively rare.

The **demonstration effect** is also an aspect of the *direct* socio-cultural impact of tourism. Tourists influence the behaviour of the host population by their example. This is an area where tourism development is at a distinct disadvantage when compared with the use of alternative industries as a means to economic development. Tourism is a product that requires simultaneous production and consumption. Although international tourism may be seen as an export industry, in the same way as, say, oil or automobiles, it has the disadvantage that the consumer must visit the place of production (the factory) in order to consume it. This means that tourism will bring with it the physical presence of tourists and this will stimulate changes in the behaviour and dress style of the host population.

It is not even necessary for tourists to come into direct contact with members of the host population for the demonstration effect to take place. Those members of the host population who are influenced by the behaviour of the tourists are likely to influence other members of their community by their changed attitudes and behaviour. This can be classified as an *indirect* socio-cultural impact. Moreover, if tourism development is successful, new employment opportunities created by the increased activity will be the harbinger of social change in the same way that any form of economic development will change the consumption habits, the location and the behaviour of the local population. These changes will be stimulated further by the introduction of new or enhanced forms of communications, transport and infrastructure primarily provided for tourism development. These latter factors may also be considered to be *indirect* socio-cultural impacts but this time they are associated with many types of economic development, not just tourism. However, the diversity of productive sectors associated directly and indirectly with the tourism industry is such that these types of socio-cultural impacts will probably be more widely spread as a result of tourism development than any other industry.

As an economy grows and develops there will probably be an increase in income levels and the proportion of the population involved in the monetised sector. This will alter the consumption patterns of the local population. Such changes, if they include consumer durables such as television, videos and radio, will expose the local population to a greater range of wants and, in so doing, speed up the process of social change. These effects, because they are a result of increased income levels and consumer spending, may be seen as being *induced* socio-cultural impacts. This latter type of socio-cultural impact will also be evident irrespective of the type of economic catalyst that generated the development and is not uniquely attributable to tourism development.

The magnitude of the direct socio-cultural impact associated with tourism development will also be determined by the extent of the difference in socio-cultural characteristics between hosts and guests. Inskeep (1991) suggests that these differences include:

- basic value and logic system;
- religious beliefs;
- traditions;
- customs;
- lifestyles;
- behavioural patterns;
- dress codes;
- sense of time budgeting; and
- attitudes towards strangers.

To add further complexity to our understanding of the problems, the speed of development and change will have an important role in determining the magnitude of the socio-cultural changes because time allows for the process of adaptation. Compounding the issue further is the fact that the tourists' cultures when abroad (it is probable that the tourists will represent several different cultures) are different from the tourists' cultures at home. In other words, tourists often take on different attitudes and adopt different codes of behaviour when they are on vacation and away from their normal environment.

As discussed earlier, the socio-cultural impacts associated with tourism can be either positive or negative. One of the positive impacts highlighted by de Kadt was the exchange of cultural information, ideas and beliefs. But tourism can also be used to help stimulate interest in, and conserve aspects of, the host's cultural heritage such as in Petra, Jordan, York in the UK and Machu Picchu (the lost city of the Incas) in Peru. This is a significant positive socio-cultural impact and extends over ancient monuments, historic sites, arts, crafts and cultural ceremonies and rituals. If tourists appreciate the cultural heritage of a destination, that appreciation can stimulate the hosts' pride in their heritage and foster local crafts, traditions and customs.

The negative socio-cultural impacts are sometimes the result of *direct* contact and the demonstration effect and these can distort the traditional crafts and customs into shorter, commercialised events that offer the host community little in the way of rich cultural experience. Negative socio-cultural impacts can also be generated if the tourism development is not managed properly and the full economic potential of that development is not realised. For instance, foreign employment in tourism-related jobs and foreign investment in tourism projects both add to the local resentment of tourism development. The exclusion of hosts from certain tourist facilities (such as private beaches, casinos and transport services such as the Sky Train in Bangkok where locals have been excluded by high prices and limited flexibility off the tourism route) will further increase the pressure of resentment and may create conflict between the host population and the tourists.

As with any form of economic development, the new income-earning opportunities created by tourism development are unlikely to be evenly distributed across the destination. This may give rise to some members of the host community feeling resentful and antagonistic towards tourism development. Tourism destinations such as Jamaica in the Caribbean have experienced social problems because tourism development was confined to the north and western coast, although more recently attempts have been made to redress this imbalance. In tourism's favour, it is generally developed in areas where there is little in the way of competing industries (particularly manufacturing); therefore it helps provide employment opportunities in areas where they may be most needed. The creation of job opportunities with higher wage rates than those paid by the more traditional industries of fishing and agriculture can create social pressures between hosts who occupy these posts and their families and peers who do not.

A major problem can also occur because of a real (and sometimes only apparent) difference in wealth between the tourists and their hosts. It is true that there are occasions when the tourists are generally much wealthier than the hosts with whom they come into contact. However, this difference may be exacerbated by the fact that tourists exhibit spending patterns and behaviour that is very different from their norm, simply because they are on vacation. The normal spending habits of tourists is not information readily available to the average host. Furthermore, the difference in wealth between tourist and host may not be as severe a problem as initially perceived given the fact that the vast majority of international tourism takes place between industrialised countries and not between industrialised and developing countries.

When attempting to measure the level of irritation generated by tourist–host contact, Doxey (1975) drew up the following Index:

1. **The level of euphoria** – the initial thrill and enthusiasm that comes along with tourism development results in the fact that the tourist is made welcome.

2. **The level of apathy** – once tourism development is under way and the consequential expansion has taken place, the tourist is taken for granted and is now seen only as a source of profit-taking. What contact is made between host and guest is done on a commercial and formal footing.

3. **The level of irritation** – as the industry approaches saturation point, the hosts can no longer cope with the number of tourists without the provision of additional facilities.

4. **The level of antagonism** – the tourist is now seen as the harbinger of all ills, hosts are openly antagonistic towards tourists and tourists are regarded as being there to be exploited.

5. **The final level** – during the above process of 'development' the host population has forgotten that all they once regarded as being special was exactly the same thing that attracted the tourist, but in the rush to develop tourism circumstances have changed. The social impact has been comprehensive and complete and the tourists will move to different destinations.

Although we have discussed a wide range of approaches to the study of the socio-cultural impact of tourism, there are some very strong common strands. If the typology used by Valene Smith is linked to the host–guest interaction suggested by Doxey, within the framework proposed by Butler and Plog then the commonality can be seen. Figure 9.2 shows each of these theories combined within a two-dimensional frame.

Although Figure 9.2 presents the various approaches within a single framework, the framework is a static one. This means that it is still hampered by the fact that the dynamics of the process are not reflected and thus its practical applicability is severely limited.

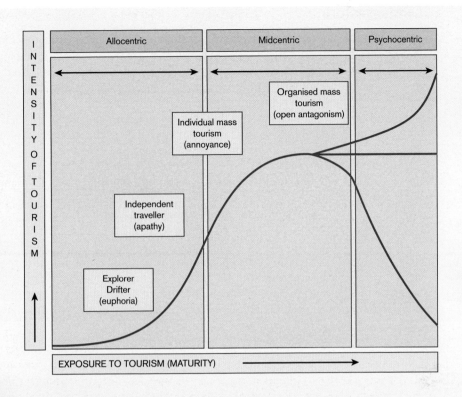

| Figure 9.2 | The approaches to studying the socio-cultural impact of tourism |

# SOME GENERAL NEGATIVE SOCIO-CULTURAL IMPACTS OF TOURISM

There is a wide variety of ways in which the development and operation of tourism can create social tensions and impact on the integrity of the local culture. The most obvious and direct effect is the bringing together of two different cultures and this is an issue that threads its way throughout this chapter. However, the socio-cultural impact of tourism may arise from some general but less obvious factors.

## Economic factors

The majority of tourism activity takes place between the industrialised economies of the world. However, where tourism takes place between the industrialised and the less developed destinations or regions, there can be an enormous imbalance of economic power between the tourists and the hosts. Where tourists are much wealthier than the people with whom they come into contact there is likely to be some attempt at emulation as well as some resentment. This may be reflected in behaviour, dress and spending patterns. Furthermore, where tourism results in the migration of labour from rural to urban areas and attracts workers from the traditional sectors, there could be a growing inequality in the wealth of the local residents as some of them enjoy the higher wages of the tourism sector. This can also lead to social tensions. But it should be borne in mind that the latter channel of economic inequality will be present with any form of economic development.

The tax burden on the local residents may be increased in order to meet the growing demands for better infrastructure (roads, water supply, sewage treatment, etc.). Where tourism drives improved infrastructure without the costs being reflected in the tourism product, there will be growing social tension as residents may struggle to meet the higher tax demands.

## Labour factors

The economic factors demonstrated how tourism can attract workers from other industries. The level of antagonism with respect to tourism can be exacerbated where the employment opportunities for workers within the tourism industry are limited to lower level, front-line workers. In such cases the senior and middle management positions are filled by experienced staff from outside the country (often from the country that has provided either the investment or the tourists). Even where a significant proportion of the managerial staff are locals, their contact with other non-local staff and the tourists may cause a change in their consumption habits so that they have a high propensity to consume imported goods.

Although tourism may be an industry that is associated with higher wages and salaries than the more traditional industries such as farming and fishing, there are many cases where the working conditions are found to be less than desirable. Child labour, casual contracts, part-time jobs with no training are all too common. The International Labour Organization (ILO) estimate that some 10–15% of all employees in the tourism industry are below the age of 18. Children under the age of 12 are frequently employed in developed and developing countries to work in tourism-related businesses. This, again, is not unique to tourism as child labour has always been apparent in the primary sectors (such as agriculture) and manufacturing sectors (such as textiles). Tourism, because of its relatively high use of female labour and also its dependency upon land usage, can bring with it some far-reaching socio-cultural impacts.

## MINI CASE STUDY 9.1
Travel philanthropy on course to benefit Maasai people in Tanzania

### By Apolinari Tairo, eTN, 26 August 2010

TANZANIA (eTN) – Clad in their traditional attire, the Maasai women are found selling beads and locally-made jewelry and bracelets to the tourists camping and visiting in their location within the Loliondo area in northern Tanzania.

Beads, necklaces, and scepters made in different colors, along with bracelets, are the most attractive locally-made jewelry by the Maasai women folks and which most tourists visiting the area want to buy.

The Maasai are the most interesting people in Tanzania because of their lifestyle, which until today has remained intact and unchanged for a number of centuries.

Most of the Maasai people live in Arusha region of northern Tanzania, the area which is the tourist hub in East Africa. But the Maasai beliefs have confined them to cattle-keeping, with less interest in modern lifestyles and education.

Travel philanthropy is currently changing the Maasai life with more benefits from tourist companies, which are operating in the Loliondo area, where a section of companies are running hunting and photographic safaris.

The Enyuata Women's Collaborative is a living example of Maasai women who are going to benefit from travel philanthropy initiatives. From just ten women, the Enyuata Women Group now has more than 100 members who are aiming for the stars. Enyuata Women's Collaborative members are looking to benefit from tourists who pass through their village, Sukenya, heading to Loliondo-based tourist camps. The Maasai women members of Enyuata Collaborative have planned to start a community health initiative in their area soon. Enyuata chairwoman, Nairotiai Parmeres, has been happy to see many more tourists calling at their road-side stalls packed with traditional artifacts.

Unlike most communities in Tanzania, the Maasai people in the Loliondo area live in a harsh environment, sharing the semi-arid land with wild animals, where water, better roads, health services, and schools have been lacking for decades. Only four-wheel tourist and heavy-duty vehicles can enter the Loliondo Maasai area on ground. Most tourists prefer to fly there with light aircraft.

Chairman of the Ngorongoro District Council Mr. Simon Soinda said more tourist companies are greatly needed to help the Maasai people, saying this would make them change from their traditional lifestyle to a modern life. Non-Government Organizations (NGOs) from across the world are being accused of reaping donor money in the name of Maasai communities, with no or little help in changing their lifestyles through provision of modern education and other social services. Those NGOs have been operating within the Maasai communities with little or no changes observed to alleviate the Maasai communities from ignorance and abject poverty.

Over 65,000 animals out of 380,000 cattle in the Ngorongoro District died last year due to a dry spell, which hit a big part of northern Tanzania, said Elias Wawa Lali, the Ngorongoro District Commissioner. This situation caused more sufferings to the Maasai communities whose entire life depends on cattle. Cattle are a symbol of wealth for the Maasai communities, whose modern education and agriculture are a far dream to reach.

Travel philanthropy in the Sukenya village and the rest of the Loliondo area is going to change the current life situation the Maasai people are living with today. Tourists visiting the area have contributed, through their host companies, significant portions of their spending. It is anticipated that Maasai communities will benefit through direct financing from tourists visiting the Sukenya village in the forms of provisions of water; construction of classrooms and teachers' houses; and a subsidy for teachers' salaries.

Despite travel philanthropic support to the Maasai for education, a big challenge remains on how to encourage Maasai parents to relieve their children from caring for the cattle on dry grass pastures in favor of school and learning.

Tanzania Conservation Limited (TCL) has committed a travel philanthropic contribution from 700 tourists who are expected to visit the Sukenya village before the end of this year. If successful, the Maasai communities in the village will reap not less than US$14,000 that will go to the village directly. Each tourist camping with Tanzania Conservation Limited will be encouraged to contribute US$20 to the village. The company, TCL, is currently financing construction of teachers' modern houses at a cost of US$30,000.

Enaboishu Warriors Group, that is made up of 15 Maasai youths, is the other beneficiary of travel philanthropy from TCL. The group members entertain tourists during the evenings, and each member gets a token of US$10 just after a few minutes of traditional performance. A Maasai story-teller is the other beneficiary of travel philanthropy from TCL. She gets a token of US$30 after telling her local Maasai cultural story about wildlife, cattle, or a lifestyle.

Land conflicts between the Maasai communities and wildlife institutions, including the government-controlled wildlife areas, remains at the top of the problems facing the Maasai as they strive to maintain their old cultures, taking cattle as a symbol of wealth and polygamy as a pride.

European-based NGOs are said to be fueling the conflict between the Maasai communities who are herding their livestock in the Ngorongoro Conservation Area, where the attractive Ngorongoro Crater is located.

The fight between the Maasai versus Tanzania government over the land ownership inside Ngorongoro Conservation Area has attracted the Tanzanian president Jakaya Kikwete to direct the Maasai people to look for better and more productive methods in keeping their livestock and to avoid environmental hazards within the rich wildlife Ngorongoro, which has been listed as a World Heritage Site.

*Source*: http://www.eturbonews.com/18140/travel-philanthropy-course-benefit-maasai-people-tanzania (accessed 6 June 2012)

## DISCUSSION QUESTIONS

1. What are the positive and negative aspects involved when translating culture to tourists in the ways that the Maasai are attempting? Draw on your understanding of the different phases of tourism development and tourism typology studies to support your discussion.

2. Would it be better, from a socio-cultural point of view, to isolate tourists from the local population by putting them into private resorts or to integrate them by developing tourism into existing sites?

3. What policies could be implemented to ensure that the Maasai tribe fully benefits from the outcome of the above scheme, what controls would you implement and what indicators would you monitor to ensure that the scheme is working effectively?

## Behavioural and demonstration factors

If the tourists are not aware of, or care for, the local customs they may behave in a way that creates severe social friction between tourists and residents and, ultimately between the residents themselves. The planet is rich in customs and every custom gives the tourist an opportunity to adapt to the local norms or to insult their hosts, often without ever knowing that they have done so. Slurping of soup may be seen as the result of poor table manners in the UK but is an expression of appreciation in China; putting your chopsticks vertically into the bowl of rice in Japan is a symbol of death and is usually only seen in funeral ceremonies; showing the soles of your shoes is considered offensive in a number of countries including Thailand and Iran; inappropriate dress in Muslim countries can cause offence, so too can inappropriate consumption (such as alcohol) or nude sunbathing in countries that may be conservative in this respect.

There are many destinations in the Middle East, the Far East, the Caribbean and the South Pacific that would find the lack of adherence to local social behaviour codes difficult to tolerate. Those that are exposed to such inappropriate behaviour or dress codes may find that, over time, they come to accept them and even emulate such behaviour, causing tension between the residents.

## Resource use factors

A great deal of tourism is concerned with real estate development and this places high demands on land use. These demands compete with alternative local use and often result in land price inflation. Where land price inflation occurs it can create social tensions as local residents are priced out of the market for local houses and apartments.

Environmental and cultural damage resulting from tourism can lead to significant social tensions. This is a common problem in areas where there are heritage sites and examples can be found in places like Paphos, where there was open pilfering by the tourists and residents from the site of the Byzantium Fort. It is not only the man-made heritage that is being stolen; precious and irreplaceable fossils in areas such as the Petrified Forest of Arizona are also subject to looting by smugglers and tourists. Similarly, where the social tensions increase there can be vandalism and wilful damage to heritage sites.

Competition between locals and tourist businesses for local resources is commonplace, such as the use of a beach or mountain area. The economics of the situation gives the tourist businesses the upper hand in such competitions and the locals often find that their use of the facilities are removed or downgraded.

# SOME SPECIFIC NEGATIVE SOCIO-CULTURAL IMPACTS OF TOURISM

## Sex

The fact that tourists will travel abroad to enjoy uninhibited casual sexual encounters is not a new phenomenon. Sexual exploitation has grown as rapidly as tourism in many destinations. The early European tourists were to some extent motivated by the liberal attitude towards sex in some of the Third World countries they visited. More recently, a major tourism market has grown up around **sex tourism** and destinations such as Thailand, Gambia and some of the Central European countries have actively marketed the sexual content of their products. The proliferation of **AIDS** has done much to dampen the rapid growth of this element of the tourism industry but it is still a significant part of the market. It is questionable whether tourism created the social disruption associated with the sex trade or whether the sex trade has stimulated the tourism market. But, as with all forms of prostitution, it is impossible to be conclusive as to the rights and wrongs of either party. Certainly the growth of paedophile activity is one element of the tourist industry that is outlawed in many tourist-generating countries and can only be pursued under the guise of international tourism. The United Nations defines sex tourism relating to children to be 'tourism organised with the primary purpose of facilitating the effecting of a commercial sexual relationship with a child'. The growth of such activities is often supported by a network of facilitators ranging from pimps and brothels through to the seemingly more respectable taxi drivers and hotel workers. The Internet has only added to the problem by creating an international communication network that can market these services on an international scale. So prolific is this problem that agencies such as ECPAT have been set up to campaign against child prostitution. The acronym stands for 'End Child Prostitution, Child Pornography and Trafficking of Children for Sexual Purposes'.

Sex tourism is prolific in many destinations and covers all permutations from males seeking females, females in search of males, same-sex encounters and even catering for those in search of group sex or those trying to fulfil fetish desires of some sort or other. All forms of sex tourism carry with them dangers not only to the participants but also to the destinations and tourist-originating communities as a whole.

Given the current world where AIDS and other sexually transmitted diseases are prevalent one would have thought that the development of the tourism based on offering sexual activities would have been in decline. However, many tourists, particularly those from industrialised countries, may expect to relax their sexual morals during a vacation and this can lead to a thin line being drawn between destinations that are primarily trading on sex and those that offer an environment wherein tourists can relax their sexual morals. Certainly there seems to be no limit in the imagination or permutations of sexual offerings associated in some tourism destinations. Furthermore, sex tourism is often linked with organised crime, making destinations that use sex as a tourist attraction vulnerable to a wide range of serious consequences.

## Crime

The link between tourism and crime is hard to establish. Many writers, such as Mathieson and Wall (1982), have suggested the link but find it hard to establish whether crime increases simply because of the increased population density (urbanisation) or whether it is more specifically associated with tourism. Clearly the presence of large numbers of tourists carrying relatively large sums of money and valuables with them provides a source for illegal activities including drugs trafficking, robbery and violence. Brazil, Florida and Jamaica are just three of the many destinations that have been the subject of international press coverage because of acts of violent crimes against tourists. Tourists are sometimes obvious victims of crime where they are clearly identifiable by language or colour and can be expected to be carrying significant sums of money with them.

Tourism is often the catalyst for the growth of gaming activities and a number of destinations have used casino developments as a means of attracting tourist spending. Unless properly monitored and controlled, such developments can induce social behaviour that is detrimental to social cohesion.

Where hotels attempt to protect their guests by the use of armed agents this can often inflame the social tension between tourists and local residents.

## Health

The problem of AIDS has already been mentioned. However, there are other less newsworthy diseases that can be transmitted when people from different communities interact, such as the recording of more than 8,500 cases of malaria in the UK largely through tourists and **VFR** traffic. Although often not fatal, these illnesses can cause social and economic stress to the host population who may have less immunity to the diseases than the tourist population. Where tourism growth is rapid and unplanned there can be infrastructure failures that lead to health hazards. Tourism activity can also be suddenly curtailed by outbreaks of health scares such as those related to SARS, Avian Flu, Swine Flu and Foot and Mouth Disease. The media are highly influential in the way that tourists and tour operators respond to outbreaks of disease, for instance during the outbreak of SARS (2002/3) the media created an image of an outbreak of pandemic proportions and some destinations, such as Malaysia, suffered severely even though they did not have a single registered case of SARS. In the UK, during an outbreak of Foot and Mouth Disease (2001), the image of the UK was severely damaged by pictures and videos of mountains of sheep and cattle carcasses being burned in an attempt to curtail the spread of the disease which closed off large swathes of the British countryside. Although agriculture was compensated to some degree by the government for its losses, the same was not true for tourism where many businesses fell victim to the closure of the countryside.

## Slum tourism

Slum tourism, where relatively wealthy tourists visit areas of extreme poverty is not a new phenomenon and was something that was practised back in Victorian England and subsequently in the USA, when wealthy people visited some of the deprived areas of London or Manhattan to see how poor people lived. Organised tours to slums, Favelas or Townships are now given greater publicity, with some notable destinations such as those found in India, Brazil and South Africa. This type of tourism raises some moral and ethical questions regarding the 'zooism' aspects of visitors going to observe people living in squalid conditions. However, if operated ethically, such forms of tourism can generate income and employment opportunities to those living under conditions of extreme poverty and can act as a catalyst to further development. Again the impact of tourism can be on the visitors as well as the hosts, and visits to areas of extreme poverty and deprivation can change the attitudes and behaviour of the relatively wealthy visitors towards poor people.

## Dark tourism

Dark or 'Thanotourism' refers to the more macabre side of the tourism industry where tourists visit sites where shocking events have occurred. It covers a spectrum of darkness in that some events can be very distant, such as the eruption of Mt. Vesuvius in AD 79 which destroyed Pompeii which has been a major tourist attraction for more than 200 years. Tourists can go and visit the area and not only see some of the buildings that were excavated, but also see representations of figures of people who died in excruciating circumstances. In contrast to this, the site of the Twin Towers in New York City (Ground Zero) went from being a site of mass death in September 2001 to being a major tourist attraction with over 3 million visitors in 2002. Sites such as Auschwitz, where over a million Jews or 'enemies of the state' were transported, or as small as a quiet village in England (Soham), where two schoolgirls were murdered, attract tourists in their thousands. There are clearly issues relating to the moral and ethical underpinning of such forms of tourism and where the line is drawn between what is human curiosity and what is exploitation. (Issues relating to dark tourism are discussed in greater detail in Chapter 12.)

## Other aspects

Following the lead of Cohen (1988), it is possible to categorise the key themes that characterise the interface between culture and tourism. There are a variety of ways in which such categories can be constructed but the following issues reflect the major concerns that are currently being debated:

- **Commodification** – where the demands of tourism lead to the mutation and sometimes destruction of the meaning of cultural performances and events. Tourists are likely to have different time-frames and expectations from local residents and this may result in religious rituals and traditional ethnic customs and rites being changed to suit the needs and wishes of tourists. This process is sometimes referred to as reconstructed ethnicity.

- **Staged authenticity** – where 'pseudo-events' are presented to satisfy tourists' needs for new (simulated) experiences, such as the Fijian firewalkers (see below).

- **Standardisation** – where the tourists' search for the familiar leads to a loss of cultural diversity.

- **Alien cultural experiences of tourists** – which examines the apparent inability to enjoy meaningful cultural experiences without travelling to different environments.

## Commodification

Commodification is a long-standing criticism relating to tourism's effect on culture and art. Crafts, ceremonies and rituals are often driven into an exploitation stance, abbreviated, made more colourful, more dramatic and spectacular in order to capture the attention and imagination of an audience that often does not possess the underlying knowledge/experience that would make the unadapted version appealing. Countless examples can and have been cited, from the sale of concrete paving slabs with carvings of Bob Marley on them in Jamaica, the *Bula Fiji* carved wooden knives and clubs, to the Polynesian dances of Western Samoa and the limbo dancers of the Caribbean. Where culture becomes a commodity for financial transactions it is difficult to be objective. Although it is true that the demands of people from alien cultures who are operating on a very tight and sometimes fixed time budget are very different from the local demands, it is sometimes this foreign demand that enriches and/or preserves decaying and dying skills and performances.

## Staged authenticity

With growing public awareness regarding cultural and ethnic differences there has been increasing demand for tourism products that offer cultural authenticity, that is, environments where the tourists can 'get behind the scenes' to meet and observe the real people. Although, in the Plog sense, this may be considered a great leap forward in perception and understanding by volume tourists and a movement back from the psychocentric scale of the tourist market, it can also be regarded as being a signal for impending cultural devastation for some destinations. This represents the social impact dilemma of post-1980 tourism development.

In order to differentiate their product from other tourism products on the market destinations have highlighted environmental, climatic and cultural differences. In this last instance, they are using their cultural heritage as a promotional device to attract increasing numbers of tourists. Although this may be considered to be a positive step in achieving greater awareness concerning cultural differences and, perhaps, a greater empathy between tourist and host, it also exposes a deeper layer of the sociological structure and thereby risks further 'contamination'.

However, there are ways of differentiating the tourism product, providing tourists with sufficient cultural exposure to satisfy their demands while preserving the true cultural identity of the host population. One such way is the use of staged authenticity whereby the host population provides a more realistic performance of cultural heritage than existed before, but still ensures that the tourists do not manage to penetrate behind the stage curtains. Figure 9.3 demonstrates the concept and dangers of staged authenticity.

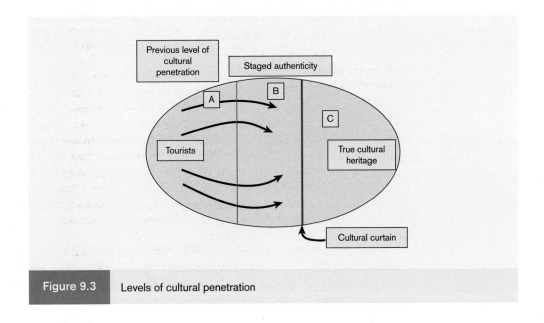

**Figure 9.3**   Levels of cultural penetration

In Figure 9.3 the arena is divided into three distinct areas:

**A** – the previous level of tourist penetration into the host culture;

**B** – the new level of cultural penetration that is considered to be authentic by the tourist but is, in fact, staged authenticity; and

**C** – the true cultural heritage of the host society that maintains its integrity by keeping tourists on the other side of the firewall curtain.

Although effective in the short term, this approach to cultural impact containment can lead to increasing levels of penetration when the firewall curtains are continually retreating in order to provide greater tourist experiences and diversity within a competitive market. Even if the social firewall does not retreat there is a danger that some of the tourists will manage to penetrate beyond the curtain. Eventually there will be nowhere for the host population to maintain the integrity of their culture. There is an additional danger in the form of a *gradual* cultural impact. The very act of staging the authenticity of the culture can blur the true boundaries of the local heritage and, in so doing, distort the cultural heritage that is being maintained behind the firewall curtain.

It has also been argued that the so-called authenticity of culture is a fleeting moment in the development calendar. Culture is a dynamic living concept and changes continually in order to capture and embrace the needs of society in the present time period. From this point of view culture continually runs through a process of being invented and reinvented and so, in this sense, all of culture can be defined as staged authenticity.

An example of the dynamics of cultural performances can be seen in the Fijian firewalkers. Like the limbo dancers of the Caribbean, the firewalkers of Fiji are, today, almost exclusively found in cultural centres or hotels. In fact, they can be found wherever tourists are willing to exchange money for the privilege of watching these ancient customs that are packaged and transformed into dinner-side entertainment.

The Fijians who perform the ritual known as *Vilavilairevo* (which translates literally as 'jumping into the oven') accept that the walking across the heated stones of a *lovo* (earth oven) is now a commercial event. It is rarely performed as a sign of respect for powerful and important visitors and never as a commemorative ritual to celebrate (and test the legend of) *Tui Qualita*. Nor does it any longer signify the conquering of the *lovo* in which a defeated warrior may be buried and baked. The tourists who visit Fiji often have no prior information about the origin of this particular form of firewalking but it does little to detract from the spectacular and impressive displays. The fact that the tourists, in spite of any narrative that may accompany the firewalking events, are unaware of the true meaning and significance of the ritual does not mean that tourism's mutation of the custom has created a gulf between host and visitor. That gulf existed prior to the performance and may well be one of the reasons why the tourist chose that destination. The commercialisation of the event in itself is also not wholly bad in that it generates much-needed currency for communities and, given its redundancy as part of modern-day Fijian culture, preserves a custom and instils pride in the history and culture of the Fiji people.

## Standardisation

Tourists, although they may search for unfamiliar environments and cultures, often search for familiar facilities. Examples such as McDonald's demonstrate this effect quite clearly. This introduces a number of factors into the development scenario. First, there is the development of superstructure that might be quite different from that normally found in the local environment. Secondly, the operation of those facilities may introduce work practices and systems that are different from those normally found in the local economy, particularly their employment structures and conditions as well as their purchasing strategies. Finally, by building familiar structures within unfamiliar environments there is a loss of diversity that is as real to the socio-cultural environment as the loss of a species may be to biodiversity. This issue becomes more problematic as you move into the high-volume tourist markets where destinations must not appear too strange if they wish to capture large segments of the market.

| Photograph 9.2 | Firewalking for tourists in Fiji. |
| --- | --- |
| | *Source*: Danita Delimont Creative/Alamy Images |

### Alien cultural experiences of tourists

This issue revolves around the apparent inability of tourists to take part in or enjoy meaningful cultural experiences within their home environment. As with many of the aspects that underlie the motivation of tourists, it is not so much the inability of tourists to enjoy meaningful cultural experiences within their home environment – indeed many do so without even recognising the fact – it is more the reflection that tourists search for different – or *alien* – experiences. The desire to experience different climatic conditions (sun, rain or snow) and different environmental surroundings (deserts, rainforests, cities or rolling green fields) is willingly accepted. Therefore, it is not an absurd proposition to suggest that tourists may actively seek out cultural experiences that are deliberately different from their norm – indeed such motivation is becoming an increasingly important aspect of twenty-first-century tourism.

## SOME GENERAL POSITIVE SOCIO-CULTURAL IMPACTS ASSOCIATED WITH TOURISM

### Tourism fosters local pride

Tourism can inspire pride in a destination's heritage. Often we forget the value of the things that surround us and only when seen through the eyes of tourists do we revalue our culture. Ceremonies and rituals become jaded over time and can lose their appeal to local residents. Tourism can put new life into such ceremonies and make them come alive once more. The same is true regarding old skills and crafts that, without tourism, may have ceased to exist in a modern world where they lose relevance. Of course, it can be argued that if these skills or crafts were past their sell-by date and would have ceased to exist then they should be allowed to have a peaceful natural death and not be preserved as something that is 'quaint' for the sake of tourism.

## Tourism for socio-cultural awareness and peace

Tourism takes people to new places and broadens their understanding and knowledge of other cultures and environments. This is an educational process and is an important part of the industry. If channelled properly this education can lead to a greater awareness, sympathy and admiration for other societies. This cultural exchange that takes place between tourists and local residents can help foster peace between communities. So strong is the belief in the relationship between tourism and peace that in 1986 the International Institute for Peace through Tourism (IIPT) was set up. The IIPT has organised several conferences since its inception and in November 2000 made the Amman Declaration that set out the fundamental objectives of the IIPT and those that were aligned to the movement. This was ratified by more than 450 delegates from 60 countries and included the chief executive officers of 22 major international tourism corporations. The Amman Declaration was a far-reaching document that attempts to incorporate socio-cultural, environmental and economic objectives under a single banner.

## Tourism provides shared infrastructure

When tourism is developed in a destination the local infrastructure is often enhanced to meet the needs of this development. The local community can find that the quality of their life is significantly enhanced through being able to enjoy this improved infrastructure. This can be as simple as the increased health afforded by improved water supply and sewage treatment to the more complex issues surrounding the provision of an airport and access to regular international flights. New sporting venues, entertainment facilities, restaurants and a better range of food and beverages available for consumption are just some of the many positive side effects that tourism can create for the local population.

## Tourism can provide direct socio-cultural support

The tourism industry can provide much-needed funds to help restore heritage sites or conserve natural and cultural sites. Examples of such good practice can be found on the Tour Operators Initiative website (**http://www.toinitiative.org/index.php?id=48**). They include examples such as the Travel Walji's case, where the company is not only providing direct financial support to conservation in the Karakorum region of South Asia but is also providing indirect support to the area through its tourism development aid.

Tourism can yield enormous socio-cultural benefits as well as devastating costs. The net effect depends upon the responsibility exercised by the various stakeholders of the industry, including the public and private sectors as well as the tourists and residents. To be able to evaluate the net socio-cultural benefits of tourism it is necessary to be able to measure the benefits and costs in an objective and acceptable framework.

# METHODS OF MEASURING THE SOCIO-CULTURAL IMPACT OF TOURISM

## Data collection

The socio-cultural factors influenced by tourist activities are, in general, the most difficult ones to measure and quantify. Whereas the economic and many of the environmental indicators do lend themselves to objective measurement, the socio-cultural impacts are often highly qualitative and subjective in nature. The nature of socio-cultural impacts can range from those impacts that are obvious and measurable, such as the outbreak of particular types of disease and/or infection, to those that are hard to identify and measure such as changes in customs and codes of conduct. On the other hand, there are those impacts that may be identifiable, such as increased crime rates, drug abuse and prostitution, but are difficult to attribute to tourism rather than to other factors of influence (such as media intrusion).

There is a wide range of data sources that may be utilised in order to examine the social impact of tourism. It is important to recognise that some of these data may not be exclusively related to tourism activity. Where causes of variable changes are multivariate then deeper analysis must be undertaken in order to filter out other influences. Complete filtering is unlikely to be possible.

Data collection sources can be categorised into primary and secondary. Primary data can be collected by undertaking household and visitor surveys. This method of data collection is time-consuming and costly. It is also sometimes difficult to maintain the appropriate level of objectivity and the resident awareness questionnaires require very careful construction if they are to provide data that are both unbiased and in a form that is user-friendly. Other forms of primary data collection include the interviewing of **focus groups, key informants, Delphi analyses** and participant observation. Table 9.2 distinguishes between interview/questionnaire/Delphi approaches and those that use observation techniques.

**Table 9.2** Data from different sources

| Indicators (changes in) | Primary data | | Secondary data | |
|---|---|---|---|---|
| | Survey | Observe | Data | Media |
| Crime rates/levels | × | | × | × |
| Prostitution | | × | × | × |
| Drug abuse | × | | × | × |
| Promiscuity | × | × | × | × |
| Gambling | × | | × | × |
| Family relationships | × | | × | × |
| Social values | × | × | × | × |
| Creative expressions | × | × | | × |
| Traditional ceremonies | × | × | | × |
| Safety levels | × | | × | |
| Health | × | | × | |
| Community organisations | × | | × | × |
| Infrastructure | × | × | × | × |
| Collective lifestyles | × | × | | × |
| Economic independence | × | | × | × |
| Population dispersion | × | | × | |
| Cultural commercialisation | × | × | × | × |
| Host/tourist hostility | × | | × | × |
| Demonstration effects | × | × | | |
| Economic and social dualism | × | | × | × |
| Psychological stress | × | | × | × |
| Living standards | × | | × | × |

There are a variety of secondary sources for gathering information with respect to socio-cultural impacts. These include criminal activity statistics, notification of infectious diseases statistics, employment and unemployment data, newspaper reports/articles and other media coverage. Some of these data are quantitative in nature whereas others are quite subjective and care must be taken in the interpretation. Table 9.2 distinguishes between those data that are collected, assimilated and tabulated for other purposes, and information (largely qualitative) that can be gleaned from scanning past and present newspaper cuttings, television and radio news and documentary programmes and other media forms of covering current affairs.

The two fundamental means of assessing socio-cultural impacts in a destination are by surveying both tourists and local residents. There are several factors that should be taken into account when undertaking a local resident survey.

First, it is important, as with all sampling procedures, to obtain a representative sample of the population. This may seem obvious, but several social impact studies have relied entirely upon random sampling of the immediate population (those directly in the vicinity of the tourist facilities). In order to gauge the true impact and its level of penetration it is important that the survey population is seen as being wider than this. Secondly, it is important to establish whether or not the respondent correctly identifies who is a tourist. The misperception as to what constitutes a tourist can render local resident surveys misleading. Thirdly, in areas subject to seasonality, it is also important to undertake the survey at different times of the year. Quite often a good indicator of the magnitude of the social impact of tourism is how quickly the levels of awareness, resentment and other characteristics decline once the peak season recedes. Where there is a significant level of decline shortly after the peak season one can assume that the impacts, although severe during the peak period, are not too deeply embedded in the local population. Where remedial action is required in visitor management flows or **infrastructural investment**, there is every chance that these actions will be successful. If the levels of resentment continue to run high during the off-peak periods then there is a distinct possibility that any remedial action will need to be fundamental, even to the point of reducing the peak levels of tourism flows.

In order to complement the work that has already been undertaken in the field of economic and environmental impacts and to provide a common framework for the analysis of socio-cultural impacts, researchers at Bournemouth University have attempted to embed the process of socio-cultural impacts within the economic and environmental model structure. The inclusion of socio-cultural impacts within such a model allows for the direct, indirect and induced impacts to be considered as well as providing a vehicle for the study of social and cultural changes as a result of other (non-tourism-related) factors.

At this point in time the number of socio-cultural variables that can be included at such a detailed and quantifiable level are limited but include indicators such as:

- the ratio of tourists to host population;
- the number of contacts between hosts and guests for transactions;
- the number of contacts between hosts and guests while sharing facilities;
- the number of contacts between hosts and guests for socio-cultural purposes;
- differences between host and guest age distributions;
- percentage of local population coming into contact with tourists;
- percentage of population working in tourism-related industries weighted by indirect and induced employment;
- tourist/host clustering; and
- the nature of tourism.

The above data should be collected and analysed at relatively frequent intervals. Some of these data are readily available in most countries and systems can be put into place to show those ratios on a weekly or monthly basis. Others are more difficult to acquire and may only be available at discrete time intervals.

## CONCLUSION

This chapter has examined the nature and determinants of the socio-cultural impacts associated with tourism development. In so doing, the nature of the tourism development process has been explored together with the influence of socio-economic factors in driving the development of tourism. The typological studies undertaken by researchers such as Smith and Plog have provided a framework which facilitates the further development of socio-cultural impact methodologies and that framework can be used to show the commonalities of the models suggested by Butler and Doxey. But, it was noted, this framework is static and is severely limited by the nature of the variables used. The development of tourism can have specific implications for incidents of crime and health, as well as influencing the individual and collective lifestyles of the local population. It was also noted that there are positive aspects to tourism's socio-cultural impacts and that these should not be neglected when evaluating the performance of tourism in a given destination. It is also important to recognise the fact that tourists can also transmit socio-cultural impacts back to the populations of the originating countries.

The problems associated with measuring either the desirability of preserving the cultural heritage of a destination or determining how this is influenced by the presence of tourists make it a difficult area of research. The staged authenticity approach to tourism development can provide a firewall in order to maintain the integrity of the local cultural heritage. However, staged authenticity can also act as a catalyst for further cultural penetration and form the 'thin end of the wedge' for further intrusion.

There are data available that can be used to analyse the magnitude and direction of socio-cultural impacts and these were examined in order to suggest a framework for an integrated tourism impact model.

## SELF-CHECK QUESTIONS

1. What are the major approaches to studying the socio-cultural impacts of tourism?

2. What models have been put forward to explain the development of tourism and its impact on the local population?

3. What are the main socio-cultural dangers associated with using sex tourism or gambling as platforms for tourism development?

4. Identify three direct positive socio-cultural impacts of tourism and three indirect negative socio-cultural impacts of tourism.

5. What are the major difficulties involved in measuring the socio-cultural impacts of tourism and what sources of data are available?

## YOUTUBE

### Cultural impacts

Cornwall: The Impact of Tourism. Three separate identities speak about how tourism affects their profession, and how they feel about being a fish in an ocean of travellers.
**http://www.youtube.com/watch?v=KPIGqCJWXpk**

'Death in Venice: is tourism killing or saving the city?'
**http://www.youtube.com/watch?v=XJeKs2dUxD4**

Alex Saragoza – Tourist or Traveler? The Impact of Tourism in Mexico and Cuba
**http://www.youtube.com/watch?v=l9ivZdC-P3I**

# REFERENCES AND FURTHER READING

Butler, R.W. (1980) 'The concept of a tourist area cycle of evolution: implications for management of resources', *Canadian Geographer* **24**(1), 5–12.

Cohen, E. (1984) 'The sociology of tourism: approaches, issues and findings', *Annual Review of Sociology* **10**, 373–92.

Cohen, E. (1988) 'Authenticity and commoditization in tourism', *Annals of Tourism Research* **15**, 371–86.

Deery, M. Jaogo, L., and Fredline, L. (2012) 'Rethinking social impacts of tourism research: A new research agenda', *Tourism Management*, **33**(1), 64–73.

De Kadt, E. (ed.) (1979) *Tourism: Passport to Development?*, Oxford University Press, New York.

Doxey, G.V. (1975) 'When enough's enough: the natives are restless in Old Niagara', *Heritage Canada* **2**(2), 26–7.

Gill, A. and Williams, P. (1994) 'Managing growth in mountain tourism communities', *Tourism Management* **15**(3), 212–20.

Inskeep, E. (1991) *Tourism Planning: An Integrated and Sustainable Development Approach*, Van Nostrand Reinhold, New York.

Jafari, J. (1987) 'Tourism models: the sociocultural aspects', *Tourism Management*, **8**(2), 151–9.

Mathieson, A. and Wall, G. (1982) *Tourism: Economic, Physical and Social Impacts*, Longman, Harlow.

Murphy, P.E. (1985) *Tourism: A Community Approach*, Methuen, New York.

Plog, S.C. (1977) 'Why destination areas rise and fall in popularity', in Kelly, E.M. (ed.) *Domestic and International Tourism*, Institute of Certified Travel Agents, Wellesley, MA.

Plog, S.C. (2004) *Leisure Travel: A Marketing Handbook*, Pearson Prentice Hall, Upper Saddle River, NJ.

Price, M.F. (1992) 'Patterns of the development of tourism in mountain environments', *Geojournal* **27**(1), 87–96.

Smith, V.L. (1989) *Hosts and Guests: The Anthropology of Tourism*, 2nd edn, University of Pennsylvania Press, Philadelphia.

Stokowski, P.A. (1996) *Riches and Regrets: Betting on Gambling in Two Colorado Mountain Towns*, University Press of Colorado, Niwot.

Stokowski, P.A. (2000) 'Assessing social impacts of resource-based recreation and tourism', pp. 265–74, in Gartner, W.C. and Lime, D.W. (eds), *Trends in Outdoor Recreation, Leisure and Tourism*, CABI, Wallingford.

Stymeist, D.H. (1996) 'Transformation of Vilavilairevo in tourism', *Annals of Tourism Research* **23**(1), pp. 1–18.

## MAJOR CASE STUDY 9.1
### Tourists behaving badly

## TOURISTS FOR BETTER OR WORSE?

Destinations want tourists! Most want tourists to come to their destination and to spend their money so that they earn income, foreign exchange and create employment opportunities. But all tourists are not the same either from an economic or a socio-cultural point of view. There have been many articles in the media about tourists' bad behaviour over the years. So who are the worst tourists to invite to your destination? The short answer is 'it depends who you ask!'.

According to regular polls undertaken at sites such as the one run by Expedia, the French do quite well at being voted the world's worst tourists, largely because of behaviour such as poor tipping, impoliteness and unwillingness to attempt to speak the local language. According to a report in *Time* (http://www.time.com/time/world/article/0,8599,1909526,00.html) the French did not even manage to come in the top two for being best dressed, having lost out to the Italians and their runners up, the British, which must raise some eyebrows somewhere and perhaps raises question marks about the methodology used to come up with these results!

According to an article which appeared in the *Daily Mail* (http://www.dailymail.co.uk/news/article-1209411/ Russians-snatch-worst-tourists-crown-Germans– hiding-sunloungers-ROOMS.html) it's not the French who top the list as the world's worst tourists, it is the Russians who head up the leader board for being the most rude tourists, a mantle often worn by the Germans (according to the British). For many years now the British have complained about German tourists putting their towels on sunbeds/loungers even before dawn has arrived in order to reserve them, but apparently, according to this article, the Russians take the process several notches further by taking the sun loungers to their rooms overnight! But the Russians were not voted first simply for their sun lounger antics, they were also deemed to be without any fashion sense, to eat most of the food in all-inclusive venues (even stocking up bags to take food away), to possess poor table manners and to be rude to staff at hotels and in restaurants.

A poll undertaken by LivingSocial (http://corporate. livingsocial.com/inthenews/articles/174) across five countries, claims that even the Americans themselves think that Americans make the worst tourists, followed by the Chinese and then the French. However, when they asked the Irish, the response was that the British make the worst tourists, and when British are asked they argue that the Germans are the worst tourists. There is clearly a lot of political bias and stereotyping going on in all of these polls.

Given the issues relating to the behaviour of tourists and the impact that this has not only on the image of the country of origin but also on the culture of the hosting community, China has made explicit efforts to create 'better tourists' – see the following case study.

## CHINA'S CAMPAIGN FOR CIVILIZED TOURISM: WHAT TO DO WHEN TOURISTS BEHAVE BADLY

Jenny Chio, Emory University

In October 2006, a campaign for civilized tourism (*wenming lüyou*) was formally inaugurated by the China Central Spiritual Civilization Steering Committee, the central state body devoted to the regulation, promotion and creation of well-behaved, well-regarded Chinese people. Two sets of rules were issued: one for Chinese traveling overseas and one for Chinese traveling within the country. This campaign was a large-scale, nationally publicized effort centered around rules for Chinese tourist behavior abroad and domestically and intended as part of broader 'civilized behavior' improvement programs developed prior to the 2008 Beijing Olympics. Nevertheless, the impetus for creating guidelines for tourists was also rooted in the increasing number of reports of 'bad behavior' committed by Chinese tourists overseas from years prior (see the chapter by Pál Nyíri in the 2009 volume, *Asia on Tour*, edited by Tim Winter, Peggy Teo and T.C. Chang, as well as Nyíri 2010, *Mobility and Cultural Authority in Contemporary China*).

Official tourism statistics from 2000 onward attest to huge surges in the numbers of Chinese tourists traveling both internationally and domestically, with figures now indicating that on average (though certainly not in practice) there are 1.5 tourist trips taken per year per person in the country. Yet while travel is considered to inculcate desirable benefits for the development of modern Chinese individuals, the emergence in the 2000s of stories of the badly behaved Chinese tourists abroad put a damper on this upbeat association between travel, individual quality and national character. Most recently in May 2010, a German newspaper reported acts of bullying and name-calling by Chinese tourists trying to enter the German Pavilion at the 2010 Shanghai Expo (*Sueddeutsche Zeitung*, May 18, 2010).

### Civilizing the tourist

The China Central Spiritual Civilization Steering Committee took the matter of unattractive tourist behavior seriously in 2006, issuing a document in August titled 'Plans for Raising the Civilized Quality of Chinese Tourists.' Furthermore, the Spiritual Civilization Steering Committee and the National Tourism Administration jointly issued a call for stories and submissions on 'uncivilized tourist behavior' and 'suggestions for quality tourist behavior.' By September, they reported having received over 30,000 entries and three million hits (Zhongguo Wenming Wang 2006). The Central Spiritual Civilization Committee published the top 10 bad behaviors of Chinese tourists abroad, the top 10 bad behaviors of domestic Chinese tourists, and a list of 20 suggestions for raising the civilized quality of tourists on September 20, 2006 (www.godpp.gov.cn). At the top of the list for bad habits was spitting and littering (directed at Chinese tourists going both abroad and domestically), and the number-one piece of advice for tourists was to pay more attention to media reports on what constituted ideal, good behavior.

Indeed, national media sources have been central to the campaign, both in terms of broadcasting official policies and in promoting, or pointing a finger at, certain behaviors. An article from the *Beijing Youth Daily* newspaper, published in September 2006, ran the headline 'How Do Foreigners See Chinese Tourists?' and recounted the unbecoming antics by Chinese tourists as reported in Thai, Malaysian, and US media outlets (Zhongguo Wenming Wang 2006). Photographs of tourists behaving inappropriately were posted online, captioned with statements such as 'Although China's tourism industry is developing, the teaching of civilized tourism is still deficient' (**www.chinanews.com**, October 2, 2006).

Thus, amid much official publicity and attention from both domestic and international news outlets, the guidelines for tourist behavior were published online and in print as booklets and posters on October 2, 2006, during the National Day Golden Week Holiday. Separate guidelines were issued for Chinese tourists traveling internationally and domestic Chinese tourists (available at **www.wenming.cn**). Travel agencies were responsible for giving each of their tourists a guidebook prior to commencing a tour, and posters with the guidelines were displayed in airports, airline ticketing offices and other relevant travel industry locations.

According to the guidelines, improving one's civilized qualities required only small changes to everyday behaviors; among other regulations, out-bound Chinese tourists were reminded to 'be polite and respectful,' 'wear appropriate clothes and don't spit,' 'let women and the elderly go first,' and to 'be quiet while eating' (Zhongguo Wenming Wang 2006). For domestic tourists, the guidelines included an emphasis on environmental protection and admonishments against littering and spitting, as well as reminders to protect ancient heritage objects, to respect religious traditions and not to insist on taking pictures with foreign tourists. According to an article in the New Capital Newspaper (Xin Jing Bao), tourism, and by extension the quality (suzhi) of Chinese tourists, was a matter of image management and symbolized the quality of both individuals and the nation as a whole. Thus, only when domestic tourists were civilized would outbound tourists also be civilized (Xin Jing Bao 2006).

These regulatory mechanisms of Chinese tourist behavior illuminate how ideas of national character and individual development are bound up in the moral discourses of tourism and travel as a means of governance, not only socially but also politically in terms of China's relationships with other nations. But, according to Chinese blogger Wu Fei, 'the "poor overseas image" [of Chinese tourists] comes about because there has been no move to cultivate a good domestic image. . . . So to change the image of Chinese people abroad is not merely a matter that can be handled by passing out "Notes for Going Abroad" to international tourists' (translated version at **www.danwei.org**). Wu points out the additional, rather obvious, fact that the Chinese who can afford to travel abroad, and whose behaviors are thus at the source of the poor image of Chinese tourists overseas, are the wealthy and, more often than not, the urban – not the rural peasants or domestic migrant workers who are frequently targeted as 'lacking quality' in national discourses of population quality (themes also explored in a recent volume of the journal positions: east asia cultural critique 17[3]).

## The underbelly of mobility

It could be argued, then, that raising the quality of China's rural, increasingly mobile socio-economic under class is the key to improving on future Chinese tourists – domestic or international. With the right amount of guidance and economic development, these 'low quality' populations might eventually become wealthy enough to travel and, by that time, they would also be socialized into being good tourists. After all, national level attention to tourist behaviors in 2006 coincided with renewed efforts to promote tourism as a part of rural development. The joint proclamation of 2006 as the Year of Rural Tourism and the beginning of the national campaign to 'Build a New Socialist Countryside' aimed at not only increasing rural incomes but also improving the social character of rural people.

While not an entirely new idea, this emphasis on rural development-cum-tourism brought with it new slogans, new declarations and new policy statements. The Year of Rural Tourism was to bring forth, according to its slogan, 'New Villages, New Tourism, New Experiences, New Customs.' According to numerous Chinese reports and scholarly articles, rural tourism was a part of the longer challenge and struggle to build a New Socialist Countryside. However, these rural development programs in 2006 were premised on the expectation that rural people themselves would not travel, at least for the time being; they could better their economic and social conditions by staying put and being visited by presumably higher quality, urban tourists.

The campaign to improve Chinese tourist behaviors at home and abroad thus points toward the underbelly of mobility in contemporary China – the implicit moral distinctions between who should travel and who should not, and what is appropriate behavior toward one's fellow countrymen and countrywomen or toward utterly foreign others. Regulating tourist behavior, at home or abroad, shifts the focus of human movement away from earlier concerns over if people move and toward the broader, less concrete matter of how people are mobile. To consider mobility as morally charged is to acknowledge that the ways in which human mobilities emerge and exist hold consequences that extend beyond the economic or strictly functional. The guidelines for tourists were in equal parts an attempt to shape individual behaviors and a projection of moral values for a mainstream, Chinese leisure class that would represent all of China to the world through its mobility as tourists.

The governance of Chinese tourists underscores the centrality of mobility as a key social analytic in experiences of modernity in China today, where tourism becomes a justification for social engineering. Through public 'shaming' vis-à-vis an online competition for the worst cases of tourist behavior and rolling out blanket guidelines to be enforced by profit-driven operators within the tourism industry itself, China's campaign for civilized tourism illuminates how the politics of difference are unavoidably entangled in the morality of mobility. Tourists are not exempt from these debates, and the guidelines for tourist behavior issued by the Chinese government clearly demonstrated that, at least in some opinions, certain people needed to work harder at being leisurely in just the right ways.

*Jenny Chio is Assistant Professor of Anthropology at Emory University, in Atlanta, Georgia (USA). She has conducted long-term fieldwork on tourism, rural social transformation, ethnicity and heritage, and visual culture in China since 2006. She is also an ethnographic filmmaker.*

*Source*: Reproduced by permission of the American Anthropological Association from *Anthropology News*, Volume 51, Issue 8, pages 14–15, November 2010. Not for sale or further reproduction.

## DISCUSSION QUESTIONS

1. Tourism brings together people from different cultural backgrounds, whether that is rural people visiting urban areas as part of domestic tourism or international visitors coming from foreign lands. To what extent does the responsibility of ensuring that the negative cultural impacts are mitigated fall upon the tourists or the host communities?

2. How can the coming together of different cultures provide strong beneficial effects whilst minimising any negative effects?

3. Can you legislate effectively against bad tourist behaviour?

4. The case study highlights the behaviour of individuals as a major concern when looking at socio-cultural impacts of tourism. However, serious socio-cultural impacts can be created by organisations and these are not addressed by attempts such as this from China. Discuss.

# CHAPTER 10
## SUSTAINABLE TOURISM

### LEARNING OUTCOMES

This chapter focuses on the long-term tourism issues relating to the development and operation of tourism activities and issues related to climate change and how it may affect tourism. It is intended to provide you with:

- an understanding of the concept of sustainability and an appreciation of the difficulties associated with trying to derive a universally acceptable definition;

- an appreciation of how the sustainability issue pervades all aspects of the tourism process and applies to all of the **stakeholders** involved in the tourism process;

- an understanding of the concept of carrying capacity and the difficulties involved in applying that concept in the real world;

- an understanding of the impact of climate change;

- an insight into the simulation models used to predict climate change and its effects on tourism; and

- an understanding of how destinations may mitigate the effects of, or adapt to climate change.

Photograph: Leptis Magna, Libya © Helen Savill

# INTRODUCTION

This chapter investigates the concept, definition and practical applications of sustainable tourism. Sustainability has become a fashionable term with respect to tourism development and operation. However, even though sustainable development was discussed by those interested in agriculture and forestry centuries ago and the modern usage of the term can be traced back 40 years or so, there is still a significant amount of confusion relating to its meaning and whether or not it is achievable with respect to tourism. The chapter looks at the historical background of sustainability and how it applies to tourism activity. Following a debate about the origin of the term and its definition in general, the implications of the concept for tourism are considered. The threshold levels of destinations are examined under the heading of carrying capacity, a fundamental aspect of sustainability. Carrying capacity is associated with economic, environmental and social impacts as well as the ability of the tourism product to withstand degradation as flows increase. Finally, the chapter examines climate change and how that may impact on the long-run development of tourism around the world.

# HISTORICAL BACKGROUND

Sustainability is one of the most common concepts used in modern tourism development discussions. At the same time it is also one of the least understood concepts and both academics and practitioners are still a very long way from reaching a consensus regarding its definition. The analytical framework of sustainability is broad, encompassing economics, environmental and socio-cultural issues while using ethics and the platforms of intra- and inter-generational equity as the instruments of the debate. Type '**sustainable development**' into an Internet search engine and you will find 22 million results (this would have achieved only 4.5 million results five years ago). Sustainable tourism produces 6.5 million listings (four times the number just five years ago) and there are literally hundreds of definitions of sustainability. Although finding its roots in agriculture with the notion of sustainable yield (the Holy Grail of Forestry) in the Middle Ages, the movement towards today's sustainable development platform can be traced back to the late nineteenth century when the first formal signs of concern about planet Earth manifested themselves in the formation of protection societies and national parks (Yellowstone National Park, USA, 1872; Royal Society for the Protection of Birds, UK, 1889; National Trust, UK, 1894). National Parks were formed in many Commonwealth countries (Australia, Canada and New Zealand) towards the later stages of the nineteenth century and within the UK at the start of the twentieth century. Economics has never been far away from the issues of sustainability because of its focus upon the optimum use of scarce resources, and sustainability issues have been explored for the best part of a century. The 1960s were a catalytic decade that saw the first major movements towards mass concern for the planet, perhaps in response to the post-war period of rapid economic development and the realisation of the planet's fragility fuelled by the first images of Earth from space. The early 1970s witnessed the first United Nations (UNEP) Conference on the Human Environment (Stockholm, 1972), which produced an action plan for the environment based on:

1. the global environmental assessment programme (Earthwatch);
2. environmental management activities; and
3. international measures to support the national and international actions of assessment and management.

The Stockholm Conference resulted in the commissioning of the World Conservation Strategy (WCS) (1980), which can be seen as the implementation arm of the human environmental action plan in the way it focused on how development and conservation could work together. The next landmark in the pathway to sustainability was the Brundtland Report (1987: ix), which stated that one of its primary goals was to:

> help define shared perceptions of long-term environmental issues and the appropriate efforts needed to deal successfully with the problems of protecting and enhancing the environment, a long-term agenda for action during the coming decades, and aspirational goals of the world community.

The Brundtland Report has been criticised on the grounds that many of its predictions and concerns did not materialise, but it provided an invaluable platform for the debate on the north–south poverty divide as well as underscoring the global concerns that had been the outcome of the Stockholm Conference. Within five years of the Brundtland Report the Earth Summit was held in Rio de Janeiro (1992) putting down a landmark for sustainability in the form of a broad action strategy that is known as Agenda 21. The good intentions that came out of the 1992 Summit still apply today; what has been lacking has been any significant action to implement the resolutions that came out of the Summit and this was the main focus of the Johannesburg Summit a decade later (2002). Unfortunately, a significant amount of the momentum built up to overcome the inertia of dealing with sustainable development issues has been brushed aside by the global economic crisis that started in 2008. It seems to be a sad fact that economic imperatives are always more urgent and carry greater weight with governments than sustainability imperatives.

Any form of production and consumption will have sustainability implications and therefore the debate on sustainable development should rightly encompass all forms of activity. Tourism in particular comes under the sustainability spotlight because (a) production and consumption tends to take place in areas where the natural or man-made resources are fragile (for example, areas of natural beauty, coastal areas, heritage buildings, etc.) and (b) the environment and culture are often used as a major component of the product without being subject to the price mechanisms that apply to many natural resources.

# DEFINITIONS OF SUSTAINABILITY IN GENERAL

The Brundtland Report (1987) defined sustainability to be 'meeting the needs of the present generation without compromising the ability of future generations to meet their own needs' and it went on to identify some basic principles of sustainability. These identified needs were to:

a) take a holistic approach to planning and strategy;

b) protect the environment (biodiversity) and man-made heritage;

c) preserve the essential ecological processes;

d) facilitate and engage public participation;

e) ensure that productivity can be sustained into the long-term future; and

f) provide for a better level of fairness and opportunity between different countries.

The challenge is at its greatest when looking at the last identified need (f) in the context of all of the other needs listed. There is a conflict unless (f) can be achieved by reducing the resources currently used by industrialised countries. The increasing pressures placed on the world's resources have been underscored by the dramatic increase in demand for minerals and fossil fuel by the emerging BRIC (Brazil, Russia, India and China) economies. Thus, there is a debate between intra-generational equity and inter-generational equity. If the latter objective is pursued without concern for the former then there is an implicit assumption that the distribution of wealth and opportunity in the present day is somehow optimal and this is not a point that many would be able to defend.

There are many definitions of sustainability that range from the early definitions proposed by Coomer (1979), which suggested that a sustainable society is not a no-growth society but one that lives within the self-perpetuating limits of its own environment, through the WCS (IUCN, 1980) definition that focused its attention on maintaining the essential ecological processes, to the more recent suggestion by Choucri (1997), who argues that it is the process of managing social demands without eroding life support properties or mechanisms of social cohesion or resilience.

The vagueness of the definitions and the hypocrisy that often accompanies international organisations that have flaunted sustainable development on the global stage, have undermined the principles of sustainable development and done little to enhance the implementation of sustainable practices (Butcher, 1997). To be effective any objective must possess certain characteristics. They should be clear, unambiguous, non-conflicting, measurable and achievable. The reality of sustainable development as it has been defined to date is that it fails on nearly all of these counts. On that basis alone sustainable development cannot be considered to be achievable.

The term 'sustainable development' could be replaced by terms such as 'wise use', 'sound planning' or 'responsible development' as they have in the past, but even here it is too vague and still lacks any mechanism by which it could be measured or achieved. Economists could argue that all resources should be properly costed and included within the market process so that rational decisions can be made on the basis of complete information. But the issue is much wider than the economics of the environment; the planet's heritage and culture are also part of the system and these too should be included within the decision-making processes.

The responsibility of pursuing sustainability is also a matter of some importance because it is not simply the responsibility of the international organisations or the governments that support them. Industry and consumers have a key role to play in recognising the importance of social responsibility and long-term objectives. Yet both are driven by short-term needs and objectives that work counter to the long-term goals of sound planning and sustainability.

The proponents of sustainability can be subdivided into two schools of thought: those that may be classified as strong or full sustainable supporters and those that may be deemed to be weak or partial sustainable supporters. In order to examine the two schools it is necessary to define the different types of resource that are subject to depletion or degradation. Simplistically we can categorise them into four types of capital stock:

1. Human – the population, welfare, health, workforce, educational and skill base.
2. Physical – productive capital such as machinery, equipment, buildings.
3. Environmental – man-made and natural resources, biodiversity.
4. Socio-cultural – well-being, social cohesion, empowerment, equity, cultural heritage.

These four categories of capital stock are shown in Figure 10.1. In reality there are significant overlaps between these categories. However, they do serve to explain the differences between the two schools of thought and the concept of sustainability.

At any point in time there is a given stock of each form of capital. These capital stocks can be used for production that will be either consumed or invested back into the capital stock. The strong sustainability proponents would argue that sustainability meant that the level of each of these individual capital stocks must be maintained for future generations. The weak sustainability proponents would argue that the total capital stock (i.e. the sum of all four categories) must be maintained but that it is possible to deplete one stock in order to increase another. Clearly some of the capital stocks are responsive to investment. Education and health services are two ways of improving the quality of the population and workforce and this stock can be increased over time by such investment. In the long term there are likely to be diminishing returns to such investments. The physical capital stock is that capital used for productive purposes and this can and is being invested in all the time both for replacement purposes and for new investment to increase productive capacity. Some aspects of the environmental capital can respond to investment, the creation of national parks, cleaning up rivers, preventing air and noise pollution being examples on the natural environment side, and, with respect to the built environment, the construction of new homes, shopping malls, hotels, etc. However, there is clearly a trade-off between these two elements of the environmental stock. Bridging the environmental capital stock with the socio-cultural stock there is also scope for investment in temples and monuments. Finally, with respect

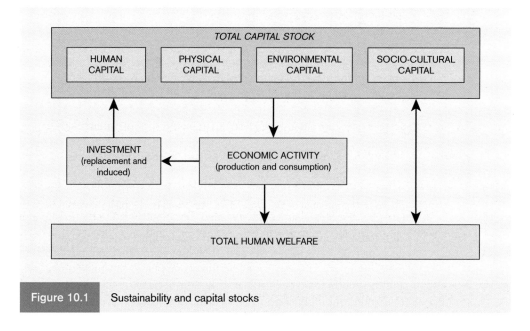

| Figure 10.1 | Sustainability and capital stocks |

to the socio-cultural capital stock it is possible to invest in customs and traditions by training and raising the profiles of them within the local population and to visitors to ensure their continuity.

If the strong sustainability approach is adopted there is a serious question mark over any form of production because, although it is possible to invest in some of the capital stocks and to restore their levels, it is not possible to increase the level of others without adopting a no-growth stance. For instance, new physical capital cannot be created without depleting some of the environmental capital stocks. Wherever land or raw materials are used this represents a depletion of that capital stock and unless alternative land or raw materials can be recovered from elsewhere such a process will have a finite future and cannot be sustained.

# DEFINITIONS OF SUSTAINABLE TOURISM

The difficulty of coming up with an acceptable definition for sustainability in general is mirrored in the efforts to define sustainable tourism. Using the Brundtland definition as its starting point, the World Tourism Organization defined sustainable tourism thus:

> **Sustainable tourism development** meets the needs of present tourists and host regions while protecting and enhancing opportunity for the future. It is envisaged as leading to management of all resources in such a way that economic, social, and aesthetic needs can be fulfilled while maintaining cultural integrity, essential ecological processes, and biological diversity, and life support systems.

There have been many variations of this definition used by regions and countries around the world. For instance, the Organization of East Caribbean States (OECS) provides the following definition:

> The optimal use of natural and cultural resources for national development on an equitable and self-sustaining basis to provide a unique visitor experience and an improved quality of life through partnership among government, the private sector and communities.

Whichever definition of the hundreds that have been published seems most relevant, the key factors that come out of the debate on definitions of sustainability are that sustainability requires appropriate consideration of the long-term economic, environmental, socio-cultural and political well-being of all stakeholders, and that to achieve such long-term goals requires the engagement of all of the stakeholders involved in the production and consumption process.

# SUSTAINABILITY OF TOURISM

Tourism is not an industry that sits easily within the concept of sustainability. International tourism, for instance, involves major transport components, cultural mixes and fierce resource competition. Examining each aspect of sustainability with respect to tourism activity and development paints a depressing picture.

## Economic aspects working against sustainable tourism

To work within the parameters of 'wise or responsible use' or 'sustainability' it is important that the net long-term economic benefits are optimal. The economic impact of tourism (discussed in Chapter 7) means that tourism competes with other industries for factors of production, and as such it can create price inflation, driving up the cost of resources, land and labour. It attracts workers from rural areas who may have been employed in traditional industries causing output levels in those industries to fall. Scarce investment funds may be attracted to the tourism industry on the promise of rapid returns and foreign exchange inflows. This can distort the allocation of resources in the longer term and lead to structural unemployment. Where tourism development takes place in industrialised urban areas the above may not present severe obstacles, but to less developed countries or sparsely populated regions the effects associated with the development of tourism can be economically traumatic.

## Environmental aspects working against sustainable tourism

Airlines are responsible for a major aspect of air pollution and the vast majority of air transport is for tourism purposes. Tourism is about real estate development and so it competes for land use and depletes the natural environmental stock as it does so. Tourism activities can be severely disruptive to biodiversity from the extreme activities of hunting and fishing to the less obvious disruptions through wildlife observing and hill walking. The spectacular is often headline material, such as the effects of boats, anchors and pollution on the coral reefs in the Caribbean. The unusual also captures headlines, such as visitors to the Antarctic, the degradation of the environment at Everest Base Camp, and the erosion of ancient monuments. The increased presence of tourists in the tombs of the Valley of the Kings, Egypt can raise the humidity levels by several percentage points and this increases the erosion from pollutants. The less spectacular is no less devastating, such as the increased use of fossil fuels for energy consumption and water desalination, and the construction of roads, airports and sea ports to cater for the travel of tourists. The introduction of large numbers of visitors to environmentally fragile areas will always be accompanied by tension between the natural environment and tourism.

## Socio-cultural aspects working against sustainable tourism

Tourists, whether they come from the explorers that Valene Smith suggests adapt to local norms or the mass tourists who do not adapt at all, will always have socio-cultural impacts on the local community. They may be through natural curiosity where the empathetic visitor is intrigued by local customs and traditions so they go to observe and that observation can set in motion a commercialisation process that will sooner or later change the events. Or it could be the psychocentric visitor who wishes no surprises, does not wish to get involved but, through the demonstration effect of their behaviour, dress and customs, alters the corresponding behaviour, dress and customs of the local residents. Because tourism requires the tourists to visit the destination these negative impacts are bound to be a threat.

Irrespective of the difficulties encountered when trying to define sustainable tourism in a usable and acceptable manner, there are approaches that can be taken to mitigate some of the threats to the long-term viability of the industry. One approach is to set limits on the future growth of tourism in each destination. This would not necessarily improve the net benefits derived from tourism for any destination and in a destination where tourism was already creating problems it would not secure its long-term viability. Another approach is to change the behaviour of the

| Photograph 10.1 | Ecocamp in Chile. |
| --- | --- |
| | *Source*: Blaine Harrington III/Alamy Images |

stakeholders in the tourism industry to make the products currently provided more sustainable. This could involve better socio-cultural and environmental management within businesses together with better awareness and behaviour from tourists towards the destination's environment and culture. It would also probably require some changes to the economic structure and power balance between the businesses involved in the supply chain of tourism products so that local factors were fully and equitably included within the market processes. The third approach is to replace the current (unsustainable) tourism products with new products that are sustainable.

To be successful it is likely that a combination of all three approaches will be necessary. That is, there will need to be a change in the behaviour of stakeholders, with businesses, tourists and local residents behaving more responsibly, with limits or thresholds being placed on developments and activities (carrying capacity) and with new products being introduced that have greater empathy with the local environment and culture. The following discussion examines the issues surrounding the identification of carrying capacity for a destination.

## Thresholds and carrying capacity

The fact that tourism activity impacts on the social, cultural, environmental and economic aspects of a destination brings with it significant implications for sustainability. Even with a more aware tourism industry or more environmentally friendly types of tourism activity there will be thresholds beyond which the negative impacts may easily outweigh the net economic benefits. It would be unrealistic to assume that these impacts could be eliminated altogether and, therefore, the volume of tourists and the type of activity they pursue will have a direct implication for sustainability. If it is assumed that there are both positive and negative impacts associated with tourism and that the net effects are likely to diminish as the volume of tourism increases there will be certain thresholds beyond which additional tourists will create unacceptable net impacts (economically, environmentally or socially). Exceeding these thresholds is likely to affect every facet of tourism development. For instance, exceeding:

- physical thresholds will limit the volume of tourist flows and expose tourists to safety hazards;
- environmental thresholds will also limit the tourist flows by creating secondary problems, such as health hazards, or detract from the attractiveness of a destination;

- social and cultural thresholds will generate resentment and antagonism towards tourists from the host population;
- tourist flow thresholds will affect the satisfaction levels of tourists and cause them to search elsewhere for a better product; and
- economic thresholds will result in the misallocation of resources and factors of production.

The main challenge is to find the level of the thresholds beyond which tourism should not venture. As with the definitions of sustainability, defining these thresholds and the carrying capacity implied by them is a difficult task. Scientists from a wide range of specialist fields have attempted, with varying degrees of success, to provide a working definition of carrying capacity. For instance, ecologists might define carrying capacity as 'the population of an identified species which can be supported throughout the foreseeable future, within a defined habitat, without causing permanent damage to the ecosystem upon which it is ultimately dependent'. If this type of definition is transferred to the human species some modifications must be made unless the 'defined habitat' is taken to be the planet as a whole. That is, the territorial boundaries are not unique or limiting in terms of the ability of the species' population to survive. What happens within one territorial boundary may well influence the long-term viability of the species in others.

With respect to tourism, one approach is to adopt Hardin's (1991) formulation of human impact and simply transfer it to tourism such as that set out below:

tourism's impact = tourist population × tourist impact, per capita

However, this is not sufficient and such a definition fails to reflect the variety of influences relating to the nature of the tourist activity, the vulnerability of the destination, technological changes and so on.

Carrying capacity has been defined as 'the maximum number of people who can use a site without an unacceptable alteration in the physical environment and without an unacceptable decline in the quality of experience gained by visitors' (Mathieson and Wall, 1982). Note that the use of words like 'acceptable' means that there will be alterations and decline and this means that sustainability in its purest sense will not be achieved. Note also that the term 'tourist presence' is used as opposed to the simpler notion of tourist numbers. This is because it is necessary, when attempting to identify the levels of carrying capacity, to weight the absolute numbers of tourist arrivals to take account of a number of factors as follows:

- the average length of stay;
- the characteristics of the tourists and hosts;
- the geographical concentration of tourists;
- the degree of seasonality;
- the types of tourism activity;
- the accessibility of specific sites;
- the level of infrastructure use and its spare capacity;
- the extent of spare capacity among the various productive sectors of the economy.

Another aspect rarely touched upon in the literature is the fact that different tourists interact with each other in different ways. For example, destinations in the Caribbean, such as St Lucia, draw their tourists from a variety of countries, but the majority of tourists come from the US market and a significant number come from European countries. The problem here is the fact that the Caribbean is a relatively inexpensive destination for the American market, which is close by, whereas it is a relatively expensive destination for the European market, because of the high cost of transport involved in the package. This means that European tourists are more likely to be from a higher socio-economic grouping than their American counterparts. This problematic mix can shorten the **tourist satisfaction** ratings quite significantly, suggesting that, from the tourists' point of view, carrying capacity may be as much influenced by the mix of tourists as by their absolute number.

When attempting to determine or identify carrying capacity, it is essential that tourism presence is measured in some unambiguous manner. One possibility is to discuss carrying capacity in terms of *tourism units*, where a tourism unit is a standardised concept based upon tourist numbers weighted by some composite factor derived from the above influencing elements. In this way each destination is likely to have different carrying capacity levels. However, the derivation of some standardised unit is difficult. For example, there are problems to be encountered if the number of day visitors is to be incorporated into the overall tourist numbers. This is because day visitors tend to be associated with different levels of impact per hour per tourist from those of their staying counterparts. The shorter the stay of tourists the more pressing will be the sense of time budgeting and the higher will be the level of expenditure per unit of time.

Composite indicators can be constructed to provide some insight into the threshold levels of tourism activity. For instance, McElroy (2004) discusses the strengths and limitations of a Tourism Penetration Index (TPI) for selected Caribbean islands where the index is based on per capita visitor spend, average daily density of visitors (in aggregate) and hotel rooms per square kilometre. The use of such indices is highly questionable given that they do not take into account temporal variations (seasonality), the spatial spread and size of the island (which influences the density indicator) and the retention of revenue from tourism. Many other factors could also be included, such as the geographical spread of economic activity, the nature of visitor host interactions, etc., but these data are expensive and time-consuming.

Carrying capacity definitions tend to include the term 'acceptable' and the question that needs to be asked is to whom should a change be acceptable or unacceptable? If, as in the case of social impacts, the host population is the body that should consider the acceptability of developments, how is this reflected in policies? In a perfectly democratic political system, then, we could argue that the residents would be able to register their views on proposed developments. However, such perfect democracy may be hard to find. Furthermore, much tourism development is driven by the private sector, which may take a much narrower perspective on the issues surrounding development and hold quite different views about acceptable levels of development.

The issue becomes even more complex with respect to any environmental carrying capacity. Who should consider and vote on the acceptability, or otherwise, of a project that brings environmental impacts? The environment itself may signify changes and species of flora and fauna may suffer from development but they do not have a vote. How will environmental acceptability be considered and voiced within the planning framework?

The above issues relate to all aspects of carrying capacity, with the exception of the acceptability of developments to tourists. Visitor satisfaction surveys are frequently undertaken by many destinations to monitor acceptability. Furthermore, if the carrying capacity in this respect is exceeded, tourists will vote with their feet and go elsewhere.

In spite of the problems involved in converting a theoretical definition of carrying capacity into an operational tool, it does fit in well with modern development strategies that increasingly incorporate attempts to impose some constraints on the level of development to prevent damaging impacts on the environment and society or to avoid the risk of over-dependence.

## The dynamics of carrying capacity

The literature on carrying capacity, rather like the literature on tourism development planning, gives the impression that it is in some way static or absolute. The very word 'capacity' makes one think of a specific level like filling the seats on a boat or an aircraft, but nothing could be further from the truth. Carrying capacity is an extremely fluid and dynamic concept. As with many human traits, exposure to stimuli brings with it a degree of acceptability. Socio-cultural tolerance levels change over time with gradual exposure to tourists. If, for example, a small island destination goes from 100 to 1 million tourists in the space of a year it is likely that the socio-cultural, economic and environmental impacts will be devastating. Take the same destination and increase the volume of tourists by the same amount over a 50-year period and the discernible impact is likely to be far less. People become accustomed to change – it does not make the change any less, but it does make it more acceptable. Economies too are better at adjusting to structural change that takes place over a long time period, rather than dealing with rapid changes. Sufficient time will allow for the necessary linkages and support services to be put in place and, in consequence, allow the destination to optimise its benefits from tourism. Even the environment, or at least the local population's concern for it, may be better able to cope if change comes slowly and proper visitor management systems can be implemented to mitigate negative impacts.

In effect the carrying capacity of today will not be the carrying capacity of tomorrow. In the 1950s few of the top tourist destinations in the world could have imagined the volume of tourists that they are playing host to today. This dynamic characteristic of carrying capacity, together with the difficulty in finding a universally acceptable definition, has resulted in some bodies, such as the United States National Park Service, choosing to adopt an alternative terminology, that of **limits of acceptable change** (LAC), as their planning indicator.

Therefore, carrying capacity is a dynamic concept in the sense that the threshold levels that determine carrying capacity are likely to grow over time, providing that the development of tourism is sound. Unplanned rapid development could easily result in low tolerance levels and carrying capacities of much lower values.

## Other factors influencing carrying capacity

In addition to the characteristics of the tourists and their hosts, there are a number of other factors that will influence the carrying capacity of a destination. It has already been noted that the speed of change is an important factor. The difference between the tourists and hosts is also an important consideration. It is not the absolute characteristics of either population group that is important, but the relative difference. This is one reason why domestic tourism is often, but not always, more acceptable than international tourism in terms of the socio-cultural impacts.

If the demographic profiles of tourists are similar to those of the host population, particularly in relation to age distribution, socio-economic grouping and religion, then the socio-cultural impact of increasing tourist numbers is likely to be relatively low. On the other hand, major differences in any of these factors can result in significant socio-cultural impacts even though the number of tourists in both scenarios is the same.

The fact that there are four broad groups of capacity indicators – economic, environmental, socio-cultural and tourist satisfaction levels – gives rise to some difficulty in establishing exactly what the carrying capacity of a specific destination may be. It is likely that, for any given destination, the carrying capacity will be reached in just one of these areas before it is reached in the rest. Thus, a destination may find that tourism activity brings pressure to, say, the local ecosystem before it creates any significant threats to the social structure, the culture or the economy. This means that, regardless of the threshold limits in these latter areas, the carrying capacity for this destination is dictated by the vulnerability of the ecosystem. In order to move away from the qualitative to the quantitative approach for determining carrying capacity it is necessary to delineate the different areas of study (outlined below) and examine the processes by which carrying capacity is determined and how it may change over time.

## The process of scoping the various aspects of carrying capacity

Figure 10.2 outlines the process by which carrying capacity is influenced and can be assessed. The diagram shows the broad groups of factors that determine carrying capacity along with the different stages that can influence the magnitude and direction of the impacts and hence the carrying capacity. The different areas of the flow diagram are set out under the following subheadings.

### Local factors

There are many local factors that will influence the magnitude and direction of impacts but what is important, besides the nature of the local factors, is the relative difference between the local factors and the tourist counterparts and the speed of change. Looking at individual factors we can see how complex the issues are.

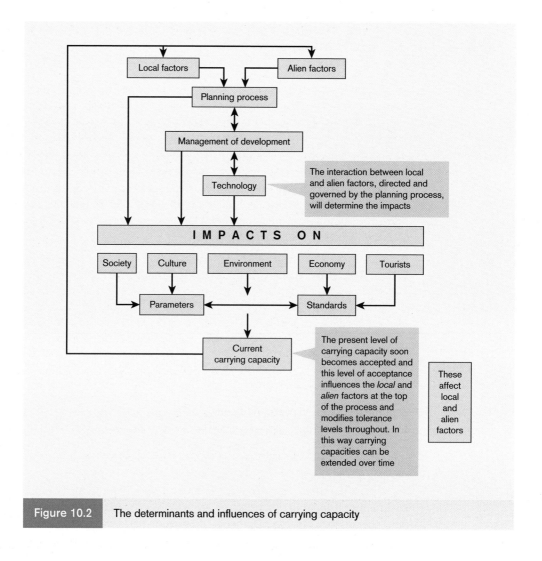

| **Figure 10.2** | The determinants and influences of carrying capacity |

### Social structure

The social structure of the destination is vital in determining the scale and nature of any impacts. For example, taking two extreme views, the social structures of London, New York and Sydney are more able to absorb and tolerate the presence of tourists than cities such as Apia in Western Samoa or Port Louis in Mauritius. The former can tolerate the presence of tourists without incurring any significant changes to their social structures because those changes have already occurred. They are larger in population and cosmopolitan in structure, making them more adaptable to change. The latter have relatively small populations, the extended family system is still largely intact (particularly in Apia) and they are not as cosmopolitan in structure. Therefore, some societies can accept large-volume tourism with little obvious effect while others cannot. In general, the smaller the local population, the more dramatic will be the social impact of tourism, particularly if that tourism is based upon large-volume tourist flows.

### Cultural heritage

The cultural heritage of a destination is very important when attempting to determine the impact and carrying capacity. The more unusual the cultural background, the more attractive a destination may become to potential tourists. Ironically, the more unusual the cultural background, the more likely it is to be adversely affected by the presence of tourists. The end result is either the destruction of the cultural heritage or, more probably, the distortion of the local culture through staged authenticity and the over-commercialisation of cultural features and traditions, such as dances and costumes, religious ceremonies, arts and crafts. The destination can soon be in danger of becoming a caricature of itself.

### Environment

The environment *will* be changed by the presence of tourists no matter how sympathetic they may be or how carefully the tourism activity is planned. The environment can be either artificial or natural. In general the former is more resilient to tourism impacts than the latter. Environmental change is inevitable and will be more obvious and pronounced in those areas that are sparsely populated and not subject to frequent high-volume tourist visits. The more fragile and unique an environment, the more vulnerable it is to change from the presence of humans. It is important to remember that the environment is also changed by many factors, not just tourism, and it is often difficult to isolate those effects created by tourists from those created by other factors.

### Economic structure

The economic structure will determine the benefits and costs associated with tourism activity. In general, the more developed and industrialised the economy, the more robust and adaptable it will be. As economies grow and diversify, so too do the skills of the workforce. This, together with a more refined capital system, allows such economies to respond and adapt to the changes brought by tourism. These countries will be able to secure the greatest benefits from tourism activity while incurring the minimum costs. In contrast, economies that are not sophisticated may find that rapid developments in tourism can distort the allocation of resources quite drastically and set up importation habits that may be difficult to break in the future.

Tourism development, particularly rapid development, tends to be resort-based and this may bring with it the economic problems associated with:

- migration from rural to urban areas; and
- the transfer of labour from traditional industries to tourism and its related industries.

Economies have to be mature to be able to adjust to these pressures.

### Political structure

The political structure can affect the impacts of tourism and its carrying capacity in a number of ways. To begin with, political instability will deter tourists and therefore hinder tourism development. Some groups of tourists are more sensitive to political instability than others but few tourists are unaffected by the prospect of political instability. The political structure may also have direct influences upon tourism development if, in reflecting the ideals and beliefs of the population, it is decided that tourism development should be constrained or even discouraged. Some countries limit tourism development by restricting the number of visas issued within any given year (Bhutan, for example), whereas others may increase the costs of obtaining visas or make the acquisition of visas difficult, thereby restricting them to only the most determined. The political openness may well reflect the willingness of society to welcome tourism development and this may either raise or lower the carrying capacity thresholds.

### Resources

The availability of local resources (labour, capital, land, etc.) is likely to have a major influence on the acceptability and desirability of tourism development, and even on the form that development takes. Where resources are scarce, competition for them will be high and the opportunity cost of using these resources for tourism will also be high. The local infrastructure is also part of the resource base. If tourism development means that the local infrastructure will be over-utilised then this will create a capacity constraint (at least in the short term) that may well become operative before any of the other carrying capacity constraints are approached. If the infrastructure is over-utilised because of tourism development then this may well breed resentment and hostility among the local population, and then the social impact of tourism will create a carrying capacity constraint.

On a more positive note, tourism development may well result in an improved infrastructure, which will be available for the use of hosts as well as tourists, and this may enhance the lives of the local community.

## Alien factors

### *Tourist characteristics*

Clearly, the characteristics of the tourists who visit any given destination are an important factor in determining the social and cultural impact of tourism on the host community. For instance, tourists who belong to the mass or charter groups are more likely to have a greater social and cultural impact than those who belong to the explorer, adventurer and ethnic tourist categories. The former tends to demand Western amenities and bring their culture with them without adapting to the local norms and customs. The latter tend to be far more sympathetic towards local customs and traditions and actively seek them out as part of their vacation experience. This, however, is not always the case. The important factor is the relative difference between tourists and hosts. The greater the difference between the host's and the tourist's social and cultural backgrounds, the greater the impact and consequent change. Tourist characteristics also include visitor expenditure patterns, mode of transport, structure and size of party, age, educational background, income and purpose of visit. All of these factors will influence the nature and magnitude of the impacts on the host community.

Carrying capacity is centred on tolerance levels:

- how tolerant the ecological system is to tourist intrusion and activity, as well as those activities created as a result of tourism activity;
- how tolerant the socio-cultural structure is to the introduction of foreign cultures, ideals and beliefs; and
- how much tolerance there is within the economic structure.

However, carrying capacity is also about the tolerance levels of the tourists. A destination that is considered to be overcrowded by the tourists has exceeded its carrying capacity and, in consequence, will find its tourist arrivals diminishing or the composition of tourists changing. The composition of tourists may change as the destination lowers prices in an attempt to shore up falling numbers. The tolerance level of tourists introduces a further complication into the issue of determining carrying capacity. Different categories of tourists will display different levels of tolerance with respect to deviations from their expected experience.

Figure 10.3 demonstrates how tolerance levels associated with different types of tourist and within different types of resort may change. The figure represents two planes. The horizontal plane depicts the nature and characteristics of the destination with a range moving from the fragile and vulnerable, such as Antarctica, through the vulnerable but less fragile areas, such as the Galapagos Islands, to the more organised and controlled but nevertheless vulnerable game parks, such as those found in Kenya, right through to the full-blown totally dedicated destinations such as Hawaii and Benidorm in Spain.

The vertical plane represents the type of tourist and ranges from the explorer to the mass tourist as you move down the plane. The diagonal line running from the top left-hand corner through to the bottom right-hand corner demonstrates the 'fit' between tourist and destination. Thus, starting in the top right-hand corner we find that the explorer will seek out the fragile but exclusive destinations such as Antarctica. At the bottom left-hand corner, reading across the horizontal plane and down the vertical plane we find that the mass tourist will seek out the no-surprise destinations such as Benidorm. The range along the line between these two polar extremes also shows the 'fit' between the characteristics of the tourist and the destination. The dotted lines that run alongside the central diagonal line represent the tolerance levels. By this we mean that each type of tourist will be associated with an average given level of tolerance with respect to how closely a destination may match their expectations. Thus, explorers may generally be regarded as being fairly intolerant of significant deviations from their expectations. If the destination does not live up to expectations they will quickly seek alternative destinations. At the other extreme, mass tourists are generally more tolerant of deviations from the expected. Thus, the corridor of tolerance increases in size as we move away from the top left-hand corner. The tolerance levels of destinations can also be seen in this diagram in the sense that the central diagonal line still shows the 'fit' between tourist and destination, but the corridor of tolerance may

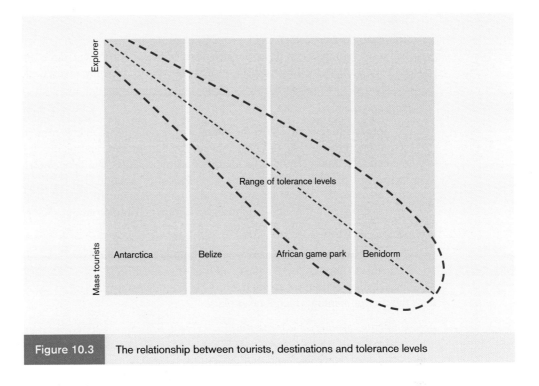

| Figure 10.3 | The relationship between tourists, destinations and tolerance levels |

also relate to the destination's tolerance to changes in tourism. Fragile destinations are unable to cope with significant changes in the volume of tourism whereas the more commercial purpose-built destinations are more able to absorb such deviations.

### Types of tourist activity

The types of tourist activity pursued will be closely linked to the characteristics of the tourists who take part in them. However, the presence of certain activities, such as gambling, can bring specific social problems and stresses that are far greater in magnitude than those associated with the same number of tourists undertaking different activities. Gambling can bring with it increased risks to the host community (and to other tourists) in terms of exposure to prostitution, drugs and crime. All of these factors will help create much lower carrying capacities than might normally be associated with tourism. It need not be just the emotive cases of gambling and prostitution that can limit the carrying capacity. Destinations with very fragile ecosystems or with, say, rare bird species, may suffer more severely at the hands of the special interest groups who would actively seek out and disturb the habitats, albeit unintentionally.

### Planning, management and technology

Planning is concerned with the organisation of factors in order to manipulate future events. The management of tourism is the process by which plans are put into practice. Changes in technology will have direct and indirect effects on the difficulties associated with the planning and management tasks. Given the interaction between local and alien factors within the host environment, the planning and management process should aim to secure the maximum positive benefits (as dictated by the planning objectives) while incurring the minimum costs. Figure 10.2 shows that the planning, management and technology factors act as a funnel between the 'raw' interaction of the local and alien factors and the impact that this interaction has on the destination. The more successful the planning and management, the lower will be the levels of negative impacts and the greater will be the carrying capacity. The dynamic nature of this process is such that suitable developments combined with appropriate visitor flow management will 'naturally' select the required tourist market segments, while allowing the local factors the amount of time and space needed to adapt to the alien factors. The end result is a destination that can enjoy both growth and sustainability (growth + sustainability = development).

Impacts

The local and alien factors, manipulated by planning and the management of tourism development, will result in impacts on the social structure, culture, environment and economy, and upon other tourists. Impacts are the yardsticks of carrying capacity, but they are derived variables. The task to the planner and tourism management specialists is to ensure that the appropriate impacts occur.

### Parameters

The impacts that occur reflect the nature and magnitude of change brought about by the interaction between tourists and hosts, given the management and planning that has been implemented. The parameters can be identified as the changes that take place to the local and alien factors as a result of different levels and types of interaction. They are *factual* in the sense that they are devoid of value judgements and simply relate tourist host interaction and tourist presence to changes in the social, cultural, environmental and economic factors.

### Standards

The standards may be seen as acceptable limits applied to the parameters. They refer to the value judgements imposed by the host and tourist populations with respect to how much a variable may change without incurring irreversible or undesirable damage to the nature of tourism and the environment in which it takes place.

### Carrying capacity determination

Carrying capacity is the dependent variable. It is not possible to overemphasise the word 'variable' because it is not a fixed value based on tourist presence. The dynamic nature of carrying capacity is based upon the changing tolerance levels of each of the determining factors as a result of both exposure and management.

The feedback over time, between carrying capacity and the local and alien factors, will be responsible for increasing/decreasing the magnitude of acceptable tourist presence. The carrying capacity will also feed back into the planning and management stages in order to inform and enhance the processes of visitor and destination management.

If the carrying capacity is exceeded with respect to any of the impact areas, the tourism development process will be hindered and the development may be considered unsustainable. The damage created by exceeding the carrying capacity may be related to any of the impact areas or in terms of tourist satisfaction, but the end result will be the same. Either the destination will experience diminishing numbers as its tourism industry declines – tourists pursuing alternative destinations – or the mix of tourist arrivals may change, making it increasingly difficult for the destination to achieve its declared planning objectives.

The vulnerability of different destinations to the presence of tourists is a major factor in setting the limits of acceptable standards. To illustrate this point the plight of World Heritage Sites can be examined. The very nature of World Heritage Sites means that they are not only finite but also irreplaceable and the successful management of such sites is vital. The World Heritage Convention requires that the international community cooperates to ensure that measures taken to protect and conserve these sites are effective. The management of these sites is almost always translated into access control. For instance, the management of Keoladeo National Park in India relies upon the access provided by the restricted number of trained guides or by bicycles and specified trails set out for the 100,000 tourists that visit each year. In other areas more arbitrary, but still restrictive, limits are set, such as the 11,800 visitors per annum allowed to view the resident gorilla families, and accommodation within the park is limited to two lodges owned and controlled by the government. Alternative strategies can also be used, such as the spacing of tourist visits, or restrictions based on a specific aspect of a destination in order to manage its overall tourism development.

## Measurement criteria

Carrying capacity is subject to multiple determination and, as such, each of the separate components must be investigated. Tables 10.1 and 10.2 are provided to give some guidance to the variables that may be measured, the thresholds that may be encountered and the effects of over-exploitation.

| Table 10.1 | Variables and thresholds | |
|---|---|---|

| Impact on | Variable | Threshold(s) |
|---|---|---|
| **Economy** | | |
| Dependency | Contribution to GNP | Diversity/imports |
| Finance | Level of investment | Availability of funds |
| Labour | Employment | Shortages/training |
| Price inflation | Consumer price index | Social costs/distribution |
| Wealth | Income growth/distribution | Wage inflation/imports |
| **Environment** | | |
| Changes | Species/populations | Extinction/balance of population |
| Hazards | Fires, erosion, pollution | Costs/risks |
| Viability of wildlife | Urbanisation | Land usage/species count |
| **Physical resources** | | |
| Access | Cost/time/volume | Congestion/hazards |
| Accommodation | Number/size/quality | Occupancy |
| Attractions | Number/size/type | Access/available land |
| Land | Proportion of land usage | Land price inflation |
| Transportation | Cost/capacity | Congestion/hazards |
| Infrastructure | Investment/quality | Capacity/health risks |
| **Political framework** | | |
| Strategies | Goals range/scope | Conflicts, goals missed |
| Resources | Expenditure/revenue | Budgetary deficits |
| Cooperation | Partnerships | Lack of participation/funds |
| **Society/culture** | | |
| Population | Migration | Distribution/infrastructure |
| Living standards | Real income/wealth | Inflation |
| Values | Crime/drugs/health | Social disruption/costs |
| Traditions | Participation/quality | Occurrence/characteristics |

Clearly, understanding the implications for each of the indicators is an important aspect of being able to determine the thresholds of successful tourism development. As mentioned earlier in this chapter, setting limits on tourism activity is only one aspect of striving towards successful tourism development. Destinations can also work towards changing the behaviour of the stakeholders involved in the tourism process either by creating an appropriate economic framework or by investing in awareness campaigns. They can also encourage the development of more sustainable forms of tourism activity. Given that both of these strategies work towards meeting tourism demand in a way that minimises the net negative impacts they can be considered within the same framework.

## Sustainable tourism products

Terms such as **eco-tourism** and **alternative tourism** have taken a prominent position in tourism literature (academic and marketing) since they were introduced in the mid-1980s. Eco-tourism has been misused as a term both intentionally, as a marketing ploy, and unintentionally due to a lack of understanding and, in common with the term sustainability, there has been considerable debate about an acceptable definition. Wight (2001) points out that the World Tourism Organization estimated that some 10–15% of global tourism could be classified as eco-tourism in 1997. However, within that same year the WTO revised this estimate to 20%. It is hard to find any credibility in these proportions given the dominance of mass tourism in total global tourism activities. Eco-tourism is unequivocally linked to natural tourism attractions rather

| Table 10.2 | Scale of development and its effect on impacts and carrying capacity | |
| --- | --- | --- |
| **Effect on** | **Small-scale dispersed** | **Large-scale concentrated** |
| **Accommodation** | | |
| Range of products | Highly limited | Diverse |
| Range of prices | Low/medium | Low/medium/expensive |
| Seasonality | Peaked | Wider but more problematic |
| Size of business | SME | SME to international |
| Ownership | Local | Non-local |
| **Characteristics of facilities** | | |
| Range | Highly limited | Diverse |
| Finance | Local | Mixed local/foreign |
| Usage | Peaked | High volume |
| Need for support | Low | High |
| **Labour market** | | |
| Demand/supply | Learning by doing | Demand for high skills |
| | Local labour | Mixed local/migrant labour |
| | Constrained by local supply | Increased migration |
| **Transport** | | |
| Infrastructure | Limited | High but congestion during |
| Supplier | Private sector | peaks |
| Stimulating supply | Low-level effect | Greater public supply |
| | | High-level effect |

# MINI CASE STUDY 10.1
## Sustainable tourism in the Srepok Wilderness Area, Cambodia

Local people and endangered animals such as elephants, tigers and wild water buffalo should benefit from a unique wildlife ecotourism initiative in Southeast Asia led by IIED and WWF in Cambodia.

## BACKGROUND

A serious decline in species' populations in the last few decades due to unsustainable harvesting and habitat loss has prompted urgent action from the government, WWF and other local partners to address this trend. These groups, along with IIED, have identified high-value low-impact wildlife ecotourism as a means of securing the future of these species and their ecosystem through generating financing for conservation activities and supporting local livelihoods as well as ensuring the financial sustainability of the protected area.

The project was designed under the premise that the local communities that are dependent on the use of natural resources within the Srepok Wilderness Area (SWA) are some of Cambodia's poorest. Also, these communities represent the best chance for genuine conservation of key species within the SWA – they know the species, the area and their own poverty reduction needs.

Communities are unwittingly part of the problem; over-harvesting species and degrading the ecosystem within the SWA so that key species cannot persist. Therefore, the project aims to build awareness, and to create the environment necessary to make sure that costs of avoiding harvesting and other environmentally damaging activities are at least balanced with the benefits received from other sources.

The original Darwin Initiative-funded project successfully piloted community-based monitoring in the 3,500 square kilometre SWA. Its success led to calls from the Cambodian government and NGOs for replication in other Protected Areas. Work is now building on the project's initial success to scale up work in SWA and

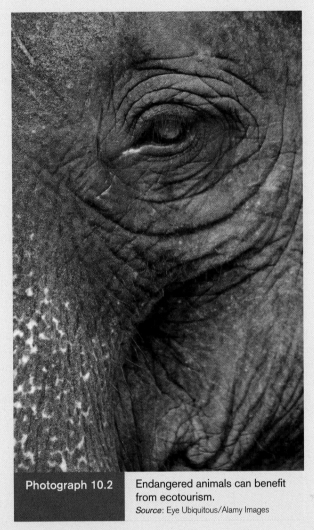

| Photograph 10.2 | Endangered animals can benefit from ecotourism. |
|---|---|

*Source*: Eye Ubiquitous/Alamy Images

expanding activities into the Eastern Plains Landscape (EPL) of protected areas and biodiversity corridors. This is as part of an ecosystem approach that aims to safeguard 15,000 square kilometres of globally important tropical dry forest habitat in Cambodia.

One unequivocal success was a Management-Oriented Monitoring System (MOMS) pilot led by community rangers in SWA which clearly shows potential replicability throughout the region. The next step is to train community-monitoring teams across EPL to conduct MOMS independently as a means of building stronger support for conservation activities.

Further, this project will expand capacity-building by the provincial Wildlife Ecotourism Management Board (WEMB). It will also develop a community tourism homestay initiative and environmental awareness and education activities. All of these activities begun under the first DI grant, but need extra momentum to expand to the landscape level.

*Source*: http://www.iied.org/sustainable-tourism-srepok-wilderness-area-cambodia (accessed 7 June 2012)

## DISCUSSION QUESTIONS

1. Tourism development can be harnessed to help drive sustainability where communities and practices are under threat from non-tourism factors. Is such a strategy likely to be viable?

2. What are the longer term dangers presented by adopting this Cambodian strategy?

3. This sustainable tourism strategy can provide wider long-term benefits to rural communities in developing countries but the opportunity costs may be significant. Discuss.

than their man-made counterparts and environmental sustainability is often found to be a core component of such a product's definition. However, it is also accepted that many definitions of eco-tourism include some reference to indigenous cultural sustainability. According to Weaver (2004), a further factor that is associated with definitions of eco-tourism relates to their educational or learning opportunity components. Once all of these aspects are incorporated into a single tourism product it can be seen that eco-tourism will not appeal to the masses at present. The masses seek sand, sea, sun vacations within a wide variety of areas that may or may not also be areas of outstanding natural beauty. Eco-tourism demands a high level of interpretation whereas the mass tourism product does not. This is not to say that mass tourism products would not benefit from greater interpretation.

Both eco-tourism and alternative tourism imply small-scale, indigenous low-key activities. Where the former holds the preservation of the natural environment at its core, the latter may not necessarily do so. Indeed, the latter may simply be at the beginning of the tourism development process for a destination soon to be enveloped in a more commercial package as the product develops. Eco-tourism suggests that it has in place constraints that will prevent or inhibit uncontrolled development. However, both forms of tourism activity can provide a temporary runway for the take-off of the destination as it moves towards mass tourism. There is no product currently on the market that could come close to being classified as mass sustainable tourism. The presence of large numbers of tourists in high densities with the necessary infrastructure for transportation and public health and safety defies the laws of sustainability.

The 1980s also saw the emergence of the 'Three Rs' being applied to sustainability in the corporate world. The fact that the corporate world was even thinking about sustainability was a huge leap forward, although the cynics would argue that they were paying lip-service to a concept that would pay dividends in terms of increased sales. Tour operators such as Thomsons did not find sustainable tourism products to be the 'hot' products that this line of thinking promised. The three Rs were:

**Reduce**

**Reuse**

**Recycle**

The very fact that these words were being used in corporate circles represents a major shift in attitudes towards the environment and social responsibility. Middleton (1998) expanded this list to 10 Rs:

**Recognise**

**Refuse**

**Replace**

**Reduce**

**Reuse**

**Recycle**

**Re-engineer**

**Retrain**

**Reward**

**Re-educate**

Although some of the additional Rs may be considered to be contrived and there is considerable overlap between several of them, the list does serve to show just how far away the three Rs were from presenting a significant step towards sustainability. Furthermore, a major **R** in the form of 'Responsibility' was not included in the Middleton list. Middleton's marketing approach provides some good examples of the issues relating to sustainable tourism.

# SUSTAINABILITY AS A STRATEGY

In spite of the difficulties involved in trying to find an acceptable definition for sustainability that will have practical value and the enormous problems in trying to measure crucial factors such as a destination's carrying capacity, there is a way forward. Sustainability more than anything else involves a process of recognition and responsibility. Recognition that the resources which are used to produce the tourism products are vulnerable. Responsibility for the wise use of these resources rests across all stakeholders from the governments and planners, through the industry that delivers the product, to the tourists and their hosts who temporarily coexist within the destination. A sustainable strategy must engage all of the stakeholders in the planning of tourism. The involvement of local resident participation is as difficult to achieve in practice as trying to get the industry to behave in a more environmentally and socially sympathetic manner.

From an environmental point of view there have been numerous attempts at trying to 'green' the industry. These attempts have been in the form of awareness campaigns through to certification schemes but none of them has been successful to date. The major problem has been the failure of the companies and organisations that have touted their certification programmes to demonstrate to the industry that certification truly saves them money or generates additional demand. Tourists are still largely driven by the pleasure factors of the product rather than their social and environmental conscience. Therefore consumers must share their responsibility because without a demonstrable demand for certified green products the certification process will not be embraced by the industry without some form of supporting legislation. The certification companies have by and large failed to put credible programmes into the marketplace because the enforcement that must accompany certification is expensive and time-consuming, making it an unwelcome burden on the industry. The only effective way of providing such certification schemes would be through a non-profit public sector body in the same way that health and safety standards are enforced.

The only practical way forward from a planning point of view is to develop integrated impact-modelling tools. One such tool was developed by staff at the International Centre for Tourism and Hospitality, Bournemouth University. It demonstrates the use of fully integrated impact software and provides a valuable planning tool that demonstrates the interrelatedness between each of the different types of impact, analyses them within a unified framework and allows these impacts to be examined from either forecasted future impacts or from those drawn as hypothetical case studies.

Economic sustainability for tourism requires holistic planning across all industrial sectors. It must also reach beyond the destination to make sure that intermediaries such as tour operators are not able to circumvent or put undue pressure on the planning processes. The formation of partnership chains throughout the industry would be one way to achieve this but is unlikely ever to happen given the competitiveness of the tourism industry and the predominance of SMEs. The quality of the tourism product demands staff training that is universally acceptable and the economic environment must make environmentally and socio-culturally sound behaviour the best economic choice.

Environmental sustainability in tourism requires greater awareness and knowledge about the impacts and ways of translating those impacts into the economic marketplace. The responsibility of tourists and businesses must be made clear and there needs to be a legislative system that penalises failure to abide by those systems. The indirect and induced environmental consequences of activities must be included in the calculation of their market prices but it must also be recognised that environmental and social systems change over time as a natural consequence of development and such changes need to be accommodated.

Tourism is also fundamentally dependent upon the climate in which it takes place and climates are subject to dynamic process. There has been much discussion about climate change over the past couple of decades and a great deal of debate about whether the climate changes we are currently experiencing are the result of cyclical effects or whether they are the result of human activities. Irrespective of the source of climate change, such changes will, in the long term, bring fundamental changes to the way in which tourism activity takes place. Tourists have a 'comfort zone' where the climate is appropriate to the activities they are pursuing. At its extremes, skiers require a climate that produces snow as much as sunbathers require one that has plenty of sun rays. The vast majority of tourism activity requires a climate that is within the 'comfort zone' of tourists so that they can do whatever activities they wish to pursue in comfort. Therefore the issue of climate change is an important one when considering the long-term sustainability of the tourism industry in each region of the world.

# CLIMATE CHANGE AND TOURISM

The earth's climate has demonstrably changed since pre-industrial times (before 1750) and is anticipated to continue changing for centuries to come. The most recent scientific, technical and socio-economic information produced worldwide relevant to the understanding of climate change is periodically reviewed and assessed by the Intergovernmental Panel on Climate Change (IPCC). In its latest report that was published in 2007, the IPCC declared that 'Warming of the climate system is unequivocal, as is now evident from observations of increases in global average air and ocean temperatures, widespread melting of snow and ice, and rising global average sea level'. The global mean temperature has increased approximately 0.76°C between the end of the nineteenth century and the beginning of the twenty-first. Most of the temperature change observed since the middle of the twentieth century can very likely be attributed to human activities that are increasing greenhouse gas concentrations in the atmosphere. Tourism is one of the human activities that contributes directly to climate change. In 2005, it was responsible for an estimated 5% of total $CO_2$ emissions, 40% of which are caused by aviation and 35% by other modes of transport. Air travel needs to be seen as the most problematic global environmental impact of tourism. The increasing trends for short breaks and more distant destinations add to this problem, with flights getting longer and far more frequent.

Tourism is a highly climate-sensitive economic sector, as a result of its close connections to the environment and climate itself. Indeed, the impacts of a changing climate are already becoming evident at destinations around the world, making clear that climate change is not a remote issue for tourism. The capacity of the tourism sector to adapt to climate change is relatively high because of tourism's dynamic nature. Therefore there will be important opportunities for tourism to reduce the vulnerability of communities to climate change through sustainable development.

The following section provides an overview of the main types of impacts of climate change on tourism and the regions that are most vulnerable. It also presents some of the main avenues for adaptation that are open to tourism stakeholders.

## Climate change impacts on tourism

Tourism businesses and the destinations in which they operate are clearly sensitive to climate variability and change. For example, changes in temperature, precipitation, wind speed, humidity or snow depth may have a direct effect on (i) the feasibility of tourism and recreation activities, and/or (ii) levels of safety associated with participation in tourism and recreation activities, and/or (iii) the quality of the experiences of those who participate in them. Modifications in any of these three aspects may cause participants to alter the frequency, duration, timing and/or location of future activity, or even to shift participation to an entirely different activity altogether. Climate defines the length and quality of tourism seasons and plays a major role in destination choice. In addition, climate affects a wide range of environmental resources that are critical to tourism, such as snow depth, biodiversity and stocks of fresh water. It also influences various facets of tourism operations, including heating, cooling and snowmaking. All in all, there are four broad categories of climate change impacts that could affect the competitiveness and sustainability of tourism destinations: direct climatic impacts; indirect environmental change impacts; indirect societal change impacts; and policy responses of other sectors, such as mitigation policy.

## Direct climatic impacts

Direct impacts include changes in the frequencies and patterns of extreme weather events, and changes in climate-related push and pull factors. In addition, costs for heating and cooling, as well as snowmaking, are directly linked to thermal conditions, which are changing. Adequate climatic conditions are key for all types of tourism activities, ranging from conventional beach tourism to special interest segments. As a result, the redistribution of climatic assets among tourism regions will be one of the most prominent impacts of projected climate change. Changes in the length and quality of climate-dependent tourism seasons (i.e. sun-and-sea or ski holidays) could have considerable implications for competitive relationships between destinations and, therefore, the profitability of tourism enterprises.

Substantial shifts in the world's climate suitability patterns have been projected. Some studies indicate that, towards the end of the century, the Mediterranean region is expected to become much less attractive for tourism in summer and more attractive in the shoulder seasons of spring and autumn. At the same time, northern Europe, the traditional source regions of the majority of tourists to the Mediterranean, is projected to become more suitable for tourist activities year round, particularly in the summer. As a result, more of these tourists might opt to stay within their own region, and more people from the south might decide to escape hot summer temperatures in the Mediterranean by travelling to northern Europe during the summer months. In North America, the number of cities in the USA with excellent conditions in the winter months is likely to increase, so that southern Florida and Arizona could face increasing competition for winter sun holiday travellers. Other world regions may have the potential for an even more substantive redistribution of climate resources for tourism than North America and Europe. In particular, the tropics may be vulnerable, although no detailed analyses for these regions have been performed so far.

## Indirect impacts from environmental change

Climate change also has an impact on tourism in more subtle and indirect ways, through changes in the environment and through changes in society. Environmental and climatic conditions are such critical resources for tourism that any changes will have an inevitable effect on the industry. Changes in water availability and snow cover, biodiversity loss, degradation of the aesthetics of destination landscapes, coastal impacts, damage to infrastructure and the increasing incidence of vector-borne diseases all impact on tourism in various ways.

A significant share of tourism takes place in warm, dry and sunny places, where water availability already acts as a constraint for tourism development. Climate change is likely to intensify this problem, as for major tourism regions such as the Caribbean and the Mediterranean rainfall levels are projected to decrease further. Competition for water will intensify between different uses, including drinking water (residential population), irrigation (agriculture) and swimming pools and golf courses (tourism). Globally, tourism accounts for only a tiny contribution to water demand, but locally it can be significant. The tourism industry is generally considered to be wasteful with regard to water. Specific segments such as golf tourism can have an enormous impact on water withdrawals. An 18-hole golf course can consume a few hundred million or even billion cubic metres of water per year.

Ironically, climate change is also projected to increase the likelihood of heavy precipitation and other extreme weather events. As a result, the tourism sector is likely to be affected not only by water shortages, but also by water excesses such as floods, which will impact on both natural and cultural heritage attractions in many regions. The higher frequency and higher intensity of natural hazards such as flooding, coastal erosion and more frequent hurricanes and tropical storms will also damage tourism facilities and infrastructure. In fact, this is already happening. The higher frequencies and intensities of hurricanes and other phenomena seem to play a significant role in the marked increase in insured losses from natural catastrophes that has occurred over recent years. Insurability may soon become an issue for businesses operating in high-risk areas such as flood plains and coastal areas.

Nature and biodiversity constitute important resources for tourism that will be strongly affected by climate change. The existence of certain endemic animal populations, birdsong, the flowering of plants, coral reefs, the type and cover of forests and other facets of biodiversity will be affected by climate change. Between 20% and 30% of plant and animal species assessed are likely to be at risk of extinction if increases in global average temperature exceed 1.5–2.5°C. Among other things, this will alter landscape aesthetics, a factor that greatly influences destination choice. In Tanzania and Kenya, park managers have noticed that changing climate conditions are affecting the migration of the wildebeest herds, in terms of both timing and route. Witnessing this great migration is one of the primary reasons for tourists to visit East Africa.

The health of millions of people will also be put at risk by projected climate change, particularly in those regions that have a low adaptive capacity. Countries identified as having the lowest adaptive capacity are predominantly in Sub-Saharan Africa and developing countries in Asia. The greatest impacts are likely to be caused by proportionally small increases in diseases that currently have major impacts already and will become even more widely prevalent. Examples include diarrhoea, malnutrition and malaria and other so-called vector-borne diseases transmitted by mosquitoes, flies and other vectors. These health impacts will compromise some destinations' ability to cater adequately for tourism, and will also affect tourists themselves, who will be exposed to new health risks when travelling.

## Indirect impacts from societal change

Climate change is thought to pose a risk to future economic growth and to the political stability of some nations. According to the influential Stern Review (2006), there could be an eventual permanent reduction in consumption per capita of 20% later in the twenty-first century or early twenty-second century, if we do nothing to slow down climate change. Any reductions of global GDP due to climate change would be likely to have negative implications for anticipated future growth in tourism spending.

Tourism, as discussed in Chapter 12, is known to be sensitive to security issues. Regional climate change can bring about the degradation of fresh water resources, declining food production, increased storm-related disasters and trans-boundary environmental migration. All of these impacts could overwhelm local capacities to respond to them and result in violence and the destabilisation of fragile governments. Climate change-associated security risks have been identified in a number of regions where tourism is highly important to the local economies, such as the Caribbean and Central America, Mediterranean and North Africa and China.

## Impacts from (mitigation) policies in other sectors

The Stern Review notes that tackling climate change is a pro-growth strategy for the longer term, with the benefits of strong, early action considerably outweighing the costs of doing nothing. It is also clear that in order to achieve the large emissions reductions needed to avoid 'dangerous' climate change, absolute emission reductions will eventually be required of the aviation sector, and aviation mitigation policies will therefore become increasingly relevant to international tourism. National or international mitigation policies – that is, policies that seek to reduce greenhouse gas emissions – have an impact on tourist behaviour in a number of ways: by increasing the costs of travel and perhaps real income through inflation, and by fostering environmental attitudes and changes in travel behaviour.

Climate change policy initiatives such as carbon trading are likely to increase transport costs enough to outweigh economic savings achieved through efficiency gains. Leisure travellers and short-haul travellers appear to be more sensitive to such price increases than business travellers and those on long-haul trips. One reason for this may be that there are more choices and possibilities for substitution for shorter trips compared with longer ones. In addition, tourists who can afford long-distance holidays are likely to be wealthier than average. An increase in air fares may not have an immediate effect (i.e. tourists cannot or do not want to change their plans quickly), but over time tourists will learn to avoid the more expensive option of air travel and become more aware of alternative transport options, such as buses, trains and cars.

In common with the role played by the perception of tourists towards travel risk, their perception with respect to transport, particularly air travel and its carbon footprint, is possibly more important than tourists' responses to price changes. Again, as with terrorist attacks (see Chapter 12), there is a key role played by the media that influences tourists' behaviour in response to climate change. Cheap air travel has increasingly come to be viewed as a 'right' that people appreciate and do not want to give up. Examples of this can be found in the concerns about the impact of 'anti-travel' sentiments in Europe, and concerns about the costs of carbon taxes or other mitigation policies have been expressed in Australia, New Zealand and Asian long-haul destinations. Some studies even conclude that a 'psychology of denial' exists in terms of people's awareness of air travel's contribution to climate change.

## Impacts on vulnerable destination types

The positive and negative impacts of climate change on the tourism sector will vary substantially by market segment and geographic region. There will be 'winners and losers' at the business, destination and nation level. In order to minimise associated risks and capitalise upon new opportunities, all tourism businesses and destinations will need to adapt to climate change in a sustainable manner. The vulnerability of tourism is of particular concern to those areas where tourism constitutes the major livelihood of local communities (dependency). The following section looks at the potential impacts of climate change on three major destination types with established vulnerabilities: mountains, islands and coastal zones, and natural and cultural heritage areas.

### Mountain and winter sports destinations

Mountain regions are important destinations for global tourism, and snow cover and pristine mountain landscapes are their principal attractions. These features are also very vulnerable to climate change. Sensitive mountain environments will be altered by climate change, with implications for their attractiveness for nature-based tourism, as well as for the frequency and magnitude of natural hazards.

The impact of climate change on the snow-based sports tourism industry is potentially severe. The industry has been repeatedly identified as being at risk regarding global climate change, because of the close linkage between economic performance and climate. The key climate change impacts of interest to the winter sports industry relate to natural snow reliability and also technical snow reliability (i.e. cold temperatures to make snow). The latter is important in areas where snowmaking is almost universal among ski areas and covers a high proportion of terrain suitable for skiing.

Known vulnerabilities exist in a range of European and North American countries, but the projected impacts on destinations in these nations vary in magnitude and relate to different time horizons. The Australian and Scottish ski industries could disappear completely if some of the projections relating to moderate or high warming scenarios over the next 50 years materialise. Within most regional markets, however, the probable consequence of climate change will be limited to a contraction in the number of ski operators and destinations. In practice, the higher-altitude destinations are likely to expand at the expense of the lower-altitude ones.

A recent study conducted for the Organization for Economic Cooperation and Development suggests that the number of ski areas in the European Alps that are considered 'naturally snow reliable' will drop from 609 (91%) to 404 (61%) under a +2°C warming scenario and would further decline to 202 (30%) under a +4°C warming scenario. By comparison, climate change scenarios for the European Alps project an annual warming of 2.3 to 3.3°C by mid-century and 2.9 to 5.3°C by the end of the twenty-first century. Warming is even more pronounced in the winter months.

Developments in natural snow reliability do not tell the whole story. Evidence from North America suggests that advanced snowmaking systems substantially lower the vulnerability of ski areas. Such systems may be beneficial for a ski area as a whole, but require investments that may be too large for individual actors. This may partly explain why advanced snowmaking systems are less common in Europe than in North America, where ski resorts tend to be more integrated.

Snowmaking is no solution for snowmobiling, which is another major snow-based winter sport in North America. Snowmobiling is completely reliant on natural snowfall, which makes this industry much more vulnerable to climate change than the ski industry. Under the rapid climate change scenarios, a reliable snowmobile season will disappear from most regions of eastern North America within 50 years.

## Impacts on islands and in coastal zones

Islands and coastal zones are among the most vulnerable types of tourist destinations with respect to climate change. They are likely to experience an increased intensity and frequency of extreme events, sea-level rise, increased climate variability, changes in ocean circulation and changes in natural ecosystems. It is very likely that the most immediate and significant of these will be changes in the nature of extreme events (e.g. flooding, tropical cyclones, storm surges, heatwaves) and climatic variability (e.g. droughts, and prevailing winds accelerating coastal erosion). Coastal areas are particularly vulnerable to extreme wind events. Major wind-storm disasters and the losses generated by them have increased drastically in recent decades. Extreme events can destroy ecosystems, such as mangrove forests, tropical forests and coral reefs. Coral reefs especially are a crucial resource for tourism and other sectors. In many destinations, reefs are the key pull factor for tourists as a visitor attraction and can be considered a major economic asset. The increase in sea surface temperature and increasing acidity of the water will impact on marine life and coral reefs and erode these assets.

Given that most tourism activities take place in coastal zones, sea-level rise is of major importance to tourism. It aggravates coastal erosion and leads to the loss of beaches. Sea-level rise is primarily a consequence of the expansion of sea water (warmer water takes up more space); the continued melting of mountain glaciers and small ice caps add to this. Further global sea-level rise could range from 20 to 60 cm by 2100.

Even small rises in sea level will result in significant erosion, increased flood hazard, contamination of freshwater aquifers, loss of protective coral reefs, mangrove areas and sand beaches. In small island regions especially, much of the biological diversity and most of the population, agricultural land and capital assets are located in these areas and are, therefore, at risk. Among these vulnerable islands are major tourism destinations. In the Indian Ocean, the Maldives average only 1.5 metres above sea level and projected rates of sea level rise are likely to inundate large areas of the different islands and atolls. Other low-lying islands, such as the Bahamas and Kiribati, face similar problems.

## MINI CASE STUDY 10.2
For Dominica, adaptation best option to combat climate change

### By Desmond Brown

ROSEAU, Dominica, Jun 6, 2012 (IPS) – It has been dubbed the 'Nature Isle' of the Caribbean, its craggy and dense rain forests, usually covered with fog, bearing testament to how cool temperatures can be here.

But in recent times, Dominica, an island located between the French dependencies of Martinique and Guadeloupe in the Lesser Antilles, and more so its capital, Roseau, have been experiencing sweltering heat of 31 degrees Celsius or higher. Officials blame the temperatures on climate change and global warming.

'This is . . . probably one of the most obvious effects of climate change that we experience on a daily basis,' Kenneth Darroux, environment minister, told IPS.

'Gone are the days when people thought that climate change was just a figment of the imagination of a few mad scientists,' he said. 'We are actually starting to feel the effects now, and the science is proving correct.'

The island has seen a marked change in seasonal temperatures and rain cycles. Darroux said climate change is already costing Dominica millions of dollars annually in lost crops and disaster response.

The findings of a new report, to be released at the Rio+20 summit later in June, said Latin America and the Caribbean face annual damages in the order of 100 billion US dollars by 2050 from diminishing agricultural yields, disappearing glaciers, flooding, droughts and other events triggered by a warming planet.

On the positive side, the cost of investments in adaptation to address these impacts is much smaller, in the order of one-tenth the physical damages, according to the study, jointly produced by the Inter-American Development Bank (IDB), the Economic Commission of Latin America and the Caribbean (ECLAC) and the World Wildlife Fund (WWF).

However, the study also notes that forceful reductions in global emissions of greenhouse gases are needed to avert some of the potentially catastrophic longer term consequences of climate change.

## HARNESSING FUNDS

Countries would need to invest an additional 110 billion US dollars per year over the next four decades to decrease per capita carbon emissions to levels consistent with global climate stabilisation goals, the report estimates.

Darroux said Dominica intends to cash in on some of the millions of dollars available to help countries deal with the climate change and its effects.

He noted that once local officials became aware of the potentially devastating impact climate change could have on the environment and the large volume of funds potentially available to mitigate such devastation, the government moved swiftly to set up an Environment Ministry following general elections in 2009.

In December 2011, Darroux announced that Dominica was in the process of formulating a Low-Carbon Climate-Resilient Development Strategy that he later explained took a two-pronged approach.

'While we work towards combating the impacts of climate change, it also looks at incorporating climate change projects in the whole scope of national development,' Darroux said. 'It also serves as a means of attracting financing. We have heard about the much elusive billions of dollars out there so right now this strategy is actually a way of harnessing these funds.'

He explained that the strategy incorporates multiple national government policy papers, identifying a number of priority areas that climate change and the effects of climate change are most likely to affect, including agriculture, fisheries, eco-tourism and green energy.

This particular strategy may be new, but the government has actually been combating the effects of climate change for years by building sea defense walls and river defense walls to protect coastal villages, roads and properties against storm surges and other potentially damaging phenomena such as rising sea levels and erratic tropical storms.

'Our terrain makes us very vulnerable,' Darroux said, noting that a lot of the country's infrastructure is located along the coast. The country is also highly prone to landslides.

## MORE VICTIM THAN PERPETRATOR

While Latin America and the Caribbean contribute only 11 percent of the emissions that cause global warming, the region is particularly vulnerable to global warming's effects, given its dependence on natural resources and the presence of bio-climate hotspots such as the Amazon basin, the Caribbean coral biome, coastal wetlands and fragile mountain ecosystems, says the new report to be released Rio+20.

These effects can be felt in agriculture, exposure to tropical diseases and changing rainfall patterns, among other areas. The value of the loss of net agricultural exports is estimated to fall between 30 billion and 52 billion US dollars in 2050.

The study notes that the cost of adaptation is a mere fraction of the cost of the actual physical impacts, conservatively estimated at .2 percent of GDP for the region. Adaptation efforts would also offer significant development benefits, from enhanced water and food security to improved air quality and less vehicle congestion, ultimately reducing their net costs.

The Environmental Coordinating Unit has been doing its best to spread the climate change message to the general population, the unit's director, Lloyd Pascal, told IPS.

'We've produced calendars that we distribute throughout the schools across the island; we make sure that every government department receives a calendar,' he said, adding that they also engaged in media outreach and public awareness work.

While Pascal is not satisfied that every corner of Dominica has received the message, he said that nevertheless, based on three severe events that occurred last year, 'we are sure that more people are aware of the effects of climate change now than when we started in 1995'.

*Source*: http://ipsnews.net/news.asp?idnews=108060 (accessed 7 June 2012)

## DISCUSSION QUESTIONS

1. The destinations most vulnerable to the negative impacts of climate change are also the ones least able to meet the adaptation and mitigation costs. What strategies can be used to help such vulnerable destinations?

2. The acceptance of the effects of climate change may mean that some destinations should diversify into industries that are not so vulnerable to changes in the climate. Is this an unreasonable observation when looking at SIDS?

### Impacts on natural and cultural heritage

The natural environment is often a very important determinant of tourism demand. Landscape ranks among the most important factors in destination choice, and tourists are attracted to national parks because they represent an aesthetically pleasing and healthy environment with interesting flora and fauna. The impact of climate change on biodiversity and natural landscapes may have a negative influence on their amenity value and hence on visitor numbers. Coral bleaching is a case in point. Its effects on visitation could be assessed by studying the impacts of the bleaching events in the 1990s and 2000s. Most studies concluded that the impact of bleaching were limited, presumably because of the divers' low levels of awareness of bleaching. Whether the impacts remain limited after sustained periods of bleaching is an open question.

For some types of tourism, the loss of individual species is important, rather than the loss of scenic beauty. Sportfishing, for example, depends upon specific types of fish that require specific climatic conditions. Changes in these conditions will lead to financial damage for the sportfishing industry, which for the US have been estimated at US$320 million per year or more in the 2050s.

Cultural heritage includes considerations of built heritage (historic and architectural), archaeological heritage and socio-cultural heritage. The most obvious impact of climate change on cultural heritage is the direct effect of rising sea level on structures near coasts that may be flooded or damaged by coastal erosion. Increased rainfall resulting in rising water tables will also have an effect on the foundations or the fabric of buildings. Saving vulnerable sites from climate change, including world famous destinations such as Venice, will in many cases be very costly.

## Implications for tourism demand patterns

The response of tourists to the complexity of destination impacts will determine how tourism demand patterns will be affected by climate change. Climate, the natural environment and personal safety are three primary factors in destination choice, and climate change is anticipated to have significant impacts on all three of these factors. Climate is also a principal driver of seasonality in demand, which has been described as one of the most problematic features of the tourism industry.

Weather and climate are of universal importance in defining destination attractiveness and central motivators in the selection of holiday destination and the timing of discretionary travel. Temperature and sunshine have been found to influence travel patterns and tourism expenditures. In addition, the weather conditions experienced at the destination are believed to influence holiday satisfaction. As climate is an important resource for tourists, projected changes in the distribution of climate resources are forecast to have important consequences for tourism.

Translating these projected changes in climate resources into projected changes in tourist visitation has proved to be very difficult. Our understanding of how tourists respond to climate variability and change is very limited, and the effect of perceived versus real changes has hardly been explored. In addition, it is uncertain if and how institutions such as school holidays will respond to climate change. Rigid institutions may limit tourists to adaptation through destination choice, whereas flexible institutions may open up the possibility of going on holiday in a different season. For many destinations, coping with climate change will be much easier in this latter scenario.

Simulation models have been used to explore the potential impact of climate change on the level of aggregated international tourism. Anticipated impacts include a gradual shift in preferred destinations to higher latitudes and to higher elevations in mountainous areas. Tourists from temperate nations that currently dominate international travel (e.g. northern Europe) are expected to spend more holidays in their home country or nearby, adapting their travel patterns to take advantage of new climatic opportunities closer to home. This shift in travel patterns would have three important implications: proportionally more tourism spending in temperate nations, proportionally less spending in warmer nations now frequented by tourists from temperate regions, and a modest net reduction in total international tourist numbers.

The above studies assume the existence of certain temperature thresholds, above which further temperature increases lead to deterioration in the level of attraction of specific destinations. Little is known about such thresholds, however; for instance, about what tourists perceive to be 'too hot' for any particular tourism destination. Equally little is known about the role of tourist perceptions of the environmental impacts of global climate change at destinations. Perceptions of coral bleaching, glacier losses or reduced wildlife prevalence may be more important for tourism demand than the actual changes that occur. Information on tourist climate preferences and key thresholds, and tourist perceptions are important knowledge gaps that need to be addressed if potential long-range shifts in tourist demand are to be more accurately forecast.

## Adaptation to climate change

Regardless of the level of success of efforts to reduce emissions, a certain amount of climate change is unavoidable. Even if emissions were reduced to zero today, the global average temperature would still increase by another 0.6 °C. The IPCC has therefore indicated that there is a need for societies around the world, and economic sectors like tourism, to adapt to climate change in the decades ahead. Adaptation to climate change refers to an adjustment in natural or human systems in response to actual or expected climatic stimuli or their effects, which moderates harm or exploits beneficial opportunities.

The tourism industry is known to be remarkably resilient to shocks. Recent disasters from which tourism has quickly recovered include SARS, terrorist attacks and the Asian tsunami. The resilience and dynamic nature of the tourism industry suggests a relatively high climate change adaptive capacity within the sector as a whole. Many stakeholders in the industry are highly optimistic about their ability to cope with the effects of climate change. This optimism may not be warranted, however, as climate change may bring major impacts that the stakeholders do not have prior experience with.

There are several key barriers to adaptation. While acknowledging the reality and seriousness of climate change, many stakeholders have no clue how climate change might affect their businesses or activities. There is a real or perceived gap between the long timeframes associated with climate change and the short timeframes of business activities. In addition, there is a gap between the broad-scale projections produced by climate models and the very local conditions experienced by the stakeholders. Large parts of the tourism industry are relatively poorly organised, consisting of SMEs with limited human and financial resources to invest in a good understanding of the relevance of climate change for their business. Importantly, the tourism industry is very image sensitive and is very cautious about even acknowledging concerns about climate change risks for fear of adversely affecting destination or business reputation. Many businesses are therefore inclined to adapt quietly rather than publicly express their worries. Not wanting to be or appear proactive the industry tends to expect public authorities to take the lead.

In general, adaptive capacity is thought to vary between the sub-sectors of the tourism industry. Tourists have the greatest adaptive capacity, with relative freedom to avoid destinations impacted by climate change or to shift the timing of travel to avoid unfavourable climate conditions. Large tour operators, which do not own the infrastructure, are also in a good position to adapt to changes at the destination level because they can respond to clients' demands and provide information to influence clients' travel choices. Destination communities and tourism operators with large investments in immobile capital assets (e.g. hotel, resort complex, marina or casino) have the lowest adaptive capacity.

The new risks introduced by climate change pose additional challenges to the design of new tourism infrastructures. Similarly, existing infrastructure may have to be modified if current performance standards are inconsistent with the changed climatic conditions. For example, tourist accommodation in tropical areas should be built or retro-fitted to be cyclone-proof, withstanding both high average wind speeds and extreme conditions. Early-warning systems can help to reduce risks further.

Some climate-related risks cannot be avoided by any adaptation measures. In such cases, insurance is critical. It enables the industry to spread the burdens of such risks. In time, some risks may become uninsurable, however, as the insurance industry faces the prospect of a growth in the number and size of claims as a consequence of climate change. In fact, the insurance industry is already implementing risk-reduction strategies. A number of insurers in the USA recently decided to reduce coverage in Florida and the Gulf of Mexico. Such changes in insurability will have major implications for future tourism reinvestment in and development of disaster-prone regions such as the Caribbean.

Adaptation is not limited to technical or behavioural measures; it can also include management of tourism's natural resource base. Conservation of biodiversity and maintenance of ecosystem structure and function are important climate change adaptation strategies. Establishing and enforcing protected areas is generally considered to be one of the most appropriate strategies for ensuring that terrestrial, freshwater and marine ecosystems are resilient to the additional pressures arising from climate change.

Protecting the natural environment can also help to reduce the risk of avalanches and rock slides in mountain destinations. These destinations also have a wide range of climate change adaptation options available to cope with reduced natural snowfall and to take advantage of longer warm-weather tourism seasons. The importance of snowmaking as an adaptation to climate variability and change cannot be overstated. In eastern North America and Australia, snowmaking is almost universal among ski operators. In other ski regions such as Western Europe, western North America, East Asia and South America, snowmaking is not as extensively used, but is continuing to grow.

The sustainability of some adaptation strategies has been questioned. Glacier preservation and expansion of ski areas into higher elevations have been criticised for harming fragile ecosystems and reducing landscape amenities. Communities and environmental organisations have expressed concern about the extensive water and energy use associated with snowmaking, and about the chemical additives involved in the process. For some ski operators, snowmaking may be uneconomic altogether, because of the elevated costs of energy, infrastructure and water.

Product and market diversification are common adaptation strategies to cope with the business challenges of pronounced tourism seasonality. Many ski resorts have made substantial investments to provide alternative activities for non-skiing visitors (e.g. snowmobiling, indoor pools, health and wellness spas, retail stores). A number of former ski resorts have further diversified their business operations to become 'four season resorts', offering non-winter activities such as golf, boating and white-water rafting, mountain biking, paragliding, horseback riding and indoor skiing. Product diversification is also a key adaptation option for island and coastal destinations. Many of them seek to become less dependent on beach tourism and other climate-sensitive activities by adding golf courses, cultural heritage sites and shopping malls to their portfolio.

Climate change risk management should be integrated into business practices relating to revenue and cost, assets and liabilities, and the wider supply chain. As the above sections show, tourism businesses, entrepreneurs and investors can improve their management of climate change risks, independent from the adaptation policies undertaken at an institutional level (e.g. international organisations, national governments or communities). This includes managing vulnerabilities to direct impacts from climate change, and those to changes in the resource or customer bases. For example, business planning might benefit from an understanding of which markets might react most strongly to temperature increases or to the negative perception of air travel.

## CONCLUSION

Sustainablity is an integral part of modern day tourism development, in spite of the difficulties associated with achieving it or even defining it. Sustainable strategies are now at the forefront of the tourism agenda.

Climatic change adds to the factors that influence perceived travel risk and major environmental events such as tsunamis, earthquakes and hurricanes attract a great deal of media attention. Destinations can adapt to climatic change within limits by building infrastructure and superstructure designed to withstand extreme weather conditions, developing tourism facilities on land with higher elevations or away from areas that are known to be more at risk of temperature or rainfall levels that exceed the threshold of acceptability exhibited by tourists, but this is a slow and very expensive process. Some businesses, such as intermediaries, are better able to adapt to climatic change whereas others have no room at all for adaptation. The only certain thing is that travel-related risk has always been a part of the industry, it has become more important over the past couple of decades and is likely to continue to influence tourists' decision making in an increasingly significant way.

## SELF-CHECK QUESTIONS

1. Define sustainability.
2. What are the major obstacles to achieving sustainable development?
3. What methods can be used to make tourism more sustainable than it is at present?
4. What is meant by the term 'carrying capacity'?
5. What are the major direct and indirect impacts of climate change on tourism destinations?
6. How might tourism destinations adapt to climate change and what are the limitations to such adaptations?

## YOUTUBE

### Sustainability

How Sustainability relates to Tourism and Economic Development South Carolina
**http://www.youtube.com/watch?v=u6WkoRtEjMQ**

One Planet Tourism, a film by the Cornwall Sustainable Tourism Project (CoaST)
**http://www.youtube.com/watch?v=F4H5AosDk8s**

Sustainable Tourism 2012
**http://www.youtube.com/watch?v=qsZgB90pOrc**

Sustainable Tourism – VisitScotland
**http://www.youtube.com/watch?v=8oKm3E63Z4**

## Climate Change

Climate change and tourism in Lapland
**http://www.youtube.com/watch?v=V5jpGkovKlw**

UQ School of Tourism Seminar Series – The Future of Tourism: A climate change perspective (Part 1)
**http://www.youtube.com/watch?v=NbvL_5X65J0**

UQ School of Tourism Seminar Series – The Future of Tourism: A climate change perspective (Part 2)
**http://www.youtube.com/watch?v=0t39rdytynk**

UQ School of Tourism Seminar Series – The Future of Tourism: A climate change perspective (Part 3)
**http://www.youtube.com/watch?v=BcuHGFPOXuU**

UQ School of Tourism Seminar Series – The Future of Tourism: A climate change perspective (Part 4)
**http://www.youtube.com/watch?v=41GXdFlGp1Y**

Scotland's ski industry faces up to climate change
**http://www.youtube.com/watch?v=uz4jMtvJ_mU**

Caribbean Climate Change Let's Adapt!
**http://www.youtube.com/watch?v=O8tDmdNCACE**

# REFERENCES AND FURTHER READING

Brundtland, G. (ed.) (1987) *Our Common Future: World Commission on Environment and Development*, Oxford University Press, Oxford.

Butcher, J. (1997) 'Sustainable development or development', pp. 27–38 in Stabler, M.J. (ed.) *Tourism Sustainability – Principles to Practice*, CAB International, Wallingford.

Butler, R.W. (1997) 'The concept of carrying capacity for tourism destinations', pp. 11–22 in Cooper, C.P. and Wanhill, S.R.C. (eds), *Tourism Development: Environmental and Community Issues*, Wiley, Chichester.

Choucri, N. (1997) 'Global system for sustainable development research TDP-MIT', Unpublished notes, MIT, Cambridge, MA, January.

Ciscar, J.-M., Iglesias, A., Feyen, L., Szabo, L., Regermorter, D. V., Amelung, B., Nicholls, R., Watkiss, P., Christenson, O.B., Dankers, R. Garrote, L., Goodess, C.M., Hunt, A. Moreno, A., Richards, J. and Soria, A. (2011) 'Physical and economic consequences of climate change in Europe', *PNAS* **108**(7), 2678–83.

Coomer, J. (1979) 'The nature of the quest for a sustainable society', in Coomer, J. (ed.), *Quest for a Sustainable Society*, Pergamon Press, Oxford.

Duval, D. (ed.) (2004) *Tourism in the Caribbean: Trends, Development, Prospects*, in the series edited by M. Hall, Contemporary Geographies of Leisure, Tourism and Mobility, Routledge, London.

European Commission (2009) *White Paper Adapting to Climate Change. Towards a European Framework for Action*, COM (2009) 147 final.

Gartner, W. and Lime, D. (eds) (2000) *Trends in Outdoor Recreation, Leisure and Tourism*, CABI, New York.

Hardin, G. (1991) 'The tragedy of the unmanaged commons: population and the disguises of providence', in Andelson, R.V. (ed.), *Commons Without Tragedy: Protecting the Environment from Overpopulation – A New Approach*, Barnes and Noble Books, Savage, MD.

IUCN, UNEP and WWF (1980) 'World conservation strategy: living resource conservation for sustainable development', IUCN, Gland, Switzerland.

Johnson, P. and Thomas, B. (1994) 'The notion of capacity in tourism: a review of the issues', pp. 297–308 in Cooper, C.P. and Lockwood, A. (eds), *Progress in Tourism, Recreation and Hospitality Management*, Wiley, Chichester.

Mathieson, A. and Wall, G. (1982) *Tourism: Economic, Physical and Social Impacts*, Longman, Harlow.

McElroy, J. (2004) 'Global perspectives of Caribbean tourism', pp. 39–56 in Duval, D.T. (ed.), *Tourism in the Caribbean*, Routledge, London.

Middleton, V.T.C. with Hawkins, R. (1998) *Sustainable Tourism: A Marketing Perspective*, Butterworth Heinemann, Oxford.

Stern Review (2006) at **http://webarchive.nationalarchives.gov.uk/+/http://www.hm-treasury. gov.uk/stern_review_report.htm**

Weaver, D.B. (2004) 'Manifestations of ecotourism', pp. 172–86 in Duval, D.T. (ed.), *Tourism in the Caribbean*, Routledge, London.

Wight, P. (2001) 'Ecotourists: not a homogenous market segment', in Weaver, D. (ed.), *The Encyclopaedia of Ecotourism*, CABI, Wallingford.

# MAJOR CASE STUDY 10.1
## A sustainable tourism investment model

Bournemouth University, working with WWF and UNEP developed a new approach to measuring the economic and environmental impacts associated with tourism investment and combined it with a model framework that is intended to drive tourism businesses towards greater economic and environmental efficiency. Adopting the robustness of input–output technology but overcoming its shortages by developing an online rolling year on year model to ensure that the model is dynamic in nature, the new system has three interfaces, each intended to optimise the activities of the stakeholders involved in the tourism industry.

## WHAT DOES THE MODEL DO?

By providing a focus for stakeholders to measure and compare their economic, business and environmental performance with others in their sector, the model creates an 'environment of competitive efficiency' to drive existing and new businesses to a more efficient and sustainable future.

Through its engagement of the private sector on a *quid pro quo* basis, the model provides detailed information about the impact of their business on the local economy and environment and how well it is performing compared with other businesses in its sector. The model provides potential investors with a series of data that are designed to allow them to determine how they might perform in the market and the impacts of their project.

For the public sector the model provides an economic and environmental overview for policy and planning decisions.

The overall aim of the model is to place economic and environmental efficiency at centre stage of economies and to drive towards a more sustainable future (see Figure 10.4).

## FEATURES OF THE MODEL

- The model is web-based, providing password-protected access wherever users are located. Registration to gain access is compulsory and once registered, users are confined to those data relevant to their sector.

- The model provides macro and micro information on performance indicators, benchmarks, impacts and forecasts.

- All sectors, not just tourism-related sectors, can engage with the model, helping to drive sustainability across a broad front.

- The interaction of users with the model gives the stakeholders ownership.

- The model will self-perpetuate by maintaining the integrity of the data through the engagement of stakeholders – a sustainable, sustainable model!

- Time series views of performance indicators show how efficiency improvements are achieved over time.

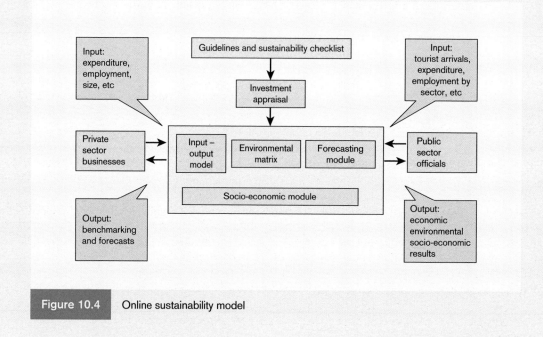

**Figure 10.4**    Online sustainability model

## WHO BENEFITS FROM THE MODEL?

The model benefits all stakeholders by helping drive forward not only a more environmentally sound economy, but also a more efficient and competitive one.

### Businesses

Irrespective of the size of businesses, from large hotels to small cafés, from taxis to airlines, all sectors will be able to examine how they compare with the minimum, average and maximum performers in their sector and modify their business activities to compete.

### Investors

Investors will be able to see how well the sector is performing before they invest, establish if the local economy will support their investment and examine the likely impacts of their investment on the local economy and its environment.

### Destinations

The public sector will benefit because they will be able to see a detailed overview of the economy, determine the likely impacts of proposed investments and to explore what if . . .? scenarios.

### Residents and employees

The local population will benefit from the increased robustness of the local economy, the sustainability of businesses and by reducing the negative environmental consequences associated with the growth of the tourism industry.

## DISCUSSION QUESTIONS

1.  An online rolling model that is regenerated each year overcomes many of the limitations of the input–output framework, but what limitations remain?

2.  What are the dangers of giving ownership of the sustainability model to the stakeholders and how might they be mitigated?

3.  What planning and policy features could be extracted from such a model and how can the information be used to guide marketing strategies?

## TOURISM AS I SEE IT
Sustainability

Someone famously said that 'an elephant is a very hard thing to define, but if you see one coming down the street you know what it is'. It's rather the same about sustainability and tourism – we've stopped describing it and started to engage it.

20 years ago at the 1992 Rio Earth Summit – when the modern approach to 'sustainable development' was set out in 'Agenda 21' – the focus was on preserving the planet's resources and for our sector it was very much ecotourism and the conservation, adventure, nature niche, often translated as 'take pictures; leave footprints'. Our industry was not seen as a major polluter so was under limited pressure to embrace the new sustainability mindset.

Ten years later at the Johannesburg World Summit on Sustainable Development the mood had shifted from planet to people and poverty. Against the background of the Millennium Development Goals we moved on to a broader idea of responsible tourism with an emphasis on ensuring that local populations don't suffer from tourism's influx and a growing focus on creating economic benefits and jobs.

Now at Rio+20 we have seen another 'sustainability' shift to green growth – a geopolitical paradigm to respond to the big social, economic, environment and climate challenges of today and the population-driven resource challenges on the horizon. Not so much a defined set of initiatives, guidelines or even policies but a multi-decade journey to create sustainable consumption, production and investment patterns for every activity on the planet.

Our industry has also begun to come of age as a mainstream sector with recognition of its socio-economic importance by the G20. At the same time the climate and economically driven rethink of the last decade has broadened our environmental engagement, highlighting carbon impacts – particularly from transport – and with increasing attention on local jobs as well as lifestyle impacts in terms of lower carbon, more conservation, resource efficiency and inclusion. Increasingly the 'travelism' phenomena – tourism, transport and local impacts – will be linked with this new mainstream sustainability.

Geoffrey Lipman
President, ICTP International. Council of Tourism Partners.
Geoffrey also holds Professorial appointments at European institutions.

# CHAPTER 11
## TOURISM AND DEVELOPMENT PLANNING

### LEARNING OUTCOMES

The objectives of this chapter are to ensure that you:

- understand how tourism fits into the general theories of economic development;

- understand the importance of integrated tourism planning and development, development planning layers and the role of the community in this respect;

- understand how approaches such as Visioning, SWOT, STEP and PESTEL can add value to the planning process and the likely success of strategies;

- are able to identify characteristics of the tourism product that have implications for tourism planning and development; and

- can outline the major steps involved in the tourism planning and development process.

Photograph: South Beach, Miami, Florida, USA © Kelly Miller

## INTRODUCTION

Any form of economic development requires careful planning if it is to be successful in achieving the implicit or explicit objectives that underlie the development. In this chapter we show that tourism development, because it is a multi-sector activity and because it brings with it the environmental, social and economic impacts discussed in Chapters 7–9, requires considerable planning if it is to be successful and sustainable (see Chapter 10). The role of tourism within the major general economic development theories is examined. We also show that the development of tourism will not be optimal if it is not undertaken as a partnership that engages all of the stakeholders rather than being left entirely in the hands of the private sector. The private sector tends to be associated with a myopic view that is focused upon short-term profits whereas the public sector is often associated with a conservative approach towards development. We therefore identify in this chapter that tourism development planning requires careful cooperation and coordination of both the public and private sectors together with the engagement of the local community. This chapter also demonstrates that the emphasis of tourism development planning has moved away from the rigid 'grand design' master plan in favour of more flexible and reactive development plans. This change in approach is due, in no small way, to the recognition that development is not a finite concept. Development is infinite and takes place in an ever-changing environment. Therefore development plans should attempt to facilitate the desired objectives while taking into account the changing factors that influence not only the objectives but also the means of achieving them.

# TOURISM AND ECONOMIC DEVELOPMENT THEORIES

There have been a number of theories put forward to explain the process of economic development (see Nafziger, 1997). A few of the more influential economic development theories in their time include:

- The English classical theory of economic stagnation.
- Marx's historical approach.
- Rostow's identification of stages of economic growth.
- Vicious circles of demand/supply and investment.
- Balanced and unbalanced growth theories.
- Theories of dependence.

It is possible to examine the main threads of these theories in order to identify whether or not there is a role for tourism within the more general theories of economic development, although it should be noted that since the 1970s there has been a tendency to move away from the grand theoretical notions of economic development and instead use a more specific, case-by-case, approach. Nevertheless, it can be helpful to look at the characteristics of tourism development within a framework of general economic development.

## English classical theory of economic stagnation

This theory grew out of the classical writings of early economists Malthus, Mill and Ricardo. To understand the concept of the theory it needs to be noted that such writers were very much influenced by Newtonian physics with its belief that life was never random and was ordered by some 'grand design'. Of the various assumptions employed by the classical economists, the operation of this theory can best be seen by focusing upon just two of them: that in the event of no technological progress, output was constrained by the scarcity of land, and the law of diminishing returns.

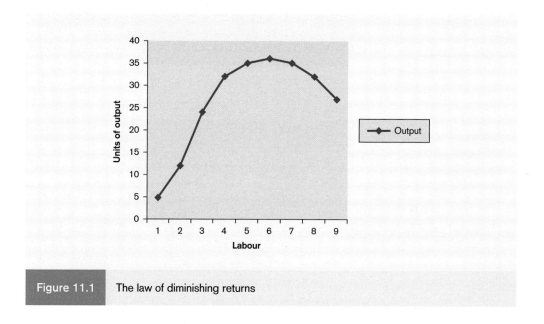

| Figure 11.1 | The law of diminishing returns |

In Figure 11.1 it can be seen that additional units of labour with a fixed amount of land increase output per unit of labour significantly when the labour is increased from 1 to 3. However, when a fourth unit of labour is added the increase in output, although positive, is not as great as the previous increase. The increase in output achieved when the fifth and sixth units of labour are added becomes progressively less. If more than six units of labour are added the output starts to decline as diseconomies of large scale are experienced.

The theory also suggests that the long-term wage rate, the natural wage rate, was at the subsistence level. Therefore, in spite of short-term deviations from the natural wage rate, it would always tend to return to the natural level.

Under this theory, if food production increases, wages rise and the extra food available means that the population becomes healthier and grows. As the population increases there are more mouths to feed and more units of labour with the fixed supply of land. As the labour force is increased the average wage rate falls and continues to do so until the subsistence wage rate is reached. If the wage rate falls below subsistence level then the population declines and the scarcity of labour forces the average wage rate back up to its natural level. Given the lack of any technological progress, the only way to mitigate the diminishing returns is to increase the capital accumulation per worker. But even here, the classical economists had tied themselves into an economic straitjacket. The need to acquire profits and interest payments in return for increased capital stocks requires the existence of increased availability of surplus value (output less the cost of labour) but the diminishing returns assumption means that the surplus diminishes and hence the return on capital. With diminishing returns on capital there is reduced incentive to increase the capital per worker and the route to economic stagnation and decline is set. There are good grounds for viewing the English classical theory as a theory of doom and gloom.

The flaws in the theory are many and include the neglect of technological progress that can greatly multiply the output per worker. Also, the assumption that population growth was uniquely determined by prosperity is found to be wanting, particularly in industrialised countries where voluntary birth control has stabilised population levels. The ownership of capital and land is not necessarily the prerogative of the private capital owners. State ownership of capital and land may result in a different set of objectives that may allow continued growth.

## Marx's historical approach to development

Marx's historical materialism approach to development is framed within a dynamic world rather than being based on the static scenario used by the classical economists. Within this dynamic view of development, changing technology, enhanced organisation of production and the development of human skills all work together to provide lubricant for the engine of change. The world, as seen by Marx and Engels, moved naturally from **feudalism** to **capitalism** to **socialism** and then to **communism**. The economic consequences of the rise to capitalism include demand expanding more slowly than productive capacity and an increase in monopolistic power that forces out small businesses, creating a segment of the population of workers who are without property. The dynamics of this results in what Marx referred to as a reserve army of unemployed that acts as a buffer to absorb the shocks as the economy expands and contracts during business cycles. The result is a series of crises where the ownership of productive capacity is repeatedly challenged by the educated proletariat until communism is established and socialism through the state becomes redundant.

There are a number of flaws in Marx's view of economic development, including the observed facts, that revolution when the proletariat took the state happened in Russia rather than the West at a time when Russia was one of the least developed capitalistic countries in Europe. The theory relies upon there being a conflict of the objectives held by capitalists and those held by the proletariat. If there is no conflict and both sides realise that they can prosper if they both decide to share a fast-growing output then the dynamism of Marx's theory takes a serious blow. In spite of this, Marx's theory still finds a great deal of support from those either discontented with the distribution of wealth in their country or worried about the threats of the recent trends towards globalisation and the dominance of multinational corporations.

## Rostow's theory of growth and development

The processes of change identified within Marx's dynamic world were not evenly distributed. If a historical view is taken, the existence of the pre-capitalist societies was spread over long periods of time with little evidence of significant changes to economic life. It was the recognition that there were five distinct stages through which economies pass as they develop that led to Rostow identifying the stages in his influential work (Rostow, 1990). The five stages were:

1. The (pre-industrial) traditional society.
2. The preconditions for economic take-off.
3. Economic take-off.
4. Self-sustained drive towards maturity.
5. The age of mass consumption.

Rostow's work was more a collection of identified sequential trends rather than a theory. The tenet of Rostow's paper is that there is a natural inertia that needs to be overcome before self-sustained development takes place. This inertia is overcome by a build-up of transport investment; enhanced organisation and production in agriculture; and increased imports – particularly capital. These three factors Rostow refers to as the preconditions for take-off. The preconditions were deemed to have been met when countries experience a rapid increase in net investment, have a major leading economic sector with strong linkages to other sectors and have in place the necessary infrastructure to support the development of modern industries.

Once the preconditions for take-off have been met and take-off has started, the economy is deemed to be on a route of self-sustained consistent growth. This stage is associated with migration from rural to urban areas, a developed labour force and a state system that provides stability. This process of self-sustained growth will continue until it matures into a stage of mass consumption where the ownership of durable goods such as automobiles, white goods and other equipment is considered to be the norm.

Rostow's view of economic development was more influential within government circles, where it presumably struck some familiar chords in US government offices, than it has within academic circles. Rostow's academic peers received his theory with mixed views and it was severely criticised by some as being too vague, overly simple and impossible to test. His theory was also criticised on the basis that it lumped together a wide range of countries under the category of traditional economies irrespective of their resources, history or structure. The theory relating to the role played by net investment in breaking down the natural inertia of economies is not supported by empirical evidence and there is no demonstrable reason as to why the components of each stage should not occur at any time in the development process rather than only in the stage to which Rostow refers. A fundamental criticism of Rostow's theory is that it implicitly assumes that development today will mirror the development process that was experienced by today's developed countries. This ignores the effects of international linkages and trade as well as assuming that today's developing countries all have the same objectives for development as were pursued by the industrialised countries of today.

## Vicious circles of demand/supply and investment

This theoretical approach suggests that countries are poor because they always have been. The poverty leading to poverty premise can be examined from either the demand side or the supply side in order to arrive at the same conclusion. From the demand side it is suggested that if a country is poor then the levels of income will be low. This means that the level of demand for goods and services will also be low and therefore there is no incentive for entrepreneurs to invest in additional productive capacity. This means that the amount of capital per worker remains low, productivity remains low, and this sustains the link between low income and low demand. From a supply side there is a suggestion that low income levels present few opportunities for saving and this means that there is little in the way of capital availability to invest in productive capacity. With low investment there is low capital per worker and this maintains the low productivity which leads to low income and savings.

These mechanisms are appealing from the point of view of simplicity but it is their simplicity that gives most cause for concern. The link between income levels and savings at national level is not as obvious as this theory suggests. Corporate saving is an important element of total savings and in many cases the marginal propensity to consume may not be significantly higher than in industrialised countries where there are constant forces trying to induce consumers to spend more. The simplicity of the theories also suggests a level of volatility that is not apparent in national economies. For instance, a small injection of additional demand would lead to the opportunity to invest in additional capital per worker, leading to additional productivity, higher income levels and higher demand. This would expand the economy out of its poverty trap.

## Balanced and unbalanced growth approaches

These theories are variants of a theme and relate to whether development occurs across all sectors or whether there is development in a few leading sectors that will act as a catalyst for development across the economy as a whole. The balanced growth theory suggests that it is not possible to overcome the natural inertia in a stagnant economy by investing in and developing only a few export sectors. There is indivisibility in infrastructure that requires a broader development platform if it is to be successful and investment decisions often have linkages with other investment decisions without which they would not be viable. As an alternative there is the suggestion that unbalanced growth, where investment occurs in just a few leading sectors, is far more achievable with resources of developing countries and that these leading sectors will drag the other sectors up in their wake.

## Dependency theory of development

The dependency theory of economic development suggests that the ability of an economy to achieve autonomous development is determined by its dependency upon other capitalist countries. The greater the dependency upon other capitalist economies the lower the ability to achieve economic development. Proponents of this theory cite the colonial periods as evidence of foreign powers exploiting less developed countries in order to grow richer as a result of their relationship – even to the point of de-industrialising them. There are many instances where colonialism can be seen to have had such a negative impact on a colony's economic development, although it is often difficult to determine how much development would have taken place without colonialism. Furthermore, there are many countries that were never colonised and that have remained underdeveloped, such as Afghanistan and Ethiopia. Nevertheless, there are few people who would argue that colonialism and dependency did not lead to the suffocating of indigenous development forces through:

- migration of workers from rural to colonial organised urban areas;
- 'cropping' the best workforce members to work in colonial offices;
- foreign trade on unfair terms; and
- opening of local markets to foreign companies.

## The development theories and tourism's role

Within the English classical theory of development there is no clear role for any industry beyond the limits imposed by the scarcity of land. Tourism development is a form of real estate development and as such it will add to the pressures on the use of land without providing a way of breaking down the constraining factors associated with diminishing returns.

As a vehicle or catalyst of change, there is a clear role for tourism within Marx's theory of development. Tourism can speed up the process of change because it has product characteristics (see below) that enable it to develop quickly and help the transfer process perhaps from capitalism through to socialism and eventually communism. However, there are elements of the industry that thrive on exploiting economies of large-scale production (natural monopolies such as airlines) that would resist the movement from capitalism to more egalitarian-based systems. But, overall, tourism can be seen as an excellent driving force for economic, social and political change.

If the role of tourism is examined with respect to Rostow's stages of economic development there is clearly a strong role that can be played by tourism. The development of the transport and infrastructure, together with the import of capital, that is seen as a precondition for take-off is a fundamental part of most tourism development. Thus tourism can be used as a catalyst to overcome the inertia of developing countries. The organisation of agricultural production is also often associated with the injection of the additional demand presented by tourism development.

Tourism could play a significant role within the vicious circle theory of development simply by either injecting additional demand into an economy or providing a stimulus to investment. The introduction of tourism under this theory of development would result in an expanding economy when viewed from either a demand or a supply side.

In either the balanced or unbalanced growth theory approaches there is a clear role for tourism within the theories, either as part of the overall broad balanced approach to development or as one of the leading sectors in an unbalanced approach. Why tourism would be chosen as a lead sector within the unbalanced approach to development can be found in the extent of linkages that tourism has with other industries within an economy. Often they are far more widely spread and of deeper significance than those traditionally found with primary goods markets such as agriculture or fishing.

It is not difficult to relate modern-day tourism traits to the dependency theory of development. There are often fears about dependency on tourism as an industry and as a dependency upon foreign suppliers (particularly tour operators and transport companies) as they are the lifeline of tourism development. As such the dependency theory is more an explanation of underdevelopment rather than one that tries to explain development. There is a role for tourism but it can be either a stimulant or an inhibitor of development depending upon ownership of the tourism establishment.

In summary, of the major theories that have attempted to enhance our understanding of the economic development of countries, there is a major role that can be played by tourism except in the case of the English classical theory where there is little scope for any industrial sector other than the latitude offered by the availability of land and its relationship with population (see Table 11.1). Tourism leads the global economy as an engine of development as we enter the twenty-first century. Its growth performance has been nothing short of astonishing over the last

| Table 11.1 | The role for tourism in major development theories | |
|---|---|---|
| **Theories** | | **A role for tourism** |
| English classical theory | | × |
| Marx's theory | | ✓ |
| Rostow's theory of growth | | ✓ |
| Vicious circle theory | | ✓ |
| Balanced/unbalanced | | ✓ |
| Dependency theory | | ✓ |

half of the twentieth century. The result of this is that tourism is a development option that most governments fondly embrace.

When the discussion turns to 'sustainable' development the key economic development theories discussed above are all found to be lacking as they do not encompass the environmental and socio-cultural aspects that must be considered if sustainability is to be explored. Nor does the market system fully reflect the true cost of resources upon which so much of tourism depends. (This is a topic that is explored in Chapters 6 and 8.)

# INTEGRATED PLANNING AND DEVELOPMENT

When planning for the development of an industry or an economy the planners and policy makers may take a proactive stance and develop strategies to secure the desired development path. This approach requires deep and thorough understanding of not only the local economy and its structure, limitations and strengths, but also the probable effects of external factors, how they may impinge on the local development process and what form these external effects are likely to take. Alternatively, one can adopt the reactive stance of chaos theory. This approach is based upon the premise that there are too many variables, internally and externally, to be able to plan. These variables cannot be controlled nor can they be predicted with sufficient levels of accuracy. Therefore, it is better to develop reactive schemes so as to be in good order to meet the unexpected rather than to attempt a proactive but indeterminable development path. This latter approach involves training policy makers to react (like pilots are trained using flight simulators) so that their reactions develop in positive and enlightened ways. However, both proactive and reactive approaches make use of other approaches, such as analogies. Pilots are trained to fly to predetermined paths and schedules while, at the same time, they are trained to be able to react sensibly to unexpected events. The same may be said about tourism development planning. To rely purely on reactive policy solutions is to forsake the prospect of optimising tourism development.

A second issue that has given rise to much academic debate since the 1990s is the notion of sustainable development (see Chapter 10). Although much that has been said about sustainable development is sound from an academic viewpoint, it is neither innovative nor radical. The notion that we must look forward to future generations when we are planning to consume finite resources today is commendable and such notions should also be transferred to all other production and consumption activities, not just tourism. Furthermore, the term 'sustainable development' is a misnomer and has led to much confusion. Development has sometimes been confused with the concept of growth and it is *this* misunderstanding that has caused the increased volume of literature to be published proclaiming the call for sustainable development. In reality, development has to be sustainable to be classified as development at all, otherwise it is short-term growth. Most textbooks that attempt a definition of development include some statement about self-sustained growth. However, the allocation of finite resources to productive activities is not sustainable unless technological inventions and innovations can find alternative resources in the future. There is a

**Photograph 11.1** Intensive tourism development.
*Source*: Image broker/Alamy Images

**Photograph 11.2** Low-intensity tourism development: the Kuelap archaeological complex, Peru. Tourism here is relatively small scale, but on the rise.
*Source*: Yolka/Shutterstock.com

danger in inhibiting specific forms of tourism activities in order to reduce the immediate impacts of tourism in the short term because such remedial actions may unleash far more devastating and less sustainable impacts in the future. Clearly, there is no simple answer to the sustainability debate, only to state that development planning has *always* been concerned with sustainability issues and it is only 'bad' planning that has given so much impetus to these recent debates.

## Tourism and development

If tourism is to be incorporated into a country's development plan it must be organised and developed according to a strategy constructed on sound foundations. These foundations should take account of the coordination of the tourism-related sectors, and the supply and demand for the tourism product. The process of development planning involves a wide cross-section of participants who may bring with them goals that are conflicting. Furthermore, different stakeholders may well bring with them incompatible perceptions about the industry and the development process itself. Before looking at the process of tourism development planning it is worth considering some of the advantages and disadvantages associated with selecting tourism as a catalyst for general development.

### Tourism product characteristics

The tourism product is unique in terms of the range and diversity of activities encompassed. Few products can compete with the wide variety of activities included under the heading of tourism. Tourists can add to this uniqueness by bringing their own extra dimension to the product. Furthermore, the tourism product must be consumed within the geographical boundaries of the destination in which it is offered. The producers of the tourism product, however, are not always confined to the local economy and in this growing age of globalisation tourism may include transport businesses, accommodation owners, tour operators, travel agents and information providers that are based outside of the destination. As with any personal service, production and consumption occur simultaneously and, in the case of tourism, such production affects most other sectors (directly and indirectly) of the economy. As seen elsewhere in this book, this **simultaneity of production** and consumption also creates specific social (and to some extent, environmental) impacts not normally associated with the production of other goods and services.

### Tourism as a means of wealth redistribution

Tourism is widely recognised as one of the fastest earners of foreign exchange and one of the most effective income redistribution factors in many countries. Although able to provide strong redistribution effects within an economy when residents of urban areas spend some of their income in the less populated poorer regions of their country, it has been disappointing as a vehicle to redress the global economic imbalance between North and South. Nevertheless, it has provided a valuable source of foreign exchange to the smaller developing countries that find it difficult to compete in the tangible goods markets.

Domestic tourism is a very effective means of redistributing income between different areas within a national economy. This is because tourism tends to take place in the more sparsely populated scenic areas where there is little in the way of manufacturing industry. Therefore tourism provides the opportunity to create employment and income in areas with limited alternative sources. Thus, English residents head for Cornwall, the Peak District, Scotland and Wales for the domestic trips, the French leave Paris en masse in August and generally head south. The mass exodus of people out of the cities throughout Europe, the Americas and Australia during the main vacation periods is evidence of this domestic redistribution at work.

The literature on international tourism as a means of income redistribution is somewhat deceptive. Many of the articles written about tourism development tend to focus upon economically, environmentally and/or socially vulnerable destinations. This is because they provide a more visible stage on which to examine each of the consequences of tourism development. However, in reality, the vast bulk of international tourist movement takes place between industrialised

## MINI CASE STUDY 11.1
A strategy and action plan for sustainable tourism in the Broads 2011–2015

The Broads is an area of waterways located on the East Coast of the UK across the counties of Norfolk and Suffolk. It is a well-established tourist destination with the navigable waterways providing the focus of the attraction. They are managed and planned in the same way as national parks and the administrative authority has similar powers and responsibilities as National Park Authorities in the UK. The SWOT matrix (Figure 11.2) was set out in the 2011–2015 Strategy and Action Plan published by the Broads Authority.

| Strengths | Weaknesses |
|---|---|
| • The UK's premier waterspace and wetland and a member of the family of National Parks<br>• Excellent offer for motor cruising and sailing with extensive access to uninterrupted waterways of high quality<br>• An established destination in its own right with strong links to Norwich<br>• Easy access to markets in south east and east of England – numerous/affluent<br>• High conservation value of wetland with opportunities for casual encounters with wildlife<br>• Visitor attractions including wildlife-related attractions<br>• Many opportunities to get on to water for all levels of ability and experience<br>• Presence of good quality, smaller, serviced accommodation<br>• High volume, improving quality of non-serviced accommodation<br>• Improving quality of food offer and use of local produce<br>• Some creative and entrepreneurial operators<br>• Heritage themes and features strongly associated with landscape – windmills, wherries, churches<br>• Strong offer for angling and sailing<br>• Good rail access and network<br>• Good climate with high sunshine/low rainfall | • Geographically fragmented land with division between northern and southern Broads and poor communication links<br>• Organisational fragmentation of product delivery and related information provision<br>• Knowing about opportunities to get near and on to water<br>• Patchy quality of facilities and services<br>• Low volume and recognition of larger serviced accommodation<br>• Over-concentration of growth in north west<br>• Overlapping destinations<br>• Lack of cycling infrastructure<br>• Perception of boating as too risky for some and too safe (boring) for others<br>• Angling not available year round |
| **Opportunities** | **Threats** |
| • Growing awareness of established Broads brand<br>• A developing Broads Tourism forum and opportunities for B2B innovation<br>• Strong domestic market in a range of sectors of importance to the Broads<br>• Growing market interest in outdoor activities, including water-based, and health and well-being<br>• Appeal to those with limited mobility of water-based activities and gentle gradients<br>• Visitor volumes present on the coast<br>• Active voluntary sector making strong contribution to conservation management and to the visitor experience<br>• Non-public landowners may be less affected by public sector cuts<br>• Potential to engage with local communities | • Viability of enterprises<br>• Uncertainty about future capacity of Broads Authority<br>• General public sector funding cuts<br>• Longer recession<br>• Climate change – flooding, saltwater intrusion, water levels, changing weather<br>• Any increase in restrictions on development in flood plain<br>• Possible impact of pressure on wildlife and communities and implications for response to development proposals<br>• Competition from other destinations/cruising areas including acquisition of Blakes/Hoseasons by global operator<br>• Any deterioration in water quality |

**Figure 11.2**  SWOT matrix
*Source*: http://www.broads-authority.gov.uk/broads/live/authority/strategy/Tourism_Strategy_for_the_Broads_2011.pdf Page 28 (accessed 6 June 2012)

## DISCUSSION QUESTION

Comment on how planning may be able to address the strengths, weaknesses, opportunities and threats identified in the SWOT matrix from the Broads Strategy Action Plan.

countries. To support this viewpoint it can be noted that in 2002 more than 88% of total international tourist arrivals in Europe came from other European countries and that globally more than 80% of international tourist arrivals tend to be residents within the region where they arrive. In terms of the North–South debate, tourists escape the industrialised countries to visit other industrialised countries and the South enjoys little in the way of a significant share of the wealth created by tourism. This is a fact that should be borne in mind when examining the global consequences of tourism development.

## Tourism as a labour-intensive industry

Tourism, in common with most personal service industries, is labour intensive. For developing countries with surplus labour and for industrialised countries with high levels of unemployment, tourism provides an effective means of generating employment opportunities. In general, at a time when the labour:capital ratio is moving strongly against labour in most production industries, the importance of the labour-absorbing qualities of tourism cannot be overlooked. However, in many countries there are labour shortages and it is not uncommon to find these countries importing labour to work in their tourism industries. Under such circumstances one might question whether these countries have a comparative advantage in tourism and whether or not their factors of production would be better employed in alternative industries.

Even in those situations where there is an abundance of labour it may be the case that there are other factors of production that provide arguments in favour of development routes other than through tourism. Where there are clear indications that the local destination would benefit from the employment created by tourism, this view should be tempered by the characteristics of the labour force generally associated with tourism-related establishments. The employment profile of large hotels, for example, tends to yield a relatively flat occupational pyramid such as that shown in Figure 11.3. This means that middle and senior management posts are relatively scarce compared with the high number of low-skill employees. Such an occupational pyramid results in a lack of career development and, consequently, a lack of staff motivation. A point also worthy of consideration is the predominance of females and young people employed in tourism-related establishments.

Attempts have been made to increase the height of the occupational pyramid by, for example, the introduction of departments and layers of middle management posts in luxury hotels. This, it was hoped, would provide a much-needed impetus to career prospects and motivation. However, recent experience suggests that there has been a reversal of this trend with 'de-layering' and the career development prospects in large hotels are not significantly different from that exhibited three decades ago. Thus, although tourism may provide a quick and ready means of increasing the number of employed people in the local economy, its contribution to long-term development may be questionable. To expand this argument further it is necessary to consider the secondary employment effects associated with tourism development and here one can find a much broader range of skill requirements and career development paths. Therefore, although

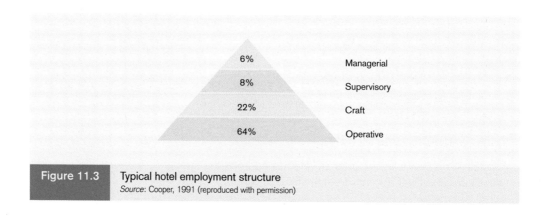

| | |
|---|---|
| 6% | Managerial |
| 8% | Supervisory |
| 22% | Craft |
| 64% | Operative |

**Figure 11.3**  Typical hotel employment structure
*Source*: Cooper, 1991 (reproduced with permission)

the direct employment effects of tourism may be subject to some limiting characteristics, the indirect effects do not suffer in the same way.

## Tourism and on-the-job training

The development of travel and hospitality skills in the local labour market is unlikely to make large demands on educational resources. The educational qualifications of those employed in the accommodation sector are heavily weighted in favour of those with only a rudimentary education. This is undesirable both from the point of view of the future of the industry and in terms of the overall development of the destination. There is often an urgent need for training and education at all levels in both the private and public sectors. However, industry often chooses to ignore this need and to enjoy the benefits of a cheap and plentiful labour market, and the public sector is often more concerned with the short-term goal of achieving employment opportunities rather than the development of a well-educated and qualified labour force. There is an unquestionable need for education and training in the tourism and hospitality industries and the reliance upon untrained labour with on-the-job training is responsible for many poor-quality tourism products. These destinations fail to compete with high-quality tourism destinations that, in consequence, are able to charge higher prices and enjoy more buoyant demand for their products.

The poor quality and inadequate education and training related to the tourism and hospitality industries is an aspect that has been known for almost two decades, as Table 11.2 demonstrates. From a short-term growth point of view rather than as a development option, this educational profile has both positive and negative implications. On the positive side it means that the labour force for tourism growth can be mobilised relatively quickly. The training can be undertaken on the job, which means that units of labour can be brought in quickly from either the unemployed or, as is often the case in developing countries, from agriculture and fishing industries. On the negative side, the lack of educational qualifications found in tourism-related businesses means that the growth of tourism does not necessarily result in a more educated labour force – one of the factors perceived to be an important ingredient in the economic development process.

## The structure of the tourism industry

One of the more notable features of the tourism industry is the proportion of the total businesses that are classified as small and medium-sized enterprises (SMEs). The nature of tourism as a personal service industry tends to make it attractive to individual and family entrepreneurs. The proliferation of small businesses brings with it both advantages and disadvantages. In the first instance it facilitates quick start-ups and flexible supply sources that can respond rapidly to fluctuations in demand. It is also an industry that, from the outside, does not appear technically daunting and thus encourages budding entrepreneurs to enter the industry. There are few **barriers to entry** in the sense that businesses can be started with small amounts of investment

| Table 11.2 | Level of training in tourism | |
|---|---|---|
| **Level** | **Accommodation (%)** | **Supplementary activities (%)** |
| University | 1 | 3 |
| Other higher education | 4 | 5 |
| Secondary | | |
| Higher | 30 | 45 |
| Lower | 34 | 40 |
| No qualifications | 31 | 7 |

*Source*: WTO, 1980

and there is room for **product differentiation** to provide some monopolistic power to the smallest businesses. However, these advantages can also be the source of the industry's worst problems in terms of:

- inadequate staff training (unstructured informal training);
- too high a debt/equity ratio leading to business failure (borrowing on the goodwill of the business); and
- inefficiency problems because of a failure to capitalise on economies of large-scale production.

Although the vast majority of business establishments in tourism may be considered to be SMEs, a significant proportion of the total output of the industry is attributable to the larger national and multinational corporations. Nevertheless, there is certainly scope for a wide range of business structures within tourism, from bed and breakfast units through to international hotel chains, from independent sightseeing flight operators to national airline giants. Each type of business has its own operating characteristics, with a tendency for the smaller firms to be more labour intensive and dependent upon local suppliers, to the larger companies that make extensive use of capital and bulk purchase from a global warehouse.

## Protectionism

The simultaneity of production and consumption of tourism means that the tourist must travel to the destination to enjoy the product. This makes tourism unique as an export industry. The consumers of international tourism (the importing country) often fail to recognise their tourist spending overseas as an import and hence do not see it as a serious threat to the level of employment in their own countries. Thus, tourism tends to escape the danger of being singled out for **protectionism** or trade retaliation, except as part of a general macro-economic policy which restricts foreign exchange allowances to correct balance of payment problems. Having said that, it is often the existence of foreign exchange restrictions in many of the developing regions of the world that explains the relatively slow rates of growth in interregional tourism (as, for example, in South-East Asia). Similarly, when countries are faced with currency crises (such as the UK in the 1960s and 1970s and Malaysia in the 1990s) the governments of the day imposed restrictions on the amount of currency that outbound tourists could convert. In the global financial crisis that started in 2008 industries not associated with protectionism are a valuable tool to combat the effects of recession.

## Multitude of industries

Tourism is a composite industry product. That is, it is composed of the output of the travel, accommodation and food and beverage, retail, entertainment sectors plus many others. This means that its economic and development impacts are felt quite widely from the initial impact onwards. It also tends to suggest that tourism has strong linkages with many other sectors of the economy and it is the strength of these linkages that determines the value of the output, income and employment multipliers associated with tourist expenditure.

The variety of industries included under the umbrella of tourism means that there are a variety of employment opportunities generated by tourism activity. This may stimulate the labour market and the delivery of vocational training.

## Price flexibility

Many developing countries are dependent upon the world market prices for primary agricultural produce for their foreign exchange receipts. That is, the prices of, say, cocoa, sugar, rice, etc., are determined in world commodity markets where individual countries have very little say in determining the final price of the goods. Tourism, on the other hand, provides a source of foreign exchange that is subject to some degree of control by the host country. Product differentiation, either through natural endowments or man-made resources, can provide some price-setting power. The greater the product differentiation that is either innate or can be engineered, the greater the **monopolistic power** and hence the greater freedom a destination has in setting its own price. Product differentiation can be based on natural factors, ranging from broad aspects such as climate (Florida, Bermuda and Iceland as examples) to specific natural attractions (such as Victoria Falls, Great Barrier Reef and Grand Canyon). Differentiation can also be achieved through socio-cultural aspects, heritage (such as the Pyramids of Egypt, the Great Wall of China and Stonehenge in the UK) and even in terms of the quality of the tourism product itself. Basically, it does not matter what aspect is used to differentiate the product providing there is sufficient demand for it. However, tourism is also highly **price competitive**.

## Price competitive

The bulk of the tourism market, which is resort tourism, is extremely price sensitive and, consequently, internationally competitive. The effects of currency fluctuations on the number of international arrivals and the volume of tourist expenditure adequately demonstrate this fact. Although most mass tourism destinations claim a high degree of product differentiation, a brief examination of the major tour operators' brochures selling sun, sand and sea products will show that the major battleground is fought not on hotels, the quality of beaches or the sea, but the price of the package. Price competition is a fundamental feature of the budget tourism market for both destinations and operators.

## Seasonality

A striking feature of tourism in many countries is the way in which the level of activity fluctuates throughout the year. This is not a characteristic unique to tourism – agriculture is also an industry used to seasonal fluctuations in activity – but the majority of industries are not subject to the degree of seasonality experienced by tourism establishments. Seasonality in tourism can be caused by either supply factors, such as those mentioned above, or demand factors such as the availability of tourists to travel at different times of the year. For instance, international holiday packages aimed at attracting family groups from Europe or the USA would need to bear in mind that the availability of most families will be determined by the school holidays. The effect of this can be seen by searching for flight costs during school term periods and those during school holiday periods. The latter tend to be associated with a premium price tag. Therefore the forces of seasonality attack the consumption of the product from both sides of the market – demand and supply.

Irrespective of the cause of the seasonality in the tourism industry, it tends to be reflected in:

- employment (casual/seasonal staff);
- investment (low annual returns on capital);
- pricing policies (discounted off-season prices).

From an economics point of view, any business subject to seasonal fluctuations in demand for its output is faced with a dilemma. If it purchases sufficient resources to meet the peak load demand, then it will have to carry spare productive capacity for the remainder of the year. If it gauges its resources according to the average level of demand it will spend part of the year carrying spare capacity and be unable to meet the peak-load demand level. Alternatively, it can take on variable resources (staff) to meet the peak-load demand and then shed these variable factors of resources during the off-season. Although attractive from the point of view of the profit and loss account, this widely practised solution does nothing to improve employer/employee relations. Also, there is an inherent waste in taking on staff each year on a temporary basis, investing in human resources (by training) and then losing that investment at the end of the main season.

In order to offset some of the costs associated with seasonality many hotels and operators offer holidays for off-season periods with heavily discounted prices. By offering lower prices it is possible to induce visitors to a destination at a time when they would otherwise not visit. However, there are limits to such discounting. First, the revenue that establishments receive during the off-season must *at least* cover the variable costs of production. If this is the case then, by opening in the off-season, they will be able to maintain their staff and, perhaps, make some contribution to their **fixed costs**. Secondly, the discounting of off-season packages should not be so great as to damage the desirability of the main season product.

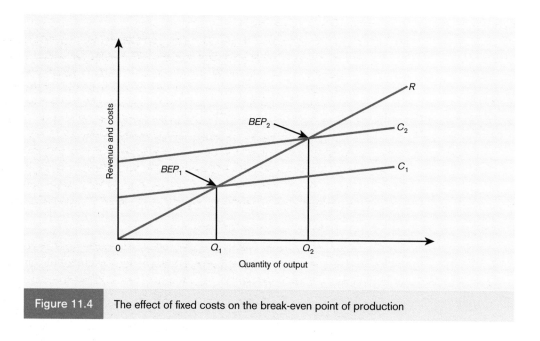

| Figure 11.4 | The effect of fixed costs on the break-even point of production |

There are also destinations that do not suffer much from seasonal variations and this provides them with a competitive advantage by allowing them to operate at a higher throughput of tourist activity across the year without suffering from as much socio-cultural and environmental impacts as their seasonal competitors.

### High operating leverage/fixed costs

Many of the tourism-related industries are subject to high levels of fixed costs. That is, there is a large capital element that must be committed before any output is produced. In industries subject to this type of cost structure (e.g. airlines and hotels) the volume of sales becomes the all-important factor. This aspect is shown in Figure 11.4, where the vertical axis measures revenue and costs, and the horizontal axis depicts the quantity of output produced during the time period under consideration. The break-even output for the non-tourism industry is represented by Q1 whereas Q2 shows the break-even output for the tourism industry. The cost curve $C_1$ relates to the cost function of a non-tourism industry and $C_2$ relates to the cost function of a typical tourism-related industry. We can see that both industries are subject to the same variable-cost structures (that is why the two cost functions run parallel to each other) but the tourism-related industry is subject to a higher fixed-cost element. The end result is that the break-even point for the tourism-related industry ($BEP_2$) is much higher than that for the non-tourism industry, thus the volume of output becomes all important for high fixed-cost industries. The break-even point refers to that level of revenue and output that will just cover the costs involved in producing the output.

The preoccupation with volume displayed by industries that have high operating leverages can also influence the mindset of the national tourist organisations. Many tourist destinations base their tourism development plans on volume figures. Countries the world over tend to celebrate the fact that visitor numbers exceed some *magical* annual threshold and many countries still express the targets/objectives of their development plans in terms of bed spaces and tourist nights. However, the presence of tourists in itself is not the main objective of any of these destinations. The primary aims are economic and the indicators of performance and targets should be expressed in economic rather than volume figures and/or constrained by environmental or social indicator values.

Clearly, there is overwhelming evidence to support the view that there are a number of factors related to the tourism industry which make it an attractive development option. But some of these factors may make it less attractive if they are not controlled or alleviated by proper planning.

# DEVELOPMENT PLANNING LAYERS

Tourism development planning can take place at international, national and sub-national levels.

## International tourism planning

At the international level organisations such as the WTO, EU, OECD, Caribbean Tourism Organisation (CTO) and the Tourism Council for the South Pacific (TCSP) all undertake, albeit limited, forms of tourism planning. This level of planning is often weak in structure, detail and enforcement. It is generally provided in guideline form in order to assist the member states.

## National tourism planning

National tourism planning encapsulates the tourism development plans for a country as a whole but often includes specific objectives for particular sub-national regions or types of areas within the national boundary. The plans manifest themselves in a variety of forms including:

- tourism policy;
- marketing strategies;
- taxation structure;
- incentive/grant schemes;
- legislation (e.g. employment, investment, repatriation of profits);
- infrastructure developments;
- external and internal transport systems and organisations; and
- education/training and manpower programmes.

## Regional/local tourism planning

Regional and local tourism planning deals with specific issues that affect a sub-national area. It tends to be much more detailed and specific than its national counterpart and can vary quite significantly from area to area. For instance, there may be areas where tourism development is to be encouraged and others where specific types of tourism facilities, such as a casino, are actively discouraged. Such plans may relate to a state within a country, to a county, a city or even a local resort area.

However, there are constraints on how different regional plans can be from other regional plans or from the national plan. Certainly they should not detract from the overall aims and objectives of the national plan or those of another region. Ideally, the sub-national plans should work in harmony with the national plan as far as local conditions will allow.

Plans at all levels should include consideration of how information is transferred to the consumer – the tourist. It should also be borne in mind that what you *do not* tell the tourist is often as vital as what you *do* tell them. This is particularly true from the point of view of visitor management when attempts are made to direct the tourists towards some specific regions but deter them from visiting others. Such information can be disseminated through a variety of media including the Internet, which is becoming increasingly important as a tool for tourism development and marketing. However, traditionally the following media have been used:

- visitor orientation centres;
- tourist information centres;
- advertising brochures, maps, magazine articles and broadcasting;
- self-guided tours and trails;
- official guides;
- posters and displays.

The above can all be seen as a means to visitor awareness and can be used to support more formal programmes run by tourism officials. In the globalised world in which we now live the cooperation, coordination and co-integration of the different planning levels is not only more feasible than it was in the middle of last century, it is more vital and is likely to be one of the characterising trends of tourism planning as we move forward from 2012.

# THE TOURISM DEVELOPMENT PLANNING PROCESS

The concept of planning is concerned with organising some future events in order to achieve pre-specified objectives. The pre-specified objectives are clearly fundamental and start from the question: 'Why do we want to develop tourism?' Of course there are many reasons and the economic reasons often prevail. However, even when there is a green light to go ahead and develop tourism from an economic perspective there are still many questions that have to be asked and these can often be identified and debated during a 'Visioning Exercise'. A visioning exercise is where the key stakeholders are brought together to discuss and agree on what it is they envisage for their destination. What are the activities that are acceptable, which activities would not be acceptable, what is the scale of the development, the limits to acceptable development, etc. Often these visioning exercise lead to the crystallisation of the tourism development objectives which are discussed below.

Integrated planning and development is a form of comprehensive planning: comprehensive because it integrates all forms of planning – economic, physical, social and cultural. Planning should not be seen as a static concept, rather it attempts to deploy the best strategy in a world of changing internal and external influences. Although planning as a dynamic concept can take a variety of forms, there is a consistent structure that can be applied to the process of planning. That structure is set out in Figure 11.5.

## Study recognition and preparation

The study recognition and preparation are really concerned with the recognition by the planning authorities (normally the government), private industry and the local community that tourism is a desirable development option, together with some awareness of the constraints within which it must develop. The fact that it is recognised that a strategy is required is an important indication that the government and people are aware of the complexity of the tourism industry and its need for coordination.

## Setting of objectives or goals for the strategy

In order to design a development plan successfully it is necessary to have a clear understanding of the objectives that are to be achieved by the development of tourism. A common mistake in tourism development planning is to lose sight of the reasons why tourism has been selected as a development option. If it is the case that tourism is seen as the most appropriate vehicle for generating foreign exchange and employment opportunities, these goals should be embedded in the development strategy from the start. This helps to avoid the problems encountered when the objectives are set down in terms of visitor numbers or annual guest nights.

Some major objectives, commonly found in tourism development plans, are set out below:

- To develop a tourism sector that, in all respects and at all levels, is of high quality, though not necessarily of high cost.
- To encourage the use of tourism for both cultural and economic exchange.
- To distribute the economic benefits of tourism, both direct and indirect, as widely and to as many of the host community as feasible.
- To preserve cultural and natural resources as part of tourism development and facilitate this through architectural and landscape design which reflect local traditions.

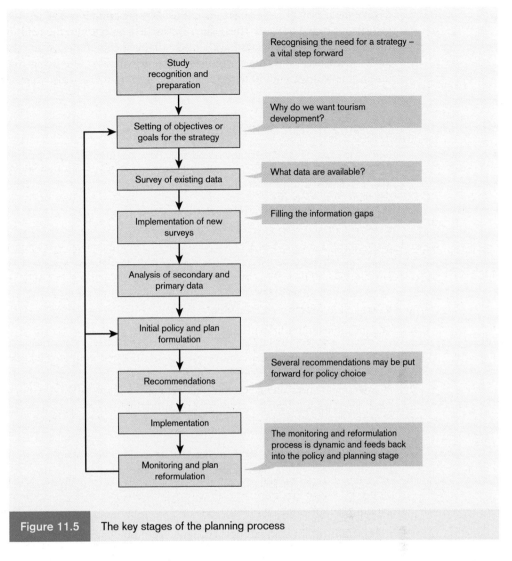

**Figure 11.5**    The key stages of the planning process

- To appeal to a broad cross-section of international (and domestic) tourists through policies and programmes of site and facility development.
- To maximise foreign exchange earnings to ensure a sound balance of payments.
- To attract high-spending 'upmarket' tourists.
- To increase employment opportunities.
- To aid peripheral regions by raising incomes and employment, thus slowing down or halting emigration.

It is important that the objectives set out in the development plan are *clear, unambiguous, non-conflicting* and *achievable*. We can see from the above list of objectives that these examples are not specific in nature, thus it would be difficult to assess whether or not the objective had indeed been achieved. Also, some of the objectives may be conflicting, particularly those relating to the type of tourist to be attracted and their desired impact. Where the objectives are vague and/or conflicting, the tourism development plan is doomed to failure from the start.

## Survey of existing data

Before setting out on the data collection stage it is vital to undertake an existing data search. Although this may sound obvious, there are many instances where data that are crucial to tourism development planning are collected and held by government agencies not expressly concerned with the planning process. Thus, when researchers go out into the field to collect **primary data** they are told that businesses have already supplied this information. The authors have come across incidences where no fewer than five hotel surveys were being conducted concurrently. This is not only wasteful in terms of time and resources, but it also depletes the goodwill of the business community.

## Implementation of new surveys

Once the existing data are known and the scope of the planning objectives have been set, the information gap can be filled by undertaking primary data collection. The data requirements for development planning are quite comprehensive and include:

- tourist characteristics/travel patterns;
- tourist attractions;
- accommodation facilities;
- other tourist facilities;
- land availability and use;
- economic structure – all sectors;
- education and training needs and provisions;
- environmental indicators;
- socio-cultural characteristics;
- investment and available capital – all sectors;
- public and private sector organisations; and
- relevant legislation and regulation.

All of the above factors are considered with respect to both their existing states and their projected states within the development plan's timescale.

The survey of existing data and primary data collection should generate an awareness of the importance of good-quality data for planning, management and monitoring purposes. The authorities should implement a long-term strategy of data enhancement by setting up a management information system that is flexible enough to accommodate the collection of new data when they become available and to encompass issues not necessarily identified within the current strategy.

## Analyses

Once the objectives have been formulated, the analytical framework chosen will determine the precise sets of data to be collected. Once collected, the data are analysed by considering a wide range of issues. The major issues to be considered generally fall into four subject areas:

1. **Asset evaluation.** This area of analysis examines the existing and potential stock of assets, the ways in which they can be developed and the probable constraints on that development. The asset evaluation should also include an appraisal of the infrastructure in order to determine whether or not further investment is required. The asset evaluation should begin with a broad approach, looking at assets across a wide range of sectors and their alternative uses. The evaluation could then be focused to concentrate on the tourism-related assets and how they should be best employed within that framework.

2. **Market analysis.** The market analysis is clearly a crucial component of a sound development plan. The market analysis undertaken during tourism development planning is sometimes too narrow in scope to be of optimum use. Initial issues that need to be addressed concern global, regional and country market trends by type of tourism activity. Another fundamental question is 'Why do tourists come to this destination?' Too many development plans of the past have relied upon the assumption of constant market share and this is not a valid assumption. To appraise the development plans, attempts must be made to determine whether or not

the proposed developments are appropriate, the markets that are likely to be attracted by these developments and the price level or **tariff structure** that should be adopted. The market analysis must also incorporate a study of developments in competitive markets and/or in competitive modes of transport. Generally these issues will be tackled within a competitive and comparative advantage study that incorporates a SWOT analysis.

3. **Development planning.** A major issue to be studied under this heading is the time phasing of the development plan in order to ensure successful implementation. The possible sources of funding of the development are examined and the appropriate level of foreign funding (if any) is calculated. The analysis section encompasses all issues, such as the number of foreign employees, the marketing strategy to be adopted, investment incentives, organisational structures and training programmes.

4. **Impact analyses.** The impact analyses should be all-embracing, covering issues such as the probable effects that the development will have on the host community and the environment, the economic implications in terms of key indicators (employment, income, government revenue and foreign exchange flows) and the probable economic rates of return. Analyses should also examine the risks involved and the sensitivity of the results to changing assumptions. The integration of economic, environmental and socio-cultural impact analyses is a vital advancement to tourism planning tools which took place in the closing years of the twentieth century. The incorporation of a forecasting model, so that future economic, environmental and social impacts can be assessed, is equally crucial. Tourism researchers are constantly striving to develop enhanced planning tools for use in tourism development and models, such as those developed within the International Centre for Tourism and Hospitality Research, Bournemouth University, will play a major part in providing the framework for future tourism planning exercises.

The analyses set out above are of both a quantitative and qualitative nature and most of these issues must be faced before a move can be made towards formulating policy recommendations. The resilience of the strategies can be tested through the use of SWOT, PESTEL, STEP, PEST analyses to explore the weaknesses, strengths, opportunities and threats which exist that could benefit or detract from the strategies. The framework for such tests takes into account the following dimensions:

Political factors

Stability of the government and the dynamics of change.

Legislation, including labour, environmental, planning, social and constitutional laws.

Media freedom, corruption and bureaucracy.

Trading legislation together with regulation and deregulation.

Economic factors

GDP, changes in growth, inflation, interest rates.

Income distribution and growth.

Fluctuations in activity, internal and external.

Imports, exports, exchange rates and globalisation.

Labour demand and supply, training, unemployment rates.

Social factors

Population dynamics: age distribution, gender.

Education, career development, employment profiles.

Health awareness and social mobility.

Safety, security and risk management.

Religion, work ethics, etc.

Technological factors

Research and development activities, rates of technological change.

New technologies, incentives, transfer of technologies.

Infrastructural developments.

Environmental factors

Resource usage and depletion.

Protection of identified species and areas.

Climate change effects, including extreme weather events.

Pollution and clean-up strategies.

Legal factors

Legal changes (internal and external) such as anti-trust/monopolies legislation.

Trading, consumer and employment legislation.

Discrimination law (internal and external).

By assessing the different factors and the creation of alternative scenarios on how they may affect the destination and, more importantly, how they might affect the performance of the recommended strategies, policy makers can assess the corridors of likely outcomes from the strategies. The SWOT and PESTEL approaches can also be used earlier in the planning process to help identify those aspects that might create development opportunities (opportunities) and those aspects that give rise to concern (threats) in the future.

## Policy and plan formulation

The results from the analyses of the survey data are unlikely to yield a unique solution and, instead, will tend to suggest a number of possibilities for development strategies. The process from here is one of formulating draft plans on the basis of each policy option derived from the analyses. The alternative plans are then evaluated in terms of their potential economic, physical and socio-cultural costs and benefits, together with any possible problem areas that may result from the implementation of each plan. The plans that achieve the most objectives while not exposing the destination to potentially serious problems are then selected and drawn up in full. Finally, a 'preferred' plan is drafted for policy consideration.

## Recommendations

The preferred plan that has been selected on the basis of the analyses, having now been completed in detail, is submitted to the authorities by the planning team. This submission is sent to the authorities, together with recommendations concerning the optimum methods of developing tourism in the destination and, in so doing, achieving the plan's objectives. It is more than likely that the planning team will present the authorities with a selection of recommendations that all fulfil the requirements of the preferred plan. It is at this stage that feedback between the authorities and the development plan team is essential in order to focus attention on issues where attention is needed and to play down areas where it is not. During the process of these discussions the final development plan is formulated. Therefore, the recommendations stage should really be regarded as a period of dialogue between the planning team and the policy makers.

## Implementation of the plan

The methods of implementing the development plan will have been considered throughout most stages of its construction. Thus, during the secondary data survey stage attention will have been paid to many aspects that relate to implementation – such as the existing legislative and regulatory frameworks. By the time that the implementation stage is reached, all of the necessary legislation and regulation controls will have been brought into effect. Furthermore, the methods used to facilitate public debate and discussions relating to the development will have been devised and enquiry and appeal mechanisms will be in place. During the implementation stage particular attention will need to be paid to the phasing of the plan and the critical path analyses will have highlighted areas that may be the cause of concern.

## Monitoring and reformulation

Once the development plan has been implemented it must be closely monitored in order to detect any deviations that may occur from the projected path of development. Any such deviations – and there will probably be some – must be analysed in order to assess how they will affect the development plan and its objectives. Once this secondary analysis has been completed, the research team can report back to the authorities with recommendations as to how the plan and its policy recommendations should be modified in order to stay on target. External and internal factors may influence the performance of the strategy and it is important that the monitoring systems enable the research team to be fully informed about all relevant changes. Furthermore, even with the best-laid plans, unexpected events do occur and it is here that the reactive policy skills of the research team and policy makers come into play. For instance, there could be outbreaks of disease that are of international headline importance (the outbreak of the plague in India, the foot-and-mouth crisis in the UK), terrorist activities (Bali, Cairo, London, Madrid and New York) or a destination may be deemed to be unsafe by governments (such as – at various times – Cyprus, Indonesia, Saudi Arabia and Sri Lanka) that cause the international flows of tourists to deviate from their expected path. Even positive developments in competing countries, such as the liberalisation of South Africa, can have unforeseen effects on other destinations. It is important that the research team is aware of how sensitive the strategy is to each of the conceivable variables and how best to react to such events. Even then the tourism plan is likely to face inconceivable events where the research team and policy makers will have to rely upon intuition.

## The development plan team

The development plan team will need considerable expertise and experience in the formulation of such plans. In general, the team will consist of four groups of specialists, falling into the broad categories of technical services, marketing specialists, planners and economists. In more detail, the likely spread of specialist skills will include:

- market analysts;
- physical planners;
- economists;
- environmental scientists;
- infrastructure engineers;
- transport engineers;
- social scientists;
- draughtsmen and designers; and
- legal experts.

The plan will be constructed over a period of time and this time can be broken down into five distinct phases.

1. **Identification and inventory of the existing situation**. This phase includes:
   a) characteristics and structure of current consumer demand;
   b) study of consumer choice;
   c) current land use, land tenure and land-use control;

**d)** existing natural and artificial attractions;

**e)** ecosystem factors – particularly those considered to be vulnerable;

**f)** economic structures and the capacity thresholds of industries;

**g)** labour force skill mix and educational base, together with availability;

**h)** accommodation facilities;

**i)** tourist services facilities;

**j)** infrastructure facilities and their capacities;

**k)** transport facilities and their capacities;

**l)** graphic presentation of physical inventory.

The above data will be used to establish the adequacy of existing structures and facilities, the classification and cost organisation of existing facilities (together with an index of standards currently achieved), and the economic impact of present tourism activity. This then leads on to the second phase.

2. **Forecasts for the future.** This phase will include forecasts of future demand and probable tourist movements and needs. This will be complemented by an analysis of the implications of these forecasts for future production levels of each relevant service and good, together with the infrastructural requirements. Anticipated standards of service will be examined and the economic forecasts of local repercussions will be estimated.

3. **Plan formulation.** The formulation of the plan will include proposed programmes of market organisation and promotion, comprehensive land-use and control planning, detailed infrastructural plans and the economic, environmental and social evaluations associated with the proposed development plan. Again it is likely to include a graphic presentation of land use and infrastructure, together with a mapping of social impacts and the constraints imposed by the environmental considerations.

4. **Specific project development.** This phase will include an analysis of specific policies and projects for marketing and tourism management. The physical planners and architects will draw up selections of alternative layouts relating to specific projects and alternative solutions to infrastructural development problems will be developed. Costs of the alternative projects and infrastructural schemes will be assessed, along with the economic analysis of the various possible investment projects. Once the specific projects have been selected from the various alternatives these will, again, be subject to graphic presentations. The local environmental issues will be assessed and methods of alleviating problems will be set out. Examples of environmental planning actions could be broadly based, such as the treatment of raw sewage and the maintenance of water quality, or highly specific, such as the planned periodic movements of footpaths to prevent serious erosion. Matters relating to visitor orientation programmes, visitor management and interpretation will all be considered and set out within this phase.

5. **Implementation.** The implementation programme will be set into motion with construction and supervision, technical and managerial assistance in tourism development projects, and financial analysis, and the recommended infrastructure investment programme will commence. The implementation stage will include the setting up of the continuing monitoring and re-evaluation activities to ensure that the strategy is performing optimally and so that adjustments can be made swiftly if the circumstances (internally or externally) change.

# TOURISM DEVELOPMENT PLANNING: WHEN IT GOES WRONG

Even the best-laid plans can be knocked off course or fail because of unexpected events. Disaster management is an important element of modern-day planning and tourism is subject to a wide range of disasters, including earthquakes, hurricanes, outbreaks of infectious diseases and acts of terrorism. A large number of tourism development plans are, to varying degrees, unsuccessful.

Given the fact that such plans operate in an environment that is constantly changing because of forces acting outside the control of the authorities, often outside the geographical area of the destination, perhaps this is not surprising. For instance, the terrorist attacks on the USA on 11 September 2001 have changed tourism flows in ways that have severely damaged the tourism development plans of many Caribbean states. However, many plans fail as a result of inadequacies in the development plans themselves. Discussions about this latter type of failure can be broken down into two categories: failure at the design stage and failure at the implementation stage.

## Design stage plan failure

Many of the tourism development plans that fail do so because, at the design stage, they follow no more than the basic formulation of tourism development. Consider the basic tourism development plan in Figure 11.6. A plan of this structure will provide a general framework for state and municipal/local investments and will help to guide and evaluate the proposals of private developers. However, this type of plan structure lacks the analytical detail and scope necessary for a successful tourism development plan. Quite often this absence of analytical components is a reflection of the planning bodies that carry out the construction of the plan, bodies lacking in planning expertise and experience.

More importantly, the plan does not give a clear statement with respect to its objectives – objectives must be achievable, unambiguous and non-conflicting. The plan also fails to take into account the wider issues relating to environmental and social impacts because it is driven uniquely by its financial returns. One of the dangers of drawing up development plans in order to seek external funding is that the myopic view of financial profit and loss accounts may cause the planners to overlook some of the fundamental issues involved. This may well result in a plan that will fail financially as well as structurally.

The development plan takes no consideration of the impact of tourism on the host community, the environment and the economy. The projects are only evaluated on a financial basis (profit and loss accounts) and take no account of social costs and benefits.

Too much emphasis is placed upon physical development, i.e. supply-led tourism development, without proper consideration of returns to capital investments and effects on the market. The plan structure fails to make adequate market assessment. The global approach of examining tourist flows from the tourist-generating countries and projecting forward to future time periods under the assumption that all destinations will receive their fair share, fails to address

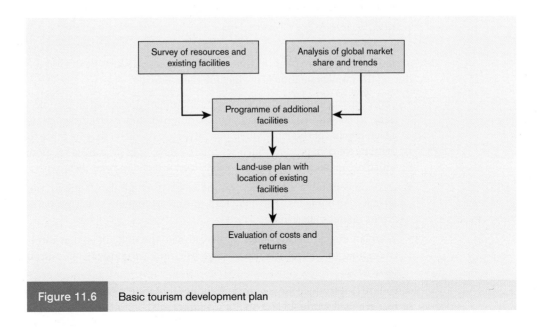

**Figure 11.6**　Basic tourism development plan

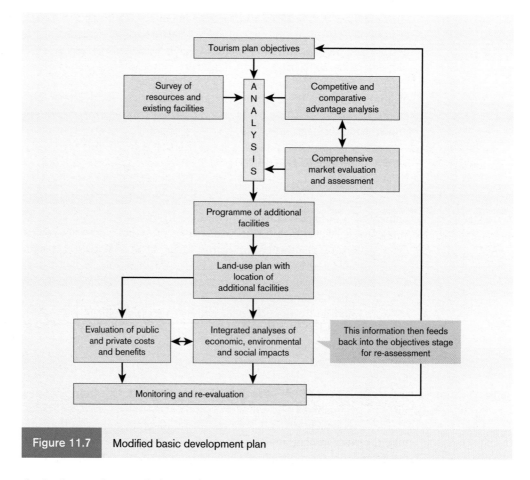

**Figure 11.7** Modified basic development plan

the fundamental issue of *why people want to come to this particular destination*. Unless this issue is addressed future projections can be wildly off target.

Taking the above points into account, the basic development plan structure can be modified as in Figure 11.7.

## Implementation stage plan failure

Problems encountered at the implementation stage are largely, but not exclusively, concerned with miscalculations regarding the use of land and the control of land usage. Tourism is, after all, an activity largely involved in real estate development. The type of land difficulties encountered during the implementation stage include the following:

- Those that actually undertake the development are sometimes more concerned with real estate speculation rather than the operation of tourist facilities. Thus, the motivation for development (particularly when incentives are on offer) may be more to do with capital gain than the tourism product. Such speculative development can lead to poorly designed facilities which are inefficient to operate, or facilities situated in poor locations.

- Development often takes place on the basis of a high debt/equity ratio using land values as security for the loans. This may lead to financial failure when property sales and operating profits do not materialise.

- The planning authorities often underestimate the difficulties that can be encountered when attempting to control the use of land. The only certain way of controlling land usage is by ownership.

- Failure to introduce the required planning legislation quickly enough to implement the development plan, or the lack of ability to enforce such legislation.

- If the specific sites earmarked for development are 'leaked' prior to the implementation of the development plan, land speculation and price inflation is likely to follow. This will alter the economic evaluations and may turn a viable project into a certain failure.

Other problems that may be encountered include the following:

- Failure to coordinate intermediaries in the travel trade, private sector development and public sector provision. Tour operators are an extremely influential component of the tourism process. If left to market forces then oligopolist behaviour can put severe pressure on the economic profitability and local benefits derived from tourism will suffer. Lack of coordination between public and private sectors can result in supply bottlenecks, affecting most aspects of the tourism product, damaging the economic benefits associated with the tourism activity, adversely affecting visitor satisfaction, and consequently causing the plan to miss its targets.
- Poor communications and infrastructure.
- Inadequate procedures to deal with public opposition and representations concerning the proposed development. A lack of such a mechanism can slow the development process down considerably and result in plan failure.

One of the most common scenarios from unsound tourism planning policies is over-exploitation – when the carrying capacity thresholds of a destination are exceeded, such as in Aya Napa in Cyprus where the local population was displaced by tourism development or Benidorm in Spain during the rapid growth stages that created pressures on infrastructure, water supply, health and safety. Such excesses tend to lead to a decline in the quality of the tourism product and, ultimately, to a decline in the 'quality' of tourists, i.e. tourists associated with greater undesirable impacts and lower spend. Under such circumstances the destination may find some or all of the following indicators:

- ecological imbalance through overuse of resources;
- outbreaks of diseases through infrastructural failure;
- congestion, queues and economic inefficiencies;
- deterioration of natural and artificial environment through overuse;
- resentment towards tourists;
- increases in criminal activities; and
- destruction of host community's values.

Although some of the above problems can be alleviated, such as improving the infrastructure to reduce the health risks of water and sewage treatment failure, some of them cannot. The effects of over-exploitation can be minimised, however, by diverting pressures. For instance, ecological imbalances can be tackled by:

- appropriate visitor flow management;
- fencing off areas subject to overuse;
- providing alternative routes and facilities for tourists to relieve others;
- dispersing tourists over wider or to different areas;
- zoning tourism-related activities;
- educating tourists and hosts to limit socio-cultural damage; and
- encouraging more positive local involvement in tourism activities.

One of the most well-tried techniques is that of access control – the volume or flow of tourists can be controlled economically, through prices, or physically, through closures, limiting parking facilities, transport or issuing quotas.

There are, of course, dangers associated with these remedial actions. For instance, dispersing tourists to other areas or to a wider area can sow the seeds for greater long-term problems if the source of the over-exploitation is not harnessed. Dispersing tourists temporally by extending the tourist season can reduce the time that some destinations need to recover from the industry's activities. Redirecting tourism flows may alleviate damaged areas in the short term, but only to replace them with newly damaged areas in the longer term. Such dispersion can also conflict with the prime objectives of the tourism plan. Zoning brings with it many limitations and problems, particularly in border areas. Therefore, when the remedial actions are implemented they should be seen as short-term alleviation methods until the true source of the problems can be tackled.

Finally, the issue of quality should be embedded in all aspects of tourism development planning. The issue of quality is vital for successful tourism development and should manifest itself in the structure and nature of the plans, the educational institutions that train the management and labour force and the monitoring and evaluation of the tourism development process. There are destinations, such as Mauritius and some Indonesian resorts, that owe their competitive advantage to the 'quality' of their tourism product and use 'quality' as a means of product differentiation. Quality should not be confused with high price or up-market tourism. It is just as important to strive for quality in a bed and breakfast or one-star hotel as it is in a five-star hotel or resort. However, when quality is the only factor leading to a competitive edge, then the development of the destination is vulnerable because quality is replicable by other destinations. This means that quality should be considered as a vital part of any tourism development strategy if the strategy is to achieve long-term success.

## CONCLUSION

Tourism, as an industry, fits well into the various economic development theories that have been put forward over the past couple of centuries. The only theory that does not provide a positive role for tourism in achieving general economic development is the English classical theory which provides little hope for any industry. The remaining theories all suggest that tourism would be a useful component of general economic development.

The successful development of tourism requires the construction of a development plan or strategy that is flexible and thorough. Flexibility is required in order to adjust and reformulate in response to internal and external changes. Thoroughness is required because of the complexity of the tourism industry and the economic, environmental and social consequences of its development. The issue of 'sustainability' is no more than sound planning because development requires that the path chosen is one that is in some way sustainable. Although the process of tourism development planning will be specific from destination to destination there are processes that need to be followed at national and sub-national levels and these processes provide the framework for tourism development planning.

Tourism development plan failure, when it occurs, is likely to be attributable to failures at either the design stage (inadequate planning structure) or the implementation stage. Both forms of failure are common but in many instances there are remedial actions that may be taken to alleviate some of the problems encountered by failure. Finally, it is important that authorities have contingency plans in place to deal with unexpected events that may knock the tourism strategy off-course.

## SELF-CHECK QUESTIONS

1. Which theories of economic development provide the best basis for tourism as a catalyst for economic development?

2. What are the major steps, and their sequence, that need to be undertaken as part of the planning process?

3. What reasons can be cited to explain tourism development plan failure at the design stage?

4. Why do tourism master plans/strategies fail at the implementation stage?

5. List the characteristics of the tourism product that influence its attractiveness as a development option. In so doing identify whether the characteristic provides a positive or negative influence when considering tourism as a development option.

# REFERENCES AND FURTHER READING

Ashworth, G. and Dietvorst, A. (1995) *Tourism and Spatial Transformations: Implications for Policy and Planning*, CAB, Oxford.

Bodlender, J. and Gerty, M. (1992) *Guidelines on Tourism Investment*, WTO, Madrid.

Chopra, S. (1991) *Tourism and Development in India*, Ashish, New York.

Cooper, C. (1991) *Progress in Tourism, Recreation and Hospitality Management*, Wiley, Chichester.

De Kadt, E. (1979) *Tourism, Passport to Development*, Oxford University Press, Oxford.

Edgell, D. (1990) *International Tourism Policy*, Van Nostrand Reinhold, New York.

Hall, C.M. and Jenkins, J.M. (1994) *Tourism and Public Policy*, Routledge, London.

Inskeep, E. (1993) *National and Regional Planning, Methodologies and Case Studies*, WTO/Routledge, Madrid/London.

Inskeep, E. and Kallenberger, M. (1992) *An Integrated Approach to Resort Development*, WTO, Madrid.

Jansen-Verbeke, M. (1998) *Leisure, Recreation and Tourism in Inner Cities*, Routledge, London.

Johnson, P. and Thomas, B. (eds) (1992) *Perspectives on Tourism Policy*, Mansell, London.

Kinniard, V.H. and Hall, D.R. (eds) (1994) *Tourism Development: The Gender Dimension*, Belhaven, London.

Lawson, F. (1995) *Hotels and Resorts: Planning, Design and Refurbishment*, Butterworth Heinemann, Oxford.

Murphy, P. (1997) *Quality Management in Urban Tourism*, Wiley, New York.

Nafziger, E.W. (1997) *The Economics of Developing Countries*, 3rd edn, Prentice Hall, Upper Saddle River, NJ.

Rostow, W.W. (1990) *Stages of Economic Growth: A Non-Communist Manifesto*, 3rd edn, Cambridge University Press, Cambridge.

WTO (1980) *Tourism and Employment: Enhancing the Status of Tourism Professions*, WTO, Madrid.

# MAJOR CASE STUDY 11.1
## Republic of Kenya Ministry of Tourism Strategic Plan 2008–2012

Kenya Vision 2030 is the country's new development blueprint covering the period 2008 to 2030. It aims to transform Kenya into a newly industrialising, 'middle-income country providing a high quality life to all its citizens by the year 2030'. The Vision has been developed through an all inclusive and participatory stakeholder consultative process, involving Kenyans from all parts of the country. It has also benefited from suggestions by some of the leading local and international experts on how the newly industrializing countries around the world have made the leap from poverty to widely-shared prosperity and equity.

The Vision is anchored on three 'pillars': the economic, the social and the political. The adoption of the Vision by Kenya comes after the successful implementation of the Economic Recovery Strategy for Wealth and Employment

Creation (ERS) which has enabled the country's economy to revert back to the path of rapid growth since 2002, when GDP grew from a low of 0.6% rising gradually to 6.1% in 2006 and 6.3% in the first quarter of 2007.

The economic pillar aims to achieve an economic growth rate of 10% per annum by 2012. Six priority sectors have been targeted to raise the national GDP growth rate to 10% by 2012. Tourism has been listed as the leading player of the six sectors. Others include Agriculture and Livestock, Wholesale and Retail Trade, Manufacturing, Business Process Outsourcing and Financial Services.

The social pillar seeks to build a just, cohesive and equitable social development in a clean and secure environment. The political pillar aims to realise an issue-based, people-centred, result-oriented and accountable democratic system that respects the rule of law, and protects the rights and freedoms of every individual in Kenyan society. The Kenya Vision 2030 is to be implemented in successive five-year Medium-Term Plans, with the first one covering the period 2008–2012.

The Ministry of Tourism's Strategic Plan for fiscal years 2008/9–2012/13 takes into account the Ministry's commitment to achieve the tourism sector goals as spelt out in Vision 2030 and the Medium Term Plan (2008–2012). These goals are to:

(a) increase international visitors from 1.8 million in 2007 to 3 million in 2012;

(b) increase average spending per visitor from Kshs 40,000 in 2006 to Kshs 70,000 by 2012;

(c) treble annual national earnings from Kshs 65.4 billion in 2007 to Kshs 200 billion by 2012.

The plan outlines the major strategic objectives to be implemented within the plan period and provides implementation strategies, activity implementation plans, monitoring and evaluation plan, financial requirements projections and proposes a new Ministry structure. The plan also envisages mobilisation of resources beyond Central Government's budgetary allocations and outlines some of the potential sources of funds and how they will be identified. It is projected that the Ministry will require an estimated Kshs 116 billion to implement its strategies and activities over the Plan period.

The Ministry's objectives and the requisite strategies needed to actualize the tourism sector goals are:

## Objective 1: To formulate and implement an appropriate policy and legal framework for the development of the tourism sector

The objective will be achieved through the following strategies:

● Finalize and facilitate the enactment of the National Tourism Bill.

● Operationalize the Tourism Act.

● Harmonize and enhance coordination of tourism development and service delivery.

## Objective 2: To develop new products and diversify source markets

The strategies for achieving this objective are:

● Develop and diversify tourism products

● Broaden the source markets.

## Objective 3: To increase tourism revenue from Ksh. 65 billion in 2007 to Ksh. 200 billion by 2012

This objective will be accomplished by implementing the following strategies:

● Increase the number of international tourists from 1.8 to 3 million.

● Increase the number of domestic bednights from 1.8 to 3.6 million.

● Increase average spending per visitor from Kshs 40,000 to Kshs 70,000.

## Objective 4: To offer and maintain internationally accepted standards of tourist service

The strategies for achieving this objective are:

● Review the hotel and restaurant classification criteria.

● Coordinate compliance with regulations and standards.

## Objective 5: To enhance safety and security of tourists

This objective will be accomplished by pursuing the following strategies:

● Develop capacity of the Tourist Police Unit (TPU) and Kenya Wildlife Service (KWS) rangers.

● Enhance capacity of crisis management centre.

● Coordinate management of beach activities.

## Objective 6: To enhance and sustain the financial resources for the tourism sector

The strategies for achieving this objective are:

● Establish a sustainable funding mechanism for the sector.

● Mobilize resources from external sources.

● Improve efficiency of resource utilization.

## Objective 7: To attract, develop and retain competent and motivated staff

This objective will be accomplished by pursuing the following strategies:

- Upgrade skills in the workforce
- Rationalize staff capacity.
- Improve work environment.
- Mainstream public sector integrity programme.

### Objective 8: To reduce tourism resource conflict

This objective will be accomplished by pursuing the following strategies:

- Promote tourism area management.
- Enhance community based tourism.

### Objective 9: To enhance tourism information management and research capacity

This objective will be attained by pursuing the following strategies:

- Improve use of ICT in tourism sector.
- Establish tourism research centre.
- Enhance publicity and information flow on tourism.

Implementation of the objectives and strategies outlined above will enable the Ministry to harness its resources and to take advantage of the opportunities existing in the dynamic tourism sector and address pertinent challenges as outlined later in this Plan. This will in turn propel the Ministry to higher levels of performance and realization of its mission and vision for the benefit of all stakeholders (Republic of Kenya, Ministry of Tourism, Strategic Plan 2008–2012, pp. vii–x).

*Source*: http://www.tourism.go.ke/ministry.nsf/doc/STRATEGIC_PLAN_2008%20-%202012.pdf/$file/STRATEGIC_PLAN_2008%20-%202012.pdf

## DISCUSSION QUESTIONS

1. What do you think the strengths and weaknesses are of the strategic plan drawn up by the Kenyan Ministry? What opportunities might they take advantage of to fulfil their objectives and what threats are posed both internally and externally that may undermine their plan?

2. What issues would you identify and raise with respect to the objectives of the strategy?

## TOURISM PLANNING AS I SEE IT . . .

International benchmarking of high-performing tourism destinations consistently highlight the importance of having an ambitious vision, a clear understanding of the destination's values with an unambiguous strategy to guide tourism planning and development. Having strong leadership with a focused, well-resourced, destination management organisation is fundamentally important for successfully driving the implementation of the strategy.

Clearly, this process has to involve all stakeholders within the touristic system in a public:private sector partnership. It is no coincidence, however, to report that the more successful destination organisation models are those that are private sector led. The UNWTO acknowledges that this is the case, recognising that the private sector is, ultimately, more dynamic, more aware of market demands and less risk averse.

This type of private sector-led, public sector-supported partnership approach is evident around the world. Good examples include: Park City (Utah), Jackson Hole (Wyoming), Lausanne and Montreux Vevey (Switzerland), Turku (Finland) and Oslo (Norway).

In the UK and, indeed, in a number of other countries, these lessons from international best practice are ignored. All too often tourism planning remains the prerogative of the public sector. Local government officials and civil servants dominate the destination planning process. They pay lip service to industry engagement, ignoring, or failing to understand, the basic principles of destination management.

Under these constrained conditions tourism is lagging. The result is inevitable: a stagnant tourism economy lacking in innovation and investment.

We exist in increasingly competitive and turbulent times. Strategic planning for tourism needs fresh ideas and creativity. It needs a dynamic that only the informed and enlightened private sector can bring. It is the role of the public sector to create the environment to allow ambition, aspiration in vision and strategy to be enacted.

**PROFESSOR TERRY STEVENS**
**MANAGING DIRECTOR, STEVENS & ASSOCIATES**

# CHAPTER 12
## TOURISM, CRISES AND DISASTER MANAGEMENT

### LEARNING OUTCOMES

This chapter will provide you with:

- an understanding of travel risk and travel risk perceptions;
- an understanding of how travel risk perceptions can affect travel decisions;
- an insight into how negative events (natural or man-made) may impact on destinations and the length of time needed to recover from such events; and
- an overview of the literature in terms of responses to crises.

## INTRODUCTION

Tourism, like any industry, does not operate in a vacuum and is subject to shocks and disruptions caused by a host of different factors (see the chapters on marketing and planning). In fact, tourism is more susceptible to shocks and disruptions than many industries because (a) it is a highly perishable service sector industry, (b) it requires the consumers to travel to the destination in order for tourism to take place, and (c) a large part of the industry depends upon the environment in which it takes place. The characteristics of tourism provide additional pressures in the sense that tourists often travel to new destinations on the basis of what they have heard from others or found out from the media and other forms of communication. The image or perception that tourists have of a destination can be dramatically altered if there is suddenly a major disaster, either natural, such as a tsunami, hurricane or an earthquake, or man-made, such as political unrest, crime, etc. This chapter examines the impacts of such disasters on tourists' perceptions and actions and on the destinations that are subjected to them. A PEST analysis can show that there are many factors affecting tourism and disasters can impact on any of those factors (see Chapter 11). These events are often outside the control of the local or national tourism industry, but planners can implement policies and responses that can either mitigate the effect of a crisis or develop sectors in such a way that they adapt to the dangers to reduce future impacts.

The first half of this chapter examines the issues relating to disasters and travel risk perceptions, whereas the latter half looks at the managerial issues relating to coping with disasters.

# NATURAL AND MAN-MADE DISASTERS AND THE TOURISM INDUSTRY

Tourism is directly or indirectly disrupted by natural disasters such as hurricanes, tsunamis and earthquakes (such as earthquakes in Taiwan 1999; Hurricane Katrina on the North Central Gulf Coast, USA 2005; the tsunami in March 2011 off the Pacific coast of Tōhoku) or man-made disasters such as terrorist attacks, political unrest, civil wars, kidnapping and on-going crime (such as the 9/11 attacks in the USA, Arab Spring since January 2011, drug cartel struggles in Mexico, kidnapping of tourists in Kenya in September 2011). The immediate effects of natural disasters can be the destruction of tourist infrastructure such as transportation, communication, electricity, water and waste disposal systems together with damage to the tourism superstructure, including accommodation and recreation facilities. The effects of man-made disasters may be similar, including damage to the infrastructure and superstructure (9/11; Beirut 1975–1990) or may simply damage the image of the destination (this will be discussed later in this chapter).

The impact that events may have on consumer demand depends upon a wide variety of factors, including the intensity or magnitude of the event, the frequency of events (and thus the likelihood of a recurrence) and whether tourists are the focus of the event. Furthermore, the same event doesn't necessarily have the same impact on different destinations. This depends on a series of other variables such as the stage of tourism development, the political relations between the affected destination and its generating market (i.e. travel warnings issued by governments in the originating country) the relationship with international media, as the way in which events are portrayed can determine the impact they have on the perceptions of consumers. Finally, all tourists are not alike and different tourists will respond in different ways to events and their tolerance of travel-related risks.

Similarly, the period of time that it takes a destination to recover fully from a negative incident will be determined by the time taken to reconstruct damaged infrastructure and superstructure and the ability of the media (and the resources put into them) to reassure visitors that the risk of recurrence has been reduced or eliminated. Developing countries may find it difficult to recover quickly as they may not have the economic diversity or resources to fund such recovery strategies. There is also a dilemma facing tourist destinations subjected to serious events when the government wishes to try and secure international help and resources to assist with recovery and consequently highlights the extent of the damage that has occurred, whereas the industry may wish to play down the level of damage and get back to 'business as normal' because they need the tourists to return as quickly as possible in order to maintain their operations.

In addition to the direct effects of a disaster, destinations may suffer further long-term damage to the tourism industry because tourists may perceive there to be a lack of safety and security measures to protect them. Generally speaking, the perception of travel-related risk is an image based on the likelihood of negative consequences associated with visiting a destination. Risk is not a tangible aspect of travel; it is what tourists perceive and experience during the process of purchasing and consuming tourism-related services. Travel risk perception is a major factor influencing the decision-making process with regard to the choice of destination and the purchase of tourism services. Tourism is a part of the service sector with unique characteristics (intangibility, inseparability, variability and perishability) which intensify the perceived risk when compared to the purchase of tangible goods. In addition, tourism gives rise to other risk elements, such as the possibility of poor weather, unfriendly communities, disruptions to travel through industrial action, inedibility of local food, acts of terrorism, crime, political unrest disease and natural disasters. These factors can all influence the level of perceived risk experienced by tourists and hence their decision to travel.

The nature of risk during the tourism decision and consumption process is such that if the level of perceived risk is greater than some personal threshold limit, the tourist may try to reduce exposure to this risk by not travelling or travelling elsewhere. Normally, this threshold value is reached more quickly for a discretionary tourism product than, say, for a tangible good (you can always send the dysfunctional washing machine back to the seller but this is not the case with tourism). However, risk perceptions are not generally formed on factual data or calculated risk indices and it is the image that is being measured against the threshold, rather than the actuality, which means that perception is everything. Thus, it does not matter how incorrect or wrong a perception of risk may be, it will still influence the behaviour of the potential tourist in exactly the same way that decisions would be affected by real changes in the level of risk from actual events. Therefore the perception of risk has a direct impact and can, in effect, generate much greater losses than those that may be caused by the original event itself.

The media to which potential tourists are exposed, and the choice of words that the media use to communicate an event can determine the levels of risk perception. For example, when there is a disruption by a group or by an individual, the media tend to point to the fact that this disruption is caused by a particular terrorist group or by an individual for personal reasons. The former tends to have a more profound effect on the public's perception of risk than the latter as it may seem more likely to reoccur.

Tourists may well perceive acts of terrorism to be a higher risk than natural disasters when travelling to specific destinations. In some regions, natural disasters are relatively rare and, unlike many acts of terrorism, are not specifically centred on tourists. Therefore, when tourists are considering a trip to the more politically volatile areas, such as some countries in the Middle East, they are likely to be far more concerned about man-made disasters than they are about natural disasters. Conversely, when travelling to the Caribbean during hurricane season tourists may be more aware of the risks relating to natural disasters than they are about acts of terrorism.

## DESTINATION RISK

Some destinations may appear to be associated with greater travel risks than others. For instance, Europe may be perceived to be a classically safe destination and relatively free from serious crime; however, Latin America may be seen as being more prone to acts related to organised crime. Some countries in the Middle East have experienced political unrest for sustained periods and hence travel to the Middle East may seem to travellers to carry a higher level of risk than travel to non-Middle Eastern destinations. Some unfortunate countries seem to suffer from an abundance of both natural and man-made risks (e.g. Indonesia) which is likely to keep their name in the media and raise the profile of risk to potential travellers. Researchers found that perceived risk has a stronger influence with respect to tourists avoiding a particular region than it has on the decision of planning to visit one. For example, those perceiving terrorism as a risk may be more likely to avoid travelling to the Middle East.

# MINI CASE STUDY 12.1
## March 2011, disaster in Japan

Almost six years after the December 2004 earthquake in the Indian Ocean, which generated a tidal wave that affected countries from Indonesia to Africa, a major earthquake off the Pacific coast of Tōhoku in March 2011, triggered a series of tsunami waves that reached heights of up to 40.5 metres and travelled up to 10 kilometres inland when it struck Japan. The death toll exceeded 15,000 and there are still 4,000 people missing.

The tsunami in turn created a nuclear disaster resulting in mass evacuation. Some foreign governments recommended that their citizens evacuate the affected area distancing themselves at least 80 kilometres (50 miles) from the plant. The full damage to the infrastructure included the collapse of almost 130,000 buildings and serious damage to more than 250,000 buildings and some damage to a further 700,000 buildings. Around 4.4 million households in north-eastern Japan found themselves to be without electricity and 1.5 million without water. The other industries were urged to reduce their energy consumption so that the national power grid could supply the basic necessities to support people. The earthquake and subsequent tsunami caused extensive and severe structural damage in north-eastern Japan, including severe damage to highways and rail tracks as well as triggering fires and floods. The Japanese Prime Minister, Naoto Kan, said: 'In the 65 years after the end of World War II, this is the toughest and the most difficult crisis for Japan' **(http://statistics.unwto. org/sites/all/files/pdf/tsa_data.pdf).**

Tourism accounted for around 2.1% of Japan's total GDP in 2011, which is still short of the 2007 peak as the country felt the effects of the global financial crisis and the March 2011 earthquake and tsunami. Following the tsunami, tourist arrivals fell 27% compared with the corresponding figure for 2010 (see Figures 12.1 and 12.2). In February 2012, almost a year after the earthquake, tourist arrivals were still 19% lower than the corresponding figures for 2010.

The early evidence shows that Japan has suffered a significant fall in the number of international visitors coming from the West, although tourists from China have continued to arrive. Unlike Thailand, which offered financial incentives to restore tourism activity following civil unrest, Japan has relied more upon extensive marketing campaigns but, even here, some of the campaigns have included offers of free flights to Japan.

*Source*: http://news.bbc.co.uk/1/hi/programmes/fast_track/9628697.stm

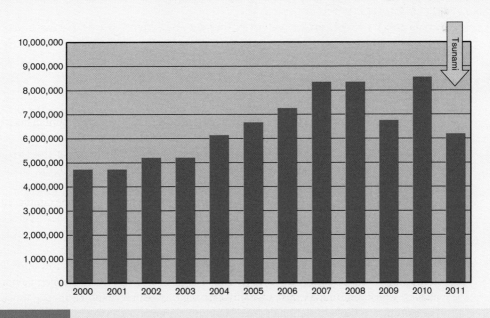

| Figure 12.1 | Visitor arrivals, Japan, 2000–2011 |

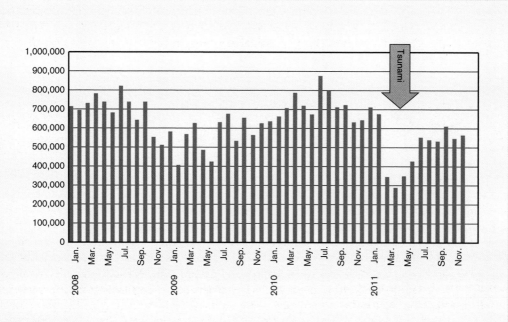

| Figure 12.2 | Monthly visitor arrivals to Japan, 2008–2011 |

## DISCUSSION QUESTIONS

1. The 2011 earthquake and tsunami severely damaged the north-east coastal area of Japan. Why do you think that the tourists have continued to stay away from Japan's tourist areas in the post-tsunami period?

2. Marketing campaigns immediately following crises are not always effective. Why do you think this is the case?

3. Why do you think that the Japanese earthquake and tsunami did not affect Chinese tourist arrivals as much as their European counterparts?

## TOURISM AND TERRORISM

Tourism is not only susceptible to natural disasters it is also affected by man-made disasters, such as the outbreak of war, political unrest and terrorism (e.g. the Balkan Wars of the 1990s, 9/11 New York and Washington, the Arab Spring 2010–2012). Some of the terrorist attacks targeted tourists directly, such as the Bali bombings in 2002 (Indonesia), the Luxor attacks in 1997 (Egypt). It is expected that attacks directed at tourists are likely to have a more prolonged effect than those not directed at tourists but this is not always the case. For example, although the attacks in Kenya in 2002 were specifically targeted at tourists, they were seen as a one-off attack directed at Israeli tourists and so the after-effects, in terms of the number of tourists travelling to Kenya, were quite minimal (Morakabati, 2007).

Terrorists have recognised that their activities can feed a media that is hungry for spectacular news and this gives the perpetrators a high profile and much publicity. Al-Qaeda style attacks, which aim to maximise casualties, have attracted international media, especially when the victims are Western nationals. The literature abounds with papers looking at the effects of the media on tourists' travel risk perceptions, and identifies that where the attacks are directed towards tourists there tends to be a lasting effect on risk perceptions. Most of these events have entered the tourists' decision-making process, generating fear and insecurity to travellers and creating a barrier to travel. In addition to the openly stated fear of personal harm, there can be a more general lack of interest in travel, which masks this underlying fear. Tourists may well perceive acts of terrorism to be a higher risk than natural disasters when travelling to specific destinations.

The perception of travel-related risk associated with terrorism has changed in recent times as a result of the change in the magnitude and frequency of attacks. Where attacks in the past have been relatively small-scale, the events of 9/11 (2001), the Bali bombings (2002, 2005), the Madrid bombings (2004), incidents in Turkey and Egypt (2005) and the attacks on the London transport network (2005) have all made the risk of terrorism a part of the international travel scene. The extent to which tourists perceive the risk from terrorist acts often depends on the region to which they are travelling, the characteristics of the traveller and how recently a terrorist incident has taken place.

## Impacts of negative events

While no destination is immune to disasters, the time period necessary for recovery varies significantly from destination to destination. There are a number of factors that can explain why it may take one destination longer to recover from a disaster than another destination, including the timing of the attack, the stage of development of the tourism industry, the scale of the attack, the frequency of attacks and the responses made after an attack. Figure 12.3 shows the impact of various terrorist attacks aimed at the tourism industries in six selected countries by looking at tourist arrivals during and after the terrorist attack.

Figure 12.4 shows tourist arrivals for six countries in three years, where '−1' is the year before a terrorist attack, '0' is the year during which the terrorist attack took place and '+1' is the year after the terrorist attack. It is interesting to see that the countries fall into two groups, with Egypt, Indonesia and the USA all ending up with a similar decline in the number of tourist arrivals, whereas Kenya, Spain and the UK end up with increased numbers of arrivals compared with the situation prior to the attacks. One explanation of this clustering of results could be the fact that in Egypt and Indonesia the attacks were focused mainly on international visitors whereas the attacks in Madrid and London were centred on the transport systems. The USA attack was unprecedented and shocked the world whereas the victims of the Kenya attack were predominantly Israeli visitors. In isolation it is difficult to attribute these differences to specific factors and, of course, they are not unrelated in that the 9/11 event was followed by the Bali bombings and then Egypt, Madrid and the UK a few years later. Questions to be asked include: do tourists come to accept the risk of terrorism as more and more events take place, or are they more

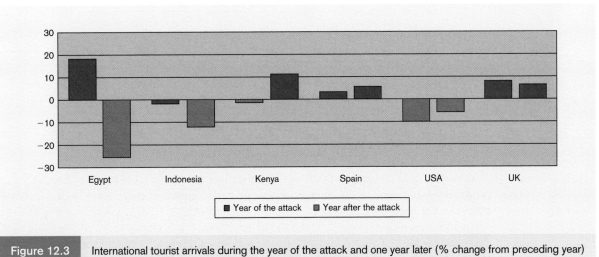

**Figure 12.3**  International tourist arrivals during the year of the attack and one year later (% change from preceding year)

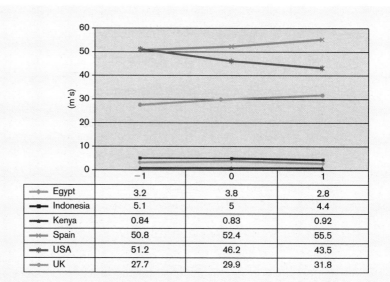

| | −1 | 0 | 1 |
|---|---|---|---|
| Egypt | 3.2 | 3.8 | 2.8 |
| Indonesia | 5.1 | 5 | 4.4 |
| Kenya | 0.84 | 0.83 | 0.92 |
| Spain | 50.8 | 52.4 | 55.5 |
| USA | 51.2 | 46.2 | 43.5 |
| UK | 27.7 | 29.9 | 31.8 |

**Figure 12.4**  Arrivals where −1 is the year before the attack, 0 is the year of the attack and 1 is a year after the attack

confident with the tighter security that follows? Also, it should be borne in mind that all of these countries invested heavily in enhanced marketing campaigns following the events and it may be more helpful to examine tourist expenditure as well as the number of arrivals.

When the tourism industry is under pressure and trying to recover from a negative shock, it is not surprising to find tour operators and destinations reducing prices to make the destination more competitive and attract a wider range of visitors. Therefore, one would expect to see that the fall in the volume of tourist expenditure is greater than the fall in the number of tourist arrivals. Figure 12.5 shows the patterns of change in tourist receipts for the same countries that were shown in Figure 12.3 and Figure 12.4 (with the exception of Egypt). This confirms that the three countries that suffered the greatest impact in terms of the drop in tourist arrivals suffered a slightly greater proportional drop in tourist receipts, whereas those countries that were able to maintain or increase the number of tourist arrivals also enjoyed an increase in tourist receipts. Figure 12.6 shows the temporal effects of the events of 9/11 on the average room rates in New York City.

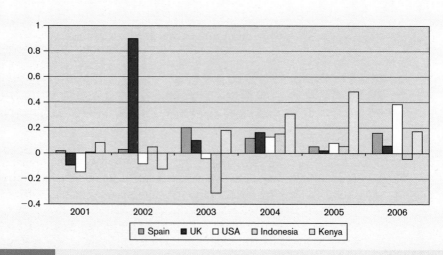

**Figure 12.5**  International tourism receipts (% change 2000–2006)

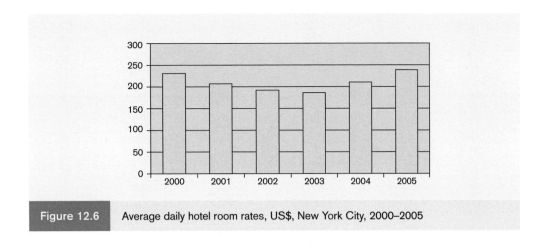

| Figure 12.6 | Average daily hotel room rates, US$, New York City, 2000–2005 |

The fall in tourist expenditure can be observed by looking at some of the component prices of travel such as the cost of airline tickets and hotel rates. As an example, air fares fell dramatically after 9/11 in order to try and coax travellers back on to aircraft amid fears of further attacks. Further, the growth of the low-cost airlines only helped underscore the fall in the cost of travel at a time when oil prices were rapidly increasing. Hotel prices were also being offered at bargain basement prices. For instance, if the average daily room rates for New York hotels are examined it can be seen that there is a marked effect following the events of 9/11. In 2000 the average daily room rate in New York was US$233. Even though the terrorist attacks on the Twin Towers did not occur until September 2001, the average daily room rate fell for that year to just US$204 and the true underlying rate was not revealed until 2003 when rates fall to US$193. The room rates were kept low throughout 2002, 2003 and 2004, to maintain occupancy levels and the pre-attack average room rate was not restored until 2005 (see Figure 12.6).

Of course, the frequency of terrorist attacks affects the perceptions that travellers have about the risk associated with travel. Indonesia, for example, has been subjected to two significant terrorist attacks, the first in 2002 and the second in 2005, not to mention the 2004 tsunami. Does this make Indonesia a risky place in the minds of potential tourists?

# RISK PERCEPTION

Generally speaking, the perception of travel-related risk experienced by an individual will be determined by a variety of factors, including the individual's aversion to risk, their consideration of what may occur as a result of their decisions or behaviour, the potential scale of a threat, the probability of incidence and, often more importantly, the media's coverage of earlier events or threats. If the individual or a close friend/relative has been exposed to high-risk situations prior to the decision-making process then this is likely to have a significant influence on an individual's perception of risk.

There are many aspects of the tourism product that give rise to risk and upon which travellers' perceptions will be formed. For instance, even the product itself is an unknown to the first-time visitor and holds an element of risk in that it may not live up to the tourist's expectations. Travel is fraught with risks in terms of accidents, getting lost, disruptions through industrial action, the effect of the weather on the transport system and acts of terrorism. Even the destination may hold risks in terms of health, crime, being an unfriendly environment or finding that an onward flight or the hotel is overbooked. Some of these risks may not figure strongly in some people's minds whereas they may be the central focus for some travellers.

| Table 12.1 | Examples of divergence between actual and perceived top risk countries | |
| --- | --- | --- |
| **Type of risk** | **Perception[1]** | **Actual[2]** |
| Health risks | India | Thailand |
| | China | Egypt |
| | Thailand | Caribbean |
| Crime risks (theft, fraud, etc) | USA | Thailand |
| | Italy | South Africa |
| | Spain | Caribbean |

*Source*: [1]Morakabati, 2007; [2]Norwich Union Insurance Report, 2006

Risk during the tourism decision and consumption process involves the uncertainty about whether there will be a difference between the expected and the actual outcomes of decisions or actions. Risk perceptions are often formed in ways that do not reflect reality, but it is the perceptions that are important because they will guide the decision. Thus, it does not matter how incorrect or wrong a perception of risk may be, it will still influence the behaviour of the potential tourist in exactly the same way that decisions would be affected by changes in the level of actual risk.

In a recent study of travel risk perceptions it was found that there was little correlation between the perceptions of travellers and the frequency and magnitude of claims experienced by a major insurance company. Table 12.1 shows the top three countries for travel risk as perceived by travellers (based on a survey of 730 travellers from a wide range of countries of origin) and the top three countries/regions in terms of actual travel insurance claims from a leading travel insurance company.

## Types of disasters

In spite of the impact that crisis events may have on all aspects of the tourism industry the academic debate on this issue is relatively recent and compared to other areas of tourism research has not received a great deal of attention. Fewer than 10 books have been written on tourism and disaster management in the past decade and the number of journal articles on this topic is not particularly large. At a theoretical level many gaps remain and aside from the pioneering work of Faulkner (2001), gaps in how tourism is affected and how destinations should respond remain. Other and arguably less important areas of tourism research including heritage and even tourism and peace have generated specialist journals. This is not the case in the area of tourism crisis research and this highlights a major gap.

Both man-made and natural disasters can have direct and indirect impacts on tourism activity:

- by affecting the destination through loss of infrastructure and superstructure;
- by creating an image that the particular destination is not safe, and this perception tends to have a long-lasting effect.

Natural disasters can create catastrophic results such as the extensive destruction of infrastructure and superstructure (Indian Ocean Tsunami in 2004; Japan's earthquake and tsunami in 2011) on a scale (spatial aspect) that is beyond the control of man. The scale of destruction of man-made disasters is often more limited. For example, terrorists often attack transportation systems (or use transportation systems in the case of 9/11). Sometimes human acts result in disasters that are beyond the control of human capacity, for example Chernobyl or the oil spill in the Gulf of Mexico (see Chapter 8). The difference between the terrorist attacks and these latter man-made disasters is the degree of maliciousness associated with them.

| Photograph 12.1 | Remembrance ceremony on the first anniversary of the 11 September 2001 terrorism attacks in the US. Terrorism impacts on residents and tourists. |
|---|---|

*Source*: Jeremy Hogan/Alamy Images

Chernobyl and the Gulf oil spill are more related to incompetence and errors in judgement than a deliberate attempt to bring chaos. The required response also differs between the two types of events.

Terrorist attacks, wars or other types of political instability can create a wider image and affect a region rather than a specific country. For instance, the Middle East as a region is painted with an image of conflict, social unrest and terrorism. Tourists' geographical knowledge is often unclear and they tend to associate a disturbance in one country with travel risks for the whole region, and nowhere is this more apparent than the Middle East. For example, in the early 1990s, during the Gulf War, some of the news bulletins were broadcast from Cyprus and this created an image that Cyprus was in or in close proximity to the war zone; thus tourist arrivals dropped in Cyprus from 3.38 million in 1990 to 2.94 million in 1991.

Further distinctions can be made between disasters in the sense that some disasters can be minimised through the implementation of early warning systems. For instance, natural disasters such as hurricanes or typhoons can be identified and prepared for whereas others (such as earthquakes or terrorist attacks) give little or no warnings before the disaster occurs. This gives rise to the distinction where some types of disasters are known as python events (slow but inevitable) whereas others are known as cobra events (sudden and unexpected). Another difference between types of disasters is that natural disasters are often seen as being one-off events whereas terrorist attacks can be seen as being part of a series of events.

In the case of natural disasters, there is also a conflicting issue between host and tourists when both are affected. Holidaymakers in hotels expect to be looked after by the staff, whereas in reality an earthquake may devastate local towns and villages and staff will be focused on the safety of their own families. From the employees' perspective it seems to be a challenge to expect staff to prioritise guests over their own families. From a tourist perspective they have few if any local connections, do not know the area well and may not be able to even speak the local language. Without access to local emergency response information tourists are particularly vulnerable.

| Photograph 12.2 | Natural disaster. Cancun Caribbean houses after hurricane storm crash disaster. |
| --- | --- |

*Source*: Holbox/Shutterstock.com

One important aspect of disaster management is the ability to prepare for events in the first place and, should such events occur, to be able to respond to them (see Figure 12.7). The organisations responsible for planning for disasters and responding to them are likely to include different entities and the roles which these organisations take are likely to be fluid, changing as

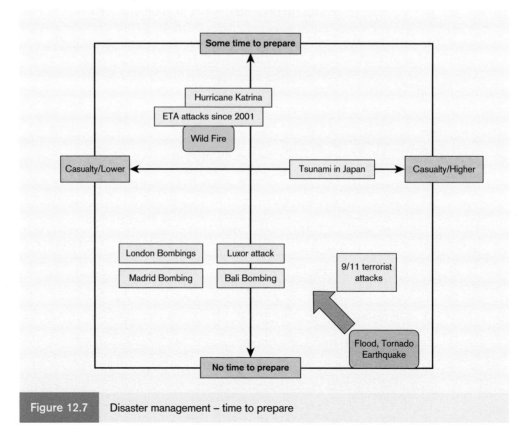

| Figure 12.7 | Disaster management – time to prepare |
| --- | --- |

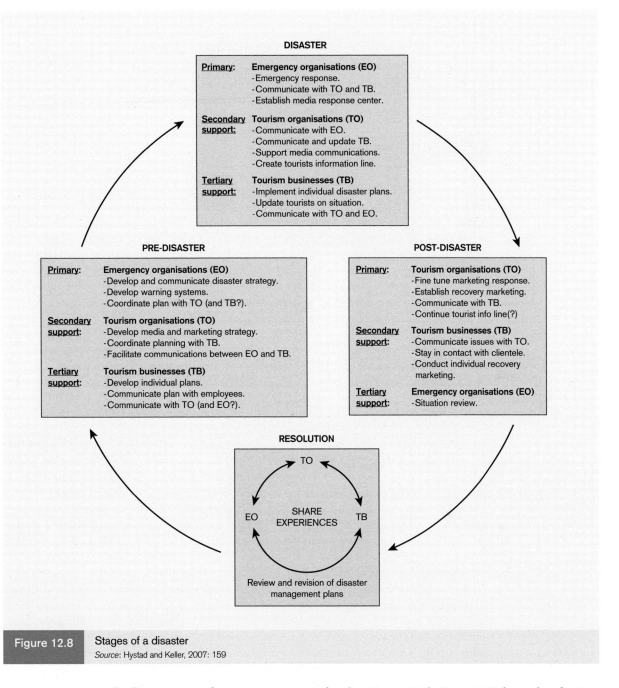

| Figure 12.8 | Stages of a disaster |
|---|---|
| | *Source*: Hystad and Keller, 2007: 159 |

the disaster moves from one stage to another (see Figure 12.8). Figure 12.7 shows that the time needed to prepare for a disaster depends on the type of disaster. However, with an Al-Qaeda type of disaster there is unlikely to be any time to prepare because the perpetrators are attempting to cause the maximum loss of life. Other types of terrorist activities, such as by ETA in Spain, tend to provide warnings prior to the attacks as their aim is not to maximise the human collateral but to disrupt services and damage infrastructure/superstructure. In the case of natural python-type disasters, such as hurricanes, when the stakeholders can see the disaster coming there is an aspect of predictability, but it depends on the sophistication of the early warning systems. However, in spite of good early warning systems, poor planning can result in a poor response performance (such as Hurricane Katrina in USA).

Disaster time phases can be divided into three distinct periods: pre-disaster, during or imme-diately after disaster and post-disaster. For management, there are two approaches that tourism destinations and businesses can take when faced with scenarios of disasters – they can strategise

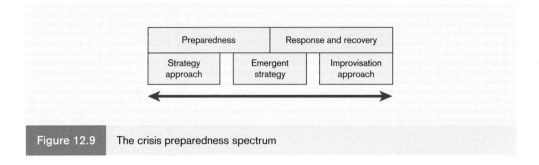

Figure 12.9    The crisis preparedness spectrum

or improvise (see Figure 12.9). The strategise approach demands planning and forecasting so that future events can be predicted and built into operational systems (Porter, 1980; Prahalad and Hamel, 1990) whereas the improvise approach adopts the view that you can't plan for what you do not know and that extrapolating from the past will not equip you for the future (Ansoff, 1991; Fredrickson, 1984; Minzberg, 1990, 1991, 1994). Others have even gone so far as to suggest that taking the strategy approach can be detrimental when faced with a crisis (Cunha, 2004). Counter to this view, Hosie (2006) suggests that crises demand preparation, response and recovery planning while others have gone so far as to argue that organisations (and by inference destinations) that do not have a plan of action in case of crises are unlikely to remain in existence. The days of static plans are long gone. The increased rate of change in the business environment and its accompanying volatility pushes businesses away from rigid top-down planning approaches in favour of more flexible reactive planning approaches. These flexible planning systems form the basis of emergent strategies where plans evolve through a process of learning as a result of events. Thus, the businesses strategies are dynamic processes that are continually monitoring the environment in which they operate and the strategies are reformulated on the basis of what is discovered.

Flexibility is at its height when considering the improvisation approach. It would be incorrect to simply assume that improvisation is based on a 'make it up as you go along' strategy as it relies on there being a learning process to understand the environment in which the business is operating. Because disaster management, particularly during the response stage, is dealing with the unknown in many cases, improvisation is clearly an important element of any disaster management strategy. This does not mean that it should not occur within a more planned disaster strategy. In reality, the approaches from traditional strategy to improvisation are polar extremes of the same spectrum.

Authors such as Drabek (1995), Kash and Darling (1998), Faulkner (2001), Glaesser (2003) and Ritchie (2004) have suggested that proactive planning within the industry is a rarity (although the large multinationals may have site-specific plans) and, in 2011, a thorough examination of the UNISDR and UNWTO Survey databases only served to reinforce this view. Furthermore, not all plans are the same – a wide variation is found between the structure and approaches of different plans. In addition stakeholder views can differ even within destinations; there can be conflicting signals between the public sector and the private sector in the immediate aftermath of a disaster, when the government may wish to communicate internationally on the scale of the damage as it goes in search of international aid, whereas the private sector may want the world to know that it is 'business as usual' to kick-start the recovery process. There is a need for proactive plans and those plans should include and engage all stakeholders.

There are many different actions that can be taken according to the types of disasters. When there is time to prepare for an imminent disaster, planners can build up and plan for the dissemination of information (communication). This means that SMEs and larger organisations can take action based on this information, such as coordinating different bodies and ensuring that casualties are kept to a minimum, through the evacuation of tourists, stopping incoming flows, mitigating infrastructure and superstructure damage (such as shutting down nuclear reactors), ensuring the availability of food and shelter, and the availability of mobile and satellite phones, etc.

But the situation is far worse when the event occurs without warning – for example, when terrorists attack a transportation system and this results in fatalities. By definition, in such events there is no time to evacuate because, by its very nature, the attack occurs before response teams can be deployed or warnings can be given.

Responses to disasters can be divided into two main categories: firstly there are responses that actually deal with immediate needs, such as responses by emergency services and security forces. The second area of response that creates problems is when the government and industry try to restore public confidence. Dealing with so many conflicting stories coming from a variety of sources can be a major headache for the authorities. In the pre-social media period governments could get away with limiting the information made available to reduce the risk of panicking the public or generating overreactions. However, the evolution of social media, with its instant and unregulated information, means that governments must ensure that accurate and timely information is made available.

It is common to see that governments issue travel warning advisories to their citizens if a disaster has occurred in a specific country. Travel advisories result in tour operators pulling tourists out of a destination and stopping the inflow of tourists. Once the disaster has passed and the local environment is safe for tourism to resume it is important that such travel advisories are lifted as quickly as possible. However, governments sometimes err on the side of caution and it can take some time for these travel advisories to be lifted. Once lifted it is important for the industry in the affected destination to resume business as normal as quickly as possible. Marketing campaigns, including inviting the media and tour operators from tourist-generating markets, is a tried and tested way of getting the information out that the destination is now safe and back to normal. This is more of a challenge when the scale of the event is large or there has been a frequent series of events. Biermann (2001) suggested that it takes time for the public to build up confidence in a destination and that images from the media repeatedly showing the event or the reconstruction of infrastructure and superstructure keep the event firmly in the mind of the potential tourists. The period of time (attention life cycle) when a disaster is in the minds of potential tourists can be quite fleeting and tourists traditionally have short memories, their attention being diverted to the 'next' crisis being highlighted by the media. During the time when the disaster is fresh in the minds of tourists even the most vigorous marketing campaigns are unlikely to be effective.

Other challenges arise from promotional campaigns, as they might change the demographics of tourists through attracting different types of market. Such changes may lead to a fall in the average tourist spending levels or they may attract tourists who are associated with greater negative environmental and socio-cultural impacts. This can damage the long-term net returns to tourism activity. For destinations that are highly dependent upon tourism for their economic well-being such changes can have major effects, especially on the poorer segments of the host population.

Overall, the best strategy is to deal with the issues in an overt and effective manner so that potential tourists can feel secure in booking vacations. The thing about tourism is that it is a consumption that is based on 'faith' in the sense that consumers are booking something that they have not tried and can't take back if they don't like it. Therefore, they need a great deal of reassurance that it will be what they expect it to be. Also, tourists are not always the best people to evaluate the true risk associated with travel – after 9/11 many US residents chose to drive to their destinations in the USA and many more people were killed on the roads than died as a result of 9/11 – the risk of being killed per mile as an air passenger is negligible (unless you are one of the few that are killed) but people have elevated risk perceptions associated with air transport.

Bringing home the benefits of travel, showing the positives and demonstrating the number of satisfied tourists is an excellent way of making tourism go viral and spreading the word, especially given the effect of social media. Confidence when dealing with crises and demonstrating the fact that as a destination they are fully equipped to handle any crisis without the destination looking as if it is operating under siege are essential ingredients for reassuring potential tourists. At the end of the day tourism is an incredibly resilient industry and with sufficient stability the tourists will return.

## CONCLUSION

This chapter examined how vulnerable the tourism industry can be to the impacts of negative events which are beyond its control. Because tourists have to travel to destinations in order to consume tourism products, they step into a world that can quickly become transformed into something outside of their comfort zone. At the destination they may be less familiar with the supporting networks around them and this can generate higher perceptions of risk and make them more susceptible to shocks and disruptions. The nature of leisure tourism also means that potential tourists may not be willing to sacrifice any of their civil liberty, safety and security when there are alternative destinations that may pose fewer perceived risks.

The types of events that could disrupt tourism flows were examined under two distinct headings, man-made and natural disasters. Many studies have measured the effects of both types of negative events, but in general they find that the severity of impact will likely depend on the magnitudes of the events and their frequency of occurrence. It was also suggested that the stage of tourism development was an influencing factor where 'newer' destinations were likely to suffer more severely from a negative event than the more mature destinations that had built up a more robust profile and image. Tourists, however, have a relatively short memory span and unless constantly reminded by the media tend to forget events especially if they are deemed to be small scale and one-off. Even the larger scale events have proved not to have lasting effects on a destination.

In terms of the management of disaster events it was suggested that there are two main categories of events: Python Events which are relatively slow in occurring and give the authorities some time to take pre-event actions, such as evacuating an area prior to a major storm or hurricane, and Cobra Events which limit the disaster management to responding to the impacts of events where there has been little or no warnings, such as earthquakes or terrorist attacks. In this latter case the authorities are focused on recovery rather than preparation, although preparations can be undertaken in terms of implementing building regulations, simulating events and responses etc. This suggests that planning can be pro-active and reactive, however, pro-active approaches can be costly and require significant amounts of resources which may deter the countries with fewer resources available to them from implementing pro-active systems.

## SELF-CHECK QUESTIONS

1. What are the different factors that influence travel risk and travel-risk perceptions?
2. What factors are likely to determine the impact of terrorist attacks on tourism destinations?
3. How can regional (e.g. Asia, Middle East) tourism suffer when only one or two countries within that region are in conflict?

## YOUTUBE

### Crisis (disaster management)

Bournemouth University's Disaster Management Centre
**http://www.youtube.com/watch?v=poTnxwLz7d8**

Qld tourism struggles in wake of floods
**http://www.youtube.com/watch?v=UfRgIoU2aAY**

Japan's Earthquake, Tsunami May Affect Hawaii's Key Industry
**http://www.youtube.com/watch?v=LwVYQHXw_AY**

UHERO: Tsunami Effect On Tourism
**http://www.youtube.com/watch?v=7O9LbZekjVg**

Bangkok in need of more tourists
**http://www.youtube.com/watch?v=BXVWaVENX1w**

Disaster Management Amid Cruise Sinking
**http://www.youtube.com/watch?v=bD6IlygWGLk**

# REFERENCES AND FURTHER READING

Abegg, B., Agrawala, S., Crick, F. and de Montfalcon, A. (2007) 'Climate change impacts and adaptation in winter tourism', pp. 25–60 in S. Agrawala (ed.), *Climate Change in the European Alps: Adapting Winter Tourism and Natural Hazards Management*, OECD, Paris.

Agrawala, S. (ed.) (2007) *Climate Change in the European Alps: Adapting Winter Tourism and Natural Hazards Management*, OECD, Paris.

Amelung, B. and Viner, D. (2006) 'Mediterranean tourism: exploring the future with the tourism climatic index', *Journal of Sustainable Tourism* **14**(4), 349–66.

Amelung, B., Nicholls, S. and Viner, D. (2007) 'Implications of global climate change for tourism flows and seasonality', *Journal of Travel Research* **45**(3), 285–96.

Ansoff, H.I. (1991) 'Critique of Henry Mintzberg's the design school: reconsidering the basic premises of strategic management'. In *Strategic Management Journal* **12**(6), 449–62.

Associated Press (2011) 'US breaks with Japan over power plant warnings'. 16 March at **http://abcnews.go.com/US/wireStory?id=13149441#.T15CaoEu15Y.** (accessed 12 March 2012).

BBC (2011) Roland Buerk 'Japan earthquake: Tsunami hits north-east' 11 March. Archived from the original on 11 March 2011 at **http://www.bbc.co.uk/news/world-asia-pacific-12709598** (accessed 12 March 2011).

Becken, S. (2005) 'Harmonizing climate change adaptation and mitigation: The case of tourist resorts in Fiji', *Global Environmental Change – Part A* **15**(4), 381–93.

Becken, S. and Hay, J. (2007) *Tourism and Climate Change – Risks and Opportunities*, Channel View, Cleveland.

CNN (2011a) 'Japanese PM: 'Toughest' crisis since World War II', CNN, 13 March. Archived from the original on 12 April 2011 at **http://edition.cnn.com/2011/WORLD/asiapcf/03/13/japan.quake/index.html?iref=NS1** (accessed 12 March 2012).

CNN (2011b) '3 nuclear reactors melted down after quake, Japan confirms', 7 June. Archived from the original on 9 June 2011 at **http://www.cnn.com/2011/WORLD/asiapcf/06/06/japan.nuclear.meltdown/index.html** (accessed 6 June 2011).

CNN Wire Staff (2011) 'Japan: 3 nuclear reactors melted down – news story – KTVZ Bend', **Ktvz.com** 6 June. Archived from the original on 28 July 2011 at **http://www.ktvz.com/news/28143212/detail.html.** (accessed 7 September 2011).

Cunha, M.P. (2004) 'Organisational time: a dialectical view', *Organisation* **11**(2), 271–96.

Drabek, T.E. (1995) 'Disaster responses within the tourist industry', *International Journal of Mass Emergencies and Disasters* **13**(1), 7–23.

Dubois, G. and Ceron, J.-P. (2006) 'Tourism/leisure greenhouse gas emissions forecasts for 2050: factors for change in France', *Journal of Sustainable Tourism* **14**(2), 172–91.

Faulkner, B. (2001), 'Towards a framework for tourism disaster management', *Tourism Management*, **22**, 135–47.

Fredrickson, J.W. (1984) 'The comprehensiveness of strategic decision processes: extension, observation, future directions', *Academy of Management Journal* **27**(2), 445–66.

Glaesser, D. (2003) *Crisis management in the tourism industry*. Amsterdam: Butterworth.

Gössling, S. and Hall, C.M. (2005) 'Uncertainties in predicting tourist flows under scenarios of climate change', *Climatic Change* **79**(3–4), 163–73.

Gössling, S., Peeters, P., Ceron, J.-P., Dubois, G., Patterson, T. and Richardson, R.B. (2005) 'The eco-efficiency of tourism', *Ecological Economics* **54**(4), 417–34.

Hamilton, J.M., Maddison, D. and Tol, R.S.J. (2005) 'Climate change and international tourism: A simulation study', *Global Environmental Change* **15**(3), 253–66.

Hosie, P. (2006) *Human Resource Development: Proactive Preparation to Manage Crises*, School of Management, Curtin Business School Working Paper Series, 15.

Hystad, P.W. and Keller, P.C. (2007) 'Towards a Destination Tourism Disaster Management Framework: Longterm Lessons from a Forest Fire Disaster', *Tourism Management* **29**, 151–62.

IPCC (2007a) *Climate Change 2007: The Physical Science Basis.* Contribution of Working Group I to the Fourth Assessment Report of the Intergovernmental Panel on Climate Change (Solomon, S., Qin, D., Manning, M., Chen, Z., Marquis, M., Averyt, K.B., Tignor, M. and Miller, H.L. (eds)), Cambridge University Press, Cambridge and New York.

IPCC (2007b) 'Sumary for policymakers', in Parry, M.L., Canziani, O.F., Palutikof, J.P., van der Linden, P.J. and Hanson, C.E. (eds), *Climate Change 2007: Impacts, Adaptation and Vulnerability.* Contribution of Working Group II to the Fourth Assessment Report of the Intergovernmental Panel on Climate Change, Cambridge University Press, Cambridge and New York.

*Journal of Sustainable Tourism* **14**(4), 2006. Special issue: Tourism and its Interactions with Climate Change. Guest Editor: David Viner.

Kash, T.J. and Darling, J.R. (1998) 'Crisis management: prevention, diagnosis and intervention', *Leadership and Organization Development Journal* **19**(4), 179–86.

Knowles, T., Diamantis, D., El-Mourhabi, J. (2004) *The Globalisation of Tourism and Hospitality: A strategic perspective*, Cengage Learning, p. 35.

Makdisi, S., Fattah, Z. and Limam, I. (2007) 'Determinants of economic growth in the MENA countries', in Nugent, J.B. and Pesaran, H. (eds.), *Explaining Growth in the Middle East, Contributions to Economic Analysis*, Netherlands, Elsevier, pp. 31–60.

Mastny, L. (2002) 'Travelling light: new paths for international tourism', Worldwatch Paper 159, Washington DC.

Mintzberg, H. (1990) 'The Design School: Reconsidering the Basic Premises of Strategic Management', *Strategic Management Journal* **11**(3), 171–95.

Mintzberg, H. (1991) 'Learning 1, Planning 0, Reply to Igor Ansoff', *Strategic Management Journal* **12**(6), 463–6.

Mintzberg, H. (1994) *The rise and fall of strategic planning*, New York, Free Press.

Morakabati, Y. (2007) 'Tourism, Travel Risk and Travel Risk Perceptions', PhD Thesis, Bournemouth University, 2007.

Morakabati, Y. (2011) 'Deterrents to tourism development in Iran', *International Journal of Tourism Research* **13**, 103–23.

Morakabati, Y. (2012) 'Tourism in the Middle East: Conflicts, Crises and Economic Diversification, Some Critical Issues', 23 April, DOI: 10.1002/jtr. 1882.

NASP (2003) 'Responding to Natural Disasters: Helping children and families, Information for school crisis teams' at **http://www.nasponline.org/resources/crisis_safety/naturaldisaster_teams_ho.aspx**

Norwich Union Insurance Report (2006) *Daily Telegraph*, 11 July.

NPR Staff and Wires (2011) 'Millions of stricken Japanese lack water, food, heat', NPR, 14 March. Archived from the original on 12 April 2011 at **http://www.npr.org/2011/03/14/134527591/millions-of-stricken-japanese-lack-water-food-heat** (accessed 16 March 2011).

OECD (2006) *Climate Change and Winter Tourism. Report on Adaptation* at **http://www.oecd.org/dataoecd/58/4/37776193.pdf**

Peeters, P. (2007) *Tourism and Climate Change Mitigation – Methods, Greenhouse Gas Reductions and Policies*, NHTV Academics Studies No. 6, NHTV, Breda.

Porter, M.E. (1980) *Competitive Strategy*, New York, Free Press.

Prahalad, C.K. and Hamel, G. (1990) 'The core competence of the corporation', *Harvard Business Review* **68**(3), 79–91.

Ritchie, B.W. (2004) 'Chaos, crisis and disaster: A strategic approach to crisis management in the tourism industry', *Tourism Management* **25**, 669–83.

Syed, Saira 16 March (2011) 'Japan quake: infrastructure damage will delay recovery' *BBC News*, 16 March. Archived 17 March 2011 at WebCite (accessed 18 March 2011).

Scott, D., Amelung, B., Becken, S., Ceron, J.-P., Dubois, G., Gössling, S., Peeters, P. and Simpson,

M. (2007) *Climate Change and Tourism: Responding to Global Challenges*, WTO, Madrid and UNEP, Paris.

Scott, D., McBoyle, G. and Schwartzentruber, M. (2004) 'Climate change and the distribution of climatic resources for tourism in North America', *Climate Research* **27**(2), 105–17.

Stern, N. (2006) *The Economics of Climate Change: The Stern Review*, Cambridge University Press, Cambridge.

World Bank (2012). Available from **http://databank.worldbank.org/ddp/home.do**

# MAJOR CASE STUDY 12.1
Is there more than a risk of sunburn in the Middle East?

The Middle East can be seen as a region of extremes. It is home to some of the richest and poorest nations in the world and the words oil and Arab World are so closely associated that they are often used interchangeably (Makdisi, 2007). The region's future is sometimes described in terms of disputes related to territory, oil and water. Oil and water are resources that are critical to the region from the point of view of economic and physical sustainability (Morakabati, 2012).

The Middle East region has the world's largest share of oil and gas reserves (see Figure 12.10) and 99% of the region's reserves are found in the Persian Gulf.

However, oil and gas resources are not renewable and are depleting quickly as the demand for them continues to increase to record levels. The region will find it difficult to fund investment into other industries once the oil and gas revenues have ceased and this is therefore seen as a last resort for the future economic development of the Middle East. However, the Middle East is also bestowed with some of the most desirable assets for tourism development, including a favourable climate and a wealth of heritage sites.

In the decade following the turn of the twenty-first century tourist arrivals to the Middle East increased 2.5 times in spite of the conflicts and negative images generated about the region. During that same period of time visitors to Europe increased 1.2 times. However, the share of world tourism attributable to the Middle East has failed to increase significantly, remaining at the 6.4% compared to Europe's 50.7% (see Figure 12.11).

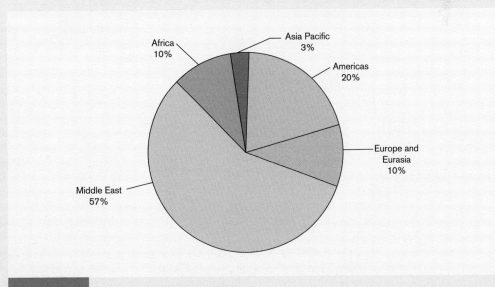

**Figure 12.10**   Oil reserves by region, 2009

The recent events in and around the region have only confirmed the image of conflict and unrest and the media paints the Middle East as a landscape of terrorism and conflict. The negative images are compounded further by issues relating to the violation of human rights, discrimination against women and sometimes distorted religious fundamentalism occurring in some countries in the region (Morakabati, 2012).

Tourism is an industry that not only needs a good supply of labour and investment; it also requires an image that builds confidence, first in the mindset of tour operators and second in the minds of the potential tour-

ists. Safety and security are fundamental ingredients for successful tourism development. Figure 12.12 shows how negative events are associated with downturns in tourist arrivals to the Middle East.

The negative events have had a clear impact on the growth of tourist arrivals but the global financial crisis that started in 2008 has had a much more severe effect as tourists have had to reassess their spending in the light of downturns in real discretionary income.

A survey of UK travellers revealed that travel risk perceptions and attitudes towards travelling to the region are affected by events. As Figure 12.13 shows,

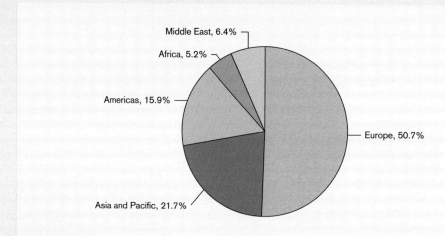

**Figure 12.11**   International tourist arrivals by region, % of total world arrivals

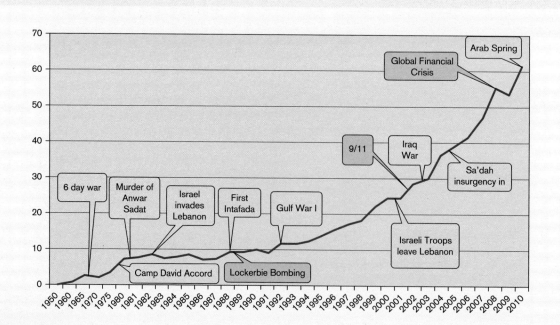

**Figure 12.12**   Tourist arrivals to the Middle East, 1950–2010
*Source*: Morakabati, 2012; UNWTO, 2012

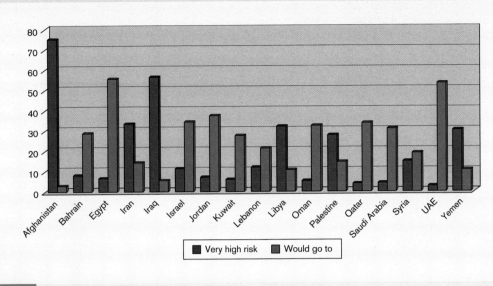

| Figure 12.13 | UK tourist attitudes and risk perceptions, by country, 2010 |
|---|---|

*Source*: Morakabati, 2011

the higher the risk the more negative the attitude towards travelling to the region. For example, the respondents saw the United Arab Emirates to be associated with less risk and were consequently more willing to travel there. With respect to Iraq they saw the country as a high-risk destination and did not wish to go there.

## DISCUSSION QUESTIONS

1. 'Negative events don't always affect the attraction of a destination (the pull factors).' Discuss this statement using an example of your choice.

2. 'The public's perception about a destination of their choice will be a reflection of what information is distributed by the media.' Do you agree with this statement? Do you think the media is responsible for people's perceptions of travel-related risk?

3. When can you say that a destination has fully recovered from the impact of a negative event? Explain your answer. What can be done to improve the speed of recovery?

# PART 3

## THE TOURISM SECTOR

Photograph: Tatopani, Nepal © Graham Meyer

# INTRODUCTION

In Part 3 we turn our attention to the tourism sector and public sector organisations that influence and support tourism demand and supply. We have adopted an analytical and evaluative approach to this section, identifying the main sub-sectors that, when combined, constitute the tourism sector. We have focused generally on providing insights into the operating characteristics, trends and issues that dominate tourism and, specifically, upon attractions, accommodation, the organisation and management of events, intermediaries, transportation, public sector organisations and their role in policy making. Although these do not represent an exhaustive range of enterprises, they do illustrate the dominant characteristics of the tourism sector and demonstrate key operational practices.

Leiper defined the tourism 'industry' as 'the range of businesses and organisations involved in delivering the tourism product' and, in the light of his model of the tourism system, these businesses and organisations represent a key element. However, despite the unique nature of tourism and the differing attributes of the individual sectors, there are common characteristics, trends and issues that are evident across the board:

- The low level of *concentration* in a sector where small businesses dominate despite the fact that a relatively few, large corporations have market prominence.

- The high ratio of *fixed costs* to variable costs which has considerable implications for financial stability and which dominates tactical and strategic operation.

- The high levels of customer contact, demanding staff to be highly trained in both operational aspects and customer care.

- The low levels of technological adoption across much of the sector for small and medium-sized enterprises.

- The general lack of marketing and human resource management expertise remains a constraint in all sectors of tourism, albeit to varying degrees.

- The importance of location vis-à-vis access to markets.

- The **perishable** nature of the product for all tourism sectors demands continued investment in reservation and yield management systems.

- The prevalence of seasonal and irrational demand patterns, involving enterprises in the use of promotional and pricing strategies.

- The inconsistent adoption of the principles of sustainability, environmental auditing and EIA techniques.

- The increasing degree of **vertical**, **horizontal** and **diagonal integration** throughout the sector.

- The increasing adoption of *collaboration* within and across the various segments of the tourism sector.

- The traditional outlook of service industries and, arguably, the so-called 'under-management' of the tourism sector which means that the sector as a whole is vulnerable to ideas and takeovers from other industrial sectors.

- Conversely, the increasing professionalism of the sector.

These are issues and difficulties that dominate tourism as a whole, irrespective of sub-sector. Nevertheless, it is also possible to isolate the key sectors and attribute more detailed and precise characteristics to each; thus, we have divided this section into six chapters. This said, it is important that the reader should understand the complex linkages and interrelationships that exist between the various individual tourism sectors and the mutual dependency of one sector on the next. It is the objective of this section, therefore, to highlight these complex relationships and to explore the implications of these on tourism as a whole.

In Chapter 13, the focus of attention is on the attractions segment of the tourism sector, incorporating natural and artificial attractions. Attractions are integral to the tourism product, often providing the primary motivation for tourist visits, yet they continue to receive a patchy and undisciplined coverage in the literature. We use this chapter to explore many of the issues associated with the development and management of attractions as well as to consider some of the possible visitor management techniques that may be implemented to address the adverse social, cultural and environmental impacts of tourism at both natural and artificial sites.

Chapter 14 is concerned with accommodation, perhaps the most visible and ubiquitous of all sectors of tourism. The scope and size of the sector is explored and the relationship between this sub-sector and the complete tourism product is discussed. We also evaluate many of the key issues that are currently influencing the accommodation sector such as hotel consortia, yield management, the role of information technology, the new-found emphasis on environmental issues and the role and importance of quality and branding.

Chapter 15 reflects the growing influence of events in tourism more broadly and their specific contribution to the development and marketing of destinations. In order to leverage maximum benefit from the organisation and management of events, the chapter introduces the nature of events management and the reasons behind its growth, the diversity of the types of events in existence and a synthesis of contemporary developments within the sector. The chapter concludes with an introduction to event legacies and the increasing focus on sustainability within the events market.

Chapter 16 introduces and reviews the role of intermediaries in the packaging and distribution of the tourism product. The distribution of the tourism product is unusual in so far as it is achieved, almost exclusively, by intermediaries, rendering the distribution channel extremely competitive and susceptible to fierce power struggles and damaging price wars. The structure of the distribution channel and the respective roles of intermediaries make the distribution of the tourism product very risky, particularly in light of the precarious economics of tour operation/ wholesaling and the intense financial pressures that dominate their operation. The chapter also explores more recent online and social media developments and the increasing consolidation and concentration of tourism intermediaries.

Chapter 17 concentrates on transportation for tourism and offers a thorough review of the issues which dominate this sector. Particular emphasis is placed on the changing competitive framework with a focus on the development of low-cost airlines and the continued expansion and popularity of cruising.

In Chapter 18, we concentrate on those public sector organisations that are crucial to tourism and discuss the role of governmental intervention in tourism. We consider the importance of public sector involvement in tourism and review its current, and changing, role: increasingly, the public sector is withdrawing from tourism and private sector organisations are being encouraged to step in. However, it is argued here that, while tourism must involve participation and funding by the private sector, there are many clear and powerful reasons why the public sector must remain involved:

- Many core tourist attractions – such as landscapes, culture and built heritage and architecture – are public goods and, to this end, public sector involvement is at least desirable and at best crucial.

- Many activities such as planning, research, resource allocation, management and regulation can be undertaken most effectively – and most impartially – by the public sector.

- The lack of expertise in the tourism sector in certain key areas (such as marketing), and the domination of small businesses with inadequate funds to promote themselves sufficiently, provides a compelling argument for continued involvement of the public sector.

We also use this chapter to demonstrate the global and local policy frameworks for tourism and to provide an overview of the likely administrative structure of a national tourist office (NTO). In addition, the impact of the public sector in respect of its demand and revenue management roles (marketing, promotion and information provision) and its supply and cost management roles (planning controls, building regulations, land-use decisions, market regulation, market research, and planning and investment incentives) are also considered in detail.

It is clear that, while the individual sectors of tourism are interlinked and, to some extent, are mutually dependent upon each other, there is a potential for conflict within and between sectors. This may be attributed to the fact that each sector is working to its own agenda with a view to its own profit maximisation. One of the primary objectives of the public sector, therefore, is to temper overambitious individual providers and sectors and to provide a strategic approach to product development, distribution and marketing for the overall benefit of the destination. However, it may be argued that the intermediaries are perhaps the most powerful determinants of the ultimate success or failure of a destination in terms of revenue, market share and visitor numbers, since it is in the hands of the intermediaries that influence is exerted most directly on tourism demand.

In the next six chapters, we explore many of the key issues in respect of the above and provide the reader with a greater understanding and appreciation of the tourism sector, its core business and its operating practices.

## TOURISM AS I SEE IT

Tourism is a serious economic driver – in Manchester it is worth almost £6 billion per annum, where we refer to it increasingly in its wider context as the 'visitor economy'. With new localism, the demise of regional development structures and a dearth of public sector funding, the tourism industry, more than ever, needs to get its act together!

In Manchester, we have created something called the Manchester Visitor Economy Forum which takes a collective responsibility in addressing visitor economy challenges, meeting the opportunities and ensuring a strategic fit with wider economic strategies. The Forum doesn't consist of tourism professionals, it consists of professionals from the visitor economy with senior representation from the constituent sectors – transport, local authorities, conference venues, hotels, the independent sector, universities, airport, sport, culture, city centre management and visitor attractions.

It is this collaborative (and true partnership) approach that will ensure that we continue to grow the visitor economy for the benefit of all and strive towards success. The visitor economy comprises everything that makes up the total visitor experience. It's about marketing (which needs to be original and distinctive) and improving the quality of the visitor experience which needs to reflect local distinctiveness and authenticity. Action oriented networks will need to be created to fall in behind unifying strategies and will cover the full range of the visitor economy ensuring it acts in a coordinated and concerted way. The visitor economy can influence and help shape planning and public policy but we need to ensure that it is treated seriously – civic leadership is key and these decision makers need to 'get it'!

**Paul Simpson, Managing Director – Visit Manchester**

# CHAPTER 13

## ATTRACTIONS

### LEARNING OUTCOMES

Attractions are an integral part of the tourism product and, in this chapter, we focus on providing you with:

- a review of the nature, purpose and classification of attractions;

- a discussion of the roles and responsibilities of the public and private sectors in respect of the development and management of tourist attractions;

- a consideration of all issues associated with the management of attractions;

- an analysis of environmental issues in respect of attractions; and

- an evaluation of strategies that have been developed with a view to alleviating environmental and visitor impacts of tourism at attractions.

Photograph: Colosseum, Rome, Italy © Sundus Pasha

## INTRODUCTION

For many tourist destinations around the world, it is their attractions that serve as the catalyst for tourist visits. Attractions are numerous, diverse, fragmented geographically and often have limited resources at their disposal for purposes of management. In order to shed some light on the management complexity and diversity of development of attractions this chapter is broken down into three main sections. The first section introduces the nature and purpose of attractions, their characteristics and issues pertinent to both natural and man-made attractions. The second section builds on this foundation by exploring a range of issues relating to their development. The third and final section concentrates on the management of attractions with issues of ownership, the problems of cost structure, pricing and revenue generation, the employment and training of staff, and attempts to counter seasonality featuring strongly. It also outlines the variety of visitor management techniques in existence and attempts made by operators of attractions to manage visitor impacts in a more sustainable manner. This leads on to the issue of sustainable tourism development in which the object is to manage tourism growth in a manner that ensures that tourists do not destroy by pressure of numbers the very attractions they come to see. In this discussion, the choice – or balance – between regulation and market solutions is discussed, with a closing discussion on the impact on attraction authenticity of 'modern' attraction management.

# THE NATURE AND PURPOSE OF ATTRACTIONS

Attractions provide the single most important reason for leisure tourism to a destination. Many of the components of the tourist trip – for example, transport and accommodation – are demands derived from the consumer's desire to enjoy what a destination has to offer in terms of 'things to see and do'. Thus a tourist attraction is a focus for recreational and, in part, educational activity undertaken by both day and stay visitors that is frequently shared with the domestic resident population. Every region and every town boasts at least one attraction, adding to its appeal as a destination. Attractions also serve a variety of different purposes, since for many their origins had nothing to do with tourism. For example, attractions often have an explicit educational purpose, are frequently central to the protection, or in fact creation, of cultural identities, and can contribute to the conservation and protection of many historic sites. This variety of 'sense of purpose' is important in that it helps explain why attractions are often so difficult to manage, especially those that fall within the domain of the public sector, such as museums. They frequently have to accommodate the numerous wishes of their stakeholders, the various expectations of different visitor groups (often from different countries), meet the needs of owners or trustees, and serve on occasion as **attraction 'icons'** for national governments in international marketing strategies. Examples of the latter are the use of images of the Colosseum when marketing Rome, the use of Table Mountain when marketing South Africa, or the Houses of Parliament when promoting London and the UK overseas.

In addition to the above, there are many examples where attractions have played a catalytic role in the regeneration of an area or destination. The success of the Guggenheim Museum in Bilbao, Spain and the National Museum of New Zealand and its contribution to the development of Wellington as a destination are two examples of 'best practice'. Such **'flagship'** attractions can be used to pull in visitors, meet needs of local residents and develop stronger tourism activities within the destination. While a destination rarely survives long term on the basis of one attraction, it can be the key pump-primer in more sustainable development of a destination. Flagship attractions need not be iconic or characteristic of the destination: it is their ability to attract visitors that is their main benefit (Weidenfeld, 2010).

**Photograph 13.1**  Table Mountain, which identifies Cape Town, South Africa, in any international marketing and publicity material
*Source*: Gordon Bell/Shutterstock.com

With such diversity present within the attractions sector, the uniform definition and categorisation of attractions has proved elusive, as has the ability of many attractions to share 'best practice' both from attractions of a similar kind and from attractions elsewhere around the globe. The fact that tourist attractions may be shared with the host community can give rise to conflict in popular destinations, where tourism is perceived to cause problems of crowding, traffic congestion, environmental damage and litter. There can thus be little doubt that the management of tourist attractions is a challenging activity with so many publics to please.

## Characteristics of attractions

There are many different types of attraction, and a number of attempts have been made to classify them. Classification is possible along a number of different dimensions:

- ownership;
- capacity;
- **market or catchment area**;
- permanency;
- type.

Early attempts at classification were according to type, distinguishing between natural resources and artificial 'man-made' features or products. Man-made features were as follows:

- Cultural – religion, modern culture, museums, art galleries, architecture, archaeological sites.
- Traditions – folklore, animated culture, festivals.
- Events – sports activities and cultural events.

Natural resources included national parks, wildlife, viewpoints and outstanding natural phenomena such as Uluru (Ayers Rock) in Australia or the Niagara Falls in Ontario, Canada. Classification by type is the most common way in which countries collect attraction statistics, but here some form of permanency is required so that public access can be controlled

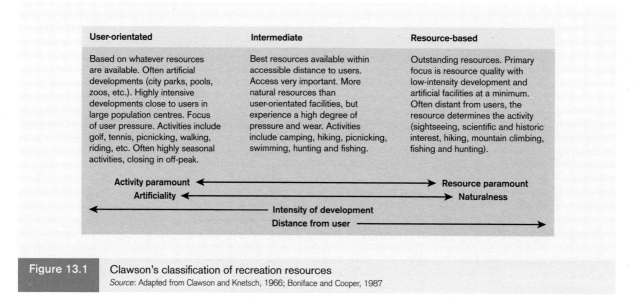

**Figure 13.1**   Clawson's classification of recreation resources
*Source*: Adapted from Clawson and Knetsch, 1966; Boniface and Cooper, 1987

and measured, which implies that even some iconic attractions are never listed in official statistics.

An alternative and more complex approach is that designed by Clawson and Knetsch (1966) and shown in Figure 13.1. In one diagram, Clawson and Knetsch linked the classification of attractions in a spatial sense, according to their proximity to markets, to their level of uniqueness and to their intensity of use. Clawson's approach is flexible and best utilised as a way of thinking about attractions. For example, a major historic building is clearly a resource-based attraction, but it may extend its market by adding a user-orientated element, such as a leisure park or garden development, as has occurred with many of the stately homes and palaces in Britain and continental Europe.

In this chapter, for purposes of analytical convenience, we have adopted the more recent classification shown in Figure 13.2. Although not exhaustive, Figure 13.2 identifies the principal features of classification used in various settings and demonstrates the diversity of the attraction product around the world. At the core of the recent classification rests the core product offered by the attraction, which represents the resources/attributes that attract visitors in the first place. Also within the core are those aspects of the attraction which contribute to its presentation, such as interpretation, and generation of additional income and revenue streams – a facet of most attractions irrespective of their natural or man-made origins. Going further, it will be appreciated that this basic classification may be subdivided again into attractions which are site-specific because of the physical location of facilities and therefore act as a destination, and attractions which are temporary because they are events. International events that are regarded as world class normally stand alone as **hallmark events**, while others may be used to complement site-specific attractions. It is what is happening at the time that is usually more important for events than their location, so **mega-events**, such as the Olympics, and exhibitions, for example world trade fairs, may move around the globe. However, some hallmark events do evolve in and become specific to their location, so that they become branded by it. Thus several of the most spectacular events in the form of parades or carnivals have become associated with major cities, for example the Rio Carnival, the Pamplona Bull Run in Spain or the Calgary Stampede in Alberta. This is because cities provide access to a large market and have the economic base to support them. Similarly, important religious festivals are often connected with locations that are considered the foundations of the faith, such as Mecca and Jerusalem. In this respect, the growth in cultural tourism is encouraging many destinations to try and turn important events in the local calendar into hallmark events as a means of developing tourism as evidenced in Mini Case Study 13.1.

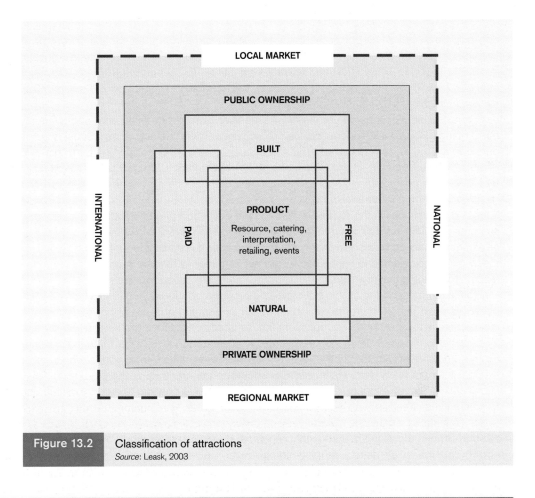

| Figure 13.2 | Classification of attractions |
| --- | --- |
| | *Source*: Leask, 2003 |

## MINI CASE STUDY 13.1
### Savonlinna Opera Festival

In many instances festivals and events are designed to augment the tourist product of a destination. Hallmark events are stand-alone products because it is what is happening at the time that is important rather than their location. However, some become branded by their location and in so doing contribute greatly to the image of the destination through becoming an iconic attraction. Such an example is the Savonlinna Opera Festival, an annual event that takes place every July in Olavinlinna Castle, which adjoins the town of Savonlinna in the Etelä-Savo region, a lake area of Eastern Finland, but in this case location choice is highly relevant. What determines the establishment of most music festivals is the place and the setting and for Savonlinna the setting is the courtyard of a medieval castle, with exceptional acoustics, that juts out into a lake. One can compare this to the Dalhalla Opera Festival in mid Sweden, which is located in an old quarry that has its own natural lake and, again, first-class acoustics.

The history of the Savonlinna Opera Festival dates back to 1912 when it was founded by the famous Finnish soprano Aino Ackté (1876–1944), thus making it one of the oldest European music festivals. Unfortunately, the Savonlinna Festival was swallowed up in the maelstrom of World War I and then caught up in the political turmoil between Finland and Russia, so it did not appear again until 1930. In the recessionary period of the 1930s and with war clouds again on the horizon, this revival was short-lived. But memories of the Festival lingered on in the town, and after a period of close on four decades, it was started again in 1967 with the production of Beethoven's *Fidelio*. The artistic revival of the Festival is considered by the management team to date from the production of Mozart's *Magic Flute* during the 1973 season. At that time the Festival lasted only one week, but it has progressed now to a stable formula of three weeks of own productions of four to five operas over 24–26 performances, some concerts and one week when it hosts a guest company (initiated in 1987 with the Estonian Theatre Company from Tallin). To accomplish this task, the Festival has a full-time staff of 12 and three craftsmen in its workshop, with total employment rising to some 660 persons during the season, including its own chorus and orchestra.

Opera is recognised as one of the most expensive of the performing arts, and sums of US$500,000 per performance in the major opera houses are not uncommon. Equally, public subsidy per attendance by far outstrips any other performing art. This is because it is 'a 19th century art form that has built into it 19th century cost assumptions' (Lord Guthrie, English Arts Council, 1995). By this is meant that costs are dictated by a long-gone composer and his/her librettist, and there is little the artistic director can do about this without radically changing the experience, which would be self-defeating if it fails to attract audiences. Thus the traditions and conventions in the repertoire lead to high costs and prices in today's market, despite relatively high amounts of public subsidy given to enable the art form to survive. Many cultural activities are risky and have, as a consequence, an uncertain financial return, because it is difficult for consumers to know which production they would enjoy most, and hence banks may not lend money for new productions, even to good credit risks. It is not for nothing that investors in the performing arts are called 'Angels'!

From a tourism standpoint, it is externalities generated by 'off-site' visitor expenditure that are often contemplated as most important in the evaluation of the performing arts. With the exception of most of the USA, where there is reliance on private sponsorship, major cities do subsidise their artistic companies, because it is evident that in today's tourism market no city can claim to be world class without a first-class cultural centre. From a human welfare perspective, cultural activities are public 'merit' goods which generate consumption externalities for society as a whole, such as adding to the creativity of the population, quality of life, identity, social criticism, aesthetics, pluralism and so forth; values that provide, to a considerable degree, the rationale for cultural measures and are legitimate arguments for public provision or subsidy.

As a charitable organisation, the underlying philosophy of the Festival is one of service to the public at large through offering a quality experience that is comparable to any other world-class venues. However, the experience is constrained by the requirement to break even 'one year with another' from a variety of revenue sources, of which nearly 70% comes from ticket sales, the remainder being made up of public subsidy, sponsorship and commercial trading of opera recordings, guest performances and so on. This means that despite the many operas that exist, in order to meet revenue targets, most opera companies position the bulk of their work around a popular few, either in the form of new productions or revivals. These are the operas that are popular with audiences worldwide and can be relied on to fill seats. Audiences tend to fall dramatically for contemporary opera even at reduced ticket prices. These aspects are reflected in the artistic policy of the Festival:

- one new production every year;
- one new opera every three years;
- carrying over some (popular) operas from previous years;
- a guest company performing two (usually popular) operas in the last week.

In this the Festival office is attempting to balance artistic endeavour against prudential financial management. The potential monetary risks from changing the repertoire are high; hence the marketing concentrates on retaining existing customers, bringing in around 70–75% repeat business every Festival. The management is cautious about experimenting with tradition and new ventures. For example, some years ago the Festival launched a winter season for one week, which proved to be very damaging financially. On the other hand, while repeats of popular operas sell well, venues do not get the same critical acclaim as they would for new productions or totally new operas. It may thus be appreciated that the skill in managing the performing arts is about maintaining a balance between filling seats, controlling costs and artistic integrity.

The success of the Opera Festival witnessed the establishment of a summer ballet event in 2002 and the opening of a new concert and conference centre and a holiday home fair. From the perspective of the municipality, cultural tourism has become the catalyst for the establishment of arts amenities for the town, as well as drawing in new businesses through building a successful image of the area as a place to live and work. The town has around 28,000 inhabitants, but being a popular tourist resort, the population rises to around 100,000 during the main season when the Festival is running. An indirect measure of the importance of the Festival to the town's tourism sector can be gauged from the expansion of flights between Helsinki and Savonlinna to five flights per day during the period of the Festival, dropping to two flights per day afterwards. Success breeds success and the Festival organisers continue to augment the product by adding new events such as an international singing competition, and arranging opera packages through selected tour operators.

*Source*: Updated from Wanhill, 2006

## DISCUSSION QUESTIONS

1. The popular view of opera is that it is an elite art form, so to what extent should it be subsidised from the public purse, if at all, given the many other calls on government money, such as health, welfare and education?

2. The pricing process for opera seats is similar to other arts venues. Suggest the various criteria that may be used to set seat prices.

3. Cultural values and economic values do not necessarily go together, yet cultural change is irreversible. Should art forms of the past be preserved if most people do not suffer any great sense of loss if they disappear?

Complementarity of events and site-specific attractions may be achieved by staging a festival of the countryside to enhance the appeal of a country park, and similarly for the performance of a Shakespeare tragedy in the courtyard of a historic castle. Events are also used to give animation to object-orientated attractions, such as museums, to encourage new and repeat visitors, particularly in the off-season. Hallmark events are frequently used to raise the image of a destination, a factor that lies behind the very competitive bidding for the Olympic Games, which had a lasting impact on the international perception of Barcelona in 1992. It is considered that the Games held in Sydney in 2000 were equally successful and have been perceived as a 10-year marketing investment for Australia. They are, however, very costly activities and within two years of winning the bid, the budget for the London Olympics in 2012 had risen from £2.5 billion to nearly £10 billion, but it is seen as a major regeneration project for East London.

The extent to which attractions are in fact 'natural' or 'man-made' represents the next stage of classification. Natural attractions include country parks in Britain, lakes in Canada, mountains in Switzerland and the coast in Spain, for example. Man-made attractions, however, are more commonly the results of the history and culture of a country which leaves a legacy of historic monuments and buildings, but also includes specially created entertainment complexes such as theme parks, of which the most well known are the Walt Disney parks, originating in California, but now reproduced in Florida, Tokyo, Paris, Hong Kong, with one further park due to open soon in Shanghai (Braun and Soskin, 2010). One could, in fact, go one stage further and subdivide the man-made category into those attractions that were created specifically for tourism, such as Disney's theme parks, and those that were created originally for purposes other than tourism. Historic houses, castles and monuments would all come under this category of man-made attraction. It is these types of attractions in particular that often have the greatest challenges in maintaining their **authenticity**, the addition of cafés, restaurants and gift shops for purposes of income generation often diluting the 'purity' of the attraction product, but they are essential for meeting the requirements of the average visitor.

The varying approaches to the management of natural and man-made attractions and the different pressures they have to face help explain their inclusion here. For example, while the Grand Canyon may have management objectives that focus on conservation issues and the management of visitors, theme parks have at their core objectives of entertainment and income generation. The division between natural resources and artificial attractions, however, is not always clear-cut. Many natural attractions require considerable inputs of infrastructure and management in order to use them for tourism purposes. This is the case for water parks, ski resorts, safari parks, aquaria and many attractions based on nature. This infrastructure may also be put in place to protect the resource from environmental damage. In many countries, it is no longer possible to have open public access to many forests. Specific sites are designated for cars, caravans and camping, and there are colour-coded trails for walkers.

Man-made attractions that are the legacy of history and culture also share with natural resources the fact that they cannot be reproduced without considerable expense and alterations to their authenticity, unlike attractions designed principally for entertainment. They therefore deserve greater protection and management input to guard against excessive use. Such attractions are commonly in the control of the state. A good example is Stonehenge in the UK, which exhibits all the features of being resource-based and non-reproducible, so that for some time too many visitors have threatened it. Measures to resolve this have included the construction of a new visitor centre some distance from the monument and putting a cordon around the stones to prevent them being further defaced by touching and, in some instances, chipping of the stones by capricious visitors. From this it follows that when looking at the development of attractions, we can place them on a scale that has at one end those that have been built or designed for visitor purposes such as family recreation parks, which are in the minority, and, at the other, cultural resources and facilities that were neither for visitors nor can be adapted for them. The bulk of attractions would then be spread out between these two poles.

The next basis upon which classification can be attributed is the pricing policy adopted for access to attractions, that is whether or not access is free or an admission charge is required. Many countries around the world offer free access to their national museums, galleries and monuments – such attractions considered by governments to be the national heritage of the population at large (tax concessions are often also connected to such a strategy). This is not always the case, however, with the decline of the public purse sometimes serving as the catalyst for the levy of admission charges at previously 'free' attractions. Understandably, the contrasting objectives between the public and private owners of attractions affects the operational and management approaches adopted. More recent studies, however, suggest that the increasingly competitive markets that attractions now find themselves in are leading to greater commonality of management practice, because once paying visitors are introduced to attractions in the public and voluntary sectors, then pressure builds up for the visitor experience, in support of admissions, to become the marketed output, as in the commercial sector. This is something that is often resisted by the curatorial staff of these attractions, who are rightly concerned about the authenticity of the visitor experience. For example, in the 1980s, the Victoria and Albert Museum was heavily criticised for using the marketing strap-line 'Ace caff with rather a nice museum attached!' to stimulate a reappraisal of the museum by the public, a marketing strategy that would be considered quite acceptable today.

The market in which the attraction draws its visitors represents the final classification in Figure 13.2. For example, while Universal Studios' theme parks may have an international audience, since they are based on the global film industry, the Eden Project in England a national audience, and the wineries of Western Australia a regional audience, the majority of attractions have a much smaller local audience. Clearly the nature of the market and the volume of visitors may well determine the nature and management of the product offering, particularly with regard to pricing, visitor spend and interpretation.

## Natural attractions

In the instance of natural features it is often the quality of the resource that provides the attraction, whereby location becomes secondary. Their appeal is both national and international. Thus tourists come from all over the globe to enjoy the Himalayas in Nepal, the Blue Ridge Mountains of Virginia, or the Ring of Kerry in Southern Ireland. Traditionally, water-based resources, either coastlines or lakes, have always been the most important tourism resource and still are, but with more frequent holiday-taking, the countryside and panoramic scenery have witnessed increasing usage. However, natural amenities are not only confined to the landscape but also include, for example, climate (which accounts for the dominant tourist flows still being North–South to sun resorts), vegetation, forests and wildlife.

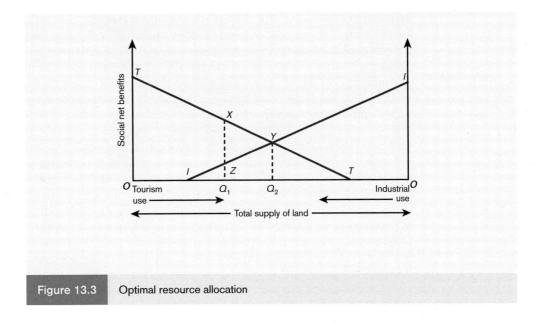

**Figure 13.3**    Optimal resource allocation

The most common aspect of natural resources is that they are generally fixed in supply and are able to provide only a limited amount of services in any given time period. But in many cases, the services provided by this fixed stock of natural amenities can be put to several different uses. Thus if it is proposed to increase the land available for tourism and recreation purposes, it may often be at the expense of other land users, say, industry. There is therefore a trade-off that must take place to ensure that the resource is used to the best advantage of society. This is demonstrated in Figure 13.3, where the vertical axis represents the **social net benefits** (social benefits less social costs) of using a given area of land for tourism or industrial purposes. The schedule *TT* illustrates how these net benefits decline as more land is made available for tourism, and similarly for the schedule *II* which applies to industrial use. At $Q_1$ the social net benefit from the last portion of land devoted to industry is measured by the distance $ZQ_1$, while that for tourism use is given by $XQ_1$. Clearly, the net benefits obtainable from tourism use are much greater than those that can be gained from industrial use and so it will pay society to switch land from industrial designation to tourist use. The optimal point will be at $Q_2$ where the net social benefits from each use are equalised. By undertaking such a move, society increases social net benefits by the amount $XYZ$, for the total gain from tourism use is $XQ_1Q_2Y$ but this must be offset by a loss to industry of $ZQ_1Q_2Y$.

The essence of land-use planning and the legislation that enforces it is to determine some optimal allocation in the manner shown by Figure 13.3. In this way land is zoned for a variety of uses, from tourism and recreation through to urban development, and when disputes occur as to use it is customary to hold some form of public inquiry in which the benefits and costs of alternative choices are evaluated to reach an appropriate decision. Most governments maintain strict planning controls on alternative uses of land, whether it is publicly or privately owned. Thus social considerations via the political process are the main driving force behind land allocation; for example, the planning of the London Olympics involved the relocation of a number of firms away from East London. In the case of privately owned land, social choice may be enforced through compulsory purchase by the state. In some cases the stark choice presented in Figure 13.3 is nullified in practice because multiple land use is possible. National Parks in Britain, such as the Lake District, for example, include residential, farming, forestry, recreational activities and small-scale production within their boundaries.

## Market failure and public provision

One of the problems concerning the provision of outdoor areas for leisure purposes on a large scale is that they are rarely commercially viable in terms of the investment costs and operating expenditure necessary to establish and maintain them (see Bracalente et al. 2011). The reasons for this lie in their periodic use (weekends and holidays) and the political and administrative difficulties of establishing private markets in what are perceived by the public as gifts of nature. This suggests that, if left to market forces, the result is more likely to be under-provision of natural resources for leisure purposes rather than over-provision. Yet there are considerable social benefits to be enjoyed by the population from the availability of recreational amenities and in the control of land use to prevent unsightly development spoiling the beauty of the landscape.

Economists ascribe the term **market failure** to situations of the kind outlined above and in such circumstances it is common for the state to make the necessary provision. Thus some 85% of outdoor recreation areas in the USA are owned by the federal government, with the object of encouraging consumption and protecting the resource for the enjoyment of future generations. Public facilities made available for the purpose of encouraging consumption are termed merit goods, to indicate that the facilities are socially needed even if the willingness to pay for them in the marketplace is somewhat limited. The recognition of this principle in the USA goes back to 1872 with the enactment of the Yellowstone National Park. In Britain, planning and development for tourism purposes is largely a post-1945 phenomenon, commencing with the National Parks and Access to the Countryside Act in 1949, though it was not until the 1960s that positive action in the field of tourism and recreation provision really got going. The worldwide growth of tourism has prompted many other countries to enact similar legislation to manage natural resources in a way that will sustain their use for consumption, while at the same time providing protection against overuse.

There is another aspect of state provision: the so-called **public or collective good**. The principal feature of such goods or services is that it is not realistically possible to exclude individuals from consumption once they have been made available. Private markets for these goods would quickly disintegrate because the optimal strategy for the individual consumer is to wait until someone else pays for the good and then to reap the benefits for nothing. Thus if the good or service is to be provided at all, it may be consumed by everyone without exception and normally without charge at the point of use. The natural environment is a typical example of a public good and the growing pressure of tourist development has created concern for the environment in a number of countries. The point at issue is that public goods form no part of the private costs facing the tourism developer and are therefore open to abuse through overuse. In response the state, in addition to enforcing collective provision out of taxation, regulates individual behaviour through legislation to preserve environmental amenity. For example, in Bermuda tourists are not allowed to hire cars, but only mopeds, while on the Greek island of Rhodes, vehicles are banned from the touristically attractive town of Lindos. Mauritius has a planning law that restricts buildings to a height no greater than the palm trees. In practice, this means hotels of only two storeys and thus permits adequate screening on the seaward side. Where legislation is considered impractical, or overly restrictive, then the approach is to try to change behaviour through educational awareness campaigns. The purpose of such codes is to disseminate information and persuade tourists that on their own volition they should avoid damage to the environment and adverse socio-cultural impacts. These codes apply not only to visitors; there are also industry codes to educate staff and the business community in the recycling of materials and respect for the environment, as well as codes for the host community to help in understanding tourism and the benefits it brings, so as to encourage better relationships between hosts and guests.

## Managing the attraction resource

Given a fixed amount of natural resources for leisure purposes, it is only possible to alter the supply by adopting different use patterns. Critical to this is the generally accepted premise that tourists should not destroy through excessive use the natural features that they came to enjoy. This view is encapsulated in the concept of sustainable tourism development, which argues that economic growth is only acceptable if it can maintain, at a minimum, the stock of tourist assets intact from one generation to another. Emphasis tends to be placed on the natural environment because it cannot be directly substituted for artificial facilities, and the danger of irreversible damage appears more likely. This danger is also present with man-made attractions such as historic artefacts, but

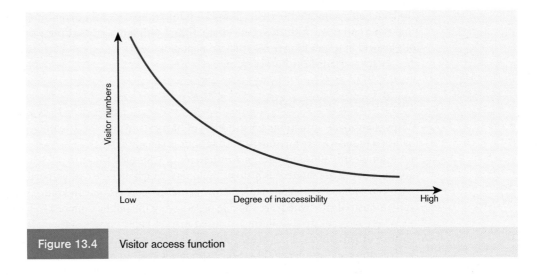

| Figure 13.4 | Visitor access function |

here the concept is more subjective in that it has to do with authenticity – namely, at what point does repair and replacement of stone, say, on a historic monument owing to erosion and visitor damage, mean that it is no longer authentic? This is further complicated by the fact that perception seems to vary according to the nature of the historic artefact under consideration – whether it is glassware, tapestry, a sculpture or features of a building.

It has already been noted that the application of capital, labour and management to the natural environment is often necessary to render them suitable for tourist use, as in the case of a beach resource. This permits more intensive use of the beach provided that the necessary safeguards are put in place to prevent over-exploitation of the free availability of the resource in its role as a public good. One way of achieving this is to restrict accommodation provision to match the desired density of the population on the beach. A high-quality resort would aim at allocating 20 square metres per person, compared with 10 square metres per person for a budget resort. In other situations, the degree of inaccessibility may be used to control visitor numbers. This is illustrated in Figure 13.4, which demonstrates the inverse relationship between visitor numbers and difficulties of access and is also indicated in Clawson's classification (Figure 13.1). This inverse relationship may be due to time, distance or restrictions imposed by the managing authority. For example, with natural attractions that draw visitors both at the national and international level, it is common for the authorities to implement 'park and ride' schemes so as to control the flow of cars in the area. Another popular strategy is the use of **honey pots**, whereby a variety of attractions, shops, restaurants and accommodation is clustered around one or two viewpoints to create a complex capable of absorbing a high population density.

The honey pot concept augments natural attractions with artificial, user-orientated attractions capable of drawing visitors away from the rest of the natural resource area. It is well known, for example, that the demand for domestic tourism and recreation facilities arises, in the main, from urban areas but that pressures on attractions and rural areas generally decrease with distance from city centres. Hence greater opportunities for protection and management of natural sanctuaries for wildlife and vegetation can be found by locating them in areas remote from urban environments. As the city centre is approached so there is a need to provide purpose-built facilities to cope with day excursions and weekend trips. Depending on the climate and country these will include seaside or lakeside resorts, mountain resorts, health centres, spas, and themed and nature parks. Within the city boundary there will be a requirement for town parks, and sport and leisure complexes. Thus as the volume of leisure demand increases so the need to augment natural attractions with artificial facilities arises. In this respect, cities such as Amsterdam, St Petersburg and Istanbul have always been great magnets for tourists because of their historical and cultural resources. For these same reasons, cities everywhere are becoming tourist destinations in their own right rather than just places where people live and work.

Today's better-educated traveller is looking for experiences that combine educational interest and entertainment, with the result that cultural tourism is expanding worldwide and, with it, the growth in urban tourism, so that no major city today can count itself as world class unless it has an acknowledged cultural centre.

## Man-made attractions

Many man-made attractions are products of history and culture. The range of museums and art galleries in the world's top tourist destinations is usually extensive and many are subject-specific, for example, the Rijksmuseum in Amsterdam or Chicago's Museum of Science and Industry. In addition to this are numerous historic buildings, which include castles, palaces, churches, houses and even completely walled medieval towns such as Carcassonne in France, as well as a variety of early industrial sites which are capable of satisfying the public's interest in bygone times.

Where old industrial buildings, disused market halls, railway stations and docks are located close to urban centres, it has been quite common to convert them into tourist zones which serve both visitors and residents alike. Since shopping is an important tourist activity, the focus has been on speciality shopping – as in Faneuil Hall, Boston – intermingled with hotels, leisure attractions and also business facilities – a convention centre, exhibition hall or trade centre. In this way, tourism has replaced manufacturing and distribution industries which have left the inner core for more spacious and cheaper locations on the outskirts of the city, and has proved to be a feasible economic option for urban regeneration, as in the development of Baltimore's Inner Harbor, South Street Seaport, New York, Darling Harbour, Sydney and Birmingham's Gas Street Basin in the UK.

Over and above the attractions left by historical legacy, there are numerous engineered attractions whose principal role is one of entertainment. Such attractions are user-orientated and are capable of handling thousands of visitors per day: they include theme and leisure parks, sporting venues, theatres and all-weather holiday centres. Theme parks will also include an educational function – for example, Futurescope in France – as well as providing exciting 'white knuckle' rides in the form of roller coasters, runaway trains, log flumes and oscillating 'pirate' ships.

One of the most famous theme parks (in the true sense), Colonial Williamsburg in Virginia, USA, is a living museum. It was originated by establishing an old city within a new one and by the staff creating a time capsule of the colonial period of America through role play and using the technology of the day. Its success has drawn in a range of partners to propagate the cultural richness of the state of Virginia. A similar recreation has taken place at Beamish in the north of England. The museum has been positioned at a time just before World War I and staff demonstrate the technology and converse with visitors in the way of life of that period. As far as possible the houses, shops, transport system, goods and artefacts are genuine articles of the time that have been brought to the site from all parts of the UK. In this manner, Beamish and Colonial Williamsburg have crossed the boundary between a theme park and a museum. In so doing they have captured the public's imagination by allowing participation. The public is now attuned to experiencing the sights and sounds of the era being witnessed, which gives opportunities for using technology creatively to enhance the visitor experience. We know that ultimately it is the visitor experience that is the marketed output of tourist attractions. The acceptance of the content and style of this experience is determined by fashion, which has its own dynamic that is born out of the spirit of enquiry and competition within society to alter its patterns of consumption and value systems.

To this extent, animals in captivity in the form of zoos or safari parks are no longer acceptable to many people and there is a marked decline of interest in static attractions and object-orientated museums, unless they are national collections or they are best presented in this way, as for example jewellery. The quest for improving the attraction experience forces theme and leisure park operators to install more complicated rides and challenging entertainment as the public seeks to increase the skill content of their consumption. Similarly, historic properties, museums and gardens change their displays and feature special exhibitions/events to maintain interest. Some attractions are fortunate enough to be able to tie themselves to regular events aimed at an enthusiast market, for example automobile rallies, for which demand is more or less continuous.

**YOUTUBE**
Natural and man-made attractions

Discover Ireland – Discover Natural and Manmade Delights
http://www.youtube.com/watch?v=oqsflYlSuh8

Western Australia Perth
http://www.youtube.com/watch?v=5miGr-R10PU

Mountains of Norway (Preikestolen, Preacher's Pulpit or Pulpit Rock)
http://www.youtube.com/watch?v=26R9g4v_ByE

Natural Attractions in Fort Lauderdale, Florida
http://www.youtube.com/watch?v=AilGcDstNQY

New York Tourist Attractions – Visit New York's Top Tourist Attractions FREE
http://www.youtube.com/watch?v=wzw0PGi4r64

## Developing attractions

Already it is clear that the range of attractions is extensive and that there are numerous variations in respect of the product concept or creativity of the design and its appeal. This we will term the **imagescape** to match the use of the word 'imagineers' by the Disney Corporation when describing its designers. The concept is based on the fact that all attractions, in some part, measure their performance by the number of visitors, the quality of the experience they give them, and the memories that they take home to ensure repeat visits or the spread of word-of-mouth recommendation. To enhance the experience, the modern approach is to place tangible objects, say a thrill ride or a collection of museum artefacts (despite their intrinsic value), within the context of a specific theme or image in a particular setting or environment: hence the word 'imagescape'.

This approach is consistent with the post-industrial societal views espoused by Pine and Gilmore (1999) in their seminal publication *The Experience Economy*, where it is argued that the production system should be re-engineered to add value through marketing experiences. This implies producing services with attached goods, rather than the traditional mass production process in which commodities are uniformly produced and sold on price. In this way, customers are able to receive a package that relates to their needs. Following this viewpoint, Figure 13.5

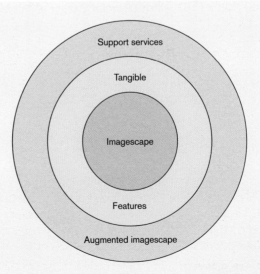

| Figure 13.5 | The attraction product |
| --- | --- |
| | *Source*: Wanhill, 2008 |

offers an abstract perspective of an attraction product where the core element is represented by the 'imagescape' – the idea of which is to communicate the fundamental nature of the visitor experience to the potential target markets. Clearly a variety of 'imagescapes' are possible. Examples may include 'art and media', 'childhood', 'fame and notoriety', the 'human body', 'myths and fantasy', the 'natural world' and 'war and conflict', to name but a few.

The core is surrounded by commodities and services, which are combined to add value through experiences that generate memorable mood benefits (and in consequence attachment) for the visitor and support the core, in the manner of a 'product wrapper'. For example, within the performing arts, facilities such as retailing, restaurants and bars, cloakrooms, first aid, special needs access, queue management, handling complaints and car parking, as well as an augmented imagescape, are provided to ensure that all customer experiential requirements are met. Components of the latter include: friends'/patrons' associations, behind the scenes tours, inclusive dining, pre-show talks and presentations.

## The attraction development process

When contemplating attraction development the ideal process from a demand standpoint is one of Market → Imagescape → Location. In reality, however, this demand-led sequential process is seldom implemented, only applying to **'footloose' attractions** that have flexibility across all three aspects in order to generate economic success. Given that most attraction developments are constrained more often than not by their location, type and ownership, a more common process – especially in the instance of regeneration – is one of Location → Imagescape → Market (see Figure 13.6), which raises the danger of 'talking up the market' to justify the development.

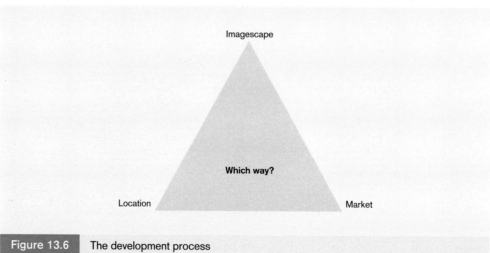

| Figure 13.6 | The development process |
|---|---|

*Source*: Wanhill, 2008

Several millennium projects sponsored by the Heritage Lottery Fund in the UK went this way and some had to close. This reflects the fact that location, imagescape and market are inextricably bound up with one another. If site selection becomes at most a second choice, this throws greater weight on to the market–imagescape mix in order to achieve visitor numbers commensurate with notions of the economic viability of the attraction. How in reality these three factors are balanced clearly depends upon the overriding objectives of the attraction and the status of its owners.

## The market–imagescape mix

What is clear from the above is that both market and imagescape are inextricably linked to each other vis-à-vis the development of attractions, as evidenced in Figure 13.7. The type of attraction which carries the least commercial risk is that identified in the first quadrant (QI), that of **'me too' attraction development**. The fact that parallel attractions already exist in the marketplace ensures that the creators of the attraction are able to benefit from previous market performance and the passage of trends over a specified time period. One of the dangers of 'me too' developments is that assumptions are often made, incorrectly, that if a concept works in one location then it will automatically work elsewhere. It is also a problem in some countries with the overdevelopment of heritage attractions – often perceived as a 'quick win' for politicians, but frequently short of visitors after the initial spurt of interest. Before giving the 'green light' to such attractions it is advisable to evaluate the likely displacement of visitors from other attractions and so anticipate the genuine additionality, if any, to the destination in question.

Success in delivering **'grand inspiration' attractions** in QII is clearly dependent on the imagescape meeting the needs and expectations of the market. Pre-market evaluation of the concept is difficult in that the market is frequently unaware of what the concept will look like. In terms of assessment, a common strategy in this area is to try to reverse the project evaluation sequence by estimating the volume of visitors needed to make the project both feasible and viable at a price the market is prepared to pay.

Even if this is successful, however, there still remain the problems of raising finance and finding a suitable location. The fact that most available land is owned by the public sector is a hindrance in that very few local or regional authorities have the vision to foresee the positive impact of such attractions. Equally, many developers have experienced and recognised the ability of local pressure groups to 'kill off' sound project proposals.

**'New version' attractions** in QIII represent on the one hand a reformulation of the attraction product, yet preserving the existing imagescape, because the current public has become too familiar with it and, on the other hand, expansion to new locations and access to new markets. The expansion of the Disney concept to Japan, Paris and Hong Kong represents a good example

| Image<br>Market | Current | New |
|---|---|---|
| Current | Q I<br>'Me too'<br>attraction | Q II<br>'Grand inspiration'<br>attraction |
| New | Q III<br>'New version'<br>attraction | Q IV<br>'Wonder'<br>attraction |

**Figure 13.7**  The attraction market–imagescape mix
Source: Wanhill, 2008

of the latter type of development. Such developments are supply-led, as they are generating demand in spatial terms where it has not been previously and so there is a need for substantial market research and forecasting in order to take account of both short-term conditions and longer-term ones. Yet there is no guarantee of success, as realised by the financial difficulties of Disneyland Paris, so that in the case of Hong Kong Disney was careful to lay the bulk of the investment on the government of Hong Kong. For established attractions, meeting the needs of new and future markets may require a much greater leap forward in terms of imagescape development for the new version to be successful, something that was achieved successfully by the opening of the Guggenheim in Bilbao.

Those attractions that carry with them the highest level of risk are labelled **'wonder' attractions,** as identified in QIV. This type of attraction represents projects on a grand scale that deliver significant economic impacts on their location. Because the development of such attractions contains considerable risk and uncertainty, it is fair to say that very few examples of attraction development would sit in this category: Disney's EPCOT (opened in 1982) and Sydney's Opera House (opened in 1973) are two examples of success, though only after a financial struggle, particularly the Opera House, which came in 10 years late and 14 times over budget. London's Millennium Dome is an example of how a part regeneration development can go off course! This can be attributed to political interference and a lack of clarity in the marketplace of what it was supposed to be. It was designed as a celebration for the year 2000, but was judged by the press as a commercial attraction, so that the outturn of 6.5 million visitors for the year as against a forecast of 12 million was declared a financial 'disaster' in the media and the political arena, and an embarrassment to the British government. With the clear majority of all attraction developments achieving annual attendance levels of 200,000 and below, it is no surprise that investments of the above scale are few and far between. The risks are high and the funding required is such that they tend to proceed with the support of governments and large leisure corporations working in partnership. That said, if the balance is right the potential benefits to accrue from success are considerable. With regard to the innovation process with 'wonder' attractions, the departure from existing imagescapes is common in that the new attraction often sets the standard for others to follow and is an inspiration for subsequent development. With such a large investment from the public sector, the development of the Titanic Quarter in Belfast in the UK will hopefully serve as a catalyst for further development across Belfast's historic shipyards and docklands.

## MINI CASE STUDY 13.2
### Big build projects: Titanic Belfast

Titanic Belfast is Northern Ireland's newest visitor attraction that opened on 31 March 2012, ahead of the centenary of the tragic sinking of RMS *Titanic* during its maiden voyage on 15 April 1912. It is located on Queens Island alongside the actual slipway where the ship first entered the water and next to the drawing offices of Harland and Wolff where it was conceived and designed, and in close proximity to the company's shipyards where it was built. At a cost of £97 million, this is Northern Ireland's most expensive visitor attraction, designed to create the wow factor and provide Northern Ireland with international standout, as well as position the city of Belfast as a destination with a distinct maritime heritage. The visitor attraction presents visitors with a mix of education and entertainment; transporting them back to Belfast in the early decades of the past century where they see the ship being designed and built, allowing them to get up close and personal to a replica of the ship's rudder and its engines, gazing at life on the *Titanic* from the activities on deck to looking in on first to third class passengers; retelling the story of striking the iceberg and the hours leading up to its tragic sinking; the inquiries that followed and the discovery of the wreckage on the sea bed. The entertainment dimension is provided through simulated rides and fully interactive panel displays and flooring within many of the attraction's 'galleries'.

| Photograph 13.2 | Titanic Belfast. |
| --- | --- |
| | *Source*: Ros Drinkwater/Rex Features |

Belfast as a city has witnessed a major transformation over the past three decades; from a closed city of the late 1980s to a thriving short-break destination at present. However, it has lacked a major visitor attraction and the opening of Titanic Belfast provides the city with a 'must see' visitor attraction that will cater to all markets: domestic and international, holiday, business and VFR. According to a recent report by the Northern Ireland Audit Office, it is the most expensive visitor attraction built in Europe and it is anticipated that to break even it will have to receive over its lifetime (20–25 years) 290,000 visitors per year. During the first 10 months of operation some 600,000 visitors passed through the attraction.

## DISCUSSION QUESTIONS

In light of the above description of Titanic Belfast, consider the following questions.

1. Should a destination invest in such a level of capital spend on one iconic build?
2. What necessary steps should the company charged with running the visitor attraction take to ensure that visitor numbers remain above the required level to ensure financial viability?
3. Is a 'build it and they will come' philosophy a wise one to create international standout for destinations?
4. Can Titanic Belfast survive as a visitor attraction beyond the immediate interest of leading up to the centenary?
5. Consider the role of the creating the 'wow factor' and building the 'iconic' in marketing destinations?

*Source*: Professor Stephen Boyd, Department of Hospitality and Tourism Management, University of Ulster

In trying to develop a successful attraction, the discussion above leads to the conclusion that the creativity of the imagescape has to connect to the needs and expectations of the market. In the majority of cases, attractions as a product group tend to defy business logic in that they are frequently supply-driven with many being developed for purposes other than tourism and in other economic sectors. Although this is maybe obvious with regard to many public attractions such as museums, monuments and historic houses, it is also true for many themed attractions such as Disney, in that the Disney characters were established icons long before the development of the theme parks in California and Florida. This, and to a large extent the future of attraction development, appears to lie with new developments that customers recognise by association with known products: the development of corporate brand attractions being a perfect example of this, such as the Guinness Storehouse in Dublin, Ireland and Niketown in the USA. Investments of this kind may be regarded as **brand extensions or stretching**.

# MANAGING ATTRACTIONS

The sheer diversity, geographic fragmentation, varying pattern of ownership and funding, scale and market–imagescape mix are such that the management of visitor attractions can be a very complex and demanding proposition (Leask, 2010). This applies especially with regard to attempts made to date in developing a cohesive national strategy for visitor attractions, which in turn creates a sound strategic platform for the management of individual attractions. Work by Middleton (2003) outlines those conditions where a national strategy for visitor attractions would be beneficial. Such conditions include:

- the destabilising effects of a sudden massive injection of unanticipated capital into an already saturated market;
- where large, newly opened projects are putting established attractions at a significant disadvantage;
- instances of major expenditure on other major urban regeneration projects;
- situations where there is a steady decline of local authority annual revenue funding for traditional attractions such as museums and galleries;
- where the industry structure is one in which the great majority of attractions are small businesses, with only a very small percentage of larger attractions capable managerially and financially of marketing themselves professionally and organising their own data collection; and
- where there is a lack of management information and where the attractions sector is populated by more non-commercial 'public' institutions than by commercial 'private' businesses.

If the majority of the above conditions are in place, Middleton identifies seven key components that ought to be considered for action recommendations in any national strategy for visitor attractions. The seven factors are:

- the collection and dissemination of effective research on a comparable basis and which covers both demand- and supply-side perspectives;
- application of expertise to the analysis and communication of trends and their implications in terms that the majority of smaller attractions will be able to understand and respond;
- advice, and perhaps support, on assessing quality of visits and providing customer assurance via benchmarking initiatives;
- collection and dissemination of good practice examples in visitor attraction management and operations;
- coordination and possibly funding for/provision of training and management development;
- influence over funding bodies concerning the criteria they apply to bids from new and existing attractions including advice to government on the way in which taxes in the sector are imposed and collected; and
- influence and advice to public sector bodies, especially local authorities, that they may consider in relation to their own decisions on planning and funding activities for attractions in their areas.

Moving away from the notion of a national strategy, however, a number of issues are fundamental to the day-to-day management of visitor attractions.

## Economic aspects

As with natural resources, a great many man-made tourist attractions, because of their histor-ical legacy, are not commercially owned. They are owned by central government, in the case of national collections, quasi-public bodies which are at an 'arm's length' from the government, local government and voluntary bodies in the form of charitable trusts. Ownership status is in fact one of the key determinants of attraction management. Leask (2003: 11) for example, concludes that ownership proved to be a 'key independent variable with regard to determining the entire approach to attraction management'. This was particularly the case for 'managing revenue and overall yield, visitor management strategies and the management of environmental impacts at attractions'.

## Issues of ownership

### Public ownership

Publicly owned attractions may receive all or a substantial part of their funds from general taxation, either directly or via grant-in-aid for quasi-public bodies. They are thus provided in the manner of a **merit good** and as a result impose a degree of coercion on everyone, as individuals are not free to adjust the amounts that are made available. This is shown by Figure 13.8: the schedule $SS$ is the quantity of, say, museum services supplied to each person as a result of public provision. The distance $0t$ represents the amount of income forgone per person in terms of tax and $A$ the demand curve of individual A and similarly for $B$. At a tax cost $0t$, A demands only $Q_A$ museum services while B demands $Q_B$ Clearly, the supply of services exceeds A's demand by $XY$, but falls below B's demand by $YZ$. It follows therefore that public provision is likely to generate political debate and lobbying as individuals try to alter the amounts produced to suit their own requirements. In market-orientated economies the trend has been towards charging for national museums in order to cut public expenditure, though there is still resistance among certain sections of the community, including museum managers, who feel that museums have a public obligation requirement. As a consequence, only voluntary admission donations have been introduced in some instances, with a recom-mended minimum contribution, while other museums have simply refused to charge for admission in exchange for tax breaks, and those that are free still make charges for special exhibitions.

It is evident from the above discussion that the classification of goods and services into public and private provision is by no means clear-cut. It is up to society to decide upon the dividing

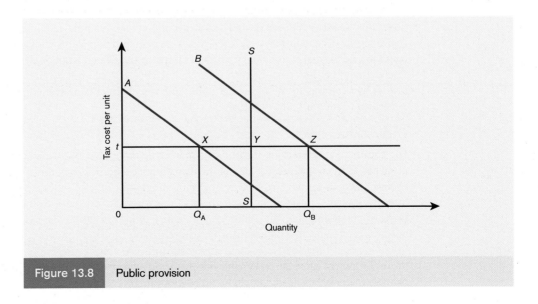

| Figure 13.8 | Public provision |

line through the political process. Nevertheless, governments do have to make everyday decisions on which projects to promote. This is particularly true of tourist attractions, because they are frequently sponsored by local authorities and voluntary organisations that look to central government for grant assistance. To aid decision making, economists have devised the analytical framework of cost–benefit analysis, which takes a wider and longer look at project decisions. The diversity of tourism expenditure is such that the most feasible method of assessing government support is to look at the impact that spending by visitors to the attraction has on local income and employment via the multiplier process. Implicit in this process is the requirement that the normal financial checks will be undertaken to ascertain whether the project is able to sustain itself operationally: if not, then it will need permanent subsidy if it is to proceed.

## Voluntary organisations

Many museums and events have arisen out of the collections or interests of a group of enthusiasts who come together to provide for themselves and others collective goods and services which are unlikely to have any widespread commercial appeal (market failure) and are equally unlikely to be of sufficient importance to attract central provision by the state. These organisations are in effect clubs and normally have non-profit aims. But, in contrast to the public sector, they are not able to raise funds from taxation and so in the long run must cover their costs out of income. Yet, unlike the private commercial sector, many find their income source is not made up principally of admission charges and visitor spending inside the attraction, and those that do will have a different pricing policy than commercial operators. Membership fees, gifts and bequests often take on a far greater significance in the income statement. As a consequence, recruiting new members to share the collective visitor experience is a priority task for these organisations.

As these voluntary associations grow in size, there comes a point where it pays them to be incorporated as charitable trusts. By law, this can usually only be for the purposes of education, religion, relief of the poor, or the public good, and allows them to qualify for public funding and tax relief for capital and revenue expenses. One of the most well-known examples of the latter in the UK is the National Trust, which was started in 1895 with the object of protecting places of historic and natural significance for the nation. The Trust maintains a wide range of historic properties, parks and woodlands, and is an institutional model that has been copied elsewhere. Acquisition has normally been via bequests from previous owners together with substantial endowments that provide the economic foundations for the organisation. Given the breadth of its facilities, with the potential of taking on more, it has a policy of expanding membership, since its objective, as with any other club, is to encourage consumption among like-minded persons. However, it is also careful to hedge the demand risk by receiving income from a variety of sources: admission charges from non-members, shops and catering, grants and donations, sponsorship, events and services rendered, for example, lecture programmes. On the cost side, like other voluntary societies, the Trust benefits from some labour inputs and materials being provided free of charge. An events example is the Sealed Knot Society, which undertakes re-enactment battles of the English Civil War (1642–1651). Similarly, there are several military history associations in the USA that undertake re-enactments of events that took place in the American Civil War (1861–1865).

## Commercial sector

For commercial attractions the rules of market economics apply. They are required to make profits so as to contribute a return on the capital invested. In theory this return, at a minimum, should be equal to the current cost of raising money for investment purposes, and for new or 'venture' projects considerably more. In situations where attractions are owned by multi-product firms or conglomerates, the ability of the facility to contribute to the cash flow of the overall business is often given a higher priority than return on capital. Production industries frequently have long lead times between incurring costs and receiving revenues. In these circumstances, the ownership of subsidiaries capable of generating ready cash inflows into the organisation on a daily and weekly basis can contribute greatly to total financial stability.

The principal economic concerns of most commercial attractions are the same ones that face many other tourist enterprises, namely their cost structure and the seasonal nature of demand. Furthermore, for user-orientated attractions, fashions and tastes also play a considerable part. As noted earlier, theme park owners have to add new rides and replace old ones long before they are physically worn out simply to maintain attendances. Historic properties and museums can fall back on the intrinsic value of their buildings and collections, but even here presentation and interpretation have become more important. The Major Case Study at the end of this chapter provides a very pertinent example of commercial theme park attraction development and identifies many of the contemporary issues and future challenges faced by commercial attraction operators.

## Costs

Typically, the cost structure of tourist attractions is made up of a high level of fixed, and therefore unavoidable, costs in relation to the operational or variable costs of running the enterprise. The main component of the fixed costs is the capital investment required to establish the attraction in the first place and capital additions from new development. The economic consequence of having a high level of fixed costs is to raise the break-even point in terms of sales or visitor numbers, as shown in Figure 13.9. The revenue line from sales to visitors over a given time period is represented by $R$. The lines $C_1$ and $C_2$ are total cost schedules according to different visitor numbers: the slope of these cost schedules is determined by the variable costs incurred per visitor (marginal costs) and where they cut the revenue and costs axis determines the level of fixed costs. It may easily be seen that with overall fixed costs of $F_1$ the break-even point ($BEP_1$), which is at the intersection of $R$ and $C_1$, is achieved at $V_1$ level of visitors. If fixed costs are set at $F_2$, then the number of visitors needed to break even rises substantially to $V_2$, which increases the amount of risk in the successful running of the operation. This also has an impact on location, because for user-orientated attractions population catchment areas in terms of ease of access to the site are of prime importance. The greater the visitor numbers required in order for an attraction project to break even, the fewer are the number of acceptable locations. It follows from this that government initiatives to stimulate the development of tourist attractions largely hinge, for their success, on the amount of assistance that can be given to help with the capital costs of starting up the project. This assistance may be in the form of cash grants, subsidised ('soft') loans, shared ownership, the provision of benefits-in-kind such as land, infrastructure and access routes or a combination of any of these. For example, the site for Disneyland Paris was

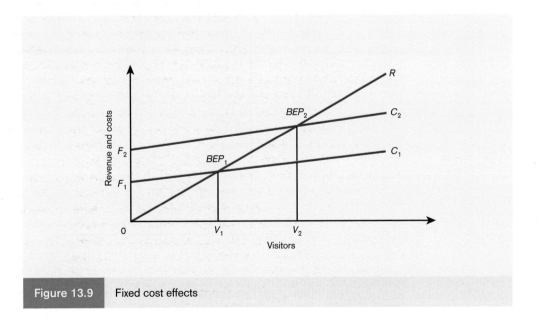

**Figure 13.9**    Fixed cost effects

obtained at 1971 agricultural prices, in spite of the fact that it had already been zoned for urban development. As a rule, cash grants are perceived by the commercial sector as the most effective form of financial help.

## Pricing policy

Figure 13.10 examines the normative economics of the appropriate pricing rules that may be followed. $D$ is the demand schedule and market economics dictate that private operators should attempt to optimise profitability, which is achieved by equating marginal revenue generated from an additional sale ($MR$) to marginal cost ($MC$), setting an adult admission rate of $P_1$ and attracting $V_1$ visitors – pricing according to 'what the market will bear'. In practice, contestable market conditions may give rise to limits on the price level and ease of entry will erode excessive profits.

The public sector, which has the interest of the economy at large, is faced with two economically efficient choices: free at the point of use, which results in a demand level of $V_4$, or setting admission equal to $MC$, implying a charge $P_2$ for $V_2$ visitors. The former typically applies to outdoor recreation areas or for attractions whose consumption the state wishes to encourage, while the latter is appropriate for state museums, where exclusion from consumption is possible. Equating $P_2$ to $MC$ is the optimal pricing rule that would be obtained under perfect competition and represents the most efficient use of economic resources, for the price level is both lower and output greater than under monopolistic competition. Figure 13.10 depicts $MC$ lying above $AC$, but it is common in attractions for $MC$ to be small and lying below $AC$, which implies that even if governments charge for admission to public museums, they will still have to be subsidised directly from taxation if they are to survive.

The appropriate policy for the voluntary sector, if it wants to distribute maximum benefits to its members, while being mindful of its not-for-profit charitable objectives, is one of average cost pricing, setting a price $P_3$ to generate $V_3$ users, where $V_3$ may be interpreted in practice as visitors who are members and non-members. Generally, such operators tend to be 'fixed-price' organisations, in that should demand increase in circumstances of limited capacity they will accumulate waiting lists for membership and extend facilities, rather than seek monopoly rents by raising dues. The optimum sized club is at the lowest point on the $AC$ curve, so in Figure 13.10 it could be that attendance will be restricted to members and guests only at $V_5$, which is off the demand curve, and so $V_3 - V_5$ will be the waiting list for potential members, who may be allowed to attend as non-members. However, as noted earlier, voluntary organisations often provide their labour at little or no cost, due to their non-economic mission. Thus their cost curves could be lower and their optimum greater than that shown in Figure 13.10.

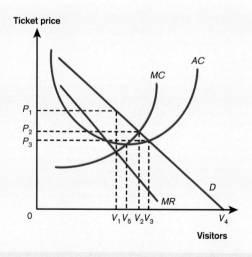

| Figure 13.10 | Pricing rules by organisation |

A common approach to voluntary society membership is the two-part tariff, where the annual fee is designed to cover fixed costs and there is an ongoing charge to meet usage costs for meetings and activities. In the commercial sector the annual fee is commonly segmented by membership category to extract the maximum willingness to pay (WTP). Thus, through pricing policy, the pattern of ownership can alter the financial outcomes of an attraction and the nature of competition. A valid criticism of the not-for-profit sector, whether it is public or voluntary, is that it has the inclination to try and do too much, because the management looks to meet perceived needs rather than market demand. To take a simple analogy; if people are asked if they want more of a collective good, then, in the absence of a price system, they will surely vote 'Yes', putting the onus of the public sector to meet these needs, as there is a political incentive to do so. Failing public sector attractions rightly raise scorn from commercial operators who argue that if public funding and project inflation results in a situation where there is no relationship between the cost of delivering and what the customer actually pays, then this is a case of predatory pricing (technically defined as price less than the average variable costs of provision) in an over-supplied market that is likely to harm them commercially. Governments are sensitive to this kind of criticism and as a rule avoid trying to compete 'head on' with the private sector.

The effects of having high fixed costs also spill over into pricing policy. The difference between the price charged for admission to an attraction and the variable or marginal cost of providing the visitor experience for the customer is the contribution margin per customer towards paying the fixed costs and meeting targets on profitability. As shown in Figure 13.11, where the contribution margin desired is low because fixed costs are low, the marginal cost of supplying an additional unit is relatively high and so provides a good guide to setting the price level. This is known as cost-orientated pricing. On the other hand, where there are high fixed costs, the admission charge has to be set considerably above the **marginal cost** of provision, in order to ensure a high contribution margin to meet the financial costs of servicing the investment that has been sunk into the attraction. In this instance, the marginal cost of provision is no longer a good guide to pricing and the enterprise is forced to take a market-orientated stance in its pricing policy. The difference between the admissions price and marginal cost is the range of price discretion that the business has, for it must cover its operating costs in the short run but may take a longer-term perspective in terms of how it might cover its fixed costs. By seeking out a range of different market segments with a variety of different prices, including discounts for volume sales and long-term contracts, the commercial attraction operator will try to optimise the yield (the difference between price and marginal cost) on the site's assets. This is termed **yield management**. It is the same principle as haggling in tourist markets, where the trader assesses each visitor's ability to settle the bargain. (The range of pricing strategies and their marketing aspects are discussed in Chapter 21.) For performing arts venues, once the repertoire is fixed then the marginal cost per seat falls to zero,

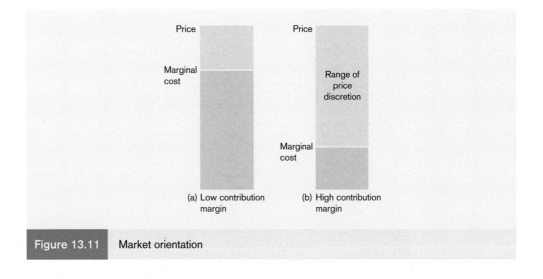

**Figure 13.11**    Market orientation

so yield management is effectively **revenue management**, hence major cities often have discount ticket booths located in 'theatreland' to dispose of surplus tickets for today's performances, since any price greater than zero represents a contribution to fixed expenses.

## Managing people

The perception of attractions in recent years vis-à-vis employment has changed in that many jobs in the sector are no longer viewed as low paid and seasonal but represent opportunities that offer real benefits and long-term development. This is reflected in a gradual improvement in good management, recruitment, training, appraisal procedures and the development of career structures. Many of these points were noted by Swarbrooke in 2002 when identifying those issues deemed important for the future success of managing visitor attractions. It was noted also that attractions would have to contend with flatter organisational structures and the empowerment of staff, an increased emphasis on quality and a growth in performance-related pay for valued employees.

Despite recognition of much of the above by many attractions, there still remains across the leisure sector in the UK a considerable skills gap. This was noted by Keep and Mayhew (1999) whereby, in particular, information technology and customer care skills were deemed to be lacking, with little evidence of training for volunteers. These points were also noted by Watson and McCracken (2002, 2003) in their study of attractions in Scotland. A number of key environmental factors were highlighted as significant drivers for future change, notably developments in technology, legislative changes (including requirements on health, safety and employment issues) and external socio-economic trends. Irrespective of one's particular viewpoint, it is clear that attractions need to continue to acquire more professional approaches to the recruitment, development and overall management of people if the sector as a whole is going to sustain growth and popularity in the years to come, and at best catch up with more 'professional' sector neighbours (such as transportation, intermediaries and the hospitality sector) in managing their workforce.

## Managing seasonality

Seasonality becomes an issue in tourist attractions because the product, the visitor experience, cannot be stored. This being the case, it is peak demand that determines capacity and user-orientated attractions are frequently designed to a standard based on a fixed number of days per annum when capacity is likely to be reached or exceeded. This implies that at most times of the year the attraction has too much capacity. The level of investment is therefore more than what would be required if the product was storable. In turn, seasonality can affect pricing policy, as presented in Figure 13.12. SS is the supply schedule representing the incremental

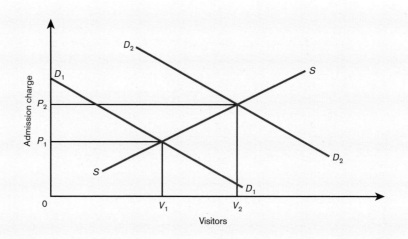

**Figure 13.12**    Seasonal demand

cost of expanding visitor numbers. $D_2D_2$ is the demand for the visitor experience in the main season, while $D_1D_1$ is the off-season demand. Market clearing requires a policy of seasonal price differentiation, charging $P_2$ in the main season and $P_1$ in the off-season. However, in practice many attraction managers are opposed to seasonal pricing because, they argue, it simply reacts on customers' perceived value for money. Visitors feel that they are being overcharged because they are unable to come in the off-season. To counter this perception problem, attraction operators tend to narrow seasonal price ranges and offer additional product benefits, in the form of free entrance to different parts of the site, to those visitors coming when the attraction is not busy.

Another method of smoothing the difference in prices is to charge a two-part tariff. Instead of the major contribution to fixed costs being borne by main season visitors, the admission price is made up of a fixed charge to meet the requirement to cover fixed costs in the long term and a variable charge depending on the level of usage. While most attractions pay attention to segmented pricing techniques for groups, senior citizens, children and schools, the dictates of yield management do require operators to address the seasonal and spatial limitations of demand in their pricing policy.

## Managing visitors

Price has often been used as a method of regulating demand and enforcing exclusivity, as in luxury resorts such as Malibu and the Maldives, or in luxury hotels, for example the Mandarin and Shangri La hotels in Asia. To be able to use price to limit the number of visitors requires that consumption should be excludable – only those who pay can benefit from the visitor experience. But this is frequently deemed undesirable in the case of natural resources or the historical and cultural artefacts of a country, either because they are public goods, so that it is not practical to exclude consumption, or because they are merit goods whereby it is to the benefit of society that consumption should be encouraged. Even commercial attractions would have difficulty in using price as the sole regulator of visitor numbers. In any one year such attractions have a variety of peaks and troughs, which would therefore entail a whole range of different prices. In Western economies, the public does not respond well to wildly fluctuating prices and so all attractions resort to some non-price methods to manage visitor flows.

A number of possible actions exist to manage visitors at busy times and thereby avoid congestion and improve the visitor experience. These start with marketing and information provision and go through to techniques that can influence the visitor's behaviour on the site. Some attractions have adopted deliberate demarketing at peak times, but where they are nationally or internationally known this is only of limited effectiveness. First-time visitors to capital cities nearly always want to see the principal landmarks: Prague Castle in the Czech Republic, the Grand Palace in Bangkok and the Empire State Building in New York City. The first step at any site is to deal with car and bus traffic, if only to prevent congestion building up and blocking main roads. Once on site, visitors can be channelled using internal transport systems, for example land trains, where distances involve a considerable amount of walking. For theme parks, queue management is often necessary for popular attractions and rides, so that excessive waiting does not detract from the visitor's enjoyment. This may be achieved by ensuring that the queue line passes through a stimulating environment, with the ability to view the attraction as the latter is approached, by providing entertainers and by using markers to indicate the length of time people will have to wait at different stages of the queue.

## Environmental impacts

The concern for the tourism environment, be it natural or artificial, is linked with the notion of sustainable development (as discussed in detail in Chapter 8). Rarely in history has any society willingly absorbed the imposition of a variety of outside cultures upon it, yet, in the interests of generating local economic activity and employment, this is precisely what host communities

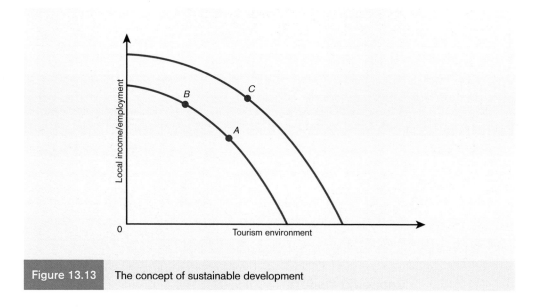

| Figure 13.13 | The concept of sustainable development |

are expected to do with regard to the development of tourism. The situation is depicted in Figure 13.13. Suppose the local economy is positioned at *A* and the desire is to increase employment. The adverse consequence is where such a policy can only be accomplished by a move from *A* to *B*, which trades off employment against environmental quality. The concept of sustainable tourism development used here argues that economic growth and environmental quality are not mutually exclusive events. By changes in technology to improve the use of resources, compensating for the running down of some resources, controlling waste and managing visitor flows to prevent or repair damage to non-renewable tourism resources, it is possible to reach a position such as *C* in Figure 13.13.

Going 'green' can build a platform for long-term growth by offering a better tourist product, saving resources and raising the public's perception of the tourism industry. Sustainable development thus offers a way to escape the 'limits to growth' syndrome illustrated by a move from *A* to *B*, by searching out a way forward that will maintain community well-being. But care of the environment is more than just preservation or protection: some of the key principles that should govern environmental policy for the implementation of any tourism development plan are:

- recognition of a two-way relationship between tourism and the environment, yielding possibilities of conservation through tourism;
- visitor management to reduce pressure;
- environmental improvement for the benefit of residents and visitors;
- sensitive development that respects and, if possible, enhances the environment;
- responsible operation through ecologically sound practice in tourism businesses and the means of travel.

The significant feature that is not always given the coverage it deserves in the media is the existence of this two-way relationship between tourism and the environment, as illustrated in Table 13.1. The tendency in the discussion of the impacts of tourism has been to give weight to the negative aspects of tourism on the environment rather than the positive opportunities that are available.

### Regulation or market solutions?

The question posed is how should the mechanism for sustainable development work? In market-orientated economies the policy preference is for solutions based on the principle

| Tourism to environment | Environment to tourism |
|---|---|
| **Opportunities** | **Opportunities** |
| Commercial returns for preservation of built environment and natural heritage | Fine scenery and heritage as visitor attractions |
| New use for redundant buildings and land | Eco-tourism based on environmental appreciation |
| Increased awareness and support for conservation | |
| **Threats** | **Threats** |
| Intrusive development | Off-putting, drab environments |
| Congestion | Pollution hazards on beaches, in water, and in rural and urban areas |
| Disturbance and physical damage | |
| Pollution and resource consumption | Intrusive developments by other industries |

Table 13.1     Tourism in relation to the environment

that the **polluter should pay**, thus prices should reflect not only the economic costs of provision but also the social costs. The different approaches to the impact of visitors on the tourism environment are shown in Figure 13.14. *DD* is the demand schedule and at low rates of tourist consumption, say, $V_1$, the social cost per unit (*SC*) is equal to the economic cost (*EC*) of usage. Thus up to $V_1$ current consumption does not interfere with future consumption or damage the resource. If only current demand is considered then the resource would be used to a level $V_2$ with visitor expenditure settling at point *B*. This results in resource depletion to the extent that *SC* is as high as point *A*. The market solution is to drive consumption back to $V_3$ by imposing a tourist tax *CE* on usage to compensate for the renewal cost of the resource.

The difficulty with market solutions is that, as discussed elsewhere, many natural attractions have public good properties whereby consumption is non-excludable and there is an element of

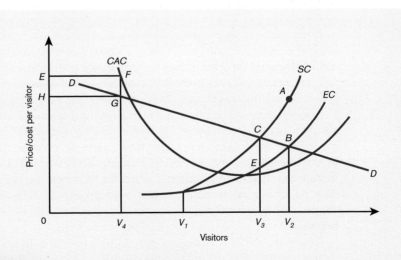

Figure 13.14     Control versus market solutions

public resistance to charging for a nation's heritage which is presumed to belong to all, although some museums and galleries do discriminate between domestic and foreign visitors, through having, say, a local residents' 'privilege' card. In such situations there is little choice other than to control visitor flows by influencing behaviour and/or to follow a programme of continual repair and maintenance. The significant aspect of many environmental matters is that the assets involved do not pass through the marketplace and the sheer number of agents involved in tourism, both public and private, with very different objectives and performance measures, make it virtually impossible to achieve concerted action other than through a regulating agency that has the force of law, which leaves little scope for market economics. The British experience, for example, has been that rarely have visitors or tourist businesses been charged directly for the social and environmental costs generated by their actions at the destination. The money is paid indirectly through general taxation and most of the burden of coping with congestion, litter and visitor management falls on the public sector, particularly local authorities. To this extent the government tries to take account of the influx of visitors in its support grant for local provision of public services. This is not to say that the 'polluter pays' principle through the application of 'green' taxes may not be appropriate in certain circumstances. Thus the Australian authorities raise a specific charge on visitors to the Great Barrier Reef, a popular destination that is under considerable environmental pressure, and the UK's Air Passenger Duty is claimed to be a tax to compensate for the greenhouse gas emissions caused by air transport.

The pure conservation solution requires that demand is driven back to $V_1$ by simply limiting the number of visitors, so that no social costs are incurred whatsoever and any social benefits that may be gained by expanding demand to $V_3$ are ignored. Such a position contrasts strongly with the ideas expressed in Table 13.1 and may be morally repugnant since it may conflict with the desirability of development for the welfare of the local community. A more extreme situation, one in which society becomes over-zealous in its actions, is depicted by $V_4$ in Figure 13.14. *CAC* represents the combined average cost curve of the tourism plant in the community. If demand is forced back to $V_4$ it may be seen that this plant is no longer viable, for the average cost of supply (point *F*) is greater than the average visitor spend (point *G*), and so in order to survive in the longer term the tourism enterprises have to be subsidised by an amount *EFGH*. One of the paradoxes of tourism is that those who do not see that their income is directly dependent on the tourism industry are frequently opposed to it, yet closing down the tourism plant reverses the multiplier process. Quite soon local businesses and employment are affected, and the economic rationale for the community may be impaired, which can affect the very jobs of those who are opposed to tourism development.

Regulation and market solutions to manage the tourism environment are not necessarily mutually exclusive. A compromise is to assign quotas at the conservation level $V_1$ to tourist enterprises, but at the same time allowing market forces to work by levying a graduated environmental charge on those businesses exceeding their quotas, or, in regulatory terms, requirements to undertake compensating environmental projects when businesses apply for planning permission to expand. The object here is to position society as near as possible to point *C* in Figure 13.14. To ensure that allocations are adjusted in an optimal manner, businesses are allowed to buy and sell quotas so as to reach a level appropriate to their own organisation. Currently, it is the excessive production of greenhouse gases that is causing most concern, which is why these principles have been embodied in carbon trading schemes devised by the EU. Destinations such as Canada, Ireland, New Zealand and Scotland, where the landscape is recognised as a major visitor attraction, are looking to innovative carbon offset projects to maintain their competitive position. The concept of a carbon-neutral destination is one that is considered to have significant tourism benefits.

Clearly, the model depicted in Figure 13.14 is not static. In times of growth this is of benefit, for it is politically less painful to refuse planning permission for new projects than it is to regulate existing operators. Over time it is expected that new technologies for maintenance and repair, and improved visitor management techniques, will enable the *SC* schedule to be shifted to the right. This should allow a greater number of visitors to be handled at a lower cost to the environment, which is the essence of the sustainable tourism development argument depicted in Figure 13.13.

## Attraction authenticity

It is the concern of social researchers that tourists should be given a genuine appreciation of the destination they are visiting. In too many cases, it is argued, tourists are given the impression that the destination is some idyllic fantasy world, and that they are fooled into this by attractions, particularly events, that are staged and may have little relevance to the culture of the country. Thus the tourists do not see the real landscape and way of life of the host community. This implies a loss of authenticity in the visitor experience. However, authenticity from the tourists' perspective is subjective and is of differing importance to different market segments. Some tourists do not want an authentic experience: the purpose of going to leisure or theme parks to participate on the rides is for entertainment and excitement.

The ideal situation is considered to be where both the host community and the visitor see the experience as authentic. However, given mass tourism flows, it is virtually impossible to meet the curiosity of visitors without staging events and certain aspects of historic attractions. Many historic properties in Britain stage period tableaux to give visitors an impression of what living was like at those times. The visitor knows that they are staged, yet at the same time every effort is made by the provider to give the most authentic representation possible, even including the reproduction of smells, as in the Jorvik Centre in York, which places visitors in a 'time car' to travel around the re-creation of a Viking village. Authenticity becomes questionable when the destination tries to conceal the staging of an event by giving visitors the impression that what they are seeing is real, when in fact it may be an artificially created event or belong to a time gone by and have no place in the current life of the community. Historic and cultural staging presents the visitor with the salient features of a community's heritage and reduces the need for encroaching on the private space of the host population. It may also generate pride and interest among the local community that has previously taken these aspects for granted.

# CONCLUSION

Attractions are an integral – and important – component of the tourism product. As we note in early chapters, certain attractions are so alluring in their own right that they provide the sole motivation for a visit. However, for most attractions to survive and flourish, other elements of the tourism product must also be on offer at a destination, at a complementary level, quality and price, to support the attraction and to provide the tourist with the necessary supporting infrastructure and superstructure.

As an area of investigation and study, tourist attractions are becoming increasingly important. Their contribution to the overall tourism product has been recognised and, as new technology-based innovations have been applied in this domain, the profile of many tourist attractions has risen dramatically.

Attractions remain the focal point for new visitor management and control techniques that aim to alleviate the pressure of large numbers of tourists and to ensure natural resources are protected and sustained.

While there remains a debate about the effectiveness of these strategies, there also exists discord as to who should be responsible for investing in the development and maintenance of resources that are enjoyed by many groups, including the local community. The role of the public sector versus the private sector in attraction investment and management has become an important issue as both strive to balance the oft-conflicting needs of user groups and to enhance the quality of the attraction experience for all.

## SELF-CHECK QUESTIONS

1. With reference to the contents of this chapter, what would you see as the main customer segments that are attracted to national parks?

2. In classifying attractions, how would you compare theme parks to, say, museums?

3. What are the main factors affecting the establishment of a new large-scale theme park attraction?

4. LEGOLANDs are a reflection of the LEGO toy. What other themed attractions are reflections of industrially-produced products? Consider the advantages and disadvantages of this type of development.

5. To what extent do you consider publicly funded mega attractions, such as the Titanic Belfast, are likely to continue as a viable means of developing destinations at a time of economic austerity in many countries around the world?

## REFERENCES AND FURTHER READING

Boniface, B. and Cooper, C. (1987) *The Geography of Travel and Tourism*, Heinemann, London.

Bracalente, B., Chirieleison, C., Cossignani, M. and Ferrucci, L. (2011) 'The economic impact of cultural events: the Umbria Jazz music festival', *Tourism Economics* **17**, 1235–56.

Braun, B. and Soskin, M. (2010) 'Disney's return to theme park dominance in Florida', *Tourism Economics* **16**, 235–50.

Clawson, M. and Knetsch, J. (1966) *The Economics of Outdoor Recreation*, Johns Hopkins University Press, Baltimore, MD.

Keep, E. and Mayhew, K. (1999) *The Leisure Sector*, Skills Task Force Research Paper No. 6, DfEE Publications, London.

Leask, A. (2003) 'The nature and purpose of visitor attractions', pp. 5-15 in Fyall, A., Garrod, B. and Leask, A. (eds), *Managing Visitor Attractions: New Directions*, Elsevier, Oxford.

Leask, A. (2008) 'The nature and purpose of visitor attractions', pp. 3–15 in Fyall, A., Garrod, B., Leask, A. and Wanhill, S. (eds), *Managing Visitor Attractions: New Directions*, Butterworth Heinemann, Oxford.

Leask, A (2010) 'Progress in visitor attraction research: towards more effective management', *Tourism Management* **31**, 155–66.

Lennon, J. (2004) 'Revenue management and customer forecasts: a bridge too far for the UK visitor attraction sector?', *Journal of Revenue and Pricing Management* **2**, 338–52.

Middleton, V.T.C. (2003) 'A national strategy for visitor attractions', pp. 270–83 in Fyall, A., Garrod, B. and Leask, A. (eds), *Managing Visitor Attractions: New Directions*, Butterworth Heinemann, Oxford.

Murphy, P.E. (1985) *Tourism: A Community Approach*, Methuen, London.

Pine II, B. and Gilmore, J. (1999) *The Experience Economy*, Harvard Business School Press, Cambridge, MA.

Swarbrooke, J. (2002) *The Development and Management of Visitor Attractions*, Butterworth Heinemann, Oxford.

Wanhill, S. (2006) 'Some economics of staging festivals: the case of opera festivals', *Tourism, Culture and Communication* **6**(2), 137–49.

Wanhill, S. (2008) 'Interpreting the development of the visitor attraction product', pp. 16–35 in Fyall, A., Garrod, B., Leask, A. and Wanhill, S. (eds), *Managing Visitor Attractions: New Directions,* 2nd edn, Elsevier, Oxford.

Watson, S. and McCracken, M. (2002) 'No attraction in strategic thinking: perceptions on current and future skills need for visitor attraction managers', *International Journal of Tourism Research* **4**(5), 367–78.

Watson, S. and McCracken, M. (2003) 'Visitor attractions and human resource management', pp. 171–84 in Fyall, A., Garrod, B. and Leask, A. (eds), *Managing Visitor Attractions: New Directions,* Butterworth Heinemann, Oxford.

Weidenfeld, A (2010) 'Iconicity and "flagshipness" of tourist attractions', *Annals of Tourism Research* **37**, 851–54.

# MAJOR CASE STUDY 13.1
Developing a theme park

## BACKGROUND

The theme parks of today are the modern form of the travelling fairs of yesteryear, which are now limited in number as they have been made somewhat obsolete by technology, laws on safety and duties of care to the public, and the increase in leisure expenditure that has reduced the need to travel from one market to another to capture limited spending power. Of the traditional amusement parks the earliest, which still exists today, is the 'Bakken', Copenhagen, which dates from 1583. It is still a traditional funfair drawing mainly on the 1.5 million population of Greater Copenhagen. It has some 60 concessionaires and entry is free, so visitor numbers of 2.6 million are only broad estimates. However, it is generally acknowledged that it was Walt Disney at Anaheim, California, in 1955 who acted as the catalyst for redirecting the concept of amusement parks and fairgrounds of former times into a fantasy-provoking atmosphere. Built at a cost of some US$17 million, it was the largest park investment that had ever been made and broke the mould of traditional amusement park development, the latter dating from Chicago's Columbian Exposition of 1893. As is common with new ideas, there were many sceptics who were unable to see how an amusement park without any of the traditional attractions, such as a Ferris Wheel or Tunnel of Love, could be successful. They listed a catalogue of perceived mistakes that would end in failure, for instance having only one entrance, which could cause excessive congestion for visitors, the lack of traditional revenue earners, and the amount of space devoted to non-revenue-earning Main Street USA. But Disney swept aside his critics: the park brought in 3.8 million guests in its first year, a figure that reached 13.9 million in 2000 and 16.0 million in 2010, and the Walt Disney Corporation is now the accepted standard that most look to for inspiration, along with the creativity that can be found in Universal

Photograph 13.3 | The Wizarding World of Harry Potter at Islands of Adventure, Orlando, Florida
*Source*: KeystoneUSA-ZUMA/Rex Features

Studios, which is able to theme rides and attractions around its most successful films. However, the financial failure of Disneyland Paris (see Chapter 20) showed that even Disney is not infallible.

## THEME PARK CONCEPTS

A suitable definition of a theme park is 'a family amusement complex orientated towards a range of subjects or historical periods, combining the continuity of costuming and architecture with entertainment through rides and other attractions, catering and merchandising, to provoke an experience for the imagination'. Irrespective of the imagescape or size, the underlying principle of the theme park product is to provide a pleasurable day out for the family, and is founded on resolving a long-established market research outcome, that families cannot stay together for more than two to three hours without bickering, unless a variety of activities are provided.

Normally, such facilities have a pay-one-price (POP) admission charge and differ from traditional amusement parks, in that they tend to be on open sites outside towns and cities, and have high management standards and finish in a themed environment, where everything is centrally owned as opposed to being made up of a large number of concessionaires. In the manner of long-established parks, they may offer 'optional' pricing in the form of free or low cost entry general admission (GA) and a 'pay-as-you-go' system, or the opportunity to buy an all-inclusive ticket or book of tickets, although these days it can all be done with an electronic 'swipe' card or wrist band.

## PARK DEVELOPMENT

The initial stage of the development process involves generating the original idea, getting a firm definition of the imagescape, understanding of the economic viability of the project, organising the ownership group and producing the master plan. Whatever is envisaged has to be commensurate with target markets and their willingness to pay. Beyond the master plan lies careful management of the design and construction process to keep to timelines and budgets, and establishing an operational plan prior to opening. The goal is to bring everything together for a successful opening day, for in the entertainment world it is very difficult for projects to recover from a poor start.

Planning a theme park is normally centred on the first and fifth years of operation, the latter being the design standard when park operations should have settled and the future of the park is established, which then gives the opportunity for any venture capital funds to sell on their interests. The market potential is made up of the resident population in the specified catchment area, visitors to the area and groups; the latter includes schools, company outings, clubs and associations. Because parks are seeking to maximise their attendance levels, they calculate the population catchment area within a specified drive time of up to two hours for cars and three to four hours for coach, bus or train. For example, the

LEGO Corporation plans its parks along the following guidelines:

- Prospective locations are in regions where toy sales are substantial and there is strong brand awareness.
- They are family parks for children aged 2–13 years and the investment of some US$200–250 million requires a resident catchment area of around 20 million, with about 50% or more being target families.
- An established tourist area yielding a steady flow of visitors to meet a design level of around 1.5 million guests.
- Attractive rural surroundings with planning permission for leisure development.
- Minimum site requirement of 40 hectares.
- Locally available support services in terms of suppliers and general tourist infrastructure.

When calculating the market penetration rates for the park, in order to ascertain likely visitor numbers, account has to be taken of disposable income, accessibility, competing attractions, the appeal of the imagescape and the level of capitalisation required to ensure that visitors have a variety of activities to enjoy during their stay and want to return. The latter is termed the 'warranted' level of investment. Generally speaking, US parks have a greater level of warranted investment and thus higher penetration rates than European parks. In part, this can also be explained by closer proximity of parks to each other in Europe, which means greater competition through overlapping catchment areas. In addition, US parks have a larger percentage of admissions as groups than Europe: established parks should generate 35–50% of their market as groups.

Theme park modelling may best be understood by taking the example illustrated in Table 13.2. The park is assumed to be year-round, but has some seasonality; the peak month being July, with an anticipated 308,000 guests in the design year. There are eight weekend/holiday days in July and 23 weekdays, with attendance at weekend days being 2.5 times those of weekdays. From this it follows that the design day is $308,000 \times 2.5/(2.5 \times 8 + 23) = 17,907$ guests. As a rule, seasonal parks may expect to have a design day of 1–2% of annual attendances. The design day is used to determine the time period in which the 'peak in ground' number would occur. The latter is arrived at by first recording likely hourly arrival rates during opening hours and then deducting departure patterns, recorded on the same basis, from arrivals; this tends to be in the range of 70–85%. Let this value be 75% of the design day, occurring late in the morning, to give a peak in ground of 13,430 upon which the infrastructure, facilities and attractions in the park will

| Table 13.2 | Design characteristics for a theme park | |
|---|---|---|
| Item | Year 1 | Design Year 5 |
| Population catchment | 14,000,000 | 14,000,000 |
| Penetration rate | 6% | 11% |
| Visitor numbers | 840,000 | 1,540,000 |
| Peak month of July | 168,000 | 308,000 |
| Design day | 9,767 | 17,907 |
| Peak in ground | 7,326 | 13,430 |
| Average entertainment units/hr | 1.5 | 1.5 |
| Total entertainment units/hr | 10,988 | 20,145 |
| Average attraction throughput/hr | 750 | 750 |
| Mean number of attractions | 14 | 26 |
| Allowing for 25% waiting time | 17 | 32 |

be based. The industry standard is that, given queuing time, 'walk-around' time and miscellaneous activities, the average guest should participate in 1.5 to 2.5 entertainment units per hour, the lower figure being typical in dry parks (with a spread of 1.2–1.8), with a higher figure being more appropriate for water parks. Taking 1.5 as the standard, then this park should have an hourly operating capacity of $1.5 \times 13,430 = 20,145$ entertainment units. Major roller coasters have ride throughputs that range from one to two thousand entertainment units per hour (the Disney model is based on approximately 1,600 per hour), but the simple provision of, say, 14 coasters is not the planning answer!

While some park operators, such as Six Flags and Wet 'n Wild, specialise in 'white knuckle' rides, the largest and best parks provide a mix of rides and shows to entertain the whole family. This will reduce average hourly throughput, for while an average coaster ride may only last in the order of two minutes (the larger ones as long as four minutes), a show can be up to a half-hour in length and family-style rides tend to have a smaller capacity. Applying an overall hourly throughput standard of 750 entertainment units indicates a 'nominal' provision of 26 attractions made up of, say, five key or 'anchor' rides that can be the focus for promotion, a mixture of 15 medium-sized round rides and capacity filling flat rides that appeal to young children, and six live shows, play areas and virtual reality attractions to round out the mix. The advantage of the latter is in terms of both cost and space, thus one can expect that a simulated ride will cost about one-tenth of the equivalent high-tech ride.

Seasonal conditions imposed by the weather and marked peaks in attendances affect capacity usage and question the viability of developments under these circumstances. The solution is to reduce the number of anchor rides and replace them with attractions that only require a moderate outlay and to increase the amount of 'soft' capacity, say in terms of seating for shows and films. As an example, the Legoland parks have a great deal of additional capacity in the form of workshops where model-makers are on display and give advice to visitors, and Miniland, which is an exhibition of their art, is a passive visual activity that can absorb a variable number of people. As well as increasing the utilisation of the rest of the park, a programme of events is also a way of adding to existing capacity without incurring long-term overheads.

## QUEUES

In spite of improvements in the design of queues as part of the fabric of the attraction, the number one guest complaint is usually paying higher entrance fees, only to wait for hours for a two-minute key ride. Traditional solutions have been to try to manage visitor flows around the park to smooth arrival patterns at the various attractions and increasing capacity. The most recent direction has been the introduction of timed/priority ticketing, for the anchor rides, such as Disney's Fast Pass, Universal's Express and Six Flags' Flash Pass. By renting a hand-held wireless device (Q-bot), guests can reserve their place in line for a number of rides and attractions. Adding to capacity means taking account of the variability in the standard 1.5 entertainment units. On average, visitors should expect to spend about 25% of their stay queuing, the exception being at peak times, but if 1.5 is the mean of a symmetric probability distribution, then only 50% of peak in-ground activities would be covered. From statistical quality control theory, the Camp-Meidell inequality shows that for symmetrical distributions the probability of an outcome that is greater than, say, $x$ standard deviations from the mean is $1/(4.5x^2)$ even if the exact probability distribution is unknown. The spread 1.2–1.8 indicates a standard deviation of 0.3 units, so a value of 1.8 (plus one standard deviation) would account for 78% of the distribution, and by interpolation 1.77 would take in 75% of peak in-ground requirements. This will raise the number of attractions at design level in Table 13.2 from 26 to 32. It is a matter of economic planning (to keep within the warranted level of investment) as to whether higher capacity rides will be added so as to maintain the design level at 26, or whether some rides may be phased in as visitor numbers adjust to the park's design year, which tends to happen, or whether dealing solely with queuing at the anchor rides will be sufficient. It is to be noted that the benefits of reducing waiting times go beyond customer satisfaction, as more time is now available to spend in the restaurants and shops.

## THEMING

Theming allows designers to give new meaning to attractions, park facilities and infrastructure, and can cost as much again or more than the attractions themselves. It tells a story that transports the visitor to another place. To be effective, the message is continually repeated in the imagescape of each zone so as to have the highest visitor impact and reinforce the entertainment value through the illusion and sense of role-play created by the use of different storylines and settings. Beyond this there are a number of more specific advantages:

- Park operators are in continual touch with the main ride and attraction manufacturers, so that there is a broad element of similarity in terms of what is on offer.
- Theming allows parks to develop a sense of individuality and product differentiation and create competitive advantage if it is a popular and well-recognised imagescape.
- A perception of quality is created.
- A memorable environment serves to increase the probability of return.
- Events may be themed for certain target markets and times, say Halloween and Christmas, to raise attendances.
- The imagescapes provide passive entertainment for seniors and family members with young children who may not wish to participate in the anchor rides,

but enjoy watching others, particularly members of their group, having a good time.

- Themed entertainment and waiting spots make queuing a less frustrating experience.
- Well themed areas, restaurants and shops can help in managing visitor flows by increasing walk-around time as well as raising secondary spend.
- Merchandise may be coordinated to themes to encourage purchase.

## THE MASTER PLAN

Once the number of rides has been agreed, they are evaluated for their place on the master layout, their suitability for the range of imagescapes proposed in the park and their contribution to the balance of the experience provided by each zone. A popular layout is the 'Hub and Spoke System', where the hub is a central facility offering restaurants, shopping, arcades, entertainment, conference rooms and other amenities (benefiting from economies of scale in infrastructure provision), while the spokes are the themed areas connecting the visitor experience. Locating refreshment points, souvenir sales and amenities appropriate to the imagescape in each zone is also necessary in order to create additional spending opportunities and allow flexibility of provision in accordance with the daily and seasonal fluctuations of visitor numbers. It is likely that the master plan will go through several iterations in refining the details, so as to optimise the park's creative appeal, effectiveness and affordability, and ensure that no particular cultural habits are overlooked, for example the tendency of the family to always lunch together in a fixed one-hour period, as in France. Of course, it is possible to over-design a park, so a normal tenet is that the 'soft' costs for professional services, pre-opening expenses and other incidental costs should not exceed 30% of the total investment.

## IMPLEMENTATION

Implementation requires setting out the master plan in a time schedule. It outlines a series of dates, termed milestones, within which activities and tasks have to be completed to advance the park to its opening in a reasonable time frame, which would be around two years for the example illustrated in Table 13.2. The project manager's job is to assign responsibility to accomplish each task to the development team and to ensure they hold to the goals and objectives of the master schedule. These tasks will encompass: raising finance, obtaining planning permissions from public authorities, construction and ride procurement, and operational planning.

The latter includes the recruitment and training of staff, marketing, the progression of shows and entertainment, and arranging the various support services, such as ticketing, catering, merchandising and matters concerning the health and safety of guests.

The development process does not stop at the design year: parks encourage repeat visits through festivals and events, re-theming old attractions and spending some 5–10% of their initial attraction investment on launching new rides, preferably to offer something new every year. A working rule of thumb is to put aside for reinvestment the equivalent of depreciation each year. Annual developments are usually fairly modest, but the larger parks do compete in trying to have several 'firsts' in their portfolios and therefore introduce major attractions every two or three years to boost custom, though few can compete with the Universal's Wizarding World of Harry Potter at US$265 million.

*Source*: Updated from Wanhill, 2008

## DISCUSSION QUESTIONS

1. Taking the example in Table 13.2, describe the kinds of attractions you would think appropriate to fill out the mix.

2. Branded parks such as Disneylands, Legolands and Universal Studios seem to be continuously successful. What are the reasons for this?

3. To what extent does the 'hybrid' nature of the theme parks limit international expansion?

# CHAPTER 14
## ACCOMMODATION

### LEARNING OUTCOMES

During this chapter, we will focus on the accommodation sector and some of the issues that currently influence it. The learning objectives for this chapter, therefore, may be defined as:

- identifying and assessing the scope of the accommodation sector of the hospitality industry;
- understanding the structure of the accommodation sector, the role of brands and the different ownership models that predominate;
- assimilating the sector's historical development and the effect of this on today's operation; and
- discussing some of the key issues that dominate the sector today and that will influence its future development.

Photograph: Casa Batlló, Barcelona, Spain © Sundus Pasha

# INTRODUCTION

Accommodation or lodging is, by a long way, the largest and most ubiquitous sub-sector within the tourism economy. With few exceptions, tourists require a location where they can rest and revive during their travels through, or stay within, a tourism destination. We can therefore see that accommodation is an important support facility in Leiper's destination region and, with few exceptions, commercial accommodation facilities are found wherever tourists venture. Of course, there is great diversity in the size, type and organisation of this accommodation. This diversity ranges through:

- accommodation that provides for one or more guests in simple, home-style facilities, the 'bed and breakfast', to 'bedroom factories', hotels that operate with a capacity to cater for up to 5,000 guests;
- accommodation in a very basic, functional form, or in extreme luxury and opulence;
- ownership which can be private and informal, or accommodation that may be provided within units operated by major multinational organisations; and
- accommodation that meets the needs of guests with varying requirements and motivations for travel – for example, business, conventions, leisure and pilgrimage.

In short, accommodation is characterised by extreme heterogeneity and any attempt to generalise about the sector must take this into account.

In this chapter, we are primarily concerned with those establishments and organisations that provide places of rest and revival on a commercial and organised basis. We therefore give rather less consideration to lodging in the VFR sector where accommodation is, usually, within the family or friend's home being visited – this contrasts with what we might describe as the 'commercial home' within which paying guests are taken into a personal home on a business basis (Di Domenico and Lynch, 2007). Although VFR is, in many countries, the most important tourist motivation, its value to the commercial accommodation sector is generally more limited.

This chapter, therefore, is mainly concerned with:

- fully or partially serviced accommodation such as hotels, motels, rhyokan (a Japanese-style lodging house), aparthotels, guest houses, bed and breakfasts, and farmhouses;
- self-catering accommodation such as apartments, country cottages, gites, campus accommodation, camping and static caravan sites, and timeshare;
- accommodation support facilities where provision is made for campers, caravanners and trailer owners who bring their own accommodation with them, in other words mobile sites; and
- accommodation within mobile transportation such as cruise ships, ferries, trains and airliners.

These accommodation types vary in their importance and contribution to both domestic and international tourism. There are also close links between accommodation providers and other sectors within tourism where the cross-sectoral characteristics of tourism organisations are increasing with integration in the tourism industry. For example, hotels have always been major providers of food service but this role has, as we shall see, changed significantly in recent years. Hotels are also, however, major providers of leisure, sporting and entertainment facilities as well as business and conference services. Likewise, accommodation's relationship with transportation is of long standing but it is increasing in its sophistication and complexity, as transport providers recognise that accommodation can be an attraction to guests in its own right and not just a necessary service to be provided en route.

## ACCOMMODATION AND THE TOURISM PRODUCT

In the context of the tourism sector in general, accommodation rarely has a place or rationale in its own right. It is rare for a tourist to select to stay in a hotel or other form of accommodation for its own sake. Rather, the choice is made because the accommodation provides a support service for the wider motivation that has brought the visitor to the destination, whether for business or leisure purposes. It is arguable that some resort hotels may fall outside this generalisation in that guests may choose to stay at Greenbriars or Gleneagles because of the accommodation experience that such hotels provide but, generally, this motivation will be coupled with the desire to avail themselves of a wider tourism product within the resort or locality. That said, an emerging trend in many destinations is for the need to provide the discerning tourist with an innovative or even unusual mix of accommodation in which to stay. In such instances, 'unusual places to stay' become the essence of the visit experience rather than as an ancillary product or service.

Ultimately, accommodation is a necessary component in the development of tourism within any destination that seeks to serve visitors other than day-trippers. The quality and range of accommodation available will both reflect and influence the range of visitors to a location. As such, achieving the appropriate balance of accommodation to meet the destination's strategic tourism development objectives can be a challenge. It is arguable, for example, that the inability of traditional destinations such as the Isle of Man to create new market opportunities in the wake of the decline of its traditional visitor base (family holidays) was directly linked to its old and inflexible accommodation stock. We can identify situations where accommodation is seen as part of the overall tourism infrastructure without which tourists will not visit the location. It therefore also assists in attracting wider investment in the tourism product at the locality. For example, the province of Newfoundland, in Canada, built four hotels in strategic locations as part of its tourism development strategy in the early 1980s. Accommodation can also feature as an element in wider economic development strategies. The town of Akueryi, in Iceland, built and operates a hotel at a deficit because it is seen as an essential support facility for wider economic development, particularly in the fisheries sector. More recently, the phenomenal growth in hotel construction in the likes of Dubai and parts of coastal China represent perfect examples of where accommodation is an integral but varied role in the wider development of tourism.

Accommodation also plays an important role in the overall economic contribution which tourism makes at a local and national level. It is difficult to generalise about the proportion of total tourist expenditure that is allocated to accommodation because this varies greatly according to the market, accommodation type and nature of product purchased. As a very general rule, perhaps 33% of total trip expenditure is allocated to this sector but this varies greatly between different market segments. It decreases in the case of fully inclusive packages to, for example, the Mediterranean resorts where intermediaries negotiate low-cost bulk purchases of apartments or hotel rooms. By contrast, the proportion may be considerably higher in the case of domestic tourism where transportation costs are, generally, lower than is the case with international travel. Accommodation may be sold as a **loss leader** to promote expenditure on other components of the tourism product in casino and other specialist resorts. Off-season offers are frequently promoted whereby hotel rooms are provided 'free' on condition that guests purchase a specified minimum in terms of food and beverages. This strategy recognises important dimensions of the accommodation sector:

- demand is highly volatile and fluctuates on a seasonal and weekly basis; and
- accommodation can act as the catalyst for a range of additional sales opportunities within complex tourism and hospitality businesses – traditionally, casino hotels have discounted accommodation in anticipation of generating considerable profits from customers at the gaming tables, while golfing hotels may seek to generate profits from green fees rather than room revenues.

Indeed, accommodation pricing in general is a complex and, sometimes, controversial area. Rack room rates (those formally published as the price of the room) are rarely achieved and extensive discounting for group bookings, advance reservations and corporate contracts are widespread. Fixed pricing is generally only successful and commonplace within the budget hotel sector. Yield, measured against potential, often runs at little more than 60% in the mid- to upper-market levels of the hotel industry in some countries, although locations such as Hong Kong are very different and see occupancy percentage rates running in the high 80s and above, with some in the high 90s. Yield maximisation systems are in place, within most large companies, in order to ensure that achieved rates are designed to optimise occupancy potential. Managing contracts in order to maximise yield is also an important strategy for accommodation units with the objective of replacing low-yield groups or aircrew business with higher yield business or fully inclusive tour (FIT) guests.

# DEFINING THE ACCOMMODATION SECTOR

## Hotels

Hotels are undoubtedly the most significant and visible sub-sector within accommodation or lodging. Although a highly varied collection of properties in most countries, hotels are the tourism sub-sector that provides the greatest total employment in global terms and probably accounts for the highest level of receipts. The traditional view of a hotel was an establishment providing accommodation as well as food and beverage services to short-stay guests on a paying basis. This view has influenced most attempts to define hotels. But, as we shall see later in this chapter, this is a somewhat inadequate description in view of the growth of ancillary activities commonly associated with the hotel sector (leisure, business, etc.) and the withdrawal of many hotel companies from the operation of food and beverage services entirely.

In many countries of the world, hotel businesses are dominated by small, family-owned operations, which have developed hand-in-hand with the tourism sector often earlier in the twentieth century and, in particular, since 1945. Thus, the typical hotel business is represented by 30-bedroom seafront establishments in resorts, country house hotels or the wide range of city properties. This small business sector has declined in importance in recent years, faced with the challenge of branded multiple operators offering a range of products from budget to luxury. The cost of reinvestment in order to meet changing consumer demand combined with the marketing and operational challenges posed by technology have forced many hotels of this kind out of business. Those that do survive successfully in the contemporary tourism industry do so because they have recognised the importance of niche marketing by tailoring their products and services to meet the specific niche requirements of identified market groups. An important survival strategy for small, independent hotels is membership of a marketing consortium representing similar operations at a national or international level. Best Western and Golden Tulip are two of the best-known international **consortia**.

The group or chain component of the hotel sub-sector accounts for upwards of 10% of the property stock in most European countries but this figure is much higher in South-East Asia and in North America. In terms of the bedroom inventory of most countries, the percentage penetration of groups/chains is rather greater:

- up to 40% of the total in the UK; and
- over 60% in the USA.

This reflects the fact that hotels that are part of multiples tend to be considerably larger (and generally more recently built) than independents. The almost universal trend in the hotel sub-sector is for multiples to gain market share from independent operators within expanding markets.

Ownership and management of hotels reflect the growing complexity of business formats within the private sector generally. There are three major operating models with various combinations:

1. Hotel companies may *own and operate* the hotels that are marketed under their name or they may have a part equity stake in the property.

2. Alternatively, the hotel may be operated and owned by a *franchise partner* – this is a rapidly growing business format, especially within the budget market. Franchises may be operated at an individual property level or as part of a master franchise arrangement whereby a company owns or operates a large number of properties, typically at a national or regional level, under the umbrella of an established brand or brands.

**3.** Finally, the hotel company may *manage the property on behalf of an owner* – this is a common format at the top end of the international market, to be found in the portfolios of major companies such as Hilton, Hyatt, Inter-Continental and Marriott.

A major influence on the publicly quoted hotel sector in recent years has been that of increasingly focused performance demands placed upon operators by stock market investors. In the past, especially in Europe, average return on investment within the hotel sector was considerably below that achieved in other industrial and service sectors. This reflects in part the small business structure of hotel companies as well as perceptions of an operating culture that sets hotels apart from other businesses – one where the focus was on hospitality rather than profitability. The view was that the two were, in some way, incompatible. This perception lost its primacy in North America some time before influencing the European industry. The success of many Asian companies in combining the two objectives of profitable service and excellence has led to change in Europe as well. Companies such as Accor, Marriott and Premier Travel Inn, each owners and operators of a portfolio of different hotel brands, now operate to profit criteria designed to satisfy City interests as their first priority.

## Boutique hotels

One of the newest forms of accommodation, first popularised in the USA and UK, is the boutique hotel which relates to accommodation normally of a highly individual, quality and full-service hotel, frequently on a distinct theme. One example of such a hotel is The Chocolate Boutique Hotel in Bournemouth on the south coast of England which, as the name suggests, expressly offers guests a chocolate extravaganza (see **http://www.thechocolateboutiquehotel .co.uk/**). Although they often vary in size, boutique hotels tend to be located in the main cities with their ultimate point of differentiation being the need to avoid the uniformity of corporate hotels. That said, a number of the larger chains are beginning to include boutique-style hotels in their portfolios as they begin to recognise the market appeal, especially among discerning travellers, of this type of accommodation.

## Guest houses, bed and breakfasts, farmhouse accommodation, inns

This sub-sector brings together a number of different types of operation with the common characteristics of offering accommodation plus some food and beverage (often just breakfast) in a small, family-style environment. Such properties may provide many similar facilities to smaller hotels, although the category also includes simple and limited operations where guests may share facilities and, indeed, meals with their hosts.

Internationally there are significant contrasts in the operation of this sub-sector:

- In the UK, bed and breakfast and guest house enterprises are not significantly different, although the former require fewer controls in order to operate. Indeed, it is a sub-sector where many operators take guests on a seasonal or sporadic basis and, as a result, can offer a flexible accommodation resource to a city or locality, available for use as and when required, but without large fixed costs, particularly in terms of labour. Although with a heritage of being a cheaper alternative to small and niche hotels, the bed and breakfast or guest house has gradually closed the gap in terms of perceived quality in relation to expectation and price.

**YOUTUBE**
Boutique hotels

Boutique Hotel Internet Marketing Case Study
http://www.youtube.com/watch?v=1cfdCGZqkac

- Bed and breakfast enterprises in the USA, however, tend to be rather more sophisticated in their approach and comprehensive in their services. In European terms, they resemble inns or small hotels and are frequently members of national or regional marketing consortia.

- In Canada, inns are similar and can be grouped together on a themed or regional basis for marketing purposes. The Historic Inns of Atlantic Canada is one example and membership depends upon a number of criteria, of which one is age – all properties must have been built before 1930. Some Canadian inns offer very sophisticated facilities. One example is the Spruce Pine Acres Country Inn in Port au Port, Newfoundland, which is a modern, purpose-built facility with just six bedrooms, but its services also include a licensed dining room, a well-equipped meeting room and full electronic business provision.

Farmhouse accommodation is a central component in the growing international agri-tourism movement. Not only has this become a major feature of tourism development in a number of countries such as Ireland and New Zealand, but it is also a component in the development plans of countries in Eastern Europe and Asia. Accommodation is, generally, similar to that afforded by bed and breakfast operations but the context is different. Provision is usually within a working farm environment and guests may be able to participate in various aspects of the agricultural working routine as part of their stay. Marketing of farmhouse accommodation includes consortia operating at a national and/or international level.

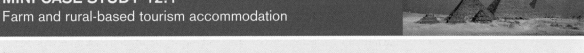

## MINI CASE STUDY 12.1
Farm and rural-based tourism accommodation

Farm and rural-based tourism accommodation is of increasing appeal to many markets, especially families, where you get the combined benefits of comfortable, friendly and highly hospitable accommodation and an authentic, natural and rural holiday experience. Such provision is popular in many countries around the world, including the UK, with parts of Italy and France well endowed with quality farm and rural-based accommodation. In many ways, Italy is at the forefront of such initiatives, with many parts of the country well stocked with quality accommodation where visitors can switch off, relax and enjoy the natural environment and be at one with nature. Such an experience also offers visitors a chance to experience local food and drink and see how the local population live and eat – including the making of authentic pasta!

India, not traditionally well known for such a provision, is also now tapping into this relatively niche form of accommodation for those wishing to escape the demands of the cities and avoid the 'sameness' of some of

**Photograph 14.1**   Making pasta.
*Source*: Corbis Bridge/Alamy Images

| Photograph 14.2 | Agritourism in Italy.
*Source*: MARKA/Alamy Images |

the larger, more corporate-style of hotels. One such example is the picturesque Rutu Farm which offers visitors an exceptional experience in an idyllic setting at the foothills of Panchgani, approximately 1.5 hours drive from Pune. Not only can you benefit from the rural beauty of the area but you are also able to experience the religious side of life in rural India. Unsurprisingly, although televisions are available in a common dining area, no televisions are evident in the bedrooms. As for WiFi and Internet connectivity, neither represent part of the farm and rural tourism experience!

## DISCUSSION QUESTIONS

1. What markets are likely to be particularly interested in farm and rural-based holidays?
2. How may the saturation of new technologies in most parts of everyday life impact on the future appeal of an authentic farm and rural-based holiday in the future?
3. What may be some of the benefits and drawbacks of 'branding' farm and rural-based accommodation?

Small, independent operators across this sub-sector face significant challenges from the growing budget hotel sector, especially in Europe. In physical product terms, there may be considerable similarities between the two in terms of their bedrooms – indeed, budget properties may well exceed the competition in this respect. For example, the growth of the budget sector has forced the generally unregulated family-style property in the UK to upgrade their facilities or to cease operating. As a result, many such operations now provide en-suite bathrooms, multi-channel television and tea- and coffee-making facilities.

### Self-catering accommodation – apartments, cottages, gîtes, etc.

Self-catering accommodation is an important and varied component of the lodging sector within tourism. Essentially, what such properties have in common is a combination of accommodation with additional recreational areas and the facility to prepare food on a personal basis.

Apartments form a major element within the accommodation available in many Mediterranean resorts but the sector also includes:

- individual cottages and gîtes – frequently adapted from normal residential use; and
- purpose-built cottage colonies developed and marketed as a distinct brand – for example, Rent an Irish Cottage, established in 1968 by Shannon Development (a public sector body) but subsequently sold off to private interests in the early 1990s.

Self-catering holiday accommodation may be rented as part of a vacation package, through an agency or independently directly from the owner. Alternatively, holiday accommodation owner-ship is a major component in the tourism industries of some countries and specific destinations. This is so much so in some places that in the off-season communities can be just a fraction of those at peak periods. In some countries, ownership of a country or beach cottage is common-place and not confined to the wealthy, as in Scandinavia – for example, Norway with the seaside or mountain *hutte*. Where holiday homes are not purpose-built but purchased within the normal housing environment, they can create considerable distortion to the local property market and resentment within local communities through rising prices that exclude younger residents from the local housing market. North and West Wales and the coastal regions of Cornwall are exam-ples of areas where holiday homes from time to time have become a sensitive political issue. In Denmark, the ownership of second homes is confined to people residing in the country for taxa-tion purposes, which excludes the offshore ownership that can be found in many Mediterranean destinations. (The community issues arising from second-home ownership are reviewed and discussed in more detail in Part 2, dealing with the impacts of tourism.)

It is quite common for local residents' homes to form the accommodation for self-catering vacations. This may be through a number of mechanisms:

- House-swap schemes, by which a family from, say, Sweden, exchanges homes for a month with counterparts (often in the same professional or work area) from Canada; the exchange may include use of vehicles and responsibility for pets as well as accommodation.
- Major events can also prompt local residents to vacate their homes in favour of visitors on a pay basis – SW19 in London experiences much of this during Wimbledon tennis fortnight, as does the village of Silverstone during the British Formula 1 Grand Prix weekend.

## Campus accommodation

Campus accommodation includes facilities that are used both within and outside the tourism sector. For much of the time, most campus accommodation is used on a semi-permanent basis by students, as many readers of this book will know. However, increasingly, universities and colleges seek to utilise a resource that is underused during major periods of the year when students are on vacation. Accommodation is, therefore, widely used not only for conference and meetings purposes, but also as a leisure location, especially by campuses close to scenic or vacation areas. In addition, some campuses include permanent hotel-style facilities, designed for short-term visitors such as those attending executive development modules in business schools. Generally, the trend is towards upgrading facilities in campus accommodation so that its use for non-student lets is competitive with other accommodation providers. The marketing of campus facilities is also now professional – in Scotland, an umbrella organisation, the Scottish Universi-ties Accommodation Consortium, is responsible for supporting this aspect.

## Time-share and fractional ownership

Time-share or fractional ownership is a form of period-constrained (i.e. one or two weeks a year) self-catering holiday home ownership, which provides additional benefits to owners in the form of possible access to similar properties in resorts throughout the world through exchange consortia. Many time-share properties also provide a range of additional services and facilities, including food service and sports/recreation so that they have much in common with resort hotels. Pressure selling of timeshare has gained the sector a bad reputation in some countries.

## Youth accommodation

Youth travel is an important, growing and little researched sector of the tourism market. The extent of such travel and the specific facilities designed to meet its needs vary greatly between countries. Young people tend to utilise accommodation at the low-cost end of the market – bed and breakfasts, youth hostels such as those run by the Youth Hostel Association (YHA), Young Men's Christian Association (YMCA) and Young Women's Christian Association (YWCA) and their local equivalents as well as camp sites. Books such as *Cheap Sleeps Europe* (Wood, 2005) and *Eastern Europe on a Shoestring* (Stanley, 1997) provide information and listings of establishments with quality guidance based on user experience. Such information across the accommodation range is also increasingly available via web blogs which give potential customers a very direct source of information on guest experiences in establishments.

Specialist accommodation providers to the youth market, such as youth hostels in many countries, YMCA/YWCAs and backpacker hostels in Australia, have moved from offering simple, frequently dormitory-style accommodation, to providing greater comfort, a more sophisticated product and more comprehensive services. In some cases, there is little to distinguish these providers from equivalently priced hotel products – the YMCA in Hong Kong is a good example. These trends reflect changing youth market demand, expectations and travel experience together with the increasing affluence of young people in many countries.

## Camping and caravan sites

An important component in the domestic and international tourism of many countries is that where visitors bring their own accommodation to the destination in the form of tents, caravans or trailers. The accommodation levels provided on these sites has improved greatly from the camping experience of earlier generations but is still restricted in terms of space and privacy. An important provider, within tourism, is the sub-sector offering sites for campers or caravanners. Such sites may be basic fields with few if any utilities provided or sophisticated resort locations including a range of comfort services as well as leisure, food service and retail options. While camping stereotypes often conjure up images of low-value tourism, more recent developments in camping and caravanning are very much at the upper end of the market with the camping 'experience' enjoyed by high- as well as low-end markets.

Some sites offer permanently sited tents or caravans and tourists travel to the locations for a one- or two-week stay. Companies such as Eurocamp package these site holidays in Mediterranean locations for north European clients on very much the same basis as hotel or apartment-based fully inclusive packages. Permanent caravan sites include vehicles for short-term let, as well as those owned by visitors who may use the accommodation on a regular basis throughout the season.

## Medical facility accommodation

This area is not normally seen as part of the tourism industry although facilities in hospitals, especially private institutions, are close to the best available within tourism accommodation. However, some specialist medical facilities also offer quality accommodation to relatives and friends. This may be true of premium children's hospitals, for example.

**YOUTUBE**
New Zealand!

New Zealand brand new camping van
http://www.youtube.com/watch?v=w4Sg72o6_m8

Nursing homes and other long-stay facilities for the elderly, likewise, are not normally associated with tourism. However, this market has attracted increasing attention from hotel companies such as Accor and Marriott which have developed a long-stay product for the seniors market which is a hybrid of a luxury hotel and a nursing home, offering medical as well as leisure facilities within the one establishment.

In Eastern Europe, countries such as Romania have spa tourism where resorts offer integrated medical treatment and hotel accommodation at all levels from the very basic to the very luxurious.

## Cruise liners and ferries

Long-distance passenger liners were, of course, the main form of transport for those wishing for transatlantic or intercontinental travel in the era that preceded the development of wide-bodied jets. Such liners provided functional accommodation to all but first-class passengers, designed as a necessary facility and ancillary to the prime purpose of transport. Likewise, ferries provided functional but limited accommodation services.

The growth of cruising from European and North American ports in the 1960s grew as an alternative use for the now-redundant liners and little attempt was made to alter the form of accommodation or the attendant facilities provided. Accommodation management also retained a marine and functional ethos. The building of dedicated cruise ships has changed the focus of on-board services from one where the main purpose was transport to an environment where the cruise itself became equally important to the destinations visited. The popularity of the 'cruise to nowhere' concept in South-East Asia testifies to this. Modern cruise ships have more in common with all-inclusive resorts than with traditional marine transport. From an accommodation perspective, they are designed to offer comfort, facilities and service comparable to that of equivalent resort hotels. Indeed, the terminology used and the culture is that of hotel services. Ferries, too, have changed in a similar way, particularly those offering longer services between, for example, the UK and Scandinavia or Spain.

## Trains and aircraft

Although luxuriously appointed accommodation as part of train travel has a long history, the more common model was akin to seaborne comfort. The natural constraints of space which railways impose on sleeping accommodation are difficult to overcome and, as a result, most overnight sleeper facilities remain basic and functional. However, there has been a revival of luxury, on-train accommodation, spearheaded by companies such as the Orient Express in Europe and between Singapore and Bangkok, as well as by a number of operators in India, Australia and South Africa. These trains, either modernised versions of old rolling stock or purpose-built, provide hotel comforts to the maximum permitted by space constraints.

Aircraft are faced with similar space constraints in providing sleeping accommodation for regular fare-paying passengers. A number of first-class products make claims to provide bed-like comfort for long-haul travellers, with similar provision but on a lower scale for business class. However, by comparison with their hotel equivalents, even the best of these products is akin to dormitory-style accommodation with a lack of real space or individual privacy, though the new Airbus 380, which is the world's largest passenger jet and can seat up to 800 passengers, offers considerable variations in configurations to raise the level of comfort. Most customer airlines are planning for 555 seats in a three-cabin layout.

## Visiting friends and relatives

While outside the commercial accommodation sector, VFR tourists generally, but not exclusively, utilise facilities within the homes of their family or friends. As a result, their economic contribution to a community or region may be limited but, nonetheless, VFR constitutes a major element within the tourism industries of many countries, especially domestic tourism. In many developed countries, as family ties continue to weaken, it is likely that fewer and fewer people may use the VFR option. Where the return home is to a society that is markedly different from

**YOUTUBE**
Trends and new types of accommodation

Emerging Trends in the Hotel Industry
http://www.youtube.com/watch?v=QTVGrFWAkjo

2011 Annual Trends® In the Hotel Industry
http://www.youtube.com/watch?v=VQ0_3ofKJXw

Future of Travel Industry Google Travel and Tourism Conference Keynote by Futurist
Dr Patrick
http://www.youtube.com/watch?v=L1C1chw1l4U

Husky Sledding from Tipi Base Camp
http://www.youtube.com/watch?v=pjsxxFkVx0I

Treehouse holidays in Kent UK
http://www.youtube.com/watch?v=fi3lDKt3RRI

The Ice Hotel – Sweden
http://www.youtube.com/watch?v=0NmLaFDJXKU

that where the tourists originate (for example, Afro- or Irish-American visitors to their roots), it is quite likely that commercial accommodation providers will be used for VFR trips, although payment may well be by the host family rather than the visitors.

# THE DISTINCTIVE NATURE OF ACCOMMODATION

In addition to the heterogeneous nature of the accommodation industry discussed above, the hospitality and accommodation sector is distinct from other industries in three areas.

The first of these areas is the concept that hospitality and accommodation comprise both tangible and intangible factors. The tangible aspects of hospitality and accommodation would include the physical surroundings, the equipment needed to provide hospitality and accommodation, the decor, the location and perhaps the food and beverages that were consumed by the guest. The management of the tangible aspects of hospitality and accommodation are complex and guests will make judgements concerning the appearance and surroundings of a commercial accommodation provider in comparison to their expectations. Similarly, while the provision of food and beverages at its most basic level merely satisfies essential human needs, the dining experience often forms an integral aspect of the overall accommodation experience and the provision of food and beverages is considered important as it will influence a staying guest's lasting memories. In addition, the management of food and beverages is further complicated by the guest's not unreasonable expectation to be provided with food and beverages that have been appropriately and hygienically produced and served.

In comparison, the intangible aspects of hospitality and accommodation are potentially much more complicated than the tangible aspects and would include the atmosphere present in an establishment and, importantly, the service that the consumers of the product experience.

Most hospitality and accommodation products are a combination of both tangible objects and intangible performances or experiences. The tangible/intangible emphasis will depend on both the accommodation provider and the activity. For example, a guest's experience in a hotel restaurant will involve the combined effect of numerous intangible activities – including the acquisition of supplies, the preparation of the meal and the serving of the meal. The tangible components behind all this – the building, the interior decor, the kitchen equipment, the table, the chairs, the cutlery and of course the food items are obviously necessary for the service, but it is the intangible service activities that make up the key product offering. On the other hand, while there will be greater emphasis on intangible aspects concerning the concierge activity in a hotel, it is the tangible aspects of accommodation provision that will outweigh the intangibles.

The second area concerns the inseparability of the production and consumption of goods and services in the hospitality and accommodation sector. Essentially this means that the guest has to be present during the production and consumption of the accommodation provision – the guest has to be present during the overnight stay. This is in contrast to the provision of a physical good, such as a washing machine, that may be manufactured in China but consumed in the UK.

The concept of inseparability in the provision of goods and services in the hospitality and accommodation sector further means that the goods and services consumed by the guest or customer have no lasting value. While it is recognised that the guest will benefit from staying in a hotel overnight, apart from the memory of the stay the guest will experience no lasting physical benefit from the experience. Similarly, eating a meal in a hospitality provider will satisfy the customer's hunger; however, that customer will start to feel hungry again in four or five hours. Compare this to the purchase of a washing machine that will continue performing the task for which it was bought for a number of years.

The third area that distinguishes accommodation from other industries is the fact that it is immediately perishable. Essentially this means that accommodation cannot be stored and if it is not sold for any given night, the opportunity for the sale is lost forever. Even if all subsequent nights are full due to a sudden surge in demand, lost revenue from the previous empty night can never be recovered. Demand, therefore, plays an especially significant role in the production and delivery of accommodation. In certain accommodation situations where demand is steady, for example in public institutions, the concept of perishability does not pose a significant problem. However, the majority of accommodation providers experience seasonal fluctuations in demand, which affect both the management of accommodation provision and the nature of the investment. For example, in high latitude destinations where the main summer season is short, it is very difficult to justify more than basic hotel provision and in peripheral areas only chalet-style or static caravan developments may be justified.

# THE MANAGEMENT OF COMMERCIAL ACCOMMODATION

While it is recognised that the management of commercial accommodation provision is a complicated business and it is beyond the scope of this chapter to discuss all aspects of this activity, this section aims to highlight two fairly unique aspects of the management of such businesses.

First, the concept of overbooking is relatively common within commercial accommodation. Overbooking is the act of selling more rooms than are actually available in an attempt to ensure that the accommodation element of the business is full. This activity has increased in popularity due to the number of reservation cancellations and no-shows that are experienced in commercial accommodation provision. For example, according to the reservation system, a hotel might be fully booked; however, guests' plans may change, resulting in their cancelling their reservation, or not informing the hotel and just not turning up. Depending on the time of year, the level of cancellations and no-shows might be as high as 15%, and in order to combat this, hotels will regularly overbook by a similar amount.

Overbooking is, however, a sensitive activity and should a guest with a reservation turn up and not obtain a room then, technically, the hotel has breached the contract with that guest. Due to potential legal liability and the substantial damage to the hotel's reputation and goodwill, some hotels have completely eliminated the practice of intentional overbooking. Others continue to take that risk in an effort to ensure that their hotel is completely full, but safeguard themselves by making out-booking arrangements with other properties, usually with an upgrade for the guest to compensate for the inconvenience.

Secondly, and in an effort more closely to manage the reservation system and as a means of ensuring the maximum number of rooms are full at any given time, accommodation providers have increasingly been adopting concepts such as yield or revenue management. Donaghy et al. (1995) consider that yield management is a revenue maximisation technique which aims to increase the net yield (or revenue) through the predicted allocation of available accommodation capacity to predetermined market segments at optimum price. First developed in the airline industry (which also suffers from acute perishability), yield or, as it is more commonly known today, revenue management (Schwartz, 2003) has been adopted by many commercial accommodation providers. Essentially yield management means that the accommodation provider sells accommodation to the right people at the right price and at the right time. Practically speaking, the accommodation provider might examine historical reservation charts in an effort to identify periods of low demand. Thereafter, rooms that have proved difficult to sell in the past will be subject to marketing, advertising and discounting as a means of stimulating demand. The accommodation provider will adopt a flexible pricing policy based on the number of rooms available and the demand for those rooms. Indeed the cost of accommodation might increase the closer to the date the reservation is made. Thus it is usual for guests to be paying a variety of rates for staying in the same type of room, in the same hotel, on the same night. This activity will also assist accommodation providers in identifying periods of high demand and ensuring that rooms are not sold at a discounted rate, thus maximising yield.

# SECTORAL OVERLAP

The accommodation sector may or may not exist in organisational isolation from other sectors of the tourism economy. In other words, there are operations that provide accommodation facilities and nothing else to their customers – some budget hotel products, self-catering cottages and campsites are examples of businesses where there may be minimal horizontal integration with other activities in tourism. By contrast, there are operations where accommodation is just one of a range of integrated tourism services provided by the one organisation. All-inclusive resorts and cruise ships, offering a wide range of entertainment, leisure, retail and food service facilities in addition to accommodation, provide good examples. The problem, from a definitional point of view, is that terms in the accommodation area are used very loosely so that the word 'hotel' may be employed to describe a small, family-owned bed and breakfast establishment, a budget hotel, a luxury country house property or an integrated resort such as Gleneagles in Scotland. As a result, official definitions are rarely of much value and are mainly used in order to regulate or grade the sector.

An important trend, in the hotel sector, is the disaggregation of accommodation from other aspects of hotel services, particularly in the moderate and economy sectors of the marketplace. The customer may not always be aware of this disaggregation because it frequently represents a business rather than a service arrangement. Both Hallam and Baum (1996) and Espino et al. (2006) discuss the growing trend towards outsourcing food and beverage services within hotels, either to individual operators or to branded chain restaurants, allowing some hotel companies to concentrate on high-yield, low-cost accommodation provision while ensuring that their customers have access to appropriate food service opportunities. Other concepts, such as Embassy All-Suites in the USA, and Travelodge in the budget sector in the UK, have been designed as almost exclusively accommodation providers, encouraging guests to make use of external food service, leisure and entertainment facilities. This disaggregation process appears to represent a growing trend in the tourism industry at one end of the market. At the other end, increasingly sophisticated integrated all-inclusive resort provision points in the opposite direction.

# SECTOR ORIGINS AND THE INFLUENCE OF THE USA

Accommodation has been a travel requirement since the first trading, missionary and pilgrimage routes were established in Asia and Europe in pre-Christian times. The basis of such accommodation was, generally, non-paying with travellers provided with a roof and sustenance as part of religious obligation or in the hope that similar hospitality might be offered to the host in the future. Possibly the first reference to commercial accommodation provision in Europe comes from thirteenth-century Florence but an identifiable commercial accommodation sector cannot really be identified until the late eighteenth century when coaching inns in Britain developed in response to organised stagecoach travel and the first large hotels were opened in France and the USA. The dawn of the railway era stimulated hotel development in many countries of Europe and elsewhere and the railway companies were among the main promoters of hotel building, proximate or integral to main termini in cities such as New York, London or Edinburgh. In many respects, these were the first hotel multiples or chains with which we are familiar today.

The latter half of the nineteenth century also saw increased travel stimulate the development of some of the great luxury hotels of the major capital cities of the world, many of which continue to set standards of luxury for the industry today. Hotels such as the Waldorf Astoria in New York, the Savoy, Dorchester and Claridges in London and the Ritz in Paris all date from this era. Raffles in Singapore and the Taj Mahal in Mumbai, while somewhat different in the motivation for their establishment, also date from the same period and represent a tradition of European-style accommodation or hotel-keeping which provided the dominant model until superseded by the American approach in the late 1940s and early 1950s. At the other end of the luxury scale, the growth of popular and accessible tourism options in most industrialised countries stimulated the development of low-cost seaside accommodation in resorts such as Deauville, Douglas, Blackpool and Atlantic City.

The post-1945 period saw the development of the American model of accommodation management and operations. Dominated, in its early days, by concepts of standardisation, risk-avoidance and the application of Fordian principles of mass production, the American model is one that has spawned most of the major hotel corporations which increasingly dominate the international accommodation sector: Hilton, Hyatt, Holiday Inn, Sheraton and InterContinental all have their origins in this concept of the hotel, although not all the companies in question are American-owned today.

The American influence on the contemporary accommodation or lodging sector has been profound and it is arguable that this source continues to dominate new ideas, products and systems. The European concept of professional hospitality has been very important, especially in translating service from the *mine host* environment of the small hospitality business into larger organisations in all parts of the world. Similarly, the more recent influence of Asian service cannot be underestimated. The American contribution has been to apply successive industrial models to the accommodation sector and thus create the foundations of an industrial sector from what was a loose amalgam of small business enterprises. While the American influence has been most noticeable within the hotel sector, the impact has been felt in other sub-sectors such as bed and breakfast and cruise liners. The American influence has been wide-ranging and we will only address a selection of examples here.

- The mass mobility of millions of Americans, previewed in the 1930s and a true reality in the post-1945 era, created roadside demand for value and informal accommodation which led to the motel concept, the forerunner of today's chain budget or economy lodge. With minimum service, these largely family-run operations were opened along all main highways in the country and established a new form of accessible and low-cost accommodation available to a segment of the population which, previously, had been unable to afford conventional hotels. The heyday of the motel was the 1940s and 1950s before they were overtaken by the chain or franchise alternatives of the major lodging companies. However, the old-style, independent motel is still to be found in more remote parts of the USA – a journey along Highway 1 through Maine and to the Canadian border passes a large number of such businesses to which few changes or compromises to modernity have been made since their opening some 50 years ago.

- The creation of the standardised chain offering common services, prices and reducing the risk in accommodation choice for the frequent traveller is commonly attributed to Kemmons Wilson and the foundation of the Holiday Inn chain in 1952. Wilson developed the idea for Holiday Inns as a result of the unpredictable quality and prices of motels that he had experienced (Nickson, 1997). As a result of this, Holiday Inns were based and developed on the notion of concept standardisation, to ensure operational control and guest consistency.

Wilson also introduced franchising into the accommodation sector on a large scale for the first time, thus facilitating rapid growth for his concept and, at the same time, applying strict operating standards and consistency to a previously unregulated area of the tourism industry.

- Holiday Inn was one example of the growth of hotel chains or groups, some standardised and some not, which became an important feature of the American lodging industry – household names such as Hilton, Hyatt, InterContinental, Marriott and Sheraton all have their origins from this period when multiple hotel operations were unusual elsewhere in the world and, where they existed, rarely operated under the banner of a common brand name.

- The strength of the emerging American hotel chains, coupled with US-led commercial and travel growth, created the first major wave of internationalisation in the accommodation sector. Nickson (1997) talks about this in terms of the *American way*, whereby the certainties offered to the American hotel chains in their home country encouraged them to export the same processes abroad.

- It is arguable that the major impact of this early internationalisation in the hotel sector was to create models and set standards which newer, non-American entrants into this market have adopted and enhanced, without ever losing the key flavour of their origins. Nickson argues that recent dilution of American ownership in the international hotel sector represents a shift of influence to Asia and Europe in terms of the sector's culture. Given the strength of early American influence on what we know today as the international hotel, this argument is, at least, open to debate.

- Finally, in this context, the American lodging model has given respectability to minimalism in terms of service and services within the accommodation sector. American lodgings, from motels onwards, have increasingly accepted the business benefits of the separation of food service from accommodation in operational and ownership terms (Hallam and Baum, 1996) or, indeed, its total elimination, which is commonplace in the modern budget or economy property.

The accommodation sector today is moving from traditions that were predominantly national to a more international stage, although the truly global accommodation brand, in the sense of Coca-Cola or Kellogg's, remains some way off. Companies are, increasingly, looking to investment that is international in focus so as to create brand awareness on a larger scale, to the benefit of domestic businesses and those in the countries of investment. American companies are developing elsewhere because of perceived saturation in the marketplace at home where reinvestment in tired mid-market, franchised properties is of greater need than the creation of additional capacity. European and Asian companies see the opportunity to bring the distinctive flavour of their brands (for example, Novotel and Mandarin Oriental) to new markets. Competition in the accommodation sector, therefore, increasingly exists at an international level but is complemented by strengthening and upgrading of many independent or small chain operators at a local level.

# QUALITY ISSUES AND GRADING IN THE ACCOMMODATION SECTOR

In common with all areas of tourism, the accommodation sector in any one location is a product of local and global forces representing historical, political, economic, socio-cultural and technological factors. The interplay of these environmental determinants is the main cause of the sector's heterogeneity.

**YOUTUBE**
Branding and accommodation

3 Key Elements of a World Class Hotel Brand
http://www.youtube.com/watch?v=DynjtjpaMVA

Comparison, therefore, becomes difficult between sub-sectors within accommodation and between operations in different countries and regions of the world. There are few meaningful frameworks or criteria that can compare the physical product attributes and ambience of, for example, Ashford Castle in the west of Ireland with its focus on the traditional in the style of the landed aristocracy and the ultra-modernity of the Ritz-Carlton, Millenia, Singapore, situated in the heart of that urbanised city state. Both offer excellence within their own location and context but their physical product is completely different. Where comparison may be ventured is in terms of service quality but this dimension presents numerous problems of, in particular, subjective assessment.

Quality comparisons are attempted through various accommodation grading and classification schemes. These generally operate on a national or regional basis within countries and may be run by either public (e.g. tourist board) or private sector (e.g. the Automobile Association (AA) or the American Automobile Association (AAA)) organisations. Attempts to introduce transnational systems within, for example, the EU have failed largely because of diversity within the industry of each country.

Accommodation classification or grading may be applied to all sub-sectors but is predominantly used with respect to hotels, guesthouses, farmhouse accommodation, bed and breakfast establishments and campsites. There is a difference in focus and purpose between classification and grading:

- **Classification** may be defined as 'the assignment of hotels to a categorical rating according to type of property, facilities, and amenities offered' (Gee, 1994). This is the traditional focus of most schemes.
- **Grading,** in contrast, emphasises quality dimensions. In practice, most national or commercially operated schemes concentrate on classification with quality perceived to be an *add-on* which does not impact upon the star rating of an establishment.

The purposes of accommodation classification are varied. They include:

- *standardisation* – to establish a system of uniform service and product quality that helps to create an orderly travel market distribution system for buyers and sellers;
- *marketing* – to advise travellers on the range and types of accommodation available within a destination as a means of promoting the destination and encouraging healthy competition in the marketplace;
- *consumer protection* – to ensure that accommodation meets minimum standards of accommodation, facilities and service within classification and grade definitions;
- *revenue generation* – to provide revenue from licensing, the sale of guidebooks and so forth;
- *control* – to provide a system for controlling general industry quality; and
- *investment incentive* – to give operators incentive to upgrade their facilities and services, in order to meet grading/classification criteria.

Accommodation classification, however, is not without problems. One of these relates to the subjectivity of judgement involved in assessing many key aspects of both the tangible and intangible elements of the accommodation experience such as personal service or the quality of products. As a consequence, many classification schemes concentrate, primarily, on the physical and quantifiable attributes of operations, determining level of grade on the basis of features such as:

- room size;
- room facilities, especially whether en suite or not; and
- availability of services – laundry, room service, 24-hour reception.

However, this is commonly done without any attempt to assess the quality of such provision or the consistency of its delivery. Other problems with classification schemes include:

- political pressures to offer classification and grading towards the top end of the spectrum to most hotels, thus creating a top-heavy structure;

- the cost of administering and operating a comprehensive classification assessment scheme, especially where subjective, intangible dimensions are to be included;
- industry objections to state-imposed, compulsory schemes; and
- the tendency of classification schemes to encourage standardisation rather than individual excellence within hotels.

In addition to the above, there is the growing trend in some parts of the world to encourage self-proclaimed grading to the extent that in Dubai you now have the world's first seven-star hotel!

Quality and quality assessment are rooted in the culture and context of the country in which they are located. As a result, a five-star or de luxe hotel in South-East Asia will be significantly different from a property that purports equivalence in Turkey or the UK. At best (and even this is debatable), classification can provide a guide to national standards. Even this is not always the case. In Spain, for example, the level of tax that a hotel pays is related to its grade, with five-star properties paying more than twice the amount of four-star hotels. As a consequence, there are few five-star hotels in Spain and a clustering of four-star properties covering a wide range of standards. Hotels such as Sofitel, InterContinental and Crowne Plaza are classified as four star when, elsewhere in Europe, these hotel brands would attract higher levels. Indeed, neighbouring Sofitel and Novotel properties in Madrid are both classified as four star, making a mockery of parent company Accor's branding intentions where they are clearly differentiated.

Probably the major difficulty faced by hotel classification schemes in Europe and North America is how to include the growing number of budget or economy hotels within schemes without creating unworkable ambiguities. The modern budget or economy hotel room contains a comprehensive range of simple but comfortable furnishings and facilities in a spacious, clean and modern environment. The comfort to be found in such rooms is primarily related to the physical product and is, generally, offered with minimum levels of service. One effect of the growth within this sector has been to create very real problems for hotel classification systems, which find it difficult to accommodate physical comfort with the absence of services available to the guest.

Budget hotels in Europe are a response to changing customer needs and expectations and their importance can be dated from the mid-1980s. Prior to their development, the consumer in search of low-cost accommodation would have patronised one of the large number of small, independent hotels, guesthouses or bed and breakfast establishments, generally at the unclassi-fied, one- or two-star level, to be found in all Western European countries. Products and services were very varied – just the problem faced by Kemmons Wilson in the USA some 30 years previously. The option of quality, low-cost and modern accommodation in the form of budget hotels, branded under names such as Formule 1, Travelodge, Premier Inn and Campanile, has moved a significant volume of demand away from traditional operators and resulted in both widespread upgrading of facilities and business failure in this sector.

As a consequence, the overall quality of bedroom accommodation in the lower-priced segments of the Western European lodging industry has improved significantly over the past two decades. The quality gap between this sector of the market, measured in physical product terms, and that provided by mid- to upper-sector hotels (three to five stars) has decreased greatly as a result and, with the growing impact of low-cost technology, this is a gap that is likely to narrow further. It is a reasonable expectation that, just as en-suite facilities, hot beverage equipment, international direct dialling (IDD) telephones and satellite television services are virtually the norm throughout much of the accommodation range, additional benefits (fax, Internet and especially wifi) will become available to properties at all levels and simultaneously.

The challenge for higher priced and graded accommodation providers, therefore, is to ensure clear market differentiation between their offering and that of the budget sector. However, as up to 50% of the custom of budget hotels in the UK is from the business market, this suggests that, at present, they are not particularly successful in doing so. The key differentiation that they are able to offer, given that physical attributes no longer provide such clear water, is that of service in its widest sense. There is considerable evidence that there is an accommodation market that is able and willing to pay considerably more for the benefits that attentive, individualised and problem-solving service provides. Balmer and Baum (1993) provide a theoretical explanation for this, based on the work of Herzberg.

Accommodation organisations place increasing emphasis on their ability to respond positively to the service demands of their customers and companies such as Ritz Carlton and Marriott have established international reputations for their focus on service.

# THE ACCOMMODATION SECTOR AND ENVIRONMENTAL ISSUES

The accommodation sector is not one that we generally think of as evoking images of pollution and environmental degradation. However, the structure of the sector, with operational units widely dispersed in some of the most fragile natural environments as well as within ancient and historic cities, means that its environmental impact can be very significant at both macro and micro levels. Indeed, visitors' fascination with the most fragile natural, historic and cultural environments may create demand for accommodation in locations that, otherwise, would be totally off the beaten track.

The accommodation sector's impact, in environmental terms, is varied and complex. The key areas are included under the following subheadings.

## Water use

Tourists are high consumers of water and many major tourist destinations are located in areas of potential or actual water shortage. Much of the water that visitors use during their time is within accommodation units – for baths, showers, in the swimming pool, laundry, maintaining green and attractive garden areas and sports facilities such as golf courses. Generally, tourists are less likely to visit destinations or stay in accommodation where there are restrictions on the use of water or where its quality is sub-standard. However, the long-term impact of unregulated water use by tourists can be very significant. In parts of southern Spain, for example, the permanent lowering of the water table affects other economic activities, notably agriculture. Likewise, rice farmers in Phuket, Thailand have had restrictions placed on their cropping seasons in order to preserve water for tourists. Sectors of the accommodation industry have responded to the pressures of a finite water supply and also the increasing tendency to charge businesses for consumption by activating varied water conservation measures. Towel reuse opportunities are in place in many hotels, whereby guests are asked to indicate which of their towels require laundering and which can be reused. Some hotels, such as the Holiday Inn in Phuket, has its own water treatment plant which permits sufficient treatment of waste water to allow for its use in the hotel's gardens and leisure facilities.

## Energy use

Reducing energy use, whether for heating in a winter climate or air-conditioning in hot climates, has clear environmental as well as financial savings to the business concerned (Shiming and Burnett, 2012). The *Hong Kong Guide* identifies practical routes to energy conservation within all departments of hotels. Computer technology permits the more effective control of energy, whether heat, air-conditioning or light, and it is possible, for example, to close down rooms, corridors or whole blocks automatically if vacated by guests.

## Recycling

Reuse of paper products from reception and administrative areas, replacement of individual shampoo sachets in bathrooms with dispensers and the avoidance of disposable tableware are examples of how the accommodation sector can recycle items normally bound for disposal.

## Waste disposal

Accommodation operations, especially large hotels, create large amounts of liquid and solid waste, which requires sensitive disposal. In some situations, especially small island locations such as the Maldives, disposal is a major problem and solid waste may need to be shipped off island for disposal. In some countries, hotels quite freely dispose of liquid waste directly into the sea or rivers. This can be seriously damaging to health and the environment.

## Fragile nature

Hotels and other accommodation units located within fragile natural environments (such as safari lodges) pose major threats to the fauna and flora of such locations. Such environments need to be managed with appropriate sensitivity so that guests are not disappointed in their experience but, at the same time, their presence does not destroy the very resource they have come to experience.

The critical concern here is one of the education of both employees within accommodation units and of their guests in the importance of environmental sensitivity and responsibility. The accommodation sector's role, in environmental and conservation terms, is not entirely negative. The contribution to the conservation and, indeed, enhancement of historic houses and castles in many parts of the world, adapted for hotel use, cannot be ignored for these are properties which may otherwise not have found another suitable use without conversion to accommodation facilities.

# INFORMATION TECHNOLOGY AND THE ACCOMMODATION SECTOR

In common with all other areas of services and, indeed, most areas of tourism, the accommodation sector is increasingly influenced by developments in the information and communications technology field. In many respects, technology has permitted the creation of highly labour-efficient and quality product budget or economy units by centralising all non-customer contact functions (reservations, marketing, finance) and allowing the property to concentrate on the delivery of a limited but consistent product. Technology impacts both at the unit level, within accommodation, and in terms of macro marketing and financial aspects:

- **Unit level.** Technology is the key to the efficient management of resources at unit level – energy, stock, human and financial. The training implications for effective use of technology in the small accommodation business is an issue that is not widely recognised.

- **Macro level.** The significant development at this level is the increasing dominance of the global distribution system (GDS) as the lead method of securing market share and marketing advantage for major accommodation brands. At the same time, cost of participation within GDS means that small companies and independent operators have had difficulty from this technology-driven avenue of reaching key customers unless they were able to establish sufficient market presence through participation in an established consortium such as Best Western.

- **The Internet.** This has allowed small operators to bypass the power of the GDS, either directly through their website, via email or through locally organised reservation bureaux that arrange bookings online. For example, it is rare for small hotels or bed and breakfast establishments to take in passing trade. Most guests arrive from prior bookings, if only by email. From the perspective of consumers, this has opened up a much wider choice of accommodation, allowing the small operator the chance to 'niche' market his or her product. Perhaps one of the biggest influences on the sector in recent years is the emergence of platforms such as **LastMinute.com** that enable suppliers of accommodation to manage and 'off-load' accommodation stock in order to maximise capacity, without losing sight of the impact of revenue per available room (RevPAR).

Although to many, Facebook, Twitter and YouTube remain primarily for social pleasure, the use of such social networking sites for business is increasing exponentially. For those investing both time and resources in leveraging business benefit from their implementation, the customer-driven orientation of the sites is influencing not just marketing communication activity but the entire value chain, with all accommodation providers over time being driven to re-examine their business practices. In the domain of marketing, the growing prevalence of online communities that facilitate consumers (or guests) to exchange information about products or services, and to compare prices among competitors, has resulted in a rapid loss of control by marketers as to how their products and services are presented to potential customers. Through reviews and customer-generated content, sophisticated algorithms are driving the use of social media by the sector, with the attraction of real-time feedback being of particular benefit. The use of embedded videos on YouTube enable customers to view accommodation before deciding to purchase and they are then, if satisfied, able to share their accommodation experience with friends and so contribute to the phenomenon of electronic word-of-mouth recommendation.

Social media can also be used to gather market research either through 'listening' to consumer sites or through gaining access to unfiltered feedback from customers. Accommodation providers can also engage proactively in customer 'dialogues' through online forums which quite often can facilitate benchmarking against competitors. One warning for all users of social media, however, is the need to ensure that all employees have clear guidelines as to how to use, and not to use, such sites as the ease with which unwarranted comments can go 'viral' is such that once released the damage is often very difficult to contain, to the detriment of all concerned. For selling, the use of social media offers genuine cost-effective benefits, with many accommodation providers now in a position to commence a conversation with potential customers as soon as they press the 'like' button. Starwood already has Facebook pages for over 1,000 of its hotel properties across its full range of brands!

## HUMAN RESOURCES AND THE ACCOMMODATION SECTOR

Service-intensive businesses within accommodation are also labour intensive and are always likely to remain so. This is despite considerable improvements in:

- productivity through use of technology;
- training;
- systems efficiency; and
- management effectiveness.

There are few significant labour-saving initiatives that can drastically reduce the level of employment in, say, housekeeping. By contrast, the budget or economy sector is able to provide a quality product without significant service levels through minimising the level of staffing employed.

In spite of significant changes to the use and productivity of labour within the sector, accommodation remains an area that provides employment opportunities for a wide range of skills and aptitudes, reflecting not only the diversity of businesses that operate under the accommodation umbrella but also the variety of tasks that working in the sector demands. In many communities, accommodation businesses contribute socially by providing employment opportunities for people who would find it difficult to work in other sectors of the economy. Accommodation also provides relatively easy access to employment for new immigrants (legal and illegal) as well as those entering the labour market for the first time (school leavers, students). These positive dimensions must be counterbalanced by recognition of perceived and actual problems with respect to work conditions, pay and general industry image issues, especially in developed countries. These issues and their wider human resource implications are addressed in detail elsewhere (Baum, 2006; Janta et al., 2011, 2012; Joppe, 2012).

# CONCLUSION

In this chapter, we have addressed the largest and, arguably, the most important sub-sector within tourism at a domestic and international level. The purpose of the chapter has been to demonstrate the position of accommodation within the wider tourism sector and to show how its diversity meets the requirements of virtually all tourism market groups. The origins of the accommodation sector are considered and the dominant influence of the US model of commercial hospitality discussed. Issues such as standardisation, the management of standards and the accommodation sector's environmental responsibilities are addressed.

Accommodation is a rapidly changing sector within tourism and, as a consequence, it is an area where many businesses are casualties in the face of competition from new products and service/product standards. It is unlikely that the pace of change will slow in the foreseeable future with the sector, like all others, determined to ensure that it continues to meet the increasing experiential demands of its guests.

# SELF-CHECK QUESTIONS

1. In what ways has the accommodation sector changed since 1945 and what effect has this had on the wider tourism industry?

2. Account for the diversity in the accommodation sector between different countries and regions.

3. Given its diversity, how can the accommodation sector provide meaningful comparisons of quality?

4. Review and discuss the key issues facing the accommodation sector and their likely impact in the future.

5. What are the benefits, to the small independent hotel, of participation in a marketing consortium?

6. What strategies can small-to-medium sized accommodation providers adopt to compete effectively with the larger chain operators?

7. What are the unique characteristics of accommodation? Can you think of any other special features that characterise the accommodation industry that are not found in other service businesses?

# REFERENCES AND FURTHER READING

Balmer, S. and Baum, T. (1993) 'Applying Herzberg's hygiene factors to the changing accommodation environment: the application of motivational theory to the field of guest satisfaction', *International Journal of Contemporary Hospitality Management* **5**(2), 32–5.

Baum, T. (2006) *Human Resource Management for Tourism, Hospitality and Leisure: An International Perspective*, International Thomson, London.

Di Domenico, M. and Lynch, P.A. (2007) 'Host/guest encounters in the commercial home', *Leisure Studies* **26**(3), 321–38.

Donaghy, D., McMahon, U. and McDowell, D. (1995) 'Yield management: An overview', *International Journal of Hospitality Management* **14**(2), 139–50.

Espino, T., Lai, P. and Baum, T. (2006) 'Make or buy service operations in the hotel businesses. An empirical application in Scotland', Proceedings of Euroma Conference, Glasgow, June.

Gee, C. (1994) *International Hotels: Development and Management*, Educational Institute of the American Hotel and Motel Association, East Lansing, MI.

Hallam, G. and Baum, T. (1996) 'Contracting out food and beverage operations in hotels: a comparative study of practice in North America and the United Kingdom', *International Journal of Hospitality Management* **15**(1), 41–50.

Janta, H., Ladkin, A., Brown, L. and Lugosi, P. (2011) 'Employment experiences of Polish migrant workers in the UK hospitality sector', *Tourism Management* **32**(5), 1006–19.

Janta, H., Lugosi, P., Brown, L. and Ladkin, A. (2012) 'Migrant networks, language learning and tourism employment', *Tourism Management* **33**(2), 431–9.

Joppe, M. (2012) 'Migrant workers: challenges and opportunities in addressing tourism labour shortages', *Tourism Management* **33**(3), 662–71.

Nickson, D. (1997), 'Continuity or change in the international hotel industry', pp. 213–28 in Foley, M., Lennon, J. and Maxwell G. (eds), *Hospitality, Tourism and Leisure Management: Issues in Strategy and Culture*, Cassell, London.

Schwartz, Z. (2003) 'Hotel revenue management with group discount room rates', *Journal of Hospitality and Tourism Research* **27**(1), 24–47.

Shiming, D. and Burnett, J. (2012) 'Energy use and management in hotels in Hong Kong', *International Journal of Hospitality Management* **21**(4), 371–80.

Stanley, D. (1997) *Eastern Europe on a Shoestring*, Lonely Planet, London.

STB (1996) *Quality Assurance*, Scottish Tourist Board, Inverness.

Wood, K. (2005) *Cheap Sleeps Europe: The Definitive Guide to Cheap Accommodation*, Robson Books, London.

# MAJOR CASE STUDY 14.1
## Hilton worldwide

## INTRODUCTION

From very humble origins in Cisco, Texas in 1919, where Conrad Hilton purchased his very first hotel, The Mobley, and in Dallas, again in Texas, where in 1925 the first formally named Hilton opened, Hilton Worldwide (formerly Hilton Hotels Corporation) is today a major global hospitality company. Owned by the Blackstone Group, a private equity firm, Hilton Worldwide today operates 633,238 rooms in 3,843 properties across 88 countries and is ranked as the 36th largest private company in the United States. In 2011 alone, Hilton Worldwide became the fastest growing major hotel company, opened 170 hotels and signed management or franchised agreements on more than 320 hotels. Within its portfolio of leading brands are included the likes of the Waldorf Astoria Hotels & Resorts (21 in 8 countries), Conrad Hotels & Resorts (17 in 13 countries), Hilton Hotels & Resorts (553 in 77 countries), DoubleTree by Hilton (281 in 24 countries), Embassy Suites Hotels (212 in 7 countries), Hilton Garden Inn (538 in 13 countries) as well as Hampton Inn and Hampton Inn & Suites, Homewood Suites by Hilton,

Home2 Suites by Hilton and Hilton Grand Vacations. The latter is of particular interest as it now hosts in excess of 176,000 members across five countries: the USA, Canada, Mexico, Portugal and Scotland. Hilton Worldwide is thus very much a leading player in the global hospitality industry!

## THE EARLY INNOVATOR

Returning to its early days, Hilton was always at the leading edge of innovation in the hospitality. Although not perhaps appearing as radical today, back in 1927 cold running water and air-conditioning in the public rooms was deemed to be a major leap forward. Similarly, when the Roosevelt Hilton in New York City became the first hotel in the world to install televisions in guest rooms in 1947, this was a widely recognised 'step change' in the hospitality 'product' and was one that many competing hoteliers felt obliged to follow. The same could also be said about the launch in 1948 of Hilton's multi-hotel reservations system, an innovation that soon served as the catalyst for the modern-day reservation system. This was soon followed by the launch of Hilton's first international property in 1949 when Hilton International was 'born' with the opening of the Caribe Hilton in Puerto Rico; the beginning of an international dynasty that continues to go from strength to strength.

The exponential success of Hilton was such that Conrad Hilton became the first ever hotelier to appear on the cover of *Time* magazine, while he later became the first to appear twice when he appeared in the July issue in 1963. Much of this was attributed to his dedication to customer service and ability to be one step ahead of the game. This was evidenced in 1970 when Hilton became the first NYSE-listed company to enter the domestic gaming business with the purchase of the Flamingo Hotel and the Las Vegas International. A little later in 1973, Hilton developed the first centralised reservation service using computer technology, HILTRON, which unites all Hilton hotels. Quite incredibly, this landmark system, the most sophisticated computerised hotel reservation referral and reporting system in the industry, served the company right up to the end of the 1990s. After the launch of its sophisticated reservation service, perhaps the next biggest customer service landmark was the launch of Hilton HHonors, its first guest loyalty programme in 1987. This was enhanced further in 1994 when Hilton HHonors Reward Exchange enabled travellers to earn both points and air miles and so bring together two of the most potent components of the wider tourism product. Today, Hilton HHonors has over 30 million members with 3.5 million joining in 2011 alone!

With the launch of its first website, **http://www .hilton.com**, in 1995 and its new reservation system, HILSTAR, in 1999, innovation continued apace as Hilton entered the new millennium. For example, it launched Hilton Worldwide Resorts in 2002, its first collection of premium resorts and exotic vacation experiences, while in 2006 Hilton Hotels Corporation and Hilton International were reunited, and also launched its first ever application for mobile devices. This new innovation enabled guests to make reservations, check-in, search hotels, view HHonors account activity, book HHonors reward stays and order Hilton Requests upon Arrival amenities. And, not wishing to miss out on the social media frenzy occurring at the time, Hilton became the first major hotelier to reach 50,000 fans on Facebook! And, finally, bringing things up to the present, Hilton Hotels formally became Hilton Hotels & Resorts and introduced a refreshed brand logo soon after Hilton Hotels Corporation changed its name to Hilton Worldwide.

## HILTON WORLDWIDE

For the future, Hilton Worldwide has four key strategic priorities which will drive the business forward over the next decade: aligning its culture and organisation; maximising performance across the enterprise; strengthening and expanding its brands and commercial services platform; and, perhaps above all, expanding its global footprint. With a significant number of its development pipeline of nearly 900 hotels comprising about 130,000 rooms now outside of the USA and Canada, the international ambitions of the company are very much in evidence, with a particular focus on Asia/Pacific, Europe, the Middle East and Latin America – all of these being markets where traditionally Hilton has been under-penetrated when compared to its footprint in the USA. Across the regions, growth really is quite impressive. For example, there are plans in place to double its footprint in Latin America, the Caribbean and Europe, to triple the number of properties in Asia Pacific and increase nine-fold the number of new hotels in China!

Interest in China, although perhaps obvious in view of the sheer number of opportunities on the horizon, remains impressive. Hilton, recognising the need to adapt to the needs of local markets, is considering launching a brand targeted specifically at Chinese travellers, as it seeks to keep pace with its rivals in what very soon is likely to become the world's single largest hotel market. One particular rival is the InterContinental Hotels Group PLC (IHG.LN), which is currently the market leader in China with around 160 hotels and a similar number in the pipeline. To cater to the specific needs of the Chinese market, IHG.LN plan to launch 'Hualuxe' in 2013–14, the new hotels incorporating tea houses, Chinese gardens and noodle bars. IHG's ambitions are big in that it expects Hualuxe to reach 100 cities within 15 to 20 years, with further growth to follow in Asia's other booming economies. Rather than focusing too much on its competitors, however, Hilton Worldwide is now firmly focused on the opportunities to be gained from tapping into what in 2025 will be the largest market in the world with approximately 6 million hotel rooms – a figure that will double by 2039.

## A SENSE OF CORPORATE RESPONSIBILITY

Although global expansion is a key strategic priority, Hilton Worldwide remains committed to the green and broader sustainability agendas. For example, Hilton Worldwide now boasts a number of key partnerships that seek to inculcate a step change in its broader responsibilities as a corporate citizen. For example, while Good360 connects hotels donating high-quality used goods to charitable organisations, the Global Soap project repurposes soap from Hilton Worldwide hotels to vulnerable populations in developing countries. With regard to cost savings, the company saved more than US$74 million in utility costs as a result of reducing energy use by 6.6%, carbon outputs by 7.85%, waste output by 19% and water use by 3.8%.

*Source*: http://www.hiltonworldwide.com (accessed 28 May 2012)

## DISCUSSION QUESTIONS

1. Hilton Worldwide is clearly a successful global company in a very competitive global market. What specific strengths do you think underpin its growth in recent years?

2. International expansion brings with it many opportunities. It does, however, also bring with it many challenges. What do you consider to be the biggest challenges for Hilton Worldwide as it seeks to expand globally and what particular challenges lie ahead in China, soon to become the world's largest single hospitality market?

3. Hilton Worldwide has a very successful portfolio of branded hotel products. What may be some of the benefits and drawbacks from the adoption of a more 'umbrella' form of branding?

4. Developing a strong sense of corporate responsibility is a highly laudable goal and is one that many major corporations are currently developing. What can Hilton Worldwide do to embed such a goal in the minds of its customers and how may such an approach impact on their future patterns of buying behaviour?

# CHAPTER 15
## EVENTS MANAGEMENT

### LEARNING OUTCOMES

The focus of this chapter is on event management, its growth as a sector of study in the service industry and its importance within tourism. By the end of this chapter, therefore, you will be:

- familiar with the nature of events management and its growth;
- aware of the diversity of the types of events and how they are classified;
- familiar with events management as a field of study;
- aware of contemporary developments within the sector;
- introduced to event legacies and the growing focus on sustainability within the events market.

Photograph: Paralympics stadium, 2012, London, UK © Kelly Miller

## INTRODUCTION

Events management has become one of the fastest growing industries in the world and consequently has led to many educational institutions delivering tailored courses in events studies, in a variety of forms, within their curriculum. It is, according to Bowdin et al. (2011), the convergence of project management theory to the creation and development of festivals, events and conferences to reflect a more professional approach. Because events management is an internationally developing field, this chapter is devoted to addressing the field's global reach. It is now a rapidly expanding, multi-million pound industry ranging from small community festivals to large mega events, yet there remains no formal research undertaken to measure its total growth. Separate sectors of the events industry such as the MICE (meetings, incentives, conferences and exhibitions) sector, conduct their own research but there are no all-encompassing events growth indicators that demonstrate its complete reach.

The use of events is considered to be one type of strategic marketing tool used by corporate entities, with product launches, press conferences, promotional events, sales symposia and incentive events all featuring in integrated marketing communications plans. Other corporate events include road shows, grand opening events, award ceremonies, launch parties, fashion shows etc. Many companies hire professional event agencies external to the organisation as they often do not have in-house expertise – hence the title of professional event manager. Furthermore, out of the expansion has come the birth of an events industry with an associated demand for training and certification. This is where the roles of event educators and event practitioners have come into being.

To understand the context in which it is now a taught programme at university level, it is necessary to examine the historical growth through centuries of advances to modern-day contemporary developments. Within this expansion it has been necessary to add structure to the classification of the numerous types of events, with a consequent introduction to many of the key authors in the field. The future direction sees an increase in interest around how the events sector diversifies further, the legacies that are left from events, and a drive to improve the sustainability of the events industry, all of which feature within this chapter.

## THE HISTORICAL DEVELOPMENT OF EVENTS

> A special event is a onetime or infrequently occurring event outside the normal programme or activities of the sponsoring or organising body. To the customer, a special event is an opportunity for a leisure, social or cultural experience outside the normal range of choices or beyond the everyday experience.
>
> (Getz, 1991: 44)

Events have been occurring throughout the world for centuries as man has found ways to celebrate the phases of the moon, through life cycles of birth, marriage and death to historical and cultural celebrations (Bowdin et al., 2011). In the UK the early folk festivals were associated with Plough Monday, May Day, Midsummer Day and Harvest Home, as the changing seasons and country life were responsible for many festivals and events. With several of the traditions and pastimes of the countryside now disappearing, however, how many of these events and festivals will continue is open to debate.

Modern-day celebrations include New Year's Eve (Old Father Time), Guy Fawkes, Halloween and Christmas Day. Today, using the UK as an example, this is a country becoming more culturally diverse, with many newcomers bringing both customs and traditions to the country which have now become a part of wider British heritage. Other celebrations are increasingly appearing within the country, such as Chanukah, Divali, Chinese New Year and Passover. Similarly, festivals and cultural events have spread throughout the world in conjunction with immigration and displacement of peoples as culture has always played a huge part in the rituals and ceremonies that have taken place for centuries. Changes in society have influenced these events yet many still remain the same.

Wood (2002) suggests that events came about through the commercialisation of popular celebrations and that with the increase in work through industrialisation, people were often too tired to celebrate and therefore celebration had to become a separate entity away from work. This is partly the reason why in 1871 bank holidays in the UK became lawful while the monarch still has the power, with governmental approval, to grant additional days such as for Silver, Golden and Diamond Jubilee celebrations.

People wish to identify important happenings in their lives through celebration, especially key moments marking rites of passage such as bar mitzvahs, twenty-first birthday celebrations, marriages and anniversaries. Momentous public events become milestones by which people measure their private lives, i.e. 'before the Royal Wedding'; 'after the Manchester Commonwealth Games'. In addition, occasional events help to mark eras and define milestones: 1966 World Cup, 1997 Hong Kong Handover Ceremony, 2002 FIFA World Cup South Korea, Shanghai World Expo 2010, London 2012 Olympic Games.

Celebrations continue to take place both in public and private and even in an age where criticism is levied on people who seem to have 'lost touch with common religious beliefs and social norms of the past, there is still the need for social events to mark the local and domestic details of our lives' (Bowdin et al., 2011: 2). Goldblatt (1997) argues that the term 'celebration' also relates to education and marketing and therefore encompasses all aspects of human life, so a further term to use for a more comprehensive definition is 'to perform'. Pine and Gilmore (1999) and Shone and Parry (2001) agree that events have expanded into the leisure and commercial marketplace, thus becoming part of the burgeoning 'experience economy'. In the world today events are central to people's culture more than ever and with increases in disposable income and with greater amounts of leisure time being available to many in developed countries since the late 1940s, there has been a surge in events from all spectrums of society. This includes governments which capitalise on the economic development opportunities, marketing and national pride, through to corporations and businesses which wish to promote image and awareness along with community groups and individuals that organise events for their shared interests, to charities using events on a local, national and global basis to raise not just funds but also awareness for their causes.

## Birth of the events industry

The structure of events and their operation varies across this diverse industry. Each event is a one-off, unique occurrence for the client, therefore being a very important occasion, which rests on the shoulders of the event planner. The client is known as the 'primary stakeholder' and their wants, needs and budget are all variable and discussed with the event planner. The two will then typically engage in a series of meetings and conversations to organise the event and, from that, a finalised event will emerge. This event is often set out in a written contract or memorandum

### YOUTUBE

Careers in Event Management
http://www.youtube.com/watch?v=Y_-NvzzMtTk&feature=related

Career advice on becoming an event manager by Rachael Bee
http://www.youtube.com/watch?v=q7OkRA42qgc&feature=related

Events Management at Bournemouth University
http://www.youtube.com/watch?v=KKhX_iywF_Y

Opening Ceremony – Innsbruck 2012
http://www.youtube.com/watch?v=NhshLl7oyRl

Olympic Games through history
http://www.youtube.com/watch?v=ABvGkUcluUU

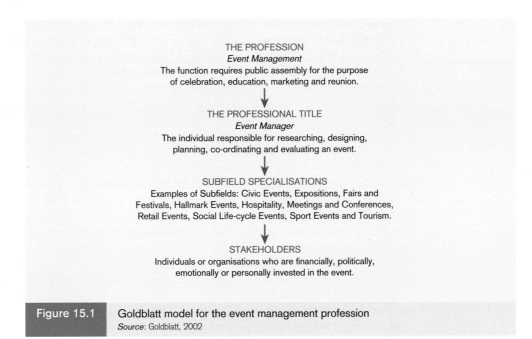

THE PROFESSION
*Event Management*
The function requires public assembly for the purpose
of celebration, education, marketing and reunion.

↓

THE PROFESSIONAL TITLE
*Event Manager*
The individual responsible for researching, designing,
planning, co-ordinating and evaluating an event.

↓

SUBFIELD SPECIALISATIONS
Examples of Subfields: Civic Events, Expositions, Fairs and
Festivals, Hallmark Events, Hospitality, Meetings and Conferences,
Retail Events, Social Life-cycle Events, Sport Events and Tourism.

↓

STAKEHOLDERS
Individuals or organisations who are financially, politically,
emotionally or personally invested in the event.

| Figure 15.1 | Goldblatt model for the event management profession |
|---|---|
| | *Source:* Goldblatt, 2002 |

of understanding between the parties involved. This works to protect both the client and the event manager, and to rule out any misunderstandings concerning the formalities of the event. These written contracts may vary but will be universal in the underlying structure. The details of the final contract, including any changes, are then converted into a 'run sheet', detailing the list of occurrences for the event. This is presented in a formal way for the event coordinator or manager to run the event. The run sheet reflects the base contract and is a tabulated version of the plan, in hard copy. Furthermore, the growth in the industry has necessitated some formal type of training and the recognition of career paths within the profession as seen in Figure 15.1.

## Typologies of events

With the events industry being so large, it therefore requires some form of categorising of events into groups with their own distinct definitions. Many writers have categorised events including Allen (2002), Getz (1991, 2007), Goldblatt (2008), Hall (1992), Ritchie (1984) and Watt (1998). According to Van der Wagen (2001), the relative size of events varies from those large world-wide events, called mega events, such as the Olympic Games, through to hallmark events which are designed to appeal to a specific tourism destination or region and which can have a positive financial impact on the city, to major events which are of local interest with large numbers of participants as well as gathering significant tourism revenues. Minor events include all other categories of events. The bigger the event the greater the impact on the economy, especially trade, transport and tourism (Yeoman et al., 2004).

Events are also classified by type, including sporting, special events, entertainment, art and cultural, commercial, marketing and promotional events, and meetings, conventions and exhibitions. Sporting events include those that attract sportsmen and women from the highest levels from all over the world, from the Olympic Games to smaller local sporting competitions and celebrations. In New Zealand the recent hosting of the Rugby World Cup in 2011 was a major factor for increased tourism, media coverage and economic impact, much like the hosting of the 2000 Olympic Games was for the whole of Australia, not just the host city of Sydney. According to Allen et al. (2005) major events are classified as attracting significant local interest and large numbers of participants.

However, prior to this one of the first authors to categorise events was Ritchie in 1984, who classified events according to their religious, cultural, commercial, sporting or political emphasis.

However, subsequently, few authors classified events according to their social or economic importance as their significance can change according to the perspective of the viewer – be they the organiser, the host community, the stakeholder or the visitor. Despite this, Ritchie further wrote that different cultures and Western versus non-Western attitudes will play a significant role in this perception. Global cultures have different ways of celebrating their traditions based on their religious and cultural values, which helps make the events business one of the most culturally diverse industries operating today.

Special events are classified as being unique and, for the client, 'an opportunity for a leisure, social or cultural experience outside the normal range of choices or beyond everyday experience' (Getz, 1997: 5). Special events can range from weddings to festivals, including entertainment, culture and arts, and are usually community events that can attract any number of people from 50 to 500,000.

The largest sector within events, other than mega events, is the MICE industry which is fast becoming a very dominant part of the hospitality sector – one which is instrumental in enhancing levels of occupancy in many tourism destinations. These can often suffer severe bed shortages in shoulder tourism periods or excess supply during times of economic downturn as the capacity has been built up to cope with the greatest levels of demand. Events can therefore complement and support other sectors of the leisure industry. Shone and Parry (2001) classify according to complexity and uncertainty along a two-dimensional grid structure, thus understanding the demands made by each event upon its organisers, with the concept of size often dictating the experience sought by the organiser. Getz (1997), in his model (Figure 15.2), also uses a simple approach to the classification of event genres, and its narrowness of classification has for a long time been accepted by the events industry as being the most useful model for identification purposes.

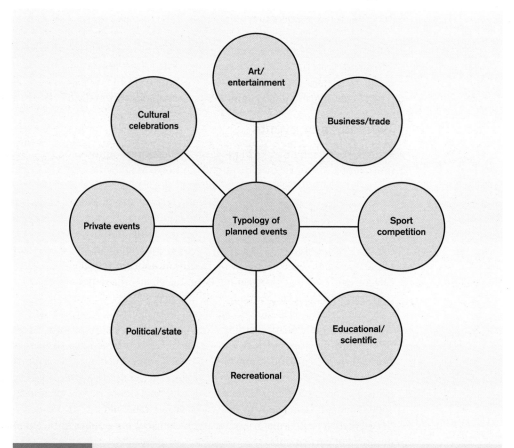

| Figure 15.2 | Typology of planned events |
|---|---|
| | *Source*: Adapted from Getz, 1997 |

Another useful classification of types of event genre and descriptions of what each category entails can be found in the table developed by Julia Rutherford Silvers out of the EMBOK (Event Management Body of Knowledge) international global project (Table 15.1). This classification is part of the process to develop their on-going EMBOK framework: 'To create a framework of the knowledge and processes used in event management that may be customized to meet the needs of various cultures, governments, education programs, and organizations' **(http://www.embok.org/)**.

| Table 15.1 | The event genre of event management |
| --- | --- |
| **Business and corporate events** | Any event that supports business objectives, including management functions, corporate communications, training, marketing, incentives, employee relations and customer relations, scheduled alone or in conjunction with other events. |
| **Cause-related and fundraising events** | An event created by or for a charitable or cause-related group for the purpose of attracting revenue, support and/or awareness, scheduled alone or in conjunction with other events. |
| **Exhibitions, expositions and fairs** | An event bringing buyers and sellers and interested persons together to view and/or sell products, services and other resources to a specific industry or the general public, scheduled alone or in conjunction with other events. |
| **Entertainment and leisure events** | A one-time or periodic, free or ticketed performance or exhibition event created for entertainment purposes, scheduled alone or in conjunction with other events. |
| **Festivals** | A cultural celebration, either secular or religious, created by and/or for the public, scheduled alone or in conjunction with other events. (Many festivals include bringing buyer and seller together in a festive atmosphere.) |
| **Government and civic events** | An event comprised of or created by or for political parties, communities or municipal or national government entities, scheduled alone or in conjunction with other events. |
| **Hallmark events** | An event of such significance and/or scope that its image or stature assures national and international recognition and interest. |
| **Marketing events** | A commerce-orientated event to facilitate bringing buyer and seller together or to create awareness of a commercial product or service, scheduled alone or in conjunction with other events. |
| **Meeting and convention events** | The assembly of people for the purpose of exchanging information, debate or discussion, consensus or decisions, education and relationship building, scheduled alone or in conjunction with other events. |
| **Social/life-cycle events** | A private event, by invitation only, celebrating or commemorating a cultural, religious, communal, societal or life-cycle occasion, scheduled alone or in conjunction with other events. |
| **Sports events** | A spectator or participatory event involving recreational or competitive sport activities, scheduled alone or in conjunction with other events. |

*Source*: http://www.juliasilvers.com/embok/EMBOK_structure_update.htm

The EMBOK classification is the most comprehensive framework to date as it includes events used by charities to raise awareness and funds. However, events can actually belong in more than one classification at the same time. For example, sports events can be fundraising events as well as being classified as sports; incentive meetings can be business and corporate events, as well as meetings and conferences.

Special events are an important classification of events. Shone and Parry (2001: 4) offer a definition that they believe both defines and classifies such events: 'special events are that phenomenon arising from those non-routine occasions which have leisure, cultural, personal or organizational objectives set apart from the normal activity of daily life, whose purpose is to enlighten, celebrate, entertain or challenge the experience of a group of people'. In addition, they write that for an event to be classified as such, it will have eight characteristics: uniqueness, perishability, labour intensiveness, fixed-time scales, intangibility, personal interaction, ambience and ritual or ceremony. These eight characteristics are a blend of the ideas and typologies of many key event writers supporting the view that an event is unique and different and, whilst it is true that events can be repeated, the participants, the surroundings and the audience all combine to make the event unique each time. This also accounts for its perishability, in that facilities unused or provided for a specific event cannot be 'stored' for reuse as the opportunity has either been lost or is too unique to be repeated. This is an important concept when studying events management as each event becomes unique through the combination of tangible elements such as the entertainment, decor and catering with the intangibles of service, supporting Shone and Parry's eight characteristics. This is seen in the Concerto Group, which quotes in its mission statement: 'Working in partnership to exceed expectations through innovation, enthusiasm and vision' **(http://www.concertogroup.co.uk)**.

## Events education

Events management education has been through a trajectory of rapid growth over the last 20 years. Growth has been driven by a significant increase in demand for more professional skills to support the growing field of events management practitioners. The increasing presence of events in strategic business plans as well as government initiatives is more common than ever. Due in part to the onset of integrating technology in everyday lives, planned events allow for people to converge in meaningful ways to achieve common goals such as raised awareness, sales potential, information sharing, education gathering and relationship building. Each of these activities is facilitated by planned events. Along the way, the needs of the field of event management have dictated that professionalisation in the field is needed in an increasing number of business environments. As a result, the emergence of specialised offerings in events education have developed in many countries around the world.

The George Washington University in Washington DC was one of the first to offer a certificate programme at university level in event management (Bowdin *et al.*, 2011). This was delivered in 1994. In the UK context, Leeds Metropolitan University launched the first ever Events Management degree in 1996.

The options for event management education courses have continued to expand ever since. Courses now come in a variety of different credit bearing options such as diplomas, foundation degrees, degrees and masters level. This is a result of a surge in the field of events management coming into its own as a profession, and therefore meeting a need to offer professional qualifications (Goldblatt, 2000).

The span of events management education could be said to encompass a number of areas. Degree and diploma bearing institutions may offer any combination of the following areas in their courses, and this does not represent an exhaustive list: marketing, consumer behaviour, financial management, event management, strategy and leadership, health and safety, feasibility studies, human resources and event volunteering, event bidding, creative media, social media, client proposals, economics, design and production, exhibitions and conferences, planning mega-events, event policy, risk management etc.

Comparatively, specialist skills such as crowd management and health and safety are known to crop up as one-off certificate bearing qualifications applied to them by some institutions and

## MINI CASE STUDY 15.1
The story of Beach Break Live – then and now

| Photograph 15.1 | Beach Break Live. |
| --- | --- |
| | *Source*: With kind permission from Mary Beth Gouthro |

Beach Break Live is the festival brain child of Celia Norowzian and Ian Forshew. They were university students themselves when they created this 'uni student only' music festival which they called Beach Break Live in Cornwall in June 2007. After accumulating £40,000 in debt with that venture, they remained undeterred and began planning a second one for 2008. Now in its 7th year, the June 2013 version of Beach Break Live is due to be held once again in Pembrey Country Park (Cefn Sidan Beach) in Carmarthenshire Wales, and has grown from 1,000 guests in their first year to an expected crowd of 20,000 to descend upon the much-expanded music festival again in 2013.

The journey to festival success hasn't always been an easy one for Celia and Ian. After hosting the first in 2007, they took stock of their debt position and knew that investment needed to be explored. Therefore, they soon took their business idea before BBC's *Dragon's Den* in the autumn of 2007 to try and attract investors in their venture. They positioned Beach Break Live as a 'uni student only', end-of-exam gathering where head-lining bands and surfboards would meet, drawing their market to a 3-day extravaganza for those weary-eyed students in time to celebrate the close of an academic year and to kick off summer in the ideal month of June. Much to their surprise, this dynamic duo were offered investment proposals from each of the five members of the *Dragon's Den* panel. On the back of this success, they were then offered a more intriguing investment offer from Outgoing Travel based in Manchester. Beach Break Live continues with the investment support of this company since 2007. They have also spun off their own festival recruitment agency under the name Seed Staff (see **www.seedstaff.com**).

It hasn't all been smooth sailing for Beach Break Live over time. In their 3rd year, they had planned the beach-side festival for an idyllic location in Cornwall. Much to their dismay, and long after much of the planning had been established and put in place in terms of licensing, health and safety, and artist line-up confirmed, representatives from Cornwall County Council removed the already-granted licence to host the festival from BBL with only two weeks to go, citing safety and traffic concerns voiced by a development planning sub-committee of the council. With no alternative venues in place so close to the start of the festival, the organising team along with Celia and Ian were looking at the very real possibility of having to cancel the festival they had been planning for close to a year. As it happened and after a lot of long nights, phone calls and endless coffee, the festival was quickly re-located to Kent, on a site that was not exactly next to a beach, but rather a zoo! Thankfully, most of the ticket holders planning to take in the Cornwall location followed Beach Break Live to their 'new' site, and experienced many of the same things they came to hear or like about the festival previously – an attractive artist line-up, cool chill out space, themed tents and dance nights. This was in addition to a wide variety of socially-responsible vendors selling regional organic products and services, as well as providing an inviting and fun campground space for its revellers.

## DISCUSSION QUESTIONS

1. Is Beach Break Live addressing a gap in the 'event' market? If so, how does it do this?

2. Celia and Ian as festival/event entrepreneurs took risks conceptualising a festival for a low-spending student market. How do you think they addressed this in their business planning?

3. In its third year, Beach Break Live had to re-locate the festival with just days to go before it was due to start, re-locating 300 miles away from its original site venue. What made them successful in drawing most of their ticket holders to the new venue, in such a short window of time?

4. Is the future of Beach Break Live viable in the festival market going forward? Discuss.

professional organisations. However, it is the UK that has probably experienced the most growth in offering credit bearing courses by way of university degrees. In 2012 there were over 70 higher education and further education institutions in the UK offering event management courses at the foundation degree level through to Masters Level at colleges and universities. Some of these are labelled as Event Management degrees, yet others are offered in combination with specialisms such as drama, arts, performance, media production, tourism, hospitality, sports, journalism, and geography and at varying qualification offerings i.e. foundation degrees, 3 year degrees and sand-wich degrees. Courses continue to crop up across the globe with similar offerings now found in countries such as India, China, Singapore, United Arab Emirates and the United States. In any one of these areas, events education is delivered in different formats (e.g. executive training, skills training, accreditation) and also partner scenarios with existing degree providers e.g. UK univer-sities with those in China, along with distance learning and Masters level certification.

Organisations such as AEME (Association of Event Management Educators (**www.aeme.org**)) based in the UK is committed to raising the profile of events education through the sharing of good practice, research and education. Its membership is made up of institutions with degree bearing powers in the field of events management, as well as professional practitioners e.g. marketing agencies. This mix of professional input serves to move the events field forward in a productive way with subject specialism core to its focus.

Deriving from academic disciplines raises areas of field of study. For example, the study of tourism was embedded in the discipline of geography as a specialisation within it. Today, many schools and universities offer courses specialising in tourism. As events are an important sector within tourism economies and activity, it too has evolved as a specialist area for a field of study within the service sector.

Event studies therefore, is considered to be a related field of study, and has also evolved within the professionalisation of event management. It is defined by Getz (2007, p.2) as 'the academic field devoted to creating knowledge and theory about planned events. The core phenomenon is the experience of planned events, and meanings attached to them'. Getz includes all those events that are planned in some level within this definition, ranging the full scope from festivals, religious celebrations, sport, political, business (exhibitions, conventions), educational, arts and entertainment. Much that is discussed in the literature relates to the economic and marketing function of events, but equally the social and cultural importance of planned events is also meant to be considered in the wider domain of Events Studies. Researchers in academic settings around the world, from Asia to America and from Europe to the South Pacific are actively engaged in research activity on the subject and the significance of events in our everyday lives, both on personal and professional levels.

University graduates typically leave with the following skills:

- Can demonstrate a critical understanding of the principles and methods of working appropriate to the events industries.
- Have developed the cognitive abilities of critical evaluation, analysis and synthesis.
- Can demonstrate practical management skills relevant to events management.
- Are self-reliant, self-disciplined learners capable of working in an interdisciplinary environment.
- Are able to meet the challenges presented by a career in a national or international environment.
- Possess academic curiosity and the appropriate academic foundations for further study and training. (**www.bournemouth.ac.uk**)

Below is a list of some UK and international event industry associations that inform the field and professional practice more widely:

- British Exhibition Contractors Association **www.beca.org.uk**
- British Association of Conference Destinations **www.bacd.org.uk**
- Eventia – the events industry association  **www.eventia.org.uk**
- Meeting Industry Association **www.mia-uk.org**
- Events Industry Alliance **www.eventsindustryalliance.com**
- Meeting Planners International  **www.mpiweb.org**
- International Special Events Society **www.ises.com**
- International Congress & Convention Association **www.iccaworld.com**
- International Festivals & Events Association **www.ifea.com**
- European Association of Event Centers **www.evvc.org**
- The Event Services Association **www.tesa.org.uk**
- National Outdoor Events Association **www.noea.org.uk**
- Society of Event Organisers **www.seoevent.co.uk**
- Association of British Professional Conference Organisers **www.abpco.org**

## Contemporary event developments – Olympic Games

Whilst the study of events management encompasses all sizes and genres of event, the undisputed biggest event management project in the world is the modern Olympics. Not only is it a celebration of sport, it is also a global phenomenon that is responsible for creating jobs, generating media coverage, involving huge investment in infrastructure, encompassing project management of an unprecedented scale and complexity. It is the epitome of event management. It is

## YOUTUBE

Events management at Bournemouth University
**http://www.youtube.com/watch?v=KKhX_iywF_Y**

important when studying the Olympics to understand the rituals, myths, history and symbolism that is so unique within the Olympic movement, which, whilst developing from the ancient traditions of the original Games, still apply in its modern form. Many similarities still exist in the physical preparations but also in many of the underlying messages too, notwithstanding some of the controversies of recent times. Many of the social, cultural and political values from the origins of the Games also still apply today and the similarities are part of the values and traditions that survive within the movement; yet the differences highlight changes in society, not least the commercialism that has become a byword for the Games in recent years.

The Games are more than just a sporting spectacle and should also be viewed as a cultural festival, with the Cultural Olympiad forming an integral part of each host city's preparations. However, the operational requirements of sport, and in particular the elitism of the sports, tend to overshadow the aspirations of the Olympic values. Baron de Coubertin's (the founder of the modern revival of the Games) vision matched the global visions of the nineteenth century: the internationalisation and rule-based management of sports developing alongside the philosophy of Olympism with the training and application of both body and mind symbolising human potential. However, the preparations and endeavours of today's modern athletes and their physiologists, psychologists and other trainers, should also be recognised as superhuman endeavour that may not always result in medal glory.

However, with planning a project of the size and magnitude of the Olympics comes a range of impacts on a global scale, both positive and negative. Numerous studies have been undertaken into the economic impacts of hosting the Games and especially since the Lillehammer Winter Games of 1994 a greater importance has been given to the environmental impacts. In recent years an increasing focus has begun to emerge on the social impacts, and this is beginning to produce some conflicting research in a newly emerging area as more authors suggest ways of measuring largely intangible variables. All events, including the Olympics, take place in a cultural and social context and these impacts are often proportional to the size and complexity of the event, thereby leading to the assumption that the impacts of the Olympics will always be the greatest.

## Events legacies and sustainable events

In the study of events, and their evaluation, consideration must always be given to the long-term legacy impacts, which may be indirect and subtle (Getz, 2007), as well as the short-term impacts. Many key event authors (Andersson et al., 1999; Getz, 1991; Hall, 1997; Ritchie, 2000) discuss the impacts than can arise from event legacies, acknowledging that they are not always positive and can have negative consequences (Sadd and Jones, 2008; Sadd, 2010). Often the true impacts of event legacies are either not apparent as they are hard to measure (i.e. social impacts) or they are overshadowed by the positive tangible benefits (i.e. economic impacts). It is imperative to understand the social implications of all events and this is often undertaken through resident surveys, although these mean little unless they are undertaken longitudinally over a period of time before, during and after an event to study the changes. These changes are very subjective and can differ from one resident to another but the suggestion is to undertake a social impact audit before any event to maximise the positive and minimise the negative social impacts. Examples of positive social impacts include increases in civic pride and community cohesion and negative

## YOUTUBE

Youth Olympic Games Innsbruck 2012 – Opening Ceremony
**http://www.youtube.com/watch?v=NhshLl7oyRl**

Olympic Games through history
**http://www.youtube.com/watch?v=ABvGkUcluUU**

ones include displacement and relocations, loss of facilities and increased levels of crime. Doxey's 1975 model is often used as a longitudinal measure of a resident population's reaction to tourism developments in their local area and it is also now used to measure the impacts of events that take place on a regular basis in the same area. Doxey's model measures the relationship between the impacts of events and residents' attitudes toward the event attendees, passing through a series of stages from 'euphoria', through 'apathy' and 'irritation' to 'antagonism', as perceived costs exceed the expected benefits. The scope of events legacies encompass the economic, environmental, physical and technological legacies, with many costs being hidden or other impacts, such as increased tourism receipts, masking the true cost of the event (Getz, 1999). Other potential legacies include outcomes in terms of the built and physical environment, public life, politics and culture, sporting facilities, education and information, and symbols, memory and history (Cashman, 2006). Preuss's (2006) legacy typology is divided into positive and negative legacies, identified along three legacy dimensions of planned, positive and degree of quantifiable structure within the legacy planning. However, he does not implicitly recognise how intangible elements can have an even greater impact/outcome (Ritchie, 2000), or the indirect and subtle intangible impacts analogy (Getz, 2008), though he does include tangible legacies in the form of community spirit and popular memory. Furthermore, he does believe that the psychological, social, cultural and political legacies are more subjective and therefore more difficult to quantify and measure accurately. He argues that the social and psychological factors are sometimes the most valuable in terms of enhancing long-term well-being and the lifestyle of host residents.

## Growth of the role of social media in events

Given the onset of social media in the 2000s through MySpace, Facebook, Twitter, etc., their importance as an element in events presence has only intensified. Given its adoption by growing numbers of Internet users worldwide, social media has in some instances become the reason for hosting events (e.g. flash mobs). As a marketing tool, companies and organisations have staged spontaneous events, often in very public places (airports, public parks, train station forecourts) as a method to promote their products and services (e.g. mobile phone companies, energy drinks). Outside of this, many events use Facebook in the promotion of events and to communicate informal and formal messages about those people and organisations hosting them. In its present form, Facebook has the facility for users to create event pages, and invite attendees. Promotional material as well as informal chat space for questions on an event is facilitated in this part of Facebook.

Twitter is another medium by which events are promoted and commented on. Equally, Twitter as an online tool is oftentimes used to relay real-time information on events, as a way of communicating with participants, for example at conferences. It can also be used so that remote participants from around the globe can interact in group sessions, for example the employees within a global company. Social media has also been the platform on which other events are planned and executed. For example, groups wishing to organise a political protest or demonstration are able to mobilise their supporters effectively and quickly through social media. The UK was subject to riots in August 2011 and word of these events was spread by means of social media and mobile communications. A global example of political events planned globally in 2011 also coordinated with the aid of social media was the 'occupy protest' (Occupy Wall Street, Occupy London). This protest movement initially intended to protest against economic and social inequality in society, and it then spread across the world to other countries such as Spain, Israel, South Africa and Cyprus.

Events from now and going into the future will very much be based around, or should be based around, the generation of good content, whether it is a PR stunt or a more experiential-based event with a large amount of direct interaction with consumers/customers. Due to the ever-increasing ways of spreading messages across platforms, if an event can create content which users choose to actively share on social media sites then that can be a story in itself and, more importantly, as this is the ultimate requirement of any event, result in a large return on investment for the client. Sites such as Facebook, Twitter, Tumblr are obviously the first things consumers, customers and event managers think of in terms of sharing content, but mobile is very much the future and, if they do not already, events need to look to mobile platforms as an integral part of planning future events. Mobile research will show that it is the up-and-coming segment in marketing/advertising. It won't be too long before people use their phones for everything, from checking into hotels, making payments, and events need to look at ways of using this development. They are also very much a platform for viewing content – with PR stories and newspaper coverage the main way for brands to get an immediate (and measurable) return on investment, events need to be very responsive to current trends and hooks in the media.

## Predictions for the future of events

In 2000 a conference was held in Sydney Australia, entitled 'Events beyond 2000 – setting the agenda' which brought together most of the leading academics and authors on events at that time. One of the keynote addresses was given by Joe Jeff Goldblatt, and in his talk entitled 'A future for event management: the analysis of major trends impacting the emerging profession' he predicted the major trends that would impact on the event profession over the next 25 years. Now that we are half-way through his timescale of predictions it is prudent to see which have come true. He split his predictions into three categories of environmental, technological and human resource and gave five-year period changes. By 2015 he believed that for human resource issues, more women would enter management roles within the events business (a verifiable trend), there would be a shorter working week (not in the events field) and a proliferation of funeral events as the population expands yet people request life celebrations as opposed to more traditional religious ceremonies (not conclusive). In relation to technology, he predicted we would capitalise on e-commerce (advancements evolve daily in the twenty-first century), broadband offering real-time live (virtual events) and 24-hour complete systems integration whereby event attendance is a full participation event over a long time period from before, during and after (beginning to emerge). With regard to environmental issues the big change is state intervention in setting environmental management standards, especially in relation to global warming (true, with BS 8901 the industry standard in the UK).

What, however, are his future predictions for the industry? Regarding environmental issues he believes water shortages will result in more recycling and purification systems at events and advances in medical care will see a wider age span of people involved with and enjoying events. Considering human resource issues, the future predictions include machines replacing some of the more traditional event functions, with event staff therefore becoming more specialised, and the ageing population remaining mentally active for longer. Finally, from the technology standpoint, he predicts that by 2025 we will see interplanetary events and robots being involved in event production – an interesting and exciting prediction.

Whether you believe in these predictions or not, the truth is that many of his forecasts from 2000 to 2015 have come to fruition. What is clear is the role that technology and social media will have within the event management industry (and the earlier section on social media confirms this).

## CONCLUSION

The growth of events as an industry and the integral demand for the study of event management as a profession has led to many academic texts being devoted to this topic alone. Therefore it is acknowledged that just one chapter here has limited scope. However, we have attempted to provide an overview of the synergy between the study of tourism and events. This is particularly true as much of the theoretical underpinning used within the study of events comes from other disciplines, none more so than the study of tourism. Similarly, the study of events also encompasses hospitality, retail, sports, leisure, science, psychology, anthropology – the list seems endless. The growth of the events business and the volume of people employed within all the facets of the industry, including the educational arm, show how important the study of this industry is.

## SELF-CHECK QUESTIONS

1. What are the principal classifications of events?
2. What are the differences between 'hallmark' and 'mega' events?
3. Identify five key trends impacting on the future development of events.
4. Why is the management of events now considered a profession?
5. What are the important developments in social media in relation to events management?

## REFERENCES AND FURTHER READING

Allen, J. (2002) *The Business of Event Planning*, John Wiley & Sons, Ontario, Canada.

Allen, J., O'Toole, W., McDonnell, I. and Harris, R. (2005) *Festival and Special Event Management,* 3rd edn, John Wiley & Sons, Milton, Queensland, Australia.

Andersson, T.D., Persson, C., Sahlberg, B. and Strom, L.-I. (1999) *The Impact of Mega-Events*, European Tourism Research Institute, Ostersund, Sweden.

Bowdin, G., Allen, J., O'Toole, W., Harris, R. and McDonnell, I. (2011) *Events Management*, Oxford, Butterworth-Heinemann.

Cashman, R. (2006) *The Bitter Sweet Awakening – The Legacy of the Sydney 2000 Olympic Games*, Sydney, Walla Walla Press.

Doxey, G.V. (1975) 'A causation theory of visitor–resident irritants: methodology and research inferences', pp. 195–8, in *Proceedings of the 6th Annual Conference of The Travel Research Association*, Travel and Tourism Research Association, San Diego, CA.

Getz, D. (1991). *Festivals, Special Events and Tourism*, Van Nostrand Reinhold, New York.

Getz, D. (1997) *Event Management and Event Tourism*. NY, USA, Cognizant Communications Group.

Getz, D. (2007) *Event Studies – Theory, Research and Policy for Planned Events,* Butterworth-Heinemann, Oxford.

Goldblatt, J.J. (1997) *Special Events: Best Practices in Modern Event Management*, 2nd edn, John Wiley & Sons, New York.

Goldblatt, J.J. (2000) 'A future for event management: the analysis of major trends impacting the emerging profession', in *Events Beyond 2000 – Setting the Agenda,* Proceedings of the Conference on Evaluation, Research and Education, 13–14 July.

Goldblatt, J.J. (2002) *Special Events: 21st Century Global Events Management*, 3rd edn, Wiley, New York.

Goldblatt, J.J. (2008) *Special Events: Event Leadership for a New World*, 5th edn, John Wiley & Sons, Hoboken, NJ.

Hall, C.M. (1992) *Hallmark Tourist Events: Impacts, Management, and Planning,* Belhaven Press, London.

Hall, C.M. (1997) 'Mega-events and their legacies', in P.E. Murphy (ed.), *Quality Management in Urban Tourism,* John Wiley & Sons, Chichester.

Hede, A. (2007) 'Managing special events in the new era of triple bottom line', *Event Management* **11**(1–2), 13–22.

MRG (2008) *Town Centre Master Vision,* evaluation of the effect of an evening event in the town on business levels and customer perceptions, Bournemouth University, Bournemouth, UK.

Narayan, D. (1999) *Bonds and Bridges: Social Capital and Poverty*, Poverty Group, PREM.

Pine, B.J. and Gilmore, J.H. (1999) *The Experience Economy: Work is a Theatre and Every Business a Stage,* Harvard Business School Press, Boston.

Preuss, H. (2006) 'Lasting effects of major sporting events', in *idrottsforum.org/artiklar,* Malmo, idrottsvetenskap.

Ritchie, J.R.B. (1984) 'Assessing the impact of hallmark events', *Journal of Travel Research* **23**(1), 2–11.

Ritchie, J.R.B. (2000) 'Turning 16 days into 16 years through Olympic legacies', *Event Management* **6**, 155–65.

Sadd, D. and Jones, I. (2008) 'Implications and issues for London site residents', *London Journal of Tourism, Sport and Creative Studies* **1**(1), 22–9.

Sadd, D. (2010) 'What is event led regeneration? Are we confusing terminology or will London 2012 be the first Games to truly benefit the local existing population?', *Event Management* **13**(4), 265–75.

Shone, A. and Parry, B. (2001) *Successful Event Management: A Practical Handbook,* 2nd edn, Thomson, London.

Small, K., Carlsen, J., Robertson, M. and Ali-Knight, J. (2007) 'Social dimensions of community festivals. An application of factor analysis in the development of the Social Impact Perception (SIP) scale', *Event Management* **11**, 45–55.

Van der Wagen, L. (2001) *Event Management for Tourism, Cultural, Business and Sporting Events,* Lynn Van der Wagen Hospitality Press, Melbourne, Australia.

Watt, D.C. (1998) *Event Management in Leisure and Tourism,* Longman, London.

Wood, E.H. (2002) 'Events, civic pride and attitude change in post-industrial town: evaluating the effect of local authority events on residents' attitudes to the Blackburn region'. Paper presented at *Events & Place Making Conference,* University of Technology, Sydney, July.

Wood, E. (2006) 'Measuring the social impacts of local authority events: a pilot study for a civic pride scale', *International Journal Non-profit Voluntary Sectors* **11**(3), 165–79.

Yeoman, I., Robertson, M., Ali-Knight, J., Drummond, S. and McMahon-Beattie, U. (2004) *Festival and Events Management: An International Arts and Cultural Perspective,* Elsevier Butterworth-Heinemann, Oxford.

# MAJOR CASE STUDY 15.1
## Bournemouth Air Festival

**Photograph 15.2** Bournemouth International Air Festival, UK, 2013.
*Source*: With kind permission from Joanna Milner

## INTRODUCTION

The Bournemouth Air Festival represents an interesting case study to analyse socio-cultural impacts. Events play a significant role in the enhancement of an image of an area and the provision of services to the benefit of tourists and the local community; none more so than in Bournemouth, a UK seaside resort in the south of England which attracts in excess of 5 million day visitors per annum.

In the 1980s Bournemouth was identified as a town with a lack of sense of belonging as a result of the restructuring of UK cities. In response local government looked towards events as a means to foster a sense of community and pride in the town and to transform it into a place of entertainment. Bournemouth is a large coastal resort town in the county of Dorset on the southern coast of England which, according to the 2011 census, has a population of 168,100, making it the largest settlement in Dorset. With the neighbouring historic towns of Poole and Christchurch, Bournemouth forms the South East Dorset conurbation, which has a total population of approximately 400,000. Founded in 1810 by Lewis Tregonwell, Bournemouth's growth accelerated with the arrival of the railway, becoming a recognised town in 1870. Many wealthy Victorians then built grand summer homes in the town and over time, with the development of railways and latterly cars, the resort became known as a place to visit, firstly to escape the living conditions in industrial towns and secondly to help those with breathing and chest problems to convalesce. Gradually the supply of hotels and boarding houses expanded and the town became a popular holiday resort for domestic tourism, for which it is still well known today. In addition, the town now supports a thriving financial services industry as well as being a major supplier of educational services.

Since 1997 the town has been administered by a unitary authority, meaning that it has autonomy from Dorset County Council. The local authority is Bournemouth Borough Council. Bournemouth's location has made it a popular destination for tourists and the town is also a regional centre of business – home of the Bournemouth International Centre and financial companies that include Liverpool Victoria, Nationwide and J.P. Morgan. In a 2007 survey by First Direct, Bournemouth was found to be the happiest place in the UK, with 82% of people questioned saying they were happy with their lives. Historically Bournemouth relied on three main industries – tourism, education and finance – yet in response to the Bournemouth Tourism Management Board objective in 2008 to 'establish a major event to attract tourists to the area' it was decided to consider an air festival. Board members therefore visited air festivals in Sunderland, Eastbourne and Southend to research the concept (MRG, 2008). It was identified as a major spectacle to attract tourist numbers as 'Military and civil airshows in the UK remain second only to football in terms of spectator numbers' (MRG, 2008). Over 1.3 million people attended the Air Festival in 2009 and the focus in this case study is to identify the impacts on the quality of life of the residents of Bournemouth and the surrounding area. The air show lasts four days, takes place on one beach, attracts a million spectators, involves day and night entertainment including dusk aerial displays, 16 hours of flying displays, pyrotechnics, live music and circus entertainers. The festival brings more than £30 million into the local economy. The Royal Navy, RAF and Army all bring vital assets to make the show bigger and better each year.

Those responsible for the operational management of the Air Festival are the existing core team of four within the Council Events Group. They have overall responsibility for the external organisational management, event development and delivery of any events held on council-owned/managed facilities, including all parks, buildings and the seafront itself. They have a portfolio that includes the four-day Air Festival providing an injection of over £30 million to the local economy as well as meeting a diversity of commercial and community objectives. The Air Festival has become the major project for the team and the visitor numbers have increased over the three years since it began. Whilst there are many impacts of hosting such an event, this case study examines in detail some of the identified social impacts and suggests ways of maximising those that are positive and trying to minimise those that are considered negative.

## SOCIO-CULTURAL IMPACTS

A review of the impacts seen as a result of studying the events over four days for three consecutive years has shown that the biggest positive impacts are:

### 1. Pride

Pride in the local areas is identified as the main positive socio-cultural impact. Wood (2006) identifies the importance of civic pride and how local authorities should attempt to evaluate the users' perception of the success of the event by measuring the attitude of the consumers to the event, the value of the event to the local authority and finally the consumer perception of the region. The research to date (MRG, 2008) identifies an increase in pride for the respondents at hosting an event of this scale in their town, plus welcoming the additional income that the event brings to the town which is then reinvested in the local community.

### 2. Profile of Bournemouth

The Bournemouth Air Festival aims to raise the profile of Bournemouth as a tourist destination and to attract future tourists to the area through local, national and international coverage in the media.

### 3. Tourist and leisure amenities

The Festival maintains the quality of local tourist and leisure amenities which the local people can enjoy, including restaurants, attractions and entertainment venues. Positive perceptions of the town have increased through the new facilities and improvements to existing facilities.

### 4. Free event with mass appeal

The strap line for the Bournemouth Air Festival is 'By the Sea and Completely Free', which engages local residents to come to the Festival. The research further identifies that the audience of the event is widely spread across gender and ages and attendees come from local and regional audiences. The mass appeal of the event ensures a broad appeal from a socio-cultural perspective for the local residents.

# NEGATIVE IMPACTS

## 1. Negative media coverage

The Bournemouth Air Festival has been affected by over-hanging cloud cover in 2010, severe flash floods in 2011 and the fatal accident involving a Red Arrow fighter jet in 2011, all of which attracted national media attention. This has implications for users attending events and shows the power of the media and social networking sites to spread these messages and stories too quickly for the organisers to control. A concerted effort was made by the organisers to manage the media in 2011 and to leverage this in a positive manner for the 2012 show.

## 2. Noise pollution

Due to the nature of the event the noise of the displays over a four-day period can have a negative impact on local residents and animals in the area. The greatest impact is on some of the more vulnerable members of society. This could be managed by the organisers by coordinating the timings of the noisy exhibitions and minimising the impact on the community through consul-tation and effective communication.

## 3. Overcrowding

It is important for the event organisers to monitor the capacity that the town can adequately cater for, bearing in mind the infrastructure, parking and amenities. It is said that negative impacts from tourism events occur when the volume of visitor numbers is greater than the environment's ability to cope with these numbers, known as the limits of acceptable change (LAC).

## Socio-cultural event mitigation strategies

Socio-cultural capital has grown in importance in recent years and refers to norms and social relations embedded in social structures of societies that enable people to coordinate action to achieve desired goals (Narayan, 1999). The social capital gained can be related to the Bournemouth Air Festival regarding the positive impacts to the local community.

## Recommended strategies to maximise positive impacts

- To engage with the local residents and integrate them into the future planning of the event in order to continue to foster pride in the event and community cohesion. To increase the scope of researching resi-dents in the local area by targeting residents within a 15 kilometre radius of the festival to derive more representative feedback.
- To continue to develop the profile of Bournemouth Air Festival and determine what capacity can be catered for.

- To ensure residents make use of the new amenities for the area.
- To adopt the Social Impact Evaluation Framework (adapted from Small et al., 2007: 69) to adopt a longer term strategic approach to effectively managing the future sustainability of the festival.

## Organisations must work to minimise the negative social impacts

- To develop a strategy to deal with social media.
- To develop a contingency plan for inclement weather that can affect the event and put forward a possible replacement to ensure the sustainability of the event.
- To develop crowd management strategies to ensure the town can cope with the increased numbers of visitors to the event as it grows in maturity so as not to alienate the local residents of Bournemouth.

# CONCLUSION

A cost–benefit strategy could be adopted by the local authority to determine whether the money invested in the event and the benefits outweigh the negative impacts of the event. This represents an opportunity cost that may have been devoted to another need in the community. This is particularly relevant at the present time with the increased pressure on local government spending. The Bournemouth Air Festival is an exciting event for the town but it needs to be managed care-fully to ensure the future sustainability and success of the event. Therefore measuring the triple bottom line through the economic, social and environmental impact is important. Hede (2007) identifies the importance of integrating the triple-bottom-line concept into the plan-ning stages to ensure successful future planning of special events. It is recommended that the Bournemouth Air Festival team develop a strategy of measuring the social impacts that can be compared and analysed over time to ensure the future sustainability of the event in the future and support from the local community.

*Source*: Case study written with Pearl Morrison, Bournemouth University

# DISCUSSION QUESTIONS

1. What other possible social impacts could the Air Festival produce?
2. Can the festival keep growing without more negative social and environmental impacts?
3. In what ways could the festival encourage repeat visits from the local community?
4. How can you measure the social impacts on the host population?

# CHAPTER 16

## INTERMEDIARIES

### LEARNING OUTCOMES

The focus of the chapter is the packaging and distribution of the tourism product. By the end of this chapter, therefore, you will:

- be familiar with the nature and structures of intermediation and the arguments for and against disintermediation of distribution channels in tourism;

- be aware of the increasing consolidation and concentration of tourism intermediaries;

- have an understanding of recent online developments and be aware of the emergence and significance of social media in the context of intermediaries and travel booking behaviour;

- be familiar with the operating characteristics, roles and functions of retail travel agents and tour operators;

- have an understanding of the process of distribution; and

- be aware of the financial constraints on the operation of intermediaries and the difficulties these inflict.

Photograph: Aleppo Souk, Syria © Helen Savill

# INTRODUCTION

In this chapter we show that the principal role of intermediaries is to bring buyers and sellers together. For travel and tourism, intermediation comes about through tour operators or wholesalers assembling the components of the tourist trip into a package and retailing the latter through travel agents, who deal directly with the public. However, as this chapter shows, this is not the only way by which the tourist product reaches the customer and we discuss several other distribution channels. The structure of intermediation is complicated by the fact that some retail agents and some of the principal suppliers, such as airlines, also act as tour wholesalers. Much of this trend has been driven by online developments and the rapid adoption of electronic technologies in facilitating the supply of and demand for tourism products. Online travel trends will be explored in this chapter and their impact on the traditional industry will be examined, as will the emergence and significance of social media.

In this context, the chapter outlines the roles played by the retail travel agent and the tour operator respectively. We point out the differences between the North American and European travel trade systems, although our main emphasis is on the commonality of the underlying principles governing their activity. The conceptual aspects of tour operation are relatively straightforward but the implementation requires considerable organisation and planning, particularly in view of the time lags involved. We therefore discuss the main stages of tour operation in some detail. Finally, the factors making for market dominance are analysed.

# THE NATURE OF INTERMEDIATION

In all industries the task of **intermediaries** is to transform goods and services from a form that consumers do not want into a product that they do want. For everyday household requirements, this is performed mainly through holding bulk supplies and breaking these down into amounts required by individuals, as well as bringing the goods to the marketplace. In tourism the situation is somewhat different, for it is quite possible to buy the components of the tourism trip (accommodation, transport, excursions and entertainment) directly from producers. This dispenses with the need for an intermediary. Traditionally, this has not happened to any great degree because the linkages (termed distribution channels) between the suppliers of tourism products and their potential customers are imperfect, and so the output of the travel intermediary is what is termed a *search* good, since it offers consumers the opportunity of avoiding the effort and cost of undertaking the production activity. However, as will be mentioned throughout this chapter, the information communications technology (ICT) revolution in recent years has made it easier, through the growth of low-cost airlines, the provision of supplier websites and the use of online social networks, for experienced travellers to assemble their own itineraries and drive, through their user-generated content, the general direction of the sector.

Thus, from the perspective of economics, the role of intermediaries is to improve distribution channels and so make markets by bringing buyers and sellers together. It is argued that distribution channels often both influence consumer behaviour by branding the product and thereby supplying a **credence** good, as well as determining the ability of the industry to respond to consumers' requests efficiently in terms of the product as a search good. In this manner, distribution channels quite clearly help determine the competitiveness of suppliers and destinations. The bulk of this work falls upon the tour operator or wholesaler who packages the main components of the tourist trip (legally not fewer than two) into a single product and sells this at one price through retail travel agents or, particularly in North America, airline sales offices. This identifies the tour operator as the **principal** (a trade term) economic entity and not merely as the **agent** selling on commission. The latter role is that of the retail travel agent, who provides an outlet for the actual sales of tours, tickets and travel services, such as insurance or foreign exchange, to the public.

## Benefits

By making markets, travel intermediaries bestow benefits on producers, consumers and the destination. These benefits include the following:

**Producers:**

- Are able to sell in bulk and so transfer risk to the tour operator, though wholesalers do attempt to cover themselves by a variety of agreements and release clauses. The latter may vary from four or more weeks to seven days.
- Can reduce promotion costs by focusing on the travel trade, rather than consumer promotion, which is much more expensive.

**Consumers:**

- Can avoid search and transaction costs in both time and money by being able to purchase an inclusive tour.
- Gain from the specialist knowledge of the tour operator and the fact that the uncertainties of travel are minimised. For example, cruising and coach tours are attractive to senior citizens because the holiday starts the moment they board the ship or coach.
- Often gain most from lower prices, notably in the case of resorts dealing with large numbers of visitors as in the Mediterranean, Mexico, Florida and Hawaii. In such destinations wholesalers are able through their buying power to negotiate discounts of up to 60% off the normal tariff.

**Destinations:**

- Especially in developing countries where budgets are limited, may benefit considerably from the international marketing network of tour operators. However, it is naïve to expect, as some countries do, that this should be a responsibility of these companies, particularly as the Internet has made it so much easier for national tourist organisations (NTOs) to promote their tourist areas.

Clearly some disadvantages do exist. For the producer, use of intermediaries will reduce margins, and their degree of marketing control and influence over the process of distribution, although they would hope to make this up in improved business performance. It is also likely that ultimate customer service will be beyond their control, with most attention being directed at the channel intermediaries rather than the end consumer. For the consumer, further concentration and consolidation of tourism intermediaries may actually reduce choice and increase prices. For destinations, if they become overly dependent on intermediaries for bookings, they are very much susceptible to the 'whims' and 'vagaries' of the marketplace, and the ability of intermediaries to influence consumer choice by 'switch' selling to more profitable locations.

## Structure

A schematic diagram of the structure of distribution channels is shown in Figure 16.1. Independent travellers put their own itinerary together. This they can do by purchasing the key components of accommodation and transport directly from suppliers, from their own outlets or websites, or via the retail travel agent in the high street or through their website. It is common in domestic tourism for consumers to purchase their trip requirements directly because they usually have good product knowledge and ready access to a telephone, if not the Internet, to make reservations. However, in order to boost the market for the domestic product in the UK, the national and regional tourist boards have produced travel brochures which they distribute in a number of ways: directly through the mail or 'downloads' in response to enquiries or from a mailing list (termed direct response marketing), through tourist information centres (TICs), or by persuading the travel trade to give commissionable brochures rack space in their shops. These brochures simply give the public a portfolio of products to choose from, which avoids the tourist boards being classified as 'organisers' according to the 1992 EU Package Travel Directive that regulates provision within Europe, protects consumers and adds credence to the product.

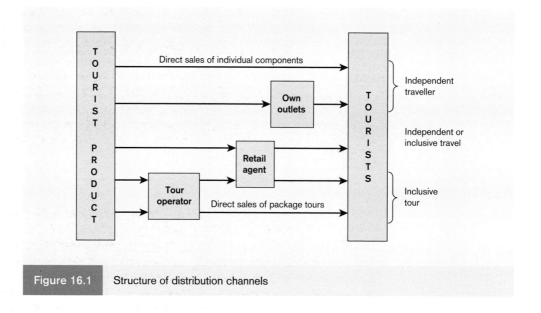

| **Figure 16.1** | Structure of distribution channels |

It has been common for airlines, bus and shipping companies to have their own outlets in large cities from which the public may purchase travel products directly, though less so today in the face of developments in information communication technologies, most notably the Internet. Airlines have been particularly keen to secure their presence in the market by locating offices on flagship sites in capital cities. These serve both the trade and the public, and are especially important in world cities such as Bangkok, Berlin, London or New York where not only are there large numbers of business travellers, but also many overseas holidaymakers travelling independently. International hotel chains and hotel marketing consortia also use individual establishments for selling rooms in other properties belonging to the group. This has become routine with the advent of modern reservation systems.

The founding companies of today's travel trade, Thomas Cook (see Major Case Study 16.1) and American Express, are both travel agents and wholesalers, with both demonstrating an increasing online presence, and so history is on the side of the retail agent that buys directly from producers. Through agency agreements (which, in the United States, are requirements set by what have been historically termed conferences representing the domestic and international airlines, shipping companies and railways), retailers sell the individual components of the trip, such as transport tickets, accommodation and excursions, but they may also put together their own brand of tours, over-brand another tour operator's brochure or have a specialist wholesaler put together a brochure for them. Such own branding is a practice that has been traditionally more common in North America than in Europe, as has been the use of travel counsellors in agencies to assemble specially tailored packages for clients.

Traditionally, travel agents have made the bulk of their money from selling **inclusive tours** and airline tickets, though the situation regarding the latter has changed, because the major full-service carriers, in the face of competition from low-cost carriers, have cut their distribution costs by removing commissions to travel agents and global distribution systems (GDSs) in an effort to lower their bottom-line costs. Agents have responded to this by charging a handling fee to customers. In Europe most inclusive tours are associated with foreign travel, whereas in North America domestic trips are the dominant source of inclusive tour sales. The importance of business travel has led to the growth of agencies, usually belonging to a chain, dealing solely with this aspect of tourism, to the extent of providing 'implants', albeit electronically, in major corporations solely for the purpose of covering their corporate travel needs, including arranging meetings, conventions and incentive travel awarded to staff. More recently banks and major corporations have organised travel departments to serve not only their own needs, but also those of their privileged (high net-wealth) customers.

Photograph 16.1 | Thomas Cook, holidaymaking in the 1950s. Although a major player in the business of travel intermediation, Thomas Cook has over 160 years of travel industry experience.
*Source*: Thomas Cook Archives

The most common way of distributing foreign holiday travel in Europe is still through inclusive tours packaged by tour operators and sold by travel agents, despite the Internet, social media, digital TV and the proliferation of call centres, which permit holiday packages to be marketed directly to the public by wholesalers. At one stage it was thought that a number of developments ranging from commission capping by a number of international airlines, the growth of 'no-frills' airlines, increasing computer literacy and confidence among consumers and the rapid proliferation in e-ticketing would lead to the demise of the traditional travel agent but to date many still exist with many markets, especially the elderly, still preferring to deal with an intermediary rather than going direct (Buhalis, 2003). That said, many tour operators in Europe do have **direct-sell** brands within their portfolio, which currently amount to around 40% of their turnover, and the expectation is that this will rise to 70% in the next few years. Within North America, the domestic nature of the product is such that online bookings are already over 70% for the major travel companies.

Although direct selling of foreign tours has been slow to capture the public's attention and is still behind that of products purchased by more time-honoured means, it has also been put forward that the increasing sophistication of the travelling public, combined with the ease of making reservations, would lead to the demise of the package holiday and **disintermediation** of the tourism distribution system. Principals in this instance may be a tour operator, a hotel or a transport company. While it is true that more people are travelling independently, evidence to

**YOUTUBE**
Trends

Travel Trends – Peter Cochrane on the Changing World Travel Market
http://www.youtube.com/watch?v=Pa-UYJbLC8c

What drives Travel Agent influences
http://www.youtube.com/watch?v=OTvXMEvUtk4

date, as noted above, suggests that traditional purchasing patterns will continue in many markets (especially 'grey' markets and those on a low budget), for it still remains the case that operators can negotiate cheaper arrangements through their bulk purchasing power, they are also able to respond to the public's demands by building in more options to their package offers and they are bound by economic regulations that offer quality assurance and security to the customer. It is not so much that we are looking at disintermediation in the wake of the ICT revolution but **reintermediation** as the industry adjusts its strategic positioning and continues to reinvent itself.

## Integration, consolidation and concentration

The term **integration** is an economic concept describing formal linking arrangements between one organisation and another. **Vertical integration** is where the linking occurs along the production process, for example when an airline establishes its own tour operating company. This would be an example of vertical integration forwards into the marketplace, of which the most common in terms of intermediaries is where a tour wholesaler acquires through merger or purchase a retail travel chain.

Tour operators owning airlines provide an example of vertical integration backwards and this is also common among scheduled airlines, which form alliances with (and even own) multinational hotel chains and surface transport companies to secure trading advantages over their rivals. One of the widest range of integrated activities may be found in the French conglomerate Groupe Accor. Originally known for its hotel operations, Groupe Accor's interests now include all aspects of tourism, as can be seen in Figure 16.2.

Looking at developments over time, it appears that the degree of vertical integration varies with the **product life cycle**. We illustrate this in Figure 16.3. At the early stage of development, as in the case of Thomas Cook, there is a high degree of vertical integration as there are few suppliers. But as demand expands so specialists develop to increase the efficiency of the distribution channel. Operators are bound together by their mutual interest in helping the market to grow. As the market matures, competitive pressures for market share force companies to seek the benefits of forming vertical links. These include:

- economies of scale through the linking of complementary activities, investing in new technologies and improved management expertise in, say, foreign exchange transactions, forecasting and marketing;
- cutting out the intermediary by being able to control costs and quality standards under the umbrella of one organisation;
- securing supplies and increasing buying power; and
- protecting market position by guaranteeing retail outlets on prime high street sites.

It is important to note that vertical integration forwards does not necessarily have to come about through ownership. Control may be exercised by franchising. This is a licensing agreement whereby the parent company grants another, usually smaller, firm the right to sell its products and use its brand name, but in return the firm should not sell the products of its competitors. In Germany, the package holiday business was developed by the major retail groups, such as

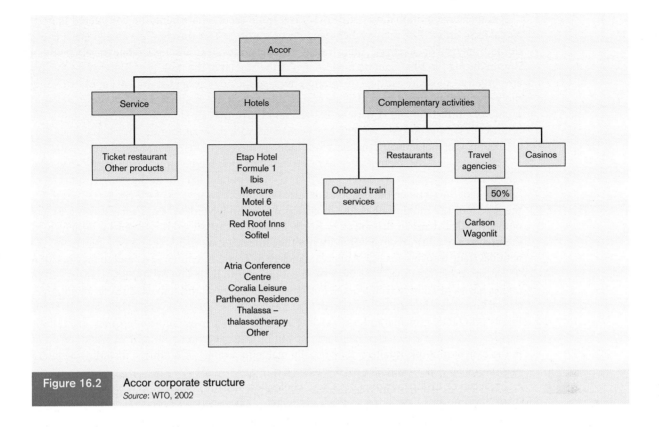

Figure 16.2    Accor corporate structure
*Source*: WTO, 2002

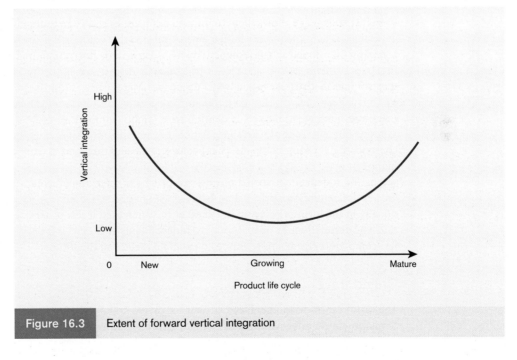

Figure 16.3    Extent of forward vertical integration

Karstadt, Neckermann and Quelle in the 1960s. They already had the advantage of retail shops and mail order systems to distribute their products. Owing to stricter cartel laws, further expansion through vertical integration was difficult, so they developed market power through mutual shareholding agreements and a system of tied agency licensing, which gave them exclusive outlets for their products and protected their profit margins.

Another organisational aspect of the travel trade sector that should be considered is *horizontal integration*. This occurs when two tour operators or two travel agents amalgamate, either through merger or takeover. This strategy was very prevalent amongst retail travel chains in Britain during the 1980s and became known as the 'march of the multiples'. The reasons for this are similar to those for vertical integration but also include the spatial dimension of extending the geographical spread of outlets to ensure representation in all regions. Thomas Cook and Lunn Poly in Britain, and American Express and Carlson Wagonlit Travel (which acquired the historically famous Ask Mr. Foster travel agency network that was founded in 1888) in the USA, are examples of major chains that have traditionally increased their geographical representation.

For the retailers, horizontal integration strengthens their buying power with regard to wholesalers. They support this by developing their own corporate identity in the design and style of operation of their branch outlets, so as to raise the public's awareness of the company. Naturally, the march of the multiples has drawn criticism from independent travel agents owing to loss of their market share. In Britain, as in North America, many small travel agencies have formed themselves into consortia to give themselves the same negotiating power as the multiples and the national trade associations, the American Society of Travel Agents (ASTA) and the Association of British Travel Agents (ABTA), have been enthusiastic in their support for independents. Both bodies have a mission to facilitate the business of selling travel through effective representation, shared knowledge and the enhancement of professionalism. They seek a retail travel marketplace that is profitable, growing and a rewarding place to work, invest and do business. Large tour operators have also grown by amalgamation, but instead of enforcing a uniform brand image, as in the case of multiple retailers, they usually maintain a range of products, including acquired brands, to meet the consumer's need for choice.

Criticism of major tour operators and wholesalers usually comes from destinations, particularly those in less-developed countries. The latter have expressed concern over the strength of the economic buying power of large wholesalers, which allows them to obtain prices below those that would occur in markets where competition prevails. It is further argued that their specialist knowledge allows them to influence consumer choice in tourism-generating countries and so gives them the opportunity to switch sales to destinations that are more profitable to the company. Continued integration activity, be it vertical or horizontal, in addition to increasing numbers of mergers and acquisitions has led to further consolidation and concentration of tourism intermediaries, especially in Europe (see Major Case Study 16.1).

The major beneficiaries of consolidation are clearly consumers and shareholders, with consumers in a number of markets benefiting from highly competitive price wars and shareholders in terms of their rising stock values. A note of caution is necessary here, however, as the cost of consolidation for some companies has been excessive and threatens to damage their very existence in the future.

For the independent sector businesses, of which there remain many, the future demands greater differentiation, and an ability to deal with barriers that increase with consolidation, most notably in the form of price wars. Whether it is increased levels of service provision or a focus on niche destinations or travel products, independents are likely to experience more, rather than less competition from an ever more consolidated sector in the future.

## Online travel

The significant development and growth of **online travel**, predominantly on the back of the development of information technologies and telecommunications plus phenomenal growth of the Internet and electronic commerce, has been one of the great success stories for tourism generally, and tourism intermediaries in particular (Berne et al., 2012; Buhalis and Law, 2008; Ho et al., in press). The volume of online tourism-related transactions is anticipated to reach over half of all e-transactions in the near future, with considerable implications for intermediaries and their competitors across the wider tourism industry – and none more so than for the four major GDSs which still dominate the distribution of travel products, notably Sabre and Worldspan, which dominate in the USA, and Galileo and Amadeus, which are market leaders in Europe. Back in 1996, Sabre was the first GDS to venture online with its launch of **Travelocity .com**, a virtual agency. At the same time, **Expedia.com** was launched by USA Networks. This was then followed by Amadeus.net in 1997 by Amadeus Global Travel Distribution and the purchase of **TRIP.com** by Galileo International in 2000. After just three years in operation, **Travelocity .com** and **Expedia.com** were among the 10 largest US distributors of travel products in terms of revenue. In Europe, **lastminute.com** was launched in 1998 and **eBookers.com** in 1999, demonstrating that new methods of online communication were able to cross entry barriers to a market previously outside the scope of new players.

One of the biggest contributors to the growth in the purchase of e-tickets has been the rise of discount 'no-frills' airlines, especially across the USA and Europe, and their replication elsewhere in Asia and Australia. The principal catalysts for change were Southwest Airlines in the United States and easyJet and Ryanair in the UK and Ireland respectively, leading to AirAsia in Malaysia and Virgin Blue in Australia. For airlines generally, although they are subject to the same rules as travel agencies, they often are able to offer special rates and exclusive deals and so motivate consumers to purchase tickets directly rather than via a travel agent. This incredible growth has been in a remarkably short time period and reflects most dramatically how certain parts of the wider tourism industry have capitalised on changing trends in technology and their greater acceptance by the consumer. In response to the fierce competition from the 'no-frills' carriers and the growth of virtual intermediaries, many international airlines are coming together in order to compete head-on with the new players. For example, in December 2001, the virtual intermediary Opodo was launched by nine European airlines with an initial focus on the German, French, Italian and British markets. Collectively, Air France, British Airways, Lufthansa, Alitalia, Iberia, KLM, Aer Lingus, Finnair and Austrian Airlines have used Amadeus technology to develop a serious competitor to existing players. One cautionary note is the move by some airlines to withdraw commissions to online agencies. Although this may represent a temporary initiative it does introduce an element of uncertainty for the future relationship between producers and intermediaries in their efforts to find the most effective and cost-efficient means of reaching the final consumer.

The fact that there remains in some parts of the market much caution with regard to the use of virtual intermediaries explains in part the development of **'click-and-mortar' agencies**, whereby a combination of online and offline services – often in the form of a network of traditional travel agencies and/or call centres – is a strategic response to the concerns of many. In addition, many traditional players are now developing the reverse, as part of the reintermediation process, in that they are developing a web presence to complement their traditional business.

In addition to the above, and consistent with traditional intermediaries and the wider tourism industry, consolidation is occurring also in the virtual marketplace. Clearly, the speed with which online travel has developed is remarkable. The speed with which consolidation has begun to impact on the structure of the industry is even more remarkable, however, in that in the space

## YOUTUBE
### Online travel agencies and social media

Jordan Senior Travelers Jordan Tour Operators Jordan Holidays
http://www.youtube.com/watch?v=SGft2J1iGTM

Technology and Tourism, Royal Roads University School of Tourism and Hospitality Management Adjunct Professor, Rod Harris
http://www.youtube.com/watch?v=werONqfzxik

Dr Ian Yeoman – SME panel discussion – The Future with High Speed Broadband conference
http://www.youtube.com/watch?v=8aL1lSRA7nU

of seven to eight years a number of the new players are now rewriting the rules of competition for the established conglomerates.

## Social media

One of the most dramatic trends in recent years both generally and in the specific context of travel is the emergence of social media (i.e. Facebook, Twitter, YouTube). The exponential growth in the use and influence of social media has served as a suitable catalyst for change among many intermediaries that are now far more aware of the needs and expectations of the market through their 'conversations' with customers and through the user-generated content provided on sites such as TripAdvisor (see Mini-Case Study 16.1) and Priceline which provide transparency to the entire process with regard to quality, levels of satisfaction and perhaps most significantly prices.

## MINI CASE STUDY 16.1
### TripAdvisor

Launched in February 2000, TripAdvisor is a website that helps customers gather travel information on places to visit at the same time as offering customers a vehicle to post reviews and opinions for the entire world to see. TripAdvisor today attracts more than 69 million monthly visitors across 20 popular travel brands which include **http://www.tripadvisor.com**, **http://www.familyvacationcritic.com**, **http://www.independenttraveler.com** and **http://www.travel-library.com** among others. While **http://www.tripadvisor.com** attracts the vast majority of web visits, the diversity of the rest of TripAdvisor's travel brands are integral to the company's expansion and current dominance in the market. This dominance is reflected in the figures that show over 60 million travel reviews and opinions from around the world, 1.6 million businesses, over 100,000 destinations, 600,000 hotels, 198,000 attractions and 858,000 restaurants. Perhaps more amazing is the fact that more than 40 new contributions are posted every minute while over 90% of all topics posted on the forums are replied to in 24 hours.

Much of TripAdvisor's early success can be attributed to the fact that it was a very early adopter of user-generated content. With the website free to access, it is the users who provide the majority of the information while the website is supported by a business model which is driven by advertising. With revenues in excess of $486 million in 2010 and now employing in excess of 1,300 staff, TripAdvisor has grown through a combination of innovative use of the web and acquisition. Claiming to be one of the world's largest social travel networks, TripAdvisor now offers a connection to Facebook that enables users to read reviews from those in their own online world. Although there have been a number of challenges to TripAdvisor for the posting of unsubstantiated anonymous reviews, TripAdvisor actively seeks out bad practice and to date has black-listed many hotels for suspicious reviews.

TripAdvisor has a number of key features and is constantly innovating to maintain its position as the market leader. For example, its 'Instant Personalization' feature with Facebook allows users to seek advice from their Facebook friends while 'Reviews at a Glance' enables users to get a quick snapshot of the general traveller sentiment regarding a place or property. As well as 'Mobile City Guides', a 'Vacation Rental Calculator' and 'Quick Guides', TripAdvisor now offers users videos, maps, popularity indexes and price rate checks that collectively provide the traveller with all the information they need, free of charge, to conduct their trips, vacations or business travel!

*Source*: http://www.TripAdvisor.co.uk (accessed 29 May 2012)

### DISCUSSION QUESTIONS

1. TripAdvisor clearly offers the user many benefits. How can it be used to the advantage of tourism suppliers such as hotels and car rental operators in their own marketing strategies?

2. Are there any travel products that are not suited to the TripAdvisor treatment?

3. To what extent does TripAdvisor benefit larger, corporate players in the tourism industry rather than the majority SMEs in most destinations?

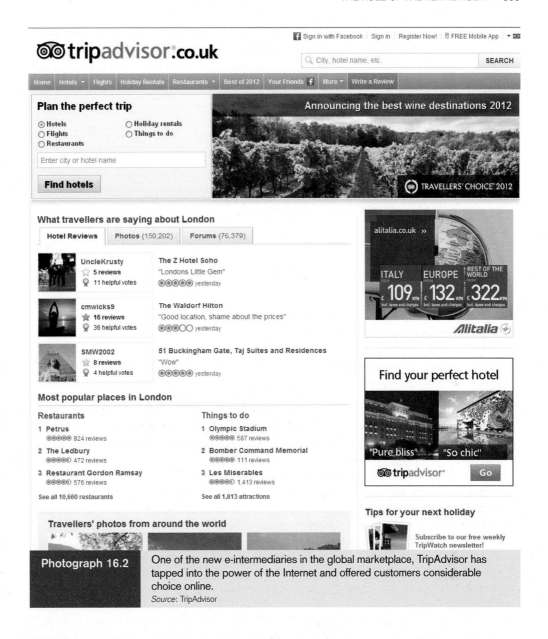

**Photograph 16.2** One of the new e-intermediaries in the global marketplace, TripAdvisor has tapped into the power of the Internet and offered customers considerable choice online.
*Source*: TripAdvisor

## THE ROLE OF THE RETAIL AGENT

Notwithstanding, the primary task of travel agents is to supply the public with travel services. This they do on behalf of their suppliers or principals. An agent may also offer travel-related services such as insurance or foreign exchange. For providing these services, the agent is rewarded by commission from the principals. Traditionally, commission amounts to 10% of the selling price, but this is normally 1% or 2% less for hotel bookings and rail travel, while, as noted earlier, major airlines have moved to a zero commission model, so that agents now charge the customer a booking fee. Insurance will usually generate commission of around 30% and car hire can, on occasions, make considerably more than the basic 10%. Sales of travellers' cheques and currency will yield no more than about 2%. However, by dealing with preferred suppliers and achieving specified sales targets, agents can achieve '**overrides**', which are extra commission amounting to about 2.5% of sales. The fast changing nature of this sector in the new arena of **e-intermediaries** implies that commission rates and what is commissionable in the future, both for traditional and virtual players, is likely to be the subject of continual negotiation and debate, with all rates going down rather than up.

How a retail travel agency should set about discharging its primary function is a matter for discussion. Where an agent has no wholesaling function and therefore does not share in the risk of tour production by holding stock, it is suggested that the agent's main concern should be the choice of location to ensure ready availability of the principal's products in the marketplace. The agent has access to a principal's stock through the reservation system and here efficiency is important. The customer expects instant confirmation and staff at the agency do not want to waste time with repeated telephone calls. Instant availability on a computer screen permits the staff in the traditional agency to share the booking process with the customer to reinforce the buying decision. This approach to the role of the retailer likens the agent to a 'filling station' for travel: creating demand is the responsibility of the principals. If demand is given, then controlling costs is the best way for the agent to maintain profitability.

An alternative view argues that the acquisition of product knowledge and the assumption of the risks involved in assessing the extent and nature of demand is the job of the agent. The agent should thus take on the role of a travel counsellor to give the public impartial advice and seek to generate business in the local market area. Many countries have national associations for travel agents that also act as regulating bodies that encourage this approach through their respective codes of business practice, such as ABTA in Britain and ASTA in the USA. Likewise, these bodies link with the United Federation of Travel Agents' Associations (UFTAA), which acts internationally and liaises closely with the International Air Transport Association (IATA).

It has already been noted that the counselling role has been far more prevalent in North America than in Europe. It appears that in Europe the tour operator's brochure, together with advertising and promotion, and more recently use of the web, has held greater sway in destination choice, thus conforming to the filling station model. However, the process of reintermediation in Europe has seen travel agents changing their ways of operating by harnessing ICT to their own advantage through Sabre's Travelocity and Galileo's range of agency web products. These have allowed agents to have full access to air, rail, hotel and car rental reservations, so as to put together independent inclusive tours (IITs) for their customers, thus moving them firmly in the direction of travel counsellors, remaining as agents and not principals, yet acting like tour operators. They are able to compete with the large companies by buying seats on an ad hoc basis from low cost carriers in the main, charters or even scheduled airlines for 'upmarket' tours. Figure 16.4 represents a conceptual model of the process and factors influencing agents' destination recommendations. Concern has been expressed about the impartiality of advice in that while agents want to meet their clients' needs they are also mindful of the different rates of commission on offer and any bonuses. In the case of corporate chains, this is known as 'switch' or 'directional' selling and can be described as a 'sale or attempted sale by a vertically integrated travel agent of the foreign package holidays of its linked tour operator, in preference to the holidays of other operators' (MMC, 1998: 4). This anti-competitive practice is against the 'level playing field' concept required by regulating bodies and the consumer has recourse to complaint procedures, which act as a constraint on such activities. However, one has to accept that agents will give prominence on their shelves to the products of their principals.

## Retail agency economics

Traditionally the retail travel trade has been characterised by ease of entry. This is because the retailer carries no stock and so capitalisation is relatively low. All that is required is a suitable shop front and the acquisition of agency agreements from tour operators to sell their products. It is then up to the marketing skill of the agent to establish the business within the locality. If the agent wishes to offer air transport services worldwide, which is essential for dealing with business travel, then it is necessary that the agent holds a licence from IATA. This requires a thorough investigation of the agency by IATA, particularly the qualifications and experience of the staff.

In the USA virtually all retailers are members of both IATA and the Airlines Reporting Corporation (ARC), which allows them to sell both international and domestic air tickets. ARC is an airline-owned company serving the travel industry with financial services, data products and services, ticket distribution, and settlement in the United States, Puerto Rico and the US Virgin Islands. An ARC appointment is essential for retail agents in the USA and normally enables an agent to obtain other licences without difficulty.

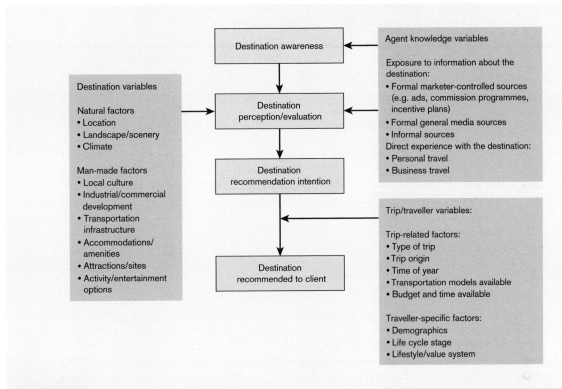

**Figure 16.4** Conceptual model of the process and factors influencing agents' destinations recommendations
*Source*: Hudson et al., 2001

A representative breakdown of the operating accounts of a medium to large travel agent is shown in Table 16.1. The example is drawn on European experience and is standardised to 1 million currency units of turnover. Table 16.1 gives an indication of the items that enter the **operating account** and shows that inclusive tours and ticket sales, of which the majority continue to be airline tickets, are by far the most important sales items. Transport tickets, other than for airlines, include sales arising from acting as an agent for rail, shipping and coach companies. Miscellaneous includes independent bookings of accommodation, excursions, ground handling services, theatres, etc., foreign exchange transactions and the sale of travel goods such as luggage, sports items, first aid kits and travel clothes.

The most important item of income to the agent is commission and, since there exists considerable pressure on commissions in some markets, it will be appreciated that the ability of the agent to generate turnover is crucial, particularly for the independent retailer. The latter has been trebly squeezed: first, by fierce competition from the multiples and virtual intermediaries, secondly, from the fact that the relative cost of holidays has fallen in real terms while overheads have been generally increasing and, thirdly, from zero commissioning of airline tickets; however, low capitalisation has enabled them to adjust to these changes. The major item of 'Other income' in the revenue statement is charges for ticket provision, but this also includes interest earned on clients' deposit money. For accounting purposes the latter is a profit item, which is only indirectly sales-related. It could be excluded here and added into the net income statement afterwards.

The largest item of cost is remuneration to staff (including payments to directors or owners). The difficulty that independent agents experience in trying to expand turnover has tended to make them cost-orientated in the operation of their businesses. Controlling costs, especially for the smaller agent, has been the short-term recipe for survival and this in turn has served to keep staff salaries low, which creates difficulties in both attracting experienced staff and retaining existing staff when compared to multiples, but with their changing role they can no longer afford not to invest in new technology and staff professionalism. Administration costs include: printing,

| Table 16.1 | Travel agency operating accounts |
|---|---|

| Item | Currency units |
|---|---|
| **Sales** | |
| Independent inclusive and package tours | 640,000 |
| Transport tickets | 269,000 |
| Insurance | 10,000 |
| Car hire | 4,000 |
| Miscellaneous | 77,000 |
| **Total** | 1,000,000 |
| **Revenue** | |
| Commission | 69,000 |
| Other income | 32,000 |
| **Total** | 101,000 |
| **Costs** | |
| Payroll expenses | 46,500 |
| Communications | 11,000 |
| Advertising | 4,000 |
| Energy | 2,000 |
| Administration | 7,000 |
| Repairs and maintenance | 500 |
| Accommodation expenses | 12,500 |
| Depreciation | 2,500 |
| **Total** | 86,000 |
| **Net income** | 15,000 |

*Source*: Trade information

stationery, insurance, bonding levy, legal and professional fees, bank charges, accounting and record keeping, and any travel that may be incurred. Accommodation expenses refer to charges arising from occupation of the premises.

Although the independent retailer can compete with the multiple and virtual intermediary on the basis of the level of personal service, the argument for raising commission rates has always been a strong one. The difficulty is that in a competitive environment higher commission rates may simply be countered by the multiples and virtual intermediaries offering larger discounts and so independents must look to their own ability for creating personalised packages and stocking exclusive products for their survival. Under pressure from the budget airlines the multiples are already closing down high street branches in favour of increasing direct sales via the Internet.

It is interesting to note, however, that in the UK TUI suggest that the costs of its stores in relation to the costs of running social media sites is not as disadvantageous as one would think. The volume of sales from its stores, the cost-efficient nature of its store operations and the opportunity stores provide in cross-selling other travel options can result in a highly efficient retail operation alongside, rather than in competition with, the use of social media.

# THE ROLE OF THE TOUR OPERATOR/WHOLESALER

Despite the growth of urban tourism since the 1980s to the world's major cities, the dominant international leisure tourism flows are still short haul to sun resorts, although the falling cost of long-haul travel has made previously considered exotic destinations more accessible. Therefore, it is not surprising that much of the work of tour operators and wholesalers is bound up in providing single destination inclusive or package holidays. Multi-centred holidays are more common on long-haul travel where the period of stay may extend to three weeks. There is still a buoyant market for coach tours, which were the main form of inclusive holiday before the arrival of low-priced air travel in the 1950s, although Vladimir Raitz took the first group of holidaymakers on a tour by air to Corsica in 1949 (their accommodation was in tents). It was operated by Hickie Borman and would be considered today as a tailor-made package and therefore outside the EU 1992 definition of a 'prearranged' inclusive tour. That same year Raitz founded the British company Horizon Holidays (later acquired by Thomson), which is considered to be the first business to introduce the modern form of package holiday when, in 1950, in order to circumvent exchange controls by paying the whole price in the country of origin, Horizon marketed combined transport and accommodation arrangements to Corsica (Bray and Raitz, 2001).

At its most fundamental, tour operating is a process of combining aircraft seats and beds in hotels (or other forms of accommodation), in a manner that will make the purchase price attractive to potential holidaymakers. As we noted earlier, tour wholesalers achieve this through bulk buying which generates economies of scale that can be passed on to the customer. Despite the increasing popularity in the use of operators' websites, the most essential link in this process remains the tour operator's brochure, which communicates the holiday product to the customer. The brochure must include within it:

- illustrations which provide a visual description of the destination and the holiday;
- copy, which is a written description of the holiday to help the customer match the type of product to his or her lifestyle; and
- price and departure panels which give the specifications of the holiday for different times of the season, duration of stay and the variety of departure points.

Large tour operators and wholesalers normally sell a wide portfolio of tours and therefore have a range of brochures. For instance, there will be separate brochures for summer sun and winter sun holidays, ski holidays, long-haul travel and short breaks. Popular destinations will have tour operators' brochures dealing solely with holidays to that country or region, and the number has continued to grow. Research has shown that the place to visit is often the first holiday decision made by some travellers. The brochure is designed to encourage customers to buy and may be the only information they might have concerning the resort until they arrive there, though more and more are obtaining information over the Internet even if they are not booking directly by this means. However, the brochure cannot be a comprehensive travel guide. The number of pages is limited by considerations of cost and size, and operators try to put as much detail about accommodation and resorts as they can in the space available, but in so doing they must also conform to the legal requirements of the consumer protection legislation that exists in the country where the brochure is marketed. Clearly, the contents of the brochure must be consistent with the brand image each operator is trying to convey, as they will each be competing for the customer's attention on travel agents' brochure racks.

## Principal stages of tour operating/wholesaling

Although the conceptual principles of tour operating are easy to follow – linking transport and accommodation to produce a package that can be offered in a brochure – the practicalities of the tour-operating cycle require careful planning, preparation and coordination. For example, media advertising in support of the brochure must be booked well in advance, particularly if numerous channels are to be used. The process of brochure production is initiated early on in the cycle to ensure that printing deadlines are met. There are myriad tasks to be performed, not only by separate divisions within the tour company, but also by outside contractors. The task of coordinating all these activities usually falls upon the marketing department.

Because of the complexity of organising package trips, there are tour operators and wholesalers who do not put together their own programme. They simply contract the work out to a wholesaler and pass on the bookings as they come in. An example of this is organisations known as *affinity groups*. They range from travel clubs whose members may have ethnic ties with particular countries, to professional associations that may arrange to have their meetings in different parts of the world.

Figure 16.5 presents a stylised layout of an operating cycle for a large-scale summer programme selling 1 million or more holidays. From initial research to the commencement of sales, the period spans some 14 months and, to first departures, 21 months. For winter programmes and short breaks, which are normally smaller in volume, the corresponding preparation periods are somewhat less. The example shown should not be taken as definitive since, by nature of the very many activities that are being performed and the differing objectives of tour companies, there will always be variances on timings – for example, spreading the season into April or curtailing it at the end of September or in mid-October.

## Research

Key outcomes of research are the forecasts of overall market size and the changing patterns of holiday-taking. These will assist in the selection of destinations, which in turn will be constrained by conditions of access, the extent of the tourist infrastructure and the political climate of the host country. In terms of destination choice, a specialist tour operator is able to respond far more quickly to changing market conditions than the volume or mass tour operator. The latter usually has long-term commitments to existing destinations which may include capital tied up in resorts. From destination choice, the research process will enable the operator to derive a market strategy, whereby one of four main options is possible. The first, market penetration, suggests that the destination continues to appeal to existing markets with the same product but through more manipulation of the elements of the marketing mix. The second, product development, suggests that the destination develops a new product to appeal to its existing market while, third, market development suggests that the existing destination product is targeted to new segments within the wider market. Finally, destinations could diversify in that they develop totally new products for new markets – a strategy that brings with it slightly higher risk than the preceding three strategy options.

## Capacity planning

The market forecasts can be used to plan total capacity, which, together with the market strategy, will set tour specifications by type, destination and volume. Once the tour programme has been planned, negotiations for beds and aircraft or coach seats may take place. Bed contracts may take two forms: an allocation (also referred to as an allotment) or a guarantee (also referred to as a commitment). An allocation operates on a sale-or-return basis with an appropriate release date. This type of contract is usually negotiated with medium-grade hotels and above, where opportunities for resale are generally easier. The risk is thus transferred from the tour operator/wholesaler to the hotelier. In turn the hotelier covers this risk by making contracts with several operators and quoting variable rates. With a guarantee, the wholesaler agrees to pay for the beds whether they are sold or not. Such a commitment naturally brings with it a cheaper rate than an allotment and is commonly applied for traditional destinations that enjoy high demand, or to self-catering properties for the purpose of obtaining exclusive contracts. As a rule, guarantee contracts would be below 20% of a tour operator's portfolio.

Aircraft seats may be contracted in a variety of ways. The largest tour operators and wholesalers are likely to have their own charter airline. The world's largest charter airline is Thomsonfly which is owned by the TUI group. Some scheduled airlines, notably in the USA and Europe, also have tour wholesaling divisions or companies and many provide charter services. In other circumstances, the tour operator may contract an aircraft for the whole season (a 'time charter'), for specified flights (a 'whole plane charter'), or purchase a block of seats on a scheduled service or a chartered airline (a 'part charter'). The use of scheduled services tends to be for specialist tours (which are often escorted) or tailor-made packages for customers. As scheduled flights, even using codesharing, are likely to work on a break-even 'load factor' of 70% or less, airlines are prepared to give good discounts for inclusive tour excursion fares, which they make available through air-brokers, termed 'consolidators', to the advantage of agents putting together IITs.

| ACTIVITY | Year 1 Aug | S | O | N | D | Year 2 Jan | F | M | A | M | J | J | A | S | O | N | D | Year 3 Jan | F | M | A | M | J | J | A | S | O |
|---|---|---|---|---|---|---|---|---|---|---|---|---|---|---|---|---|---|---|---|---|---|---|---|---|---|---|---|
| **Research** | | | | | | | | | | | | | | | | | | | | | | | | | | | |
| • Review market performance | × | × | | | | | | | | | | | | | | | | | | | | | | | | | |
| • Forecast market trends | × | × | | | | | | | | | | | | | | | | | | | | | | | | | |
| • Select and compare new and existing destinations | | | × | × | | | | | | | | | | | | | | | | | | | | | | | |
| • Determine market strategy | | | | × | × | | | | | | | | | | | | | | | | | | | | | | |
| **Capacity planning** | | | | | | | | | | | | | | | | | | | | | | | | | | | |
| • Tour specifications | | | | | | × | × | | | | | | | | | | | | | | | | | | | | |
| • Negotiate with and contract suppliers | | | | | | | × | × | × | × | × | | | | | | | | | | | | | | | | |
| **Financial evaluation** | | | | | | | | | | | | | | | | | | | | | | | | | | | |
| • Determine exchange rates | | | | | | | | | | | × | × | | | | | | | | | | | | | | | |
| • Estimate future selling prices | | | | | | | | | | | × | × | | | | | | | | | | | | | | | |
| • Finalise tour prices | | | | | | | | | | × | | | | | | | | | | | | | | | | | |
| **Marketing** | | | | | | | | | | | | | | | | | | | | | | | | | | | |
| • Brochure planning and production | | | | | | | × | × | × | × | × | | | | | | | | | | | | | | | | |
| • Brochure distribution and launch | | | | | | | | | | | | | × | | | | | | | | | | | | | | |
| • Media advertising and sales promotion | | | | | | | | | | | | | × | × | × | × | × | × | × | × | × | × | | | | | |
| • Market stimulation | | | | | | | | | | | | × | | | | | | | | | | | | | | | |
| **Administration** | | | | | | | | | | | | | | | | | | | | | | | | | | | |
| • Recruit reservation staff | | | | | | | | | | | | | × | | | | | | | | | | | | | | |
| • Establish reservation system | | | | | | | | | | | | | | × | × | × | × | × | | | | | | | | | |
| • Receive reservations by telephone and view data | | | | | | | | | | | | | | × | × | × | × | × | × | × | × | × | × | | | | |
| • Tour accounting and documentation | | | | | | | | | | | | | | | × | × | × | × | × | × | × | × | × | × | × | × | × |
| • Recruit resort staff | | | | | | | | | | | | | | | | | | | × | × | | | | | | | |
| **Tour management** | | | | | | | | | | | | | | | | | | | | | | | | | | | |
| • Customer care at resort | | | | | | | | | | | | | | | | | | | | | | × | × | × | × | × | × |
| • Customer correspondence | | | | | | | | | | | | | | | | | | | | | | × | × | × | × | × | × |
| • Payment of suppliers | | | | | | | | | | | | | | | | | | | | | | × | × | × | | | |

**Figure 16.5** Tour-operating cycle of an abroad summer programme

Where an operator has an own carrier or is contracted for a time charter, it is important to maximise the utilisation of the aircraft. The underlying principle is that aircraft should be operated back to back, namely that the plane should fly out with a new tour group and return with the previous group. Empty flights (known as 'empty legs') will arise at the beginning and end of the season, and these must be allowed for in the costing of seats. In summer the aircraft is likely to be used for three return trips or 'rotations' per day (two in winter) following the flight patterns shown in Figure 16.6. Aircraft may be used to rotate from one point of departure to a range of destinations or from a variety of departure points to one destination, or a combination of the two.

However, in the interests of protecting scheduled airlines from unfair competition through charter airlines taking their normal traffic at peak times, aviation authorities have usually imposed operating restrictions on charter use. These may include the following:

- The trip must be an inclusive tour, which implies the provision of accommodation as well as an airline seat.
- Airport terminals used by passengers must be the same on both the outward and return journeys.
- The air ticket must be for a round trip and is neither transferable nor part-usable in the sense that the holder may not use the return portion without having first travelled on the outbound flight.

## Financial evaluation

We can see from Figure 16.5 that tour operators and wholesalers have to finalise prices some eight months or more before the first tour departs. Apart from the usual hazards of forecasting so far in advance, there are several inherent risks that must be accounted for. These are:

- contracts with local suppliers are commonly made in the currency of the destination country;
- the currency for payment of airlines is usually US dollars;
- airlines maintain the right to raise prices in response to increases in aviation fuel costs; and
- alterations in dues, taxes or fees levied by governments.

Tour operators and wholesalers cover these risks (termed **hedging**) by trying to build in anticipated changes in exchange rates for the purposes of determining tour prices and then buying forward the foreign exchange required at an agreed rate in order to meet contractual obligations, and by bringing in surcharges at the point of final billing of customers. Because the latter have

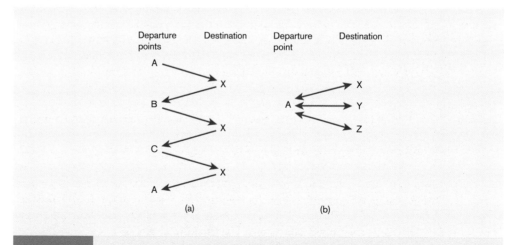

| Figure 16.6 | Time charter aircraft flight patterns: (a) 'w' pattern; (b) radial pattern |

proved unpopular, operators have tried to avoid their negative impact by offering no-surcharge guarantees, limiting the amount of surcharge liability, or offering cancellation options. In this context, it is worth noting that surcharges are often regulated by codes of conduct issued by the trade association and/or consumer protection legislation, as in the EU Package Travel Directive, which requires that latest date for price revisions (about a month before departure) must be included in the contract and that any significant alterations to the contract give the customer the right of cancellation without incurring penalties.

## Marketing

Brochure production starts several months prior to the publication date with initial agreements about printing arrangements. It is usual for the layout of the brochure to be undertaken by a specialist design studio following the guidelines laid down by the tour operator's own staff. A variety of styles may be considered before the final choice is made. Particular attention is paid to the front cover to make sure that it conveys the right message to the target market segment and to ensure that it is likely to stand out on the travel agent's brochure racks. The draft final document is scrutinised for errors and corrected, with the pricing panels being left to the last possible moment before full production, to allow for any unforeseen economic changes.

It is important for the brochure to be launched well before the summer season starts because there is a section of the market that likes to book early in order to guarantee the destination and to take advantage of any promotional prices. The pattern of brochure distribution depends on the nature of the tours being offered and a trade-off between the costs of sending to all agents in order to maximise brochure exposure and limiting the number of outlets in the knowledge that the majority of the business will come from a minority of agents. Specialist wholesalers offering high-priced trips will restrict the number of retailers and in so doing convey the message of product exclusiveness to the customer. In any event, they are unlikely to be in a position to support a large network of travel agents. For cost-effective reasons even mass tour operators limit the number of agents they appoint and, as indicated previously, very large wholesalers often have their own retail travel chain to distribute their products.

Monitoring the progress of advertising and sales campaigns is achieved through booking patterns. Typically operators are looking for capacity utilisation factors of 85–90% in order to break even. Past experience enables wholesalers to establish reference booking patterns so as to compare actual with predicted bookings. Tour operators/wholesalers reserve the right to cancel or 'consolidate' holidays, for example merging flights or combining itineraries and switching accommodation, if the demand take-up is insufficient. This makes it relatively easy for operators to test new products in their brochures. However, on the supply side, merging charter flights is not normally feasible for a summer programme after January because of the cost of airline cancellation charges. Large operators benefit here by having their own airlines.

On the demand side, consolidation is a common source of annoyance to customers and leaves the travel agent with the unenviable task of advising his or her clients of the changes. Tour operators defend this practice on the grounds that if they were unable to use cancellation or consolidation to reduce overcapacity, then the average price of a holiday would rise. Underestimating demand is less of a difficulty because there is usually some flexibility in the system for procuring extra flights and accommodation. On the other hand, tour operators protect themselves against cancellation by their clients. Refunds are normally arranged on a sliding scale, so that the cancellation of a holiday six or seven weeks before departure may result only in a lost deposit, but after that the amount of the purchase price returned falls relatively sharply to zero for a cancellation only a day or so before departure.

Owing to the negative effects of consolidation on customers and the wider impacts this may have on public relations, tour operators and wholesalers prefer to use market stimulation techniques to boost sluggish booking patterns. Such tactical (as opposed to strategic) marketing methods will depend upon the time available and may vary from increasing advertising expenditure through special discounts for booking by a certain time, to substantial price cuts some six to four weeks before departure. Critical to obtaining last-minute sales is a network of retailers linked into the operator's own computer reservation system so that price promotions may be quickly communicated to the travelling public via this distribution channel, as well as own website postings and distribution to e-intermediaries. Consumers, in turn, have recognised the bargains on offer and these have, over the years, encouraged later booking.

### Administration

Owing to the seasonal nature of tour operation, the extra staff required to run the reservation system and represent the operator/wholesaler overseas are recruited and trained when needed, with only a core being employed all year. Frequently the same staff come and work for the same operator every year, which reduces the need for training.

The reservation system holds the tour operator's stock of holidays and careful attention is paid to matching the information held by the system to that contained in the brochure. Normally, travel agents make direct bookings through computer terminals in their own offices, but many agents still have to make telephone connections for clarification of the product on offer and to meet additional requests from increasingly knowledgeable clients.

### Tour management

Specialist tour operators are most likely to offer escorted tours whereby a tour manager accompanies holidaymakers throughout the whole of their journey in order to oversee arrangements. For the volume package tour market, the function of the operator's resort representative is to host the tour. This involves meeting the tourists when they arrive and ensuring that the transfer procedures to the places of accommodation go smoothly. The representative will be expected to spend some time at the resort before the start of the season checking facilities, noting any variations from the brochure and, with the authority of the company, requesting discrepancies to be put right. During the holiday, the representative is required to be available to guests at the various hotels to give advice and deal with the many problems that may arise, as well as supervising (and sometimes organising) social activities and excursions, where they earn commission on sales.

After the holiday the operator/wholesaler will receive customer correspondence that will include compliments, suggestions and complaints. Most correspondence can be dealt with by a standard letter and justified complaints may receive a small refund. For serious complaints, national travel associations may offer arbitration services which can reconcile disputes before steps are taken to instigate legal proceedings.

## Tour operator economics

We have already considered many of the economic aspects of tour operation in our discussion of the benefits of intermediation and the way in which a tour programme is put together. Essentially the mass tour operator or wholesaler relies on the economies of scale generated by bulk purchase and this in turn allows individual packages to be competitively priced to the consumer on the basis of a high take-up rate of offers made.

Once the tour operator/wholesaler is committed to a programme, the financial risks are substantial, irrespective of tactical risk-avoidance strategies such as late release clauses, surcharges and consolidation. This is because most of the costs of running the programme, if it is to run at all, are unavoidable and therefore fixed. The marginal or variable costs of selling an extra holiday are very small, which accounts for the large discounts on offer for 'late-availability' trips that give the customer only a short period of notice (sometimes just a few days) before departure.

### Leverage

The financial structure of tour operation is illustrated in Figure 16.7. $R$ is the revenue line which increases with the level of capacity utilisation and $C_1$ the total cost line attributable to running the tour programme. It may be seen that $C_1$ cuts the revenue and costs axis some way above the point of origin. The latter is caused by the high level of fixed costs in relation to the variable costs of tour operation. The financial term for this is a 'high operating leverage', which is a characteristic of tour operation. By way of contrast, $C_2$ is a total cost line, which has a low operating leverage: fixed costs are relatively small when compared to the steeply rising variable costs.

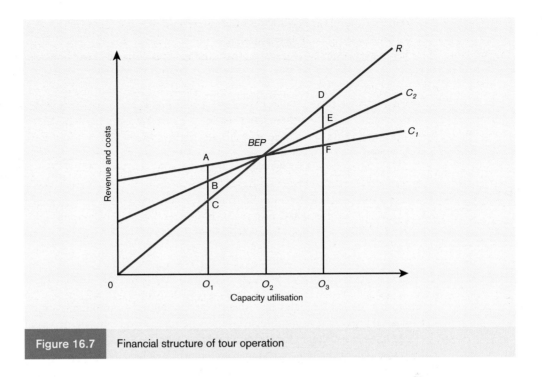

| Figure 16.7 | Financial structure of tour operation |

Consider a tour operator which is planning a break-even capacity utilisation level of $O_2$, but demand is such that $O_3$ holidays are sold. Clearly, $O_3$ is well above the break-even point ($BEP$) and so the operator makes substantial profits, as shown by the difference DF between $R$ and $C_1$. A firm that has a low operating leverage would not do so well, as can be seen from the difference DE between $R$ and $C_2$. Conversely, if the tour operator did not manage to achieve targeted break-even sales and the realised utilisation was some way below the required level, say $O_1$, the losses AC can be severe and may result in the collapse of the operator. We show in Figure 16.7 that a firm with a low operating leverage would not be so badly affected, for AB is much less than AC.

There is thus considerable financial risk associated with large-scale tour operation and this acts as a deterrent to entry. It is important to realise that once a tour programme has been arranged and the day of departure is near, then even costs that were once variable now become fixed, so operators are willing to discount heavily at the last minute in order to make a contribution to their fixed expenses. Specialist operators cover this risk by dealing with niche markets, and using scheduled airline services and high-grade hotels for which reservations may be readily cancelled if the minimum number of confirmed bookings for the tour is not met. The major tour operators address this financial risk by securing their market position through vertically integrating their operation both forwards and backwards. The **tied agency** scheme in Germany was particularly effective in allowing the large tour operators to profit from their market position.

While ICT developments have led to a proliferation of small tour operators purchasing the components of a package on an ad hoc basis, it is in the middle ground, among wholesalers which have neither their own aircraft (and so must purchase a whole or part charter) nor their own retail network, that the financial risk tends to be at its highest. These are the tour operators that are most likely to go out of business when demand falters and whose numbers have been falling in recent years. To safeguard the public from lost holidays or from being stranded abroad when a tour operator collapses, responsible governments have legislation requiring operating licences, for example, the UK Air Travel Organisers Licence (ATOL), which was initiated in 1972, and bonding arrangements through a bank or an approved insurer, though the fund is not always sufficient to meet the losses or extra expenses incurred.

| Table 16.2 | Sales structure of a large tour operator |
|---|---|

| Sales | Percentages |
|---|---|
| Summer inclusive tours | 45 |
| Winter inclusive tours | 30 |
| Short breaks and Others | 20 |
| Excursions and insurance | 4 |
| Interest on deposits | 1 |
| **Total** | **100** |

*Source*: Trade information

## Sales mix

During the 1950s holiday tourism was largely centred around the traditional summer break at a coastal resort, but rising affluence, longer holiday periods and an increasing desire to travel have led to an expansion in the degree of market segmentation. Tour operators and wholesalers have responded to changing consumer preferences by diversifying their portfolios of products. This in turn has helped to spread risk and generate all-year business. Thus most major tour operators have winter and summer programmes.

Table 16.2 presents the sales mix that would be appropriate for a large European operator offering summer sun holidays to short-haul (less than five hours' flying time) Mediterranean resorts. Most holiday movements in Europe are still towards beach destinations in summertime, though winter holidays have increased their market share in response to more frequent holiday-taking, as well as short breaks and other trips, such as minimum rated packages (effectively the transport cost only) for those having their own holiday accommodation. Budget airlines have been strong competitors for the latter market.

## Pricing

A taxonomy of different approaches to price-setting may be found in Chapter 21, but here it is sufficient to note that the price of an inclusive holiday in a wholesaler's brochure will be bounded above by what the market will bear and below by the cost of providing the holiday, and that over time a pricing process and structure, which becomes the model for most operators, tends to establish itself. Thus customers expect exclusive holidays and tailor-made packages to be relatively expensive and so price is used as an indicator of quality, which in turn gives the tour operator the opportunity of securing higher margins. The volume market for inclusive tours is sold competitively on price, so costs and capacity utilisation have greater significance. Hence operators will consider a range of offers, taking account of factors such as:

- seasonal effects – the range of variation between low- and peak-season prices is usually around 20 to 30%;
- exchange rate movements;
- competitors' prices and the degree of product differentiation and brand value;
- load factors;
- component costs and their complexity, for example, supplements for extended stay;
- promotional pricing to encourage early booking and late-availability discounts;
- market segmentation pricing, with special offers for senior citizens, young people and families with children below a certain age; and
- discounts for affinity group travel.

The price structure for a typical mass market inclusive tour undertaken within Europe is shown in Table 16.3. Competition keeps profit margins low, and so the emphasis is on volume sales and cost control to sustain net income. In these circumstances, the importance of hedging on foreign exchange is readily appreciated, because uncovered fluctuations in exchange rates may easily erode slender profit margins. This does not entirely remove the risk, for the tour operator/wholesaler still has to predict the amount of business going to each destination.

## Air seats

For wholesalers who operate their own airlines or secure whole plane or time charters, an important element in determining the tour price is the costing of an air seat. This is calculated from the following formula:

$$s = \frac{dR}{(d-1)LN} + t$$

where $s$ = unit seat cost per round trip, $d$ = number of aircraft departures, $R$ = aircraft cost per rotation, $L$ = load factor, $N$ = number of seats per flight and $t$ = airport tax.

As an example, consider an aircraft of 350 seats contracted on a time charter for 30 departures. The rotation cost is calculated at 45,000 currency units, the load factor at 90% and airport tax is ascertained to be 20 currency units. By substitution into the above formula, the unit seat cost per return flight is:

$$s = \frac{30 \times 45,000}{29 \times 0.9 \times 350} + 20$$
$$= 168$$

Note that the number of departures in the denominator of the equation is reduced by 1 to allow for empty legs.

| Table 16.3 | Price structure of a 14-night inclusive tour |
|---|---|

| Item | Percentages |
|---|---|
| **Price** | 100 |
| **Direct costs** | |
| Accommodation | 41 |
| Air seat (including taxes) | 32 |
| Transfers, excursions, etc. | 3 |
| Agent's commission | 10 |
| **Total** | 86 |
| **Gross margin** | 14 |
| **Indirect costs** | |
| Payroll expenses | 4 |
| Marketing | 3 |
| Office expenses | 2 |
| **Total** | 9 |
| **Net income** | |
| Trading profit | 5 |
| Interest on deposits | 1 |
| **Total** | 6 |

*Source*: Trade information

## Strategic positioning

History has shown that while there are no major constraints on entry into travel wholesaling, the mass holiday market in any country tends to be dominated by only a handful of companies. The tour operator/wholesaler has no monopoly over airline seats or hotel beds and product standards are easy to emulate. This being the case, the lessons of success indicate strategic market positions secured by a combination of the following factors:

- economies of scale through bulk purchase and volume distribution;
- low-cost distribution network, particularly IT direct sales, together with national coverage;
- developing new products and markets, and adopting new technologies;
- competitive pricing;
- multi-branding to attract different market segments; and
- product differentiation to avoid competing on price alone.

As with major retail stores and supermarket chains, volume throughput and national presence are critical to the success of a mass tour operator. This being the case, in a European context it is unlikely that any wholesaler can compete effectively, particularly on price, in the mass market segment with sales of under a million holidays. When account is taken of the organisation structure needed and bonding requirements of around 10% of turnover if belonging to a recognised trade association with its own reserve fund, but as much as 25% otherwise (EU Package Travel Directive), it will be appreciated that the costs of entry into the volume market do act as a considerable deterrent. However, once the volume market has been penetrated, the substantial fixed costs involved are easily transferable to rival operations.

The factors giving rise to a winning strategy are also the cause of a high degree of sales concentration in the tour operation industry, leaving small operators to create their own distinctive market share through specialised holidays. The economics of the industry are such that this situation is one that can only continue: markets are **contestable** and the large operators are prepared to defend their market position by diversifying their products, even into specialist areas, by multi-branding to reach economic sales levels in particular markets quickly, by undertaking price wars and generally enforcing the success criteria outlined above. This of course is subject to legislation on competition policy in their source markets, termed **anti-trust legislation** in the USA.

# CONCLUSION

We have used this chapter to review the way in which the individual elements of the tourism product may be packaged together for convenience and then distributed to the market efficiently. There are important variations in the way in which this procedure is executed in different regions of the world but, as a result of the predominant North–South flow in tourism, it is the northern countries of the world that have developed the most sophisticated network of distribution to satisfy the volume of market demand.

However, it is important to remember that the distribution of the tourism product is the aspect of the tourism system that has changed most rapidly over recent years as new technology permeates the marketplace and direct access to the tourism product becomes even more prevalent. The counter to this is the way the travel trade has been able to reshape itself to meet these changes.

# SELF-CHECK QUESTIONS

1. Review and discuss the roles of travel agencies and tour operators.
2. Identify the benefits and drawbacks of further consolidation and concentration in the distribution channel in tourism.

3. Compare and contrast differences in the distribution of the tourism product between the USA and Europe.

4. Identify potential threats to the continued dominance of travel agencies and tour operators and assess the likely impact of technological progress in respect of distribution.

5. What is the likely future balance between traditional forms of tour operations and web-based models?

6. How is the increased use of social media sites likely to change the sector in the near-to-mid future?

7. What are the implications of 'switch selling' for both the tourism intermediary and the consumer?

## REFERENCES AND FURTHER READING

Berne, C., Garcia-Gonzalez, M. and Mugica, J. (2012) 'How ICT shifts the balance of tourism distribution channels', *Tourism Management* **33**(1), 205–14.

Bray, R. and Raitz, V. (2001) *Flight to the Sun: the Story of the Holiday Revolution*, Continuum, London.

Buhalis, D. (2003) *eTourism: Information Technology for Strategic Tourism Management*, Pearson Education, Harlow.

Buhalis, D. and Law, R. (2008) 'Progress in information technology and tourism management: 20 years on and 10 years after the Internet – the state of eTourism research', *Tourism Management* **29**(4), 609–23.

Ho, C.-I., Lin, M.-H. and Chen, H.-M. (2012) 'Web users' behavioural patterns of tourism information search: from online to offline', *Tourism Management* **33**(6), 1468–82.

Horner, S. and Swarbrooke, J. (2004) *International Cases in Tourism Management*, Elsevier Butterworth Heinemann, Oxford.

Hudson, S., Snaith, T., Miller, G. and Hudson, P. (2001) 'Travel retailing: "switch selling" in the UK', pp. 172–84 in Buhalis, D. and Laws, E. (eds), *Tourism Distribution Channels: Practices, Issues and Transformations*, Continuum, London.

MMC (1998) *Foreign Package Holidays*, HMSO, London.

WTO (2002) *Tourism in the Age of Alliances, Mergers and Acquisitions*, WTO, Madrid.

# MAJOR CASE STUDY 16.1
## Thomas Cook Group plc – a changing landscape

With its origins going back as far as the mid-1800s, Thomas Cook grew from a one-man excursion 'organiser' to what is today one half of Europe's second largest travel operator. Thomas Cook's first European tour took place during the summer of 1855 whereupon two significant innovations arose. The first, the hotel coupon, enabled travellers to pay for hotel accommodation and meals instead of using money. The second, the circular note, proved to be the forerunner for the travellers' cheque, which enabled tourists to obtain local currency in exchange for a paper note issued by Thomas Cook. After a turbulent period of development in the early 1900s, Thomas Cook benefited considerably from the post-war holiday boom, which saw 1 million Britons travelling abroad by 1950. Although Thomas Cook remained the largest and most successful company in the industry, the 1960s brought with it ever-increasing competition from numerous new players which sought to undercut Thomas Cook. Acquired by a consortium of the former Midland Bank, Trust House Forte and the Automobile Association in 1972, a number of radical changes were implemented to withstand the competitive threat – including its again highly innovative Money Back Guarantee scheme in 1974. Thomas Cook later became a wholly owned subsidiary of the Midland Bank Group and began to concentrate on the long-haul, rather than short-haul package tours market.

After celebrating 150 years of operation in 1991, Thomas Cook was acquired from the Midland Bank by Westdeutsche Landesbank (WestLB), Germany's third largest bank, and LTU Group, Germany's leading charter airline, in 1992. Eventually, Thomas Cook became a wholly owned subsidiary of WestLB before entering a period of rapid growth which saw the acquisition of Sunworld, Time Off and Flying Colours in quick succession. This period of growth for Thomas Cook then culminated in merger with Carlson Leisure Group's UK travel interests and the subsequent formation of JMC in 1999.

The new millennium saw the acquisition of Thomas Cook by C&N Touristik AG, an acquisition which was eventually approved by the European Community in March 2001. Recognising the heritage and respect for the global travel brand that is Thomas Cook, C&N Touristik AG renamed itself Thomas Cook AG and was able to benefit fully from being one of the most recognised and most respected brands in the world. A few years later, Thomas Cook AG merged with MyTravel which had its origins going back to the north of England in the early 1970s. The combined 'value' for the new group in 2006 was just under £8,000 million, with a combined total of 19.1 million passengers, 2,926 retail outlets, 97 aircraft and just under 33,000 employees. At the time, the new company was debt-free and had high financial reserves so was in a strong position to proactively participate in further market consolidation in Europe.

Today, Thomas Cook has expanded to become one of the world's leading leisure travel groups with sales of nearly £10 billion, 23.6 million customers, operating in six geographic segments in 22 countries and is number one or number two in all core markets. In many of these markets Thomas Cook has increasing levels of controlled distribution, increasing levels of Internet usage and is recording operating profit margins from between 1% and 9%.

More recently, however, the name (and share price) of Thomas Cook has been besmirched a little in response to a number of difficulties being experienced in what, it has to be said, is a very challenging market position. Ever since the financial turmoil of 2007 and 2008, economies throughout the Western world have struggled to maintain growth with many, including the UK, suffering economic recession. One of the consequences of such economic turmoil has been the arrival of the 'staycation' effect whereby millions of people who under normal economic conditions would travel abroad, many undoubtedly with Thomas Cook, have decided to take their holidays at home rather than incur the costs of overseas travel. Hence, although highly beneficial to the domestic tourism industry, the significant decline in the outbound market has had devastating consequences for Thomas Cook. Although it is not easy to pinpoint exactly where things have gone wrong, the 'staycation' effect only being one contributory variable, with the problems in Tunisia and Egypt also an issue, the costs and complexities of previous mergers and acquisitions have increasingly come under the spotlight, as has the ease with which computer systems and online platforms have been brought together in a seamless manner to the benefit of customers.

One of the principal causes for concern has been the collapse in its share price whereby the overall value of the company fell to £120 million, quite a contrast compared to its 2006 level post-merger with MyTravel. Over the winter period of 2011, Thomas Cook was obliged to borrow in excess of £200 million to keep the company afloat, while the £1.4 billion deal with a number of large banking institutions struck early in 2012 has given the company much-needed breathing space as it seeks to tackle its debt of approximately £900 million. Over 200 branches were identified for closure over a two-year period while, since March 2011, the company's shares lost an amazing 90% of their stock market value! Even more worrying perhaps was the Civil Aviation Authority's concerns as to whether Thomas Cook could fulfil its obligations under the Air Travel Organiser's Licensing (ATOL) agreement and whether there were any potential grounds for revoking its Air Operator's Certificate (AOC).

For the future, Thomas Cook's strategy is focused on strengthening its core business and investing in areas of considered future growth, which include independent travel, travel-related financial services and other opportunities via mergers, acquisitions and partnerships. As with the early origins of the company, Thomas Cook remains committed to making customers' dreams come true, albeit in an environment where the harsh realities of the economic landscape are a wake-up call for both company and customers alike!

*Source*: Horner and Swarbrooke, 2004, http://www.thomascook.com/about-us/ (accessed 28 May 2012)

# DISCUSSION QUESTIONS

1. Despite its very rich travel heritage and its iconic status in the world of travel, Thomas Cook has struggled to come to terms with the vagaries of the market. Do you consider this to be mere 'blip' or do you consider there to be more fundamental shifts in the outbound travel market that will shape things further in the years to come?

2. Thomas Cook has invested significant sums in the future of independent travel. Do you think that this reflects the end of mass outbound travel or does it merely reflect substantial growth in the use of technology and social media which in turn has facilitated the boom in independent travel?

3. Where do you see the future growth markets for Thomas Cook and what markets are likely to see enhanced levels of disinvestment over the next three to five years?

4. What is the single biggest threat to tour operations of the scale of Thomas Cook: changing patterns of purchasing behaviour, economic turmoil, external crises or advances in technology?

# CHAPTER 17
## TRANSPORTATION

### LEARNING OUTCOMES

The primary objective of this chapter is to demonstrate the importance of transportation to the overall tourism product and to illustrate their interdependence. Transport is responsible not only for physically moving tourists from the main originating areas to the destination, but also for their mobility once they arrive at the destination. Different modes of transport impose different environmental costs on society, while transport will become an increasingly significant contributor to greenhouse gas emissions. On completion of this chapter, you will have:

- an understanding of the major modes of transportation for tourism, their relative importance and the competitive advantages and disadvantages of each;

- an appreciation of the influence of political developments on transportation for tourism;

- a knowledge of the purpose and impact of regulation in transportation;

- an awareness of the externalities imposed by transport and their impacts on tourism;

- an appreciation of transport's contribution to greenhouse gas (GHG) emissions; and

- an understanding of transport as a tourist attraction.

Photograph: South Beach, Miami, Florida, USA © Kelly Miller

## INTRODUCTION

Tourism is about being elsewhere and, in consequence, the main function of transport in the tourism system (Leiper 1990) is one of transit, carrying tourists between generating regions and the tourist destination regions. The relationship is two sided. Tourism demand is important for the financial viability of transport operators whilst adequate transportation infrastructure offering access from generating markets is one of the most important prerequisites for the development of a tourist destination (see Prideaux, 2004).

Mass tourism has traditionally been developed in areas with extensive transportation networks that have the capacity to handle additional irregular tourism-related demand in peak periods. The transport infrastructure attracts tourism infrastructure, so at most destinations worldwide the traveller can find adequate hospitality and leisure facilities close to transportation terminals. Traditionally hotels developed at main railway stations in the nineteenth century and at airports in the twentieth century.

On the other hand, tourism demand has stimulated the rapid development of transportation. As the number of tourists requiring safe, quick and comfortable transport to destinations at a reasonable cost increased, the transportation industry has had to adjust in order to accommodate this demand. In response, technology has developed new vehicles with improved speeds, increased capacity and lower operating costs.

In this chapter we provide a framework for the analysis of passenger transportation operations for tourism. We identify the elements of the transportation system, examine issues such as regulation of transport and its environmental impacts, and perform a competitive analysis for the major modes of transportation. Finally, the chapter illustrates the major future political, environmental and economic challenges for tourist transportation.

## TRANSPORT AS A COMPONENT OF THE TOURIST PRODUCT

Transportation is an essential element of the tourist product in three ways:

- the means to reach the destination;
- a necessary means of movement at the destination;
- in a minority of instances it is the actual tourism attraction or activity.

### Transport as transit

By far the most important contribution of transport is as a means of transit between the main tourism originating regions and the destination. This accounts for 90% of tourist use of transport. It is a derived demand, which is not undertaken for its own sake but merely as a means of getting from the tourism-generating region to the tourism destination. This can produce significant operational difficulties because the transport operator has little control over the demand for such services. The busiest tourism routes are those which link originating regions, which display high levels of income and leisure time, with popular tourist destinations. For example, there remain large traffic flows between affluent countries of northern Europe and countries with Mediterranean resorts in southern Europe and North Africa. The future prospects for such routes are more a function of the relative affluence of the former and attractiveness of the latter than they are of any actions taken by the transport operator.

The busiest tourism routes also tend to be shorter distances. Domestic trips exceed the number of international trips and short-haul trips are more frequent than longer-haul trips as the lower requirement of disposable time and income enable more frequent consumption. Table 17.1 illustrates the pattern for EU holiday trips.

| Table 17.1 | Number of tourism journeys by EU-25 citizens in 2000 (%) |
|------------|-----------------------------------------------------------|

| Type of journey | % |
|-----------------|-----|
| Domestic | 61 |
| Intra-EU 25 | 29 |
| Europe outside EU | 04 |
| Intercontinental | 06 |
| **Total** | 100 |

*Source*: Peeters et al., 2007

Tourism is a fragile industry and traffic flows can undergo significant change instantaneously as a result of a natural catastrophe, conflict or political instability such as that displayed by the fall in transatlantic air travel in the immediate aftermath of events post-9/11. Leisure transport flows between northern Europe and North African countries such as Egypt and Tunisia have been affected by the political instability of the summer of 2011, the so-called 'Arab Spring'.

Not only is the size of demand outside the control of the transport operator, so too are the patterns of demand. The derived nature of transport demand means that factors such as climate, restrictions to vacation entitlement from work, religious festivals and the dates of school holidays all influence when the demand for tourism transport occurs, creating peaks and troughs. For cold climate regions such as northern Europe there are clear periods of peak seasonal demand from June to mid-August, but within this pattern there are more subtle peaks, particularly day of the week peaks. In many destinations such as the UK, Denmark or the ski resorts of the Alpine region of North Tyrol and Salzburg there is a preference to travel on Saturdays for main holidays, heavily influenced by accommodation providers, many of which only accept Saturday to Saturday bookings. The growth of short weekend-break holidays has contributed to Friday travelling peaks on some modes of transport, notably rail and express coaches.

These peak periods of demand create operational problems because, like many service industries, transport production cannot be stored, it is consumed at the point of production. Therefore to meet demand at peak periods the transport operator has to provide extra capacity which may then be underutilised during the **off-peak** periods. If one is not careful, serving peak demand can become unprofitable. Transport operators must take care to ensure the revenue earned (which could be over a relatively short peak period) exceeds the full costs of providing the capacity, including all fixed costs, which are incurred over the whole year. The most commonly cited examples of **peak** capacity are related to fleet size. Coach companies, rail operators and airlines all have potential for the fleet size to be determined by the peak season, with some vehicles not really required to meet levels of demand in the off-peak season. However, the operational problems extend to other elements of the transport system such as the terminal. For example, Palma airport (Majorca), which handles over 21 million passengers per annum, has four passenger terminals, but only fully utilises them during the peak summer season when it becomes one of the busiest airports in Europe.

Transport operators have only limited powers to increase levels of demand or to influence patterns of demand. Their most powerful tool is price. For instance, very low prices can be used to generate or stimulate additional demand during the off-peak period. Nevertheless, very low fares to Majorca in January may be able to increase demand for air services during that off-peak month, but will not generate passenger numbers to match those of the peak period and, with the low fares, overall yields will also be low. Operators can also charge higher fares for peak days of demand or peak times of demand to reduce fluctuations. UK rail operators have used higher leisure fares for travel on Fridays and charge different fares for different times of day. A perusal of online rail information sites such as **http://www.nationalrail.co.uk/** demonstrate that the lowest leisure fares on rail are only offered for specific trains where demand is lower. Many charter airlines in Europe have charged higher fares for Saturday travel, although, as this chapter will demonstrate, the timing of when the booking is made is now more influential than the day of travel.

Despite being a derived demand, transport for transit can be viewed as part of the leisure experience, with the journey being an important leisure component for some categories of visitor. The view from the coach or the excitement of flying are examples of potential enjoyment. However, for the business traveller, transport may be seen as a necessary evil, a disutility which must be experienced to reach the destination. The degree to which travel is part of the leisure experience has been analysed as a continuum. It is influenced by:

- the mode of transport. Some modes are intrinsically more enjoyable than others;
- the personality of the tourist;
- the frequency with which the tourist uses that mode;
- the group with which one travels. Supervising young children will for instance add stress to the journey.

However, increases in traffic result in increased congestion, contributing to unscheduled and unacceptable levels of delay that reduce the pleasure gained from travelling for a range of modes such as driving (still often portrayed as a pleasure activity by motoring manufacturers in their advertising campaigns) and air travel. While still very rare, instances of air rage and road rage are increasing.

## Transport at the destination

Once at the destination, visitors make use of taxis, rental cars, scheduled bus and coach services, rail and, dependent on the destination, even ferries. For longer-haul holidays where the country is seen as the destination area, scheduled domestic air may be used and rail should increase in significance. Travel in the destination area accounts for around 10% of tourist use of transport. This of course involves tourists sharing scheduled local transport services not specifically designed for tourist use with the local population. Sometimes this provides an ideal fit, with the two markets complementing each other. This is true of tourism to major cities such as Amsterdam, Helsinki, Boston and Brisbane where tourism demand for bus and metro services tends to commence after 9.30–10.00 am when the peak period of local use for commuting to work is over. Therefore tourists provide an opportunity for the transport operator to earn additional revenue at a time when there is spare capacity. Special off-peak travel tickets have been developed which allow unlimited travel but only after the morning peak. This can help the operator segment the two markets, although some conflicts between local and tourist use during the early evening peak may occur. Increasingly some operators, especially rail operators in the UK are limiting off-peak tickets on trains in the evening peak.

In other locations there can be conflicts between tourist and local requirements. The vintage bus fleet in Malta, currently in the process of being replaced through a process of major fleet investment, is more attractive to tourists than the local population, although ticketing policy does not reflect the needs of tourist users well. Visitor expenditure figures illustrate the importance of transport as an element of the product. Transport at the destination can represent as much as 15% of international visitor expenditure within a large country such as Indonesia.

Some transport operators in destination areas tailor products specifically for tourism, such as the half-day and whole-day coach excursion to attractions in the surrounding region. Sightseeing tours on the top of a double-deck bus with the roof removed are familiar sights in many destination areas, particularly cities. Having first begun in capital cities such as London, the concept has over recent years expanded and in 2012 City Sightseeing, the largest global operator of such tours, was operating in 96 destinations in 29 countries over six continents, although the UK (30 destinations) and the rest of Europe (50 destinations in 19 countries dominate) (see **http://www .city-sightseeing.com/tours/united-kingdom.htm**). These tours do give the tourist mobility around the destination area and tickets are valid all day so one can hop on and hop off. However, for many the vehicle itself becomes the attraction and perhaps that rightly falls under the next section.

Another development, pioneered in the USA, are 'Duck Tours', which undertake a sightseeing tour using a World War II amphibian landing craft, with a short water-based section included on the tour route.

### Transport as the tourist attraction

Increasingly, there are instances of transport, both within and between countries, becoming an attractive tourist product in its own right. The largest mass market is the cruise industry (see Major Case Study 17.1). Other examples include:

- railway products – the Palace on Wheels (India), the Blue Train (South Africa), the Venice Simplon-Orient-Express (Europe), and the Eastern & Oriental Express (South-East Asia);
- sea products – day trips by ferry;
- canal cruises in a narrow boat.

## COMPONENTS OF THE TRANSPORTATION SYSTEM

We can identify four basic elements in any transportation system, namely:

- the way;
- the terminal;
- the vehicle; and
- motive power.

These elements vary for each transportation mode but performance is dependent on the interaction of these four elements. Speed, capacity, safety, security and even perceived quality of service for each mode is dictated by the weakest element in the system.

### The way

The way is the medium of travel over which the vehicle operates. Railways and inland waterways restrict vehicle movement to specific pathways, while road offers a much greater degree of vehicle flexibility over the route network. At first sight air and sea would appear to allow unlimited flexibility but international regulations and conventions dictate otherwise. Significant areas of airspace over a country are reserved solely for military use and the civil airspace is delineated into air corridors and controlled by **air traffic control** (ATC) systems, such as NATS in the UK, utilising sophisticated computer systems and comprehensive radar coverage. Likewise, although less rigorous, there are designated shipping lanes. In considering transport modes, the availability of the way is very important and requires considerable investment.

A shortage in capacity leads to inefficient services, congestion and unscheduled delays. Currently in the UK congestion on the rail network has resulted in reduced numbers of services on some routes in an attempt to improve reliability. In contrast, in mainland Europe rail use has been encouraged by expanded rail capacity with the addition of new high-speed lines. The first, the Train à Grand Vitesse (TGV) line between Paris and Lyon was developed between 1976 and 1981 but investment in high-speed rail in Europe has increased dramatically in recent years. Three new lines opened in 2007 and the European network expected to double to 4,000 kilometres by 2020 (Mintel, 2008) with an EU target to triple the high-speed rail network by 2030 (COM, 2011). Traffic congestion on roads is a phenomenon familiar to many in developed and developing countries.

### The terminal

Public transport terminals give the passenger access to the vehicle, or act as an interchange between different modes of transport. Not all modes need to have sophisticated terminals; buses and coaches for instance can and do operate from roadside locations, although town and city

centre terminals are often more substantive. Perhaps the most complex terminal is an airport and the dramatic growth in air transport worldwide has witnessed the development of many new airports in recent years (Hong Kong, Kuala Lumpur and Athens) and expansion of others (Terminal 5 at Heathrow).

In fact, most terminals are becoming integrated transportation points as they can act as interchanges where travellers can transfer between vehicles or modes. Switzerland has examples of integrated rail and air transport, with rail termini at the airports of Zurich and Geneva linked to main rail routes and then the post-bus to the final destination. Airports can be used as transfer points between aircraft, often organised into the well-structured patterns of arrival and departures required for hub airports in the hub-and-spoke route networks initially developed in the deregulated US domestic market, but also must interface with other modes of travelling, such as the car, coach or train.

The design of terminals and the amenities they offer depend heavily upon the type of journey and mode of transportation involved, as does the length of time spent at the terminal. Air will generally require the longest visit, with arrival at the airport required one to two hours (or even longer where security measures dictate) prior to scheduled departure. Travellers will also tend to allow excess time for infrequently undertaken long-distance rail journeys, whereas arrival will be just in time for shorter, frequent and familiar rail journeys such as commuting. The basic requirement is for toilet facilities and light refreshment, although the length of time the passenger is held as a captive customer creates retail opportunities which airport terminals seek to exploit fully, with up to 60% of airport revenue from retail activity. This share appears to be falling in European airports following the abolition of duty free sales for passengers travelling within the EU in June 1999 (Graham, 2008). Main line city centre termini for intercity rail traffic have also sought to exploit retail opportunities (Liverpool Street and Victoria Stations in London).

For private transport such as the car there is still a requirement for the user to access the vehicle and for the vehicle to access the way, although there is no designated terminal where this must happen. The relative importance of the terminal is often and easily overlooked. The comfort and convenience of the journey can be influenced as much by the experience at the terminal as by the experience on the vehicle. Airlines seek to gain a competitive advantage for high-yield first and business class passengers with the use of VIP lounges. Airports also demonstrate the importance of the terminal in the capacity of the overall transport network. All terminals need sufficient capacity for both vehicular movements and also for passenger movement. In the case of the airport these activities are separated. The vehicle movements are airside, predominantly measured as **air traffic movements** (ATMs) and catered for by runways (together with the capacity of ATC). The number of runways, the use and availability of taxiways, the number of parking stands for aircraft and the number of exit points on the runway for smaller aircraft which do not need the full length of the runway all dictate the number of ATMs an airport can handle each hour. Shortage of capacity to meet forecast demand at London airports from around 2015 (DfT, 2009) have led to controversial proposals to develop additional runways (DfT, 2003; DfT 2006), which are again under review following a change of government. A mis-match of ATC capacity and runway capacity can result in aircraft having to circle busy airports for significant amounts of time awaiting a landing slot, a process known as stacking.

Passenger capacity is a function of the terminal facilities to handle the passengers carried by the ATMs. Essential facilities include check-in, baggage handling and baggage reclaim, passport, immigration and customs controls as well as the shopping and refreshment facilities. Since 1985 virtually all increases in airport capacity in London have been achieved by the development of more terminals. However, squeezing more capacity into airports brings its own problems. Maximum runway throughput can only be achieved with queuing aircraft (on the ground for takeoff and in stacks for landing) which itself affects reliability (Graham, 2008). Airlines publish longer scheduled flight times to allow for the delays in an attempt to retain punctuality and yet despite this over 25% of flights from many European airports such as Madrid, Rome, Paris (Charles De Gaulle – CDG – and Orly) as well as London are over 15 minutes late. The position in the USA is equally difficult, with congestion well documented. Additional runway capacity will be a major requirement in many destinations if growth rates are to be maintained.

## The vehicle

The carrying unit is the actual transportation medium: the vehicle that facilitates the movement. The nature of vehicles has been influenced by numerous factors, which include travel demand and technological developments, as well as the other elements of the mode, particularly motive power. In the past few decades developments have occurred in the carrying units which have enabled greater speed, and usually, but not always, resulted in greater efficiency and sometimes improved consumer comfort. Executive-style coaches with on-board services, airline-style reclining seats on trains and railway-viewing cars and flat seats in airline business class are all examples of improved comfort.

Vehicle size has shown a mixed picture between modes. Economies of scale, in both construction and operation, have resulted in the introduction of increasingly larger cruise ships (Major Case Study 17.1). The Airbus A380 has a capacity of 555 passengers in tri-class seating, and is designed to serve heavily trafficked routes, especially if there are capacity problems at the airports, enabling airlines to reduce unit costs and carry more passengers per ATM. However, this technological advance has not been without its setbacks and the number of airports which can accommodate the A380 is far fewer than the 200-plus airports that can handle a Boeing 747. Airports have to upgrade their infrastructure by widening and strengthening runways, repositioning taxiways, lengthening baggage carousel belts and redesigning or even rebuilding the terminal fingers and air bridges between the terminal and the plane. It is a clear illustration of how developments in one component of the transport system (the vehicle) impacts on another component (the terminal).

There is a fundamental difference of opinion between the two main manufacturers, Airbus and Boeing. Boeing has dropped its project for a larger aircraft on the grounds that the trend in large deregulated markets such as the US domestic market is for airlines to offer more frequent services on linear services with smaller aircraft. Boeing's strategy has been on developing a fuel-efficient medium-sized jet, 787, the Dreamliner, which the manufacturer premiered in July 2007 but is only now entering commercial production in 2012. The range of three aircraft will have between 210 and 330 seats, but with some 50% of their primary structure made from composite materials, they are of light weight and 20% more fuel-efficient than current competitor models. Airlines will require both types of aircraft, but the two manufacturers clearly disagree as to the type and size of aircraft that will make up the bulk of airline orders over the next 20 years.

## Motive power

Finally, and perhaps the most important, motive power is the key element in transportation development. Natural power of horse-drawn carriages and sailing vessels provided the initial energy for transportation. The expansion of steam power provided the opportunity for the introduction of steamships and railways which were such a driving force behind the creation of mass tourism in Europe, while the internal combustion engine stimulated the development of road and air transportation. Finally, jet propulsion enabled air transportation to be competitively priced and gave aircraft speed, range and increased vehicle size. The combination of speed (which allowed the vehicle to make more return trips each 24 hours) and increased vehicle size dramatically reduced operating costs per seat km (Doganis, 2010), enabling these savings to be passed on to the consumer in the form of lower fares. Not all technological advances led to increased efficiency. Concorde, which was withdrawn from passenger service in 2003, had relatively poor productivity despite its very high speed, largely as a result of the low vehicle capacity (approximately 100 seats) and was only viable operating predominantly a business service with a premium fare. Likewise the Hovercraft offered high-speed sea crossings but a combination of high fuel consumption and poor reliability in rough weather prevented its development into the mass mode that was predicted in the 1960s.

Speed of travel has largely stabilised in the last decade with no major technological advances. Naturally the speed for any mode is governed by the interaction of the various components. Cars can move faster than 70 mph (100 km per hour) but limitations of the way mean that maximum speed limits are required for the safety of other road users (both car drivers and where there is no segregation pedestrians, cyclists and so forth). The rail industry even more clearly demonstrates the limitations the way imposes on vehicle speeds. Most of the alignment of the UK national rail network dates back to the nineteenth century when they were constructed. While new high-speed rail vehicles have been developed, this technology, pioneered by the **Train à Grande Vitesse** (TGV) network in France, cannot be adopted onto existing track due to track alignment and particularly the angle of bends. The solution of matching the vehicle speed to the way is to build a new high-speed rail link, as adopted with the development of the TGV in France and copied in much of Europe including the UK with the opening of the first phase of the high-speed Channel Tunnel rail link in 2003 and the proposals for a new high-speed rail link, HS2, between London and Birmingham by 2025.

Attempts to run faster trains over existing track is a much more technologically difficult project, although the development of tilting trains, first attempted by the ill-fated **advanced passenger train** (APT) project in the UK in the early 1980s, is now coming to fruition with Virgin's Pendolino trains. Amtrak's attempts to introduce high-speed trains in the US market, where rail has a significantly lower share than Europe, ran into technical difficulties, although the journey time from New York to Boston has been reduced from five hours to four with speeds of up to 150 mph.

The recent history of transport for tourism is characterised by changes in technology but the emphasis is moving to more environmental considerations (Table 17.2). Engine technology has resulted in more fuel-efficient engines helping to reduce emissions, including greenhouse gases ($CO_2$). Car engine efficiency has improved by around 1.5% per annum and the rate of technical progress is accelerating; some governments have further encouraged this by imposing strict new emission regulations on manufacturers for new cars (see for example European Commission 2009 Regulation EC No 443/2009 which set new statutory levels for 2012).

| Table 17.2 | | The historical development of tourism: recent changes in transport | | | |
|---|---|---|---|---|---|
| | **1930s** | **1940s–1950s** | **1960s–1970s** | **1980s–1990s** | **2000 on** |
| Air | Civil aviation established<br>Travel is expensive and limited | Propeller technology<br>Travel still limited<br>Basic terminals<br>400–480 km/h | Jet aircraft<br>Boeing 707<br>Cheap fuel<br>800–950 km/h<br>Charters take off | Wide-bodied jet 747<br>Extended range<br>Fuel efficient<br>No increases in speed except Concorde | Concorde withdrawn<br>Megacarriers emerge of 500–800 seats<br>More fuel-efficient carriers – Boeing Dreamliner |
| Sea | Ocean liners and cruises<br>Short sea ferry speed less than 40 km/h | Little competition from air<br>No increase in speed | Air overtakes sea on N. Atlantic<br>Hovercraft and faster craft being developed | Fly–cruise established<br>Larger and more comfortable ferries<br>Fast catamarans developed | Even larger cruise ships (Project Genesis) |
| Road | Cars 55 km/h<br>Coaches develop | Cars 100 km/h | Cars used for domestic tourism<br>Speed 115 km/h | Speed limits in USA<br>Rise in car ownership rates<br>Urban congestion<br>Green fuel<br>Improved coaches | LPG powered and hybrid vehicles |
| Rail | Steam era<br>Speed exceed cars | Railways at peak | Electrification<br>Cuts in rail systems: some resorts isolated | High-speed networks develop in Europe<br>Business products offered – memorabilia and steam | Even faster trains to 300 kph |

The last two decades have seen quieter engines, particularly in the case of aircraft, where new EU regulations regarding noise emissions are being phased in.

There are two key factors driving the development of fuel-efficient technology. These include the unpredictability of the cost of fuel. The price of crude oil is volatile, often influenced by specific major incidents:

- In 1973–74, the Arab–Israeli War.
- In 1978–79 the Iranian crisis.
- In 1991 the Gulf War.
- War in Afghanistan in 2001.
- War in Iraq in 2003.

The volatility of oil prices was demonstrated in April 2008 when the price of keresone reached record high levels which generated record losses for airlines despite their attempts to recover some of the increased costs through fuel surcharges. Although the price fluctuates, long-term trends are upward. For example, aviation fuel has become an increasing component of airline operating costs, rising rapidly over recent years from just over 14% of operating costs in 2000 to over 25% in 2007 (Doganis, 2010).

Furthermore, oil is a finite resource. Whilst estimates of the remaining global reserves vary, and oil exploration continues to search for new sources, there is broad agreement that conventional oil will decline between 2020 and 2030 (Becken and Lennox, 2012) with production from non-OPEC countries having peaked. Consequently the price of oil is forecast to rise in real terms as this resource becomes scarcer.

The second factor is the need to reduce transport's contribution to greenhouse gas (GHG) emissions, particularly $CO_2$. Currently transport in the EU is 97% dependent on fossil fuels (COM, 2009) and the European Commission has set a target for a 10% share from renewable energy sources. The scope to achieve this will differ for different modes of transport but the main options include biofuels and electric propulsion, although the environmental gains from the latter depend on the degree to which electricity generation itself is from non-carbon sources such as renewables or nuclear. Rail is clearly a low-carbon option, particularly where electric propulsion is widespread. There remain significant barriers to the mass adoption of electric cars. There are currently only around 1,000 electric cars in the UK with an estimated price of €40,000 for a car with a 300-kilometre range, around double the cost of a conventional vehicle. A second barrier to their mass adoption is the continued lack of associated infrastructure, particularly recharging points, and they are not well suited to long journeys, due to their limited range. The bus and coach industry have adopted biodiesel in some countries and there has been some progress in the use of biofuels for aviation. Following an inaugural flight by Virgin Atlantic between London (Heathrow) and Amsterdam in February 2008 where one of the four engines was powered by a biofuel manufactured from Brazilian babassu nuts, a number of other experimental flights have been undertaken by Air New Zealand, KLM, Continental and JAL trialling a range of biofuel sources including algae, babassu, switchgrass and jatropha in combination with regular jet fuel. The technology is still in its developmental stage and the cost is high. The longer-term impacts of aviation biofuels will be dependent on its performance during continued trials, the quantities that can realistically be produced and the price once the technology progresses to mass production, although the EU has set a target for low-carbon sustainable fuels in aviation to reach 40% by 2050 (COM, 2011).

# COMPETITOR ANALYSIS

The most obvious way of analysing transport is by mode. There are four major modes:

- road;
- rail;
- water;
- air.

The choice of mode of transport is related to the type of person as well as the purpose of travel, although visitor types are no longer as homogeneous as previously assumed. Some leisure passengers will elect to travel business class and a significant percentage of passengers using low-cost airlines are business passengers. Table 17.3 provides an indicative structure for modal choice. Factors influencing modal choice include:

- distance;
- length of stay;
- status and comfort;
- safety;
- price;
- geographical location of origin or destination, especially remote or peripheral destinations;
- availability;
- reliability;
- frequency of service;
- convenience;
- flexibility.

Increasingly transport operators are attempting to identify segments of demand for which specific categories of service will appeal. In Europe coaches now offer degrees of comfort and service unheard of in the 1970s and express coach services in the UK now offer WiFi while ferry companies have become expert in organising varied itineraries for motoring holidays.

**Table 17.3**   Mode of transport and visitor type with examples of product types

| Visitor type | Road | | Air | | | Sea/water | | Railways |
|---|---|---|---|---|---|---|---|---|
| | Car | Coach | Scheduled | Charter | Low cost carriers | Ferry | Cruise | |
| Holiday – inclusive tour | Car hire Fly–drive | Coach tour | Packages – long haul – city break | Long/medium/short-haul packages | | Ferry package | Cruise | Orient Express |
| – independent | Touring private car | Scheduled coach | Self packaging – Internet | Seat only to – villa – second home | Short-haul and city break – accommodation booked by Internet independently – second home | Private car | | 7- or 14-day ticket InterRail |
| Business and conference | Company car | Executive coach | Fully flexible fare | | On frequent short-haul routes (30% of passengers) | High speed catamaran | | TGV or Bullet Train |
| VFR | Private car | Scheduled | Cheapest fare | Group travel | Cheap fares | Private car | | Excursion fare Group fare |
| Other special and common interest, e.g. religion | Car hire Private car | Service Coach charter | Cheap or flexible fare | | | | | |
| Same-day visitors (excursion) | Private car | Scheduled excursion fare | Scheduled excursion fare | Special flights | Domestic routes | Coach/car excursion | Local day cruise | Day excursion fare |

| Table 17.4 | Main modes of transport for holiday trips of 4+ nights by residents in the EU-27: 2008 (%) | | |
|---|---|---|---|
| **Mode** | **Domestic holidays** | **International holidays** | **Total holidays** |
| Car | 76 | 28 | 56 |
| Rail | 12 | 03 | 09 |
| Bus/coach | 06 | 06 | 07 |
| Air | 04 | 58 | 26 |
| Sea | 02 | 04 | 03 |
| **Total** | **100** | **100** | **100** |

*Source*: Eurostat, 2010

International tourism travel is dominated by air and domestic tourism by private car, although this will vary between countries influenced by spatial factors and by the level of economic development. Table 17.4 shows the modal split for tourism travel for European Union countries, where the car is an important mode for short-haul international trips on mainland Europe where distances can be low. There are significant variations in modal share among the EU-27 countries. Air accounts for over 50% of holiday trips from the UK and Eire, reflecting that they are islands, and is also very high for Denmark, Estonia and Latvia but is very low for Bulgaria. Rail has a relatively low share for holiday tourism, although it is higher for Poland (18%) and France (13%), the latter benefiting from a large land area and a well-established high-speed TGV network. Bus and coach has a low market share, although market shares of over 20% are recorded in the less developed countries of Bulgaria and Slovakia. Sea, as a main mode of transport is rare with the exception of Greece, where travel to and from island destinations results in 18% of the modal split.

## Road transport

The car dominates road transport. It is almost the perfect tool for tourist use, offering the following attractions:

- control of the route and the stops en route;
- control of departure times;
- door-to-door flexibility;
- the ideal capacity for families;
- the ability to carry baggage and equipment easily;
- the ability to use the vehicle for accommodation in the case of recreational vehicles and caravans;
- privacy;
- the freedom to use the vehicle once the destination is reached; and
- the low perceived cost.

Some nations tend to utilise cars much more than others for recreation and tourism. This reflects levels of economic development, which influences levels of car ownership among the population, but also is dependent upon geography (average distances travelled for tourist trips), climate and the cost, quality and availability of alternatives. Nevertheless, the car share is very high in developed countries. Trips by car account for approximately 90% of the pleasure/personal and business trips taken by Canadian and US residents, for almost 60% of the total holiday trips in Europe and over 70% of all UK domestic holiday trips.

Growth rates of traffic in the latter half of the twentieth century have been phenomenal. For instance, in the UK the modal share of car for all journey purposes has grown from 35% of all passenger kilometres in 1955 to 84% by 2010 (DfT, 2011). However, over the same period both disposable time and disposable income have increased, resulting in far more travel overall so the increase in vehicle kilometres is eight-and-a-half fold. Likewise traffic volume in the USA increased by 76% between 1980 and 2000. The leisure and tourism share of all this traffic is not insubstantial. Around 13% of all passenger kilometres are accounted for by holiday trips, but day trip excursions and appropriate VFR traffic would increase the 'tourism' share to nearer 30% of all kilometres. Peeters et al. (2007) estimate that tourism accounts for between 15% and 20% of passenger kilometres travelled in Europe by surface modes of transport. More recently, road traffic growth has slowed in a number of developed countries. Passenger kilometres have been virtually stagnant in the UK, with a total growth of 2% between 2000 and 2010 (DfT, 2011). This mirrors similar trends in Belgium, The Netherlands and Germany, perhaps indicating that car travel is approaching saturation (Robbins and Dickinson, 2007).

These high rates of car use are now considered unsustainable by governments in many developed countries as car users are imposing huge costs on others which they do not directly pay for (termed **externalities**). The contribution of cars to greenhouse gas emissions is high at around 18% of the total UK emissions despite improving engine efficiency. Cars also affect local air quality and produce particulates which are linked to asthma and other respiratory complaints, and generate huge costs to society in terms of congestion, road accidents and visual intrusion. Large numbers of vehicles can reduce the attractiveness of tourist destinations, most particularly popular rural locations such as national parks.

Traffic growth rates in developing countries where levels of car ownership are lower will continue at high rates, driven by economic growth coupled with significant population growth. Ironically, higher levels of car ownership can be seen as proof of economic success by governments and yet the externalities of car use are equally problematic.

The UK government has set out a number of policies to reduce car dependency. The concept of road pricing, charging the motorist directly for using the most congested parts of the road network at the most congested times, has gained ground. The introduction in February 2003 of congestion charging for a central core area of London between 0700 and 1830 on weekdays has attracted international attention. While it is not the first road pricing scheme, schemes such as Singapore's pre-date it, it is the first on this scale. Early results exceeded expectations, with traffic falls of 18% and congestion reduced by 30% over the first year of operation. Stockholm trialled a similar scheme for six months in 2006 and, following a referendum, implemented it on a permanent basis in August 2007.

Other forms of road pricing are aimed at long-distance travel in the form of motorway/autobahn/interstate highway tolls. They have a relatively long history in Europe and the USA and were introduced in the UK for the first time in 2003 (M6 Toll), and again charges can be used as a tool to manage traffic growth. UK policy options include combining both elements into an electronic national road pricing scheme using satellite technology, although such a scheme is not on the current agenda and will require a strong political will, over 1.75 million UK residents signed an electronic petition against electronic road pricing in 2007. Road pricing has the advantage of narrowing the price advantage of the car over other forms of transport by placing a greater element of car use costs at the point of use. Currently the point of use cost of a car is very low (petrol costs plus perhaps a little extra for vehicle maintenance) and the price advantage is enhanced for family groups of 3–5 people. However, if the cost of car travel rises too steeply, there are fears that tourism growth rates may slow or even move into decline.

## YOUTUBE

Car Rental Orlando
http://www.youtube.com/watch?v=9_5pjZlWV3A

## The coach

In many developed countries the scheduled bus and coach networks have seen a significant decline in passenger numbers. However, the coach still plays a role in the tourism market, divided into three sectors. First, scheduled long-distance coaches are used as an alternative usually to rail or car to travel to the destination, although long-distance coach services in the USA (for instance Greyhound and Trailways) are in direct competition with air. This mode is particularly useful for short- and medium-distance journeys. It has traditionally attracted very price-sensitive consumers, most notably students, lower occupational or social groups and the over-50s market. Beyond a certain threshold distance, lack of comfort and the relatively slower speed compared with other modes has to be traded off against cheaper and more attractive pricing structures. The coach network is more dense than the rail network, offering more destinations, and can be quicker than rail in areas where there has been investment in new roads versus an ageing rail system (northern Portugal). For some destinations it may be the only public transport alternative. In the UK the extensive National Express network has seen a significant rise in competition on main routes from **MegaBus.com** which has in particular targeted a student market with e-ticketing and departure points at university campuses.

The second sector is the coach tour. Again the market traditionally attracts an over-50s market, but often from higher socio-economic groups and also passengers from car-owning households. The break from driving, the scenic views from the coach and the social interaction with the other coach passengers are all attractions for this type of holiday.

The third sector is the hired coach. This has traditionally been employed at the destination by groups for transfers to and from the terminal, most notably on inclusive tour holidays. In addition, sightseeing trips and tours are normally conducted by coaches or minibuses. Safaris in particular use the adapted microbus for sightseeing and game watching, such as in Kenya.

The importance of the coach market can be overlooked. It is estimated coaches carried 860 million US passengers in 2000 with the vast majority (90%) carried on privately hired vehicles.

## Rail transport

Overall the rail share of travel for holiday purposes is traditionally not high (Table 17.4). However, the rail shares for certain corridors (especially high-speed lines) are higher as they include business and conference traffic. Railway termini are often located in city centre locations in contrast to airports, which are often located 20 or 30 kilometres away from the centre. This increases their attraction for this market and a major competitive advantage is city centre to city centre journey times compared with air. Beyond a certain distance, some visitors see rail as being too cumbersome and tiring and it is then that notions of adventure and sightseeing take over as the attractions of the rail mode. However, the traditional model demonstrated in Figure 17.1 is

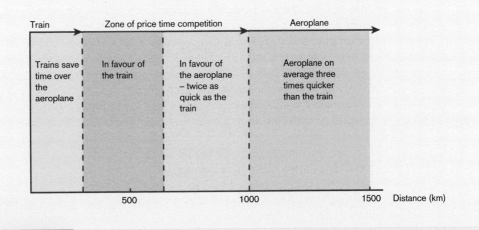

| Figure 17.1 | Competition between the aeroplane and the high-speed train on international routes in Europe |

*Source*: Adapted from *Business Travel World*, May 1997

beginning to break down in Europe, with rail services losing out to low-cost air carriers on many routes at distances significantly below 500 kilometres. One factor contributing to this is price. Rail has very high fixed costs (track, signalling, engineering costs), which either result in high fares (UK) or high levels of subsidy (France, Germany) or a combination of both. Another disadvantage over air is the difficulty in booking online through tickets on international rail journeys (see Dickinson et al., 2010b), although rail operators are beginning to address this and develop integrated systems. Railteam, an alliance of Europe's seven high-speed rail operators, aims to provide better coordinated services with better connecting services and much better coordinated online ticketing systems.

Trains are a relatively 'green' form of travel in terms of both fuel efficiency and emissions, although the performance of ageing diesel trains has been criticised. Electric trains are much more fuel-efficient than cars per passenger kilometre travelled. Rail also has a hugely better safety record than car travel. The scope for rest and relaxation of travel by train, and the ability the use the travel time productively on the train are additional advantages although high-quality services rarely extend throughout the whole network, so journeys involving a change from main high-speed lines to branch lines are more variable. The luxury and comfort attributes of rail are most prominent on journeys between 200 to 500 kilometres between major cities, although airlines are currently making inroads in that market in Europe. The traditional market for the train has been regarded as the independent holiday visitor, particularly the VFR category; they may also attract a significant 'fear of flying' market.

## Sea transport

In broad terms, we can divide water-borne transport into short sea ferry transport and ocean-going cruises. Other categories exist, such as inland waterway craft and small pleasure craft, but assume less significance as a means of transport as they are more destination products in their own right. Cruising should also be thought of as a holiday product as much as a mode of transport. Ferry services, which include or exclude vehicles, can provide lifeline services to islands as well as a focus for visitors. Catamarans tend to be faster than conventional forms of ship technology but, in general (unless for short sea commuting such as between Hong Kong and Macau), business visitors tend to choose other modes of transport. Geographical factors tend to determine the provision of ferry transport, leaving some destinations heavily dependent upon such links. Examples include:

- Aegean island-hopping or travel to and from the Greek mainland; or
- channel crossings such as the English Channel, Irish Sea, the Cook Strait between the North and South islands of New Zealand, and the Baltic Sea.

As far as the transportation of vehicles and merchandise is required on short sea crossings, ferries offer inexpensive, reliable and safe services. Ferry transportation is the only possibility in the case of remote and small islands which have no airport. This situation can be found in Greece, where there are only 15 airports to serve 95 inhabited islands, a coastline of 14,854 kilometres and 750 ports and anchorages. In this case, large ferries provide coastal shipping services linking the mainland ports and islands as well as the islands with each other. Piraeus port handles 21.5 million ferry passengers per annum, of whom around 11.5 million are domestic passengers, and is therefore a very important facility in the provision of tourism transport services. Furthermore, smaller regional ferries undertake transportation between the islands, especially during the summer peak period.

However, in many cases, air can be a viable alternative to sea transportation between larger islands and the mainland. The main advantage of ferry operators when compared with air transportation is price, combined with the fact that passengers can carry their own vehicles and use them at the destination. The popularity of motoring holidays and self-drive packages, as well as the introduction of roll on–roll off facilities, which enables the ports to handle a much greater volume of vehicles, demonstrates the increase of passenger demand for ferry services.

In Europe, the gradual liberalisation of air transportation, the decrease of air fares, the construction of the Channel Tunnel and the development of alternative modes of travel have forced the ferry companies to improve the luxury of their vessels considerably, to increase the cruising speed, to increase their size and to install leisure facilities. Routes with longer crossings can enhance the leisure facilities – casinos, cabaret bars, cabins – to offer a consumer-orientated service.

Modern vessels, such as the wave-piercing catamaran and hydrofoils, have been introduced on some routes in recent decades. Their main aim is to offer a shorter crossing time than the traditional ferry service. Their speed is up to three times that of a conventional ferry, while they have a great manoeuvrability, fast turn-around in port and need minimum dock facilities. However, these vessels are:

- much more expensive than the ferries;
- vulnerable in rough seas and strong winds;
- noisy; and
- environmentally insensitive, with higher $CO_2$ emissions and wave actions that contribute to coastal erosion.

## Air transport

Travelling by air is probably the most important transportation innovation of the twentieth century. It has enabled the transportation of passengers in the shortest time and it has boosted the demand for long-haul trips, for which there is no realistic alternative mode of transport. In fact, no part of the world is now more than 24 hours' flying time from any other part. International tourist arrivals by air have grown dramatically, producing global growth rates for air travel of between 5% and 6% per annum between 1970 and 2000 (Gössling and Peeters, 2007). Although these very high rates have receded over the last two years as the economic recession has impacted on demand for air services, most forecasts predict continuing longer-term global air traffic growth rates of 4.7–5% per annum (Symth and Christodoulou, 2011). Therefore air transportation has gained a very significant share of the transportation market, especially for movements over 500 kilometres as Table 17.4 indicates for Europe. As new aircraft, such as the Boeing 747-400 series and now the A380, have come into operation, the range for air travel has been extended to up to 15,000 kilometres for non-stop flights.

Scheduled airlines offer a safe, convenient, reliable, frequent and relatively consumer-orientated product; airlines attract business travellers, who appreciate the speed and flexibility between the various flights, especially on popular routes, as well as the leisure passengers who enjoy the ability to arrive at the destination quickly, and without spending time and money en route. Air transport requires sophisticated and comprehensive ground services and terminal facilities. Airlines offer a number of incentives for their loyal customers through various 'frequent flyer' programmes. Traditionally, air transportation was the most expensive mode, especially for the short-haul routes, but this has changed over recent years with the introduction of new business models. Leisure passengers have always been offered lower fares. The main holiday routes in Europe between the industrialised north to Mediterranean destinations in the south were served by charter airlines from the 1960s (discussed below). For scheduled airlines a limited range of promotional fares were available but these included restrictions such as limited or no opportunities for alterations on the travel arrangements and advance purchase such as the **advanced purchase excursion fare** (APEX), standby, and other forms of **instant purchase fares** (IPEX). However, air transport was very heavily regulated and the availability of such tickets were controlled. Following the process of liberalisation and deregulation (discussed below) in a number of important aviation markets, airlines were given much greater freedom over their route structure and their fare structure to operate commercially and attempt to achieve maximum yield by taking account of potential demand and supply factors. More sophisticated yield management has emerged, assisted by Internet booking and e-ticketing. Following on from developments in the USA, Europe has seen the emergence of low-cost, no-frills airlines and the model is gradually being adopted, sometimes with modifications, in other markets.

## Low-cost airlines

The term low cost is often associated with budget airlines or no-frills carriers. The concept developed in the USA following deregulation of air services in 1978, pioneered by Southwest Airlines. The concept transferred to Europe in the mid-1990s with the emergence of several carriers copying the Southwest approach between 1995 and 1998. Outside Europe and the USA adoption of the low-cost model has been slower. However, since 1999 there has been the emergence of carriers in Australia, Canada (albeit with very low market share), East Asia and the Pacific, South Africa and Latin America. Virgin Blue, a wholly owned subsidiary of the Virgin Group, was launched in 2000. Now rebranded Virgin Australia, it is Australia's second airline and operates to 54 destinations carrying almost 18.5 million passengers (16 million on domestic routes). Other low-cost carriers to emerge include WestJet (Canada), Kulula.com (South Africa) and Gol Transportes Aerosand (Brazil). In 2001 there were five LCCs operating in Asia and the Pacific region, all on domestic routes, but this had increased to 30 airlines by 2008, including some international routes.

Southwest Airlines was set up in 1971 to operate services within Texas. Its home base was the subsidiary airport in Dallas (Love Field), which was much closer to downtown Dallas than the main airport Dallas Fort Worth, an irony considering the subsequent criticism levelled at low-cost carriers, particularly in Europe, over the use of airports up to 100 kilometres from town centres. Its strategy from the first was to offer low fares and high point-to-point frequencies on short-haul routes within Texas. Following deregulation of the US domestic market in 1978 it cautiously expanded into services between states, concentrating predominantly on short flights of two to four hours which it could serve with a single type of Boeing 737 aircraft (Lawton, 2002), selecting routes where there was no competition. Today it is America's largest airline (passengers carried) and in January 2010 announced a profit for the 37th consecutive year, in marked contrast to other US airlines. The driving force behind this success are very low costs. Doganis (2006: 176) indicates that low-cost carriers can achieve costs per seat at around 40% of the costs of full service airlines on short-to medium-haul routes (2–4 hours). Its current average flight length is 653 miles or 1 hour 52 minutes (Southwest Airlines, 2010).

There are a number of texts that show how low-cost carriers achieve their low operating costs. Doganis (2006) offers the most detailed analysis, although the strategies summarised below are also covered by Duval (2007), Groß and Schröder (2007), Hanlon (2007), Lawton (2002) and Page (2009) among others. Some differences have emerged between low-cost carriers, but by and large they will feature most of the following:

- **Operation from secondary airports at major cities or from regional airports**

This generates two distinct sets of savings:

  - Landing charges and operating costs are lower. Many airports offer discounts, and the volume of traffic that low-cost airlines can bring to small airports is so attractive that some moved beyond discounts to offering subsidies. In Europe, subsidies offered by airports owned by the public sector have been ruled as being anti-competitive and unlawful following legal judgments on Ryanair's agreements with Charleroi Airport in Belgium and the now discontinued service to Strasbourg.

- The use of uncongested airports enables very rapid turnaround time (often under 30 minutes), maximising aircraft utilisation productivity.

- **Standardised fleet, initially on one aircraft type**

This brings the following savings:

  - Reduces maintenance costs, although in most cases maintenance is outsourced. The volume of spares and hence storage costs are also reduced.
  - Reduces pilot and cabin crew training costs.

However, as the airline expands and diversifies into routes of varying length and different characteristics, the fleet may diversify to two or three configurations of this aircraft type.

- **Maximise aircraft capacity**
  - Operating a single class of seating.
  - Adopting a low seat pitch (29–31 inches), which is acceptable to passengers on short flights.
  - Utilising galley space freed up by not providing free food and for additional seating.

- **Minimise in-flight costs**
  - By not offering free food and beverages on board but charging for these services.
  - By operating with the minimum number of cabin crew allowed by safety regulations.
  - By not offering pre-assigned seating at check-in.
  - Adherence to very strict baggage limits and, charging for baggage destined for the hold.
  - By minimising ex-gratia payments to customers in carriage. In the event of delay and cancellation the airline will offer the minimum subsistence and compensation that it can under its statutory obligations, plus a refund of the fare paid or a place on the next available flight which might be some days hence.

- **Reduce sales and distribution costs**
  - Online bookings.
  - No commission paid to agents.

In Europe the third phase of liberalisation became operational in 1997, paving the way for the emergence of low-cost airlines. Although Ryanair began in 1985 between Waterford Ireland to London Gatwick at a time when the regulatory regime between the UK and Ireland was liberal it did not expand to non-UK–Irish routes until deregulation in 1997. Following a visit to Southwest Airlines in the early 1990s, it decided it had to reduce its cost base along the lines pioneered by Southwest, since when it has displayed phenomenal growth. By 2009 it had 1,300 routes linking 44 bases carrying 72 million passengers, making it the largest international airline in the world (and the fifth largest in total) in terms of passengers carried. Clearly, because it focuses on shorter routes, it is not the largest airline in terms of passenger kilometres. EasyJet, the largest low-cost airline in the UK, began operations in 1995 based at Luton with two aircraft on two routes and by 2010 operated 552 routes across 30 countries carrying 50.3 million passengers.

The evidence from both the USA and Europe is that the very low fares of low-cost carriers has both attracted passengers from the higher-cost full-service airlines and also generated significant new traffic. Contrary to popular belief, they also carry business passengers, although the number varies significantly from route to route, attracted in part by the high frequency on some routes.

Full-service airlines are beginning to copy a number of the operating strategies of the low-cost carriers in an attempt to control costs, most notably e-ticketing, automated check-in and reducing or even eliminating the meals service on shorter-haul routes, particularly routes from regional airports. While full-service carriers will have to retain important short-haul services, particularly into their main hub airports to facilitate passengers **interlining** to their more profitable long-haul services, many commentators have forecast increased withdrawal from other short-haul routes.

They find it difficult to compete on cost, not least because of their use of congested primary airports, making quick turn around and high aircraft utilisation difficult to achieve. British Airways (BA) divested itself of BA Connect, its regional airline business, to Flybe in 2007.

One interesting reaction from some scheduled carriers was the development of their own low-cost operations either to counter the competition from other low-cost airlines or because it might be profitable. Examples include Go, set up in 1998 by BA, Buzz (2000) by KLM, United Airlines with Ted in the United States in 2004, Thai Airways with Nok in Thailand in 2004 and Air Canada and Tango in 2001. Most of these were short-lived experiments, and Go was acquired by easyJet, Buzz by Ryanair and Tango (2004) and Ted (2009) ceased operations.

The inexorable growth of low-cost airlines has shown signs of slowing down, partially as a result of the global recession and partially due to the very high cost of crude oil and its impact on operating costs. That said, Ryanair is to expand operations and create an estimated 1,000 jobs as part of its regional airport expansion in the UK, with airports in Liverpool, Manchester and East Midlands benefiting significantly from this growth.

There has been increasing debate as to whether the low-cost no-frills principles of operation can be applied to long-haul services. Following increased competition from new low-cost carriers in the USA, Southwest has extended its operations to routes of over 1,000 kilometres and its longest route is Philadelphia to Oakland (3,626 kilometres). Nevertheless, most observers have come to the conclusion the model will not transfer well for a number of reasons. On routes where there is a significant level of high fare paying first class and business class passengers on the full-service carriers, the fares that these carriers can charge for economy services are very competitive, whereas the cost savings achievable over full-service airlines on long-haul services will be lower, perhaps 20–25% (see Francis et al., 2007 for a fuller analysis). Full-service airlines already achieve high vehicle utilisation and there are limits as to the minimum acceptable seat pitch for longer flights. The omens for a successful long-haul low-cost service are not good. Attempts to operate low-cost services on long-haul routes include Zoom, which operated services from the UK to Canada/US, and Oasis, which operated between the UK and Hong Kong. Both services ceased operations in 2008. Previous failures for low-cost services on the transatlantic route include Laker's Skytrain in 1982 and People's Express in the mid-1980s. Most recently Air Asia X suspended its low-cost long-haul services from Kuala Lumpur to London and Paris from March 2012.

## Charter airlines

Charter flights are utilised widely to facilitate the movement of holidaymakers on package tours, although up to 20% of passengers are carried on 'seat only' arrangements. Most charter airlines are owned by tour operators which attempt to integrate their operations vertically, such as Thomson Airways and Thomson Holidays in the UK. Charter airlines offer ad hoc transportation services, although in peak seasons they operate to a timetable, which although not formally published is known to tour operators. Services are characterised by:

- minimal flexibility in altering flights;
- flying at inconvenient and therefore not busy hours for the terminal and achieving very high utilisation of the plane over a 24-hour period;

## YOUTUBE

Trends and technologies at the Air Transport IT Summit 2011
http://www.youtube.com/watch?v=3j3QZLWlXII

Mark Pilling on the 2011 Air Transport IT Summit
http://www.youtube.com/watch?v=eGwqcLC_6_Q

- reduced seat pitch to fit in as many seats as possible;
- consolidation of flights if not fully booked;

The higher **load factor** achieved on **charter services** (90%) compared with **scheduled services** (averaging 70%) is the final factor explaining the substantial difference in the unit cost of production and the price at which the product can be sold. For a more detailed analysis of charter airline costs see Doganis (2010).

Charter airlines held a substantial share (almost 50%) of the short-haul intra-European market in the 1980s, with the dominant pattern of demand being the carrying of tourists from north Europe to the resorts and tourist destinations in the south. However, they have lost substantive market share since the mid-1990s as a result of direct competition from the low-cost carriers, although they remain important, still carrying around of 29% of air passengers from the UK. Charter airline seat costs per kilometre are probably below those of low-cost airlines and yet it is the latter that have achieved rapid growth over the last 10 years. The trend towards independent holidays, growing second home ownership and direct booking on the Internet have all contributed to the declining appeal of the package holiday and therefore the performance of charter airlines. Charter airlines have developed a number of strategies for their future survival and development. Some, like Monarch, have diversified to become hybrid airlines which offer scheduled services using the same low-cost model, although on some routes they still carry predominantly passengers on an inclusive tour. This strategy also enables them to compete more successfully for the seat-only traveller. Most charter airlines have also diversified into long-haul routes, for which their more varied fleet is well suited and where they compete solely with full-service carriers.

## Business and leisure travel

People who travel for their economic activities and therefore have their fares paid by their employers require maximum flexibility in order to be able to alter their travelling arrangements at short notice. Services, terminals and aircraft have to be designed to facilitate the function of the busy business traveller. It is estimated that business travellers account for about 30% of all international air traffic.

Leisure travellers' share of air transportation has increased rapidly during the recent decades. Leisure travellers have much more time and they do not necessarily require very high-quality services. They are free to make their holiday arrangements well in advance and thus they do not need flexibility. However, unlike the business traveller they do pay their own fares and therefore they are price conscious. The development of specific leisure fares by scheduled airlines as well as the charter airlines in Europe appeared to cater for the needs of this market adequately until the emergence of low-cost carriers demonstrated otherwise.

# POLITICAL INFLUENCES ON TRANSPORT FOR TOURISM

International tourist movements are affected by the activities of governments. Barriers to communication, apart from distance, include border controls, the need for visas or transit visas and customs controls. For rail and road the boundary between nations is the place of border control, and for sea transport the land/sea interface or the port is the point of control; however, for air transport the airport terminal, wherever located, is the processing point.

The concept of sovereignty of airspace versus the freedom of the high seas has always been a factor limiting and influencing provision of transport for tourism by air. Rail transport across and between nations, apart from gauge differences, has usually been relatively smooth compared with quota regulations for coaches in transit or entering other countries. The motorist has been affected by the insurance requirements for a Green Card and international driving licences, but in parts of Europe such barriers as border controls and restraints have all but disappeared.

Because of its very nature, air developed as a complex and political industry. Airlines are important within the national economy for foreign exchange and for fare payments from foreign travellers, and historically the majority of international airlines were wholly or majority owned by their national governments with some exceptions, most notably in the US and Latin America but also Scandinavian Airlines System (SAS) and Air Afrique. Many 'flag carriers' have been subsidised by governments and are seen to be prestige companies. The size of an airline is not necessarily related to the size of traffic potential of that country; the example of KLM illustrates this point. Although the dominance of state-owned airlines began to change from the mid-1980s, the process was gradual and by 2004 there remained over 70 airlines where the state remained the sole or majority shareholder (Doganis, 2006).

# REGULATION OF COMPETITION

Since their inception, transport modes have been subject to regulation by governments. A regulatory environment usually consists of two distinct sets of controls, qualitative and quantitative. The quality controls focus on issues of safety and good practice and are necessary for safety and technical reasons. Quantity controls are legal and economic forms of regulation where the regulator controls competition, capacity and fares. Such controls protect incumbent operators, sometimes the state-owned operators described in the previous section or so-called 'pioneer operators', which incur development costs to set up routes but are then vulnerable to another operator moving in without those costs to recoup. This was the basis of bus and coach legislation in the UK, which had been heavily regulated from 1930 until deregulation of coaches in 1980, followed by the deregulation of the bus industry in 1985. The US (1982), Scandinavia, Portugal and Greece have all followed. Railways tend to be natural national monopolies and to be state-owned and subsidised, but in Europe there has been privatisation in several countries following the European Commission Directive 91/440/EEC, although competition between train operators has proved impractical in most instances and the industry remains regulated.

Policies on regulation have tended to focus on air transport to a greater degree than other modes as international aviation has been regulated since its emergence as a significant economic activity. International air law is a factor that controls the extent to which national airlines may operate. In the United States the so-called anti-trust provisions have always existed to prevent the development of price fixing, cartels and collusion between competitors. In Europe, under the Treaty of Rome, transport has been deemed to be subject to competition rules and the European Commission has outlawed agreements between pairs of national carriers which pool their capacity and revenues, and still judges whether potential mergers of airlines are anti-competitive or not.

The conflicts between regulation and deregulation reflect differences in philosophy and ideology. Supporters of regulation argue that it provides a stable, planned, comprehensive network of transport services. Competition can lead to the demise of some routes, perhaps socially necessary services, which protected operators had retained through cross-subsidy from profitable routes. However, supporters of deregulation believe that free market competition is a much more efficient allocator of resources, matching supply with demand, than planners and regulators. They argue that regulation creates inertia where planned networks fail to respond to changing patterns of demand.

A second concern over a regulated market is the protection the transport provider receives from the regulator to operate as a monopoly or duopoly, which encourages inefficiency and poor operating practices. Regulated markets are characterised by high wage costs, over staffing, generous working conditions, high fares and poor customer service. The pressure of competition in a deregulated market benefits customers as the competition creates more efficient operators with much more effective cost control leading to lower fares. Competition should also lead to improved quality of service as multiple operators compete for customers.

## Impacts of aviation deregulation

The Airline Deregulation Act 1978 was introduced in President Carter's era for domestic services in the United States and led to the development of the first open skies policy. The Civil Aeronautics Board (CAB) was phased out as a regulatory body devising policy. Its role had been to devise regulations on conditions of service such as frequency and capacity, on exit and entry into operation and on fares and prices. Such matters then became the subject of free competition within the US domestic environment. Up until the late 1970s the International Airline Transport Association (IATA) was the *de facto* controlling body worldwide, being a trade association for airlines, though in reality it represented governments as well. However, ever since the famous Show Cause Order where the IATA had to show good cause why it should be exempt from the US anti-trust provisions, this body has lost its stature and strength to implement fare structures to protect its high-cost member airlines. IATA's influence varies from continent to continent and it is still strong in parts of Africa and Latin America.

The regulatory framework for international air services was established by the Chicago Convention of 1944. The so-called 'five freedoms of movement' giving technical and traffic rights to airlines are still important for international movements. These are outlined in Figure 17.2. Subsequent to the Chicago Convention, sixth, seventh and eighth freedoms have been formulated. However a truly multilateral agreement was not reached at Chicago so a series of bilateral arrangements, termed air service agreements (ASAs), emerged between governments to complement it and establish the detailed regulations for international services. National governments approve and license carriers nominated to fly between the home country and an overseas destination; fares are fixed by reference to IATA conference machinery or between respective governments. There were huge numbers of ASAs, for example in 2003, EU members operated some 1,500 ASAs, the United Kingdom alone had 149 (House of Lords, 2003).

The extent to which US domestic policies have been translated to overseas situations has been limited. Within the USA, as a result of fierce competition, instability arose when a great number of air carriers entered the market and the fares reached their lowest levels. However, in the following years only a few carriers could survive and most of the small or weak airlines were

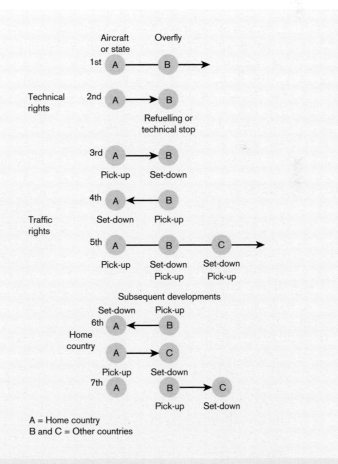

**Figure 17.2**    The five freedoms of the air as agreed at the Chicago Convention, 1944

absorbed or merged with the stronger ones, and ironically the industry is more concentrated today than it was in 1978. Nevertheless, whilst there have been some disadvantages, such as the loss of some thinly trafficked routes to small airports, overall there have been increased traffic levels and lower fares. The emergence of Southwest Airlines and the low-cost model is clearly an important outcome. Interestingly the pattern of travel changed as most airlines (although not Southwest Airlines) operated a hub and spoke network. In 1978 around 80% of US domestic passengers were able to fly direct to their destination without an interchange, yet by 2000 this had fallen to 64% (Page, 2009).

European skies were quite reluctant to open up to complete deregulation. This is partly because of the public sector's role in the airline industry as well as the social role of the carriers to maintain uneconomic routes in the peripheral areas for social reasons. After three directives from the European Commission, the development of true **cabotage** (eighth freedom)arrangements, with Europe emerging as a single aviation market, finally happened on 1 April 1997. Again the major impact has been the emergence of low-cost airlines driving traffic growth.

There is another issue which involves the agreements made between the United States and the EU over air traffic between the two. Historically, there were separate bilateral agreements between the US and different European countries but in 2002 the European Court of Justice declared that the EU has the right to govern and negotiate agreements between the whole EU region with foreign countries such as the USA. The EU–US Open Skies agreement was signed in April 2008 and:

- Removed restrictions on route rights so any EU airline can fly from any EU city to any US city.

- Any US airline can fly into any EU airport and from there on to a third destination.

- EU airlines can fly between any US city and any city in a non-EU country which is a member of the European Common Aviation Area (ECAA).

- US airlines can own 49% of the voting rights in European airlines whereas European airlines can only hold 25% of the voting rights in US airlines (Pitfield, 2009).

The current agreement continues to favour US airlines. It allows cabotage for US airlines in the EU whereas European airlines have no access to routes in the US domestic market. The differing regulations over foreign ownership of European and US airlines is also unbalanced. (For a more detailed review see the Special Issue of *The Journal of Air Transport Management*, 2009, Volume 15.)

# FUTURE TRENDS

In this section we provide an analysis of the external environment and its impact on the future trends of tourism transportation.

## Globalisation and integration

Globalisation is one of the major trends in the international tourism industry and involves a convergence in tastes, preferences and products. The global firm is one that capitalises on this trend and produces standardised products contributing to the homogenisation of the world tourism market. Essentially this means an increase in worldwide business between multinational corporations irrespective of the geographical location and can lead to the virtual firm as a transport operator.

The truly global carrier, as some have predicted, has not really emerged, in part due to wishes by governments and other trading blocs to retain national sovereignty as vested in their national carriers and enforced by the regulatory environment. However, there has been a further consolidation of strategic and marketing alliances and an integration of services and operations as an alternative approach to gain some influence over, access to and feeder traffic from regions that an airline would not otherwise have. Airlines are forging strategic alliances to both increase their market reach and control costs. Motivating factors include:

- the maturity of domestic traffic;
- the competition for terminal space and slots;
- the need for extensive networks worldwide;
- the necessity for economies of scale in airline operation;
- the control of the new distribution channels (CRS); and
- the gradual deregulation in world transportation.

There are many examples of the globalisation of airlines. For example British Airways:

- has franchise operations such as with British Mediterranean Airways;
- in 1992 bought a stake in US Air, which it decided to sell in 1996, but after several failed attempts over 10 years established a transatlantic alliance with American Airlines in 2010;
- had joint business venture with Qantas from 1995–2013;
- merged with Iberia in 2010;
- is a major player in the Oneworld Alliance of 11 airlines and has codeshare agreements with alliance and some non-alliance carriers.

Other alliances include the Star Alliance, which at its inception in 1997 comprised the founder members Thai, Air Canada, United, Lufthansa and SAS, and in 2009 had 23 members, and Skyteam with nine members. Objectives include:

- integrate products and connecting services;
- offer common check-in and reservation services;
- share airport lounge services; and
- share marketing, communications and rewards services.

The trend towards globalisation has been seen in respect of numerous attempts to merge. To date, few attempts have been successful, especially in the European context due to great pride in government ownership and national sovereignty. There have been notable examples of bankruptcy in the early 2000s in the form of Sabena, the Belgian flag carrier, and Swissair, which later re-emerged as Swiss International Airlines. In 2004 the merger of Air France and KLM was finally approved by the competition regulators in Brussels and Washington and, as stated above, British Airways and Iberia in 2010. Whilst the European market is displaying the economic pressures that produce a more concentrated industry that has been a key feature of US deregulation, the political pressures will prevent it becoming as concentrated as the US.

## Environmental policies

The environment will become the biggest challenge to tourism transport over the coming decade. It is not easy to measure tourism's contribution to global warming, although Peeters (2007) estimates it at 4–10% worldwide, with tourism's contribution in the developed world somewhat higher (10–20%). There is a growing body of literature which confirms transport as the dominant contributor to tourism's environmental impacts. Høyer (2000) calculates that travel to and from the Tyrol region in Austria, together with local transport within the destination area, is responsible for between 40% and 60% of tourism's total environmental impact on the region. A case study of Amsterdam, where international tourist arrivals by air form a significant share of the overall market, estimates the transport contribution at a higher figure of 70%, although local transport around the destination accounts for a mere 1%. In contrast, the share of accommodation is estimated at 21% and visiting attractions and other leisure facilities account for a relatively small 8% of environmental impacts (Peeters and Schouten, 2005).

Concern has been expressed about the continued growth of both car traffic and air traffic and in particular their contribution to greenhouse gasses and other noxious emissions. Already policies of restraint on car use are being explored and introduced by various governments and the introduction of congestion charging in London appears to show that policies of constraint can be both successful and, perhaps more importantly, politically popular. There are some concerns that for certain large department stores turnover has been reduced by up to 9%, but there are other factors in play (not least a reduction in North American visitors to the UK post-9/11) and the majority of businesses are reporting increased turnover. Other similar schemes appear inevitable.

The position with regard to air travel is more mixed. Air transport accounts for approximately 3.5% of global $CO_2$ but the forecast growth of air traffic estimates that $CO_2$ emissions from aviation will double over the next 15 years, and that calculation allows for continued improvements in aviation technology and more efficient aircraft. Air transport will account for 6–10% of $CO_2$ emissions by 2050, at a time when many other sectors are actually reducing $CO_2$ emissions in line with government targets, and yet most governments still retain a 'predict and provide' approach (see Mini Case Study 17.1). Such is the relative economic importance placed on air transport (it is estimated that London Heathrow alone accounts for 1% of the UK's GDP) government is attempting to meet demand for air services where and when it arises, leading to the decision to expand airports. Environmental groups argue that there should be some form of pollution taxation and the view that aviation fuel should not be zero rated for VAT is gaining ground. The impact of air transport on the environment will emerge as a large-scale controversial topic over the coming years. Increases in environmental taxes or airport charges will disproportionately affect the cost structures of fast-growing low-cost carriers and fares will have to rise.

## Slow travel

One potential response to develop low-impact, low-carbon tourism is the small but growing niche market of slow travel. The concept, developed out of the slow food movement which started in Italy in 1986, is about the quality of the tourist experience. Most definitions of slow travel have three components:

- the pleasure of the journey is an important dimension of the holiday experience;
- travel is conducted at a slow pace to enjoy more fully the places visited and engage with the local population and culture to produce a more rewarding tourist experience;
- using modes of transport with a low carbon intensity (Dickinson et. al., 2010a; Dickinson and Lumsdon, 2010).

The concept is attracting growing interest as a potential growth area and also as a potential alternative to high-carbon air tourism, although low carbon emissions is not the primary motivation for many participants, even if it is a beneficial outcome.

## MINI CASE STUDY 17.1
Tourism and the environment: mixed signals from the government

### REDUCING EMISSIONS

The 1997 World Climate Change Conference in Kyoto established binding reductions on GHG emissions. The treat was ratified by 166 countries in 2005, and although longer-term objectives were set out, binding targets were only established up until 2012. The signatories included significant omissions, most notably the US. Despite subsequent summits there are no binding agreements beyond 2012 although there is broad agreement on objectives.

The UK government is committed to reducing greenhouse gas emissions, particularly $CO_2$ emissions. The Kyoto protocol set the UK a target of 12.5% reduction over 1990 levels, but the UK set itself a more ambitious target to reduce emissions by 20% over 1990 levels by the year 2010, and passed the UK Climate Change Act in 2008 committing itself to an 80% reduction over 1990 levels by 2050. In the event, the most recent assessment is that the UK is broadly on target, having achieved a reduction of 16% by 2010, with further significant reductions in 2011 indicating emissions are now 23% below 1990 levels (DECC, 2012). Interestingly this was achieved with an overall reduction in energy consumption of only 5%. There are six GHG gasses but $CO_2$ is by far the most important, accounting for about 84% of the UK's GHG emissions.

Despite this positive picture there remain significant barriers to achieving the 2050 targets. Much of the reduction in emissions was achieved in the energy supply sector where there have been improvements in electricity generation and a move away from coal to less energy-intensive fuels – the so-called dash for gas – and it is questionable whether reductions in this sector will continue at this level. However, the most significant concern is that there have been no emission reductions in the transport sector, where GHG emissions are virtually unchanged since 1990.

International aviation and shipping are excluded from these figures as these sectors were omitted from the Kyoto protocol. Aviation may seem a small player in terms of worldwide $CO_2$ emissions with a 3.5% global share, but aviation emissions are rising fast when all other sectors are reducing their $CO_2$ emissions. By 2050 aviation's share could reach 24% of UK emissions. The UK government is aware of its significance and was prominent for the inclusion of aviation in phase III of the EU Emissions Trading Scheme (EU ETS) from 2013 and will seek the inclusion of international aviation in future treaties to replace Kyoto.

## AVIATION POLICY AND EMISSIONS

The DfT forecasts continued growth in the demand for air transport services. There has been a five-fold increase in air travel over the last 30 years and the government forecasts that it will increase from this very high figure by a further two or three times over the next 30 years. It is estimated that at least half the population fly once a year.

How should the government deal with these forecasts? What are the options? One obvious option is to control the demand for aviation growth. Much of the additional air traffic is holiday/leisure traffic and more of it is outbound (UK residents flying abroad) than inbound (overseas visitors to the UK), which produces a tourism deficit. Furthermore, much of the extra traffic is for short-break additional holidays, encouraged by the low fares from the low-cost airlines. Long journeys of a short duration are very carbon-intensive.

There are news stories, admittedly not yet supported by hard statistical evidence, that as a result of global warming more Germans are opting to take beach holidays on the Baltic Coast in Germany (travelling by train) as an alternative to Mediterranean holidays by air. They are seeking to benefit from global warming, in the form of higher temperatures and improved climate in the Baltic, while significantly reducing their own carbon footprint. Likewise, more UK residents took domestic holidays in the UK in 2010 and 2011, although this may be more related to the economic recession rather than a longer-term travel trend.

One option to deflate aviation demand is a range of environmental taxes. Currently there is no Value Added Tax (VAT) on aviation and aviation fuel is not taxed. New 'green' taxes would raise the price of air tickets, which is likely to reduce the demand for travel. Other ideas include increasing efficiency by charging an additional tax to the airlines for every empty seat on an aircraft that lands or takes off. The logic is that this will result in fuller aircraft, so an increase in passengers does not also have to result in an increase in the number of flights. In reality, load factors are already high and in any event it may encourage some airlines to offer very cheap promotional fares where sales are low.

## PREDICT AND PROVIDE – ENCOURAGING INCREASED EMISSIONS?

The previous government's response was to develop additional airport capacity (DfT, 2003, 2006). This is most urgently required for airports in the London area. Capacity at London Heathrow is being dramatically increased from the current 69 million passengers per annum to over 90 million passengers per annum with the construction of Terminal 5 and the replacement of Terminals 1 and 2 but further expansion beyond that requires additional runway capacity including controversially a third runway at Heathrow.

This expansionist policy approach is an attempt to meet all the forecast demand, in essence predict and build. However, it provides the government with a dilemma. It permits, even encourages, aviation growth at a level to produce much increased $CO_2$ emissions unless there is some form of technological miracle, and this will impact on the target reduction of 80% by 2050, and requires other sectors to achieve reductions well in excess of 80% to compensate. The proposal appeared to be in direct conflict with the Climate Change Act, encouraging rather than discouraging emissions by providing such levels of capacity. Yet aviation is clearly very important to the UK economy and the current government, which opposed the expansion when in opposition, is now also reviewing airport capacity.

The importance of government leadership in issues of GHG emissions cannot be overstated. There is a wide body of recent research which seeks to explain why frequent flying has become habitual, socially acceptable and even desirable, even though awareness of its harmful environmental consequences is growing. Converting environmental concern into action and behavioural change is a major challenge (Anable et al., 2006) and one prominent justification for continued personal frequent flying is that responsibility for policy and leadership lies with others, such as government and industry (see for example Cohen et al., 2011; Dickinson et al., 2010b; or Hares et al., 2010). Individual actions to forgo air travel are seen as incidental and futile (Dickinson et al., 2010b). In the meantime, the conflicting messages from government of strict emission targets encouraging personal carbon reduction whilst planning significant airport expansion blur an overall environmental vision.

## DISCUSSION QUESTIONS

1. What are the main policy options to reduce $CO_2$ emissions from aviation?
2. In what ways do you think the aviation industry can make a positive contribution to sustainable development?
3. What actions can we as individuals take to reduce our carbon footprint from international travel?

## CONCLUSION

As tourism demand grows, transportation – and indeed transportation infrastructure – will become increasingly important. New technology in respect of every aspect of transportation will be influential, and the transport industry of the future will supply visitors with ticketless travel, smart card technology for payment, and also perhaps for visa and passport purposes in certain country groups.

However, the transport industry for tourism has many issues confronting it as the numbers of visitors worldwide increase. All forms of transport pollute the environment and some will never be able to develop totally green policies. Airlines will still burn kerosene and create noise. Trains can be electrically operated, but ultimately rely on nuclear or fossil fuels. Coaches and cars burn fossil fuels and seaborne craft likewise, except leisure craft that are wind-driven. As other suppliers of the elements of the tourist product develop more environmentally friendly policies and practices, operators must be seen as natural polluters in the foreseeable future – whether curbs on transport operators that pollute will affect the price or availability of transport for tourism remains to be seen.

## SELF-CHECK QUESTIONS

1. What is the purpose of government regulation of transport? Is it desirable?
2. Compare and contrast the environmental impacts of different modes of transport.
3. List the components of a transport system and illustrate how the overall performance of a mode of transport is governed by the relative strengths and weaknesses of each.
4. Explore how transport demand in destination areas brings benefits to public transport operators. Does it also bring conflicts or problems?
5. What do airlines gain from membership of inter-airline alliances?

# REFERENCES AND FURTHER READING

Anable, J. Lane, B. and Kelay, T. (2006) *An Evidence Based Review of Public Attitudes to Climate Change and Transport Behaviour*, Department for Transport, Stationery Office, London.

Becken, S. and Lennox, J. (2012) 'Implications of a long-term increase in oil prices for tourism', *Tourism Management* **33**(1), 133–42.

CLIA (2006) *Cruise Industry Overview: Marketing Edition*, Cruise Line International Association, New York.

CLIA (2010) *Cruise Industry Overview: Marketing Edition*, Cruise Line International Association, New York at **http://www.cruising.org/sites/default/files/misc/2010FINALOV.pdf**

Cohen, S.A. Higham, J.A.S. and Cavaliere, C.T. (2011) 'Binge flying behavioural addiction and climate change', *Annals of Tourism Research* **38**(3), 1070–89.

COM (2009) *A Sustainable Future for Transport – Towards an Integrated, Technology-led and User Friendly System*, European Commission, Luxembourg.

COM (2011) *A Sustainable Future for Transport – Towards an Integrated, Technology-led and User Friendly System*, European Commission, Luxembourg.

DECC (2012) *Statistical Release – 2011 UK Greenhouse Gas Emissions, Provisional Figures and 2010 UK Greenhouse Gas Emissions, Final Figures by Fuel Type and End-User*, at **http://www.decc.gov.uk/assets/decc/11/stats/climate-change/4817-2011-uk-greenhousegas-emissions-provisional-figur.pdf**

Dickinson, J. and Lumsdon, L. (2010) *Slow Travel and Tourism*, Earthscan, London.

Dickinson, J.E. Lumsdon, L.M. and Robbins, D. (2010a) 'Slow travel: issues for tourism and climate change', *Journal of Sustainable Tourism* **19**(3), 281–300.

Dickinson, J.E., Robbins, D., Lumsdon, L. (2010b) 'Holiday travel discourses and climate change', *Journal of Transport Geography* **18**(3), 482–9.

DfT (2003) *The Future of Air Transport*, Stationery Office, London.

DfT (2006) *The Future of Air Transport Progress Report*, Stationery Office, London.

DfT (2009) *UK Air Passenger Demand and $CO_2$ Forecasts*, Stationery Office, London.

DfT (2011) *Transport Statistics Great Britain*, Stationery Office, London.

Doganis, R. (2006) *The Airline Business*, 2nd edn, Routledge, London.

Doganis, R. (2010) *Flying Off Course: The Economics of International Airlines*, 4th edn, Routledge, London.

Dowling, R.K. (ed.) (2006) *Cruise Tourism: Issues, Impacts, Cases*, CABI Publishing, Wallingford.

Duval, D.T. (2007) *Tourism and Transport – Modes, Networks and Flows*, Channel View Publications, Clevedon.

Eurostat (2010) *Tourism Statistics in the European Statistical System*, European Commission, Luxembourg.

Francis, G. Dennis, N. Ison, S. and Humphreys, I. (2007) 'The transferability of the low-cost model to long-haul airline operations', *Tourism Management* **28**(2), 391–8.

Gössling, S. and Peeters, P. (2007). 'It does not harm the environment! An analysis of industry discourses on tourism, air travel and the environment', *Journal of Sustainable Tourism* **15**(4), 402–17.

Graham, A. (2008) *Managing Airports: An International Perspective*, 3rd edn, Butterworth Heinemann, Oxford.

Groβ, S. and Schröder, A. (eds.) (2007) *Handbook of Low Cost Airlines: Strategies, Business Processes and Market Environment*, Erich Schmidt Verlag, Berlin.

Hanlon, P. (2007) *Global Airlines – Competition in a Transnational Industry*, Butterworth Heinemann, Oxford.

Hares, A. Dickinson, J.E. and Wilkes, K. (2010) 'Climate change and the air travel decisions of UK tourists', *Journal of Transport Geography* **18**(3), 466–73.

Høyer, K.G. (2000) 'Sustainable tourism or sustainable mobility? The tourism case', *Journal of Sustainable Tourism* **8**(2), 147–60.

House of Lords Select Committee on European Union (2003) *Open Skies or Open Markets*, Seventeenth Report. Available from **http://www.publications.parliament.uk/pa/ld200203/ldselect/ldeucom/92/9203.htm**

Lawton, T. (2002) *Cleared for Take-off: Structure and Strategy in the Low Fare Airline Business*, Ashgate, Aldershot.

Leiper, N. (1990) *Tourism Systems: An Interdisciplinary Perspective*. Occasional Paper 2, Auckland, Massey University Department of Management Systems.

Lester, J. and Weeden, C. (2004) 'Stakeholders, the natural environment and the future of Caribbean cruise tourism', *International Journal of Tourism Research* **6**(1), 39–50.

Mintel (2003) 'Cruises', *Leisure Intelligence*, April.

Mintel (2008) *Rail Travel – Europe*, London, Mintel.

Page, S.J. (2009) *Transport and Tourism*, Elsevier, Oxford.

Peeters, P. (2007) 'Mitigating tourism's contribution to climate change – an introduction', pp. 11–26 in Peeters, P. (ed.), *Tourism and Climate Change Mitigation: Methods, Greenhouse Gas Reductions and Policies*, NHTV, Breda.

Peeters, P. and Schouten, F. (2005) 'Reducing the ecological footprint of inbound tourism and transport to Amsterdam', *Journal of Sustainable Transport* **14**(2), 157–71.

Peeters, P. Szimba, E. and Duijnisveld, M. (2007) 'European tourism transport and the main environmental impacts', *Journal of Transport Geography* **15**(2), 83–93.

Peisley, T. (2006) *The Future of Cruising – Boom or Bust: A Worldwide Analysis to 2015*, Seatrade Communications Ltd, Colchester.

Peisley, T. (2010) *Cruising at the Crossroads – A Worldwide Analysis to 2025*, Seatrade Communications Ltd, Colchester.

Pitfield, D.E. (2009) 'The assessment of the EU–US Open Skies Agreement: the counterfactual and other difficulties', *Journal of Air Transport Management*, **15**, 308–14.

Prideaux, B (2004) 'Transport and destination development', pp. 79–92, in Lumsdon L. and Page, S. (eds), *Tourism and Transport: Issues and Agenda for the New Millennium*, Elsevier, Oxford.

Robbins, D.K. and Dickinson, J.E. (2007) 'Achieving domestic tourism growth and simultaneously reducing car dependency: the illusive prize', pp. 169–88 in Peeters, P. (ed.), *Tourism and Climate Change Mitigation: Methods, Greenhouse Gas Reductions and Policies*, NHTV, Breda.

Southwest Airlines (2010) **http://www.southwest.com/html/about-southwest/history/fact-sheet.html**

Symth, A. and Christodoulou, G. (2011). 'Maturity in the passenger airline industry? Revisiting the evidence and addressing maturity in forecasting the future market for air travel', Paper presented at European Transport Conference, Glasgow. Available from **http://www.etcproceedings.org/paper/maturity-in-the-passenger-airline-industry-revisiting-the-evidence-and-address**

Wood, R. (2000) 'Caribbean cruise tourism: globalization at sea', *Annals of Tourism Research* **27**(2), 345–70.

Wood, R. (2004) 'Cruise ships: deterritorialized destinations', pp. 133–45 in Lumsdon, L. and Page, S. (eds), *Tourism and Transport*, Elsevier, Oxford.

# MAJOR CASE STUDY 17.1
## The cruise ship industry

The cruise ship industry has grown into a genuine form of mass tourism over the last 30 years. The measurement of cruise-taking can be quite misleading, as the usual figure quoted is the number of cruises taken (Table 17.5). However, there is a very significant difference in terms of consumption and economic impact between a passenger on a short cruise of say 3–4 days and a passenger cruising for 14 days or longer. A measure of cruise days,

as used in Table 17.6, is more illuminating. Nevertheless, the growth over the last 30 years by any measure has been staggering, with annual growth rates between 1980 and 2009 of 7% per annum, although this has been much lower since 2008 (CLIA, 2006, 2010).

To accommodate the growth there has also been substantial investment in new vessels. Growth rates in cruise capacity have averaged 7.6% between 1981 and

| Table 17.5 | Total cruise passenger market ('000) |
|---|---|

| Year | N America | UK | Rest/Europe | Rest/ World | Total | % growth |
|---|---|---|---|---|---|---|
| 1990 | 3,640 | 179 | 330 | 345 | 4,495 | |
| 1991 | 3,979 | 187 | 354 | 414 | 4,980 | 10.7 |
| 1992 | 4,136 | 219 | 407 | 490 | 5,460 | 9.6 |
| 1993 | 4,480 | 254 | 420 | 467 | 5,940 | 8.8 |
| 1994 | 4,448 | 270 | 502 | 1,196 | 6,280 | 5.7 |
| 1995 | 4,378 | 340 | 694 | 1,481 | 6,440 | 2.5 |
| 1996 | 4,656 | 416 | 785 | NA | 6,850 | 6.0 |
| 1997 | 5,051 | 522 | 928 | NA | 7,580 | 10.7 |
| 1998 | 5,428 | 663 | 902 | 850 | 8,210 | 8.3 |
| 1999 | 5,894 | 746 | 994 | 1,160 | 9,067 | 10.4 |
| 2000 | 6,882 | 754 | 1,096 | NA | 10,138 | 10.1 |
| 2001 | 6,906 | 776 | 1,130 | 1,380 | 10,192 | 0.5 |
| 2002 | 7,470 | 824 | 1,296 | 1,608 | 11,198 | 9.9 |
| 2003 | 8,195 | 963 | 1,709 | 1,474 | 12,340 | 10.2 |
| 2004 | 9,107 | 1,029 | 1,764 | 1,463 | 13,383 | 8.5 |
| 2005 | 9,919 | 1,071 | 2,054 | 1,413 | 14,457 | 8.0 |
| 2006 | 10,336 | 1,204 | 2,205 | 1,662 | 15,410 | 8.1 |
| 2007 | 10,596 | 1,335 | 2,667 | 1,824 | 16,442 | 6.6 |
| 2008 | 10,352 | 1,477 | 2,945 | 2,327 | 17,101 | 4.1 |
| 2009 | 10,459 | 1,533 | 3,409 | 2,439 | 17,840 | 4.3 |

*Source*: CLIA, 2006; Peisley, 2006, 2010

| Table 17.6 | Cruise capacty for selected destinations (CLIA members) bed days (%) |
|---|---|

| Destination | 1989 % | 1995 % | 2001 % | 2002 % | 2006 % | 2010 % |
|---|---|---|---|---|---|---|
| Caribbean | 44.5 | 42.8 | 36.6 | 42.1 | 39.2 | 34.8 |
| Alaska | 6.5 | 8.4 | 7.9 | 8.0 | 7.8 | 5.7 |
| Bahamas | | 7.7 | 7.9 | 4.5 | 7.5 | 6.5 |
| Mexico | | 4.9 | 1.9 | 5.3 | 6.4 | 4.7 |
| South America | | | 2.4 | 2.2 | 1.8 | 2.2 |
| SE Asia | | | 0.7 | 0.5 | 0.7 | 1.0 |
| Mediterranean | 7.6 | 9.7 | 12.7 | 10.2 | 12.9 | 17.8 |
| North Europe | 3.1 | 4.4 | 8.1 | 10.9 | 8.4 | 8 |
| **Total (Bed Days)** | **24,699** | **35,661** | **53,862** | **59,581** | **81,454** | **104,109** |

*Source*: CLIA, 2006, 2010

| Table 17.7 | The largest cruise ships | | | |
|---|---|---|---|---|
| Year | Vessel | Size | Capacity (passengers) | Cruise line |
| 1988 | Sovereign of the Seas | 73,000 gwt | 2,852 | Royal Caribbean |
| 1996 | Carnival Destiny | 101,353 gwt | 2,642 | Carnival |
| 1999 | Voyager of the Seas | 137,300 gwt | 3,114 | Royal Caribbean |
| 2004 | Queen Mary 2 | 150,000 gwt | 2,620 | Cunard (Carnival) |
| 2005 | Freedom of the Seas | 158,000 gwt | 3,643 | Royal Caribbean |
| 2009 | Oasis of the Seas | 225,000 gwt | 5,400 | Royal Caribbean |
| 2010 | Allure of the Seas | 225,000 gwt | 5,400 | Royal Caribbean |

*Source*: Compiled by the author

2005 (CLIA, 2006), so overall occupancy levels have been virtually unchanged. This represents huge levels of investment and 13 new vessels were delivered in 2010 alone. Occupancy levels of cruise ships are high at around 96% so there is a need for continued expansion of the fleet to accommodate the growth in demand, although some new vessels will replace older cruise ships being withdrawn, such as the *QE2*, decommissioned in 2008. However, the impact of the recession on the cruise industry resulted in a significant decline to new cruise ship build by cash-strapped companies making reduced profits. Ten new ships are on order in 2013–2015, a much reduced level of delivery compared with recent years.

The vessels are getting larger (Table 17.7). The average capacity of new vessels delivered in 2010 was in excess of 3,000 passengers and yet in 1985 only one ship had over 70,000 gwt (gross tonnage) and there were no ships over 100,000 gwt. By 2006 there were 24 ships over 100,000 gwt.

## PATTERNS OF DEMAND

The US market dominates cruise demand (Table 17.5), accounting for close to 70% of cruise passengers in 2006. However, since 2006 this market has hit a period of stagnation whereas the UK market (the world's second largest traveller-generating region) has continued to grow modestly and the rest of western Europe has demonstrated more rapid growth, reducing the North America share to 59%. Within Europe, Germany has shown the largest recent growth (over 10% in 2008–2009) and has now exceeded 1 million cruise passengers for the first time (Peisley, 2010).

Although there has been diversification of destinations by the cruise companies the Caribbean region still dominates with around 35% of all cruise days. Table 17.6 shows the main cruise destinations in 2006. However, the annual figures of capacity hide a significant pattern. There are many more cruise ships in the Caribbean between October and the following March than there are between April and September and Cruise Line International Association (CLIA) statistics show that around 62% of annual Caribbean capacity is offered between October and the following March.

The Caribbean therefore takes on huge significance for the future growth and prosperity of the global cruise industry as other important destination markets demonstrate seasonal demand. The Mediterranean has a season stretching from March to September, while other important destinations such as Alaska and North Europe (Baltic, Norwegian Fjords) have even shorter peaks during the same season. Cruise lines have found it increasingly difficult to find alternative destinations to the Caribbean between October and March. There have been some successes, such as European cruises to the Atlantic Islands, and a few select vessels embark on a three-month 'world cruise' commencing in December or January, but overall progress has been slow. South-East Asia has not grown as rapidly as many had expected, although there has been significant recent development of the market to South America. Another region showing some potential is the Middle East, with large-scale investment in Dubai as a cruise port. Nevertheless, many vessels are repositioned from seasonal markets back to the Caribbean to achieve high annual utilisation.

Following a decade of falling market share, cruise capacity in the Caribbean grew significantly in 2002 (Table 17.6) due to a significant repositioning of ships away from the Mediterranean to the Caribbean by US cruise lines as a reaction to 9/11. European destinations recovered lost ground following this initial reaction, but it does demonstrate the fragility of the industry to outside political factors.

## TRENDS IN THE INDUSTRY

- Cruise passengers are attracted from an ever-increasing range of socio-economic, income and age groups. Penetration in the North American market had been increased by a trend towards shorter cruises. Cruises of between two and five days were by far the fastest growing segment of the North American market between 1980 and 1991 but this trend has since reversed and average cruises are getting longer (Table 17.8), with the market share of short cruises stagnating at about one-third of all North American cruises. The emergence of budget cruise lines including the provision of cruises by tour operators, pioneered by Airtours in 1995 and adopted by Saga and Thomson amongst others, widened the appeal and affordability of cruising in the UK market and now accounts for 35% of all UK cruise passengers. The CLIA has reported that over 1 million children now take a cruise worldwide.

- As previously stated, vessels are getting bigger, bringing operational economies of scale to the cruise lines. This is changing the nature of the product, with fewer ports of call as the vessel becomes more of the leisure experience (the experience economy). The vast majority of the mega vessels are deployed in the Caribbean but in a strategy to enable the region to cope with this additional demand as many as six cruise brands own private uninhabited Caribbean islands.

- There has been the creation of an oligopoly following the takeover of P&O cruises by Carnival. The three largest cruise companies, Carnival Corporation, Royal Caribbean Cruises and Star Cruise Group, now account for 80% of all cruise capacity, a share which continues to grow driven by both acquisition and organic growth in the form of new vessels.

| Table 17.8 | Average length of US cruises |
|---|---|
| 1981 | 6.7 days |
| 1990 | 6.2 days |
| 1991 | 6.1 days |
| 1995 | 6.5 days |
| 2000 | 6.5 days |
| 2005 | 6.9 days |
| 2008 | 7.8 days |

*Source*: CLIA, 2010

## FUTURE PROSPECTS FOR GROWTH

The cruise industry is bullish about its future prospects. The CLIA estimates that only 20% of the US population has ever cruised. There are similar figures for the UK market. Mintel (2003) estimate that only 13% of the UK population has ever cruised and for the rest of the world the levels of penetration are even lower. Market research surveys by the CLIA show that 51 million North Americans indicate an intention to cruise in the next three years. With such a large untapped market they argue that the growth rates of the last 20 years can be sustained well into the future. They further argue that a high percentage of cruise passengers cruise again. The 'large potential untapped market' argument is convincing given past trends, and clearly cruise companies have confidence in it otherwise they would not be investing in new vessels. However, such surveys do need to be treated with some caution bearing in mind they are asking hypothetical questions about future consumption. Forecasts of future rates of growth have been slightly revised due to the slowdown in new vessel construction and 30 million cruises are now forecast for 2023 (Peisley, 2010).

## BARRIERS TO CONTINUED GROWTH

### Discounting

There is some evidence that the dramatic growth over recent years has been partially 'supply led' rather than demand led. Industry sources cite heavy discounting in both the North American and European markets. The temptation for cruise lines to discount is obvious. Once substantial investment in new vessels is made, those vessels have to be filled. There is scope for significant on-board spend, the three largest areas being at the bar, on shore-based excursions and in the casino areas of vessels. Indeed, cruise lines will argue that passenger psychology is such that a low brochure price makes marketing sense. Passengers will put substantial energy into achieving relatively small savings in the brochure price and yet while actually on the cruise itself they are far less conscious of spending levels. As new capacity has come on stream discounting by the major cruise lines has been fierce, reducing cruise line yields and affecting cruise line profitability. The concerns of the financial markets over falling profitability and the potential of future over-capacity in the market led to falls in the share price of all the major cruise companies in the early 2000s.

Over recent years yields have begun to recover from their low point of 2003 and, although discounting will continue for the foreseeable future, both revenues and profits for the two largest cruise companies increased in 2005. Carnival reported a $2.2 billion profit based on a revenue of $11 billion and RCC returned $716 million profit on a revenue of $4.9 billion. Despite this recovery a number of financial and corporate analysts question whether the compound market growth rates of around 7% can be sustained into the longer term, and whether the need for widespread discounting is evidence of a market approaching maturity, if not saturation.

## SATURATION OF CRUISE DESTINATION AREAS

Around 24 cruise line brands operate around 70 vessels in the Caribbean over the year. Berth capacity offered by cruise vessels was predicted to exceed the number of hotel beds by 2006 (Wood, 2000) and Caribbean governments are beginning to question the value of cruise activity continuing to grow at this level. The majority of the mega vessels coming on stream are destined for the Caribbean market. The number of ports the largest vessels can call at are reduced but the socio-cultural or environmental impacts of each call on small port destinations are considerable. The cruise call does bring economic benefit for the destination. The ships may require fresh water, sewage disposal facilities, bunkerage and fresh food, all offering the potential for local jobs. Passenger spend can, however, remain relatively low, perhaps $50 per passenger limited to shopping, light refreshments (perhaps lunch) and organised excursions, which if booked on board may see much of this spend retained by the cruise line.

The trend for cruise lines to purchase small uninhabited Caribbean islands may overcome some of the socio-cultural problems but reduces the economic benefit to the region. Cruise lines also argue that the trend to larger vessels is helpful in accommodating growth without a comparable increase in ship calls. Nevertheless, local governments are giving consideration to limiting cruise calls to the region along the lines of the quotas introduced in the number of cruise calls to Bermuda in the mid-1980s. It is difficult to envisage the continued growth of cruising at current levels if the Caribbean does not accommodate a fair share of future growth. The most significant issue is alternative destinations to absorb global cruise growth between October and March.

## ENVIRONMENTAL PRESSURES

Continued growth at the current levels may not represent sustainable development. A large cruise ship generates around 210,000 gallons of sewage, millions of gallons of grey water, 25,000 gallons of oily bilge water plus solid waste and hazardous waste every week. The disposal of ship waste and sewage, while more highly regulated than before, undoubtedly causes damage with such a high concentration of vessels in the Caribbean (Lester and Weeden, 2004; Wood, 2004). There is also increased pressure for additional dredging to deepen harbours to enable ports to accept the larger vessels.

Peisley (2010) argues that new international environmental regulations being introduced over the next five years including amended regulations over the introduction of fuel with sulphur additives will raise operating costs significantly.

## SECURITY

Security is an issue facing cruise lines. It is over 20 years since there was a major terrorist attack with the *Achille Lauro* hijacking, although issues of safety are being raised. It has affected some cruise itineraries, for instance potential cruise itineraries to Kenya and the Middle East have been amended due to concerns over piracy.

## HEALTH

Occasional outbreaks of illness on board cruise ships have the potential to spread rapidly in the very enclosed environment. Cruise ships attempt to enforce very high hygiene standards and there are soap and disinfectant dispensers placed in strategic locations around the ship. Nevertheless, outbreaks of noro virus will occur from time to time. In addition to the premature end of a cruise, this can bring about severe negative publicity. It also disrupts the schedule of the cruise ship, which has to be withdrawn from service immediately to undergo a deep clean.

## SAFETY

The public image of cruising was most recently influenced by the running aground and partial sinking of the *Costa Concordia* in January 2012, when 34 people died and a further 64 were injured, some seriously. Overall such incidents are rare and the cruise industry has an excellent safety record, but this accident has had major short-term impacts on the cruise industry. The share price of the parent company fell by 16.5%, partly due to the cost of the salvage operation combined with the lost income from a large cruise ship. However, the greater concern is how the incident has affected public confidence and the future demand for cruises. News stories surrounding the cause of the accident combined with the fact there had not been a muster drill prior to departure have further tarnished the image of the industry, which was not helped by a second incident of an electrical fire on the *Costa Allegra* in February 2012 in the Indian Ocean, which saw the vessel lose power and require

**Photograph 17.2**   *Allure of the Seas*, the world's largest cruise ship.
*Source*: All Canada Photos/Alamy Images

towing into the Seychelles. There is an expectation that even higher discounts may be required to fill cruise ships in 2012. It is of course far too early to conclude whether the accident will impact on longer-term growth prospects of the industry.

## CONCLUSION

The cruise industry is confident of future profitable growth. The former CEO of Princess Cruises, Peter Ratcliffe, sums up the industry view:

> **Our industry has sustainable long-term growth characteristics despite the impact of recent events on short-term trading. The key indicators of demographics, penetration, high levels of customer satisfaction and trends in leisure spend point to significant growth over the long term and increasing globalisation of the industry.**

Time will tell whether this optimistic view for continued growth is right.

*Source*: http://www.cruising.org

## DISCUSSION QUESTIONS

1. How have cruise lines widened the age and socio-economic profile of passengers?

2. What are the main benefits and disbenefits of cruise calls to the Caribbean region?

3. What are the potential barriers to the continued growth of the cruise shipping industry?

# CHAPTER 18
## PUBLIC SECTOR AND POLICY

### LEARNING OUTCOMES

The focus of this chapter is on the role of the public sector, in the shape of governmental organisations, in tourism. Specifically, upon completion, the reader will have:

- a knowledge of the key organisations globally with an interest in and influence upon tourism;

- an understanding of the key functions of NTOs and an insight into how such offices might be structured and how responsibilities are divided;

- an overview of the role of the public sector; and

- a knowledge of the instruments available to governments to manipulate demand for tourism and control the supply of it.

Photograph: Anchorage, Alaska, USA © Andrew J. Müller

# INTRODUCTION

Governments are involved with tourist organisations at both the international and national level. In the latter case they are normally the instigators for the establishment of a **national tourist organisation** (NTO), while in the former instance they are partners along with other member states in such bodies as the UN World Tourism Organization (UNWTO), the European Travel Commission (ETC), and the Pacific Asia Travel Association (PATA). All these bodies can contribute to the formation of a country's tourism policy. In this chapter we look at the overall policy framework and consider the experience of different governments in order to illustrate the changes that occur in policy, noting the very many organisations that express an interest in tourism at the national level. As national tourist offices are commonly the executive agency for government policy, their administrative structure and functions are considered in some detail. The last part of the chapter examines intervention by the public sector in tourism. Particular consideration is given to the variety of instruments governments have at their disposal to manage the direction of tourism development in the interests of the host community.

# PUBLIC POLICY FRAMEWORK

With tourism as one of the main international economic drivers in the twenty-first century, together with increasing demands from the domestic population for leisure and recreation, the industry is a development option that few governments can afford to ignore. A critical difference between tourism and many other agents of development is that of inseparability, in that tourism is consumed at the place of production, thus involving itself with the host community, and requiring some **commodification** and sharing of traditions, value systems and culture. Since the tourist industry does not control all those factors that make up the attractiveness of a destination and the impact on the host population can be considerable, it is necessary for the options concerning the development of tourism to be considered at the highest level of government and the appropriate public administrative framework put in place. As a rule the greater the importance of tourism to a country's economy the greater is the involvement of the public sector, to the point of having a government ministry with sole responsibility for tourism. While tourism can be planned to be more or less sustainable at the destination end through the range of policies analysed in this chapter, it must not be forgotten that there is the continuing issue of the 'carbon footprint' generated by domestic and international travel to the destination, arising particularly from the growth in low-cost air transport (see Chapter 17). The airlines' response has been to increase fuel efficiency and introduce composite materials that are capable of being recycled and are lighter in the air.

Beyond the national horizon, governments are involved in supporting a variety of **multinational agencies**. The official flag carrier for international tourism is the UNWTO (Mini Case Study 18.1), which is vested by the United Nations with a central and decisive role in promoting the development of responsible, sustainable and universally accessible tourism. Elsewhere there are a number of other international bodies whose activities impinge upon tourism: these include the World Bank Group – whose commercial arm is the International Finance Corporation (IFC), which takes on private sector projects, whereas its other arm, the International Bank for Reconstruction and Development (IBRD), provides government funding for **structural adjustment** and infrastructure developments – other United Nations bodies – such as the International Civil Aviation Organization (ICAO), the World Health Organization (WHO) and UNESCO – the International Air Transport Association (IATA) and the Organisation for Economic Co-operation and Development (OECD).

## MINI CASE STUDY 18.1
### The United Nations World Tourism Organization (UNWTO)

The UNWTO can trace its origins back to 1925 to a non-governmental body that after World War II became the International Union of Official Travel Organisations (IUOTO). IUOTO was made up of a mixture of private and public sector organisations dealing with the technical aspects of travel and tourism. However, by the 1960s, the growth of tourism, its international dimensions and the increasing activities of national governments in this field, necessitated the transformation of IUOTO into an intergovernmental body, the World Tourism Organization. The latter was ratified in 1974 and was empowered to deal on a worldwide basis with all matters concerning tourism and to cooperate with other competent world agencies that came under the umbrella of United Nations organisation. The prefix UN was added at the end of 2005.

The UNWTO is an operative rather than a deliberative body that pays particular attention to the interests of the developing countries in the field of tourism. Its functions include:

- helping member countries, tourist destinations and businesses maximise the positive economic, social and cultural effects of tourism;
- collecting statistics, identifying and forecasting markets;
- assisting in tourism planning as an executing agency of the United Nations Development Programme (UNDP), with emphasis on its pro-poor strategy;
- advising on the harmonisation of policies and practices;
- sponsoring education and training, and identifying funding sources;
- promoting eTourism initiatives to introduce web portals for distribution and destination management, increase security and simultaneously reduce 'hassle' for travellers;
- promoting the broader relationship of visitors to the physical and social environment, by defining sustainability as development which meets the needs of present tourists and host regions while protecting and enhancing opportunities for the future;
- encouraging the implementation of a global code of ethics for tourism for promoting peace, the observance of human rights and fundamental freedoms.

As an intergovernmental body the UNWTO's membership (currently 155 member states, seven associate members and two permanent observers) works largely in terms of political groupings that can bring pressure on the general formulation of tourism policy. In order to benefit from advances in operational practice, the UNWTO has an affiliate membership scheme (currently over 400 members) for organisations working within the tourism sector. While the general assembly of the UNWTO is largely concerned with debates on policy, the meetings of affiliate members usually take up topical issues affecting tourism, for example taxation. Some major successes of the UNWTO have been: the methodological design of the Tourism Satellite Account, which has set the standard for measuring the economic importance of tourism within the framework of the United Nations system of national accounts; working with the World Bank Group, the regional development banks and national aid agencies to place tourism amongst their key priorities for infrastructure and entrepreneurial support in relieving poverty; promoting education and women in tourism; and establishing good practice in terms of ethics and environmental standards. The latter is of particular significance and is now represented in the Global Code of Ethics for Tourism (GCET), which is a comprehensive set of principles designed to guide key players in tourism development. The Code aims to help maximise the sector's benefits while at the same time minimising negative impacts on the natural environment, society and cultural heritage. Originally adopted back in 1999, the Code represents a voluntary implementation mechanism and is recognised by the World Committee on Tourism Ethics (WCTE).

## DISCUSSION QUESTIONS

1. Consider the benefits of having a world body that has tourism as its sole sphere of interest.
2. What priorities would you attach to the range of functions covered by the UNWTO?

3. If your country is a member of the UNWTO, what benefits do the tourist authorities perceive they get from membership?
4. What may be some of the barriers, whether real or perceived, that hinder the implementation of a global code for ethics in tourism?

At a lower level, there is a variety of regional bodies such as the Organization of American States (OAS), Pacific Asia Travel Association (PATA) and the European Travel Commission (ETC). Most of their efforts are devoted to promotion and marketing, though they do provide technical assistance and promote codes of conduct to encourage travel that is respectful of other people's lives and places.

As an organisation whose membership is made up of the NTOs of Europe, the ETC provides a forum for the directors of the European NTOs to meet regularly and exchange ideas. It carries out its objective to promote the region as an attractive destination through its new web portal **visiteurope.com**, public relations, and consumer advertising and trade promotion. Prior market research determines the choice of activities and campaigns in the overseas markets. The ETC is in constant touch with the principal international agencies and people working in tourism, as well as assisting with the professional development of its members. Its work is supported by the European Commission, which sees tourism as an activity of great economic and social significance within the European Union (EU), particularly for the peripheral and somewhat poorer regions of Europe. Although a wide variety of regional disparities exist across the EU, from early on it was realised that there is a distinct tendency for the poorest regions to be situated on the outer areas of the Union and, since the late 1980s, greater emphasis has been given to stimulating small tourism firms and **indigenous development** in areas to take advantage of their natural surroundings.

Apart from the World Bank, funds for developing tourism in low-income countries may be obtained from regional banks such as the European Bank for Reconstruction and Development (EBRD) for Eastern Europe and the Commonwealth of Independent States; the Inter-American Development Bank; African Development Bank; Asian Development Bank; Arab Bank for Economic Development in Africa; East African Development Bank; and the Caribbean Development Bank. Their principles of operation are mainly for the granting of medium- or long-term loans (often with various grace periods and low rates of interest) to specific projects or to national development institutions, and providing technical assistance in project preparation. They are sometimes prepared to take a minority shareholding in investments, provided there is an option for onward selling, preferably to host country nationals.

Looking at the structure in Europe, officially the Tourism Unit in the EU comes under Directorate-General Enterprise and Industry, but the development work of Directorate-General Regional Policy also involves tourism projects as a means of overcoming **regional disparities**. With the adoption of the Single European Act (1987), there is a commitment by the EU to promote economic and **social cohesion** through actions to reduce regional disparities, and the Maastricht Treaty (1992) acknowledged, for the first time, the role of tourism in these actions. With the more recent Lisbon Treaty (2009), tourism became a specific competence of the EU, allowing the latter to support and complement actions within the member states by encouraging the creation of an atmosphere that is conducive to developing tourism enterprises and fostering cooperation between member states, while excluding any harmonisation of the legal and regulatory provisions of member states. The resources for mitigating regional differences are drawn from the structural funds, which are made up of contributions from member states with the express purposes of helping less well off regions (see Major Case Study 18.1). Alongside public monies, commercial funding of tourism projects is obtainable from the European Investment Bank.

Largely because of the new tourism powers in the Lisbon Treaty, Members of the European Parliament (MEPs) are now more engaged with European tourism policy than ever before.

Specifically, strategy is developed around the following objectives:

- stimulating competitiveness in the European tourism sector, which divides into:
  - promoting diversification of the supply of tourist services;
  - developing innovation in the tourism industry;
  - improving professional skills;
  - encouraging an extension of the tourist season;
  - consolidating the socio-economic knowledge base for tourism.
- promoting the development of sustainable, responsible and high-quality tourism;
- consolidating the image and profile of Europe as a collection of sustainable high-quality destinations;
- maximising the potential of EU policies and existing financial instruments for developing tourism.

It is important that, in developing its strategy for tourism, the European Commission does not duplicate the work of other organisations. The key aspects are:

- the intention is the creation of a 'Europe' brand in the face of falling world market share;
- development of an ICT and tourism platform to help small businesses get the most out of new technologies;
- tourism training initiatives;
- a 'virtual' tourism observatory by making research information available online;
- a European 'quality' label that brings together existing national and regional quality assurance schemes.

Ultimately, the differing nature of the tourist product within Europe leaves the Commission with little option but to assign the primary role of tourism policy to member states and proceed with tourism projects only in close partnership with national and regional bodies. The principle applied is that of **subsidiarity**, which argues for decisions to be made at the lowest level of authority so as best to meet local needs and be as close as possible to the citizen, which is seen as a requirement to safeguard democratic control of European institutions and to maintain the variety of regional differences and cultural identities.

All European countries have NTOs: some are part of government, as in France or Spain, or in Eastern Europe, while others are established independently of government but are supported by central grants and other income-generating activities, as in the UK. The case for public sector involvement in tourism rests on concepts of market failure, namely that those who argue for the market mechanism as the sole arbiter in the allocation of resources for tourism are ignoring the lessons of history and are grossly oversimplifying the complex and varied nature of the product. In an EU context, research among member states has indicated a number of sources of market failure that are the concerns of member states:

- developing tourism as a common good that collectively benefits many businesses, with the NTO acting as a broker between suppliers and potential visitors;
- infant industry development as part of regional policy (including peripheral areas), where commercial viability requires public sector support through the provision of essential infrastructure and financial incentives;
- improving the tourism product through more emphasis on research and development, and via the implementation of measures such as benchmarking good practice and training programmes for tourism workers;
- incorporating the concept of sustainable and balanced growth into tourism by taking account of socio-cultural and environmental issues in tourism planning;
- enhanced support for rural and farm tourism.

By way of contrast, the US Congress took a much more market-orientated stance and closed down the United States Travel and Tourism Administration (USTTA) in 1996, some 15 years after its establishment. In the main, the responsibility for tourism marketing and development was left with the individual states and the Travel Industry Association of America. The latter has campaigned vigorously for federal involvement in promoting the image of the USA worldwide, arguing that it should not be left to a few strong destination brands, such as Florida, New York or Hawaii, and major companies, such as Disney, Hyatt and Hertz, to 'pull the tourism train'. In the last decade, tighter visa restrictions, tougher entry procedures at immigration desks and a general increase in anti-American sentiment in the wake of the wars in Iraq and Afghanistan saw the industry losing market share, so in response the US passed the Travel Promotion Act which established the Corporation for Travel Promotion (now 'Brand USA'), a public–private marketing entity, in 2010 with responsibilities for directing the national travel and tourism strategy. The past assumption that tourists would keep coming had been found wanting.

Nevertheless, much of the tourist product in the USA is under federal control through the Department of the Interior, whose responsibilities include:

- preserving national scenic and historic areas;
- conserving, developing and utilising fish and wildlife resources;
- coordinating federal and state recreation programmes; and
- operating job corps conservation youth camps.

The Forest Service of the Department of Agriculture also takes an active role in promoting and sustaining the nation's landscape.

The US experience of changes in direction of tourism policy is not uncommon in other countries. In Britain, the Development of Tourism Act 1969 was instigated by the recognition of tourism as an important earner of foreign exchange after the devaluation of 1967. Over the years since the Act's inception, the economic policy emphasis for tourism has shifted back and forth to the extent that there is little doubt that the frequent alterations in direction have been more of a handicap than a benefit to the development of public sector tourist organisations in Britain. There have been continual changes in tourism ministers followed by one tourism review after another, all falling short of repealing the Act, but rather confining themselves to using funding as a means to curtail or expand the activities of the national boards.

On the question of financial commitment, the UNWTO has long used the rule that the minimum of 1% of a country's tourist receipts should be devoted to the NTO, but in Britain this has never been the case and the industry continually laments what it sees as the short-sighted policies of the UK Treasury that cause inadequate representation in source markets due to limitations on VisitBritain funds. With increasing devolution, the responsibilities for VisitScotland and Visit Wales have been transferred to their governing authorities (the Northern Ireland Tourist Board was established by statute in 1948 and has always been separate), which has given them much higher funding allocations, but this, it is argued, has only served to create a fragmented presence abroad and ineffective impact and waste, due to uncoordinated actions and spending. In summary, the professional view is that the UK's Department of Culture, Media and Sport, which is responsible for tourism, has repeatedly espoused policy targets, but has not created a cohesive strategy for their achievement; nor has it been able to ensure that VisitBritain can act as an adequate catalyst to implement, encourage or fund effective programmes.

For political reasons there is always the temptation for governments to switch policy direction. This gives the impression of the dynamics of change, but can, in practice, generate chaos through conflicting objectives. It takes a long time to create tourist destinations and build up market positions. It is, therefore, rather simplistic to behave as if the factors influencing such developments can be turned on and off as with a tap. One of the principal difficulties is that tourism is a diverse and fragmented industry with many different economic agents acting in their own interests (often on the basis of imperfect information), which may not be to the long-term benefit of tourism as a whole. Uncoordinated market competition can, in these circumstances, produce cyclical growth patterns, with a consequent waste of resources. This places a premium on an overall planning body such as an NTO, which is able to give a sense of direction by marketing the destination and acting as a distribution channel by drawing the attention of potential tourists and the travel trade to the products that the numerous suppliers in a country have to offer.

# ADMINISTRATIVE FRAMEWORK

There are considerable variations in the structure of the public administration of tourism, which in turn depend on the size of the tourist industry and the importance the government attaches to the various reasons advanced for public sector involvement in tourism. A generalised hierarchical structure is presented in Figure 18.1. It demonstrates a chain of direction from the governing assembly, which could be a council of ministers, a congress or a parliament, downwards to the destinations, where tourism policy and plans are implemented.

A list of some of the most common arguments put forward for government participation in tourism include:

- foreign exchange earnings and their importance for the balance of payments;
- employment creation and the need to provide education and training;
- tourism is a large and fragmented industry requiring careful coordination of development and marketing;
- the need to maximise the net benefits to the host community;
- spreading the benefits and costs equitably;
- building the image of the country as a tourist destination;
- market regulation to protect consumers and prevent unfair competition;
- the provision of public goods and infrastructure as part of the tourist product;
- protecting tourism resources and the environment;
- regulating aspects of social behaviour, for example gambling; and
- the requirement to monitor the level of tourism activity through statistical surveys.

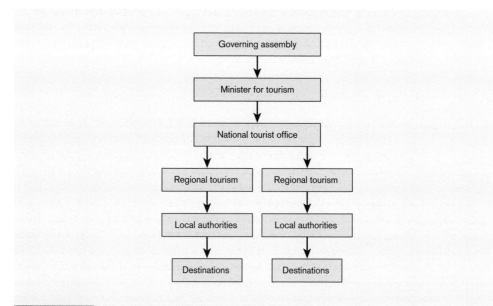

| Figure 18.1 | The public administration of tourism |

In most cases, where tourism is a significant element of economic activity, so that much weight is attributed to the arguments presented above, it is common practice to have a Ministry of Tourism. This is particularly true of island economies, which frequently form some of the world's most attractive tourist destinations. The position of the NTO within this framework may be inside or outside the ministry. In the latter case, the NTO becomes a government agency or semi-governmental body. It usually has a separate constitution, enacted by law, and a board of directors appointed from outside government which, in theory, gives independence from the political system. However, the link is maintained through the NTO being the executive arm of government policy as agreed by the ministry and public money providing the major source of funds for most NTOs. The reality is that few governments can resist giving specific policy directions for developments that are likely to influence political results in locations where the electoral outcomes are close. This allows local political parties at the destination to usurp tourism plans, either by frustrating developments or having projects inserted into plans that have a high political visibility but are of little economic worth, which results in a trail of poor value for public money that often ends in financial insolvency. Good NTOs are attuned to this and build flexibility into the planning process to deal with barely concealed electoral calculations, ensuring that they receive prior written instructions from the responsible minister before proceeding.

Some NTOs, normally termed a convention and visitor bureau (CVB), are simply private associations whose constitution is determined by their membership, which may include government representation. Income is thus raised from a variety of sources and, similar to other businesses, the existence of these bureaux is dependent on the demand for their services in the marketplace. In times of recession, such associations often have difficulty raising funds from the private sector to maintain their activities and need to have injections of public funds to continue with long-term projects.

Since the 1980s, the upsurge in market economics has seen more and more governments urging their NTOs to generate matching funds from the tourist industry. Methods to achieve this objective have included joint marketing initiatives and charging for a range of services, for example, market research reports and brokerage fees from arranging finance. However, the main obstacles to raising private sector revenue have always been the long-term and non-commercial nature of many of the tasks undertaken by NTOs. Added to this is the fact that when NTOs do embark on commercial activities they may be criticised by the private sector for unfair competition, because they are largely funded from taxation. Some countries, for example many of the island tourist destinations such as Bermuda, have recognised these difficulties and have levied specific tourist taxes on the private sector to pay for the work of the NTO – although where such taxes are not separately set aside for tourism, it can also be argued that the tourist industry is just another source of tax revenue.

## Structure of a national tourist organisation

A stylised organisational layout for an NTO, illustrating its principal divisions, is presented in Figure 18.2. This type of NTO is at 'arm's length' from the Ministry of Tourism by virtue of having its own chairman and board of directors. Where an NTO is a division of a ministry, which may have a wider portfolio of activities than just tourism, then it is usual for the director of tourism to report to the senior civil servant in the ministry rather than a board. Many NTOs have only marketing responsibilities and are designated as such, as this is considered to be their primary function, with tourism development being placed in the general portfolio of a national or regional planning authority. In these cases Figure 18.2 should not have a development division and research activity is likely to be included under the marketing division, but the industry view is that it is better served when both marketing and development are under one body, as in Figure 18.2.

Clearly, the exact structure of an NTO will depend upon the objectives laid down for it by government and the tasks the organisation has to undertake in order to meet those same objectives. For example, Visit Wales, the Welsh Assembly's tourism department, sees its principal

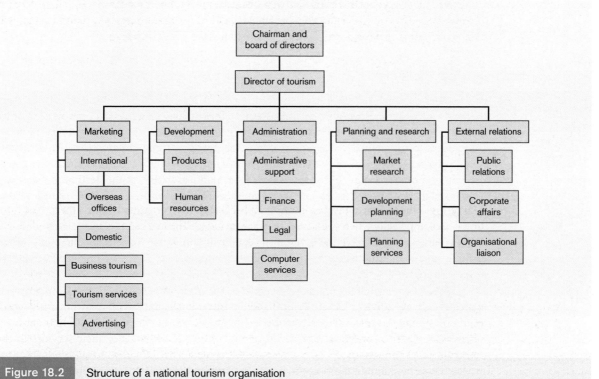

**Figure 18.2**    Structure of a national tourism organisation

role as providing leadership and strategic direction to the tourism industry in Wales, targeting resources towards priorities that will most benefit the industry, as outlined in its objectives:

- to assist in raising the quality of the tourism offer in Wales;
- to stimulate growth in the demand for Wales and to position Wales as a must-see travel destination;
- to use effective partnership working to achieve mutual benefits for Wales;
- to encourage, support and reward innovation;
- to encourage a skilled and professional workforce equipped to deliver a quality Wales experience.

For any organisation maintaining quality in the face of competition is important for retaining value. It is measured indirectly through physical and qualitative evaluation indicators as formalised in classification and grading schemes (discussed for the accommodation sector in Chapter 14). This being the case, quality evaluation will always be an inexact science and one that is resolved through expert judgement and opinion. Since NTOs do not own the tourism product they have to work in partnership with many other businesses to create a positive, distinctive and motivating identity for their country as an attractive destination in target markets. Innovation is commonly associated with new products and this is the basis on which public funding in the form of grants and subsidised loans are normally given. However, the concept is broader than this, since it may also encompass new methods of production, new sources of supply, new markets or simply improving the structure of the organisation. In sum, innovation is about new ways of doing things that add value to the business.

It is clear that NTOs are generally set multiple objectives by their political masters, which makes it difficult to maximise any one of them. Thus trying to maximise the economic gain, particularly in the short term, may not be in the long-term interests of the host community and could be at variance with the objective of protecting the natural and built environment. Managers have to become adept at creating optimal policies that satisfy a bundle of objectives, so as to minimise conflict. This makes it important that governments should not set NTOs objectives that may seriously conflict with each other. Too often governments talk of tourism quality yet measure the performance of the NTO in terms of numbers. Common examples of policy objectives that are most likely to be at variance with each other are:

- maximising foreign exchange earnings versus actions to encourage the regional dispersion of overseas visitors;
- attracting the high-spend tourist market versus policies to expand visitor numbers;
- maximising job creation through generating volume tourist flows versus conservation of the environment and heritage; and
- community tourism development versus mass tourism.

## Marketing function of NTOs

Marketing is the principal responsibility of an NTO and therefore usually forms the largest functional area, especially when overseas offices are included. The marketing division formulates the NTO's marketing strategy and is given the task of maintaining the website, producing the advertising campaign and publicity materials, and promoting sales through the media and the travel trade. The latter is achieved through the provision of 'familiarisation' visits to the destination, circulating a regular newsletter and press releases and attending a series of travel trade shows, of which the most significant are the International Travel Exchange, Berlin and the World Travel Market, London. Overseas offices are responsible for exercising the functions of the marketing division in a manner that takes particular account of the preferences of the travel trade and the potential visitors in the countries or areas where they are located. They also act as 'shop windows' where potential visitors may obtain information and brochures about the host country, though ICT developments have reduced the necessity for this. Many governments do not actively promote domestic tourism and so their NTOs have this section absent from their structure.

Business tourism often merits its own section within an NTO because of its importance in terms of tourist expenditure and the different servicing requirements of meetings, exhibitions and incentive travel groups when compared with leisure tourism. Likewise, advertising is such a key activity that it may command its own specialist group to plan campaigns and deal with outside advertising agencies. Tourism services includes a multitude of tasks, such as:

- operating a reservation system either directly through the website or, as is more common, via links to commercial providers;
- licensing and grading of hotels, restaurants and other suppliers (which may include price controls);
- handling tourist complaints, which may be formal procedures attached to licensing;
- programming festivals, events and tours; and
- managing tourist facilities provided either solely or jointly by the NTO, for example, tourist information centres (TICs) or tourist beaches as in Cyprus.

## Development function of NTOs

The development division can only have truly operational involvement if it is given funding to engage in projects with the private sector and implement training programmes and activities. If this is not the case then it can only take on a coordinating and strategic role. The former is achieved by acting as a 'one-stop shop' for prospective developers through intermediation to obtain planning permission, licences and any financial assistance or incentives from the relevant authorities. In a strategic role the development division will acquire the planning functions that have been allocated to the planning and research division in Figure 18.2. The reason for the separation in Figure 18.2 rests on the fact that an operational development division is likely to be too heavily involved in day-to-day project management to be able to incorporate long-term development planning. The latter is a research activity and therefore best located in the unit equipped for this task. The planning services section is an important addendum to the role of an NTO in that it seeks to capitalise on the expertise of the organisation to provide advice and even undertake studies for the private sector and other public bodies, for example, drawing up tourism plans for local communities.

The remaining divisions shown in Figure 18.2 are, to a large extent, self-explanatory. Administration is responsible for the internal smooth running of the NTO and will normally adjudicate on legal matters in respect of tourism legislation, including, in some countries, carrying out prosecutions. External relations is a functional area of considerable significance because the NTO is frequently the representative of the government, both at home and overseas, and has to deal with a mass of enquiries from the public, the media and commercial operators, as well as taking an active stance in public relations to support the advertising and sales promotion administered by the marketing division. It is for the latter reason that external relations may be allocated to marketing, although the tasks given to the division are usually much broader than those required by marketing, as is the case of liaison activities with a variety of public bodies and voluntary associations who have an interest in tourism.

Given the complexity of the tourist product, more recent emphasis on the liaison role of the NTO has focused on building partnerships in line with models of community tourism development, so as to bring the various stakeholders together. If the institutional framework is to function in a manner that is socially compatible, then there is a prerequisite for local involvement in the development process to encourage discussion about future directions. Cultural conflicts need to be resolved through, say, staging development and using marketing communication channels to prepare guests better for their holiday experience. From experience in less developed countries (LDCs), the greater the difference in lifestyles between hosts and guests and the less the former have been exposed to visitors, then the longer should be the period of adaptation.

# IMPACT OF THE PUBLIC SECTOR

In the light of public sector involvement with tourism, either directly through a ministry with responsibility for tourism and the NTO, or indirectly through, say, foreign policy, legal controls or the provision of infrastructure, the government has at its disposal a series of instruments that can be used to manage tourism flows to meet its policy objectives. The manner in which actions by governments influence tourism may be classified in two ways:

- demand and revenue management; and
- supply and cost management.

## Demand and revenue management

There are primarily five policy instruments used by governments to manage demand:

- marketing and promotion;
- information provision and network development;
- pricing;
- controlling access; and
- security and safety.

### Marketing and promotion

As has already been observed, marketing is the principal function of the NTO and its job is to create and protect the 'brand image' of the country/destination. The specific techniques are discussed in Part 4 of this text, so it is sufficient here to point out that the key requirements for effective marketing are clear objectives, a thorough knowledge of markets and products, and the allocation of adequate resources. It would, however, be putting the 'cart before the horse' without the product, which is generally not under the control of the NTO, hence the importance of assigning the NTO some development powers. Typically, with many other calls on the government's budget, finance officials are naturally parsimonious with regard to expenditure on marketing because of difficulties in measuring effectiveness. As a rule, the amounts spent by governments and other public organisations on destination promotion are only a fraction of what is spent in total by the private sector. One of the main reasons for this is that private enterprises are competing for market share *at the destination*, whereas governments are interested in expanding the total market *to the destination*.

The issue of marketing effectiveness is very pertinent to the earlier discussion on conflicting objectives for public sector managers. The latter normally have to satisfy a range of stakeholders, with the result that campaigns are often 'me too' watered down propositions that fail to differentiate from the rest of the 'clutter' in the marketplace and squander resources. Attempts to break though this may generate considerable controversy in the media that has political repercussions. Similarly, establishing destination identities is usually conceived as exercises in local pride, which fail as 'promotional hooks' for attracting tourists and in creating a distinctive sense of place.

## Information provision and network development

The ability of tourists to express their demands depends upon their awareness of the facilities available, particularly attractions, which are a key component of leisure tourism. For a number of years there has been government interest in creating computer-based national reservation systems. NTOs in Europe have already been operating 'Holiday Hotlines' and out-of-hours telephone information. In many countries, local tourist information centres (TICs) offer a booking service to personal callers, though still very much a manual system requiring TIC staff to telephone accommodation establishments to check availability. For example, in Britain, the TIC network was used to develop the 'Book a Bed Ahead' scheme for the independent traveller touring different parts of the country. However, as more and more bookings are being made electronically, what is ideal is a fully networked computerised reservation system (CRS). The key to penetrating the source markets from the destinations lies in using the CRS to link suitable accommodation to a range of 'things to see and do', so what is being sold is a complete holiday, not just accommodation. Although desirable, this does not necessarily mean complete packaging of other products: it is common just to use complementary suppliers in marketing and to couple this with the provision of good information on site. Others would go further and recommend a complete destination management system (DMS) that acts as a neutral facilitator and reservation system to the tourist industry, which would put small businesses on the same footing as the major corporate suppliers.

Implementation of a complete DMS via the NTO or regional tourist association is no easy task: in the past, proposals at the local level have foundered on the unwillingness of small enterprises to give commission, to make booking allocations available, competitive jealousies concerning the equity of how bookings will be distributed by operating staff and arguments over classification and grading – an essential ingredient for the inclusion in such a scheme, as in all tourist bureau publications. Such experiences suggest that a complete DMS cannot be implemented or sustained without a great deal of public sector involvement and cooperation, particularly if the ETC's ideal of Europe as a single destination is to be realised. As discussed further in Chapter 22, various systems are now available to enable potential visitors to assemble their own itineraries. The usual role of the NTO is to act as a facilitator to bookings through provision of information on its web portal that gives links to agencies providing reservation services, so that end users and resellers can access the product of the destination. By this means NTOs enable end users and resellers to search, book and pay in a single application, as well as building networks to connect businesses and consumers to TICs. The reasons why people do not book online are to do with ease of booking, credit card security, trust in the supplier and lack of consistent information, though it is becoming clear that even the smallest accommodation provider is requiring a website and email facilities because the chances of potential guests walking in without prior notification are diminishing. In this respect, the adoption of ICT is crucial, for by lowering distribution costs for suppliers and reducing search cost for consumers, via the Internet in particular, market potential is widened. Experience has shown that the ICT phenomenon has radically increased the collective market share of niche products and flattened the sales distribution pattern, producing what has been termed by writers in this field 'the long tail' that allows many more products to sustain themselves in the marketplace. Nor should travel and social media sites (referred to as eWOM sites) such as TripAdvisor, Facebook and Twitter be ignored, as they are powerful distribution channels for highlighting positive and negative feedback. Placing written and video blogs are a way of maximising online distribution. The modern tourist is able to use portable technologies such as a Tablet or Smartphone to view the destination, take advice from TripAdvisor, and book online. Interactivity with the customer to find out what they want and say through website contacts, social media chat rooms, emails and mobile phone messaging offers a new dimension to the traditional promotional mix, pushing the latter down the scale of relevance.

The evidence suggests that when planning for tourism the creation of trails or tourist circuits will enhance the visitor experience as well as regulating tourist flows. The establishment of a network of TICs and tourist information points (TIPs) at transport terminals and prominent tourist spots will both help the visitor and assist in dispersion. It is not often appreciated that it is the poorly informed visitor who is likely to contribute to crowding and traffic congestion because of a lack of knowledge about where to go and what there is to see at the destination. Normally, visitors will first look for the main attractions and then move on to lesser attractions as their length of stay increases. Giving prominence to the variety of attractions available, restricting advertising and informing excursion operators of times when congestion can be avoided are examples of the way in which information management can be used to try to relieve pressure on sensitive tourist areas.

In some countries, NTOs use the provision of information to influence tourists' behaviour, as in the PATA example noted earlier. This may come about through editing the information in the tour operator's brochure so that it does not generate unrealistic expectations about a destination and presents the tourist with an informed view of the culture of the host community. An alternative approach is a poster and leaflet campaign aimed directly at the tourist to explain the 'dos and don'ts' of acceptable behaviour – for example, several island resorts offering beach holidays produce leaflets on standards of dress and the unacceptability of wearing only swimsuits in shops, banks and so on.

### Pricing

There are several ways in which the public sector may affect the price the tourist pays for staying at a destination. The direct influence arises out of state ownership, notably in the case of attractions. Many of the most important attractions at a destination fall within the public domain (an issue that is examined in some detail in Chapter 13, which is specifically about attractions). The trend in market-orientated economies is for governments to introduce charges for publicly owned attractions. Many of the world's airlines are still owned by governments, though the trend is increasingly towards privatisation or, if not, the liberalisation of air policy, particularly in response to the rise of low-cost airlines (see Chapter 17), which, as noted earlier, has raised issues concerning greenhouse gas emissions. It is not uncommon in less developed countries to find state ownership of hotels and souvenir shops. Thus in some countries the key elements making up holiday expenditure are directly affected by the public sector, to the point of total control in the situation that existed in the former centrally planned economies of Eastern Europe.

Indirect influences come from economic directives such as foreign exchange restrictions, differential rates of sales tax, special duty free shops for tourists and price controls. Exchange restrictions are commonly employed in countries where foreign exchange is scarce and the tourist is usually compelled to change money at an overvalued exchange rate which serves to increase the real cost of the trip. Tourists are discouraged from changing money on the black market by threats of legal prosecution and severe penalties if caught. Counterfeit merchandise is also coming under scrutiny as destinations are tightening up the enforcement of copyright and trademark laws, particularly in Europe. Being fined abroad is one thing, but when returning home tourists run the risk of having their bargain priced goods confiscated and destroyed by customs. In the worst instance, the trademark owner can demand a statement of guilt, which comes with high fees.

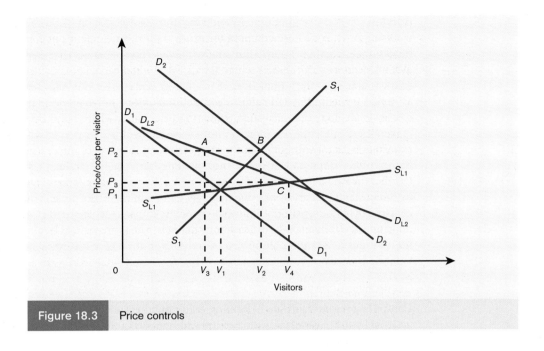

| Figure 18.3 | Price controls |

The case for price controls is advanced in terms of promoting the long-term growth of the tourist industry and preventing monopolistic exploitation of tourists through overcharging, a practice that can be damaging to the reputation of the destination. The argument for price regulation is illustrated in Figure 18.3. Initially the destination is receiving $V_1$ visitors, paying an average package price of $P_1$ for their stay, with equilibrium being determined at the intersection of the demand schedule $D_1D_1$ and the short-run supply curve $S_1S_1$. Demand expands to $D_2D_2$, which gives the opportunity for suppliers to raise prices to $P_2$, at the market equilibrium point $B$. This arises because significant parts of the tourism sector, such as airlines and hotels, are open to revenue or yield management systems, whereby market adjustment is more likely to be through price than quantity. These systems are designed to improve performance in situations where the product is relatively homogeneous and perishable, demand is seasonal, capacity is fixed in the short run and suppliers have the ability to segment the market. In simple terms this is described as 'making money while you can', as in the case of London hotels which moved to full-rate tariff during the 2012 Olympics. This can be counter-productive in circumstances where the number of competing destinations and the holiday price consciousness of travellers ensure that demand in the longer term is more sensitive to price than in the short run, as illustrated by the slope of $D_{L2}$. The price control argument says that by keeping price at $P_2$ existing suppliers will make excess profits, but this could be at the expense of the destination's market share. This is shown on Figure 18.3 as a new market equilibrium position at $A$, where visitor numbers have fallen back from $V_2$ to $V_3$. The destination is perceived as 'pricing itself out of the market'.

There is no doubt that destinations are aware of their price competitiveness and some NTOs compile a tourist price index for their own country as well as others, in order to assess their relative market position. Where governments regulate prices, the objective is to set their level at, say, $P_3$ which is sufficient to encourage the long-run growth in supply as shown by $S_{L1}$ and commensurate with market expansion to an equilibrium point such as $C$, giving a growth in visitor numbers to $V_4$. Producers, on the other hand, are prevented from making short-term excess profits.

Where price controls are enforced, they are normally a further stage in an overall market regulation package, which commences with the registration and licensing of establishments. In the case of hotels this will include classification and possibly a quality grading system. Price regulation can be found in almost all instances where the government manages capacity and therefore restricts competition. Worldwide, the most common example is the licensing and metering of taxis. Where competition exists then the argument put forward in Figure 18.3 hinges upon whether supply adjusts more quickly than demand. There have been many examples of Mediterranean resorts where the growth of bed capacity has outstripped demand and so the problem for the authorities has been more an issue of controlling standards than prices, as well as trying to prevent ruinous competition among hoteliers. In market economics there is a basic ideology that is against regulating prices and, where opportunities for suppliers to make excess profits in the short term do arise, control is often exercised informally through exhortation that it will not be in the long-term best interests of the destination. This has been termed 'maintaining rate integrity' through long-term pricing strategies, so that visitors do not feel that they are being exploited at a time when there is a high demand for the destination. On the other hand, the art of revenue management from the firm's perspective is to continuously adjust to the price sensitivity of diverse market segments, tackle pricing wars with the competition and effectively manage distribution channels. The more visitors book online, the less is the need for businesses to publish fixed price lists and the easier it is to extract the optimal price to fill up capacity.

## Controlling access

Controlling access is a means of limiting visitor numbers or channelling visitor flows. At an international level, the easiest way for a country to limit demand is by restricting the number of visas issued. Prohibiting **charter flights** is a means by which several countries have conveyed an image of exclusiveness to the market and, in some instances, have protected the **national air carrier**. At the destination, controlling access is usually concerned with protecting popular cultural sites and natural resources. Thus visitor management techniques may be used to relieve congestion at peak times and planning legislation invoked to prohibit or control the development of tourist infrastructure (particularly accommodation) near or around natural sites. (Visitor management techniques are explored in more detail in Chapter 13.)

## Safety and security

There have always been issues of criminal activities targeted at tourists, particularly in countries where there are large disparities between 'the haves and have-nots'. Older age groups are perceived as being more vulnerable, which is compounded by the fact that many tourist environments are designed for open access and some are from the past when the security of guests was not high on the agenda. Increasingly, tourist enterprises have tightened security and visitors have been given advice to make them 'streetwise'. Governments have also instituted special tourist police, as in Egypt and Brazil, and tourism victim support services, for example in Ireland and Holland.

On the supply side, the cash-rich nature of tourism operations makes them a convenient channel for money laundering from organised criminal gangs, or simply from individuals evading taxes or trying to find a safe haven for their money abroad because they have no confidence in the domestic financial system due to corrupt practices. Casinos, real estate transactions and purchases of luxury items such as jewellery are distinct favourites for money laundering activities.

Unfortunately, terrorism is much more difficult to deal with, because its causes have little to do with tourism. It is associated with political and religious fanaticism, civil wars and rich–poor income gaps that result in political turbulence in the form of mass protests, for example anti-globalisation movements, and occasional riots and shootings, in which innocent tourists may become targets. What was special about the destruction of the World Trade Center, New York in 2001 (9/11) was that tourist destinations were largely caught unawares, as few had crisis management plans to deal with the consequences for international travel flows – a situation that has now been put right in the principal destinations. On the other hand, dealing with terrorist threats also raises difficulties, in that the stringent entry policies and procedures since the terrorist attacks of 9/11 have created perceptions of an unwelcoming USA in the minds of prospective tourists, contributing to a decline in America's share of global travel.

| Photograph 18.1 | The 'Arab Spring' (Cairo, anti-government protesters, 1 February 2011). Political upheaval in a country affects people's perception of its safety as a tourist destination. |
| --- | --- |

*Source*: Mohamed Elsayyed/Shutterstock.com

## Supply and cost management

Government activity on the supply side is concerned with influencing the providers of tourist facilities and services, as opposed to demand management policies aimed at guiding the tourist's choice, controlling the costs of stay or stimulating/regulating visitor numbers. We have already stressed that the development of tourism should be regarded as a partnership between the private and public sectors. The extent of government involvement in this partnership depends upon the prevailing economic, political and social policies of a country. Where the government envisages a particular direction for tourism growth or wishes to speed up the process, it may intervene extensively in the marketplace by setting up a tourist development corporation (TDC) and assigning it the responsibility for building resorts. A well-known example of this process is the building of new resorts in Mexico, but many countries have instituted TDCs at one time or another, for example, Egypt, France, India, Malaysia, New Zealand and a number of African countries. In theory, once the resort has been built, the development corporation's function ceases and the assets are transferred to the private sector (at a price) and the local authority. This is the general trend in market-orientated economies, but in countries where there is a strong degree of central planning the TDC often maintains an operational role in running hotels and tours. Beyond this, governments may also establish a development bank with duties to provide special credit facilities for tourist projects and on-lend funds made available by multinational aid agencies. This is common in LDCs where capital funds are short and local capital markets are weak.

The methods that are frequently used by governments to influence the supply side of the tourism industry are:

- land-use planning and environmental control;
- building regulations;
- market regulation;

- market research and planning;
- taxation;
- ownership;
- education and training; and
- investment incentives.

## Land-use planning and environmental control

Control over land use is the most basic technique and arguably the one that has the greatest influence on the supply of tourist structures. All governments have a form of town and country planning legislation whereby permission is required to develop, extend or change the use of almost every piece of land. As a rule, the controls are designed to protect areas of high landscape and amenity value: for example, it is now common to restrict the proximity of buildings to the shoreline in coastal developments. The case is that the environment has an intrinsic value, which outweighs its value as a tourism asset. Its enjoyment by future generations and its long-term survival must not be prejudiced by short-term considerations. But (as noted in Chapter 13) it is possible to have conservation through tourism, by recognising the two-way flow between tourism and the environment.

Zoning of land and compulsory purchase are commonly used as a means of promoting tourism development. One of the key aspects of land control is that before any detailed site plans and future land requirements for tourism are published, the appropriate administrative organisation and legislation is in place in order to prevent speculation, land division or parcelling. Dealings or speculation in land prior to legislative control have been a common cause of failure in tourism master plans.

## Building regulations

Building regulations are used to supplement land-use control and typically cover the size of buildings, height, shape, colour and car-parking arrangements. For example, Mauritius has a rule that restricts coastal developments to two levels, roughly the height of palm trees, which permits adequate screening from the seaward side. Car parking is a matter that is not always given the attention it deserves in some resorts. To private sector operators, car parks are often considered unproductive space and so there is a tendency to avoid having to provide them, leaving visitors little alternative than to park their cars in nearby streets. This may only serve to add to traffic congestion and the annoyance of local residents. In addition to structural regulations, many countries also have protective legislation governing cultural resources such as historic buildings, archaeological remains, religious monuments, conservation areas and even whole towns.

## Market regulation

Governments pass legislation to regulate the market conduct of firms in matters of competitive practices and also to limit the degree of ownership in particular sectors of the industry to prevent the abuse of monopoly power. Governments may also regulate markets by imposing on suppliers obligations to consumers. This does not have to be legislation; it could be industry-enforced codes of conduct of the kind laid down as conditions for membership of national travel trade associations, though in Europe such codes have passed into the legislation of member states as a result of the EU Package Travel Directive.

One of the economic criteria dictating the optimal working of markets is that consumers should have complete knowledge of the choices open to them. For if consumers do not have the right to safety, to be informed, to choose or of redress and firms are not behaving according to the accepted rules of conduct, then resources will be wasted, which may be seen to be inefficient. The economic aspects of a consumer policy are shown in Figure 18.4. As the level of protection increases, so wastage or compensation payments decline, while at the same time the costs of protection increase. The optimum amount of protection is where the two schedules intersect

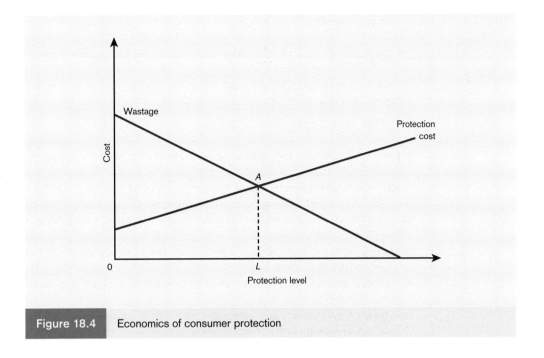

**Figure 18.4**     Economics of consumer protection

at point *A*, which defines level *L* on the axis below. This is the economic rationale: on social or political grounds the state may legislate to ensure nearly 100% protection. But the economic consequences of such an action could be to raise the supply price of the good or service to the point where the market is substantially diminished. At the consultation stage of the EU Package Travel Directive amendments were accepted to some of the proposals on the grounds that their compliance would significantly raise holiday prices.

## Market research and planning

The tourist industry usually expects the public sector to collect statistical information and carry out market surveys. There have been steps towards the creation of tourism satellite accounts as advocated by UNWTO, but generally not enough is being done, when compared to the traditional statistics collected for the extractive and manufacturing sectors of national economies. Inadequacy means that it is impossible to measure accurately the impact of tourism policy, or monitor trends in the marketplace – and the result is an incalculable loss of unrealised potential. The NTO is naturally concerned with understanding demographic and lifestyle changes in its source markets – for example, the increasing environmental awareness – and how they affect the image of the country. For their own part, governments are interested in monitoring changes in the industry and carry out research to identify the social and environmental benefits and costs of tourism. The emerging research themes that suggest themselves from the new tourism trends discussed in this text are: changes in the demographic structure and lifestyles upon tourism demand; product management and innovations in distribution facing the industry; improving the attractiveness of destinations through product development in a sustainable way by moving towards the idea of being 'carbon neutral'; and the strengthening of public/private sector partnerships.

When dealing with products that belong to the tourism sector, the transformation of invention to innovation cannot be compared to the processes seen in manufacturing. Manufacturing starts with product innovation (invention and introduction of the product), qualitative process innovation (the setting up of the manufacturing systems), and quantitative process innovation (improvements and rationalisation of the production system for mass supply). Tourism products start with the quantitative process innovation by taking established products and using them to increase the efficiency of current service production, which, in turn, leads to qualitative changes in the production system and then wholly transformed or entirely new service experiences, which are the output of the tourism industry. Thus some of the most successful visitor attractions are the result of brand extensions of products that are the output of another industrial process, as, for example, the amusement parks of the Walt Disney Corporation and the Universal Studios Recreation Group (see Chapter 13).

## Taxation

There are two main reasons why governments levy specific taxes on the tourism sector. The first is the classic argument for a **tourist tax**, namely to allocate to the supply price the external costs imposed on the host community through providing public amenities for tourists. The second is for purposes of raising revenue. Tourists are seen as part of the overall tax base and, from a political perspective, they are not voters in the destination country; therefore the welfare burden that taxes impose on consumers, which has to be considered for the domestic population, does not apply to tourists. Where residents and tourists consume goods jointly, then if tourists were less sensitive to price rises, it is possible for the tax revenue raised to more than outweigh the loss of benefit to domestic consumers.

With the growth of tourism worldwide, there has been an escalation in the number of countries levying tourist taxes and in the rates of taxation, drawing the inference that governments principally see such taxes as a source of revenue. It is not unreasonable that the tourist industry should pay taxes as in any other business and the World Travel and Tourism Council (WTTC) has argued that tax payments should be made in accordance with the following guidelines:

- **Equity**: the fair and even-handed treatment of travel and tourism with respect to the other sectors of the economy.
- **Efficiency**: the development of tax policies that have a minimal effect on the demand for travel and tourism, unless specifically imposed for the purpose of regulating tourist flows to, say, environmentally sensitive areas (see Chapter 13).
- **Simplicity**: taxes should be simple to pay and administer, so as not to disrupt the operation of the travel and tourism system.

Being aware of the competitive nature of the leisure tourism product and conscious of market share, the industry is opposed to the increasing number of discriminatory taxes on tourism, the most common forms of which are airport departure taxes, ticket taxes and taxes on hotel occupancy. Their principal argument is that they are not normally hypothecated to improvements in travel infrastructure, but submerged in the general tax take (which the industry already pays into via corporation tax, sales taxes, property taxes and income tax payment made by employees and shareholders), thus raising the price of the tourist product with no noticeable improvement in quality. Moreover, where a country has a large domestic tourism industry, a hotel occupancy tax makes it less costly for domestic tourists to switch demand to destinations abroad, as well as being more expensive for inbound tourists. Opposition can be effective; thus in 2002 the regional government of the Spanish islands of Majorca, Minorca and Ibiza introduced a tourist tax of €1 per night on all visitors. This was a way of raising funds for environmental projects, but after protests from hotel owners about the added cost of vacations on the islands and the burden of collecting the payments from guests, the bed tax was scrapped a year later. The political appeal of tourist taxes is that in the main they fall most heavily on people who do not vote on either the taxes or those who impose them. Most of the anti-tax lobby is generated by the suppliers who are concerned about competitiveness.

When it comes to raising revenue, casinos can be a very profitable source: governments have been known to take as much as 50% of the 'drop', which is the amount of money taken in from the tables. However, there are clearly many other issues to do with regulation and ethics when it comes to expanding casinos and generating tax revenues in this way.

Although a tourist tax may be paid by the guest at the hotel and collected from the hotelier, the incidence as to who bears the tax will depend on the responsiveness of demand and supply to a price change. In Figure 18.5, the imposition of a tax raises the supply price by moving the

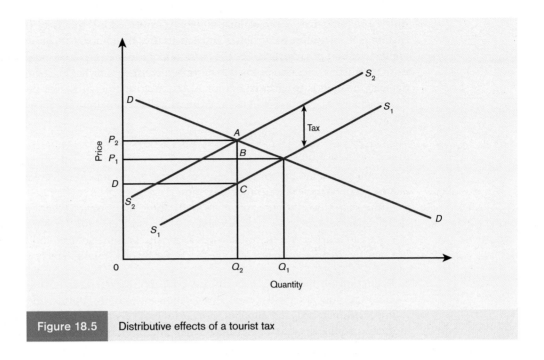

| Figure 18.5 | Distributive effects of a tourist tax |

supply curve from $S_1S_1$ to $S_2S_2$, which in turn reduces the quantity of, say, room sales demanded from $Q_1$ to $Q_2$. However, the amount of tax income raised $P_2ACD$ does not all fall on the tourists in the form of a higher price. Price rises from $P_1$ to $P_2$ only and the larger share of the incidence of the tax $P_1BCD$ falls on the supplier in the form of reduced profits. Tourists contribute $P_2ABP_1$ of the tax revenue. The less sensitive tourists are to price (something that can be reflected in a much steeper demand schedule $DD$), the greater is the ability of suppliers to pass on the tax in the form of a higher price and therefore the larger will be the share of the tax burden falling on the tourists.

## Ownership

Mention has already been made of state ownership of attractions, natural amenities and some key revenue-earning activities such as hotels, modes of transport (especially airlines) and souvenir shops. It is possible to add to this list conference centres, exhibition halls, sports and leisure complexes (including casinos) and the provision of general infrastructure. The latter may include banks, hospitals, public utilities (water and energy supplies), telecommunications, road networks, transport terminals, and education and training establishments. The arguments for public ownership of these facilities rest on their importance as essential services for any economic development, the fact that outside investors would expect such provision and economies of scale in production. Traditionally, public infrastructure and transport networks have been regarded as natural monopolies; the minimum scale of production is such as to make it impossible for more than one firm to enjoy all the economies in the market, so that even if they were not publicly owned these organisations would need to be publicly regulated. However, changes in technology are undermining the natural monopoly concept in telecommunications and power generation, reducing further the need for public ownership.

## Education and training

The provision of an educated and trained labour force to meet the demands of a modern economy has been a task that has fallen to many governments. In common with other planning activities, this requires an assessment of the current occupational distribution of the tourism workforce, which is then mapped onto the general educational level of each occupational group. Overall forecasts of economic activity for the tourist industry are then turned into workforce needs, which are compared to projections of supply from existing trends in the education system, enabling the estimation of surpluses and deficits. It is then possible to lay down a strategy for the implementation of projects in the education and training sector to bring demand and supply as close together as might be deemed practical, given the somewhat loose linkage between education and the skills base of the labour force. Actions to augment this may be the provision of low-cost housing for key workers in resort areas, as well as immigration policies to add to the quality of the workforce.

## Investment incentives

Governments around the world offer a wide range of investment incentives to developers. They may be grouped under three broad headings:

1. **Reduction of capital costs.** This includes capital grants or loans at preferential rates, interest rate relief, a moratorium on loan repayments for, say, x years, provision of infrastructure, provision of land on concessional terms, tariff exemption on construction materials and equity participation.

2. **Reduction of operating costs.** In order to improve operating viability governments may grant tax 'holidays' (5–10 years), give a labour or training subsidy, offer tariff exemption on imported materials and supplies, provide special depreciation allowances and ensure that there is double taxation or unilateral relief. The latter are government-to-government agreements that prevent an investor being taxed twice on the same profits.

3. **Investment security.** The object here is to win investors' confidence in an industry that is very sensitive to the political environment and economic climate. Action here would include guarantees against nationalisation, free availability of foreign exchange, repatriation of invested capital, profits, dividends and interest, loan guarantees, provision of work permits for 'key' personnel and the availability of technical advice.

The administration of grants or loans may be given to the NTO, a government-sponsored investment bank or the TDC. Tax matters will usually remain the responsibility of the treasury or the ministry in charge of finance. Less-developed countries are often able to attract low-cost investment funds from multinational aid agencies, which they can use to augment their existing resources for the provision of development finance.

It may be taken that policies to ensure investment security are primary requirements for attracting tourism developers. The objective of financial incentives is to improve returns to capital so as to attract developers and investors. Where there is obvious market potential the government may only have to demonstrate its commitment to tourism by providing the necessary climate for investment security. Such a situation occurred in Bermuda during the early 1970s and so, in order to prevent over-exploitation of the tourism resources, the Bermuda government imposed a moratorium on building large hotels.

The impact of financial incentives on the amount of investment is illustrated in Figure 18.6. The schedule $SS$ represents the supply of investable funds while $D_1D$ is the schedule of returns to capital employed. $D_1D$ slopes downwards from left to right as more and more investment opportunities are taken up – the declining marginal efficiency of investment. In the initial situation, equilibrium is at $A$ with the amount of investment being $I_1$ and the rate of return $i_1$.

Conditions of market failure imply that the community benefits from tourism investment are not entirely captured in the demand function $D_1D$. Optimal economic efficiency is where the demand function includes these external effects, as represented by $D_2D$. The government now implements a range of financial incentives that have the effect of raising the rate of return per unit of capital to $i_2$, moving the marginal efficiency of investment schedule to $D_2D$. The new return $i_2$ equals $(1 + s)i_1$, where $s$ is the effective rate of subsidy. If the amount of investable funds available for tourism is limited at $I_1$, then the impact of incentives serves merely to raise the return to investors by raising the equilibrium point to $B$. The loss to the government treasury is the area $i_1 AB i_2$ which equals the gain to private investors.

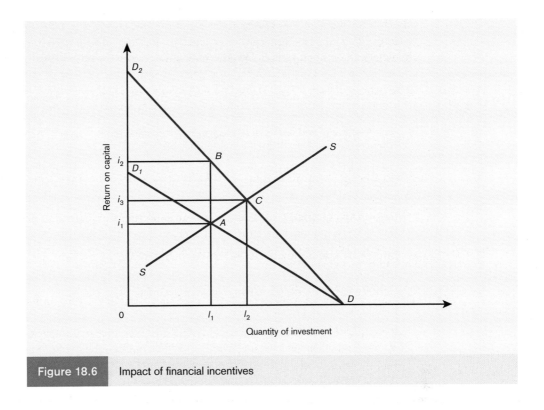

| Figure 18.6 | Impact of financial incentives |

There is no doubt that many countries have been forced by competitive pressures for foreign investment into situations that are similar to those above. Countries can become trapped in a bidding process to secure clients and as a result the variety of financial incentives multiplies together with an escalation of the rates of benefit, without evaluating their necessity or their true cost to the economy. Given that the supply of investment funds is responsive or elastic, the net effect of an incentives policy is to expand the amount of tourism projects to $I_2$ and the rate of return settles at $i_3$, the equilibrium point being $C$. The private opportunity cost of the investment funds is the area under the supply curve, $I_1\, AC\, I_2$, while the public willingness to pay for correcting for market failure is the area $I_1\, BC\, I_2$: subtracting the two areas gives a net gain represented by the area $ABC$.

It is important to note that there are frequent instances where it is gross uncertainty, as in times of recession, rather than limited potential that prevents the private sector investing. In such situations the principal role of government intervention is to act as a catalyst to give confidence to investors. Thus public funds are able to lever in private money by nature of the government's commitment to tourism and enable the market potential of an area to be realised.

In implementing a tourism investment policy the government has to decide to what extent incentives should be legislated as automatic entitlements, as against being discretionary awards. It has already been noted that automatic incentives may give too much money away, when what is required to ensure that the treasury receives maximum benefit from its funds is the application of the concept of 'project additionality'. The latter seeks to provide financial support or the equivalent benefits in kind to the point where the developer will just proceed with the project.

The implication of **additionality** is an ideal situation where all incentives are discretionary and therefore offered selectively. The legislation would be fairly general, empowering the ministry responsible for tourism to offer loans, grants, tax exemptions and equity investment as it sees fit. The granting of incentives to prospective developers is in accordance with ministerial guidelines, which are regularly reviewed in response to the level of tourism activity. To have only **discretionary incentives**, however, is a counsel of perfection. Competition for tourism investment

---

**YOUTUBE**
Public sector and policy

Tourism for all and accessibility of destinations within EU'S new tourism strategy
http://www.youtube.com/watch?v=KsdcEsamEOE

Visa-free travel and financial aid to top EU–Russia summit
http://www.youtube.com/watch?v=j4vacgdLym8

Tourism EU zone debt concerns
http://www.youtube.com/watch?v=7ZkpUBTaoX4

Greek budget woes worsen
http://www.youtube.com/watch?v=VjAw1x-2GUQ

Tourism for all and accessibility of destinations within EU's new tourism strategy
http://www.youtube.com/watch?v=KsdcEsamEOE

EU Commission Vice President Looks to Spur Muslim Tourism to Europe
http://www.youtube.com/watch?v=fspCp0xOYmA

EU plans tourism boost
http://www.youtube.com/watch?v=gaNwf5fHw44

Jamaica's tourism minister, Edmund Bartlett has outlined the background for the ministry's decision to fund the island's marketing efforts with a US$10 increase in travel taxes.
http://www.youtube.com/watch?v=WQ5sHgzSAuc

---

frequently requires countries to legislate for automatic financial help in order to attract investors in the first instance. Some countries may legislate for all the incentives discussed here; others for a subset of them. Several countries have been guilty of copying incentive legislation without any real grasp of its meaning.

The appropriateness of the various financial incentives available depends on understanding the nature of the business risk and the probable returns to the tourist industry, as well as the ability of the country to afford them. Thus developing countries may find themselves in no position to offer grants or cheap loans, which highlights the importance of contributions from aid agencies. One of the main sources of business risk in tourist enterprises is the tendency to have a high ratio of capital charges in relation to operating expenses. It is for this reason that incentives to reduce capital costs are the preferred form of assistance when the viability of the business is being considered.

# INTERVENTION POLICY

The range of policy instruments available to governments is considerable and enables the public sector to exercise varying degrees of influence over the direction of tourism development. From the perspective of the NTO charged with implementing a national development strategy, it might be thought that once the objectives have been defined then it is simply a matter of packaging the appropriate instruments to achieve the desired results. However, this ignores the political dimension. We have already discussed earlier how outside political influences at the destination level may alter policy at the top, but in any representative political system there are a number of inside influences on the governing authority.

Political parties influence the government of the day through the preparation of the manifesto, which it is the task of the minister to steer through the governing assembly. The groups putting pressure on the assembly to form policy are many. They range from the governing party itself, various statutory bodies, trade associations, trade unions, individual industries, clubs and ordinary people. Typical activities undertaken include: holding receptions at the assembly; representations to government; meetings with senior civil servants; individual lobbying of elected representatives; and evidence to government committees. The latter are the 'workhorses' of government for policy purposes, as the floor of the assembly is largely a debating chamber where matters under discussion may be secondary to the objective of 'scoring a point' over the opposition.

The membership of a government committee is normally representative of all the major political parties, with a majority in favour of the governing party for voting purposes. A committee will normally conduct its inquiry in three ways:

- invite written memoranda;
- take oral evidence from expert witnesses; and
- undertake fact-finding tours.

All evidence given to a government committee has to be received formally, since it provides the basis on which recommendations are made. The reality is that in making recommendations a committee can act only within its sphere of influence, otherwise it can appear foolish. If a particular project does not appear in the report, it is because no supporting evidence was given. In the taking of oral evidence, the presence of the press can make the questioning combative, and while this may produce headlines for some politicians, it usually serves no useful purpose. With expectations raised, it becomes impossible to have a discussion of the issues without it appearing in the press as a major row.

Generally speaking, to be accepted the recommendations of government committees have to fit into a tourism strategy that is structured around tolerable political criteria rather than tourism needs. It should be remembered that the 'status quo' in politics is a powerful force to be reckoned with. The government is unlikely to accept recommendations that are politically contentious in respect, say, of its manifesto or that require significant legislative changes or are likely to upset the Ministry of Finance. It is not surprising, therefore, that tourism professionals will often be frustrated by the direction of government policy, which may be described as 'the art of the possible' within the context of the various interest groups. At best the outcomes of government committees are improvements to policy and at worst they are a damage limitation exercise, filtering out 'bizarre' ideas.

# CONCLUSION

Around the globe governments have intervened to assist and regulate the private sector; this is because the complex nature of the tourist product makes it unlikely that private markets will satisfy all the tourism policy objectives of a country. The role of governmental organisations in the influencing of tourism supply and the manipulation of tourism demand is critical in the shaping of the tourism system. We saw how governmental involvement may influence the demand for tourism in Part 1 of this text and in this part we demonstrate the function of public sector bodies in coordinating and funding the supply aspects of the tourism product. The trend towards pure market-led economics stemming from the 1980s has led to a clawback of state involvement and the questioning of intervention as mechanisms more likely to lead to market distortions than market corrections. This was in total contrast to the concept of sustainable development, which challenges the ability of private markets to improve the distribution of income and protect the environment. The spillover benefits of tourism are well known, and, more than any other industry, tourism deals with the use of natural and cultural resources. The lessons of the past indicate that it is unwise for governments to abandon their ability to influence the direction of tourism development, and many governments have recognised this through their support for tourism as an economic regeneration activity, particularly for cities with the growth in cultural tourism. Tourism is a truly global business that has reduced the power of national governments to shield themselves from outside events, so what is required is a pragmatic approach to intervention and regulation, with an emphasis on collaboration between government agencies through international bodies. It would be convenient if there were a few instruments or levers which could be considered optimal for the implementation of tourism policy. Certainly, the tourist industry responds strongly to legislation and the availability of finance, but the tourist product varies so much around the globe that it is customary for states to adopt a bundle of instruments and adjust them over time, in response to feedback information on their workings.

## SELF-CHECK QUESTIONS

1. Why are international tourism organisations important for tourism and tourism development?

2. Suggest some of the areas in a continent of your choice that might be classified as peripheral and the features that would make them attractive for tourism development.

3. Suggest some of the non-governmental organisations in your own country that have a significant influence on tourism policy.

## REFERENCES AND FURTHER READING

Anderson, C. (2006) *The Long Tail*, R.H. Business Books, Kent.

Baud-Bovy, M. and Lawson, F. (1998) *Tourism Recreation Handbook of Planning and Design*, Architectural Press, London.

Commission of the European Communities (2006) *Regions for economic change*. Brussels, Belgium, COM (2006), 675 final.

Commission of the European Communities (2007) *Agenda for a Sustainable and Competitive European Tourism*, Office for Official Publications of the European Communities, Brussels, Belgium.

European Commission Directorate-General for Regional Policy (2004) *Working for the Regions*, Office for Official Publications of the European Communities, Luxembourg.

Dwyer, L., Forsyth, P. and Spurr, R. (2003) 'Inter-industry effects of tourism growth: implications for destination managers', *Tourism Economics* **9**(2), 117–32.

Gooroochurn, N. and Sinclair, T. (2005) 'Economics of tourism taxation: Evidence from Mauritius', *Annals of Tourism Research* **32**, 478–98.

Hall, C.M. (2000) *Tourism Planning: Policies, Processes and Relationships*, Harlow, Prentice Hall.

Holloway, J.C. (2002) *The Business of Tourism*, 6th edn, Pearson Education, Harlow.

House of Commons (1969) *Development of Tourism Act 1969*, HMSO, London.

Inskeep, E. (1991) *Tourism Planning: An Integrated and Sustainable Development Approach*, Van Nostrand Reinhold, New York.

Jamal, T.B., Stein, S.M. and Harper, T.L. (2002) 'Beyond labels: pragmatic planning in multi-stakeholder tourism-environmental conflicts', *Journal of Planning Education and Research* **22**(2), 164–77.

Jenkins, J. (2000) 'The dynamics of regional tourism organisations in New South Wales, Australia: history, structures and operations', *Current Issues in Tourism* **3**(3), 175–203.

Jensen, T. and Wanhill, S. (2002) 'Tourism's taxing times: VAT in Europe and Denmark', *Tourism Management* **23**(1), 67–79.

Mak, J. (2005) 'Tourist taxes', pp. 441–3 in J. Cordes, R. Ebel and J. Gravelle (eds), *The Encyclopedia of Taxation and Tax Policy*, Urban Institute Press, Washington, DC.

Mason, P. (2003) *Tourism Impacts, Planning and Management*, Butterworth Heinemann, Oxford.

Middleton, V.T.C. and Hawkins, R. (1998) *Sustainable Tourism: A Marketing Approach*, Butterworth Heinemann, Oxford.

Myers, J., Forsberg, P. and Holecek, D. (1997) 'A framework for monitoring global travel and tourism taxes: the WTTC Tax Barometer', *Tourism Economics* **3**(1), 5–20.

Nilsson, P., Petersen, T. and Wanhill, S. (2005) 'Public support for tourism SMEs in peripheral areas: The Arjeplog project northern Sweden', *Service Industries Journal* **25**(4), 579–99.

Palmer-Tous, T., Riera-Font, A. and Rosselló-Nadal, J. (2007) 'Taxing tourism: the case of rental cars in Mallorca', *Tourism Management*, **28**, 271–79.

Pearce, D. (1992) *Tourist Organisations*, Longman, Harlow.

Vanhove, N. (2005) *The Economics of Tourist Destinations*, Elsevier, London.

Wanhill, S. (1997) 'Peripheral area tourism: a European perspective', *Progress in Tourism and Hospitality Research* **3**(1), 47–70.

Wanhill, S. (2005). 'Investment support for tourism SMEs; a review of theory and practice', pp. 227–54 in Jones, E. and Haven, C. (eds), *Tourism SMEs, Service Quality and Destination Competitiveness*, CABI, Wallingford, England.

WTO (1993) *Sustainable Tourism Development: Guide for Local Planners*, WTO, Madrid.

# MAJOR CASE STUDY 18.1
## Tourism project assistance from the European Union

The purpose of this case study is to provide an understanding of the framework for the allocation of structural funds by the European Union; to illustrate the range of criteria against which proposals are judged and funds allocated; to offer an overview of the system in action.

## INTRODUCTION

Above the investment help offered separately by the governments of the EU, there is the pan-European programme of regional aid made available to member states through the Union's structural funds. The governing principle is that of *solidarity*, whereby the strong help the weak to improve economic convergence; that is to eliminate major disparities of wealth, and ensure a better spread of economic activities throughout the territories located within the boundaries of the Union. The morality of this principle is generally accepted by member states and therefore acted upon at a political level. In a global world it is argued that it is in the member state's own interest to act internationally.

Regional project assistance is currently given under three general funds and one that is specific to agriculture:

1. The European Regional Development Fund (ERDF), which is focused mainly on productive investment, infrastructure and local business development in less favoured regions, and is the principal vehicle for regional support.

2. The European Social Fund (ESF), which has the task of promoting jobs through investing in educational systems, vocational training and employment assistance.

3. The Cohesion Fund to promote growth-enhancing conditions and factors leading to real convergence for the least-developed member states and regions, such as transport and environmental infrastructure.

4. The European Agricultural Fund for Rural Development (EAFRD), which is targeted at improving agricultural competitiveness, managing the environment, improving the quality of rural life and diversifying the rural economy.

The European Commission recognises that the funds make a major contribution to the development of tourism in the EU and, in so doing, progress the objectives of economic and social cohesion as defined in Article 130a, Treaty of the European Union (the Maastricht Treaty), 1992. In essence, the Commission's policy for using tourism as an instrument of regional economic development is one of taking advantage of the many positive aspects of the industry, namely:

- the continuing growth in tourism worldwide;

- disadvantaged regions often have a comparative advantage in natural tourism resources;

- tourism attracts spending from outside the regions;

- tourism and culture bring people together and help tear down divides;

- tourism has important spillover benefits (multiplier effects) elsewhere in the regional economy; and

- job creation within a relatively short period of time is an important aspect of tourism development.

| Photograph 18.2 | The headquarters of the European Union in Brussels, the centre of regional policy decision making throughout the political union. |
|---|---|

*Source*: European Parliament. ASP: AEL, Avenue des Courses 15, 1050 Brussels; PHS: Association des architectes du CIC, rue du Prince royal 19, 1050

Tourism, as a part of Europe's wealth that gives identity to its regions and is a source of economic activity and new jobs, has therefore a significant presence in structural interventions. Many programmes have strands specifically devoted to the development of tourist-related infrastructure or projects, protection of heritage, promotion of festivals and so forth.

## BACKGROUND

Prior to 1988, there was no coherent system for the disbursement of the structural funds, which resulted in the dissipation of funds over many areas, thus reducing their effectiveness. Therefore, in 1988, a new regulation on the uses of the funds was adopted in preparation for the first planning period from 1989 to 1993, with lesser changes for the next interval from 1994 to 1999. The changes were based on three fundamental principles:

1. Transforming structural policy into an instrument with real economic impact by concentration on priority objectives.

2. Using a multi-annual programming approach for expenditure planning to assure member states of the stability and predictability of EU support.

3. Implementing a partnership with all the parties actively participating in structural policy, especially the regional authorities.

From 1989 onwards, member states were required to coordinate, for the first time, the use of the funds and draw together all forms of Union support, including lending by the European Investment Bank (EIB) and the European Coal and Steel Community (ECSC). This also allowed the EU to adopt a greater degree of control on the use of the funds within the sphere of integrated regional development plans put forward by member states.

In general terms, each member state prepares a National Strategic Reference Framework (NSRF) over the course of an ongoing dialogue with the Commission. This prepares the programming of funds, and replaces the previous Community Support Frameworks (CSFs) and the single programming documents (SPDs) that were used to develop a series of Operational Programmes (OPs) up to the last planning period 2000–2006. The NSRF comprises the description of the strategy of the state in question and its proposed list of OPs that it hopes to implement.

The NSRF must be sent to the Commission for adoption and appropriate validation, as well as each OP. The OPs present the priorities of the member state (and/or regions) as well as the way in which it will lead its programming. For the 2007–2013 period, some 450 OPs have been adopted by the Commission. Economic and social partners as well as civic bodies participate in the programming and management of the OPs.

In contrast to the investment incentives discussed in this chapter, which may be applied in a piecemeal manner, project promoters are only eligible for assistance from the structural funds if their schemes are included within the planning process and meet one of the Community objectives shown in Table 18.1. In the 1994–1999 planning period there were six objectives, but at the Berlin Summit, held in March 1999, the Council of Ministers agreed to amalgamate them into three for 2000–2006. With the enlargement of the Community from 15 to 25 members in 2004 and the addition of Bulgaria and Romania in January 2007, the previous Objectives 1, 2 and 3 were replaced by three new Objectives: Convergence, Regional Competitiveness and Employment, and Territorial Cooperation for the planning horizon 2007–2013.

The objectives shown in Table 18.1 are used to identify regions and allocate funds. Thus Convergence is supported by ERDF, ESF and the Cohesion Fund, Regional Competitiveness and Employment by ERDF and ESF, while ERDF is the sole fund for Territorial Cooperation.

## FUNDING POLICY

The ERDF is the principal instrument for regional intervention and the sums available dwarf the other structural funds. The method of subvention from the funds is grant aid that is conditional to the project and requires matching funding from the project promoter. The limit rate of grant is normally 50% of public expenditure, but has been raised to 85% in the case of projects in the outermost regions. The majority of projects no longer receive support at the limit rate. For tourism investment, grants are unlikely to be in excess of 45% of the investment cost and may usually be less.

Tourism projects tend to be public sector-led and the principal aspects that should be addressed when bidding for European assistance are:

- the use of the project should be 50% non-local;
- the project should result in an increase in overnight stays;
- the project should result in an increase in employment opportunities;
- the economic position of the project within the local area should be examined;
- the project should form part of a tourism strategy for the local area. Thus the project should sit within an NSRF that forms the regional strategy approved by the member state and the Commission; and
- national/regional tourist organisation support will give weight to the application.

## EVALUATION

Member states are given considerable flexibility as to how they present a proposal, which is consistent with the principle of *subsidiarity* outlined in this chapter. What follows is therefore representative of the criteria that are employed in evaluating a project proposal, namely:

| Table 18.1 | Structural funds' objectives, 2007–2013 |
| --- | --- |

| Objective | Aim |
| --- | --- |
| Convergence | To promote growth-enhancing conditions and factors leading to real convergence for the least-developed member states and regions (those whose GDP per capita is 75% or less than the EU average) |
| Regional competitiveness and employment | To strengthen the competitiveness, employment and attractiveness of regions other than those which are the most disadvantaged, by anticipating economic and social changes, promoting innovation, business spirit, protection of the environment, accessibility, adaptability and the development of inclusive labour markets |
| Territorial cooperation | To strengthen cross-border, transnational and interregional cooperation through promoting common solutions for neighbouring authorities in the fields of urban, rural and coastal development, the development of economic relations and the creation of networks of small and medium-sized enterprises (SMEs) |

- the project should be feasible in that the scheme has the capacity to generate revenues above operating costs so that it can support its own running arrangements;

- viability is assured after financial assistance in order that the project can service the capital investment costs out of its operating surplus;

- the need for structural funds support should be proven;

- displacement of visitors from other tourism businesses within the area of the Operational Programme, or from any other European-assisted area, should be minimised; and

- multiplier effects in terms of job creation should be examined.

## Impact assessment

A key political objective for public intervention lies in some loosely connected social welfare function that links tourist expenditure to local income generation and thence employment. These are the most significant factors affecting project acceptability, since the primary use of structural funds is to correct for regional imbalances. We may note that tourism and hospitality projects are usually well suited to European funding requirements because they are labour-using and commonly have a high operating leverage – that is, a relatively low level of operating costs but a high level of fixed costs caused by prior capital spending. Once the financing of the capital has been adequately taken care of, the project usually runs into surplus after three years and can maintain itself thereafter.

Tourists come to a destination for many reasons, but if the requirement is to establish the economic worth of an investment that has been assisted through European funds, the first step is to draw up a model to reflect the impact visitors have on tourist expenditure in the area.

### Methodology

Suppose that there exists a tourist destination with two attractions and a seaside. Visitors are surveyed at both attractions and on the beach to ascertain what motivated them to come to the destination. Total spending at the destination ($T$) amounts to expenditure at Attraction X ($Tx$) plus expenditure at Attraction Y ($Ty$) plus all remaining expenditure ($R$). Let the pull factor (reason for visit) for Attraction X be $a$, for Attraction Y, a value $b$, leaving $c = 1 - a - b$ as the significance of the beach. It follows therefore that attributable tourist expenditure by drawing power is:

Attraction $X = aT$
Attraction $Y = bT$
Seaside $= cT$
where $T = T_x + T_y + R$

It is proposed that European assistance should be given to Attraction X and so there is a requirement to evaluate its worth in terms of its contribution to tourist spending and employment in the area. The benefits of Attraction X ($B$) are the difference between with and without the project. The without situation is:

Attraction $X = 0$
Attraction $Y = b(T_y + R)$
Seaside $= c(T_y + R)$
$T_w = (b + c)(T_y + R)$

Hence,

$$B = T - T_w$$
$$= T - (b + c)(T_y + R) \tag{18.1}$$

Expanding $T$ gives,

$$B = T_x + a(T_y + R) \tag{18.2}$$

### Employment effects

The benefits shown in equation 18.2 are in two parts. The first term on the right-hand side is on-site expenditure and the second is off-site expenditure. The amount of off-site expenditure attributable to the attraction depends on its ability to generate visitors to Attraction Y and the area in general. This is termed the 'visitor additionality' factor. The application of employment multipliers per unit of tourist spending to equation 18.2, either on a full-time equivalent (FTE) or employment headcount basis, will give estimates of the gross employment ($E$) generated by Attraction X. These multipliers are calculated so as to measure the direct employment effects of the attraction, the indirect effects arising out of intermediate purchases made by the attraction and the induced effects on the local economy as a result of the re-spending of local incomes derived from the attraction, and similarly for off-site expenditure. Thus:

$$E = T_x e_x + aOe_o \tag{18.3}$$

Where $e_x$ is the employment multiplier appropriate to the attraction, $O$ is the sum of off-site expenditure ($T_y + R$) and $e_o$ the required employment multiplier.

However, equation 18.3 ignores any demand diversion from competitors elsewhere in the area – this is the displacement effect and in this respect it is important to define the boundary of the attraction, since the larger the area the more likely it is that the attraction could divert expenditure and employment from elsewhere. National finance ministries sometimes argue that, in the case of the economy as a whole, all expenditure, and consequently employment, is displacement and there is in effect a zero-sum game being played out in which there are only regional distribution benefits.

At a national level, the above argument assumes that market forces are moving the economy towards full employment equilibrium so that public investment expenditure, whether raised through taxation or borrowing, is simply displacing private funds in the capital market. Similarly, the operation of the attraction is displacing demand in the same or related product markets and likewise in the labour and property markets. In reality, economies do get stuck at a level of Keynesian unemployment disequilibria and one of the major objectives of regional policy is to 'kick-start' a demand-deficient economy so as to raise the level of output through the multiplier process. This discussion does not imply that displacement should be neglected so that policy decisions are made in terms of the gross effect only, but merely raises the issue that the logic of the crowding-out effect ends up with a 'do nothing' policy. Modern growth theory places emphasis on the importance of embodied technical progress so that intervention policies designed to help product improvement will affect development through raising efficiency on the supply side.

If $d$ is the proportion of locally diverted demand (or demand diverted from other assisted firms) in equation 18.2, then, from equation 18.3, net employment is:

$$N = E - dE$$
$$= (1 - d)(T_x e_x + aOe_o) \qquad (18.4)$$

Equation 18.4 forms the core of the basic evaluation model that can be used to judge in employment terms the return to public funds given to a business by way of a range of incentives.

### Case example

In Table 18.2 we present data that have been drawn from case study material on attractions, to show how the employment effects of a tourism project may be measured. The workings of Table 18.2 are along the following lines: using visitor expenditure surveys, the total expected on-site and off-site spending arising from the project is estimated, in euros, at €30,034,950.

It is at this point that the concept of visitor additionality is invoked: clearly, on-site expenditure by visitors is attributable absolutely to the attraction as the customers have demonstrated their preferences through their willingness to pay, but this is not the case with off-site spending. The extent to which off-site spending may be attributed to the attraction depends on the

| Table 18.2 | Assessing the impact of a tourist attraction |
| --- | --- |

| Item | On-site expenditure (Euros) | Off-site expenditure (Euros) |
| --- | --- | --- |
| **Visitor markets** | | |
| Stay | 2,649 790 | 15,491,080 |
| Day | 2,955, 535 | 2,637,800 |
| Local residents | 4,586, 175 | 1,714,570 |
| **Total** | 10,191, 500 | 19,843,450 |
| **Visitor additionality** | | |
| Stay | Not applicable | 10% |
| Day | Not applicable | 85% |
| Local residents | Not applicable | 100% |
| **Displacement** | | |
| Stay | 0% | 0% |
| Day | 30% | 30% |
| Local residents | 100% | 100% |
| **FTE multipliers per €10,000** | | |
| Direct | 0.0638 | 0.0524 |
| Indirect | 0.0344 | 0.0325 |
| Induced | 0.0050 | 0.0050 |
| **Total** | **0.1032** | **0.0899** |

importance of the attraction in the customer's decision to visit the location. This can only be ascertained by surveying visitors and asking about their motivations for coming to the destination. As expected, a much higher percentage is recorded for day visitors and local residents, because they normally make a specific decision to go to a place, an event or an attraction. Using the visitor additionality factors in Table 18.2 to account for attributable off-site expenditure, the gross expenditure benefits (B) from the attraction are:

$$B = €10,191,500 + (0.10 \times €15,491,080)$$
$$+ (0.85 \times €2,637,800) + (1.0 \times €1,714,570)$$
$$= €15,697,308 \qquad (18.5)$$

It is anticipated that the attraction will create 70.5 FTE jobs directly on-site, and so the required additions to this number will be the expected indirect and induced employment generated from on-site spending. The direct multiplier is not used here as it refers to the average attraction, so it is better to use the direct estimate of employment in these circumstances. Using the appropriate FTE multipliers shown in Table 18.2 and calculated as a decimal fraction of a given amount of tourist expenditure, this figure comes to $(0.0344 + 0.0050) \times €10,191,500/10,000 = 40.2$ FTE jobs. Off-site jobs amount to $0.0899 \times 5,505,808/€10,000 = 49.5$ FTE jobs, where €5,505,808 is the total of attributable off-site benefits.

Hence, the gross employment generated ($E$), in terms of FTEs, is expected to be:

$$E = 70.5 \text{ FTEs} + 40.2 \text{ FTEs} + 49.5 \text{ FTEs}$$
$$= 160.2 \text{ FTEs} \qquad (18.6)$$

So far the analysis has only measured gross FTEs likely to be generated by the attraction. The net figures have to account for what is termed displacement, which is factored into Table 18.2. Displacement has to do with the extent to which an attraction may capture tourist spending from competitors in the local area. It is estimated that 0% of staying visitors will be taken from competitors; the attraction is providing more to 'see and do' at the destination and the tourists' budgets have sufficient margin of flexibility. For day visitors, it is probable that 30% will be displaced from other attractions, while for local residents a conservative assumption is made that all expenditure will be displaced from elsewhere in the local economy. The latter assumption is overly pessimistic in practice, for household budgets are not that inflexible.

Weighting the displacement factors in Table 18.2 by the different categories of visitor spending gives an overall displacement expenditure of €7,860,045. Hence the value of $d$ is €7,860,045/€15,697,308, which is equal to 0.5007. Thus, the net employment ($N$) that can be expected to result from the attraction is:

$$N = 160.2 - 0.5007 \times 160.2$$
$$= 80.0 \text{ FTEs} \qquad (18.7)$$

It is this number of FTEs that should be used to evaluate the project's worth in public policy decision making when applications for European support or comparisons with alternative projects are being made.

## PROJECT MANAGEMENT

After the Commission has taken a decision on the OPs, the member state and its regions then have the task of implementing the programmes, i.e. selecting the thousands of projects, and monitoring and assessing them. The principle of subsidiarity devolves the monitoring function to the local level through programme management authorities in each country and/or each region. The latter are made up of representatives from central and local government, public agencies and any other interested parties, and they will be responsible for all projects within the OPs. The Commission commits the expenditure to allow the member state to start the programmes.

For every project, targets are set at the approval stage and returns must be submitted quarterly, showing the progress of each scheme against its targets. The member state is required to certify statements of expenditure and payment applications before their transmission to the Commission and to provide an auditing body to ensure the efficient running of the management and monitoring system. The Commission pays the certified expenditure and monitors each OP alongside the member state. Strategic reports are submitted by the Commission and by the member state throughout the given planning period (currently 2007–2013). It is a member state's responsibility to make site visits and evaluate project performance: these tasks usually fall to the government department responsible for administering the OP that contains the project. Member states have the responsibility to ensure that European funds are correctly spent and yield good value for money in terms of the project evaluation criteria. This responsibility is regulated by the European Court of Auditors, which has powers of examination and verification to establish that projects are:

- eligible for European funds as specified;
- managed in accordance with the European Commission's rules with regard to technical and financial controls; and
- claiming grant against justifiable expenditure.

The above verifications are undertaken by making one or two visits every year and subjecting a group of pre-selected projects to detailed checking.

## CONCLUSION

Since about 1975, the entry of the EU into regional policy, in order to create a greater convergence between the economies of the Union, has ended member states' monopoly of regional policy within their borders. Inside the Union, there is a distinct tendency for the poorest regions to be situated on the geographical periphery and the more prosperous regions, with the benefit of market access, to be centrally located. With the adoption of the Single European Act (1987), with the intention to create one market in Europe and a single currency, there is a commitment by the EU to promote economic and social cohesion through actions to reduce regional disparities. The Maastricht (1992) and Lisbon (2009) Treaties established the role of tourism in these actions.

The resources for mitigating regional differences are drawn from the structural funds, which are continually being increased, in real terms, from one planning period to another. The funds have specific objectives, as shown in Table 18.1, and support for tourism development manifests itself in regions that already have an established tourist industry, in cross-border cooperation, rural development and also where tourism has contributed to the diversification of economic activities in areas of industrial decline. Tourism programmes are seen as key activities in reducing regional imbalances. In support of this, the case study discusses the principles of structural assistance and the methodology for project evaluation, with particular emphasis on job creation, though we should be mindful of the clear intention of the European Commission to propagate tourism developments in a sustainable manner, in order to guarantee that the activity continues on a regular basis.

The division of intervention in the tourist industry between member states and the EU is always likely to remain contentious, but given the diversity of the tourist product, the Union has to work in close partnership with national and regional authorities. At the political level, this issue has been technically put to one side by Article 3b of the Maastricht Treaty, which states that:

**the Community shall take action, in accordance with the principle of subsidiarity, only if and in so far as the objectives of the proposed action cannot be sufficiently achieved by the Member States and can therefore, by reason of the scale or effects of the proposed action, be better achieved by the Community.**

## DISCUSSION QUESTIONS

1. Why is the EU concerned about regional inequalities?

2. How important is tourism in the EU in respect of its contribution to the GDP of member states and employment in the Union?

3. What are the strengths and weaknesses of positioning tourism projects within an overall strategy to guide their use as opposed to opportunistic development?

4. The nature of grant aid from the EU has been described as conditional matching funding. Other forms of grant mechanisms are lump-sum payments, which may be tied to specific projects (conditional) or just given to the overall programme (unconditional). What are the relative merits of these different systems?

5. How would you go about preparing a local area tourism strategy?

6. What are the concepts that lie behind the measurement of direct, indirect and induced income and employment multipliers?

7. The capital investment for the attraction project illustrated in Table 18.2 is €8,600,000. The European Commission decides to grant aid the scheme at 30% of the capital cost. What is the grant cost per direct FTE job created on-site, for the gross employment generated and net jobs created by the project?

8. Suppose the EU introduces a rule limiting grant support to €20,000 per net job created. How much would the project now receive in grant aid as a percentage of the capital cost?

# PART 4

## MARKETING FOR TOURISM

# INTRODUCTION

Marketing is assuming an ever more important role given the lack of stability of world markets. The tourism market will never be the same again given the new realisation that terrorism, weather-induced catastrophes and health-related problems can affect generating countries and tourist demand behaviour. The beginning of this century has produced turbulence of an economic, social and increasingly political nature. In turn this has subsequently led to changes in the consumption patterns of travel around the world. Many international tourism companies and destination markets have experienced a softening of demand and reduction in average daily expenditure. The tourism industry is volatile and demand suffers when there are economic problems on the scale we have witnessed throughout the world after the global financial banking crisis. A drop in demand was seen for both business and leisure tourists. Other historical reasons include industry factors such as over-forecasting and investing in expansion of the tourism supply side which in turn created risk and excessive debt. In addition, other events have compounded the problems of tourism companies whereby the risk of illness, such as SARS in humans or foot and mouth in animals, natural disasters such as tsunamis, ongoing terrorist activity and subsequent conflict have occurred.

All tourism activity is changing from a relaxed experience and the adventure of the trip to some apprehension of what may be the downside risk associated with travelling away from a home destination. Given the need for steady demand, the role of marketing will become increasingly important for tourism organisations operating in both public and private sectors as they continue to strive to protect and improve their market share.

The process of marketing and its management provides companies and organisations with the many complex tools to affect demand in target markets. It is a complex area that, as this section highlights, requires expertise and experience for success. In this section, we provide a comprehensive evaluation of all aspects of the management of tourism marketing, including the strategies and tools that may be applied to deliver the tourism product effectively and efficiently to satisfy the tourism consumer.

In Chapter 19, Managing Marketing for Tourism, we begin by looking at the historical development of marketing in general and how its roots have influenced the application of marketing theory to the tourism product in particular. While marketing in one form or another has been in existence for centuries, the relative recency of sophisticated techniques and an awareness of services marketing requirements have meant that current marketing is evolving rapidly to suit the needs of the tourism industry. We also introduce and discuss the characteristics of the service product such as intangibility, perishability and inseparability which, it is argued, differentiate the tourism product from others. In addition, we outline other characteristics related to the notion of risk which also distinguish the tourism product from manufactured goods. To combat the risk brought about by the characteristics of the product, the concept of quality – and its management – has become a prevailing force in tourism marketing: the lack of control over the service process, which is essentially an unpredictable human encounter, has become a prime target for the application of quality techniques to standardise the delivery of the product. We present key models in respect of the service delivery system appropriate to the tourism industry and outline some of the criticisms that have been levelled at tourism marketing.

Chapter 20, Marketing Planning, is concerned with the introduction of tactical and strategic marketing planning procedures in respect of the tourism product. We define marketing planning and emphasise its role and application to the diverse sectors which, when amalgamated, form the tourism industry. We review the benefits and purposes of marketing planning, consider the structure of a marketing plan and explore the implications of neglecting tourism marketing planning.

Chapter 21, Marketing Mix Applications, relates to the **marketing mix**. This is a key strategic tool which is integral to the effective manipulation of the tourism product and the successful implementation of marketing planning procedures. However, the fundamental starting point for the creation of a successful marketing mix strategy is the definition of target markets since this will dictate the direction of the elements of the marketing mix and provide a focus for all marketing mix decisions and activity.

The final chapter in this part, Chapter 22, provides us with an understanding of how e-tourism has led to a new way of doing business for many small as well as large companies. Tourism is an industry which is characterised by the need for intense levels of exchange of information. It is also a price-sensitive industry where cost control is important. These factors have heralded the use of information technology. As such the tourism industry has undergone rapid as well as radical change. It is therefore of vital importance that any person studying, or carrying out tourism understands the dynamics and applications associated with these changes.

Thus, Part 4 presents a comprehensive approach to the issues and considerations of the marketing of tourism, together with aspects of distribution through information technology. However, the application of marketing management techniques in the tourism industry can be hampered by a number of factors that are inherent in the nature of tourism itself:

- First, it has been suggested that while the tourism product is sufficiently distinctive to demand a unique marketing approach, the result of this has been that marketing strategies, tools and techniques in tourism are less evolved and advanced than in other industries.

- Secondly, the relative immaturity and diversity of the tourism industry has overlooked the need to take into account the unique characteristics of tourism and the complexity of its products.

- Thirdly, the predominant practice in tourism is often based upon developing managers from grass roots. The implications of this are that while they may be good generalists few have the marketing training and expertise necessary to maximise marketing potential.

- Fourthly, many enterprises in tourism are small operations which have neither the expertise nor the resources to devote to a fully fledged marketing management approach.

- Finally, the application of technology in tourism has placed a number of pressures on organisations in relation to the requirement to understand how to harness possible applications and improvements for their business.

While some of these criticisms are accurate there have been improvements and changes in the tourism industry. The unique nature of the tourism product is recognised far more by marketers and there is now a body of knowledge and a series of techniques for marketing in the service industries. These are outlined throughout the next chapters. The tourism industry does, however, create its own handicaps to effective marketing:

- Data relating to the market and to the actions of competitors are often weak or scarce.

- A short-term outlook prevails, denying a carefully structured and strategic marketing planning approach.

- Managers in tourism tend to have risen through the ranks and to be generalists. The organisation of the industry thus militates against the development of specialists in tourism marketing.

- In addition, it is important to make the point that the tourism industry is subject to governmental and European regulation of its activities, and consumer protection is well developed in tourism. These factors can be instrumental in restricting the marketing options of a tourism company.

Public sector organisations in tourism are also somewhat handicapped in adopting a true marketing orientation. It is, for example, not uncommon to find visitor and convention bureaux with the following problems:

- They may be hidebound by government personnel operating guidelines in terms of working hours and remuneration of staff.

- They may possess insufficient resources to build a presence in the marketplace, particularly in respect of the international arena and information technology.

- They may lack sufficient marketing expertise.
- They may have little or no control over the quality of the product they are marketing.

This section clearly emphasises the interlinkages that characterise the tourism industry. For example, the nature of tourism demand is inextricably linked to marketing of the product and the manipulation of the marketing mix to attract pre-identified **segments**. Moreover, marketing is also linked to the supply of tourism at the destination being marketed. Therefore, if the destination is to sustain its market share, then the range and quality of the attractions and facilities on offer need to live up to those promises as communicated to the target market(s) via the marketing process.

Marketing is, therefore, an important tool in an industry where loyalty in both the distribution chain and to the company is low. Government organisations often find it more cost-effective to market to intermediaries and carriers or enter into joint promotions rather than market directly to potential travellers. Furthermore, due to the pressures of oversupply of capacity in many sectors of the tourism industry marketing is becoming a more important function and we would contend that improving training and education among the tourism workforce, coupled with the realities of increasingly intense competition, are encouraging a new emphasis on marketing management and a greater marketing orientation within the industry.

## A MARKETING PRACTITIONER'S VIEW

**By Tom Wright who was CEO for nearly seven years of VisitBritain, the National Tourist Board, promoting Britain around the world. Before that he was Managing Director of Saga Holidays and for Scottish and Newcastle plc developing Center Parcs.**

Tourism is a massive economic driver, never more so than in the current downturn, yet tourism marketing rarely receives the long-term investment needed to grow the sector, while any such investment is often inconsistent or fragmented, as reflected by the disparate investment in devolved bodies such as the old Regional Development Agencies over the last decade.

Tourism is too often taken for granted until times of crisis when industry and government work best together. This was never more the case than following Foot and Mouth disease and then 11 September 2001 when the Million Visitor Campaign, led by VisitBritain, galvanised industry and government to deliver highly effective global campaigns with fantastic rates of return.

Offers are often key to converting interest into action, especially when a destination has a strong currency (as is the case of Switzerland at the moment) and price is the most elastic part of the tourism offer. So the most effective tourism marketing combines offers and products with a destination halo.

The rest of the world is out-investing Britain and sees tourism as a strategic industry, not just something to top up during a crisis. Tourism marketing has to be far more than promotion; it has to bring together the products, infrastructure, offers and distribution under an inspiring brand. To achieve this it needs strategic engagement across government and industry, and not just in times of crisis.

# CHAPTER 19
## MANAGING MARKETING FOR TOURISM

### LEARNING OUTCOMES

The objective of this chapter is to provide the reader with a comprehensive introduction to marketing as it relates to the tourism industry. By the end of this chapter, therefore, you will:

- understand the concept of marketing, what it is and how it has developed into its current form;
- be able to differentiate between selling and marketing;
- recognise that companies may have different business philosophies and be able to identify the implications of these differences for marketing;
- appreciate the importance of value creation as part of the process of marketing management;
- appreciate the importance of the characteristics of the service product and the implications of these differentiating characteristics for the approach an organisation might adopt for its marketing effort;
- recognise that the purchase of tourism products is associated with the need for quality management and the reduction of perceived risk; and
- be familiar with the key criticisms targeted at tourism marketing and the problems of properly utilising tourism marketing techniques.

Photograph: Stair Hole, Lulworth Cove, Dorset, UK © Peter Woowat

## INTRODUCTION

In this chapter we introduce the evolution and concept of marketing as it applies to tourism. We demonstrate that tourism marketing has emerged as a result of business and social changes which have occurred throughout the past decades as a reaction to the conditions that impinge on business operations. However, while we are able to identify different business philosophies that have influenced the adoption of a marketing orientation and the application of the marketing concept, a fuller understanding of marketing lies in the way marketing management functions in attempting to create and maximise consumer value and satisfaction. In addition, we show that marketing management related to tourism cannot ignore the principal characteristics that set tourism apart from other products. The management of tourism cannot be divorced from the management of service and quality and the tasks related to these are also explored in detail.

## WHAT IS MARKETING?

Tourism can be traced back for centuries but because the elements of the product and conditions of the marketplace have changed so enormously in the last few decades there has been a corresponding requirement for a change in business methods. This has led to the adoption and use of tourism marketing. Some believe that marketing is primarily associated with forms of promotion and communication that have been paid for out of marketing budgets. However, this is a very narrow interpretation of the activity of marketing and, as we shall see, marketing is far more than the promotion of a product. This forms only *one* aspect of marketing.

It is often stated that we live in an era of marketing, but what is marketing? One way of attempting to answer the question 'what is marketing?' is to examine accepted definitions. Although it is very easy to describe what the term marketing means, it is far more difficult to describe the practice of marketing. This is because a central tenet of marketing is the body of underlying concepts that form the general guide for organisational and managerial thinking, planning and action. Consequently, for a comprehensive understanding of marketing it is necessary to learn the underlying concepts.

## THE EVOLUTION OF MARKETING

Marketing has evolved against a background of economic and business pressures. These pressures have required an increased focus on the adoption of a series of managerial approaches based upon satisfying consumer needs. The key to the importance of marketing within tourism has been the overall level of economic growth which has historically led to improvements in living standards and led to increased travel, but more recently economies have stagnated and placed more emphasis on marketing. Also, the enlargement of the population of tourism-generating countries has slowed due to falling birth rates. The early changes among consumers led the Disney management in 1955 to launch the Disneyland theme park concept and in the same year McDonald's to open its first fast-food restaurant. In Europe an understanding of consumer change led Centre Parcs to open its first village in Holland in 1968 and in the UK in 1987. However, soon after the start of the recent financial crisis in Europe the Greek government took steps to offer better prices to attract tourists by reducing levies on transport such as ferries; the waiving of landing and taking-off fees at airports outside Athens; and overall to bring down VAT from 11% to 6.5% on tourist accommodation.

Often the need to transform tourism businesses has been forced upon the industry because of the changes that have occurred in relation to consumer and market forces. Modern tourism

CULTURE
IS
GREAT
BRITAIN

ENJOY FREE ACCESS TO THREE OF
THE WORLD'S TOP FIVE MUSEUMS

British Museum
London

visitbritain.com

| Photograph 19.1 | The marketing of Great Britain, through emphasis on culture. |
| | *Source*: UK Government Departments, with kind permission |

marketing has emerged as a business reaction to changes in the social and economic environment, with the most successful companies or tourist bodies having provided the right organisational structure and product offering for the consumer or visitor. This relies as much upon an approach or attitude to business, or the market, as it does to specific management expertise. Marketing is therefore initially a philosophy that relies on the art and science of different managerial approaches.

A survey of the literature reveals an account of the history of marketing and modern business practice as having developed in three distinct stages (adapted from Gilbert and Bailey, 1990):

1. **The production era.** This occurred when there was a belief that if products were priced cheaply enough they would be purchased. Therefore, it was important to supply products to the marketplace with the emphasis on consistently reducing costs. The focus of management was on increasing efficiency of production which involved an *inward, product-orientated* emphasis rather than an outward, market-orientated emphasis. The main focus for managers at the time was a concern for improving production capacity, financing expansion, having quality and cost control and meeting the rise in demand. The over-riding objective for management was the development of a standardised product which could be offered at the lowest price to the market. The market was characterised by a lack of problems with demand and as such managers focused on process and systems and not the customer. Nowadays, in destinations that have high demand, this approach on process, which ignores the importance of the customer, can be recognised in many aspects of the delivery of the tourism product.

2. **The sales era.** This was an evolutionary phase where companies attempted *to sell the products they had formulated without assessing the acceptability of the product or offer*. The problem is often one of a market with declining demand and surplus capacity, which in turn leads to a search for more effective means of selling. We can recognise this today in declining destinations where hotels or restaurants face greater competition, and there is often a shift to increase promotional and sales efforts to improve demand. However, there is little analysis as to the

reasons for the problems as the belief is that the product is acceptable. In the sales era companies attempted to influence demand and tailor it *to meet their supply* but primarily through simple sales techniques.

3. **The marketing era.** This era is characterised by a reversal of the preceding philosophy as organisations started to provide the products they had researched and knew they could sell, *rather* than trying to sell what they had simply produced or formulated. Organisations adopted a consumer-led approach and concentrated on improving the marketing mix. This era was effectively based upon the recognition that utilising a full range of marketing in meeting **customer needs** and providing **consumer satisfaction** proved the most *effective basis* for planning and that an organisation has to be *outward-looking* to be successful. The philosophy of this era is that tourism business activity has to recognise the customer as the central driving force of an activity that realises survival and prosperity is based upon meeting individual customer needs.

There are continuing arguments as to the dates of the above eras leading up to marketing as we need to understand it today. Moreover, some question whether they can be treated as discrete periods at all. For our purposes, in the majority of texts, the marketing era is identified to have been established from the 1950s onward. The interesting aspect of living in today's marketing era is that we can still find tourism companies which act as if they are in a preceding era. The important factors that have ushered in marketing during the past half-century are as follows:

- The increases in demand were at a lower rate than the rises in supply and production. In tourism, this culminated in an oversupply of accommodation in specific locations, and of aircraft seats on important routes as well as too many inefficient companies in the marketplace who could not survive with low levels of demand. The increase in competition and the risks associated with the tourism marketplace led to the realisation of the benefit of an increased use of marketing. In more graphic terms, the business system can be viewed as an organism that is concerned with survival and proliferation. Following this argument, when a business system is threatened it needs to take functional steps to improve the situation. As marketing can provide for tactical change and modification of the system, in times of risk where there is oversupply and market saturation, marketing assumes a much more important role.

- A number of consumers became more affluent in terms of discretionary income and therefore it was possible to develop products that could be sold using a range of non-price-sensitive attributes. This required the development of methods designed to create or change consumer attitudes and behaviour. An example of this is American Airlines development of a loyalty scheme – its AAdvantage scheme of frequent flying rewards – in 1981 in order to build repeat business, which was then copied by many other different tourism-based companies from hotels to restaurants.

- The distance between the tourism product provider and the tourist has been continually increasing due to increasing size of organisations. This led to a need for marketing research related to the gathering of information on market trends, evaluating levels of satisfaction and understanding consumer behaviour.

- New tourism and hospitality products were being launched which required more emphasis on marketing. For example, the large attractions that have been developed in different countries and the setting up of low-cost airlines have required high levels of demand to make them viable.

- As society developed, the mass market splintered into a number of sub-markets, while at the same time the mass market became increasingly difficult to reach. This was due to the increase in specialist media and the potential for a whole range of alternative leisure pursuits. The changes required improved expertise in the **segmentation** of markets and the provision of different marketing mix strategies which would maximise demand for individual segments.

# DEFINITIONS AND CONCEPTS OF MARKETING

Any conceptual definition of a business discipline is, by nature of its condensed form, a limited abstraction of values, techniques and practices which are the focus of its activity. Therefore, no single definition can be comprehensive enough to describe the true essence or complexity of marketing. Various definitions of marketing have been offered based upon the values prevalent at the time. A popular early definition utilised for many years stressed marketing as being a managerial process of providing the right product, in the right place, at the right time and at the right price. This definition is mechanistic and stresses the provision of the product offer without due regard to any of the actors or functions involved in the process.

No definition of marketing can ever disregard the importance of Philip Kotler. He has established himself as the most widely referenced proponent of general marketing theory. Kotler and Keller (2006) define marketing in a social context as: 'a societal process by which individuals and groups obtain what they need and want through creating, offering, and freely exchanging products and services of value with others'. Kotler argues that the definition has a social basis and is built on the main concepts of wants, needs, demands, satisfactions of marketing and marketers because they are central to the study of marketing. For Kotler and Keller, marketing management is, 'the art and science of choosing target markets and getting, keeping, and growing customers through creating, delivering and communicating superior customer value'. In 1984 the British Chartered Institute of Marketing defined marketing as: 'the management process responsible for identifying, anticipating and satisfying customers' requirements profitably'.

An examination of both definitions reveals significant core similarities. On comparison it is found that both stress marketing as a process. Such approaches provide a concept as one where the process is established by way of a marketing channel connecting the (tourism) organisation with its market. This is based upon management aiming to convert customer purchasing power into effective demand. In addition the British Chartered Institute clarifies the management responsibility to be one of assessment of consumer demand through the identification and anticipation of customer requirements. This denotes the importance of research and analysis as part of this process.

One important difference is that the Kotler and Keller definition is more appropriate to non-profit organisations where there is free entrance or subsidisation towards the cost of a service. It is also more fitting regarding facilitators of tourism such as tourist boards.

However, the most important aspect, and one that should be at the heart of any definition of marketing, is the emphasis placed on the consumer's needs as the origin of all of the organisation's effort. The **marketing concept** has been expressed in many succinct ways from the: 'Have it your way' from Burger King, to 'You're the boss' of United Airlines. This is the basis of the modern marketing concept whereby the principal means of success is based not only on identifying different consumer needs but also on delivering a tourist product whose experiences provide sets of satisfactions that are preferable to those of the competitors. In addition these satisfactions have to be delivered with attention to their cost-effectiveness, since marketing has to be evaluated on the basis of its efficiency of expenditure.

We have seen how the definitions of marketing lead to the marketing concept, whereby the consumer is the driving force for all business activities. Prior to the introduction and discussion about the notion of the marketing concept we will emphasise the aspects of delivering value prior to differentiating the principles and activities associated with marketing and selling.

## The concept of value within tourism

As mentioned above, the aspect of delivering superior value is an important part of the marketing management approach. This means companies have to find ways to ensure they optimise the delivery of value. As such there is a requirement for a way of uncovering the value sought by the customer, the development of that within the company and then the delivery of optimum value to the end customer (see Table 19.1).

| Table 19.1 | A system for delivering value | | |
|---|---|---|---|
| **Approaches** | **Uncovering value needs** | **Developing value** | **Delivering value** |
| **Gathering/analytical** | Data/feedback of company representatives, surveys, etc | Operations/customer interfaces and touch points | Logistics/product quality, service |
| **Organisational** | Interpretation of customer requirements and resultant expected organisational competencies | Training/motivation of staff and working with suppliers who also add quality | Improved attitudes and behaviour of employee interfaces |

The value of a tourism product incorporates a number of different aspects which include the perception of price, quality and image as well as the economic and social aspects of the consumer. Consumers of today have far more information with which to make comparisons between alternative offers. As we are dealing with perceptions, these will differ as they are based upon the available time individuals have to carry out comparisons. No one company projects a single image as this is a multi-attribute concept. Also, some individuals have a wide network of acquaintances and may consult alternative information sources in making a decision about what offer delivers more value than another. This means perceptions of value will fluctuate within the population.

Product perceived value is based upon:

- Actual price asked and the relativity to prices for the same or similar product offered elsewhere.
- Perceived quality, service and image associated with the brand/product.
- Convenience of purchasing method or channel, and its congruence to the needs of the customer.
- Consumer difficulty in ability to assess the benefits/relative price of the product.
- Experience associated with the purchase or consumption process.

It will be seen from the last point in the list above that the focus on any judgement of value for money will include intrinsic aspects, so that either the purchase itself as a pre-trip activity or the actual tourism experience can be treated as being of value for its own sake. For example, an experiential perspective may include the symbolic, hedonic and aesthetic aspects of the consumption process. This means that practical consumer judgement has to include hedonic criteria, based on an appreciation of the good or service for its own sake. As such, value can be based upon the thinking and feeling dimensions of purchase and consumption behaviour. Consumption by value criteria is based upon a multiplicity of inputs which contribute in varying ways to consumer judgement in different choice situations. In fact, tourism can be thought of as producing a **total tourist experience** that will include everything from the pre-planning, the purchase, the journey, the visit/and perhaps stay, the return journey and overall reflection on the activity. This total tourist experience involves all aspects of the offering and experience which provide sets of satisfaction and dissatisfactions related to the whole episode. Marketing has to consider all these aspects to ensure that value and satisfaction is judged to be above the tourist's expectation. A good overall experience will culminate in the tourist being an advocate for a company or destination and lead to the telling of others of their experience in a positive way.

If we consider the early success of McDonald's, the value is not simply the hamburger or fries, it is the way the service, cleanliness and speed of food production has provided an added value to the food. McDonald's customers are made up of a whole series of segments who value a fast, light and reasonably priced meal. This is all achieved by means of a great deal of planning and understanding. The company sets itself (and its franchisees) a series of high standards to achieve, which is known internally as 'QSCV'. QSCV is Quality, Service, Cleanliness and Value and provides a defined target area of value delivery for its operations. This is only one aspect that is important in the running of the company. The marketplace is dynamic and therefore McDonald's has had to renew itself constantly by introducing new menu items, which fit with the values of health and nutrition, in order to react to the changing market environment.

In order to deliver value through the delivery of lower prices the low-cost airlines need to keep operating costs significantly lower than the 'traditional' scheduled airlines in order to be successful in the niche they have selected. This is achieved through specific marketing measures such as direct booking by use of the Internet and lower costs by means of ticketless travel and online check-in rather than use of travel agents; a high utilisation of aircraft whereby time on the ground is reduced; use of cheaper secondary airports; and reduction in variable costs by not offering free meals on board.

Understanding the overall experience from a marketing perspective is extremely important. However, the marketing concept – where the consumer is the driving force for all business activities – must not be confused with a sales approach. The next section ensures that difference is understood and then we will introduce you to the notion of marketing orientation.

## THE DIFFERENCES BETWEEN MARKETING AND SELLING

By now it should be obvious to the reader that marketing and selling are not the same. This is not just a new account as, according to Drucker (1973: 64):

> Selling and marketing are antithetical rather than synonymous or even complementary. There will always, one can assume, be a need for some selling, but the aim of marketing is to make selling superfluous.

The contrast between the sales and marketing approaches highlights the importance of marketing planning and analysis related to customers and the marketplace. The sales concept focuses on products and uses selling and promotion to achieve profits through sales volume. The underlying weakness is that the sales concept does not necessarily satisfy the consumer and may only culminate in short-term, rather than long-term, company success. The marketing concept focuses on customer needs and utilises integrated marketing to achieve profits through customer satisfaction (Figure 19.1).

## DIFFERENT BUSINESS PHILOSOPHIES

As we have seen, marketing is a business philosophy that places the consumer, and his or her needs, at the forefront of all activities. For example, it is known that business travellers want frequent and reliable transport systems with sensible timings of departure and arrival. They favour priority check-in and check-out facilities and efficient, good-quality staff. Business

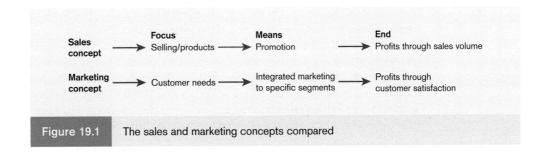

**Figure 19.1**    The sales and marketing concepts compared

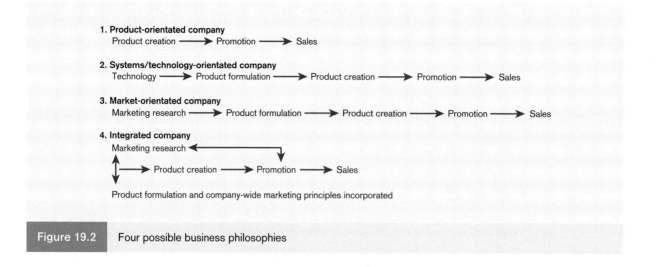

**1. Product-orientated company**
Product creation ⟶ Promotion ⟶ Sales

**2. Systems/technology-orientated company**
Technology ⟶ Product formulation ⟶ Product creation ⟶ Promotion ⟶ Sales

**3. Market-orientated company**
Marketing research ⟶ Product formulation ⟶ Product creation ⟶ Promotion ⟶ Sales

**4. Integrated company**
Marketing research ⟵
⟶ Product creation ⟶ Promotion ⟶ Sales

Product formulation and company-wide marketing principles incorporated

| Figure 19.2 | Four possible business philosophies |
| --- | --- |

travellers need to feel they can make their trips and have their meetings without any worry of delay or discomfort. Therefore, knowledge of business travellers' needs occurs only when someone takes care to identify those needs.

While it is important to recognise the importance of structuring any organisation so that its focus is upon the customer, a number of alternative philosophies can be identified (see Figure 19.2). Each of these philosophies acts as a guiding orientation and system of approaching the market, and while a product-led company may be less effective, it is still possible to identify such companies within the tourism sector.

It is important to understand the initial starting place within the chains of the individual systems in Figure 19.2, since this is the first stage in the sequence of events which clearly demonstrates the focus of the organisation's approach to effecting exchange relationships. Examples (1) and (2) can be ineffective because of problems encountered in having the wrong product for the market and, as a consequence, having to waste more resources on promotion and selling in order to achieve a sale. In these examples it is normal to find that organisations believe their products are acceptable, and that all that is required for sales to occur is the identification of prime markets and methods of selling. Such an approach to the marketplace by a destination, hotel or airline marketing department is characterised by an emphasis on pictures of empty bedrooms, bleak-looking buildings or the exterior of an aircraft. This product-led emphasis rather than one which stresses the benefits the consumer is seeking is still at the heart of a great deal of today's marketing. Quite often tourist promotional literature is devoid of scenes of tourists experiencing rest, enjoyment or good service. A product-focused philosophy is more acceptable when there is shortage or boom times, which are characterised by little competition. However, both the first two philosophies provide for inward-looking management, which concentrates on improvement within the company, rather than on outward-looking management, which concentrates on the consumer and emerging tourist needs. Pontins, which was launched in the UK in 1946, did not update its product, and more recently utilised heavy discounting due to the economic recession that led from the position of having 24 UK holiday camps and camps abroad in the 1970s to the collapse of its business when it went into administration in 2010. However, the Britannia hotel group bought Pontins with plans to improve the product offer.

Examples (3) and (4) in Figure 19.2 offer the ideal approach to organising business in the modern tourism marketplace. They are driven by research that creates an understanding of the consumer, the business and the marketplace. Research will be both secondary and primary. Information has to be collected from within and outside the company in order to establish a clear picture of the marketing environment. The integrated approach provides a sequence of events that commences with an understanding of the consumer, the competitors, the types of product that the company is capable of providing and a system that sensitises the whole organisation to a marketing orientation. The integrated system helps to ensure that methods of improving the satisfaction levels of the consumer are incorporated into each department's objectives.

Within the final two examples of company philosophy, it can be seen that the feedback process allows the marketing department to develop products as well as different forms of promotion that are right for the consumer. This establishes a more effective means of ensuring products are successful and that marketing budgets are used efficiently.

The tourism industry is spending vast sums of money on developing new attractions, improving products, building hotels and investing in technology. The only way for the risk level to be kept to a minimum is through the adoption of a marketing philosophy that provides products related to the needs of consumers.

However, all companies operate in a fiercely competitive environment that impinges upon the flexibility of management and company action. This should reinforce an approach whereby planning starts with the consumer and the market. This reflects the sovereignty of the consumer in the process. Such an approach has to be the correct strategy because it is the consumer who ultimately supports, through personal expenditure, tomorrow's tourism marketplace.

# MARKETING ORIENTATION

The dynamic nature of business activity has led to many different sales and marketing opportunities in the tourism industry. The industry has thrown off many of its traditional attitudes toward the customer. This has come about through the realisation of the importance of a marketing orientation. As such, five main areas can be identified, as follows.

1. **It is a management orientation or philosophy.** The focus of the organisation's effort is placed on the consumer as a set of guiding values, and this then leads to the customer being the centre of attention. These ideals should lead to a proactive approach in ensuring marketing efforts optimise exchange transactions within which consumers feel they have been rewarded with value and satisfaction. When customers' needs are met they are more likely to return to the cruise line, tour operator, hotel or restaurant, and, more importantly, to let others know of their satisfaction. There is the recognition that the conduct of the organisation's business must revolve around the long-term interests and satisfactions of the customers it serves. This is an outward-looking orientation which requires responsive action in relation to external political, economic, social or technological events, and competitive actions.

2. **It encourages exchange to take place.** This involves the attitudes and decisions of consumers in relation to the willingness to buy from producers or distributors. As the marketplace becomes more competitive, strategies to strengthen an existing customer base have become increasingly important in tourism as it has been recognised that long-term relationships with existing customers are less expensive to maintain than forever attempting to attract new customers. If a close long-term relationship can be achieved, the possibility is that customers are more likely to provide higher purchase patterns and lower marketing costs per customer. While the objective of marketing is to achieve enduring relationships with the customer it should also be recognised that, in some situations, short-term sales (i.e. transaction marketing) may be just as important when there is little likelihood that the customer will be a repeat purchaser. As such marketers have to develop innovative methods to encourage both exchange transactions as well as retention.

There is the need to ensure the service offers value for money, which may mean there is a requirement for creating a range of benefits over time. This has led to loyalty schemes and what is known as 'relationship marketing' (RM). Relationship marketing is an approach whereby marketers attempt to retain the customer over longer periods of time through club or loyalty programmes such as hotel, car rental or airline frequent flyer programmes. This is based upon the organisation becoming more involved with the customer as part of relationship marketing as opposed to the idea of concentrating on only a single sale or transaction (Table 19.2).

| Table 19.2 | The difference between transaction and relationship marketing |

| Transaction marketing | Relationship marketing |
| --- | --- |
| Short-term orientation: sale as end result | Long-term orientation: the sale is only the beginning |
| 'Me' orientated | 'We' orientated |
| Focus on achieving a sale | Focus on retention and repeat sales |
| Emphasis on persuasion to buy | Stress on creating positive relationships |
| Need to win, manipulation | Providing trust and service |
| Stress of conflict of achieving a new transaction and maximising benefits to own company | Partnership and cooperation to minimise defection and provide longer-term relationships (with customers or strategic alliances, joint ventures, vendor partnering, etc.) |
| Anonymous customer won by conquest in a carefully planned event but with no follow-up | Individual profile of customer known so that a continuing process of targeted communication and offers can emerge |

As part of the analogy, the RM process is available to advance relationships to higher levels of loyalty until a status is achieved whereby the customer is not only loyal but also advocates the company, the employees and service to others. RM should not be confused with brand loyalty based upon simple commitment to the product, as RM is far more complex. The rationale for RM is that it makes business sense to focus on long-term financial benefits that can accrue once a customer has been won for the first time. This is because it has been estimated to be five to ten times more expensive to recruit a new customer than to retain an existing one. Therefore, there is importance placed upon the **retention** of a customer with commercial consideration of the lifetime value of customers based upon quantity of repeat purchases. Such an approach enables the costs of acquisition and conversion of the prospect to be set against the revenues earned over the longer term. In an effective scheme sales and profits improve in direct proportion to the length of the relationship.

In relationship marketing customers will represent a diverse set of purchasing and spending patterns. However, it is important to be able to make marketing decisions which reflect the worth and potential of any one customer over a period of time. The analysis which allows this is known as **lifetime value** (LTV). Lifetime value, related to a frequent flyer programme or similar tourism loyalty scheme, allows for the measurement of the total worth to the organisation of its relationship with a particular identified customer over a period of time. This is based upon the time-related income and costs of that individual adjusted so that the future amounts are discounted in order to provide a net present value worth of the individual. Therefore, in order to make a calculation of LTV the company has to capture or estimate the costs and revenues of each relationship. The costs will be related to the acquisition, communication and any rewards or incentives given during any one year. The analysis of a frequent hotel guest or frequent flyer will reveal the profile of customers who provide high returns as well as those who are costly for the company to service. The LTV information will allow for improved decision making based upon assessing the asset value of each customer regarding:

- The assigning of appropriate acquisition allowances to attract the higher-spending customers. The profile of these individuals is utilised to identify and segment the targeting strategy.

- Improving media strategies in order to acquire higher LTV individuals. Database analysis will provide information as to the optimal allocation of marketing communications budgets to alternative media in recruitment campaigns.

- Providing selection policies for customer marketing programmes. LTV analysis will allow a division of customers into graded levels of worth to the company. This allows for different rewards and privileges to be given to the different levels or categories of customer. It also allows for the cutback in communication for those individuals who represent only break-even or loss when marketing costs are taken into consideration.

- Which individuals to contact and reactivate from the lapsed category. The database can identify the timing and worth of purchases made by individuals. If a previously higher-spending individual indicates lapsed behaviour a 'win-back' policy may be triggered. Such a reactivation allowance can be allocated based upon the likely return of the individual and their future revenue potential.

The use of data mining based upon customer records allows for the determination of the optimal level of investment in future marketing activities. Such measurement by customer can provide knowledge of purchase, purchase frequency and timing of demand.

3. **It involves long and short-term planning.** This requires the systematic organisation of strategic planning and tactical activity. In the short term an organisation does not normally have the flexibility to change rapidly even if the marketplace warrants this. The physical infrastructure of a hotel building, the skills of the workforce and other production capabilities can often only be changed marginally. Therefore, in the short term the constraints of earlier planning will restrict the choice a company or resort area may have. Because of the short-run constraints one aspect of planning which increases in importance to capacity risks is the control mechanisms for the monitoring of performance against targets. The long-term success of an organisation requires the efficient use of resources and assets, while tactical action will be required to keep plans on course. IT systems offer the opportunity to model demand and take tactical action at the earliest opportunity to sell unsold inventory or expand supply.

4. **It requires efficient, cost-effective methods.** Marketing's principal concern within any organisation has to be the delivery of maximum satisfaction and value to the customer at acceptable or minimum cost to the company so as to ensure long-term profit. The use of resources within marketing has to be both efficient and effective. The trend in the use of relationship marketing to build closer bonds and better retention with valued customers who provide repeat business is more effective than treating all customers as equal. However, in many organisations, the dilemma is that management is often judged by short-term success in relation to sales and profit performance and this places less emphasis on longer-term investment in marketing.

5. **It requires the development of an integrated company environment.** The organisation's efforts and structure must be matched with the needs of the target customers. Everybody working for the organisation must participate in a total corporate, marketing environment with each division maximising the satisfaction level of consumers. Integration is not just a smile or politeness. Barriers to serving the customer well have to be removed. The onus is on the organisation to provide organisational structures that are responsive and able to undergo change to suit customer needs. Such an environment has to be based upon a culture of customer-focused adaptation.

## TOURISM AS A SERVICE PRODUCT

With tourism, hospitality and leisure products we are dealing with a **service product** that has specific characteristics which set the product apart from the more general goods sold in the marketplace. An understanding of the complexity of the service product concept is an essential prerequisite for successful tourism marketing. This is because the emphasis is increasingly placed on the service provider to develop a deeper understanding of the linkages that correspond to consumer benefits sought and the nature of the service delivery system itself.

A starting point is an examination of the dimensions and characteristics of the service product concept. Products can be placed along a continuum of services and goods, with most products being a combination of the two. A pure service would be consultancy or teaching whereas a pure good would be a can of beans or clothing. Some products will have more service content than others, and if they are able to be placed to the left-hand side of the continuum shown in Figure 19.3, they may be termed service products.

Products

| Service | Good |
|---------|------|
| ← | → |
| Intangibility | More tangible |
| Perishability | Often storable |
| Inseparability | Standardisable |

| Figure 19.3 | Services and goods continuum |
|-------------|------------------------------|

## The characteristics of the service product

### Intangibility

The service product has the characteristic of **intangibility**, which means it cannot be easily evaluated or demonstrated in advance of its purchase. For example, a travel agent cannot allow the testing or sampling of the tourism product or a sales representative for a hotel cannot take anything but secondary material to a sales call meeting. On the other hand, a car or computer game can be tested prior to purchase, and clothing can be tried on. Much of the selling of tourism and hospitality is related to the promise of safe and timely delivery of the individual by transport companies, or comfort and good service by accommodation companies. Only a ticket, voucher or Internet reservation number is exchanged at the time of purchase. The marketers of tourism and hospitality products, therefore, face greater difficulty as the sale is based upon a promise of future benefit. Because of fixed time and space constraints staff cannot easily demonstrate the benefits of the products they are selling. The problem for the tourism service marketer is overcome by the production of a range of printed literature, videos or other means of providing cues as to the type of product on offer in an attempt to increase tangibility. In addition, there is a need to ensure marketing provides clear and well-managed branding of accommodation, transport and distribution organisations. This positions the brand name more tangibly in the mind of the consumer, in addition ensuring that the tangible aspects related to uniforms, decor and physical evidence give cues as to the quality of the service. These final points are important as marketers need to realise that there is a distinction which should be made between the degree of intangibility of the actual service and the intangibility, or lack of physical evidence, surrounding the process of this service delivery. The airline industry is an example of this where the physical evidence represents a major component of the service because the service performance characteristics of staff are supported largely by means of tangible elements such as food and drink, the cabin configuration and comfort of the seat, in-flight entertainment system, etc.

### Perishability

The characteristic of **perishability** means that service products such as tourism, unlike goods, cannot be stored for sale on a future occasion. For example, a hotel bed or an airline seat unsold or a convention centre left empty is revenue that can never be recouped. This leads to the high-risk nature of the tourism industry. Perishability is also linked to the seasonality of demand whereby some companies or destinations have high and low periods of demand and in low periods the problem of perishability is exacerbated. Marketers in the tourism and hospitality sector have to devise complex pricing and promotion policies in an attempt to sell during 'off-season' periods and create greater synchronisation of staffing levels and supply to match demand patterns. Weak demand is not the only problem as the sector is characterised by hotels, airlines, attractions, museums, galleries, etc., all of which have fixed capacity with a maximum upper level demand constraint. In peak periods the industry often has difficulty in coping with demand and therefore charges premium prices or uses queuing as a control mechanism, but in the low periods there is a need for greater marketing activity. The reaction to perishability is for marketers to try to smooth out demand curves by careful use of the marketing mix: for example, cheaper tickets for a matinee show. There is also a concentration on the use of computerised reservation systems in order to forecast the need for tactical action if demand is believed to be below expected levels, and of specialist websites to sell off last-minute availability.

### Inseparability

Service products are often referred to as having **inseparability,** which means the product is often consumed and produced simultaneously. This means that both the service provider and customer are present when the service function occurs. Because there is less opportunity to manage and pre-check a tourism or hospitality product, it can vary in the standard of its service delivery. This is sometimes characterised by authors as *heterogeneity* or *variability*. The tourism sector offers an amalgam of services which make up the delivery of the product. This occurs in a fragmented system where different organisations may have responsibility for the level of service delivery. Even for a single service such as air travel there will be the travel agent, airport checking-in agent and staff, airline staff, catering company, baggage handling staff, cabin cleaning staff, all of whom provide the single continuous flight experience. Variance occurs because of the inseparable nature of the product's delivery when the customer is part of the production system. The simultaneous process of production and consumption can lead to situations where it is difficult to ensure the overall satisfaction of consumers. For example, peak demand load cannot always be forecast and may create dissatisfaction by way of secondary problems of lack of staffing. There is also the potential problem of having groups or types of clients with conflicting needs that may result in disharmony. A couple wanting a quiet romantic anniversary dinner in a restaurant could find the evening unacceptable if a group of the local football club's supporters decide to eat at the same time. Whether on the aircraft, in the hotel, or in the restaurant there could be the clash of social values, noisiness, drunkenness, high spirits or a child crying. Staff may also have had personal problems or be feeling ill or tired, and this can affect their level of commitment to their performance of giving good service or resolving problems.

As the nature of the tourism service product is largely one of interpersonal relationships, where the performance level of staff is directly related to the satisfaction and overall experience of the consumer, there is a need for quality assurance programmes. Staff are emotional and changeable and if a high content of the product is based upon interpersonal relationships between 'strangers', as guest and service provider, it is important to ensure standardised service levels are adhered to. Quality assurance is important as a basis of planning for competitive advantage and controlling the standards of staff interactions. To reduce the problems that can be associated with inseparability there is a need for investment in company training programmes for all service staff and policy standards as to service delivery requirement.

## Other aspects of tourism as a service product

1. **Shorter exposure to service delivery.** The customer's exposure to the delivery of the service is normally of short duration. This allows only a limited time during which company personnel can build a relationship and effect repeat business.

2. **More personal.** The human aspect of 'self' is very much involved emotionally in the service encounter and as such the personal feelings created by contact service personnel are an important determinant of future demand. Therefore, it is important to recruit staff for personal qualities and then train for skills as such qualities are not easy to develop through training.

3. **Growing use of self-service.** To reduce costs and provide more timely service companies are more likely to introduce self-service buffet meals, Internet reservation technology etc. rather than interpersonal service alternatives. This requires the customer to handle the self-service process or technology appropriately and for the service not to be so complicated that there is any danger of negative consequences. An important consideration for companies using self-service processes and technology is the potential lack of personal interaction between the service employee and the customer which allows the opportunity to exceed customer service expectations.

4. **Greater significance on managing evidence.** Due to the intangible nature of the tourism product it is important to plan to deliver cues as to the positioning and quality of the offer by means of cleanliness, decor, uniforms, signage style, etc.

5. **Complementarity is greater.** The overall tourism product is often made up of an amalgam of many different services, all of which has to add up to an overall positive experience. Destinations are aware that they have to control service quality to ensure a satisfactory experience and therefore attempt to regulate tourism providers.

6. **Easier copying of services.** Services can be benchmarked and copied by other organisations due to their visibility.

# TOURISM PRODUCTS AND RISK

Tourism products are important in relation to the type of marketing they require. Tourism has developed rapidly over the past few decades, led by a marketing thrust which has created diversity of supply, focused on important consumer segments and stimulated high levels of demand. Within this development marketing has often concentrated more on improving the product than on understanding the consumer and the complexity of his or her decision processes. As uncertainty is part of the process of purchase and consumption this is often associated with personal reservations and a judgement of **perceived risk**.

A major aspect of consumer behaviour, linked to the purchase of tourism products, is the notion of risk and a consumer's judgement about the likelihood of a problem occurring. Tourism products often involve a complex decision-making process because the purchase is of relatively high risk and high involvement. However, the concept is complex given that throughout the population the threshold at which an individual perceives *economic*, *physical*, *performance* and *psychological* risk differs by age, income and experience. The concept is also related to individual feelings of uncertainty based upon the subjective possibility of any occurrence of the following types of risk.

## Economic risk

Economic risk is associated with the decision for potential tourists as to whether the product offer is of good value or not. Given the range of prices offered for short-haul flights from both no-frills and scheduled carriers there is frequently some uncertainty as to which airline to book with and which price to pay. All consumers face economic or financial risk when they purchase tourism products given that they cannot be sure whether their choice will deliver the benefits they desire. Tourism often involves the purchase of an expensive product, such as the annual holiday, that cannot easily be seen or sampled prior to consumption. This type of risk is heightened for those with low levels of disposable income, for whom the purchase represents a major expenditure and will be associated with a high level of involvement in the travel decision.

## Physical risk

Some overseas destinations may be perceived as dangerous owing to disease or crime, and some transport companies such as ferry or airline operators are thought to be safer than others. The fear of an illness such as SARS or travelling at the time of war or civil unrest is a clear indication of this concept. Some people fear flying no matter what airline they fly with, while others may reduce the perception of physical risks by selecting certain 'safer' airlines. A study by Lepp and Gibson (2003) based upon a random sample of US-born young adults found that there are seven important risk factors: health, political instability, terrorism, strange food, cultural barriers, a nation's political and religious dogma, and crime. Analysis revealed that the more experienced tourist was less likely to be concerned about terrorism. It was also found that there is a difference by gender in that women perceived a greater degree of risk regarding health and food. However, tourist role was the most significant variable, with familiarity seekers being the most risk-averse.

## Performance risk

The quality of different destinations or unknown hotel brands cannot be assessed in advance. This type of risk is associated with feelings that the product may not deliver the desired benefits. There may be substandard service encounters at airports, as part of the travel experience, at the accommodation, or any of the aspects of tourist supporting services. It is rarely possible for those who have had a bad holiday to make up for it by attempting to have another better holiday in the same year. Most consumers do not have the additional money or holiday entitlement to make good the holiday that went wrong. This heightens their awareness of the risk factors involved. One important performance risk for UK travellers is weather. The risk of poor weather while holidaying in the UK is one reason why many people travel abroad.

## Psychological risk

Status can be lost through visiting the 'wrong' country because it has no status in the minds of others, or travelling with a company that has a poor image. This risk occurs when the potential customer feels the purchase may not reflect the self-image he or she wishes to portray. This may be connected to social risk or sense of well-being, which suggests there could be a loss of social status due to the act of purchasing from a company that has a poor image. The travel to an unknown destination may also be associated with stress based upon how different the new environment may be to that of the home destination.

From a marketing point of view, the above perceptions of risks need to be minimised through product and promotion strategies. Creating and delivering information in brochures and leaflets that helps to convince the potential traveller of the reliability of the company will lessen the perception of risk. However, it is important to realise that communications by word of mouth, whereby a friend reassures another about a purchase, is a more powerful source than company-controlled literature. By acquiring information the consumer builds up mental pictures and attitudes that create the expectation of positive benefits from the travel or destination experience.

In order to achieve positive word of mouth and to create advocates for the company or a country it is important for the quality of the product to be controlled especially in relation to the process of all encounters of service delivery.

# PLANNING THE SERVICE ENCOUNTER

If we examine a systems perspective that identifies the linkage between the consumer's needs and the service delivery, we can be more aware of the management principles associated with service products. This can also be utilised in the establishment of benchmark points against which the service can be positioned.

A well-positioned service enables the organisation to achieve the following two important objectives:

- to differentiate its position so as to distinguish itself from competitors; and
- to deliver service superior to that accepted as the norm.

The above objectives allow the organisation to plan and build competitive advantage by establishing leadership principles of service standards and delivery. Once the standards are established there should be a policy to communicate and reinforce the service provision philosophy at every possible opportunity: meetings, training and internal marketing programmes, induction programmes and appraisal systems. The human resource function needs to be organised so as to ensure the different levels in Figure 19.3 are always clearly understood and reinforced through organisational culture and reward. Often services are managed on the subjective opinions of managers, when they should be based upon objective designs to ensure there is no confusion as to what needs to be achieved. Without good internal organisational procedures and relationships it is unlikely that even the best conceived of quality programmes will be successful.

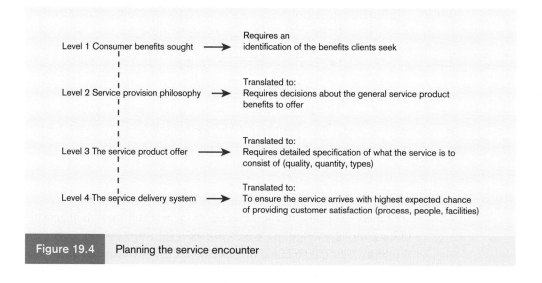

| | |
|---|---|
| Level 1 Consumer benefits sought ⟶ | Requires an identification of the benefits clients seek |
| Level 2 Service provision philosophy ⟶ | Translated to: Requires decisions about the general service product benefits to offer |
| Level 3 The service product offer ⟶ | Translated to: Requires detailed specification of what the service is to consist of (quality, quantity, types) |
| Level 4 The service delivery system ⟶ | Translated to: To ensure the service arrives with highest expected chance of providing customer satisfaction (process, people, facilities) |

**Figure 19.4**    Planning the service encounter

The levels shown in Figure 19.4 illustrate the linkages for designing a successful service delivery process. For the model to be successful the implementation process must consider the need for the following:

- Leadership and commitment by senior management based upon clear goals and a policy on quality being established and communicated to employees. There is also the need to release the appropriate resources to create changes and achieve the required results.

- All changes and objectives to be defined by the customer. All the approaches related to quality delivery and standards have to be delineated in all of the dimensions of the service delivery with reference to what customers value. What customers expect and value should consequently be incorporated into the company induction and training programmes.

- The organisation having the flexibility to change and improve service. This requires a process and systems approach to match or exceed customer expectations. Such a system may incorporate a quality audit system which applies measurement and inspection to ensure defects are corrected and the system delivers optimum quality results.

- Effective human resource management to hire those with service competencies and inclinations and then to motivate, train and educate staff to deliver the concepts of quality. This is reinforced through teamwork values and a culture that champions quality product delivery as a prerequisite for competitive advantage.

- An assessment to be made of the added value and benefit of any change rather than there being a simple cost-cutting and price-leadership strategy. The long-term benefits of any change need to be the focus of service encounter decision making.

- Quality audits and control to ensure the service meets or exceeds customer expectations.

It is crucial that an organisation creates its own quality management culture and does not simply attempt to clone a system used by a competitor. A successful service encounter approach requires honest two-way communication between management and staff which will build confidence in the implementation process. This means that staff members have to be allowed to own up to weaknesses and problems of poor quality in a supportive atmosphere where the organisation attempts to learn from weaknesses rather than to punish staff. Such methods create teamwork, confidence and commitment. However, there is also the need for competence to deliver the changes. This may require further training and seminars for staff and follow-up sessions. The recognition that there is a need to treat other members of staff as internal customers will assist the transition to a **total quality management** (TQM) system.

It is obvious that organisations have customers from within as well as without. With this in mind, if employees visualise the relationships between each other based upon supplier and customer links as a quality chain, then the question is always, 'Am I meeting the full requirements of my role?' For example, the secretary is a supplier to the boss with the need to provide timely error-free work in order to aid him or her as supplier to his or her internal customer. An organisation, therefore, is a web of internal suppliers and customers. Such chains are easily weakened or broken by faulty equipment or by fallible people. The important issue is that an internal quality chain failure will ultimately have some effect on the external customer.

# QUALITY MANAGEMENT

We cannot adequately describe the management of tourism without touching on the importance of the growing emphasis on quality management. There are four main reasons that can account for the growing relevance of quality management:

1. Organisations need to find ways of creating differential advantage by having better service levels than their competitors.

2. The increased level of consumerism and the greater media attention on quality has meant organisations have to be more responsive to quality issues. Consumers are far more aware of their rights and are less likely to suffer quietly from the results of poor quality.

3. There has been a growing sophistication of consumer markets, with the non-price factors of image, product positioning and service delivery strategies becoming more important.

4. More recently technology is one of the new applications to quality enhancement. Technology can aid service by providing higher levels of convenience, for example automatic vending or ticketing machines, pre-payment systems, or SMS mobile phone applications.

It is important for the quality of the product to be controlled, especially in relation to the process of service delivery. This is because relative quality between service providers or retailers has implications for market share and profitability. Quality is therefore one of the key components that contribute to a successful strategy. Quality has emerged as a major competitive component of a service organisation's strategy. However, when we examine the employment of the term 'quality', there is almost a superabundance of the use of this word in relation to the way management operates. There is a crusade for quality management and improvement within industry worldwide and the campaign for improved quality was rooted in the manufacturing industry prior to the adoption into the service industry. However, many individuals in the industry are still unaware of the theoretical grounding of quality management. Such management has to consider core and peripheral services which need to be developed and delivered after a careful diagnosis of customer expectations and perceptions.

## What are the key terms for quality?

There are several key concepts related to quality. Quality is the totality of relationships between service providers (functional aspects) and the features of the product (technical aspects) which are related to the delivery of satisfaction. It is therefore important to create systems of **quality control** which are checks and monitoring to ensure measurement of service delivery is taking place. To this end TQM is a holistic organisational approach which systematically attempts to enhance customer satisfaction by focusing on continuous improvements without incurring unacceptable cost increases. These improvements are part of an unending quest for excellence in all aspects of quality service delivery. Therefore, TQM has to form the values and mindset for all employees, which leads to quality being an integrated element of corporate culture. For success, quality must be the concern of all employees and the culture, therefore, should not be based upon a departmental or technical understanding of quality. Instead, the notion of quality must be disseminated to employees within the organisational structure and implemented as a systematic process extending throughout the organisation. The focus of any change in quality must be based upon external customer expectations and not internal organisational ideas.

TQM is managed by **quality assurance** arrangements whereby a system is instituted to allocate responsibility for planned and systematic activities that will ensure the product will provide the right levels of satisfaction to all concerned. A service guarantee system can provide more quality control and data capture in an organisation. This facilitates a better understanding of potential for improvement by capturing information on what is going wrong. Following this the information gathered on what goes wrong allows for a reaction in improvement of service. Some companies are now guaranteeing their service or paying out compensation with schemes such as flight delay insurance. A good service guarantee is identified as unconditional, easy to understand and communicate, meaningful, and easy to invoke in order to obtain recompense. But there is a need:

- not to promise something your customers already expect;
- not to shroud a guarantee in so many conditions that it is meaningless; or
- to offer a guarantee so mild that it is never invoked.

A guarantee can set clear standards and allow the company personnel to be clear about what the organisation stands for. If customers can complain easily, there is the benefit of collecting data on common problems that subsequently need to be addressed and eradicated. This is because a guarantee system forces the focus on why the failure occurred and what needs to be done about it to improve service quality. Moreover, a guarantee adds credibility and weight to the marketing effort of the organisation. It allows for a communication of the presence of the guarantee which may lead to a reduction in the perception of risk associated with purchase and can lead to higher levels of demand.

As a measure of whether the quality delivery complies with the planned delivery of the service a quality audit needs to take place to judge the effectiveness of the total service delivery arrangements. For a system to be audited correctly there is a need for a method of creating unbiased feedback. While a range of aspects of quality can be assessed, a number of categories exist. These may include the following, which are based upon various research that attempted to establish categories of service quality determinants:

- **Tangibles.** This will include physical evidence of the service, such as physical aspects of airline cabins, hotel bedrooms and facilities, or material the customer can see, touch, use etc., like equipment, merchandise, personnel, for example:
  - physical facilities such as extra legroom on the aircraft or size of hotel room;
  - appearance of personnel and condition of the surroundings;
  - technology or equipment used to provide the service;
  - physical representation of the service (e.g. airline loyalty card);
  - other customers in the service facility.

- **Reliability.** This involves consistency of performance and dependability. Gaining the customer's confidence is vital in service organisations. The ability of the service provider to establish a relationship of trust and faith greatly influences perceived service quality. A company should perform the service right the *first time* in order to achieve a good reputation. In many circumstances reliability is an expected dimension, as an airline should deliver this as a core service. It means the firm should honour its promises and have the ability to trust employees with the responsibility to deliver service consistently and accurately which meets policy standards, such as:

  - accuracy in a bill or charging;
  - collecting and keeping the correct records;
  - assuring confidentiality and security of any personal data held;
  - performing the service at designated time (e.g. delivery of opening or departure time promise).

- **Responsiveness.** This refers to the willingness or readiness of employees to provide service, their reaction and willingness to help customers and give timely service, such as:
  - providing complimentary drinks for a delayed flight;
  - mailing a transaction slip or sending an email or SMS text immediately;
  - calling a customer back quickly after a query or problem;
  - giving prompt service (e.g. arranging a change of itinerary, or reacting to the hotel guest's request).

- **Competence.** This concerns knowledge and courtesy of employees as well as the peace of mind that the company is to be trusted. This then delivers the assurance that employees will have the knowledge, skills and courtesy to create trust and confidence in the customer base, for example:
  - knowledge and skill of the contact personnel;
  - explaining the actual and wider service available;
  - the reputation of the organisation;
  - personal characteristics of the contact personnel;
  - confidentiality, financial and personal security.

- **Empathy.** This relates to the individualised attention to customers, the caring, individual concern and attention for others and their emotions, such as:
  - recognising and relating to regular customers;
  - learning the customer-specific requirements;
  - providing individualised service (customisation or personalisation is regarded as an essential attribute of service offerings due to the ability to tailor offers to customer-specific requirements).

The elements that could be assessed in the above could also include availability of items the customer demands; after-sales service and contact; the way telephone orders and queries are handled by contact centres; the reliability and safety of the product being sold; availability of sales literature and brochures; the number and type of items that can be demonstrated; technical knowledge of staff; the way an employee deals with a complaint, etc. In addition the organisation can use the above list as a means to assess the way in which it could develop its positioning strategy in order to distinguish itself from its competitors.

Table 19.3 indicates some of the ways in which quality can be assessed. It is important to realise that whatever system is used to audit quality at the end of the day anything which is not measured cannot be easily controlled.

Given the nature of tourism as a people-based industry with employee performance and interaction being of paramount importance, then we are dealing with a human activity where errors are inevitable. There is therefore a need to judge the benefit of increased usage and repeat

| Table 19.3 | Auditing systems |
| --- | --- |
| **Internal inspection** | **Auditing** |
| • Statistical process control based upon quality failure information and objective measures | • Internal auditors of quality<br>• External bodies |
| • Visual inspections to check against standards and consistency | • Consultants, regular users, non-user surveys and feedback |
| • Management by walking about | • Cross-department audits |
| • Quality control group feedback | • Mystery shoppers |
| • Inspection of competitors' offer and assessment of own company offer | • Content analysis of complaint and praise letters/emails and documented problems |
| | • Free telephone line feedback |

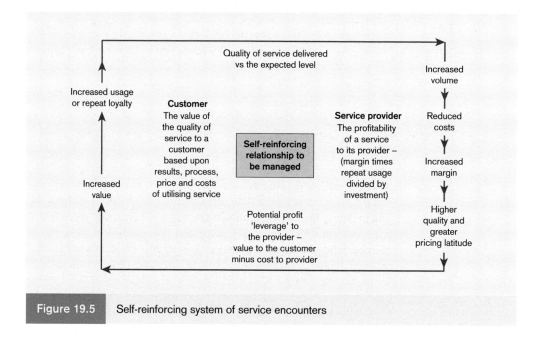

**Figure 19.5** Self-reinforcing system of service encounters

business as opposed to the loss of custom. The moment of truth or impact on the bottom line of any organisation is therefore the judgement by customers of the quality of its service. Figure 19.5 is based upon Hart, Heskett and Sasser (1990), who argue for the linkages of service encounters as creating a self-reinforcing mechanism. It indicates the relationship between the customer on the left and the service provider on the right. This overcomes the notion that improvement in quality is associated with increased costs. The model indicates that in the long-term true quality improvement leads to an improved trading position.

The above proposition is that a continuous improvement in service is not a cost but an investment in a customer who will return more profit in the long term. The premise is based upon research which indicates that the cost of acquiring a new customer is five times as high as retaining an existing customer through providing quality service. Such argument is based upon non-traditional accounting practices which stress that satisfied customers will be willing to pay higher prices owing to the service quality they have experienced and liked; there is a free advertising benefit due to the positive word-of-mouth recommendation; and there is a different cost in acquiring new customers as opposed to the benefit of retaining existing customers over longer time periods. Thus, in general, following the ideas of relationship marketing, it is suggested that to keep a customer over the long term provides important savings. On a cost–benefit basis good service quality is thought to increase revenue and reduce long-term costs.

Given that the cost of finding a new customer is far greater than that of retaining an existing one, there is growing emphasis on customer retention and relationship marketing as discussed earlier in this chapter, whereby long-term revenue can be enhanced by service recovery strategies. These include the following:

- **Training.** As service is an interpersonal performance activity then the provision of communication and customer relation skills will enhance the ability of staff to deal with the most difficult of situations. Perhaps more importantly, training will allow staff to feel confident in the service encounter transaction and allow them to deal professionally with all situations.

- **Watching for signals.** Allowing those customers who are reticent or quiet when it comes to complaints to break their silence. Organisations need the opportunity to prove their commitment to the customer through service quality measures. However, the silent customer who is not satisfied will escape company notice but may tell many acquaintances of the problem.

Some organisations provide free telephone lines for complainants or employee training to enable staff to watch, listen and report on any signals of a customer's dissatisfaction. Many organisations empower staff to provide remedial action if they suspect poor service has been experienced. Alternatively service may be tested with the use of mystery customers or satisfaction research studies.

- **Preplanning.** There is the need to analyse the service delivery process so as to anticipate those aspects of service that may exceed the tolerance level of customers. Times of peak demand or low levels of staffing may affect the judgement of the customer as to the overall level of service quality delivery. Staff can be asked to describe situations which if improved would lead to a more error-free service standard.

- **Empowerment.** A great deal of staff service delivery goes unsupervised. It is better if the front-line staff react quickly to service problem situations without the input of supervisors. The policy of identifying problems quickly and correcting them at the local level is far more effective than relying on official complaint systems or delays in a problem's resolution. A staff member who provides some extra means of satisfying a customer may allay a more difficult or serious situation. A long wait to be seated in a restaurant may be acknowledged by a reduction in the bill or free coffee. Empowerment provides an obligation to act in order to recover the situation which relies on trust of the front-line staff. This is in contrast to a system where the focus is on blame for a poor service encounter rather than timely resolution.

Good service recovery procedures allow a customer to refocus on the satisfactions received from the service delivery process rather than to question why corrective action was not taken. A problem tests the system and if a customer complaint is dealt with appropriately the customer is likely to become more loyal. If a formal complaint is made it should be treated *individually* according to the *urgency* of the complaint and customer's *value* to the organisation.

A complaint system must be in place for prompt and personal customer communication:

- to acknowledge the receipt of written/verbal complaints and to inform customers about the resolution;

| Photograph 19.2 | Service and service information are increasingly important in the product delivery. |
|---|---|

*Source*: Image Source/Alamy Images

- to keep customers fully informed with progress reports;
- to encourage customers to appeal to a higher authority within the company in case of a unsatisfactory initial resolution;
- to assign and authorise one department to be accessible at reasonable hours for complaint processing and review;
- to have a complaint system which is both user and staff friendly.

We can classify the different approaches to quality management into two categories: the product-attribute approach and the consumer-orientated approach (Gilbert and Joshi, 1992).

## The product-attribute approach

The product-attribute approach is based upon trying to match the product's conformance to standardised requirements which have been set by reference to what organisational managers think the failure point to be. Product-attribute approaches rely on trying to control the organisation's products using an internal product perspective. This relies on an inward-looking product-led approach.

## The consumer-orientated approach

It is therefore more appropriate to adopt a consumer-orientated approach which recognises that the holistic process of service delivery has to be controlled by taking into consideration the expectations and attitudes of tourism and hospitality clients. In tourism, an assessment of quality is made during the process of service delivery and this can be treated as an encounter between the customer, the service provider and the physical aspects of the place of delivery. The customer will judge the outcome of this encounter in terms of levels of satisfaction. If the starting point for management is the understanding of how quality is judged by clients then the perception processes of this judgement, as to whether a service is good or bad, can be managed. Gronroos is a leading author who has clarified this concept.

## The Gronroos model

Gronroos (1982) developed a model to explain what he called the 'missing service quality concept'. The model shown in Figure 19.6 focuses mainly on the construct of image, which represents the point at which a gap can occur between expected service and perceived service. Gronroos makes us more aware of the ways image is created from the aggregation of different aspects of technical and functional variables. By following his model of different inputs, we are alerted to the fact that we should not reduce quality to a simplistic description, but should try to understand the full range of inputs. This is because to speak just of quality gives the manager no indication of what aspects of the product should be controlled.

Gronroos argued that the function and range of resources and activities include what customers are looking for, what they are evaluating, how service quality is perceived and in what way service quality is influenced. He defined the 'perceived quality' of the service as dependent on two variables. These are 'experienced service' and 'perceived service' which collectively provide the outcome of the evaluation.

As part of his analysis, Gronroos distinguished between 'technical quality' and 'functional quality' as the components of the service image delivery:

- Technical quality refers to what the customer is actually receiving from the service. This is capable of objective measurement, as with tangible goods.
- Functional quality refers to how the technical elements of the service are transferred. We know that a customer in a restaurant will not only evaluate the quality of the food consumed but also the way in which it was delivered (the style, manner and appearance of the staff, or the ambience of the place itself). Figure 19.6 shows that the attitudes, behaviour and general service-mindedness of personnel can be influenced by management.

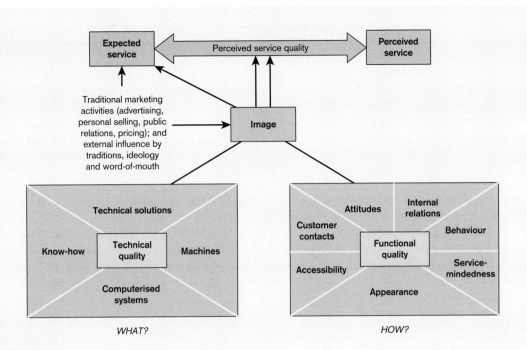

| Figure 19.6 | Managing the perceived service quality |
| --- | --- |
| | *Source*: Gronroos, 1982 |

## MINI CASE STUDY 19.1
### New York set for boom in gay weddings

*Financial Times*, 29 June 2011 by Shannon Bond

A champagne toast, a suite overlooking Fifth Avenue, an intricately crafted cake and a carriage ride through Central Park: all the elements of a classic New York wedding are included in a package the Pierre Hotel is marketing to gay couples following the legalisation of same-sex marriage. The luxury hotel is just one of many businesses advertising special deals timed to follow the state's landmark legislation – part of the city's global marketing campaign to sell New York as a gay wedding destination.

'We already had a package in mind when the city approached the hotel about its push,' said Nora Walsh, the Pierre's director of public relations. 'It was a great chance to get it out there right away. We wanted to make sure that everyone knows we're celebrating the age of modern marriage.'

New York's marriage equality act is likely to generate some $311m in revenue from weddings, tourism, taxes and licence fees for the state over the next three years, according to projections from the state senate's Independent Democratic Conference.

The city's hotels, wedding planners, caterers, photographers and other businesses are gearing up for a surge of interest following the passage of the legislation, which goes into effect in late July. 'We anticipate that the campaign, set to launch soon, will create hundreds of millions of dollars in additional economic impact to the city's $31bn tourism industry, and have a positive impact on tourism industry jobs,' said George Fertitta, the tourism bureau's chief executive. 'Every time a new state has legalised [gay] marriage, more people want to get into the business,' said Bernadette Smith, a wedding planner who specialises in ceremonies for gay clients. 'But New York is even more appealing to same-sex couples across the country because the origin of the modern gay civil rights movement is here.'

Carley Roney, editor in chief of The Knot, a wedding website, agreed. 'Yes, you can go to Vermont or New Hampshire or Massachusetts, states where gay marriage is already legal,' she said. 'It's just not as sexy as coming to New York City.' With the average cost of a wedding in New York running at more than $70,000, according to The Knot, a large proportion of that money will funnel to businesses in the city. In addition, as heterosexual marriage rates have stalled nationally, gay marriage carries the promise of expanding the market for the first time in two decades, Ms Roney said.

'The people who are high fiving themselves and chest bumping right now are the venues, which account for about half the total cost of a wedding,' she said. 'This is going to be a huge influx of money into caterers, hotels, reception halls, anyone who is in the venue rental business. That's where all the money goes.'

Smaller players in the wedding industry are also seeing a rush of interest. Annie Lawrence, an interfaith minister in Manhattan, has received about a dozen calls since Friday. 'The first couple to contact me was from Long Island. They've been together 19 years and already have the date booked,' she said. Recalling a British couple who spoke with her last month about a civil union in New Jersey, she said, 'I can't wait to tell them they can do it in New York instead.' Ms Lawrence also plans to contact couples for whom she has performed commitment ceremonies and invite them to come back to get legally married.

Ms Smith, the wedding planner, has been organising celebrations in Boston for more than seven years. When the measure came to a vote in the New York senate on Friday, she was ready. She opened an office in Manhattan and has started taking calls from excited couples – and from people looking for a job.

'I've been strategically stalking New York for a few years,' she said. 'The floodgates are opening and it's going to be a really exciting time.'

## DISCUSSION QUESTIONS

1. What are some of the future prospects for tourism given the changes in legislation where laws are allowing new marketing opportunities?

2. If you were designing a hotel website page for the above changes, which provide New York hotels with market opportunities, what brief would you give to a web design agency in order to achieve success?

3. Do you think there is a market for divorce celebrations for the hotel market – if so what marketing should be carried out to build this business?

### The Parasuraman, Zeithaml and Berry model

Parasuraman, Zeithaml and Berry (1985) also developed a model of service quality which claimed the consumer evaluates the quality of a service experience as the outcome of the difference (gap) between expected and perceived service (Figure 19.7). The model highlighted the main requirements for a service provider delivering the expected service quality. By understanding the flow of this model we believe it is possible to provide greater management control over tourist service relationships. This should lead to an improved realisation of the key points of influence on the satisfactions of the consumer.

From the model we can identify five gaps that may lead to unsuccessful service delivery.

1. **Gap between consumer expectation and management perception.** This may result from a lack of understanding of what consumers expect from a service.

2. **Gap between management perception and service quality specification.** This gap results when there is a discrepancy between what management perceives to be consumer expectations and the actual service quality specifications established. Management might not set quality standards or very clear ones, or they may be clear but unrealistic. Alternatively, the standards might be clear and realistic, but management may quite simply not be committed to enforcing them.

3. **Gap between service quality specifications and service delivery.** Even where guidelines exist for performing a service well, service delivery may not be of the appropriate quality owing to poor employee performance. Indeed, the employee plays a pivotal role in determining the quality of a service.

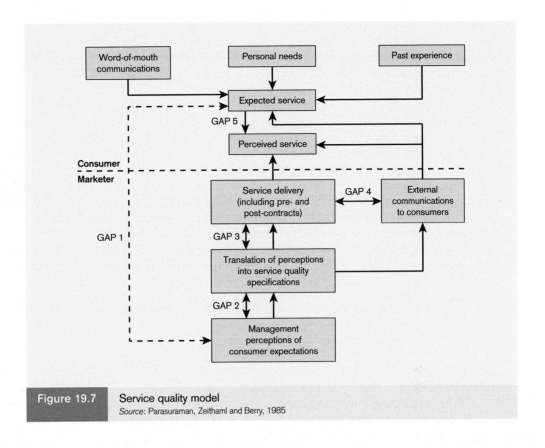

| Figure 19.7 | Service quality model |
|---|---|

Source: Parasuraman, Zeithaml and Berry, 1985

4. **Gap between service delivery and external communications.** Consumer expectations are affected by the promises made by the service provider's promotional message. Marketers must pay close attention to ensure consistency between the quality image portrayed in promotional activity and the actual quality offered.

5. **Gap between perceived service and delivered service.** This gap results when one or more of the previous gaps occur.

The focus on perceptions and expectations provides a guideline for quality management intervention strategies. To this end, on examining the model proposed by Parasuraman, Zeithaml and Berry, we believe that it has two main strengths to recommend it:

1. The model presents an entirely dyadic view of the marketing task of delivering service quality. The model alerts the marketer to consider the perceptions of both parties (marketers and consumers) in the exchange process. This can lead to many insights, such as that the company may be providing the over-delivery as well as the under-delivery of service in different areas.

2. Addressing the gaps in the model can serve as a logical basis for formulating strategies and tactics to ensure consistent experiences and expectations.

Employee performance is crucial to improving the quality of service delivery and perceived service quality. Internal marketing is a means by which companies can influence the interpersonal performance of staff. Providing promotional communications that lead staff to achieve high levels of customer care and service quality is becoming increasingly important. One poster targeted to staff read 'Good enough is not good enough', which sets the standards and aims of the company personnel above the average. This type of inward marketing provides a means to change the general attitudes of staff towards quality.

## Zone of tolerance

The **zone of tolerance** concept assumes that customers do not have expectations of a service attribute on one given level. Rather, they can tolerate a variation in their experiences and still consider them acceptable or not according to their preconceived expectations. This concept implies that customers' expectations exist on two levels, a desired level and an adequate level. The desired level reflects what level the service could be, whereas the adequate level is what customers believe it should be. The latter level is the least acceptable level of the service experience. Expectations of service delivery will obviously alter on the basis of each customer as within the delivery of services consumers will have different levels of tolerance. There is a parameter for a service zone of tolerance whereby the majority of customers will fall within a zone between the upper and lower desired and adequate levels of performance. This is not fixed as the area of the zone of tolerance can increase or decrease for individual customers depending on other variables such as alternatives provided by the competition, how much was paid and whether it represented value for money, or other differences in the company's service. It is also important to realise that there are differences between individual customers' perceptions; similarly each customer may have different expectations of one brand in comparison with another. For example, if Airline A has delivered more consistent service over time than Airline B then the expectations for the Airline A brand are higher. If Airline A service were to decline to the level consistently offered by Airline B, the customer may be more disappointed by the service received from Airline A – even though the service standards are similar.

# MANAGEMENT TASKS

A marketing orientation relies on a series of management responsibilities. To clarify the situation, marketing can be seen to provide for a business-to-customer or business-to-business interface with responsibility for specific management tasks. (These tasks are more clearly explained in Chapter 21 on the marketing mix.) However, it should be quite clear that tourism organisations without a proper commitment to a marketing orientation have little likelihood of effectively executing the marketing function.

The marketing function requires the combination of a number of related activities. Whether they are those involving staff, intermediaries or customers they are all focused on expediting transactions and relationships. The tasks itemised in Table 19.4 ensure that marketing will provide the functional inputs to deliver a sound basis for company activity. In addition this can be treated as a system which is designed to be an interface with the customer. This system is outlined in Figure 19.8.

| Table 19.4 | The business-to-customer interface |
| --- | --- |
| **Task** | **Marketing function** |
| 1. Identifying the customers' needs for a tourism-related product | → Marketing research and database analysis |
| 2. Analysing marketing opportunities | → Analysis and selection of target markets (segments) and understanding buyer/supplier relationships |
| 3. Translating needs into products | → Product planning and formulation |
| 4. Determining the product's value to the customer at different seasonal periods | → Pricing policy and creation of value delivery |
| 5. Making the product available | → Distribution policy and planning |
| 6. Informing and motivating the customer | → Promotion (communicating, advertising, sales effort and relationship scheme) |

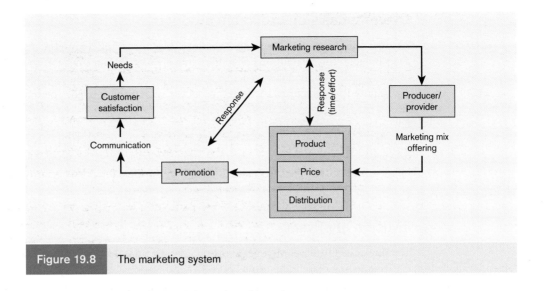

Figure 19.8 The marketing system

# THE ADOPTION OF A MARKETING ORIENTATION

The tourist industry, owing to the high service-based content of the product, has been character-ised by a history of custom and tradition. There has been a lack of vision in the industry which has meant the demise, merger and takeover of many organisations throughout the past 20 years. From the previous description of marketing and the examples presented, you should now be aware that tourism marketing involves a number of special characteristics:

- Marketing is a philosophy with the overriding value that the decision-making process of any organisation has to be led by the consumers' needs, the marketplace and the company's assets and resources.
- Successful marketing requires a special organisation structure that believes in integrating the principles of consumer orientation throughout the organisation.
- Marketing requires innovative methods of thinking and planning so that new ideas are gener-ated to take advantage of opportunities or to improve existing methods of marketing.

However, it is important to remember that while the use of marketing is expanding, as a prac-tice it is not without its critics.

# CRITICISMS OF THE MARKETING CONCEPT

There is a growing concern for protection of the environment and the adoption of business poli-cies that will enable the earth's resources to be sustained. The new values emerging are placing pressure on the underlying concepts of marketing. This is creating a great deal of debate regarding the ethical standpoint of marketing. Some of the most significant criticisms are considered in this section.

## Environmental marketing impact

Tour operators/wholesalers have continuously developed new areas, expanded successful resorts and created promotional campaigns without due regard to the cost of impacts on the area and local population (see Part 2). Alongside this there is the over-abundance of different types of outdoor promotional material, which makes a home or overseas destination less attractive. There are roadside poster sites, advertisements on taxis, messages painted on buildings, and leaflets given away and then discarded, all of which create invasive pollution.

## Overemphasis on profitable products

The marketing concept dictates that products can only be offered to the marketplace when they are profitable. This has culminated in the axing of bus and train transport routes and the disregard of low-spending individuals. Where a want exists and the marketing opportunity cannot deliver the required profit return, then the product is seldom developed. The market-based system is guided by self-interest and profit motivation. Therefore, consumer preferences are only accounted for if there is an ability to pay. These values are represented by a lack of concern for those who cannot afford a holiday, or for the supply of amenities to cater for those who are disadvantaged or handicapped. A number of changes to planning policy makes it easier with improved facilities for blind, infirm and handicapped people but this group are often of low priority in overall resort and accommodation planning.

## Invasion of privacy

The power of IT allows organisations to capture a complete range of personal information for use in targeting direct mail campaigns. As organisations begin to spend more on research there is the problem of a greater use of telephone and high street interviews. If this is for a reputable survey there is no problem but a number of companies are simply collecting information under the disguise of research to be used in further sales efforts.

A personal computer is not that personal when emails can be received which are unsolicited. It is estimated that hundreds of millions of emails are sent each day. Of these around 30% are unsolicited and form what is known as 'spam'. Spam emails are those which are not welcome and so should not have been sent. Therefore, companies should be considering permission marketing as a means to decide that a recipient is happy to receive information and messages. Good permission marketing is where the individual 'opts in' to receive the messages rather than having to tick an 'opt out' box in order not to get the mailings.

## Waste of resources on tourism marketing

Marketing is perceived as wasteful owing to the high amounts of money spent on promoting products. The money given over to tourism promotion is often associated with enticing consumers to buy products that they may not want. In addition, competitive advertising is argued to be responsible for higher costs and subsequently higher prices. It is therefore argued that if advertising were reduced, or did not exist, there would be more competition based upon price and service. The consumerist standpoint is that it would be better to spend the money on informative advertising rather than competitive advertising. It is believed the most disadvantaged tourist consumers are the ones most likely to be influenced by high expenditure on tourism marketing. The levels of marketing expenditure are quite often blamed for changing consumer attitudes and bringing about a materialistic society where status is derived from the number and type of destinations we visit, or leisure and activities we undertake. There is little doubt that marketing panders to materialistic values. However, the question is does marketing create these values, or simply appeal to the values already embedded within society as even in the most simple of societies the drive towards accumulation of possessions is the norm?

# A SOCIETAL MARKETING APPROACH

It has been argued that the pressures affecting the image of marketing need to be more carefully considered. This has culminated in the movement toward a societal concept of marketing which stresses the enhancement of the needs of society as well as the consumer. Some organisations such as brewers and distillers are creating campaigns to warn people of the excesses of drinking, but it is questionable whether they are worried as much about the customer as about the legislation that could affect their operations.

While some organisations may pay lip service to a societal concept for PR purposes, in a competitive situation many of the problems related to tourism, and its marketing, will continue. It is also important to recognise that consumers are now better educated and are competent to select products that are not creating undue problems to society. Moreover, if organisations or their products do create problems, there are articulate pressure groups and government legislation available for consumer and environmental protection.

There is growing recognition that companies need to discover approaches to the marketplace that will build a socially responsible and ethical company culture. There is a need to understand the following three basic issues:

- **Consumerism.** This is organised group pressure, by all consumers, to protect and benefit consumer groups and the environment. This means it is not solely those consumers buying from a company, it is a broad movement to bring about improved exchange relationships.

- **Corporate social responsibility.** This is the decision of a firm to conduct its business in the interest of society as a whole as well as its own interests.

- **Ethics.** This involves personal decisions on the moral principles of what would be the right or wrong activity for individual employees. These decisions will be linked to the values and culture of the organisation. Ethical values are the core beliefs and standards that will dictate the stance a company takes in relation to its marketing, such as honesty and fairness.

A truly societal marketing approach is problematic due to the need to resolve multifaceted decisions over profit, pollution, social and environmental impact concerns. However, some companies perform their marketing activities better than others and are judged in positive terms by the public. Some companies are quite good at giving something back to the industry that supports them. Since the early 1990s, United Airlines has donated some of its Boeing 727s and 737s to museums and universities in the USA. The universities turn the aircraft into hands-on classrooms for students pursuing careers in aircraft maintenance, flight or aviation administration. United's initiative on this will bring it longer-term benefits as the disposition of the public to a brand is an important aspect of contemporary marketing.

If managers are going to achieve change it is argued that they need to put themselves in the consumer's position with regard to how they or their family would feel others should treat them. The following points are relevant in this context:

1. Good business managers should be socially responsible to all stakeholders (customers, employees, suppliers, shareholders, society, etc.) related to the company or tourism offer so as to minimise social costs. They should also have regard for laws or regulations and be ethical in management decisions.

2. Managers should be honest in claims and promotions, not be deceptive or agree to misleading advertising. They should show fairness to third parties. In addition, there should not be any hidden costs – or they should identify extra costs which may be applicable. For example, hoteliers should display the prices of rooms and supplements in a prominent public position and always make their cancellation policy clear at the time of booking and have it written into their communication literature.

3. The products offered should not cause harm or unacceptable tourism impact and managers should communicate any risks which are known to be associated with any product.

4. Marketers should undertake not to adopt sales techniques under the guise of its being research (such as that associated with time-share selling). Also, it is unfair and unethical to use promotions as research when adequate stock is unavailable because the research is being used as a method of deciding on the supply requirements.

## CONCLUSION

We have demonstrated that the concept of marketing and its practical application have evolved as a result of changing business and social conditions that have emerged throughout the last century. The differences between sales and marketing were covered so that the reader will be more aware of why marketing planning and understanding the consumer is an important component of tourism marketing. In the course of this chapter we have identified different business philosophies that currently exist, the benefits of a marketing orientation and the basis of the marketing concept – including that of building relationships and delivering superior value.

The tourism product is predominately a service product with the main characteristics of intangibility, perishability and inseparability. The tourism purchase involves complex decisions related to perceptions of risk and the expectation of high levels of quality. As such there is a need for a deeper understanding of the process of TQM and consumer's expectation of service delivery standards. Finally, the use of marketing should take into account the issues surrounding the criticism of its application and as such an understanding of consumerism, social responsibility and ethics is important.

## SELF-CHECK QUESTIONS

1. Name up to three ways in which value can be added to the tourism product.
2. What are the economic benefits of adopting a relationship marketing approach to business?
3. Name three main aspects which characterise the service product.
4. Provide a list of the main types of risk which a tourist may experience.
5. What are the reasons why quality management is now more important than in the past?

## YOUTUBE

http://www.youtube.com/watch?v=biIOOPuAvTY&feature=related
Philip Kotler providing some marketing insight

http://www.youtube.com/watch?v=SD2v80TKO1E
Ethics in marketing

http://www.youtube.com/watch?v=7hbRZ3ZCyl8&feature=related
Philip Kotler on marketing in difficult economic times

http://www.youtube.com/watch?v=6DRNLHF7jRc&feature=results_main&playnext=1&list=PL4233BEA681819D3F
Provides a broad understanding of marketing

http://www.youtube.com/watch?v=cX3qVqPlopk
The link allows an understanding of how competitive forces work

## REFERENCES AND FURTHER READING

Ang, S.H., Leong, S.M. and Kotler, P. (2000) 'The Asian apocalypse: crisis marketing for consumers and businesses', *Long Range Planning* **33**(1), 97–119.

Baker, M. (1999) *The Marketing Book*, Butterworth Heinemann, Oxford.

Chartered Institute of Marketing (1984) Cookham, Berkshire.

Dann, G.M.S. (1981) 'Tourist motivation: an appraisal', *Annals of Tourism Research* **8**(2), 187–219.

Drucker, P. (1973) *Management: Tasks, Responsibilities, Practices*, Harper & Row, New York.

Economist (2001) 'Ready for take off', *Economist* **361**(8247), 52.

Economist (2002) 'So many planes, so few passengers' and 'Signs of life', *Economist* **364**(8290), 51–2, 57.

Gilbert, D.C. (1989) 'Tourism marketing – its emergence and establishment', pp. 77–90 in Cooper, C. (ed.), *Progress in Tourism, Recreation and Hospitality Management*, Vol. 1, Belhaven Press, London.

Gilbert, D.C. (1991) 'An examination of the consumer behaviour process related to tourism', pp. 78–105 in Cooper, C. (ed.), *Progress in Tourism, Recreation and Hospitality Management*, Vol. 3, Belhaven Press, London.

Gilbert, D.C. (1996) 'Relationship marketing and airline loyalty schemes', *Tourism Management* **17**(8), 575–82.

Gilbert, D.C. and Bailey, N. (1990) 'The development of marketing – a compendium of historical approaches', *Quarterly Review of Marketing* **15**(2), 6–13.

Gilbert, D.C. and Joshi, I. (1992) 'Quality management and the tourism and hospitality industry', pp. 149–68 in Cooper, C. and Lockwood, A. (eds), *Progress in Tourism, Recreation and Hospitality Management*, Vol. 4, Belhaven Press, London.

Gronroos, C. (1982) *Strategic Management and Marketing in the Service Sector*, Swedish School of Economics and Business Administration, Helsinki.

Hart, C.W.L., Heskett, J.L. and Sasser, W.E. (1990) 'The profitable part of service recovery', *Harvard Business Review* July/August, 148–56.

Hudson, S. (2008) *Tourism and Hospitality Marketing: A Global Perspective*, Sage, London. The book offers a number of chapters dealing with contemporary issues in tourism marketing as well as giving examples. There are chapters on research and consumer behaviour.

Keith, R.J. (1981) 'The marketing revolution', pp. 44–9 in Enis, B.M. and Cox, K.K. (eds), *Marketing Classics*, 4th edn, Allyn & Bacon, London.

Kotler, P. and Keller, K. (2006) *Marketing Management*, Prentice Hall, Upper Saddle River, NJ.

Kotler, P., Bowen, J. and Makens, J. (2009) *Marketing for Hospitality and Tourism*, 5th edn, Pearson, Upper Saddle River, NJ. The book draws upon the marketing material of Philip Kotler's other books and as such is based upon his pedigree which has been developed over a number of years of writing marketing textbooks. However, the examples are often better in other texts and other specialist books need to be read in conjunction with this one. This latest edition now covers electronic marketing, has case studies and provides a broad understanding of the role of marketing in hospitality and tourism. Specialist areas covered are customer quality management and destination marketing.

Lepp, A. and Gibson, H. (2003) 'Tourist roles, perceived risk and international tourism', *Annals of Tourism Research* **30**(3), 606–24.

Levitt, T. (1960) 'Marketing myopia', *Harvard Business Review* July/August, 45–56.

Lovelock, C. and Wirtz, J. (2004) *Service Marketing: People, Technology and Strategy*, 5th edn, Pearson, Upper Saddle River, NJ. This book offers insight into the challenges facing the service sector by providing a well-researched and, at the same time, practical text. Coverage is given to service processes and systems, service positioning and service management. The text questions other approaches and allows the reader to experience new material not to be found in other textbooks dealing with a similar subject area.

Martin, W. (2002) *Quality Service: What Every Hospitality Manager Needs to Know*, Prentice Hall, Harlow. This book has many applications to the hospitality and tourism sector including not only tourism, hotels and restaurants but also theme parks and clubs. The book has a number of figures and clear explanation of some of the main concepts.

Middleton, V., Fyall, A., Morgan, M. and Ranchhod, A. (2009) *Marketing in Travel and Tourism*, 4th edn, Butterworth Heinemann, Oxford. *Marketing in Travel and Tourism* explains the basic principles and practice of marketing in the contemporary setting of the new pressures affecting tourism including areas not normally found in similar texts such as NTOs. In addition, international case studies are included.

Nightingale, M. (1983) 'Determination and Control of Quality Standards in Hospitality Services', MPhil. Thesis, University of Surrey.

Parasuraman, A., Zeithaml, V.A. and Berry, L.L. (1985) 'A conceptual model of service quality and its implications for future research', *Journal of Marketing* **49**(4), 41–50.

Shaw, S. (2011) *Airline Marketing and Management*, 7th edn, Ashgate, Aldershot. This seventh edition text offers a comprehensive overview of the needs of the current airline industry to utilise and formulate marketing approaches within their sector. It includes material on terrorism, economic and regulatory pressures, as well as airline alliances. Its strength is that the book examines the structure of the airline marketplace against the major principles of marketing and provides many examples from airline practice.

Yeoman, I. and Lederer, P. (2005) 'Scottish Tourism: Scenarios and Vision', *Journal of Vacation Marketing* **11**(1), 71–87.

Zeithaml, V.A. and Bitner, M.J. (2000) *Services Marketing*, 2nd edn, Irwin McGraw-Hill, New York.

## Websites

http://www.britishairways.com/press/

http://www.easyjet.com/en/about/investorrelationsrfinancialnews.html

http://www.insights.org.uk/

# MAJOR CASE STUDY 19.1
## The case of Malta as a competitive tourist destination

One of the characteristic examples of successful implementation of promotion policies in the frame of strategic planning is that of Malta and the Maltese Islands. Malta and the Maltese islands have received great attention of research especially since the decade of the 1980s and so on (Bolssevain, 1979; Oglethorpe, 1985; Markwick, 2001; Bramwell, 2003). Situated in the central Mediterranean Sea, Malta is a small archipelago of five islands – Malta (the largest), Gozo, Comino, Comminotto (Maltese, Kemmunett) and Filfla. The last two are uninhabited. The capital city of Malta is Valletta. Its land area is only 316km² and in this restricted space live 378,000 people giving it one of the highest population densities in the world (Makhzoumi, 2000; Bramwell, 2006), hosting at the same time over 1,000,000 visitors per year (Chapman and Cassar, 2004).

Given Malta's geographical location, there are no direct connections to the European land corridors. However, due to its strategic position on the main routes of the Mediterranean Sea, Malta has a pivotal role for sea-lane connections (National Reform Programme (NRP), 2005:10). In Malta's case, tourism has been recognised as an industry for far longer than 40 years. This fact is very common, since the majority of small islands states tend to depend on tourism more than larger states do (Briguglio and Briguglio, 1996; McElroy and Olazarri, 1997). The reason for this could be associated with the competitive advantage and specialization that islands tend to have in tourism-related activities (Briguglio and Briguglio, 1996; Kerr, 2005), while some scholars support that the economic development in small islands is positively affected by the growth in tourism (Latimer, 1985; Croes, 2006). Tourism has been acknowledged as Malta's foremost economic activity generating as much as 24% of gross national product and 27% of full-time equivalent employment in the Maltese islands; this demonstrates tourism's major role in the (actual and potential) social economic and environmental scenarios in Malta, putting up pressure due to dependence, constraints and vulnerability (Mangion, 2001; NCSD, 2004: 33; UN, 2002: 47). The number of incoming tourists has increased rapidly from 1960 to 1980 followed by a large decrease in tourism inflows from 1980 to 1985. Finally, the tourists' numbers peaked rapidly again during the last half of the 1980s and the 1990s (Briguglio and Briguglio, 1996).

Define the Problem and the Solution: The Repositioning of Malta – 'Every Visit would be a Unique

Experience'. The case of Malta is not unique, but is very distinctive, since Malta is not only an island tourism destination but also a state. Although Malta is an internationally recognized tourist destination, the reconstruction and the promotion of its image policy was deemed necessary in order to face the new tendencies and challenges in the global tourist market and Place Marketing, Strategic Planning and Competitiveness retain a competitive profile towards its rivals, especially in the Mediterranean basin. This fact generates one important question: Why does a competitive destination need to plan and implement promotion policies in frequent time periods? A logical answer is that the implementation of marketing policies is related to a variety of factors that have to be investigated so that cities or regions can remain competitive and attractive on a long-term basis. Consequently, the implementation of marketing policies reflects on the place's necessity to secure their sustainable process of development, contributing positively to the local and regional economic development.

According to Ashworth and Tunbridge (2003), the three interrelated problems that Malta faced are summarized as the 'tourism problem' (the 'traditional' coast tourism vs. the 'new' tourism consumers, including cultural and heritage experiences), the 'heritage problem' (management of heritage resources focusing on the cost of preservation, renovation and continuing maintenance) and the 'development problem' (building on Malta's competitive advantage, implying that tourism, and especially heritage tourism, has been identified as such an international competitive advantage whose exploitation is thus immediately pressing). During 2004, a process of restructuring commenced at the Malta Tourism Authority (MTA), with an aim to increase the value of tourism to Malta more effectively. The MTA, set up by an Act of Parliament on 1 September 1999, has undertaken an in-depth evaluation of the Malta tourism offer. The conclusion was that Malta was no longer competitive in the basic sun and sea package due to the much extended offers by larger and often newer destinations which could handle much larger volumes. A fundamental shift was therefore set in motion, where the Malta product was redefined to rest on Malta's distinctive comparative advantage, away from the more traditional sun and sea product to one which adds 'our rich heritage' (Ashworth and Tunbridge, 2003: 5). It was clear therefore that what had basically fuelled the growth of the Maltese industry in the last decades could no longer sustain the growth and development of the industry. Malta therefore had to think creatively and to innovate in order to rejuvenate the Malta tourism offer. According to Ashworth and Tunbridge (2003: 36), the promotion of heritage tourism as an independent, rather

than an add-on activity, requires a different set of images projected to different markets using different techniques than at present. Especially, in the case of marketing, Malta has to provide more specific images than the very generalized, to more specific and interesting markets. Furthermore, advertisement placement in the markets of UK, Germany and Benelux, in particular, will need to use more upmarket media than in the current phase. In the end, the investigation of small, more profitable niche markets and the development of more effective management of tourism behaviour should be taken into serious consideration.

The MTA (2002a: 6) is therefore engaged in a process that began in 2002 and it is summarized as 'The repositioning of Malta', as a different type of destination, where 'every visit would be a unique experience'. Within the restructuring process of MTA, a new, two-pronged strategy for tourism encompassing mainstream tourism and identified niche tourism is implemented. This strategy will also outline ways of increasing private sector involvement in the management of attractions such as beaches, cultural assets and other areas. Furthermore, key heritage sites are upgraded to improve their interpretation, accessibility, conservation and promotion and finally, a branding exercise for tourism, shifting overseas marketing from a geographical market approach to a segment based approach, by focusing, not in particular geographical areas, but in particular segments of the international tourism market is implemented (NRP, 2005: 22; World Report Malta, 2006).

The MTA is responsible for Malta's single most sophisticated tourism marketing plan on a global scale (MTA, 2002b). The plan consists of a number of programmes aimed at increasing visibility in the international market and establishing a strong and positive brand image in Malta's source markets. In order to carry out such an ambitious plan, the MTA's Marketing and Promotion Directorate operates an international network of offices and representatives, commissions advertising campaigns, co-ordinates a public relations programme, supports tour operators through joint marketing activities and participates in a wide range of trade and consumer fairs. The four core axes of this tourism marketing plan include: (a) market research analysis and collection of primary data, (b) marketing and promotion, (c) strategic planning and (d) branding.

The marketing and promotion axis includes several actions (networking, advertising, public relations, etc.) that focus on the development, distribution and promotion of Malta's distinctive characteristics to its potential target markets globally. The MTA's 'overseas network' ensures that Malta's tourism industry is extremely active on a worldwide basis. Currently, the number of outstations manned by MTA officials amount to 12. The largest presence is in Malta's core markets, namely the UK, Germany, Italy, France and the Netherlands. Other offices are operational in Russia, Belgium, Sweden, Austria, the US and China. Representative offices service smaller markets. Such offices are located in the Czech Republic, Hungary, Poland, Portugal, Finland, Turkey, Cyprus, Australia and Japan (MTA, 2003).

The three core segments that amount to around 26% of national tourism inflows are: history and culture, conference and incentive travel, and sports tourism (Malta Business Bureau, 2006).

*Source*: Metaxas, T. (2009) *European Planning Studies* **17**(9), 1357–78. Adapted and reduced as an excerpt

## DISCUSSION QUESTIONS

1. Try to access the full paper to assess how Malta is to be developed and try to see what other measures are required to bring about success – for example with regard to further product development and different target segments.

2. Assess the number and position of the overseas offices and comment with reasons on whether you would target other tourist-generating areas.

3. Provide assessment of the case and indicate the strengths, weaknesses and missing opportunities it may reveal in the marketing of Malta as an island destination.

# CHAPTER 20

## MARKETING PLANNING

### LEARNING OUTCOMES

Marketing planning is crucial to organisational survival in an environment that is increasingly unpredictable and volatile. It is necessary to cope with many unprecedented social and economic changes throughout the world. This chapter therefore considers all aspects of marketing planning to ensure that, by the end of the chapter, the reader is able:

- to recognise the importance of marketing planning in respect of tourism and the implications of inefficient planning procedures;

- to understand the purposes of marketing planning in protecting the organisation and enhancing its market position;

- to appreciate the key stages of marketing planning and thus be in a better position to develop and implement a marketing plan successfully; and

- to identify the structure and content of an effective marketing plan.

Photograph: Hvar Town, Croatia © Helen Savill

## INTRODUCTION

In this chapter, we outline an approach to marketing planning in tourism and suggest that the marketing plan represents a structured guide to action. As such, it acts as a systematic method of data collection, logical analysis and objective setting of the most appropriate direction for an organisation, distributor or destination product. If a marketing plan is to be accepted by all concerned then the compilation of the plan has to involve all levels of personnel. This is because marketing plans require organisation-wide commitment if they are to be successful.

Giving the rate of change in tourism the plan must reflect the dynamic nature of the marketplace and as such the plan needs to be thought of as a loose-leaf binder rather than as a tablet of stone. This means the plan should act as a working document which can be updated or modified to take into account new opportunities, challenges or unanticipated problem situations.

## WHAT IS MARKETING PLANNING?

We all need to plan to some extent if we are to make a success of our lives. Very few Olympic medallists could be successful without a planned programme of training and events leading up to their Olympic finals and achievements. Whether it is for examinations, sports events, going on holiday or organising a party, the use of a systematic planning approach is more likely to lead to the probability that the event will be a success. Without the right approach, and a sensible plan, alternative courses of action may not have been considered and, consequently, there is the likelihood that individuals, companies or organisations may not function to their maximum potential.

Planning is the most important activity of marketing management. It should provide a common structure and focus for all of the organisation's management activities. It is therefore essential for us to understand planning in its context as the key function of management.

The tourism sector provides a combination of different products and activities, which range from the small taxi firm and guest house to the largest airline or hotel group. The concepts of change and survival are as important to the small business as they are to a destination, major international hotel chain or airline. The fact that changes will occur, and with increasing speed, is the most predictable aspect of contemporary business life. It would therefore seem sensible to become familiar with the underlying trends and forces of change that impinge on tourism business activities. This enables the management of change towards desired objectives rather than being driven blindly before the tide of market forces.

The long-term survival of any organisation is dependent on how well the business relates to its environment. This relies on devising forward plans of where an organisation, destination or product would be best placed for the future. Some of the key points relating to marketing planning may be identified as follows:

- The plan requires control over the changes that have to be made.
- It needs to allow for the exploitation of any short-term advantages and improvement on weaknesses.
- It has to promote the use of analysis, reason and evaluation as an integral part of planning procedure.

A lack of marketing planning will result in a wide range of possible consequences. For a destination, this could involve one or more of the following:

- failure to take advantage of potential growth markets and new marketing opportunities – such as increasing use of the Internet or social networking;

- lack of maintenance of demand from a spread of markets and erosion of market share due to the actions of competitors;
- demand problems in low-season periods or due to economic problems;
- low level of awareness of the destination's product offering;
- poor image of the destination;
- lack of support for cooperative marketing initiatives;
- poor or inadequate tourism information services;
- decline in quality levels below acceptable limits;
- difficulty in attracting intermediaries to market or package holidays;
- disillusionment and lack of motivation of tourism service employees.

Thus, the implementation of marketing planning procedures can be instrumental in alleviating many of the difficulties which tourism organisations may face. This is reflected in Major Case Study 20.1 which focuses on Disneyland® Resort Paris, and some of the weaknesses in the marketing planning procedures in respect of this venture.

Although planning cannot guarantee success it can make the organisation less vulnerable to market forces and unpredictable events. Perhaps the very early business casualties of tourism with the demise in the past of Laker Airways, Courtline and ILG could have been avoided if more attention had been given to planning activities by their respective managements, especially in relation to cash flow, fixed cost and expansion attributes. The customer can suffer from bad planning but from 2008 the UK government brought in a levy on each customer's holiday package price as part of a replacement of earlier bonding schemes in order to raise a fund through the Air Traffic Organisers' Licence Scheme (ATOL) to mitigate against being stranded overseas if on holiday. A recent collapse is that of the XL Group, which had flown more than 2 million passengers in 2007, a failure that resulted in 85,000 customers stranded overseas of whom 10,000 had a flight-only booking and as they were not on a package tour they were not covered by ATOL protection to bring them home. The early lower price advantage of Sir Freddie Laker's operation or the low margin approach of XL provided excellent market positions for the products, yet the weakness of financial planning played a major part in each company's downfall.

Each organisation will adopt a different approach to the task of planning based upon the way senior executives see the purpose of a **marketing plan**. The values of any organisation fall along a continuum which begins at *wait and see* as a passive position, moves through the next set of values to *prepare and predict* and finally ends with organisations that want to *make it happen* which are far more proactive in approach. An organisation will benefit more from a future that is made to happen because of the clear direction given, which provides fewer surprises for the workforce and less pressure on the requirements of company resources.

## THE MARKETING ENVIRONMENT OF THE ORGANISATION

Each and every organisation has to operate within a market environment. This environment is made up of different levels of influence that will affect the opportunities and marketing decisions that need to be made. The historical conditions affecting competition and rivalry in company markets, the values of stakeholder groups and the political, economic, social and technological changes of the wider environment all affect the likely performance of the organisation and its brands.

The organisational setting, or environment of operation, is related to the four levels identified in Table 20.1. It should be noted that the influences and pressures of the different levels shown are only taken into account by those organisations following a market-led business philosophy. At level 1 the organisation needs to be adequately resourced to be successful. As companies grow they have to be more aware of level 2 as the marketplace they operate in may become more difficult; and at level 3 there is the emphasis on creating a 'value chain' from the stakeholder participants whereby different relationships have to be fostered and reinforced in positive ways. The

| Table 20.1 | Four levels of marketing environment affecting the organisation | |
|---|---|---|
| **Level 1** | **The organisation** | Marketing sub-functions need to be well organised and integrated with other organisational functions.<br><br>Marketing has to communicate the needs of the market environment as described in the subsequent levels and marketing thinking has to dominate any strategy formulation. |
| **Level 2** | **Company markets** | Identification of domestic and international consumer markets for products/services, or industrial, intermediary or institutional markets.<br><br>The degree of rivalry and competitive activity as well as extent of consumer behaviour will affect market activity choice. |
| **Level 3** | **Organisational stakeholders** | Interest groups will affect the context of decision making, e.g. shareholders, competitors, customers, employees, unions, government, suppliers, debtors, local community or banks, all of whom may have conflicting values but have some stake in the organisation. |
| **Level 4** | **The wider environment** | Analysis is required of political, economic, social, technological, environmental and legal aspects of the marketplace (PESTEL). Interrelations of the different forces and changes in the foregoing are powerful market environment determinants. |

wider macro-environment (level 4) places pressures on management that are outside the control of the organisation. The broad categories of PESTEL (see the discussion on PESTEL further on in this chapter) involve a series of different levels of aggregation: regional, national and international, which are related to business constraints as well as opportunities. We can examine these first.

# THE PURPOSE OF THE MARKETING PLAN

The marketing plan is normally a short-term plan that will direct the organisation from one to three years. Typically, a five-year plan will be a strategic plan which is more general and less detailed than a marketing plan. **Strategic planning** involves developing and maintaining a fit between the environment, the competencies and resources of the organisation and its changing marketing opportunities. The strategic plan will concern itself more with external environmental influences and opportunities and less with the detail of the organisation's marketing activities. Strategic plans are normally either medium or long term and marketing plans are short or medium term.

The marketing plan and its compilation is able to provide a number of benefits for an organisation. The creation of a marketing plan will result in a wide range of management benefits as indicated in the following:

● To provide clear direction to the marketing operation based upon a systematic, written approach to planning and action. The planning system allows direction by virtue of requiring a written mission statement and set of objectives to be established, both of which can be transmitted to the workforce. This provides clear leadership principles and allows the workforce to know how their own efforts are essential to the achievement of desired results.

- To coordinate the resources of the organisation. This eliminates confusion and misunderstanding in order to achieve maximum cooperation. Tasks and responsibilities need to be set which clarify the direction and objectives of the organisation. To ensure there is a united effort, recommendations have to be presented in such a way that they can be fully understood at all organisational levels. The plan then acts as a master guide which will underpin all endeavours and decision making. The plan should lead to greater employee cohesion and make everyone feel part of a team in which each individual believes he or she can make a valuable contribution.

- To set targets against which progress can be measured. Quantified targets for volume or revenue provide the focus for individual, departmental or company performance. Some organisations will set targets at achievable levels whereas others will set artificially high targets to encourage enhanced employee effort. The targets, once set, act as the benchmark against which all marketing programmes are monitored.

- To minimise risk through analysis of the internal and external environment. The planning procedure allows managers to identify areas of strength and weakness so that the first can be exploited and the second surmounted. In addition, threats and opportunities can be assessed.

- To examine the various ways of targeting to different market segments. This allows for different marketing mix strategies to be appraised prior to their implementation. Estimates can be made of the likely impacts in relation to sales and revenue targets to the marketing budget. For example, targeting more segments could require an increase in sales literature which may increase cost rather than profit.

- To provide a record of the organisation's marketing policies and plans. This allows managers to check on what has been attempted in the past and to evaluate the effectiveness of previous programmes. It also provides continuity and a source of reference for new managers joining the organisation.

- To focus on longer-term business objectives. This allows the organisation to plan to be in the best position to achieve its longer-term future aims, and allows management to develop continuity of thought and action from one year to the next.

Given that you have understood the previous information on marketing then it will be agreed that organisational objectives should be based upon relevant market-centred opportunities. It is the responsibility of tourism marketers to identify these opportunities and to devise a system of planning that may lead to their exploitation. However, planning can be fraught with problems, as the next section explains.

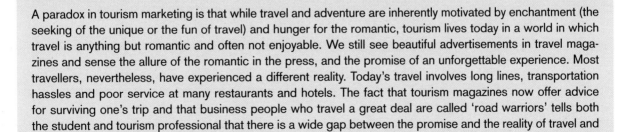

## MINI CASE STUDY 20.1
Tourism in a post-enchanted world

A paradox in tourism marketing is that while travel and adventure are inherently motivated by enchantment (the seeking of the unique or the fun of travel) and hunger for the romantic, tourism lives today in a world in which travel is anything but romantic and often not enjoyable. We still see beautiful advertisements in travel magazines and sense the allure of the romantic in the press, and the promise of an unforgettable experience. Most travellers, nevertheless, have experienced a different reality. Today's travel involves long lines, transportation hassles and poor service at many restaurants and hotels. The fact that tourism magazines now offer advice for surviving one's trip and that business people who travel a great deal are called 'road warriors' tells both the student and tourism professional that there is a wide gap between the promise and the reality of travel and tourism.

Too many in the industry live in a time warp in which travel marketing still assumes an industrial version of mass travel that may soon no longer exist in the developed world. Indeed it can be hypothesised that as travel is sold on a more massive scale, its allure decreases and the enchantment of travel fades. While land tours of the 'if it's Monday, it must be . . .' variety, with the exception of bus tours, are now passé, the advent of the mass cruise industry and the all-inclusive is still very much a current tourism success story. As the post-enchanted age of tourism continues to dawn, tourism specialists will need to consider new and innovative ways to recover something of tourism's past. An early example of the attempt to recreate enchantment in a post-enchanted age is the 'fly–drive' tour. These 'tours' permit travellers ways to personalise their trips and search for unique experiences rather than the common experience.

Despite tourism's claims to the contrary, our industry often develops its facilities, and uses the assumptions of mass marketing to judge itself. One only has to ask for some small variation at a convention meal to learn that kitchens are developed to sell a uniform product without addressing individual tastes, preferences, and/or health or religious needs. A simple survey of brochures provides us with an example of how much tourism is tied to a mass marketing design. A perusal of travel brochures demonstrates the uniformity of these brochures and it is not uncommon to see the same photo adorning the brochure of two different communities! In mass-produced tourism, the differentiated becomes undifferentiated, and reality merges with the imagination of the brochures' writers. This new world of travel has brought about all or some of the following factors which tourism professionals will need to consider:

- In a world in which no one is safe from the threat of terrorism or new illnesses such as SARS, the thrill of tourism has been tempered by the fear of travel.

- Destinations must become less dependent on brochures and other mass-produced and orientated forms of marketing. Instead, word-of-mouth advertising in which genuine emotions are displayed will act as the most effective market developer.

- Our resource of time is so limited that the pleasure traveller is now forced into a stressful search-for-fun vacation.

- Vacation groups are no longer stable. The industry must prepare itself and offer alternatives for cultural and social individualisation.

- Service is of greater importance in this post-enchanted high-tech age: business people often no longer wish to travel.

- Originality is now essential. Locales that have truly original activities that can be protected and refined will have greater tourism pull than locales seeking to replicate that which already exists elsewhere.

- Being genuine is essential. No matter what the destination offers, the post-enchanted tourist will shun the ersatz for the genuine. Locations that are 'real' and touch our emotions will have the potential of becoming major destinations.

*Source*: Abridged version of Tarlow, 2003

## DISCUSSION QUESTIONS

1. To what extent do you agree or disagree with Tarlow's assessment of current tourism and its marketing and are there other areas he could also have included?

2. How can marketing planning for tourism marketing have a positive impact on the future development of tourism given the points made by Tarlow?

3. Discuss what new forms of tourism are required for the new post-enchantment period and how your recommendations could become reality through a planning approach.

## SUCCESSFUL PLANNING

Most textbooks suggest planning is simply the following of a series of simple steps. However, the true art of planning is to understand both the human aspects and procedural necessities involved. A poor planning experience may be a function of one or more of the following issues or problems:

- **Lack of senior management support**. A lack of support from the chief executive and other senior people is a major problem and one that is difficult to resolve. Any planning approach requires senior management support if it is to be treated seriously by employees.

- **Inappropriate planning procedures**. The system of planning which is adopted may not suit the organisation. There is often the separation of different planning functions from each other that leads to a lack of integration. Therefore, the planning system often has to be designed to match the organisation and to achieve a harmony of approach between employee groups.

- **Poor planning and management**. The system of planning is often blamed when the weakness is actually poor planning and management. Sometimes there is confusion over available data or even planning terms. The requirement is for a plan to be compiled which clarifies times and responsibilities for different actions and meetings which will lead to the appropriate information and people being utilised.

- **Unpredictable external events**. Unexpected environmental changes may create adverse effects on the organisation's performance. Planning is then often blamed for not having incorporated such a scenario. Plans need to be flexible and updated when necessary.

- **Organisational and managerial acceptance**. The values of the management team will imply different acceptance levels of the plan and may ultimately determine its success or failure. There is often hostility towards plans because of the feeling of a lack of involvement in the planning process. This often occurs when the planning is left solely to a planner or it becomes a once-a-year ritual.

- **Level of detail**. Problems occur when there is an over-abundance of information which has to be filtered for its relevance. Too much detail in the early stages can produce what is sometimes termed 'paralysis analysis' which means there is a need to decide what is important and what is not at an early stage of planning.

It is distressing that those travel companies that have recognised the need for a more structured approach to planning, and subsequently adopted the formalised procedures found in the literature, seldom enjoy the advantages claimed when embarking on planning. In fact, it is often planning itself which is brought into disrepute when it fails to bring about the desired changes within an organisation.

The problems faced in marketing planning have led to a growing body of literature which indicates that organisations should do what they are good at, rather than embarking upon higher-level planning exercises. We believe this is a retrograde step because organisations should attempt to take the most logical direction and not be hampered by internal failings of the human resource aspects of implementation, lack of planning expertise or disregard of the involvement of others in the planning process. An understanding of the social aspects of the organisation is a prerequisite for successful planning. It is necessary for those involved in planning to recognise the need for involvement of all departments in the organisation in the formulation of the plan. This means that personnel are more likely to be motivated towards its successful implementation. Moreover, key personnel bring valuable knowledge and expertise to marketing plan formulation. It is also important to understand that most accomplishments in service industries, such as tourism, are made through people.

It is essential to ensure that plans are not prepared within the vacuum of one department or by a marketing team that believes it is an elite group. Structured management meetings can offer a setting where deliberation, responsibility and authority are shared and taken by all. This precludes dogmatic assertions about the particular methods of preparing and organising marketing planning.

The marketing planning system offers a structured approach to organising and coordinating the efforts and activities of those involved in deciding on the future of an organisation. However, there is no one right system for any particular tourism organisation, since organisations differ in size and diversity of operations, the values of the senior management and the expertise of those involved in the planning exercise.

# STRUCTURE OF THE MARKETING PLAN

The construction of the marketing plan is characterised by a range of headings developed by different theorists. Some authors offer a list of sections with the first headed 'SWOT issues' or 'situational analysis', the second headed 'statement of objectives and goals' or 'setting objectives', the third is 'strategy' or 'marketing programming' and the last is 'monitoring' or 'control'. We prefer to use different stages which are more easily understood by managers and students. The stages are:

1. What is it we want?
2. Where are we now?
3. Where do we want to go?
4. How do we get there?
5. Where did we get to?

These are represented in Figure 20.1. In reading the structure of the marketing planning model it is important to realise the system is not always the linear progression it appears. Quite often the process needs to involve an interplay between the various stages with the flexibility to move backwards as well as forwards. We should also understand that refinement of the plan takes place as understanding of the interconnections improves. We should not presume that perfection will be achieved until a number of drafts have been completed.

Linked to the simplistic stages above, the model of marketing planning can be described as involving:

1. Ensuring the consideration of human resources for successful planning.
2. Corporate mission and goals.
3. External and internal audit.
4. Business situation analysis.
5. Creating the objectives.
6. Providing an effective marketing mix strategy.
7. Monitoring the plan.

## The consideration of human resources for successful planning

The involvement of different departments will help reduce resistance to future changes or tasks. Continuous concern about the human aspects of planning can provide a greater possibility of the plan's success. The planner or planning team should be aware that they are only a technical service to a wider team. However, we have to be careful not to make the system too open as to be in danger of creating anarchy and loss of focus. On the other hand, the system should not be too closed, as this leads to problems of bureaucracy and apathy.

Good planning is a combination of qualitative and quantitative factors based upon creative, as well as analytical and logical thinking. As Albert Einstein once remarked: 'When I examined myself, and my methods of thought, I came to the conclusion that the gift of fantasy has meant more to me than my talent for absorbing positive knowledge.' Creative thinkers are able to bring specific benefits to the planning process such as:

- challenges to norms and assumptions and the ability to question what others automatically accept as true;
- the focus on chance and the unexpected rather than safe answers;
- the development of new ways of thinking which transform familiar ideas into more unconventional approaches and so provide new ways and means of thinking of 'taken-for-granted' situations;
- allowing individuals to make associations and so combine seemingly unrelated events, topics and ideas;

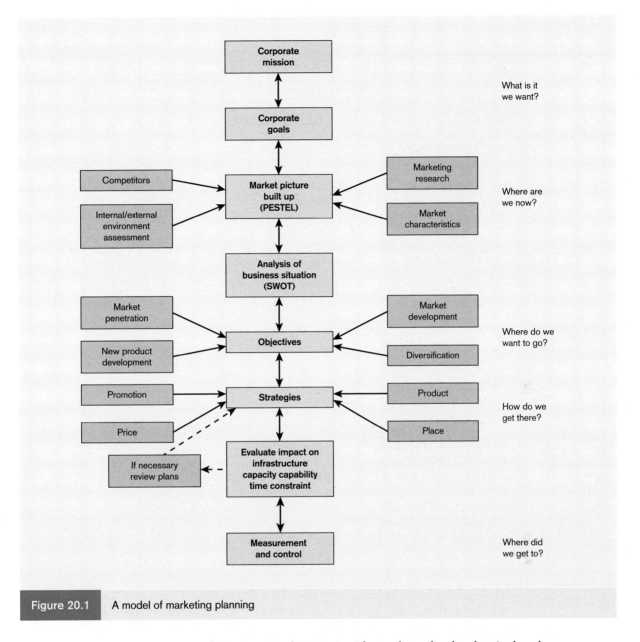

| Figure 20.1 | A model of marketing planning |

- allowing product, service and promotion ideas to be updated and revised; and
- keeping the planning function from becoming too boring and so retaining its excitement and innovation by bringing human resource values to the whole process.

One vital behavioural consideration of any plan which affects all aspects of the company is that it should not clash with the organisational culture. Such a clash can be overcome by ensuring staff values are incorporated into various stages of the planning cycle. The involvement of the full range of staff leads to a situation where the organisational culture values of staff are reflected in the 'bottom-up' comments. This helps to ensure that the plan is created as part of a process which makes it compatible with the corporate culture.

Again, we stress that organisations have to plan for the involvement level of staff. This needs to be as seriously considered as planning for the company's markets. Figure 20.2 provides one approach in dealing with the need to have marketing planning involvement at all levels.

One other important aspect of influence when including a cross-section of people in planning is their ability to hinder or help the plan. Within any company or organisation, managers'

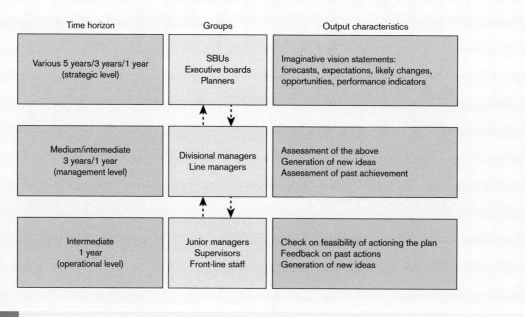

**Figure 20.2** Involvement levels for marketing planning

competence to plan will be based upon how busy they are, their preoccupation with other business matters, their career goals, their experience and their ability to think analytically. These attributes are linked to other managers' values and the cultural climate within the organisation, which may be more or less responsive to change and adaptation through adherence to the planning system.

A plan when completed should be read by far more people than actually do read it. This is often due to the lack of time of busy executives and the complexity of the plan. To overcome the problem all plans require the addition of a good management summary, written in clear, concise language, which will ensure the principal points and themes are communicated. The summary should concentrate on objectives, main target markets, opportunities and threats, key strategies and timings.

## Corporate mission and goals

It is important to understand what is expected of the plan from the long-term goals set at corporate level. The goals may be based upon the values and objectives of the key shareholders, board directors or senior managers. In some situations goals are set only after the establishment and evaluation of the marketing programmes. This is a parochial, programme-led method of planning, where management does not attempt to meet higher-level corporate goals within the planning process because managers are more prepared to settle for what they believe will work. An organisation with this approach will not investigate as broad a range of strategies as the organisation that is driven to ensure consistency with the overall corporate strategy and goals.

The most effective form of planning creates a balance between corporate direction and ensuring different levels of employee involvement (see Figure 20.2). If goals are dictated to employees, there is very little sense of ownership of the plan and a corresponding lack of motivation. Goals can be set in a functional, top-down approach or as a negotiation of goals through the combination of bottom-up and top-down processes.

The **mission statement** is a guide for employees to know what the purpose of the organisation is. The mission statement acts as a confirmation of what business the organisation is in from a consumer viewpoint. It then represents the overriding goal of the organisation. In the 2010–2013 VisitBritain's strategy the vision is to 'inspire the world to explore Britain' and the mission to 'build the value of tourism to Britain working in partnership with the industry and nations and regions'.

## External and internal audit

It is necessary to gather enough relevant information about the external and internal organisational environment to be able to construct a business and market picture of current and future pressure and trends. One important part of marketing planning is knowing what to analyse. Executives have to be careful that they do not have too limited a view of the environment. Understanding the different needs of the tourist, as illustrated by Photograph 20.1, is only one

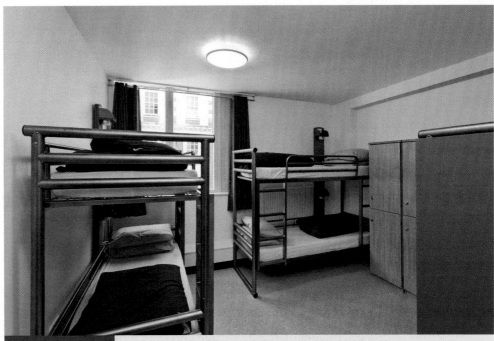

**Photograph 20.1**     Tourism marketing has to consider the different product needs of the tourist.
*Source*: top: Caro/Alamy Images, bottom: Archimage/Alamy Images

aspect which requires investigation. Market knowledge requirements are so complex these days that having checklists of necessary information is one way to help organisations in scanning the environment for the essential data related to their individual needs.

The information collected should, at the very least, form the basis of a PESTEL investigation. PESTEL analysis is an examination of the conditions of **P**olitical, **E**conomic, **S**ocial, **T**echnological, **E**nvironmental and **L**egal changes that may affect the market, the organisation and ultimately the plan. Information-gathering is part of an internal and external audit which should collect a range of information, as detailed below. In addition to incorporating these factors in the marketing plan this information should be gathered on the basis of how it affects the organisation, especially in relation to its key competitors.

## PESTEL analysis and market environment

The PESTEL analysis tool is a helpful framework approach for identifying those marketing activities that may impede or contribute to success in the macro (external) environment. It acts as an analysis for the various components of the macro environment. This includes the following:

- **Political:** taxation including VAT, subsidies to tourism, duty, tourism policies, airport regulations.
- **Economic:** inflation, unemployment, fuel costs, exchange rates, average salaries, consumption patterns (see also the market environment list below).
- **Social:** demographics, cultural differences, language barriers, holiday/leisure time entitlement, values (consumerism), lifestyle, male/female role changes, delay of first child, education, workforce changes, home-based Internet usage increases.
- **Technological:** innovations, new systems (reservations, yield management, customer relationship management), Internet, better transference of data direct to customer, mobile technology such as 3G.
- **Environmental:** global warming and diminishing natural resources, pollution issues, green holiday development, carbon footprint charges.
- **Legal:** regulation, trade laws, constraints on companies and authorities.

## Other important environmental factors

- **Total market:** size, growth, trends, value, industry structure, identify the competitors, barriers to entry, extent of under- or over-capacity of supply, marketing methods.
- **Companies:** level of investment, takeovers, promotional expenditure, redundancies, revenue, profits.
- **Product development:** trends, new product types, service enhancements, competitiveness of other companies' products.
- **Price:** levels, range, terms, practices.
- **Distribution:** patterns, trade structure, policies.
- **Promotion:** expenditure, types, communication messages, brand strengths, effectiveness of own current promotion methods.

## Understanding competition – Porter's model

The plan has to be formulated in relation to those forces which impinge on the likelihood of success. Prime among such forces is competition. The plan cannot exist in isolation from other factors. As Porter has argued (1980), it is easy to view the competition too narrowly and too pessimistically. Porter views intense competition as natural, with the state of competition depending on the relationship between five basic forces (see Figure 20.3). Porter argues that it is the collective strength of these forces that determines the ultimate profit potential of any industry. The model has become widely known as the 'five forces' model of competition.

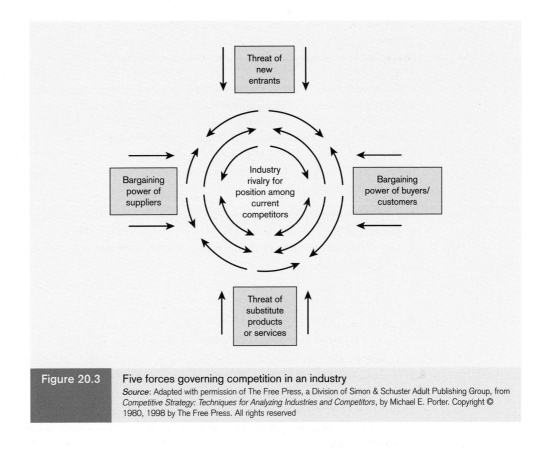

| Figure 20.3 | Five forces governing competition in an industry |
|---|---|

*Source*: Adapted with permission of The Free Press, a Division of Simon & Schuster Adult Publishing Group, from *Competitive Strategy: Techniques for Analyzing Industries and Competitors*, by Michael E. Porter. Copyright © 1980, 1998 by The Free Press. All rights reserved

The focuses of rivalry among existing competitors are (1) the outcome of rivalry; (2) the bargaining power of suppliers; (3) the bargaining power of buyers; (4) the threat of new entrants; and (5) the threat of substitute products or services. Each of these forces, in turn, can be broken down into its constituent elements. The following discussion of these forces helps with our understanding of the tourism industry and clarifies the considerations we must take into account.

### 1. Rivalry among existing competitors

Factors which might affect the nature of competitiveness or 'the jockeying for position' by the use of tactics in the industry include the following:

- the degree of concentration in the industry and the number and relative size of the competitors – the different sectors compete such as self-catering versus hotel accommodation or trains versus air travel etc.;
- if industry growth is slow there will be increased struggle for market share;
- the extent and nature of product differentiation where less differentiation leads to more of a stress on price competition;
- when fixed costs are high or the product perishable as is the case with much of the tourism industry offerings;
- capacity in relation to demand and the seasonal characteristics of demand;
- high exit barriers will keep companies competing even though they may be earning low or negative returns.

### 2. Bargaining power of suppliers

Factors relevant to the supply side of the industry will be similar to those mentioned on the customer side of the industry and thus include:

- the structure of the supplier side relative to the producer industry;
- the degree of product differentiation/substitutability;
- the potential for forward integration;
- the relative importance of the industry demand to suppliers;
- the feasibility and cost of producers switching suppliers.

### 3. Bargaining power of buyers

The bargaining power of the buyers (that is, demand for the products or services whether it is the company acting as buyer from suppliers or whether it is the final customer) is related to the following features:

- the degree of concentration relating to the relative importance of levels of demand on the customer side by comparison with that of the competing suppliers;
- the relative significance of the product or service to customers in terms of quality, expenditure and service;
- relative ease and cost of changing to new suppliers (switching costs) such as a negative cost from switching out of a loyalty scheme or time-share arrangement;
- the amount of information and knowledge possessed by buyers;
- the ability of buyers to integrate backwards;
- affluence level of buyers;
- the extent to which buyers want differentiated products.

### 4. Threat of new entrants

The ease, or difficulty, with which new producers may enter the industry affects the degree to which the structure of the industry can change due to the extra competition and the desire to gain market share. New entrants need to have some form of competitive advantage to help them succeed. For example, a new destination may have new tourism facilities and infrastructure but a successful destination will have larger promotional budgets to counteract this. The seriousness of the threat is dependent on the type of barriers to entry and on the way existing competitors will react:

- the extent to which there are economies of scale (note that airline alliances such as Star or One World can provide these);
- the amount of capital required to capture customer loyalty and create brand identification;
- the capital required for inventories and absorbing start-up costs (for example, the cost of leasing new aircraft as a no-frills airline start-up);
- existing companies may have experienced learning curve benefits with lower costs (lower costs may be important to an airline when wanting to enter a new route on a large enough scale to compete with rivals);
- the level of customer switching costs (for example, for an airline are there frequent flyer benefits or loyalty considerations?);
- the existence of government regulation and legal limitations and barriers (for example, can an airline obtain desired take-off and landing slots or obtain an air operator's licence?).

### 5. Threat of substitutes

These include:

- the availability of substitutes and willingness of buyers to utilise substitute products which have the same functional capability (for example, video conferencing rather than business travel);
- the impact on profits of close substitutes;
- the impact of the comparative price and quality of substitutes.

The above approach to industry analysis can allow a company to understand the pressures on the industry and the likely effect on the prospects for short- and longer-term success. More specifically, a company is able to take into consideration its true competitive position with regard to its opponents and can identify the possible strengths and weaknesses due to the current state of rivalry in the industry. It may then proceed to consider what level of importance should be attached to the marketing planning process in order to provide a competitive advantage and a position from which to achieve its financial objectives.

Rivalry in the airline business led to new forms of strategic alliance business model being developed in order to remain competitive. Airline alliances are based upon providing for a larger, more global business operation which has a number of possible joint benefits:

- Alliance partners can achieve more cost-effective business operations.
- Ability to offer a wider range of choice and destinations due to airline partners.
- Better utilisation of aircraft.
- Improve service by sharing lounge/airport facilities.
- Ability to offer round fares/circle fares.
- Enhanced ability to reward passengers and give quicker mileage accrual.
- More cost-effective customer retention/acquisition strategies.
- Access to larger more sophisticated passenger database.
- Sharing of communication and campaign management tools.

## Portfolio analysis

A portfolio approach allows for the analysis of an organisation's current position in relation to the marketplace, its own companies or products. A commonly used technique for consideration of the growth and share of an organisation is the Boston Consulting Group matrix (BCG). Portfolio analysis has been described as a family of techniques with BCG as the most famous (Abell and Hammond, 1979). The BCG approach has been used by a large number of planners in different marketing settings. This approach allows an organisation to classify the position of each of its strategic business units (SBUs) on one axis in terms of their market share relative to competitors and on the opposite axis to position annual industry growth. By creating a measurement based upon the scales of each of these axes, a spatial plot is derived which by the use of the creation of quadrants places each plot in a specific category. As part of the analysis, a company may identify which SBUs are dominant when compared to competitors, and whether the areas in which the company operates are growing, stable or declining. The two-by-two matrix (see Figure 20.4) describes four types of position labelled as star, question mark, cash cow and dog.

### Stars

These are SBUs or products with a high market share in a fast-growing market and, importantly, offering good prospects for growth. As such, the objective would be for an investment or protection for any SBU or product to be identified when it falls into this quadrant. The objective is to build on the strength of the position and/or to hold on to it in the face of any competition. If the organisation has a balanced portfolio, the transferring of money from a cash cow to the star SBU could be contemplated if this would create higher returns in the long run. This could be the airline route which offered the most return to the company or the destination to which a tour operator could obtain the highest demand.

### Question marks

These are SBUs or products where there is some question about their position. Spatially, there is the potential for high market growth, but there is also low market share. The objectives would be to investigate further the possibility of any future movement in the market or from the competition, creating a new position of either a star or a dog. If the question mark has the possibility of becoming a star and if the organisation has a cash cow then money should be transferred to build the question mark position with the objective of creating a star. Alternatively, a poor

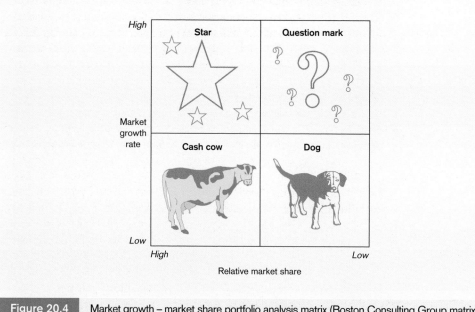

| | Figure 20.4 | Market growth – market share portfolio analysis matrix (Boston Consulting Group matrix) |
|---|---|---|

*Source*: Boston Consulting Group, www.bcg.com

outcome for the analysis may mean the objective has to be one of becoming a niche operator – or even divestment. If the unit of consideration were an overseas destination for a tour operator and a certain destination such as Florida fell into this quadrant, there may need to be an expansion of brochure space for the area and the use of increased promotion to increase demand.

### Cash cows

This category is where the SBU or product is enjoying the benefit of a high market share but in a low- or zero-growth market. The objective would be to exploit the strong, positive cash flow situation but not to devote any investment into the SBU or product apart from to ensure its maintenance. The objective is normally to hold the position and harvest money so that it can be used to grow other parts of the business. This can be the case in some seaside resort areas where a good hotel retains high-value business but the resort itself is in decline and there is no reason to expect any future increase in demand.

### Dogs

These are SBUs or products with a low market share and static or no market growth. The inference is that any future earnings are bound to be low and little or no profit will be made. The objective would be either to create a niche area for activity or to withdraw from this area of business by selling out or planning closure. If the unit of consideration were items on a restaurant menu and certain items fell into this area, there would be an argument for reducing or removing the meal types from the menu. Another example is the withdrawal of British Airways from the Dublin route as it could not compete with other lower-cost carriers.

Each of the BCG model's spatial areas allows an identification of what strategies may be most appropriate. This allows objectives to be decided upon which are in the long-term interests of the organisation as a whole, so that a balanced approach is taken which considers all aspects of an operation.

The assumption is that the higher the market share of any strategic business unit the better its long-term marketplace position, because of the probability of economies of scale, lower costs and higher profitability. In Figure 20.4 the vertical axis identifies the annual growth rate percentage of the operating market for the SBUs, companies or products being assessed. The logic of its inclusion is related to the notion that any organisation in a situation where there is high market growth will have derived benefit from the situation of buoyant development in the marketplace.

Relative market share is the horizontal axis and is used because of its ability to provide the unit of measurement as an indicator of the ability to generate cash based upon the relative position to the market leader. The measure of market share is expressed as a comparison to that of the largest competitor. This is important because it reflects market share relative to the leader and shows the degree of power the market leader has over others in the market. For example, if company 'A' had 25% share of the market and its competitor 'B' also had 25%, there is little advantage. However, the market situation is dramatically different and more favourable to 'A' if it is the market leader with a 25% share and its closest competitor has a 12.5% market share. The horizontal axis provides a relative ratio to the market leader and, therefore, the example given would create a 1:1 ratio in the first case and 1:0.5 in the second. These ratios are plotted on the horizontal axis against the market leader's share to reflect the individual positions of dominance for different units of measurement. The axis can be divided on any scale which makes sense for the market being considered but should enable the relative positions, across the range of the axis, to be plotted. As there is the use of a market leader share figure, the left-hand end of the scale will be no larger than 1 as no other SBU, product or company can exceed the size of the leader's share.

A certain amount of caution has to be applied to the indiscriminate use of portfolio analysis. At the outset it should be realised that portfolio analysis has more dimensions than simply market and market growth. In fact, one of the difficulties is to decide upon the scales for the axes. Once these are agreed, it may be difficult to obtain competitive data. With a BCG approach the spatial positioning outcome of any analysis is not necessarily related to profitability, as a high market share could be based upon low profitability if prices are lower than the competition, or vice versa. In addition, a higher market share for a company or a product may reflect a disproportionate amount of promotional expenditure which in turn could be creating unacceptable cost implications. There are conceptual and practical problems in defining both products and markets when using the matrix. While international flights to America or Asia may be a star, the main business for the airline could be suffering due to the impact of no-frills operators on European routes. Finally, a market which is growing may not be a good environmental fit, or suit the business strengths of the SBU or company. None of these weaknesses indicates there is a major problem with the BCG matrix or its principles but simply that it has to be utilised with some degree of caution. Its strength is that it allows for a more detailed analysis of the business.

### Competitive advantage

When tourism companies decide upon strategies that may offer them a higher likelihood of achieving market success they need to consider different generic routes to obtain competitive advantage. Porter (1980) describes the three generic strategies of *cost leadership* (a company that seeks, finds and exploits all sources of cost advantage – providing for a standard, no-frills package such as that successfully pioneered by Southwest Airlines in America and adopted a few years later by easyJet in the UK and other no frills carriers (see Figure 20.5)); *differentiation* (a company seeks something distinctive to set it apart from others that can bring in good profit returns – typically having attributes that are different to the competition such as the quality added value of the tour operator such as Kuoni); and a *focus* strategy (a company selects a segment of the market and targets that to the extent of excluding other segments whereby a tour company will specialise in a single type of product, such as walking holidays).

## Business situation analysis

Once sufficient information has been collected, there is the need to carry out an analysis of the business situation and this is best done by identifying the major strengths, weaknesses, opportunities and threats facing an organisation. This is the so-called 'SWOT analysis'. There is also the need to check the results of the SWOT analysis against information provided from PESTEL analysis.

The systematic analysis carried out at this stage provides the formulation of a number of assumptions about the past performance, future conditions, product opportunities, resources and service priorities which all lead to the possibility of a range of strategic options for an organisation in the tourism sector.

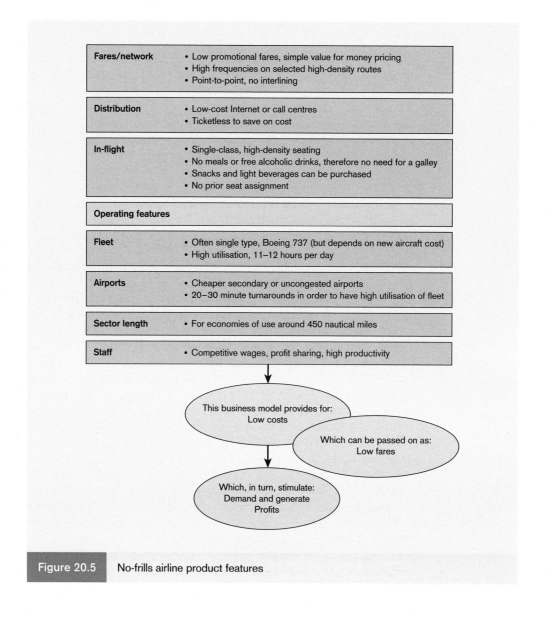

Figure 20.5    No-frills airline product features

At this stage of planning, it is possible to circulate the assumptions and forecasts to different company divisions. These should be offered as a range of alternatives. For example, if you have assumed the market will grow at $x$% and this will create £$Y$ with a specific strategy, then it is also wise to create alternative scenarios. You should estimate sales at lower and higher rates than expected so that the impact on profits can be assessed. For example, a rate of growth of $x + 2$%, given different relative cost implications, may create a profit of $1.3 \times £Y$, or alternatively $x - 2$% gives $0.7 \times £Y$. Managers can then involve their team in discussions about the relevance of the material created from the foregoing environmental scanning stage.

## Creating the objectives

Objectives are a combination of what is expected of the organisation by its shareholders or directors, and an evaluation of the options emerging out of the first stages of the planning process. The objectives should emerge as the most logical course of action for the organisation to embark upon given the detailed analysis in the preceding stages.

We also have to ensure that the objectives are not only related to volume of sales and financial objectives, but also involve broader marketing objectives. One danger in planning is that large organisations often set financial objectives in terms of growth rate in earnings per share, return on equity or investment and so on, and ignore marketing objectives such as the selection of specific segments as target markets and the improvement of products, brand image or consumer awareness. Objectives should also include the expected market share achievements because this performance may only be realistic if certain budgets are made available.

Objectives need to be a balance of the aspirational and realistic so that the organisation attempts to improve its market position within acceptable risk limits. The basic criteria for setting objectives based upon the SMART acronym is that they need to be:

- **Specific**, by being focused on the results required.
- **Measurable** for each objective set.
- **Achievable**, set against trends and market position constraints and assessed fully.
- **Realistic**, given resource constraints of time and money, etc.; and set against
- **Time limits** of when the objective(s) should be reached.

The objective stage inputs of Figure 20.1 are based upon growth strategies whereby a company is attempting to expand. Organisations will normally want to attack the market share of others by penetrating the market to increase their own share of the market. This takes place in the current markets and is normally based upon a more aggressive use of the marketing mix. The organisation may attempt to increase existing customer usage rates or attract competitors' customers. For example, Barclaycard has combined with Thomas Cook and in 2011 offered price discounts to Visa card members on holidays and insurance; and the company has utilised promotional techniques such as being able to earn extra bonus points in relation to car hire in an attempt to get their cardholders to use their cards while on holiday in preference to competitors' cards. Larger organisations or companies will try to increase sales through market development by attempting to sell current products in new markets. This may involve the addition of new locations, such as McDonald's opening outlets to compete at airports, at tourist attractions and even within office buildings. Market development may also be based upon convincing the customer to find new uses for existing products. Larger organisations or companies will try to develop markets by selling the benefits of, say, self-catering holidays to those who take hotel holidays. Organisations may also develop their markets by expanding internationally, such as Holiday Inn and the Accor group.

Objectives may also include **new product development** or diversification. The Eurostar Channel Tunnel service in 2007 improved the service by changing the London-based terminus and reduced the travelling time to Paris. The objective for this investment required intensive product research and assessment as to the incremental business from northern cities. Tour operators/wholesalers develop new destinations and airlines embark upon new air routes. Diversification has occurred where companies such as Virgin developed a new business from its retail base into an airline operation in several different countries. Hotel organisations have developed contract catering operations and vice versa. There has also been the diversification of airlines into the hotel business.

## Providing an effective marketing mix strategy

The success of the plan relies on creating the right marketing mix strategies for achieving the objectives (see Chapter 21 for a clear explanation of the different aspects of the marketing mix). The use of the marketing mix involves balancing the elements of the marketing mix to achieve the highest expected probability of meeting the plan's objectives. However, mix strategies have to be checked to ensure they are acceptable. For example, if the strategy is for expansion of a destination, say by means of price benefits, an impact or environmental analysis should be considered. Figure 20.6 shows a situation where there is no extra benefit in expanding tourist numbers since the social costs (due to extra arrivals) increase at the same rate as the benefits. Note that $Q_1$ and $Q_2$ are in exactly the same position in both parts (a) and (b) of Figure 20.6.

Figure 20.6(a) shows the relationship between demand and price for a tourism destination. If price is reduced from $P_1$ to $P_2$ then the resultant demand for the area increases from $Q_1$ to $Q_2$.

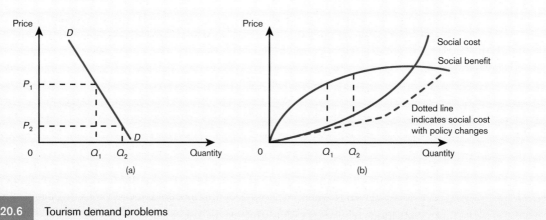

| Figure 20.6 | Tourism demand problems |
| --- | --- |

Tourism destinations can reduce the average price of visits through government policies such as allowing more charter arrivals or reducing tourist taxes. If the positions of Figure 20.6(a) are examined against the social cost and benefit curves of Figure 20.6(b) it will be seen that position $Q_2$ is no better than position $Q_1$ as the social costs (such as those depicted in Photograph 20.2) have increased at a rate that cancels out the increase in social benefits. The result is that the destination is no better off socially from an increase in arrivals and may have to check other criteria and bring in policy changes before it agrees to expansion policies.

| Photograph 20.2 | Every tourist destination has social costs that need to be managed. |
| --- | --- |

*Source*: Tommy Trenchard/Alamy Images

## Market segmentation

Emanating out of the SWOT analysis will be the objective to target specific sub-markets or what are known as segments. Market segmentation is the process of dividing the total perceived market into subsets, in each of which the potential customers have characteristics in common, which lead to similar demand needs for a product or service. The marketer has to decide upon the coverage of the target market. This can be any one of a selection from a broad mass market, a selective market segment strategy or aiming at two or more multiple segments.

Mass tourism operators selling undifferentiated European and long-haul destinations will target a very broad subset of consumers. This is because their success lies in offering a wide range of popular countries at value-for-money prices. In contrast, a specialist tour operator/wholesaler can attempt to identify a new segment or adopt an upmarket or downmarket position. A current lifestyle change is towards being healthier. The medical profession and a number of magazines and newspapers have changed attitudes to both leisure pursuits and eating habits. Both of these will have repercussions on the provision of leisure centres in hotels and resorts, activity holiday supply and spa and health products as well as be an opportunity for new product development.

### *Achieving strength of positioning*

To be successful in positioning, a company or destination has to understand how to modify the perception of the consumer by improving, reinforcing or defending its position in the market-place. Ries and Trout (1986) argue that positioning has to be correctly addressed, as it is the only way to counteract the confusion created by the communication jungle. Accordingly, Ries and Trout recommend 'the best approach in our over-communicated society is the over-simplified message'. This has to happen at the right time and as such the secret of positioning becomes the organised system for finding the window in the mind. Ries and Trout contend that: 'Positioning starts with a product. A piece of merchandise, a service, a company, an institution or even a person . . . But positioning is not what you do to a product. Positioning is what you do to the mind of the prospect. That is, you position the product in the mind of the prospect.' To achieve success at positioning the tourism product or brand there is a need to ensure the position has clarity, is credible, has consistency over time and will remain competitive in relation to the needs of the company's chosen target groups. This is explained as follows:

- **Clarity.** It is important to realise that positioning is about communicating a message to the consumer so as to spatially place the tourism service offered in their mind. This has to be based upon a clear message with no confusion. If the message is not clear the consumer will not understand what the brand or offer is about. A positioning strategy requires a clear message that most people will understand.

- **Credibility.** A positioning message has to be believable. If we claim that our travel agency offers better service than it delivers in reality, consumers may well utilise it a first time but never again. They may well feel cynical about the company claims if they find the delivery does not match the promise. This is particularly vital in the case of services where it is not possible for customers to sample an offering very easily. Also, customers have a preconceived set of relative positions already in their minds as expectations and therefore they have learnt what is possible in terms of any claim to a specific position.

- **Consistency.** It has been pointed out that positioning is all about creating an image in the mind of the consumer. Clearly for this to be achieved the message has to be consistent. If a company changes its communications policy there will be no clear messages and the public will not be able to visualise the positioning the company is attempting to occupy. Of course, it is possible to change positioning but this takes time to achieve.

- **Competitiveness.** In any decision over position there needs to be a strategic decision which positions the company relative to that of the competition (we are friendlier, larger, offer more value, have better service, more modern, safer, etc.) and this has to be accepted by the customer. Positioning the brand with a set of attributes that the customer does not care about is never going to be effective.

| Table 20.2 | Some general characteristics of segmentation strategies |
|---|---|
| **Characteristic** | **Typical classification** |
| Geographic | Region of world, country, area of country, urban, suburban, rural areas, city, town, post code, type of house or by climate type |
| Demographic | Age group, gender, education, family life cycle, ethnic group. Socio-economic classification of household based upon A, B, C1, C2, DE classifications |
| Psychographic | Lifestyle. Personality type – introvert, extrovert, high/low ego drive, independent, compulsive, gregarious, group worker |
| Usership | Non-user, current user, past user, potential user, loyalty type, heavy user, medium user, light user |
| Kind of purchase | Special occasion (honeymoon, anniversary), annual holiday trip, business travel, method of purchase (agent, direct, etc.) |
| Attitudes | Towards product area, towards brand, towards usership and use situations |
| Benefits sought | Status, convenience, luxury, economy, etc. |

### Selecting the segments to target

The identification and selection of segments will require judgement based on the analysis of different data. The purpose of segmentation is to select a segment (target market) with the best potential on a range of criteria. The objective set is then to create product benefits, features and promotional messages which will appeal to the needs of the selected segment(s). A number of characteristics are examined when deciding upon target groups as shown in Table 20.2. (See Chapter 3 on consumer behaviour for further discussion of some of these characteristics.)

In order for segmentation to be successful there is a need to apply intellectual rigour to the segmentation procedure. When a target group is identified it is prudent to use a checklist to ensure the segment offers a viable opportunity for the organisation, such as:

- **Is the segment measurable?** Progress at various stages of the segmentation activity needs to be measured. Segment composition, size, purchasing power etc. in order for assessment need to be measurable.

- **Is the segment accessible?** The targeting decision requires that individual buyers can easily be contacted through promotional messages as well as be accessible to be offered a purchase opportunity or service.

- **Is the segment substantial?** The segment must be large enough to provide a viable level of business.

- **Is the segment sustainable?** The choice of segment has to take into account whether the demand will last. Fashion and 'lifestyle' market segments are prone to change and fall into demise.

- **Is the segment actionable?** Are there any impediments to putting together a marketing mix so that the target market can be reached with a clear product positioning strategy and message which will fit the needs, aspirational ideals and behaviour of the segment?

- **Is the segment defendable?** Can the target market be defended against competitor activity if they also select the same target group, and will rivalry cause any viability problems?

Segmentation leads to positioning the service or product offer so that it is right for the target audience. This is reliant on adherence to the initial objectives and results in the final choice of the marketing mix. Once the segments have emerged from the consideration process the objectives need to be reconsidered.

If it is found that there are no problems with the objectives, and the plan is to be adopted, there has to be some assessment of whether the objectives can be achieved within specific time constraints. Competitors may be able to develop more quickly or the organisation may find it too difficult to change in a short period of time. The ability to change is often related to the availability of resources. It is necessary to question whether the resources available are sufficient to achieve the objectives (budgets, personnel, technology, existing hotels, aircraft or built facilities). If, after evaluation, it is decided the strategy is unacceptable, there is a need to review and revise the plan's objectives.

Agreeing the marketing mix strategy has to be linked to laying down task-related programmes which allocate budgets and create responsibilities and timings for the plan's implementation. There is always a need to link planning with budgeting which will allow for the adoption and execution of an effective marketing mix strategy to achieve the objectives of the plan.

## Monitoring the plan

There should be a means of monitoring the achievements of the plan so that tactical action can be taken either to get the plan back on course or to take advantage of new opportunities. There is therefore the need for the provision of assessment and measurement methods that will monitor progress towards the achievement of the plan's overall objectives. There is also the need to know what deviations from the initial objectives are acceptable. This will allow for the review and amendment of the plan on a continuous basis.

The tourism and hospitality industry has invested in reservation systems that allow a continuous flow of financial and booking pattern data. This has enabled the modelling of different performance indicators. These can include forecasts of probable load factors or occupancy levels as well as assessment of the effectiveness of regional or national sales promotion, price changes and sales representative campaigns. Nowadays, the airline and hotel sectors are applying these systems to yield management systems as a means to monitor demand and maximise the revenue from consumers.

## CONCLUSION

Marketing planning is probably the most important activity for any tourism organisation. The long-term survival of an organisation is related to the way that it understands how to assess its environment, set sensible objectives and choose logical strategies for achieving success. Utilisation of different models such as SWOT, PESTEL, Porter's five force model and the BCG model all allow for a more informed approach to the planning analysis. The conditions for maximising the advantages from planning are based upon the need to understand the human aspects of the process as well as the formalised procedures of a structured approach.

## SELF-CHECK QUESTIONS

1. Name the four levels of marketing environment and identify how these may affect the company.
2. What do the acronyms PESTEL and SWOT stand for and when should they be used?
3. List the main problems that you may encounter when producing a marketing plan.
4. What do you understand the term 'portfolio analysis' to mean?
5. Explain the concept of positioning and its relationship to target groups.

## YOUTUBE

http://www.youtube.com/watch?v=iNmiKbGFfYl
Indicates importance of data analytics TRAVELCLICK® Hotelligence360™ Hospitality Business Intelligence

http://www.youtube.com/watch?v=-pygu7vyRm4
Provides insight into the adoption of products

http://www.youtube.com/watch?v=i1qF2y3A-Ak
What needs to be considered in opening up a restaurant

http://www.youtube.com/watch?v=mYF2_FBCvXw
Michael Porter talks about the five forces and the airline industry

http://www.youtube.com/watch?v=laTzwz08M94&feature=relmfu
An understanding of a segmentation approach

# REFERENCES AND FURTHER READING

Abell, D.F. and Hammond, J.S. (1979) *Strategic Market Planning Problems and Analytical Approaches*, Prentice Hall, Englewood Cliffs, NJ.

Evans, N., Campbell, D. and Stonehouse, G. (2003) *Strategic Management for Travel and Tourism*, Butterworth Heinemann, Oxford. The text provides a comprehensive insight into strategic planning for tourism organisations. It offers approaches to the selection, evaluation and implementation of strategic planning. It is specifically written in relation to the travel and tourism industry with an explanation of strategic management applications and theory. In addition it has case studies from Southwest Airlines, Airtours, Marriott and Thomas Cook.

Gilbert, C. (2003) *Retail Marketing Management*, 2nd edn, Financial Times/Prentice Hall, Harlow.

Gilbert, D., Child, D. and Bennett, M. (2001) 'A qualitative study of the current practice of "no-frills" airlines operating in the UK', *Journal of Vacation Marketing* 7(4), 302–15.

Holloway, C. (2004) *Marketing for Tourism*, 4th edn, Prentice Hall/Financial Times, Harlow. This book provides a good introduction to different aspects of tourism marketing and especially communications. It has a large number of case studies.

IPS (2005) *International Passenger Survey*, Office of National Statistics, Cardiff.

Kotler, P. (2000) *Marketing Management – The Millennium Edition*, Prentice Hall, Upper Saddle River, NJ.

Kotler, P., Bowen, J. and Makens, J. (2009) *Marketing for Hospitality and Tourism*, 5th edn, Prentice Hall, Upper Saddle River, NJ. The book draws upon the marketing material of Philip Kotler's other books and as such is based upon his pedigree which has been developed over a number of years of writing marketing textbooks. However, the examples are often better in other texts and other specialist books need to be read in conjunction with this one. This latest edition now covers electronic marketing, has case studies and provides a broad understanding of the role of marketing in hospitality and tourism. Specialist areas covered are customer quality management and destination marketing.

McArdle, J. (1989) 'Product branding – the way forward', *Tourism Management* **10**, 201.

McDonald, M. (1989) *Marketing Plans*, Heinemann, Oxford.

McDonald, M. (2007) *Marketing Plans, How to Prepare Them, How to Use Them*, Butterworth Heinemann, Oxford. This text provides the reader with a comprehensive coverage of all the aspects of producing a successful marketing plan. The book concentrates upon the logical development of a marketing plan and only deals with the marketing concepts in a perfunctory manner so is recommended solely for understanding the marketing planning process and approach.

Mintel (2000) 'The gay holiday market', Mintel International Group, London.

Porter, M.E. (1980) *Competitive Strategy: Techniques for Analysing Industries and Competitors*, Free Press, New York.

Ries, A. and Trout, J. (1986) *Positioning: The Battle for Your Mind*, McGraw-Hill, London.

Tarlow, P. (2003) *e-Review of Tourism Research*, John Wiley & Sons, New York.

Urry, J. (1992) *The Tourist Gaze*, Sage, London.

# MAJOR CASE STUDY 20.1
Disneyland® Resort Paris

When the Disney Corporation assessed the idea of a theme park in Europe initially a site with sufficient flat land and a good climate similar to Florida was thought to be in the Alicante area of Spain. However, the area also suffered from the notorious Mistral winds. The final decision was for the French location, at Marne-la-Vallée, which could attract European visitors and has the benefit of close proximity to Paris. The location put the park within four hours' drive for around 68 million people, and two hours' flight or train journey for a further 300 million.

However, Disneyland® Resort Paris, formerly Euro Disney, became a huge embarrassment to the Walt Disney Corporation after it plunged into the red shortly after its opening in France in 1992. The initial cost of the theme park, at US$4.4 billion for its initial development represented the largest single piece of construction in Europe's history apart from the Channel Tunnel project linking England and France.

Cumulative losses at the end of 1993 exceeded US$1 billion. The loss is all the more significant given that the then Euro Disney had only achieved target attendance objectives of 9 million rather than 11 million planned 'guests' in slightly over one year of operation. The situation did not improve in 1994 when Euro Disney reported a loss for the year to the end of September of US$317 million and attendance was 10% down on levels achieved in 1993. The Walt Disney company announced it would close the park unless the banks agreed to restructure the $1 billion debt that the park's construction and operation had accumulated. The banks could have been left with massive debt and therefore agreed to write off virtually all of the next two years' interest charges, and allowed a three-year postponement of loan repayments. In return the Walt Disney company restructured its own share of the park and loan arrangements.

The question is what went wrong with the planning? The main problem can be found to lie with the planning assumptions and forecasts which did not reflect the European economy or the willingness of consumers to pay high entrance fees. There was also a mistaken belief in a flatter seasonal demand curve, which characterises demand in the USA, as a result of mid-semester or off-peak visits by parents with their children. As a result, the levels and patterns of demand never reached those anticipated by planners.

An additional problem is related to the homogeneity of European markets. Disney planners in the USA initially treated Europe as a single country, underestimating the inherent differences between the existing markets in respect of demand and importing marketing methods which had succeeded in America but which did not successfully transplant to the European context. Consequently, the American parent company was forced to accept that tourists' habits vary a great deal throughout the European context and that its prices were too high for French visitors.

As an integral part of the financial subsidisation for the development of the park, the plan had assumed that well-appointed, high-priced hotels and other property could be constructed and then sold on to entrepreneurs for considerable profits. Disney planners did not want to be faced with either the land-use problems they had experienced in the USA where extra land has had to be purchased for expansion or the financial limitations imposed in Tokyo where Japanese investors took huge profits while Disney earned 10% of gross earnings on rides and 5% on food and beverage. Consequently, the planners were concerned with attempting to maximise profit opportunities from the outset.

Disney planners overlooked the worsening economic conditions prevailing in Europe in the early 1990s which led to a severe slump in the property market for accommodation. The planners embarked on a vast property development – including hotels, shops, offices and residential housing – ignoring the severe handicap this posed of potentially unrealistic financial obligations to its American parent. The hotels were not sold as originally planned and, in addition, currency devaluation in Great Britain and Italy further depressed purchasing power, driving down demand for foreign travel.

Other planning problems materialised. The design of the hotel restaurants, for example, did not take into consideration the different tastes of the guests and were often too small, because of the belief that few Europeans would eat a full breakfast. Consequently, long waiting times and queuing problems ensued, culminating in guest dissatisfaction and complaints. The park's outlets were designed for snacking but the pattern was that at 1 o'clock there was a major demand for a reasonably substantial meal. Moreover, Disney outlets were restricted by a 'no alcohol' policy which meant the French custom of taking wine with a meal was not permissible.

The problems were further compounded by pre-opening reports by Disney that employees would have to comply with the written Disney code of dress which consisted, for women, of short fingernails, appropriate undergarments and strict policies on hairstyles. The global code based upon Disney brand values was considered an insult by the French people who believed it attacked the underlying principles in French culture of individualism and privacy. Thus, unforeseen cultural issues emerged with newspapers, such as *Le Figaro*, stating: 'Euro Disney is the very symbol of the process by which people's cultural standards are lowered and money becomes all-conquering.'

In addition, Disney characters were attacked as likely to pollute the nation's culture. Concessions were made and new emphasis was placed on European fairy-tale characters such as Snow White and Pinocchio rather than Bambi and Dumbo. Also, in order to echo French culture, the turret which the company's 'imagineers' built was modelled not on Neuschwanstein, the Bavarian castle reconstructed at Disney's other theme parks, but on a drawing from a fifteenth-century French manuscript.

Following the embarrassment of heavy losses and low levels of demand in 1993 and 1994, Disney brought in French senior management who orchestrated key developments at Euro Disney. The theme park was renamed Disneyland® Resort Paris and in 1994 a complete product reassessment and reduction programme was implemented. The number of souvenir lines was cut in half from 30,000 and restaurant menu items were also reduced from 5,400 to 2,000.

Marketing strategies were reappraised and advertising messages modified. The advertising was designed to make parents and grandparents sympathetic to their children's emotional pleasure while emphasising the adventure element for adults. Potential customers are targeted with special offers during off-peak winter months, a strategy which evolved in response to market research activity which demonstrated that levels of repeat visits were high. In addition, the promotional links with Eurostar have helped to increase the number of UK visitors.

Pricing policies were also adjusted to offer reduced entrance admission charges in the evening, for example. Job flexibility arrangements, customer care programmes and other efficiency drives were also instigated, leading to the first ever surplus for Disneyland® Resort Paris for 1995. This was related to improvements in hotel occupancy, which rose steadily from 55% in 1993 to 68% in 1995, compared with an average of roughly 60% for hotels in and around the Paris area.

The current situation is linked closely to the need to pay off the park's debts and net losses. The hope was that the addition in 2002 of Walt Disney Studios, which was modelled on the success of Universal Studios in Florida, would attract higher numbers. The recent plan of the heavily indebted group is based upon a belief of the need for further new attractions to increase visitor numbers. In 2010 Euro Disney was given permission by the French government to build a third park in the Marne-la-Vallée region to enlarge the Disneyland Paris Park. The Paris complex had a record attendance of 15.4 million visits in its 2009 financial year and hotel occupancy was relatively high at 87.3%, but down from 90.9% in 2008. However, the recent financial crisis and promotional prices lowered the expenditure of visitors, leading to a net loss of €63 million in 2009 after modest profits in 2008, which was for the first time in five years. The slip continued in 2010 when Euro Disney reported a net loss of €114.5 million in the six months to end March 2010 and a 6.5% fall in attendances.

Therefore, it is crucial that financial and marketing planning are implemented professionally if the park is to maintain its profitability and prosper in the European marketplace. This is especially important given increasing competition from other European theme parks such as Europa Park in Germany, Tivoli Gardens in Denmark, PortAventura in Spain, and Parc Asterix which is just North of Paris, France.

*Source*: Based on information from the Internet, various newspaper articles and reports.

## DISCUSSION QUESTIONS

Provide some analysis and marketing solutions for Disneyland® Resort Paris. For example:

1. See **http://www.coastergrotto.com/theme-park-attendance.jsp** and examine world trends in theme park attendance. Assess the figures and draw conclusions as to what type of park is having success. Also, look at the websites of the successful parks, and assess if there are additions that Disneyland Paris needs to adopt. If so argue in a reasoned way what these would be?

2. Is there a need to plan to attract different market segments by country and demographically, and if so how can this be achieved?

3. Examine and assess the marketing activity for Disneyland Paris on the web. Does the park need to have an improved overall marketing communication strategy targeted to potential visitors and/or past visitors? See YouTube: **http://www.youtube.com/watch?v=4bFzw5YJLmo**

# CHAPTER 21
## MARKETING MIX APPLICATIONS

### LEARNING OUTCOMES

The marketing mix offers management a set of tools that may be manipulated to meet specific objectives and attract predefined target markets. The marketing mix is the focus of this chapter and, by the end of the chapter, you will be able to:

- identify the elements that make up the marketing mix and understand how this may be applied to a tourism product;

- recognise that the management of the marketing mix generally, and promotion and pricing in particular, will be beneficial in meeting specific predetermined objectives;

- appreciate that distribution and product formulation are linked to, and influenced by, technological and structural changes in the tourism industry; and

- understand the centrality of the concept of the target market to the marketing mix.

Photograph: Kairouan Medina, Tunisia © Helen Savill

# INTRODUCTION

Anyone who purchases a tourism product has probably been influenced by a promotional campaign, assessed the product offer, considered whether they are willing to pay the price and, finally, thought about how easy it would be to buy it. Each of these aspects of purchase is carefully planned by tourism marketers in an attempt to convince potential tourists to buy their products. They are the basic ingredients of the marketing mix, the aspect of marketing that we consider in detail in this chapter.

In actual fact a great deal of tourism management involves aspects of the marketing mix. Each of the areas that make up the marketing mix involves a complex set of management decisions which have to take into account not only the individual mix strategy but also the effect of such a mix on the target market groups. A major tourism marketing task is to carefully integrate the marketing mix in order to deliver optimum value for both the trade and the consumer. This chapter will therefore provide some of the most important considerations required in the planning of the marketing mix.

# WHAT IS THE MARKETING MIX?

It is customary to accept that the marketing mix (Figure 21.1) is within the control of management and refers to decisions made in relation to the four Ps. These may be defined as:

- **P**roduct.
- **P**rice.
- **P**romotion.
- **P**lace (distribution).

There are, however, alternative approaches where authors stress the need for an expansion of these four. This is an interesting development because the four Ps were conceived by

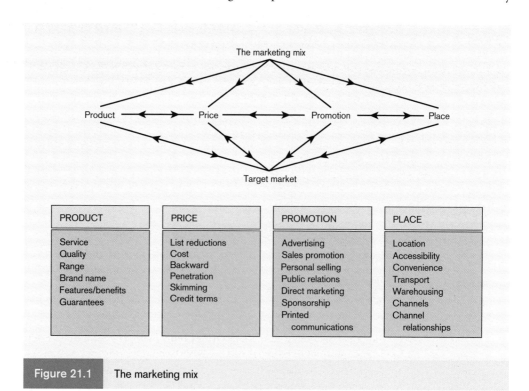

**Figure 21.1** The marketing mix

McCarthy (1978) as an abridged version of a much wider range of what were termed 'marketing ingredients'. McCarthy based the classification of his four Ps upon a whole collection of marketing ingredients offered much earlier by Borden (1965). We will discuss this later in this chapter. Kotler and Armstrong (2005) indicate that the marketing mix is one of the key concepts in modern marketing theory. They define the marketing mix as 'the set of controllable, tactical marketing tools that the firm blends to produce the response it wants in the target market'.

## Target market

The fundamental starting point for the creation of a successful marketing mix strategy is to ensure the **target market** is clearly defined. Although the target market is not part of the marketing mix, its role in dictating the different ways the mix is used makes it indistinguishable from the concept and of paramount importance. The target market is the focus for all marketing mix activity and is linked to the final selection of segments that we discussed in the previous chapter.

The market for a product is made up of actual and potential consumers. This total available group of consumers will be analysed and a decision will be made as to segments or subgroups to be targeted. The segments would probably have been identified as part of the marketing planning process (see Chapter 20 for an explanation of choosing segments) and would have emerged or been specified at the time of the setting of objectives. The specification of the target market has a number of important benefits which are discussed below.

### Benefits of targeting

Targeting facilitates the following:

- A fuller understanding of the unique characteristics and needs of the group to be satisfied is reached. The target market acts as a reference point for marketing decisions, especially as to how the marketing mix should be planned. This should lead to greater effectiveness for the mix which in turn provides for the success of the programme.

- A better understanding of a company's competitors is gained because it is possible to detect those who have made a similar selection of target markets. If an organisation does not clarify the markets it wishes to target, it may treat every other organisation in its sector as an equal competitor. Once a main competitor is identified their marketing efforts can be more closely followed – or benchmarked and then reacted to.

- An improvement is possible in an understanding of the changes and developments in the needs of the target market. Awareness is heightened due to the scrutiny focused upon the target group's actions, and reactions to slightly different forms of the marketing mix.

As we have seen with the section on segmentation in Chapter 20, target markets can be based upon a number of factors such as:

- socio-economic groups;
- geographic location;
- age;
- sex;
- income levels;
- visitor type;
- benefits sought; and
- purchase behaviour and attitudes for both the international and domestic business, holiday visitor and recreationalist.

The target market acts as the focus for tailoring the mix so that target customers will judge the overall product to be superior to that of the competition. Segmentation and target marketing are central to efficient and effective marketing activity because they are instrumental in ensuring the marketing mix strategy is tailored to meet the specific needs of different customer groups.

# PRODUCT

The effectiveness of planning the marketing mix depends as much on the ability to select the right target market as on the skill in devising a product offer which will generate high levels of satisfaction. We have to realise that the customer is looking for the right product to solve their problem of satisfying a need. Often this involves a portfolio approach. Club Mediterranée is treated as having a singular product to offer yet it has more than 80 different holiday villages in many different countries, as well as having expanded into other types of tour business. More recently Club Mediterranée utilised quality as a means to reduce its product range and improve its positioning. The service product (see Figure 21.2) is quite complex and can be thought of as being a combination of different levels with four important areas – the *core product*; *the facilitating product*; *the supporting product*; and the *augmented product*.

## Core product

Every **product** is a package of problem-solving services and tangible attributes that will be successful if the package is valued enough to satisfy a need or want. A product includes everything that the customer receives and this includes the central level of the *core product* which is made up of the delivery of benefits and features. A holiday consumer in a travel agency is looking for the benefit of relaxing in the sun and having no hassle in the journey or stay. They leave the detail of how to arrange this to the travel agent. To put it another way, buyers 'do not buy quarter inch drills; they buy quarter inch holes'. Marketing staff have to uncover the subtle benefits that the consumer seeks when utilising a retail distribution channel or purchasing a product. We know that consumers buy products for the benefits they are expected to deliver. It therefore makes sense to incorporate different additions into the product that will help to differentiate it from the comparable product offered by competitors. Adding in the right features creates a higher probability that a purchase will occur. There are the different features that are added as the tangible aspects of the product which help to differentiate it from competitors. The tangible features may be the size of the hotel entrance, the physical aspects of a destination or the comfort of the airline seat. In order to understand a product it must be understood that service products are different and as such should not be confused with other general marketing literature concepts which are less complex in their approach.

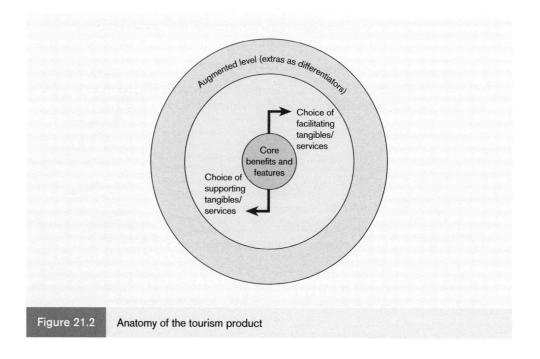

| Figure 21.2 | Anatomy of the tourism product |

## Facilitating, supporting and augmented product

The *facilitating product* aspects must be present for the customer to utilise the services of the core product. This will be the service and goods such as lift service in a high-rise hotel, receptionist and telephone operator, credit card payment facilities, signage and easy access around the destination. *Core products* require *facilitating products* but do not necessarily have to include *supporting products* (see Figure 21.2). In fact the no-frills airlines need the facilitating products of check-in and baggage handling but only provide a minimum of supporting products in order to adhere to their cost-leadership strategy. The supporting product for a scheduled full-service airline may include such extras as separate lounge area, higher employee numbers providing superior service, service to deal with children travelling and so on, as these are all supporting products which may be planned into the product offer.

The *augmented* product level is the added aspects of the product which form the extras and which can help the product compete more favourably in the marketplace. This could be achieved through sensory marketing such as creating a special atmosphere in an airline lounge area by creating garden setting spaces with birdsong and different lighting as well as having sanctuary areas of peace and quiet such as those areas and lounges at places such as Singapore's Changi airport. In fact, Changi also has a nature trail to follow. Companies should take the opportunity to consider factors such as the use of materials and the decor of public areas which will provide the atmosphere within which the customer interacts. A feature could be the inclusion of flight-delay cover. Tourism is normally associated with the risk of delayed flights, exchange rate fluctuations or insufficient snow on skiing holidays. The potential risk of flight delay or inadequate snow cover on ski slopes can be insured against holistically by the operator who passes on a small premium to its clients as part of the price of the trip. A further example is a contract agreement to hotel rates, the early buying forward of currency or advance purchase of aircraft fuel which will allow a company to offer the guarantee of no increase in a quoted price.

By complementing the basic product with special benefits that add value, the product is made more appealing to the consumer. Another method could be to negotiate on behalf of the customer and pass on the added benefits. For instance, arranging a contract with car parks near to airports in off-season periods can allow a company to offer the car-parking service free to its clients. The cost is passed on to each client as a fraction of the true cost of the service because the arrangement allows the car park to acquire business at a difficult time. Features such as free car hire, pick-up at the airport, fast check-outs, study bedrooms and free tickets to tourism attractions or the theatre are all added benefits that can be planned into the product offer. Utilising the augmented approach, the company is able to add extras which are more memorable and can act as differentiators over the competition when other aspects of facilitating and supporting products are likely to be similar between companies. The marketer needs to look constantly at how the different component parts of the overall product need improvement and change and this is sometimes referred to as the potential product in other contexts but here is seen as being within a development and renewal of existing levels, not a new level.

## Service

This is concerned with creating the level of services to be offered. For a hotel, a tour operator/ wholesaler, a restaurant or an airline, this poses the question of how much of the service should the client be expected to perform and how much should be provided by staff. For example, self-service buffet-style food operations or the personal carrying of hand luggage is now thought of as acceptable and, at times, desirable by clients. Similarly, tea- and coffee-making facilities in hotel bedrooms is now seen to be integral to the accommodation product offering, especially if the provision of room service is limited to certain hours. Service provision for air travellers now satisfies communication needs, as some airlines offer an improved business product with in-flight telephone provision, power for a personal computer and mobile phone text messages if there is any problem with a flight. Club Med has gained a positive reputation for its Gentil Organisateurs (GOs), who look after guests, and its Gentil Employés (GEs), who carry out other back office work. Interestingly these 'Gentile' terms (which mean congenial) were introduced about 30 years ago by the organisation as a way of reinforcing aspects of friendship. These developments are indicative of the relentless quest for cost-effective improvements to the service content of the tourism product. Any tourism operation is predominately service-based and has to be able to deliver high levels of service.

## Quality

Quality involves deciding on quality standards for the product and implementing a method of assurance on the performance level of staff and facilities. The management of quality is becoming an increasingly important management function (as discussed in Chapter 19) since it is crucial to create a good reputation for the quality of the product and service offered. This encourages a positive image for the company or organisation and a reputation for good quality is a major advantage in reducing the perception of risk in the minds of consumers. Tourism service providers are more likely to be successful if they can be depended upon to deliver higher levels of service than their competitors. Success through quality is often associated with the outcome of the relationship between a customer's prior expectations of service delivery and the perception of the actual service. With this in mind, Swissair aims for at least 96% of its passengers to rate the quality of its service as good or superior, otherwise it will take remedial action.

## Range

It is necessary to decide how different individual products will fit into the overall range of the organisation's products offered to the marketplace. A tour operator/wholesaler has to decide whether to include five-star or two-star hotels in their range of offerings, or whether they should operate to traditional or newly emerging destinations. More recently the cruise market has expanded and many tour operators/wholesalers have altered their product range to include cruise ships to accommodate the resurgence in demand. In fact, the introduction of new ships from the Carnival group such as Cunard's *Queen Mary 2* as the longest, tallest and heaviest passenger ship ever, bears witness to the investment in this sector.

Tourism enterprises have to decide on the range of offers and how each product fits into the product mix. Such decisions will produce change over time, as illustrated by some of the milestones in the development and change of Thomas Cook in Table 21.1. The essence of the early success of Thomas Cook in providing unique experiences is reflected in the seeking out of new experiences.

| Table 21.1 | Examples of the historical aspects of Thomas Cook |
|---|---|
| 1841 | First excursion from Leicester to Loughborough |
| 1845 | Trip to Liverpool and excursions to Wales |
| 1846 | First tours to Scotland |
| 1851 | Trips for 165,000 people to the Great Exhibition |
| 1855 | First continental tours |
| 1866 | First tours to North America |
| 1869 | First tours to the Holy Land |
| 1872 | Pioneers of round-the-world tours |
| 1874 | Traveller's cheques introduced |
| 1902 | First winter sports brochures and motor car tours |
| 1919 | The company advertises air tours |

| Table 21.1 | *(Continued)* |
|---|---|
| 1927 | First air charter, New York to Chicago for Dempsey fight |
| 1939 | First package tour to south of France |
| 1972 | Thomas Cook becomes part of the Midland Bank Group |
| 1981 | Agreement to launch euro traveller's cheques |
| 1988 | Cessation of short haul operations |
| 1989 | Direct sales operation set up |
| 1992 | Thomas Cook sold by Midland Bank to Westdeutsche Landesbank (WestLB) and the LTU Group |
| 1992 | 21.6% shareholding acquired from Owners Abroad in order to form an alliance (became First Choice) |
| 1994 | Thomas Cook corporate travel business and USA franchised travel offices sold to American Express |
| 1994 | Travel Kiosks set up to sell direct by the use of advanced technology |
| 1999 | The company rationalises and reduces the number of its sub-brands and also launches the new JMC brand |
| 2000 | The company becomes wholly owned by Thomas Cook AG (formerly C&N Touristic AG – which itself was formed as a merger of Condor and Neckermann); the sale also took place of its Global and Financial Division to Travelex |
| 2001 | Thomas Cook UK rationalised as part of a transformation programme |
| 2002 | JMC brand abandoned three years after its introduction |
| 2003 | Thomscook.com adopt a customised system for customers to personalise their travel with a build-your-own (BYO) self-packaging technology linking flights, hotels, car hire and insurance |
| 2003 | Announcement of the merger of its two charter airlines, Condor Flugdienst and Condor Berlin, the sale of some of its hotels and other assets and a large reduction in staff, in order to reduce costs |
| 2004 | The integrated business model of combining the elements of in-house airlines, tour operators and travel agents is not as sustainable given the level of independent travel driven by the success of low-cost airlines |
| 2005 | Although Thomas Cook UK business generated record profits of £51 million ($98 million), the results were affected by losses elsewhere in the group; this led to cost-cutting and selling off 12 of its fleet of Boeing 757-200 aircraft |
| 2006 | KarstadtQuelle, the German retailer, takes full control of Thomas Cook from partner Lufthansa, the German airline |
| 2007 | MyTravel (formerly Airtours), the £1.1 billion UK holiday company, and Thomas Cook (owned by KarstadtQuelle, the German group), agree a merger, with Thomas Cook owning 52% of the capital and MyTravel the remainder |
| 2008 | Thomas Cook Group acquires Canada's TriWest Travel Holdings, French tour operator Jet Tours, and UK independent travel companies hotels4u, Gold Medal and Elegant Resorts |
| 2010 | Thomas Cook Group merged with The Co-operative Travel |
| 2011 | Thomas Cook shares lose about three-quarters of their value on the London Stock Exchange after the company announced it was in talks with its banks about increasing borrowing and the need to shut some UK travel agencies |

## Brand name

A **brand** is a name, a symbol, term or design or a combination of these that marketers attempt to promote so that the brand is well known and provides added value to a product. This can lead to consumers insisting on the product by brand name and, as a consequence of the delivery of satisfaction, the achievement of brand loyalty or less price sensitivity.

The benefit of developing a strong brand is important as consumers are often prepared to pay a price premium for perceived added values related to buying well-marketed brands. The price premium, also known as *brand equity*, is the price customers are prepared to pay above the commodity value of a product or service. This being the case, well-respected brands – if well positioned and managed – can give a better return to the company. Brands with a strong personality are attractive to companies that own them and predator companies wishing to buy into their potency. A successful brand is a flag bearer as it provides visible signals of positional strength in the marketplace. There are also distribution benefits whereby a strong brand will obtain channel leverage due to customers wanting to purchase and travel agents or travel websites wanting to have inventory. In this way successful brands provide their parent companies with a competitive advantage.

Figure 21.3 illustrates the benefit of creating a strong brand which is able to add value to the company offer. A differentiated position from that of the competition with a clear identity allows the brand to achieve higher prices and higher levels of demand even in periods of recession.

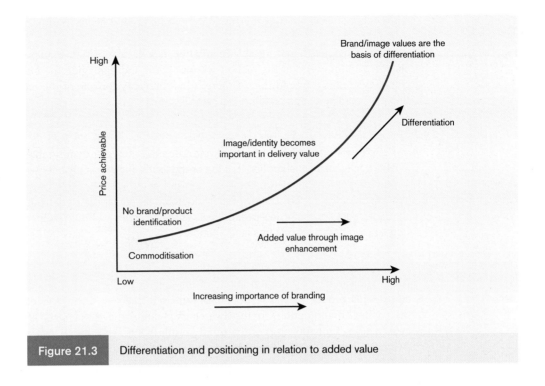

| Figure 21.3 | Differentiation and positioning in relation to added value |

A secondary consideration is that strong domestic brands provide a good base on which to build an international or global presence.

Brands, and ranges of brands, may fall into a number of different categories:

- **Family brands.** This is where each of the company's products adopts the same brand name. Examples include many of the leading hotel companies which have a family name. Accor as a leading international accommodation provider emphasises Accor as a single web page brand but offers Sofitel, Novotel, Ibis and Mercure under this group branding. Holiday Inn as part of the InterContinental hotels group offers Holiday Inn, Holiday Inn Express and Holiday Inn Club vacations with different price and quality positioning so as to attract different market segments.

- **Individual brands.** Alternatively, products offered by the same company may be branded very differently. For example, a tour operator or airline can have individual brand names within its businesses, with its long-haul, medium and budget-priced product offerings each having individual brand names unrelated to the others. In America, Hilton hotels has the independent brands of Conrad hotels, Hampton Inn, Homewood Suites and Embassy Suite, which are individual brands.

- **Own-brands.** Finally, organisations can have own-brand products. For example, some travel agents will offer the leading tour operator products but may also have their own specialist brochures with the agency brand name which is used to sell their own product.

There are strengths and weaknesses associated with each strategy. The individual brand name approach, for example, allows a company to search for the most appropriate brand name. Its weakness is that the promotional budget for each brand has to be sufficiently large to support that brand. With family brands there is a spin-off effect for each of the brands from the expenditure on any one brand. Conversely, if one of the family brands obtains poor publicity, because of association there will be damage to the other brands. For family branding, careful attention has to be given to the quality control of the products. One other benefit of family branding is that each product brand performance (PBP) can be measured against the overall family brand performance (FBP). When FBP is divided by PBP and shows an increase over time, without good reason, it may mean that the product brand needs modification, revitalisation or a detailed review.

With individual branding an organisation is able to position brands and products at the cheaper (bottom) end of the market without the brand damaging the image of the rest of the company's brands. In addition, if there is bad publicity for one of the company's brands then the other company brands do not necessarily suffer.

## Brand awareness

People will often buy a familiar brand because they are comfortable with things familiar. There may be an assumption that the brand that is familiar is probably reliable, in business to stay, and of reasonable quality. A recognised brand will thus often be selected in preference to an unknown brand. The awareness factor is particularly important in contexts in which the brand must first enter the evoked set – it must be one of the brands that are evaluated. An unknown brand usually has little chance.

(Aaker, 1991: 19)

Creating awareness of a brand is one of the biggest challenges for marketers as they need to ensure their product/brand is thought of (enters the evoked set) by customers as one of any of the available brand options. In the 'awareness pyramid' diagram (Aaker, 1991: 62), a customer's evoked set is shown by 'top of the mind' recall; this is the optimal awareness of a brand. The awareness pyramid shows brand awareness at the following levels:

- At the highest level – the apex of the pyramid, there is optimal awareness of a brand, or **Top of mind** awareness
- At the second level down there is **Brand recall**
- At the third level down there is **Brand recognition**
- At the base of the pyramid the customer is **Unaware of brand**

This pyramid is only representative as there are no established scales or measurements connected with it, but it does serve as a conceptual framework.

Marketing strategy should take the 'evoked set' into consideration because the actual choices of individual customers depend crucially upon which brands are considered and evaluated by consumers and which are not. According to research, it is found that consumers generally carry only a limited number of brands in their 'evoked set' – often no more than three to five brands. However, consumers do not necessarily select brands only from their 'evoked set' nor is their selection process logical, but if buyers recall a company's brand first the likelihood of their purchasing it increases. This concept accounts for the enormous amounts of money companies spend in buying out a well-branded competitor, to erase the visibility and reinforcement of alternative brands in the marketplace. Therefore, advertising is often aimed at facilitating the growth of brand awareness. Furthermore, it can develop an image and manipulate consumers' perception, which is fundamental to building values over and above the price–value relationship.

In addition, many consumers will select a brand with which they are familiar and which, it has been proved, is capable of providing satisfaction and quality. A recognised destination will thus often be selected over an unknown destination: 'People will often buy a familiar brand because they are comfortable with the familiar' (Aaker, 1991: 19). The awareness factor here is particularly important so a destination featured in a recent film or the coverage of an Olympics will increase customer awareness. The establishment of a strong brand image makes it more likely that the destination will be remembered and evaluated against other brands. A weak destination brand usually has little chance of entering any assessment and consequently will not be as successful.

# PRICE

The pricing policy selected for a tourism product is often directly related to the performance of its future demand. Setting the right **price** is also crucial to the profitability of the tourism enterprise. We believe that, of all the marketing mix, pricing decisions are the hardest to make. This is because prices for tourism products have to take into account the complexity created by seasonality of demand and the inherent perishability of the product. Also, within tourism there are major differences in segments such as business travellers and those taking a vacation. The relative elasticities of demand for these segments are dissimilar and price sensitivity is affected by different factors.

Figure 21.4 shows demand curves that indicate different market reactions to price change, i.e. where demand is highly responsive (or price elastic) and where demand is not price responsive (or price inelastic). Tourism industry products related to vacations are associated with an elastic demand curve, where a small increase in price creates a large fall in demand. Leisure travel is price elastic because of the following:

- The ratio of tourism prices to income is normally high. This is the case not only for overseas travel but also for leisure centres, cinemas and attractions, especially in times of recession. However, the different types of tourism demand from business travel to deciding on a secondary holiday will be associated with different elasticities. These may be as shown in Figure 21.5.

- The consumer can choose a substitute or forgo the purchase if the overall value is considered to be unacceptable.

- It is relatively easy to judge the offer of alternative brands and products, and therefore easy to switch demand to cheaper alternatives. Although price may be an indicator of quality, the consumer is able to choose between several offers, by referring, for example, to the type of aircraft they may fly on or the star rating or brand of accommodation.

Elasticity is a key element in the understanding of the demand process. It is defined as the ratio of the percentage response in the quantity sold to a percentage change in price of one of the other marketing mix elements, such as the expenditure on advertising. It therefore measures

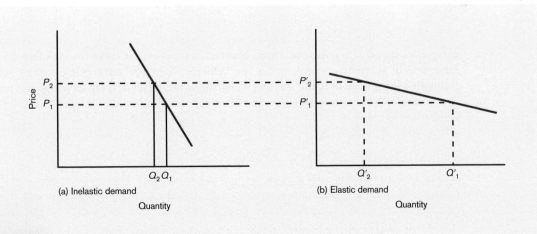

**Figure 21.4**   Price elasticity of demand

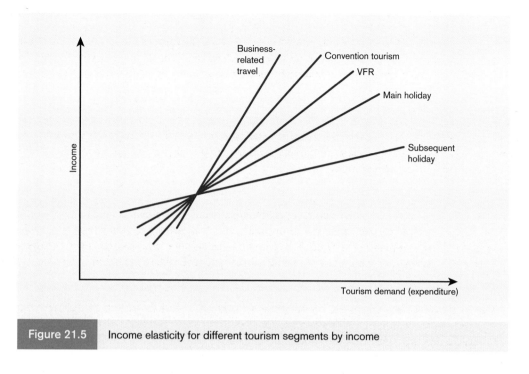

**Figure 21.5**   Income elasticity for different tourism segments by income

the sensitivity in quantity demanded to a change in the demand determinant. Mathematically, elasticity can be calculated as follows:

$$\text{Elasticity} = \frac{\text{Percentage change in quantity demanded}}{\text{Percentage change in any demand determinant}}$$

For price elasticity the denominator is simply changed to a percentage change in price. The coefficient of price elasticity is nearly always negative because the price and quantity are inversely related. This means that when the price falls, the quantity demanded tends to rise; and when price rises, the demand tends to fall. Thus the tourism marketer would be interested in the size of the coefficient as a coefficient of more than 1 indicates that demand is elastic (if price rises, demand falls significantly) and less than 1 that it is inelastic (if price rises, demand falls but only slightly).

From this it follows that the mark-up on highly competitive products such as package holidays to Spain tends to be low because the demand for such items is price elastic. In general, mark-ups should vary inversely with price elasticity of demand if profits are to be maximised.

## Factors affecting price sensitivity

A number of factors will affect the price sensitivity of products. From a marketing viewpoint a deeper understanding of price sensitivity assists with an understanding of the different target segments and the development of strategic planning. The main factors to consider are listed under the following headings.

### Perceived substitutes effect

Buyers are more sensitive the higher the product's price is in relation to another product or substitute they could purchase. Therefore, the consumer may choose a substitute or forgo the purchase if they believe the overall value is unacceptable. For example, local residents may avoid an area with higher priced shops frequented by tourists who are unaware of the alternatives.

### Unique value effect

Buyers are less sensitive to a product's price the more they value any of its attributes that differentiate it from competing products. For example, many customers are loyal to a national airline such as Thai or Singapore airlines because they perceive the airline to offer superior benefits.

### Importance of purchase effect

If the risk of the purchase increases then the price will not be the most important aspect of the purchase. This occurs when the item is an important purchase such as a honeymoon or anniversary. The greater the importance of the product, the less price sensitive (more inelastic) the purchase will be.

### Difficult comparison effect

Buyers are less sensitive to price when they find it more difficult to compare alternatives. This may lead to a demand for the more established brands, or greater destination or brand loyalty, in order to reduce the perception of risk.

### Price quality effect

A higher price may signal that the product is of superior quality. The result may be less sensitivity to price. This is not a conclusive effect as it applies to some products, while others may generate different reactions. For example, a restaurant menu at a higher price may signal improved quality but very few people would think higher priced fast-food items offered any real quality advantage.

### Expenditure effect

Buyers become more price sensitive when the expenditure is larger, either in absolute money amounts or as a percentage of their income. This may curb demand for long-haul holidays and is most prevalent in low-income households in which all expenditure is carefully controlled. This effect is also stronger and more likely to occur in times of recession.

### Fairness effect

If the buyer believes the price falls outside a band of what would be judged reasonable and fair then they become more price sensitive. With some types of products it is relatively easy to judge the offer of alternative brands and products and therefore easy to switch demand to cheaper alternatives. Consumers will perceive retailers, or the brands they stock, to be 'ripping off' customers if they exploit situations of shortage by being greedy. For example, street vendors are often seen to be selling drinks or ice creams at highly inflated prices when the temperature is extremely high.

## Problems related to price cutting

The setting of price cannot be solely concerned with the consumer. Care and attention have to be given to the reaction of the consumer as well as that of the competition. Owing to the high-risk nature of the tourism industry, a price advantage which takes market share from a competitor will often provoke a hostile repricing reaction. If Company A, in Figure 21.6(a), attempts to increase its market share by price cutting, it will need to take market share from Companies B and C. This is a situation in which C and B are likely to react by cutting their own prices. The outcome is that the market shares remain similar and can, as in the second example, lead the market to grow in volume, as in Figure 21.6(b), although not necessarily in overall revenue. The long-term result is that the market remains extremely unstable because smaller margins are being applied. In this situation an organisation has to ensure it has a high volume of business in order to exceed its break-even point. Price-cutting policies have been a feature of the tour-operating business in the UK and the example provided above helps us understand what has led to the collapse of a whole range of different companies. The following list shows the various influences on pricing in the tourism industry:

- The perishable nature of the product, which is unable to be stored until a future occasion, leads to various forms of last-minute tactical pricing.
- The high price elasticity of demand exhibited by holiday and leisure markets places emphasis on setting prices at the right levels.
- Increased price transparency due to the ease of access to price comparisons by use of the Internet and more recently by use of a mobile phone.

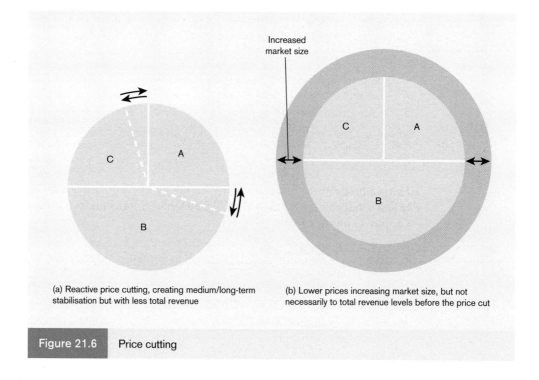

(a) Reactive price cutting, creating medium/long-term stabilisation but with less total revenue

(b) Lower prices increasing market size, but not necessarily to total revenue levels before the price cut

**Figure 21.6**    Price cutting

- The volatility of the market due to short-run fluctuations in international costs, exchange rates, oil prices and political events requires sophisticated forward planning.
- Many companies are reliant on high volumes to break even and will forgo short-run profit in order to create acceptable load factor or occupancy levels.
- Cost control is an important part of pricing policy. Many tourism enterprises have high fixed costs and price near to break-even positions. This can make them vulnerable to financial collapse or takeover if costs are not controlled.
- Some regions and countries have price controls for airline travel and hotel accommodation.
- Seasonal demand leads to peak and low-season periods, which require demand management pricing to cope with the short-run capacity problems.
- Price is associated with the psychological aspects of both quality and status. It is therefore always important to gauge the way prices or their change will be perceived by the different target segments.
- Cash flow is high due to much of the payment for tourism products being made in advance of consumption. Many tourism companies make profit on the investment of this money.

Pricing policy has to consider the above list and therefore the scope of choice is remarkably wide. The choice will probably be one or a combination of the following types of pricing.

## Cost-orientated pricing

Cost-orientated pricing refers to setting prices on the basis of an understanding of their costs.

### Cost-plus pricing

Cost-plus pricing sets prices in relation to either marginal costs or total costs including overheads. A percentage mark-up is then normally applied to reach the final price.

This form of pricing is often used for the retail outlets of tourist attractions. Its weakness as a method of pricing for tourism is that it does not take into consideration demand for the product, what prices the marketplace will bear, and it is not based upon the price levels of the competitors. Knowing the cost breakdown of the product is crucial and it is often important to have calculated the operating price of a hotel bedroom or a sector flight airline seat. This allows the marketer to know what the effect of any tactical price reduction will be.

### Rate of return

Rate of return pricing provides an organisation with an agreed rate of return on its investment. Whereas the cost-plus method concentrates on the costs associated with the running of the business, the rate of return method concentrates on the profits generated in relation to the capital invested. This approach is not appropriate for tourism enterprises as it ignores the need to link the pricing policy to the creation of a sales volume which is large enough to cover overheads and remains consistent over time.

To use either cost-plus or rate of return methods of pricing is generally not appropriate for tourism products that have to survive in a highly competitive marketplace because of the need to judge the contribution margin for different market segments so as to cover long-run costs (see Chapter 13 on attractions).

## Demand-orientated pricing

Demand-orientated pricing takes into consideration the factors of demand rather than the level of costs in order to set the price. A conference centre, for example, may charge one price for admission to a rock concert and only half that price for admission to a classical concert.

### Discrimination pricing

This is sometimes called flexible pricing and is often used in tourism where products are sold at two or more different prices. Quite often students and older people are charged lower prices at attractions, or events, than other segments. Discrimination pricing is often time-related, with cheaper drink charges in 'happy hour' periods or cheaper meal prices in the early evening prior to high-demand periods. For price discrimination to be successful it is necessary to be able to identify those segments that, without the price differentials, would be unable to purchase the product.

To obtain a high flow of business, a hotel will have to discount for customers who offer significant volume. This means that, while business travellers may benefit from corporate rates, those on vacation may be staying on tour operator/wholesaler rates.

Discrimination can also be based upon increasing the price of products that have higher potential demand. For example, if rooms in a hotel are all the same but some have good scenic views of the countryside or sea, then those rooms could be sold for a higher price.

### Backward pricing

This is a market-based method of pricing that focuses on what the consumer is willing to pay. The price is worked backwards. First, an acceptable margin is agreed upon. Next, the costs are closely monitored so that the estimated final price is deemed to be acceptable to the target segment. The objective is to set a price that matches consumer preference. If necessary an adjustment is made to the quality of the product offer or service to meet the cost-led needs of this technique.

Tour operators/wholesalers selling on a price-led basis will often contract with hotels one or two blocks back from the seafront, if this lowers the room rates making up the final price. Other methods include lowering the flight content of a holiday price by organising cheaper night flights which may also save on the first night's accommodation cost. To be successful with this method of pricing it is important to understand the psychological effects of creating products that may appeal to the price conscious. However, the holiday may not give satisfaction if the holiday experience and company are considered to be of poor quality.

### Market penetration pricing

Market penetration pricing is adopted when an organisation wants to establish itself quickly in a market. Prices are set below those of the competition in order to create high growth for the company's products. Tour operators/wholesalers, when setting up an operation to a new destination, will use market penetration pricing for that destination in the first couple of years and then, once that destination becomes better established, will slowly increase the prices.

### Psychological pricing

Companies will often price products below a round figure. This could be the changing of a menu price from say £10 to £9.95 or £9.99 to foster the perception of the price as being below that threshold at which the customer is willing to buy. Just as £9.95 may appear to be significantly less than £10, so a holiday price of £488 may seem to be more on a £400 level than a £500 level. However, there is no conclusive evidence that such pricing policies make any significant difference to profits.

### Skimming pricing

This term is used as if skimming off the cream from milk. The method is utilised when there is a shortage of supply of the product and where demand will not be dampened by charging a premium price. Luxury villas set in good locations are normally priced with higher margins than other accommodation products because of their relative shortage. Market skimming policies can only occur where there is a healthy demand or waiting lists, or to take advantage of a strong destination image such as that of the south of France.

## Pricing and the relationship to value

Whatever pricing policy is adopted, a company has to take into consideration the potential consumer's perceptual assessment. In deciding to buy a product a consumer has to be willing to give up something in order to enjoy the satisfactions of the benefits the product will deliver. This concept is more complex than it seems. The majority of tourists are looking for value when they buy a product and value is derived from the functions of quality and price, as well as the added value of the image or brand. This may be expressed as:

$$\text{Value} = \frac{\text{Quality}}{\text{Price}} + \text{Image}$$

If a consumer believes the image and quality of a product is good, he or she will be willing to make greater sacrifices in order to purchase that product. This explains how first-class travel continues to be successful on different forms of transport such as trains, aircraft and cruise ships and why leading brands or destinations are able to attract higher prices. The interrelationship between price, quality and value plays a significant role in the buying behaviour of customers. Value was grouped into four categories by Zeithaml (1988):

- value as low price;
- value as whatever is wanted from a product;
- value as the quality one gets for the price paid;
- value as what one gets for what one gives.

Zeithaml describes value as a 'trade-off between salient benefit components and sacrifice components'. Benefit components according to Zeithaml include intrinsic attributes, extrinsic attributes, perceived quality and other relevant high abstractions. This means value is a judgement about superiority and benefits delivered. Therefore, having the lowest price may not be a sufficient strategy as the best route to marketplace success.

If prices change, this can affect the consumers' quality perception. A price reduction may be associated with a belief that the company is in financial trouble, that it will have to cut service and quality, or that prices are falling and, if one waits, a price will come down even more. The value of the product is thought to have decreased because quality, by association with the changes, is observed to have fallen by a greater ratio than prices.

Alternatively, a price increase may be interpreted as the way the company is going to pay to improve the quality and service of the offer. However, some consumers may simply think that the company is being greedy and that quality has not improved. This means the consumer may judge the value to have fallen. The outcome quite often depends on how the company explains the increase in price to the consumer.

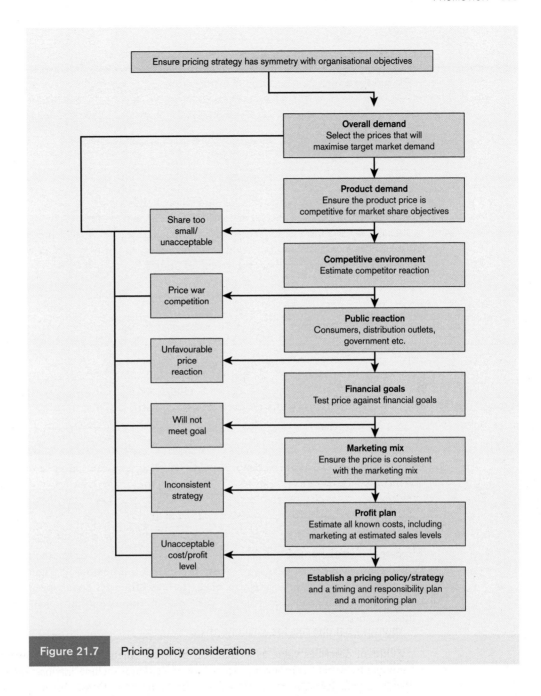

| Figure 21.7 | Pricing policy considerations |

To ensure the maximum chance of success for the pricing policy adopted there is a need to check each stage of the procedure, as in Figure 21.7. This figure identifies the important considerations required for the successful evolution of a pricing policy.

## PROMOTION

**Promotion** is the descriptive term for the mix of communication activities that tourism organisations, or tourist boards, carry out in order to influence those publics on whom their sales depend. The important groups, which need to be influenced, are not simply the target market group of current and potential customers. There is the need also to influence trade contacts such as retail agents and suppliers, as well as opinion formers such as journalists and travel writers.

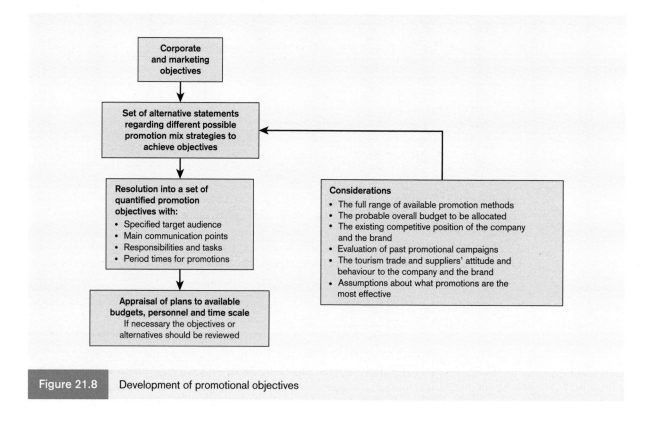

**Figure 21.8** Development of promotional objectives

Even local, national and international politicians and important professional groups may need to be influenced.

## Setting objectives

A range of promotional methods can be employed by the tourism marketer, so it is important to define what the promotion has to achieve. It is necessary to define the marketing objectives clearly so that the most effective types of promotion can be utilised. Figure 21.8 explains how promotional objectives can be developed. The mix strategies could specify a need to achieve awareness, inform, educate, create purchase action, improve loyalty, change the perception of the customer, etc.

The promotional objectives should have some precise terms in order to clarify the entire intention of the promotion and then monitor the results. This can be achieved by means of SMART objectives. SMART objectives will provide Specific, Measurable, Actionable, Realistic/ Relevant and Targeted/Timed results along the following lines:

1. The target audience or market has to be identified (by segment, geographical area, and for what products). For example, identifying the grandparents of school-age children living in London who would possibly take the children to Disneyland® Resort Paris.

2. The specific product (goods and service) to be promoted has to be identified. For example, mini break holidays in or near to France.

3. Specific goals should be set, perhaps that sales will increase by £*x*, or that attitudes to the product or brand will become more positive for the 40-plus age group. To fit with the SMART objectives these goals have to be *achievable* in that the company has to deliver to the objectives, and also *relevant* to the task required.

4. The time horizon of when the expected effect will have occurred should be stated. For example, targets should be achieved by end September of a specified year.

Taking up the example used in the list above, a SMART objective would therefore be:

> To ensure that the grandparents of children between the ages of 4 and 16, within the Greater London area, are communicated with and receive information on the France and Disneyland offers. Subsequently, sales for these products will increase by £150,000 over the previous year by 30 September.

## Promotional budget approaches

The second important step in any promotional campaign is to agree the budget. There are different approaches to agreeing budgets that may be based upon a number of criteria. It is important to realise there is no one best method to set budgets. This is because promotional campaign measurement is not straightforward, given that there is often a time lag between the campaign and any resultant demand patterns. Also, other elements in the marketing mix will affect the demand.

Various factors determine the overall promotional budget but any decision has to take into account existing or potential sales of the company. The most common approaches are objective-and-task, affordable method, percentage of sales method, and competitive parity method:

- **Objective-and-task method** – whereby the budget is related to the communications objectives. If the company needs to create awareness, change attitudes and build a brand then these objectives become the necessary tasks against which the budget is determined.

- **Affordable method** – where the first step is to produce a budgeted period forecast of the expected sales and company costs, excluding the promotional expenditure. The difference between the surplus expected and the desired profit allows for a decision over the communications budget based upon what can be afforded. This approach treats the promotional budget as a cost of business and does not encourage marketers to spend against the likelihood of future problems or as an investment to increase sales.

- **Percentage of sales method** – is an approach where the communications budget is set on the basis of a predetermined percentage of the forecasted sales. The weakness is that the method assumes the historical percentage is still relevant for the current marketplace. It also relies on accurate forecasts which provide for the chance of unacceptable error. In addition, if a company wants to build preference for a new product launch then a system of budgeting based upon the percentage of sales method may not raise the necessary budget to achieve the short-term task of ensuring awareness and acceptability. The other problem is that the method will provide for lower budgets when there is a downturn in the market or due to loss of sales based upon increased competitor activity that takes away business. This may lead to further sales decline as less and less money is spent on the company's promotional effort.

- **Competitive parity method** – allows the setting of the budget based upon both the share of market of the product or company and also the estimated expenditure level of its competitors. This method does not allow for specific marketplace opportunities as the parity level of expenditure will be held and consequently a strategic penetration of the market may not be achieved.

## Communication effects

There is always the need to plan to achieve the most effective response from the target market. An important part of the promotional effort is the building of brand and product awareness. Sometimes it will take a long time for the consumer to know about the brand and the type of products on offer.

A promotional campaign should aim to provide knowledge about the product, to ensure the consumer will feel favourable towards the product and build up preference for it. Any campaign has to sell the benefits that a customer would be seeking in a credible way so that the potential customer feels conviction and is more likely than not to make a purchase.

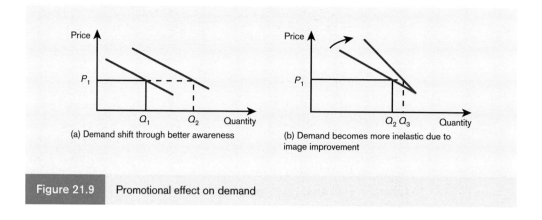

(a) Demand shift through better awareness

(b) Demand becomes more inelastic due to image improvement

| **Figure 21.9** | Promotional effect on demand |
| --- | --- |

Figure 21.9 shows how a promotional campaign could be utilised by a destination or organisation to create awareness of the benefits of the product offer. The development of a positive image will create a more price-elastic demand curve, which means the product is more resilient to price rises and does not have to rely on having lower prices than the competition. In Figure 21.10(a) $P_1Q_1$ is existing demand before a campaign has been developed to create more awareness in the target audience. At $P_1Q_2$ demand has increased because, owing to a promotional effect, more people are now aware of the product benefits which the brand or destination can deliver. At $P_1Q_3$ in Figure 21.10(b) the campaign has improved the image of the organisation or destination so that more status is derived in travelling with the brand or to a destination. This changes the shape of the demand whereby it becomes more inelastic.

Advertising and sales promotion are the most widely used forms of promotion. Because of the intrusive characteristics of these forms of promotion, most consumers relate ideas of marketing to the use of advertising or sales promotion. The other major forms include personal selling and public relations.

## Advertising

**Advertising** includes any paid form of non-personal communication through the media which details a product that has an identified sponsor. The media may include travel guides, newspapers, magazines, radio, television, direct mail, web pages and billboards.

Advertising is used to achieve a whole range of objectives which may include changing attitudes or building image, as well as achieving sales. Advertising is often described as 'above-the-line' promotion (due to the commission for the promotional activity being paid by the media company direct to the advertising agency) with all other forms of promotion, such as sales promotion or direct marketing, being termed 'below-the-line'. The difference between above and below the line is simply academic now as the emphasis is on integrating both areas, for example sales promotion and advertising working together to achieve the greatest impact. The approach is also to raise budgets for overall integrated campaigns so that expenditure accounting differences become non-existent. In addition, advertising has developed different ways of affecting the consumer. Direct mail is being used to build awareness and television is being used to sell products direct to the consumer, and therefore there is a great deal more flexibility in the use of different promotional media.

### Communication theories

Communication theorists have proposed several models to explain the way advertising works and each have some similarity. The basic underlying approach is to theorise that the individual will first move to a *knowledge state* or *awareness state* on the basis of information gained through experience and methods of communication. *Attitudes* are then formed and the importance is to move the potential purchaser to a *behavioural action* phase of purchase through desire and *conviction*. One model known as the DAGMAR model (Defining Advertising Goals for

| Photograph 21.2 | Interesting promotional pictures capture attention. |
|---|---|

*Source*: Pichugin Dmitry/Shutterstock.com

Measured Advertising Results) describes the sequence of stages through which the prospective customer has to move:

- unawareness;
- awareness;
- comprehension of the offer;
- conviction;
- action or inaction.

Through advertising, the marketer will make the potential customer aware of the company or destination and its range of offers. As part of the advertising communication process, information has to be clearly transmitted so it can be decoded and comprehended properly. The process is then to make the offer credible so that the potential customer can be moved to a favourable attitude to the product. The act of purchase may then follow.

Advertising has the potential to affect a large number of people simultaneously with a single message. The secondary effect of advertising is personal communications among consumers. This is known as the *two-step flow of communication*. The first step in the process is the communications flow from media to opinion leaders – the individuals whose attitudes, opinions, preferences and actions affect others. The second step is word-of-mouth communications from opinion leaders to others (followers). This communication can occur through personal conversation between friends or with work colleagues based upon communication about the company or product. It can also occur through non-verbal communications when someone displays video or holiday photographs. One implication of the need to achieve as much benefit as possible from the two-step model is the requirement to reach and influence opinion leaders.

## Sales promotion

**Sales promotion** involves any activity that offers an incentive to induce a desired result from potential customers, trade intermediaries or the sales force. Sales promotion campaigns will add value to the product because the incentives will ordinarily not accompany the product. For example, free wine or free accommodation offers are frequently used in sales promotion campaigns for hotel restaurants which need improved demand at certain periods. Most incentives are planned to be short term in nature.

An integral part of sales promotion is the aspect of merchandising. Merchandising includes materials used in travel agents or in-house locations to stimulate sales. For a hotel, these would include tent cards which may attempt to sell cocktails or desserts, menus, in-room material, posters and displays. Merchandising is important as a means of creating impulse purchase or reminding the consumer of what is on offer.

Sales promotion is often used in combination with other promotional tools in order to supplement the overall effort. However, it has to be remembered that it is sometimes difficult to terminate or change special promotions without causing adverse effects. Airline frequent flyer loyalty programmes are an example of this. Also, a sales promotion (or series of promotions) has to take account of the likely effect it may have on the image of the brand or outlet. For example, there may be an unanticipated surge of negative perception which may occur due to association with banal and frivolous promotions.

### Evaluation of sales promotion

To evaluate a sales promotion there should be a consideration of:

- the cost of the promotion in employee time, as well as for the cost of any merchandise, giveaway items or promotional literature;
- the increase in sales and profit, or improvement in awareness, based upon the campaign;
- whether the campaign had secondary effects of switching demand from other company products which would have been sold;
- whether there were any additional sales outside of the promotion, due to customers being attracted to the company or tourism product offer.

It is not always easy to isolate the above effects from other marketing factors, but it is always important to make some assessment of the benefit of different types of promotion.

## Personal selling

**Personal selling** is an attempt to gain benefit through face-to-face or telephone contact between the seller's representative and those people with whom the seller wants to communicate. This type of selling may be utilised by a non-profit-making tourist attraction as well as the conference manager of a large hotel.

A number of employees in travel agents or retail related to tourism are often viewed as order *takers* when they could possibly be order *procurers*. The intent of personal selling is:

- to obtain a sale – often customers enter the retail outlet after acquiring information and the salesperson needs to persuade potential customers to purchase;
- to stimulate sales of 'impulse buy' purchases by bringing attention to extra requirements such as travel insurance, car hire, excursions and airport transfers; or
- to complete a successful transaction with the customer utilising a range of sales skills.

This will leave the customer satisfied and well informed about the detail of the transaction.

| Table 21.2 | An approach to selling tourism products by a travel agent |
|---|---|
| 1. Preparing through skills and knowledge (of the travel products available and systems) | Feedback and learning from prior listening and retail agency training |
| 2. Anticipating and identifying a prospective sale based upon interaction with the customer | Having knowledge and an understanding of the needs of customers |
| 3. Method of dealing with the potential customer in order to make a recommendation | Feedback and learning from prior listening plus asking appropriate questions |
| 4. Presenting the features and benefits of the recommendation | Active selling skills and listening in order to check on acceptability of offer |
| 5. Dealing with customer concerns | Active listening in order to revise the argument or recommendation to overcome objections |
| 6. Building obligation and commitment and selling in other products (e.g. insurance) | Active listening in order to ensure the offer is acceptable and the sale can be concluded |
| 7. Establishing affinity and relationship | Reinforcement of the relationship through creating a satisfied customer |

The benefit of personal selling is that a salesperson can adapt the communication of benefits to be gained to the specific needs of the customer. The feedback process of listening to the customer's needs allows the salesperson to be flexible in his or her approach. This is made easier in a selling situation because the personal contact produces heightened awareness and attention by the customer. However, the sales functions of retailers have to be carefully handled because staff who lack empathy will be judged 'pushy'.

If we take the example of a travel agency, the retail selling process is made up of a number of the steps outlined in Table 21.2: preparing, anticipating a prospective sale, approaching, presenting, dealing with concerns, gaining commitment and establishing relationships. All these are linked into the feedback process of active listening and response.

## Public relations

**Public relations** (PR) is non-personal communication that changes opinion or achieves coverage in a mass medium and that is not paid for by the source. The coverage could include space given to a press release or favourable editorial comment. PR is important not only in obtaining editorial coverage, but also in suppressing potential bad coverage. An organisation that has good links with the media is more likely to have the opportunity to stop or moderate news that could be damaging to their organisation prior to its release.

The major benefit of PR is that it can provide and enhance an organisation's image. This is very important for service-based organisations which are reliant on a more tangible positive image in order to be successful. PR is a highly credible form of communication as people like to read 'news stories' and will believe them to be less biased than information provided in advertisements. However, editorial decisions over what is communicated will produce control over the message, its timing, placement and coverage.

Table 21.3 details the common activities undertaken as part of PR. The benefits of good PR effort and coverage emanating from this are:

- it is perceived to be impartial and acts as a neutral endorsement of the company;
- it is credible and believable as it is not identified as a paid form of promotion;
- it helps to build image of a brand and develop favourable opinions by the drip effect of the information provided;

| Table 21.3 | Activities of public relations |
| --- | --- |
| • Media information releases/contact/speeches | • Advertorials (which require PR copy along with an advertisement) |
| • Production of PR materials (videos, CDs, web information, press kits, corporate identity materials, etc.) | • In-house and customer magazines<br>• Facility visits to an overseas area (especially for travel writers), etc. |
| • PR events, media conferences and newsworthy 'stunts' | • Sponsorship and donations |
| | • Lobbying |

- it can generate interest and increased sales;
- it allows for a cost-effective means to promote special offers and sales initiatives; and
- it can possibly limit or neutralise negative or hostile opinions.

PR activity can be either planned or unplanned. Planned activity means the company attempts to retain control over the activity and news release. With unplanned activity, the company simply reacts in the most beneficial way to the chance of some publicity or to suppress a negative news item. Larger organisations will have a public relations agency or in-house department. These will attempt to influence the company's 'publics'. The 'publics' are made up of those important to the company – customers, shareholders, employees, suppliers, local community, the media and local and national government. Planned publicity will involve sending press releases and photographs to the media (trade papers, local and national press, radio and television), organising press conferences for more newsworthy events, sending letters to editors of journals or local newspapers, organising different creative 'stunts' to acquire the right tone of media coverage and making speeches (or writing articles) on informed tourism issues in order to be perceived as a well-informed company.

## Other promotional activity

There is a growing use of **sponsorship** and **direct marketing**. These do not comfortably fit into the other four promotion categories. Sponsorship is the material or financial support of a specific activity, normally but not exclusively sport, education or the arts, which does not form part of the sponsor organisation's normal business. Direct marketing is direct communication with pre-selected target groups in order to obtain an immediate response or build closer relationships. Direct marketing is used extensively by direct-sell tour operators/wholesalers such as Saga Holidays and Portland. One traditional method is direct mail, which is postal communication by an identified sponsor. This is being expanded into database marketing based upon relationship marketing practices.

In addition, because tourism is an intangible product, a great deal of promotion includes the production of printed communications such as brochures or sales leaflets. The design, compilation and printing of tourism brochures is one of the most important promotional functions. Printed communications are often costly. In fact, the printing and distribution costs of brochures constitute the largest part of most marketing budgets within the tourism industry. This is a necessary expenditure as the brochure or leaflet is the major sales tool for tour operators/wholesalers and tourism organisations.

A new means of communication is through the medium of mobile phones. Technology is proving the possibility of many new ways of access and the enjoyment of services. Mobile phones offer the opportunity to obtain locations of places of interest, parking, refreshments etc. as well as help in interpretation and understanding of any built or natural attraction. In addition, leading tourism attractions are developing games and walking tours for mobile phone use.

## Characteristics of each promotional technique

Each of the above promotional elements has the capacity to achieve a different promotional objective. While personal selling has high potency for achieving communication objectives, only a relatively small number of people can be contacted. Therefore, advertising is a more effective method of reaching a high number of people at relatively low unit cost. Public relations is more credible than advertising but organisations lack the control they have over advertising messages, which may also be repeated on a regular basis. Thus, when it is difficult to raise advertising budgets, public relations is a lower cost alternative, but it is difficult to control the timing and consistency of PR coverage. Sales promotion, such as leaflet drops that offer price discounts, may produce an initial trial for a product, such as the purchase of a leisure break in a hotel, but this type of promotion should only be used over a short-term period. Some promotions are permanent as they are related to known patterns of demand fluctuations and the 'happy hour' promotion is widely utilised in resorts to increase sales in early off-peak hours.

Each element of the promotions mix has its own strengths and weaknesses. While this may include the factors of cost, ability to target different groups and control, there are other important considerations. Figure 21.10 indicates the relative strengths of each of the four forms of promotion. They are compared on the basis of the level of awareness of the communication, its comprehension, as well as whether it can build conviction and succeed in creating action.

## Integrated marketing communications

It should be obvious that many of the activities of tourism promotion will occur in different areas of the company and with different activities taking place based upon the predilections of the individuals in control. Therefore, while it is obvious that coordination is required it is often not carried out in a systematic way. If it were, all elements of marketing communications could work in unison so as to create a whole that is greater than the sum of the parts. To ensure such impact is achieved there is a requirement for an **integrated marketing communications** (IMC) approach throughout the business. Integrated marketing communications is the process a company adopts in order to integrate and coordinate its messages and media to deliver clear reinforcing communication. However, this will only occur if the various components of the communication effort are coordinated. To achieve this the marketer has to provide policy planning guidelines which direct the efforts in every part of the organisation so that all aspects of communication will offer a reinforcement to each other.

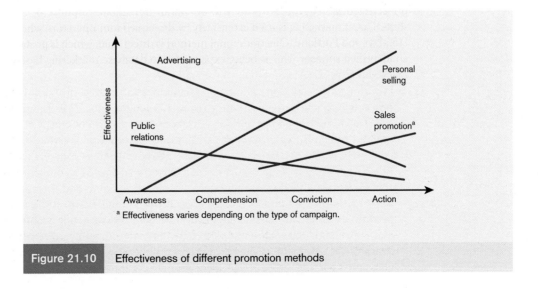

| Figure 21.10 | Effectiveness of different promotion methods |

# PLACE (DISTRIBUTION)

The special characteristics of the tourism product have led to specific forms of distribution. The tourism product is one where no transfer of ownership takes place and service is simply rented or consumed. However, prior to consumption the tourism product has to be both available and accessible. This requires a distribution system – or choice of a marketing channel. A **distribution system** is the mix of channels used to gain access, or means by which a tourism service is made available to the potential buyers of the product.

The following aspects of tourism distribution should be noted:

- There is no actual product being distributed. There are only clues given through persuasive communication about the product.

- Tourism normally involves the episode of a purchase act related to decisions over travel to a destination, the stay and return. As such the nature of travel distribution is related to entering into the production as well as consumption of the product. Therefore, the method of selling and environment within which the purchase is made becomes part of the overall tourism experience.

- Major amounts of money are allocated by the industry to the production and printing of literature as well as to its delivery direct to the customer or to the retail travel agent. Brochures and leaflets are produced in large quantities, and often the distribution cost involves an amount for warehousing and the planned despatch of packs of brochures via different modes of transport.

- Distribution of overseas holidays in the UK is now a balance of web-based services and travel agents who sell a homogeneous set of choices. These agents have important power and control over the companies that sell the products (principals). Agents decide on the brochures to display on their racks and the companies they will recommend to consumers. However, airline bookings are progressively being switched to Internet-based direct systems (see Chapter 22 for more information).

There is continuing development of CRSs (computer reservation systems) or GDSs (global distribution systems) (see Table 21.4). These offer an agent instant access to airline bookings as well as the major hotel groups, car hire and cruise lines. Such systems, utilising the Internet, allow agents to tailor holidays to suit individual client requirements and the consumer to make their own arrangements, and this is leading to increases in direct bookings. The CRSs have been led by developments from the principal airlines, with historically Galileo dominating the UK and being strong in both Europe and the USA, Amadeus being predominately strong in Europe, Sabre dominating in the USA, and, finally, Travelport, which in 2007 combined Apollo, Worldspan and Galileo and as a group has helped develop innovations for many reservation systems (see below).

- **Sabre** – founded in the 1960s by American Airlines and in 1996 Sabre became a separate legal entity of AMR (parent company of American Airlines). It has been involved in a lot of Internet-led development of booking sites (Sabre owns **Travelocity.com**, a major worldwide online travel site) and is considered to be one of the most significant and competitive GDSs due to the fact that it anticipates and takes advantage of the changes in the information economy and develops innovative practices. Sabre Global Distribution System is used by travel agencies around the world to search, price, book and ticket travel services provided by airlines, hotels, car rental companies, rail providers and tour operators. Opodo, the European equivalent of Orbitz, which is a US airline-led initiative to counteract the private reservation sites, was founded in 2001 by nine European airlines as a competitor to start-up online travel agencies. Opodo was subsequently sold off to Sabre and then Amadeus but may be the target of further buy-outs. It has faced tough competition in the UK, where it did not perform as well as **ebookers.com**, **lastminute.com** (subsequently acquired in 2005 by Sabre) and Expedia. In 2006 Sabre was sold to two private equity buyers, Silver Lake Holdings and Texas Pacific. The Sabre sale resulted in some of the world's most important travel distribution companies coming under private ownership.

| Table 21.4 | GDS – key owners of online leisure and corporate travel services | |
|---|---|---|
| **GDS** | **Leisure market** | **Corporate market** |
| Amadeus | Opodo | Amadeus e-Travel Management |
| Sabre | Travelocity, which includes:<br>Lastminute<br>World Choice Travel Zuji | GetThere<br>Travelocity Business |
| Travelport (Apollo, Galileo, Worldspan) | Travelport holds a majority stake in Orbitz, which includes:<br>CheapTickets<br>ebookers<br>HotelClub<br>RatesToGo | Traversa<br>Orbitz for Business |

*Source*: Gilbert, based upon various reports, 2012

- **Travelport** grew out of Worldspan, which was founded in 1990, and previously owned by affiliates of Delta, Northwest and TWA. Worldspan was sold to a consortium including Travelport in 2007. Worldspan successfully developed the strategies, solutions and services for web-based distribution. Worldspan helped launch the Orbitz site in 2001, which was previously a US airline alliance-led Internet site set up to counteract the successful trends in disintermediation by companies such as Travelocity, which was taking increasing revenue in commission charges and kept valuable customer data for its own purposes. Prior to this, Worldspan agreed to provide the booking engines in 1995 for Microsoft's **Expedia.com** and in 1998 for **Priceline.com**. In 2006, Galileo and Worldspan, which were Sabre's main competitors in the US, agreed to merge in a $1.4 billion deal. The Galileo merger deal is based upon the historically important use of a system which was founded in 1993 by 11 major North American and European airlines. Subscribers to Travelport's GDSs now can access Apollo, Galileo and Worldspan.

- Meanwhile, in Europe, the Amadeus group is also owned by buy-out groups. In addition, there are several minor GDSs, including SITA's Sahara, Infini (Japan), Axess (Japan), Tapas (Korea), Fantasia (South Pacific) and Abacus (Asia/Pacific) that serve smaller regional markets or countries.

The development of electronic distribution systems has strengthened the major players as the cost and adoption implications provide a barrier to entry. The current systems have standardised the channel for bookings to such an extent that small or medium-sized organisations will find it almost impossible to develop agency channel alternatives. This has implications for loss of control for smaller companies and therefore requires safeguards to ensure the owners of reservations systems do not manipulate the display or bookings procedure to favour preferred brands or those companies that can pay for prime display. However, there are those low-cost carriers such as Southwest airlines, easyJet and Ryanair that are very seldom found on reservations systems other their own, as they prefer to save on distribution costs.

## Different tourism distribution needs

There are some forms of tourism such as museums, theme parks or physical attractions where no form of prior booking is required as there is almost always excess supply available and in peak periods queuing is the method of allocation. There are other types of tourism where excess demand and more complex product packaging and financial risk create the need for sophisticated advance booking systems. The booking system enables the organisation to spread demand as the consumer can often be persuaded to arrive or travel at a different time.

In order for a tourism organisation to sell in advance of consumption and to have a record of the reservation, the company has to sell its available capacity through an inventory system. Whether it is a small guest house or large hotel, a farmhouse or cruise ship, some method of allocating capacity and creating reservations without creating overbooking is important. The timing of these bookings may range from minutes prior to departure for an aircraft or a reserved place on a train service to several years for a major conference. For these reasons, the use of a database booking system (CRS/GDS) is common in tourism. These systems combine the memory capacity of computers (to update and store information constantly) with the communication facility of telecommunications, which rapidly inform travel agents of the current capacity remaining. Such systems can then be programmed to maximise the 'yield' of the capacity as it is sold to the customer.

The next consideration is related to the location of the business. A well-located hotel, theatre or attraction will be able to pick up passing demand. In this case the consumers will find the product easily and there may be less need for a separate distribution channel. This is because the product is easily available for purchase.

In an increasingly competitive world, however, it has been necessary for most organisations to consider different forms of direct distribution. Companies are able to sell direct either from their place of location or through direct marketing methods. Many hotels organise weekend-break programmes to improve the weekend occupancy levels. These weekend packages are often promoted directly in newspapers or by email and are booked directly with the hotel.

## Development of travel agency distribution

In the UK in 2005 there was the opportunity to have access to a wide network of around 4,727 distribution outlets controlled by the Association of British Travel Agents but these have declined in number each year. The need for travel agents first arose in the 1950s due to the rapidly expanding operations of airline/ferry businesses. Transport providers required a means of distribution for their products that was more cost-effective than establishing individual networks of booking offices around the country. The subsequent development of travel agents was a direct result of the increasing consumer demand for inclusive tours from holidaymakers who were largely uneducated and unsophisticated, and therefore looked to 'experts' to facilitate the process. These agents charge commission on the sales they make and they need to hold a stock of the companies' brochures or sales literature. The travel retail agent sells a product that is both intangible and perishable and this is very different from some of the more traditional types of retail business. The bookings made for travel abroad, from the UK, are often organised through either high street travel agents for holidays or by specialist business travel agents for business travel. For many travellers, a foreign holiday was an opportunity to emulate grand lifestyles through the services of a travel agent. However, changes in education, economic, social and experiential trends are leading to new ways of purchasing. Figure 21.11 indicates the trends emanating from new distribution pressures which are now taking place in this once traditional retail arena.

The Internet and more recently mobile phones have many implications for all areas of business and every sector of society. Its effect can be seen already in the precarious balance of travel distribution. Disintermediation does not appear to be lessening the travel industry's complicated distribution network, if anything it is adding to it.

## Electronic retailing

Electronic retailing to consumers (or B2C) was first developed in the 1980s. The area is advancing at a rapid rate with retail and tourism organisations realising the growing importance of the sale of products through these new distribution channels. Electronic delivery systems do not necessarily require direct human interaction and, as such, they offer specific advantages. In principle, quality can be assured, the costs are lower, there is consumer convenience of access and distribution can be wider than normal retail channels. The key underlying reasons behind electronic retailing are consumer time poverty, consumers wanting to have more control over time and

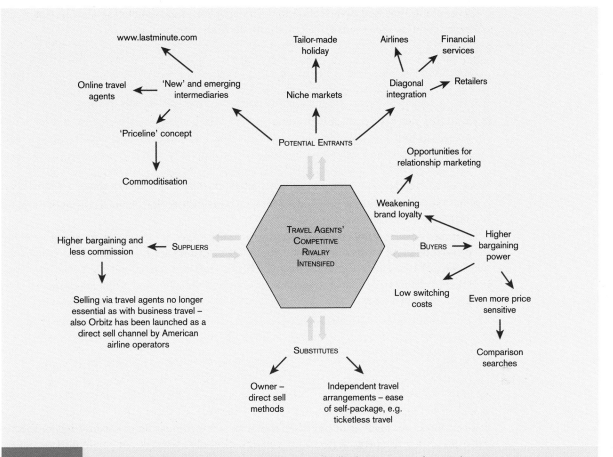

| Figure 21.11 | Application of Porter's five forces model to new distribution pressures for travel agents |
|---|---|

*Source*: Based on and application of model in *Competitive Strategy: Techniques for Analyzing Industries and Competitors*, by Michael E. Porter. 1980, 1998, The Free Press.

place of transaction, the technology convergence allowing change to take place and growing experience of the benefits of the medium.

The companies that undertake electronic business can be classified in three main ways:

1. **Virtual distributors** – these have no shops or stores or physical presence in the high street, malls or out-of-town locations. They trade exclusively on the Internet or on television and have to find new ways of attracting custom and serving consumer needs. Examples of these are **Travelocity.com** and **lastminute.com**.

2. **Two-channel distributors** – these are established companies that have developed an electronic retailing capability as a major or minor aspect of their business. For example Thomas Cook has also set up the **thomascook.com** website which it has promoted by offering special discounts or free insurance for a holiday booking.

3. **Multichannel distributors** – these are established companies which service customer needs in a number of ways, including shops, telephone/mobile ordering, the Internet, catalogues and television.

Although many observers originally felt that electronic retailing would be dominated by new *virtual* distributors, it now seems likely that the marketplace will be made up of all three categories. However, what is clear is that the Internet offers suppliers much more benefit than utilising a travel agent for their distribution. There are five main advantages associated with the Internet as a revenue channel, from which travel industry suppliers, such as hoteliers and airlines, stand to benefit if they develop more direct sales for their business. They are:

1. **Lower sales costs** – If a hotel were to sell its inventory via an online intermediary such as **www.travelweb.com** then the information need only be distributed via a switch to translate the data into a 'standard' language. However, selling with a travel agent involves a switch, a CRS and the travel agency booking fee, resulting in the hotel retaining substantially less revenue.

2. **Expanded market reach and presence** – The Internet does not recognise international borders, so tourism providers can potentially reach a world target audience. The site can be accessed 24 hours a day, which is also less restrictive. For example, an Asian customer in Hong Kong would be able to complete a transaction with an English company at a time that was convenient to them because the eight-hour time difference between the two destinations is immaterial. Also, many potential customers search the website and then make an offline booking so it is important to have the web presence.

3. **Increased customer loyalty** – The decision by tourist providers to use travel agents to facilitate the sale of their products restricts the level of contact they have with the end customer, meaning that loyalty may be developed with the retailer rather than the actual provider. However, the Internet enables travel industry suppliers to address this and take a more active part in the transaction.

4. **Leverage for other sales channels** – Cost savings from this method of distribution can be used to have multichannel strategies as lower costs in one channel can subsidise the more expensive channels, such as travel agents.

5. **Collection of databases** – Any system which is owned by the company has the benefit of collecting data on customers which can be used as part of a future relationship marketing exercise.

Given the above benefits of increased direct sales it is important that travel agents should anticipate further competition from existing businesses diversifying their portfolios to exploit a potentially lucrative market opportunity. Figure 21.12 indicates the changes taking place and the complexity of the distribution of tourism products.

## Priceline.com

**Priceline.com** has positioned itself as offering the cheapest prices on the Internet. Priceline receives requests based upon the 'name-your-own-price' system for airline tickets, rental cars, hotel rooms, long-distance calls and even new cars. Priceline then attempts to match each individual request with a supplier who is willing to fulfil the order at an agreed transaction price. Priceline creates revenue using the spread between the prices at which airlines sell discounted tickets and consumers buy them. To achieve this Priceline monitors changing airline pricing and

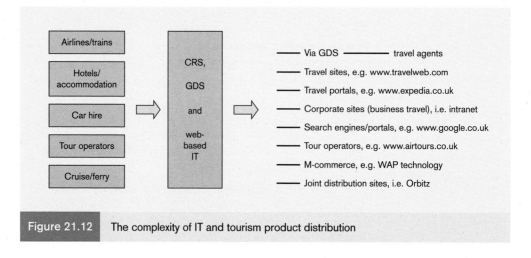

**Figure 21.12** The complexity of IT and tourism product distribution

availability on a minute-by-minute basis. Consumers have the benefit of buying at a price which offers them value for money, while sellers may be able to move otherwise unsold capacity or to generate incremental revenue. The advantage of the Priceline e-commerce business model is they have no risk of inventory as they only facilitate transactions once they receive the customer's credit card details.

To date there is evidence that the sales of airline tickets are becoming more direct but not that the British package holidaymaker is buying direct in the same way. There is little doubt that for many, the convenience of using an agent to book the holiday is an important element in the buying process. This is because a travel agent may offer greater opportunities for advice on the parallel purchase of insurance, car hire, rail travel to the airport, traveller's cheques, and so on. As Table 21.5 outlines, the travel agent still offers a number of benefits, which may be the reason more travellers have not booked direct. (See also Chapters 16 and 22 on intermediaries and e-commerce.)

However, with Expedia and Travelocity now widely known and accepted, the use of more direct systems of booking are making inroads into traditional forms of distribution. There is a

| Table 21.5 | Travel agent benefits |
|---|---|

● **Easy accessibility**

  – to a full range and wide choice of brochures; to product components of visas, traveller's cheques, insurance, etc.;

  – to agent services in every main town and city, as well as to alternative agents, products and brands.

● **Convenience**

  – for obtaining independent information and advice (surfing the Web can be very time-consuming and may not provide for the best possible purchase; and the Internet often does not allow for further questions to be asked). Agents are more likely to take on an independent consultant's role, which is not offered through direct-sell operations;

  – for making the purchase and payment for the holiday (with less perceived risk than would be the case with payment by credit card to an Internet site);

  – for making complaints and being represented by a third party if things go wrong.

● **Habit**

  – People can get into a pattern of behaviour which becomes habit-forming. However, a major campaign by direct mail from Internet direct-sell tour operators/wholesalers could change this habit as could the greater familiarity of use of the Internet for booking air tickets.

● **Security/risk**

  – Consumers feel more secure when dealing with a reputable company or agent (Internet searches involve more personal individual responsibility of the outcome of payment and choice).

● **Environment/atmosphere**

  – Travel agents offer an environment that is part of the holiday experience. The travel agency environment is the perfect setting for personal selling methods which are a powerful means of generating bookings (the Internet is a much more impersonal medium).

● **Economic**

  – Because travel agents compete on price or added value, and tour operators/wholesalers have the smallest of margins, the price between travel agent's products and those available through direct-sell channels are not significantly different.

*Source*: Adapted from Gilbert, 1990a

growing use of mobile phones to book and pay for tickets or a hotel room and to use apps that allow for links to booking engines. In addition more use of mobiles to view the destination, a brochure or video content is growing.

# THE MARKETING MIX REVISITED: ARE THE FOUR PS SUFFICIENT?

The adaptation of the marketing mix by authors such as Booms and Bitner (1981) has been based upon arguments that stress that the original marketing mix is more appropriate to manufacturing than to service companies. For example, Booms and Bitner added three extra Ps (see Figure 21.13):

- people;
- physical evidence; and
- process.

Authors such as Booms and Bitner argue that the marketing mix of four Ps is not comprehensive enough for the tourism and hospitality industry. The major difference is said to be the intangible element of human behaviour where quality and its control is of paramount importance.

We believe that there is a need for more research into the industry and its marketing before the four Ps require revision. For the present it is believed the four Ps offer an adequate framework into which the differences can be incorporated. The main task of marketers in tourism and hospitality is to understand the characteristics of the products they plan, control and manage. This will ensure that managers will attempt to control the aspects of the marketing mix which have most bearing on the satisfaction level of consumers. We provided the basis of this assessment in this chapter and Chapter 20 on marketing planning.

While it is obvious that there are differences between manufactured and service products, the framework of the four Ps is sufficient for planning purposes as physical evidence, people or process are part of the category of product or its implementation. The four categories do not presuppose the relegation of service product considerations to secondary importance. On the contrary, the four categories should ensure that within product formulation greater focus will be placed on the integration of all the different service management considerations.

| Product | Price | Place | Promotion | People | Physical evidence | Process |
|---------|-------|-------|-----------|--------|-------------------|---------|
| Range | Level | Location | Advertising | Personnel: | Environment: | Policies |
| Quality | Discounts: | Accessibility | Personal selling | training | furnishings | Procedures |
| Level | allowances | Distribution | Sales promotion | discretion | colour | Mechanisation |
| Brand name | commissions | channels | Publicity | commitment | layout | Employee |
| Service line | Payment terms | Distribution | Public relations | incentives | noise level | discretion |
| Warranty | Customer's | coverage | | appearance | Facilitating | Customer |
| After-sales | perceived | | | interpersonal | goods | involvement |
| service | value | | | behaviour | Tangible clues | Customer |
| | Quality/price | | | attitudes | | direction |
| | Differentiation | | | Other customers: | | Flow of activities |
| | | | | behaviour | | |
| | | | | degree of | | |
| | | | | involvement | | |
| | | | | customer/ | | |
| | | | | customer | | |
| | | | | contact | | |

**Figure 21.13** The marketing mix for services
*Source*: Reprinted by permission of the American Marketing Association from Booms and Bitner, 1981

## MINI CASE STUDY 21.1
The rise of accessories tourism

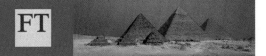

**FT, 13 October 2011, by Vanessa Friedman**

You've heard of eco-tourism, and experience tourism? Well, in a report entitled *'Around the World'* HSBC has identified yet another sub-niche in the industry: accessories tourism, or the tendency of consumers from the emerging markets to plan their trips according to where the handbags are cheapest. According to the HSBC report, there are 'increasing incentives to travel from an economic standpoint as purchasing power and currency fluctuations can play an important role as well as relative price positioning'.

OK, we all knew this was true to a certain extent: all those lines outside Louis Vuitton in Paris full of non-Parisians clearly meant something, but according to the report, this is less about status (the chic of buying from the point of origin) than economic intelligence (the savings involved). And it has reached a critical mass that is pretty hard to ignore.

To wit: Chinese tourists are now the 'third biggest spenders in the world' (Germans and Americans are first and second) but – and this is crucial – of the spending by Chinese visitors, '32 per cent of their budget' went on shopping. This is a bigger chunk than these tourists put towards on hotels or dining, and more than German or American visitors spend on stuff. As to why, well, exchange rates play a part, but taxes and duties play a bigger role.

Consider the following nugget from the report: last year, half of all handbags and 75 per cent of watches sold in Hong Kong were purchased by people from mainland China, and the savings in taxes and duties between buying in HK and buying in the mainland actually off-set the price of the plane ticket. Also popular, apparently, are watches in Switzerland, and iPads in the US.

And this isn't limited to Chinese travellers: in Florida, 'Brazil has overtaken the UK' as the source of the largest group of tourists, but those Brazilian visitors 'spent close to twice as much as British tourists' on products, partly because a $100 pair of sneakers in the US could cost $300 in Brazil. Meanwhile, according to a survey on business improvement to New York's Madison Avenue district, Brazilians are the district's number one customers, followed by British visitors and then by Chinese tourists. It's not about souvenirs; it's about savings.

What does this mean? Well, HSBC concludes that 'up to 50 per cent of sales of luxury goods in western Europe are generated by foreigners' and, in fact, 'global travel could generate as much as 30 per cent of total sales of luxury goods'. Let the shopping safaris begin.

## DISCUSSION QUESTIONS

1. Do travel brochures, tourist boards or websites offer enough information on shopping in overseas' destinations? Search the relevant information and provide a report.

2. Provide a list of countries where you think value for money at the destination will be a major benefit that the tourist would enjoy. Then identify the segments by country that would make a good target group for these countries.

3. Is there a sufficient gap in the market for organising shopping excursion tours to different destinations? Weigh up the evidence and report your findings.

It should be apparent that marketing mix decisions must be geared to achieving the objectives of the company or organisation, and should be linked to acceptability throughout the organisation. While marketing departments often lead in setting the marketing mix strategy, they should not ignore input from others and should be sensitive to views on whether the strategy will be workable from an operational standpoint.

The marketing mix offers the range and spread of alternative strategies by which a marketer can influence demand. However, while the available range is very similar for all tourism marketers, the choice is not. For example, an NTO will not normally be involved in developing products or setting prices. The process of mix formulation and balancing is quite often unique to each organisation.

For an organisation to be successful with its marketing mix, it has to develop a differential advantage which will distinguish the organisation's product offering(s) from that of the competition. Only when an organisation has built an advantage will it find that customers seek it out, in which case it is easier to create higher profits. The advantage may be based upon quality, image or product concept. Center Parcs in the UK has developed an advantage (through all-weather facilities, forest-like settings and many different activities) and the results can be seen in the high year-round demand for its product.

# DESTINATION MARKETING

Destinations rely on tourism as a major tool in the creation of economic development and support for the indigenous population. In the current environment the marketing of destinations is of considerable importance as rivalry for the tourist grows and private and public sector marketing strategies become increasingly sophisticated. When we describe destinations they are of different types (see Part 2). Originally, destinations were thought of simply as geographical areas such as a country, an island or a town. In this way destinations can be local, regional or even national: we can speak of America, California or San Francisco with each, and all, capable of being a destination. However, Batchelor (1999) characterised destinations on a continuum with one end consisting of compact product entities such as theme parks. These may be product destinations which create differing lengths of visit or stay. At the other end of the continuum we would find countries or groups of countries which are marketed as a tourism destination. In between, there are many types of destination, defined by the tourist and/or administrative bodies that assume responsibility for them, and include: (1) self-contained resorts, country club hotels, holiday villages; (2) villages, towns, cities; (3) areas with cohesive identity such as national parks; and (4) a region as defined by administrative boundaries or brand names.

The understanding of destination image is important for any destination marketing plan. Destination image has two closely interrelated components: (1) the perceptive/cognitive evaluations, which refer to the individual's own knowledge and beliefs about the destination, and (2) affective appraisals, which refer to the individual's feelings towards the destination. The two components together form a compound image which an individual will draw upon to describe a destination to others, or in order to decide upon a visit. More specifically from a cognitive point of view, the tourist destination image comprises a set of attributes that match the physical, social and built resources that a tourist destination has at its disposal. A destination offers a number of elements which allow individuals a choice of activities, and which culminate in experiences to remember on return.

Tourists form an image of a tourist destination after undergoing a process which, according to Gunn (1988), involves the following stages:

1. accumulating mental images of the destination, thus forming an organic image;
2. modifying the initial image after more information, thus forming an induced image;
3. deciding to visit the destination;
4. visiting the destination;
5. sharing the destination;
6. returning home; and
7. modifying the image on the experience in the destination.

This led Gunn to distinguish between the two types of image – *organic* and *induced*. The organic image is based on non-commercial sources of information, such as news about the destination in the mass media, education at school, information received and opinions of friends and relatives. The induced image is based on commercial sources of information, such as different forms of advertising and information from travel agents and tour operators.

The marketing of destinations is complex as we are dealing not only with the tangible inventory of physical attributes such as the natural geography, built environment and attractions, accommodation and transport facilities, but also intangible social and cultural factors. Although the destination is often the focus for all the marketing effort, it does not follow that there will be a local, regional or national agency that will take responsibility for its marketing. It is also often the case that where there is an organisation charged with destination marketing, its responsibility is based upon a fairly narrow set of powers and limited resources. Traditionally the public sector has been involved in destination marketing through NTOs, regional boards such as DMOs or local authorities but, increasingly, a trend is emerging where marketing agencies or conference and visitor bureaux are established for cities. Such agencies are often funded by a mix of private and public means.

## The marketing of destinations

The marketing of destinations is a relatively new departure for many localities, particularly at the regional and local level. At these levels the lead agency tends to be the public sector and this, in turn, has a number of implications for the marketing process which are rooted in the inability of the public sector to control the product. In addition, there is an issue here in terms of whether we should transform places where people live, work and play into *products*. We are only beginning to understand how to translate generic marketing approaches to destinations. There are some key areas to consider here:

- The images of the destination which the marketing campaigns wish to communicate should take into account the views and sensitivities of local people.
- Public sector agencies have to be even-handed in their support for businesses at the destination – it is difficult politically for them to back only 'product' winners.
- The public sector controls neither the business plans of private sector companies at the destination, nor the quality of service delivery.
- Public sector marketing organisations seldom *achieve the sale,* rather they are instrumental in attracting the consumer to the point of sale – usually a private sector company. It is therefore difficult to evaluate the effectiveness of destination marketing.
- Finally, the critical issue of resources is a constant problem for public sector marketing budgets, especially for activities which may be perceived as dispensable – such as market research – but which in reality are crucial to success in the tourism marketplace.

The traditional role of many of these approaches has been elementary. The emphasis has been confined to promotional strategies which aim to improve the destination image or to produce more positive 'mental concepts' in relation to potential as well as actual tourists. This is often related to the selection of desirable market segments that are targeted through the use of advertising, Internet home pages, direct mail, print or PR campaigns (as discussed earlier in this chapter). There is further emphasis on providing information at the destination through information posters or tourist information centres.

Destinations need to identify those product attributes that will appeal to different tourist segments and then to ensure that the promotional campaign delivers a cohesive message. There is also the need to produce a distinctive identity or 'brand' which forms the basis of the 'positioning' of a destination area, providing it with a personality and differentiating it from competitors.

De Chernatony and McDonald (1992) describe the necessary attributes of a successful brand and these may also be applied to tourism destinations:

A successful brand is an identifiable product, service, person or place augmented in such a way that the buyer, or user, perceives relevant, unique added values which match their needs most closely. Its success results from being able to sustain these added values against competitors.

Such results may be achieved through the theming of an area by linking it to a famous personality who may have lived in the area, such as a painter (Constable country such as Dedham Vale, valley of the Stour river and East Bergholt), a writer or poet (Hemingway and Cuba or Wordsworth associated with the Lake District and Grasmere), a television series or film, a historical era (Pompeii) or seasonal beauty (New England in the autumn). There are many other themes, of course, but all need to be developed with a creative flair for the tastes of the potential visitor as well as the acceptability of the theme to the media.

The involvement of tourist boards at the national and regional level is often one of facilitation. Facilitation is made up of a series of assistance schemes which support the constituent service sectors of the tourist industry forming the accommodation, transport and attraction provision of a country, region or locality. This may take the form of a set of objectives related to:

- the development of specific tourism areas or products;
- the targeting of specific segments from generating areas;
- the level of expenditure available;
- a range of promotional activities (PR, advertising, exhibitions, literature production); or
- the need for cooperative private initiatives or expenditure.

The industry is diverse and fragmented, comprising many small companies which require help in areas such as:

- the collection and use of research data;
- the organisation of trade exhibitions and shows;
- representation through overseas offices;
- the production of trade manuals, catalogues and brochures (which can have space bought by smaller companies); and
- the development of global reservation systems which can provide local information on a global basis.

The facilitation process can help create an overall brand image of a destination through the total activity which takes place. However, the marketing, through all forms of promotion, will create a specific brand image. This is beneficial if a strong brand image is created.

An area that has a strong brand image is able to:

- achieve better margins and higher prices than commodity-positioned brands;
- differentiate itself more easily from competitors;
- provide a sense of added value and so more easily entice customers to purchase;
- act as a sign and enticement to the potential traveller, which implies fulfilment of expectations;
- build repeat visits and loyalty; and
- improve the strength of its position as a status area rather than as a commodity.

A destination has an image of place associated with it. This can be based upon differences related to what is normal in both a tourist-generating area and in the culture of the destination. The differences may be real or imagined. Promotion of a destination is based on an image selected by the tourism marketer and communicated to the generating markets, often providing stereotypical images of an exotic, carefree host culture. In reality this may mask a whole set of socio-cultural realities of what life is like for the average inhabitant of a destination.

The power to portray selective images of place relies on factors such as whether a tourist is a first-time visitor or a repeat visitor and also on the amount of information the tourist has gleaned from television, films, books or friends. A destination, once branded and having communicated a distinctive image, is in a far stronger position to influence demand if problems arise of price increases, excess demand and crowding or unfavourable currency exchange rates.

The Spanish Tourist Board, faced with the loss of a strong Spanish image for its resort areas, embarked upon an exercise to reposition and rebrand the country. The history, culture, traditions and inland areas had been under-promoted and weakly communicated. The campaign from 1992 emphasised the 'Spanishness' of the country within a campaign which stressed, 'Spain – Passion for life'. The painter, Miro, was commissioned to create a logo that would reflect the fundamental spirit of Spain. He created a vibrant logo reflecting the national flag colours of yellow and red and this was used on all communication messages.

## Consumers' concept of 'self-image'

When consumers choose among brands, they rationally consider practical issues about the relative functional capabilities of all the brands on offer. At the same time, they evaluate different brand personalities, forming a view about the brand that most closely represents the image with which they wish to be associated.

Applying this to tourism, it is possible to suggest that when competing destinations are perceived as being equal and similar in terms of their physical capabilities, the brand that comes closest to enhancing the consumer's self-concept is more likely to be chosen. Consumers look to brands not only for what they can do, but also for the message they communicate about the purchaser to peer groups. Trips to Monte Carlo, for example, are chosen not just for their functional excellence, but also because they make an important statement about the traveller.

According to de Chernatony and McDonald (1992), the symbolic nature of brands increases the attraction for consumers as they:

- help set social scenes and enable people to mix with each other more easily;
- enable consumers to convey messages about themselves;
- provide a basis for a better understanding of the way people act; and
- help consumers say something to themselves.

In effect, consumers are transmitting subtle messages to others by purchasing and displaying the use of particular brands in the hope that their reference groups decode the messages in a positive and acceptable way. Consumers hold what is called their own 'self-image' and buy brands that conform to that image. Consumers, therefore, could be said to admit brands and their 'personalities' into their social circle, in much the same way as consumers enjoy having like-minded people around them. When friends or colleagues admire a holiday destination choice, the traveller feels pleased that the destination brand reinforces his or her self-image and may therefore repeat the purchase.

The economic and social situation in which consumers find themselves will dictate, to some extent, the type of image they wish to project. Through anticipating and subsequently evaluating the people that they will meet at a particular event or destination, consumers then seek brands to reflect the situational self-image that they wish to display.

## CONCLUSION

The marketing mix cannot be effective without a full understanding of the target market and the needs of each of the segments. The marketing mix is formulated and implemented to satisfy the target market. We take the marketing mix to be made up of the four Ps of product, price, promotion and place (distribution), but there are alternative approaches where authors argue for an expansion owing to the service characteristics of tourism and hospitality products. However, the additional ingredients can be included in the existing headings associated with the four Ps and, as long as the characteristics of the tourism and hospitality product are emphasised, there is little benefit in pre-dating McCarthy's late 1970s' simplification of approach.

# SELF-CHECK QUESTIONS

1. Name and describe the different product levels that may exist for a leading hotel.

2. Describe the benefits that a strong tourism brand may provide for a company.

3. Provide a list and understanding of what needs to be assessed when setting the price for a package holiday.

4. Explain the ways of deciding upon the amount of money required when raising a marketing communication budget.

5. What are the major advantages related to use of the Internet as a distribution channel?

# YOUTUBE

**http://www.youtube.com/watch?v=jjYxdrcJ4OY&feature=related**
The link provides a good overview of changing social media use

**http://www.youtube.com/watch?v=GEf7f3qLvTI**
Interesting view of brand knowledge and development

**http://www.youtube.com/watch?v=dg3ZKfF4tQ4&feature=related**
This provides insight into Disney bookings related to the social media uses

**http://www.youtube.com/watch?v=PduM85zPHDM&feature=related**
Discusses electronic channel management

**http://www.youtube.com/watch?v=4phxRH6vk-I**
Indicates tips on pricing a product

# REFERENCES AND FURTHER READING

Aaker, D.A. (1991) *Managing Brand Equity: Capitalizing on the Value of a Brand Name*, Free Press, Simon & Schuster, New York.

Aaker, D.A. and Biel, A.L. (1993) *Brand Equity and Advertising*, Lawrence Erlbaum Associates, Mahwah, NJ.

Batchelor, R. (1999) 'Strategic Marketing of Tourism Destinations', pp. 183–95 in Vellas, F. and Becherel, L. (eds), *The International Marketing of Travel and Tourism*, Macmillan Press, London.

Bierman, D. (2003) *Restoring Tourism Destinations in Crisis: A Strategic Marketing Approach*, CABI, Cambridge, MA.

Booms, B.H. and Bitner, M.J. (1981) 'Marketing strategies and organization structures for service firms', pp. 47–51 in Donnelly, J. and George, W.R. (eds), *Marketing of Services*, American Marketing Association, Chicago.

Borden, N.H. (1965) 'The concept of the marketing mix', pp. 386–97 in Schwartz, G. (ed.), *Science in Marketing*, Wiley, Chichester.

Buhalis, D. (2003) *eTourism: Information Technologies for Strategic Tourism Management*, FT/Prentice Hall, London. This book addresses the change to a digitisation of processes and value chains in the tourism industry. It offers insight into the new technological trends based upon the impacts of the information communication technology (ICT) revolution. The book adopts a strategic management and marketing perspective for tourism enterprises and destinations.

CIMtIG (2004) D. Blastland (managing director, First Choice Holidays) 'Can tour operators and travel agents survive?', Member minutes of meeting of Chartered Institute of Marketing Industry Group, January.

De Chernatony, L. and Daniels, K. (1994) 'Developing a more effective brand positioning', *Journal of Brand Management* **1**(6), 373–9.

De Chernatony, L. and McDonald, M.H.B. (1992) *Creating Powerful Brands*, Butterworth Heinemann, Oxford.

De Chernatony, L. and McWilliam, G. (1989) 'The varying nature of brands as assets', *International Journal of Advertising* **8**, 339–49.

Gilbert, D.C. (1990a) 'European product purchase methods and systems', *Service Industries Journal* **10**(4), 664–79.

Gilbert, D.C. (1990b) 'Strategic marketing planning for national tourism', *Tourism Analysis* **1**(90), 18–27.

Gunn, C. (1988) *Vacationscape: Designing Tourist Regions*, 2nd edn, Van Nostrand Reinhold, New York.

Hankinson, G. and Cowking, P. (1993) *Branding in Action: Cases and Strategies for Profitable Brand Management*, McGraw-Hill, London.

Kotler, P. and Armstrong, G. (2005) *Marketing: An Introduction*, Prentice Hall, Upper Saddle River, NJ.

Kotler, P., Bowen J. and Makens, J. (2009) *Marketing for Hospitality and Tourism*, 5th edn, Pearson, Upper Saddle River, NJ. The book draws upon the marketing material of Philip Kotler's other books and as such is based upon his pedigree which has been developed over a number of years of writing marketing textbooks. However, the examples are often better in other texts and other specialist books need to be read in conjunction with this one. This latest edition now covers electronic marketing, has case studies and provides a broad understanding of the role of marketing in hospitality and tourism. Specialist areas covered are customer quality management and destination marketing.

McArdle, J. (1989) 'Product branding – the way forward', *Tourism Management* **10**, 201.

McCarthy, E.J. (1978) *Basic Marketing: A Managerial Approach*, 6th edn, Irwin, Homewood, IL.

Middleton, V., Fyall, A., Morgan, M. and Ranchhod, A. (2009) *Marketing in Travel and Tourism*, 4th edn, Butterworth Heinemann, Oxford. *Marketing in Travel and Tourism* explains the basic principles and practice of marketing in the contemporary setting of the new pressures affecting tourism including areas not normally covered in such texts such as NTOs. In addition, international case studies are included.

Morgan, N. and Pritchard, A. (1998) *Tourism Promotion and Power: Creating Images, Creating Identities*, John Wiley & Sons, Chichester. The book is underpinned by marketing theory and does not simply deal with the more general concepts related to tourism promotion. The book offers a different approach by taking a sociological and cultural approach to tourism marketing. It focuses on contentious issues of tourism imagery by discussing issues such as gender, sexuality and race as key determinants of tourism power dimensions. The book is underpinned by good case studies which are thought-provoking.

Zeithaml, V.A. (1988) 'Consumer perceptions of price, quality, and value: a means–end model and synthesis of evidence', *Journal of Marketing* **52**(July), 2–22.

## Websites

http://www.eyefortravel.com

http://world-tourism.org/

http://wttc.org/

## MAJOR CASE STUDY 21.1
The portrayal of indigenous identity in Australian tourism brand advertising: engendering an image of extraordinary reality or staged authenticity?

## INTRODUCTION

In national tourism advertising campaigns, facets of national identity may be used to portray an image of an extraordinary world, where the ordinary rituals of home and work can be replaced by an inverted social ritual of freedom and play (Hummon, 1988). Elements of the desired identity (Van Rekom, 1997) of the nation are used to construct a favourable brand image for the consumer, differentiating and building preference among competing destination brands. A key element of a successful brand strategy is the communication of a clear and consistent positioning of the brand. But a nation offers a 'fragmented set of images, so the key is to exploit the right fragments in line with the product and the target customer group' (O'Shaughnessy and O'Shaughnessy, 2000: 58).

To portray the paradise that is the extraordinary tourist world, fragments of national identity that might be used include heritage, lifestyle or the physical environment. In multicultural nations, the benefits of cultural diversity might be celebrated, or indigenous culture may be promoted to convey the core character of the destination. National image is intertwined with the social concept of the nation, based on a shared territory, common interests and key elements of a common culture (O'Shaughnessy and O'Shaughnessy, 2000). But a nation state may be composed of multiple nations; Taylor (2001b), for example, identifies seven 'nations of Britain'. National identity, therefore, may be contested among multiple ideas of the nation, creating confusion for advertising audiences.

A recent national tourism advertising campaign for Australia, attempting to leverage off the international exposure of the Baz Luhrmann-directed movie, *Australia: The Movie,* is an example of such a contested identity portrayal. The campaign's potential success might be considered from the perspective of how Indigenous Australian identity is appropriated to create an image of the extraordinary. The presentation of Indigenous identity elements in national tourism destination advertising may prove sub-optimal when the advertising message is perceived as incongruent with prior nation brand beliefs, due to the inclusion of illegitimate or contrived brand claims; as 'unexorcised demons' may reappear to 'afflict a nation's image' (O'Shaughnessy and O'Shaughnessy, 2000: 58). MacCannell (1973)

discusses this illegitimacy in terms of staged authenticity: cultural products are staged to look authentic, focusing on pre-conceived stereotypes. The debate about the nature of authenticity is an ongoing one. The tourism sector has responded to the demand by tourists for supposed authentic experiences but the reality remains that the industry can only offer commodified authenticity in a 'packaged' format. Thus, authenticity is effectively a contradiction in terms that can never be fully achieved. Getting as close to the authentic experience as possible is all that can be reasonably expected by the paying tourist.

The purpose of this article is to explore the issue of identity portrayal for Indigenous Australians and to also propose a study to examine whether and how incongruity between the advertised national brand, based on a postcolonial and staged portrayal of Indigenous identity, and consumers' prior-held nation-brand beliefs might influence the persuasiveness of such a place branding approach. The national tourism brand is argued to offer a valuable place branding context, as the consumer may be expected to engage in a high degree of involvement and elaboration over such informational inputs in the vacation decision. This context is of interest as tourism promotion is often the loudest voice in 'branding' the nation, as the 'tourist board usually has the biggest budgets and the most competent marketers' (Anholt, 2007: 25).

Tourism place brand perceptions therefore have the potential to spill over to evaluations in other product categories. Promotion of the extraordinary, however, will be considered along with people's first-hand experience with a country, as tourists or business travelers, or indirect awareness, variously accumulated. In question here is how uncomfortable, postcolonial social challenges, such as a lack of reconciliation between conquered and conquerors, are accentuated when nation branding strategies are pursued, and how branding portrayals are perceived when the authenticity promoted is a staged or illegitimate one. The concept of authenticity is well documented in the tourism literature (Cohen, 1988; Hughes, 1995; Wang, 1999; Taylor, 2001a). Cohen (1988) observes, 'recreational tourists, whose concern with authenticity is relatively low, may well accept even a substantially staged product and experience as "authentic", but for some tourists, staged authenticity might prove less compelling'.

. . . Tourism advertising typically presents 'idealized imagery . . . shaped by the economic interests of promoters and the social psychological motives of consumers pursuing anything from status displays to self-realization' (Hummon, 1988:180). Yet the desired national destination identity aspects thrown up for the international tourist's consumption are deliberately included in order to help shape the nation's brand. Chosen tourism imagery fragments should serve to convey the extraordinary characteristics of the nation as a vacation destination and add to the values inherent in the nation brand.

. . . National identity might be expected to reflect the notion of shared imagery, but the extent to which nations do indeed represent one community with a shared imagery is questionable. 'Old-world' nations are often communities of different ethnic groups, many of which have become increasingly multicultural. 'New-world' nations, such as the countries of North and South America, South Africa, New Zealand, and Australia, have typically become multicultural as a result of colonialism, and subsequent immigration flows, where an indigenous population, variously, occupies a marginalised space and identity in the modern nation. For these indigenous communities, the imagery of one nation's identity may be far from a shared one.

*Source*: Short excerpt from Alan Pomering and Leanne White (2011) 'The portrayal of indigenous identity in Australian tourism brand', *Place Branding and Public Diplomacy* **7**(3), 165–74

## DISCUSSION QUESTIONS

1. Examine the web pages and communications of the 'New World' nations and Identify the main images being used to see if they reflect the indigenous population in sufficient detail, or whether the images are staged European models of tourist activity.

2. Should those images of Australia created for tourism, which are often not authentic, be assessed against the benefits or otherwise of creating an accepted shared imagery of the nation state in terms of its diversity and multicultural basis?

3. What brief would you give to an advertising agency if they were to brand your own country in terms of what needs to be emphasised in the images portrayed?.

# CHAPTER 22
## INFORMATION TECHNOLOGY IN TOURISM

### LEARNING OUTCOMES

In this chapter we focus on the strategic and operational role of ICTs in tourism organisations. The chapter demonstrates a wide range of eTourism concepts to provide you with:

- an understanding of the key ICT and eTourism concepts;

- an appreciation of the generic ICTs applications in the tourism industry;

- a knowledge of the basic concepts of computer reservation system and global distribution channels;

- an explanation of the key trends in Internet adoption around the world;

- an understanding of social media and their usage for engagement;

- a comprehension of the impact of the Internet and ICTs tools on the structure and components of the tourism system; and

- an appreciation of the strategic importance of ICTs and the Internet for the future of each stakeholder in the tourism industry.

Photograph: Zanzibar, Tanzania, Africa © Graham Meyer

## INTRODUCTION

ICT developments have changed the best operational and strategic practices for organisations on a global level and altered the competitiveness of enterprises and regions around the world (Buhalis and Law, 2008). eTourism defined as the application of 'information communication technologies' (ICTs) on the tourism industry has dramatically affected the strategic and operational management of tourism organisations and destinations (Buhalis, 2003). In addition, social media and Web 2.0 provided a group of Internet-based applications that allow the creation and exchange of user generated content (Kaplan and Haenlein, 2010). This enabled organisations to capitalise on user generated content (UGC) to engage dynamically with all their stakeholders. Innovative organisations such as Marriott, Hilton, easyJet and British Airways took advantage of the emerging technologies early in order to improve their operational processes and enhance their communication with consumers and stakeholders. Others emerged as a result of the Internet, including Expedia, Omena and Kayak. The Internet provided the ability to expand the customer base to cover the global population cost effectively. Large organisations, such as airlines and hotel chains, were able to access an international clientele and develop the tools to manage properties around the world at the touch of button (Egger and Buhalis, 2008). Smaller companies could also for the first time develop their 'virtual size' and offer their services to global markets (Spencer et al., 2012; O'Connor, 1999). Destinations could develop virtual representations and boost their image globally. However, several tourism organisations failed to meet the challenge that eBusiness introduced. Many of them failed to incorporate ICTs in their strategy and to appreciate the significant changes evident in the tourism industry structure caused by technology. Consequently they developed competitive disadvantages and found it increasingly difficult to maintain their position in the marketplace.

This chapter explores the main implications of the ICTs' developments in the tourism industry. It illuminates the complexity of the various types of systems and demonstrates how they fit together in the production, distribution and delivery of tourism products. The utilisation of ICTs and the Internet by different functions and sectors of the industry is examined and conclusions for the future impact of ICTs outlined.

# INFORMATION COMMUNICATION TECHNOLOGIES AS A BUSINESS TOOL

Information communication technologies (ICTs) and the Internet introduced a second industrial revolution in the late 1990s. The development and application of computerised systems accelerated rapidly and enabled their use for a wider range of business functions and activities. The enhancements in ICTs capabilities, in combination with the decrease of the size of equipment and ICT costs, improved the reliability, compatibility and interconnectivity of numerous terminals and applications (Gupta, 2000). The emergence and mainstreaming of the Internet empowered the global networking of computers, enabling individuals and organisations to access a plethora of multimedia information and knowledge sources, regardless of their location or ownership, often free of charge. Thus, almost everybody with an Internet connection can effectively access unprecedented levels of information and knowledge.

Dean et al. (2012) explain that since the day the first domain was registered in 1985, the Internet has not stopped growing. It has sailed through multiple recessions and one near-collapse and kept on increasing in use, size, reach and impact. It has ingrained itself in daily life to the extent that most of us no longer think of it as anything new or special. The Internet has become, quite simply, indispensable. By 2016, there will be 3 billion Internet users globally – almost half the world's population. The Internet economy will reach $4.2 trillion in the G-20 economies. If it were a national economy, the Internet economy would rank in the world's top five, behind only the US, China, Japan and India, and ahead of Germany. Across the G-20, it already amounted to 4.1% of GDP, or $2.3 trillion, in 2010 – surpassing the economies of Italy and Brazil. The Internet is contributing up to 8% of GDP in some economies, powering growth and creating jobs. The

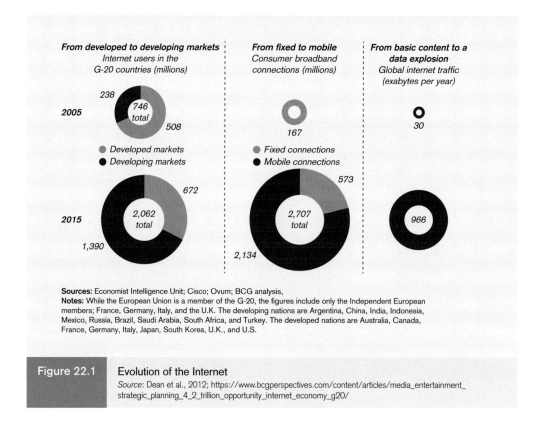

**Sources:** Economist Intelligence Unit; Cisco; Ovum; BCG analysis,
**Notes:** While the European Union is a member of the G-20, the figures include only the Independent European members; France, Germany, Italy, and the U.K. The developing nations are Argentina, China, India, Indonesia, Mexico, Russia, Brazil, Saudi Arabia, South Africa, and Turkey. The developed nations are Australia, Canada, France, Germany, Italy, Japan, South Korea, U.K., and U.S.

| Figure 22.1 | Evolution of the Internet |
|---|---|

*Source*: Dean et al., 2012; https://www.bcgperspectives.com/content/articles/media_entertainment_strategic_planning_4_2_trillion_opportunity_internet_economy_g20/

scale and pace of change is still accelerating, and the nature of the Internet – who uses it, how and for what – is changing rapidly too. Developing G-20 countries already have 800 million Internet users, more than all the developed G-20 countries combined. Social networks reach about 80% of users in developed and developing economies alike. Mobile devices – smartphones and tablets – will account for four out of five broadband connections by 2016, as demonstrated in Figure 22.1.

eBusiness can be defined as: 'the use of digital tools for business functions and processes'. It is becoming increasingly evident that eBusiness is an essential prerequisite for successful organisations in the emerging, globally networked, Internet-empowered business environment. Many organisations had to go through a major business processes re-engineering to take advantage of the emerging technologies in order to transform their processes and data handling as well as their ability to operate and to compete in the emerging global marketplace (Laudon and Laudon, 2007). At the macro level, entire economies were empowered to communicate and trade through electronic tools, determining their ability to compete within the global economy. Consequently, economies and enterprises, regardless of their size, product and geographical coverage, were affected and their competitiveness was dramatically altered.

However Minghetti and Buhalis (2009) demonstrate that there is a digital divide in the diffusion of the information and communication technologies (ICTs) in the tourism sector that often makes communities unable to improve the social and economic impacts. A number of factors lead to unequal access and use of ICTs for tourists and destinations and technical, social and motivational aspects need to be taken into consideration to enable many citizens and organisations in developed and developing countries to benefit from the technological revolution and enable markets and destinations to meet and interact effectively in a global tourism environment.

## The evolution of ICTs towards eBusiness

ICTs include not only the hardware and software required but also the groupware, netware and the intellectual capacity (humanware) to develop, program and maintain equipment (Table 22.1). Synergies emerging from the use of these systems effectively mean that information is widely

| Table 22.1 | Information communication technologies |
|---|---|

**Hardware:** Physical equipment such as mechanical, magnetic, electrical, electronic or optical devices (as opposed to computer programs or method of use)

**Software:** Prewritten detailed instructions that control the operation of a computer system or of an electronic device. Software coordinates the work of hardware components in an information system. Software may incorporate standard software such as operating systems or applications, software processes, artificial intelligence and intelligent agents, and user interfaces

**Telecommunications:** The transmission of signals over long distances, including not only data communications but also the transmission of images and voices using radio, television, telephony and other communication technologies

**Netware:** Equipment and software required to develop and support a network or an interconnected system of computers, terminals and communication channels and devices

**Groupware:** Communication tools, such as email, voice mail, fax, videoconferencing that foster electronic communication and collaboration among groups

**'Humanware':** The intellect required for the development, programming, maintenance and operation of technological development. Humanware incorporates the knowledge and expertise pool of the society

**Social media** are a group of Internet-based applications that build on the ideological and technological foundations of Web 2.0, and that allow the creation and exchange of user generated content

*Source:* Adapted from: Gupta, 2000; Laudon and Traver, 2011, Kaplan and Haenlein, 2010

available and accessible through a variety of media and locations. Mobile devices such as portable computers, mobile phones as well as digital television and self-serviced terminals/kiosks can be used to interact and perform several functions. This convergence of ICTs effectively integrates the entire range of hardware, software, groupware, netware and humanware and blurs the boundaries between equipment and software (Werthner and Klein, 1999). The emergence of Web 2.0 and social networking changed dramatically how organisations interact with their stakeholders and force them to develop new and innovative ways to engage with them.

The integration of information processing, multimedia and communications created the 'World Wide Web' (WWW), a multimedia protocol which is using the 'Internet' (the network of all networks) to enable the near instant distribution of media-rich documents (such as textual data, graphics, pictures, video and sounds) and to revolutionise the interactivity between computer users and servers. Web 2.0, a phrase coined by O'Reilly (2005) refers to a second generation of web-based services based on citizens/consumer-generated content – such as social networking sites, blogs, wikis, communication tools and folksonomies – that emphasise online collaboration and sharing among users. Increasingly the Internet is becoming a platform of data/views/knowledge creation and sharing which harness the network to get better information to all users.

Social media, such as blogs, Twitter and Facebook are increasing both their number of users every day as well as their role in the customer interaction arena. Social media are becoming particular tourism organisation destination marketing tools as they influence major markets. Organisations around the world can post valuable information, product videos, pictures, customer testimonials, create discussion forums and much more. More importantly user-generated content provides clear credentials for organisations and enables consumers to state their side of the story. Social networking offers innovative ways to develop customer relationship management strategies and engagement that can have a direct influence on a company's credibility, influence and word-of-mouth advertising. Social platforms simplify the process of connecting to consumers, and at the same time it has made publicity much more difficult to control (Hays et al., 2012; Fotis et al., 2011).

| Table 22.2 | | Web 2.0 |
| --- | --- | --- |
| **Web 1.0** | | **Web 2.0** |
| DoubleClick | → | Google AdSense |
| Ofoto | → | Flickr |
| Akamai | → | BitTorrent |
| mp3.com | → | Napster |
| Britannica Online | → | Wikipedia |
| Personal websites | → | Blogging |
| Evite | → | Upcoming.org and EVDB |
| Domain name speculation | → | Search engine optimisation |
| Page views | → | Cost per click |
| Screen scraping | → | Web services |
| Publishing | → | Participation |
| Multimap | → | Google Earth with content layers |
| Content management systems | → | Wikis |
| Directories (taxonomy) | → | Tagging ('folksonomy') |
| Stickiness | → | Syndication |

*Source*: Based on O'Reilly, 2005

O'Reilly formulates the sense of Web 2.0 as shown in Table 22.2.

As far as organisations are concerned the dynamic development of the **Internet** instituted an innovative platform for the efficient, live and timely exchange of ideas and products, whilst providing unprecedented and unforeseen opportunities for interactive marketing to all service providers. It also enabled the development of **'intranets'** ('closed', 'secured' or 'fire walled' networks) within organisations to harness the needs of internal business users, by using a single controlled, user-friendly interface to support all company data handling and processes. Increasingly enterprises need to formulate close partnerships with other members of the value-chain for the production of goods and services. As a result, **'extranets'** utilise the same principle and computer networks to enhance the interactivity and transparency between organisations and their trusted partners. This facilitates the linking and sharing of data and processes between organisations to maximise the effectiveness of the entire network.

Buhalis (2003) concluded that ICTs include 'the entire range of electronic tools, which facilitate the operational and strategic management of organisations by enabling them to manage their information, functions and processes as well as to communicate interactively with their stakeholders for achieving their mission and objectives'. Thus, ICTs emerge as an integrated system of networked equipment and software, which enables effective data processing and communication for organisational benefit towards transforming organisations to eBusinesses.

The pace of Internet adoption globally demonstrates clearly that ICTs and the Internet in particular restructure the way we live, work, shop and play. It even affects the way that governments operate and how democracy functions, as demonstrated by the political unrest in Egypt, Tunisia and in the Middle East. Millions of people worldwide rely on the Internet for home shopping, tele-entertainment, tele-working, tele-learning, tele-medical support and tele-banking. The electronic/interactive/intelligent/virtual home and enterprise has emerged gradually, facilitating the entire range of communications with the external world and supporting all functions

## MINI CASE STUDY 22.1
Internet and social media's role in democracy and political movements

The recent events in Tunisia and in Egypt clearly demonstrate the role of technology and social media in the emerging political landscape and also in how societies will operate in the future. The Internet played a direct role in mobilising protest, allowing a range of different players, at all levels and sections of society: the working class, the Internet savvy, rights campaigners, senior members of the legal profession, Muslim Brotherhood members and Coptic Christians to spread their message to their communities and mobilise them accordingly. Protesters used a range of different media to communicate with each other and to get their message across effectively and in real time. Photos and videos from mobile phones were sent live on the Internet and these were complemented by TV cameras broadcasting live footage of the unrest. Facebook and Twitter were the two tools primarily utilised for communication. Footage of protests and police repression filmed on mobile phone cameras was broadcast on social media and back to the Egyptian population via satellite channels. As channels of communication were blocked, people turned to other channels. When the Egyptian government blocked social media sites and mobile phone networks and then blocked access to the Internet, the power of the Internet became even more evident. The government's censorship truly backfired as it forced more people on to the streets to see what was really happening. Often the information shared was inaccurate and subjective but people believed it more than information from the official channels. The power of social media in organising the political and social movement and in sharing user-generated content in real time has never before been demonstrated so vividly.

*Source*: Based on: Alexander, A. (2011) 'Internet role in Egypt's protests', http://www.bbc.co.uk/news/world-middle-east-12400319 (accessed 9 February 2011) and other news sources

of everyday personal and professional life through interactive computer networks. Increasingly fast broadband connections and the fast expansion of wireless connectivity through WiFi and 4G enable both consumers and suppliers to be constantly connected and generate further opportunities and challenges.

## ICTs, competitiveness and strategy

ICTs have had a major effect on the operation, structure and strategy of organisations. Not only do they reduce both communication and operational costs, but they also enhance flexibility, interactivity, efficiency, productivity and competitiveness. Although ICTs are not a panacea and cannot guarantee financial success on their own, ignoring and under-utilising ICTs can generate significant competitive disadvantages. This is because ICTs are instrumental in ensuring efficient internal organisation, effective communication with partners and interactivity with consumers. Certain 'prerequisites' are needed to be successful, namely:

- long-term planning and strategy;
- rational management and development of hardware and software;
- re-engineering of business processes;
- top management commitment; and
- training throughout the hierarchy.

These prerequisites facilitate the achievement of sustainable competitive advantage. Failure to address these issues can jeopardise the competitiveness, prosperity and even existence of tourism organisations.

Using ICTs as a stand-alone initiative is inadequate and has to be coupled with a redesign of processes, structures and management control systems. Provided that rational and innovative planning and management is exercised constantly and consistently, ICTs can support business success. As a consequence, 'business process re-engineering' argues that yesterday's practices, traditional hierarchical and organisational structures and habitual procedures are almost irrelevant. In contrast, corporations should be able to respond to current and future challenges by having the resources and expertise to design new processes from scratch, in a timely fashion. As a result of the rapid ICT developments corporations need to convert their operations from business functions to business processes, as well as reconceive their distribution channel strategy and, even more importantly, their corporate values and culture (Tapscott, 1996). Perhaps the greatest challenge organisations face is to identify and train managers who will be effective and innovative users of ICTs and will lead technology-based decision making. *Intellect* therefore becomes a critical asset, while continuous education and training are instrumental for the innovative use of ICTs and the competitiveness of tourism organisations.

The ICT developments have introduced new best strategic and operational management practices that lead organisations to shift their orientation from product orientation to a consumer orientation that customises products and services and to adopt flexible and responsive practices in the marketplace. Success will increasingly depend on sensing and responding to rapidly changing customer needs and using ICTs for delivering the right product, at the right time, at the right price, for the right customer. To the degree that ICTs can contribute to the value chain of products and services by improving their cost position or differentiation, they reshape competitiveness and thus have strategic implications for the prosperity of the organisation (Porter, 1985, 2001). The competitiveness of both tourism enterprises and destinations will therefore increasingly depend on the ability of those organisation to use ICTs strategically and tactically to improve their positioning.

# eTOURISM: TOURISM AND INFORMATION COMMUNICATION TECHNOLOGIES

The ICT revolution has already had profound implications for the tourism sector. Poon (1993) predicted that: 'a whole system of ICTs is being rapidly diffused throughout the tourism industry and no player will escape ICTs' impacts'. Buhalis (2003) suggests that eTourism reflects the digitisation of all processes and value chains in the tourism, travel, hospitality and catering industries. At the tactical level, it includes eCommerce and applies ICTs to maximise the efficiency and effectiveness of the tourism organisation. At the strategic level, eTourism revolutionises all business processes, the entire value chain as well as the strategic relationships of tourism organisations with all their stakeholders. eTourism determines the competitiveness of the organisation by taking advantage of intranets to reorganise internal processes, extranets to develop transactions with trusted partners and the Internet to interact with all its stakeholders. The eTourism concept includes all business functions (eCommerce and eMarketing, eFinance and eAccounting, eHRM, eProcurement, eR&D and eProduction) as well as eStrategy, ePlanning and eManagement for all sectors of the tourism industry, including tourism, travel, transport, leisure, hospitality, principals, intermediaries and public sector organisations (Egger and Buhalis, 2008). Hence eTourism bundles together three distinctive disciplines: business management, information systems and management, and tourism.

Information is the *life-blood* of tourism and so technology is fundamental for the ability of the industry to operate. Unlike durable goods, intangible tourism services cannot be physically displayed or inspected at the point of sale before purchasing. They are normally bought before the time of their use and away from the place of consumption. They rely almost exclusively upon representations and descriptions by the travel trade and other intermediaries for their ability to attract consumers. Timely and accurate information, relevant to consumers' needs, is often the key to satisfaction of tourism demand. As few other activities require the generation, gathering, processing, application and communication of information for operations, ICTs are pivotal for tourism. Consequently the rapid development of tourism supply and demand makes ICTs an imperative partner for the marketing, distribution, promotion and coordination of the tourism sector. ICTs have a dramatic impact on the travel industry because they force this sector as a whole to rethink the way in which it organises its business, values or norms of behaviour and the way in which it educates its workforce (Sheldon, 1997; Poon, 1993; Buhalis, 1998; Buhalis and Law, 2008).

Hence, ICTs and the Internet have enabled tourism organisations to develop their processes and adapt their management to take advantage of the emerging digital tools and mechanisms to:

- Increase their internal efficiency and manage their capacity and yields better. For example, an airline's reservations system allows the company to manage the inventory more efficiently and the managers to increase occupancy levels. They also incorporate sophisticated yield management systems that support organisations to adjust their pricing to demand fluctuations in order to maximise their profitability (Buhalis, 2004).

- Promote their products through their websites and on search engines (Xiang et al., 2008).

- Interact effectively with consumers and personalise the product. For example, British Airways has launched the Customer Enabled BA (ceBA) strategy to enable passengers to undertake a number of processes, including booking, ticketing, check-in and seat and meal selection, from the convenience of their computer (Zoge and Buhalis, 2008).

- Revolutionise tourism intermediation and increase the points of sale. For example, Expedia, Travelocity, Lastminute.com, Orbitz and Opodo have emerged as some of the most dominant global electronic travel agencies, offering a one-stop-shop for consumers.

- Empower consumers to communicate with other consumers. For example **http://www.trip advisor.com** or **http://www.virtualtourist.com** support the exchange of destination information and tips, whilst **http://www.untied.com** or **http://www.alitaliasacks.com** enable dissatisfied customers to make their views known.

- Engage in conversation with social media, particularly on Facebook and Twitter, as well as utilise other tools such as YouTube for videos and flickr for photographs.

- Have open discussions on Twitter using hashtags and uploading media-rich content.

- Provide location-based services by incorporating data, content and multimedia information on Google Maps and Google Earth.

- Support efficient cooperation between partners in the value system. For example, Pegasus enables independent hotels to distribute their availability through their websites and other partners online whilst an extranet allows hoteliers to constantly change availability and pricing.

- Enhance the operational and geographic scope by offering strategic tools for global expansion.

## eTourism demand

The rapid growth of the volumes of travellers as well as the requirements for personalised, complex, specialised and quality products impose the need for utilisation of ICTs. Tourists have become increasingly demanding, requesting high-quality products and value for their money.

New/experienced/sophisticated/demanding travellers rely heavily on the Internet to seek information about destinations and experiences, such as price and availability, as well as to be able to communicate their needs and wishes rapidly to tourism suppliers. Consumers around the world are increasingly online and even developing countries, such as China, are soon going to be reaching penetration levels of more than 50%, as shown in Figure 22.2.

The Internet enables travellers to access reliable and accurate information as well as to undertake reservations in a fraction of the time, cost and inconvenience required by conventional methods. Thus, they improve the service quality and contribute to a higher tourist satisfaction. The Internet provides access to transparent and easily comparable information on destinations, holiday packages, travel, lodging and leisure services, as well as about their real-time prices and availability. Increasingly consumers utilise commercial and non-commercial Internet sites for planning, searching, reserving, purchasing and amending their tourism products. They can also get immediate confirmation and speedy travel documents, enabling prospective travellers

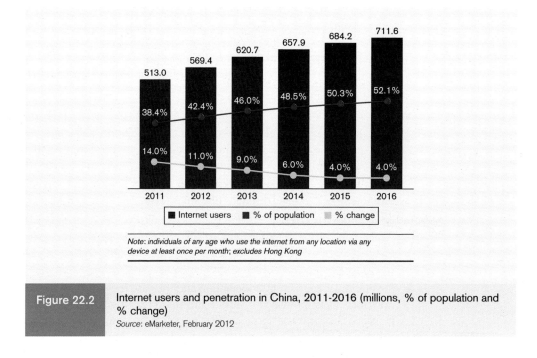

| Figure 22.2 | Internet users and penetration in China, 2011-2016 (millions, % of population and % change) |
| --- | --- |

Source: eMarketer, February 2012

to book at the 'last minute'. Experienced travellers are empowered by ICTs and use information and booking systems to improve their personal efficiency and competencies. A number of new organisations, such as Expedia, Travelocity and Lastminute.com, emerged online in the late 1990s, empowering consumers to research their travel requirements. They gradually assumed a leading global intermediation role.

The Internet has enabled consumers to access this information rapidly and increasingly the development of domain-specific search engines and meta-search engines such as Kelkoo and Kayak have introduced utter transparency in the marketplace (Wöber, 2006). In addition, consumer-generated content, through review portals such as TripAdvisor, multimedia sharing such as panoramio.com and blogs also create accessible content that increase the level of information available on a global basis (Gretzel and Yoo, 2008; Yea et al., 2009).

The use of ICTs is therefore driven by the development of complex demands, as well as by the rapid expansion and sophistication of new products, which tend to address niche market segments. There is evidence that eTourism has already taken off in several countries.

In Europe, the Internet is now more than twice as important as travel agents as an information source, although the travel trade is still very important in terms of travel distribution. It is evident now that the Internet is involved in almost 85% of holiday purchases in the UK in 2011; 53% of UK consumers research and buy holidays online, though many could be deterred by unclear pricing, according to a survey of 2,004 UK consumers commissioned by Econsultancy. The survey found that 29% of respondents don't find travel websites easy to use, and that unclear pricing is the most likely reason for abandoning purchases online; 15% said that holiday research and purchase all takes place offline, while 14% research offline before booking online. The survey also found that while just under 10% take less than a day to research their travel purchase, the majority (64%) take two weeks or more, while 26% take a week or less (Econsultancy, 2011).

Websites are also becoming incredibly influential when making decisions on destinations to visit, as increasingly consumers are searching online to help them make travel choices. Rheem's *The Empowering Inspiration* (2012) demonstrates this clearly especially for the developed US, UK and German markets (see Figure 22.3).

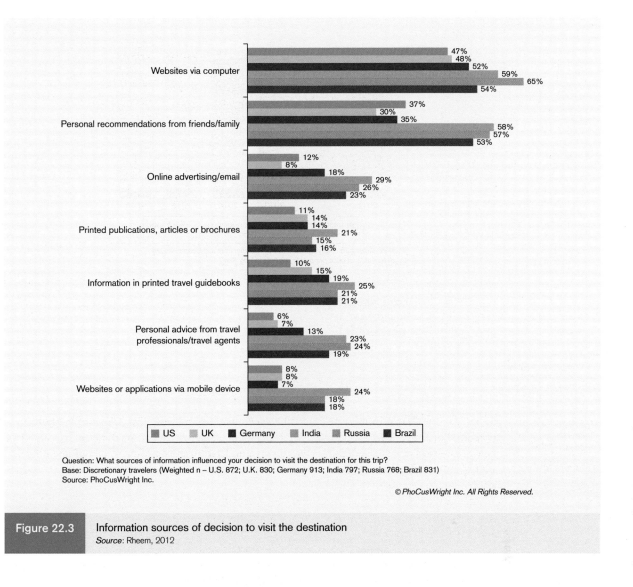

Question: What sources of information influenced your decision to visit the destination for this trip?
Base: Discretionary travelers (Weighted n – U.S. 872; U.K. 830; Germany 913; India 797; Russia 768; Brazil 831)
Source: PhoCusWright Inc.

| Figure 22.3 | Information sources of decision to visit the destination |
|---|---|
| | *Source*: Rheem, 2012 |

The report demonstrates that a range of websites is used, including search engines, online travel agency websites, travel review and provider websites as well as destination and travel guide websites (see Figure 22.4).

Smartphones are also changing the way people interact with information. The development of smartphones is a converged device bringing together telephone, personal data assistant and other functions such as music players into an integrated mobile computing platform. The proliferation of iPhones, Android-based mobiles and Blackberry enable users to access the Internet over 4G and also offer a range of applications to maximise their utility before, during and after the trip experience. With advanced wireless networks, growing worldwide adoption of web-enabled full feature phones, smartphones and tablets, travellers are already able to access information anywhere, anytime from multiple devices extending the interaction throughout the journey as demonstrated in Figure 22.5 (Rose, 2011).

Social media will be playing an increasingly important role as information sources for travellers as they increasingly appear in search engine results in the context of travel-related searches (Hays et al., 2012). Social media constitute a substantial part of the search results and therefore traditional providers of travel-related information will have to ensure that they include social media in their online marketing (Xiang and Gretzel, 2010). Looking forward, successful tourism organisations will increasingly need to rapidly identify consumer needs and to interact with

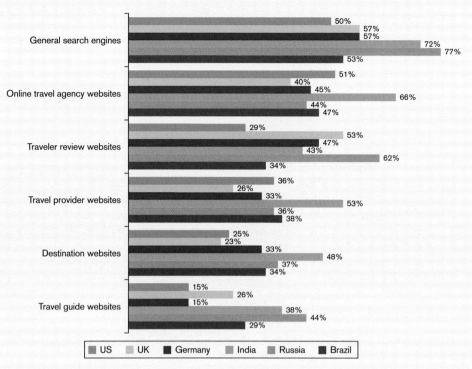

Question: What type(s) of websites did you use?
Base: Discretionary travelers who use the Internet when selecting a destination (Weighted n – U.S. 432; U.K. 429;
Germany 495; India 526; Russia 534; Brazil 497)
Source: PhoCusWright Inc.

**Figure 22.4** Websites used for destination selection
*Source*: Rheem, 2012

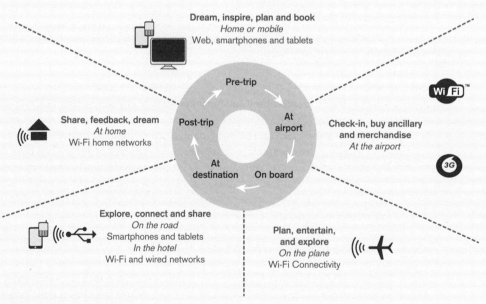

Source: Travel Tech Consulting Inc.

**Figure 22.5** Mobile's impact across the travel life cycle on a variety of decisions
*Source*: Rose, 2011

prospective clients by using comprehensive, personalised and up-to-date communication media for the design of products that satisfy tourism demand. Thus, destinations and principals need to utilise innovative communication methods in order to maintain and increase their competitiveness. They also increasingly need to engage in Web 2.0 activities and with all stakeholders that generate content for their regions and organisations.

## ICTs in tourism supply: re-engineering the tourism industry distribution

On the tourism supply side, the impacts of ICTs are evident in the production, marketing, operational and distribution functions of both the private and public sectors. The development of computerised systems facilitated the *production and management of tourism enterprises* by enabling them to handle their inventory and perform their business functions effectively and productively (Egger and Buhalis, 2008). Understandably, larger organisations took advantage of the emergent technologies earlier than smaller ones, as they had the resources to do so, and ICTs facilitated their further expansion. The ability of tourism enterprises to communicate and cooperate efficiently with remote branches, destinations, principals, agencies and to control their operational elements enabled them to expand their activities whilst reducing costs and increasing their competitiveness (Buhalis and Law, 2008). Both operational (schedule planning, pricing, inventory handling and reservations) and support (payroll, accounting, marketing) functions were improved considerably and enabled several tourism enterprises to establish their business worldwide.

In the networking era, the development of *intranets* has enabled organisations to improve their management at all levels by sharing media-rich data and processes internally. In addition, *extranets* empower cooperation between partners by enabling a certain degree of transparency and interactivity, thus increasing efficiency and productivity without compromising on security and confidentiality. This will also improve the interactivity between tourism production and distribution partners, supporting a closer cooperation towards the provision of seamless products. The *Internet* has also enabled organisations to communicate directly with consumers, enforcing a certain degree of disintermediation in the marketplace (Baggio et al., 2010).

ICTs and the Internet have pivotal implications for tourism distribution. Since the early 1970s computerised networks and electronic distribution have been leading dramatic structural changes within the tourism industry, and becoming central to the distribution mix and strategy. A *computer reservation system* (CRS) is basically a database which enables a tourism organisation to manage its inventory and make it accessible to its partners. Principals utilise CRSs to manage their inventory and distribute their capacity as well as to manage the drastic expansion of global tourism. CRSs often charge competitive commission rates while enabling flexible pricing and capacity alterations in order to adjust supply to demand fluctuations. Airlines pioneered this technology, although hotel chains and tour operators followed by developing centralised reservation systems. CRSs can therefore be characterised as the 'circulation system' of the tourism product.

From the mid-1980s, airline CRSs developed into *global distribution systems* (GDSs) by gradually expanding their geographical coverage as well as by integrating both horizontally, with other airline systems, and vertically by incorporating the entire range of principals, such as accommodation, car rentals, train and ferry ticketing, entertainment and other provisions. Sabre, Galileo, Amadeus and Worldspan are currently the strongest GDSs in the marketplace. Suppliers therefore realised that the key success factor was in systems integration through GDSs and the creation of standards that enable products to be displayed and purchased by consumers anywhere in the world. GDSs tend to have a stronger market share in the regions where their parent airlines operate, as commercial links with agencies have been exploited for the penetration of GDSs. GDSs concentrated primarily on business travel, as this was the most demanding and profitable part of the business. In the early 1990s GDSs emerged as the major driver of ICTs, as well as the backbone of the tourism industry and the single most important facilitator of ICT globalisation (Sheldon, 1993). In essence, GDSs matured from their original development as airline CRSs to travel supermarkets. Since the late 1990s GDSs have emerged as businesses in their own right, specialising in travel distribution. Many airlines have chosen to sell their shares in GDSs to improve their financial position following the cash crisis after '9/11'. Until their deregulation by the US Department of Transport in 2004, most GDSs represented the majority of principals, offering quite similar services. Their deregulation means that airlines and GDSs are free to negotiate individual deals, forcing both carriers and systems to change their relationships and their core business (Field and O'Toole, 2004).

The four global distribution systems (GDS) have processed more than 1 billion air bookings each, and another 250 million for hotels, cruises and other non-air content, generating over US$6 billion in revenues. Sabre and Amadeus own the largest civilian data-processing centres in the US and Europe respectively. The volume of global transactions through the GDS has risen 4% year-on-year to 343 million. Worldwide, the GDS reaches some 230,000 points of sale (Alford, 2006).

Merlino et al. (2010) suggest that there are currently six major global distribution systems and three GDS parent companies each owned by private equity investors. GDSs generate and process an extraordinary volume of business in both transactions and revenue. Globally the GDSs processed more than 1.1 billion transactions in 2008. That equates to just over 2,100 transactions per minute representing more than €183 billion in total personal and business travel consumption in 2008, as demonstrated in Figure 22.6.

However the emergence of the Internet has also revolutionised GDSs. They are legacy systems that may have outlived their potential. The four major systems have enjoyed an oligopoly sustained by the high entry costs required to build the IT booking systems to link airlines, hotels and car rental operators with travel agents and consumers. The Internet challenged their position dramatically as both consumers and the travel trade had the opportunity to interact with airlines

| | Amadeus | Sabre | Travelport |
|---|---|---|---|
| Owned and Operated GDSs | Amadeus | Sabre (Ownership stake in Abacus, GDS in Asia) | Apollo Galileo Worldspan |
| Net Revenue 2009 (millions)[1] | £2,461 | N/A | £1,616 |
| Employees (approx.)[2] | 9,000 | 9,000 | 5,300 |
| Ownership | BC Partners Cinven Air France Iberia Lufthansa, and publicily listed on select European exchanges (AMS) | Silver Lake, Texas Pacific Group | Blackstone Group, One Equity Partners, Technology Crossover Ventures, and Travelport management |

[1]Information sourced from company websites and public financial filings. There are other, regional GDSs, including Axess, Infini, Topas and TravelSky, which operate principally in Asia and the Middle East. Since this paper is primarily concerned with Europe, it does not address the regional GDS companies.

[2]Figures for the three GDS companies include revenues and headcount for all business units and not just the GDS business.

**Figure 22.6**  GDS key factors
Source: Merlino et al., 2010

online without using GDS infrastructure. No-frills airlines totally bypassed GDSs and used the Internet to link with consumers and the trade. Scheduled airlines have also been trying to disintermediate GDSs especially for the short haul discounted tickets in order to reduce their distribution costs.

In March 2007 British Airways' contracts with global distribution system providers expired without service interruption or BA immediately pursuing a substantially new course, as some in the industry had feared would happen. BA CEO Willie Walsh explained that the airline industry had struggled to generate levels of profitability that would be deemed acceptable. Other parts of the value chain, including the GDSs, made operating margins in the double digits. BA had fares in its European operations that started at £29, on which GDSs fees could be as high as $7.50 or about £4; after all taxes and charges, BA was left with a fare of about £2 (Boehmer and Cohen, 2007). The European eBusiness W@tch (2006) suggests that 'sales via internet platforms bear enormous cost savings for airlines compared to traditional channels via travel agencies, which usually run over GDS'. The report quotes Matthias van Leeuwen, Vice President Sales, EMEA, Lufthansa Systems Group to say 'Star Alliance member carriers currently spend an average of 12 US dollars per ticket in GDS fees. Global New Entrant (GNEs) such as G2 SwitchWorks, ITA and Farelogix have indicated to the group that they could offer the same product for 2–3 US dollars per ticket'. Therefore GDSs are forced to rethink their strategies and gradually relaunch themselves as technology platform providers for airlines and other members of the tourism industry.

The development of the Internet offered an unprecedented opportunity for distribution of multimedia information and interactivity between principals and consumers. The WWW's interlinking structure enables the provision and packaging of similarly themed information, products and services. Initially the information available on the Internet was chaotic and loosely structured, mainly due to the immaturity of ICTs and the lack of any type of standardisation.

However, the Internet provided a globally distributed infrastructure for inexpensive delivery of multimedia information, promotion and distribution of tourism. It empowered the provision and marketing of tailor-made products to meet the needs of individual tourists and, hence, it bridged tourism demand and supply in a flexible and interactive way. By the year 2007, only 13 years after the general public used the first browser, there was a certain degree of maturity evident in the marketplace. In 2012 the Internet provides the infostructure for mainstream travel distribution. This was particularly evident for organisations in well-developed economies, such as North America, Europe, Australia and North Asia. This was demonstrated by a number of indicators:

- Tourism was already one of the most successful areas of eCommerce and the sector that attracted the highest expenditure online.
- Broadband was expanded in most developed countries and enabled users to browse at faster speeds and on more secure environments.
- Most suppliers had established comprehensive and fully functional websites.
- SITA 2011 estimates that 58% of all airline bookings will be sold directly by 2014, often reaching more than 95% for low-frills carriers; 69% of airlines sell or plan to sell tickets via social media networks by 2014. 80% of airlines reach or plan to reach passengers via social networks by 2014. 15% of passengers expected to use mobile phones for check-in by 2014. All tickets issued were eTickets (SITA, 2011).
- Most hotel chains and international car rental firms were reporting a significant increase in their direct sales through their websites.
- Several key travel intermediaries emerged as global players with Expedia becoming the second largest travel agency in the world.
- A very large proportion of travellers search online before booking holidays.
- Most tourism destinations around the world had some sort of website providing information for their region whilst advanced destinations had comprehensive systems supporting itinerary building and reservations (see, for example, **http://www.australia.com**, **http://www .amsterdam.nl** or **http://www.visiteurope.com**).

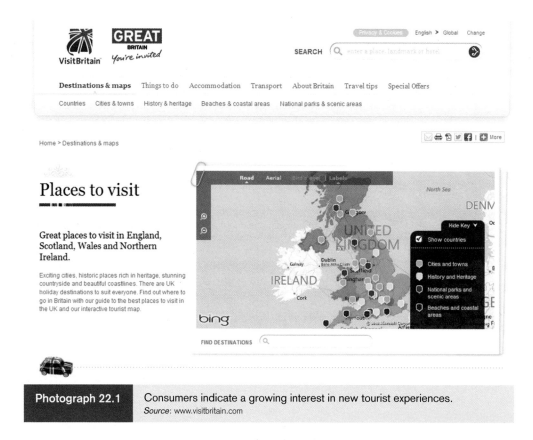

**Photograph 22.1** Consumers indicate a growing interest in new tourist experiences.
*Source*: www.visitbritain.com

Distribution is one of the few elements of the marketing mix that can still enable enterprises to improve their competitiveness and performance. ICTs enable the achievement of competitive advantage through product differentiation and/or cost advantage by increasing the unique characteristics of products, as well as efficiency throughout the production and distribution processes. ICTs increasingly transform distribution into an electronic marketplace, where access to information and ubiquity is achieved, while interactivity between principals and consumers provides major opportunities.

It is increasingly evident that many principals develop their business-to-consumer offering. They invest heavily in customer acquisition through search engine optimisation and pay-per-click on portals such as Google and Yahoo. They also invest in sophisticated customer relationship management to ensure partnerships with their clientele and customer retention. A certain degree of disintermediation of the channel is inevitable, offering both opportunities and threats for all tourism stakeholders. In addition, we can also observe a trend towards the re-intermediation of the tourism industry, as a plethora of online players emerge to bridge the gap between suppliers and customers, including hotel aggregators, electronic travel agencies and destination management organisations. In addition, meta search engines such as Kelkoo, Kayak and Sidestep enable consumers to search through a wide range of websites of both suppliers and distributors simultaneously (Wolk and Wöber, 2008).

Dynamic packaging also enables consumers to put together products and services that suit their individual tastes and to save money on the total price. The dramatic development of the Internet has instigated the re-engineering of the entire process of producing and delivering tourism products. It has also enabled the design of specialised products and promotions in order to maximise the value-added provided to individual consumers.

## A conceptual synthesis of ICTs in tourism

A conceptual synthesis of the emergent ICTs in tourism yields a multi-dimensional communication and operational framework, which will determine the future competitiveness of principals and destinations. This framework shows the paradigm shift and the business process re-engineering experienced, which has already started to radically reshape the tourism industry. Table 22.3 illustrates several examples of the intra-and inter-organisational functions facilitated by ICTs. It also shows how technologies advocate the multi-integration of the industry. Not only does this framework demonstrate the dependence of both demand and supply on ICTs, but it also illustrates that networking and interactivity will increasingly dominate tourism production and consumption. This clearly implies that players who fail to participate in the electronic marketplace will be excluded from the production and consumption functions of the industry and jeopardise their future prosperity.

| Table 22.3 | A multidimensional framework for tourism industry processes facilitated by ICTs |
|---|---|
| **Intra-organisational communications and functions** | **Inter-organisational communications and functions** |
| • Within a tourism organisation<br>  • Management and marketing<br>    strategic planning<br>    competition analysis<br>    financial planning and control<br>    marketing research<br>    marketing strategy and implementation<br>    pricing decision and tactics<br>    middle term planning and feedback<br>    management statistics/reports<br>    operational control<br>    management functions<br>  • Communication between departments<br>    networking and information exchange<br>    coordination of staff<br>    operational planning<br>    accounting/billing<br>    payroll<br>    supplies management<br>• Communication and function with remote branches<br>  coordination of operations<br>  availability/prices/information<br>  orders from headquarters/administration<br>  share of common resource databases<br>  for customer and operational information | • Tourist product suppliers and intermediaries<br>  • Pre-travel arrangements<br>    direct marketing<br>    general information<br>    availability/prices inquiries<br>    negotiations and bargaining<br>    contracting<br>    reservations and confirmations<br>    ancillary services<br>  • Travel-related documentation<br>    lists of groups/visitors<br>    receipts/documents<br>    vouchers and tickets production<br>  • Post-travel arrangements<br>    payments and commissions<br>    feedback and suggestions<br>    customer satisfaction survey<br>    complaint handling<br>    direct marketing |
| **Consumer communication with tourism industry** | **Tourism enterprise communication with non-tourism enterprises** |
| • Travel advice/general information<br>• Request availability/prices/information<br>• Reservation and confirmation<br>• Amendments for a reservation<br>• Deposits and full settlements<br>• Electronic ticketing<br>• Special interest requests/inquiries<br>• Feedback/complaints<br>• Discussions groups/fun clubs | • Other suppliers and ancillary services<br>  vaccinations<br>  travel formalities and visas<br>• Insurance companies and services<br>• Weather forecasting<br>• Banking/financial services/credit cards<br>• Remote internet provision for travellers<br>• Other business services |

# eTOURISM AND THE TOURISM INDUSTRY SECTORS

The evolution of the Internet and ICTs has propelled a 'paradigm shift' where all practices and processes had to be changed dramatically affecting the the industry structure. eTourism provides opportunities for business expansion in all geographical, marketing and operational senses. Several major factors make ICTs an integral part of the strategy for all tourism organisations:

- Economic necessity, as fierce global competition requires maximum efficiency.
- Rapid advancements in technology which provide new marketing opportunities.
- Low barriers to entry allowing many new entrants to the market.
- Improvements in ICTs' price/performance ratios which yield better productivity for capital employed in ICTs.
- Rising consumer expectations, as they become used to advanced products and expect better quality of presentation and service.

As a result of Internet developments a number of new players have come into the tourism marketplace. Perhaps the most significant change was the proliferation of no-frills airlines that use the Internet as a main distribution mechanism for direct sales. This development educated consumers that they can only find cheap fares if they go direct to the carrier online, threatening both traditional/flag carriers as well as their entire distribution system (GDSs and travel agencies). Equally, the development of major eTravel agencies such as Expedia, Travelocity, Lastminute.com, Orbitz and Opodo has created powerful 'travel supermarkets' for consumers. They provide integrated travel solutions and a whole range of value-added services, such as destination guides, weather reports and insurance. By adopting dynamic packaging, i.e. the ability to package customised trips based on bundling individual components at a discounted total price, they effectively threaten the role of tour operators and other aggregators.

What follows is an analysis of ICT and the various sectors of the tourism industry. It demonstrates the key developments and the influence of ICTs and the Internet for their internal organisation, their relationships with partners and the interaction with consumers and stakeholders.

## eAirlines

Airlines realised quite early the need for efficient, quick, inexpensive and accurate handling of their inventory and internal organisation, due to the complexity of their operations. Originally, reservations were made on manual display boards, where passengers were listed. Travel agencies had to locate the best routes and fares in manuals and then check availability and make reservation by phone, before issuing a ticket manually. In 1962, American Airlines introduced the Sabre CRS as an alternative to expand its Boeing 707 fleet by 50%. The growth of air traffic and air transportation deregulation stimulated the expansion of CRSs to gigantic computerised networks. As prices, schedules and routes were liberated, airlines could change their pricing and schedules instantly, while new airlines entered the market. CRSs enabled airlines to compete by adapting their schedule and fares to demand. To increase competitiveness, airlines developed the 'hub and spoke' systems, while their pricing became very complex and flexible. 'Fare wars' multiplied the fare structures and increased computing and communication needs, while most major CRSs installed terminals in agencies to facilitate distribution. In addition, vendor airlines biased their CRSs screens in order to give higher display priority to their own flights rather to their competitors'. The remote printing of travel documents, such as tickets and boarding passes, itineraries and invoices, as well as the sale settlements between airlines and travel agencies and partnership marketing through frequent flyer programmes were invaluable benefits supported by the emerging ICTs. CRSs were developed to global distribution systems (GDSs) and re-engineered the entire marketing and distribution processes of airlines. They essentially became strategic business units (SBU) in their own right due to their ability to generate income and to boost airlines' sales at the expense of their competitors. Many airlines sold their interests in GDSs, enabling them to operate as independent distribution companies.

Distribution is a crucial element of airlines' strategy and competitiveness, as it determines the cost and the ability to access consumers. The cost of distribution is increasing considerably and airlines find it difficult to control. Nowadays ICTs and internal CRSs are used heavily to support the Internet distribution of airline seats. These systems are at the heart of airline operational and strategic agendas (Buhalis, 2004). This is particularly the case for smaller and regional carriers as well as no-frills airlines which cannot afford GDSs' fees and aim to sell their seats at competitive prices. This has forced even traditional/full-service/flag airlines, such as British Airways and Aer Lingus, to recognise the need for re-engineering the distribution processes, costs and pricing structures. Hence, they use the Internet for:

- enhancing interactivity and building relationships with consumers and partners;
- online reservations;
- electronic ticketing;
- yield management;
- electronic auctions for last-minute seats;
- disintermediation and redesign of agency commission schemes; and
- maximising the productivity of the new electronic distribution media (Buhalis, 2004).

The Airline IT Trends Survey 2012 demonstrates that the vast majority of airlines have a three-year IT strategy that aims to reduce costs and increase efficiency. On average airlines spend around 2% of their revenue on IT. As demonstrated in Figure 22.7 airlines are investing heavily in direct sales, which, coupled with 'customer relationship management' and supporting revenue opportunities, will enable them to better control their distribution and strategic marketing.

In addition Figure 22.8 demonstrates that airlines are investing heavily in mobiles and social media to serve better their customers and reduce their distribution cost.

Increasingly airlines are relying on social media for engaging in a dialogue with their consumers and informing them before, during, and after the trip. KLM has been at the forefront of social media usage in tourism and has integrated a number of initiatives to enrich the customer experience.

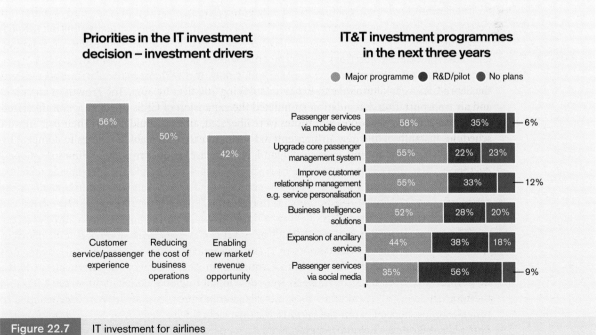

**Figure 22.7** IT investment for airlines
*Source:* SITA, 2012

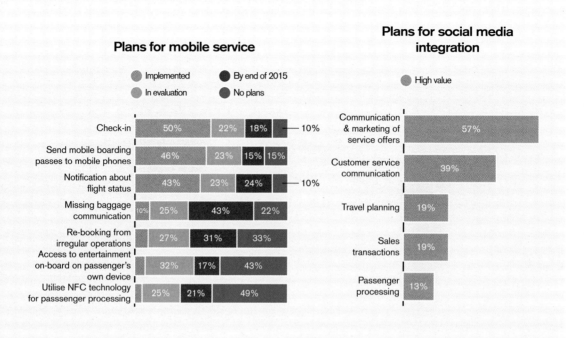

**Figure 22.8**  Airlines engaging with passengers through mobiles and social media
*Source:* SITA, 2012

## eHospitality

Technology has radically changed both operations and marketing of hotels. Hotels use ICTs in order to improve their operations, manage their inventory and maximise their profitability (O'Connor, 2008a). Their systems facilitate both in-house management and distribution through electronic media. 'Property management systems' (PMSs) coordinate front office, sales, planning and operational functions by administrating reservations and managing the hotel inventory. Moreover, PMSs integrate the 'back' and 'front' of the house management and improve general administration functions such as accounting and finance; marketing research and planning; forecasting and yield management; payroll and personnel; and purchasing. Understandably, hotel chains gain more benefits from PMSs, as they can introduce a unified system for planning, budgeting and controlling and coordinating their properties centrally. Hotels also utilise ICTs and the Internet extensively for their distribution and marketing functions. Global presence is essential in order to enable both individual customers and the travel trade to access accurate information on availability and to provide easy, efficient, inexpensive and reliable ways of making and confirming reservations. Although central reservation offices (CROs) introduced central reservations in the 1970s, it was not until the expansion of airline CRSs and the recent ICT developments that forced hotels to develop hotel CRSs in order to expand their distribution, improve efficiency, facilitate control, empower yield management, reduce labour costs and enable rapid response time to both customers and management requests. Following the development of hotel CRSs by most chains, the issue of interconnectivity with other CRSs and the Internet emerged. As a result, 'switch companies', such as Thisco and Wizcom, emerged to provide an interface between the various systems and enable a certain degree of transparency. This reduces both set-up and reservation costs, whilst facilitating reservations through several distribution channels (Emmer et al., 1993; O'Connor, 2004).

**Photograph 22.2**  KLM pioneers the use of social media.
*Source*: www.facebook.com/KLM

One of the most promising developments in hospitality is 'application service providers' (ASPs). ASPs will increasingly be more involved in hosting a number of business applications for hospitality organisations. Hotels will 'rent' the same software for a fee and will use it across the Internet. For example, some hotel firms may 'rent' their PMS software application from supplier Micros/Fidelio. ASPs are ideal for hotels, especially for smaller to mid-sized ones, that want to leverage the best vertical and enterprise support applications on the market without having to deal with the technology or pay for more functionality than needed. As they do not have extensive ICT departments and expertise, they can easily access up-to-date applications and benefit from the collective knowledge accumulated by ASP providers without having to invest extensively in technology or expertise building (Paraskevas and Buhalis, 2002).

The development of the Internet has provided more benefits as it reduces the capital and operational costs required for the representation and promotion of hotels. For example, the cost per individual booking can be reduced from US$10–15 for voice-based reservations, to US$7.50–3.50 for reservations through GDSs, to US$0.25 through the WWW. Savings can also be achieved in printing, storing, administrating and posting promotional material.

Murphy et al. (2006) use diffusion of innovations and configurational theories to investigate how website features and email responses reflect evolving Internet adoption. Internet adoption evolves from static to dynamic use, as organisations add website features and provide quality responses to customer emails. Chan and Law (2006) suggest that hotel websites are a basic requirement for an increasing number of communication and business strategies. The usability of a website, effectiveness of its interface, as well as its amount of information, ease of navigation and user friendliness, are central to the success of these strategies and an automatic website evaluation system (AWES) can provide objective and quantitative guidance to website design (Qi et al., 2010).

However, many small and medium sized, independent, seasonal and family hotels find it extremely difficult to utilise ICTs due to:

- lack of capital for purchasing hardware and software;
- lack of standardisation and professionalism;
- insufficient marketing and technology training and understanding;
- small size which multiplies the administration required by CRSs to deal with each property; and finally
- the unwillingness of proprietors to lose control over their property.

These properties are increasingly placed at a major disadvantage, as they cannot be represented in the electronic marketplace and so their future existence is jeopardised. However, they cannot afford to ignore the rapid development of ICTs and therefore should take advantage of the emergent opportunities and decreasing costs to enhance their competitiveness. It is increasingly evident that even the smallest establishments will have to take advantage of the Internet and promote themselves in the electronic marketplace. There are several solutions that can offer a cost-effective online presence. Small properties will find it difficult to continue trading unless they have an online presence as they will be invisible to consumers searching online. The establishment of destination-based collaboration ventures would perhaps enable small firms to pool resources in order to share development and operation costs. Distributing their products through the Internet would enable them to access their target markets at an affordable cost and gain benefits (Buhalis, 2003).

Technology is emerging as a critical determinant in hotel guest satisfaction and many hotels utilise technology as a value-added amenity to help promote differentiation and enhance guest satisfaction. Cobanoglu et al. (2011) found that there is evidence of a significant positive relationship between three factors – 'Business essentials for travellers', 'In-room technologies', and 'Internet access' and hotel guest's overall satisfaction.

Hoteliers gradually explore online marketing to increase their market awareness and to attract more guests and higher revenues by using techniques like website design, search engine optimisation, paid search marketing and email (O'Connor, 2008b). Hospitality executives worldwide, including general managers, revenue managers, sales and marketing managers, and other industry professionals:

- are shifting their budgets from offline to online marketing activities;
- rely more on direct to consumer bookings via their stand-alone websites compared to intermediary sites as a percentage of their overall Internet business;
- believe new media formats such as consumer-generated media and blogs will generate better ROIs than traditional banner advertising;
- rely more heavily on keyword search marketing (PPC) and search engine optimisation (SEO) than their international counterparts who favour website re-design and optimisation, and strategic linking;
- enhance their social media engagement with their consumers;
- concentrate on website optimisation, search optimisation and organic search, and website redesign to increase their ROIs;
- rely more heavily on the chain websites for franchised hotels.

HeBS (2007) concludes that hoteliers have gradually matured and now understand that long-term, strategic objectives and formats such as website redesigns and optimisations, email marketing and strategic linking produce higher return on investment than 'quick fix' solutions, such as search engine optimisation and pay per click strategies. Finally, two main strategies emerged in online distribution for hospitality, namely price parity and brand integrity. Post 9/11, many hotels around the globe were having problems filling their rooms. This was in combination with the development of online intermediaries, such as Hotels.com and Expedia, that were using the merchant model of contracting, which meant that many hotels were effectively unable to control their price on the various online outlets. This not only caused revenue loss, as prospective customers were shopping around, but also damaged their brands. Over a period of time major branded properties realised that control over pricing should be central to the marketing proposition and hence undertook a number of measures to address that. Key findings of O'Connor's (2002) study include that brands use multiple simultaneous routes to the marketplace, and that the rates offered over alternative routes have equalised. Demirciftci et al. (2010) explain that in order to further enhance a relationship of trust between the hotel company and the guest, the guest must not feel that they are being cheated by paying more because they did not know where to get the best rates. While consumer savviness is growing, the complexity of purchasing choices is growing at an even faster rate. However, there are still significant differences between rates within both direct and indirect channels.

One of the key areas that has been emerging for hotels is the management of their online reputation. Online reputation management (ORM) is the act of monitoring online conversations about your brand and executing online strategies to highlight positive, quality content while suppressing damaging content from the consumers' point of view. As the social Web is emerging as the area where consumers share product information and service experiences, and search engines consider social channels and conversations in their results listings, hoteliers find it challenging to deal with their online reputation. O'Connor (2010) explains that user-generated content is rapidly gaining traction as an input into the consumer purchase decision-making process. The development of Web 2.0 for travel and TripAdvisor in particular as the largest online network of travel consumers demonstrate the key factors of satisfaction and dissatisfaction. However, few hotels actively manage their reputation on the TripAdvisor site, despite a facility to respond to criticism or to comment on reviews.

## eTour operators

Leisure travellers often purchase 'packages', consisting of charter flights and accommodation, arranged by tour operators. Tour operators tend to pre-book these products and distribute them through brochures displayed in travel agencies. Hence, until recently in northern European countries, where tour operators dominate the leisure market, airline and hotel CRSs were rarely utilised for leisure travel. In the early 1980s, tour operators realised the benefits of ICTs in organising, promoting, distributing and coordinating their packages. The Thomson Open-line Programme (TOP) was the first real-time computer-based central reservation office in 1976. It introduced direct communication with travel agencies in 1982, and announced that reservations for Thomson Holidays would only be accepted through TOP in 1986. This move was the critical point for altering the communication processes between tour operators and travel agencies. Gradually, all major tour operators developed or acquired databases and established electronic links with travel agencies, aiming to reduce their information handling costs and increase the speed of information transfer and retrieval. This improved their productivity and capacity management whilst enhancing their services to agencies and consumers. Tour operators also utilised their CRSs for market intelligence, in order to adjust their supply to demand fluctuations, as well as to monitor the booking progress and productivity of travel agencies (Karcher, 1996).

Tour operators have been reluctant to focus on ICTs through their strategic planning. Few realise the major transformation of the marketplace, while the majority regard ICTs exclusively as a facilitator of their current operations, and as a tool to reduce their costs. However, several tour operators in Germany, Scandinavia and the UK have moved towards electronic distribution, enabling them to concentrate on niche markets by:

- offering customised packages;
- updating their brochures regularly;
- saving the 10–20% commission and reducing the costs of incentives, bonus and educational trips for travel agencies; and
- saving the cost of developing, printing, storing and distributing conventional brochures – estimated to be approximately £20 per booking.

Strategically Internet developments and dynamic packaging threatens the dominance of tour operators. Although a partial disintermediation seems inevitable, there will always be sufficient market share for tour operators who can add value to the tourism product and deliver innovative, personalised and competitive holiday packages. As ICTs will determine the future competitiveness of the industry, the distribution channel leadership and power of tour operators may be challenged should other channel members or newcomers utilise ICTs effectively to package and distribute either unique or cheaper tourism products. However, many key players including TUI have started disintegrating their packages and selling individual components directly to the consumers. In this sense they will be able to re-intermediate, by offering their vast networks of suppliers through their channels. Innovative tour operators use the Internet extensively to promote their products and to attract direct customers. They also use the internet to de-compose their packages and sell individual products. Thomson, for example, has developed a comprehensive online strategy to provide media-rich information on its website. The company supports podcasting, videocasting and has also integrated Goggle Earth geographical information data on its website. It also distributes branded content on a wide range of Internet sites such as YouTube to attract consumers to its website and to encourage them to book. It is evident therefore that tour operators that use technology innovatively will be able to provide value to their clientele and safeguard their position in the marketplace.

## eTravel agencies

ICTs are irreplaceable tools for travel agencies as they provide information and reservation facilities and support the intermediation between consumers and principals. Travel agencies operate various reservation systems, which mainly enable them to check availability and make reservations for tourism products. Until recently GDSs have been critical for business travel agencies to access information and make reservations on scheduled airlines, hotel chains, car rentals and a variety of ancillary services. GDSs help construct complicated itineraries, while they provide up-to-date schedules, prices and availability information, as well as an effective reservation method. In addition, they offered internal management modules integrating the 'back office' (accounting, commission monitor, personnel) and 'front office' (customers' history, itinerary construction, ticketing and communication with suppliers). Multiple travel agencies in particular experience more benefits by achieving better coordination and control between their remote branches and headquarters. Transactions can provide invaluable data for financial and operational control as well as for marketing research, which can analyse the market fluctuations and improve tactical decisions.

The vast majority of leisure travel agencies used 'videotext networks' to access tour operators and the reservation systems of other suppliers – such as ferry operators, railways and insurance companies. On the plus side, videotext systems are relatively inexpensive to purchase and operate, require little training and expertise and are fairly reliable. However, on the minus side, they are slow, data has to be retyped for each individual database searched, they fail to integrate with the back office, cannot interface with multimedia applications and are unable to take advantage of the emergent ICTs. Effectively, the type of agency and its clientele determine the type of ICTs utilised. Typically business travel agencies are more GDS dependent, whilst leisure agencies and holiday shops are more likely to use videotext systems (Inkpen, 1998).

The Internet has revolutionised the travel agency industry. For the first time ever, agencies had the ability to reach travel inventory directly without having to invest in time and costs for acquiring GDSs. They are able to search and book suppliers such as airlines and hotels online, increasing their bookable inventory. They also have the tools to sell their own services and to promote their organisations. However, until recently travel agencies have been reluctant to take full advantage of the ICTs, mainly due to:

- a limited strategic scope;
- deficient ICT expertise and understanding;
- low profit margins which prevents investments; and
- focus on human interaction with consumers.

Spencer et al. (2012) demonstrate that the diffusion of innovation and technology in small owner-managed travel firms depends on hierarchical structures, decision-making processes and ultimately by leadership. A number of leadership typologies predict the level of technology adoption in travel agencies.

This has resulted in a low level of integration of ICTs and capitalisation on the Internet's potential. Many agencies still do not have Internet access and are unable to access online information or suppliers. As a result, many agencies lack access to the variety of information and reservation facilities readily available to consumers and therefore their credibility in the marketplace is severely reduced, damaging their competitiveness. This may jeopardise their ability to maintain their competitiveness and consequently, they may be threatened by disintermediation (Spencer et al., 2011). Several forces intensify this threat:

- inadequate understanding by their leadership;
- consumers increasingly search information and make reservations online;
- principals aim to control distribution costs by communicating directly with consumers and by developing customer relationship management;
- commission cuts; and
- travel agencies have limited expertise as they employ inadequately trained personnel.

Gradually it is becoming evident that travel agencies around the world not only will have to utilise the Internet to access travel suppliers and information online but will also have to rely on the media to communicate with their clientele, to put the offerings forward to the marketplace and to attract business. Traditional travel agencies can use the Internet to provide extra value to their clientele by integrating additional products and services to their core products. In addition, they may use the Internet to concentrate on particular niche markets and to offer specialised services to those markets.

In contrast, new players (such as Expedia, Travelocity, Orbitz, Lastminute.com and Opodo) have already achieved a high penetration in the marketplace and have grown spectacularly. Through a number of mergers and acquisitions there are effectively five major groups that have emerged in the marketplace.

Interestingly even in areas with low Internet penetration, online travel agencies have taken off. The Chinese market is one of those markets that is growing rapidly (Li and Buhalis, 2006). For example, Ctrip.com in China is growing massively, demonstrating both the potential and the growth of the Chinese eTourism market, as shown in Table 22.4.

As location becomes less significant electronic travel agents will dominate global travel retailing. Therefore, the future of travel agencies will depend on their ability to utilise ICTs in order to increase the added value to the final tourism product and to serve their customers. Agencies that simply act as booking offices for tourism products will probably face severe financial difficulties in the future. In contrast, knowledgeable and innovative agencies, which utilise the entire range of technologies in order to provide suitable integrated tourism solutions, will add value to the tourist experience and increase their competitiveness. Traditional travel agencies will have to compete on both price and service with both suppliers and online travel agencies and will only be able to survive if they offer superior service.

## eDestinations

Destinations are amalgams of tourism products, facilities and services which compose the total tourism expertise under one brand name. Traditionally the planning, management and coordination functions of destinations have been undertaken by either the public sector (at national, regional or local level) or by partnerships between stakeholders of the local tourism industry. Destination Management Organisations are usually regarded as the main bodies held responsible for the destination's marketing (Buhalis, 1998). Many opportunities to address the destination marketing challenges lay in ICT integration – providing new marketing tools and empowering consumers who are now more independent, well informed and looking for new experiences. For the last 20 years the development of destination management systems (DMSs) has been one of the most popular solutions to address these issues. The basic version of DMS consists of product

| Table 22.4 | Ctrip.com International, Ltd. (Nasdaq: CTRP), show growth in China eCommerce in 2011 |
| --- | --- |

**Ctrip.com International, Ltd. (Nasdaq: CTRP), show growth in China eCommerce but profits fall**

Ctrip.com International, Ltd. (Nasdaq: CTRP), a leading travel service provider of hotel accommodation, airline tickets, packaged tours and corporate travel management in China, announced its unaudited financial results for the full year ended 31 December 2011.

Highlights for the full year 2011:

- Net revenues were RMB3.5 billion (US$556 million) in 2011, up 21% from 2010. In 2011, Wing On Travel and ezTravel contributed 1% to the year-on-year growth for net revenues.
- Gross margin was 77% in 2011, compared to 78% in 2010.
- Income from operations was RMB1.1 billion (US$169 million) in 2011, up 1% from 2010. Excluding share-based compensation charges (non-GAAP), income from operations was RMB1.4 billion (US$224 million) in 2011, up 9% from 2010.
- Operating margin was 30% in 2011, compared to 37% in 2010. Excluding share-based compensation charges (non-GAAP), operating margin was 40%, compared to 45% in 2010.
- Net income attributable to Ctrip's shareholders was RMB1.1 billion (US$171 million) in 2011, up 3% from 2010. Excluding share-based compensation charges (non-GAAP), net income attributable to Ctrip's shareholders was RMB1.4 billion (US$225 million), up 10% from 2010.
- Diluted earnings per ADS were RMB7.08 (US$1.12) in 2011, compared to RMB6.97 (US$1.06) in 2010. Excluding share-based compensation charges (non-GAAP), diluted earnings per ADS were RMB9.33 (US$1.48), compared to RMB8.59 (US$1.30) in 2010.
- Share-based compensation charges were RMB343 million (US$54 million), accounting for 10% of the net revenues, or RMB2.25 (US$0.36) per ADS in 2011.

For the full year ended 31 December 2011:

- Total revenues were RMB3.7 billion (US$592 million), representing a 22% increase from 2010.
- Hotel reservation revenues were RMB1.5 billion (US$236 million), representing a 16% increase from 2010. The hotel reservation revenues accounted for 40% of the total revenues in 2011, compared to 42% in 2010.
- Air ticket booking revenues were RMB1.4 billion (US$228 million), representing a 19% increase from 2010. The air ticket booking revenues accounted for 39% of the total revenues in 2011 and remained consistent with those in 2010.
- Packaged tour revenues were RMB535 million (US$85 million), representing a 41% increase from 2010. Wing On Travel and ezTravel contributed 3% to the year-on-year growth for packaged-tour revenues. The packaged tour revenues accounted for 14% of the total revenues in 2011, compared to 12% in 2010.
- Corporate travel revenues were RMB162 million (US$26 million), representing a 25% increase from 2010. The corporate travel revenues accounted for 4% of the total revenues in 2011, remaining consistent with that in 2010.
- Net revenues were RMB3.5 billion (US$556 million), representing a 21% increase from 2010. In 2011, Wing On Travel and ezTravel contributed 1% for the year-on-year growth for net revenues.
- Gross margin was 77%, compared to 78% in 2010.
- Sales and marketing expenses were RMB625 million (US$99 million), representing an increase of 38% from 2010. Excluding share-based compensation charges (non-GAAP), sales and marketing expenses accounted for 16% of the net revenues, increasing from 15% in 2010.

*Source*: http://www.iresearchchina.com/news/4004.html

database, customer database and a mechanism connecting the two (Buhalis and Law, 2008). Not only do DMSs enable coordination of a whole range of products and services offered by the local suppliers and promote them on the global scale but they also allow travellers to create a personal destination experience (Buhalis, 2003). They usually:

- provide information and undertake some marketing activities through mass media advertising;
- provide advisory service for consumers and the travel trade;

- design and distribute brochures, leaflets and guides; and
- coordinate local initiatives.

Although ICTs were never regarded as a critical instrument for the development and management of destinations, increasingly 'destination management organisations' (DMOs) use ICTs in order to facilitate the tourist experience before, during and after the visit, as well as for coordinating all partners involved in the production and delivery of tourism. Thus, not only do DMOs attempt to provide information and accept reservations for local enterprises as well as coordinate their facilities, but they also utilise ICTs to promote their tourism policy, coordinate their operational functions, increase the expenditure of tourists, and boost the multiplier effects in the local economy.

Despite the fact that studies on destination-oriented CRSs have been traced back to as early as 1968, it was not until the early 1990s that the concept of 'destination management systems' (DMSs) emerged. Even at this stage, however, most DMSs are mere facilitators of the conventional activities of tourism boards, such as information dissemination or local bookings. Several planned DMSs have failed in their development phase, mainly due to:

- inadequate financial support;
- lack of long-term vision of the developers;
- lack of understanding of industry mechanisms and interest groups;
- expensive and inappropriate technological solutions; and
- IT leading rather following tourism marketing.

This has discouraged DMO managers from investing further in the development of suitable systems (Buhalis, 1997). However, by 2004 most destinations around the world had recognised the value of the DMS concept and had some type of system offering information about their region. In the last few years DMOs have realised that it is critical for their competitiveness to develop their online presence. To the degree that tourists increasingly research their holidays online DMOs realise the need to have an inspirational website that can encourage and facilitate tourist visitation.

Using the emergent opportunities for multimedia distribution, DMSs increasingly utilise the Internet to provide interactive demonstrations of local amenities and attractions and to enable consumers to build their own itinerary based on their interests, requirements and constraints. In addition, DMSs are utilised to facilitate the management of DMOs, as well as the coordination of the local suppliers at the destination level. DMSs are particularly significant for small and medium-sized tourism enterprises which lack the capital and expertise to undertake a comprehensive marketing strategy and rely on destination authorities and intermediaries for the promotion and coordination of their products (Frew and O'Connor, 1999; WTO, 2001). Interestingly it is not only DMOs that provide destination information online but a wide range of players (Buhalis and Deimezi, 2004). Govers and Go (2006) demonstrate how destination identity can be projected only through the use of photographic imagery and narratives in an online environment in the context of marketing a fast-growing tourist destination such as Dubai. They conclude that private sector organisations, in particular hospitality and transport, are product oriented and projected images relate primarily to the specific facilities and tourist activities on offer. In contrast, the destination marketing organisation focuses on the projection of cultural identity and heritage.

The recent emergence of Web 2.0 with its ideology of openness, sharing and cooperation gives hope that there might be more affordable and easy to use marketing/information search tools. If the right information could be found by the right consumer, the sales of destinations and their enterprises could increase. Out of the five main types of Web 2.0 applications described by Constantinides and Fountain (2008) the content aggregators (allowing automatisation and customisation of information access and streaming) are the only ones that had not been researched in the tourism context so far. Content aggregators, as opposed to the rest of Web 2.0 developments which can be grouped under the term of user generated content (UGC), offer

| Table 22.5 | Average number of daily posts and total number of posts in June 2011 | | | |
|---|---|---|---|---|
| Country | Average no. of daily Facebook posts, June 2011 | Total no. of Facebook posts, June 2011 | Average no. of daily tweet(s) June 2011 | Total no. of tweet(s), June 2011 |
| Mexico | 0.33 | 10 | 0.8 | 24 |
| Malaysia | 1.53 | 46 | 2.33 | 70 |
| Germany | 0.57 | 17 | 1.1 | 33 |
| UK | 0.73 | 22 | 11.63 | 349 |
| Turkey | n/a | n/a | 0.37 | 11 |
| France | 0.5 | 15 | 0.67 | 20 |
| Spain | 0.7 | 21 | 0.77 | 23 |
| Combined | 0.73 | 131 | 2.52 | 530 |

*Source*: Hays et al., 2012

unique functionality for complete customisation of the accessed content through widget technology (Matloka and Buhalis, 2010).

Stankov et al. (2010: 112) argued that DMOs are 'beginning to realise the importance of using the power of social media. However, less than half of the 39 NTOs in the European Travel Commission were officially represented on Facebook. Hays et al. (2012) demonstrate that social media are gaining prominence as an element of destination marketing organisation (DMO) marketing strategy at a time when public sector cuts in their funding are requiring them to seek greater value in the way marketing budgets are spent. Social media offers DMOs a tool to reach a global audience with limited resources. Social media usage among top DMOs is still largely experimental and strategies vary significantly, as shown in Table 22.5.

The majority of DMOs are not currently utilising social media to their full effectiveness when it comes to the ability to interact and engage with consumers. Social media is still not widely recognised and/or respected as a vital tool in marketing strategies, and thus is frequently underfunded and/or neglected. Lastly, DMOs could benefit from becoming even more innovative and creative when it comes to their social media strategies, in order to fully differentiate these efforts from traditional marketing methods. It is also evident that the main factor for an advanced social media strategy is leadership and the simple acknowledgment that social media is a powerful method to engage dynamically with all stakeholders.

Advanced DMSs would enable destinations to achieve differentiation by theming their products and targeting niche markets. Providing accurate and realistic information would also improve the balance between the expectations and the perceived experiences for both tourists and locals, improving their interaction. This would enable destinations to integrate their offering and satisfy the needs of both indigenous people and visitors. In addition, DMSs can increase the bargaining power of local enterprises with tourism intermediaries as they enable them to explore new and innovative distribution channels. The illustration of environmentally sensitive areas as well as the demonstration of socio-cultural rituals would enable a better understanding by locals and tourists and therefore would improve the tourism impacts in the area. DMOs should benefit by implementing advanced DMSs (or destination integrated computer information reservation management systems (DICIRMS)).

Gretzel and Fesenmaier (2003) suggest that the development of knowledge-based tourism business-to-business (B2B) communities requires the adoption of a multidimensional, multi-level perspective on system design that incorporates processes of knowledge creation and transformation and takes organisational stages of effective technology use into consideration.

Integrating the management of information and knowledge flows can foster capacity building among community members towards strengthening the collective competitiveness of destinations. Open to external content DICIRMS, closely integrated with social media can rationalise destination management and marketing by supporting their promotion, distribution and operations and also by offering innovative tools for strategic management and amelioration of tourism impacts (Buhalis and Spada, 2000; WTO, 2001; Buhalis, 2003; Matloka and Buhalis, 2010; Hays et al., 2012).

# CONCLUSION – eTOURISM AND THE STRUCTURE OF THE TOURISM INDUSTRY

eTourism represents the *paradigm shift* experienced in the tourism industry as a result of the adoption of ICTs and the Internet. It is evident that all best business practices have been transformed as a result, and that each stakeholder in the marketplace is going through a redefinition of their role and scope. Both challenges and opportunities are emerging but the competitiveness of all tourism enterprises and destinations has been altered dramatically. It is evident that the 'only constant is change'. Organisations that 'compute' will be able to compete in the future. Although ICTs can introduce great benefits, especially in efficiency, coordination, differentiation and cost reduction, they are not a universal remedy and require a pervasive re-engineering of business processes, as well as strategic management vision and commitment in order to achieve their objectives.

Using Porter's (2001) five forces framework illustrates that the emergence of the Internet altered the structure of the travel industry (Porter, 2001; Buhalis and Zoge, 2007). Overall, consumers benefited the most as their bargaining power increased due to their ability to access accurate and relevant information instantly and to communicate directly with suppliers, while benefiting from lower switching costs. The Internet led to the intensification of rivalry among tourism suppliers as it introduced transparency, speed, convenience and a wide range of choice and flexibility in the marketplace. Transparency enabled buyers to increase their bargaining power by facilitating price comparisons and access to instant, inexpensive and accurate information but reduced the bargaining power of suppliers. Rivalry was further intensified because of lowered barriers to entry and because of the possibility of equal representation of small businesses. Innovative suppliers increasingly use advanced CRM to gather information on consumers' profiles and to offer tailored and value-added products whilst expanding their distribution mix widely to harness the marketplace. Suppliers should enhance their direct communications with end consumers and online intermediaries to save on costs, increase profitability and enhance their efficiency. Real-time representation facilitated instant distribution and led to bypassing the traditional distribution channels. This not only changed the structure of the tourism value system but also raised challenges for traditional intermediaries. The need for traditional intermediaries to shift their role to consumer advisors is becoming evident and unless TAs and TOs utilise Internet tools for building and delivering personalised tourism products they will be unable to compete in the future. Although the tourism industry structure has been altered dramatically it is evident that both tourism suppliers and online intermediaries should apply constant innovation, in terms of marketing techniques and technological advancements, in order to be able to offer differentiated, personalised, tailored and value-added products. The key point for sustaining their competitive advantage is to focus on their core competencies and to exploit the opportunities that technology offers to improve their strategic position in the tourism value system.

Social media is particularly relevant since tourism is an information-intensive industry. Social media will be increasingly influencing several components of consumer behaviour such as awareness, information acquisition, opinions, attitudes, but also purchase behaviour and post-purchase communications and evaluation (Fotis et al., 2011). Travellers will increasingly rely on other travellers' advice, versus guidebooks and standard print advertisements, and hence online travel communities will increase their importance in engaging consumers in conversations between consumer-to-consumer and consumer-to-producer, as well as many-to-one, one-to-many, one-to-one or many-to-many (Buhalis, 2003). This will lead to co-creation of tourism products. Marketers should use social media to try to stimulate conversation, encourage interaction and engage towards developing loyalty, generating interesting content and increasing awareness.

ICTs provide innovative strategic tools for tourism organisations and destinations to improve both their operations and positioning. Hence, the visibility and competitiveness of principals and destinations in the marketplace will increasingly be a function of the technologies and networks utilised to interact with individual and institutional customers. Unless the current tourism sector utilises the emergent ICTs, and develops a multi-channel and multi-platform strategy they will be unable to take full advantage of the emerging opportunities (Buhalis and Licata, 2002). It is safe to assume that only creative and innovative principals and destinations which apply continuous innovation in using intelligent eTourism applications and adopt their processes accordingly will be able to achieve sustainable competitive advantages in the future.

## SELF-CHECK QUESTIONS

1. How has the Internet changed the role of each player in the tourism industry?
2. What are the key factors that influence the adoption of ICTs in the tourism industry?
3. What is disintermediation and re-intermediation in tourism?
4. How do airlines change their business functions as a result of the Internet?
5. How can tourism organisations maximise their online representation?
6. What is the influence of social media?
7. How is the proliferation of mobile devices affecting tourism?
8. What are the Internet-related challenges for managing tourism brands?

## REFERENCES AND FURTHER READING

Alford, P. (2006) 'Global distribution systems – international', Mintel, May.

Baggio, R., Scott, N., Cooper, C. (2010) 'Network science: a review focused on tourism', *Annals of Tourism Research* **37**(3), 802–27.

Beekman, G. (2001) *Computer Confluence: Exploring Tomorrow's Technology*, 4th edn, Prentice Hall, New Jersey.

Boehmer, J. and Cohen, A. (2007) 'BA, GDSs still talking: business as usual despite much-hyped contractual expiration', *BTNonline magazine*, **http://www.btnonline.com/businesstravelnews/ headlines/frontpage_display.jsp?vnu_content_id=1003553031**

Buhalis, D. (1993) 'Regional integrated computer information reservation management systems as a strategic tool for the small and medium tourism enterprises', *Tourism Management* **14**(5), 366–78.

Buhalis, D. (1994) 'Information and telecommunications technologies as a strategic tool for small and medium tourism enterprises in the contemporary business environment', pp. 254–75 in Seaton, A. et al. (eds), *Tourism: The State of the Art: The Strathclyde Symposium,* J. Wiley and Sons, Chichester.

Buhalis, D. (1997) 'Information technologies as a strategic tool for economic, cultural and environmental benefits enhancement of tourism at destination regions', *Progress in Tourism and Hospitality Research* **3**(1), 71–93.

Buhalis, D. (1998) 'Strategic use of information technologies in the tourism industry', *Tourism Management* **19**(3), 409–23.

Buhalis, D. (2003) *eTourism: Information Technology for Strategic Tourism Management*, Pearson (Financial Times/Prentice Hall), London.

Buhalis, D. (2004) 'eAirlines: strategic and tactical use of ICTS in the airline industry', *Information and Management* **41**(7), 805–25.

Buhalis, D. and Deimezi, R. (2004) 'eTourism developments in Greece', *International Journal of Tourism and Hospitality Research* **5**(2), 103–30.

Buhalis, D. and Law, R. (2008) 'Progress in tourism management: twenty years on and 10 years after the internet: the state of eTourism research', *Tourism Management* **29**(4), 609–23.

Buhalis, D. and Licata, C. (2002) 'The eTourism intermediaries', *Tourism Management* **23**(3), 207–20.

Buhalis D. and O'Connor, P. (2005) 'Information communication technology – revolutionising tourism', *Tourism Recreation Research* **30**(3), 7–16.

Buhalis, D. and Spada, A. (2000) 'Destination management systems: criteria for success', *Information Technology and Tourism* **3**(1), 41–58.

Buhalis, D. and Zoge, M. (2007) 'The strategic impact of the Internet on the tourism industry', pp. 481–92 in Sigala, M., Mich, L. and Murphy, J. (eds), *ENTER 2007 Proceedings*, Ljubljana, Springer-Verlag, Wien.

Chan, S. and Law, R. (2006) 'Automatic website evaluations: the case of hotels in Hong Kong', *Journal of Information Technology and Tourism* **8**(3–4), 255–69.

Clarke, R. (2004) 'Value proposition', *Airline Business* (March), 44–5.

Cobanoglu, C., Berezina, K., Kasavana, M. and Erdem, M. (2011) 'The impact of technology amenities on hotel guest overall satisfaction', *Journal of Quality Assurance in Hospitality and Tourism*, **12**, 272–88.

Collins, G.R. and Cobanoglu, C. (2008) *Hospitality Information Technology: Learning How to Use It*, 6th edn, Kendall/Hunt, Dubuque, IA.

Connolly, D., Olsen, M. and Moore, R. (1998) 'The internet as a distribution channel', *Cornell Hotel and Restaurant Administration Quarterly* **39**(4), 42–54.

Constantinides, E. and Fountain, S.J. (2008) 'Web 2.0: conceptual foundations and marketing issues', *Journal of Direct, Data and Digital Marketing Practice* (9), 231–44.

Ctrip.com (2007) 'Ctrip.com posts impressive results', 12 February, **http://www.chinatechnews.com/2007/02/12/4986-ctripcom-posts-impressive-results/print/**

Dean, D., DiGrande, S., Field, D., Lundmark, A., O'Day, J., Pineda, J. and Zwillenberg, P. (2012) 'The Internet economy in the G-20: the $4.2 trillion growth opportunity', BCG Perspectives, 19 March, **https://www.bcgperspectives.com/content/articles/media_entertainment_strategic_planning_4_2_trillion_opportunity_internet_economy_g20/**

Demirciftci, T., Cobanoglu, C., Beldona, S. and Cummings, P. (2010) 'Room rate parity analysis across different hotel distribution channels in the US', *Journal of Hospitality Marketing and Management* **19**(4), 295–308.

eBusiness W@tch (2006) 'ICT and e-Business in the tourism industry', Sector Impact Study No. 08, European Commission, **http://www.ebusiness-watch.org/resources/tourism/SR08-2006_Tourism.pdf**

Econsultancy (2011) 'What do customers want from travel websites?', 8 February, **http://econsultancy.com/uk/blog/7134-what-do-customers-want-from-travel-websites**

Egger, R. (2010) 'Web 2.0 in tourism, a look behind the scenes – theoretical concepts and approaches', *Journal of Information Technology and Tourism* **12**(2), 125–38.

Egger, R. and Buhalis, D. (eds) (2008) *eTourism Case studies: Management and Marketing Issues in eTourism*, Butterworth-Heinemann, Oxford.

Emmer, R., Tauck, C., Wilkinson, S. and Moore, R. (1993) 'Marketing hotels using global distribution systems', *The Cornell Hotel Restaurant Administration Quarterly* **34**(6), 80–89.

Feldman, J. (1988) 'CRS and fair airline competition' *Travel and Tourism Analyst* (2), 5–22.

Fesenmaier, D. Woeber, K. and Werthner, H. (eds) (2006) *Destination Recommendation Systems: Behavioural Foundations* and *Applications*, CABI, Wallingford, UK.

Field, D. and O'Toole, K. (2004) 'Where next for the GDS?', *Airline Business* (March), 34–43.

Fotis, J., Buhalis, D. and Rossides, N. (2011) 'Social media impact on holiday travel: the case of the Russian and the FSU markets', *International Journal of Online Marketing* **1**(4), 1–19.

Frew, A. and Horam, R. (1999) 'eCommerce in the UK hotel sector: a first look', *International Journal of Hospitality Information Technology* **1**(1), 77–87.

Frew, A. and O'Connor, P. (1998) 'A comparative examination of the implementation of destination marketing system strategies: Scotland and Ireland', pp. 258–68 in Buhalis, D., Tjoa, A.M. and Jafari, J. (eds), *Information and Communications Technologies in Tourism*, ENTER 1998 Proceedings, Springer-Verlag, Wien.

Frew, A. and O'Connor, P. (1999) 'Destination marketing system strategies: refining and extending an assessment framework', pp. 398–407 in Buhalis, D. and Scherlter, W. (eds), *Information and Communications Technologies in Tourism*, ENTER 1999 Proceedings, Springer-Verlag, Wien.

Govers R. and Go, F. (2006) 'Projected destination image online: website content analysis of pictures and text', *Journal of Information Technology and Tourism* **8**(3–4), 73–89.

Gretzel, U. and Fesenmaier, D. (2003) 'Implementing a knowledge-based tourism marketing information system', *The Illinois Tourism Network* **6**(3), 245–55.

Gretzel, U. and Yoo, K. (2008) 'Use and impact of online travel reviews', pp. 35–48 in O'Connor, P. Höpken, W. and Gretzel, U. (eds), *Information and Communication Technologies in Tourism 2008*, Springer-Verlag, Wien/New York.

Gupta, U. (2000) *Information Systems: Success in the 21st Century*, Prentice Hall, New Jersey.

Hammer, M. and Champy, J. (1993) *Reengineering the Corporation: A Manifesto for Business Revolution*, Nicholas Brealey, London.

Hays, S., Page, S. and Buhalis, D. (2012) 'Social media as a destination marketing tool: its use by national tourism organisations', *Current Issues in Tourism*, **http://www.tandfonline.com/doi /abs/10.1080/13683500.2012.662215**

HeBS (2007) 'Mastering internet marketing in 2007: a benchmark survey on hotel internet marketing budget planning and best practices in hospitality', **http://www.hospitalityebusiness .com/hr/hr-Mar_05_2007_1520.html**

Inkpen, G. (1998) *Information Technology for Travel and Tourism*, 2nd edn, Addison Wesley Longman, London.

Kaplan, A. and Haenlein, M. (2010) 'Users of the world, unite! The challenges and opportunities of social media', *Business Horizons* **53**(1), 59–68.

Karcher, K. (1996) 'Re-engineering the package holiday business', pp. 221–33 in Klein, S. et al. (eds), *Information and Communication Technologies in Tourism*, Conference proceedings ENTER 1996, Spinger-Verlag, Wien.

Laudon, K. and Laudon, J. (2007) *Management Information Systems*, 10th edn, Prentice Hall, New Jersey.

Laudon, K., Traver, C. (2011) *E-Commerce 2011*, 7th edn, Pearson Education, New Jersey.

Li, L. and Buhalis, D. (2006) 'eCommerce in China: the case of travel', *International Journal of Information Management* **26**(2), 153–66.

Marcussen C. (2006) 'Internet distribution of European travel and tourism services', Research Centre of Bornholm, Denmark, **http://www.crt.dk/uk/staff/chm/trends.htm**

Matloka, J. and Buhalis, D. (2010) 'Destination marketing through user personalised content (UPC), pp. 519–30 in Gretzel, U., Law, R. and Fuchs, M. (eds), *ENTER 2010 Proceedings*, Lugano, Springer-Verlag, Wien.

Merlino, D., Quinby, D., Rasore, P. and Sileo, L. (2010) *Technology and Independent Distribution in European Travel Industry*, PhoCusWright, European Technology and Travel Services Association, **http://www.ettsa.eu/uploads/NewsEvents/ETTSA%20Study%202010% 20Single%20Pages.pdf**

Mills, M. and Law, R. (eds.) (2005) *Handbook of Consumer Behaviour, Tourism and the Internet*, Haworth Press.

Minghetti, V. and Buhalis, D. (2009) 'Digital divide in tourism', *Journal of Travel Research* **49**(3), 267–81.

Murphy, J., Schegg, R. and Olaru, D. (2006) 'Investigating the evolution of hotel internet adoption', *Journal of Information Technology and Tourism* **8**(3–4), 161–77.

Nyheim, P., McFadden, F. and Connolly, D. (2005) *Technology Strategies for the Hospitality Industry*, Pearson-Prentice Hall, New Jersey.

O'Brien, J. (1996) *Management Information Systems: Managing Information Technology in the Networked Enterprise*, Irwin, Chicago.

O'Connor, P. (1999) *Electronic Information Distribution in Tourism & Hospitality*, CAB, Oxford.

O'Connor, P. (2004) *Using Computers in Hospitality*, 3rd edn, Cassell, London.

O'Connor, P. (2002) 'An empirical analysis of hotel chain online pricing strategies', *Information Technology and Tourism* **5**(2) 65–72.

O'Connor, P. (2008a) 'Managing hospitality information technology in Europe: issues, challenges and priorities', *Journal of Hospitality Marketing & Management* **17**(1–2), 59–77.

O'Connor, P. (2008b) 'E-mail marketing by international hotel chains: an industry-practices update', *Cornell Hospitality Quarterly* **49**(1), 42–52.

O'Connor, P. (2010) 'Managing a hotel's image on TripAdvisor', *Journal of Hospitality Marketing and Management* **19**(7), 754–72.

O'Connor, P. and Frew, A. (2000) 'Evaluating electronic channels of distribution in the hotel sector: a Delphi study', *Information Technology and Tourism* **3**(3/4), 177–93.

O'Connor, P. and Horan, P. (1999) 'An analysis of web reservations facilities in the top 50 international hotel chains', *International Journal of Hospitality Information Technology* **1**(1), 77–87.

O'Connor, P. and Rafferty, J. (1997) 'Gulliver-distributing Irish tourism electronically', *Electronic Markets* **7**(2), 40–45.

O'Reilly, T. (2005) 'What is Web 2.0: design patterns and business models for the next generation of software', **http://www.oreillynet.com/pub/a/oreilly/tim/news/2005/09/30/what-is-web-20.html**

O'Toole, K. (2004) *IT Trends Survey 2003*, Airline Business/SITA, August.

Oz, E. (2000) *Management Information Systems*, 2nd edn, Thomson Learning – Course Technology, Boston.

Paraskevas, A. and Buhalis, D. (2002) 'Web-enabled ICT outsourcing for small hotels: opportunities and challenges', *Cornell Hotel and Restaurant Administration Quarterly* **43**(2), 27–39.

Peacock, M. (1995) *Information Technology in Hospitality*, Cassell, London.

Peppard, J. (ed.) (1993) *IT Strategy for Business*, Pitman, London.

Pollock, A. (1998) 'Creating intelligent destinations for wired customers', pp. 235–48 in Buhalis, D., Tjoa, A.M. and Jafari, J. (eds), *Information and Communications Technologies in Tourism*, ENTER 1998 Proceedings, Springer-Verlag, Wien.

Poon, A. (1993) *Tourism, Technology and Competitive Strategies*, CAB International, Oxford.

Porter, M. (1985) *Competitive Advantage*, Free Press, New York.

Porter, M. (1989) 'Building competitive advantage by extending information systems', *Computerworld*, 9 October, **23**(41), 19.

Porter, M. (2001) 'Strategy and the Internet', *Harvard Business Review* **103**(March), 63–78.

Porter, M. and Millar, V. (1985) 'How information gives you competitive advantage', *Harvard Business Review* **63**(4), 149–60.

Qi, S., Law, R. and Buhalis, D. (2010) 'A comparison of Chinese and international online user perceptions of the usefulness of hotel websites', *Journal of Information Technology and Tourism* **11**, 329–40.

Rheem, C. (2012) *Empowering Inspiration: The Future of Travel Search*, PhoCusWright, USA.

Robson, W. (1994) *Strategic Management and Information Systems: An Integrated Approach*, Pitman, London.

Rose, N. (2011) 'The always-connected traveller: how mobile will transform the future of air travel', Amadeus, **http://www.amadeus.com/alwaysconnectedtraveller**

Sheldon, P. (1993) 'Destination information systems', *Annals of Tourism Research* **20**(4), 633–49.

Sheldon, P. (1997) *Information Technologies for Tourism*, CAB, Oxford.

SITA (2006) *IT Trends Survey*, Airline Business, Executive Summary, **http://www.sita.aero/NR/rdonlyres/7D4B9E97-F208-44CA-95B8-72CCF702BD33/0/AirlineIT_Booklet06.pdf**

SITA (2012) *Airline IT Trends Survey 2012*, **http://www.sita.aero/file/8068/airline-it-trends-2012-executive-summary-pdf**

Smith, C. and Jenner, P. (1998) 'Tourism and the Internet', *Travel and Tourism Analyst* (1), 62–81.

Spencer, A., Buhalis, D. and Moital, D. (2012) 'A hierarchical model of technology adoption for small owner-managed travel firms: an organizational decision-making and leadership perspective', *Tourism Management* **33**(5), 1195–208.

Stankov, U., Lazic, L. and Dragicevic, V. (2010) 'The extent of use of basic Facebook user-generated content by the national tourism organizations in Europe', *European Journal of Tourism Research* **3**(2), 105–13.

Tapscott, D. (1996) *The Digital Economy: Promise and Peril in the Age of Networked Intelligence*, McGraw-Hill, New York.

Tapscott, D. and Caston, A. (1993) *Paradigm Shift: The New Promise of Information Technology*, McGraw Hill Inc, New York.

Truitt, L., Teye, V. and Farris, M. (1991) 'The role of computer reservation systems: international implications for the tourism industry', *Tourism Management* **12**(1), pp. 21–36.

Werthner, H. and Klein, S., (1999) *Information Technology and Tourism – A challenging relationship*, Springer, New York.

Wöber, K.W. (2006) 'Domain-specific search engines', pp. 205–26 in Fesenmaier, D.R., Werthner, H. and Wöber, K.W. (eds) *Destination Recommendation Systems: Behavioural Foundations and Applications*, CABI, Wallingford.

Wolk, A. and Wöber, K. (2008) 'Dimensions of tourist information needs across different European destinations according to search terms entered on a tourism-specific search engine', *Journal of Information Technology and Tourism* **10**(2), 119–31.

WTO (1995) *Global Distribution Systems in the Tourism Industry*, World Tourism Organization, Madrid.

WTO (1999) *Marketing Tourism Destinations Online: Strategies for the Information Age*, WTO, Madrid.

WTO (2001) *eBusiness for Tourism: Practical Guidelines for Destinations and Businesses*, World Tourism Organization, Madrid.

Xiang, Z. and Gretzel, U. (2010) 'Role of social media in online travel information search', *Tourism Management* **31**(2), 179–88.

Xiang, Z., Woeber, K. and Fesenmaier, D.R. (2008) 'Representation of the online tourism domain in search engines', *Journal of Travel Research* **47**(2), 137–50.

Yea, Q., Law, R. and Bin Gu, B. (2009) 'The impact of online user reviews on hotel room sales', *International Journal of Hospitality Management* **28**(1), 180–82.

Zoge, M. and Buhalis, D. (2008) 'British Airways', pp. 269–82 in Egger, R. and Buhalis, D. (eds), *eTourism Case Studies: Management and Marketing Issues in eTourism*, Butterworth-Heinemann, Oxford.

## Websites

**http://www.ifitt.org/**
IFITT's website

**http://www.eyefortravel.com/**
Commercial websites with news and white papers

**http://www.hotelmarketing.com**
Monitoring eTourism news

**http://www.etcnewmedia.com/review/default.asp?SectionID=10**
New media group collecting statistics

**http://www.traveldailynews.com**
Newsletters and new developments

**http://www.travelmole.com**
Newsletters and new developments

http://www.btnonline.com/
Newsletters and new developments

http://www.electronic-tourism.com
Newsletters and new developments and white papers

http://www.tia.org/
Information on Travel developments in the USA

http://www.hotel-online.com
Newsletters and new developments on eHospitality

http://www.internetworldstats.com
Internet World Statistics

http://www.jup.com/
http://www.forrester.com/
Internet statistics

http://www.genesys.net/
Information on tour operators and travel agencies

http://www.phocuswright.com
Commercial websites with news and white papers

http://www.waksberg.com/
Tourism research resources

http://www.world-tourism.org/
World Tourism Organization

http://www.wttc.org
World Tourism Travel Council

http://www.ih-ra.com/
International Hotel Restaurant Association

http://www.staruk.org.uk
Tourism Statistics in the UK

# GLOSSARY

**9/11** The terrorist attacks in New York and Washington, D.C. on 11 September 2001.

## A

**Acidification** The process of increasing acidity or becoming acidic.

**Additionality** When new products or facilities are introduced if they add to the total value of tourist spend then they are said to provide additionality as opposed to **displacement**.

**Advanced passenger train** Introduced in the UK in 1979 to provide fast intercity rail transport.

**Advanced purchase excursion fare** Early booking of tickets often results in lower ticket prices; also known as APEX fares.

**Advertising** Includes any paid form of non-personal communication through the media which details a product that is identifiable.

**Agenda 21** The programme action plan that came out of the 1992 Rio Summit. It was given the title Agenda 21 because of the 21 chapters dealing with a wide range of aspects relating to sustainable development.

**Agent** A business that distributes the product of principals without alteration in the main.

**AIDS** Acquired Immune Deficiency Syndrome.

**Air traffic control** The system that directs the movement of aircraft in time and space.

**Air traffic movements** Data on air traffic routes and runway utilisation, etc.

**Alternative tourism** Has a wide variety of meanings and was put forward as a response to the excesses associated with mass tourism.

**Anthropology of tourism** The study of tourism with respect to socio-cultural, linguistic and archaeological issues.

**Anti-trust legislation** US legislation against controlling trusts or monopolies influencing market competition.

**Attraction 'icons'** Those attractions that mark a destination in the mind of the tourist, giving instant association of the attraction with its location.

**Authenticity** This term is generally used to show that something is original and honest, that it is what it appears to be.

## B

**Balance of payments** Refers to the balance between foreign exchange spent and received in an economy.

**Barriers to entry** Devices designed to prevent new companies from entering an industry. The barriers may be through production secrets, scarcity of resources or through the high price of inputs.

**Biological diversity** The number, range and abundance of species living within a common environment.

**Brand** A name, a symbol, term or design or a combination of these.

**Brand extensions or stretching** The extension of product range under a single brand.

## C

**Cabotage** This refers to where overseas airlines have been given the right to fly any routes they wish from particular airports.

**Capitalism** A social system based on individual rights where goods and services are produced and exchanged with minimal government interference.

**Charter flights** See **charter services**.

**Charter services** A system of conditions over a finite period that relates to levels of service and frequency of flights in order to secure capacity.

**Classical decomposition** The process of breaking up a time series of data into its component parts.

**Click-and-mortar agencies** Established businesses with physical outlets engaging in e-commerce (Internet trade).

**Codesharing** A procedure where different airlines, who are members of an alliance, agree to pool their different airline codes into one flight so as to use up spare capacity. It is particularly common with short-haul onward connections from main airport hubs.

**Commercialisation and bastardisation** The change made to an event, skill, craft or ritual to make it more attractive to tourists.

**Commodification** The transformation of non-commercial relationships into commercial relationships.

**Communism** A society where the people are responsible for resource allocation, production and distribution. In theory, essentially classless and without a need for government.

**Comparative advantage** Where the opportunity cost of producing a specific good or service is less than it is in another country then the former is considered to have a comparative advantage in the production of that good or service. Is used as a justification for international trade.

**Conservation** Managing environmental resources in a way that optimises their contribution to the quality of life.

**Consortia** A combination or group formed in order to undertake a venture that would be beyond the resources of a single individual/company.

**Consumer satisfaction** The extent to which a company's business efforts matches or exceeds the expectations of the consumer.

**Contestable markets** Those markets where firms' conduct is not determined by market structure, but rather the need to deter entry is the main influence on performance.

**Cost–benefit analysis** Used in project appraisal to determine the monetary value of costs and benefits (to a community) relating to a project (such as an airport extension, highway, new sewage treatment plant) to see if it is worthwhile.

**Credence good** A product or service bought on trust from the supplier since it is not possible to pre-test it prior to purchase.

**Customer needs** Customer-felt state of deprivation.

**D**

**Delphi analysis** An iterative panel method of analysis where the panel members do not meet.

**Demand determinants** The factors that influence the scope and nature of travel.

**Demonstration effect** Influencing the behaviour, dress and attitudes of people through demonstration/imitation and interaction.

**Destination image** An individual's awareness of a destination made up of the cognitive evaluation of experiences, learning, emotions and perceptions.

**Destination management organisation** A destination-based organisation tasked with the responsibility of co-ordinating and managing destination activity, including planning and promotion.

**Developing countries** Countries that are defined as low- or middle-income countries by the World Bank, where living standards are thought to be low relative to high-income countries. Although there is no precise definition there are thought to be more than 125 countries with populations in excess of 1 million that have these characteristics.

**Development strategies** Approaches and plans designed to bring about the desired growth and development of tourism or an economy.

**Diagonal integration** This refers to collaboration among different service providers (such as airlines, car hire companies, tour operators and financial services companies) designed to get closer to the consumer and reduce transaction costs through economies of scope, system gains and synergies.

**Direct marketing** Direct communication with pre-selected target groups in order to obtain an immediate response or build closer relationships.

**Direct sell** The absence of **intermediaries**. Therefore the product is sold directly from the supplier to the tourist.

**Disaggregation** The degree to which the various productive sectors of the economy are broken down (e.g. the UN Standard Industrial Classification (SIC) 2, 3 or 4 digit levels of disaggregation).

**Discretionary incentives** Incentives normally linked to conditions, such as job creation in depressed areas. Can also take the form of discretionary grants.

**Disintermediation** A reduction in the amount or value of transactions that are distributed through intermediaries.

**Displacement** Refers to the amount of current revenue that is displaced by a new development. For instance, if a new five-star hotel is built in Quebec and 50% of its business is attracted from existing five-star hotels in the city then there is a 50% displacement rate.

**Distribution system** Mix of channels used to gain access or means by which a tourism service is made available to the potential buyers of the product.

**Distributive trade** Refers to all companies involved in the distribution of goods and services. The UN Standard Industrial Classification (SIC) incorporates distributive trade under heading 6 (i.e. 6.1 wholesale trade, 6.2 retail trade, 6.3 hotels and catering).

**Diversification** The broadening of the economic base by the development of different industries, and/or a strategy to achieve company growth by means of starting up or acquiring new businesses outside the existing company products or markets.

**Domestic tourism** The activity of people visiting destinations within their own country's boundaries.

**E**

**Ecological system** A collection of interconnected living beings (including humans) and the system in which they coexist such as the earth's surface.

**Economic dependence** When the costs and revenues of one country, company or project depend upon that of another.

**Econometric models** They explain movements in the data of interest in terms of a range of influencing variables.

**Economic recession** A decline in economic activity (**GDP**) that persists for at least two quarters.

**Eco-tourism** Nature-based tourism that attempts to minimise its environmental impact.

**E-intermediaries** E-intermediaries and emediaries are intermediaries that offer streamlined intermediation services across the Internet.

**Elasticities of demand and supply** The responsiveness of supply and demand to changes in prices (price elasticity) or income (income elasticity).

**Empirical studies** Studies that are based on experience, experiment or observation.

**Environmental Action Programmes** Environmental policies and strategies.

**Environmental auditing** A management system designed to mitigate environmental impacts.

**Eutrophication** The process whereby water becomes enriched with plant nutrients and this replaces the oxygen.

**Exogenous change in demand** A change in final demand brought about by changes outside the economy in question.

**Externalities** The external economic effects that are not taken into account within the normal marketplace. Can be positive (benefits) or negative (costs) and are associated with the production or consumption of goods and services.

**Extranet** Private network that is accessible only by trusted business partners using secured connections over the Internet.

**F**

**Feudalism** The social system that was prevalent in Europe from the eighth century onwards. Seen by some as control of a state by an entrenched minority for their own benefits.

**Fixed costs** Those costs that do not vary with the volume of output.

**Flagship** The chief or major one of a group, e.g. flagship attraction or hotel.

**Focus groups** A method of undertaking collective interviews that explicitly uses the group's interaction to generate results.

**'Footloose' attractions** Attractions that can be located almost anywhere where there is sufficient space, i.e. not dependent upon a specific natural resource or factor.

**G**

**GATS** The General Agreement on Trade in Services. An attempt by the World Trade Organization to liberate the trade in services in the same way that the GATT did for trade in goods.

**GDP** Gross domestic product. A key indicator of an economy's performance and is based on the total value of goods and services produced by a country within its economy.

**Global distribution system** Computer databases used by intermediaries to book tourism products.

**Global warming** The rise in the world's temperature due to the greenhouse effect.

**Globalisation** A term that refers to the process of increasing economic and communication connectivity that has occurred over the past half century. Global markets replacing national and regional markets, e.g. capital markets.

**GNI** Gross national income. The value of all income earned by residents of an economy whether it is earned within or outside the national boundary (see **GNP**).

**GNP** Gross national product. The value of all current final goods and services produced over the course of a year within an economy (which is gross domestic product [GDP]) plus the income that residents of the economy receive from outside that economy, less income paid to people that reside outside the economy.

**'Grand inspiration' attractions** Attractions that are developed as a result of an individual's dream.

**GVA** Gross Value Added. A measure of the value of goods and services produced in an area or sector of the economy.

**H**

**Hallmark events** Hallmark is generally a sign of quality, authenticity or distinguishing feature therefore a hallmark event is intended to make the destination distinctive in some way

**Hedging** A strategy that is implemented to reduce risk. An example would be for a business to take up a position in a futures market that is opposite to that held in the cash market so that risks are reduced.

**Honey pots** An expression used in tourism management whereby a viariety of attractions, shops, restaurants and accommodation are clustered at points where tourists want to visit to create a complex capable of absorbing a high population density.

**Horizontal integration** The merging of two or more businesses that are operating at the same stage of the production process.

**I**

**Imagescape** The medium or background in which people feel they live.

**Inclusive tours** The package tour.

**Indigenous development** Economic development that occurs as a result of changes within the country.

**Inflation** A persistent increase in the general price level over time resulting in a decrease in the purchasing power of a unit of currency, e.g. dollar.

**Information communication technology (ICT)** Digital tools used for business functions and processes.

**Infrastructural investment** Investment in infrastructure such as roads, airports, water supply and communications.

**Input–output model** A general equilibrium approach to measuring the effects of a change in final demand on the rest of the economy.

**Inseparability** The service product is often produced and consumed simultaneously.

**Instant purchase fares** Product is purchased at the time that the transaction takes place even though this may be well in advance of the dates of the trip.

**Institutionalised or mass tourism** A constant stream of large numbers of tourists to destinations.

**Intangibility** The tourism product cannot be easily demonstrated, assessed or tested prior to purchase.

**Integrated marketing communication** The process a company adopts in order to integrate and coordinate its messages and media to deliver clear reinforcing communication.

**Integration** The combination of businesses that are at the same or different stages of a process or distribution channel.

**Interlining** This refers to where passengers transfer from one flight to another within the same company or alliance rather than switching to an alternative company or competing alliance.

**Intermediaries** Companies or individuals that act as brokers or middlemen between the tourists and the suppliers (travel agents, tour operators).

**International tourism** The activity of people visiting destinations outside their own country's boundaries.

**Internet** Self-regulated global network of computers interconnecting independent hosts around the globe.

**Intersectoral linkages** The purchase and sale of goods and services between the various sectors of an economy – representing intermediate demand.

**Intranet** Internal communication (Local Area Network LAN or Wide Area Network WAN) network, using Internet type of interfaces accessibility only by authorised employees and protected by the company's firewall.

**Invisible export** The export of a service as opposed to a visible export which would be a tangible good. International tourist receipts are exports.

**K**

**Key informants** People able to provide collective and important viewpoints and opinions.

**L**

**Leakages** Refers to money that drops out of circulation within the local economy, either by being saved or being spent on goods and services from outside the economy.

**Lifetime value** The measurement of the total worth to the organisation of its relationship with a particular identified customer over a period of time.

**Limits of acceptable change** The acceptable level of change that an environment can suffer without irreversible degradation.

**Linear homogeneity in production** The assumption that all companies within a single sector are making the same product/service in the same way and that there are no economies of large-scale production so that the next unit of output will require exactly the same proportion of inputs as the previous unit of output.

**Load factor** The measure of business and the indicator of efficiency for transport systems, generally expressed as the percentage of available seats that are occupied on the journey.

**Loss leader** A good or service sold at less than market price in order to attract consumers.

**M**

**Marginal cost** The incremental cost of producing one more unit of a good or service. Governments tend to intervene in the marketplace for market goods by providing subsidies or directly providing them so that the consumption of such goods and services is increased.

**Marginal propensity to consume** The amount of each additional unit of income that an individual is likely to spend.

**Market failure** The inability of a market system to truly reflect the social costs and/or benefits associated with transactions, an example being the over-consumption of non-priced elements in the production process, such as the environment. In such cases, the market fails to find an efficient solution to the distribution.

**Market or catchment area** The area in which goods and services take place. Markets can also relate to the characteristics of potential purchasers and sellers such as specific segments of the population.

**Marketing concept** The marketing management philosophy that places the satisfaction of the needs of the target market as a central guiding goal.

**Marketing mix** The combination of product, price, place and promotion marketing tools that a company decides upon in order to affect consumer behaviour.

**Marketing plan** A detailed company approach to the selection of target groups and the formulation of a marketing mix to achieve marketing objectives and financial targets.

**'Me too' attraction developments** The development of an attraction on the basis of the evidence that it has worked before therefore it will work again, i.e. it ignores market saturation and displacement.

**Mega attraction** Mega is a prefix that means 1 million. These are attractions on a grand scale in terms of cost and visitor numbers that deliver significant economic impacts on their location.

**Mega events** A mega event is generally considered to be a large-scale event that has global publicity and/or is associated with large-scale impacts.

**Merit goods** Goods that are deemed to have a greater value to society than is reflected in their market price.

**Mission statement** A short statement as to the main purpose or major goal of the organisation in relation to the wider environment.

**Monopolistic power** The ability of a business to determine (to some extent) the price of the goods/services produced.

**Moving average** A series of arithmetic means constructed by taking a rolling average of a data series.

**Multinational agencies** Agencies that operate across national boundaries, such as the United Nations Development Agency.

**Multiplier analysis** An economic technique for estimating the impact of tourism on the local economy.

**N**

**National air carrier** The airline that carries the national flag, the state airline.

**National tourist organisation** The tourist authority for a state/country.

**New product development** The introduction of a good, service or idea that is perceived by customers to be new.

**New tourist** A tourist who is experienced, aware of opportunities and empowered.

**'New version' attractions** Modern-day interpretations of classic attractions, e.g. from fairgrounds to theme parks.

**O**

**OECD** Organisation for Economic Cooperation and Development. A collection of 30 member states that use the organisation as a discussion forum to further their aims for a free market system.

**Off-peak** The periods when travel and tourist activities are in less demand. Often associated with discounts to attract business.

**Online travel** The acquisition of information and the purchase of travel-related services from businesses selling on the Internet.

**Operating account** An account for day-to-day operations of the business.

**Opportunity costs** Costs a country, company or individual has to forgo in order to have something.

**Outliers** Out of the ordinary happenings in a data series, that need to be excluded from any analysis since they would skew the results.

**Overrides** Extra commission paid by airlines, hotels and other suppliers for volume bookings.

**P**

**Paid holiday entitlement** The practice of employers providing employees with time off with pay.

**Peak** The prime period of demand.

**Perceived risk** The interpretation of the seriousness of economic, physical, performance and pyschological aspects related to decision making.

**Peripheral areas** Areas away from the centre or the core.

**Perishability** A characteristic of service products implies they cannot be easily stored for future sale.

**Personal selling** An attempt to gain benefit through face-to-face or telephone contact between the seller's representative and those people with whom the seller wants to communicate.

**Polluter should pay** Philosophy that supports the view that the costs of cleaning up pollution should be borne by those who create the pollution.

**Preservation** Not using, or limiting the use of, resources so as to preserve them for future generations.

**Price** The amount of money charged for a product or service based upon what a consumer is willing to give up in return for the benefits delivered

**Price competitive** Where small changes in the price charged for a product may result in sales being won by a rival business.

**Primary data** New data gathered by the researcher for the purpose of the study.

**Principal** A trade term used to define the economic entity supplying the product.

**Product** A package of problem-solving services and tangible attributes formulated to satisfy a need or want.

**Product differentiation** Making the output of a business distinctly different from the output of competitors.

**Product life cycle** A term borrowed from biological sciences that refers to the way in which a product evolves over time.

**Project appraisal** Involves a collection of instruments (such as the internal rates of return) that can be used to determine the financial viability of a variety of projects.

**Promotion** Descriptive term for the mix of communication activities that tourism organisations carry out in order to influence those publics on whom their sales depend.

**Property management system** A computerised system for integrating all elements of hospitality information and management.

**Pro-poor tourism** Tourism strategies designed to alleviate poverty.

**Protectionism** The opposite to trade liberalisation – the imposition of tariffs or quotas to stop imports.

**Psychographic analysis** A way of categorising tourists according to their attitudes, values, behaviour and beliefs.

**Public or collective good** A public good is one that everyone feels the benefits of and from which no one can practically be excluded and is non-rival in consumption. Collective goods have similar qualities but exclusion is possible, e.g. television broadcasts started as collective goods but have largely moved into the private sector domain – this movement does not detract from the 'collective' qualities they possess and there is no suggestion that the private market achieves an efficient allocation.

**Public relations** Non-personal communication that changes opinion or achieves coverage in a mass medium and that is not paid for by the source.

**Q**

**Quality assurance** The system which assures the end customers receive a level of service with which they will be satisfied.

**Quality control** The checks against standards set to ensure the organisation achieves its quality objectives.

**R**

**Regional disparities** The differences between regions with respect to specified variables such as income, employment etc.

**Reintermediation** A term used where traditional intermediaries in a transaction are redefined and re-employed in the distribution system.

**Repatriated income** That income sent home (out of the economy) by foreign workers or companies.

**Resource allocation** The way in which resources are allocated across different uses in an economy.

**Retention** Retention of a customer is the ability to keep a customer over a period of time (by metric of at least a year) in order to maintain the company's customer base.

**Revenue management** A term used to describe the manipulation of different market segments by suppliers so as to maximise sales in order to minimise unsold product at any one time.

**S**

**Sales promotion** Involves any activity that offers an incentive to induce a desired result from potential customers, trade intermediaries or the sales force.

**Same-day visitor** A person on a brief recreational trip, not exceeding 24 hours at the destination.

**Sampling** A process of drawing in a systematic way a subset of units from a population so as to be representative of the whole.

**Scheduled services** Transport systems that operate according to strict conditions relating to frequency and scheduling.

**Seasonality** The temporal fluctuations of tourism on a daily, weekly, monthly or annual basis.

**Sectoral linkages** Refer to the transactions (sales and purchases) that take place between companies in a single economy.

**Segment** A sub-market of consumers who have been chosen as a target group and are marketed to in a different way from other sub-groups.

**Segmentation** The process of identifying the most appropriate sub-markets for the company's or destination's offer.

**Service industries** Companies that produce output in the form of services rather than goods.

**Service product** The formulation of an activity or benefit which is essentially intangible in nature and does not lead to the ownership of anything.

**Sex tourism** Defines the specific motivation of tourists to go on holiday for the purpose of engaging in short-term sexual relations.

**Simultaneity of production** Where the production of a service and its consumption occur at the same instant.

**SMEs** Small and medium-sized enterprises. (Medium – no more than 250 employees; small – no more than 50 employees; and micro – no more than 10 employees.) Turnover or balance sheet restrictions also apply.

**Social cohesion** The way in which society can work together as opposed to social divisions normally associated with gaps between the rich and the poor.

**Social net benefits** The result of deducting social costs from social benefits. Adding the term social to benefits and costs means including a broader range of factors than purely financial ones.

**Socialism** A system of social organisation whereby the state government takes responsibility for resource allocation, production and distribution.

**Socio-economic groups** Categorising people into groups by resorting to demographics (age, sex, occupation etc.).

**Sponsorship** Sponsorship is the material or financial support of a specific activity, normally but not exclusively sport, education or the arts, which does not form part of the sponsor organisation's normal business.

**Stagnation** A time period in which there is either little or no economic growth.

**Stakeholders** The groups of businesses, residents, governments and tourists who have a stake in the development of tourism.

**STEP analysis** An analysis of the environment based upon factors of society, technology, economics and politics.

**Strategic planning** A planning approach to ensure a fit between the environment, the competencies and resources of the organisation and its changing marketing opportunities.

**Structural adjustment** Policy of increasing privatisation and trade liberalisation intended to help countries generate greater wealth and reduce poverty. Has been criticised for inducing economic decline and endangering the welfare of the economically vulnerable.

**Subsidiarity** The assignment of political power to the smallest units of government.

**Supply constraints** When one sector reaches or comes close to full productive capacity it will not be able to respond fully to a further increase in demand for its output.

**Sustainable development** Development that meets the needs of the people today without compromising the ability of future generations to meet their own needs.

**Sustainable tourism development** As sustainable development but relating specifically to the tourism industry.

**T**

**Target market** A set of buyers selected as sharing similar needs or characteristics so that a company can organise a marketing mix to serve them.

**Tariff structure** The nature of the tariffs associated with imports.

**Tied agency** One who can deal only with the product or service of a single company.

**Tiger economies** The term within this book is used to refer to the East Asian economies and includes Indonesia, Hong Kong, Malaysia, Singapore, South Korea, Taiwan and Thailand. The term 'tiger' relates to the aggressive policies of the countries towards achieving rapid growth.

**Total quality management** An organisation-wide process and system of ensuring that all activities carried out adhere to pre-agreed quality standards.

**Total tourist experience** The combined stages of pre-planning, the purchase, the journey, the visit and perhaps stay, the return journey and overall reflection on the activity.

**Tourism satellite accounts** A set of accounts to show the total value to an economy of domestic and international tourism.

**Tourism system** Leiper's (1979) description of a three-part system of tourist-generating region, transit region and tourism destination region set within social, economic and environmental contexts.

**Tourist satisfaction** The rating that tourists give to their experience while on holiday.

**Tourist tax** Taxes specifically levied on tourists generally through businesses that deal with tourists. Can be entry taxes, hotel taxes or other specific tourism industry-based tax.

**Trade deficit** Occurs where a country's expenditures on imports of goods and services are greater (in value terms) than the receipts from the export of goods and services.

**Train à Grande Vitesse** TGV (literally, *high-speed train*) holds the highest speed record for a train on any national railroad.

**Travel propensity** The penetration of travel activity within a given population.

**Typologies** Classifications.

**U**

**Univariate models** Explain movements in the data of interest solely in terms of time progression.

**V**

**Value added** The amount of monetary value added to a good or service by a company before it is offered for sale.

**Vertical integration** When the same business owns establishments that are operating at more than one stage of the production, selling and delivery process.

**VFR** Visiting friends and relatives (tourist motivation).

**Y**

**Yield management** Management system that optimises the yield (returns) from a project.

**Z**

**Zone of tolerance** A customer will tolerate a range of standards in an area between desired and adequate rather than have one set standard of assessment.

# INDEX